State Rankings 2018

⊛SAGE stats

Featuring State Stats, Local Stats, and Business Stats

What is **SAGE Stats?** **SAGE Stats** is an exciting online destination for finding, mapping, comparing, and exporting statistics across a number of topics and geographic areas. In its three modules, **SAGE Stats** draws together the statistics from the *State Rankings* series of books by CQ Press (SAGE State Stats); a broad collection of data by county, city, and metro area (SAGE Local Stats); and a collection of highly detailed demographic data (including projections) and industry and labor measures available across geographical areas including ZIP Codes (SAGE Business Stats).

Featuring data from more than 250 different government and nongovernment sources and backed by a rich collection of thousands of historical, current, and projected data series on popular topics of research interest, **SAGE Stats** uniquely allows users to discover, view, and export key information measures for the 50 states and the District of Columbia, over 1,400 cities, over 3,000 counties, over 900 metro areas, and thousands of ZIP Codes.

SAGE Stats makes research easy by providing in one place annual measures dating back decades. Data series are displayed in a clear and consistent format with detailed source information. An intuitive interface lets users easily browse by location or by topic, and then compare across locations or across time.

Users can:

- Analyze data patterns by comparing across locations, data series, and time

- Create and export custom visuals including line charts, scatter plots, and maps

- Generate tables and download data for statistical research

- Toggle user display between interactive visual and tabular data view

- Engage a moveable timeline to discover trends

- Explore interactive maps featuring zoom and hover functions

- Export data across multiple years and data series

Ongoing updates to **SAGE Stats** throughout the year ensure that users have the most current data available.

Check it out online at http://data.sagepub.com/.

State Rankings 2018

A Statistical View of America

Editors

Kathleen O'Leary Morgan
and
Scott Morgan

For information:

CQ Press
An Imprint of SAGE Publications, Inc.
2455 Teller Road
Thousand Oaks, California 91320
E-mail: order@sagepub.com

SAGE Publications Ltd.
1 Oliver's Yard
55 City Road
London, EC1Y 1SP
United Kingdom

SAGE Publications India Pvt. Ltd.
B 1/I 1 Mohan Cooperative Industrial Area
Mathura Road, New Delhi 110 044
India

SAGE Publications Asia-Pacific Pte. Ltd.
3 Church Street
#10-04 Samsung Hub
Singapore 049483

Printed in the United States of America.

ISBN 978-1-5443-0065-8 (cloth)
ISBN 978-1-5443-0067-2 (paper)
ISSN 1057-3623

Acquisitions Editor: Andrew Boney
Assistant Editor: Diana Aleman
Production Editor: Tracy Buyan
Cover Designer: Michael Dubowe
Marketing Manager: Jennifer Bourque

18 19 20 21 22 10 9 8 7 6 5 4 3 2 1

Contents

Detailed Table of Contents

VI. EMPLOYMENT AND LABOR

VII. ENERGY AND ENVIRONMENT

VIII. GEOGRAPHY

IX. GOVERNMENT FINANCES: FEDERAL

X. GOVERNMENT FINANCES: STATE AND LOCAL

XIV. SOCIAL WELFARE

XV. TRANSPORTATION

Introduction and Methodology

State Rankings 2018 provides an easily accessible collection of data in a broad range of quality of life factors in the United States. In this latest 2018 edition, State Rankings compares data from the fifty states and the District of Columbia in 566 tables in the following fifteen different livability categories: agriculture, crime and law enforcement, defense, economy, education, employment and labor, energy and environment, geography, federal government finances, state and local government finances, health, households and housing, population, social welfare, and transportation.

Purpose of This Book

State Rankings 2018 translates complicated and often convoluted statistics into meaningful, easy-to-understand information. Too often there is an abundance of data but far too little information putting those data into context. This book allows researchers, legislators, policy analysts, journalists, and the general public to access information in a manner that not only provides basic facts about a state's quality of life but also gives a meaningful framework by comparing individual states against the rest of the country.

These data and rankings can be used in a variety of ways, by a variety of audiences, including the following examples:

- Policy makers can use the data to help identify areas warranting further study.
- Journalists can easily find impartial state information that puts stories into context.
- The general public can see how a particular state is faring compared to other states.
- Librarians can use the data as a quick reference to assist patrons in research and offer the sources and websites included as a starting point for finding other related data.

The comparison rankings in State Rankings 2018 provide an annual snapshot of how the states are doing in the fifteen livability categories mentioned above. There are two principle approaches to using these rankings. The first is to examine how a state is doing compared to all other states via the comparison rankings in this book. The second approach is to compare a state to itself over a given period of time. Both approaches are important to achieving a good understanding of how and whether a state is making progress. It is important to keep in mind that the rankings are not a definitive determination of which state is the "best." However, since so many issues are surrounded by emotions, tracking them by the numbers can help bring the discussion back to a more balanced, unbiased review that in the end leads to better decisions.

Data and Limitations

The data featured in State Rankings 2018 were chosen specifically by the editors from a variety of government and private sector sources. The statistics presented are intended to cover a broad array of quality-of-life subject areas, giving users of the book a solid collection of state information. Nonetheless, the statistics are not inclusive of all the possible data that might be available. The statistics in the book are the latest available from the sources. In a few cases, we have retained tables that have not been updated for several years because we believe our readers will find the data relevant, even if updates are not available. In other cases, we replaced obsolete data with new tables. Longtime users should note in particular that we have updated Government Finances: Federal with new government spending data from the OMB's USASpending.gov, but differences in methodology make those data difficult to compare with past editions.

Previous editions of the book have used the term most livable when describing states with the highest livability ranking. This term is no longer being used because it is purely descriptive—at no time do we attempt to explain why a particular state is ranking higher or lower in livability factors than others or against the national average. This explanation—currently sought by social science researchers—is beyond the scope of this book. While our selection of factors clearly affects the rankings, we believe the rankings provide a solid measurement of how the fifty states and Washington, D.C., are faring with regard to quality of life in the United States. Researchers, practitioners, and others can confidently use the data to understand livability issues and guide policy decisions.

Methodology

The comparison rankings for State Rankings 2018 are determined using the same methodology as we have used for the past twenty-plus years. The editors used the previously mentioned fifteen livability categories to select forty-three quality of life factors from a broad range of economic, educational, health-oriented, public safety, and environmental statistics. Overall comparison rankings were determined by averaging each state's ranking for each category. The scale is one to fifty, the higher the number, the higher the state is in the rankings (i.e., 50 is the best score to receive). Data used are for the most recent year for which comparable numbers are available from most states. All factors are given equal weight.

While the 566 tables provided in *State Rankings 2018* are ranked highest to lowest without any subjective determination as to whether a subject is "positive" or "negative," for the state comparison rankings, the editors do make a subjective determination as to whether something is "positive" or "negative." Twenty-five of the forty-three factors were determined to be negative, and the remaining eighteen were viewed as positive.

The reason for this division between positive and negative is that if a state ranks first in crime rate (i.e., it has the highest crime rate), its comparison ranking is reduced. Whereas if a state ranks first in per-capita personal income (i.e., it has the highest income), its comparison ranking is increased. To account for this, we subtract the rankings for the positive factors from 51 so that a state with the highest ranking in a positive factor ends up with a 50 for that factor (remember, high numbers are best).

Once we have chosen the factors and divided them into positive and negative groupings, we simply average the ranking for each state in all forty-three factors. If a state is missing data for a given factor, its standing is based on the average ranking for the remaining factors. The book uses the latest available data for each livability factor.

As an example, Maine ranks 49th in crime rate (negative factor), 46th in personal bankruptcy rate (negative factor), and ranks 7th in percent of population graduated from high school (positive factor). The 49th and 46th rankings go straight into the comparison formula, whereas the number seven ranking in percent of population graduated from high school is first subtracted from 51 with the resulting 44 going into the ranking. For these three factors for Maine, we would average 49, 46, and 44 with the result being 46.33. If these three factors were the only ones we used, then the resulting average of 46.33 would be the figure we would use to compare Maine to the other forty-nine states. However, for the *State Rankings* comparison rankings, an additional forty factors are added into the calculations before the final results are determined.

Designed with the researcher in mind, the numbers shown in *State Rankings* require no additional calculations to convert them from millions, thousands, and so on. All states are ranked on a high-to-low basis, with any ties among the states listed alphabetically for a given ranking. Negative numbers are shown in parentheses. For tables displaying national totals (as opposed to rates, per capita, etc.), a separate column is included that shows what percent of the national total each individual state's total represents. This column is headed by "% of USA." This percentage figure is particularly interesting when compared with a state's population in a given year. Rates may be per 10,000 persons, per 100,000 persons, or per some other denominator; these are clearly explained by the text following the national rate and, if necessary, the footnotes.

To further assist readers, source information and footnotes clearly are shown at the bottom of each page, while national totals, rates, and percentages are prominently displayed at the top of each table. Every other line is shaded in gray for easier reading. Numerous information-finding tools are provided: a thorough table of contents, table listings at the beginning of each chapter, and a detailed index. In addition, a roster of sources with addresses, phone numbers, and websites is found in the back of the book.

About the Editors

Kathleen O'Leary Morgan and **Scott Morgan** founded Morgan Quitno Press in 1990. They edited more than 2,700 annual state and city statistical reference publications before selling the titles to CQ Press in 2007. They also edited a monthly journal, *State Statistical Trends*, for six years. They have continued to edit a number of the publications continued by CQ Press, as well as an ever-growing online database.

Kathleen received a BS and a master's in Public Administration from the University of Kansas. She served in a number of media and legislative positions within the U.S. Department of Transportation, where she also served as deputy director of congressional affairs.

Scott received both a BS and a law degree from the University of Kansas. He previously worked on the staffs of two U.S. senators as well as the Senate Judiciary Committee. He represented the Senate on the Federal Election Commission and served as Chief Counsel for Senator Bob Dole's presidential campaign in 1988. He was Chief Counsel for Governor Mike Hayden in Kansas until 1990.

The 2018 State Rankings

RANK	STATE	AVG	17 RANK	CHANGE
44	Alabama	19.70	46	2
36	Alaska	22.88	36	0
40	Arizona	21.00	40	0
42	Arkansas	20.79	45	3
20	California	26.67	26	6
11	Colorado	29.26	10	-1
10	Connecticut	29.67	12	2
34	Delaware	23.07	25	-9
32	Florida	24.28	33	1
38	Georgia	22.40	37	-1
15	Hawaii	28.28	21	6
23	Idaho	25.42	23	0
32	Illinois	24.28	24	-8
29	Indiana	24.58	34	5
5	Iowa	31.47	5	0
17	Kansas	27.81	18	1
46	Kentucky	17.84	44	-2
50	Louisiana	15.84	50	0
9	Maine	30.16	13	4
12	Maryland	29.16	19	7
4	Massachusetts	32.67	4	0
27	Michigan	25.02	22	-5
2	Minnesota	34.21	2	0
47	Mississippi	17.70	49	2
30	Missouri	24.51	27	-3
26	Montana	25.23	28	2
7	Nebraska	31.05	7	0
43	Nevada	20.40	43	0
1	New Hampshire	36.05	1	0
8	New Jersey	30.23	9	1
48	New Mexico	17.53	47	-1
25	New York	25.33	30	5
39	North Carolina	22.33	39	0
18	North Dakota	27.67	8	-10
35	Ohio	23.05	35	0
45	Oklahoma	19.09	42	-3
28	Oregon	24.86	28	0
22	Pennsylvania	25.47	32	10
24	Rhode Island	25.37	20	-4
41	South Carolina	20.81	41	0
21	South Dakota	25.60	11	-10
37	Tennessee	22.65	38	1
31	Texas	24.35	31	0
3	Utah	33.21	6	3
6	Vermont	31.30	3	-3
19	Virginia	27.26	17	-2
14	Washington	28.79	16	2
49	West Virginia	17.47	48	-1
13	Wisconsin	28.88	14	1
15	Wyoming	28.28	15	0

RANK	STATE	AVG	17 RANK	CHANGE
1	New Hampshire	36.05	1	0
2	Minnesota	34.21	2	0
3	Utah	33.21	6	3
4	Massachusetts	32.67	4	0
5	Iowa	31.47	5	0
6	Vermont	31.30	3	-3
7	Nebraska	31.05	7	0
8	New Jersey	30.23	9	1
9	Maine	30.16	13	4
10	Connecticut	29.67	12	2
11	Colorado	29.26	10	-1
12	Maryland	29.16	19	7
13	Wisconsin	28.88	14	1
14	Washington	28.79	16	2
15	Hawaii	28.28	21	6
15	Wyoming	28.28	15	0
17	Kansas	27.81	18	1
18	North Dakota	27.67	8	-10
19	Virginia	27.26	17	-2
20	California	26.67	26	6
21	South Dakota	25.60	11	-10
22	Pennsylvania	25.47	32	10
23	Idaho	25.42	23	0
24	Rhode Island	25.37	20	-4
25	New York	25.33	30	5
26	Montana	25.23	28	2
27	Michigan	25.02	22	-5
28	Oregon	24.86	28	0
29	Indiana	24.58	34	5
30	Missouri	24.51	27	-3
31	Texas	24.35	31	0
32	Florida	24.28	33	1
32	Illinois	24.28	24	-8
34	Delaware	23.07	25	-9
35	Ohio	23.05	35	0
36	Alaska	22.88	36	0
37	Tennessee	22.65	38	1
38	Georgia	22.40	37	-1
39	North Carolina	22.33	39	0
40	Arizona	21.00	40	0
41	South Carolina	20.81	41	0
42	Arkansas	20.79	45	3
43	Nevada	20.40	43	0
44	Alabama	19.70	46	2
45	Oklahoma	19.09	42	-3
46	Kentucky	17.84	44	-2
47	Mississippi	17.70	49	2
48	New Mexico	17.53	47	-1
49	West Virginia	17.47	48	-1
50	Louisiana	15.84	50	0

Date Each State Admitted to Statehood*

ALPHA ORDER

RANK	STATE	DATE OF ADMISSION
22	Alabama	December 14, 1819
49	Alaska	January 3, 1959
48	Arizona	February 14, 1912
25	Arkansas	June 15, 1836
31	California	September 9, 1850
38	Colorado	August 1, 1876
5	Connecticut	January 9, 1788
1	Delaware	December 7, 1787
27	Florida	March 3, 1845
4	Georgia	January 2, 1788
50	Hawaii	August 21, 1959
43	Idaho	July 3, 1890
21	Illinois	December 3, 1818
19	Indiana	December 11, 1816
29	Iowa	December 28, 1846
34	Kansas	January 29, 1861
15	Kentucky	June 1, 1792
18	Louisiana	April 30, 1812
23	Maine	March 15, 1820
7	Maryland	April 28, 1788
6	Massachusetts	February 6, 1788
26	Michigan	January 26, 1837
32	Minnesota	May 11, 1858
20	Mississippi	December 10, 1817
24	Missouri	August 10, 1821
41	Montana	November 8, 1889
37	Nebraska	March 1, 1867
36	Nevada	October 31, 1864
9	New Hampshire	June 21, 1788
3	New Jersey	December 18, 1787
47	New Mexico	January 6, 1912
11	New York	July 26, 1788
12	North Carolina	November 21, 1789
39	North Dakota	November 2, 1889
17	Ohio	March 1, 1803
46	Oklahoma	November 16, 1907
33	Oregon	February 14, 1859
2	Pennsylvania	December 12, 1787
13	Rhode Island	May 29, 1790
8	South Carolina	May 23, 1788
39	South Dakota	November 2, 1889
16	Tennessee	June 1, 1796
28	Texas	December 29, 1845
45	Utah	January 4, 1896
14	Vermont	March 4, 1791
10	Virginia	June 26, 1788
42	Washington	November 11, 1889
35	West Virginia	June 20, 1863
30	Wisconsin	May 29, 1848
44	Wyoming	July 10, 1890

RANK ORDER

RANK	STATE	DATE OF ADMISSION
1	Delaware	December 7, 1787
2	Pennsylvania	December 12, 1787
3	New Jersey	December 18, 1787
4	Georgia	January 2, 1788
5	Connecticut	January 9, 1788
6	Massachusetts	February 6, 1788
7	Maryland	April 28, 1788
8	South Carolina	May 23, 1788
9	New Hampshire	June 21, 1788
10	Virginia	June 26, 1788
11	New York	July 26, 1788
12	North Carolina	November 21, 1789
13	Rhode Island	May 29, 1790
14	Vermont	March 4, 1791
15	Kentucky	June 1, 1792
16	Tennessee	June 1, 1796
17	Ohio	March 1, 1803
18	Louisiana	April 30, 1812
19	Indiana	December 11, 1816
20	Mississippi	December 10, 1817
21	Illinois	December 3, 1818
22	Alabama	December 14, 1819
23	Maine	March 15, 1820
24	Missouri	August 10, 1821
25	Arkansas	June 15, 1836
26	Michigan	January 26, 1837
27	Florida	March 3, 1845
28	Texas	December 29, 1845
29	Iowa	December 28, 1846
30	Wisconsin	May 29, 1848
31	California	September 9, 1850
32	Minnesota	May 11, 1858
33	Oregon	February 14, 1859
34	Kansas	January 29, 1861
35	West Virginia	June 20, 1863
36	Nevada	October 31, 1864
37	Nebraska	March 1, 1867
38	Colorado	August 1, 1876
39	North Dakota	November 2, 1889
39	South Dakota	November 2, 1889
41	Montana	November 8, 1889
42	Washington	November 11, 1889
43	Idaho	July 3, 1890
44	Wyoming	July 10, 1890
45	Utah	January 4, 1896
46	Oklahoma	November 16, 1907
47	New Mexico	January 6, 1912
48	Arizona	February 14, 1912
49	Alaska	January 3, 1959
50	Hawaii	August 21, 1959

Source: U.S. Bureau of the Census
   "1980 Census of Population" (vol. 1, part A, PC80-1-A)
*First thirteen states show date of ratification of Constitution.

STATE FAST FACTS

STATE	NICKNAME	CAPITAL	POPULATION*	AREA**
Alabama	Heart of Dixie	Montgomery	4,874,747	52,420
Alaska	The Last Frontier	Juneau	739,795	665,384
Arizona	Grand Canyon State	Phoenix	7,016,270	113,990
Arkansas	The Natural State	Little Rock	3,004,279	53,179
California	Golden State	Sacramento	39,536,653	163,695
Colorado	Centennial State	Denver	5,607,154	104,094
Connecticut	Constitution State	Hartford	3,588,184	5,543
Delaware	First State	Dover	961,939	2,489
Florida	Sunshine State	Tallahassee	20,984,400	65,758
Georgia	Peach State	Atlanta	10,429,379	59,425
Hawaii	Aloha State	Honolulu	1,427,538	10,932
Idaho	Gem State	Boise	1,716,943	83,569
Illinois	Land of Lincoln	Springfield	12,802,023	57,914
Indiana	Hoosier State	Indianapolis	6,666,818	36,420
Iowa	Hawkeye State	Des Moines	3,145,711	56,273
Kansas	Sunflower State	Topeka	2,913,123	82,278
Kentucky	Bluegrass State	Frankfort	4,454,189	40,408
Louisiana	Pelican State	Baton Rouge	4,684,333	52,378
Maine	Pine Tree State	Augusta	1,335,907	35,380
Maryland	Free State	Annapolis	6,052,177	12,406
Massachusetts	Bay State	Boston	6,859,819	10,554
Michigan	Great Lake State	Lansing	9,962,311	96,714
Minnesota	North Star State	St. Paul	5,576,606	86,936
Mississippi	Magnolia State	Jackson	2,984,100	48,432
Missouri	Show Me State	Jefferson City	6,113,532	69,707
Montana	Treasure State	Helena	1,050,493	147,040
Nebraska	Cornhusker State	Lincoln	1,920,076	77,348
Nevada	Silver State	Carson City	2,998,039	110,572
New Hampshire	Granite State	Concord	1,342,795	9,349
New Jersey	Garden State	Trenton	9,005,644	8,723
New Mexico	Land of Enchantment	Santa Fe	2,088,070	121,590
New York	Empire State	Albany	19,849,399	54,555
North Carolina	Tar Heel State	Raleigh	10,273,419	53,819
North Dakota	Peace Garden State	Bismarck	755,393	70,698
Ohio	Buckeye State	Columbus	11,658,609	44,826
Oklahoma	Sooner State	Oklahoma City	3,930,864	69,899
Oregon	Beaver State	Salem	4,142,776	98,379
Pennsylvania	Keystone State	Harrisburg	12,805,537	46,054
Rhode Island	Ocean State	Providence	1,059,639	1,545
South Carolina	Palmetto State	Columbia	5,024,369	32,020
South Dakota	Mount Rushmore State	Pierre	869,666	77,116
Tennessee	Volunteer State	Nashville	6,715,984	42,144
Texas	Lone Star State	Austin	28,304,596	268,596
Utah	Beehive State	Salt Lake City	3,101,833	84,897
Vermont	Green Mountain State	Montpelier	623,657	9,616
Virginia	Old Dominion	Richmond	8,470,020	42,775
Washington	Evergreen State	Olympia	7,405,743	71,298
West Virginia	Mountain State	Charleston	1,815,857	24,230
Wisconsin	Badger State	Madison	5,795,483	65,496
Wyoming	Equality State	Cheyenne	579,315	97,813

*U.S. Bureau of the Census, "Population Estimates" (December 2017, http://www.census.gov/programs-surveys/popest.html)
**Total of land and water area in square miles.

STATE SONG	STATE FLOWER	STATE TREE	STATE BIRD
Alabama	Camellia	Southern Pine	Yellowhammer
Alaska's Flag	Forget-Me-Not	Sitka Spruce	Willow Ptarmigan
Arizona	Saguaro Cactus Blossom	Palo Verde	Cactus Wren
Arkansas	Apple Blossom	Pine	Mockingbird
I Love You, California	Golden Poppy	California Redwood	California Valley Quail
Where the Columbines Grow	Rocky Mountain Columbine	Colorado Blue Spruce	Lark Bunting
Yankee Doodle Dandy	Mountain Laurel	White Oak	American Robin
Our Delaware	Peach Blossom	American Holly	Blue Hen Chicken
Swanee River	Orange Blossom	Sabal Palmetto Palm	Mockingbird
Georgia On My Mind	Cherokee Rose	Live Oak	Brown Thrasher
Hawaii Ponoi	Yellow Hibiscus	Candlenut	Nene
Here We Have Idaho	Syringa	White Pine	Mountain Bluebird
Illinois	Purple Violet	White Oak	Cardinal
On the Banks of the Wabash, Far Away	Peony	Tulip Poplar	Cardinal
The Song of Iowa	Wild Rose	Oak	Eastern Goldfinch
Home on the Range	Sunflower	Cottonwood	Western Meadowlark
My Old Kentucky Home	Goldenrod	Tulip Tree	Cardinal
Give Me Louisiana	Magnolia	Cypress	Eastern Brown Pelican
State of Maine Song	White Pine Cone and Tassel	Eastern White Pine	Chickadee
Maryland, My Maryland	Black-eyed Susan	White Oak	Baltimore Oriole
All Hail to Massachusetts	Mayflower	American Elm	Chickadee
Michigan, My Michigan	Apple Blossom	White Pine	Robin
Hail! Minnesota	Pink and White Lady's Slipper	Red Pine	Common Loon
Go, Mississippi!	Magnolia	Magnolia	Mockingbird
Missouri Waltz	Hawthorn	Dogwood	Bluebird
Montana	Bitterroot	Ponderosa Pine	Western Meadowlark
Beautiful Nebraska	Goldenrod	Cottonwood	Western Meadowlark
Home Means Nevada	Sagebrush	Single-Leaf Pinon	Mountain Bluebird
Old New Hampshire	Purple Lilac	White Birch	Purple Finch
Ode to New Jersey	Purple Violet	Red Oak	Eastern Goldfinch
O Fair New Mexico	Yucca	Pinon	Roadrunner
I Love New York	Rose	Sugar Maple	Bluebird
The Old North State	Dogwood	Pine	Cardinal
North Dakota Hymn	Wild Prairie Rose	American Elm	Western Meadowlark
Beautiful Ohio	Scarlet Carnation	Buckeye	Cardinal
Oklahoma!	Mistletoe	Redbud	Scissortailed Flycatcher
Oregon, My Oregon	Oregon Grape	Douglas Fir	Western Meadowlark
Hail! Pennsylvania	Mountain Laurel	Hemlock	Ruffed Grouse
Rhode Island	Violet	Red Maple	Rhode Island Red
Carolina	Yellow Jessamine	Palmetto	Carolina Wren
Hail, South Dakota	Pasque Flower	Black Hills Spruce	Ringnecked Pheasant
The Tennessee Waltz	Iris	Tulip Poplar	Mockingbird
Texas, Our Texas	Bluebonnet	Pecan	Mockingbird
Utah, We Love Thee	Sego Lily	Blue Spruce	Seagull
Hail, Vermont	Red Clover	Sugar Maple	Hermit Thrush
Carry Me Back to Old Virginia	Dogwood	Dogwood	Cardinal
Washington, My Home	Western Rhododendron	Western Hemlock	Willow Goldfinch
The West Virginia Hills; This Is My West Virginia; and West Virginia, My Home, Sweet Home	Big Rhododendron	Sugar Maple	Cardinal
On Wisconsin!	Wood Violet	Sugar Maple	Robin
Wyoming	Indian Paintbrush	Cottonwood	Meadowlark

I. Agriculture

Number of Farms in 2016

National Total = 2,060,000 Farms*

ALPHA ORDER					RANK ORDER			
RANK	STATE		FARMS	% of USA	RANK	STATE	FARMS	% of USA
20	Alabama		44,000	2.1%	1	Texas	241,500	11.7%
50	Alaska		760	0.0%	2	Missouri	96,800	4.7%
36	Arizona		19,600	1.0%	3	Iowa	87,000	4.2%
21	Arkansas		43,000	2.1%	4	Oklahoma	78,100	3.8%
5	California		76,700	3.7%	5	California	76,700	3.7%
27	Colorado		33,800	1.6%	6	Kentucky	76,000	3.7%
45	Connecticut		6,000	0.3%	7	Ohio	74,500	3.6%
48	Delaware		2,500	0.1%	8	Minnesota	73,300	3.6%
18	Florida		47,100	2.3%	9	Illinois	72,200	3.5%
22	Georgia		41,800	2.0%	10	Wisconsin	68,700	3.3%
44	Hawaii		7,000	0.3%	11	Tennessee	66,600	3.2%
34	Idaho		24,300	1.2%	12	Kansas	59,600	2.9%
9	Illinois		72,200	3.5%	13	Pennsylvania	58,200	2.8%
14	Indiana		57,500	2.8%	14	Indiana	57,500	2.8%
3	Iowa		87,000	4.2%	15	Michigan	51,400	2.5%
12	Kansas		59,600	2.9%	16	Nebraska	48,400	2.3%
6	Kentucky		76,000	3.7%	17	North Carolina	48,000	2.3%
31	Louisiana		26,900	1.3%	18	Florida	47,100	2.3%
41	Maine		8,200	0.4%	19	Virginia	44,800	2.2%
38	Maryland		12,300	0.6%	20	Alabama	44,000	2.1%
42	Massachusetts		7,800	0.4%	21	Arkansas	43,000	2.1%
15	Michigan		51,400	2.5%	22	Georgia	41,800	2.0%
8	Minnesota		73,300	3.6%	23	Mississippi	36,200	1.8%
23	Mississippi		36,200	1.8%	24	Washington	35,900	1.7%
2	Missouri		96,800	4.7%	25	New York	35,500	1.7%
30	Montana		27,400	1.3%	26	Oregon	34,400	1.7%
16	Nebraska		48,400	2.3%	27	Colorado	33,800	1.6%
47	Nevada		4,000	0.2%	28	South Dakota	31,000	1.5%
46	New Hampshire		4,400	0.2%	29	North Dakota	29,800	1.4%
40	New Jersey		9,100	0.4%	30	Montana	27,400	1.3%
32	New Mexico		24,600	1.2%	31	Louisiana	26,900	1.3%
25	New York		35,500	1.7%	32	New Mexico	24,600	1.2%
17	North Carolina		48,000	2.3%	33	South Carolina	24,500	1.2%
29	North Dakota		29,800	1.4%	34	Idaho	24,300	1.2%
7	Ohio		74,500	3.6%	35	West Virginia	20,600	1.0%
4	Oklahoma		78,100	3.8%	36	Arizona	19,600	1.0%
26	Oregon		34,400	1.7%	37	Utah	18,100	0.9%
13	Pennsylvania		58,200	2.8%	38	Maryland	12,300	0.6%
49	Rhode Island		1,240	0.1%	39	Wyoming	11,600	0.6%
33	South Carolina		24,500	1.2%	40	New Jersey	9,100	0.4%
28	South Dakota		31,000	1.5%	41	Maine	8,200	0.4%
11	Tennessee		66,600	3.2%	42	Massachusetts	7,800	0.4%
1	Texas		241,500	11.7%	43	Vermont	7,300	0.4%
37	Utah		18,100	0.9%	44	Hawaii	7,000	0.3%
43	Vermont		7,300	0.4%	45	Connecticut	6,000	0.3%
19	Virginia		44,800	2.2%	46	New Hampshire	4,400	0.2%
24	Washington		35,900	1.7%	47	Nevada	4,000	0.2%
35	West Virginia		20,600	1.0%	48	Delaware	2,500	0.1%
10	Wisconsin		68,700	3.3%	49	Rhode Island	1,240	0.1%
39	Wyoming		11,600	0.6%	50	Alaska	760	0.0%
						District of Columbia	0	0.0%

Source: U.S. Department of Agriculture, National Agricultural Statistics Service
"Farms and Land in Farms" (http://usda.mannlib.cornell.edu/MannUsda/viewDocumentInfo.do?documentID=1259)
*A farm is any establishment from which $1,000 or more of agricultural products were sold or would normally be sold during the year. This includes places with five or more horses, except horses in boarding stables or racetracks.

Land in Farms in 2016

National Total = 911,000,000 Acres*

RANK	STATE	ACRES	% of USA
31	Alabama	8,900,000	1.0%
44	Alaska	830,000	0.1%
14	Arizona	25,900,000	2.8%
22	Arkansas	13,700,000	1.5%
16	California	25,400,000	2.8%
9	Colorado	31,700,000	3.5%
49	Connecticut	440,000	0.0%
47	Delaware	500,000	0.1%
30	Florida	9,410,000	1.0%
29	Georgia	9,500,000	1.0%
43	Hawaii	1,120,000	0.1%
24	Idaho	11,800,000	1.3%
13	Illinois	26,700,000	2.9%
18	Indiana	14,700,000	1.6%
10	Iowa	30,500,000	3.3%
3	Kansas	45,900,000	5.0%
23	Kentucky	12,900,000	1.4%
34	Louisiana	7,750,000	0.9%
41	Maine	1,450,000	0.2%
40	Maryland	2,030,000	0.2%
46	Massachusetts	520,000	0.1%
28	Michigan	9,950,000	1.1%
14	Minnesota	25,900,000	2.8%
27	Mississippi	10,700,000	1.2%
12	Missouri	28,500,000	3.1%
2	Montana	59,700,000	6.6%
4	Nebraska	45,200,000	5.0%
37	Nevada	5,960,000	0.7%
48	New Hampshire	470,000	0.1%
45	New Jersey	720,000	0.1%
6	New Mexico	43,200,000	4.7%
36	New York	7,300,000	0.8%
32	North Carolina	8,200,000	0.9%
7	North Dakota	39,100,000	4.3%
21	Ohio	14,000,000	1.5%
8	Oklahoma	34,200,000	3.8%
17	Oregon	16,300,000	1.8%
35	Pennsylvania	7,630,000	0.8%
50	Rhode Island	70,000	0.0%
38	South Carolina	5,000,000	0.5%
5	South Dakota	43,300,000	4.8%
26	Tennessee	10,800,000	1.2%
1	Texas	129,800,000	14.2%
25	Utah	11,000,000	1.2%
42	Vermont	1,250,000	0.1%
33	Virginia	8,100,000	0.9%
18	Washington	14,700,000	1.6%
39	West Virginia	3,600,000	0.4%
20	Wisconsin	14,400,000	1.6%
11	Wyoming	30,300,000	3.3%

RANK	STATE	ACRES	% of USA
1	Texas	129,800,000	14.2%
2	Montana	59,700,000	6.6%
3	Kansas	45,900,000	5.0%
4	Nebraska	45,200,000	5.0%
5	South Dakota	43,300,000	4.8%
6	New Mexico	43,200,000	4.7%
7	North Dakota	39,100,000	4.3%
8	Oklahoma	34,200,000	3.8%
9	Colorado	31,700,000	3.5%
10	Iowa	30,500,000	3.3%
11	Wyoming	30,300,000	3.3%
12	Missouri	28,500,000	3.1%
13	Illinois	26,700,000	2.9%
14	Arizona	25,900,000	2.8%
14	Minnesota	25,900,000	2.8%
16	California	25,400,000	2.8%
17	Oregon	16,300,000	1.8%
18	Indiana	14,700,000	1.6%
18	Washington	14,700,000	1.6%
20	Wisconsin	14,400,000	1.6%
21	Ohio	14,000,000	1.5%
22	Arkansas	13,700,000	1.5%
23	Kentucky	12,900,000	1.4%
24	Idaho	11,800,000	1.3%
25	Utah	11,000,000	1.2%
26	Tennessee	10,800,000	1.2%
27	Mississippi	10,700,000	1.2%
28	Michigan	9,950,000	1.1%
29	Georgia	9,500,000	1.0%
30	Florida	9,410,000	1.0%
31	Alabama	8,900,000	1.0%
32	North Carolina	8,200,000	0.9%
33	Virginia	8,100,000	0.9%
34	Louisiana	7,750,000	0.9%
35	Pennsylvania	7,630,000	0.8%
36	New York	7,300,000	0.8%
37	Nevada	5,960,000	0.7%
38	South Carolina	5,000,000	0.5%
39	West Virginia	3,600,000	0.4%
40	Maryland	2,030,000	0.2%
41	Maine	1,450,000	0.2%
42	Vermont	1,250,000	0.1%
43	Hawaii	1,120,000	0.1%
44	Alaska	830,000	0.1%
45	New Jersey	720,000	0.1%
46	Massachusetts	520,000	0.1%
47	Delaware	500,000	0.1%
48	New Hampshire	470,000	0.1%
49	Connecticut	440,000	0.0%
50	Rhode Island	70,000	0.0%
	District of Columbia	0	0.0%

Source: U.S. Department of Agriculture, National Agricultural Statistics Service
"Farms and Land in Farms" (http://usda.mannlib.cornell.edu/MannUsda/viewDocumentInfo.do?documentID=1259)
*A farm is any establishment from which $1,000 or more of agricultural products were sold or would normally be sold during the year. This includes places with five or more horses, except horses in boarding stables or racetracks.

Average Number of Acres per Farm in 2016

National Average = 442 Acres*

ALPHA ORDER

RANK	STATE	ACRES
31	Alabama	202
8	Alaska	1,092
6	Arizona	1,321
22	Arkansas	319
21	California	331
9	Colorado	938
48	Connecticut	73
32	Delaware	200
32	Florida	200
27	Georgia	227
44	Hawaii	160
14	Idaho	486
18	Illinois	370
26	Indiana	256
20	Iowa	351
11	Kansas	770
41	Kentucky	170
25	Louisiana	288
37	Maine	177
42	Maryland	165
49	Massachusetts	67
34	Michigan	194
19	Minnesota	353
23	Mississippi	296
24	Missouri	294
2	Montana	2,179
10	Nebraska	934
4	Nevada	1,490
46	New Hampshire	107
47	New Jersey	79
3	New Mexico	1,756
29	New York	206
39	North Carolina	171
7	North Dakota	1,312
35	Ohio	188
16	Oklahoma	438
15	Oregon	474
45	Pennsylvania	131
50	Rhode Island	56
30	South Carolina	204
5	South Dakota	1,397
43	Tennessee	162
13	Texas	537
12	Utah	608
39	Vermont	171
36	Virginia	181
17	Washington	409
38	West Virginia	175
28	Wisconsin	210
1	Wyoming	2,612

RANK ORDER

RANK	STATE	ACRES
1	Wyoming	2,612
2	Montana	2,179
3	New Mexico	1,756
4	Nevada	1,490
5	South Dakota	1,397
6	Arizona	1,321
7	North Dakota	1,312
8	Alaska	1,092
9	Colorado	938
10	Nebraska	934
11	Kansas	770
12	Utah	608
13	Texas	537
14	Idaho	486
15	Oregon	474
16	Oklahoma	438
17	Washington	409
18	Illinois	370
19	Minnesota	353
20	Iowa	351
21	California	331
22	Arkansas	319
23	Mississippi	296
24	Missouri	294
25	Louisiana	288
26	Indiana	256
27	Georgia	227
28	Wisconsin	210
29	New York	206
30	South Carolina	204
31	Alabama	202
32	Delaware	200
32	Florida	200
34	Michigan	194
35	Ohio	188
36	Virginia	181
37	Maine	177
38	West Virginia	175
39	North Carolina	171
39	Vermont	171
41	Kentucky	170
42	Maryland	165
43	Tennessee	162
44	Hawaii	160
45	Pennsylvania	131
46	New Hampshire	107
47	New Jersey	79
48	Connecticut	73
49	Massachusetts	67
50	Rhode Island	56
	District of Columbia	0

Source: U.S. Department of Agriculture, National Agricultural Statistics Service
"Farms and Land in Farms" (http://usda.mannlib.cornell.edu/MannUsda/viewDocumentInfo.do?documentID=1259)
*A farm is any establishment from which $1,000 or more of agricultural products were sold or would normally be sold during the year. This includes places with five or more horses, except horses in boarding stables or racetracks.

Average per-Acre Value of Farmland in 2017

National Average = $3,080 per Acre*

ALPHA ORDER			RANK ORDER		
RANK	STATE	PER-ACRE VALUE	RANK	STATE	PER-ACRE VALUE
32	Alabama	$2,750	1	Rhode Island	$13,800
NA	Alaska**	NA	2	New Jersey	12,800
20	Arizona	4,100	3	Connecticut	11,200
26	Arkansas	3,180	4	Massachusetts	10,400
5	California	8,700	5	California	8,700
44	Colorado	1,430	6	Delaware	8,400
3	Connecticut	11,200	7	Iowa	8,000
6	Delaware	8,400	8	Illinois	7,300
11	Florida	5,700	9	Maryland	7,060
22	Georgia	3,550	10	Indiana	7,000
NA	Hawaii**	NA	11	Florida	5,700
33	Idaho	2,600	12	Ohio	5,650
8	Illinois	7,300	13	Pennsylvania	5,600
10	Indiana	7,000	14	Wisconsin	5,200
7	Iowa	8,000	15	Michigan	4,800
42	Kansas	1,850	16	Minnesota	4,750
23	Kentucky	3,420	17	New Hampshire	4,500
27	Louisiana	3,000	18	North Carolina	4,450
37	Maine	2,200	19	Virginia	4,350
9	Maryland	7,060	20	Arizona	4,100
4	Massachusetts	10,400	21	Tennessee	3,750
15	Michigan	4,800	22	Georgia	3,550
16	Minnesota	4,750	23	Kentucky	3,420
35	Mississippi	2,500	24	Vermont	3,360
25	Missouri	3,350	25	Missouri	3,350
46	Montana	920	26	Arkansas	3,180
31	Nebraska	2,900	27	Louisiana	3,000
45	Nevada	1,110	27	South Carolina	3,000
17	New Hampshire	4,500	27	Washington	3,000
2	New Jersey	12,800	30	New York	2,980
48	New Mexico	530	31	Nebraska	2,900
30	New York	2,980	32	Alabama	2,750
18	North Carolina	4,450	33	Idaho	2,600
43	North Dakota	1,840	34	West Virginia	2,570
12	Ohio	5,650	35	Mississippi	2,500
41	Oklahoma	1,900	36	Oregon	2,310
36	Oregon	2,310	37	Maine	2,200
13	Pennsylvania	5,600	38	South Dakota	2,180
1	Rhode Island	13,800	39	Texas	2,090
27	South Carolina	3,000	40	Utah	2,070
38	South Dakota	2,180	41	Oklahoma	1,900
21	Tennessee	3,750	42	Kansas	1,850
39	Texas	2,090	43	North Dakota	1,840
40	Utah	2,070	44	Colorado	1,430
24	Vermont	3,360	45	Nevada	1,110
19	Virginia	4,350	46	Montana	920
27	Washington	3,000	47	Wyoming	660
34	West Virginia	2,570	48	New Mexico	530
14	Wisconsin	5,200	NA	Alaska**	NA
47	Wyoming	660	NA	Hawaii**	NA
				District of Columbia**	NA

Source: U.S. Department of Agriculture, National Agricultural Statistics Service
   "Land Values and Cash Rents" (http://usda.mannlib.cornell.edu/MannUsda/viewDocumentInfo.do?documentID=1446)
*Value of farmland and buildings in nominal dollars.
**Not applicable or available.

Percent Change in Average per-Acre Value of Farmland: 2016 to 2017

National Percent Change = 2.3% Increase*

ALPHA ORDER

RANK	STATE	PERCENT CHANGE
19	Alabama	1.9
NA	Alaska**	NA
3	Arizona	7.9
11	Arkansas	4.3
1	California	10.1
34	Colorado	0.7
36	Connecticut	0.0
36	Delaware	0.0
5	Florida	5.6
10	Georgia	4.4
NA	Hawaii**	NA
12	Idaho	4.0
27	Illinois	1.4
17	Indiana	2.1
19	Iowa	1.9
24	Kansas	1.6
17	Kentucky	2.1
13	Louisiana	3.4
7	Maine	5.3
36	Maryland	0.0
36	Massachusetts	0.0
36	Michigan	0.0
32	Minnesota	1.1
29	Mississippi	1.2
25	Missouri	1.5
16	Montana	2.2
23	Nebraska	1.7
36	Nevada	0.0
13	New Hampshire	3.4
36	New Jersey	0.0
19	New Mexico	1.9
36	New York	0.0
36	North Carolina	0.0
35	North Dakota	0.5
33	Ohio	0.9
5	Oklahoma	5.6
9	Oregon	5.0
22	Pennsylvania	1.8
36	Rhode Island	0.0
36	South Carolina	0.0
15	South Dakota	3.1
27	Tennessee	1.4
4	Texas	6.6
25	Utah	1.5
29	Vermont	1.2
29	Virginia	1.2
7	Washington	5.3
36	West Virginia	0.0
2	Wisconsin	9.5
36	Wyoming	0.0

RANK ORDER

RANK	STATE	PERCENT CHANGE
1	California	10.1
2	Wisconsin	9.5
3	Arizona	7.9
4	Texas	6.6
5	Florida	5.6
5	Oklahoma	5.6
7	Maine	5.3
7	Washington	5.3
9	Oregon	5.0
10	Georgia	4.4
11	Arkansas	4.3
12	Idaho	4.0
13	Louisiana	3.4
13	New Hampshire	3.4
15	South Dakota	3.1
16	Montana	2.2
17	Indiana	2.1
17	Kentucky	2.1
19	Alabama	1.9
19	Iowa	1.9
19	New Mexico	1.9
22	Pennsylvania	1.8
23	Nebraska	1.7
24	Kansas	1.6
25	Missouri	1.5
25	Utah	1.5
27	Illinois	1.4
27	Tennessee	1.4
29	Mississippi	1.2
29	Vermont	1.2
29	Virginia	1.2
32	Minnesota	1.1
33	Ohio	0.9
34	Colorado	0.7
35	North Dakota	0.5
36	Connecticut	0.0
36	Delaware	0.0
36	Maryland	0.0
36	Massachusetts	0.0
36	Michigan	0.0
36	Nevada	0.0
36	New Jersey	0.0
36	New York	0.0
36	North Carolina	0.0
36	Rhode Island	0.0
36	South Carolina	0.0
36	West Virginia	0.0
36	Wyoming	0.0
NA	Alaska**	NA
NA	Hawaii**	NA
	District of Columbia**	NA

Source: U.S. Department of Agriculture, National Agricultural Statistics Service
 "Land Values and Cash Rents" (http://usda.mannlib.cornell.edu/MannUsda/viewDocumentInfo.do?documentID=1446)
*Value of farmland and buildings in nominal dollars.
**Not applicable or available.

Net Farm Income in 2016

National Total = $61,525,439,000*

ALPHA ORDER

RANK	STATE	FARM INCOME	% of USA
22	Alabama	$933,614,000	1.5%
47	Alaska	(947,000)	0.0%
15	Arizona	1,416,705,000	2.3%
24	Arkansas	860,532,000	1.4%
1	California	13,894,461,000	22.6%
19	Colorado	1,098,620,000	1.8%
48	Connecticut	(4,839,000)	0.0%
33	Delaware	351,833,000	0.6%
9	Florida	2,063,448,000	3.4%
10	Georgia	1,814,872,000	2.9%
44	Hawaii	36,758,000	0.1%
11	Idaho	1,666,566,000	2.7%
7	Illinois	2,272,999,000	3.7%
14	Indiana	1,467,127,000	2.4%
5	Iowa	2,560,606,000	4.2%
8	Kansas	2,235,135,000	3.6%
20	Kentucky	996,883,000	1.6%
30	Louisiana	595,458,000	1.0%
49	Maine	(61,047,000)	0.0%
32	Maryland	362,606,000	0.6%
50	Massachusetts	(68,271,000)	0.0%
42	Michigan	54,290,000	0.1%
17	Minnesota	1,237,699,000	2.0%
26	Mississippi	751,268,000	1.2%
13	Missouri	1,533,232,000	2.5%
27	Montana	735,866,000	1.2%
2	Nebraska	3,784,464,000	6.2%
41	Nevada	76,071,000	0.1%
43	New Hampshire	51,371,000	0.1%
37	New Jersey	184,579,000	0.3%
25	New Mexico	797,040,000	1.3%
28	New York	723,476,000	1.2%
6	North Carolina	2,456,104,000	4.0%
21	North Dakota	937,357,000	1.5%
31	Ohio	442,274,000	0.7%
18	Oklahoma	1,213,099,000	2.0%
23	Oregon	914,984,000	1.5%
29	Pennsylvania	716,601,000	1.2%
46	Rhode Island	9,369,000	0.0%
40	South Carolina	125,178,000	0.2%
16	South Dakota	1,371,790,000	2.2%
36	Tennessee	191,861,000	0.3%
3	Texas	3,389,982,000	5.5%
34	Utah	292,127,000	0.5%
38	Vermont	169,831,000	0.3%
35	Virginia	262,379,000	0.4%
4	Washington	2,773,955,000	4.5%
45	West Virginia	36,665,000	0.1%
12	Wisconsin	1,653,061,000	2.7%
39	Wyoming	146,344,000	0.2%

RANK ORDER

RANK	STATE	FARM INCOME	% of USA
1	California	$13,894,461,000	22.6%
2	Nebraska	3,784,464,000	6.2%
3	Texas	3,389,982,000	5.5%
4	Washington	2,773,955,000	4.5%
5	Iowa	2,560,606,000	4.2%
6	North Carolina	2,456,104,000	4.0%
7	Illinois	2,272,999,000	3.7%
8	Kansas	2,235,135,000	3.6%
9	Florida	2,063,448,000	3.4%
10	Georgia	1,814,872,000	2.9%
11	Idaho	1,666,566,000	2.7%
12	Wisconsin	1,653,061,000	2.7%
13	Missouri	1,533,232,000	2.5%
14	Indiana	1,467,127,000	2.4%
15	Arizona	1,416,705,000	2.3%
16	South Dakota	1,371,790,000	2.2%
17	Minnesota	1,237,699,000	2.0%
18	Oklahoma	1,213,099,000	2.0%
19	Colorado	1,098,620,000	1.8%
20	Kentucky	996,883,000	1.6%
21	North Dakota	937,357,000	1.5%
22	Alabama	933,614,000	1.5%
23	Oregon	914,984,000	1.5%
24	Arkansas	860,532,000	1.4%
25	New Mexico	797,040,000	1.3%
26	Mississippi	751,268,000	1.2%
27	Montana	735,866,000	1.2%
28	New York	723,476,000	1.2%
29	Pennsylvania	716,601,000	1.2%
30	Louisiana	595,458,000	1.0%
31	Ohio	442,274,000	0.7%
32	Maryland	362,606,000	0.6%
33	Delaware	351,833,000	0.6%
34	Utah	292,127,000	0.5%
35	Virginia	262,379,000	0.4%
36	Tennessee	191,861,000	0.3%
37	New Jersey	184,579,000	0.3%
38	Vermont	169,831,000	0.3%
39	Wyoming	146,344,000	0.2%
40	South Carolina	125,178,000	0.2%
41	Nevada	76,071,000	0.1%
42	Michigan	54,290,000	0.1%
43	New Hampshire	51,371,000	0.1%
44	Hawaii	36,758,000	0.1%
45	West Virginia	36,665,000	0.1%
46	Rhode Island	9,369,000	0.0%
47	Alaska	(947,000)	0.0%
48	Connecticut	(4,839,000)	0.0%
49	Maine	(61,047,000)	0.0%
50	Massachusetts	(68,271,000)	0.0%
	District of Columbia	0	0.0%

Source: U.S. Department of Agriculture, Economic Research Service
"Farm Sector Financial Indicators, State Rankings"
(http://www.ers.usda.gov/data-products/farm-income-and-wealth-statistics.aspx)
*Net farm income is a measure of the net value of production in a given year. It is determined by subtracting total production expenses from gross farm income.

Net Farm Income per Operation in 2016

National Average = $30,056 per Operation*

	ALPHA ORDER			RANK ORDER	
RANK	STATE	PER OPERATION	RANK	STATE	PER OPERATION
24	Alabama	$21,210	1	California	$181,057
48	Alaska	(1,092)	2	Delaware	140,800
5	Arizona	72,655	3	Nebraska	78,456
28	Arkansas	20,097	4	Washington	77,301
1	California	181,057	5	Arizona	72,655
12	Colorado	32,830	6	Idaho	68,526
47	Connecticut	(803)	7	North Carolina	51,300
2	Delaware	140,800	8	South Dakota	44,704
9	Florida	43,800	9	Florida	43,800
10	Georgia	43,357	10	Georgia	43,357
42	Hawaii	5,280	11	Kansas	37,730
6	Idaho	68,526	12	Colorado	32,830
15	Illinois	31,450	13	New Mexico	31,608
20	Indiana	25,600	14	North Dakota	31,488
17	Iowa	29,484	15	Illinois	31,450
11	Kansas	37,730	16	Maryland	29,535
35	Kentucky	13,090	17	Iowa	29,484
23	Louisiana	22,176	18	Oregon	26,544
49	Maine	(7,434)	19	Montana	26,148
16	Maryland	29,535	20	Indiana	25,600
50	Massachusetts	(8,777)	21	Wisconsin	24,150
46	Michigan	970	22	Vermont	23,256
30	Minnesota	16,944	23	Louisiana	22,176
25	Mississippi	20,720	24	Alabama	21,210
32	Missouri	15,876	25	Mississippi	20,720
19	Montana	26,148	26	New York	20,394
3	Nebraska	78,456	27	New Jersey	20,224
29	Nevada	19,370	28	Arkansas	20,097
38	New Hampshire	11,663	29	Nevada	19,370
27	New Jersey	20,224	30	Minnesota	16,944
13	New Mexico	31,608	31	Utah	16,416
26	New York	20,394	32	Missouri	15,876
7	North Carolina	51,300	33	Oklahoma	15,330
14	North Dakota	31,488	34	Texas	13,962
40	Ohio	6,016	35	Kentucky	13,090
33	Oklahoma	15,330	36	Wyoming	13,060
18	Oregon	26,544	37	Pennsylvania	12,314
37	Pennsylvania	12,314	38	New Hampshire	11,663
39	Rhode Island	7,504	39	Rhode Island	7,504
43	South Carolina	5,100	40	Ohio	6,016
8	South Dakota	44,704	41	Virginia	5,792
44	Tennessee	2,916	42	Hawaii	5,280
34	Texas	13,962	43	South Carolina	5,100
31	Utah	16,416	44	Tennessee	2,916
22	Vermont	23,256	45	West Virginia	1,750
41	Virginia	5,792	46	Michigan	970
4	Washington	77,301	47	Connecticut	(803)
45	West Virginia	1,750	48	Alaska	(1,092)
21	Wisconsin	24,150	49	Maine	(7,434)
36	Wyoming	13,060	50	Massachusetts	(8,777)
				District of Columbia**	NA

Source: CQ Press using data from U.S. Department of Agriculture, Economic Research Service
   "Farm Sector Financial Indicators, State Rankings"
      (http://www.ers.usda.gov/data-products/farm-income-and-wealth-statistics.aspx)
*Calculated by multiplying average acres per farm by average net farm income per acre.
**Not applicable.

Net Farm Income per Acre in 2016

National Average = $68 per Acre*

ALPHA ORDER

RANK	STATE	PER ACRE
14	Alabama	$105
47	Alaska	(1)
26	Arizona	55
24	Arkansas	63
2	California	547
30	Colorado	35
48	Connecticut	(11)
1	Delaware	704
5	Florida	219
6	Georgia	191
32	Hawaii	33
9	Idaho	141
18	Illinois	85
15	Indiana	100
19	Iowa	84
28	Kansas	49
21	Kentucky	77
21	Louisiana	77
49	Maine	(42)
8	Maryland	179
50	Massachusetts	(131)
45	Michigan	5
29	Minnesota	48
23	Mississippi	70
27	Missouri	54
43	Montana	12
19	Nebraska	84
42	Nevada	13
13	New Hampshire	109
4	New Jersey	256
40	New Mexico	18
16	New York	99
3	North Carolina	300
39	North Dakota	24
33	Ohio	32
30	Oklahoma	35
25	Oregon	56
17	Pennsylvania	94
11	Rhode Island	134
38	South Carolina	25
33	South Dakota	32
40	Tennessee	18
37	Texas	26
36	Utah	27
10	Vermont	136
33	Virginia	32
7	Washington	189
44	West Virginia	10
12	Wisconsin	115
45	Wyoming	5

RANK ORDER

RANK	STATE	PER ACRE
1	Delaware	$704
2	California	547
3	North Carolina	300
4	New Jersey	256
5	Florida	219
6	Georgia	191
7	Washington	189
8	Maryland	179
9	Idaho	141
10	Vermont	136
11	Rhode Island	134
12	Wisconsin	115
13	New Hampshire	109
14	Alabama	105
15	Indiana	100
16	New York	99
17	Pennsylvania	94
18	Illinois	85
19	Iowa	84
19	Nebraska	84
21	Kentucky	77
21	Louisiana	77
23	Mississippi	70
24	Arkansas	63
25	Oregon	56
26	Arizona	55
27	Missouri	54
28	Kansas	49
29	Minnesota	48
30	Colorado	35
30	Oklahoma	35
32	Hawaii	33
33	Ohio	32
33	South Dakota	32
33	Virginia	32
36	Utah	27
37	Texas	26
38	South Carolina	25
39	North Dakota	24
40	New Mexico	18
40	Tennessee	18
42	Nevada	13
43	Montana	12
44	West Virginia	10
45	Michigan	5
45	Wyoming	5
47	Alaska	(1)
48	Connecticut	(11)
49	Maine	(42)
50	Massachusetts	(131)

District of Columbia**	NA

Source: CQ Press using data from U.S. Department of Agriculture, Economic Research Service
   "Farm Sector Financial Indicators, State Rankings"
   (http://www.ers.usda.gov/data-products/farm-income-and-wealth-statistics.aspx)
*Net farm income is a measure of the net value of production in a given year. It is determined by subtracting total production expenses from gross farm income.
**Not applicable.

Farm Income: Cash Receipts from Commodities in 2016

National Total = $356,534,369,000*

ALPHA ORDER

RANK	STATE	FARM INCOME	% of USA
27	Alabama	$4,951,074,000	1.4%
50	Alaska	33,905,000	0.0%
29	Arizona	4,155,423,000	1.2%
16	Arkansas	8,214,594,000	2.3%
1	California	46,036,034,000	12.9%
23	Colorado	6,128,719,000	1.7%
46	Connecticut	514,256,000	0.1%
39	Delaware	1,205,648,000	0.3%
18	Florida	7,743,975,000	2.2%
14	Georgia	8,430,255,000	2.4%
43	Hawaii	648,558,000	0.2%
20	Idaho	7,109,927,000	2.0%
6	Illinois	16,096,415,000	4.5%
10	Indiana	10,119,297,000	2.8%
2	Iowa	26,529,033,000	7.4%
7	Kansas	15,355,365,000	4.3%
24	Kentucky	5,443,637,000	1.5%
34	Louisiana	2,823,356,000	0.8%
45	Maine	527,730,000	0.1%
36	Maryland	2,094,248,000	0.6%
47	Massachusetts	386,878,000	0.1%
19	Michigan	7,417,038,000	2.1%
5	Minnesota	17,094,652,000	4.8%
25	Mississippi	5,206,836,000	1.5%
13	Missouri	8,900,078,000	2.5%
30	Montana	3,677,602,000	1.0%
3	Nebraska	21,522,236,000	6.0%
44	Nevada	596,250,000	0.2%
48	New Hampshire	209,939,000	0.1%
40	New Jersey	1,024,838,000	0.3%
33	New Mexico	2,861,687,000	0.8%
26	New York	5,052,760,000	1.4%
9	North Carolina	10,536,714,000	3.0%
17	North Dakota	8,114,621,000	2.3%
15	Ohio	8,364,978,000	2.3%
22	Oklahoma	6,189,725,000	1.7%
28	Oregon	4,593,591,000	1.3%
21	Pennsylvania	6,346,684,000	1.8%
49	Rhode Island	72,080,000	0.0%
35	South Carolina	2,119,484,000	0.6%
12	South Dakota	9,351,793,000	2.6%
32	Tennessee	3,297,548,000	0.9%
4	Texas	20,897,606,000	5.9%
37	Utah	1,657,833,000	0.5%
41	Vermont	785,934,000	0.2%
31	Virginia	3,334,126,000	0.9%
11	Washington	9,917,791,000	2.8%
42	West Virginia	690,107,000	0.2%
8	Wisconsin	10,759,487,000	3.0%
38	Wyoming	1,392,026,000	0.4%

RANK ORDER

RANK	STATE	FARM INCOME	% of USA
1	California	$46,036,034,000	12.9%
2	Iowa	26,529,033,000	7.4%
3	Nebraska	21,522,236,000	6.0%
4	Texas	20,897,606,000	5.9%
5	Minnesota	17,094,652,000	4.8%
6	Illinois	16,096,415,000	4.5%
7	Kansas	15,355,365,000	4.3%
8	Wisconsin	10,759,487,000	3.0%
9	North Carolina	10,536,714,000	3.0%
10	Indiana	10,119,297,000	2.8%
11	Washington	9,917,791,000	2.8%
12	South Dakota	9,351,793,000	2.6%
13	Missouri	8,900,078,000	2.5%
14	Georgia	8,430,255,000	2.4%
15	Ohio	8,364,978,000	2.3%
16	Arkansas	8,214,594,000	2.3%
17	North Dakota	8,114,621,000	2.3%
18	Florida	7,743,975,000	2.2%
19	Michigan	7,417,038,000	2.1%
20	Idaho	7,109,927,000	2.0%
21	Pennsylvania	6,346,684,000	1.8%
22	Oklahoma	6,189,725,000	1.7%
23	Colorado	6,128,719,000	1.7%
24	Kentucky	5,443,637,000	1.5%
25	Mississippi	5,206,836,000	1.5%
26	New York	5,052,760,000	1.4%
27	Alabama	4,951,074,000	1.4%
28	Oregon	4,593,591,000	1.3%
29	Arizona	4,155,423,000	1.2%
30	Montana	3,677,602,000	1.0%
31	Virginia	3,334,126,000	0.9%
32	Tennessee	3,297,548,000	0.9%
33	New Mexico	2,861,687,000	0.8%
34	Louisiana	2,823,356,000	0.8%
35	South Carolina	2,119,484,000	0.6%
36	Maryland	2,094,248,000	0.6%
37	Utah	1,657,833,000	0.5%
38	Wyoming	1,392,026,000	0.4%
39	Delaware	1,205,648,000	0.3%
40	New Jersey	1,024,838,000	0.3%
41	Vermont	785,934,000	0.2%
42	West Virginia	690,107,000	0.2%
43	Hawaii	648,558,000	0.2%
44	Nevada	596,250,000	0.2%
45	Maine	527,730,000	0.1%
46	Connecticut	514,256,000	0.1%
47	Massachusetts	386,878,000	0.1%
48	New Hampshire	209,939,000	0.1%
49	Rhode Island	72,080,000	0.0%
50	Alaska	33,905,000	0.0%
	District of Columbia	0	0.0%

Source: U.S. Department of Agriculture, Economic Research Service
"Farm Sector Financial Indicators, State Rankings" (www.ers.usda.gov/data-products/farm-income-and-wealth-statistics.aspx)
*Commodities include crops and livestock.

Farm Income: Crops in 2016

National Total = $193,676,145,000

ALPHA ORDER

RANK	STATE	FARM INCOME	% of USA
33	Alabama	$1,069,584,000	0.6%
50	Alaska	27,871,000	0.0%
22	Arizona	2,637,301,000	1.4%
16	Arkansas	3,499,923,000	1.8%
1	California	35,587,080,000	18.4%
28	Colorado	1,968,727,000	1.0%
40	Connecticut	346,886,000	0.2%
42	Delaware	276,590,000	0.1%
11	Florida	6,082,408,000	3.1%
19	Georgia	3,139,990,000	1.6%
38	Hawaii	496,231,000	0.3%
21	Idaho	2,809,522,000	1.5%
3	Illinois	13,807,853,000	7.1%
9	Indiana	6,740,729,000	3.5%
2	Iowa	14,428,948,000	7.5%
10	Kansas	6,375,154,000	3.3%
23	Kentucky	2,495,799,000	1.3%
30	Louisiana	1,793,695,000	0.9%
44	Maine	230,660,000	0.1%
35	Maryland	868,401,000	0.4%
43	Massachusetts	270,970,000	0.1%
15	Michigan	4,507,936,000	2.3%
4	Minnesota	10,007,904,000	5.2%
25	Mississippi	2,188,661,000	1.1%
14	Missouri	4,743,410,000	2.4%
26	Montana	2,046,208,000	1.1%
5	Nebraska	9,374,861,000	4.8%
46	Nevada	151,384,000	0.1%
48	New Hampshire	95,959,000	0.0%
34	New Jersey	906,424,000	0.5%
37	New Mexico	710,819,000	0.4%
29	New York	1,965,131,000	1.0%
18	North Carolina	3,323,202,000	1.7%
8	North Dakota	7,003,448,000	3.6%
13	Ohio	5,333,033,000	2.8%
31	Oklahoma	1,350,597,000	0.7%
20	Oregon	3,115,862,000	1.6%
24	Pennsylvania	2,433,396,000	1.3%
49	Rhode Island	48,544,000	0.0%
36	South Carolina	850,553,000	0.4%
12	South Dakota	5,717,841,000	3.0%
27	Tennessee	1,980,862,000	1.0%
6	Texas	7,742,694,000	4.0%
39	Utah	412,866,000	0.2%
45	Vermont	202,096,000	0.1%
32	Virginia	1,134,376,000	0.6%
7	Washington	7,440,617,000	3.8%
47	West Virginia	141,513,000	0.1%
17	Wisconsin	3,450,689,000	1.8%
41	Wyoming	340,937,000	0.2%

RANK ORDER

RANK	STATE	FARM INCOME	% of USA
1	California	$35,587,080,000	18.4%
2	Iowa	14,428,948,000	7.5%
3	Illinois	13,807,853,000	7.1%
4	Minnesota	10,007,904,000	5.2%
5	Nebraska	9,374,861,000	4.8%
6	Texas	7,742,694,000	4.0%
7	Washington	7,440,617,000	3.8%
8	North Dakota	7,003,448,000	3.6%
9	Indiana	6,740,729,000	3.5%
10	Kansas	6,375,154,000	3.3%
11	Florida	6,082,408,000	3.1%
12	South Dakota	5,717,841,000	3.0%
13	Ohio	5,333,033,000	2.8%
14	Missouri	4,743,410,000	2.4%
15	Michigan	4,507,936,000	2.3%
16	Arkansas	3,499,923,000	1.8%
17	Wisconsin	3,450,689,000	1.8%
18	North Carolina	3,323,202,000	1.7%
19	Georgia	3,139,990,000	1.6%
20	Oregon	3,115,862,000	1.6%
21	Idaho	2,809,522,000	1.5%
22	Arizona	2,637,301,000	1.4%
23	Kentucky	2,495,799,000	1.3%
24	Pennsylvania	2,433,396,000	1.3%
25	Mississippi	2,188,661,000	1.1%
26	Montana	2,046,208,000	1.1%
27	Tennessee	1,980,862,000	1.0%
28	Colorado	1,968,727,000	1.0%
29	New York	1,965,131,000	1.0%
30	Louisiana	1,793,695,000	0.9%
31	Oklahoma	1,350,597,000	0.7%
32	Virginia	1,134,376,000	0.6%
33	Alabama	1,069,584,000	0.6%
34	New Jersey	906,424,000	0.5%
35	Maryland	868,401,000	0.4%
36	South Carolina	850,553,000	0.4%
37	New Mexico	710,819,000	0.4%
38	Hawaii	496,231,000	0.3%
39	Utah	412,866,000	0.2%
40	Connecticut	346,886,000	0.2%
41	Wyoming	340,937,000	0.2%
42	Delaware	276,590,000	0.1%
43	Massachusetts	270,970,000	0.1%
44	Maine	230,660,000	0.1%
45	Vermont	202,096,000	0.1%
46	Nevada	151,384,000	0.1%
47	West Virginia	141,513,000	0.1%
48	New Hampshire	95,959,000	0.0%
49	Rhode Island	48,544,000	0.0%
50	Alaska	27,871,000	0.0%
	District of Columbia	0	0.0%

Source: U.S. Department of Agriculture, Economic Research Service
"Farm Sector Financial Indicators, State Rankings" (www.ers.usda.gov/data-products/farm-income-and-wealth-statistics.aspx)

Farm Income: Livestock in 2016

National Total = $162,858,224,000*

ALPHA ORDER

RANK	STATE	FARM INCOME	% of USA
16	Alabama	$3,881,490,000	2.4%
50	Alaska	6,034,000	0.0%
30	Arizona	1,518,122,000	0.9%
11	Arkansas	4,714,671,000	2.9%
4	California	10,448,954,000	6.4%
13	Colorado	4,159,992,000	2.6%
44	Connecticut	167,370,000	0.1%
39	Delaware	929,058,000	0.6%
28	Florida	1,661,567,000	1.0%
9	Georgia	5,290,265,000	3.2%
45	Hawaii	152,327,000	0.1%
12	Idaho	4,300,405,000	2.6%
25	Illinois	2,288,562,000	1.4%
18	Indiana	3,378,568,000	2.1%
3	Iowa	12,100,085,000	7.4%
5	Kansas	8,980,211,000	5.5%
22	Kentucky	2,947,838,000	1.8%
38	Louisiana	1,029,661,000	0.6%
43	Maine	297,070,000	0.2%
35	Maryland	1,225,847,000	0.8%
47	Massachusetts	115,908,000	0.1%
23	Michigan	2,909,102,000	1.8%
8	Minnesota	7,086,748,000	4.4%
21	Mississippi	3,018,175,000	1.9%
14	Missouri	4,156,668,000	2.6%
29	Montana	1,631,394,000	1.0%
2	Nebraska	12,147,375,000	7.5%
42	Nevada	444,866,000	0.3%
48	New Hampshire	113,980,000	0.1%
46	New Jersey	118,414,000	0.1%
27	New Mexico	2,150,868,000	1.3%
19	New York	3,087,629,000	1.9%
7	North Carolina	7,213,512,000	4.4%
36	North Dakota	1,111,173,000	0.7%
20	Ohio	3,031,945,000	1.9%
10	Oklahoma	4,839,128,000	3.0%
31	Oregon	1,477,729,000	0.9%
15	Pennsylvania	3,913,288,000	2.4%
49	Rhode Island	23,536,000	0.0%
33	South Carolina	1,268,931,000	0.8%
17	South Dakota	3,633,952,000	2.2%
32	Tennessee	1,316,686,000	0.8%
1	Texas	13,154,912,000	8.1%
34	Utah	1,244,967,000	0.8%
40	Vermont	583,838,000	0.4%
26	Virginia	2,199,750,000	1.4%
24	Washington	2,477,174,000	1.5%
41	West Virginia	548,594,000	0.3%
6	Wisconsin	7,308,798,000	4.5%
37	Wyoming	1,051,089,000	0.6%

RANK ORDER

RANK	STATE	FARM INCOME	% of USA
1	Texas	$13,154,912,000	8.1%
2	Nebraska	12,147,375,000	7.5%
3	Iowa	12,100,085,000	7.4%
4	California	10,448,954,000	6.4%
5	Kansas	8,980,211,000	5.5%
6	Wisconsin	7,308,798,000	4.5%
7	North Carolina	7,213,512,000	4.4%
8	Minnesota	7,086,748,000	4.4%
9	Georgia	5,290,265,000	3.2%
10	Oklahoma	4,839,128,000	3.0%
11	Arkansas	4,714,671,000	2.9%
12	Idaho	4,300,405,000	2.6%
13	Colorado	4,159,992,000	2.6%
14	Missouri	4,156,668,000	2.6%
15	Pennsylvania	3,913,288,000	2.4%
16	Alabama	3,881,490,000	2.4%
17	South Dakota	3,633,952,000	2.2%
18	Indiana	3,378,568,000	2.1%
19	New York	3,087,629,000	1.9%
20	Ohio	3,031,945,000	1.9%
21	Mississippi	3,018,175,000	1.9%
22	Kentucky	2,947,838,000	1.8%
23	Michigan	2,909,102,000	1.8%
24	Washington	2,477,174,000	1.5%
25	Illinois	2,288,562,000	1.4%
26	Virginia	2,199,750,000	1.4%
27	New Mexico	2,150,868,000	1.3%
28	Florida	1,661,567,000	1.0%
29	Montana	1,631,394,000	1.0%
30	Arizona	1,518,122,000	0.9%
31	Oregon	1,477,729,000	0.9%
32	Tennessee	1,316,686,000	0.8%
33	South Carolina	1,268,931,000	0.8%
34	Utah	1,244,967,000	0.8%
35	Maryland	1,225,847,000	0.8%
36	North Dakota	1,111,173,000	0.7%
37	Wyoming	1,051,089,000	0.6%
38	Louisiana	1,029,661,000	0.6%
39	Delaware	929,058,000	0.6%
40	Vermont	583,838,000	0.4%
41	West Virginia	548,594,000	0.3%
42	Nevada	444,866,000	0.3%
43	Maine	297,070,000	0.2%
44	Connecticut	167,370,000	0.1%
45	Hawaii	152,327,000	0.1%
46	New Jersey	118,414,000	0.1%
47	Massachusetts	115,908,000	0.1%
48	New Hampshire	113,980,000	0.1%
49	Rhode Island	23,536,000	0.0%
50	Alaska	6,034,000	0.0%
	District of Columbia	0	0.0%

Source: U.S. Department of Agriculture, Economic Research Service
   "Farm Sector Financial Indicators, State Rankings" (www.ers.usda.gov/data-products/farm-income-and-wealth-statistics.aspx)
*Includes livestock products.

Farm Income: Government Payments in 2016

National Total = $12,979,677,000*

ALPHA ORDER

RANK	STATE	FARM INCOME	% of USA
24	Alabama	$168,552,000	1.3%
43	Alaska	18,058,000	0.1%
29	Arizona	110,739,000	0.9%
9	Arkansas	494,918,000	3.8%
18	California	240,813,000	1.9%
20	Colorado	233,881,000	1.8%
49	Connecticut	7,096,000	0.1%
44	Delaware	17,607,000	0.1%
35	Florida	69,136,000	0.5%
12	Georgia	444,366,000	3.4%
47	Hawaii	12,081,000	0.1%
25	Idaho	158,281,000	1.2%
1	Illinois	1,109,459,000	8.5%
5	Indiana	648,105,000	5.0%
2	Iowa	1,079,694,000	8.3%
7	Kansas	598,261,000	4.6%
27	Kentucky	128,875,000	1.0%
16	Louisiana	297,203,000	2.3%
45	Maine	14,523,000	0.1%
38	Maryland	44,771,000	0.3%
48	Massachusetts	8,233,000	0.1%
22	Michigan	195,406,000	1.5%
6	Minnesota	647,394,000	5.0%
14	Mississippi	316,994,000	2.4%
13	Missouri	443,680,000	3.4%
19	Montana	235,107,000	1.8%
4	Nebraska	804,027,000	6.2%
32	Nevada	81,487,000	0.6%
37	New Hampshire	57,928,000	0.4%
46	New Jersey	12,178,000	0.1%
34	New Mexico	73,321,000	0.6%
30	New York	106,369,000	0.8%
23	North Carolina	180,057,000	1.4%
8	North Dakota	566,367,000	4.4%
11	Ohio	473,842,000	3.7%
15	Oklahoma	309,006,000	2.4%
26	Oregon	142,260,000	1.1%
33	Pennsylvania	77,296,000	0.6%
50	Rhode Island	1,530,000	0.0%
31	South Carolina	91,524,000	0.7%
10	South Dakota	474,544,000	3.7%
28	Tennessee	112,220,000	0.9%
3	Texas	978,914,000	7.5%
39	Utah	41,039,000	0.3%
42	Vermont	19,973,000	0.2%
36	Virginia	60,207,000	0.5%
21	Washington	233,215,000	1.8%
41	West Virginia	35,093,000	0.3%
17	Wisconsin	265,265,000	2.0%
40	Wyoming	38,779,000	0.3%

RANK ORDER

RANK	STATE	FARM INCOME	% of USA
1	Illinois	$1,109,459,000	8.5%
2	Iowa	1,079,694,000	8.3%
3	Texas	978,914,000	7.5%
4	Nebraska	804,027,000	6.2%
5	Indiana	648,105,000	5.0%
6	Minnesota	647,394,000	5.0%
7	Kansas	598,261,000	4.6%
8	North Dakota	566,367,000	4.4%
9	Arkansas	494,918,000	3.8%
10	South Dakota	474,544,000	3.7%
11	Ohio	473,842,000	3.7%
12	Georgia	444,366,000	3.4%
13	Missouri	443,680,000	3.4%
14	Mississippi	316,994,000	2.4%
15	Oklahoma	309,006,000	2.4%
16	Louisiana	297,203,000	2.3%
17	Wisconsin	265,265,000	2.0%
18	California	240,813,000	1.9%
19	Montana	235,107,000	1.8%
20	Colorado	233,881,000	1.8%
21	Washington	233,215,000	1.8%
22	Michigan	195,406,000	1.5%
23	North Carolina	180,057,000	1.4%
24	Alabama	168,552,000	1.3%
25	Idaho	158,281,000	1.2%
26	Oregon	142,260,000	1.1%
27	Kentucky	128,875,000	1.0%
28	Tennessee	112,220,000	0.9%
29	Arizona	110,739,000	0.9%
30	New York	106,369,000	0.8%
31	South Carolina	91,524,000	0.7%
32	Nevada	81,487,000	0.6%
33	Pennsylvania	77,296,000	0.6%
34	New Mexico	73,321,000	0.6%
35	Florida	69,136,000	0.5%
36	Virginia	60,207,000	0.5%
37	New Hampshire	57,928,000	0.4%
38	Maryland	44,771,000	0.3%
39	Utah	41,039,000	0.3%
40	Wyoming	38,779,000	0.3%
41	West Virginia	35,093,000	0.3%
42	Vermont	19,973,000	0.2%
43	Alaska	18,058,000	0.1%
44	Delaware	17,607,000	0.1%
45	Maine	14,523,000	0.1%
46	New Jersey	12,178,000	0.1%
47	Hawaii	12,081,000	0.1%
48	Massachusetts	8,233,000	0.1%
49	Connecticut	7,096,000	0.1%
50	Rhode Island	1,530,000	0.0%
	District of Columbia	0	0.0%

Source: U.S. Department of Agriculture, Economic Research Service
"Farm Sector Financial Indicators, State Rankings" (www.ers.usda.gov/data-products/farm-income-and-wealth-statistics.aspx)
*Government payments made directly to farmers in cash.

Acres Planted in 2017

National Total = 319,136,000 Acres*

ALPHA ORDER

RANK	STATE	ACRES	% of USA
30	Alabama	2,280,000	0.7%
NA	Alaska**	NA	NA
38	Arizona	690,000	0.2%
15	Arkansas	7,169,000	2.2%
27	California	3,045,000	1.0%
17	Colorado	6,246,000	2.0%
46	Connecticut	71,000	0.0%
40	Delaware	465,000	0.1%
35	Florida	1,144,000	0.4%
24	Georgia	3,633,000	1.1%
49	Hawaii	0	0.0%
21	Idaho	4,195,000	1.3%
4	Illinois	22,850,000	7.2%
10	Indiana	12,170,000	3.8%
1	Iowa	24,511,000	7.7%
2	Kansas	23,833,000	7.5%
18	Kentucky	5,981,000	1.9%
26	Louisiana	3,235,000	1.0%
44	Maine	232,000	0.1%
32	Maryland	1,648,000	0.5%
45	Massachusetts	111,000	0.0%
16	Michigan	6,375,000	2.0%
6	Minnesota	19,711,000	6.2%
22	Mississippi	4,159,000	1.3%
9	Missouri	13,533,000	4.2%
13	Montana	9,129,000	2.9%
7	Nebraska	19,686,000	6.2%
41	Nevada	401,000	0.1%
47	New Hampshire	61,000	0.0%
42	New Jersey	317,000	0.1%
37	New Mexico	901,000	0.3%
28	New York	2,800,000	0.9%
20	North Carolina	4,422,000	1.4%
3	North Dakota	23,687,000	7.4%
11	Ohio	10,080,000	3.2%
12	Oklahoma	9,871,000	3.1%
31	Oregon	2,088,000	0.7%
23	Pennsylvania	3,758,000	1.2%
48	Rhode Island	8,000	0.0%
33	South Carolina	1,504,000	0.5%
8	South Dakota	17,572,000	5.5%
19	Tennessee	4,891,000	1.5%
5	Texas	21,759,000	6.8%
36	Utah	939,000	0.3%
43	Vermont	262,000	0.1%
29	Virginia	2,684,000	0.8%
25	Washington	3,629,000	1.1%
39	West Virginia	673,000	0.2%
14	Wisconsin	7,758,000	2.4%
34	Wyoming	1,480,000	0.5%

RANK ORDER

RANK	STATE	ACRES	% of USA
1	Iowa	24,511,000	7.7%
2	Kansas	23,833,000	7.5%
3	North Dakota	23,687,000	7.4%
4	Illinois	22,850,000	7.2%
5	Texas	21,759,000	6.8%
6	Minnesota	19,711,000	6.2%
7	Nebraska	19,686,000	6.2%
8	South Dakota	17,572,000	5.5%
9	Missouri	13,533,000	4.2%
10	Indiana	12,170,000	3.8%
11	Ohio	10,080,000	3.2%
12	Oklahoma	9,871,000	3.1%
13	Montana	9,129,000	2.9%
14	Wisconsin	7,758,000	2.4%
15	Arkansas	7,169,000	2.2%
16	Michigan	6,375,000	2.0%
17	Colorado	6,246,000	2.0%
18	Kentucky	5,981,000	1.9%
19	Tennessee	4,891,000	1.5%
20	North Carolina	4,422,000	1.4%
21	Idaho	4,195,000	1.3%
22	Mississippi	4,159,000	1.3%
23	Pennsylvania	3,758,000	1.2%
24	Georgia	3,633,000	1.1%
25	Washington	3,629,000	1.1%
26	Louisiana	3,235,000	1.0%
27	California	3,045,000	1.0%
28	New York	2,800,000	0.9%
29	Virginia	2,684,000	0.8%
30	Alabama	2,280,000	0.7%
31	Oregon	2,088,000	0.7%
32	Maryland	1,648,000	0.5%
33	South Carolina	1,504,000	0.5%
34	Wyoming	1,480,000	0.5%
35	Florida	1,144,000	0.4%
36	Utah	939,000	0.3%
37	New Mexico	901,000	0.3%
38	Arizona	690,000	0.2%
39	West Virginia	673,000	0.2%
40	Delaware	465,000	0.1%
41	Nevada	401,000	0.1%
42	New Jersey	317,000	0.1%
43	Vermont	262,000	0.1%
44	Maine	232,000	0.1%
45	Massachusetts	111,000	0.0%
46	Connecticut	71,000	0.0%
47	New Hampshire	61,000	0.0%
48	Rhode Island	8,000	0.0%
49	Hawaii	0	0.0%
NA	Alaska**	NA	NA
	District of Columbia**	NA	NA

Source: U.S. Department of Agriculture, National Agricultural Statistics Service
   "Crop Production: 2017 Summary" (January 2018)
      (http://usda.mannlib.cornell.edu/MannUsda/viewDocumentInfo.do?documentID=1047)
*Estimated totals.
**No acreage or not available.

Acres Harvested in 2017

National Total = 303,015,000 Acres*

ALPHA ORDER

RANK	STATE	ACRES	% of USA
30	Alabama	2,180,000	0.7%
NA	Alaska**	NA	NA
37	Arizona	677,000	0.2%
15	Arkansas	6,972,000	2.3%
28	California	2,653,000	0.9%
17	Colorado	5,876,000	1.9%
46	Connecticut	67,000	0.0%
40	Delaware	439,000	0.1%
35	Florida	1,124,000	0.4%
25	Georgia	3,276,000	1.1%
49	Hawaii	0	0.0%
22	Idaho	4,064,000	1.3%
4	Illinois	22,694,000	7.5%
10	Indiana	12,085,000	4.0%
1	Iowa	24,300,000	8.0%
2	Kansas	22,943,000	7.6%
18	Kentucky	5,786,000	1.9%
26	Louisiana	3,190,000	1.1%
44	Maine	228,000	0.1%
34	Maryland	1,385,000	0.5%
45	Massachusetts	108,000	0.0%
16	Michigan	6,272,000	2.1%
5	Minnesota	19,447,000	6.4%
21	Mississippi	4,102,000	1.4%
9	Missouri	13,277,000	4.4%
12	Montana	8,339,000	2.8%
6	Nebraska	19,372,000	6.4%
41	Nevada	380,000	0.1%
47	New Hampshire	60,000	0.0%
42	New Jersey	309,000	0.1%
39	New Mexico	665,000	0.2%
27	New York	2,740,000	0.9%
20	North Carolina	4,290,000	1.4%
3	North Dakota	22,832,000	7.5%
11	Ohio	9,955,000	3.3%
13	Oklahoma	7,928,000	2.6%
31	Oregon	2,050,000	0.7%
23	Pennsylvania	3,638,000	1.2%
48	Rhode Island	8,000	0.0%
32	South Carolina	1,452,000	0.5%
8	South Dakota	16,394,000	5.4%
19	Tennessee	4,751,000	1.6%
7	Texas	17,607,000	5.8%
36	Utah	914,000	0.3%
43	Vermont	256,000	0.1%
29	Virginia	2,564,000	0.8%
24	Washington	3,549,000	1.2%
38	West Virginia	667,000	0.2%
14	Wisconsin	7,522,000	2.5%
33	Wyoming	1,406,000	0.5%

RANK ORDER

RANK	STATE	ACRES	% of USA
1	Iowa	24,300,000	8.0%
2	Kansas	22,943,000	7.6%
3	North Dakota	22,832,000	7.5%
4	Illinois	22,694,000	7.5%
5	Minnesota	19,447,000	6.4%
6	Nebraska	19,372,000	6.4%
7	Texas	17,607,000	5.8%
8	South Dakota	16,394,000	5.4%
9	Missouri	13,277,000	4.4%
10	Indiana	12,085,000	4.0%
11	Ohio	9,955,000	3.3%
12	Montana	8,339,000	2.8%
13	Oklahoma	7,928,000	2.6%
14	Wisconsin	7,522,000	2.5%
15	Arkansas	6,972,000	2.3%
16	Michigan	6,272,000	2.1%
17	Colorado	5,876,000	1.9%
18	Kentucky	5,786,000	1.9%
19	Tennessee	4,751,000	1.6%
20	North Carolina	4,290,000	1.4%
21	Mississippi	4,102,000	1.4%
22	Idaho	4,064,000	1.3%
23	Pennsylvania	3,638,000	1.2%
24	Washington	3,549,000	1.2%
25	Georgia	3,276,000	1.1%
26	Louisiana	3,190,000	1.1%
27	New York	2,740,000	0.9%
28	California	2,653,000	0.9%
29	Virginia	2,564,000	0.8%
30	Alabama	2,180,000	0.7%
31	Oregon	2,050,000	0.7%
32	South Carolina	1,452,000	0.5%
33	Wyoming	1,406,000	0.5%
34	Maryland	1,385,000	0.5%
35	Florida	1,124,000	0.4%
36	Utah	914,000	0.3%
37	Arizona	677,000	0.2%
38	West Virginia	667,000	0.2%
39	New Mexico	665,000	0.2%
40	Delaware	439,000	0.1%
41	Nevada	380,000	0.1%
42	New Jersey	309,000	0.1%
43	Vermont	256,000	0.1%
44	Maine	228,000	0.1%
45	Massachusetts	108,000	0.0%
46	Connecticut	67,000	0.0%
47	New Hampshire	60,000	0.0%
48	Rhode Island	8,000	0.0%
49	Hawaii	0	0.0%
NA	Alaska**	NA	NA
	District of Columbia**	NA	NA

Source: U.S. Department of Agriculture, National Agricultural Statistics Service
   "Crop Production: 2017 Summary" (January 2018)
      (http://usda.mannlib.cornell.edu/MannUsda/viewDocumentInfo.do?documentID=1047)
*Estimated totals.
**No acreage or not available.

Acres Harvested: Corn in 2017

National Total = 82,703,000 Acres*

ALPHA ORDER

RANK	STATE	ACRES	% of USA
28	Alabama	235,000	0.3%
NA	Alaska**	NA	NA
40	Arizona	32,000	0.0%
19	Arkansas	595,000	0.7%
31	California	80,000	0.1%
14	Colorado	1,300,000	1.6%
NA	Connecticut**	NA	NA
29	Delaware	171,000	0.2%
38	Florida	37,000	0.0%
27	Georgia	245,000	0.3%
NA	Hawaii**	NA	NA
30	Idaho	115,000	0.1%
2	Illinois	10,950,000	13.2%
6	Indiana	5,190,000	6.3%
1	Iowa	12,900,000	15.6%
5	Kansas	5,200,000	6.3%
15	Kentucky	1,220,000	1.5%
21	Louisiana	490,000	0.6%
NA	Maine**	NA	NA
23	Maryland	420,000	0.5%
NA	Massachusetts**	NA	NA
13	Michigan	1,890,000	2.3%
4	Minnesota	7,630,000	9.2%
20	Mississippi	500,000	0.6%
8	Missouri	3,250,000	3.9%
34	Montana	65,000	0.1%
3	Nebraska	9,300,000	11.2%
NA	Nevada**	NA	NA
NA	New Hampshire**	NA	NA
33	New Jersey	70,000	0.1%
37	New Mexico	43,000	0.1%
22	New York	485,000	0.6%
17	North Carolina	840,000	1.0%
9	North Dakota	3,230,000	3.9%
10	Ohio	3,130,000	3.8%
26	Oklahoma	305,000	0.4%
36	Oregon	44,000	0.1%
16	Pennsylvania	920,000	1.1%
NA	Rhode Island**	NA	NA
25	South Carolina	325,000	0.4%
7	South Dakota	5,080,000	6.1%
18	Tennessee	710,000	0.9%
12	Texas	2,240,000	2.7%
41	Utah	20,000	0.0%
NA	Vermont**	NA	NA
24	Virginia	340,000	0.4%
31	Washington	80,000	0.1%
39	West Virginia	33,000	0.0%
11	Wisconsin	2,930,000	3.5%
35	Wyoming	63,000	0.1%

RANK ORDER

RANK	STATE	ACRES	% of USA
1	Iowa	12,900,000	15.6%
2	Illinois	10,950,000	13.2%
3	Nebraska	9,300,000	11.2%
4	Minnesota	7,630,000	9.2%
5	Kansas	5,200,000	6.3%
6	Indiana	5,190,000	6.3%
7	South Dakota	5,080,000	6.1%
8	Missouri	3,250,000	3.9%
9	North Dakota	3,230,000	3.9%
10	Ohio	3,130,000	3.8%
11	Wisconsin	2,930,000	3.5%
12	Texas	2,240,000	2.7%
13	Michigan	1,890,000	2.3%
14	Colorado	1,300,000	1.6%
15	Kentucky	1,220,000	1.5%
16	Pennsylvania	920,000	1.1%
17	North Carolina	840,000	1.0%
18	Tennessee	710,000	0.9%
19	Arkansas	595,000	0.7%
20	Mississippi	500,000	0.6%
21	Louisiana	490,000	0.6%
22	New York	485,000	0.6%
23	Maryland	420,000	0.5%
24	Virginia	340,000	0.4%
25	South Carolina	325,000	0.4%
26	Oklahoma	305,000	0.4%
27	Georgia	245,000	0.3%
28	Alabama	235,000	0.3%
29	Delaware	171,000	0.2%
30	Idaho	115,000	0.1%
31	California	80,000	0.1%
31	Washington	80,000	0.1%
33	New Jersey	70,000	0.1%
34	Montana	65,000	0.1%
35	Wyoming	63,000	0.1%
36	Oregon	44,000	0.1%
37	New Mexico	43,000	0.1%
38	Florida	37,000	0.0%
39	West Virginia	33,000	0.0%
40	Arizona	32,000	0.0%
41	Utah	20,000	0.0%
NA	Alaska**	NA	NA
NA	Connecticut**	NA	NA
NA	Hawaii**	NA	NA
NA	Maine**	NA	NA
NA	Massachusetts**	NA	NA
NA	Nevada**	NA	NA
NA	New Hampshire**	NA	NA
NA	Rhode Island**	NA	NA
NA	Vermont**	NA	NA
	District of Columbia**	NA	NA

Source: U.S. Department of Agriculture, National Agricultural Statistics Service
   "Crop Production: 2017 Summary" (January 2018)
      (http://usda.mannlib.cornell.edu/MannUsda/viewDocumentInfo.do?documentID=1047)
*Estimated totals. Acres harvested for grain.
**No acreage or not available.

Acres Harvested: Soybeans in 2017

National Total = 89,522,000 Acres*

ALPHA ORDER

RANK	STATE	ACRES	% of USA
24	Alabama	345,000	0.4%
NA	Alaska**	NA	NA
NA	Arizona**	NA	NA
11	Arkansas	3,500,000	3.9%
NA	California**	NA	NA
NA	Colorado**	NA	NA
NA	Connecticut**	NA	NA
27	Delaware	158,000	0.2%
31	Florida	14,000	0.0%
28	Georgia	150,000	0.2%
NA	Hawaii**	NA	NA
NA	Idaho**	NA	NA
1	Illinois	10,550,000	11.8%
5	Indiana	5,940,000	6.6%
2	Iowa	9,940,000	11.1%
9	Kansas	5,110,000	5.7%
15	Kentucky	1,940,000	2.2%
18	Louisiana	1,250,000	1.4%
NA	Maine**	NA	NA
22	Maryland	495,000	0.6%
NA	Massachusetts**	NA	NA
12	Michigan	2,270,000	2.5%
3	Minnesota	8,090,000	9.0%
13	Mississippi	2,170,000	2.4%
6	Missouri	5,910,000	6.6%
NA	Montana**	NA	NA
7	Nebraska	5,670,000	6.3%
NA	Nevada**	NA	NA
NA	New Hampshire**	NA	NA
29	New Jersey	99,000	0.1%
NA	New Mexico**	NA	NA
25	New York	265,000	0.3%
16	North Carolina	1,690,000	1.9%
4	North Dakota	7,050,000	7.9%
10	Ohio	5,090,000	5.7%
19	Oklahoma	640,000	0.7%
NA	Oregon**	NA	NA
21	Pennsylvania	585,000	0.7%
NA	Rhode Island**	NA	NA
23	South Carolina	390,000	0.4%
8	South Dakota	5,610,000	6.3%
17	Tennessee	1,660,000	1.9%
26	Texas	185,000	0.2%
NA	Utah**	NA	NA
NA	Vermont**	NA	NA
20	Virginia	590,000	0.7%
NA	Washington**	NA	NA
30	West Virginia	26,000	0.0%
14	Wisconsin	2,140,000	2.4%
NA	Wyoming**	NA	NA

RANK ORDER

RANK	STATE	ACRES	% of USA
1	Illinois	10,550,000	11.8%
2	Iowa	9,940,000	11.1%
3	Minnesota	8,090,000	9.0%
4	North Dakota	7,050,000	7.9%
5	Indiana	5,940,000	6.6%
6	Missouri	5,910,000	6.6%
7	Nebraska	5,670,000	6.3%
8	South Dakota	5,610,000	6.3%
9	Kansas	5,110,000	5.7%
10	Ohio	5,090,000	5.7%
11	Arkansas	3,500,000	3.9%
12	Michigan	2,270,000	2.5%
13	Mississippi	2,170,000	2.4%
14	Wisconsin	2,140,000	2.4%
15	Kentucky	1,940,000	2.2%
16	North Carolina	1,690,000	1.9%
17	Tennessee	1,660,000	1.9%
18	Louisiana	1,250,000	1.4%
19	Oklahoma	640,000	0.7%
20	Virginia	590,000	0.7%
21	Pennsylvania	585,000	0.7%
22	Maryland	495,000	0.6%
23	South Carolina	390,000	0.4%
24	Alabama	345,000	0.4%
25	New York	265,000	0.3%
26	Texas	185,000	0.2%
27	Delaware	158,000	0.2%
28	Georgia	150,000	0.2%
29	New Jersey	99,000	0.1%
30	West Virginia	26,000	0.0%
31	Florida	14,000	0.0%
NA	Alaska**	NA	NA
NA	Arizona**	NA	NA
NA	California**	NA	NA
NA	Colorado**	NA	NA
NA	Connecticut**	NA	NA
NA	Hawaii**	NA	NA
NA	Idaho**	NA	NA
NA	Maine**	NA	NA
NA	Massachusetts**	NA	NA
NA	Montana**	NA	NA
NA	Nevada**	NA	NA
NA	New Hampshire**	NA	NA
NA	New Mexico**	NA	NA
NA	Oregon**	NA	NA
NA	Rhode Island**	NA	NA
NA	Utah**	NA	NA
NA	Vermont**	NA	NA
NA	Washington**	NA	NA
NA	Wyoming**	NA	NA
	District of Columbia**	NA	NA

Source: U.S. Department of Agriculture, National Agricultural Statistics Service
  "Crop Production: 2017 Summary" (January 2018)
    (http://usda.mannlib.cornell.edu/MannUsda/viewDocumentInfo.do?documentID=1047)
*Estimated totals.
**No acreage or not available.

Acres Harvested: Wheat in 2017

National Total = 37,586,000 Acres*

ALPHA ORDER

RANK	STATE	ACRES	% of USA
32	Alabama	100,000	0.3%
NA	Alaska**	NA	NA
30	Arizona	107,000	0.3%
27	Arkansas	125,000	0.3%
22	California	182,000	0.5%
7	Colorado	2,029,000	5.4%
NA	Connecticut**	NA	NA
35	Delaware	69,000	0.2%
38	Florida	14,000	0.0%
34	Georgia	70,000	0.2%
NA	Hawaii**	NA	NA
10	Idaho	1,104,000	2.9%
14	Illinois	470,000	1.3%
20	Indiana	240,000	0.6%
41	Iowa	8,000	0.0%
1	Kansas	6,950,000	18.5%
18	Kentucky	310,000	0.8%
39	Louisiana	13,000	0.0%
NA	Maine**	NA	NA
21	Maryland	185,000	0.5%
NA	Massachusetts**	NA	NA
16	Michigan	425,000	1.1%
9	Minnesota	1,135,000	3.0%
36	Mississippi	25,000	0.1%
13	Missouri	540,000	1.4%
3	Montana	4,665,000	12.4%
11	Nebraska	1,020,000	2.7%
40	Nevada	10,000	0.0%
NA	New Hampshire**	NA	NA
37	New Jersey	17,000	0.0%
26	New Mexico	135,000	0.4%
27	New York	125,000	0.3%
17	North Carolina	375,000	1.0%
2	North Dakota	6,310,000	16.8%
15	Ohio	435,000	1.2%
4	Oklahoma	2,900,000	7.7%
12	Oregon	763,000	2.0%
24	Pennsylvania	150,000	0.4%
NA	Rhode Island**	NA	NA
33	South Carolina	75,000	0.2%
8	South Dakota	1,196,000	3.2%
19	Tennessee	275,000	0.7%
5	Texas	2,350,000	6.3%
29	Utah	120,000	0.3%
NA	Vermont**	NA	NA
25	Virginia	145,000	0.4%
6	Washington	2,140,000	5.7%
42	West Virginia	4,000	0.0%
23	Wisconsin	170,000	0.5%
31	Wyoming	105,000	0.3%

RANK ORDER

RANK	STATE	ACRES	% of USA
1	Kansas	6,950,000	18.5%
2	North Dakota	6,310,000	16.8%
3	Montana	4,665,000	12.4%
4	Oklahoma	2,900,000	7.7%
5	Texas	2,350,000	6.3%
6	Washington	2,140,000	5.7%
7	Colorado	2,029,000	5.4%
8	South Dakota	1,196,000	3.2%
9	Minnesota	1,135,000	3.0%
10	Idaho	1,104,000	2.9%
11	Nebraska	1,020,000	2.7%
12	Oregon	763,000	2.0%
13	Missouri	540,000	1.4%
14	Illinois	470,000	1.3%
15	Ohio	435,000	1.2%
16	Michigan	425,000	1.1%
17	North Carolina	375,000	1.0%
18	Kentucky	310,000	0.8%
19	Tennessee	275,000	0.7%
20	Indiana	240,000	0.6%
21	Maryland	185,000	0.5%
22	California	182,000	0.5%
23	Wisconsin	170,000	0.5%
24	Pennsylvania	150,000	0.4%
25	Virginia	145,000	0.4%
26	New Mexico	135,000	0.4%
27	Arkansas	125,000	0.3%
27	New York	125,000	0.3%
29	Utah	120,000	0.3%
30	Arizona	107,000	0.3%
31	Wyoming	105,000	0.3%
32	Alabama	100,000	0.3%
33	South Carolina	75,000	0.2%
34	Georgia	70,000	0.2%
35	Delaware	69,000	0.2%
36	Mississippi	25,000	0.1%
37	New Jersey	17,000	0.0%
38	Florida	14,000	0.0%
39	Louisiana	13,000	0.0%
40	Nevada	10,000	0.0%
41	Iowa	8,000	0.0%
42	West Virginia	4,000	0.0%
NA	Alaska**	NA	NA
NA	Connecticut**	NA	NA
NA	Hawaii**	NA	NA
NA	Maine**	NA	NA
NA	Massachusetts**	NA	NA
NA	New Hampshire**	NA	NA
NA	Rhode Island**	NA	NA
NA	Vermont**	NA	NA
	District of Columbia**	NA	NA

Source: U.S. Department of Agriculture, National Agricultural Statistics Service
   "Crop Production: 2017 Summary" (January 2018)
     (http://usda.mannlib.cornell.edu/MannUsda/viewDocumentInfo.do?documentID=1047)
*Estimated totals.
**No acreage or not available.

Cattle on Farms in 2018

National Total = 94,399,000 Cattle*

ALPHA ORDER

RANK	STATE	CATTLE	% of USA
23	Alabama	1,340,000	1.4%
49	Alaska	14,000	0.0%
31	Arizona	1,000,000	1.1%
17	Arkansas	1,760,000	1.9%
4	California	5,200,000	5.5%
10	Colorado	2,850,000	3.0%
44	Connecticut	50,000	0.1%
48	Delaware	17,000	0.0%
18	Florida	1,630,000	1.7%
30	Georgia	1,070,000	1.1%
42	Hawaii	144,000	0.2%
12	Idaho	2,400,000	2.5%
29	Illinois	1,150,000	1.2%
33	Indiana	870,000	0.9%
7	Iowa	4,000,000	4.2%
3	Kansas	6,300,000	6.7%
14	Kentucky	2,160,000	2.3%
34	Louisiana	820,000	0.9%
43	Maine	82,000	0.1%
41	Maryland	193,000	0.2%
45	Massachusetts	38,000	0.0%
27	Michigan	1,160,000	1.2%
13	Minnesota	2,350,000	2.5%
32	Mississippi	930,000	1.0%
6	Missouri	4,450,000	4.7%
11	Montana	2,550,000	2.7%
2	Nebraska	6,800,000	7.2%
37	Nevada	465,000	0.5%
46	New Hampshire	37,000	0.0%
47	New Jersey	29,000	0.0%
20	New Mexico	1,510,000	1.6%
21	New York	1,480,000	1.6%
35	North Carolina	810,000	0.9%
15	North Dakota	1,860,000	2.0%
25	Ohio	1,300,000	1.4%
5	Oklahoma	5,100,000	5.4%
26	Oregon	1,270,000	1.3%
19	Pennsylvania	1,620,000	1.7%
50	Rhode Island	5,000	0.0%
39	South Carolina	340,000	0.4%
7	South Dakota	4,000,000	4.2%
16	Tennessee	1,830,000	1.9%
1	Texas	12,500,000	13.2%
36	Utah	800,000	0.8%
40	Vermont	260,000	0.3%
21	Virginia	1,480,000	1.6%
27	Washington	1,160,000	1.2%
38	West Virginia	395,000	0.4%
9	Wisconsin	3,500,000	3.7%
24	Wyoming	1,320,000	1.4%

RANK ORDER

RANK	STATE	CATTLE	% of USA
1	Texas	12,500,000	13.2%
2	Nebraska	6,800,000	7.2%
3	Kansas	6,300,000	6.7%
4	California	5,200,000	5.5%
5	Oklahoma	5,100,000	5.4%
6	Missouri	4,450,000	4.7%
7	Iowa	4,000,000	4.2%
7	South Dakota	4,000,000	4.2%
9	Wisconsin	3,500,000	3.7%
10	Colorado	2,850,000	3.0%
11	Montana	2,550,000	2.7%
12	Idaho	2,400,000	2.5%
13	Minnesota	2,350,000	2.5%
14	Kentucky	2,160,000	2.3%
15	North Dakota	1,860,000	2.0%
16	Tennessee	1,830,000	1.9%
17	Arkansas	1,760,000	1.9%
18	Florida	1,630,000	1.7%
19	Pennsylvania	1,620,000	1.7%
20	New Mexico	1,510,000	1.6%
21	New York	1,480,000	1.6%
21	Virginia	1,480,000	1.6%
23	Alabama	1,340,000	1.4%
24	Wyoming	1,320,000	1.4%
25	Ohio	1,300,000	1.4%
26	Oregon	1,270,000	1.3%
27	Michigan	1,160,000	1.2%
27	Washington	1,160,000	1.2%
29	Illinois	1,150,000	1.2%
30	Georgia	1,070,000	1.1%
31	Arizona	1,000,000	1.1%
32	Mississippi	930,000	1.0%
33	Indiana	870,000	0.9%
34	Louisiana	820,000	0.9%
35	North Carolina	810,000	0.9%
36	Utah	800,000	0.8%
37	Nevada	465,000	0.5%
38	West Virginia	395,000	0.4%
39	South Carolina	340,000	0.4%
40	Vermont	260,000	0.3%
41	Maryland	193,000	0.2%
42	Hawaii	144,000	0.2%
43	Maine	82,000	0.1%
44	Connecticut	50,000	0.1%
45	Massachusetts	38,000	0.0%
46	New Hampshire	37,000	0.0%
47	New Jersey	29,000	0.0%
48	Delaware	17,000	0.0%
49	Alaska	14,000	0.0%
50	Rhode Island	5,000	0.0%
	District of Columbia	0	0.0%

Source: U.S. Department of Agriculture, National Agricultural Statistics Service
"Cattle" (http://usda.mannlib.cornell.edu/MannUsda/viewDocumentInfo.do?documentID=1017)
*As of January 1, 2018.

Milk Cows on Farms in 2016

National Total = 9,328,000 Milk Cows*

ALPHA ORDER

RANK	STATE	MILK COWS	% of USA
43	Alabama	7,000	0.1%
50	Alaska	300	0.0%
13	Arizona	196,000	2.1%
45	Arkansas	6,000	0.1%
1	California	1,762,000	18.9%
15	Colorado	151,000	1.6%
34	Connecticut	19,000	0.2%
47	Delaware	5,000	0.1%
19	Florida	123,000	1.3%
25	Georgia	84,000	0.9%
48	Hawaii	2,400	0.0%
4	Idaho	595,000	6.4%
21	Illinois	94,000	1.0%
14	Indiana	184,000	2.0%
12	Iowa	213,000	2.3%
16	Kansas	146,000	1.6%
27	Kentucky	58,000	0.6%
39	Louisiana	12,000	0.1%
32	Maine	30,000	0.3%
28	Maryland	48,000	0.5%
39	Massachusetts	12,000	0.1%
8	Michigan	419,000	4.5%
7	Minnesota	461,000	4.9%
41	Mississippi	10,000	0.1%
24	Missouri	88,000	0.9%
37	Montana	14,000	0.2%
26	Nebraska	60,000	0.6%
32	Nevada	30,000	0.3%
37	New Hampshire	14,000	0.2%
43	New Jersey	7,000	0.1%
9	New Mexico	315,000	3.4%
3	New York	620,000	6.6%
29	North Carolina	46,000	0.5%
35	North Dakota	16,000	0.2%
11	Ohio	265,000	2.8%
31	Oklahoma	37,000	0.4%
18	Oregon	125,000	1.3%
5	Pennsylvania	529,000	5.7%
49	Rhode Island	800	0.0%
36	South Carolina	15,000	0.2%
20	South Dakota	115,000	1.2%
30	Tennessee	42,000	0.5%
6	Texas	475,000	5.1%
22	Utah	92,000	1.0%
17	Vermont	130,000	1.4%
23	Virginia	90,000	1.0%
10	Washington	276,000	3.0%
42	West Virginia	9,000	0.1%
2	Wisconsin	1,279,000	13.7%
45	Wyoming	6,000	0.1%

RANK ORDER

RANK	STATE	MILK COWS	% of USA
1	California	1,762,000	18.9%
2	Wisconsin	1,279,000	13.7%
3	New York	620,000	6.6%
4	Idaho	595,000	6.4%
5	Pennsylvania	529,000	5.7%
6	Texas	475,000	5.1%
7	Minnesota	461,000	4.9%
8	Michigan	419,000	4.5%
9	New Mexico	315,000	3.4%
10	Washington	276,000	3.0%
11	Ohio	265,000	2.8%
12	Iowa	213,000	2.3%
13	Arizona	196,000	2.1%
14	Indiana	184,000	2.0%
15	Colorado	151,000	1.6%
16	Kansas	146,000	1.6%
17	Vermont	130,000	1.4%
18	Oregon	125,000	1.3%
19	Florida	123,000	1.3%
20	South Dakota	115,000	1.2%
21	Illinois	94,000	1.0%
22	Utah	92,000	1.0%
23	Virginia	90,000	1.0%
24	Missouri	88,000	0.9%
25	Georgia	84,000	0.9%
26	Nebraska	60,000	0.6%
27	Kentucky	58,000	0.6%
28	Maryland	48,000	0.5%
29	North Carolina	46,000	0.5%
30	Tennessee	42,000	0.5%
31	Oklahoma	37,000	0.4%
32	Maine	30,000	0.3%
32	Nevada	30,000	0.3%
34	Connecticut	19,000	0.2%
35	North Dakota	16,000	0.2%
36	South Carolina	15,000	0.2%
37	Montana	14,000	0.2%
37	New Hampshire	14,000	0.2%
39	Louisiana	12,000	0.1%
39	Massachusetts	12,000	0.1%
41	Mississippi	10,000	0.1%
42	West Virginia	9,000	0.1%
43	Alabama	7,000	0.1%
43	New Jersey	7,000	0.1%
45	Arkansas	6,000	0.1%
45	Wyoming	6,000	0.1%
47	Delaware	5,000	0.1%
48	Hawaii	2,400	0.0%
49	Rhode Island	800	0.0%
50	Alaska	300	0.0%
	District of Columbia	0	0.0%

Source: U.S. Department of Agriculture, National Agricultural Statistics Service
  "Milk Production, Disposition and Income: 2016 Summary" (April 2017)
    (http://usda.mannlib.cornell.edu/MannUsda/viewDocumentInfo.do?documentID=1105)
*Average number during year. Excludes heifers not yet fresh.

Milk Production in 2016

National Total = 212,436,000,000 Pounds of Milk*

ALPHA ORDER

RANK	STATE	POUNDS	% of USA
46	Alabama	92,000,000	0.0%
50	Alaska	3,500,000	0.0%
13	Arizona	4,788,000,000	2.3%
47	Arkansas	79,000,000	0.0%
1	California	40,469,000,000	19.0%
15	Colorado	3,923,000,000	1.8%
34	Connecticut	408,000,000	0.2%
45	Delaware	95,500,000	0.0%
20	Florida	2,503,000,000	1.2%
23	Georgia	1,830,000,000	0.9%
48	Hawaii	34,900,000	0.0%
4	Idaho	14,665,000,000	6.9%
22	Illinois	1,903,000,000	0.9%
14	Indiana	4,151,000,000	2.0%
12	Iowa	5,034,000,000	2.4%
16	Kansas	3,329,000,000	1.6%
27	Kentucky	1,048,000,000	0.5%
40	Louisiana	169,000,000	0.1%
33	Maine	630,000,000	0.3%
29	Maryland	956,000,000	0.5%
39	Massachusetts	215,000,000	0.1%
5	Michigan	10,876,000,000	5.1%
8	Minnesota	9,666,000,000	4.6%
41	Mississippi	144,000,000	0.1%
26	Missouri	1,373,000,000	0.6%
36	Montana	295,000,000	0.1%
25	Nebraska	1,399,000,000	0.7%
32	Nevada	660,000,000	0.3%
37	New Hampshire	284,000,000	0.1%
44	New Jersey	122,000,000	0.1%
9	New Mexico	7,711,000,000	3.6%
3	New York	14,765,000,000	7.0%
28	North Carolina	965,000,000	0.5%
35	North Dakota	345,000,000	0.2%
11	Ohio	5,532,000,000	2.6%
31	Oklahoma	692,000,000	0.3%
18	Oregon	2,593,000,000	1.2%
6	Pennsylvania	10,820,000,000	5.1%
49	Rhode Island	14,000,000	0.0%
38	South Carolina	250,000,000	0.1%
19	South Dakota	2,546,000,000	1.2%
30	Tennessee	696,000,000	0.3%
7	Texas	10,773,000,000	5.1%
21	Utah	2,095,000,000	1.0%
17	Vermont	2,724,000,000	1.3%
24	Virginia	1,723,000,000	0.8%
10	Washington	6,650,000,000	3.1%
43	West Virginia	134,000,000	0.1%
2	Wisconsin	30,123,000,000	14.2%
42	Wyoming	139,800,000	0.1%

RANK ORDER

RANK	STATE	POUNDS	% of USA
1	California	40,469,000,000	19.0%
2	Wisconsin	30,123,000,000	14.2%
3	New York	14,765,000,000	7.0%
4	Idaho	14,665,000,000	6.9%
5	Michigan	10,876,000,000	5.1%
6	Pennsylvania	10,820,000,000	5.1%
7	Texas	10,773,000,000	5.1%
8	Minnesota	9,666,000,000	4.6%
9	New Mexico	7,711,000,000	3.6%
10	Washington	6,650,000,000	3.1%
11	Ohio	5,532,000,000	2.6%
12	Iowa	5,034,000,000	2.4%
13	Arizona	4,788,000,000	2.3%
14	Indiana	4,151,000,000	2.0%
15	Colorado	3,923,000,000	1.8%
16	Kansas	3,329,000,000	1.6%
17	Vermont	2,724,000,000	1.3%
18	Oregon	2,593,000,000	1.2%
19	South Dakota	2,546,000,000	1.2%
20	Florida	2,503,000,000	1.2%
21	Utah	2,095,000,000	1.0%
22	Illinois	1,903,000,000	0.9%
23	Georgia	1,830,000,000	0.9%
24	Virginia	1,723,000,000	0.8%
25	Nebraska	1,399,000,000	0.7%
26	Missouri	1,373,000,000	0.6%
27	Kentucky	1,048,000,000	0.5%
28	North Carolina	965,000,000	0.5%
29	Maryland	956,000,000	0.5%
30	Tennessee	696,000,000	0.3%
31	Oklahoma	692,000,000	0.3%
32	Nevada	660,000,000	0.3%
33	Maine	630,000,000	0.3%
34	Connecticut	408,000,000	0.2%
35	North Dakota	345,000,000	0.2%
36	Montana	295,000,000	0.1%
37	New Hampshire	284,000,000	0.1%
38	South Carolina	250,000,000	0.1%
39	Massachusetts	215,000,000	0.1%
40	Louisiana	169,000,000	0.1%
41	Mississippi	144,000,000	0.1%
42	Wyoming	139,800,000	0.1%
43	West Virginia	134,000,000	0.1%
44	New Jersey	122,000,000	0.1%
45	Delaware	95,500,000	0.0%
46	Alabama	92,000,000	0.0%
47	Arkansas	79,000,000	0.0%
48	Hawaii	34,900,000	0.0%
49	Rhode Island	14,000,000	0.0%
50	Alaska	3,500,000	0.0%
	District of Columbia	0	0.0%

Source: U.S. Department of Agriculture, National Agricultural Statistics Service
   "Milk Production, Disposition and Income: 2016 Summary" (April 2017)
      (http://usda.mannlib.cornell.edu/MannUsda/viewDocumentInfo.do?documentID=1105)
*Excludes milk suckled by calves.

Milk Production per Milk Cow in 2016

National Average = 22,774 Pounds of Milk per Cow*

ALPHA ORDER			RANK ORDER		
RANK	STATE	POUNDS	RANK	STATE	POUNDS
49	Alabama	13,143	1	Colorado	25,980
50	Alaska	11,667	2	Michigan	25,957
5	Arizona	24,429	3	Idaho	24,647
48	Arkansas	13,167	4	New Mexico	24,479
12	California	22,968	5	Arizona	24,429
1	Colorado	25,980	6	Washington	24,094
21	Connecticut	21,474	7	New York	23,815
35	Delaware	19,100	8	Iowa	23,634
30	Florida	20,350	9	Wisconsin	23,552
19	Georgia	21,786	10	Nebraska	23,317
45	Hawaii	14,542	11	Wyoming	23,300
3	Idaho	24,647	12	California	22,968
32	Illinois	20,245	13	Kansas	22,801
16	Indiana	22,560	14	Utah	22,772
8	Iowa	23,634	15	Texas	22,680
13	Kansas	22,801	16	Indiana	22,560
37	Kentucky	18,069	17	South Dakota	22,139
47	Louisiana	14,083	18	Nevada	22,000
23	Maine	21,000	19	Georgia	21,786
33	Maryland	19,917	20	North Dakota	21,563
38	Massachusetts	17,917	21	Connecticut	21,474
2	Michigan	25,957	22	Montana	21,071
25	Minnesota	20,967	23	Maine	21,000
46	Mississippi	14,400	24	North Carolina	20,978
43	Missouri	15,602	25	Minnesota	20,967
22	Montana	21,071	26	Vermont	20,954
10	Nebraska	23,317	27	Ohio	20,875
18	Nevada	22,000	28	Oregon	20,744
31	New Hampshire	20,286	29	Pennsylvania	20,454
40	New Jersey	17,429	30	Florida	20,350
4	New Mexico	24,479	31	New Hampshire	20,286
7	New York	23,815	32	Illinois	20,245
24	North Carolina	20,978	33	Maryland	19,917
20	North Dakota	21,563	34	Virginia	19,144
27	Ohio	20,875	35	Delaware	19,100
36	Oklahoma	18,703	36	Oklahoma	18,703
28	Oregon	20,744	37	Kentucky	18,069
29	Pennsylvania	20,454	38	Massachusetts	17,917
39	Rhode Island	17,500	39	Rhode Island	17,500
41	South Carolina	16,667	40	New Jersey	17,429
17	South Dakota	22,139	41	South Carolina	16,667
42	Tennessee	16,571	42	Tennessee	16,571
15	Texas	22,680	43	Missouri	15,602
14	Utah	22,772	44	West Virginia	14,889
26	Vermont	20,954	45	Hawaii	14,542
34	Virginia	19,144	46	Mississippi	14,400
6	Washington	24,094	47	Louisiana	14,083
44	West Virginia	14,889	48	Arkansas	13,167
9	Wisconsin	23,552	49	Alabama	13,143
11	Wyoming	23,300	50	Alaska	11,667
				District of Columbia**	NA

Source: U.S. Department of Agriculture, National Agricultural Statistics Service
  "Milk Production, Disposition and Income: 2016 Summary" (April 2017)
    (http://usda.mannlib.cornell.edu/MannUsda/viewDocumentInfo.do?documentID=1105)
*Excludes milk suckled by calves.
**Not applicable.

Hogs and Pigs on Farms in 2017

National Total = 73,229,900 Hogs and Pigs*

ALPHA ORDER				RANK ORDER			
RANK	STATE	HOGS AND PIGS	% of USA	RANK	STATE	HOGS AND PIGS	% of USA
30	Alabama	57,000	0.1%	1	Iowa	22,800,000	31.1%
47	Alaska	1,500	0.0%	2	North Carolina	9,000,000	12.3%
24	Arizona	160,000	0.2%	3	Minnesota	8,500,000	11.6%
26	Arkansas	131,000	0.2%	4	Illinois	5,350,000	7.3%
27	California	95,000	0.1%	5	Indiana	4,000,000	5.5%
15	Colorado	750,000	1.0%	6	Nebraska	3,600,000	4.9%
44	Connecticut	2,700	0.0%	7	Missouri	3,400,000	4.6%
37	Delaware	6,000	0.0%	8	Ohio	2,900,000	4.0%
33	Florida	15,000	0.0%	9	Oklahoma	2,200,000	3.0%
29	Georgia	80,000	0.1%	10	Kansas	2,100,000	2.9%
39	Hawaii	5,000	0.0%	11	South Dakota	1,560,000	2.1%
NA	Idaho**	NA	NA	12	Pennsylvania	1,240,000	1.7%
4	Illinois	5,350,000	7.3%	13	Michigan	1,180,000	1.6%
5	Indiana	4,000,000	5.5%	14	Texas	1,030,000	1.4%
1	Iowa	22,800,000	31.1%	15	Colorado	750,000	1.0%
10	Kansas	2,100,000	2.9%	16	Mississippi	570,000	0.8%
18	Kentucky	405,000	0.6%	17	Utah	540,000	0.7%
37	Louisiana	6,000	0.0%	18	Kentucky	405,000	0.6%
41	Maine	4,500	0.0%	19	Wisconsin	300,000	0.4%
32	Maryland	26,000	0.0%	20	Tennessee	235,000	0.3%
36	Massachusetts	7,500	0.0%	20	Virginia	235,000	0.3%
13	Michigan	1,180,000	1.6%	22	South Carolina	185,000	0.3%
3	Minnesota	8,500,000	11.6%	23	Montana	179,000	0.2%
16	Mississippi	570,000	0.8%	24	Arizona	160,000	0.2%
7	Missouri	3,400,000	4.6%	25	North Dakota	147,000	0.2%
23	Montana	179,000	0.2%	26	Arkansas	131,000	0.2%
6	Nebraska	3,600,000	4.9%	27	California	95,000	0.1%
48	Nevada	500	0.0%	28	Wyoming	90,000	0.1%
43	New Hampshire	3,400	0.0%	29	Georgia	80,000	0.1%
34	New Jersey	12,500	0.0%	30	Alabama	57,000	0.1%
46	New Mexico	1,600	0.0%	31	New York	48,000	0.1%
31	New York	48,000	0.1%	32	Maryland	26,000	0.0%
2	North Carolina	9,000,000	12.3%	33	Florida	15,000	0.0%
25	North Dakota	147,000	0.2%	34	New Jersey	12,500	0.0%
8	Ohio	2,900,000	4.0%	35	Oregon	9,000	0.0%
9	Oklahoma	2,200,000	3.0%	36	Massachusetts	7,500	0.0%
35	Oregon	9,000	0.0%	37	Delaware	6,000	0.0%
12	Pennsylvania	1,240,000	1.7%	37	Louisiana	6,000	0.0%
45	Rhode Island	2,000	0.0%	39	Hawaii	5,000	0.0%
22	South Carolina	185,000	0.3%	39	West Virginia	5,000	0.0%
11	South Dakota	1,560,000	2.1%	41	Maine	4,500	0.0%
20	Tennessee	235,000	0.3%	42	Vermont	3,700	0.0%
14	Texas	1,030,000	1.4%	43	New Hampshire	3,400	0.0%
17	Utah	540,000	0.7%	44	Connecticut	2,700	0.0%
42	Vermont	3,700	0.0%	45	Rhode Island	2,000	0.0%
20	Virginia	235,000	0.3%	46	New Mexico	1,600	0.0%
NA	Washington**	NA	NA	47	Alaska	1,500	0.0%
39	West Virginia	5,000	0.0%	48	Nevada	500	0.0%
19	Wisconsin	300,000	0.4%	NA	Idaho**	NA	NA
28	Wyoming	90,000	0.1%	NA	Washington**	NA	NA
					District of Columbia	0	0.0%

Source: U.S. Department of Agriculture, National Agricultural Statistics Service
   "Quarterly Hogs and Pigs" (http://usda.mannlib.cornell.edu/MannUsda/viewDocumentInfo.do?documentID=1086)
*As of December 1, 2017.
**Not available. Figures for Idaho and Washington withheld to avoid disclosing data for individual operations. The two states combined had 51,000 hogs and pigs.

Chickens in 2016

National Total = 8,776,700,000 Chickens*

ALPHA ORDER

RANK	STATE	CHICKENS	% of USA
2	Alabama	1,070,100,000	12.2%
NA	Alaska***	NA	NA
NA	Arizona***	NA	NA
3	Arkansas	1,009,400,000	11.5%
NA	California**	NA	NA
NA	Colorado***	NA	NA
NA	Connecticut***	NA	NA
11	Delaware	252,500,000	2.9%
18	Florida	63,200,000	0.7%
1	Georgia	1,367,100,000	15.6%
NA	Hawaii***	NA	NA
NA	Idaho***	NA	NA
NA	Illinois**	NA	NA
NA	Indiana**	NA	NA
NA	Iowa**	NA	NA
NA	Kansas***	NA	NA
8	Kentucky	300,300,000	3.4%
NA	Louisiana**	NA	NA
NA	Maine***	NA	NA
7	Maryland	303,500,000	3.5%
NA	Massachusetts***	NA	NA
NA	Michigan**	NA	NA
20	Minnesota	48,400,000	0.6%
5	Mississippi	739,400,000	8.4%
9	Missouri	293,000,000	3.3%
NA	Montana***	NA	NA
NA	Nebraska**	NA	NA
NA	Nevada***	NA	NA
NA	New Hampshire***	NA	NA
NA	New Jersey**	NA	NA
NA	New Mexico***	NA	NA
NA	New York**	NA	NA
4	North Carolina	818,700,000	9.3%
NA	North Dakota***	NA	NA
17	Ohio	88,000,000	1.0%
13	Oklahoma	209,700,000	2.4%
NA	Oregon**	NA	NA
14	Pennsylvania	185,700,000	2.1%
NA	Rhode Island***	NA	NA
12	South Carolina	244,700,000	2.8%
NA	South Dakota***	NA	NA
15	Tennessee	175,200,000	2.0%
6	Texas	629,500,000	7.2%
NA	Utah***	NA	NA
NA	Vermont***	NA	NA
10	Virginia	269,100,000	3.1%
NA	Washington**	NA	NA
16	West Virginia	90,300,000	1.0%
19	Wisconsin	54,100,000	0.6%
NA	Wyoming***	NA	NA

RANK ORDER

RANK	STATE	CHICKENS	% of USA
1	Georgia	1,367,100,000	15.6%
2	Alabama	1,070,100,000	12.2%
3	Arkansas	1,009,400,000	11.5%
4	North Carolina	818,700,000	9.3%
5	Mississippi	739,400,000	8.4%
6	Texas	629,500,000	7.2%
7	Maryland	303,500,000	3.5%
8	Kentucky	300,300,000	3.4%
9	Missouri	293,000,000	3.3%
10	Virginia	269,100,000	3.1%
11	Delaware	252,500,000	2.9%
12	South Carolina	244,700,000	2.8%
13	Oklahoma	209,700,000	2.4%
14	Pennsylvania	185,700,000	2.1%
15	Tennessee	175,200,000	2.0%
16	West Virginia	90,300,000	1.0%
17	Ohio	88,000,000	1.0%
18	Florida	63,200,000	0.7%
19	Wisconsin	54,100,000	0.6%
20	Minnesota	48,400,000	0.6%
NA	Alaska***	NA	NA
NA	Arizona***	NA	NA
NA	California**	NA	NA
NA	Colorado***	NA	NA
NA	Connecticut***	NA	NA
NA	Hawaii***	NA	NA
NA	Idaho***	NA	NA
NA	Illinois**	NA	NA
NA	Indiana**	NA	NA
NA	Iowa**	NA	NA
NA	Kansas***	NA	NA
NA	Louisiana**	NA	NA
NA	Maine***	NA	NA
NA	Massachusetts***	NA	NA
NA	Michigan**	NA	NA
NA	Montana***	NA	NA
NA	Nebraska**	NA	NA
NA	Nevada***	NA	NA
NA	New Hampshire***	NA	NA
NA	New Jersey**	NA	NA
NA	New Mexico***	NA	NA
NA	New York**	NA	NA
NA	North Dakota***	NA	NA
NA	Oregon**	NA	NA
NA	Rhode Island***	NA	NA
NA	South Dakota***	NA	NA
NA	Utah***	NA	NA
NA	Vermont***	NA	NA
NA	Washington**	NA	NA
NA	Wyoming***	NA	NA
	District of Columbia***	NA	NA

Source: U.S. Department of Agriculture, National Agricultural Statistics Service
   "Poultry - Production and Value: 2016 Summary" (April 2017)
      (http://usda.mannlib.cornell.edu/MannUsda/viewDocumentInfo.do?documentID=1130)

*Broilers. Total includes numbers for states not shown separately but excludes states producing less than 500,000 birds. **These states produced a combined total of 564,800,000 chickens. They are combined to avoid disclosing individual operations. National total does not include chickens used for egg production. ***Produces fewer than 500,000 chickens or are not available.

Eggs Produced in 2016

National Total = 101,952,700,000 Eggs*

ALPHA ORDER

RANK	STATE	EGGS	% of USA
15	Alabama	2,110,700,000	2.1%
NA	Alaska**	NA	NA
NA	Arizona**	NA	NA
10	Arkansas	3,411,400,000	3.3%
9	California	3,473,500,000	3.4%
21	Colorado	1,364,000,000	1.3%
NA	Connecticut**	NA	NA
NA	Delaware**	NA	NA
14	Florida	2,364,100,000	2.3%
6	Georgia	4,893,800,000	4.8%
NA	Hawaii**	NA	NA
NA	Idaho**	NA	NA
19	Illinois	1,534,700,000	1.5%
3	Indiana	8,910,400,000	8.7%
1	Iowa	13,608,000,000	13.3%
NA	Kansas**	NA	NA
22	Kentucky	1,304,100,000	1.3%
30	Louisiana	541,000,000	0.5%
NA	Maine**	NA	NA
25	Maryland	795,900,000	0.8%
34	Massachusetts	40,600,000	0.0%
7	Michigan	3,963,900,000	3.9%
12	Minnesota	2,813,900,000	2.8%
20	Mississippi	1,391,900,000	1.4%
11	Missouri	3,208,900,000	3.1%
33	Montana	135,900,000	0.1%
13	Nebraska	2,570,200,000	2.5%
NA	Nevada**	NA	NA
NA	New Hampshire**	NA	NA
NA	New Jersey**	NA	NA
NA	New Mexico**	NA	NA
17	New York	1,673,800,000	1.6%
8	North Carolina	3,729,500,000	3.7%
NA	North Dakota**	NA	NA
2	Ohio	9,546,000,000	9.4%
28	Oklahoma	692,000,000	0.7%
27	Oregon	732,000,000	0.7%
4	Pennsylvania	8,212,400,000	8.1%
NA	Rhode Island**	NA	NA
24	South Carolina	1,141,700,000	1.1%
29	South Dakota	594,200,000	0.6%
31	Tennessee	394,500,000	0.4%
5	Texas	5,571,800,000	5.5%
23	Utah	1,271,400,000	1.2%
35	Vermont	38,400,000	0.0%
26	Virginia	782,300,000	0.8%
16	Washington	2,006,500,000	2.0%
32	West Virginia	287,100,000	0.3%
18	Wisconsin	1,618,800,000	1.6%
NA	Wyoming**	NA	NA

RANK ORDER

RANK	STATE	EGGS	% of USA
1	Iowa	13,608,000,000	13.3%
2	Ohio	9,546,000,000	9.4%
3	Indiana	8,910,400,000	8.7%
4	Pennsylvania	8,212,400,000	8.1%
5	Texas	5,571,800,000	5.5%
6	Georgia	4,893,800,000	4.8%
7	Michigan	3,963,900,000	3.9%
8	North Carolina	3,729,500,000	3.7%
9	California	3,473,500,000	3.4%
10	Arkansas	3,411,400,000	3.3%
11	Missouri	3,208,900,000	3.1%
12	Minnesota	2,813,900,000	2.8%
13	Nebraska	2,570,200,000	2.5%
14	Florida	2,364,100,000	2.3%
15	Alabama	2,110,700,000	2.1%
16	Washington	2,006,500,000	2.0%
17	New York	1,673,800,000	1.6%
18	Wisconsin	1,618,800,000	1.6%
19	Illinois	1,534,700,000	1.5%
20	Mississippi	1,391,900,000	1.4%
21	Colorado	1,364,000,000	1.3%
22	Kentucky	1,304,100,000	1.3%
23	Utah	1,271,400,000	1.2%
24	South Carolina	1,141,700,000	1.1%
25	Maryland	795,900,000	0.8%
26	Virginia	782,300,000	0.8%
27	Oregon	732,000,000	0.7%
28	Oklahoma	692,000,000	0.7%
29	South Dakota	594,200,000	0.6%
30	Louisiana	541,000,000	0.5%
31	Tennessee	394,500,000	0.4%
32	West Virginia	287,100,000	0.3%
33	Montana	135,900,000	0.1%
34	Massachusetts	40,600,000	0.0%
35	Vermont	38,400,000	0.0%
NA	Alaska**	NA	NA
NA	Arizona**	NA	NA
NA	Connecticut**	NA	NA
NA	Delaware**	NA	NA
NA	Hawaii**	NA	NA
NA	Idaho**	NA	NA
NA	Kansas**	NA	NA
NA	Maine**	NA	NA
NA	Nevada**	NA	NA
NA	New Hampshire**	NA	NA
NA	New Jersey**	NA	NA
NA	New Mexico**	NA	NA
NA	North Dakota**	NA	NA
NA	Rhode Island**	NA	NA
NA	Wyoming**	NA	NA
	District of Columbia	0	0.0%

Source: U.S. Department of Agriculture, National Agricultural Statistics Service
"Poultry - Production and Value: 2016 Summary" (April 2017)
(http://usda.mannlib.cornell.edu/MannUsda/viewDocumentInfo.do?documentID=1130)
*Includes hatching and market (table) eggs. **These states produced a combined 5,223,400,000 eggs. They are combined to avoid disclosing individual operations.

II. Crime and Law Enforcement

I. Arrests:

Important Note Regarding Arrest Numbers

The state arrest numbers reported by the FBI and shown on page 57 are only from those law enforcement agencies that submitted complete arrests reports for 12 months in 2016. The arrest rates were calculated by the editors using population totals provided by the FBI for those jurisdictions reporting. Reports from law enforcement agencies in Illinois and the District of Columbia were insufficient to calculate rates. Reports from Kansas, Mississippi, New York, and Vermont represented less than 60 percent of their state population. Rates for these states should be interpreted with caution.

V. Juveniles:

Important Note Regarding Juvenile Arrest Rates

The juvenile arrest rates shown on page 58 were calculated by the editors as follows:

The state arrest numbers reported by the FBI are only from those law enforcement agencies that submitted complete arrests reports for 12 months in 2016. Included in the FBI report are population totals of these reporting jurisdictions by state. Using these FBI population figures, we first determined what percentage the FBI numbers represented of each state's total resident population. Next, using 2016 Census state estimates for 10- to 17-year-olds, we multiplied the percentages derived from the FBI population figures into the Census Bureau's total juvenile population counts. The resulting juvenile population is the base that was used to determine juvenile arrests per 100,000 juvenile population. The national rate was calculated in the same manner.

Reports from law enforcement agencies in Illinois and the District of Columbia were insufficient to calculate rates. Reports from Kansas, Mississippi, New York, and Vermont represented less than 60 percent of their state population. Rates for these states should be interpreted with caution.

Crimes in 2016

National Total = 9,167,220 Crimes*

ALPHA ORDER

RANK	STATE	CRIMES	% of USA
20	Alabama	168,717	1.8%
43	Alaska	30,546	0.3%
11	Arizona	238,177	2.6%
28	Arkansas	113,536	1.2%
1	California	1,173,313	12.8%
19	Colorado	169,897	1.9%
36	Connecticut	72,585	0.8%
42	Delaware	31,091	0.3%
3	Florida	640,442	7.0%
5	Georgia	349,779	3.8%
38	Hawaii	46,998	0.5%
40	Idaho	33,043	0.4%
7	Illinois	316,887	3.5%
15	Indiana	197,954	2.2%
35	Iowa	74,176	0.8%
34	Kansas	89,086	1.0%
29	Kentucky	106,999	1.2%
17	Louisiana	180,400	2.0%
44	Maine	23,448	0.3%
21	Maryland	165,355	1.8%
25	Massachusetts	131,480	1.4%
12	Michigan	233,181	2.5%
26	Minnesota	130,533	1.4%
33	Mississippi	90,743	1.0%
14	Missouri	201,523	2.2%
41	Montana	31,652	0.3%
37	Nebraska	48,457	0.5%
32	Nevada	95,542	1.0%
45	New Hampshire	22,672	0.2%
22	New Jersey	159,702	1.7%
31	New Mexico	96,141	1.0%
4	New York	377,775	4.1%
8	North Carolina	314,771	3.4%
48	North Dakota	19,219	0.2%
6	Ohio	332,786	3.6%
23	Oklahoma	134,155	1.5%
24	Oregon	131,715	1.4%
10	Pennsylvania	262,042	2.9%
46	Rhode Island	22,468	0.2%
16	South Carolina	185,148	2.0%
47	South Dakota	20,632	0.2%
13	Tennessee	231,209	2.5%
2	Texas	886,480	9.7%
30	Utah	97,061	1.1%
50	Vermont	11,537	0.1%
18	Virginia	173,942	1.9%
9	Washington	275,858	3.0%
39	West Virginia	43,855	0.5%
27	Wisconsin	128,878	1.4%
49	Wyoming	12,835	0.1%

RANK ORDER

RANK	STATE	CRIMES	% of USA
1	California	1,173,313	12.8%
2	Texas	886,480	9.7%
3	Florida	640,442	7.0%
4	New York	377,775	4.1%
5	Georgia	349,779	3.8%
6	Ohio	332,786	3.6%
7	Illinois	316,887	3.5%
8	North Carolina	314,771	3.4%
9	Washington	275,858	3.0%
10	Pennsylvania	262,042	2.9%
11	Arizona	238,177	2.6%
12	Michigan	233,181	2.5%
13	Tennessee	231,209	2.5%
14	Missouri	201,523	2.2%
15	Indiana	197,954	2.2%
16	South Carolina	185,148	2.0%
17	Louisiana	180,400	2.0%
18	Virginia	173,942	1.9%
19	Colorado	169,897	1.9%
20	Alabama	168,717	1.8%
21	Maryland	165,355	1.8%
22	New Jersey	159,702	1.7%
23	Oklahoma	134,155	1.5%
24	Oregon	131,715	1.4%
25	Massachusetts	131,480	1.4%
26	Minnesota	130,533	1.4%
27	Wisconsin	128,878	1.4%
28	Arkansas	113,536	1.2%
29	Kentucky	106,999	1.2%
30	Utah	97,061	1.1%
31	New Mexico	96,141	1.0%
32	Nevada	95,542	1.0%
33	Mississippi	90,743	1.0%
34	Kansas	89,086	1.0%
35	Iowa	74,176	0.8%
36	Connecticut	72,585	0.8%
37	Nebraska	48,457	0.5%
38	Hawaii	46,998	0.5%
39	West Virginia	43,855	0.5%
40	Idaho	33,043	0.4%
41	Montana	31,652	0.3%
42	Delaware	31,091	0.3%
43	Alaska	30,546	0.3%
44	Maine	23,448	0.3%
45	New Hampshire	22,672	0.2%
46	Rhode Island	22,468	0.2%
47	South Dakota	20,632	0.2%
48	North Dakota	19,219	0.2%
49	Wyoming	12,835	0.1%
50	Vermont	11,537	0.1%
	District of Columbia	40,799	0.4%

Source: CQ Press using reported data from the Federal Bureau of Investigation
"Crime in the United States 2016" (Uniform Crime Reports, September 25, 2017, https://ucr.fbi.gov/)
*Includes murder, rape (legacy definition), robbery, aggravated assault, burglary, larceny-theft, and motor vehicle theft.

Crime Rate in 2016

National Rate = 2,836.9 Crimes per 100,000 Population*

ALPHA ORDER

RANK	STATE	RATE
8	Alabama	3,469.3
2	Alaska	4,117.2
9	Arizona	3,436.5
4	Arkansas	3,799.4
25	California	2,989.3
21	Colorado	3,066.5
43	Connecticut	2,029.5
14	Delaware	3,265.6
19	Florida	3,107.1
11	Georgia	3,392.5
13	Hawaii	3,289.9
44	Idaho	1,963.2
31	Illinois	2,475.4
26	Indiana	2,984.3
35	Iowa	2,366.3
22	Kansas	3,064.2
32	Kentucky	2,411.5
3	Louisiana	3,853.4
49	Maine	1,761.0
28	Maryland	2,748.3
45	Massachusetts	1,930.3
37	Michigan	2,348.6
36	Minnesota	2,364.7
23	Mississippi	3,036.2
12	Missouri	3,307.4
24	Montana	3,036.1
29	Nebraska	2,540.9
15	Nevada	3,249.6
50	New Hampshire	1,698.6
48	New Jersey	1,785.6
1	New Mexico	4,620.0
46	New York	1,913.2
20	North Carolina	3,102.3
30	North Dakota	2,535.7
27	Ohio	2,865.3
10	Oklahoma	3,419.2
16	Oregon	3,217.7
42	Pennsylvania	2,049.7
40	Rhode Island	2,126.7
6	South Carolina	3,732.0
34	South Dakota	2,383.9
7	Tennessee	3,476.1
17	Texas	3,181.7
18	Utah	3,181.1
47	Vermont	1,847.1
41	Virginia	2,067.9
5	Washington	3,785.0
33	West Virginia	2,395.0
38	Wisconsin	2,230.2
39	Wyoming	2,192.1

RANK ORDER

RANK	STATE	RATE
1	New Mexico	4,620.0
2	Alaska	4,117.2
3	Louisiana	3,853.4
4	Arkansas	3,799.4
5	Washington	3,785.0
6	South Carolina	3,732.0
7	Tennessee	3,476.1
8	Alabama	3,469.3
9	Arizona	3,436.5
10	Oklahoma	3,419.2
11	Georgia	3,392.5
12	Missouri	3,307.4
13	Hawaii	3,289.9
14	Delaware	3,265.6
15	Nevada	3,249.6
16	Oregon	3,217.7
17	Texas	3,181.7
18	Utah	3,181.1
19	Florida	3,107.1
20	North Carolina	3,102.3
21	Colorado	3,066.5
22	Kansas	3,064.2
23	Mississippi	3,036.2
24	Montana	3,036.1
25	California	2,989.3
26	Indiana	2,984.3
27	Ohio	2,865.3
28	Maryland	2,748.3
29	Nebraska	2,540.9
30	North Dakota	2,535.7
31	Illinois	2,475.4
32	Kentucky	2,411.5
33	West Virginia	2,395.0
34	South Dakota	2,383.9
35	Iowa	2,366.3
36	Minnesota	2,364.7
37	Michigan	2,348.6
38	Wisconsin	2,230.2
39	Wyoming	2,192.1
40	Rhode Island	2,126.7
41	Virginia	2,067.9
42	Pennsylvania	2,049.7
43	Connecticut	2,029.5
44	Idaho	1,963.2
45	Massachusetts	1,930.3
46	New York	1,913.2
47	Vermont	1,847.1
48	New Jersey	1,785.6
49	Maine	1,761.0
50	New Hampshire	1,698.6

District of Columbia	5,989.6

Source: CQ Press using reported data from the Federal Bureau of Investigation
"Crime in the United States 2016" (Uniform Crime Reports, September 25, 2017, https://ucr.fbi.gov/)
*Includes murder, rape (legacy definition), robbery, aggravated assault, burglary, larceny-theft, and motor vehicle theft.

Percent Change in Crime Rate: 2015 to 2016

National Percent Change = 1.3% Decrease*

ALPHA ORDER				RANK ORDER		
RANK	STATE	PERCENT CHANGE		RANK	STATE	PERCENT CHANGE
14	Alabama	0.7		1	Vermont	18.4
2	Alaska	17.1		2	Alaska	17.1
20	Arizona	0.0		3	New Mexico	6.3
16	Arkansas	0.5		4	Colorado	4.1
32	California	(1.9)		4	Illinois	4.1
4	Colorado	4.1		6	Wyoming	3.7
25	Connecticut	(0.8)		7	South Dakota	2.7
9	Delaware	2.1		8	Oklahoma	2.6
46	Florida	(4.9)		9	Delaware	2.1
37	Georgia	(2.3)		10	Montana	1.9
45	Hawaii	(3.8)		11	Iowa	1.2
17	Idaho	0.4		11	Nebraska	1.2
4	Illinois	4.1		13	Michigan	0.8
17	Indiana	0.4		14	Alabama	0.7
11	Iowa	1.2		14	Washington	0.7
36	Kansas	(2.2)		16	Arkansas	0.5
22	Kentucky	(0.2)		17	Idaho	0.4
28	Louisiana	(1.4)		17	Indiana	0.4
49	Maine	(9.8)		17	North Carolina	0.4
40	Maryland	(3.2)		20	Arizona	0.0
48	Massachusetts	(6.8)		21	Rhode Island	(0.1)
13	Michigan	0.8		22	Kentucky	(0.2)
44	Minnesota	(3.7)		23	Oregon	(0.4)
39	Mississippi	(3.1)		23	Virginia	(0.4)
26	Missouri	(1.2)		25	Connecticut	(0.8)
10	Montana	1.9		26	Missouri	(1.2)
11	Nebraska	1.2		26	Ohio	(1.2)
40	Nevada	(3.2)		28	Louisiana	(1.4)
50	New Hampshire	(13.0)		28	Utah	(1.4)
47	New Jersey	(5.2)		30	West Virginia	(1.7)
3	New Mexico	6.3		31	Texas	(1.8)
42	New York	(3.3)		32	California	(1.9)
17	North Carolina	0.4		32	North Dakota	(1.9)
32	North Dakota	(1.9)		34	Wisconsin	(2.0)
26	Ohio	(1.2)		35	South Carolina	(2.1)
8	Oklahoma	2.6		36	Kansas	(2.2)
23	Oregon	(0.4)		37	Georgia	(2.3)
42	Pennsylvania	(3.3)		38	Tennessee	(2.9)
21	Rhode Island	(0.1)		39	Mississippi	(3.1)
35	South Carolina	(2.1)		40	Maryland	(3.2)
7	South Dakota	2.7		40	Nevada	(3.2)
38	Tennessee	(2.9)		42	New York	(3.3)
31	Texas	(1.8)		42	Pennsylvania	(3.3)
28	Utah	(1.4)		44	Minnesota	(3.7)
1	Vermont	18.4		45	Hawaii	(3.8)
23	Virginia	(0.4)		46	Florida	(4.9)
14	Washington	0.7		47	New Jersey	(5.2)
30	West Virginia	(1.7)		48	Massachusetts	(6.8)
34	Wisconsin	(2.0)		49	Maine	(9.8)
6	Wyoming	3.7		50	New Hampshire	(13.0)

District of Columbia	0.8

Source: CQ Press using reported data from the Federal Bureau of Investigation
   "Crime in the United States 2016" (Uniform Crime Reports, September 25, 2017, https://ucr.fbi.gov/)
*Includes murder, rape (legacy definition), robbery, aggravated assault, burglary, larceny-theft, and motor vehicle theft.

Violent Crimes in 2016

National Total = 1,248,185 Violent Crimes*

ALPHA ORDER

RANK	STATE	CRIMES	% of USA
17	Alabama	25,355	2.0%
38	Alaska	5,670	0.5%
12	Arizona	31,745	2.5%
27	Arkansas	15,863	1.3%
1	California	171,243	13.7%
23	Colorado	18,047	1.4%
35	Connecticut	7,921	0.6%
40	Delaware	4,757	0.4%
3	Florida	86,630	6.9%
8	Georgia	40,009	3.2%
41	Hawaii	4,245	0.3%
42	Idaho	3,686	0.3%
5	Illinois	54,581	4.4%
15	Indiana	26,195	2.1%
33	Iowa	8,785	0.7%
30	Kansas	10,719	0.9%
32	Kentucky	9,841	0.8%
16	Louisiana	26,014	2.1%
48	Maine	1,536	0.1%
14	Maryland	27,910	2.2%
18	Massachusetts	25,141	2.0%
6	Michigan	43,561	3.5%
29	Minnesota	12,777	1.0%
34	Mississippi	8,011	0.6%
13	Missouri	30,974	2.5%
43	Montana	3,676	0.3%
39	Nebraska	5,294	0.4%
22	Nevada	19,495	1.6%
45	New Hampshire	2,478	0.2%
20	New Jersey	21,550	1.7%
28	New Mexico	14,210	1.1%
4	New York	72,594	5.8%
10	North Carolina	37,006	3.0%
47	North Dakota	1,817	0.1%
11	Ohio	33,429	2.7%
26	Oklahoma	17,118	1.4%
31	Oregon	10,370	0.8%
9	Pennsylvania	39,247	3.1%
46	Rhode Island	2,410	0.2%
19	South Carolina	24,220	1.9%
44	South Dakota	3,491	0.3%
7	Tennessee	41,374	3.3%
2	Texas	117,533	9.4%
36	Utah	7,003	0.6%
50	Vermont	935	0.1%
24	Virginia	17,530	1.4%
21	Washington	21,205	1.7%
37	West Virginia	6,368	0.5%
25	Wisconsin	17,158	1.4%
49	Wyoming	1,375	0.1%

RANK ORDER

RANK	STATE	CRIMES	% of USA
1	California	171,243	13.7%
2	Texas	117,533	9.4%
3	Florida	86,630	6.9%
4	New York	72,594	5.8%
5	Illinois	54,581	4.4%
6	Michigan	43,561	3.5%
7	Tennessee	41,374	3.3%
8	Georgia	40,009	3.2%
9	Pennsylvania	39,247	3.1%
10	North Carolina	37,006	3.0%
11	Ohio	33,429	2.7%
12	Arizona	31,745	2.5%
13	Missouri	30,974	2.5%
14	Maryland	27,910	2.2%
15	Indiana	26,195	2.1%
16	Louisiana	26,014	2.1%
17	Alabama	25,355	2.0%
18	Massachusetts	25,141	2.0%
19	South Carolina	24,220	1.9%
20	New Jersey	21,550	1.7%
21	Washington	21,205	1.7%
22	Nevada	19,495	1.6%
23	Colorado	18,047	1.4%
24	Virginia	17,530	1.4%
25	Wisconsin	17,158	1.4%
26	Oklahoma	17,118	1.4%
27	Arkansas	15,863	1.3%
28	New Mexico	14,210	1.1%
29	Minnesota	12,777	1.0%
30	Kansas	10,719	0.9%
31	Oregon	10,370	0.8%
32	Kentucky	9,841	0.8%
33	Iowa	8,785	0.7%
34	Mississippi	8,011	0.6%
35	Connecticut	7,921	0.6%
36	Utah	7,003	0.6%
37	West Virginia	6,368	0.5%
38	Alaska	5,670	0.5%
39	Nebraska	5,294	0.4%
40	Delaware	4,757	0.4%
41	Hawaii	4,245	0.3%
42	Idaho	3,686	0.3%
43	Montana	3,676	0.3%
44	South Dakota	3,491	0.3%
45	New Hampshire	2,478	0.2%
46	Rhode Island	2,410	0.2%
47	North Dakota	1,817	0.1%
48	Maine	1,536	0.1%
49	Wyoming	1,375	0.1%
50	Vermont	935	0.1%
	District of Columbia	8,083	0.6%

Source: CQ Press using reported data from the Federal Bureau of Investigation
    "Crime in the United States 2016" (Uniform Crime Reports, September 25, 2017, https://ucr.fbi.gov/)
*Violent crimes are offenses of murder, rape (legacy definition), robbery, and aggravated assault.

Violent Crime Rate in 2016

National Rate = 386.2 Violent Crimes per 100,000 Population*

ALPHA ORDER

RANK	STATE	RATE
7	Alabama	521.5
1	Alaska	764.2
12	Arizona	458.1
6	Arkansas	530.8
14	California	436.3
28	Colorado	325.8
45	Connecticut	221.5
9	Delaware	499.6
18	Florida	420.3
21	Georgia	388.0
30	Hawaii	297.2
46	Idaho	219.0
16	Illinois	426.4
20	Indiana	394.9
34	Iowa	280.3
23	Kansas	368.7
44	Kentucky	221.8
5	Louisiana	555.7
50	Maine	115.3
11	Maryland	463.8
22	Massachusetts	369.2
13	Michigan	438.7
41	Minnesota	231.4
36	Mississippi	268.1
8	Missouri	508.3
26	Montana	352.6
35	Nebraska	277.6
3	Nevada	663.0
48	New Hampshire	185.7
38	New Jersey	241.0
2	New Mexico	682.9
24	New York	367.6
25	North Carolina	364.8
39	North Dakota	239.8
33	Ohio	287.8
14	Oklahoma	436.3
37	Oregon	253.3
29	Pennsylvania	307.0
43	Rhode Island	228.0
10	South Carolina	488.2
19	South Dakota	403.3
4	Tennessee	622.0
17	Texas	421.9
42	Utah	229.6
49	Vermont	149.7
47	Virginia	208.5
32	Washington	290.9
27	West Virginia	347.8
31	Wisconsin	296.9
40	Wyoming	234.8

RANK ORDER

RANK	STATE	RATE
1	Alaska	764.2
2	New Mexico	682.9
3	Nevada	663.0
4	Tennessee	622.0
5	Louisiana	555.7
6	Arkansas	530.8
7	Alabama	521.5
8	Missouri	508.3
9	Delaware	499.6
10	South Carolina	488.2
11	Maryland	463.8
12	Arizona	458.1
13	Michigan	438.7
14	California	436.3
14	Oklahoma	436.3
16	Illinois	426.4
17	Texas	421.9
18	Florida	420.3
19	South Dakota	403.3
20	Indiana	394.9
21	Georgia	388.0
22	Massachusetts	369.2
23	Kansas	368.7
24	New York	367.6
25	North Carolina	364.8
26	Montana	352.6
27	West Virginia	347.8
28	Colorado	325.8
29	Pennsylvania	307.0
30	Hawaii	297.2
31	Wisconsin	296.9
32	Washington	290.9
33	Ohio	287.8
34	Iowa	280.3
35	Nebraska	277.6
36	Mississippi	268.1
37	Oregon	253.3
38	New Jersey	241.0
39	North Dakota	239.8
40	Wyoming	234.8
41	Minnesota	231.4
42	Utah	229.6
43	Rhode Island	228.0
44	Kentucky	221.8
45	Connecticut	221.5
46	Idaho	219.0
47	Virginia	208.5
48	New Hampshire	185.7
49	Vermont	149.7
50	Maine	115.3

District of Columbia 1,186.7

Source: CQ Press using reported data from the Federal Bureau of Investigation
    "Crime in the United States 2016" (Uniform Crime Reports, September 25, 2017, https://ucr.fbi.gov/)
*Violent crimes are offenses of murder, rape (legacy definition), robbery, and aggravated assault.

Percent Change in Violent Crime Rate: 2015 to 2016

National Percent Change = 3.4% Increase*

RANK	STATE	PERCENT CHANGE
4	Alabama	13.1
7	Alaska	9.7
3	Arizona	15.1
26	Arkansas	4.1
26	California	4.1
11	Colorado	8.0
29	Connecticut	2.8
34	Delaware	1.3
50	Florida	(7.0)
25	Georgia	4.2
2	Hawaii	25.6
15	Idaho	6.5
5	Illinois	13.0
18	Indiana	5.5
16	Iowa	5.6
45	Kansas	(2.8)
24	Kentucky	4.3
21	Louisiana	5.0
48	Maine	(4.2)
36	Maryland	0.4
47	Massachusetts	(3.3)
8	Michigan	9.4
39	Minnesota	0.1
32	Mississippi	1.7
23	Missouri	4.4
22	Montana	4.6
14	Nebraska	6.6
45	Nevada	(2.8)
44	New Hampshire	(1.8)
49	New Jersey	(4.4)
13	New Mexico	7.4
41	New York	(1.1)
12	North Carolina	7.5
43	North Dakota	(1.6)
33	Ohio	1.4
20	Oklahoma	5.2
40	Oregon	(0.2)
37	Pennsylvania	0.3
42	Rhode Island	(1.3)
35	South Carolina	0.7
9	South Dakota	9.2
31	Tennessee	2.4
19	Texas	5.4
29	Utah	2.8
1	Vermont	33.7
9	Virginia	9.2
16	Washington	5.6
28	West Virginia	3.6
37	Wisconsin	0.3
6	Wyoming	9.9

RANK	STATE	PERCENT CHANGE
1	Vermont	33.7
2	Hawaii	25.6
3	Arizona	15.1
4	Alabama	13.1
5	Illinois	13.0
6	Wyoming	9.9
7	Alaska	9.7
8	Michigan	9.4
9	South Dakota	9.2
9	Virginia	9.2
11	Colorado	8.0
12	North Carolina	7.5
13	New Mexico	7.4
14	Nebraska	6.6
15	Idaho	6.5
16	Iowa	5.6
16	Washington	5.6
18	Indiana	5.5
19	Texas	5.4
20	Oklahoma	5.2
21	Louisiana	5.0
22	Montana	4.6
23	Missouri	4.4
24	Kentucky	4.3
25	Georgia	4.2
26	Arkansas	4.1
26	California	4.1
28	West Virginia	3.6
29	Connecticut	2.8
29	Utah	2.8
31	Tennessee	2.4
32	Mississippi	1.7
33	Ohio	1.4
34	Delaware	1.3
35	South Carolina	0.7
36	Maryland	0.4
37	Pennsylvania	0.3
37	Wisconsin	0.3
39	Minnesota	0.1
40	Oregon	(0.2)
41	New York	(1.1)
42	Rhode Island	(1.3)
43	North Dakota	(1.6)
44	New Hampshire	(1.8)
45	Kansas	(2.8)
45	Nevada	(2.8)
47	Massachusetts	(3.3)
48	Maine	(4.2)
49	New Jersey	(4.4)
50	Florida	(7.0)
	District of Columbia	(5.4)

Source: CQ Press using reported data from the Federal Bureau of Investigation
  "Crime in the United States 2016" (Uniform Crime Reports, September 25, 2017, https://ucr.fbi.gov/)
*Violent crimes are offenses of murder, rape (legacy definition), robbery, and aggravated assault.

Murders in 2016

National Total = 17,250 Murders*

RANK	STATE	MURDERS	% of USA
17	Alabama	407	2.4%
39	Alaska	52	0.3%
18	Arizona	380	2.2%
26	Arkansas	216	1.3%
1	California	1,930	11.2%
27	Colorado	204	1.2%
35	Connecticut	78	0.5%
38	Delaware	56	0.3%
3	Florida	1,111	6.4%
5	Georgia	681	3.9%
43	Hawaii	35	0.2%
40	Idaho	49	0.3%
4	Illinois	1,054	6.1%
16	Indiana	439	2.5%
37	Iowa	71	0.4%
32	Kansas	111	0.6%
21	Kentucky	260	1.5%
11	Louisiana	554	3.2%
46	Maine	20	0.1%
15	Maryland	481	2.8%
30	Massachusetts	134	0.8%
10	Michigan	598	3.5%
33	Minnesota	101	0.6%
23	Mississippi	238	1.4%
12	Missouri	537	3.1%
42	Montana	36	0.2%
40	Nebraska	49	0.3%
25	Nevada	224	1.3%
48	New Hampshire	17	0.1%
19	New Jersey	372	2.2%
29	New Mexico	139	0.8%
9	New York	630	3.7%
6	North Carolina	678	3.9%
49	North Dakota	15	0.1%
8	Ohio	654	3.8%
22	Oklahoma	245	1.4%
31	Oregon	113	0.7%
7	Pennsylvania	661	3.8%
44	Rhode Island	29	0.2%
20	South Carolina	366	2.1%
45	South Dakota	27	0.2%
13	Tennessee	486	2.8%
2	Texas	1,478	8.6%
36	Utah	72	0.4%
50	Vermont	14	0.1%
14	Virginia	484	2.8%
28	Washington	195	1.1%
34	West Virginia	81	0.5%
24	Wisconsin	229	1.3%
46	Wyoming	20	0.1%

RANK	STATE	MURDERS	% of USA
1	California	1,930	11.2%
2	Texas	1,478	8.6%
3	Florida	1,111	6.4%
4	Illinois	1,054	6.1%
5	Georgia	681	3.9%
6	North Carolina	678	3.9%
7	Pennsylvania	661	3.8%
8	Ohio	654	3.8%
9	New York	630	3.7%
10	Michigan	598	3.5%
11	Louisiana	554	3.2%
12	Missouri	537	3.1%
13	Tennessee	486	2.8%
14	Virginia	484	2.8%
15	Maryland	481	2.8%
16	Indiana	439	2.5%
17	Alabama	407	2.4%
18	Arizona	380	2.2%
19	New Jersey	372	2.2%
20	South Carolina	366	2.1%
21	Kentucky	260	1.5%
22	Oklahoma	245	1.4%
23	Mississippi	238	1.4%
24	Wisconsin	229	1.3%
25	Nevada	224	1.3%
26	Arkansas	216	1.3%
27	Colorado	204	1.2%
28	Washington	195	1.1%
29	New Mexico	139	0.8%
30	Massachusetts	134	0.8%
31	Oregon	113	0.7%
32	Kansas	111	0.6%
33	Minnesota	101	0.6%
34	West Virginia	81	0.5%
35	Connecticut	78	0.5%
36	Utah	72	0.4%
37	Iowa	71	0.4%
38	Delaware	56	0.3%
39	Alaska	52	0.3%
40	Idaho	49	0.3%
40	Nebraska	49	0.3%
42	Montana	36	0.2%
43	Hawaii	35	0.2%
44	Rhode Island	29	0.2%
45	South Dakota	27	0.2%
46	Maine	20	0.1%
46	Wyoming	20	0.1%
48	New Hampshire	17	0.1%
49	North Dakota	15	0.1%
50	Vermont	14	0.1%
	District of Columbia	139	0.8%

Source: Reported data from the Federal Bureau of Investigation
   "Crime in the United States 2016" (Uniform Crime Reports, September 25, 2017, https://ucr.fbi.gov/)
*Includes nonnegligent manslaughter.

Murder Rate in 2016

National Rate = 5.3 Murders per 100,000 Population*

RANK	STATE	RATE
3	Alabama	8.4
11	Alaska	7.0
22	Arizona	5.5
10	Arkansas	7.2
26	California	4.9
31	Colorado	3.7
44	Connecticut	2.2
18	Delaware	5.9
23	Florida	5.4
14	Georgia	6.6
41	Hawaii	2.5
36	Idaho	2.9
4	Illinois	8.2
14	Indiana	6.6
43	Iowa	2.3
30	Kansas	3.8
18	Kentucky	5.9
1	Louisiana	11.8
49	Maine	1.5
5	Maryland	8.0
46	Massachusetts	2.0
17	Michigan	6.0
48	Minnesota	1.8
5	Mississippi	8.0
2	Missouri	8.8
32	Montana	3.5
40	Nebraska	2.6
7	Nevada	7.6
50	New Hampshire	1.3
28	New Jersey	4.2
12	New Mexico	6.7
34	New York	3.2
12	North Carolina	6.7
46	North Dakota	2.0
21	Ohio	5.6
16	Oklahoma	6.2
37	Oregon	2.8
25	Pennsylvania	5.2
38	Rhode Island	2.7
8	South Carolina	7.4
35	South Dakota	3.1
9	Tennessee	7.3
24	Texas	5.3
42	Utah	2.4
44	Vermont	2.2
20	Virginia	5.8
38	Washington	2.7
27	West Virginia	4.4
29	Wisconsin	4.0
33	Wyoming	3.4

RANK	STATE	RATE
1	Louisiana	11.8
2	Missouri	8.8
3	Alabama	8.4
4	Illinois	8.2
5	Maryland	8.0
5	Mississippi	8.0
7	Nevada	7.6
8	South Carolina	7.4
9	Tennessee	7.3
10	Arkansas	7.2
11	Alaska	7.0
12	New Mexico	6.7
12	North Carolina	6.7
14	Georgia	6.6
14	Indiana	6.6
16	Oklahoma	6.2
17	Michigan	6.0
18	Delaware	5.9
18	Kentucky	5.9
20	Virginia	5.8
21	Ohio	5.6
22	Arizona	5.5
23	Florida	5.4
24	Texas	5.3
25	Pennsylvania	5.2
26	California	4.9
27	West Virginia	4.4
28	New Jersey	4.2
29	Wisconsin	4.0
30	Kansas	3.8
31	Colorado	3.7
32	Montana	3.5
33	Wyoming	3.4
34	New York	3.2
35	South Dakota	3.1
36	Idaho	2.9
37	Oregon	2.8
38	Rhode Island	2.7
38	Washington	2.7
40	Nebraska	2.6
41	Hawaii	2.5
42	Utah	2.4
43	Iowa	2.3
44	Connecticut	2.2
44	Vermont	2.2
46	Massachusetts	2.0
46	North Dakota	2.0
48	Minnesota	1.8
49	Maine	1.5
50	New Hampshire	1.3
	District of Columbia	20.4

Source: Reported data from the Federal Bureau of Investigation
   "Crime in the United States 2016" (Uniform Crime Reports, September 25, 2017, https://ucr.fbi.gov/)
*Includes nonnegligent manslaughter.

Percent of Murders Involving Firearms in 2016

National Percent = 73.0% of Murders*

<table>
<tr><td colspan="3">ALPHA ORDER</td><td colspan="3">RANK ORDER</td></tr>
<tr><td>RANK</td><td>STATE</td><td>PERCENT</td><td>RANK</td><td>STATE</td><td>PERCENT</td></tr>
<tr><td>NA</td><td>Alabama**</td><td>NA</td><td>1</td><td>Illinois</td><td>84.9</td></tr>
<tr><td>3</td><td>Alaska</td><td>82.7</td><td>2</td><td>Mississippi</td><td>83.1</td></tr>
<tr><td>25</td><td>Arizona</td><td>67.6</td><td>3</td><td>Alaska</td><td>82.7</td></tr>
<tr><td>20</td><td>Arkansas</td><td>72.2</td><td>4</td><td>Indiana</td><td>82.5</td></tr>
<tr><td>22</td><td>California</td><td>70.9</td><td>5</td><td>Louisiana</td><td>82.0</td></tr>
<tr><td>27</td><td>Colorado</td><td>67.3</td><td>6</td><td>Missouri</td><td>81.7</td></tr>
<tr><td>31</td><td>Connecticut</td><td>63.2</td><td>7</td><td>Georgia</td><td>80.8</td></tr>
<tr><td>16</td><td>Delaware</td><td>73.2</td><td>8</td><td>Kentucky</td><td>79.6</td></tr>
<tr><td>NA</td><td>Florida**</td><td>NA</td><td>9</td><td>South Carolina</td><td>77.4</td></tr>
<tr><td>7</td><td>Georgia</td><td>80.8</td><td>10</td><td>Maryland</td><td>76.3</td></tr>
<tr><td>40</td><td>Hawaii</td><td>54.3</td><td>11</td><td>New Jersey</td><td>74.7</td></tr>
<tr><td>46</td><td>Idaho</td><td>36.2</td><td>12</td><td>Michigan</td><td>74.2</td></tr>
<tr><td>1</td><td>Illinois</td><td>84.9</td><td>12</td><td>Pennsylvania</td><td>74.2</td></tr>
<tr><td>4</td><td>Indiana</td><td>82.5</td><td>14</td><td>Wisconsin</td><td>73.5</td></tr>
<tr><td>33</td><td>Iowa</td><td>60.6</td><td>15</td><td>Tennessee</td><td>73.3</td></tr>
<tr><td>30</td><td>Kansas</td><td>63.5</td><td>16</td><td>Delaware</td><td>73.2</td></tr>
<tr><td>8</td><td>Kentucky</td><td>79.6</td><td>16</td><td>Nebraska</td><td>73.2</td></tr>
<tr><td>5</td><td>Louisiana</td><td>82.0</td><td>18</td><td>Texas</td><td>73.1</td></tr>
<tr><td>39</td><td>Maine</td><td>55.0</td><td>19</td><td>Virginia</td><td>73.0</td></tr>
<tr><td>10</td><td>Maryland</td><td>76.3</td><td>20</td><td>Arkansas</td><td>72.2</td></tr>
<tr><td>29</td><td>Massachusetts</td><td>64.4</td><td>21</td><td>Ohio</td><td>72.1</td></tr>
<tr><td>12</td><td>Michigan</td><td>74.2</td><td>22</td><td>California</td><td>70.9</td></tr>
<tr><td>33</td><td>Minnesota</td><td>60.6</td><td>23</td><td>North Carolina</td><td>70.8</td></tr>
<tr><td>2</td><td>Mississippi</td><td>83.1</td><td>24</td><td>Oklahoma</td><td>70.4</td></tr>
<tr><td>6</td><td>Missouri</td><td>81.7</td><td>25</td><td>Arizona</td><td>67.6</td></tr>
<tr><td>42</td><td>Montana</td><td>50.0</td><td>26</td><td>Nevada</td><td>67.5</td></tr>
<tr><td>16</td><td>Nebraska</td><td>73.2</td><td>27</td><td>Colorado</td><td>67.3</td></tr>
<tr><td>26</td><td>Nevada</td><td>67.5</td><td>28</td><td>Washington</td><td>65.1</td></tr>
<tr><td>42</td><td>New Hampshire</td><td>50.0</td><td>29</td><td>Massachusetts</td><td>64.4</td></tr>
<tr><td>11</td><td>New Jersey</td><td>74.7</td><td>30</td><td>Kansas</td><td>63.5</td></tr>
<tr><td>33</td><td>New Mexico</td><td>60.6</td><td>31</td><td>Connecticut</td><td>63.2</td></tr>
<tr><td>37</td><td>New York</td><td>58.4</td><td>32</td><td>West Virginia</td><td>61.8</td></tr>
<tr><td>23</td><td>North Carolina</td><td>70.8</td><td>33</td><td>Iowa</td><td>60.6</td></tr>
<tr><td>38</td><td>North Dakota</td><td>57.1</td><td>33</td><td>Minnesota</td><td>60.6</td></tr>
<tr><td>21</td><td>Ohio</td><td>72.1</td><td>33</td><td>New Mexico</td><td>60.6</td></tr>
<tr><td>24</td><td>Oklahoma</td><td>70.4</td><td>36</td><td>Utah</td><td>59.2</td></tr>
<tr><td>41</td><td>Oregon</td><td>51.0</td><td>37</td><td>New York</td><td>58.4</td></tr>
<tr><td>12</td><td>Pennsylvania</td><td>74.2</td><td>38</td><td>North Dakota</td><td>57.1</td></tr>
<tr><td>45</td><td>Rhode Island</td><td>41.4</td><td>39</td><td>Maine</td><td>55.0</td></tr>
<tr><td>9</td><td>South Carolina</td><td>77.4</td><td>40</td><td>Hawaii</td><td>54.3</td></tr>
<tr><td>47</td><td>South Dakota</td><td>33.3</td><td>41</td><td>Oregon</td><td>51.0</td></tr>
<tr><td>15</td><td>Tennessee</td><td>73.3</td><td>42</td><td>Montana</td><td>50.0</td></tr>
<tr><td>18</td><td>Texas</td><td>73.1</td><td>42</td><td>New Hampshire</td><td>50.0</td></tr>
<tr><td>36</td><td>Utah</td><td>59.2</td><td>44</td><td>Vermont</td><td>42.9</td></tr>
<tr><td>44</td><td>Vermont</td><td>42.9</td><td>45</td><td>Rhode Island</td><td>41.4</td></tr>
<tr><td>19</td><td>Virginia</td><td>73.0</td><td>46</td><td>Idaho</td><td>36.2</td></tr>
<tr><td>28</td><td>Washington</td><td>65.1</td><td>47</td><td>South Dakota</td><td>33.3</td></tr>
<tr><td>32</td><td>West Virginia</td><td>61.8</td><td>48</td><td>Wyoming</td><td>31.6</td></tr>
<tr><td>14</td><td>Wisconsin</td><td>73.5</td><td>NA</td><td>Alabama**</td><td>NA</td></tr>
<tr><td>48</td><td>Wyoming</td><td>31.6</td><td>NA</td><td>Florida**</td><td>NA</td></tr>
<tr><td></td><td></td><td></td><td></td><td>District of Columbia</td><td>77.2</td></tr>
</table>

Source: CQ Press using reported data from the Federal Bureau of Investigation
"Crime in the United States 2016" (Uniform Crime Reports, September 25, 2017, https://ucr.fbi.gov/)
*Of the 15,028 murders in 2016 for which supplemental data were received by the F.B.I. There were an additional 2,222 murders for which the type of murder weapon was not reported to the F.B.I. Includes nonnegligent manslaughter. National and state percents based on reporting jurisdictions only.
**Not available.

Rapes in 2016

National Total = 95,730 Rapes*

ALPHA ORDER					RANK ORDER			
RANK	STATE	RAPES	% of USA		RANK	STATE	RAPES	% of USA
24	Alabama	1,385	1.4%		1	California	10,149	10.6%
36	Alaska	757	0.8%		2	Texas	9,858	10.3%
11	Arizona	2,452	2.6%		3	Florida	5,528	5.8%
21	Arkansas	1,545	1.6%		4	Michigan	5,114	5.3%
1	California	10,149	10.6%		5	New York	4,569	4.8%
9	Colorado	2,619	2.7%		6	Ohio	4,141	4.3%
38	Connecticut	561	0.6%		7	Illinois	3,635	3.8%
48	Delaware	221	0.2%		8	Pennsylvania	3,233	3.4%
3	Florida	5,528	5.8%		9	Colorado	2,619	2.7%
10	Georgia	2,528	2.6%		10	Georgia	2,528	2.6%
41	Hawaii	447	0.5%		11	Arizona	2,452	2.6%
39	Idaho	529	0.6%		12	Washington	2,259	2.4%
7	Illinois	3,635	3.8%		13	North Carolina	2,086	2.2%
17	Indiana	1,851	1.9%		14	Tennessee	1,991	2.1%
34	Iowa	922	1.0%		15	Virginia	1,965	2.1%
33	Kansas	971	1.0%		16	Missouri	1,884	2.0%
29	Kentucky	1,174	1.2%		17	Indiana	1,851	1.9%
25	Louisiana	1,328	1.4%		18	Minnesota	1,731	1.8%
46	Maine	300	0.3%		19	South Carolina	1,711	1.8%
27	Maryland	1,266	1.3%		20	Massachusetts	1,592	1.7%
20	Massachusetts	1,592	1.7%		21	Arkansas	1,545	1.6%
4	Michigan	5,114	5.3%		22	Oklahoma	1,509	1.6%
18	Minnesota	1,731	1.8%		23	Wisconsin	1,458	1.5%
35	Mississippi	905	0.9%		24	Alabama	1,385	1.4%
16	Missouri	1,884	2.0%		25	Louisiana	1,328	1.4%
43	Montana	414	0.4%		26	Nevada	1,292	1.3%
37	Nebraska	738	0.8%		27	Maryland	1,266	1.3%
26	Nevada	1,292	1.3%		28	Oregon	1,261	1.3%
42	New Hampshire	423	0.4%		29	Kentucky	1,174	1.2%
32	New Jersey	1,089	1.1%		30	New Mexico	1,117	1.2%
30	New Mexico	1,117	1.2%		31	Utah	1,116	1.2%
5	New York	4,569	4.8%		32	New Jersey	1,089	1.1%
13	North Carolina	2,086	2.2%		33	Kansas	971	1.0%
47	North Dakota	256	0.3%		34	Iowa	922	1.0%
6	Ohio	4,141	4.3%		35	Mississippi	905	0.9%
22	Oklahoma	1,509	1.6%		36	Alaska	757	0.8%
28	Oregon	1,261	1.3%		37	Nebraska	738	0.8%
8	Pennsylvania	3,233	3.4%		38	Connecticut	561	0.6%
45	Rhode Island	328	0.3%		39	Idaho	529	0.6%
19	South Carolina	1,711	1.8%		40	West Virginia	468	0.5%
44	South Dakota	379	0.4%		41	Hawaii	447	0.5%
14	Tennessee	1,991	2.1%		42	New Hampshire	423	0.4%
2	Texas	9,858	10.3%		43	Montana	414	0.4%
31	Utah	1,116	1.2%		44	South Dakota	379	0.4%
50	Vermont	124	0.1%		45	Rhode Island	328	0.3%
15	Virginia	1,965	2.1%		46	Maine	300	0.3%
12	Washington	2,259	2.4%		47	North Dakota	256	0.3%
40	West Virginia	468	0.5%		48	Delaware	221	0.2%
23	Wisconsin	1,458	1.5%		49	Wyoming	150	0.2%
49	Wyoming	150	0.2%		50	Vermont	124	0.1%
						District of Columbia	401	0.4%

Source: Reported data from the Federal Bureau of Investigation
"Crime in the United States 2016" (Uniform Crime Reports, September 25, 2017, https://ucr.fbi.gov/)
*Although the definition of rape was revised in 2013 the FBI continues to release estimates based on the legacy definition for comparison purposes to previous years. The legacy definition used for these figures is "Forcible rape is the carnal knowledge of a female forcibly and against her will. Assaults or attempts to commit rape by force or threat of force are included. However, statutory rape without force and other sex offenses are excluded."

Rape Rate in 2016

National Rate = 29.6 Rapes per 100,000 Population*

ALPHA ORDER

RANK	STATE	RATE
29	Alabama	28.5
1	Alaska	102.0
13	Arizona	35.4
3	Arkansas	51.7
35	California	25.9
5	Colorado	47.3
49	Connecticut	15.7
43	Delaware	23.2
33	Florida	26.8
40	Georgia	24.5
21	Hawaii	31.3
19	Idaho	31.4
30	Illinois	28.4
32	Indiana	27.9
28	Iowa	29.4
17	Kansas	33.4
34	Kentucky	26.5
30	Louisiana	28.4
45	Maine	22.5
46	Maryland	21.0
41	Massachusetts	23.4
4	Michigan	51.5
19	Minnesota	31.4
26	Mississippi	30.3
24	Missouri	30.9
8	Montana	39.7
9	Nebraska	38.7
6	Nevada	43.9
18	New Hampshire	31.7
50	New Jersey	12.2
2	New Mexico	53.7
44	New York	23.1
47	North Carolina	20.6
16	North Dakota	33.8
12	Ohio	35.7
10	Oklahoma	38.5
25	Oregon	30.8
38	Pennsylvania	25.3
22	Rhode Island	31.0
15	South Carolina	34.5
7	South Dakota	43.8
27	Tennessee	29.9
13	Texas	35.4
11	Utah	36.6
48	Vermont	19.9
41	Virginia	23.4
22	Washington	31.0
36	West Virginia	25.6
39	Wisconsin	25.2
36	Wyoming	25.6

RANK ORDER

RANK	STATE	RATE
1	Alaska	102.0
2	New Mexico	53.7
3	Arkansas	51.7
4	Michigan	51.5
5	Colorado	47.3
6	Nevada	43.9
7	South Dakota	43.8
8	Montana	39.7
9	Nebraska	38.7
10	Oklahoma	38.5
11	Utah	36.6
12	Ohio	35.7
13	Arizona	35.4
13	Texas	35.4
15	South Carolina	34.5
16	North Dakota	33.8
17	Kansas	33.4
18	New Hampshire	31.7
19	Idaho	31.4
19	Minnesota	31.4
21	Hawaii	31.3
22	Rhode Island	31.0
22	Washington	31.0
24	Missouri	30.9
25	Oregon	30.8
26	Mississippi	30.3
27	Tennessee	29.9
28	Iowa	29.4
29	Alabama	28.5
30	Illinois	28.4
30	Louisiana	28.4
32	Indiana	27.9
33	Florida	26.8
34	Kentucky	26.5
35	California	25.9
36	West Virginia	25.6
36	Wyoming	25.6
38	Pennsylvania	25.3
39	Wisconsin	25.2
40	Georgia	24.5
41	Massachusetts	23.4
41	Virginia	23.4
43	Delaware	23.2
44	New York	23.1
45	Maine	22.5
46	Maryland	21.0
47	North Carolina	20.6
48	Vermont	19.9
49	Connecticut	15.7
50	New Jersey	12.2
	District of Columbia	58.9

Source: Reported data from the Federal Bureau of Investigation
   "Crime in the United States 2016" (Uniform Crime Reports, September 25, 2017, https://ucr.fbi.gov/)
*Although the definition of rape was revised in 2013 the FBI continues to release estimates based on the legacy definition for comparison purposes to previous years. The legacy definition used for these figures is "Forcible rape is the carnal knowledge of a female forcibly and against her will. Assaults or attempts to commit rape by force or threat of force are included. However, statutory rape without force and other sex offenses are excluded."

Rapes (Revised Definition) in 2016

National Total = 130,603 Rapes*

ALPHA ORDER

RANK	STATE	RAPES	% of USA
24	Alabama	1,916	1.5%
36	Alaska	1,053	0.8%
11	Arizona	3,290	2.5%
20	Arkansas	2,143	1.6%
1	California	13,702	10.5%
9	Colorado	3,555	2.7%
38	Connecticut	763	0.6%
48	Delaware	308	0.2%
3	Florida	7,598	5.8%
10	Georgia	3,509	2.7%
41	Hawaii	619	0.5%
39	Idaho	719	0.6%
7	Illinois	4,908	3.8%
17	Indiana	2,501	1.9%
35	Iowa	1,247	1.0%
33	Kansas	1,312	1.0%
29	Kentucky	1,641	1.3%
25	Louisiana	1,816	1.4%
46	Maine	412	0.3%
26	Maryland	1,756	1.3%
21	Massachusetts	2,128	1.6%
4	Michigan	7,125	5.5%
19	Minnesota	2,348	1.8%
34	Mississippi	1,277	1.0%
16	Missouri	2,554	2.0%
43	Montana	578	0.4%
37	Nebraska	994	0.8%
27	Nevada	1,733	1.3%
42	New Hampshire	582	0.4%
32	New Jersey	1,453	1.1%
30	New Mexico	1,526	1.2%
5	New York	6,260	4.8%
13	North Carolina	2,849	2.2%
47	North Dakota	342	0.3%
6	Ohio	5,589	4.3%
22	Oklahoma	2,039	1.6%
28	Oregon	1,721	1.3%
8	Pennsylvania	4,433	3.4%
45	Rhode Island	442	0.3%
18	South Carolina	2,387	1.8%
44	South Dakota	509	0.4%
15	Tennessee	2,714	2.1%
2	Texas	13,367	10.2%
31	Utah	1,520	1.2%
50	Vermont	178	0.1%
14	Virginia	2,737	2.1%
12	Washington	3,077	2.4%
40	West Virginia	657	0.5%
23	Wisconsin	1,979	1.5%
49	Wyoming	205	0.2%

RANK ORDER

RANK	STATE	RAPES	% of USA
1	California	13,702	10.5%
2	Texas	13,367	10.2%
3	Florida	7,598	5.8%
4	Michigan	7,125	5.5%
5	New York	6,260	4.8%
6	Ohio	5,589	4.3%
7	Illinois	4,908	3.8%
8	Pennsylvania	4,433	3.4%
9	Colorado	3,555	2.7%
10	Georgia	3,509	2.7%
11	Arizona	3,290	2.5%
12	Washington	3,077	2.4%
13	North Carolina	2,849	2.2%
14	Virginia	2,737	2.1%
15	Tennessee	2,714	2.1%
16	Missouri	2,554	2.0%
17	Indiana	2,501	1.9%
18	South Carolina	2,387	1.8%
19	Minnesota	2,348	1.8%
20	Arkansas	2,143	1.6%
21	Massachusetts	2,128	1.6%
22	Oklahoma	2,039	1.6%
23	Wisconsin	1,979	1.5%
24	Alabama	1,916	1.5%
25	Louisiana	1,816	1.4%
26	Maryland	1,756	1.3%
27	Nevada	1,733	1.3%
28	Oregon	1,721	1.3%
29	Kentucky	1,641	1.3%
30	New Mexico	1,526	1.2%
31	Utah	1,520	1.2%
32	New Jersey	1,453	1.1%
33	Kansas	1,312	1.0%
34	Mississippi	1,277	1.0%
35	Iowa	1,247	1.0%
36	Alaska	1,053	0.8%
37	Nebraska	994	0.8%
38	Connecticut	763	0.6%
39	Idaho	719	0.6%
40	West Virginia	657	0.5%
41	Hawaii	619	0.5%
42	New Hampshire	582	0.4%
43	Montana	578	0.4%
44	South Dakota	509	0.4%
45	Rhode Island	442	0.3%
46	Maine	412	0.3%
47	North Dakota	342	0.3%
48	Delaware	308	0.2%
49	Wyoming	205	0.2%
50	Vermont	178	0.1%
	District of Columbia	532	0.4%

Source: Reported data from the Federal Bureau of Investigation
"Crime in the United States 2016" (Uniform Crime Reports, September 25, 2017, https://ucr.fbi.gov/)
*The definition of rape was revised in 2013 to "Penetration, no matter how slight, of the vagina or anus with any body part or object, or oral penetration by a sex organ of another person, without the consent of the victim. Attempts or assaults to commit rape are also included; however, statutory rape and incest are excluded." This revised definition includes both male and female victims and drops "forcible" from the title.

Rape Rate (Revised Definition) in 2016

National Rate = 40.4 Rapes per 100,000 Population*

ALPHA ORDER

RANK	STATE	RATE
29	Alabama	39.4
1	Alaska	141.9
15	Arizona	47.5
4	Arkansas	71.7
37	California	34.9
5	Colorado	64.2
49	Connecticut	21.3
42	Delaware	32.4
34	Florida	36.9
40	Georgia	34.0
19	Hawaii	43.3
20	Idaho	42.7
31	Illinois	38.3
32	Indiana	37.7
28	Iowa	39.8
16	Kansas	45.1
33	Kentucky	37.0
30	Louisiana	38.8
45	Maine	30.9
46	Maryland	29.2
44	Massachusetts	31.2
3	Michigan	71.8
22	Minnesota	42.5
20	Mississippi	42.7
25	Missouri	41.9
8	Montana	55.4
9	Nebraska	52.1
6	Nevada	58.9
18	New Hampshire	43.6
50	New Jersey	16.2
2	New Mexico	73.3
43	New York	31.7
48	North Carolina	28.1
16	North Dakota	45.1
12	Ohio	48.1
10	Oklahoma	52.0
24	Oregon	42.0
38	Pennsylvania	34.7
26	Rhode Island	41.8
12	South Carolina	48.1
7	South Dakota	58.8
27	Tennessee	40.8
14	Texas	48.0
11	Utah	49.8
47	Vermont	28.5
41	Virginia	32.5
23	Washington	42.2
35	West Virginia	35.9
39	Wisconsin	34.2
36	Wyoming	35.0

RANK ORDER

RANK	STATE	RATE
1	Alaska	141.9
2	New Mexico	73.3
3	Michigan	71.8
4	Arkansas	71.7
5	Colorado	64.2
6	Nevada	58.9
7	South Dakota	58.8
8	Montana	55.4
9	Nebraska	52.1
10	Oklahoma	52.0
11	Utah	49.8
12	Ohio	48.1
12	South Carolina	48.1
14	Texas	48.0
15	Arizona	47.5
16	Kansas	45.1
16	North Dakota	45.1
18	New Hampshire	43.6
19	Hawaii	43.3
20	Idaho	42.7
20	Mississippi	42.7
22	Minnesota	42.5
23	Washington	42.2
24	Oregon	42.0
25	Missouri	41.9
26	Rhode Island	41.8
27	Tennessee	40.8
28	Iowa	39.8
29	Alabama	39.4
30	Louisiana	38.8
31	Illinois	38.3
32	Indiana	37.7
33	Kentucky	37.0
34	Florida	36.9
35	West Virginia	35.9
36	Wyoming	35.0
37	California	34.9
38	Pennsylvania	34.7
39	Wisconsin	34.2
40	Georgia	34.0
41	Virginia	32.5
42	Delaware	32.4
43	New York	31.7
44	Massachusetts	31.2
45	Maine	30.9
46	Maryland	29.2
47	Vermont	28.5
48	North Carolina	28.1
49	Connecticut	21.3
50	New Jersey	16.2

	District of Columbia	78.1

Source: Reported data from the Federal Bureau of Investigation
"Crime in the United States 2016" (Uniform Crime Reports, September 25, 2017, https://ucr.fbi.gov/)
*The definition of rape was revised in 2013 to "Penetration, no matter how slight, of the vagina or anus with any body part or object, or oral penetration by a sex organ of another person, without the consent of the victim. Attempts or assaults to commit rape are also included; however, statutory rape and incest are excluded." This revised definition includes both male and female victims and drops "forcible" from the title.

Robberies in 2016

National Total = 332,198 Robberies*

RANK	STATE	ROBBERIES	% of USA
23	Alabama	4,686	1.4%
40	Alaska	850	0.3%
15	Arizona	7,055	2.1%
33	Arkansas	2,120	0.6%
1	California	54,789	16.5%
26	Colorado	3,528	1.1%
30	Connecticut	2,703	0.8%
36	Delaware	1,359	0.4%
4	Florida	20,175	6.1%
8	Georgia	12,205	3.7%
38	Hawaii	994	0.3%
47	Idaho	213	0.1%
5	Illinois	17,827	5.4%
13	Indiana	7,330	2.2%
37	Iowa	1,148	0.3%
34	Kansas	1,671	0.5%
27	Kentucky	3,369	1.0%
19	Louisiana	5,576	1.7%
45	Maine	266	0.1%
9	Maryland	10,289	3.1%
20	Massachusetts	5,365	1.6%
14	Michigan	7,120	2.1%
25	Minnesota	3,728	1.1%
31	Mississippi	2,397	0.7%
16	Missouri	6,570	2.0%
45	Montana	266	0.1%
39	Nebraska	946	0.3%
17	Nevada	6,340	1.9%
43	New Hampshire	427	0.1%
11	New Jersey	8,984	2.7%
29	New Mexico	2,737	0.8%
3	New York	22,316	6.7%
10	North Carolina	9,336	2.8%
48	North Dakota	181	0.1%
6	Ohio	12,523	3.8%
28	Oklahoma	3,162	1.0%
32	Oregon	2,278	0.7%
7	Pennsylvania	12,326	3.7%
42	Rhode Island	540	0.2%
24	South Carolina	4,035	1.2%
44	South Dakota	272	0.1%
12	Tennessee	7,813	2.4%
2	Texas	33,317	10.0%
35	Utah	1,541	0.5%
49	Vermont	106	0.0%
21	Virginia	4,803	1.4%
18	Washington	5,651	1.7%
41	West Virginia	720	0.2%
22	Wisconsin	4,706	1.4%
50	Wyoming	59	0.0%

RANK	STATE	ROBBERIES	% of USA
1	California	54,789	16.5%
2	Texas	33,317	10.0%
3	New York	22,316	6.7%
4	Florida	20,175	6.1%
5	Illinois	17,827	5.4%
6	Ohio	12,523	3.8%
7	Pennsylvania	12,326	3.7%
8	Georgia	12,205	3.7%
9	Maryland	10,289	3.1%
10	North Carolina	9,336	2.8%
11	New Jersey	8,984	2.7%
12	Tennessee	7,813	2.4%
13	Indiana	7,330	2.2%
14	Michigan	7,120	2.1%
15	Arizona	7,055	2.1%
16	Missouri	6,570	2.0%
17	Nevada	6,340	1.9%
18	Washington	5,651	1.7%
19	Louisiana	5,576	1.7%
20	Massachusetts	5,365	1.6%
21	Virginia	4,803	1.4%
22	Wisconsin	4,706	1.4%
23	Alabama	4,686	1.4%
24	South Carolina	4,035	1.2%
25	Minnesota	3,728	1.1%
26	Colorado	3,528	1.1%
27	Kentucky	3,369	1.0%
28	Oklahoma	3,162	1.0%
29	New Mexico	2,737	0.8%
30	Connecticut	2,703	0.8%
31	Mississippi	2,397	0.7%
32	Oregon	2,278	0.7%
33	Arkansas	2,120	0.6%
34	Kansas	1,671	0.5%
35	Utah	1,541	0.5%
36	Delaware	1,359	0.4%
37	Iowa	1,148	0.3%
38	Hawaii	994	0.3%
39	Nebraska	946	0.3%
40	Alaska	850	0.3%
41	West Virginia	720	0.2%
42	Rhode Island	540	0.2%
43	New Hampshire	427	0.1%
44	South Dakota	272	0.1%
45	Maine	266	0.1%
45	Montana	266	0.1%
47	Idaho	213	0.1%
48	North Dakota	181	0.1%
49	Vermont	106	0.0%
50	Wyoming	59	0.0%
	District of Columbia	3,480	1.0%

Source: Reported data from the Federal Bureau of Investigation
"Crime in the United States 2016" (Uniform Crime Reports, September 25, 2017, https://ucr.fbi.gov/)
*Robbery is the taking or attempting to take anything of value by force or threat of force.

Robbery Rate in 2016

National Rate = 102.8 Robberies per 100,000 Population*

ALPHA ORDER				RANK ORDER		
RANK	STATE	RATE		RANK	STATE	RATE
19	Alabama	96.4		1	Nevada	215.6
11	Alaska	114.6		2	Maryland	171.0
16	Arizona	101.8		3	Delaware	142.7
31	Arkansas	70.9		4	California	139.6
4	California	139.6		5	Illinois	139.3
34	Colorado	63.7		6	New Mexico	131.5
29	Connecticut	75.6		7	Texas	119.6
3	Delaware	142.7		8	Louisiana	119.1
18	Florida	97.9		9	Georgia	118.4
9	Georgia	118.4		10	Tennessee	117.5
32	Hawaii	69.6		11	Alaska	114.6
49	Idaho	12.7		12	New York	113.0
5	Illinois	139.3		13	Indiana	110.5
13	Indiana	110.5		14	Missouri	107.8
42	Iowa	36.6		14	Ohio	107.8
35	Kansas	57.5		16	Arizona	101.8
28	Kentucky	75.9		17	New Jersey	100.4
8	Louisiana	119.1		18	Florida	97.9
47	Maine	20.0		19	Alabama	96.4
2	Maryland	171.0		19	Pennsylvania	96.4
26	Massachusetts	78.8		21	North Carolina	92.0
30	Michigan	71.7		22	Wisconsin	81.4
33	Minnesota	67.5		23	South Carolina	81.3
25	Mississippi	80.2		24	Oklahoma	80.6
14	Missouri	107.8		25	Mississippi	80.2
45	Montana	25.5		26	Massachusetts	78.8
40	Nebraska	49.6		27	Washington	77.5
1	Nevada	215.6		28	Kentucky	75.9
43	New Hampshire	32.0		29	Connecticut	75.6
17	New Jersey	100.4		30	Michigan	71.7
6	New Mexico	131.5		31	Arkansas	70.9
12	New York	113.0		32	Hawaii	69.6
21	North Carolina	92.0		33	Minnesota	67.5
46	North Dakota	23.9		34	Colorado	63.7
14	Ohio	107.8		35	Kansas	57.5
24	Oklahoma	80.6		36	Virginia	57.1
37	Oregon	55.6		37	Oregon	55.6
19	Pennsylvania	96.4		38	Rhode Island	51.1
38	Rhode Island	51.1		39	Utah	50.5
23	South Carolina	81.3		40	Nebraska	49.6
44	South Dakota	31.4		41	West Virginia	39.3
10	Tennessee	117.5		42	Iowa	36.6
7	Texas	119.6		43	New Hampshire	32.0
39	Utah	50.5		44	South Dakota	31.4
48	Vermont	17.0		45	Montana	25.5
36	Virginia	57.1		46	North Dakota	23.9
27	Washington	77.5		47	Maine	20.0
41	West Virginia	39.3		48	Vermont	17.0
22	Wisconsin	81.4		49	Idaho	12.7
50	Wyoming	10.1		50	Wyoming	10.1
					District of Columbia	510.9

Source: Reported data from the Federal Bureau of Investigation
   "Crime in the United States 2016" (Uniform Crime Reports, September 25, 2017, https://ucr.fbi.gov/)
*Robbery is the taking or attempting to take anything of value by force or threat of force.

Aggravated Assaults in 2016

National Total = 803,007 Aggravated Assaults*

RANK	STATE	ASSAULTS	% of USA
13	Alabama	18,877	2.4%
38	Alaska	4,011	0.5%
12	Arizona	21,858	2.7%
22	Arkansas	11,982	1.5%
1	California	104,375	13.0%
23	Colorado	11,696	1.5%
35	Connecticut	4,579	0.6%
40	Delaware	3,121	0.4%
3	Florida	59,816	7.4%
9	Georgia	24,595	3.1%
44	Hawaii	2,769	0.3%
42	Idaho	2,895	0.4%
5	Illinois	32,065	4.0%
17	Indiana	16,575	2.1%
32	Iowa	6,644	0.8%
29	Kansas	7,966	1.0%
34	Kentucky	5,038	0.6%
14	Louisiana	18,556	2.3%
49	Maine	950	0.1%
19	Maryland	15,874	2.0%
16	Massachusetts	18,050	2.2%
7	Michigan	30,729	3.8%
30	Minnesota	7,217	0.9%
36	Mississippi	4,471	0.6%
11	Missouri	21,983	2.7%
41	Montana	2,960	0.4%
39	Nebraska	3,561	0.4%
24	Nevada	11,639	1.4%
45	New Hampshire	1,611	0.2%
25	New Jersey	11,105	1.4%
28	New Mexico	10,217	1.3%
4	New York	45,079	5.6%
8	North Carolina	24,906	3.1%
47	North Dakota	1,365	0.2%
18	Ohio	16,111	2.0%
21	Oklahoma	12,202	1.5%
31	Oregon	6,718	0.8%
10	Pennsylvania	23,027	2.9%
46	Rhode Island	1,513	0.2%
15	South Carolina	18,108	2.3%
43	South Dakota	2,813	0.4%
6	Tennessee	31,084	3.9%
2	Texas	72,880	9.1%
37	Utah	4,274	0.5%
50	Vermont	691	0.1%
27	Virginia	10,278	1.3%
20	Washington	13,100	1.6%
33	West Virginia	5,099	0.6%
26	Wisconsin	10,765	1.3%
48	Wyoming	1,146	0.1%

RANK	STATE	ASSAULTS	% of USA
1	California	104,375	13.0%
2	Texas	72,880	9.1%
3	Florida	59,816	7.4%
4	New York	45,079	5.6%
5	Illinois	32,065	4.0%
6	Tennessee	31,084	3.9%
7	Michigan	30,729	3.8%
8	North Carolina	24,906	3.1%
9	Georgia	24,595	3.1%
10	Pennsylvania	23,027	2.9%
11	Missouri	21,983	2.7%
12	Arizona	21,858	2.7%
13	Alabama	18,877	2.4%
14	Louisiana	18,556	2.3%
15	South Carolina	18,108	2.3%
16	Massachusetts	18,050	2.2%
17	Indiana	16,575	2.1%
18	Ohio	16,111	2.0%
19	Maryland	15,874	2.0%
20	Washington	13,100	1.6%
21	Oklahoma	12,202	1.5%
22	Arkansas	11,982	1.5%
23	Colorado	11,696	1.5%
24	Nevada	11,639	1.4%
25	New Jersey	11,105	1.4%
26	Wisconsin	10,765	1.3%
27	Virginia	10,278	1.3%
28	New Mexico	10,217	1.3%
29	Kansas	7,966	1.0%
30	Minnesota	7,217	0.9%
31	Oregon	6,718	0.8%
32	Iowa	6,644	0.8%
33	West Virginia	5,099	0.6%
34	Kentucky	5,038	0.6%
35	Connecticut	4,579	0.6%
36	Mississippi	4,471	0.6%
37	Utah	4,274	0.5%
38	Alaska	4,011	0.5%
39	Nebraska	3,561	0.4%
40	Delaware	3,121	0.4%
41	Montana	2,960	0.4%
42	Idaho	2,895	0.4%
43	South Dakota	2,813	0.4%
44	Hawaii	2,769	0.3%
45	New Hampshire	1,611	0.2%
46	Rhode Island	1,513	0.2%
47	North Dakota	1,365	0.2%
48	Wyoming	1,146	0.1%
49	Maine	950	0.1%
50	Vermont	691	0.1%
	District of Columbia	4,063	0.5%

Source: Reported data from the Federal Bureau of Investigation
"Crime in the United States 2016" (Uniform Crime Reports, September 25, 2017, https://ucr.fbi.gov/)
*Aggravated assault is an attack for the purpose of inflicting severe bodily injury.

Aggravated Assault Rate in 2016

National Rate = 248.5 Aggravated Assaults per 100,000 Population*

ALPHA ORDER

RANK	STATE	RATE
7	Alabama	388.2
1	Alaska	540.6
12	Arizona	315.4
4	Arkansas	401.0
19	California	265.9
29	Colorado	211.1
44	Connecticut	128.0
10	Delaware	327.8
15	Florida	290.2
26	Georgia	238.5
31	Hawaii	193.8
37	Idaho	172.0
23	Illinois	250.5
24	Indiana	249.9
28	Iowa	212.0
18	Kansas	274.0
48	Kentucky	113.5
5	Louisiana	396.4
50	Maine	71.3
21	Maryland	263.8
20	Massachusetts	265.0
14	Michigan	309.5
43	Minnesota	130.7
39	Mississippi	149.6
9	Missouri	360.8
16	Montana	283.9
32	Nebraska	186.7
6	Nevada	395.9
47	New Hampshire	120.7
45	New Jersey	124.2
2	New Mexico	491.0
27	New York	228.3
25	North Carolina	245.5
34	North Dakota	180.1
42	Ohio	138.7
13	Oklahoma	311.0
38	Oregon	164.1
34	Pennsylvania	180.1
40	Rhode Island	143.2
8	South Carolina	365.0
11	South Dakota	325.0
3	Tennessee	467.3
22	Texas	261.6
41	Utah	140.1
49	Vermont	110.6
46	Virginia	122.2
36	Washington	179.7
17	West Virginia	278.5
33	Wisconsin	186.3
30	Wyoming	195.7

RANK ORDER

RANK	STATE	RATE
1	Alaska	540.6
2	New Mexico	491.0
3	Tennessee	467.3
4	Arkansas	401.0
5	Louisiana	396.4
6	Nevada	395.9
7	Alabama	388.2
8	South Carolina	365.0
9	Missouri	360.8
10	Delaware	327.8
11	South Dakota	325.0
12	Arizona	315.4
13	Oklahoma	311.0
14	Michigan	309.5
15	Florida	290.2
16	Montana	283.9
17	West Virginia	278.5
18	Kansas	274.0
19	California	265.9
20	Massachusetts	265.0
21	Maryland	263.8
22	Texas	261.6
23	Illinois	250.5
24	Indiana	249.9
25	North Carolina	245.5
26	Georgia	238.5
27	New York	228.3
28	Iowa	212.0
29	Colorado	211.1
30	Wyoming	195.7
31	Hawaii	193.8
32	Nebraska	186.7
33	Wisconsin	186.3
34	North Dakota	180.1
34	Pennsylvania	180.1
36	Washington	179.7
37	Idaho	172.0
38	Oregon	164.1
39	Mississippi	149.6
40	Rhode Island	143.2
41	Utah	140.1
42	Ohio	138.7
43	Minnesota	130.7
44	Connecticut	128.0
45	New Jersey	124.2
46	Virginia	122.2
47	New Hampshire	120.7
48	Kentucky	113.5
49	Vermont	110.6
50	Maine	71.3
	District of Columbia	596.5

Source: Reported data from the Federal Bureau of Investigation
"Crime in the United States 2016" (Uniform Crime Reports, September 25, 2017, https://ucr.fbi.gov/)
*Aggravated assault is an attack for the purpose of inflicting severe bodily injury.

Property Crimes in 2016

National Total = 7,919,035 Property Crimes*

ALPHA ORDER

ALPHA ORDER | | | | RANK ORDER | | | |

RANK	STATE	CRIMES	% of USA	RANK	STATE	CRIMES	% of USA
20	Alabama	143,362	1.8%	1	California	1,002,070	12.7%
43	Alaska	24,876	0.3%	2	Texas	768,947	9.7%
11	Arizona	206,432	2.6%	3	Florida	553,812	7.0%
28	Arkansas	97,673	1.2%	4	Georgia	309,770	3.9%
1	California	1,002,070	12.7%	5	New York	305,181	3.9%
19	Colorado	151,850	1.9%	6	Ohio	299,357	3.8%
36	Connecticut	64,664	0.8%	7	North Carolina	277,765	3.5%
42	Delaware	26,334	0.3%	8	Illinois	262,306	3.3%
3	Florida	553,812	7.0%	9	Washington	254,653	3.2%
4	Georgia	309,770	3.9%	10	Pennsylvania	222,795	2.8%
38	Hawaii	42,753	0.5%	11	Arizona	206,432	2.6%
40	Idaho	29,357	0.4%	12	Tennessee	189,835	2.4%
8	Illinois	262,306	3.3%	13	Michigan	189,620	2.4%
14	Indiana	171,759	2.2%	14	Indiana	171,759	2.2%
35	Iowa	65,391	0.8%	15	Missouri	170,549	2.2%
33	Kansas	78,367	1.0%	16	South Carolina	160,928	2.0%
29	Kentucky	97,158	1.2%	17	Virginia	156,412	2.0%
18	Louisiana	154,386	1.9%	18	Louisiana	154,386	1.9%
44	Maine	21,912	0.3%	19	Colorado	151,850	1.9%
22	Maryland	137,445	1.7%	20	Alabama	143,362	1.8%
27	Massachusetts	106,339	1.3%	21	New Jersey	138,152	1.7%
13	Michigan	189,620	2.4%	22	Maryland	137,445	1.7%
24	Minnesota	117,756	1.5%	23	Oregon	121,345	1.5%
31	Mississippi	82,732	1.0%	24	Minnesota	117,756	1.5%
15	Missouri	170,549	2.2%	25	Oklahoma	117,037	1.5%
41	Montana	27,976	0.4%	26	Wisconsin	111,720	1.4%
37	Nebraska	43,163	0.5%	27	Massachusetts	106,339	1.3%
34	Nevada	76,047	1.0%	28	Arkansas	97,673	1.2%
45	New Hampshire	20,194	0.3%	29	Kentucky	97,158	1.2%
21	New Jersey	138,152	1.7%	30	Utah	90,058	1.1%
32	New Mexico	81,931	1.0%	31	Mississippi	82,732	1.0%
5	New York	305,181	3.9%	32	New Mexico	81,931	1.0%
7	North Carolina	277,765	3.5%	33	Kansas	78,367	1.0%
47	North Dakota	17,402	0.2%	34	Nevada	76,047	1.0%
6	Ohio	299,357	3.8%	35	Iowa	65,391	0.8%
25	Oklahoma	117,037	1.5%	36	Connecticut	64,664	0.8%
23	Oregon	121,345	1.5%	37	Nebraska	43,163	0.5%
10	Pennsylvania	222,795	2.8%	38	Hawaii	42,753	0.5%
46	Rhode Island	20,058	0.3%	39	West Virginia	37,487	0.5%
16	South Carolina	160,928	2.0%	40	Idaho	29,357	0.4%
48	South Dakota	17,141	0.2%	41	Montana	27,976	0.4%
12	Tennessee	189,835	2.4%	42	Delaware	26,334	0.3%
2	Texas	768,947	9.7%	43	Alaska	24,876	0.3%
30	Utah	90,058	1.1%	44	Maine	21,912	0.3%
50	Vermont	10,602	0.1%	45	New Hampshire	20,194	0.3%
17	Virginia	156,412	2.0%	46	Rhode Island	20,058	0.3%
9	Washington	254,653	3.2%	47	North Dakota	17,402	0.2%
39	West Virginia	37,487	0.5%	48	South Dakota	17,141	0.2%
26	Wisconsin	111,720	1.4%	49	Wyoming	11,460	0.1%
49	Wyoming	11,460	0.1%	50	Vermont	10,602	0.1%
					District of Columbia	32,716	0.4%

Source: Reported data from the Federal Bureau of Investigation
"Crime in the United States 2016" (Uniform Crime Reports, September 25, 2017, https://ucr.fbi.gov/)
*Property crimes are offenses of burglary, larceny-theft, and motor vehicle theft.

Property Crime Rate in 2016

National Rate = 2,450.7 Property Crimes per 100,000 Population*

ALPHA ORDER

RANK	STATE	RATE
13	Alabama	2,947.8
3	Alaska	3,353.0
10	Arizona	2,978.4
5	Arkansas	3,268.6
27	California	2,553.0
19	Colorado	2,740.7
42	Connecticut	1,808.0
17	Delaware	2,766.0
22	Florida	2,686.8
7	Georgia	3,004.5
8	Hawaii	2,992.7
43	Idaho	1,744.2
34	Illinois	2,049.0
24	Indiana	2,589.4
33	Iowa	2,086.0
21	Kansas	2,695.5
31	Kentucky	2,189.7
4	Louisiana	3,297.7
46	Maine	1,645.7
29	Maryland	2,284.5
47	Massachusetts	1,561.1
39	Michigan	1,909.9
32	Minnesota	2,133.3
16	Mississippi	2,768.1
15	Missouri	2,799.1
23	Montana	2,683.5
30	Nebraska	2,263.3
25	Nevada	2,586.6
50	New Hampshire	1,512.9
49	New Jersey	1,544.6
1	New Mexico	3,937.1
48	New York	1,545.6
20	North Carolina	2,737.5
28	North Dakota	2,295.9
26	Ohio	2,577.5
9	Oklahoma	2,982.9
11	Oregon	2,964.4
44	Pennsylvania	1,742.7
40	Rhode Island	1,898.7
6	South Carolina	3,243.8
36	South Dakota	1,980.6
14	Tennessee	2,854.1
18	Texas	2,759.8
12	Utah	2,951.5
45	Vermont	1,697.4
41	Virginia	1,859.4
2	Washington	3,494.1
35	West Virginia	2,047.2
38	Wisconsin	1,933.3
37	Wyoming	1,957.3

RANK ORDER

RANK	STATE	RATE
1	New Mexico	3,937.1
2	Washington	3,494.1
3	Alaska	3,353.0
4	Louisiana	3,297.7
5	Arkansas	3,268.6
6	South Carolina	3,243.8
7	Georgia	3,004.5
8	Hawaii	2,992.7
9	Oklahoma	2,982.9
10	Arizona	2,978.4
11	Oregon	2,964.4
12	Utah	2,951.5
13	Alabama	2,947.8
14	Tennessee	2,854.1
15	Missouri	2,799.1
16	Mississippi	2,768.1
17	Delaware	2,766.0
18	Texas	2,759.8
19	Colorado	2,740.7
20	North Carolina	2,737.5
21	Kansas	2,695.5
22	Florida	2,686.8
23	Montana	2,683.5
24	Indiana	2,589.4
25	Nevada	2,586.6
26	Ohio	2,577.5
27	California	2,553.0
28	North Dakota	2,295.9
29	Maryland	2,284.5
30	Nebraska	2,263.3
31	Kentucky	2,189.7
32	Minnesota	2,133.3
33	Iowa	2,086.0
34	Illinois	2,049.0
35	West Virginia	2,047.2
36	South Dakota	1,980.6
37	Wyoming	1,957.3
38	Wisconsin	1,933.3
39	Michigan	1,909.9
40	Rhode Island	1,898.7
41	Virginia	1,859.4
42	Connecticut	1,808.0
43	Idaho	1,744.2
44	Pennsylvania	1,742.7
45	Vermont	1,697.4
46	Maine	1,645.7
47	Massachusetts	1,561.1
48	New York	1,545.6
49	New Jersey	1,544.6
50	New Hampshire	1,512.9
	District of Columbia	4,802.9

Source: Reported data from the Federal Bureau of Investigation
"Crime in the United States 2016" (Uniform Crime Reports, September 25, 2017, https://ucr.fbi.gov/)
*Property crimes are offenses of burglary, larceny-theft, and motor vehicle theft.

Percent Change in Property Crime Rate: 2015 to 2016

National Percent Change = 2.0% Decrease*

ALPHA ORDER				RANK ORDER		
RANK	STATE	PERCENT CHANGE		RANK	STATE	PERCENT CHANGE
22	Alabama	(1.2)		1	Alaska	18.9
1	Alaska	18.9		2	Vermont	17.2
28	Arizona	(2.0)		3	New Mexico	6.1
15	Arkansas	(0.1)		4	Colorado	3.7
35	California	(2.9)		5	Wyoming	3.0
4	Colorado	3.7		6	Illinois	2.4
22	Connecticut	(1.2)		7	Delaware	2.2
7	Delaware	2.2		7	Oklahoma	2.2
45	Florida	(4.6)		9	Montana	1.5
37	Georgia	(3.0)		9	South Dakota	1.5
47	Hawaii	(6.0)		11	Iowa	0.7
16	Idaho	(0.3)		12	Nebraska	0.6
6	Illinois	2.4		13	Washington	0.3
17	Indiana	(0.4)		14	Rhode Island	0.0
11	Iowa	0.7		15	Arkansas	(0.1)
29	Kansas	(2.1)		16	Idaho	(0.3)
20	Kentucky	(0.7)		17	Indiana	(0.4)
32	Louisiana	(2.4)		17	North Carolina	(0.4)
49	Maine	(10.2)		17	Oregon	(0.4)
41	Maryland	(3.9)		20	Kentucky	(0.7)
48	Massachusetts	(7.5)		21	Michigan	(0.9)
21	Michigan	(0.9)		22	Alabama	(1.2)
44	Minnesota	(4.1)		22	Connecticut	(1.2)
39	Mississippi	(3.5)		24	Virginia	(1.4)
29	Missouri	(2.1)		25	Ohio	(1.5)
9	Montana	1.5		26	Utah	(1.7)
12	Nebraska	0.6		27	North Dakota	(1.9)
38	Nevada	(3.3)		28	Arizona	(2.0)
50	New Hampshire	(14.2)		29	Kansas	(2.1)
46	New Jersey	(5.3)		29	Missouri	(2.1)
3	New Mexico	6.1		31	Wisconsin	(2.3)
40	New York	(3.8)		32	Louisiana	(2.4)
17	North Carolina	(0.4)		33	South Carolina	(2.5)
27	North Dakota	(1.9)		34	West Virginia	(2.6)
25	Ohio	(1.5)		35	California	(2.9)
7	Oklahoma	2.2		35	Texas	(2.9)
17	Oregon	(0.4)		37	Georgia	(3.0)
41	Pennsylvania	(3.9)		38	Nevada	(3.3)
14	Rhode Island	0.0		39	Mississippi	(3.5)
33	South Carolina	(2.5)		40	New York	(3.8)
9	South Dakota	1.5		41	Maryland	(3.9)
43	Tennessee	(4.0)		41	Pennsylvania	(3.9)
35	Texas	(2.9)		43	Tennessee	(4.0)
26	Utah	(1.7)		44	Minnesota	(4.1)
2	Vermont	17.2		45	Florida	(4.6)
24	Virginia	(1.4)		46	New Jersey	(5.3)
13	Washington	0.3		47	Hawaii	(6.0)
34	West Virginia	(2.6)		48	Massachusetts	(7.5)
31	Wisconsin	(2.3)		49	Maine	(10.2)
5	Wyoming	3.0		50	New Hampshire	(14.2)
					District of Columbia	2.4

Source: Reported data from the Federal Bureau of Investigation
  "Crime in the United States 2016" (Uniform Crime Reports, September 25, 2017, https://ucr.fbi.gov/)
*Property crimes are offenses of burglary, larceny-theft, and motor vehicle theft.

Burglaries in 2016

National Total = 1,515,096 Burglaries*

ALPHA ORDER

RANK	STATE	BURGLARIES	% of USA
16	Alabama	34,065	2.2%
42	Alaska	4,053	0.3%
12	Arizona	37,736	2.5%
23	Arkansas	23,771	1.6%
1	California	188,304	12.4%
22	Colorado	23,903	1.6%
36	Connecticut	10,045	0.7%
41	Delaware	5,023	0.3%
3	Florida	100,325	6.6%
6	Georgia	63,344	4.2%
40	Hawaii	6,017	0.4%
39	Idaho	6,318	0.4%
8	Illinois	47,989	3.2%
15	Indiana	34,097	2.3%
33	Iowa	15,030	1.0%
34	Kansas	14,364	0.9%
25	Kentucky	20,834	1.4%
14	Louisiana	34,667	2.3%
43	Maine	4,003	0.3%
21	Maryland	24,692	1.6%
28	Massachusetts	19,193	1.3%
11	Michigan	39,568	2.6%
30	Minnesota	18,606	1.2%
24	Mississippi	23,354	1.5%
18	Missouri	31,710	2.1%
44	Montana	3,934	0.3%
38	Nebraska	6,444	0.4%
29	Nevada	18,850	1.2%
48	New Hampshire	2,963	0.2%
20	New Jersey	25,284	1.7%
31	New Mexico	17,281	1.1%
10	New York	39,821	2.6%
4	North Carolina	72,082	4.8%
46	North Dakota	3,243	0.2%
5	Ohio	66,883	4.4%
19	Oklahoma	29,103	1.9%
32	Oregon	16,866	1.1%
13	Pennsylvania	35,520	2.3%
45	Rhode Island	3,788	0.3%
17	South Carolina	32,976	2.2%
47	South Dakota	3,000	0.2%
9	Tennessee	40,312	2.7%
2	Texas	148,740	9.8%
35	Utah	12,836	0.8%
49	Vermont	2,103	0.1%
26	Virginia	20,018	1.3%
7	Washington	49,180	3.2%
37	West Virginia	9,301	0.6%
27	Wisconsin	19,425	1.3%
50	Wyoming	1,771	0.1%

RANK ORDER

RANK	STATE	BURGLARIES	% of USA
1	California	188,304	12.4%
2	Texas	148,740	9.8%
3	Florida	100,325	6.6%
4	North Carolina	72,082	4.8%
5	Ohio	66,883	4.4%
6	Georgia	63,344	4.2%
7	Washington	49,180	3.2%
8	Illinois	47,989	3.2%
9	Tennessee	40,312	2.7%
10	New York	39,821	2.6%
11	Michigan	39,568	2.6%
12	Arizona	37,736	2.5%
13	Pennsylvania	35,520	2.3%
14	Louisiana	34,667	2.3%
15	Indiana	34,097	2.3%
16	Alabama	34,065	2.2%
17	South Carolina	32,976	2.2%
18	Missouri	31,710	2.1%
19	Oklahoma	29,103	1.9%
20	New Jersey	25,284	1.7%
21	Maryland	24,692	1.6%
22	Colorado	23,903	1.6%
23	Arkansas	23,771	1.6%
24	Mississippi	23,354	1.5%
25	Kentucky	20,834	1.4%
26	Virginia	20,018	1.3%
27	Wisconsin	19,425	1.3%
28	Massachusetts	19,193	1.3%
29	Nevada	18,850	1.2%
30	Minnesota	18,606	1.2%
31	New Mexico	17,281	1.1%
32	Oregon	16,866	1.1%
33	Iowa	15,030	1.0%
34	Kansas	14,364	0.9%
35	Utah	12,836	0.8%
36	Connecticut	10,045	0.7%
37	West Virginia	9,301	0.6%
38	Nebraska	6,444	0.4%
39	Idaho	6,318	0.4%
40	Hawaii	6,017	0.4%
41	Delaware	5,023	0.3%
42	Alaska	4,053	0.3%
43	Maine	4,003	0.3%
44	Montana	3,934	0.3%
45	Rhode Island	3,788	0.3%
46	North Dakota	3,243	0.2%
47	South Dakota	3,000	0.2%
48	New Hampshire	2,963	0.2%
49	Vermont	2,103	0.1%
50	Wyoming	1,771	0.1%
	District of Columbia	2,361	0.2%

Source: Reported data from the Federal Bureau of Investigation
"Crime in the United States 2016" (Uniform Crime Reports, September 25, 2017, https://ucr.fbi.gov/)
*Burglary is the unlawful entry of a structure to commit a felony or theft. Attempts are included.

Burglary Rate in 2016

National Rate = 468.9 Burglaries per 100,000 Population*

ALPHA ORDER

RANK	STATE	RATE
7	Alabama	700.5
14	Alaska	546.3
15	Arizona	544.4
2	Arkansas	795.5
23	California	479.8
26	Colorado	431.4
46	Connecticut	280.9
17	Delaware	527.6
22	Florida	486.7
11	Georgia	614.4
28	Hawaii	421.2
34	Idaho	375.4
35	Illinois	374.9
19	Indiana	514.0
24	Iowa	479.5
21	Kansas	494.1
25	Kentucky	469.6
5	Louisiana	740.5
43	Maine	300.6
31	Maryland	410.4
45	Massachusetts	281.8
32	Michigan	398.5
39	Minnesota	337.1
3	Mississippi	781.4
18	Missouri	520.4
33	Montana	377.4
38	Nebraska	337.9
10	Nevada	641.1
49	New Hampshire	222.0
44	New Jersey	282.7
1	New Mexico	830.4
50	New York	201.7
6	North Carolina	710.4
27	North Dakota	427.9
13	Ohio	575.9
4	Oklahoma	741.7
30	Oregon	412.0
47	Pennsylvania	277.8
36	Rhode Island	358.6
9	South Carolina	664.7
37	South Dakota	346.6
12	Tennessee	606.1
16	Texas	533.8
29	Utah	420.7
40	Vermont	336.7
48	Virginia	238.0
8	Washington	674.8
20	West Virginia	507.9
41	Wisconsin	336.1
42	Wyoming	302.5

RANK ORDER

RANK	STATE	RATE
1	New Mexico	830.4
2	Arkansas	795.5
3	Mississippi	781.4
4	Oklahoma	741.7
5	Louisiana	740.5
6	North Carolina	710.4
7	Alabama	700.5
8	Washington	674.8
9	South Carolina	664.7
10	Nevada	641.1
11	Georgia	614.4
12	Tennessee	606.1
13	Ohio	575.9
14	Alaska	546.3
15	Arizona	544.4
16	Texas	533.8
17	Delaware	527.6
18	Missouri	520.4
19	Indiana	514.0
20	West Virginia	507.9
21	Kansas	494.1
22	Florida	486.7
23	California	479.8
24	Iowa	479.5
25	Kentucky	469.6
26	Colorado	431.4
27	North Dakota	427.9
28	Hawaii	421.2
29	Utah	420.7
30	Oregon	412.0
31	Maryland	410.4
32	Michigan	398.5
33	Montana	377.4
34	Idaho	375.4
35	Illinois	374.9
36	Rhode Island	358.6
37	South Dakota	346.6
38	Nebraska	337.9
39	Minnesota	337.1
40	Vermont	336.7
41	Wisconsin	336.1
42	Wyoming	302.5
43	Maine	300.6
44	New Jersey	282.7
45	Massachusetts	281.8
46	Connecticut	280.9
47	Pennsylvania	277.8
48	Virginia	238.0
49	New Hampshire	222.0
50	New York	201.7
	District of Columbia	346.6

Source: Reported data from the Federal Bureau of Investigation
"Crime in the United States 2016" (Uniform Crime Reports, September 25, 2017, https://ucr.fbi.gov/)
*Burglary is the unlawful entry of a structure to commit a felony or theft. Attempts are included.

Larceny-Thefts in 2016

National Total = 5,638,455 Larceny-Thefts*

ALPHA ORDER				RANK ORDER			
RANK	STATE	THEFTS	% of USA	RANK	STATE	THEFTS	% of USA
22	Alabama	97,574	1.7%	1	California	637,010	11.3%
43	Alaska	17,766	0.3%	2	Texas	551,151	9.8%
11	Arizona	150,275	2.7%	3	Florida	410,352	7.3%
29	Arkansas	66,747	1.2%	4	New York	250,968	4.5%
1	California	637,010	11.3%	5	Georgia	219,625	3.9%
19	Colorado	108,336	1.9%	6	Ohio	212,807	3.8%
34	Connecticut	47,512	0.8%	7	Illinois	194,407	3.4%
42	Delaware	19,791	0.4%	8	North Carolina	190,377	3.4%
3	Florida	410,352	7.3%	9	Pennsylvania	174,228	3.1%
5	Georgia	219,625	3.9%	10	Washington	173,187	3.1%
38	Hawaii	31,082	0.6%	11	Arizona	150,275	2.7%
41	Idaho	20,962	0.4%	12	Tennessee	134,404	2.4%
7	Illinois	194,407	3.4%	13	Michigan	129,876	2.3%
15	Indiana	122,931	2.2%	14	Virginia	126,606	2.2%
35	Iowa	45,378	0.8%	15	Indiana	122,931	2.2%
31	Kansas	57,066	1.0%	16	Missouri	120,544	2.1%
30	Kentucky	66,438	1.2%	17	South Carolina	114,032	2.0%
18	Louisiana	109,380	1.9%	18	Louisiana	109,380	1.9%
44	Maine	17,134	0.3%	19	Colorado	108,336	1.9%
21	Maryland	100,919	1.8%	20	New Jersey	101,540	1.8%
26	Massachusetts	79,088	1.4%	21	Maryland	100,919	1.8%
13	Michigan	129,876	2.3%	22	Alabama	97,574	1.7%
24	Minnesota	90,422	1.6%	23	Oregon	91,286	1.6%
32	Mississippi	55,054	1.0%	24	Minnesota	90,422	1.6%
16	Missouri	120,544	2.1%	25	Wisconsin	82,337	1.5%
40	Montana	21,299	0.4%	26	Massachusetts	79,088	1.4%
37	Nebraska	31,994	0.6%	27	Oklahoma	75,779	1.3%
36	Nevada	44,017	0.8%	28	Utah	67,834	1.2%
45	New Hampshire	16,360	0.3%	29	Arkansas	66,747	1.2%
20	New Jersey	101,540	1.8%	30	Kentucky	66,438	1.2%
33	New Mexico	52,907	0.9%	31	Kansas	57,066	1.0%
4	New York	250,968	4.5%	32	Mississippi	55,054	1.0%
8	North Carolina	190,377	3.4%	33	New Mexico	52,907	0.9%
48	North Dakota	12,195	0.2%	34	Connecticut	47,512	0.8%
6	Ohio	212,807	3.8%	35	Iowa	45,378	0.8%
27	Oklahoma	75,779	1.3%	36	Nevada	44,017	0.8%
23	Oregon	91,286	1.6%	37	Nebraska	31,994	0.6%
9	Pennsylvania	174,228	3.1%	38	Hawaii	31,082	0.6%
46	Rhode Island	14,674	0.3%	39	West Virginia	25,677	0.5%
17	South Carolina	114,032	2.0%	40	Montana	21,299	0.4%
47	South Dakota	12,639	0.2%	41	Idaho	20,962	0.4%
12	Tennessee	134,404	2.4%	42	Delaware	19,791	0.4%
2	Texas	551,151	9.8%	43	Alaska	17,766	0.3%
28	Utah	67,834	1.2%	44	Maine	17,134	0.3%
50	Vermont	8,217	0.1%	45	New Hampshire	16,360	0.3%
14	Virginia	126,606	2.2%	46	Rhode Island	14,674	0.3%
10	Washington	173,187	3.1%	47	South Dakota	12,639	0.2%
39	West Virginia	25,677	0.5%	48	North Dakota	12,195	0.2%
25	Wisconsin	82,337	1.5%	49	Wyoming	8,889	0.2%
49	Wyoming	8,889	0.2%	50	Vermont	8,217	0.1%
					District of Columbia	27,382	0.5%

Source: Reported data from the Federal Bureau of Investigation
  "Crime in the United States 2016" (Uniform Crime Reports, September 25, 2017, https://ucr.fbi.gov/)
*Larceny-theft is the unlawful taking of property without use of force, violence, or fraud. Attempts are included. Motor vehicle thefts are excluded.

Larceny-Theft Rate in 2016

National Rate = 1,745.0 Larceny-Thefts per 100,000 Population*

ALPHA ORDER			RANK ORDER		
RANK	STATE	RATE	RANK	STATE	RATE
15	Alabama	2,006.3	1	New Mexico	2,542.4
2	Alaska	2,394.7	2	Alaska	2,394.7
10	Arizona	2,168.1	3	Washington	2,376.3
6	Arkansas	2,233.6	4	Louisiana	2,336.3
29	California	1,623.0	5	South Carolina	2,298.5
20	Colorado	1,955.3	6	Arkansas	2,233.6
42	Connecticut	1,328.5	7	Oregon	2,230.0
12	Delaware	2,078.7	8	Utah	2,223.2
16	Florida	1,990.8	9	Hawaii	2,175.8
11	Georgia	2,130.1	10	Arizona	2,168.1
9	Hawaii	2,175.8	11	Georgia	2,130.1
47	Idaho	1,245.4	12	Delaware	2,078.7
31	Illinois	1,518.6	13	Montana	2,043.0
23	Indiana	1,853.3	14	Tennessee	2,020.7
37	Iowa	1,447.6	15	Alabama	2,006.3
19	Kansas	1,962.9	16	Florida	1,990.8
34	Kentucky	1,497.4	17	Missouri	1,978.4
4	Louisiana	2,336.3	18	Texas	1,978.1
45	Maine	1,286.8	19	Kansas	1,962.9
27	Maryland	1,677.4	20	Colorado	1,955.3
49	Massachusetts	1,161.0	21	Oklahoma	1,931.4
44	Michigan	1,308.1	22	North Carolina	1,876.2
28	Minnesota	1,638.1	23	Indiana	1,853.3
24	Mississippi	1,842.1	24	Mississippi	1,842.1
17	Missouri	1,978.4	25	Ohio	1,832.3
13	Montana	2,043.0	26	Nebraska	1,677.6
26	Nebraska	1,677.6	27	Maryland	1,677.4
35	Nevada	1,497.1	28	Minnesota	1,638.1
48	New Hampshire	1,225.7	29	California	1,623.0
50	New Jersey	1,135.2	30	North Dakota	1,608.9
1	New Mexico	2,542.4	31	Illinois	1,518.6
46	New York	1,271.0	32	Wyoming	1,518.2
22	North Carolina	1,876.2	33	Virginia	1,505.1
30	North Dakota	1,608.9	34	Kentucky	1,497.4
25	Ohio	1,832.3	35	Nevada	1,497.1
21	Oklahoma	1,931.4	36	South Dakota	1,460.4
7	Oregon	2,230.0	37	Iowa	1,447.6
41	Pennsylvania	1,362.8	38	Wisconsin	1,424.8
40	Rhode Island	1,389.0	39	West Virginia	1,402.3
5	South Carolina	2,298.5	40	Rhode Island	1,389.0
36	South Dakota	1,460.4	41	Pennsylvania	1,362.8
14	Tennessee	2,020.7	42	Connecticut	1,328.5
18	Texas	1,978.1	43	Vermont	1,315.6
8	Utah	2,223.2	44	Michigan	1,308.1
43	Vermont	1,315.6	45	Maine	1,286.8
33	Virginia	1,505.1	46	New York	1,271.0
3	Washington	2,376.3	47	Idaho	1,245.4
39	West Virginia	1,402.3	48	New Hampshire	1,225.7
38	Wisconsin	1,424.8	49	Massachusetts	1,161.0
32	Wyoming	1,518.2	50	New Jersey	1,135.2

District of Columbia 4,019.8

Source: Reported data from the Federal Bureau of Investigation
"Crime in the United States 2016" (Uniform Crime Reports, September 25, 2017, https://ucr.fbi.gov/)
*Larceny-theft is the unlawful taking of property without use of force, violence, or fraud. Attempts are included. Motor vehicle thefts are excluded.

Motor Vehicle Thefts in 2016

National Total = 765,484 Motor Vehicle Thefts*

ALPHA ORDER

RANK	STATE	THEFTS	% of USA
23	Alabama	11,723	1.5%
39	Alaska	3,057	0.4%
10	Arizona	18,421	2.4%
32	Arkansas	7,155	0.9%
1	California	176,756	23.1%
9	Colorado	19,611	2.6%
33	Connecticut	7,107	0.9%
45	Delaware	1,520	0.2%
3	Florida	43,135	5.6%
5	Georgia	26,801	3.5%
35	Hawaii	5,654	0.7%
42	Idaho	2,077	0.3%
7	Illinois	19,910	2.6%
14	Indiana	14,731	1.9%
36	Iowa	4,983	0.7%
34	Kansas	6,937	0.9%
27	Kentucky	9,886	1.3%
25	Louisiana	10,339	1.4%
49	Maine	775	0.1%
21	Maryland	11,834	1.5%
31	Massachusetts	8,058	1.1%
6	Michigan	20,176	2.6%
30	Minnesota	8,728	1.1%
38	Mississippi	4,324	0.6%
11	Missouri	18,295	2.4%
40	Montana	2,743	0.4%
37	Nebraska	4,725	0.6%
18	Nevada	13,180	1.7%
47	New Hampshire	871	0.1%
24	New Jersey	11,328	1.5%
22	New Mexico	11,743	1.5%
15	New York	14,392	1.9%
12	North Carolina	15,306	2.0%
43	North Dakota	1,964	0.3%
8	Ohio	19,667	2.6%
20	Oklahoma	12,155	1.6%
17	Oregon	13,193	1.7%
19	Pennsylvania	13,047	1.7%
44	Rhode Island	1,596	0.2%
16	South Carolina	13,920	1.8%
46	South Dakota	1,502	0.2%
13	Tennessee	15,119	2.0%
2	Texas	69,056	9.0%
29	Utah	9,388	1.2%
50	Vermont	282	0.0%
28	Virginia	9,788	1.3%
4	Washington	32,286	4.2%
41	West Virginia	2,509	0.3%
26	Wisconsin	9,958	1.3%
48	Wyoming	800	0.1%

RANK ORDER

RANK	STATE	THEFTS	% of USA
1	California	176,756	23.1%
2	Texas	69,056	9.0%
3	Florida	43,135	5.6%
4	Washington	32,286	4.2%
5	Georgia	26,801	3.5%
6	Michigan	20,176	2.6%
7	Illinois	19,910	2.6%
8	Ohio	19,667	2.6%
9	Colorado	19,611	2.6%
10	Arizona	18,421	2.4%
11	Missouri	18,295	2.4%
12	North Carolina	15,306	2.0%
13	Tennessee	15,119	2.0%
14	Indiana	14,731	1.9%
15	New York	14,392	1.9%
16	South Carolina	13,920	1.8%
17	Oregon	13,193	1.7%
18	Nevada	13,180	1.7%
19	Pennsylvania	13,047	1.7%
20	Oklahoma	12,155	1.6%
21	Maryland	11,834	1.5%
22	New Mexico	11,743	1.5%
23	Alabama	11,723	1.5%
24	New Jersey	11,328	1.5%
25	Louisiana	10,339	1.4%
26	Wisconsin	9,958	1.3%
27	Kentucky	9,886	1.3%
28	Virginia	9,788	1.3%
29	Utah	9,388	1.2%
30	Minnesota	8,728	1.1%
31	Massachusetts	8,058	1.1%
32	Arkansas	7,155	0.9%
33	Connecticut	7,107	0.9%
34	Kansas	6,937	0.9%
35	Hawaii	5,654	0.7%
36	Iowa	4,983	0.7%
37	Nebraska	4,725	0.6%
38	Mississippi	4,324	0.6%
39	Alaska	3,057	0.4%
40	Montana	2,743	0.4%
41	West Virginia	2,509	0.3%
42	Idaho	2,077	0.3%
43	North Dakota	1,964	0.3%
44	Rhode Island	1,596	0.2%
45	Delaware	1,520	0.2%
46	South Dakota	1,502	0.2%
47	New Hampshire	871	0.1%
48	Wyoming	800	0.1%
49	Maine	775	0.1%
50	Vermont	282	0.0%
	District of Columbia	2,973	0.4%

Source: Reported data from the Federal Bureau of Investigation
   "Crime in the United States 2016" (Uniform Crime Reports, September 25, 2017, https://ucr.fbi.gov/)
*Includes the theft or attempted theft of a self-propelled vehicle. Excludes motorboats, construction equipment, airplanes, and farming equipment.

Motor Vehicle Theft Rate in 2016

National Rate = 236.9 Motor Vehicle Thefts per 100,000 Population*

ALPHA ORDER

RANK	STATE	RATE
19	Alabama	241.1
5	Alaska	412.1
13	Arizona	265.8
20	Arkansas	239.4
2	California	450.3
7	Colorado	354.0
28	Connecticut	198.7
33	Delaware	159.7
26	Florida	209.3
15	Georgia	259.9
6	Hawaii	395.8
43	Idaho	123.4
36	Illinois	155.5
24	Indiana	222.1
34	Iowa	159.0
21	Kansas	238.6
23	Kentucky	222.8
25	Louisiana	220.8
49	Maine	58.2
29	Maryland	196.7
44	Massachusetts	118.3
27	Michigan	203.2
35	Minnesota	158.1
39	Mississippi	144.7
11	Missouri	300.3
14	Montana	263.1
17	Nebraska	247.8
3	Nevada	448.3
48	New Hampshire	65.3
42	New Jersey	126.6
1	New Mexico	564.3
47	New York	72.9
38	North Carolina	150.8
16	North Dakota	259.1
32	Ohio	169.3
9	Oklahoma	309.8
8	Oregon	322.3
46	Pennsylvania	102.1
37	Rhode Island	151.1
12	South Carolina	280.6
30	South Dakota	173.6
22	Tennessee	227.3
17	Texas	247.8
10	Utah	307.7
50	Vermont	45.1
45	Virginia	116.4
4	Washington	443.0
40	West Virginia	137.0
31	Wisconsin	172.3
41	Wyoming	136.6

RANK ORDER

RANK	STATE	RATE
1	New Mexico	564.3
2	California	450.3
3	Nevada	448.3
4	Washington	443.0
5	Alaska	412.1
6	Hawaii	395.8
7	Colorado	354.0
8	Oregon	322.3
9	Oklahoma	309.8
10	Utah	307.7
11	Missouri	300.3
12	South Carolina	280.6
13	Arizona	265.8
14	Montana	263.1
15	Georgia	259.9
16	North Dakota	259.1
17	Nebraska	247.8
17	Texas	247.8
19	Alabama	241.1
20	Arkansas	239.4
21	Kansas	238.6
22	Tennessee	227.3
23	Kentucky	222.8
24	Indiana	222.1
25	Louisiana	220.8
26	Florida	209.3
27	Michigan	203.2
28	Connecticut	198.7
29	Maryland	196.7
30	South Dakota	173.6
31	Wisconsin	172.3
32	Ohio	169.3
33	Delaware	159.7
34	Iowa	159.0
35	Minnesota	158.1
36	Illinois	155.5
37	Rhode Island	151.1
38	North Carolina	150.8
39	Mississippi	144.7
40	West Virginia	137.0
41	Wyoming	136.6
42	New Jersey	126.6
43	Idaho	123.4
44	Massachusetts	118.3
45	Virginia	116.4
46	Pennsylvania	102.1
47	New York	72.9
48	New Hampshire	65.3
49	Maine	58.2
50	Vermont	45.1
	District of Columbia	436.5

Source: Reported data from the Federal Bureau of Investigation
"Crime in the United States 2016" (Uniform Crime Reports, September 25, 2017, https://ucr.fbi.gov/)
*Includes the theft or attempted theft of a self-propelled vehicle. Excludes motorboats, construction equipment, airplanes, and farming equipment.

Rate of Consumer Fraud Complaints in 2016

National Rate = 819.8 Complaints per 100,000 Population*

ALPHA ORDER

RANK	STATE	RATE
6	Alabama	809.0
47	Alaska	358.9
19	Arizona	656.9
34	Arkansas	519.0
10	California	713.1
23	Colorado	609.1
24	Connecticut	590.4
8	Delaware	797.5
1	Florida	1,305.6
2	Georgia	1,136.6
46	Hawaii	403.8
39	Idaho	463.4
25	Illinois	576.7
28	Indiana	562.8
48	Iowa	342.5
36	Kansas	503.4
33	Kentucky	539.7
12	Louisiana	701.9
41	Maine	423.7
7	Maryland	807.7
30	Massachusetts	547.2
3	Michigan	1,083.3
37	Minnesota	470.7
22	Mississippi	609.3
11	Missouri	706.5
40	Montana	441.2
44	Nebraska	411.9
5	Nevada	872.0
27	New Hampshire	563.8
21	New Jersey	636.7
16	New Mexico	667.9
26	New York	567.3
20	North Carolina	641.2
50	North Dakota	284.7
17	Ohio	664.8
35	Oklahoma	518.7
31	Oregon	546.8
18	Pennsylvania	659.2
15	Rhode Island	682.1
14	South Carolina	700.8
49	South Dakota	320.6
9	Tennessee	767.3
4	Texas	952.3
42	Utah	417.9
45	Vermont	405.4
13	Virginia	701.3
29	Washington	554.7
32	West Virginia	543.3
38	Wisconsin	465.9
43	Wyoming	416.2

RANK ORDER

RANK	STATE	RATE
1	Florida	1,305.6
2	Georgia	1,136.6
3	Michigan	1,083.3
4	Texas	952.3
5	Nevada	872.0
6	Alabama	809.0
7	Maryland	807.7
8	Delaware	797.5
9	Tennessee	767.3
10	California	713.1
11	Missouri	706.5
12	Louisiana	701.9
13	Virginia	701.3
14	South Carolina	700.8
15	Rhode Island	682.1
16	New Mexico	667.9
17	Ohio	664.8
18	Pennsylvania	659.2
19	Arizona	656.9
20	North Carolina	641.2
21	New Jersey	636.7
22	Mississippi	609.3
23	Colorado	609.1
24	Connecticut	590.4
25	Illinois	576.7
26	New York	567.3
27	New Hampshire	563.8
28	Indiana	562.8
29	Washington	554.7
30	Massachusetts	547.2
31	Oregon	546.8
32	West Virginia	543.3
33	Kentucky	539.7
34	Arkansas	519.0
35	Oklahoma	518.7
36	Kansas	503.4
37	Minnesota	470.7
38	Wisconsin	465.9
39	Idaho	463.4
40	Montana	441.2
41	Maine	423.7
42	Utah	417.9
43	Wyoming	416.2
44	Nebraska	411.9
45	Vermont	405.4
46	Hawaii	403.8
47	Alaska	358.9
48	Iowa	342.5
49	South Dakota	320.6
50	North Dakota	284.7
	District of Columbia	1,474.5

Source: Federal Trade Commission, Consumer Sentinel
  "Consumer Sentinel Network Data Book for January - December 2016" (March 2017, http://www.ftc.gov/sentinel/)
*National rate includes complaints not shown by state. Rates include "other" complaints but do not include identity theft or "Do Not Call" registry complaints.

Rate of Identity Theft Complaints in 2016

National Rate = 123.4 Complaints per 100,000 Population*

ALPHA ORDER

RANK	STATE	RATE
36	Alabama	82.4
25	Alaska	96.1
10	Arizona	126.2
39	Arkansas	77.2
4	California	139.5
15	Colorado	112.0
6	Connecticut	137.9
3	Delaware	155.9
2	Florida	166.8
11	Georgia	124.0
50	Hawaii	55.2
37	Idaho	80.1
5	Illinois	138.0
40	Indiana	76.8
44	Iowa	68.1
31	Kansas	87.1
45	Kentucky	65.3
42	Louisiana	69.7
29	Maine	87.9
7	Maryland	137.1
19	Massachusetts	107.0
1	Michigan	175.6
18	Minnesota	107.2
38	Mississippi	79.6
8	Missouri	136.1
43	Montana	68.2
35	Nebraska	83.1
9	Nevada	135.8
23	New Hampshire	101.3
16	New Jersey	111.5
24	New Mexico	96.9
22	New York	102.3
25	North Carolina	96.1
47	North Dakota	61.3
27	Ohio	94.8
33	Oklahoma	85.1
20	Oregon	105.3
17	Pennsylvania	109.7
13	Rhode Island	115.1
28	South Carolina	89.5
49	South Dakota	58.1
32	Tennessee	86.0
12	Texas	119.2
34	Utah	83.2
46	Vermont	62.0
21	Virginia	104.3
14	Washington	114.0
48	West Virginia	59.7
30	Wisconsin	87.5
41	Wyoming	74.6

RANK ORDER

RANK	STATE	RATE
1	Michigan	175.6
2	Florida	166.8
3	Delaware	155.9
4	California	139.5
5	Illinois	138.0
6	Connecticut	137.9
7	Maryland	137.1
8	Missouri	136.1
9	Nevada	135.8
10	Arizona	126.2
11	Georgia	124.0
12	Texas	119.2
13	Rhode Island	115.1
14	Washington	114.0
15	Colorado	112.0
16	New Jersey	111.5
17	Pennsylvania	109.7
18	Minnesota	107.2
19	Massachusetts	107.0
20	Oregon	105.3
21	Virginia	104.3
22	New York	102.3
23	New Hampshire	101.3
24	New Mexico	96.9
25	Alaska	96.1
25	North Carolina	96.1
27	Ohio	94.8
28	South Carolina	89.5
29	Maine	87.9
30	Wisconsin	87.5
31	Kansas	87.1
32	Tennessee	86.0
33	Oklahoma	85.1
34	Utah	83.2
35	Nebraska	83.1
36	Alabama	82.4
37	Idaho	80.1
38	Mississippi	79.6
39	Arkansas	77.2
40	Indiana	76.8
41	Wyoming	74.6
42	Louisiana	69.7
43	Montana	68.2
44	Iowa	68.1
45	Kentucky	65.3
46	Vermont	62.0
47	North Dakota	61.3
48	West Virginia	59.7
49	South Dakota	58.1
50	Hawaii	55.2

	District of Columbia	198.5

Source: Federal Trade Commission, Consumer Sentinel

"Consumer Sentinel Network Data Book for January - December 2016" (March 2017, http://www.ftc.gov/sentinel/)

*National rate includes complaints not shown by state. Rates do not include consumer fraud or "Do Not Call" registry complaints.

Reported Arrest Rate in 2016

National Rate = 3,316.0 Reported Arrests per 100,000 Population*

ALPHA ORDER

RANK	STATE	RATE
15	Alabama	4,064.6
16	Alaska	3,989.1
14	Arizona	4,125.9
7	Arkansas	4,743.6
40	California	2,867.6
11	Colorado	4,506.3
41	Connecticut	2,843.4
24	Delaware	3,529.0
23	Florida	3,532.0
39	Georgia	2,928.5
37	Hawaii	2,961.1
21	Idaho	3,545.1
NA	Illinois**	NA
28	Indiana	3,333.9
26	Iowa	3,414.0
33	Kansas	3,107.2
6	Kentucky	4,759.7
10	Louisiana	4,587.4
31	Maine	3,271.7
25	Maryland	3,513.7
49	Massachusetts	1,851.7
43	Michigan	2,639.1
45	Minnesota	2,586.1
2	Mississippi	5,528.5
13	Missouri	4,175.8
38	Montana	2,947.7
17	Nebraska	3,967.2
12	Nevada	4,283.3
18	New Hampshire	3,707.9
27	New Jersey	3,371.9
4	New Mexico	5,172.3
46	New York***	2,558.9
19	North Carolina	3,691.0
9	North Dakota	4,622.9
47	Ohio	2,387.6
35	Oklahoma	3,002.0
22	Oregon	3,536.1
36	Pennsylvania	2,967.3
44	Rhode Island	2,602.5
29	South Carolina	3,301.3
1	South Dakota	5,979.1
3	Tennessee	5,256.7
34	Texas	3,030.7
20	Utah	3,676.5
48	Vermont	2,314.6
30	Virginia	3,289.4
42	Washington	2,640.7
32	West Virginia	3,176.1
8	Wisconsin	4,631.7
5	Wyoming	5,131.8

RANK ORDER

RANK	STATE	RATE
1	South Dakota	5,979.1
2	Mississippi	5,528.5
3	Tennessee	5,256.7
4	New Mexico	5,172.3
5	Wyoming	5,131.8
6	Kentucky	4,759.7
7	Arkansas	4,743.6
8	Wisconsin	4,631.7
9	North Dakota	4,622.9
10	Louisiana	4,587.4
11	Colorado	4,506.3
12	Nevada	4,283.3
13	Missouri	4,175.8
14	Arizona	4,125.9
15	Alabama	4,064.6
16	Alaska	3,989.1
17	Nebraska	3,967.2
18	New Hampshire	3,707.9
19	North Carolina	3,691.0
20	Utah	3,676.5
21	Idaho	3,545.1
22	Oregon	3,536.1
23	Florida	3,532.0
24	Delaware	3,529.0
25	Maryland	3,513.7
26	Iowa	3,414.0
27	New Jersey	3,371.9
28	Indiana	3,333.9
29	South Carolina	3,301.3
30	Virginia	3,289.4
31	Maine	3,271.7
32	West Virginia	3,176.1
33	Kansas	3,107.2
34	Texas	3,030.7
35	Oklahoma	3,002.0
36	Pennsylvania	2,967.3
37	Hawaii	2,961.1
38	Montana	2,947.7
39	Georgia	2,928.5
40	California	2,867.6
41	Connecticut	2,843.4
42	Washington	2,640.7
43	Michigan	2,639.1
44	Rhode Island	2,602.5
45	Minnesota	2,586.1
46	New York***	2,558.9
47	Ohio	2,387.6
48	Vermont	2,314.6
49	Massachusetts	1,851.7
NA	Illinois**	NA
	District of Columbia**	NA

Source: CQ Press using reported data from the Federal Bureau of Investigation
"Crime in the United States 2016" (Uniform Crime Reports, September 25, 2017, https://ucr.fbi.gov/)
*By law enforcement agencies submitting complete reports to the F.B.I. for 12 months in 2016. These rates based on population estimates for areas under the jurisdiction of those agencies reporting. Arrest rate based on the F.B.I. estimate of total arrests is 3,299.7 reported and unreported arrests per 100,000 population.
**Not available. ***New York's figure does not include New York City.

Reported Juvenile Arrest Rate in 2016

National Rate = 2,585.7 Reported Arrests per 100,000 Juvenile Population*

ALPHA ORDER				RANK ORDER		
RANK	STATE	RATE		RANK	STATE	RATE
46	Alabama	1,226.2		1	Wisconsin	7,263.6
34	Alaska	2,351.4		2	South Dakota	6,049.7
16	Arizona	3,394.5		3	Wyoming	6,000.7
25	Arkansas	2,724.0		4	North Dakota	5,467.0
44	California	1,448.2		5	Nebraska	4,710.0
6	Colorado	4,217.7		6	Colorado	4,217.7
35	Connecticut	2,297.3		7	Louisiana	4,209.1
9	Delaware	3,935.1		8	Montana	4,113.2
20	Florida	3,057.1		9	Delaware	3,935.1
30	Georgia	2,480.8		10	Maryland	3,715.7
23	Hawaii	2,736.9		11	Iowa	3,650.4
15	Idaho	3,447.7		12	Minnesota	3,642.0
NA	Illinois**	NA		13	Utah	3,593.6
27	Indiana	2,670.8		14	Pennsylvania	3,560.1
11	Iowa	3,650.4		15	Idaho	3,447.7
37	Kansas	2,181.4		16	Arizona	3,394.5
47	Kentucky	1,225.5		17	Tennessee	3,325.9
7	Louisiana	4,209.1		18	Missouri	3,236.4
24	Maine	2,733.5		19	New Hampshire	3,071.4
10	Maryland	3,715.7		20	Florida	3,057.1
48	Massachusetts	1,123.0		21	Oregon	2,924.3
43	Michigan	1,765.1		22	Nevada	2,760.6
12	Minnesota	3,642.0		23	Hawaii	2,736.9
29	Mississippi	2,482.2		24	Maine	2,733.5
18	Missouri	3,236.4		25	Arkansas	2,724.0
8	Montana	4,113.2		26	South Carolina	2,681.6
5	Nebraska	4,710.0		27	Indiana	2,670.8
22	Nevada	2,760.6		28	New Mexico	2,604.4
19	New Hampshire	3,071.4		29	Mississippi	2,482.2
41	New Jersey	1,993.1		30	Georgia	2,480.8
28	New Mexico	2,604.4		31	North Carolina	2,457.6
40	New York***	2,014.1		32	Rhode Island	2,428.9
31	North Carolina	2,457.6		33	Ohio	2,421.6
4	North Dakota	5,467.0		34	Alaska	2,351.4
33	Ohio	2,421.6		35	Connecticut	2,297.3
36	Oklahoma	2,263.1		36	Oklahoma	2,263.1
21	Oregon	2,924.3		37	Kansas	2,181.4
14	Pennsylvania	3,560.1		38	Texas	2,067.9
32	Rhode Island	2,428.9		39	Virginia	2,036.9
26	South Carolina	2,681.6		40	New York***	2,014.1
2	South Dakota	6,049.7		41	New Jersey	1,993.1
17	Tennessee	3,325.9		42	Washington	1,917.6
38	Texas	2,067.9		43	Michigan	1,765.1
13	Utah	3,593.6		44	California	1,448.2
45	Vermont	1,386.5		45	Vermont	1,386.5
39	Virginia	2,036.9		46	Alabama	1,226.2
42	Washington	1,917.6		47	Kentucky	1,225.5
49	West Virginia	892.7		48	Massachusetts	1,123.0
1	Wisconsin	7,263.6		49	West Virginia	892.7
3	Wyoming	6,000.7		NA	Illinois**	NA
					District of Columbia**	NA

Source: CQ Press using reported data from the Federal Bureau of Investigation
"Crime in the United States 2016" (Uniform Crime Reports, September 25, 2017, https://ucr.fbi.gov/)
*By law enforcement agencies submitting complete reports to the F.B.I. for 12 months in 2016. Arrests of youths 17 years and younger divided into population of 10 to 17 year olds.
**Not available.
***New York's figure does not include New York City.

Prisoners in State Correctional Institutions: Year End 2016

National Total = 1,316,205 State Prisoners*

ALPHA ORDER

RANK	STATE	PRISONERS	% of USA
15	Alabama	28,883	2.2%
42	Alaska	4,434	0.3%
9	Arizona	42,320	3.2%
27	Arkansas	17,537	1.3%
2	California	130,390	9.9%
23	Colorado	19,981	1.5%
29	Connecticut	14,957	1.1%
38	Delaware	6,585	0.5%
3	Florida	99,974	7.6%
4	Georgia	53,627	4.1%
40	Hawaii	5,602	0.4%
35	Idaho	8,252	0.6%
8	Illinois	43,657	3.3%
18	Indiana	25,546	1.9%
34	Iowa	9,031	0.7%
32	Kansas	9,920	0.8%
20	Kentucky	23,022	1.7%
13	Louisiana	35,682	2.7%
47	Maine	2,404	0.2%
22	Maryland	19,994	1.5%
33	Massachusetts	9,403	0.7%
10	Michigan	41,122	3.1%
31	Minnesota	10,592	0.8%
25	Mississippi	19,192	1.5%
14	Missouri	32,461	2.5%
44	Montana	3,814	0.3%
41	Nebraska	5,302	0.4%
30	Nevada	13,757	1.0%
46	New Hampshire	2,818	0.2%
24	New Jersey	19,786	1.5%
37	New Mexico	7,055	0.5%
6	New York	50,716	3.9%
12	North Carolina	35,697	2.7%
49	North Dakota	1,791	0.1%
5	Ohio	52,175	4.0%
17	Oklahoma	26,871	2.0%
28	Oregon	15,166	1.2%
7	Pennsylvania	49,244	3.7%
45	Rhode Island	3,103	0.2%
21	South Carolina	20,858	1.6%
43	South Dakota	3,831	0.3%
16	Tennessee	28,203	2.1%
1	Texas	163,703	12.4%
39	Utah	6,182	0.5%
50	Vermont	1,735	0.1%
11	Virginia	37,813	2.9%
26	Washington	19,104	1.5%
36	West Virginia	7,162	0.5%
19	Wisconsin	23,377	1.8%
48	Wyoming	2,374	0.2%

RANK ORDER

RANK	STATE	PRISONERS	% of USA
1	Texas	163,703	12.4%
2	California	130,390	9.9%
3	Florida	99,974	7.6%
4	Georgia	53,627	4.1%
5	Ohio	52,175	4.0%
6	New York	50,716	3.9%
7	Pennsylvania	49,244	3.7%
8	Illinois	43,657	3.3%
9	Arizona	42,320	3.2%
10	Michigan	41,122	3.1%
11	Virginia	37,813	2.9%
12	North Carolina	35,697	2.7%
13	Louisiana	35,682	2.7%
14	Missouri	32,461	2.5%
15	Alabama	28,883	2.2%
16	Tennessee	28,203	2.1%
17	Oklahoma	26,871	2.0%
18	Indiana	25,546	1.9%
19	Wisconsin	23,377	1.8%
20	Kentucky	23,022	1.7%
21	South Carolina	20,858	1.6%
22	Maryland	19,994	1.5%
23	Colorado	19,981	1.5%
24	New Jersey	19,786	1.5%
25	Mississippi	19,192	1.5%
26	Washington	19,104	1.5%
27	Arkansas	17,537	1.3%
28	Oregon	15,166	1.2%
29	Connecticut	14,957	1.1%
30	Nevada	13,757	1.0%
31	Minnesota	10,592	0.8%
32	Kansas	9,920	0.8%
33	Massachusetts	9,403	0.7%
34	Iowa	9,031	0.7%
35	Idaho	8,252	0.6%
36	West Virginia	7,162	0.5%
37	New Mexico	7,055	0.5%
38	Delaware	6,585	0.5%
39	Utah	6,182	0.5%
40	Hawaii	5,602	0.4%
41	Nebraska	5,302	0.4%
42	Alaska	4,434	0.3%
43	South Dakota	3,831	0.3%
44	Montana	3,814	0.3%
45	Rhode Island	3,103	0.2%
46	New Hampshire	2,818	0.2%
47	Maine	2,404	0.2%
48	Wyoming	2,374	0.2%
49	North Dakota	1,791	0.1%
50	Vermont	1,735	0.1%
	District of Columbia**	NA	NA

Source: U.S. Department of Justice, Bureau of Justice Statistics
"Prisoners in 2016" (January 2018, NCJ 251149, http://bjs.ojp.usdoj.gov/)
*As of December 31, 2016. Totals reflect all prisoners, including those sentenced to a year or less and those unsentenced.
National total does not include 189,192 prisoners under federal jurisdiction. State and federal prisoners combined total 1,505,397.
**Responsibility for sentenced felons in D.C. was transferred to the Federal Bureau of Prisons in 2001.

State Prisoner Imprisonment Rate in 2016

National Rate = 397 State Prisoners per 100,000 Population*

ALPHA ORDER

RANK	STATE	RATE
6	Alabama	571
37	Alaska	281
4	Arizona	585
5	Arkansas	583
32	California	331
28	Colorado	356
35	Connecticut	290
17	Delaware	428
11	Florida	481
10	Georgia	512
41	Hawaii	254
16	Idaho	435
29	Illinois	341
23	Indiana	384
36	Iowa	286
32	Kansas	331
9	Kentucky	518
1	Louisiana	760
50	Maine	137
34	Maryland	329
49	Massachusetts	156
19	Michigan	414
48	Minnesota	191
3	Mississippi	624
8	Missouri	532
27	Montana	364
38	Nebraska	274
12	Nevada	460
44	New Hampshire	211
43	New Jersey	221
31	New Mexico	335
40	New York	256
30	North Carolina	339
42	North Dakota	234
13	Ohio	449
2	Oklahoma	673
26	Oregon	367
24	Pennsylvania	383
47	Rhode Island	192
20	South Carolina	408
15	South Dakota	440
18	Tennessee	422
7	Texas	563
45	Utah	201
46	Vermont	197
14	Virginia	448
39	Washington	259
22	West Virginia	392
24	Wisconsin	383
21	Wyoming	406

RANK ORDER

RANK	STATE	RATE
1	Louisiana	760
2	Oklahoma	673
3	Mississippi	624
4	Arizona	585
5	Arkansas	583
6	Alabama	571
7	Texas	563
8	Missouri	532
9	Kentucky	518
10	Georgia	512
11	Florida	481
12	Nevada	460
13	Ohio	449
14	Virginia	448
15	South Dakota	440
16	Idaho	435
17	Delaware	428
18	Tennessee	422
19	Michigan	414
20	South Carolina	408
21	Wyoming	406
22	West Virginia	392
23	Indiana	384
24	Pennsylvania	383
24	Wisconsin	383
26	Oregon	367
27	Montana	364
28	Colorado	356
29	Illinois	341
30	North Carolina	339
31	New Mexico	335
32	California	331
32	Kansas	331
34	Maryland	329
35	Connecticut	290
36	Iowa	286
37	Alaska	281
38	Nebraska	274
39	Washington	259
40	New York	256
41	Hawaii	254
42	North Dakota	234
43	New Jersey	221
44	New Hampshire	211
45	Utah	201
46	Vermont	197
47	Rhode Island	192
48	Minnesota	191
49	Massachusetts	156
50	Maine	137
	District of Columbia**	NA

Source: U.S. Department of Justice, Bureau of Justice Statistics
"Prisoners in 2016" (January 2018, NCJ 251149, http://bjs.ojp.usdoj.gov/)
*Figures as of December 31, 2016. Includes only inmates sentenced to more than one year. Does not include federal imprisonment rate of 53 prisoners per 100,000 population. State and federal combined imprisonment rate is 450 prisoners per 100,000 population.
**Responsibility for sentenced felons in D.C. was transferred to the Federal Bureau of Prisons in 2001.

Percent Change in Number of State Prisoners: 2015 to 2016

National Percent Change = 1.0% Decrease*

ALPHA ORDER

RANK	STATE	PERCENT CHANGE
45	Alabama	(6.3)
47	Alaska	(16.9)
22	Arizona	(0.9)
24	Arkansas	(1.0)
11	California	0.6
19	Colorado	(0.3)
43	Connecticut	(5.4)
24	Delaware	(1.0)
28	Florida	(1.4)
6	Georgia	2.7
40	Hawaii	(4.7)
7	Idaho	2.5
NA	Illinois**	NA
46	Indiana	(6.6)
8	Iowa	2.1
11	Kansas	0.6
2	Kentucky	6.1
30	Louisiana	(1.9)
3	Maine	5.5
38	Maryland	(3.7)
42	Massachusetts	(5.2)
37	Michigan	(3.5)
30	Minnesota	(1.9)
10	Mississippi	1.5
14	Missouri	0.4
5	Montana	3.5
27	Nebraska	(1.3)
NA	Nevada**	NA
35	New Hampshire	(2.7)
36	New Jersey	(3.4)
21	New Mexico	(0.7)
32	New York	(2.0)
34	North Carolina	(2.5)
18	North Dakota	(0.2)
16	Ohio	(0.1)
44	Oklahoma	(5.9)
NA	Oregon**	NA
26	Pennsylvania	(1.2)
39	Rhode Island	(4.5)
19	South Carolina	(0.3)
1	South Dakota	7.5
15	Tennessee	0.1
16	Texas	(0.1)
41	Utah	(4.8)
22	Vermont	(0.9)
29	Virginia	(1.5)
4	Washington	4.5
11	West Virginia	0.6
9	Wisconsin	1.7
33	Wyoming	(2.1)

RANK ORDER

RANK	STATE	PERCENT CHANGE
1	South Dakota	7.5
2	Kentucky	6.1
3	Maine	5.5
4	Washington	4.5
5	Montana	3.5
6	Georgia	2.7
7	Idaho	2.5
8	Iowa	2.1
9	Wisconsin	1.7
10	Mississippi	1.5
11	California	0.6
11	Kansas	0.6
11	West Virginia	0.6
14	Missouri	0.4
15	Tennessee	0.1
16	Ohio	(0.1)
16	Texas	(0.1)
18	North Dakota	(0.2)
19	Colorado	(0.3)
19	South Carolina	(0.3)
21	New Mexico	(0.7)
22	Arizona	(0.9)
22	Vermont	(0.9)
24	Arkansas	(1.0)
24	Delaware	(1.0)
26	Pennsylvania	(1.2)
27	Nebraska	(1.3)
28	Florida	(1.4)
29	Virginia	(1.5)
30	Louisiana	(1.9)
30	Minnesota	(1.9)
32	New York	(2.0)
33	Wyoming	(2.1)
34	North Carolina	(2.5)
35	New Hampshire	(2.7)
36	New Jersey	(3.4)
37	Michigan	(3.5)
38	Maryland	(3.7)
39	Rhode Island	(4.5)
40	Hawaii	(4.7)
41	Utah	(4.8)
42	Massachusetts	(5.2)
43	Connecticut	(5.4)
44	Oklahoma	(5.9)
45	Alabama	(6.3)
46	Indiana	(6.6)
47	Alaska	(16.9)
NA	Illinois**	NA
NA	Nevada**	NA
NA	Oregon**	NA
	District of Columbia***	NA

Source: U.S. Department of Justice, Bureau of Justice Statistics
"Prisoners in 2016" (January 2018, NCJ 251149, http://bjs.ojp.usdoj.gov/)
*From December 31, 2015 to December 31, 2016. Includes inmates sentenced to more than one year and those sentenced to a year or less or with no sentence. The percent change in number of prisoners under federal jurisdiction during the same period was an 3.7% decrease. The combined state and federal decrease was 1.4%. **Not available.
***Responsibility for sentenced felons in D.C. was transferred to the Federal Bureau of Prisons in 2001.

Prisoners under Sentence of Death as of July 1, 2017 (NAACP)

National Total = 2,755 State Prisoners*

ALPHA ORDER					RANK ORDER			
RANK	STATE	PRISONERS	% of USA		RANK	STATE	PRISONERS	% of USA
4	Alabama	191	6.9%		1	California	746	27.1%
NA	Alaska**	NA	NA		2	Florida	374	13.6%
8	Arizona	125	4.5%		3	Texas	243	8.8%
18	Arkansas	32	1.2%		4	Alabama	191	6.9%
1	California	746	27.1%		5	Pennsylvania	169	6.1%
27	Colorado	3	0.1%		6	North Carolina	152	5.5%
NA	Connecticut**	NA	NA		7	Ohio	144	5.2%
NA	Delaware**	NA	NA		8	Arizona	125	4.5%
2	Florida	374	13.6%		9	Nevada	82	3.0%
12	Georgia	61	2.2%		10	Louisiana	73	2.6%
NA	Hawaii**	NA	NA		11	Tennessee	62	2.3%
24	Idaho	8	0.3%		12	Georgia	61	2.2%
NA	Illinois**	NA	NA		13	Mississippi	48	1.7%
20	Indiana	12	0.4%		14	Oklahoma	47	1.7%
NA	Iowa**	NA	NA		15	South Carolina	41	1.5%
22	Kansas	10	0.4%		16	Kentucky	33	1.2%
16	Kentucky	33	1.2%		16	Oregon	33	1.2%
10	Louisiana	73	2.6%		18	Arkansas	32	1.2%
NA	Maine**	NA	NA		19	Missouri	24	0.9%
NA	Maryland**	NA	NA		20	Indiana	12	0.4%
NA	Massachusetts**	NA	NA		21	Nebraska	11	0.4%
NA	Michigan**	NA	NA		22	Kansas	10	0.4%
NA	Minnesota**	NA	NA		23	Utah	9	0.3%
13	Mississippi	48	1.7%		24	Idaho	8	0.3%
19	Missouri	24	0.9%		24	Washington	8	0.3%
29	Montana	2	0.1%		26	Virginia	5	0.2%
21	Nebraska	11	0.4%		27	Colorado	3	0.1%
9	Nevada	82	3.0%		27	South Dakota	3	0.1%
31	New Hampshire	1	0.0%		29	Montana	2	0.1%
NA	New Jersey**	NA	NA		29	New Mexico	2	0.1%
29	New Mexico	2	0.1%		31	New Hampshire	1	0.0%
NA	New York**	NA	NA		31	Wyoming	1	0.0%
6	North Carolina	152	5.5%		NA	Alaska**	NA	NA
NA	North Dakota**	NA	NA		NA	Connecticut**	NA	NA
7	Ohio	144	5.2%		NA	Delaware**	NA	NA
14	Oklahoma	47	1.7%		NA	Hawaii**	NA	NA
16	Oregon	33	1.2%		NA	Illinois**	NA	NA
5	Pennsylvania	169	6.1%		NA	Iowa**	NA	NA
NA	Rhode Island**	NA	NA		NA	Maine**	NA	NA
15	South Carolina	41	1.5%		NA	Maryland**	NA	NA
27	South Dakota	3	0.1%		NA	Massachusetts**	NA	NA
11	Tennessee	62	2.3%		NA	Michigan**	NA	NA
3	Texas	243	8.8%		NA	Minnesota**	NA	NA
23	Utah	9	0.3%		NA	New Jersey**	NA	NA
NA	Vermont**	NA	NA		NA	New York**	NA	NA
26	Virginia	5	0.2%		NA	North Dakota**	NA	NA
24	Washington	8	0.3%		NA	Rhode Island**	NA	NA
NA	West Virginia**	NA	NA		NA	Vermont**	NA	NA
NA	Wisconsin**	NA	NA		NA	West Virginia**	NA	NA
31	Wyoming	1	0.0%		NA	Wisconsin**	NA	NA
						District of Columbia**	NA	NA

Source: NAACP Legal Defense and Educational Fund, Inc., Criminal Justice Project
"Death Row USA, Summer 2017" (http://naacpldf.org/death-row-usa)
*Total does not include 61 federal prisoners or five military prisoners under sentence of death. Four prisoners are sentenced to death in more than one state and are counted twice.
**No death penalty as of November 9, 2016.

Rate of State and Local Police Officers in 2016

National Rate = 22 Officers per 10,000 Population*

ALPHA ORDER

RANK	STATE	RATE
9	Alabama	23
46	Alaska	16
21	Arizona	21
15	Arkansas	22
35	California	18
29	Colorado	20
15	Connecticut	22
21	Delaware	21
29	Florida	20
21	Georgia	21
15	Hawaii	22
38	Idaho	17
4	Illinois	25
35	Indiana	18
38	Iowa	17
15	Kansas	22
38	Kentucky	17
3	Louisiana	29
38	Maine	17
9	Maryland	23
7	Massachusetts	24
38	Michigan	17
38	Minnesota	17
7	Mississippi	24
9	Missouri	23
38	Montana	17
33	Nebraska	19
38	Nevada	17
15	New Hampshire	22
2	New Jersey	30
9	New Mexico	23
1	New York	38
15	North Carolina	22
21	North Dakota	21
29	Ohio	20
21	Oklahoma	21
48	Oregon	15
21	Pennsylvania	21
9	Rhode Island	23
9	South Carolina	23
33	South Dakota	19
4	Tennessee	25
29	Texas	20
49	Utah	14
46	Vermont	16
21	Virginia	21
49	Washington	14
35	West Virginia	18
21	Wisconsin	21
4	Wyoming	25

RANK ORDER

RANK	STATE	RATE
1	New York	38
2	New Jersey	30
3	Louisiana	29
4	Illinois	25
4	Tennessee	25
4	Wyoming	25
7	Massachusetts	24
7	Mississippi	24
9	Alabama	23
9	Maryland	23
9	Missouri	23
9	New Mexico	23
9	Rhode Island	23
9	South Carolina	23
15	Arkansas	22
15	Connecticut	22
15	Hawaii	22
15	Kansas	22
15	New Hampshire	22
15	North Carolina	22
21	Arizona	21
21	Delaware	21
21	Georgia	21
21	North Dakota	21
21	Oklahoma	21
21	Pennsylvania	21
21	Virginia	21
21	Wisconsin	21
29	Colorado	20
29	Florida	20
29	Ohio	20
29	Texas	20
33	Nebraska	19
33	South Dakota	19
35	California	18
35	Indiana	18
35	West Virginia	18
38	Idaho	17
38	Iowa	17
38	Kentucky	17
38	Maine	17
38	Michigan	17
38	Minnesota	17
38	Montana	17
38	Nevada	17
46	Alaska	16
46	Vermont	16
48	Oregon	15
49	Utah	14
49	Washington	14
	District of Columbia	55

Source: CQ Press using data from U.S. Bureau of the Census, Governments Division
"Annual Survey of Public Employment and Payroll" (https://www.census.gov/data/datasets.html)
*Full-time equivalent as of March 2016. Does not include employees of police departments who are not officers.

Per Capita State and Local Government Expenditures for Police Protection in 2015
National Per Capita = $328*

ALPHA ORDER

RANK	STATE	PER CAPITA
35	Alabama	$261
1	Alaska	492
22	Arizona	312
43	Arkansas	234
3	California	426
14	Colorado	337
16	Connecticut	331
9	Delaware	375
10	Florida	373
38	Georgia	251
19	Hawaii	321
36	Idaho	259
8	Illinois	389
49	Indiana	183
41	Iowa	241
32	Kansas	273
50	Kentucky	151
13	Louisiana	340
48	Maine	194
4	Maryland	412
12	Massachusetts	356
39	Michigan	247
14	Minnesota	337
40	Mississippi	245
28	Missouri	284
25	Montana	296
45	Nebraska	228
5	Nevada	396
24	New Hampshire	303
11	New Jersey	371
16	New Mexico	331
2	New York	484
21	North Carolina	317
30	North Dakota	280
26	Ohio	294
33	Oklahoma	270
23	Oregon	305
27	Pennsylvania	291
6	Rhode Island	391
42	South Carolina	236
44	South Dakota	229
29	Tennessee	281
34	Texas	269
46	Utah	227
16	Vermont	331
31	Virginia	275
36	Washington	259
47	West Virginia	204
20	Wisconsin	318
7	Wyoming	390

RANK ORDER

RANK	STATE	PER CAPITA
1	Alaska	$492
2	New York	484
3	California	426
4	Maryland	412
5	Nevada	396
6	Rhode Island	391
7	Wyoming	390
8	Illinois	389
9	Delaware	375
10	Florida	373
11	New Jersey	371
12	Massachusetts	356
13	Louisiana	340
14	Colorado	337
14	Minnesota	337
16	Connecticut	331
16	New Mexico	331
16	Vermont	331
19	Hawaii	321
20	Wisconsin	318
21	North Carolina	317
22	Arizona	312
23	Oregon	305
24	New Hampshire	303
25	Montana	296
26	Ohio	294
27	Pennsylvania	291
28	Missouri	284
29	Tennessee	281
30	North Dakota	280
31	Virginia	275
32	Kansas	273
33	Oklahoma	270
34	Texas	269
35	Alabama	261
36	Idaho	259
36	Washington	259
38	Georgia	251
39	Michigan	247
40	Mississippi	245
41	Iowa	241
42	South Carolina	236
43	Arkansas	234
44	South Dakota	229
45	Nebraska	228
46	Utah	227
47	West Virginia	204
48	Maine	194
49	Indiana	183
50	Kentucky	151

| | District of Columbia | 869 |

Source: CQ Press using data from U.S. Bureau of the Census, Governments Division
"2015 State and Local Government Finances" (http://www.census.gov/govs/local/)
*Direct general expenditures.

Per Capita State and Local Government Expenditures for Corrections in 2015

National Per Capita = $239*

ALPHA ORDER

RANK	STATE	PER CAPITA
46	Alabama	$153
1	Alaska	470
14	Arizona	251
28	Arkansas	197
2	California	392
17	Colorado	235
29	Connecticut	195
4	Delaware	320
26	Florida	201
22	Georgia	224
48	Hawaii	152
25	Idaho	206
38	Illinois	175
46	Indiana	153
49	Iowa	141
34	Kansas	177
33	Kentucky	178
16	Louisiana	242
43	Maine	159
7	Maryland	308
42	Massachusetts	162
13	Michigan	252
39	Minnesota	172
41	Mississippi	167
44	Missouri	157
12	Montana	261
15	Nebraska	249
18	Nevada	234
50	New Hampshire	138
21	New Jersey	230
5	New Mexico	319
6	New York	313
34	North Carolina	177
32	North Dakota	179
40	Ohio	170
30	Oklahoma	191
8	Oregon	281
11	Pennsylvania	265
27	Rhode Island	200
44	South Carolina	157
24	South Dakota	207
37	Tennessee	176
23	Texas	210
34	Utah	177
18	Vermont	234
9	Virginia	280
18	Washington	234
31	West Virginia	185
10	Wisconsin	267
3	Wyoming	365

RANK ORDER

RANK	STATE	PER CAPITA
1	Alaska	$470
2	California	392
3	Wyoming	365
4	Delaware	320
5	New Mexico	319
6	New York	313
7	Maryland	308
8	Oregon	281
9	Virginia	280
10	Wisconsin	267
11	Pennsylvania	265
12	Montana	261
13	Michigan	252
14	Arizona	251
15	Nebraska	249
16	Louisiana	242
17	Colorado	235
18	Nevada	234
18	Vermont	234
18	Washington	234
21	New Jersey	230
22	Georgia	224
23	Texas	210
24	South Dakota	207
25	Idaho	206
26	Florida	201
27	Rhode Island	200
28	Arkansas	197
29	Connecticut	195
30	Oklahoma	191
31	West Virginia	185
32	North Dakota	179
33	Kentucky	178
34	Kansas	177
34	North Carolina	177
34	Utah	177
37	Tennessee	176
38	Illinois	175
39	Minnesota	172
40	Ohio	170
41	Mississippi	167
42	Massachusetts	162
43	Maine	159
44	Missouri	157
44	South Carolina	157
46	Alabama	153
46	Indiana	153
48	Hawaii	152
49	Iowa	141
50	New Hampshire	138

District of Columbia		212

Source: CQ Press using data from U.S. Bureau of the Census, Governments Division
"2015 State and Local Government Finances" (http://www.census.gov/govs/local/)
*Direct general expenditures.

Per Capita State and Local Government Expenditures for Judicial and Legal Services in 2015
National Per Capita = $137*

ALPHA ORDER

RANK	STATE	PER CAPITA
44	Alabama	$86
1	Alaska	354
17	Arizona	149
49	Arkansas	71
5	California	206
19	Colorado	136
2	Connecticut	220
3	Delaware	210
31	Florida	112
31	Georgia	112
5	Hawaii	206
23	Idaho	128
26	Illinois	124
46	Indiana	81
34	Iowa	111
35	Kansas	110
28	Kentucky	116
14	Louisiana	151
47	Maine	76
13	Maryland	152
15	Massachusetts	150
30	Michigan	115
25	Minnesota	126
45	Mississippi	82
43	Missouri	88
9	Montana	163
42	Nebraska	91
12	Nevada	158
39	New Hampshire	101
8	New Jersey	171
11	New Mexico	160
4	New York	207
48	North Carolina	72
21	North Dakota	133
15	Ohio	150
41	Oklahoma	96
9	Oregon	163
18	Pennsylvania	143
22	Rhode Island	132
49	South Carolina	71
40	South Dakota	99
36	Tennessee	109
38	Texas	104
28	Utah	116
26	Vermont	124
37	Virginia	108
20	Washington	134
23	West Virginia	128
31	Wisconsin	112
7	Wyoming	200

RANK ORDER

RANK	STATE	PER CAPITA
1	Alaska	$354
2	Connecticut	220
3	Delaware	210
4	New York	207
5	California	206
5	Hawaii	206
7	Wyoming	200
8	New Jersey	171
9	Montana	163
9	Oregon	163
11	New Mexico	160
12	Nevada	158
13	Maryland	152
14	Louisiana	151
15	Massachusetts	150
15	Ohio	150
17	Arizona	149
18	Pennsylvania	143
19	Colorado	136
20	Washington	134
21	North Dakota	133
22	Rhode Island	132
23	Idaho	128
23	West Virginia	128
25	Minnesota	126
26	Illinois	124
26	Vermont	124
28	Kentucky	116
28	Utah	116
30	Michigan	115
31	Florida	112
31	Georgia	112
31	Wisconsin	112
34	Iowa	111
35	Kansas	110
36	Tennessee	109
37	Virginia	108
38	Texas	104
39	New Hampshire	101
40	South Dakota	99
41	Oklahoma	96
42	Nebraska	91
43	Missouri	88
44	Alabama	86
45	Mississippi	82
46	Indiana	81
47	Maine	76
48	North Carolina	72
49	Arkansas	71
49	South Carolina	71
	District of Columbia	159

Source: CQ Press using data from U.S. Bureau of the Census, Governments Division
"2015 State and Local Government Finances" (http://www.census.gov/govs/local/)
*Direct general expenditures. Includes courts, prosecution and legal services, and public defense.

III. Defense

Homeland Security Grants in 2017

National Total = $982,000,000*

ALPHA ORDER

RANK	STATE	GRANTS	% of USA
29	Alabama	$3,752,000	0.4%
29	Alaska	3,752,000	0.4%
14	Arizona	9,731,000	1.0%
29	Arkansas	3,752,000	0.4%
2	California	182,817,500	18.6%
18	Colorado	6,800,000	0.7%
24	Connecticut	3,962,000	0.4%
29	Delaware	3,752,000	0.4%
8	Florida	19,040,500	1.9%
9	Georgia	15,220,000	1.5%
29	Hawaii	3,752,000	0.4%
29	Idaho	3,752,000	0.4%
3	Illinois	84,501,500	8.6%
22	Indiana	4,962,000	0.5%
29	Iowa	3,752,000	0.4%
29	Kansas	3,752,000	0.4%
24	Kentucky	3,962,000	0.4%
24	Louisiana	3,962,000	0.4%
29	Maine	3,752,000	0.4%
13	Maryland	10,348,500	1.1%
7	Massachusetts	22,898,000	2.3%
10	Michigan	11,821,000	1.2%
15	Minnesota	9,142,000	0.9%
29	Mississippi	3,752,000	0.4%
19	Missouri	6,799,000	0.7%
29	Montana	3,752,000	0.4%
29	Nebraska	3,752,000	0.4%
21	Nevada	6,589,000	0.7%
29	New Hampshire	3,752,000	0.4%
6	New Jersey	28,371,000	2.9%
29	New Mexico	3,752,000	0.4%
1	New York	255,053,000	26.0%
17	North Carolina	8,309,000	0.8%
29	North Dakota	3,752,000	0.4%
12	Ohio	10,518,000	1.1%
29	Oklahoma	3,752,000	0.4%
20	Oregon	6,659,100	0.7%
5	Pennsylvania	30,637,500	3.1%
29	Rhode Island	3,752,000	0.4%
29	South Carolina	3,752,000	0.4%
29	South Dakota	3,752,000	0.4%
24	Tennessee	3,962,000	0.4%
4	Texas	60,476,000	6.2%
23	Utah	4,752,000	0.5%
29	Vermont	3,752,000	0.4%
16	Virginia	8,428,500	0.9%
11	Washington	11,656,000	1.2%
29	West Virginia	3,752,000	0.4%
24	Wisconsin	3,962,000	0.4%
29	Wyoming	3,752,000	0.4%

RANK ORDER

RANK	STATE	GRANTS	% of USA
1	New York	$255,053,000	26.0%
2	California	182,817,500	18.6%
3	Illinois	84,501,500	8.6%
4	Texas	60,476,000	6.2%
5	Pennsylvania	30,637,500	3.1%
6	New Jersey	28,371,000	2.9%
7	Massachusetts	22,898,000	2.3%
8	Florida	19,040,500	1.9%
9	Georgia	15,220,000	1.5%
10	Michigan	11,821,000	1.2%
11	Washington	11,656,000	1.2%
12	Ohio	10,518,000	1.1%
13	Maryland	10,348,500	1.1%
14	Arizona	9,731,000	1.0%
15	Minnesota	9,142,000	0.9%
16	Virginia	8,428,500	0.9%
17	North Carolina	8,309,000	0.8%
18	Colorado	6,800,000	0.7%
19	Missouri	6,799,000	0.7%
20	Oregon	6,659,100	0.7%
21	Nevada	6,589,000	0.7%
22	Indiana	4,962,000	0.5%
23	Utah	4,752,000	0.5%
24	Connecticut	3,962,000	0.4%
24	Kentucky	3,962,000	0.4%
24	Louisiana	3,962,000	0.4%
24	Tennessee	3,962,000	0.4%
24	Wisconsin	3,962,000	0.4%
29	Alabama	3,752,000	0.4%
29	Alaska	3,752,000	0.4%
29	Arkansas	3,752,000	0.4%
29	Delaware	3,752,000	0.4%
29	Hawaii	3,752,000	0.4%
29	Idaho	3,752,000	0.4%
29	Iowa	3,752,000	0.4%
29	Kansas	3,752,000	0.4%
29	Maine	3,752,000	0.4%
29	Mississippi	3,752,000	0.4%
29	Montana	3,752,000	0.4%
29	Nebraska	3,752,000	0.4%
29	New Hampshire	3,752,000	0.4%
29	New Mexico	3,752,000	0.4%
29	North Dakota	3,752,000	0.4%
29	Oklahoma	3,752,000	0.4%
29	Rhode Island	3,752,000	0.4%
29	South Carolina	3,752,000	0.4%
29	South Dakota	3,752,000	0.4%
29	Vermont	3,752,000	0.4%
29	West Virginia	3,752,000	0.4%
29	Wyoming	3,752,000	0.4%
	District of Columbia	56,933,500	5.8%

Source: CQ Press using data from U.S. Department of Homeland Security
"FY 2017 Homeland Security Grant Program (HSGP)" (https://www.fema.gov/media-library/assets/documents/131992)
*For fiscal year 2017. National total includes $7,182,400 in grants to U.S. territories. The Homeland Security Grant Program (HSGP) includes three sub-grant programs: State Homeland Security Program (SHSP), Urban Area Security Initiative (UASI), and Operation Stonegarden (OPSG). Law Enforcement Terrorism Prevention Activities (LETPA) allocations are a 25 percent subset of the SHSP and UASI allocations.

Per Capita Homeland Security Grants in 2017

National Per Capita = $2.99*

ALPHA ORDER				RANK ORDER		
RANK	STATE	PER CAPITA		RANK	STATE	PER CAPITA
46	Alabama	$0.77		1	New York	$12.85
5	Alaska	5.07		2	Illinois	6.60
30	Arizona	1.39		3	Wyoming	6.48
33	Arkansas	1.25		4	Vermont	6.02
7	California	4.62		5	Alaska	5.07
34	Colorado	1.21		6	North Dakota	4.97
38	Connecticut	1.10		7	California	4.62
9	Delaware	3.90		8	South Dakota	4.31
41	Florida	0.91		9	Delaware	3.90
29	Georgia	1.46		10	Montana	3.57
16	Hawaii	2.63		11	Rhode Island	3.54
19	Idaho	2.19		12	Massachusetts	3.34
2	Illinois	6.60		13	New Jersey	3.15
48	Indiana	0.74		14	Maine	2.81
35	Iowa	1.19		15	New Hampshire	2.79
31	Kansas	1.29		16	Hawaii	2.63
43	Kentucky	0.89		17	Pennsylvania	2.39
44	Louisiana	0.85		18	Nevada	2.20
14	Maine	2.81		19	Idaho	2.19
24	Maryland	1.71		20	Texas	2.14
12	Massachusetts	3.34		21	West Virginia	2.07
35	Michigan	1.19		22	Nebraska	1.95
25	Minnesota	1.64		23	New Mexico	1.80
32	Mississippi	1.26		24	Maryland	1.71
37	Missouri	1.11		25	Minnesota	1.64
10	Montana	3.57		26	Oregon	1.61
22	Nebraska	1.95		27	Washington	1.57
18	Nevada	2.20		28	Utah	1.53
15	New Hampshire	2.79		29	Georgia	1.46
13	New Jersey	3.15		30	Arizona	1.39
23	New Mexico	1.80		31	Kansas	1.29
1	New York	12.85		32	Mississippi	1.26
45	North Carolina	0.81		33	Arkansas	1.25
6	North Dakota	4.97		34	Colorado	1.21
42	Ohio	0.90		35	Iowa	1.19
40	Oklahoma	0.95		35	Michigan	1.19
26	Oregon	1.61		37	Missouri	1.11
17	Pennsylvania	2.39		38	Connecticut	1.10
11	Rhode Island	3.54		39	Virginia	1.00
47	South Carolina	0.75		40	Oklahoma	0.95
8	South Dakota	4.31		41	Florida	0.91
50	Tennessee	0.59		42	Ohio	0.90
20	Texas	2.14		43	Kentucky	0.89
28	Utah	1.53		44	Louisiana	0.85
4	Vermont	6.02		45	North Carolina	0.81
39	Virginia	1.00		46	Alabama	0.77
27	Washington	1.57		47	South Carolina	0.75
21	West Virginia	2.07		48	Indiana	0.74
49	Wisconsin	0.68		49	Wisconsin	0.68
3	Wyoming	6.48		50	Tennessee	0.59

District of Columbia   82.04

Source: CQ Press using data from U.S. Department of Homeland Security
"FY 2017 Homeland Security Grant Program (HSGP)" (https://www.fema.gov/media-library/assets/documents/131992)
*For fiscal year 2017. National per capita does not include grants to U.S. territories. The Homeland Security Grant Program (HSGP) includes three sub-grant programs: State Homeland Security Program (SHSP), Urban Area Security Initiative (UASI), and Operation Stonegarden (OPSG). Law Enforcement Terrorism Prevention Activities (LETPA) allocations are a 25 percent subset of the SHSP and UASI allocations.

U.S. Department of Defense Expenditures in 2016

National Total = $304,130,236,000*

ALPHA ORDER

RANK	STATE	EXPENDITURES	% of USA
13	Alabama	$8,803,865,865	2.9%
33	Alaska	1,264,175,606	0.4%
11	Arizona	9,465,055,712	3.1%
43	Arkansas	338,703,740	0.1%
1	California	32,977,026,967	10.8%
17	Colorado	5,674,941,822	1.9%
4	Connecticut	14,222,273,291	4.7%
49	Delaware	167,872,046	0.1%
5	Florida	14,004,642,555	4.6%
12	Georgia	9,288,937,106	3.1%
28	Hawaii	1,938,085,080	0.6%
44	Idaho	242,102,947	0.1%
18	Illinois	5,590,394,480	1.8%
23	Indiana	3,016,864,706	1.0%
36	Iowa	1,163,340,186	0.4%
38	Kansas	807,063,040	0.3%
15	Kentucky	5,794,454,391	1.9%
31	Louisiana	1,593,644,871	0.5%
29	Maine	1,722,848,278	0.6%
6	Maryland	13,423,295,717	4.4%
10	Massachusetts	9,705,444,559	3.2%
24	Michigan	2,910,001,119	1.0%
19	Minnesota	3,799,723,354	1.2%
21	Mississippi	3,686,805,490	1.2%
8	Missouri	10,219,272,694	3.4%
46	Montana	209,379,802	0.1%
41	Nebraska	633,683,163	0.2%
32	Nevada	1,507,974,267	0.5%
37	New Hampshire	1,159,215,300	0.4%
16	New Jersey	5,679,797,165	1.9%
34	New Mexico	1,214,274,173	0.4%
14	New York	5,966,682,617	2.0%
25	North Carolina	2,597,171,717	0.9%
47	North Dakota	203,389,512	0.1%
20	Ohio	3,728,095,837	1.2%
22	Oklahoma	3,116,014,210	1.0%
39	Oregon	676,590,911	0.2%
7	Pennsylvania	11,499,327,993	3.8%
40	Rhode Island	671,310,143	0.2%
26	South Carolina	2,504,786,411	0.8%
48	South Dakota	196,225,175	0.1%
30	Tennessee	1,714,998,616	0.6%
3	Texas	28,533,522,115	9.4%
35	Utah	1,165,742,178	0.4%
42	Vermont	365,412,133	0.1%
2	Virginia	31,857,315,547	10.5%
9	Washington	9,716,487,972	3.2%
45	West Virginia	222,514,242	0.1%
27	Wisconsin	2,474,023,606	0.8%
50	Wyoming	117,900,643	0.0%

RANK ORDER

RANK	STATE	EXPENDITURES	% of USA
1	California	$32,977,026,967	10.8%
2	Virginia	31,857,315,547	10.5%
3	Texas	28,533,522,115	9.4%
4	Connecticut	14,222,273,291	4.7%
5	Florida	14,004,642,555	4.6%
6	Maryland	13,423,295,717	4.4%
7	Pennsylvania	11,499,327,993	3.8%
8	Missouri	10,219,272,694	3.4%
9	Washington	9,716,487,972	3.2%
10	Massachusetts	9,705,444,559	3.2%
11	Arizona	9,465,055,712	3.1%
12	Georgia	9,288,937,106	3.1%
13	Alabama	8,803,865,865	2.9%
14	New York	5,966,682,617	2.0%
15	Kentucky	5,794,454,391	1.9%
16	New Jersey	5,679,797,165	1.9%
17	Colorado	5,674,941,822	1.9%
18	Illinois	5,590,394,480	1.8%
19	Minnesota	3,799,723,354	1.2%
20	Ohio	3,728,095,837	1.2%
21	Mississippi	3,686,805,490	1.2%
22	Oklahoma	3,116,014,210	1.0%
23	Indiana	3,016,864,706	1.0%
24	Michigan	2,910,001,119	1.0%
25	North Carolina	2,597,171,717	0.9%
26	South Carolina	2,504,786,411	0.8%
27	Wisconsin	2,474,023,606	0.8%
28	Hawaii	1,938,085,080	0.6%
29	Maine	1,722,848,278	0.6%
30	Tennessee	1,714,998,616	0.6%
31	Louisiana	1,593,644,871	0.5%
32	Nevada	1,507,974,267	0.5%
33	Alaska	1,264,175,606	0.4%
34	New Mexico	1,214,274,173	0.4%
35	Utah	1,165,742,178	0.4%
36	Iowa	1,163,340,186	0.4%
37	New Hampshire	1,159,215,300	0.4%
38	Kansas	807,063,040	0.3%
39	Oregon	676,590,911	0.2%
40	Rhode Island	671,310,143	0.2%
41	Nebraska	633,683,163	0.2%
42	Vermont	365,412,133	0.1%
43	Arkansas	338,703,740	0.1%
44	Idaho	242,102,947	0.1%
45	West Virginia	222,514,242	0.1%
46	Montana	209,379,802	0.1%
47	North Dakota	203,389,512	0.1%
48	South Dakota	196,225,175	0.1%
49	Delaware	167,872,046	0.1%
50	Wyoming	117,900,643	0.0%
	District of Columbia	3,887,430,578	1.3%

Source: U.S. Office of Management and Budget, USAspending.gov
"Prime Award Spending Data Summary" (https://www.usaspending.gov/, as of January 26, 2018)
*Total includes $20,690,135,000 in U.S. territories and in expenditures not distributed by state. Expenditures allocated based on place of performance of a contract. Includes Contracts, Grants, Direct Payments, Insurance, and "Other." This source replaces a previous data series, "Atlas/Data Abstract for the United States", and definitions may differ.

Per Capita U.S. Department of Defense Expenditures in 2016

National Per Capita = $876*

ALPHA ORDER				RANK ORDER		
RANK	STATE	PER CAPITA		RANK	STATE	PER CAPITA
4	Alabama	$1,811		1	Connecticut	$3,964
5	Alaska	1,705		2	Virginia	3,807
8	Arizona	1,370		3	Maryland	2,228
50	Arkansas	113		4	Alabama	1,811
19	California	839		5	Alaska	1,705
15	Colorado	1,026		6	Missouri	1,678
1	Connecticut	3,964		7	Massachusetts	1,422
46	Delaware	176		8	Arizona	1,370
22	Florida	678		9	Hawaii	1,357
16	Georgia	901		9	Washington	1,357
9	Hawaii	1,357		11	Kentucky	1,306
48	Idaho	144		12	Maine	1,295
30	Illinois	436		13	Mississippi	1,235
29	Indiana	455		14	Texas	1,040
33	Iowa	372		15	Colorado	1,026
39	Kansas	278		16	Georgia	901
11	Kentucky	1,306		17	Pennsylvania	899
34	Louisiana	340		18	New Hampshire	868
12	Maine	1,295		19	California	839
3	Maryland	2,228		20	Oklahoma	795
7	Massachusetts	1,422		21	Minnesota	688
38	Michigan	293		22	Florida	678
21	Minnesota	688		23	Rhode Island	636
13	Mississippi	1,235		24	New Jersey	633
6	Missouri	1,678		25	Vermont	584
44	Montana	202		26	New Mexico	582
35	Nebraska	332		27	Nevada	513
27	Nevada	513		28	South Carolina	512
18	New Hampshire	868		29	Indiana	455
24	New Jersey	633		30	Illinois	436
26	New Mexico	582		31	Wisconsin	429
37	New York	301		32	Utah	390
42	North Carolina	256		33	Iowa	372
40	North Dakota	269		34	Louisiana	340
36	Ohio	321		35	Nebraska	332
20	Oklahoma	795		36	Ohio	321
47	Oregon	168		37	New York	301
17	Pennsylvania	899		38	Michigan	293
23	Rhode Island	636		39	Kansas	278
28	South Carolina	512		40	North Dakota	269
43	South Dakota	229		41	Tennessee	260
41	Tennessee	260		42	North Carolina	256
14	Texas	1,040		43	South Dakota	229
32	Utah	390		44	Montana	202
25	Vermont	584		45	Wyoming	201
2	Virginia	3,807		46	Delaware	176
9	Washington	1,357		47	Oregon	168
49	West Virginia	121		48	Idaho	144
31	Wisconsin	429		49	West Virginia	121
45	Wyoming	201		50	Arkansas	113

District of Columbia 5,681

Source: CQ Press using data from U.S. Office of Management and Budget, USAspending.gov
"Prime Award Spending Data Summary" (https://www.usaspending.gov/, as of January 26, 2018)
*National per capita excludes expenditures and population for territories and undistributed amounts. Expenditures allocated based on place of performance of a contract. Includes Contracts, Grants, Direct Payments, Insurance, and "Other." This source replaces a previous data series, "Atlas/Data Abstract for the United States", and definitions may differ.

U.S. Department of Defense Expenditures as a Percent of Total Federal Government Expenditures in 2016
National Percent = 9.5%*

ALPHA ORDER

RANK	STATE	PERCENT
14	Alabama	13.2
8	Alaska	15.8
14	Arizona	13.2
48	Arkansas	1.5
17	California	11.4
12	Colorado	14.4
4	Connecticut	19.1
42	Delaware	2.5
21	Florida	8.2
13	Georgia	14.3
5	Hawaii	17.4
47	Idaho	2.0
24	Illinois	6.9
44	Indiana	2.3
30	Iowa	5.0
30	Kansas	5.0
26	Kentucky	6.5
34	Louisiana	4.5
11	Maine	14.8
2	Maryland	20.1
9	Massachusetts	15.6
36	Michigan	3.8
33	Minnesota	4.7
10	Mississippi	15.0
3	Missouri	19.3
42	Montana	2.5
29	Nebraska	5.2
20	Nevada	8.5
16	New Hampshire	12.0
19	New Jersey	9.3
28	New Mexico	5.3
36	New York	3.8
35	North Carolina	4.1
50	North Dakota	0.3
32	Ohio	4.9
18	Oklahoma	11.0
46	Oregon	2.1
27	Pennsylvania	5.9
23	Rhode Island	7.5
38	South Carolina	3.2
39	South Dakota	2.9
44	Tennessee	2.3
6	Texas	16.8
22	Utah	8.0
25	Vermont	6.7
1	Virginia	33.6
7	Washington	16.7
48	West Virginia	1.5
39	Wisconsin	2.9
41	Wyoming	2.8

RANK ORDER

RANK	STATE	PERCENT
1	Virginia	33.6
2	Maryland	20.1
3	Missouri	19.3
4	Connecticut	19.1
5	Hawaii	17.4
6	Texas	16.8
7	Washington	16.7
8	Alaska	15.8
9	Massachusetts	15.6
10	Mississippi	15.0
11	Maine	14.8
12	Colorado	14.4
13	Georgia	14.3
14	Alabama	13.2
14	Arizona	13.2
16	New Hampshire	12.0
17	California	11.4
18	Oklahoma	11.0
19	New Jersey	9.3
20	Nevada	8.5
21	Florida	8.2
22	Utah	8.0
23	Rhode Island	7.5
24	Illinois	6.9
25	Vermont	6.7
26	Kentucky	6.5
27	Pennsylvania	5.9
28	New Mexico	5.3
29	Nebraska	5.2
30	Iowa	5.0
30	Kansas	5.0
32	Ohio	4.9
33	Minnesota	4.7
34	Louisiana	4.5
35	North Carolina	4.1
36	Michigan	3.8
36	New York	3.8
38	South Carolina	3.2
39	South Dakota	2.9
39	Wisconsin	2.9
41	Wyoming	2.8
42	Delaware	2.5
42	Montana	2.5
44	Indiana	2.3
44	Tennessee	2.3
46	Oregon	2.1
47	Idaho	2.0
48	Arkansas	1.5
48	West Virginia	1.5
50	North Dakota	0.3

	District of Columbia	12.5

Source: CQ Press using data from U.S. Office of Management and Budget, USAspending.gov
"Prime Award Spending Data Summary" (https://www.usaspending.gov/, as of January 26, 2018)
*National percent excludes expenditures and population for territories and undistributed amounts. Expenditures allocated based on place of performance of a contract. Includes Contracts, Grants, Direct Payments, Insurance, and "Other." This source replaces a previous data series, "Atlas/Data Abstract for the United States", and definitions may differ.

U.S. Active Duty Military Personnel Stationed in the United States in 2016

National Total = 1,021,370 Personnel*

ALPHA ORDER

RANK	STATE	PERSONNEL	% of USA
24	Alabama	7,904	0.8%
17	Alaska	17,243	1.7%
16	Arizona	18,598	1.8%
31	Arkansas	3,953	0.4%
1	California	123,603	12.1%
10	Colorado	34,930	3.4%
30	Connecticut	4,050	0.4%
32	Delaware	3,355	0.3%
6	Florida	52,023	5.1%
5	Georgia	62,501	6.1%
8	Hawaii	37,374	3.7%
33	Idaho	3,338	0.3%
18	Illinois	15,882	1.6%
42	Indiana	922	0.1%
48	Iowa	219	0.0%
13	Kansas	22,270	2.2%
11	Kentucky	32,563	3.2%
20	Louisiana	14,623	1.4%
47	Maine	333	0.0%
12	Maryland	28,392	2.8%
40	Massachusetts	1,980	0.2%
41	Michigan	1,053	0.1%
46	Minnesota	498	0.0%
23	Mississippi	9,758	1.0%
19	Missouri	15,512	1.5%
34	Montana	3,289	0.3%
27	Nebraska	6,228	0.6%
22	Nevada	10,397	1.0%
45	New Hampshire	518	0.1%
28	New Jersey	5,911	0.6%
21	New Mexico	12,123	1.2%
14	New York	20,313	2.0%
3	North Carolina	96,170	9.4%
25	North Dakota	7,157	0.7%
26	Ohio	6,440	0.6%
15	Oklahoma	20,252	2.0%
44	Oregon	532	0.1%
38	Pennsylvania	2,358	0.2%
37	Rhode Island	3,021	0.3%
9	South Carolina	36,613	3.6%
35	South Dakota	3,246	0.3%
39	Tennessee	2,014	0.2%
2	Texas	117,553	11.5%
29	Utah	4,104	0.4%
50	Vermont	115	0.0%
4	Virginia	87,984	8.6%
7	Washington	44,148	4.3%
49	West Virginia	142	0.0%
43	Wisconsin	643	0.1%
36	Wyoming	3,030	0.3%

RANK ORDER

RANK	STATE	PERSONNEL	% of USA
1	California	123,603	12.1%
2	Texas	117,553	11.5%
3	North Carolina	96,170	9.4%
4	Virginia	87,984	8.6%
5	Georgia	62,501	6.1%
6	Florida	52,023	5.1%
7	Washington	44,148	4.3%
8	Hawaii	37,374	3.7%
9	South Carolina	36,613	3.6%
10	Colorado	34,930	3.4%
11	Kentucky	32,563	3.2%
12	Maryland	28,392	2.8%
13	Kansas	22,270	2.2%
14	New York	20,313	2.0%
15	Oklahoma	20,252	2.0%
16	Arizona	18,598	1.8%
17	Alaska	17,243	1.7%
18	Illinois	15,882	1.6%
19	Missouri	15,512	1.5%
20	Louisiana	14,623	1.4%
21	New Mexico	12,123	1.2%
22	Nevada	10,397	1.0%
23	Mississippi	9,758	1.0%
24	Alabama	7,904	0.8%
25	North Dakota	7,157	0.7%
26	Ohio	6,440	0.6%
27	Nebraska	6,228	0.6%
28	New Jersey	5,911	0.6%
29	Utah	4,104	0.4%
30	Connecticut	4,050	0.4%
31	Arkansas	3,953	0.4%
32	Delaware	3,355	0.3%
33	Idaho	3,338	0.3%
34	Montana	3,289	0.3%
35	South Dakota	3,246	0.3%
36	Wyoming	3,030	0.3%
37	Rhode Island	3,021	0.3%
38	Pennsylvania	2,358	0.2%
39	Tennessee	2,014	0.2%
40	Massachusetts	1,980	0.2%
41	Michigan	1,053	0.1%
42	Indiana	922	0.1%
43	Wisconsin	643	0.1%
44	Oregon	532	0.1%
45	New Hampshire	518	0.1%
46	Minnesota	498	0.0%
47	Maine	333	0.0%
48	Iowa	219	0.0%
49	West Virginia	142	0.0%
50	Vermont	115	0.0%
	District of Columbia	8,173	0.8%

Source: U.S. Department of Defense
"Demographics 2016" (http://www.militaryonesource.mil/footer?content_id=279104)
*Includes 6,019 not shown by state. Numbers reflect where the personnel are stationed.

U.S. Selected Reserve Personnel Stationed in the United States in 2016

National Total = 793,560 Personnel*

ALPHA ORDER

RANK	STATE	PERSONNEL	% of USA
11	Alabama	20,065	2.5%
42	Alaska	4,664	0.6%
24	Arizona	14,685	1.9%
30	Arkansas	11,541	1.5%
1	California	57,374	7.2%
27	Colorado	13,756	1.7%
37	Connecticut	6,902	0.9%
41	Delaware	5,156	0.6%
3	Florida	36,733	4.6%
7	Georgia	26,990	3.4%
34	Hawaii	9,308	1.2%
39	Idaho	5,335	0.7%
9	Illinois	24,874	3.1%
14	Indiana	19,148	2.4%
31	Iowa	11,083	1.4%
32	Kansas	10,761	1.4%
28	Kentucky	12,501	1.6%
13	Louisiana	19,485	2.5%
48	Maine	3,943	0.5%
18	Maryland	18,707	2.4%
22	Massachusetts	15,408	1.9%
23	Michigan	15,069	1.9%
16	Minnesota	18,846	2.4%
21	Mississippi	16,379	2.1%
12	Missouri	19,532	2.5%
46	Montana	4,488	0.6%
38	Nebraska	6,392	0.8%
36	Nevada	7,750	1.0%
47	New Hampshire	4,273	0.5%
20	New Jersey	17,592	2.2%
40	New Mexico	5,167	0.7%
5	New York	29,206	3.7%
10	North Carolina	22,365	2.8%
44	North Dakota	4,494	0.6%
6	Ohio	28,051	3.5%
26	Oklahoma	13,833	1.7%
33	Oregon	9,752	1.2%
4	Pennsylvania	31,306	3.9%
45	Rhode Island	4,489	0.6%
19	South Carolina	18,301	2.3%
43	South Dakota	4,632	0.6%
17	Tennessee	18,749	2.4%
2	Texas	54,142	6.8%
29	Utah	11,794	1.5%
49	Vermont	3,917	0.5%
8	Virginia	25,999	3.3%
15	Washington	19,112	2.4%
35	West Virginia	8,048	1.0%
25	Wisconsin	14,436	1.8%
50	Wyoming	2,911	0.4%

RANK ORDER

RANK	STATE	PERSONNEL	% of USA
1	California	57,374	7.2%
2	Texas	54,142	6.8%
3	Florida	36,733	4.6%
4	Pennsylvania	31,306	3.9%
5	New York	29,206	3.7%
6	Ohio	28,051	3.5%
7	Georgia	26,990	3.4%
8	Virginia	25,999	3.3%
9	Illinois	24,874	3.1%
10	North Carolina	22,365	2.8%
11	Alabama	20,065	2.5%
12	Missouri	19,532	2.5%
13	Louisiana	19,485	2.5%
14	Indiana	19,148	2.4%
15	Washington	19,112	2.4%
16	Minnesota	18,846	2.4%
17	Tennessee	18,749	2.4%
18	Maryland	18,707	2.4%
19	South Carolina	18,301	2.3%
20	New Jersey	17,592	2.2%
21	Mississippi	16,379	2.1%
22	Massachusetts	15,408	1.9%
23	Michigan	15,069	1.9%
24	Arizona	14,685	1.9%
25	Wisconsin	14,436	1.8%
26	Oklahoma	13,833	1.7%
27	Colorado	13,756	1.7%
28	Kentucky	12,501	1.6%
29	Utah	11,794	1.5%
30	Arkansas	11,541	1.5%
31	Iowa	11,083	1.4%
32	Kansas	10,761	1.4%
33	Oregon	9,752	1.2%
34	Hawaii	9,308	1.2%
35	West Virginia	8,048	1.0%
36	Nevada	7,750	1.0%
37	Connecticut	6,902	0.9%
38	Nebraska	6,392	0.8%
39	Idaho	5,335	0.7%
40	New Mexico	5,167	0.7%
41	Delaware	5,156	0.6%
42	Alaska	4,664	0.6%
43	South Dakota	4,632	0.6%
44	North Dakota	4,494	0.6%
45	Rhode Island	4,489	0.6%
46	Montana	4,488	0.6%
47	New Hampshire	4,273	0.5%
48	Maine	3,943	0.5%
49	Vermont	3,917	0.5%
50	Wyoming	2,911	0.4%
	District of Columbia	4,116	0.5%

Source: U.S. Department of Defense
"Demographics 2016" (http://www.militaryonesource.mil/footer?content_id=279104)
*Numbers reflect where the personnel are stationed.

Veterans in 2017

National Total = 19,998,799 Veterans*

ALPHA ORDER

RANK	STATE	VETERANS	% of USA
20	Alabama	369,962	1.8%
45	Alaska	68,719	0.3%
13	Arizona	507,706	2.5%
29	Arkansas	222,286	1.1%
1	California	1,681,730	8.4%
17	Colorado	403,327	2.0%
34	Connecticut	184,302	0.9%
44	Delaware	71,845	0.4%
3	Florida	1,525,400	7.6%
9	Georgia	697,127	3.5%
41	Hawaii	112,304	0.6%
39	Idaho	122,067	0.6%
10	Illinois	628,254	3.1%
16	Indiana	409,836	2.0%
31	Iowa	206,430	1.0%
32	Kansas	194,186	1.0%
27	Kentucky	295,390	1.5%
28	Louisiana	284,074	1.4%
40	Maine	114,020	0.6%
19	Maryland	389,640	1.9%
24	Massachusetts	323,253	1.6%
11	Michigan	589,326	2.9%
23	Minnesota	327,629	1.6%
33	Mississippi	191,411	1.0%
15	Missouri	442,579	2.2%
43	Montana	91,336	0.5%
38	Nebraska	130,126	0.7%
30	Nevada	218,406	1.1%
42	New Hampshire	105,390	0.5%
22	New Jersey	355,766	1.8%
35	New Mexico	158,994	0.8%
5	New York	776,522	3.9%
7	North Carolina	730,357	3.7%
48	North Dakota	51,677	0.3%
6	Ohio	774,935	3.9%
26	Oklahoma	303,205	1.5%
25	Oregon	303,689	1.5%
4	Pennsylvania	819,185	4.1%
47	Rhode Island	63,250	0.3%
18	South Carolina	402,596	2.0%
46	South Dakota	65,335	0.3%
14	Tennessee	470,390	2.4%
2	Texas	1,584,844	7.9%
37	Utah	134,313	0.7%
50	Vermont	43,191	0.2%
8	Virginia	725,028	3.6%
12	Washington	560,200	2.8%
36	West Virginia	142,694	0.7%
21	Wisconsin	363,898	1.8%
49	Wyoming	47,220	0.2%

RANK ORDER

RANK	STATE	VETERANS	% of USA
1	California	1,681,730	8.4%
2	Texas	1,584,844	7.9%
3	Florida	1,525,400	7.6%
4	Pennsylvania	819,185	4.1%
5	New York	776,522	3.9%
6	Ohio	774,935	3.9%
7	North Carolina	730,357	3.7%
8	Virginia	725,028	3.6%
9	Georgia	697,127	3.5%
10	Illinois	628,254	3.1%
11	Michigan	589,326	2.9%
12	Washington	560,200	2.8%
13	Arizona	507,706	2.5%
14	Tennessee	470,390	2.4%
15	Missouri	442,579	2.2%
16	Indiana	409,836	2.0%
17	Colorado	403,327	2.0%
18	South Carolina	402,596	2.0%
19	Maryland	389,640	1.9%
20	Alabama	369,962	1.8%
21	Wisconsin	363,898	1.8%
22	New Jersey	355,766	1.8%
23	Minnesota	327,629	1.6%
24	Massachusetts	323,253	1.6%
25	Oregon	303,689	1.5%
26	Oklahoma	303,205	1.5%
27	Kentucky	295,390	1.5%
28	Louisiana	284,074	1.4%
29	Arkansas	222,286	1.1%
30	Nevada	218,406	1.1%
31	Iowa	206,430	1.0%
32	Kansas	194,186	1.0%
33	Mississippi	191,411	1.0%
34	Connecticut	184,302	0.9%
35	New Mexico	158,994	0.8%
36	West Virginia	142,694	0.7%
37	Utah	134,313	0.7%
38	Nebraska	130,126	0.7%
39	Idaho	122,067	0.6%
40	Maine	114,020	0.6%
41	Hawaii	112,304	0.6%
42	New Hampshire	105,390	0.5%
43	Montana	91,336	0.5%
44	Delaware	71,845	0.4%
45	Alaska	68,719	0.3%
46	South Dakota	65,335	0.3%
47	Rhode Island	63,250	0.3%
48	North Dakota	51,677	0.3%
49	Wyoming	47,220	0.2%
50	Vermont	43,191	0.2%
	District of Columbia	27,875	0.1%

Source: U.S. Department of Veteran Affairs
  "Veteran Data and Information" (http://www.va.gov/vetdata/Veteran_Population.asp)
*Estimates based on 2016 data. Includes 185,571 veterans in U.S. territories or other countries.

Percent of Adult Population Who Are Veterans in 2017

National Percent = 7.9%*

ALPHA ORDER				RANK ORDER		
RANK	STATE	PERCENT		RANK	STATE	PERCENT
12	Alabama	9.8		1	Alaska	12.4
1	Alaska	12.4		2	Montana	11.2
18	Arizona	9.6		3	Virginia	11.1
16	Arkansas	9.7		4	Maine	10.6
48	California	5.6		4	Wyoming	10.6
20	Colorado	9.4		6	South Carolina	10.4
44	Connecticut	6.5		7	Oklahoma	10.2
18	Delaware	9.6		8	Hawaii	10.0
23	Florida	9.3		8	New Mexico	10.0
27	Georgia	8.9		8	South Dakota	10.0
8	Hawaii	10.0		11	Washington	9.9
12	Idaho	9.8		12	Alabama	9.8
45	Illinois	6.4		12	Idaho	9.8
36	Indiana	8.1		12	New Hampshire	9.8
30	Iowa	8.6		12	West Virginia	9.8
27	Kansas	8.9		16	Arkansas	9.7
30	Kentucky	8.6		16	Nevada	9.7
39	Louisiana	8.0		18	Arizona	9.6
4	Maine	10.6		18	Delaware	9.6
35	Maryland	8.3		20	Colorado	9.4
47	Massachusetts	5.9		20	Missouri	9.4
42	Michigan	7.6		20	Oregon	9.4
40	Minnesota	7.7		23	Florida	9.3
34	Mississippi	8.4		23	North Carolina	9.3
20	Missouri	9.4		25	Nebraska	9.1
2	Montana	11.2		25	Tennessee	9.1
25	Nebraska	9.1		27	Georgia	8.9
16	Nevada	9.7		27	Kansas	8.9
12	New Hampshire	9.8		27	North Dakota	8.9
49	New Jersey	5.1		30	Iowa	8.6
8	New Mexico	10.0		30	Kentucky	8.6
50	New York	5.0		30	Ohio	8.6
23	North Carolina	9.3		33	Vermont	8.5
27	North Dakota	8.9		34	Mississippi	8.4
30	Ohio	8.6		35	Maryland	8.3
7	Oklahoma	10.2		36	Indiana	8.1
20	Oregon	9.4		36	Pennsylvania	8.1
36	Pennsylvania	8.1		36	Wisconsin	8.1
43	Rhode Island	7.5		39	Louisiana	8.0
6	South Carolina	10.4		40	Minnesota	7.7
8	South Dakota	10.0		40	Texas	7.7
25	Tennessee	9.1		42	Michigan	7.6
40	Texas	7.7		43	Rhode Island	7.5
46	Utah	6.3		44	Connecticut	6.5
33	Vermont	8.5		45	Illinois	6.4
3	Virginia	11.1		46	Utah	6.3
11	Washington	9.9		47	Massachusetts	5.9
12	West Virginia	9.8		48	California	5.6
36	Wisconsin	8.1		49	New Jersey	5.1
4	Wyoming	10.6		50	New York	5.0

District of Columbia 5.0

Source: CQ Press using data from U.S. Department of Veteran Affairs
"Veteran Data and Information" (http://www.va.gov/vetdata/Veteran_Population.asp)
*Estimates based on 2016 data. National figures does not include veterans in U.S. territories or other countries. Percent calculated with population 18 years old and older in 2016.

U.S. Military Fatalities in Iraq and Afghanistan as of January 31, 2018

National Total = 6,930 Fatalities*

ALPHA ORDER

RANK	STATE	FATALITIES	% of USA
25	Alabama	105	1.5%
44	Alaska	26	0.4%
13	Arizona	155	2.2%
29	Arkansas	89	1.3%
1	California	747	10.8%
26	Colorado	104	1.5%
39	Connecticut	47	0.7%
49	Delaware	19	0.3%
3	Florida	349	5.0%
9	Georgia	220	3.2%
43	Hawaii	37	0.5%
36	Idaho	50	0.7%
7	Illinois	257	3.7%
12	Indiana	157	2.3%
32	Iowa	73	1.1%
31	Kansas	76	1.1%
23	Kentucky	113	1.6%
20	Louisiana	125	1.8%
36	Maine	50	0.7%
22	Maryland	124	1.8%
17	Massachusetts	128	1.8%
8	Michigan	227	3.3%
27	Minnesota	97	1.4%
30	Mississippi	80	1.2%
15	Missouri	144	2.1%
41	Montana	40	0.6%
33	Nebraska	61	0.9%
35	Nevada	54	0.8%
41	New Hampshire	40	0.6%
20	New Jersey	125	1.8%
34	New Mexico	57	0.8%
4	New York	300	4.3%
11	North Carolina	191	2.8%
48	North Dakota	20	0.3%
6	Ohio	281	4.1%
18	Oklahoma	127	1.8%
24	Oregon	110	1.6%
5	Pennsylvania	294	4.2%
50	Rhode Island	17	0.2%
27	South Carolina	97	1.4%
46	South Dakota	24	0.3%
16	Tennessee	140	2.0%
2	Texas	612	8.8%
38	Utah	49	0.7%
44	Vermont	26	0.4%
10	Virginia	200	2.9%
14	Washington	151	2.2%
40	West Virginia	41	0.6%
18	Wisconsin	127	1.8%
47	Wyoming	22	0.3%

RANK ORDER

RANK	STATE	FATALITIES	% of USA
1	California	747	10.8%
2	Texas	612	8.8%
3	Florida	349	5.0%
4	New York	300	4.3%
5	Pennsylvania	294	4.2%
6	Ohio	281	4.1%
7	Illinois	257	3.7%
8	Michigan	227	3.3%
9	Georgia	220	3.2%
10	Virginia	200	2.9%
11	North Carolina	191	2.8%
12	Indiana	157	2.3%
13	Arizona	155	2.2%
14	Washington	151	2.2%
15	Missouri	144	2.1%
16	Tennessee	140	2.0%
17	Massachusetts	128	1.8%
18	Oklahoma	127	1.8%
18	Wisconsin	127	1.8%
20	Louisiana	125	1.8%
20	New Jersey	125	1.8%
22	Maryland	124	1.8%
23	Kentucky	113	1.6%
24	Oregon	110	1.6%
25	Alabama	105	1.5%
26	Colorado	104	1.5%
27	Minnesota	97	1.4%
27	South Carolina	97	1.4%
29	Arkansas	89	1.3%
30	Mississippi	80	1.2%
31	Kansas	76	1.1%
32	Iowa	73	1.1%
33	Nebraska	61	0.9%
34	New Mexico	57	0.8%
35	Nevada	54	0.8%
36	Idaho	50	0.7%
36	Maine	50	0.7%
38	Utah	49	0.7%
39	Connecticut	47	0.7%
40	West Virginia	41	0.6%
41	Montana	40	0.6%
41	New Hampshire	40	0.6%
43	Hawaii	37	0.5%
44	Alaska	26	0.4%
44	Vermont	26	0.4%
46	South Dakota	24	0.3%
47	Wyoming	22	0.3%
48	North Dakota	20	0.3%
49	Delaware	19	0.3%
50	Rhode Island	17	0.2%
	District of Columbia	10	0.1%

Source: U.S. Department of Defense, Defense Casualty Analysis System
  "U.S. Military Casualties" (https://dcas.dmdc.osd.mil/dcas/pages/report_sum_all.xhtml)
*Total includes 115 deaths of soldiers from U.S. territories. Total does not include deaths of United Kingdom soldiers or other coalition nations. Includes 5,407 combat and 1,523 noncombat deaths. Includes 4,484 deaths in Iraq, 2,393 deaths in Afghanistan, and 53 deaths fighting Islamic State in Syria and Iraq.

Rate of U.S. Military Fatalities in Iraq and Afghanistan as of January 31, 2018

National Rate = 2.1 Fatalities per 100,000 Population*

ALPHA ORDER

RANK	STATE	RATE
28	Alabama	2.2
5	Alaska	3.5
28	Arizona	2.2
8	Arkansas	3.0
38	California	1.9
38	Colorado	1.9
50	Connecticut	1.3
34	Delaware	2.0
44	Florida	1.7
32	Georgia	2.1
16	Hawaii	2.6
10	Idaho	2.9
34	Illinois	2.0
20	Indiana	2.4
24	Iowa	2.3
16	Kansas	2.6
19	Kentucky	2.5
12	Louisiana	2.7
4	Maine	3.7
34	Maryland	2.0
38	Massachusetts	1.9
24	Michigan	2.3
44	Minnesota	1.7
12	Mississippi	2.7
20	Missouri	2.4
2	Montana	3.8
6	Nebraska	3.2
43	Nevada	1.8
8	New Hampshire	3.0
49	New Jersey	1.4
12	New Mexico	2.7
48	New York	1.5
38	North Carolina	1.9
16	North Dakota	2.6
20	Ohio	2.4
6	Oklahoma	3.2
12	Oregon	2.7
24	Pennsylvania	2.3
46	Rhode Island	1.6
38	South Carolina	1.9
11	South Dakota	2.8
32	Tennessee	2.1
28	Texas	2.2
46	Utah	1.6
1	Vermont	4.2
20	Virginia	2.4
34	Washington	2.0
24	West Virginia	2.3
28	Wisconsin	2.2
2	Wyoming	3.8

RANK ORDER

RANK	STATE	RATE
1	Vermont	4.2
2	Montana	3.8
2	Wyoming	3.8
4	Maine	3.7
5	Alaska	3.5
6	Nebraska	3.2
6	Oklahoma	3.2
8	Arkansas	3.0
8	New Hampshire	3.0
10	Idaho	2.9
11	South Dakota	2.8
12	Louisiana	2.7
12	Mississippi	2.7
12	New Mexico	2.7
12	Oregon	2.7
16	Hawaii	2.6
16	Kansas	2.6
16	North Dakota	2.6
19	Kentucky	2.5
20	Indiana	2.4
20	Missouri	2.4
20	Ohio	2.4
20	Virginia	2.4
24	Iowa	2.3
24	Michigan	2.3
24	Pennsylvania	2.3
24	West Virginia	2.3
28	Alabama	2.2
28	Arizona	2.2
28	Texas	2.2
28	Wisconsin	2.2
32	Georgia	2.1
32	Tennessee	2.1
34	Delaware	2.0
34	Illinois	2.0
34	Maryland	2.0
34	Washington	2.0
38	California	1.9
38	Colorado	1.9
38	Massachusetts	1.9
38	North Carolina	1.9
38	South Carolina	1.9
43	Nevada	1.8
44	Florida	1.7
44	Minnesota	1.7
46	Rhode Island	1.6
46	Utah	1.6
48	New York	1.5
49	New Jersey	1.4
50	Connecticut	1.3

District of Columbia — 1.4

Source: CQ Press using data from U.S. Department of Defense, Defense Casualty Analysis System
"U.S. Military Casualties" (https://dcas.dmdc.osd.mil/dcas/pages/report_sum_all.xhtml)
*National rate does not include deaths of soldiers from U.S. territories. Includes combat and noncombat deaths. Calculated with 2017 population estimates.

U.S. Military Wounded in Iraq and Afghanistan as of January 31, 2018

National Total = 52,669 Wounded*

ALPHA ORDER

RANK	STATE	WOUNDED	% of USA
18	Alabama	864	1.6%
46	Alaska	159	0.3%
14	Arizona	1,160	2.2%
29	Arkansas	650	1.2%
1	California	4,869	9.2%
22	Colorado	822	1.6%
35	Connecticut	424	0.8%
50	Delaware	84	0.2%
3	Florida	2,510	4.8%
9	Georgia	1,494	2.8%
43	Hawaii	208	0.4%
36	Idaho	391	0.7%
7	Illinois	1,758	3.3%
15	Indiana	1,107	2.1%
31	Iowa	625	1.2%
30	Kansas	626	1.2%
27	Kentucky	747	1.4%
21	Louisiana	833	1.6%
41	Maine	323	0.6%
28	Maryland	681	1.3%
20	Massachusetts	834	1.6%
8	Michigan	1,633	3.1%
26	Minnesota	754	1.4%
33	Mississippi	444	0.8%
13	Missouri	1,187	2.3%
40	Montana	327	0.6%
39	Nebraska	337	0.6%
37	Nevada	379	0.7%
42	New Hampshire	298	0.6%
24	New Jersey	771	1.5%
34	New Mexico	425	0.8%
4	New York	2,330	4.4%
10	North Carolina	1,447	2.7%
49	North Dakota	117	0.2%
5	Ohio	2,043	3.9%
19	Oklahoma	857	1.6%
23	Oregon	795	1.5%
6	Pennsylvania	2,001	3.8%
45	Rhode Island	170	0.3%
25	South Carolina	757	1.4%
44	South Dakota	194	0.4%
16	Tennessee	1,019	1.9%
2	Texas	4,366	8.3%
32	Utah	458	0.9%
47	Vermont	152	0.3%
12	Virginia	1,207	2.3%
11	Washington	1,292	2.5%
38	West Virginia	365	0.7%
17	Wisconsin	917	1.7%
48	Wyoming	150	0.3%

RANK ORDER

RANK	STATE	WOUNDED	% of USA
1	California	4,869	9.2%
2	Texas	4,366	8.3%
3	Florida	2,510	4.8%
4	New York	2,330	4.4%
5	Ohio	2,043	3.9%
6	Pennsylvania	2,001	3.8%
7	Illinois	1,758	3.3%
8	Michigan	1,633	3.1%
9	Georgia	1,494	2.8%
10	North Carolina	1,447	2.7%
11	Washington	1,292	2.5%
12	Virginia	1,207	2.3%
13	Missouri	1,187	2.3%
14	Arizona	1,160	2.2%
15	Indiana	1,107	2.1%
16	Tennessee	1,019	1.9%
17	Wisconsin	917	1.7%
18	Alabama	864	1.6%
19	Oklahoma	857	1.6%
20	Massachusetts	834	1.6%
21	Louisiana	833	1.6%
22	Colorado	822	1.6%
23	Oregon	795	1.5%
24	New Jersey	771	1.5%
25	South Carolina	757	1.4%
26	Minnesota	754	1.4%
27	Kentucky	747	1.4%
28	Maryland	681	1.3%
29	Arkansas	650	1.2%
30	Kansas	626	1.2%
31	Iowa	625	1.2%
32	Utah	458	0.9%
33	Mississippi	444	0.8%
34	New Mexico	425	0.8%
35	Connecticut	424	0.8%
36	Idaho	391	0.7%
37	Nevada	379	0.7%
38	West Virginia	365	0.7%
39	Nebraska	337	0.6%
40	Montana	327	0.6%
41	Maine	323	0.6%
42	New Hampshire	298	0.6%
43	Hawaii	208	0.4%
44	South Dakota	194	0.4%
45	Rhode Island	170	0.3%
46	Alaska	159	0.3%
47	Vermont	152	0.3%
48	Wyoming	150	0.3%
49	North Dakota	117	0.2%
50	Delaware	84	0.2%
	District of Columbia	30	0.1%

Source: U.S. Department of Defense, Defense Casualty Analysis System
"U.S. Military Casualties" (https://dcas.dmdc.osd.mil/dcas/pages/report_sum_all.xhtml)
*Total includes 4,278 wounded soldiers from U.S. territories. Total does not include wounded soldiers of United Kingdom or other coalition nations. Only includes wounded in action. Includes 32,252 wounded in Iraq, 20,355 wounded in Afghanistan, and 62 wounded fighting the Islamic State in Syria and Iraq.

IV. Economy

Gross Domestic Product in 2016

National Total = $18,511,499,000,000*

ALPHA ORDER

RANK	STATE	G.D.P.	% of USA
27	Alabama	$205,625,000,000	1.1%
46	Alaska	50,404,000,000	0.3%
21	Arizona	305,849,000,000	1.7%
34	Arkansas	121,383,000,000	0.7%
1	California	2,622,731,000,000	14.2%
19	Colorado	322,644,000,000	1.7%
23	Connecticut	259,918,000,000	1.4%
41	Delaware	71,453,000,000	0.4%
4	Florida	926,049,000,000	5.0%
9	Georgia	531,302,000,000	2.9%
38	Hawaii	84,671,000,000	0.5%
42	Idaho	68,377,000,000	0.4%
5	Illinois	796,012,000,000	4.3%
16	Indiana	347,249,000,000	1.9%
29	Iowa	185,183,000,000	1.0%
32	Kansas	150,576,000,000	0.8%
28	Kentucky	196,681,000,000	1.1%
24	Louisiana	236,999,000,000	1.3%
43	Maine	59,295,000,000	0.3%
15	Maryland	382,437,000,000	2.1%
11	Massachusetts	505,776,000,000	2.7%
13	Michigan	490,238,000,000	2.6%
17	Minnesota	339,096,000,000	1.8%
36	Mississippi	108,495,000,000	0.6%
22	Missouri	299,113,000,000	1.6%
48	Montana	46,227,000,000	0.2%
35	Nebraska	117,446,000,000	0.6%
33	Nevada	146,278,000,000	0.8%
39	New Hampshire	77,208,000,000	0.4%
8	New Jersey	575,331,000,000	3.1%
37	New Mexico	93,594,000,000	0.5%
3	New York	1,500,055,000,000	8.1%
10	North Carolina	521,621,000,000	2.8%
45	North Dakota	53,453,000,000	0.3%
7	Ohio	626,622,000,000	3.4%
30	Oklahoma	181,278,000,000	1.0%
25	Oregon	228,886,000,000	1.2%
6	Pennsylvania	719,834,000,000	3.9%
44	Rhode Island	57,529,000,000	0.3%
26	South Carolina	209,859,000,000	1.1%
47	South Dakota	48,354,000,000	0.3%
18	Tennessee	331,868,000,000	1.8%
2	Texas	1,599,283,000,000	8.6%
31	Utah	157,671,000,000	0.9%
50	Vermont	31,091,000,000	0.2%
12	Virginia	492,932,000,000	2.7%
14	Washington	476,770,000,000	2.6%
40	West Virginia	72,861,000,000	0.4%
20	Wisconsin	313,088,000,000	1.7%
49	Wyoming	38,328,000,000	0.2%

RANK ORDER

RANK	STATE	G.D.P.	% of USA
1	California	$2,622,731,000,000	14.2%
2	Texas	1,599,283,000,000	8.6%
3	New York	1,500,055,000,000	8.1%
4	Florida	926,049,000,000	5.0%
5	Illinois	796,012,000,000	4.3%
6	Pennsylvania	719,834,000,000	3.9%
7	Ohio	626,622,000,000	3.4%
8	New Jersey	575,331,000,000	3.1%
9	Georgia	531,302,000,000	2.9%
10	North Carolina	521,621,000,000	2.8%
11	Massachusetts	505,776,000,000	2.7%
12	Virginia	492,932,000,000	2.7%
13	Michigan	490,238,000,000	2.6%
14	Washington	476,770,000,000	2.6%
15	Maryland	382,437,000,000	2.1%
16	Indiana	347,249,000,000	1.9%
17	Minnesota	339,096,000,000	1.8%
18	Tennessee	331,868,000,000	1.8%
19	Colorado	322,644,000,000	1.7%
20	Wisconsin	313,088,000,000	1.7%
21	Arizona	305,849,000,000	1.7%
22	Missouri	299,113,000,000	1.6%
23	Connecticut	259,918,000,000	1.4%
24	Louisiana	236,999,000,000	1.3%
25	Oregon	228,886,000,000	1.2%
26	South Carolina	209,859,000,000	1.1%
27	Alabama	205,625,000,000	1.1%
28	Kentucky	196,681,000,000	1.1%
29	Iowa	185,183,000,000	1.0%
30	Oklahoma	181,278,000,000	1.0%
31	Utah	157,671,000,000	0.9%
32	Kansas	150,576,000,000	0.8%
33	Nevada	146,278,000,000	0.8%
34	Arkansas	121,383,000,000	0.7%
35	Nebraska	117,446,000,000	0.6%
36	Mississippi	108,495,000,000	0.6%
37	New Mexico	93,594,000,000	0.5%
38	Hawaii	84,671,000,000	0.5%
39	New Hampshire	77,208,000,000	0.4%
40	West Virginia	72,861,000,000	0.4%
41	Delaware	71,453,000,000	0.4%
42	Idaho	68,377,000,000	0.4%
43	Maine	59,295,000,000	0.3%
44	Rhode Island	57,529,000,000	0.3%
45	North Dakota	53,453,000,000	0.3%
46	Alaska	50,404,000,000	0.3%
47	South Dakota	48,354,000,000	0.3%
48	Montana	46,227,000,000	0.2%
49	Wyoming	38,328,000,000	0.2%
50	Vermont	31,091,000,000	0.2%
	District of Columbia	126,478,000,000	0.7%

Source: U.S. Department of Commerce, Bureau of Economic Analysis
    "Gross Domestic Product Data" (http://www.bea.gov/iTable/index_regional.cfm)
*G.D.P. is the market value of goods and services produced by the labor and property located in a state. It is the state counterpart to the nation's Gross Domestic Product. This was formerly known as Gross State Product (G.S.P.).

Percent Change in Gross Domestic Product: 2012 to 2016
(Adjusted to Constant 2009 Dollars)
National Percent Change = 8.3% Increase*

ALPHA ORDER

RANK	STATE	PERCENT CHANGE
33	Alabama	3.7
50	Alaska	(12.6)
21	Arizona	7.0
30	Arkansas	5.8
1	California	15.2
4	Colorado	13.1
48	Connecticut	(0.3)
21	Delaware	7.0
6	Florida	11.6
8	Georgia	11.3
19	Hawaii	7.4
7	Idaho	11.5
33	Illinois	3.7
18	Indiana	8.3
9	Iowa	10.2
42	Kansas	2.3
37	Kentucky	3.6
49	Louisiana	(0.6)
38	Maine	3.5
29	Maryland	6.0
24	Massachusetts	6.9
17	Michigan	8.4
13	Minnesota	8.9
45	Mississippi	1.1
33	Missouri	3.7
21	Montana	7.0
12	Nebraska	9.5
20	Nevada	7.2
25	New Hampshire	6.8
40	New Jersey	3.4
38	New Mexico	3.5
32	New York	3.9
15	North Carolina	8.6
44	North Dakota	1.7
26	Ohio	6.7
13	Oklahoma	8.9
16	Oregon	8.5
26	Pennsylvania	6.7
33	Rhode Island	3.7
9	South Carolina	10.2
31	South Dakota	5.6
11	Tennessee	9.6
5	Texas	13.0
2	Utah	14.4
43	Vermont	1.9
41	Virginia	2.9
3	Washington	14.2
46	West Virginia	0.7
28	Wisconsin	6.4
47	Wyoming	0.2

RANK ORDER

RANK	STATE	PERCENT CHANGE
1	California	15.2
2	Utah	14.4
3	Washington	14.2
4	Colorado	13.1
5	Texas	13.0
6	Florida	11.6
7	Idaho	11.5
8	Georgia	11.3
9	Iowa	10.2
9	South Carolina	10.2
11	Tennessee	9.6
12	Nebraska	9.5
13	Minnesota	8.9
13	Oklahoma	8.9
15	North Carolina	8.6
16	Oregon	8.5
17	Michigan	8.4
18	Indiana	8.3
19	Hawaii	7.4
20	Nevada	7.2
21	Arizona	7.0
21	Delaware	7.0
21	Montana	7.0
24	Massachusetts	6.9
25	New Hampshire	6.8
26	Ohio	6.7
26	Pennsylvania	6.7
28	Wisconsin	6.4
29	Maryland	6.0
30	Arkansas	5.8
31	South Dakota	5.6
32	New York	3.9
33	Alabama	3.7
33	Illinois	3.7
33	Missouri	3.7
33	Rhode Island	3.7
37	Kentucky	3.6
38	Maine	3.5
38	New Mexico	3.5
40	New Jersey	3.4
41	Virginia	2.9
42	Kansas	2.3
43	Vermont	1.9
44	North Dakota	1.7
45	Mississippi	1.1
46	West Virginia	0.7
47	Wyoming	0.2
48	Connecticut	(0.3)
49	Louisiana	(0.6)
50	Alaska	(12.6)

District of Columbia   5.5

Source: CQ Press using data from U.S. Department of Commerce, Bureau of Economic Analysis
"Gross Domestic Product Data" (http://www.bea.gov/iTable/index_regional.cfm)
*G.D.P. is the market value of goods and services produced by the labor and property located in a state. It is the state counterpart to the nation's Gross Domestic Product. This was formerly known as Gross State Product (G.S.P.). Adjusted for inflation using chained 2009 dollars.

Average Annual Change in Gross Domestic Product: 2012 to 2016
(Adjusted to Constant 2009 Dollars)
National Annual Percent Change = 1.6% Increase*

RANK	STATE	PERCENT CHANGE	RANK	STATE	PERCENT CHANGE
33	Alabama	0.7	1	California	2.9
50	Alaska	(2.6)	2	Utah	2.7
19	Arizona	1.4	2	Washington	2.7
30	Arkansas	1.1	4	Colorado	2.5
1	California	2.9	4	Texas	2.5
4	Colorado	2.5	6	Florida	2.2
48	Connecticut	(0.1)	6	Georgia	2.2
19	Delaware	1.4	6	Idaho	2.2
6	Florida	2.2	9	Iowa	2.0
6	Georgia	2.2	9	South Carolina	2.0
19	Hawaii	1.4	11	Nebraska	1.8
6	Idaho	2.2	11	Tennessee	1.8
33	Illinois	0.7	13	Minnesota	1.7
17	Indiana	1.6	13	North Carolina	1.7
9	Iowa	2.0	13	Oklahoma	1.7
42	Kansas	0.5	13	Oregon	1.7
33	Kentucky	0.7	17	Indiana	1.6
48	Louisiana	(0.1)	17	Michigan	1.6
33	Maine	0.7	19	Arizona	1.4
28	Maryland	1.2	19	Delaware	1.4
19	Massachusetts	1.4	19	Hawaii	1.4
17	Michigan	1.6	19	Massachusetts	1.4
13	Minnesota	1.7	19	Montana	1.4
45	Mississippi	0.2	19	Nevada	1.4
33	Missouri	0.7	25	New Hampshire	1.3
19	Montana	1.4	25	Ohio	1.3
11	Nebraska	1.8	25	Pennsylvania	1.3
19	Nevada	1.4	28	Maryland	1.2
25	New Hampshire	1.3	28	Wisconsin	1.2
33	New Jersey	0.7	30	Arkansas	1.1
33	New Mexico	0.7	30	South Dakota	1.1
32	New York	0.8	32	New York	0.8
13	North Carolina	1.7	33	Alabama	0.7
44	North Dakota	0.3	33	Illinois	0.7
25	Ohio	1.3	33	Kentucky	0.7
13	Oklahoma	1.7	33	Maine	0.7
13	Oregon	1.7	33	Missouri	0.7
25	Pennsylvania	1.3	33	New Jersey	0.7
33	Rhode Island	0.7	33	New Mexico	0.7
9	South Carolina	2.0	33	Rhode Island	0.7
30	South Dakota	1.1	41	Virginia	0.6
11	Tennessee	1.8	42	Kansas	0.5
4	Texas	2.5	43	Vermont	0.4
2	Utah	2.7	44	North Dakota	0.3
43	Vermont	0.4	45	Mississippi	0.2
41	Virginia	0.6	46	West Virginia	0.1
2	Washington	2.7	47	Wyoming	0.0
46	West Virginia	0.1	48	Connecticut	(0.1)
28	Wisconsin	1.2	48	Louisiana	(0.1)
47	Wyoming	0.0	50	Alaska	(2.6)

	District of Columbia	1.1

Source: CQ Press using data from U.S. Department of Commerce, Bureau of Economic Analysis
"Gross Domestic Product Data" (http://www.bea.gov/iTable/index_regional.cfm)
*G.D.P. is the market value of goods and services produced by the labor and property located in a state. It is the state counterpart to the nation's Gross Domestic Product. This was formerly known as Gross State Product (G.S.P.). Adjusted for inflation using chained 2009 dollars.

Per Capita Gross Domestic Product in 2016

National Per Capita = $57,239*

ALPHA ORDER

RANK	STATE	PER CAPITA
46	Alabama	$42,305
6	Alaska	67,974
44	Arizona	44,270
48	Arkansas	40,620
7	California	66,742
18	Colorado	58,343
4	Connecticut	72,447
2	Delaware	75,001
40	Florida	44,831
30	Georgia	51,515
15	Hawaii	59,265
47	Idaho	40,700
12	Illinois	62,015
27	Indiana	52,344
16	Iowa	59,147
29	Kansas	51,785
43	Kentucky	44,336
32	Louisiana	50,574
41	Maine	44,575
11	Maryland	63,478
3	Massachusetts	74,120
36	Michigan	49,352
14	Minnesota	61,374
50	Mississippi	36,342
37	Missouri	49,106
42	Montana	44,507
13	Nebraska	61,567
35	Nevada	49,767
19	New Hampshire	57,833
10	New Jersey	64,079
39	New Mexico	44,880
1	New York	75,622
31	North Carolina	51,357
5	North Dakota	70,747
26	Ohio	53,914
38	Oklahoma	46,230
23	Oregon	56,017
21	Pennsylvania	56,294
24	Rhode Island	54,398
45	South Carolina	42,312
22	South Dakota	56,125
33	Tennessee	49,909
20	Texas	57,312
28	Utah	51,792
34	Vermont	49,877
17	Virginia	58,582
9	Washington	65,482
49	West Virginia	39,844
25	Wisconsin	54,234
8	Wyoming	65,528

RANK ORDER

RANK	STATE	PER CAPITA
1	New York	$75,622
2	Delaware	75,001
3	Massachusetts	74,120
4	Connecticut	72,447
5	North Dakota	70,747
6	Alaska	67,974
7	California	66,742
8	Wyoming	65,528
9	Washington	65,482
10	New Jersey	64,079
11	Maryland	63,478
12	Illinois	62,015
13	Nebraska	61,567
14	Minnesota	61,374
15	Hawaii	59,265
16	Iowa	59,147
17	Virginia	58,582
18	Colorado	58,343
19	New Hampshire	57,833
20	Texas	57,312
21	Pennsylvania	56,294
22	South Dakota	56,125
23	Oregon	56,017
24	Rhode Island	54,398
25	Wisconsin	54,234
26	Ohio	53,914
27	Indiana	52,344
28	Utah	51,792
29	Kansas	51,785
30	Georgia	51,515
31	North Carolina	51,357
32	Louisiana	50,574
33	Tennessee	49,909
34	Vermont	49,877
35	Nevada	49,767
36	Michigan	49,352
37	Missouri	49,106
38	Oklahoma	46,230
39	New Mexico	44,880
40	Florida	44,831
41	Maine	44,575
42	Montana	44,507
43	Kentucky	44,336
44	Arizona	44,270
45	South Carolina	42,312
46	Alabama	42,305
47	Idaho	40,700
48	Arkansas	40,620
49	West Virginia	39,844
50	Mississippi	36,342

District of Columbia   184,819

Source: CQ Press using data from U.S. Department of Commerce, Bureau of Economic Analysis
"Gross Domestic Product Data" (http://www.bea.gov/iTable/index_regional.cfm)
*G.D.P. is the market value of goods and services produced by the labor and property located in a state. It is the state counterpart to the nation's Gross Domestic Product. This was formerly known as Gross State Product (G.S.P.).

Percent Change in Per Capita Gross Domestic Product: 2012 to 2016
(Adjusted to Constant 2009 Dollars)
National Percent Change = 5.3% Increase*

ALPHA ORDER

RANK	STATE	PERCENT CHANGE
34	Alabama	2.7
50	Alaska	(13.8)
42	Arizona	1.1
22	Arkansas	4.5
1	California	11.6
14	Colorado	5.9
45	Connecticut	0.2
33	Delaware	3.0
20	Florida	4.8
6	Georgia	7.0
21	Hawaii	4.7
15	Idaho	5.8
24	Illinois	4.3
7	Indiana	6.8
2	Iowa	8.1
41	Kansas	1.5
37	Kentucky	2.4
48	Louisiana	(2.3)
30	Maine	3.3
26	Maryland	3.8
22	Massachusetts	4.5
4	Michigan	7.9
11	Minnesota	6.1
43	Mississippi	1.0
35	Missouri	2.6
31	Montana	3.2
8	Nebraska	6.6
44	Nevada	0.4
16	New Hampshire	5.7
36	New Jersey	2.5
27	New Mexico	3.7
32	New York	3.1
24	North Carolina	4.3
49	North Dakota	(5.8)
11	Ohio	6.1
13	Oklahoma	6.0
28	Oregon	3.4
8	Pennsylvania	6.6
28	Rhode Island	3.4
19	South Carolina	4.9
40	South Dakota	1.8
10	Tennessee	6.3
16	Texas	5.7
5	Utah	7.1
38	Vermont	2.2
45	Virginia	0.2
3	Washington	8.0
39	West Virginia	2.1
18	Wisconsin	5.4
47	Wyoming	(1.3)

RANK ORDER

RANK	STATE	PERCENT CHANGE
1	California	11.6
2	Iowa	8.1
3	Washington	8.0
4	Michigan	7.9
5	Utah	7.1
6	Georgia	7.0
7	Indiana	6.8
8	Nebraska	6.6
8	Pennsylvania	6.6
10	Tennessee	6.3
11	Minnesota	6.1
11	Ohio	6.1
13	Oklahoma	6.0
14	Colorado	5.9
15	Idaho	5.8
16	New Hampshire	5.7
16	Texas	5.7
18	Wisconsin	5.4
19	South Carolina	4.9
20	Florida	4.8
21	Hawaii	4.7
22	Arkansas	4.5
22	Massachusetts	4.5
24	Illinois	4.3
24	North Carolina	4.3
26	Maryland	3.8
27	New Mexico	3.7
28	Oregon	3.4
28	Rhode Island	3.4
30	Maine	3.3
31	Montana	3.2
32	New York	3.1
33	Delaware	3.0
34	Alabama	2.7
35	Missouri	2.6
36	New Jersey	2.5
37	Kentucky	2.4
38	Vermont	2.2
39	West Virginia	2.1
40	South Dakota	1.8
41	Kansas	1.5
42	Arizona	1.1
43	Mississippi	1.0
44	Nevada	0.4
45	Connecticut	0.2
45	Virginia	0.2
47	Wyoming	(1.3)
48	Louisiana	(2.3)
49	North Dakota	(5.8)
50	Alaska	(13.8)

District of Columbia   (1.6)

Source: CQ Press using data from U.S. Department of Commerce, Bureau of Economic Analysis
"Gross Domestic Product Data" (http://www.bea.gov/iTable/index_regional.cfm)

*G.D.P. is the market value of goods and services produced by the labor and property located in a state. It is the state counterpart to the nation's Gross Domestic Product. This was formerly known as Gross State Product (G.S.P.). Adjusted for inflation using chained 2009 dollars.

State Exports in 2016

National Total = $1,451,010,700,000*

RANK	STATE	EXPORTS	% of USA		RANK	STATE	EXPORTS	% of USA
22	Alabama	$20,422,130,000	1.4%		1	Texas	$231,106,720,000	15.9%
41	Alaska	4,347,500,000	0.3%		2	California	163,512,850,000	11.3%
19	Arizona	22,016,240,000	1.5%		3	Washington	79,559,490,000	5.5%
35	Arkansas	5,707,470,000	0.4%		4	New York	76,720,210,000	5.3%
2	California	163,512,850,000	11.3%		5	Illinois	59,757,900,000	4.1%
33	Colorado	7,580,280,000	0.5%		6	Michigan	54,713,480,000	3.8%
25	Connecticut	14,394,220,000	1.0%		7	Florida	52,049,370,000	3.6%
40	Delaware	4,532,420,000	0.3%		8	Ohio	49,298,840,000	3.4%
7	Florida	52,049,370,000	3.6%		9	Louisiana	48,418,790,000	3.3%
11	Georgia	35,644,330,000	2.5%		10	Pennsylvania	36,484,390,000	2.5%
50	Hawaii	795,490,000	0.1%		11	Georgia	35,644,330,000	2.5%
39	Idaho	4,876,800,000	0.3%		12	Indiana	34,654,960,000	2.4%
5	Illinois	59,757,900,000	4.1%		13	Tennessee	31,432,680,000	2.2%
12	Indiana	34,654,960,000	2.4%		14	South Carolina	31,321,940,000	2.2%
27	Iowa	12,115,440,000	0.8%		15	New Jersey	31,222,790,000	2.2%
30	Kansas	10,181,350,000	0.7%		16	North Carolina	30,161,260,000	2.1%
17	Kentucky	29,199,160,000	2.0%		17	Kentucky	29,199,160,000	2.0%
9	Louisiana	48,418,790,000	3.3%		18	Massachusetts	25,891,740,000	1.8%
45	Maine	2,875,270,000	0.2%		19	Arizona	22,016,240,000	1.5%
32	Maryland	9,658,230,000	0.7%		20	Oregon	21,752,610,000	1.5%
18	Massachusetts	25,891,740,000	1.8%		21	Wisconsin	21,021,230,000	1.4%
6	Michigan	54,713,480,000	3.8%		22	Alabama	20,422,130,000	1.4%
23	Minnesota	19,202,450,000	1.3%		23	Minnesota	19,202,450,000	1.3%
29	Mississippi	10,494,720,000	0.7%		24	Virginia	16,313,180,000	1.1%
26	Missouri	13,934,620,000	1.0%		25	Connecticut	14,394,220,000	1.0%
47	Montana	1,360,100,000	0.1%		26	Missouri	13,934,620,000	1.0%
34	Nebraska	6,380,350,000	0.4%		27	Iowa	12,115,440,000	0.8%
31	Nevada	9,763,160,000	0.7%		28	Utah	12,077,720,000	0.8%
42	New Hampshire	4,143,020,000	0.3%		29	Mississippi	10,494,720,000	0.7%
15	New Jersey	31,222,790,000	2.2%		30	Kansas	10,181,350,000	0.7%
43	New Mexico	3,631,620,000	0.3%		31	Nevada	9,763,160,000	0.7%
4	New York	76,720,210,000	5.3%		32	Maryland	9,658,230,000	0.7%
16	North Carolina	30,161,260,000	2.1%		33	Colorado	7,580,280,000	0.5%
36	North Dakota	5,313,340,000	0.4%		34	Nebraska	6,380,350,000	0.4%
8	Ohio	49,298,840,000	3.4%		35	Arkansas	5,707,470,000	0.4%
37	Oklahoma	5,047,880,000	0.3%		36	North Dakota	5,313,340,000	0.4%
20	Oregon	21,752,610,000	1.5%		37	Oklahoma	5,047,880,000	0.3%
10	Pennsylvania	36,484,390,000	2.5%		38	West Virginia	5,045,390,000	0.3%
46	Rhode Island	2,277,830,000	0.2%		39	Idaho	4,876,800,000	0.3%
14	South Carolina	31,321,940,000	2.2%		40	Delaware	4,532,420,000	0.3%
48	South Dakota	1,223,350,000	0.1%		41	Alaska	4,347,500,000	0.3%
13	Tennessee	31,432,680,000	2.2%		42	New Hampshire	4,143,020,000	0.3%
1	Texas	231,106,720,000	15.9%		43	New Mexico	3,631,620,000	0.3%
28	Utah	12,077,720,000	0.8%		44	Vermont	2,989,760,000	0.2%
44	Vermont	2,989,760,000	0.2%		45	Maine	2,875,270,000	0.2%
24	Virginia	16,313,180,000	1.1%		46	Rhode Island	2,277,830,000	0.2%
3	Washington	79,559,490,000	5.5%		47	Montana	1,360,100,000	0.1%
38	West Virginia	5,045,390,000	0.3%		48	South Dakota	1,223,350,000	0.1%
21	Wisconsin	21,021,230,000	1.4%		49	Wyoming	1,098,110,000	0.1%
49	Wyoming	1,098,110,000	0.1%		50	Hawaii	795,490,000	0.1%
						District of Columbia	1,330,670,000	0.1%

ALPHA ORDER

RANK ORDER

Source: U.S. Bureau of the Census
"State Trade Data" (http://www.census.gov/foreign-trade/statistics/state/)
*Based on the state from which the merchandise starts its journey to the port of export; that is, the data reflect the transportation origin of exports. Total includes exports from Puerto Rico, Virgin Islands, and exports with unidentified origin.

Per Capita State Exports in 2016

National Per Capita = $4,283*

ALPHA ORDER

RANK	STATE	PER CAPITA
16	Alabama	$4,202
7	Alaska	5,863
31	Arizona	3,187
42	Arkansas	1,910
17	California	4,161
47	Colorado	1,371
18	Connecticut	4,012
12	Delaware	4,757
37	Florida	2,520
28	Georgia	3,456
50	Hawaii	557
34	Idaho	2,903
14	Illinois	4,656
10	Indiana	5,224
20	Iowa	3,870
25	Kansas	3,501
5	Kentucky	6,582
2	Louisiana	10,332
39	Maine	2,161
45	Maryland	1,603
22	Massachusetts	3,794
8	Michigan	5,508
27	Minnesota	3,476
24	Mississippi	3,515
38	Missouri	2,288
48	Montana	1,309
29	Nebraska	3,345
30	Nevada	3,322
32	New Hampshire	3,103
26	New Jersey	3,478
44	New Mexico	1,741
21	New York	3,868
33	North Carolina	2,970
4	North Dakota	7,032
15	Ohio	4,242
49	Oklahoma	1,287
9	Oregon	5,324
35	Pennsylvania	2,853
40	Rhode Island	2,154
6	South Carolina	6,315
46	South Dakota	1,420
13	Tennessee	4,727
3	Texas	8,282
19	Utah	3,967
11	Vermont	4,796
41	Virginia	1,939
1	Washington	10,927
36	West Virginia	2,759
23	Wisconsin	3,641
43	Wyoming	1,877

RANK ORDER

RANK	STATE	PER CAPITA
1	Washington	$10,927
2	Louisiana	10,332
3	Texas	8,282
4	North Dakota	7,032
5	Kentucky	6,582
6	South Carolina	6,315
7	Alaska	5,863
8	Michigan	5,508
9	Oregon	5,324
10	Indiana	5,224
11	Vermont	4,796
12	Delaware	4,757
13	Tennessee	4,727
14	Illinois	4,656
15	Ohio	4,242
16	Alabama	4,202
17	California	4,161
18	Connecticut	4,012
19	Utah	3,967
20	Iowa	3,870
21	New York	3,868
22	Massachusetts	3,794
23	Wisconsin	3,641
24	Mississippi	3,515
25	Kansas	3,501
26	New Jersey	3,478
27	Minnesota	3,476
28	Georgia	3,456
29	Nebraska	3,345
30	Nevada	3,322
31	Arizona	3,187
32	New Hampshire	3,103
33	North Carolina	2,970
34	Idaho	2,903
35	Pennsylvania	2,853
36	West Virginia	2,759
37	Florida	2,520
38	Missouri	2,288
39	Maine	2,161
40	Rhode Island	2,154
41	Virginia	1,939
42	Arkansas	1,910
43	Wyoming	1,877
44	New Mexico	1,741
45	Maryland	1,603
46	South Dakota	1,420
47	Colorado	1,371
48	Montana	1,309
49	Oklahoma	1,287
50	Hawaii	557
	District of Columbia	1,944

Source: CQ Press using data from U.S. Bureau of the Census
"State Trade Data" (http://www.census.gov/foreign-trade/statistics/state/)
*Based on the state from which the merchandise starts its journey to the port of export; that is, the data reflect the transportation origin of exports. National figure does not include population or exports from Puerto Rico, Virgin Islands, and exports with unidentified origin.

State Imports in 2016

National Total = $2,187,804,880,000*

ALPHA ORDER

ALPHA ORDER

RANK	STATE	IMPORTS	% of USA	RANK	STATE	IMPORTS	% of USA
23	Alabama	$22,132,100,000	1.0%	1	California	$410,182,750,000	18.7%
48	Alaska	2,094,150,000	0.1%	2	Texas	229,294,260,000	10.5%
25	Arizona	19,654,490,000	0.9%	3	Michigan	134,946,980,000	6.2%
37	Arkansas	7,828,870,000	0.4%	4	New York	130,072,200,000	5.9%
1	California	410,182,750,000	18.7%	5	Illinois	121,529,420,000	5.6%
30	Colorado	12,225,470,000	0.6%	6	New Jersey	108,133,130,000	4.9%
24	Connecticut	21,319,130,000	1.0%	7	Georgia	86,185,410,000	3.9%
38	Delaware	7,556,380,000	0.3%	8	Pennsylvania	77,163,820,000	3.5%
10	Florida	73,625,970,000	3.4%	9	Tennessee	75,285,040,000	3.4%
7	Georgia	86,185,410,000	3.9%	10	Florida	73,625,970,000	3.4%
45	Hawaii	2,930,990,000	0.1%	11	Ohio	64,263,910,000	2.9%
39	Idaho	4,493,920,000	0.2%	12	Indiana	49,536,710,000	2.3%
5	Illinois	121,529,420,000	5.6%	13	North Carolina	47,041,180,000	2.2%
12	Indiana	49,536,710,000	2.3%	14	Washington	46,997,330,000	2.1%
36	Iowa	8,233,910,000	0.4%	15	Kentucky	40,001,590,000	1.8%
31	Kansas	11,157,310,000	0.5%	16	South Carolina	36,107,340,000	1.7%
15	Kentucky	40,001,590,000	1.8%	17	Massachusetts	33,801,450,000	1.5%
18	Louisiana	32,423,700,000	1.5%	18	Louisiana	32,423,700,000	1.5%
43	Maine	3,353,810,000	0.2%	19	Maryland	30,687,940,000	1.4%
19	Maryland	30,687,940,000	1.4%	20	Minnesota	27,023,840,000	1.2%
17	Massachusetts	33,801,450,000	1.5%	21	Virginia	25,872,700,000	1.2%
3	Michigan	134,946,980,000	6.2%	22	Wisconsin	22,429,040,000	1.0%
20	Minnesota	27,023,840,000	1.2%	23	Alabama	22,132,100,000	1.0%
28	Mississippi	13,970,940,000	0.6%	24	Connecticut	21,319,130,000	1.0%
27	Missouri	17,205,940,000	0.8%	25	Arizona	19,654,490,000	0.9%
42	Montana	3,489,590,000	0.2%	26	Oregon	17,596,280,000	0.8%
41	Nebraska	3,556,500,000	0.2%	27	Missouri	17,205,940,000	0.8%
32	Nevada	10,559,950,000	0.5%	28	Mississippi	13,970,940,000	0.6%
34	New Hampshire	8,611,270,000	0.4%	29	Utah	12,989,240,000	0.6%
6	New Jersey	108,133,130,000	4.9%	30	Colorado	12,225,470,000	0.6%
47	New Mexico	2,290,270,000	0.1%	31	Kansas	11,157,310,000	0.5%
4	New York	130,072,200,000	5.9%	32	Nevada	10,559,950,000	0.5%
13	North Carolina	47,041,180,000	2.2%	33	Rhode Island	8,748,390,000	0.4%
46	North Dakota	2,563,750,000	0.1%	34	New Hampshire	8,611,270,000	0.4%
11	Ohio	64,263,910,000	2.9%	35	Oklahoma	8,487,350,000	0.4%
35	Oklahoma	8,487,350,000	0.4%	36	Iowa	8,233,910,000	0.4%
26	Oregon	17,596,280,000	0.8%	37	Arkansas	7,828,870,000	0.4%
8	Pennsylvania	77,163,820,000	3.5%	38	Delaware	7,556,380,000	0.3%
33	Rhode Island	8,748,390,000	0.4%	39	Idaho	4,493,920,000	0.2%
16	South Carolina	36,107,340,000	1.7%	40	Vermont	3,704,330,000	0.2%
49	South Dakota	1,031,070,000	0.0%	41	Nebraska	3,556,500,000	0.2%
9	Tennessee	75,285,040,000	3.4%	42	Montana	3,489,590,000	0.2%
2	Texas	229,294,260,000	10.5%	43	Maine	3,353,810,000	0.2%
29	Utah	12,989,240,000	0.6%	44	West Virginia	3,331,450,000	0.2%
40	Vermont	3,704,330,000	0.2%	45	Hawaii	2,930,990,000	0.1%
21	Virginia	25,872,700,000	1.2%	46	North Dakota	2,563,750,000	0.1%
14	Washington	46,997,330,000	2.1%	47	New Mexico	2,290,270,000	0.1%
44	West Virginia	3,331,450,000	0.2%	48	Alaska	2,094,150,000	0.1%
22	Wisconsin	22,429,040,000	1.0%	49	South Dakota	1,031,070,000	0.0%
50	Wyoming	876,560,000	0.0%	50	Wyoming	876,560,000	0.0%
					District of Columbia	486,780,000	0.0%

Source: U.S. Bureau of the Census
"State Trade Data" (http://www.census.gov/foreign-trade/statistics/state/)
*Based on where the merchandise is destined, as known at the time of entry summary filing. If the contents of the shipment are destined to more than one state, territory, or possession, or if the entry summary represents a consolidated shipment, the state of destination is that with the greatest aggregate value.

Per Capita State Imports in 2016

National Per Capita = $6,633*

ALPHA ORDER

RANK	STATE	PER CAPITA
26	Alabama	$4,553
38	Alaska	2,824
36	Arizona	2,845
41	Arkansas	2,620
4	California	10,438
43	Colorado	2,211
19	Connecticut	5,942
10	Delaware	7,932
32	Florida	3,564
7	Georgia	8,356
45	Hawaii	2,052
39	Idaho	2,675
5	Illinois	9,468
11	Indiana	7,467
40	Iowa	2,630
30	Kansas	3,837
6	Kentucky	9,017
13	Louisiana	6,919
42	Maine	2,521
21	Maryland	5,094
22	Massachusetts	4,954
1	Michigan	13,585
23	Minnesota	4,891
24	Mississippi	4,680
37	Missouri	2,825
34	Montana	3,360
46	Nebraska	1,864
31	Nevada	3,593
16	New Hampshire	6,450
2	New Jersey	12,044
50	New Mexico	1,098
14	New York	6,557
25	North Carolina	4,632
33	North Dakota	3,393
20	Ohio	5,529
44	Oklahoma	2,164
27	Oregon	4,306
17	Pennsylvania	6,035
8	Rhode Island	8,272
12	South Carolina	7,280
49	South Dakota	1,197
3	Tennessee	11,322
9	Texas	8,217
28	Utah	4,267
18	Vermont	5,943
35	Virginia	3,075
15	Washington	6,455
47	West Virginia	1,822
29	Wisconsin	3,885
48	Wyoming	1,499

RANK ORDER

RANK	STATE	PER CAPITA
1	Michigan	$13,585
2	New Jersey	12,044
3	Tennessee	11,322
4	California	10,438
5	Illinois	9,468
6	Kentucky	9,017
7	Georgia	8,356
8	Rhode Island	8,272
9	Texas	8,217
10	Delaware	7,932
11	Indiana	7,467
12	South Carolina	7,280
13	Louisiana	6,919
14	New York	6,557
15	Washington	6,455
16	New Hampshire	6,450
17	Pennsylvania	6,035
18	Vermont	5,943
19	Connecticut	5,942
20	Ohio	5,529
21	Maryland	5,094
22	Massachusetts	4,954
23	Minnesota	4,891
24	Mississippi	4,680
25	North Carolina	4,632
26	Alabama	4,553
27	Oregon	4,306
28	Utah	4,267
29	Wisconsin	3,885
30	Kansas	3,837
31	Nevada	3,593
32	Florida	3,564
33	North Dakota	3,393
34	Montana	3,360
35	Virginia	3,075
36	Arizona	2,845
37	Missouri	2,825
38	Alaska	2,824
39	Idaho	2,675
40	Iowa	2,630
41	Arkansas	2,620
42	Maine	2,521
43	Colorado	2,211
44	Oklahoma	2,164
45	Hawaii	2,052
46	Nebraska	1,864
47	West Virginia	1,822
48	Wyoming	1,499
49	South Dakota	1,197
50	New Mexico	1,098
	District of Columbia	711

Source: CQ Press using data from U.S. Bureau of the Census
    "State Trade Data" (http://www.census.gov/foreign-trade/statistics/state/)
*Based on where the merchandise is destined, as known at the time of entry summary filing. If the contents of the shipment are destined to more than one state, territory, or possession, or if the entry summary represents a consolidated shipment, the state of destination is that with the greatest aggregate value. National figure does not include population or imports from Puerto Rico, Virgin Islands, and imports with unidentified origin.

Personal Income in 2016

National Total = $15,912,777,000,000*

ALPHA ORDER

RANK	STATE	INCOME	% of USA
26	Alabama	$189,161,974,000	1.2%
48	Alaska	41,283,275,000	0.3%
20	Arizona	280,120,037,000	1.8%
34	Arkansas	118,697,988,000	0.7%
1	California	2,212,691,221,000	13.9%
17	Colorado	288,103,337,000	1.8%
23	Connecticut	247,886,635,000	1.6%
44	Delaware	45,574,410,000	0.3%
4	Florida	947,207,472,000	6.0%
12	Georgia	434,677,178,000	2.7%
39	Hawaii	71,946,077,000	0.5%
41	Idaho	66,433,410,000	0.4%
5	Illinois	663,338,023,000	4.2%
19	Indiana	285,863,662,000	1.8%
30	Iowa	144,195,709,000	0.9%
31	Kansas	137,305,437,000	0.9%
28	Kentucky	172,713,808,000	1.1%
24	Louisiana	198,025,102,000	1.2%
42	Maine	58,655,433,000	0.4%
15	Maryland	349,266,576,000	2.2%
11	Massachusetts	437,551,353,000	2.7%
10	Michigan	439,361,467,000	2.8%
18	Minnesota	287,249,809,000	1.8%
35	Mississippi	106,052,785,000	0.7%
22	Missouri	261,547,770,000	1.6%
45	Montana	44,772,870,000	0.3%
36	Nebraska	95,411,344,000	0.6%
32	Nevada	128,089,633,000	0.8%
38	New Hampshire	74,687,026,000	0.5%
7	New Jersey	549,835,795,000	3.5%
37	New Mexico	80,064,958,000	0.5%
3	New York	1,176,080,244,000	7.4%
13	North Carolina	428,638,808,000	2.7%
46	North Dakota	41,404,978,000	0.3%
8	Ohio	517,918,190,000	3.3%
29	Oklahoma	167,502,814,000	1.1%
27	Oregon	185,839,645,000	1.2%
6	Pennsylvania	648,694,472,000	4.1%
43	Rhode Island	53,272,444,000	0.3%
25	South Carolina	196,049,325,000	1.2%
47	South Dakota	41,398,241,000	0.3%
16	Tennessee	288,169,968,000	1.8%
2	Texas	1,289,310,024,000	8.1%
33	Utah	124,871,199,000	0.8%
50	Vermont	31,219,885,000	0.2%
9	Virginia	445,461,657,000	2.8%
14	Washington	397,772,297,000	2.5%
40	West Virginia	67,061,987,000	0.4%
21	Wisconsin	270,225,982,000	1.7%
49	Wyoming	32,270,465,000	0.2%

RANK ORDER

RANK	STATE	INCOME	% of USA
1	California	$2,212,691,221,000	13.9%
2	Texas	1,289,310,024,000	8.1%
3	New York	1,176,080,244,000	7.4%
4	Florida	947,207,472,000	6.0%
5	Illinois	663,338,023,000	4.2%
6	Pennsylvania	648,694,472,000	4.1%
7	New Jersey	549,835,795,000	3.5%
8	Ohio	517,918,190,000	3.3%
9	Virginia	445,461,657,000	2.8%
10	Michigan	439,361,467,000	2.8%
11	Massachusetts	437,551,353,000	2.7%
12	Georgia	434,677,178,000	2.7%
13	North Carolina	428,638,808,000	2.7%
14	Washington	397,772,297,000	2.5%
15	Maryland	349,266,576,000	2.2%
16	Tennessee	288,169,968,000	1.8%
17	Colorado	288,103,337,000	1.8%
18	Minnesota	287,249,809,000	1.8%
19	Indiana	285,863,662,000	1.8%
20	Arizona	280,120,037,000	1.8%
21	Wisconsin	270,225,982,000	1.7%
22	Missouri	261,547,770,000	1.6%
23	Connecticut	247,886,635,000	1.6%
24	Louisiana	198,025,102,000	1.2%
25	South Carolina	196,049,325,000	1.2%
26	Alabama	189,161,974,000	1.2%
27	Oregon	185,839,645,000	1.2%
28	Kentucky	172,713,808,000	1.1%
29	Oklahoma	167,502,814,000	1.1%
30	Iowa	144,195,709,000	0.9%
31	Kansas	137,305,437,000	0.9%
32	Nevada	128,089,633,000	0.8%
33	Utah	124,871,199,000	0.8%
34	Arkansas	118,697,988,000	0.7%
35	Mississippi	106,052,785,000	0.7%
36	Nebraska	95,411,344,000	0.6%
37	New Mexico	80,064,958,000	0.5%
38	New Hampshire	74,687,026,000	0.5%
39	Hawaii	71,946,077,000	0.5%
40	West Virginia	67,061,987,000	0.4%
41	Idaho	66,433,410,000	0.4%
42	Maine	58,655,433,000	0.4%
43	Rhode Island	53,272,444,000	0.3%
44	Delaware	45,574,410,000	0.3%
45	Montana	44,772,870,000	0.3%
46	North Dakota	41,404,978,000	0.3%
47	South Dakota	41,398,241,000	0.3%
48	Alaska	41,283,275,000	0.3%
49	Wyoming	32,270,465,000	0.2%
50	Vermont	31,219,885,000	0.2%
	District of Columbia	51,842,801,000	0.3%

Source: U.S. Department of Commerce, Bureau of Economic Analysis
"Annual State Personal Income" (http://www.bea.gov/iTable/index_regional.cfm)
*The national total shown here is the sum of the state estimates. It differs from the national income and product accounts
(NIPA) estimate of personal income because it omits the earnings of federal civilian and military personnel stationed abroad and
of U.S. residents employed abroad temporarily by private U.S. firms.

Percent Change in Personal Income: 2015 to 2016

National Percent Change = 2.3% Increase*

ALPHA ORDER

RANK	STATE	PERCENT CHANGE
26	Alabama	2.0
46	Alaska	(1.0)
7	Arizona	3.6
23	Arkansas	2.1
5	California	3.7
29	Colorado	1.9
40	Connecticut	1.2
19	Delaware	2.6
14	Florida	3.0
4	Georgia	3.9
10	Hawaii	3.3
9	Idaho	3.5
34	Illinois	1.6
10	Indiana	3.3
42	Iowa	1.0
43	Kansas	0.5
37	Kentucky	1.4
46	Louisiana	(1.0)
14	Maine	3.0
7	Maryland	3.6
19	Massachusetts	2.6
18	Michigan	2.8
21	Minnesota	2.4
23	Mississippi	2.1
34	Missouri	1.6
23	Montana	2.1
34	Nebraska	1.6
14	Nevada	3.0
17	New Hampshire	2.9
22	New Jersey	2.2
37	New Mexico	1.4
33	New York	1.7
13	North Carolina	3.2
48	North Dakota	(1.4)
29	Ohio	1.9
50	Oklahoma	(2.5)
3	Oregon	4.2
32	Pennsylvania	1.8
37	Rhode Island	1.4
10	South Carolina	3.3
40	South Dakota	1.2
5	Tennessee	3.7
44	Texas	0.4
1	Utah	5.2
26	Vermont	2.0
26	Virginia	2.0
2	Washington	4.7
45	West Virginia	(0.3)
29	Wisconsin	1.9
49	Wyoming	(2.2)

RANK ORDER

RANK	STATE	PERCENT CHANGE
1	Utah	5.2
2	Washington	4.7
3	Oregon	4.2
4	Georgia	3.9
5	California	3.7
5	Tennessee	3.7
7	Arizona	3.6
7	Maryland	3.6
9	Idaho	3.5
10	Hawaii	3.3
10	Indiana	3.3
10	South Carolina	3.3
13	North Carolina	3.2
14	Florida	3.0
14	Maine	3.0
14	Nevada	3.0
17	New Hampshire	2.9
18	Michigan	2.8
19	Delaware	2.6
19	Massachusetts	2.6
21	Minnesota	2.4
22	New Jersey	2.2
23	Arkansas	2.1
23	Mississippi	2.1
23	Montana	2.1
26	Alabama	2.0
26	Vermont	2.0
26	Virginia	2.0
29	Colorado	1.9
29	Ohio	1.9
29	Wisconsin	1.9
32	Pennsylvania	1.8
33	New York	1.7
34	Illinois	1.6
34	Missouri	1.6
34	Nebraska	1.6
37	Kentucky	1.4
37	New Mexico	1.4
37	Rhode Island	1.4
40	Connecticut	1.2
40	South Dakota	1.2
42	Iowa	1.0
43	Kansas	0.5
44	Texas	0.4
45	West Virginia	(0.3)
46	Alaska	(1.0)
46	Louisiana	(1.0)
48	North Dakota	(1.4)
49	Wyoming	(2.2)
50	Oklahoma	(2.5)

District of Columbia		4.4

Source: U.S. Department of Commerce, Bureau of Economic Analysis
   "Annual State Personal Income" (http://www.bea.gov/iTable/index_regional.cfm)
*Based on revised 2015 figures.

Per Capita Personal Income in 2016

National Per Capita = $49,246*

ALPHA ORDER				RANK ORDER		
RANK	**STATE**	**PER CAPITA**		**RANK**	**STATE**	**PER CAPITA**
47	Alabama	$38,896		1	Connecticut	$69,311
8	Alaska	55,646		2	Massachusetts	64,235
42	Arizona	40,415		3	New Jersey	61,472
43	Arkansas	39,722		4	New York	59,563
6	California	56,374		5	Maryland	58,052
14	Colorado	51,999		6	California	56,374
1	Connecticut	69,311		7	New Hampshire	55,954
21	Delaware	47,869		8	Alaska	55,646
27	Florida	45,953		9	Wyoming	55,116
40	Georgia	42,159		10	North Dakota	54,627
18	Hawaii	50,363		11	Washington	54,579
45	Idaho	39,470		12	Virginia	52,957
15	Illinois	51,817		13	Minnesota	52,038
34	Indiana	43,097		14	Colorado	51,999
26	Iowa	46,000		15	Illinois	51,817
23	Kansas	47,228		16	Pennsylvania	50,742
46	Kentucky	38,926		17	Rhode Island	50,427
38	Louisiana	42,298		18	Hawaii	50,363
31	Maine	44,053		19	Nebraska	50,029
5	Maryland	58,052		20	Vermont	49,984
2	Massachusetts	64,235		21	Delaware	47,869
30	Michigan	44,253		22	South Dakota	47,834
13	Minnesota	52,038		23	Kansas	47,228
50	Mississippi	35,484		24	Wisconsin	46,762
36	Missouri	42,926		25	Texas	46,274
35	Montana	42,947		26	Iowa	46,000
19	Nebraska	50,029		27	Florida	45,953
32	Nevada	43,567		28	Oregon	45,399
7	New Hampshire	55,954		29	Ohio	44,593
3	New Jersey	61,472		30	Michigan	44,253
48	New Mexico	38,474		31	Maine	44,053
4	New York	59,563		32	Nevada	43,567
39	North Carolina	42,244		33	Tennessee	43,326
10	North Dakota	54,627		34	Indiana	43,097
29	Ohio	44,593		35	Montana	42,947
37	Oklahoma	42,692		36	Missouri	42,926
28	Oregon	45,399		37	Oklahoma	42,692
16	Pennsylvania	50,742		38	Louisiana	42,298
17	Rhode Island	50,427		39	North Carolina	42,244
44	South Carolina	39,517		40	Georgia	42,159
22	South Dakota	47,834		41	Utah	40,925
33	Tennessee	43,326		42	Arizona	40,415
25	Texas	46,274		43	Arkansas	39,722
41	Utah	40,925		44	South Carolina	39,517
20	Vermont	49,984		45	Idaho	39,470
12	Virginia	52,957		46	Kentucky	38,926
11	Washington	54,579		47	Alabama	38,896
49	West Virginia	36,624		48	New Mexico	38,474
24	Wisconsin	46,762		49	West Virginia	36,624
9	Wyoming	55,116		50	Mississippi	35,484
					District of Columbia	76,108

Source: U.S. Department of Commerce, Bureau of Economic Analysis
"Annual State Personal Income" (http://www.bea.gov/iTable/index_regional.cfm)
*The national figure is based on the sum of the state estimates. It differs from the national income and product accounts
(NIPA) estimate of personal income because it omits the earnings of federal civilian and military personnel stationed abroad and
of U.S. residents employed abroad temporarily by private U.S. firms.

Percent Change in Per Capita Personal Income: 2015 to 2016

National Percent Change = 1.6% Increase*

ALPHA ORDER				RANK ORDER		
RANK	STATE	PERCENT CHANGE		RANK	STATE	PERCENT CHANGE
22	Alabama	1.8		1	Maryland	3.2
47	Alaska	(1.6)		2	Hawaii	3.1
18	Arizona	2.0		2	Utah	3.1
22	Arkansas	1.8		4	California	3.0
4	California	3.0		4	Indiana	3.0
43	Colorado	0.2		6	Maine	2.9
31	Connecticut	1.4		6	Washington	2.9
26	Delaware	1.7		8	Georgia	2.8
36	Florida	1.1		8	Tennessee	2.8
8	Georgia	2.8		10	Michigan	2.7
2	Hawaii	3.1		11	New Hampshire	2.6
29	Idaho	1.6		12	Oregon	2.4
19	Illinois	1.9		13	Vermont	2.3
4	Indiana	3.0		14	Massachusetts	2.2
40	Iowa	0.6		15	Mississippi	2.1
41	Kansas	0.5		15	New Jersey	2.1
35	Kentucky	1.2		15	North Carolina	2.1
46	Louisiana	(1.3)		18	Arizona	2.0
6	Maine	2.9		19	Illinois	1.9
1	Maryland	3.2		19	Pennsylvania	1.9
14	Massachusetts	2.2		19	South Carolina	1.9
10	Michigan	2.7		22	Alabama	1.8
26	Minnesota	1.7		22	Arkansas	1.8
15	Mississippi	2.1		22	New York	1.8
32	Missouri	1.3		22	Ohio	1.8
36	Montana	1.1		26	Delaware	1.7
39	Nebraska	0.9		26	Minnesota	1.7
38	Nevada	1.0		26	Wisconsin	1.7
11	New Hampshire	2.6		29	Idaho	1.6
15	New Jersey	2.1		30	Virginia	1.5
32	New Mexico	1.3		31	Connecticut	1.4
22	New York	1.8		32	Missouri	1.3
15	North Carolina	2.1		32	New Mexico	1.3
47	North Dakota	(1.6)		32	Rhode Island	1.3
22	Ohio	1.8		35	Kentucky	1.2
50	Oklahoma	(2.9)		36	Florida	1.1
12	Oregon	2.4		36	Montana	1.1
19	Pennsylvania	1.9		38	Nevada	1.0
32	Rhode Island	1.3		39	Nebraska	0.9
19	South Carolina	1.9		40	Iowa	0.6
42	South Dakota	0.4		41	Kansas	0.5
8	Tennessee	2.8		42	South Dakota	0.4
45	Texas	(1.2)		43	Colorado	0.2
2	Utah	3.1		43	West Virginia	0.2
13	Vermont	2.3		45	Texas	(1.2)
30	Virginia	1.5		46	Louisiana	(1.3)
6	Washington	2.9		47	Alaska	(1.6)
43	West Virginia	0.2		47	North Dakota	(1.6)
26	Wisconsin	1.7		49	Wyoming	(2.1)
49	Wyoming	(2.1)		50	Oklahoma	(2.9)
					District of Columbia	2.7

Source: U.S. Department of Commerce, Bureau of Economic Analysis
"Annual State Personal Income" (http://www.bea.gov/iTable/index_regional.cfm)
*Based on revised 2015 figures.

Disposable Personal Income in 2016

National Total = $13,954,415,000,000*

ALPHA ORDER

RANK	STATE	INCOME	% of USA
26	Alabama	$170,965,496,000	1.2%
46	Alaska	37,648,880,000	0.3%
18	Arizona	251,655,286,000	1.8%
34	Arkansas	107,118,046,000	0.8%
1	California	1,894,449,472,000	13.6%
19	Colorado	251,637,921,000	1.8%
23	Connecticut	209,097,152,000	1.5%
44	Delaware	40,460,817,000	0.3%
4	Florida	842,097,112,000	6.0%
11	Georgia	385,470,008,000	2.8%
39	Hawaii	64,180,141,000	0.5%
41	Idaho	59,733,886,000	0.4%
5	Illinois	578,257,534,000	4.1%
17	Indiana	256,164,926,000	1.8%
30	Iowa	128,684,139,000	0.9%
31	Kansas	123,207,014,000	0.9%
28	Kentucky	153,968,785,000	1.1%
24	Louisiana	180,234,202,000	1.3%
42	Maine	52,520,278,000	0.4%
15	Maryland	302,028,646,000	2.2%
13	Massachusetts	369,129,739,000	2.6%
9	Michigan	389,097,732,000	2.8%
20	Minnesota	246,993,263,000	1.8%
35	Mississippi	97,226,118,000	0.7%
22	Missouri	232,029,251,000	1.7%
45	Montana	39,804,055,000	0.3%
36	Nebraska	85,482,066,000	0.6%
32	Nevada	114,667,821,000	0.8%
38	New Hampshire	66,842,270,000	0.5%
7	New Jersey	474,050,961,000	3.4%
37	New Mexico	72,893,314,000	0.5%
3	New York	976,963,215,000	7.0%
12	North Carolina	379,644,174,000	2.7%
48	North Dakota	37,448,437,000	0.3%
8	Ohio	460,684,349,000	3.3%
29	Oklahoma	151,438,264,000	1.1%
27	Oregon	161,420,569,000	1.2%
6	Pennsylvania	571,407,019,000	4.1%
43	Rhode Island	47,181,783,000	0.3%
25	South Carolina	176,201,139,000	1.3%
47	South Dakota	37,574,050,000	0.3%
16	Tennessee	263,572,018,000	1.9%
2	Texas	1,159,251,326,000	8.3%
33	Utah	110,866,026,000	0.8%
50	Vermont	27,987,100,000	0.2%
10	Virginia	388,547,830,000	2.8%
14	Washington	354,418,094,000	2.5%
40	West Virginia	60,587,029,000	0.4%
21	Wisconsin	238,433,014,000	1.7%
49	Wyoming	29,008,573,000	0.2%

RANK ORDER

RANK	STATE	INCOME	% of USA
1	California	$1,894,449,472,000	13.6%
2	Texas	1,159,251,326,000	8.3%
3	New York	976,963,215,000	7.0%
4	Florida	842,097,112,000	6.0%
5	Illinois	578,257,534,000	4.1%
6	Pennsylvania	571,407,019,000	4.1%
7	New Jersey	474,050,961,000	3.4%
8	Ohio	460,684,349,000	3.3%
9	Michigan	389,097,732,000	2.8%
10	Virginia	388,547,830,000	2.8%
11	Georgia	385,470,008,000	2.8%
12	North Carolina	379,644,174,000	2.7%
13	Massachusetts	369,129,739,000	2.6%
14	Washington	354,418,094,000	2.5%
15	Maryland	302,028,646,000	2.2%
16	Tennessee	263,572,018,000	1.9%
17	Indiana	256,164,926,000	1.8%
18	Arizona	251,655,286,000	1.8%
19	Colorado	251,637,921,000	1.8%
20	Minnesota	246,993,263,000	1.8%
21	Wisconsin	238,433,014,000	1.7%
22	Missouri	232,029,251,000	1.7%
23	Connecticut	209,097,152,000	1.5%
24	Louisiana	180,234,202,000	1.3%
25	South Carolina	176,201,139,000	1.3%
26	Alabama	170,965,496,000	1.2%
27	Oregon	161,420,569,000	1.2%
28	Kentucky	153,968,785,000	1.1%
29	Oklahoma	151,438,264,000	1.1%
30	Iowa	128,684,139,000	0.9%
31	Kansas	123,207,014,000	0.9%
32	Nevada	114,667,821,000	0.8%
33	Utah	110,866,026,000	0.8%
34	Arkansas	107,118,046,000	0.8%
35	Mississippi	97,226,118,000	0.7%
36	Nebraska	85,482,066,000	0.6%
37	New Mexico	72,893,314,000	0.5%
38	New Hampshire	66,842,270,000	0.5%
39	Hawaii	64,180,141,000	0.5%
40	West Virginia	60,587,029,000	0.4%
41	Idaho	59,733,886,000	0.4%
42	Maine	52,520,278,000	0.4%
43	Rhode Island	47,181,783,000	0.3%
44	Delaware	40,460,817,000	0.3%
45	Montana	39,804,055,000	0.3%
46	Alaska	37,648,880,000	0.3%
47	South Dakota	37,574,050,000	0.3%
48	North Dakota	37,448,437,000	0.3%
49	Wyoming	29,008,573,000	0.2%
50	Vermont	27,987,100,000	0.2%
	District of Columbia	43,984,660,000	0.3%

Source: U.S. Department of Commerce, Bureau of Economic Analysis
  "Annual State Personal Income" (http://www.bea.gov/iTable/index_regional.cfm)
*Disposable personal income is personal income less personal tax and nontax payments. It is the income available to persons for spending or saving.

Per Capita Disposable Personal Income in 2016

National Per Capita = $43,185*

ALPHA ORDER

RANK	STATE	PER CAPITA
46	Alabama	$35,154
4	Alaska	50,747
42	Arizona	36,308
43	Arkansas	35,846
11	California	48,266
13	Colorado	45,418
1	Connecticut	58,465
22	Delaware	42,498
27	Florida	40,854
40	Georgia	37,387
15	Hawaii	44,927
45	Idaho	35,490
14	Illinois	45,171
34	Indiana	38,619
26	Iowa	41,052
23	Kansas	42,379
48	Kentucky	34,701
36	Louisiana	38,498
30	Maine	39,445
5	Maryland	50,200
2	Massachusetts	54,190
32	Michigan	39,191
18	Minnesota	44,746
50	Mississippi	32,531
38	Missouri	38,081
37	Montana	38,181
16	Nebraska	44,823
33	Nevada	39,002
6	New Hampshire	50,077
3	New Jersey	52,999
47	New Mexico	35,028
8	New York	49,478
39	North Carolina	37,415
9	North Dakota	49,407
28	Ohio	39,665
35	Oklahoma	38,597
31	Oregon	39,434
19	Pennsylvania	44,696
20	Rhode Island	44,662
44	South Carolina	35,516
21	South Dakota	43,415
29	Tennessee	39,628
24	Texas	41,606
41	Utah	36,335
17	Vermont	44,808
12	Virginia	46,191
10	Washington	48,630
49	West Virginia	33,088
25	Wisconsin	41,261
7	Wyoming	49,545

RANK ORDER

RANK	STATE	PER CAPITA
1	Connecticut	$58,465
2	Massachusetts	54,190
3	New Jersey	52,999
4	Alaska	50,747
5	Maryland	50,200
6	New Hampshire	50,077
7	Wyoming	49,545
8	New York	49,478
9	North Dakota	49,407
10	Washington	48,630
11	California	48,266
12	Virginia	46,191
13	Colorado	45,418
14	Illinois	45,171
15	Hawaii	44,927
16	Nebraska	44,823
17	Vermont	44,808
18	Minnesota	44,746
19	Pennsylvania	44,696
20	Rhode Island	44,662
21	South Dakota	43,415
22	Delaware	42,498
23	Kansas	42,379
24	Texas	41,606
25	Wisconsin	41,261
26	Iowa	41,052
27	Florida	40,854
28	Ohio	39,665
29	Tennessee	39,628
30	Maine	39,445
31	Oregon	39,434
32	Michigan	39,191
33	Nevada	39,002
34	Indiana	38,619
35	Oklahoma	38,597
36	Louisiana	38,498
37	Montana	38,181
38	Missouri	38,081
39	North Carolina	37,415
40	Georgia	37,387
41	Utah	36,335
42	Arizona	36,308
43	Arkansas	35,846
44	South Carolina	35,516
45	Idaho	35,490
46	Alabama	35,154
47	New Mexico	35,028
48	Kentucky	34,701
49	West Virginia	33,088
50	Mississippi	32,531
	District of Columbia	64,572

Source: U.S. Department of Commerce, Bureau of Economic Analysis
"Annual State Personal Income" (http://www.bea.gov/iTable/index_regional.cfm)
*Disposable personal income is personal income less personal tax and nontax payments. It is the income available to persons for spending or saving.

Median Household Income in 2016

National Median = $56,889*

ALPHA ORDER				RANK ORDER		
RANK	STATE	INCOME		RANK	STATE	INCOME
45	Alabama	$45,051		1	New Hampshire	$75,767
4	Alaska	73,449		2	Maryland	75,167
33	Arizona	53,314		3	Connecticut	73,621
46	Arkansas	44,929		4	Alaska	73,449
13	California	64,133		5	Hawaii	69,889
9	Colorado	66,595		6	Minnesota	69,329
3	Connecticut	73,621		7	Massachusetts	68,336
24	Delaware	58,283		8	New Jersey	67,944
40	Florida	49,132		9	Colorado	66,595
37	Georgia	51,725		10	Utah	66,278
5	Hawaii	69,889		11	Washington	66,095
31	Idaho	54,339		12	Virginia	65,261
19	Illinois	59,412		13	California	64,133
36	Indiana	52,486		14	Vermont	60,876
17	Iowa	59,775		15	Oregon	60,142
29	Kansas	55,517		16	North Dakota	59,964
48	Kentucky	43,889		17	Iowa	59,775
47	Louisiana	43,897		18	Nebraska	59,422
38	Maine	51,559		19	Illinois	59,412
2	Maryland	75,167		20	Pennsylvania	59,355
7	Massachusetts	68,336		21	Rhode Island	59,125
30	Michigan	54,901		22	Wyoming	58,661
6	Minnesota	69,329		23	New York	58,412
50	Mississippi	39,218		24	Delaware	58,283
26	Missouri	57,457		25	Wisconsin	58,274
32	Montana	53,642		26	Missouri	57,457
18	Nebraska	59,422		27	Texas	56,650
34	Nevada	52,887		28	South Dakota	55,665
1	New Hampshire	75,767		29	Kansas	55,517
8	New Jersey	67,944		30	Michigan	54,901
44	New Mexico	47,157		31	Idaho	54,339
23	New York	58,412		32	Montana	53,642
39	North Carolina	50,878		33	Arizona	53,314
16	North Dakota	59,964		34	Nevada	52,887
35	Ohio	52,763		35	Ohio	52,763
42	Oklahoma	48,822		36	Indiana	52,486
15	Oregon	60,142		37	Georgia	51,725
20	Pennsylvania	59,355		38	Maine	51,559
21	Rhode Island	59,125		39	North Carolina	50,878
41	South Carolina	48,944		40	Florida	49,132
28	South Dakota	55,665		41	South Carolina	48,944
43	Tennessee	47,864		42	Oklahoma	48,822
27	Texas	56,650		43	Tennessee	47,864
10	Utah	66,278		44	New Mexico	47,157
14	Vermont	60,876		45	Alabama	45,051
12	Virginia	65,261		46	Arkansas	44,929
11	Washington	66,095		47	Louisiana	43,897
49	West Virginia	42,605		48	Kentucky	43,889
25	Wisconsin	58,274		49	West Virginia	42,605
22	Wyoming	58,661		50	Mississippi	39,218
					District of Columbia	70,386

Source: U.S. Bureau of the Census
  "Historical Income Tables" (http://www.census.gov/topics/income-poverty/income/data/tables.html)
*This is a 3-year-average of inflation-adjusted single-year medians for the years 2014 through 2016.

Regional Price Parities in 2015

National Index = 100.0*

ALPHA ORDER

RANK	STATE	RATIO
49	Alabama	86.8
8	Alaska	105.6
25	Arizona	96.2
48	Arkansas	87.4
3	California	113.4
11	Colorado	103.2
6	Connecticut	108.7
14	Delaware	100.4
16	Florida	99.5
32	Georgia	92.6
1	Hawaii	118.8
30	Idaho	93.4
15	Illinois	99.7
35	Indiana	90.7
39	Iowa	90.3
38	Kansas	90.4
46	Kentucky	88.6
36	Louisiana	90.6
19	Maine	98.0
5	Maryland	109.6
7	Massachusetts	106.9
29	Michigan	93.5
22	Minnesota	97.4
50	Mississippi	86.2
43	Missouri	89.3
27	Montana	94.8
36	Nebraska	90.6
19	Nevada	98.0
9	New Hampshire	105.0
3	New Jersey	113.4
28	New Mexico	94.4
2	New York	115.3
34	North Carolina	91.2
33	North Dakota	92.3
44	Ohio	89.2
41	Oklahoma	89.9
17	Oregon	99.2
21	Pennsylvania	97.9
18	Rhode Island	98.7
39	South Carolina	90.3
47	South Dakota	88.2
41	Tennessee	89.9
24	Texas	96.8
23	Utah	97.0
13	Vermont	101.6
12	Virginia	102.5
10	Washington	104.8
45	West Virginia	88.9
31	Wisconsin	93.1
25	Wyoming	96.2

RANK ORDER

RANK	STATE	RATIO
1	Hawaii	118.8
2	New York	115.3
3	California	113.4
3	New Jersey	113.4
5	Maryland	109.6
6	Connecticut	108.7
7	Massachusetts	106.9
8	Alaska	105.6
9	New Hampshire	105.0
10	Washington	104.8
11	Colorado	103.2
12	Virginia	102.5
13	Vermont	101.6
14	Delaware	100.4
15	Illinois	99.7
16	Florida	99.5
17	Oregon	99.2
18	Rhode Island	98.7
19	Maine	98.0
19	Nevada	98.0
21	Pennsylvania	97.9
22	Minnesota	97.4
23	Utah	97.0
24	Texas	96.8
25	Arizona	96.2
25	Wyoming	96.2
27	Montana	94.8
28	New Mexico	94.4
29	Michigan	93.5
30	Idaho	93.4
31	Wisconsin	93.1
32	Georgia	92.6
33	North Dakota	92.3
34	North Carolina	91.2
35	Indiana	90.7
36	Louisiana	90.6
36	Nebraska	90.6
38	Kansas	90.4
39	Iowa	90.3
39	South Carolina	90.3
41	Oklahoma	89.9
41	Tennessee	89.9
43	Missouri	89.3
44	Ohio	89.2
45	West Virginia	88.9
46	Kentucky	88.6
47	South Dakota	88.2
48	Arkansas	87.4
49	Alabama	86.8
50	Mississippi	86.2

District of Columbia 117.0

Source: U.S. Department of Commerce, Bureau of Economic Analysis
"Annual State Personal Income" (http://www.bea.gov/iTable/index_regional.cfm)
*Regional Price Parities (RPPs) are regional price levels expressed as a percentage of the overall national price level for a given year. The price levels are determined by the average prices paid by consumers for the mix of goods and services consumed in each region. Taking the ratio of RPPs shows the difference in price levels across regions.

Real Personal Income in 2015

National Total = $14,201,214,855,000*

RANK	STATE	INCOME	% of USA		RANK	STATE	INCOME	% of USA
25	Alabama	$195,452,631,000	1.4%		1	California	$1,722,484,479,000	12.1%
48	Alaska	36,128,188,000	0.3%		2	Texas	1,214,289,983,000	8.6%
21	Arizona	256,979,514,000	1.8%		3	New York	917,151,194,000	6.5%
32	Arkansas	121,669,620,000	0.9%		4	Florida	845,853,489,000	6.0%
1	California	1,722,484,479,000	12.1%		5	Illinois	599,033,719,000	4.2%
22	Colorado	250,730,306,000	1.8%		6	Pennsylvania	595,297,259,000	4.2%
23	Connecticut	206,195,453,000	1.5%		7	Ohio	521,565,717,000	3.7%
47	Delaware	40,517,080,000	0.3%		8	New Jersey	434,172,511,000	3.1%
4	Florida	845,853,489,000	6.0%		9	Michigan	418,263,016,000	2.9%
11	Georgia	413,487,155,000	2.9%		10	North Carolina	416,783,294,000	2.9%
41	Hawaii	53,634,286,000	0.4%		11	Georgia	413,487,155,000	2.9%
40	Idaho	62,929,901,000	0.4%		12	Virginia	389,776,518,000	2.7%
5	Illinois	599,033,719,000	4.2%		13	Massachusetts	364,869,850,000	2.6%
17	Indiana	279,042,126,000	2.0%		14	Washington	331,734,311,000	2.3%
30	Iowa	144,733,243,000	1.0%		15	Tennessee	282,940,999,000	2.0%
31	Kansas	138,204,575,000	1.0%		16	Maryland	281,577,828,000	2.0%
27	Kentucky	175,847,875,000	1.2%		17	Indiana	279,042,126,000	2.0%
24	Louisiana	202,060,615,000	1.4%		18	Missouri	263,977,182,000	1.9%
42	Maine	53,175,179,000	0.4%		19	Minnesota	263,443,155,000	1.9%
16	Maryland	281,577,828,000	2.0%		20	Wisconsin	260,424,235,000	1.8%
13	Massachusetts	364,869,850,000	2.6%		21	Arizona	256,979,514,000	1.8%
9	Michigan	418,263,016,000	2.9%		22	Colorado	250,730,306,000	1.8%
19	Minnesota	263,443,155,000	1.9%		23	Connecticut	206,195,453,000	1.5%
35	Mississippi	110,274,651,000	0.8%		24	Louisiana	202,060,615,000	1.4%
18	Missouri	263,977,182,000	1.9%		25	Alabama	195,452,631,000	1.4%
45	Montana	42,299,488,000	0.3%		26	South Carolina	192,405,011,000	1.4%
36	Nebraska	94,791,230,000	0.7%		27	Kentucky	175,847,875,000	1.2%
33	Nevada	116,047,364,000	0.8%		28	Oklahoma	174,885,093,000	1.2%
39	New Hampshire	63,219,735,000	0.4%		29	Oregon	164,530,065,000	1.2%
8	New Jersey	434,172,511,000	3.1%		30	Iowa	144,733,243,000	1.0%
37	New Mexico	76,585,238,000	0.5%		31	Kansas	138,204,575,000	1.0%
3	New York	917,151,194,000	6.5%		32	Arkansas	121,669,620,000	0.9%
10	North Carolina	416,783,294,000	2.9%		33	Nevada	116,047,364,000	0.8%
46	North Dakota	41,623,729,000	0.3%		34	Utah	111,953,020,000	0.8%
7	Ohio	521,565,717,000	3.7%		35	Mississippi	110,274,651,000	0.8%
28	Oklahoma	174,885,093,000	1.2%		36	Nebraska	94,791,230,000	0.7%
29	Oregon	164,530,065,000	1.2%		37	New Mexico	76,585,238,000	0.5%
6	Pennsylvania	595,297,259,000	4.2%		38	West Virginia	69,264,332,000	0.5%
43	Rhode Island	48,683,143,000	0.3%		39	New Hampshire	63,219,735,000	0.4%
26	South Carolina	192,405,011,000	1.4%		40	Idaho	62,929,901,000	0.4%
44	South Dakota	42,435,269,000	0.3%		41	Hawaii	53,634,286,000	0.4%
15	Tennessee	282,940,999,000	2.0%		42	Maine	53,175,179,000	0.4%
2	Texas	1,214,289,983,000	8.6%		43	Rhode Island	48,683,143,000	0.3%
34	Utah	111,953,020,000	0.8%		44	South Dakota	42,435,269,000	0.3%
50	Vermont	27,559,789,000	0.2%		45	Montana	42,299,488,000	0.3%
12	Virginia	389,776,518,000	2.7%		46	North Dakota	41,623,729,000	0.3%
14	Washington	331,734,311,000	2.3%		47	Delaware	40,517,080,000	0.3%
38	West Virginia	69,264,332,000	0.5%		48	Alaska	36,128,188,000	0.3%
20	Wisconsin	260,424,235,000	1.8%		49	Wyoming	31,387,637,000	0.2%
49	Wyoming	31,387,637,000	0.2%		50	Vermont	27,559,789,000	0.2%
						District of Columbia	38,843,575,000	0.3%

ALPHA ORDER — RANK ORDER

Source: U.S. Department of Commerce, Bureau of Economic Analysis
"Annual State Personal Income" (http://www.bea.gov/iTable/index_regional.cfm)
*Real personal income is personal income at Regional Price Parities (RPPs) divided by the national Personal Consumption Expenditure price index (a measure of U.S. inflation). RPPs are regional price levels expressed as a percentage of the overall national price level for a given year. The price levels are determined by the average prices paid by consumers for the mix of goods and services consumed in each region. Taking the ratio of RPPs shows the difference in price levels across regions.

Percent Change in Real Personal Income: 2014 to 2015

National Percent Change = 4.7% Increase*

ALPHA ORDER

RANK	STATE	PERCENT CHANGE
26	Alabama	4.0
26	Alaska	4.0
14	Arizona	5.4
43	Arkansas	2.5
3	California	7.2
17	Colorado	4.8
44	Connecticut	2.1
6	Delaware	6.2
4	Florida	7.0
15	Georgia	5.1
19	Hawaii	4.6
8	Idaho	5.7
32	Illinois	3.6
30	Indiana	3.7
37	Iowa	3.4
46	Kansas	1.2
30	Kentucky	3.7
41	Louisiana	2.7
40	Maine	3.0
17	Maryland	4.8
6	Massachusetts	6.2
11	Michigan	5.5
22	Minnesota	4.3
45	Mississippi	1.3
38	Missouri	3.3
20	Montana	4.5
41	Nebraska	2.7
1	Nevada	7.5
23	New Hampshire	4.2
16	New Jersey	4.9
32	New Mexico	3.6
23	New York	4.2
8	North Carolina	5.7
50	North Dakota	(3.4)
32	Ohio	3.6
49	Oklahoma	(2.4)
2	Oregon	7.3
32	Pennsylvania	3.6
23	Rhode Island	4.2
8	South Carolina	5.7
28	South Dakota	3.8
11	Tennessee	5.5
38	Texas	3.3
4	Utah	7.0
32	Vermont	3.6
20	Virginia	4.5
11	Washington	5.5
47	West Virginia	1.0
28	Wisconsin	3.8
48	Wyoming	0.5

RANK ORDER

RANK	STATE	PERCENT CHANGE
1	Nevada	7.5
2	Oregon	7.3
3	California	7.2
4	Florida	7.0
4	Utah	7.0
6	Delaware	6.2
6	Massachusetts	6.2
8	Idaho	5.7
8	North Carolina	5.7
8	South Carolina	5.7
11	Michigan	5.5
11	Tennessee	5.5
11	Washington	5.5
14	Arizona	5.4
15	Georgia	5.1
16	New Jersey	4.9
17	Colorado	4.8
17	Maryland	4.8
19	Hawaii	4.6
20	Montana	4.5
20	Virginia	4.5
22	Minnesota	4.3
23	New Hampshire	4.2
23	New York	4.2
23	Rhode Island	4.2
26	Alabama	4.0
26	Alaska	4.0
28	South Dakota	3.8
28	Wisconsin	3.8
30	Indiana	3.7
30	Kentucky	3.7
32	Illinois	3.6
32	New Mexico	3.6
32	Ohio	3.6
32	Pennsylvania	3.6
32	Vermont	3.6
37	Iowa	3.4
38	Missouri	3.3
38	Texas	3.3
40	Maine	3.0
41	Louisiana	2.7
41	Nebraska	2.7
43	Arkansas	2.5
44	Connecticut	2.1
45	Mississippi	1.3
46	Kansas	1.2
47	West Virginia	1.0
48	Wyoming	0.5
49	Oklahoma	(2.4)
50	North Dakota	(3.4)

District of Columbia   8.2

Source: U.S. Department of Commerce, Bureau of Economic Analysis
"Annual State Personal Income" (http://www.bea.gov/iTable/index_regional.cfm)
*Real personal income is personal income at Regional Price Parities (RPPs) divided by the national Personal Consumption Expenditure price index (a measure of U.S. inflation). RPPs are regional price levels expressed as a percentage of the overall national price level for a given year. The price levels are determined by the average prices paid by consumers for the mix of goods and services consumed in each region. Taking the ratio of RPPs shows the difference in price levels across regions.

Per Capita Real Personal Income in 2015

National Per Capita = $44,255*

ALPHA ORDER

RANK	STATE	PER CAPITA
39	Alabama	$40,267
7	Alaska	48,973
45	Arizona	37,694
37	Arkansas	40,858
25	California	44,173
20	Colorado	46,016
1	Connecticut	57,520
29	Delaware	42,917
33	Florida	41,781
38	Georgia	40,540
46	Hawaii	37,634
44	Idaho	38,074
13	Illinois	46,657
31	Indiana	42,197
17	Iowa	46,359
10	Kansas	47,547
42	Kentucky	39,743
28	Louisiana	43,277
41	Maine	39,998
12	Maryland	46,969
3	Massachusetts	53,782
32	Michigan	42,173
9	Minnesota	48,052
49	Mississippi	36,889
27	Missouri	43,444
35	Montana	40,985
5	Nebraska	50,054
40	Nevada	40,242
11	New Hampshire	47,530
8	New Jersey	48,590
50	New Mexico	36,814
16	New York	46,445
34	North Carolina	41,532
2	North Dakota	54,997
22	Ohio	44,943
23	Oklahoma	44,757
36	Oregon	40,881
15	Pennsylvania	46,537
19	Rhode Island	46,119
43	South Carolina	39,308
6	South Dakota	49,463
30	Tennessee	42,902
24	Texas	44,269
48	Utah	37,435
26	Vermont	44,019
14	Virginia	46,582
18	Washington	46,330
47	West Virginia	37,622
21	Wisconsin	45,151
4	Wyoming	53,512

RANK ORDER

RANK	STATE	PER CAPITA
1	Connecticut	$57,520
2	North Dakota	54,997
3	Massachusetts	53,782
4	Wyoming	53,512
5	Nebraska	50,054
6	South Dakota	49,463
7	Alaska	48,973
8	New Jersey	48,590
9	Minnesota	48,052
10	Kansas	47,547
11	New Hampshire	47,530
12	Maryland	46,969
13	Illinois	46,657
14	Virginia	46,582
15	Pennsylvania	46,537
16	New York	46,445
17	Iowa	46,359
18	Washington	46,330
19	Rhode Island	46,119
20	Colorado	46,016
21	Wisconsin	45,151
22	Ohio	44,943
23	Oklahoma	44,757
24	Texas	44,269
25	California	44,173
26	Vermont	44,019
27	Missouri	43,444
28	Louisiana	43,277
29	Delaware	42,917
30	Tennessee	42,902
31	Indiana	42,197
32	Michigan	42,173
33	Florida	41,781
34	North Carolina	41,532
35	Montana	40,985
36	Oregon	40,881
37	Arkansas	40,858
38	Georgia	40,540
39	Alabama	40,267
40	Nevada	40,242
41	Maine	39,998
42	Kentucky	39,743
43	South Carolina	39,308
44	Idaho	38,074
45	Arizona	37,694
46	Hawaii	37,634
47	West Virginia	37,622
48	Utah	37,435
49	Mississippi	36,889
50	New Mexico	36,814

District of Columbia   57,943

Source: U.S. Department of Commerce, Bureau of Economic Analysis
   "Annual State Personal Income" (http://www.bea.gov/iTable/index_regional.cfm)
*Real personal income is personal income at Regional Price Parities (RPPs) divided by the national Personal Consumption Expenditure price index (a measure of U.S. inflation). RPPs are regional price levels expressed as a percentage of the overall national price level for a given year. The price levels are determined by the average prices paid by consumers for the mix of goods and services consumed in each region. Taking the ratio of RPPs shows the difference in price levels across regions.

Percent Change in Per Capita Real Personal Income: 2014 to 2015

National Percent Change = 3.9% Increase*

ALPHA ORDER

RANK	STATE	PERCENT CHANGE
24	Alabama	3.8
19	Alaska	3.9
19	Arizona	3.9
42	Arkansas	2.1
1	California	6.3
38	Colorado	2.9
40	Connecticut	2.3
6	Delaware	5.2
6	Florida	5.2
19	Georgia	3.9
19	Hawaii	3.9
12	Idaho	4.4
24	Illinois	3.8
33	Indiana	3.4
38	Iowa	2.9
47	Kansas	0.9
33	Kentucky	3.4
41	Louisiana	2.2
36	Maine	3.1
13	Maryland	4.3
3	Massachusetts	5.7
5	Michigan	5.5
26	Minnesota	3.7
46	Mississippi	1.4
36	Missouri	3.1
30	Montana	3.6
43	Nebraska	2.0
4	Nevada	5.6
15	New Hampshire	4.1
9	New Jersey	4.8
26	New Mexico	3.7
15	New York	4.1
10	North Carolina	4.7
50	North Dakota	(5.5)
32	Ohio	3.5
49	Oklahoma	(3.2)
2	Oregon	5.8
30	Pennsylvania	3.6
15	Rhode Island	4.1
13	South Carolina	4.3
35	South Dakota	3.2
10	Tennessee	4.7
44	Texas	1.5
6	Utah	5.2
26	Vermont	3.7
19	Virginia	3.9
18	Washington	4.0
44	West Virginia	1.5
26	Wisconsin	3.7
48	Wyoming	0.0

RANK ORDER

RANK	STATE	PERCENT CHANGE
1	California	6.3
2	Oregon	5.8
3	Massachusetts	5.7
4	Nevada	5.6
5	Michigan	5.5
6	Delaware	5.2
6	Florida	5.2
6	Utah	5.2
9	New Jersey	4.8
10	North Carolina	4.7
10	Tennessee	4.7
12	Idaho	4.4
13	Maryland	4.3
13	South Carolina	4.3
15	New Hampshire	4.1
15	New York	4.1
15	Rhode Island	4.1
18	Washington	4.0
19	Alaska	3.9
19	Arizona	3.9
19	Georgia	3.9
19	Hawaii	3.9
19	Virginia	3.9
24	Alabama	3.8
24	Illinois	3.8
26	Minnesota	3.7
26	New Mexico	3.7
26	Vermont	3.7
26	Wisconsin	3.7
30	Montana	3.6
30	Pennsylvania	3.6
32	Ohio	3.5
33	Indiana	3.4
33	Kentucky	3.4
35	South Dakota	3.2
36	Maine	3.1
36	Missouri	3.1
38	Colorado	2.9
38	Iowa	2.9
40	Connecticut	2.3
41	Louisiana	2.2
42	Arkansas	2.1
43	Nebraska	2.0
44	Texas	1.5
44	West Virginia	1.5
46	Mississippi	1.4
47	Kansas	0.9
48	Wyoming	0.0
49	Oklahoma	(3.2)
50	North Dakota	(5.5)

District of Columbia   6.4

Source: U.S. Department of Commerce, Bureau of Economic Analysis
    "Annual State Personal Income" (http://www.bea.gov/iTable/index_regional.cfm)
*Real personal income is personal income at Regional Price Parities (RPPs) divided by the national Personal Consumption Expenditure price index (a measure of U.S. inflation). RPPs are regional price levels expressed as a percentage of the overall national price level for a given year. The price levels are determined by the average prices paid by consumers for the mix of goods and services consumed in each region. Taking the ratio of RPPs shows the difference in price levels across regions.

Personal Consumption Expenditures in 2016

National Total = $12,816,386,000,000*

ALPHA ORDER				RANK ORDER			
RANK	STATE	EXPENDITURES	% of USA	RANK	STATE	EXPENDITURES	% of USA
27	Alabama	$152,397,000,000	1.2%	1	California	$1,641,724,000,000	12.8%
46	Alaska	36,758,000,000	0.3%	2	Texas	1,018,027,000,000	7.9%
17	Arizona	239,680,000,000	1.9%	3	New York	926,168,000,000	7.2%
34	Arkansas	92,984,000,000	0.7%	4	Florida	796,537,000,000	6.2%
1	California	1,641,724,000,000	12.8%	5	Illinois	534,750,000,000	4.2%
19	Colorado	236,296,000,000	1.8%	6	Pennsylvania	522,697,000,000	4.1%
23	Connecticut	173,447,000,000	1.4%	7	New Jersey	438,030,000,000	3.4%
45	Delaware	40,813,000,000	0.3%	8	Ohio	434,951,000,000	3.4%
4	Florida	796,537,000,000	6.2%	9	Michigan	390,497,000,000	3.0%
10	Georgia	357,332,000,000	2.8%	10	Georgia	357,332,000,000	2.8%
39	Hawaii	64,460,000,000	0.5%	11	Massachusetts	354,085,000,000	2.8%
42	Idaho	56,642,000,000	0.4%	12	Virginia	350,198,000,000	2.7%
5	Illinois	534,750,000,000	4.2%	13	North Carolina	342,753,000,000	2.7%
18	Indiana	236,353,000,000	1.8%	14	Washington	312,817,000,000	2.4%
30	Iowa	115,999,000,000	0.9%	15	Maryland	269,223,000,000	2.1%
33	Kansas	104,615,000,000	0.8%	16	Minnesota	242,489,000,000	1.9%
28	Kentucky	147,697,000,000	1.2%	17	Arizona	239,680,000,000	1.9%
26	Louisiana	160,025,000,000	1.2%	18	Indiana	236,353,000,000	1.8%
41	Maine	57,281,000,000	0.4%	19	Colorado	236,296,000,000	1.8%
15	Maryland	269,223,000,000	2.1%	20	Missouri	228,648,000,000	1.8%
11	Massachusetts	354,085,000,000	2.8%	21	Tennessee	227,596,000,000	1.8%
9	Michigan	390,497,000,000	3.0%	22	Wisconsin	224,143,000,000	1.7%
16	Minnesota	242,489,000,000	1.9%	23	Connecticut	173,447,000,000	1.4%
35	Mississippi	90,261,000,000	0.7%	24	South Carolina	165,036,000,000	1.3%
20	Missouri	228,648,000,000	1.8%	25	Oregon	162,684,000,000	1.3%
44	Montana	42,956,000,000	0.3%	26	Louisiana	160,025,000,000	1.2%
36	Nebraska	74,320,000,000	0.6%	27	Alabama	152,397,000,000	1.2%
32	Nevada	106,364,000,000	0.8%	28	Kentucky	147,697,000,000	1.2%
38	New Hampshire	65,151,000,000	0.5%	29	Oklahoma	129,390,000,000	1.0%
7	New Jersey	438,030,000,000	3.4%	30	Iowa	115,999,000,000	0.9%
37	New Mexico	74,290,000,000	0.6%	31	Utah	107,142,000,000	0.8%
3	New York	926,168,000,000	7.2%	32	Nevada	106,364,000,000	0.8%
13	North Carolina	342,753,000,000	2.7%	33	Kansas	104,615,000,000	0.8%
47	North Dakota	36,552,000,000	0.3%	34	Arkansas	92,984,000,000	0.7%
8	Ohio	434,951,000,000	3.4%	35	Mississippi	90,261,000,000	0.7%
29	Oklahoma	129,390,000,000	1.0%	36	Nebraska	74,320,000,000	0.6%
25	Oregon	162,684,000,000	1.3%	37	New Mexico	74,290,000,000	0.6%
6	Pennsylvania	522,697,000,000	4.1%	38	New Hampshire	65,151,000,000	0.5%
43	Rhode Island	44,850,000,000	0.3%	39	Hawaii	64,460,000,000	0.5%
24	South Carolina	165,036,000,000	1.3%	40	West Virginia	63,022,000,000	0.5%
48	South Dakota	34,164,000,000	0.3%	41	Maine	57,281,000,000	0.4%
21	Tennessee	227,596,000,000	1.8%	42	Idaho	56,642,000,000	0.4%
2	Texas	1,018,027,000,000	7.9%	43	Rhode Island	44,850,000,000	0.3%
31	Utah	107,142,000,000	0.8%	44	Montana	42,956,000,000	0.3%
49	Vermont	29,761,000,000	0.2%	45	Delaware	40,813,000,000	0.3%
12	Virginia	350,198,000,000	2.7%	46	Alaska	36,758,000,000	0.3%
14	Washington	312,817,000,000	2.4%	47	North Dakota	36,552,000,000	0.3%
40	West Virginia	63,022,000,000	0.5%	48	South Dakota	34,164,000,000	0.3%
22	Wisconsin	224,143,000,000	1.7%	49	Vermont	29,761,000,000	0.2%
50	Wyoming	23,611,000,000	0.2%	50	Wyoming	23,611,000,000	0.2%
					District of Columbia	38,720,000,000	0.3%

Source: U.S. Department of Commerce, Bureau of Economic Analysis
"Personal Consumption Expenditures by State" (http://www.bea.gov/iTable/index_regional.cfm)
*PCE by state is the state counterpart of the Nation's personal consumption expenditures (PCE). PCE represents the goods and services purchased by or on behalf of households, plus the purchases of nonprofit institutions serving households. For each state and for the District of Columbia, personal consumption expenditures are those expenditures made by or on behalf of residents. These expenditures include expenditures on activities outside of the state.

Per Capita Personal Consumption Expenditures in 2016

National Per Capita = $39,664*

ALPHA ORDER				RANK ORDER		
RANK	STATE	PER CAPITA		RANK	STATE	PER CAPITA
48	Alabama	$31,336		1	Massachusetts	$51,981
2	Alaska	49,547		2	Alaska	49,547
39	Arizona	34,580		3	New Jersey	48,972
49	Arkansas	31,117		4	New Hampshire	48,810
17	California	41,827		5	Connecticut	48,497
15	Colorado	42,648		6	North Dakota	48,225
5	Connecticut	48,497		7	Vermont	47,648
14	Delaware	42,868		8	New York	46,906
28	Florida	38,644		9	Hawaii	45,123
38	Georgia	34,657		10	Maryland	44,748
9	Hawaii	45,123		11	Minnesota	43,930
44	Idaho	33,653		12	Maine	43,021
18	Illinois	41,772		13	Washington	42,922
36	Indiana	35,633		14	Delaware	42,868
31	Iowa	37,005		15	Colorado	42,648
34	Kansas	35,984		16	Rhode Island	42,454
45	Kentucky	33,288		17	California	41,827
42	Louisiana	34,181		18	Illinois	41,772
12	Maine	43,021		19	Virginia	41,632
10	Maryland	44,748		20	Montana	41,204
1	Massachusetts	51,981		21	Pennsylvania	40,886
25	Michigan	39,332		22	Wyoming	40,327
11	Minnesota	43,930		23	Oregon	39,742
50	Mississippi	30,200		24	South Dakota	39,475
29	Missouri	37,526		25	Michigan	39,332
20	Montana	41,204		26	Nebraska	38,970
26	Nebraska	38,970		27	Wisconsin	38,788
33	Nevada	36,177		28	Florida	38,644
4	New Hampshire	48,810		29	Missouri	37,526
3	New Jersey	48,972		30	Ohio	37,449
35	New Mexico	35,699		31	Iowa	37,005
8	New York	46,906		32	Texas	36,537
43	North Carolina	33,779		33	Nevada	36,177
6	North Dakota	48,225		34	Kansas	35,984
30	Ohio	37,449		35	New Mexico	35,699
47	Oklahoma	32,978		36	Indiana	35,633
23	Oregon	39,742		37	Utah	35,114
21	Pennsylvania	40,886		38	Georgia	34,657
16	Rhode Island	42,454		39	Arizona	34,580
46	South Carolina	33,266		40	West Virginia	34,418
24	South Dakota	39,475		41	Tennessee	34,219
41	Tennessee	34,219		42	Louisiana	34,181
32	Texas	36,537		43	North Carolina	33,779
37	Utah	35,114		44	Idaho	33,653
7	Vermont	47,648		45	Kentucky	33,288
19	Virginia	41,632		46	South Carolina	33,266
13	Washington	42,922		47	Oklahoma	32,978
40	West Virginia	34,418		48	Alabama	31,336
27	Wisconsin	38,788		49	Arkansas	31,117
22	Wyoming	40,327		50	Mississippi	30,200
					District of Columbia	56,843

Source: U.S. Department of Commerce, Bureau of Economic Analysis
  "Personal Consumption Expenditures by State" (http://www.bea.gov/iTable/index_regional.cfm)
*PCE by state is the state counterpart of the Nation's personal consumption expenditures (PCE). PCE represents the goods and services purchased by or on behalf of households, plus the purchases of nonprofit institutions serving households. For each state and for the District of Columbia, personal consumption expenditures are those expenditures made by or on behalf of residents. These expenditures include expenditures on activities outside of the state.

Percent Change in Personal Consumption Expenditures: 2015 to 2016

National Percent Change = 4.0% Increase*

ALPHA ORDER

RANK	STATE	PERCENT CHANGE
42	Alabama	2.7
47	Alaska	2.3
26	Arizona	3.6
20	Arkansas	3.9
5	California	4.9
2	Colorado	5.4
37	Connecticut	2.9
33	Delaware	3.2
9	Florida	4.6
12	Georgia	4.4
3	Hawaii	5.1
3	Idaho	5.1
24	Illinois	3.7
26	Indiana	3.6
35	Iowa	3.1
40	Kansas	2.8
23	Kentucky	3.8
45	Louisiana	2.6
33	Maine	3.2
20	Maryland	3.9
12	Massachusetts	4.4
16	Michigan	4.0
9	Minnesota	4.6
42	Mississippi	2.7
37	Missouri	2.9
15	Montana	4.1
16	Nebraska	4.0
7	Nevada	4.8
29	New Hampshire	3.5
30	New Jersey	3.4
37	New Mexico	2.9
16	New York	4.0
14	North Carolina	4.3
50	North Dakota	0.2
42	Ohio	2.7
48	Oklahoma	1.8
8	Oregon	4.7
35	Pennsylvania	3.1
31	Rhode Island	3.3
11	South Carolina	4.5
24	South Dakota	3.7
20	Tennessee	3.9
16	Texas	4.0
1	Utah	6.2
40	Vermont	2.8
26	Virginia	3.6
5	Washington	4.9
46	West Virginia	2.5
31	Wisconsin	3.3
49	Wyoming	1.4

RANK ORDER

RANK	STATE	PERCENT CHANGE
1	Utah	6.2
2	Colorado	5.4
3	Hawaii	5.1
3	Idaho	5.1
5	California	4.9
5	Washington	4.9
7	Nevada	4.8
8	Oregon	4.7
9	Florida	4.6
9	Minnesota	4.6
11	South Carolina	4.5
12	Georgia	4.4
12	Massachusetts	4.4
14	North Carolina	4.3
15	Montana	4.1
16	Michigan	4.0
16	Nebraska	4.0
16	New York	4.0
16	Texas	4.0
20	Arkansas	3.9
20	Maryland	3.9
20	Tennessee	3.9
23	Kentucky	3.8
24	Illinois	3.7
24	South Dakota	3.7
26	Arizona	3.6
26	Indiana	3.6
26	Virginia	3.6
29	New Hampshire	3.5
30	New Jersey	3.4
31	Rhode Island	3.3
31	Wisconsin	3.3
33	Delaware	3.2
33	Maine	3.2
35	Iowa	3.1
35	Pennsylvania	3.1
37	Connecticut	2.9
37	Missouri	2.9
37	New Mexico	2.9
40	Kansas	2.8
40	Vermont	2.8
42	Alabama	2.7
42	Mississippi	2.7
42	Ohio	2.7
45	Louisiana	2.6
46	West Virginia	2.5
47	Alaska	2.3
48	Oklahoma	1.8
49	Wyoming	1.4
50	North Dakota	0.2

District of Columbia	4.5

Source: U.S. Department of Commerce, Bureau of Economic Analysis
   "Personal Consumption Expenditures by State" (http://www.bea.gov/iTable/index_regional.cfm)
*PCE by state is the state counterpart of the Nation's personal consumption expenditures (PCE). PCE represents the goods and services purchased by or on behalf of households, plus the purchases of nonprofit institutions serving households. For each state and for the District of Columbia, personal consumption expenditures are those expenditures made by or on behalf of residents. These expenditures include expenditures on activities outside of the state.

Percent Change in Per Capita
Personal Consumption Expenditures: 2015 to 2016
National Percent Change = 3.2% Increase*

ALPHA ORDER			RANK ORDER		
RANK	STATE	PERCENT CHANGE	RANK	STATE	PERCENT CHANGE
42	Alabama	2.5	1	Hawaii	4.9
47	Alaska	1.7	2	California	4.2
46	Arizona	1.9	3	Utah	4.1
10	Arkansas	3.5	4	Illinois	4.0
2	California	4.2	4	Massachusetts	4.0
9	Colorado	3.6	4	New York	4.0
21	Connecticut	3.1	7	Michigan	3.9
43	Delaware	2.4	7	Minnesota	3.9
33	Florida	2.8	9	Colorado	3.6
16	Georgia	3.2	10	Arkansas	3.5
1	Hawaii	4.9	10	Kentucky	3.5
16	Idaho	3.2	10	Maryland	3.5
4	Illinois	4.0	13	Indiana	3.3
13	Indiana	3.3	13	Nebraska	3.3
39	Iowa	2.6	13	New Jersey	3.3
33	Kansas	2.8	16	Georgia	3.2
10	Kentucky	3.5	16	Idaho	3.2
44	Louisiana	2.3	16	North Carolina	3.2
29	Maine	3.0	16	Pennsylvania	3.2
10	Maryland	3.5	16	Rhode Island	3.2
4	Massachusetts	4.0	21	Connecticut	3.1
7	Michigan	3.9	21	Montana	3.1
7	Minnesota	3.9	21	New Hampshire	3.1
38	Mississippi	2.7	21	South Carolina	3.1
39	Missouri	2.6	21	Vermont	3.1
21	Montana	3.1	21	Virginia	3.1
13	Nebraska	3.3	21	Washington	3.1
33	Nevada	2.8	21	Wisconsin	3.1
21	New Hampshire	3.1	29	Maine	3.0
13	New Jersey	3.3	29	Tennessee	3.0
33	New Mexico	2.8	29	West Virginia	3.0
4	New York	4.0	32	Oregon	2.9
16	North Carolina	3.2	33	Florida	2.8
50	North Dakota	0.1	33	Kansas	2.8
39	Ohio	2.6	33	Nevada	2.8
49	Oklahoma	1.4	33	New Mexico	2.8
32	Oregon	2.9	33	South Dakota	2.8
16	Pennsylvania	3.2	38	Mississippi	2.7
16	Rhode Island	3.2	39	Iowa	2.6
21	South Carolina	3.1	39	Missouri	2.6
33	South Dakota	2.8	39	Ohio	2.6
29	Tennessee	3.0	42	Alabama	2.5
44	Texas	2.3	43	Delaware	2.4
3	Utah	4.1	44	Louisiana	2.3
21	Vermont	3.1	44	Texas	2.3
21	Virginia	3.1	46	Arizona	1.9
21	Washington	3.1	47	Alaska	1.7
29	West Virginia	3.0	48	Wyoming	1.6
21	Wisconsin	3.1	49	Oklahoma	1.4
48	Wyoming	1.6	50	North Dakota	0.1
				District of Columbia	2.9

Source: U.S. Department of Commerce, Bureau of Economic Analysis

"Personal Consumption Expenditures by State" (http://www.bea.gov/iTable/index_regional.cfm)

*PCE by state is the state counterpart of the Nation's personal consumption expenditures (PCE). PCE represents the goods and services purchased by or on behalf of households, plus the purchases of nonprofit institutions serving households. For each state and for the District of Columbia, personal consumption expenditures are those expenditures made by or on behalf of residents. These expenditures include expenditures on activities outside of the state.

Bankruptcy Filings in 2017

National Total = 790,830 Bankruptcies*

ALPHA ORDER

RANK	STATE	BANKRUPTCIES	% of USA
10	Alabama	27,160	3.4%
50	Alaska	460	0.1%
18	Arizona	15,682	2.0%
26	Arkansas	10,635	1.3%
1	California	72,446	9.2%
23	Colorado	12,475	1.6%
34	Connecticut	5,654	0.7%
40	Delaware	2,858	0.4%
4	Florida	43,504	5.5%
3	Georgia	47,408	6.0%
44	Hawaii	1,388	0.2%
37	Idaho	3,771	0.5%
2	Illinois	51,768	6.5%
12	Indiana	23,639	3.0%
35	Iowa	4,308	0.5%
32	Kansas	6,711	0.8%
19	Kentucky	15,672	2.0%
22	Louisiana	13,518	1.7%
43	Maine	1,450	0.2%
16	Maryland	17,271	2.2%
31	Massachusetts	8,458	1.1%
9	Michigan	30,607	3.9%
27	Minnesota	9,744	1.2%
24	Mississippi	12,063	1.5%
15	Missouri	18,141	2.3%
45	Montana	1,314	0.2%
36	Nebraska	4,058	0.5%
30	Nevada	8,760	1.1%
42	New Hampshire	1,840	0.2%
11	New Jersey	26,716	3.4%
38	New Mexico	3,340	0.4%
8	New York	32,349	4.1%
21	North Carolina	14,454	1.8%
48	North Dakota	788	0.1%
5	Ohio	37,614	4.8%
28	Oklahoma	9,366	1.2%
29	Oregon	9,078	1.1%
14	Pennsylvania	22,281	2.8%
41	Rhode Island	2,262	0.3%
33	South Carolina	6,492	0.8%
46	South Dakota	1,058	0.1%
7	Tennessee	35,423	4.5%
6	Texas	35,518	4.5%
25	Utah	11,531	1.5%
49	Vermont	567	0.1%
13	Virginia	22,741	2.9%
20	Washington	15,057	1.9%
39	West Virginia	3,305	0.4%
17	Wisconsin	17,213	2.2%
47	Wyoming	989	0.1%

RANK ORDER

RANK	STATE	BANKRUPTCIES	% of USA
1	California	72,446	9.2%
2	Illinois	51,768	6.5%
3	Georgia	47,408	6.0%
4	Florida	43,504	5.5%
5	Ohio	37,614	4.8%
6	Texas	35,518	4.5%
7	Tennessee	35,423	4.5%
8	New York	32,349	4.1%
9	Michigan	30,607	3.9%
10	Alabama	27,160	3.4%
11	New Jersey	26,716	3.4%
12	Indiana	23,639	3.0%
13	Virginia	22,741	2.9%
14	Pennsylvania	22,281	2.8%
15	Missouri	18,141	2.3%
16	Maryland	17,271	2.2%
17	Wisconsin	17,213	2.2%
18	Arizona	15,682	2.0%
19	Kentucky	15,672	2.0%
20	Washington	15,057	1.9%
21	North Carolina	14,454	1.8%
22	Louisiana	13,518	1.7%
23	Colorado	12,475	1.6%
24	Mississippi	12,063	1.5%
25	Utah	11,531	1.5%
26	Arkansas	10,635	1.3%
27	Minnesota	9,744	1.2%
28	Oklahoma	9,366	1.2%
29	Oregon	9,078	1.1%
30	Nevada	8,760	1.1%
31	Massachusetts	8,458	1.1%
32	Kansas	6,711	0.8%
33	South Carolina	6,492	0.8%
34	Connecticut	5,654	0.7%
35	Iowa	4,308	0.5%
36	Nebraska	4,058	0.5%
37	Idaho	3,771	0.5%
38	New Mexico	3,340	0.4%
39	West Virginia	3,305	0.4%
40	Delaware	2,858	0.4%
41	Rhode Island	2,262	0.3%
42	New Hampshire	1,840	0.2%
43	Maine	1,450	0.2%
44	Hawaii	1,388	0.2%
45	Montana	1,314	0.2%
46	South Dakota	1,058	0.1%
47	Wyoming	989	0.1%
48	North Dakota	788	0.1%
49	Vermont	567	0.1%
50	Alaska	460	0.1%
	District of Columbia	738	0.1%

Source: CQ Press using data from Administrative Office of the U.S. Courts
"Table F-2, U.S. Bankruptcy Courts" (http://www.uscourts.gov/Statistics/BankruptcyStatistics.aspx)
*For 12 months through September 2017. Includes business (23,109) and non-business (767,721) filings. Includes all chapters of bankruptcy. National total includes 9,187 bankruptcies in U.S. territories.

Personal Bankruptcy Rate in 2017

National Rate = 233 Personal Bankruptcies per 100,000 Population*

ALPHA ORDER

RANK	STATE	RATE
1	Alabama	551
50	Alaska	57
22	Arizona	216
8	Arkansas	347
30	California	176
23	Colorado	215
37	Connecticut	152
19	Delaware	241
28	Florida	199
3	Georgia	446
48	Hawaii	95
25	Idaho	213
4	Illinois	397
7	Indiana	349
39	Iowa	132
21	Kansas	224
8	Kentucky	347
16	Louisiana	280
46	Maine	102
17	Maryland	279
43	Massachusetts	118
11	Michigan	302
32	Minnesota	169
5	Mississippi	396
12	Missouri	292
42	Montana	119
26	Nebraska	206
15	Nevada	283
40	New Hampshire	131
14	New Jersey	288
35	New Mexico	154
35	New York	154
38	North Carolina	136
47	North Dakota	99
10	Ohio	317
20	Oklahoma	233
23	Oregon	215
33	Pennsylvania	168
26	Rhode Island	206
41	South Carolina	126
44	South Dakota	116
2	Tennessee	521
44	Texas	116
6	Utah	366
49	Vermont	85
18	Virginia	262
29	Washington	198
31	West Virginia	175
13	Wisconsin	290
34	Wyoming	166

RANK ORDER

RANK	STATE	RATE
1	Alabama	551
2	Tennessee	521
3	Georgia	446
4	Illinois	397
5	Mississippi	396
6	Utah	366
7	Indiana	349
8	Arkansas	347
8	Kentucky	347
10	Ohio	317
11	Michigan	302
12	Missouri	292
13	Wisconsin	290
14	New Jersey	288
15	Nevada	283
16	Louisiana	280
17	Maryland	279
18	Virginia	262
19	Delaware	241
20	Oklahoma	233
21	Kansas	224
22	Arizona	216
23	Colorado	215
23	Oregon	215
25	Idaho	213
26	Nebraska	206
26	Rhode Island	206
28	Florida	199
29	Washington	198
30	California	176
31	West Virginia	175
32	Minnesota	169
33	Pennsylvania	168
34	Wyoming	166
35	New Mexico	154
35	New York	154
37	Connecticut	152
38	North Carolina	136
39	Iowa	132
40	New Hampshire	131
41	South Carolina	126
42	Montana	119
43	Massachusetts	118
44	South Dakota	116
44	Texas	116
46	Maine	102
47	North Dakota	99
48	Hawaii	95
49	Vermont	85
50	Alaska	57

District of Columbia 101

Source: CQ Press using data from Administrative Office of the U.S. Courts
"Table F-2, U.S. Bankruptcy Courts" (http://www.uscourts.gov/Statistics/BankruptcyStatistics.aspx)
*For 12 months through September 2017. National rate does not include bankruptcies or population in U.S. territories. Includes all nonbusiness bankruptcies.

Percent Change in Personal Bankruptcy Rate: 2016 to 2017

National Percent Change = 2.1% Decrease*

ALPHA ORDER				RANK ORDER		
RANK	STATE	PERCENT CHANGE		RANK	STATE	PERCENT CHANGE
7	Alabama	3.8		1	North Dakota	19.3
2	Alaska	9.6		2	Alaska	9.6
26	Arizona	(2.3)		3	Wyoming	8.5
15	Arkansas	0.9		4	New York	7.7
45	California	(5.9)		5	Delaware	7.6
47	Colorado	(6.9)		5	Mississippi	7.6
34	Connecticut	(3.8)		7	Alabama	3.8
5	Delaware	7.6		8	New Jersey	3.6
49	Florida	(10.8)		9	Kansas	3.2
27	Georgia	(2.4)		10	Texas	2.7
32	Hawaii	(3.1)		11	New Hampshire	2.3
35	Idaho	(4.5)		12	Oklahoma	2.2
44	Illinois	(5.7)		13	Kentucky	2.1
37	Indiana	(4.6)		14	Pennsylvania	1.2
20	Iowa	(0.8)		15	Arkansas	0.9
9	Kansas	3.2		16	Ohio	0.3
13	Kentucky	2.1		17	New Mexico	0.0
31	Louisiana	(2.8)		17	West Virginia	0.0
48	Maine	(10.5)		19	Maryland	(0.4)
19	Maryland	(0.4)		20	Iowa	(0.8)
39	Massachusetts	(4.8)		21	Wisconsin	(1.0)
30	Michigan	(2.6)		22	Minnesota	(1.2)
22	Minnesota	(1.2)		23	Missouri	(1.4)
5	Mississippi	7.6		24	Nebraska	(1.9)
23	Missouri	(1.4)		25	Virginia	(2.2)
39	Montana	(4.8)		26	Arizona	(2.3)
24	Nebraska	(1.9)		27	Georgia	(2.4)
42	Nevada	(5.0)		27	Tennessee	(2.4)
11	New Hampshire	2.3		27	Utah	(2.4)
8	New Jersey	3.6		30	Michigan	(2.6)
17	New Mexico	0.0		31	Louisiana	(2.8)
4	New York	7.7		32	Hawaii	(3.1)
46	North Carolina	(6.8)		33	South Dakota	(3.3)
1	North Dakota	19.3		34	Connecticut	(3.8)
16	Ohio	0.3		35	Idaho	(4.5)
12	Oklahoma	2.2		35	Vermont	(4.5)
41	Oregon	(4.9)		37	Indiana	(4.6)
14	Pennsylvania	1.2		37	Rhode Island	(4.6)
37	Rhode Island	(4.6)		39	Massachusetts	(4.8)
43	South Carolina	(5.3)		39	Montana	(4.8)
33	South Dakota	(3.3)		41	Oregon	(4.9)
27	Tennessee	(2.4)		42	Nevada	(5.0)
10	Texas	2.7		43	South Carolina	(5.3)
27	Utah	(2.4)		44	Illinois	(5.7)
35	Vermont	(4.5)		45	California	(5.9)
25	Virginia	(2.2)		46	North Carolina	(6.8)
50	Washington	(12.0)		47	Colorado	(6.9)
17	West Virginia	0.0		48	Maine	(10.5)
21	Wisconsin	(1.0)		49	Florida	(10.8)
3	Wyoming	8.5		50	Washington	(12.0)

District of Columbia   5.2

Source: CQ Press using data from Administrative Office of the U.S. Courts
  "Table F-2, U.S. Bankruptcy Courts" (http://www.uscourts.gov/Statistics/BankruptcyStatistics.aspx)
*Twelve months ending in September 2016 to 12 months ending in September 2017. National rate does not include bankruptcies or population in U.S. territories. Includes all nonbusiness bankruptcies.

2018 State Business Tax Climate Index

National Average Score = 5.18*

RANK	STATE	SCORE
35	Alabama	4.79
3	Alaska	7.21
21	Arizona	5.21
39	Arkansas	4.59
48	California	3.71
18	Colorado	5.41
44	Connecticut	4.32
15	Delaware	5.51
4	Florida	6.86
36	Georgia	4.69
27	Hawaii	5.08
20	Idaho	5.22
29	Illinois	4.99
9	Indiana	5.98
40	Iowa	4.53
23	Kansas	5.15
33	Kentucky	4.91
42	Louisiana	4.37
28	Maine	5.00
43	Maryland	4.36
22	Massachusetts	5.20
12	Michigan	5.64
46	Minnesota	4.21
24	Mississippi	5.13
16	Missouri	5.44
6	Montana	6.28
25	Nebraska	5.10
5	Nevada	6.46
7	New Hampshire	6.16
50	New Jersey	3.35
34	New Mexico	4.86
49	New York	3.60
11	North Carolina	5.76
30	North Dakota	4.97
45	Ohio	4.24
32	Oklahoma	4.91
10	Oregon	5.80
26	Pennsylvania	5.08
41	Rhode Island	4.48
37	South Carolina	4.67
2	South Dakota	7.47
14	Tennessee	5.58
13	Texas	5.61
8	Utah	5.98
47	Vermont	4.16
31	Virginia	4.92
17	Washington	5.42
19	West Virginia	5.33
38	Wisconsin	4.63
1	Wyoming	7.82

RANK	STATE	SCORE
1	Wyoming	7.82
2	South Dakota	7.47
3	Alaska	7.21
4	Florida	6.86
5	Nevada	6.46
6	Montana	6.28
7	New Hampshire	6.16
8	Utah	5.98
9	Indiana	5.98
10	Oregon	5.80
11	North Carolina	5.76
12	Michigan	5.64
13	Texas	5.61
14	Tennessee	5.58
15	Delaware	5.51
16	Missouri	5.44
17	Washington	5.42
18	Colorado	5.41
19	West Virginia	5.33
20	Idaho	5.22
21	Arizona	5.21
22	Massachusetts	5.20
23	Kansas	5.15
24	Mississippi	5.13
25	Nebraska	5.10
26	Pennsylvania	5.08
27	Hawaii	5.08
28	Maine	5.00
29	Illinois	4.99
30	North Dakota	4.97
31	Virginia	4.92
32	Oklahoma	4.91
33	Kentucky	4.91
34	New Mexico	4.86
35	Alabama	4.79
36	Georgia	4.69
37	South Carolina	4.67
38	Wisconsin	4.63
39	Arkansas	4.59
40	Iowa	4.53
41	Rhode Island	4.48
42	Louisiana	4.37
43	Maryland	4.36
44	Connecticut	4.32
45	Ohio	4.24
46	Minnesota	4.21
47	Vermont	4.16
48	California	3.71
49	New York	3.60
50	New Jersey	3.35
	District of Columbia	4.20

Source: The Tax Foundation
"State Business Tax Climate Index" (October 2017, https://taxfoundation.org/state-business-tax-climate-index-2018/)
*This index looks at levels of taxation and complexity of compliance to compare the states on how "business friendly" each state is compared to the others. The scale for each factor considered is one to ten, with ten being the "best." Rankings are based on unrounded scores and reflect those of The Tax Foundation.

Fortune 500 Companies in 2017

National Total = 500 Companies*

ALPHA ORDER					RANK ORDER			
RANK	STATE	COMPANIES	% of USA		RANK	STATE	COMPANIES	% of USA
36	Alabama	1	0.2%		1	New York	54	10.8%
37	Alaska	0	0.0%		2	California	53	10.6%
24	Arizona	4	0.8%		3	Texas	50	10.0%
22	Arkansas	6	1.2%		4	Illinois	36	7.2%
2	California	53	10.6%		5	Ohio	25	5.0%
17	Colorado	10	2.0%		6	Virginia	23	4.6%
9	Connecticut	18	3.6%		7	New Jersey	21	4.2%
30	Delaware	2	0.4%		7	Pennsylvania	21	4.2%
11	Florida	17	3.4%		9	Connecticut	18	3.6%
11	Georgia	17	3.4%		9	Minnesota	18	3.6%
37	Hawaii	0	0.0%		11	Florida	17	3.4%
30	Idaho	2	0.4%		11	Georgia	17	3.4%
4	Illinois	36	7.2%		11	Michigan	17	3.4%
21	Indiana	7	1.4%		14	Massachusetts	13	2.6%
28	Iowa	3	0.6%		15	North Carolina	12	2.4%
30	Kansas	2	0.4%		16	Tennessee	11	2.2%
28	Kentucky	3	0.6%		17	Colorado	10	2.0%
30	Louisiana	2	0.4%		17	Missouri	10	2.0%
37	Maine	0	0.0%		17	Washington	10	2.0%
24	Maryland	4	0.8%		20	Wisconsin	9	1.8%
14	Massachusetts	13	2.6%		21	Indiana	7	1.4%
11	Michigan	17	3.4%		22	Arkansas	6	1.2%
9	Minnesota	18	3.6%		23	Oklahoma	5	1.0%
37	Mississippi	0	0.0%		24	Arizona	4	0.8%
17	Missouri	10	2.0%		24	Maryland	4	0.8%
37	Montana	0	0.0%		24	Nebraska	4	0.8%
24	Nebraska	4	0.8%		24	Rhode Island	4	0.8%
30	Nevada	2	0.4%		28	Iowa	3	0.6%
37	New Hampshire	0	0.0%		28	Kentucky	3	0.6%
7	New Jersey	21	4.2%		30	Delaware	2	0.4%
37	New Mexico	0	0.0%		30	Idaho	2	0.4%
1	New York	54	10.8%		30	Kansas	2	0.4%
15	North Carolina	12	2.4%		30	Louisiana	2	0.4%
37	North Dakota	0	0.0%		30	Nevada	2	0.4%
5	Ohio	25	5.0%		30	Oregon	2	0.4%
23	Oklahoma	5	1.0%		36	Alabama	1	0.2%
30	Oregon	2	0.4%		37	Alaska	0	0.0%
7	Pennsylvania	21	4.2%		37	Hawaii	0	0.0%
24	Rhode Island	4	0.8%		37	Maine	0	0.0%
37	South Carolina	0	0.0%		37	Mississippi	0	0.0%
37	South Dakota	0	0.0%		37	Montana	0	0.0%
16	Tennessee	11	2.2%		37	New Hampshire	0	0.0%
3	Texas	50	10.0%		37	New Mexico	0	0.0%
37	Utah	0	0.0%		37	North Dakota	0	0.0%
37	Vermont	0	0.0%		37	South Carolina	0	0.0%
6	Virginia	23	4.6%		37	South Dakota	0	0.0%
17	Washington	10	2.0%		37	Utah	0	0.0%
37	West Virginia	0	0.0%		37	Vermont	0	0.0%
20	Wisconsin	9	1.8%		37	West Virginia	0	0.0%
37	Wyoming	0	0.0%		37	Wyoming	0	0.0%
					District of Columbia		2	0.4%

Source: Fortune magazine
"Fortune 500" (June 15, 2017)
*By state where each company's headquarters is located.

V. Education

(Continued)

(Continued)

Estimated Percent of School-Age Population in Public Schools in 2016

National Percent = 93.7%*

ALPHA ORDER				RANK ORDER		
RANK	STATE	PERCENT		RANK	STATE	PERCENT
29	Alabama	92.5		1	West Virginia	101.2
5	Alaska	99.4		2	Texas	100.5
24	Arizona	93.0		3	Vermont	100.0
10	Arkansas	95.6		4	Oklahoma	99.7
21	California	94.3		5	Alaska	99.4
6	Colorado	97.3		6	Colorado	97.3
19	Connecticut	94.7		7	Utah	96.9
41	Delaware	90.2		8	New Jersey	96.3
30	Florida	92.4		9	Maine	95.8
14	Georgia	94.9		10	Arkansas	95.6
50	Hawaii	84.1		10	Iowa	95.6
38	Idaho	90.8		12	Kansas	95.2
16	Illinois	94.8		13	Michigan	95.0
40	Indiana	90.7		14	Georgia	94.9
10	Iowa	95.6		14	South Carolina	94.9
12	Kansas	95.2		16	Illinois	94.8
23	Kentucky	93.4		16	Massachusetts	94.8
46	Louisiana	89.5		16	Nevada	94.8
9	Maine	95.8		19	Connecticut	94.7
45	Maryland	89.6		20	Virginia	94.4
16	Massachusetts	94.8		21	California	94.3
13	Michigan	95.0		22	Wyoming	94.0
30	Minnesota	92.4		23	Kentucky	93.4
33	Mississippi	91.5		24	Arizona	93.0
38	Missouri	90.8		25	New Hampshire	92.9
48	Montana	88.3		26	Nebraska	92.8
26	Nebraska	92.8		26	New Mexico	92.8
16	Nevada	94.8		28	Washington	92.6
25	New Hampshire	92.9		29	Alabama	92.5
8	New Jersey	96.3		30	Florida	92.4
26	New Mexico	92.8		30	Minnesota	92.4
42	New York	89.8		30	Rhode Island	92.4
35	North Carolina	91.3		33	Mississippi	91.5
43	North Dakota	89.7		33	Tennessee	91.5
43	Ohio	89.7		35	North Carolina	91.3
4	Oklahoma	99.7		35	Wisconsin	91.3
37	Oregon	91.1		37	Oregon	91.1
49	Pennsylvania	87.5		38	Idaho	90.8
30	Rhode Island	92.4		38	Missouri	90.8
14	South Carolina	94.9		40	Indiana	90.7
47	South Dakota	88.4		41	Delaware	90.2
33	Tennessee	91.5		42	New York	89.8
2	Texas	100.5		43	North Dakota	89.7
7	Utah	96.9		43	Ohio	89.7
3	Vermont	100.0		45	Maryland	89.6
20	Virginia	94.4		46	Louisiana	89.5
28	Washington	92.6		47	South Dakota	88.4
1	West Virginia	101.2		48	Montana	88.3
35	Wisconsin	91.3		49	Pennsylvania	87.5
22	Wyoming	94.0		50	Hawaii	84.1

District of Columbia 108.6

Source: CQ Press using data from U.S. Department of Education, National Center for Education Statistics
    "ElSi Table Generator" (http://nces.ed.gov/ccd/elsi/)
*Estimate based on 2016 Census population estimates for 5- to 17-year-olds compared to estimated 2015-2016 school year public school student membership. Student membership figures include counts for pre-kindergarten programs. Figures higher than 100 percent reflect using different sources for population and for student membership.

Regular Public Elementary and Secondary School Districts in 2016

National Total = 13,584 Districts*

ALPHA ORDER

RANK	STATE	DISTRICTS	% of USA
34	Alabama	134	1.0%
43	Alaska	53	0.4%
22	Arizona	234	1.7%
23	Arkansas	233	1.7%
1	California	1,058	7.8%
27	Colorado	178	1.3%
30	Connecticut	169	1.2%
48	Delaware	19	0.1%
41	Florida	67	0.5%
24	Georgia	180	1.3%
50	Hawaii	1	0.0%
36	Idaho	115	0.8%
3	Illinois	854	6.3%
17	Indiana	294	2.2%
13	Iowa	336	2.5%
15	Kansas	307	2.3%
29	Kentucky	173	1.3%
40	Louisiana	69	0.5%
19	Maine	248	1.8%
47	Maryland	24	0.2%
21	Massachusetts	239	1.8%
7	Michigan	542	4.0%
14	Minnesota	332	2.4%
33	Mississippi	144	1.1%
8	Missouri	518	3.8%
12	Montana	404	3.0%
20	Nebraska	245	1.8%
49	Nevada	18	0.1%
24	New Hampshire	180	1.3%
6	New Jersey	601	4.4%
38	New Mexico	89	0.7%
4	New York	690	5.1%
36	North Carolina	115	0.8%
28	North Dakota	175	1.3%
5	Ohio	622	4.6%
9	Oklahoma	516	3.8%
26	Oregon	179	1.3%
10	Pennsylvania	500	3.7%
46	Rhode Island	32	0.2%
39	South Carolina	84	0.6%
31	South Dakota	150	1.1%
32	Tennessee	146	1.1%
2	Texas	1,026	7.6%
45	Utah	41	0.3%
18	Vermont	291	2.1%
35	Virginia	130	1.0%
16	Washington	301	2.2%
42	West Virginia	55	0.4%
11	Wisconsin	424	3.1%
44	Wyoming	48	0.4%

RANK ORDER

RANK	STATE	DISTRICTS	% of USA
1	California	1,058	7.8%
2	Texas	1,026	7.6%
3	Illinois	854	6.3%
4	New York	690	5.1%
5	Ohio	622	4.6%
6	New Jersey	601	4.4%
7	Michigan	542	4.0%
8	Missouri	518	3.8%
9	Oklahoma	516	3.8%
10	Pennsylvania	500	3.7%
11	Wisconsin	424	3.1%
12	Montana	404	3.0%
13	Iowa	336	2.5%
14	Minnesota	332	2.4%
15	Kansas	307	2.3%
16	Washington	301	2.2%
17	Indiana	294	2.2%
18	Vermont	291	2.1%
19	Maine	248	1.8%
20	Nebraska	245	1.8%
21	Massachusetts	239	1.8%
22	Arizona	234	1.7%
23	Arkansas	233	1.7%
24	Georgia	180	1.3%
24	New Hampshire	180	1.3%
26	Oregon	179	1.3%
27	Colorado	178	1.3%
28	North Dakota	175	1.3%
29	Kentucky	173	1.3%
30	Connecticut	169	1.2%
31	South Dakota	150	1.1%
32	Tennessee	146	1.1%
33	Mississippi	144	1.1%
34	Alabama	134	1.0%
35	Virginia	130	1.0%
36	Idaho	115	0.8%
36	North Carolina	115	0.8%
38	New Mexico	89	0.7%
39	South Carolina	84	0.6%
40	Louisiana	69	0.5%
41	Florida	67	0.5%
42	West Virginia	55	0.4%
43	Alaska	53	0.4%
44	Wyoming	48	0.4%
45	Utah	41	0.3%
46	Rhode Island	32	0.2%
47	Maryland	24	0.2%
48	Delaware	19	0.1%
49	Nevada	18	0.1%
50	Hawaii	1	0.0%
	District of Columbia	1	0.0%

Source: U.S. Department of Education, National Center for Education Statistics
"Digest of Education Statistics 2017" (http://nces.ed.gov/programs/digest/index.asp)
*For school year 2015-2016. Regular school districts are agencies responsible for providing free public education for school-age children residing within their jurisdiction. Included in these figures are districts that reported having no students. This can occur when a small district has no pupils or contracts with another district to educate the students under its jurisdiction.

Private Elementary and Secondary Schools in 2016

National Total = 34,576 Schools*

RANK	STATE	SCHOOLS	% of USA
27	Alabama	352	1.0%
48	Alaska	53	0.2%
31	Arizona	320	0.9%
29	Arkansas	333	1.0%
1	California	3,425	9.9%
19	Colorado	604	1.7%
24	Connecticut	422	1.2%
46	Delaware	97	0.3%
4	Florida	2,201	6.4%
10	Georgia	1,217	3.5%
41	Hawaii	142	0.4%
33	Idaho	255	0.7%
7	Illinois	1,498	4.3%
6	Indiana	1,664	4.8%
21	Iowa	509	1.5%
34	Kansas	210	0.6%
30	Kentucky	329	1.0%
20	Louisiana	578	1.7%
40	Maine	143	0.4%
15	Maryland	764	2.2%
16	Massachusetts	755	2.2%
13	Michigan	886	2.6%
23	Minnesota	473	1.4%
36	Mississippi	182	0.5%
14	Missouri	867	2.5%
44	Montana	122	0.4%
28	Nebraska	346	1.0%
39	Nevada	146	0.4%
32	New Hampshire	259	0.7%
9	New Jersey	1,269	3.7%
37	New Mexico	171	0.5%
5	New York	1,939	5.6%
17	North Carolina	646	1.9%
49	North Dakota	49	0.1%
8	Ohio	1,356	3.9%
35	Oklahoma	183	0.5%
25	Oregon	413	1.2%
2	Pennsylvania	2,741	7.9%
42	Rhode Island	131	0.4%
26	South Carolina	375	1.1%
47	South Dakota	72	0.2%
22	Tennessee	502	1.5%
3	Texas	2,398	6.9%
38	Utah	162	0.5%
45	Vermont	113	0.3%
12	Virginia	951	2.8%
18	Washington	642	1.9%
43	West Virginia	128	0.4%
11	Wisconsin	1,054	3.0%
50	Wyoming	36	0.1%

RANK	STATE	SCHOOLS	% of USA
1	California	3,425	9.9%
2	Pennsylvania	2,741	7.9%
3	Texas	2,398	6.9%
4	Florida	2,201	6.4%
5	New York	1,939	5.6%
6	Indiana	1,664	4.8%
7	Illinois	1,498	4.3%
8	Ohio	1,356	3.9%
9	New Jersey	1,269	3.7%
10	Georgia	1,217	3.5%
11	Wisconsin	1,054	3.0%
12	Virginia	951	2.8%
13	Michigan	886	2.6%
14	Missouri	867	2.5%
15	Maryland	764	2.2%
16	Massachusetts	755	2.2%
17	North Carolina	646	1.9%
18	Washington	642	1.9%
19	Colorado	604	1.7%
20	Louisiana	578	1.7%
21	Iowa	509	1.5%
22	Tennessee	502	1.5%
23	Minnesota	473	1.4%
24	Connecticut	422	1.2%
25	Oregon	413	1.2%
26	South Carolina	375	1.1%
27	Alabama	352	1.0%
28	Nebraska	346	1.0%
29	Arkansas	333	1.0%
30	Kentucky	329	1.0%
31	Arizona	320	0.9%
32	New Hampshire	259	0.7%
33	Idaho	255	0.7%
34	Kansas	210	0.6%
35	Oklahoma	183	0.5%
36	Mississippi	182	0.5%
37	New Mexico	171	0.5%
38	Utah	162	0.5%
39	Nevada	146	0.4%
40	Maine	143	0.4%
41	Hawaii	142	0.4%
42	Rhode Island	131	0.4%
43	West Virginia	128	0.4%
44	Montana	122	0.4%
45	Vermont	113	0.3%
46	Delaware	97	0.3%
47	South Dakota	72	0.2%
48	Alaska	53	0.2%
49	North Dakota	49	0.1%
50	Wyoming	36	0.1%
	District of Columbia	93	0.3%

Source: U.S. Department of Education, National Center for Education Statistics
   "Characteristics of Private Schools in the United States" (https://nces.ed.gov/pubsearch/pubsinfo.asp?pubid=2017073)
*For school year 2015-2016. Includes private schools that provide instruction for one or more grades kindergarten through 12 (or comparable ungraded levels).

Private Elementary and Secondary School Enrollment in 2016

National Total = 4,903,596 Students*

RANK	STATE	STUDENTS	% of USA		RANK	STATE	STUDENTS	% of USA
22	Alabama	63,920	1.3%		1	California	544,800	11.1%
49	Alaska	4,518	0.1%		2	New York	461,297	9.4%
29	Arizona	46,252	0.9%		3	Florida	325,425	6.6%
34	Arkansas	30,607	0.6%		4	Pennsylvania	271,234	5.5%
1	California	544,800	11.1%		5	Texas	269,157	5.5%
27	Colorado	47,875	1.0%		6	Illinois	231,275	4.7%
24	Connecticut	60,353	1.2%		7	Ohio	222,863	4.5%
41	Delaware	17,310	0.4%		8	New Jersey	172,214	3.5%
3	Florida	325,425	6.6%		9	Georgia	168,718	3.4%
9	Georgia	168,718	3.4%		10	Louisiana	152,955	3.1%
31	Hawaii	41,703	0.9%		11	Michigan	151,909	3.1%
43	Idaho	13,901	0.3%		12	Indiana	149,460	3.0%
6	Illinois	231,275	4.7%		13	Wisconsin	126,035	2.6%
12	Indiana	149,460	3.0%		14	Maryland	122,189	2.5%
25	Iowa	59,419	1.2%		15	North Carolina	110,106	2.2%
33	Kansas	37,835	0.8%		16	Missouri	110,040	2.2%
23	Kentucky	61,766	1.3%		17	Virginia	109,991	2.2%
10	Louisiana	152,955	3.1%		18	Massachusetts	105,960	2.2%
42	Maine	17,273	0.4%		19	Washington	83,322	1.7%
14	Maryland	122,189	2.5%		20	Tennessee	79,902	1.6%
18	Massachusetts	105,960	2.2%		21	Minnesota	68,496	1.4%
11	Michigan	151,909	3.1%		22	Alabama	63,920	1.3%
21	Minnesota	68,496	1.4%		23	Kentucky	61,766	1.3%
32	Mississippi	38,168	0.8%		24	Connecticut	60,353	1.2%
16	Missouri	110,040	2.2%		25	Iowa	59,419	1.2%
45	Montana	9,604	0.2%		26	South Carolina	48,393	1.0%
30	Nebraska	43,985	0.9%		27	Colorado	47,875	1.0%
38	Nevada	19,166	0.4%		28	Oregon	47,127	1.0%
36	New Hampshire	19,993	0.4%		29	Arizona	46,252	0.9%
8	New Jersey	172,214	3.5%		30	Nebraska	43,985	0.9%
37	New Mexico	19,571	0.4%		31	Hawaii	41,703	0.9%
2	New York	461,297	9.4%		32	Mississippi	38,168	0.8%
15	North Carolina	110,106	2.2%		33	Kansas	37,835	0.8%
48	North Dakota	6,404	0.1%		34	Arkansas	30,607	0.6%
7	Ohio	222,863	4.5%		35	Oklahoma	26,977	0.6%
35	Oklahoma	26,977	0.6%		36	New Hampshire	19,993	0.4%
28	Oregon	47,127	1.0%		37	New Mexico	19,571	0.4%
4	Pennsylvania	271,234	5.5%		38	Nevada	19,166	0.4%
39	Rhode Island	18,104	0.4%		39	Rhode Island	18,104	0.4%
26	South Carolina	48,393	1.0%		40	Utah	17,636	0.4%
47	South Dakota	8,758	0.2%		41	Delaware	17,310	0.4%
20	Tennessee	79,902	1.6%		42	Maine	17,273	0.4%
5	Texas	269,157	5.5%		43	Idaho	13,901	0.3%
40	Utah	17,636	0.4%		44	West Virginia	12,951	0.3%
46	Vermont	9,335	0.2%		45	Montana	9,604	0.2%
17	Virginia	109,991	2.2%		46	Vermont	9,335	0.2%
19	Washington	83,322	1.7%		47	South Dakota	8,758	0.2%
44	West Virginia	12,951	0.3%		48	North Dakota	6,404	0.1%
13	Wisconsin	126,035	2.6%		49	Alaska	4,518	0.1%
50	Wyoming	1,488	0.0%		50	Wyoming	1,488	0.0%
						District of Columbia	15,856	0.3%

ALPHA ORDER — RANK ORDER

Source: U.S. Department of Education, National Center for Education Statistics
"Characteristics of Private Schools in the United States" (https://nces.ed.gov/pubsearch/pubsinfo.asp?pubid=2017073)
*For school year 2015-2016. Includes private schools that provide instruction for one or more grades kindergarten through 12 (or comparable ungraded levels).

Public Elementary and Secondary Schools in 2016

National Total = 98,466 Schools*

ALPHA ORDER

RANK	STATE	SCHOOLS	% of USA
24	Alabama	1,509	1.5%
44	Alaska	508	0.5%
15	Arizona	2,285	2.3%
32	Arkansas	1,088	1.1%
1	California	10,303	10.5%
19	Colorado	1,862	1.9%
27	Connecticut	1,369	1.4%
50	Delaware	223	0.2%
4	Florida	4,322	4.4%
14	Georgia	2,297	2.3%
49	Hawaii	290	0.3%
38	Idaho	744	0.8%
5	Illinois	4,175	4.2%
18	Indiana	1,921	2.0%
28	Iowa	1,349	1.4%
29	Kansas	1,320	1.3%
23	Kentucky	1,541	1.6%
26	Louisiana	1,390	1.4%
42	Maine	611	0.6%
25	Maryland	1,437	1.5%
19	Massachusetts	1,862	1.9%
7	Michigan	3,469	3.5%
11	Minnesota	2,478	2.5%
34	Mississippi	1,076	1.1%
13	Missouri	2,424	2.5%
37	Montana	823	0.8%
33	Nebraska	1,085	1.1%
41	Nevada	662	0.7%
45	New Hampshire	490	0.5%
10	New Jersey	2,588	2.6%
36	New Mexico	884	0.9%
3	New York	4,824	4.9%
9	North Carolina	2,603	2.6%
43	North Dakota	526	0.5%
6	Ohio	3,619	3.7%
22	Oklahoma	1,800	1.8%
31	Oregon	1,242	1.3%
8	Pennsylvania	3,019	3.1%
48	Rhode Island	313	0.3%
30	South Carolina	1,248	1.3%
40	South Dakota	698	0.7%
21	Tennessee	1,859	1.9%
2	Texas	8,826	9.0%
35	Utah	1,033	1.0%
47	Vermont	314	0.3%
17	Virginia	2,133	2.2%
12	Washington	2,427	2.5%
38	West Virginia	744	0.8%
16	Wisconsin	2,255	2.3%
46	Wyoming	370	0.4%

RANK ORDER

RANK	STATE	SCHOOLS	% of USA
1	California	10,303	10.5%
2	Texas	8,826	9.0%
3	New York	4,824	4.9%
4	Florida	4,322	4.4%
5	Illinois	4,175	4.2%
6	Ohio	3,619	3.7%
7	Michigan	3,469	3.5%
8	Pennsylvania	3,019	3.1%
9	North Carolina	2,603	2.6%
10	New Jersey	2,588	2.6%
11	Minnesota	2,478	2.5%
12	Washington	2,427	2.5%
13	Missouri	2,424	2.5%
14	Georgia	2,297	2.3%
15	Arizona	2,285	2.3%
16	Wisconsin	2,255	2.3%
17	Virginia	2,133	2.2%
18	Indiana	1,921	2.0%
19	Colorado	1,862	1.9%
19	Massachusetts	1,862	1.9%
21	Tennessee	1,859	1.9%
22	Oklahoma	1,800	1.8%
23	Kentucky	1,541	1.6%
24	Alabama	1,509	1.5%
25	Maryland	1,437	1.5%
26	Louisiana	1,390	1.4%
27	Connecticut	1,369	1.4%
28	Iowa	1,349	1.4%
29	Kansas	1,320	1.3%
30	South Carolina	1,248	1.3%
31	Oregon	1,242	1.3%
32	Arkansas	1,088	1.1%
33	Nebraska	1,085	1.1%
34	Mississippi	1,076	1.1%
35	Utah	1,033	1.0%
36	New Mexico	884	0.9%
37	Montana	823	0.8%
38	Idaho	744	0.8%
38	West Virginia	744	0.8%
40	South Dakota	698	0.7%
41	Nevada	662	0.7%
42	Maine	611	0.6%
43	North Dakota	526	0.5%
44	Alaska	508	0.5%
45	New Hampshire	490	0.5%
46	Wyoming	370	0.4%
47	Vermont	314	0.3%
48	Rhode Island	313	0.3%
49	Hawaii	290	0.3%
50	Delaware	223	0.2%
	District of Columbia	228	0.2%

Source: U.S. Department of Education, National Center for Education Statistics
   "ElSi Table Generator" (http://nces.ed.gov/ccd/elsi/)
*For school year 2015-2016.

Enrollment in Public Elementary and Secondary Schools in 2016

National Total = 50,327,015 Students*

ALPHA ORDER

RANK	STATE	STUDENTS	% of USA
24	Alabama	743,789	1.5%
47	Alaska	132,477	0.3%
13	Arizona	1,109,040	2.2%
33	Arkansas	492,132	1.0%
1	California	6,226,737	12.4%
19	Colorado	899,112	1.8%
30	Connecticut	537,933	1.1%
45	Delaware	134,847	0.3%
3	Florida	2,792,234	5.5%
6	Georgia	1,757,237	3.5%
41	Hawaii	181,995	0.4%
38	Idaho	292,277	0.6%
5	Illinois	2,041,779	4.1%
15	Indiana	1,046,757	2.1%
31	Iowa	508,014	1.0%
32	Kansas	495,884	1.0%
27	Kentucky	686,598	1.4%
25	Louisiana	718,711	1.4%
42	Maine	181,613	0.4%
20	Maryland	879,601	1.7%
17	Massachusetts	964,026	1.9%
10	Michigan	1,536,231	3.1%
22	Minnesota	864,384	1.7%
34	Mississippi	487,200	1.0%
18	Missouri	919,234	1.8%
43	Montana	145,319	0.3%
37	Nebraska	316,014	0.6%
35	Nevada	467,527	0.9%
40	New Hampshire	182,425	0.4%
11	New Jersey	1,408,845	2.8%
36	New Mexico	335,694	0.7%
4	New York	2,711,626	5.4%
9	North Carolina	1,544,934	3.1%
48	North Dakota	108,644	0.2%
8	Ohio	1,716,585	3.4%
26	Oklahoma	692,878	1.4%
29	Oregon	576,407	1.1%
7	Pennsylvania	1,717,414	3.4%
44	Rhode Island	142,014	0.3%
23	South Carolina	763,533	1.5%
46	South Dakota	134,253	0.3%
16	Tennessee	1,001,235	2.0%
2	Texas	5,301,477	10.5%
28	Utah	647,870	1.3%
50	Vermont	87,866	0.2%
12	Virginia	1,283,590	2.6%
14	Washington	1,087,030	2.2%
39	West Virginia	277,452	0.6%
21	Wisconsin	867,800	1.7%
49	Wyoming	94,717	0.2%

RANK ORDER

RANK	STATE	STUDENTS	% of USA
1	California	6,226,737	12.4%
2	Texas	5,301,477	10.5%
3	Florida	2,792,234	5.5%
4	New York	2,711,626	5.4%
5	Illinois	2,041,779	4.1%
6	Georgia	1,757,237	3.5%
7	Pennsylvania	1,717,414	3.4%
8	Ohio	1,716,585	3.4%
9	North Carolina	1,544,934	3.1%
10	Michigan	1,536,231	3.1%
11	New Jersey	1,408,845	2.8%
12	Virginia	1,283,590	2.6%
13	Arizona	1,109,040	2.2%
14	Washington	1,087,030	2.2%
15	Indiana	1,046,757	2.1%
16	Tennessee	1,001,235	2.0%
17	Massachusetts	964,026	1.9%
18	Missouri	919,234	1.8%
19	Colorado	899,112	1.8%
20	Maryland	879,601	1.7%
21	Wisconsin	867,800	1.7%
22	Minnesota	864,384	1.7%
23	South Carolina	763,533	1.5%
24	Alabama	743,789	1.5%
25	Louisiana	718,711	1.4%
26	Oklahoma	692,878	1.4%
27	Kentucky	686,598	1.4%
28	Utah	647,870	1.3%
29	Oregon	576,407	1.1%
30	Connecticut	537,933	1.1%
31	Iowa	508,014	1.0%
32	Kansas	495,884	1.0%
33	Arkansas	492,132	1.0%
34	Mississippi	487,200	1.0%
35	Nevada	467,527	0.9%
36	New Mexico	335,694	0.7%
37	Nebraska	316,014	0.6%
38	Idaho	292,277	0.6%
39	West Virginia	277,452	0.6%
40	New Hampshire	182,425	0.4%
41	Hawaii	181,995	0.4%
42	Maine	181,613	0.4%
43	Montana	145,319	0.3%
44	Rhode Island	142,014	0.3%
45	Delaware	134,847	0.3%
46	South Dakota	134,253	0.3%
47	Alaska	132,477	0.3%
48	North Dakota	108,644	0.2%
49	Wyoming	94,717	0.2%
50	Vermont	87,866	0.2%
	District of Columbia	84,024	0.2%

Source: U.S. Department of Education, National Center for Education Statistics
"ElSi Table Generator" (http://nces.ed.gov/ccd/elsi/)
*For school year 2015-2016.

Public Elementary and Secondary School Teachers in 2016

National Total = 3,151,496 Teachers*

ALPHA ORDER

RANK	STATE	TEACHERS	% of USA
28	Alabama	40,766	1.3%
49	Alaska	7,832	0.2%
24	Arizona	47,944	1.5%
30	Arkansas	35,804	1.1%
2	California	263,475	8.4%
22	Colorado	51,798	1.6%
25	Connecticut	43,772	1.4%
47	Delaware	8,962	0.3%
4	Florida	182,586	5.8%
8	Georgia	113,031	3.6%
42	Hawaii	11,747	0.4%
39	Idaho	15,656	0.5%
5	Illinois	129,948	4.1%
20	Indiana	57,675	1.8%
31	Iowa	35,687	1.1%
29	Kansas	40,035	1.3%
27	Kentucky	41,902	1.3%
17	Louisiana	58,469	1.9%
40	Maine	14,857	0.5%
16	Maryland	59,414	1.9%
13	Massachusetts	71,969	2.3%
12	Michigan	84,181	2.7%
21	Minnesota	55,985	1.8%
32	Mississippi	32,175	1.0%
14	Missouri	67,635	2.1%
44	Montana	10,412	0.3%
35	Nebraska	23,308	0.7%
36	Nevada	22,702	0.7%
41	New Hampshire	14,770	0.5%
7	New Jersey	114,969	3.6%
37	New Mexico	21,722	0.7%
3	New York	206,086	6.5%
10	North Carolina	99,355	3.2%
46	North Dakota	9,195	0.3%
9	Ohio	101,742	3.2%
26	Oklahoma	42,452	1.3%
33	Oregon	29,086	0.9%
6	Pennsylvania	120,893	3.8%
43	Rhode Island	10,631	0.3%
23	South Carolina	50,237	1.6%
45	South Dakota	9,638	0.3%
15	Tennessee	66,488	2.1%
1	Texas	347,329	11.0%
34	Utah	28,348	0.9%
48	Vermont	8,338	0.3%
11	Virginia	90,255	2.9%
19	Washington	57,942	1.8%
38	West Virginia	19,664	0.6%
18	Wisconsin	58,185	1.8%
50	Wyoming	7,653	0.2%

RANK ORDER

RANK	STATE	TEACHERS	% of USA
1	Texas	347,329	11.0%
2	California	263,475	8.4%
3	New York	206,086	6.5%
4	Florida	182,586	5.8%
5	Illinois	129,948	4.1%
6	Pennsylvania	120,893	3.8%
7	New Jersey	114,969	3.6%
8	Georgia	113,031	3.6%
9	Ohio	101,742	3.2%
10	North Carolina	99,355	3.2%
11	Virginia	90,255	2.9%
12	Michigan	84,181	2.7%
13	Massachusetts	71,969	2.3%
14	Missouri	67,635	2.1%
15	Tennessee	66,488	2.1%
16	Maryland	59,414	1.9%
17	Louisiana	58,469	1.9%
18	Wisconsin	58,185	1.8%
19	Washington	57,942	1.8%
20	Indiana	57,675	1.8%
21	Minnesota	55,985	1.8%
22	Colorado	51,798	1.6%
23	South Carolina	50,237	1.6%
24	Arizona	47,944	1.5%
25	Connecticut	43,772	1.4%
26	Oklahoma	42,452	1.3%
27	Kentucky	41,902	1.3%
28	Alabama	40,766	1.3%
29	Kansas	40,035	1.3%
30	Arkansas	35,804	1.1%
31	Iowa	35,687	1.1%
32	Mississippi	32,175	1.0%
33	Oregon	29,086	0.9%
34	Utah	28,348	0.9%
35	Nebraska	23,308	0.7%
36	Nevada	22,702	0.7%
37	New Mexico	21,722	0.7%
38	West Virginia	19,664	0.6%
39	Idaho	15,656	0.5%
40	Maine	14,857	0.5%
41	New Hampshire	14,770	0.5%
42	Hawaii	11,747	0.4%
43	Rhode Island	10,631	0.3%
44	Montana	10,412	0.3%
45	South Dakota	9,638	0.3%
46	North Dakota	9,195	0.3%
47	Delaware	8,962	0.3%
48	Vermont	8,338	0.3%
49	Alaska	7,832	0.2%
50	Wyoming	7,653	0.2%
	District of Columbia	6,789	0.2%

Source: U.S. Department of Education, National Center for Education Statistics
"ElSi Table Generator" (http://nces.ed.gov/ccd/elsi/)
*For school year 2015-2016. Counts are full-time equivalent figures.

Pupil-Teacher Ratio in Public Elementary and Secondary Schools in 2016

National Ratio = 16.0 Pupils Per Teacher*

ALPHA ORDER

RANK	STATE	RATIO
8	Alabama	18.3
12	Alaska	16.9
2	Arizona	23.1
36	Arkansas	13.8
1	California	23.6
11	Colorado	17.4
45	Connecticut	12.3
25	Delaware	15.1
22	Florida	15.3
17	Georgia	15.6
19	Hawaii	15.5
7	Idaho	18.7
16	Illinois	15.7
10	Indiana	18.2
30	Iowa	14.2
42	Kansas	12.4
14	Kentucky	16.4
45	Louisiana	12.3
48	Maine	12.2
29	Maryland	14.8
39	Massachusetts	13.4
8	Michigan	18.3
21	Minnesota	15.4
25	Mississippi	15.1
37	Missouri	13.6
34	Montana	14.0
37	Nebraska	13.6
4	Nevada	20.6
42	New Hampshire	12.4
45	New Jersey	12.3
19	New Mexico	15.5
41	New York	13.2
17	North Carolina	15.6
49	North Dakota	11.8
12	Ohio	16.9
15	Oklahoma	16.3
5	Oregon	19.8
30	Pennsylvania	14.2
39	Rhode Island	13.4
24	South Carolina	15.2
35	South Dakota	13.9
25	Tennessee	15.1
22	Texas	15.3
3	Utah	22.9
50	Vermont	10.5
30	Virginia	14.2
6	Washington	18.8
33	West Virginia	14.1
28	Wisconsin	14.9
42	Wyoming	12.4

RANK ORDER

RANK	STATE	RATIO
1	California	23.6
2	Arizona	23.1
3	Utah	22.9
4	Nevada	20.6
5	Oregon	19.8
6	Washington	18.8
7	Idaho	18.7
8	Alabama	18.3
8	Michigan	18.3
10	Indiana	18.2
11	Colorado	17.4
12	Alaska	16.9
12	Ohio	16.9
14	Kentucky	16.4
15	Oklahoma	16.3
16	Illinois	15.7
17	Georgia	15.6
17	North Carolina	15.6
19	Hawaii	15.5
19	New Mexico	15.5
21	Minnesota	15.4
22	Florida	15.3
22	Texas	15.3
24	South Carolina	15.2
25	Delaware	15.1
25	Mississippi	15.1
25	Tennessee	15.1
28	Wisconsin	14.9
29	Maryland	14.8
30	Iowa	14.2
30	Pennsylvania	14.2
30	Virginia	14.2
33	West Virginia	14.1
34	Montana	14.0
35	South Dakota	13.9
36	Arkansas	13.8
37	Missouri	13.6
37	Nebraska	13.6
39	Massachusetts	13.4
39	Rhode Island	13.4
41	New York	13.2
42	Kansas	12.4
42	New Hampshire	12.4
42	Wyoming	12.4
45	Connecticut	12.3
45	Louisiana	12.3
45	New Jersey	12.3
48	Maine	12.2
49	North Dakota	11.8
50	Vermont	10.5
	District of Columbia	12.4

Source: U.S. Department of Education, National Center for Education Statistics
"ElSi Table Generator" (http://nces.ed.gov/ccd/elsi/)
*For school year 2015-2016. Based on full-time equivalency counts of teachers.

Estimated Average Salary of Public School Teachers in 2017
(National Education Association)
National Average = $58,950*

ALPHA ORDER

RANK	STATE	SALARY
36	Alabama	$48,868
6	Alaska	68,138
44	Arizona	47,403
37	Arkansas	48,616
2	California	78,711
46	Colorado	46,506
4	Connecticut	72,561
13	Delaware	60,214
35	Florida	49,407
23	Georgia	54,602
16	Hawaii	57,674
42	Idaho	47,504
12	Illinois	61,602
32	Indiana	50,554
21	Iowa	55,443
41	Kansas	47,984
26	Kentucky	52,339
33	Louisiana	50,000
30	Maine	51,077
7	Maryland	66,961
3	Massachusetts	77,804
10	Michigan	62,200
18	Minnesota	57,346
49	Mississippi	42,925
40	Missouri	48,293
29	Montana	51,422
27	Nebraska	52,338
17	Nevada	57,376
19	New Hampshire	57,253
5	New Jersey	69,623
43	New Mexico	47,500
1	New York	79,637
34	North Carolina	49,837
28	North Dakota	51,618
20	Ohio	57,000
48	Oklahoma	45,245
11	Oregon	61,631
9	Pennsylvania	65,863
8	Rhode Island	66,477
38	South Carolina	48,598
50	South Dakota	42,668
39	Tennessee	48,456
25	Texas	52,575
45	Utah	47,244
14	Vermont	60,187
31	Virginia	51,049
24	Washington	54,147
47	West Virginia	45,701
22	Wisconsin	54,998
15	Wyoming	58,650

RANK ORDER

RANK	STATE	SALARY
1	New York	$79,637
2	California	78,711
3	Massachusetts	77,804
4	Connecticut	72,561
5	New Jersey	69,623
6	Alaska	68,138
7	Maryland	66,961
8	Rhode Island	66,477
9	Pennsylvania	65,863
10	Michigan	62,200
11	Oregon	61,631
12	Illinois	61,602
13	Delaware	60,214
14	Vermont	60,187
15	Wyoming	58,650
16	Hawaii	57,674
17	Nevada	57,376
18	Minnesota	57,346
19	New Hampshire	57,253
20	Ohio	57,000
21	Iowa	55,443
22	Wisconsin	54,998
23	Georgia	54,602
24	Washington	54,147
25	Texas	52,575
26	Kentucky	52,339
27	Nebraska	52,338
28	North Dakota	51,618
29	Montana	51,422
30	Maine	51,077
31	Virginia	51,049
32	Indiana	50,554
33	Louisiana	50,000
34	North Carolina	49,837
35	Florida	49,407
36	Alabama	48,868
37	Arkansas	48,616
38	South Carolina	48,598
39	Tennessee	48,456
40	Missouri	48,293
41	Kansas	47,984
42	Idaho	47,504
43	New Mexico	47,500
44	Arizona	47,403
45	Utah	47,244
46	Colorado	46,506
47	West Virginia	45,701
48	Oklahoma	45,245
49	Mississippi	42,925
50	South Dakota	42,668
	District of Columbia	76,131

Source: National Education Association, Washington, D.C.
"Rankings and Estimates" (Copyright © 2017, NEA, http://www.nea.org/home/44479.htm)
*Estimates for school year 2016-2017 for classroom teachers.

Average Teacher's Salary as a Percent of Average Annual Pay in 2016

National Average = 109.1% of Average Annual Pay*

ALPHA ORDER

RANK	STATE	PERCENT
30	Alabama	110.0
4	Alaska	126.5
47	Arizona	95.7
19	Arkansas	116.5
11	California	120.3
50	Colorado	88.3
32	Connecticut	109.7
27	Delaware	110.9
38	Florida	104.8
35	Georgia	107.3
12	Hawaii	119.5
18	Idaho	117.2
33	Illinois	108.9
23	Indiana	113.6
9	Iowa	122.3
29	Kansas	110.1
17	Kentucky	117.9
36	Louisiana	106.0
14	Maine	118.9
21	Maryland	114.8
21	Massachusetts	114.8
7	Michigan	123.7
37	Minnesota	105.2
25	Mississippi	112.3
39	Missouri	104.2
5	Montana	126.0
14	Nebraska	118.9
10	Nevada	121.3
34	New Hampshire	108.3
28	New Jersey	110.7
26	New Mexico	111.1
20	New York	116.0
41	North Carolina	103.5
39	North Dakota	104.2
14	Ohio	118.9
44	Oklahoma	102.7
8	Oregon	123.0
6	Pennsylvania	124.7
3	Rhode Island	128.9
24	South Carolina	113.3
43	South Dakota	102.8
45	Tennessee	102.5
46	Texas	96.0
42	Utah	103.1
1	Vermont	132.2
48	Virginia	92.9
49	Washington	90.4
30	West Virginia	110.0
13	Wisconsin	119.3
2	Wyoming	129.4

RANK ORDER

RANK	STATE	PERCENT
1	Vermont	132.2
2	Wyoming	129.4
3	Rhode Island	128.9
4	Alaska	126.5
5	Montana	126.0
6	Pennsylvania	124.7
7	Michigan	123.7
8	Oregon	123.0
9	Iowa	122.3
10	Nevada	121.3
11	California	120.3
12	Hawaii	119.5
13	Wisconsin	119.3
14	Maine	118.9
14	Nebraska	118.9
14	Ohio	118.9
17	Kentucky	117.9
18	Idaho	117.2
19	Arkansas	116.5
20	New York	116.0
21	Maryland	114.8
21	Massachusetts	114.8
23	Indiana	113.6
24	South Carolina	113.3
25	Mississippi	112.3
26	New Mexico	111.1
27	Delaware	110.9
28	New Jersey	110.7
29	Kansas	110.1
30	Alabama	110.0
30	West Virginia	110.0
32	Connecticut	109.7
33	Illinois	108.9
34	New Hampshire	108.3
35	Georgia	107.3
36	Louisiana	106.0
37	Minnesota	105.2
38	Florida	104.8
39	Missouri	104.2
39	North Dakota	104.2
41	North Carolina	103.5
42	Utah	103.1
43	South Dakota	102.8
44	Oklahoma	102.7
45	Tennessee	102.5
46	Texas	96.0
47	Arizona	95.7
48	Virginia	92.9
49	Washington	90.4
50	Colorado	88.3

District of Columbia	84.9

Source: CQ Press using data from National Education Association, Washington, D.C.
"Rankings and Estimates" (Copyright © 2017, NEA, http://www.nea.org/home/44479.htm)
"Quarterly Census of Employment and Wages" (http://www.bls.gov/cew/home.htm)
*Average of public elementary and secondary teacher salary for school years 2015-2016 and 2016-2017 compared to each state's 2016 average annual pay for all workers covered by federal unemployment.

Percent of Public School Fourth Graders Proficient or Better in Reading in 2015
National Percent = 35%*

RANK	STATE	PERCENT
43	Alabama	29
40	Alaska	30
40	Arizona	30
38	Arkansas	32
48	California	28
15	Colorado	39
4	Connecticut	43
21	Delaware	37
15	Florida	39
33	Georgia	34
43	Hawaii	29
26	Idaho	36
30	Illinois	35
9	Indiana	40
18	Iowa	38
30	Kansas	35
9	Kentucky	40
43	Louisiana	29
26	Maine	36
21	Maryland	37
1	Massachusetts	50
43	Michigan	29
15	Minnesota	39
49	Mississippi	26
26	Missouri	36
21	Montana	37
9	Nebraska	40
43	Nevada	29
2	New Hampshire	46
4	New Jersey	43
50	New Mexico	23
26	New York	36
18	North Carolina	38
21	North Dakota	37
18	Ohio	38
35	Oklahoma	33
33	Oregon	34
7	Pennsylvania	41
9	Rhode Island	40
35	South Carolina	33
30	South Dakota	35
35	Tennessee	33
39	Texas	31
9	Utah	40
3	Vermont	45
4	Virginia	43
9	Washington	40
40	West Virginia	30
21	Wisconsin	37
7	Wyoming	41

RANK ORDER

RANK	STATE	PERCENT
1	Massachusetts	50
2	New Hampshire	46
3	Vermont	45
4	Connecticut	43
4	New Jersey	43
4	Virginia	43
7	Pennsylvania	41
7	Wyoming	41
9	Indiana	40
9	Kentucky	40
9	Nebraska	40
9	Rhode Island	40
9	Utah	40
9	Washington	40
15	Colorado	39
15	Florida	39
15	Minnesota	39
18	Iowa	38
18	North Carolina	38
18	Ohio	38
21	Delaware	37
21	Maryland	37
21	Montana	37
21	North Dakota	37
21	Wisconsin	37
26	Idaho	36
26	Maine	36
26	Missouri	36
26	New York	36
30	Illinois	35
30	Kansas	35
30	South Dakota	35
33	Georgia	34
33	Oregon	34
35	Oklahoma	33
35	South Carolina	33
35	Tennessee	33
38	Arkansas	32
39	Texas	31
40	Alaska	30
40	Arizona	30
40	West Virginia	30
43	Alabama	29
43	Hawaii	29
43	Louisiana	29
43	Michigan	29
43	Nevada	29
48	California	28
49	Mississippi	26
50	New Mexico	23

District of Columbia	27

Source: U.S. Department of Education, National Center for Education Statistics
"The Nation's Report Card: Reading 2015" (http://nces.ed.gov/nationsreportcard/)
*There are four achievement levels: Below Basic, Basic, Proficient, and Advanced. Proficient represents solid academic mastery for 4th graders. Students reaching this level have demonstrated competency over challenging subject matter, including subject matter knowledge, application of such knowledge to real-world situations, and analytical skills appropriate to the subject matter.

Percent of Public School Eighth Graders
Proficient or Better in Reading in 2015
National Percent = 33%*

ALPHA ORDER

RANK	STATE	PERCENT
46	Alabama	26
33	Alaska	31
33	Arizona	31
43	Arkansas	27
40	California	28
9	Colorado	38
4	Connecticut	43
33	Delaware	31
36	Florida	30
36	Georgia	30
46	Hawaii	26
12	Idaho	37
25	Illinois	35
12	Indiana	37
17	Iowa	36
25	Kansas	35
17	Kentucky	36
48	Louisiana	23
17	Maine	36
12	Maryland	37
1	Massachusetts	46
32	Michigan	32
6	Minnesota	40
49	Mississippi	20
17	Missouri	36
12	Montana	37
9	Nebraska	38
43	Nevada	27
2	New Hampshire	45
5	New Jersey	41
49	New Mexico	20
30	New York	33
36	North Carolina	30
28	North Dakota	34
17	Ohio	36
39	Oklahoma	29
17	Oregon	36
7	Pennsylvania	39
25	Rhode Island	35
40	South Carolina	28
28	South Dakota	34
30	Tennessee	33
40	Texas	28
9	Utah	38
3	Vermont	44
17	Virginia	36
12	Washington	37
43	West Virginia	27
7	Wisconsin	39
17	Wyoming	36

RANK ORDER

RANK	STATE	PERCENT
1	Massachusetts	46
2	New Hampshire	45
3	Vermont	44
4	Connecticut	43
5	New Jersey	41
6	Minnesota	40
7	Pennsylvania	39
7	Wisconsin	39
9	Colorado	38
9	Nebraska	38
9	Utah	38
12	Idaho	37
12	Indiana	37
12	Maryland	37
12	Montana	37
12	Washington	37
17	Iowa	36
17	Kentucky	36
17	Maine	36
17	Missouri	36
17	Ohio	36
17	Oregon	36
17	Virginia	36
17	Wyoming	36
25	Illinois	35
25	Kansas	35
25	Rhode Island	35
28	North Dakota	34
28	South Dakota	34
30	New York	33
30	Tennessee	33
32	Michigan	32
33	Alaska	31
33	Arizona	31
33	Delaware	31
36	Florida	30
36	Georgia	30
36	North Carolina	30
39	Oklahoma	29
40	California	28
40	South Carolina	28
40	Texas	28
43	Arkansas	27
43	Nevada	27
43	West Virginia	27
46	Alabama	26
46	Hawaii	26
48	Louisiana	23
49	Mississippi	20
49	New Mexico	20
	District of Columbia	19

Source: U.S. Department of Education, National Center for Education Statistics
     "The Nation's Report Card: Reading 2015" (http://nces.ed.gov/nationsreportcard/)
*There are four achievement levels: Below Basic, Basic, Proficient, and Advanced. Proficient represents solid academic mastery for 8th graders. Students reaching this level have demonstrated competency over challenging subject matter, including subject matter knowledge, application of such knowledge to real-world situations, and analytical skills appropriate to the subject matter.

Percent of Public School Fourth Graders Proficient or Better in Mathematics in 2015
National Percent = 39%*

ALPHA ORDER

RANK	STATE	PERCENT
50	Alabama	26
39	Alaska	35
29	Arizona	38
44	Arkansas	32
48	California	29
18	Colorado	43
21	Connecticut	41
33	Delaware	37
20	Florida	42
39	Georgia	35
29	Hawaii	38
29	Idaho	38
33	Illinois	37
4	Indiana	50
14	Iowa	44
21	Kansas	41
25	Kentucky	40
46	Louisiana	30
21	Maine	41
25	Maryland	40
1	Massachusetts	54
42	Michigan	34
2	Minnesota	53
46	Mississippi	30
29	Missouri	38
21	Montana	41
9	Nebraska	46
44	Nevada	32
3	New Hampshire	51
6	New Jersey	47
49	New Mexico	27
39	New York	35
14	North Carolina	44
10	North Dakota	45
10	Ohio	45
33	Oklahoma	37
33	Oregon	37
10	Pennsylvania	45
33	Rhode Island	37
38	South Carolina	36
25	South Dakota	40
25	Tennessee	40
14	Texas	44
14	Utah	44
18	Vermont	43
6	Virginia	47
6	Washington	47
43	West Virginia	33
10	Wisconsin	45
5	Wyoming	48

RANK ORDER

RANK	STATE	PERCENT
1	Massachusetts	54
2	Minnesota	53
3	New Hampshire	51
4	Indiana	50
5	Wyoming	48
6	New Jersey	47
6	Virginia	47
6	Washington	47
9	Nebraska	46
10	North Dakota	45
10	Ohio	45
10	Pennsylvania	45
10	Wisconsin	45
14	Iowa	44
14	North Carolina	44
14	Texas	44
14	Utah	44
18	Colorado	43
18	Vermont	43
20	Florida	42
21	Connecticut	41
21	Kansas	41
21	Maine	41
21	Montana	41
25	Kentucky	40
25	Maryland	40
25	South Dakota	40
25	Tennessee	40
29	Arizona	38
29	Hawaii	38
29	Idaho	38
29	Missouri	38
33	Delaware	37
33	Illinois	37
33	Oklahoma	37
33	Oregon	37
33	Rhode Island	37
38	South Carolina	36
39	Alaska	35
39	Georgia	35
39	New York	35
42	Michigan	34
43	West Virginia	33
44	Arkansas	32
44	Nevada	32
46	Louisiana	30
46	Mississippi	30
48	California	29
49	New Mexico	27
50	Alabama	26

| | District of Columbia | 31 |

Source: U.S. Department of Education, National Center for Education Statistics
    "The Nation's Report Card: Mathematics 2015" (http://nces.ed.gov/nationsreportcard/)
*There are four achievement levels: Below Basic, Basic, Proficient, and Advanced. Proficient represents solid academic mastery for 4th graders. Students reaching this level have demonstrated competency over challenging subject matter, including subject matter knowledge, application of such knowledge to real-world situations, and analytical skills appropriate to the subject matter.

Percent of Public School Eighth Graders Proficient or Better in Mathematics in 2015
National Percent = 32%*

ALPHA ORDER

RANK	STATE	PERCENT
50	Alabama	17
28	Alaska	32
18	Arizona	35
44	Arkansas	25
40	California	27
14	Colorado	37
16	Connecticut	36
34	Delaware	30
41	Florida	26
38	Georgia	28
34	Hawaii	30
23	Idaho	34
28	Illinois	32
7	Indiana	39
14	Iowa	37
26	Kansas	33
38	Kentucky	28
49	Louisiana	18
18	Maine	35
18	Maryland	35
1	Massachusetts	51
36	Michigan	29
2	Minnesota	48
46	Mississippi	22
32	Missouri	31
7	Montana	39
11	Nebraska	38
41	Nevada	26
3	New Hampshire	46
3	New Jersey	46
47	New Mexico	21
32	New York	31
26	North Carolina	33
7	North Dakota	39
18	Ohio	35
45	Oklahoma	23
23	Oregon	34
16	Pennsylvania	36
28	Rhode Island	32
41	South Carolina	26
23	South Dakota	34
36	Tennessee	29
28	Texas	32
11	Utah	38
5	Vermont	42
11	Virginia	38
7	Washington	39
47	West Virginia	21
6	Wisconsin	41
18	Wyoming	35

RANK ORDER

RANK	STATE	PERCENT
1	Massachusetts	51
2	Minnesota	48
3	New Hampshire	46
3	New Jersey	46
5	Vermont	42
6	Wisconsin	41
7	Indiana	39
7	Montana	39
7	North Dakota	39
7	Washington	39
11	Nebraska	38
11	Utah	38
11	Virginia	38
14	Colorado	37
14	Iowa	37
16	Connecticut	36
16	Pennsylvania	36
18	Arizona	35
18	Maine	35
18	Maryland	35
18	Ohio	35
18	Wyoming	35
23	Idaho	34
23	Oregon	34
23	South Dakota	34
26	Kansas	33
26	North Carolina	33
28	Alaska	32
28	Illinois	32
28	Rhode Island	32
28	Texas	32
32	Missouri	31
32	New York	31
34	Delaware	30
34	Hawaii	30
36	Michigan	29
36	Tennessee	29
38	Georgia	28
38	Kentucky	28
40	California	27
41	Florida	26
41	Nevada	26
41	South Carolina	26
44	Arkansas	25
45	Oklahoma	23
46	Mississippi	22
47	New Mexico	21
47	West Virginia	21
49	Louisiana	18
50	Alabama	17

	District of Columbia	19

Source: U.S. Department of Education, National Center for Education Statistics
   "The Nation's Report Card: Mathematics 2015" (http://nces.ed.gov/nationsreportcard/)
*There are four achievement levels: Below Basic, Basic, Proficient, and Advanced. Proficient represents solid academic mastery for 8th graders. Students reaching this level have demonstrated competency over challenging subject matter, including subject matter knowledge, application of such knowledge to real-world situations, and analytical skills appropriate to the subject matter.

Percent of Population Graduated from High School in 2016

National Percent = 87.5%*

ALPHA ORDER				RANK ORDER		
RANK	STATE	PERCENT		RANK	STATE	PERCENT
46	Alabama	85.1		1	Wyoming	93.2
2	Alaska	93.1		2	Alaska	93.1
37	Arizona	86.7		3	Minnesota	92.9
41	Arkansas	86.0		4	Montana	92.8
50	California	82.4		4	New Hampshire	92.8
13	Colorado	91.4		6	North Dakota	92.4
17	Connecticut	90.5		7	Maine	92.3
27	Delaware	89.3		8	Vermont	92.1
34	Florida	87.4		9	Hawaii	92.0
39	Georgia	86.4		10	Wisconsin	91.9
9	Hawaii	92.0		11	Iowa	91.8
19	Idaho	90.4		12	Utah	91.7
30	Illinois	88.8		13	Colorado	91.4
32	Indiana	88.4		14	South Dakota	91.2
11	Iowa	91.8		15	Nebraska	90.9
17	Kansas	90.5		16	Washington	90.8
44	Kentucky	85.7		17	Connecticut	90.5
47	Louisiana	84.4		17	Kansas	90.5
7	Maine	92.3		19	Idaho	90.4
23	Maryland	90.1		19	Massachusetts	90.4
19	Massachusetts	90.4		19	Michigan	90.4
19	Michigan	90.4		22	Oregon	90.3
3	Minnesota	92.9		23	Maryland	90.1
48	Mississippi	84.1		23	Pennsylvania	90.1
26	Missouri	89.6		25	Ohio	90.0
4	Montana	92.8		26	Missouri	89.6
15	Nebraska	90.9		27	Delaware	89.3
41	Nevada	86.0		27	New Jersey	89.3
4	New Hampshire	92.8		27	Virginia	89.3
27	New Jersey	89.3		30	Illinois	88.8
45	New Mexico	85.4		31	Rhode Island	88.5
40	New York	86.3		32	Indiana	88.4
35	North Carolina	87.3		33	Oklahoma	87.8
6	North Dakota	92.4		34	Florida	87.4
25	Ohio	90.0		35	North Carolina	87.3
33	Oklahoma	87.8		36	Tennessee	87.0
22	Oregon	90.3		37	Arizona	86.7
23	Pennsylvania	90.1		38	South Carolina	86.6
31	Rhode Island	88.5		39	Georgia	86.4
38	South Carolina	86.6		40	New York	86.3
14	South Dakota	91.2		41	Arkansas	86.0
36	Tennessee	87.0		41	Nevada	86.0
49	Texas	82.9		41	West Virginia	86.0
12	Utah	91.7		44	Kentucky	85.7
8	Vermont	92.1		45	New Mexico	85.4
27	Virginia	89.3		46	Alabama	85.1
16	Washington	90.8		47	Louisiana	84.4
41	West Virginia	86.0		48	Mississippi	84.1
10	Wisconsin	91.9		49	Texas	82.9
1	Wyoming	93.2		50	California	82.4
					District of Columbia	90.5

Source: U.S. Bureau of the Census
"2016 American Community Survey-Table S1501" (http://www.census.gov/programs-surveys/acs/)
*Persons age 25 and older. Includes equivalency status.

Projected Public High School Graduates in 2018

National Total = 3,297,050 Graduates*

ALPHA ORDER

RANK	STATE	GRADUATES	% of USA
24	Alabama	45,100	1.4%
47	Alaska	7,940	0.2%
16	Arizona	66,760	2.0%
33	Arkansas	30,970	0.9%
1	California	426,140	12.9%
22	Colorado	56,300	1.7%
29	Connecticut	36,440	1.1%
45	Delaware	8,780	0.3%
4	Florida	173,290	5.3%
9	Georgia	104,820	3.2%
42	Hawaii	11,060	0.3%
38	Idaho	18,940	0.6%
5	Illinois	138,320	4.2%
14	Indiana	68,200	2.1%
32	Iowa	33,590	1.0%
31	Kansas	33,610	1.0%
25	Kentucky	44,380	1.3%
26	Louisiana	42,120	1.3%
41	Maine	12,340	0.4%
20	Maryland	58,670	1.8%
15	Massachusetts	66,880	2.0%
10	Michigan	101,490	3.1%
21	Minnesota	57,950	1.8%
34	Mississippi	28,230	0.9%
18	Missouri	61,250	1.9%
44	Montana	9,300	0.3%
36	Nebraska	22,150	0.7%
35	Nevada	23,720	0.7%
40	New Hampshire	13,340	0.4%
11	New Jersey	96,510	2.9%
37	New Mexico	19,520	0.6%
3	New York	186,250	5.6%
8	North Carolina	108,230	3.3%
48	North Dakota	7,080	0.2%
7	Ohio	120,010	3.6%
27	Oklahoma	40,810	1.2%
30	Oregon	35,100	1.1%
6	Pennsylvania	120,760	3.7%
43	Rhode Island	9,350	0.3%
23	South Carolina	46,180	1.4%
46	South Dakota	8,180	0.2%
17	Tennessee	63,720	1.9%
2	Texas	341,620	10.4%
28	Utah	37,680	1.1%
50	Vermont	5,810	0.2%
12	Virginia	88,470	2.7%
13	Washington	70,640	2.1%
39	West Virginia	18,140	0.6%
19	Wisconsin	61,230	1.9%
49	Wyoming	5,870	0.2%

RANK ORDER

RANK	STATE	GRADUATES	% of USA
1	California	426,140	12.9%
2	Texas	341,620	10.4%
3	New York	186,250	5.6%
4	Florida	173,290	5.3%
5	Illinois	138,320	4.2%
6	Pennsylvania	120,760	3.7%
7	Ohio	120,010	3.6%
8	North Carolina	108,230	3.3%
9	Georgia	104,820	3.2%
10	Michigan	101,490	3.1%
11	New Jersey	96,510	2.9%
12	Virginia	88,470	2.7%
13	Washington	70,640	2.1%
14	Indiana	68,200	2.1%
15	Massachusetts	66,880	2.0%
16	Arizona	66,760	2.0%
17	Tennessee	63,720	1.9%
18	Missouri	61,250	1.9%
19	Wisconsin	61,230	1.9%
20	Maryland	58,670	1.8%
21	Minnesota	57,950	1.8%
22	Colorado	56,300	1.7%
23	South Carolina	46,180	1.4%
24	Alabama	45,100	1.4%
25	Kentucky	44,380	1.3%
26	Louisiana	42,120	1.3%
27	Oklahoma	40,810	1.2%
28	Utah	37,680	1.1%
29	Connecticut	36,440	1.1%
30	Oregon	35,100	1.1%
31	Kansas	33,610	1.0%
32	Iowa	33,590	1.0%
33	Arkansas	30,970	0.9%
34	Mississippi	28,230	0.9%
35	Nevada	23,720	0.7%
36	Nebraska	22,150	0.7%
37	New Mexico	19,520	0.6%
38	Idaho	18,940	0.6%
39	West Virginia	18,140	0.6%
40	New Hampshire	13,340	0.4%
41	Maine	12,340	0.4%
42	Hawaii	11,060	0.3%
43	Rhode Island	9,350	0.3%
44	Montana	9,300	0.3%
45	Delaware	8,780	0.3%
46	South Dakota	8,180	0.2%
47	Alaska	7,940	0.2%
48	North Dakota	7,080	0.2%
49	Wyoming	5,870	0.2%
50	Vermont	5,810	0.2%
	District of Columbia	3,820	0.1%

Source: U.S. Department of Education, National Center for Education Statistics
"Digest of Education Statistics 2016" (http://nces.ed.gov/programs/digest/index.asp)
*Projected for school year 2017-2018 as of May 2017. Excludes persons receiving high school equivalency certificates.

Adjusted Cohort Graduation Rate for Public High Schools in 2016

National Average = 84.1%*

ALPHA ORDER

RANK	STATE	PERCENT
16	Alabama	87.1
47	Alaska	76.1
43	Arizona	79.5
17	Arkansas	87.0
30	California	83.0
45	Colorado	78.9
15	Connecticut	87.4
25	Delaware	85.5
37	Florida	80.7
44	Georgia	79.4
32	Hawaii	82.7
40	Idaho	79.7
25	Illinois	85.5
19	Indiana	86.8
1	Iowa	91.3
23	Kansas	85.7
7	Kentucky	88.6
46	Louisiana	78.6
17	Maine	87.0
12	Maryland	87.6
13	Massachusetts	87.5
40	Michigan	79.7
35	Minnesota	82.2
34	Mississippi	82.3
6	Missouri	89.0
24	Montana	85.6
4	Nebraska	89.3
49	Nevada	73.6
9	New Hampshire	88.2
2	New Jersey	90.1
50	New Mexico	71.0
38	New York	80.4
22	North Carolina	85.9
13	North Dakota	87.5
29	Ohio	83.5
36	Oklahoma	81.6
48	Oregon	74.8
21	Pennsylvania	86.1
31	Rhode Island	82.8
33	South Carolina	82.6
28	South Dakota	83.9
8	Tennessee	88.5
5	Texas	89.1
27	Utah	85.2
11	Vermont	87.7
20	Virginia	86.7
40	Washington	79.7
3	West Virginia	89.8
9	Wisconsin	88.2
39	Wyoming	80.0

RANK ORDER

RANK	STATE	PERCENT
1	Iowa	91.3
2	New Jersey	90.1
3	West Virginia	89.8
4	Nebraska	89.3
5	Texas	89.1
6	Missouri	89.0
7	Kentucky	88.6
8	Tennessee	88.5
9	New Hampshire	88.2
9	Wisconsin	88.2
11	Vermont	87.7
12	Maryland	87.6
13	Massachusetts	87.5
13	North Dakota	87.5
15	Connecticut	87.4
16	Alabama	87.1
17	Arkansas	87.0
17	Maine	87.0
19	Indiana	86.8
20	Virginia	86.7
21	Pennsylvania	86.1
22	North Carolina	85.9
23	Kansas	85.7
24	Montana	85.6
25	Delaware	85.5
25	Illinois	85.5
27	Utah	85.2
28	South Dakota	83.9
29	Ohio	83.5
30	California	83.0
31	Rhode Island	82.8
32	Hawaii	82.7
33	South Carolina	82.6
34	Mississippi	82.3
35	Minnesota	82.2
36	Oklahoma	81.6
37	Florida	80.7
38	New York	80.4
39	Wyoming	80.0
40	Idaho	79.7
40	Michigan	79.7
40	Washington	79.7
43	Arizona	79.5
44	Georgia	79.4
45	Colorado	78.9
46	Louisiana	78.6
47	Alaska	76.1
48	Oregon	74.8
49	Nevada	73.6
50	New Mexico	71.0

| | District of Columbia | 69.2 |

Source: U.S. Department of Education, National Center for Education Statistics
"ED Data Express" (http://eddataexpress.ed.gov/index.cfm)
*The Adjusted Cohort Graduation Rate (ACGR) is the number of students who graduate in four years with a regular high school diploma divided by the number of students who form the adjusted cohort for the graduating class. From the beginning of 9th grade, students who are entering that grade for the first time form a cohort that is "adjusted" by adding any students who subsequently transfer into the cohort and subtracting any students who subsequently transfer out, emigrate to another country, or die.

Adjusted Cohort Graduation Rate for Public High School Economically Disadvantaged Students in 2016
National Average = 77.6%*

ALPHA ORDER

RANK	STATE	PERCENT
12	Alabama	80.9
43	Alaska	68.4
25	Arizona	76.7
8	Arkansas	83.8
16	California	79.0
46	Colorado	67.8
25	Connecticut	76.7
30	Delaware	76.0
35	Florida	74.4
33	Georgia	75.3
22	Hawaii	77.9
39	Idaho	71.9
25	Illinois	76.7
6	Indiana	85.0
7	Iowa	83.9
23	Kansas	77.5
3	Kentucky	85.6
36	Louisiana	72.9
20	Maine	78.0
15	Maryland	79.2
18	Massachusetts	78.4
47	Michigan	67.1
44	Minnesota	68.2
17	Mississippi	78.8
11	Missouri	82.1
28	Montana	76.4
10	Nebraska	82.2
50	Nevada	66.7
28	New Hampshire	76.4
9	New Jersey	82.7
49	New Mexico	66.9
37	New York	72.8
13	North Carolina	80.6
40	North Dakota	71.0
38	Ohio	72.0
31	Oklahoma	75.9
45	Oregon	68.1
20	Pennsylvania	78.0
34	Rhode Island	74.8
1	South Carolina	87.7
48	South Dakota	67.0
4	Tennessee	85.5
2	Texas	86.0
32	Utah	75.6
14	Vermont	80.0
19	Virginia	78.1
41	Washington	70.2
4	West Virginia	85.5
24	Wisconsin	77.4
42	Wyoming	69.1

RANK ORDER

RANK	STATE	PERCENT
1	South Carolina	87.7
2	Texas	86.0
3	Kentucky	85.6
4	Tennessee	85.5
4	West Virginia	85.5
6	Indiana	85.0
7	Iowa	83.9
8	Arkansas	83.8
9	New Jersey	82.7
10	Nebraska	82.2
11	Missouri	82.1
12	Alabama	80.9
13	North Carolina	80.6
14	Vermont	80.0
15	Maryland	79.2
16	California	79.0
17	Mississippi	78.8
18	Massachusetts	78.4
19	Virginia	78.1
20	Maine	78.0
20	Pennsylvania	78.0
22	Hawaii	77.9
23	Kansas	77.5
24	Wisconsin	77.4
25	Arizona	76.7
25	Connecticut	76.7
25	Illinois	76.7
28	Montana	76.4
28	New Hampshire	76.4
30	Delaware	76.0
31	Oklahoma	75.9
32	Utah	75.6
33	Georgia	75.3
34	Rhode Island	74.8
35	Florida	74.4
36	Louisiana	72.9
37	New York	72.8
38	Ohio	72.0
39	Idaho	71.9
40	North Dakota	71.0
41	Washington	70.2
42	Wyoming	69.1
43	Alaska	68.4
44	Minnesota	68.2
45	Oregon	68.1
46	Colorado	67.8
47	Michigan	67.1
48	South Dakota	67.0
49	New Mexico	66.9
50	Nevada	66.7
	District of Columbia	69.3

Source: U.S. Department of Education, National Center for Education Statistics
"ED Data Express" (http://eddataexpress.ed.gov/index.cfm)
*The Adjusted Cohort Graduation Rate (ACGR) is the number of students who graduate in four years with a regular high school diploma divided by the number of students who form the adjusted cohort for the graduating class. From the beginning of 9th grade, students who are entering that grade for the first time form a cohort that is "adjusted" by adding any students who subsequently transfer into the cohort and subtracting any students who subsequently transfer out, emigrate to another country, or die.

Adjusted Cohort Graduation Rate for Public High School Students with Limited English Proficiency in 2016
National Average = 66.9%*

ALPHA ORDER

RANK	STATE	PERCENT
30	Alabama	64.0
41	Alaska	55.0
50	Arizona	32.0
2	Arkansas	86.0
14	California	72.0
34	Colorado	61.4
25	Connecticut	67.0
11	Delaware	73.0
33	Florida	62.0
40	Georgia	56.5
19	Hawaii	69.0
11	Idaho	73.0
16	Illinois	71.9
17	Indiana	71.0
3	Iowa	81.0
5	Kansas	77.4
21	Kentucky	68.0
47	Louisiana	43.0
4	Maine	78.0
45	Maryland	48.0
29	Massachusetts	64.1
13	Michigan	72.1
31	Minnesota	63.2
28	Mississippi	65.0
21	Missouri	68.0
35	Montana	59.0
41	Nebraska	55.0
48	Nevada	42.6
14	New Hampshire	72.0
8	New Jersey	74.7
24	New Mexico	67.4
49	New York	37.8
38	North Carolina	57.0
19	North Dakota	69.0
44	Ohio	50.0
36	Oklahoma	58.0
43	Oregon	53.0
32	Pennsylvania	62.7
9	Rhode Island	74.0
6	South Carolina	76.0
38	South Dakota	57.0
6	Tennessee	76.0
10	Texas	73.7
26	Utah	66.0
21	Vermont	68.0
46	Virginia	45.4
37	Washington	57.8
1	West Virginia	93.0
26	Wisconsin	66.0
18	Wyoming	70.0

RANK ORDER

RANK	STATE	PERCENT
1	West Virginia	93.0
2	Arkansas	86.0
3	Iowa	81.0
4	Maine	78.0
5	Kansas	77.4
6	South Carolina	76.0
6	Tennessee	76.0
8	New Jersey	74.7
9	Rhode Island	74.0
10	Texas	73.7
11	Delaware	73.0
11	Idaho	73.0
13	Michigan	72.1
14	California	72.0
14	New Hampshire	72.0
16	Illinois	71.9
17	Indiana	71.0
18	Wyoming	70.0
19	Hawaii	69.0
19	North Dakota	69.0
21	Kentucky	68.0
21	Missouri	68.0
21	Vermont	68.0
24	New Mexico	67.4
25	Connecticut	67.0
26	Utah	66.0
26	Wisconsin	66.0
28	Mississippi	65.0
29	Massachusetts	64.1
30	Alabama	64.0
31	Minnesota	63.2
32	Pennsylvania	62.7
33	Florida	62.0
34	Colorado	61.4
35	Montana	59.0
36	Oklahoma	58.0
37	Washington	57.8
38	North Carolina	57.0
38	South Dakota	57.0
40	Georgia	56.5
41	Alaska	55.0
41	Nebraska	55.0
43	Oregon	53.0
44	Ohio	50.0
45	Maryland	48.0
46	Virginia	45.4
47	Louisiana	43.0
48	Nevada	42.6
49	New York	37.8
50	Arizona	32.0
	District of Columbia	64.0

Source: U.S. Department of Education, National Center for Education Statistics
    "ED Data Express" (http://eddataexpress.ed.gov/index.cfm)
*The Adjusted Cohort Graduation Rate (ACGR) is the number of students who graduate in four years with a regular high school diploma divided by the number of students who form the adjusted cohort for the graduating class. From the beginning of 9th grade, students who are entering that grade for the first time form a cohort that is "adjusted" by adding any students who subsequently transfer into the cohort and subtracting any students who subsequently transfer out, emigrate to another country, or die.

Adjusted Cohort Graduation Rate for Public High School Students with Disabilities in 2016
National Average = 65.5%*

ALPHA ORDER				RANK ORDER		
RANK	STATE	PERCENT		RANK	STATE	PERCENT
43	Alabama	54.1		1	Arkansas	84.3
44	Alaska	54.0		2	New Jersey	78.8
22	Arizona	69.0		3	Montana	78.0
1	Arkansas	84.3		4	Texas	77.9
28	California	66.0		5	Kansas	77.5
39	Colorado	57.2		5	Missouri	77.5
29	Connecticut	65.2		7	West Virginia	77.0
26	Delaware	67.0		8	Oklahoma	74.4
32	Florida	61.6		9	Pennsylvania	74.1
40	Georgia	56.6		10	New Hampshire	73.0
36	Hawaii	59.0		11	Indiana	72.0
34	Idaho	60.0		11	Maine	72.0
17	Illinois	70.5		11	Vermont	72.0
11	Indiana	72.0		14	Kentucky	71.9
19	Iowa	70.0		15	Massachusetts	71.8
5	Kansas	77.5		15	Tennessee	71.8
14	Kentucky	71.9		17	Illinois	70.5
48	Louisiana	46.6		18	Utah	70.2
11	Maine	72.0		19	Iowa	70.0
27	Maryland	66.9		19	Nebraska	70.0
15	Massachusetts	71.8		21	Ohio	69.6
42	Michigan	55.4		22	Arizona	69.0
33	Minnesota	60.8		23	North Carolina	68.9
49	Mississippi	34.7		24	Wisconsin	68.5
5	Missouri	77.5		25	North Dakota	68.0
3	Montana	78.0		26	Delaware	67.0
19	Nebraska	70.0		27	Maryland	66.9
50	Nevada	29.3		28	California	66.0
10	New Hampshire	73.0		29	Connecticut	65.2
2	New Jersey	78.8		30	Wyoming	65.0
31	New Mexico	61.9		31	New Mexico	61.9
46	New York	52.6		32	Florida	61.6
23	North Carolina	68.9		33	Minnesota	60.8
25	North Dakota	68.0		34	Idaho	60.0
21	Ohio	69.6		34	South Dakota	60.0
8	Oklahoma	74.4		36	Hawaii	59.0
41	Oregon	55.5		36	Rhode Island	59.0
9	Pennsylvania	74.1		38	Washington	58.7
36	Rhode Island	59.0		39	Colorado	57.2
47	South Carolina	52.1		40	Georgia	56.6
34	South Dakota	60.0		41	Oregon	55.5
15	Tennessee	71.8		42	Michigan	55.4
4	Texas	77.9		43	Alabama	54.1
18	Utah	70.2		44	Alaska	54.0
11	Vermont	72.0		45	Virginia	53.9
45	Virginia	53.9		46	New York	52.6
38	Washington	58.7		47	South Carolina	52.1
7	West Virginia	77.0		48	Louisiana	46.6
24	Wisconsin	68.5		49	Mississippi	34.7
30	Wyoming	65.0		50	Nevada	29.3
					District of Columbia	50.0

Source: U.S. Department of Education, National Center for Education Statistics
  "ED Data Express" (http://eddataexpress.ed.gov/index.cfm)
*The Adjusted Cohort Graduation Rate (ACGR) is the number of students who graduate in four years with a regular high school diploma divided by the number of students who form the adjusted cohort for the graduating class. From the beginning of 9th grade, students who are entering that grade for the first time form a cohort that is "adjusted" by adding any students who subsequently transfer into the cohort and subtracting any students who subsequently transfer out, emigrate to another country, or die.

ACT Average Composite Score in 2017

National Average = 21.0*

ALPHA ORDER

RANK	STATE	AVERAGE SCORE
45	Alabama	19.2
37	Alaska	19.8
40	Arizona	19.7
43	Arkansas	19.4
14	California	22.8
27	Colorado	20.8
3	Connecticut	25.2
6	Delaware	24.1
37	Florida	19.8
24	Georgia	21.4
47	Hawaii	19.0
16	Idaho	22.3
24	Illinois	21.4
15	Indiana	22.6
18	Iowa	21.9
22	Kansas	21.7
36	Kentucky	20.0
42	Louisiana	19.5
4	Maine	24.3
12	Maryland	23.6
2	Massachusetts	25.4
6	Michigan	24.1
23	Minnesota	21.5
49	Mississippi	18.6
30	Missouri	20.4
32	Montana	20.3
24	Nebraska	21.4
50	Nevada	17.8
1	New Hampshire	25.5
9	New Jersey	23.9
40	New Mexico	19.7
5	New York	24.2
46	North Carolina	19.1
32	North Dakota	20.3
17	Ohio	22.0
43	Oklahoma	19.4
20	Oregon	21.8
11	Pennsylvania	23.7
8	Rhode Island	24.0
48	South Carolina	18.7
20	South Dakota	21.8
37	Tennessee	19.8
28	Texas	20.7
32	Utah	20.3
12	Vermont	23.6
10	Virginia	23.8
18	Washington	21.9
30	West Virginia	20.4
29	Wisconsin	20.5
35	Wyoming	20.2

RANK ORDER

RANK	STATE	AVERAGE SCORE
1	New Hampshire	25.5
2	Massachusetts	25.4
3	Connecticut	25.2
4	Maine	24.3
5	New York	24.2
6	Delaware	24.1
6	Michigan	24.1
8	Rhode Island	24.0
9	New Jersey	23.9
10	Virginia	23.8
11	Pennsylvania	23.7
12	Maryland	23.6
12	Vermont	23.6
14	California	22.8
15	Indiana	22.6
16	Idaho	22.3
17	Ohio	22.0
18	Iowa	21.9
18	Washington	21.9
20	Oregon	21.8
20	South Dakota	21.8
22	Kansas	21.7
23	Minnesota	21.5
24	Georgia	21.4
24	Illinois	21.4
24	Nebraska	21.4
27	Colorado	20.8
28	Texas	20.7
29	Wisconsin	20.5
30	Missouri	20.4
30	West Virginia	20.4
32	Montana	20.3
32	North Dakota	20.3
32	Utah	20.3
35	Wyoming	20.2
36	Kentucky	20.0
37	Alaska	19.8
37	Florida	19.8
37	Tennessee	19.8
40	Arizona	19.7
40	New Mexico	19.7
42	Louisiana	19.5
43	Arkansas	19.4
43	Oklahoma	19.4
45	Alabama	19.2
46	North Carolina	19.1
47	Hawaii	19.0
48	South Carolina	18.7
49	Mississippi	18.6
50	Nevada	17.8
	District of Columbia	24.2

Source: The American College Testing Program (Copyright © 2017)
    "Average ACT Scores by State" (http://www.act.org/newsroom/)
*The ACT score range is 1 to 36. Slightly more than two million 2017 U.S. high school graduates took the test. Caution should be used in using ACT scores to compare states. The percentage of high graduates taking the test varies greatly from one state to another. For example, all graduates are required to take the test in seventeen states but, in Maine, only 8 percent of graduates took the test.

Education Expenditures by State and Local Governments in 2015

National Total = $937,027,332,000*

ALPHA ORDER					RANK ORDER			

RANK	STATE	EXPENDITURES	% of USA	RANK	STATE	EXPENDITURES	% of USA
24	Alabama	$13,328,361,000	1.4%	1	California	$115,757,949,000	12.4%
40	Alaska	3,665,092,000	0.4%	2	Texas	80,471,284,000	8.6%
19	Arizona	15,364,198,000	1.6%	3	New York	79,581,962,000	8.5%
33	Arkansas	8,189,058,000	0.9%	4	Florida	40,314,065,000	4.3%
1	California	115,757,949,000	12.4%	5	Pennsylvania	38,915,490,000	4.2%
20	Colorado	15,177,835,000	1.6%	6	Illinois	37,950,445,000	4.1%
25	Connecticut	13,080,970,000	1.4%	7	New Jersey	34,797,991,000	3.7%
41	Delaware	3,614,405,000	0.4%	8	Ohio	33,725,615,000	3.6%
4	Florida	40,314,065,000	4.3%	9	Michigan	28,886,212,000	3.1%
10	Georgia	26,148,686,000	2.8%	10	Georgia	26,148,686,000	2.8%
44	Hawaii	3,232,559,000	0.3%	11	Virginia	25,085,236,000	2.7%
45	Idaho	3,185,835,000	0.3%	12	North Carolina	24,802,832,000	2.6%
6	Illinois	37,950,445,000	4.1%	13	Massachusetts	21,868,223,000	2.3%
18	Indiana	16,795,438,000	1.8%	14	Washington	21,698,682,000	2.3%
29	Iowa	10,833,260,000	1.2%	15	Maryland	19,521,342,000	2.1%
31	Kansas	9,183,051,000	1.0%	16	Wisconsin	17,721,300,000	1.9%
27	Kentucky	11,945,199,000	1.3%	17	Minnesota	17,027,342,000	1.8%
26	Louisiana	12,633,485,000	1.3%	18	Indiana	16,795,438,000	1.8%
42	Maine	3,402,978,000	0.4%	19	Arizona	15,364,198,000	1.6%
15	Maryland	19,521,342,000	2.1%	20	Colorado	15,177,835,000	1.6%
13	Massachusetts	21,868,223,000	2.3%	21	Missouri	15,045,996,000	1.6%
9	Michigan	28,886,212,000	3.1%	22	Tennessee	14,164,049,000	1.5%
17	Minnesota	17,027,342,000	1.8%	23	South Carolina	13,742,406,000	1.5%
34	Mississippi	7,933,774,000	0.8%	24	Alabama	13,328,361,000	1.4%
21	Missouri	15,045,996,000	1.6%	25	Connecticut	13,080,970,000	1.4%
48	Montana	2,809,154,000	0.3%	26	Louisiana	12,633,485,000	1.3%
36	Nebraska	6,652,161,000	0.7%	27	Kentucky	11,945,199,000	1.3%
37	Nevada	5,888,383,000	0.6%	28	Oregon	11,465,229,000	1.2%
39	New Hampshire	3,930,883,000	0.4%	29	Iowa	10,833,260,000	1.2%
7	New Jersey	34,797,991,000	3.7%	30	Oklahoma	10,143,590,000	1.1%
35	New Mexico	6,739,104,000	0.7%	31	Kansas	9,183,051,000	1.0%
3	New York	79,581,962,000	8.5%	32	Utah	8,694,287,000	0.9%
12	North Carolina	24,802,832,000	2.6%	33	Arkansas	8,189,058,000	0.9%
46	North Dakota	2,941,104,000	0.3%	34	Mississippi	7,933,774,000	0.8%
8	Ohio	33,725,615,000	3.6%	35	New Mexico	6,739,104,000	0.7%
30	Oklahoma	10,143,590,000	1.1%	36	Nebraska	6,652,161,000	0.7%
28	Oregon	11,465,229,000	1.2%	37	Nevada	5,888,383,000	0.6%
5	Pennsylvania	38,915,490,000	4.2%	38	West Virginia	5,266,709,000	0.6%
43	Rhode Island	3,275,000,000	0.3%	39	New Hampshire	3,930,883,000	0.4%
23	South Carolina	13,742,406,000	1.5%	40	Alaska	3,665,092,000	0.4%
50	South Dakota	2,244,828,000	0.2%	41	Delaware	3,614,405,000	0.4%
22	Tennessee	14,164,049,000	1.5%	42	Maine	3,402,978,000	0.4%
2	Texas	80,471,284,000	8.6%	43	Rhode Island	3,275,000,000	0.3%
32	Utah	8,694,287,000	0.9%	44	Hawaii	3,232,559,000	0.3%
49	Vermont	2,546,431,000	0.3%	45	Idaho	3,185,835,000	0.3%
11	Virginia	25,085,236,000	2.7%	46	North Dakota	2,941,104,000	0.3%
14	Washington	21,698,682,000	2.3%	47	Wyoming	2,875,619,000	0.3%
38	West Virginia	5,266,709,000	0.6%	48	Montana	2,809,154,000	0.3%
16	Wisconsin	17,721,300,000	1.9%	49	Vermont	2,546,431,000	0.3%
47	Wyoming	2,875,619,000	0.3%	50	South Dakota	2,244,828,000	0.2%
					District of Columbia	2,762,245,000	0.3%

Source: U.S. Bureau of the Census, Governments Division
"2015 State and Local Government Finances" (http://www.census.gov/govs/local/)
*Direct general expenditures for higher, secondary, elementary, and, "other" education. Includes capital outlays.

Per Capita State and Local Government Expenditures for Education in 2015

National Per Capita = $2,919*

ALPHA ORDER

RANK	STATE	PER CAPITA
33	Alabama	$2,748
1	Alaska	4,966
46	Arizona	2,259
32	Arkansas	2,752
21	California	2,966
31	Colorado	2,790
8	Connecticut	3,640
7	Delaware	3,828
49	Florida	1,989
40	Georgia	2,564
45	Hawaii	2,266
50	Idaho	1,932
23	Illinois	2,951
42	Indiana	2,541
10	Iowa	3,474
14	Kansas	3,160
36	Kentucky	2,701
35	Louisiana	2,705
41	Maine	2,563
11	Maryland	3,253
13	Massachusetts	3,219
26	Michigan	2,912
15	Minnesota	3,105
37	Mississippi	2,658
43	Missouri	2,478
34	Montana	2,732
9	Nebraska	3,513
48	Nevada	2,042
22	New Hampshire	2,955
6	New Jersey	3,884
12	New Mexico	3,236
4	New York	4,015
44	North Carolina	2,470
5	North Dakota	3,896
27	Ohio	2,906
39	Oklahoma	2,598
29	Oregon	2,855
18	Pennsylvania	3,042
16	Rhode Island	3,102
30	South Carolina	2,809
38	South Dakota	2,628
47	Tennessee	2,149
24	Texas	2,931
25	Utah	2,913
3	Vermont	4,078
20	Virginia	2,998
19	Washington	3,034
28	West Virginia	2,863
17	Wisconsin	3,077
2	Wyoming	4,906

RANK ORDER

RANK	STATE	PER CAPITA
1	Alaska	$4,966
2	Wyoming	4,906
3	Vermont	4,078
4	New York	4,015
5	North Dakota	3,896
6	New Jersey	3,884
7	Delaware	3,828
8	Connecticut	3,640
9	Nebraska	3,513
10	Iowa	3,474
11	Maryland	3,253
12	New Mexico	3,236
13	Massachusetts	3,219
14	Kansas	3,160
15	Minnesota	3,105
16	Rhode Island	3,102
17	Wisconsin	3,077
18	Pennsylvania	3,042
19	Washington	3,034
20	Virginia	2,998
21	California	2,966
22	New Hampshire	2,955
23	Illinois	2,951
24	Texas	2,931
25	Utah	2,913
26	Michigan	2,912
27	Ohio	2,906
28	West Virginia	2,863
29	Oregon	2,855
30	South Carolina	2,809
31	Colorado	2,790
32	Arkansas	2,752
33	Alabama	2,748
34	Montana	2,732
35	Louisiana	2,705
36	Kentucky	2,701
37	Mississippi	2,658
38	South Dakota	2,628
39	Oklahoma	2,598
40	Georgia	2,564
41	Maine	2,563
42	Indiana	2,541
43	Missouri	2,478
44	North Carolina	2,470
45	Hawaii	2,266
46	Arizona	2,259
47	Tennessee	2,149
48	Nevada	2,042
49	Florida	1,989
50	Idaho	1,932
	District of Columbia	4,106

Source: CQ Press using data from U.S. Bureau of the Census, Governments Division
"2015 State and Local Government Finances" (http://www.census.gov/govs/local/)
*Direct general expenditures for higher, secondary, elementary, and, "other" education. Includes capital outlays.

Expenditures for Education as a Percent of All State and Local Government Expenditures in 2015
National Percent = 33.0%*

ALPHA ORDER

RANK	STATE	PERCENT
12	Alabama	36.0
49	Alaska	24.9
26	Arizona	34.1
17	Arkansas	35.0
47	California	28.2
36	Colorado	32.1
18	Connecticut	34.9
8	Delaware	37.3
47	Florida	28.2
4	Georgia	38.6
50	Hawaii	23.9
45	Idaho	30.1
29	Illinois	33.1
25	Indiana	34.2
13	Iowa	35.9
7	Kansas	37.5
38	Kentucky	32.0
40	Louisiana	31.1
42	Maine	30.7
27	Maryland	33.9
43	Massachusetts	30.5
11	Michigan	36.1
33	Minnesota	32.3
39	Mississippi	31.4
21	Missouri	34.4
34	Montana	32.2
1	Nebraska	40.0
46	Nevada	29.2
6	New Hampshire	37.6
5	New Jersey	38.5
36	New Mexico	32.1
41	New York	30.9
28	North Carolina	33.3
32	North Dakota	32.4
14	Ohio	35.4
14	Oklahoma	35.4
43	Oregon	30.5
22	Pennsylvania	34.3
31	Rhode Island	32.5
16	South Carolina	35.2
22	South Dakota	34.3
34	Tennessee	32.2
3	Texas	39.0
2	Utah	39.8
9	Vermont	36.8
10	Virginia	36.4
30	Washington	32.6
19	West Virginia	34.7
19	Wisconsin	34.7
22	Wyoming	34.3

RANK ORDER

RANK	STATE	PERCENT
1	Nebraska	40.0
2	Utah	39.8
3	Texas	39.0
4	Georgia	38.6
5	New Jersey	38.5
6	New Hampshire	37.6
7	Kansas	37.5
8	Delaware	37.3
9	Vermont	36.8
10	Virginia	36.4
11	Michigan	36.1
12	Alabama	36.0
13	Iowa	35.9
14	Ohio	35.4
14	Oklahoma	35.4
16	South Carolina	35.2
17	Arkansas	35.0
18	Connecticut	34.9
19	West Virginia	34.7
19	Wisconsin	34.7
21	Missouri	34.4
22	Pennsylvania	34.3
22	South Dakota	34.3
22	Wyoming	34.3
25	Indiana	34.2
26	Arizona	34.1
27	Maryland	33.9
28	North Carolina	33.3
29	Illinois	33.1
30	Washington	32.6
31	Rhode Island	32.5
32	North Dakota	32.4
33	Minnesota	32.3
34	Montana	32.2
34	Tennessee	32.2
36	Colorado	32.1
36	New Mexico	32.1
38	Kentucky	32.0
39	Mississippi	31.4
40	Louisiana	31.1
41	New York	30.9
42	Maine	30.7
43	Massachusetts	30.5
43	Oregon	30.5
45	Idaho	30.1
46	Nevada	29.2
47	California	28.2
47	Florida	28.2
49	Alaska	24.9
50	Hawaii	23.9
	District of Columbia	22.2

Source: CQ Press using data from U.S. Bureau of the Census, Governments Division
"2015 State and Local Government Finances" (http://www.census.gov/govs/local/)
*Direct general expenditures for higher, secondary, elementary, and "other" education as a percent of all direct general expenditures. Includes capital outlays.

State and Local Government Expenditures for Elementary and Secondary Education in 2015
National Total = $610,857,320,000*

ALPHA ORDER

RANK	STATE	EXPENDITURES	% of USA
26	Alabama	$7,508,621,000	1.2%
40	Alaska	2,654,389,000	0.4%
25	Arizona	7,732,726,000	1.3%
32	Arkansas	5,021,308,000	0.8%
1	California	72,362,324,000	11.8%
22	Colorado	9,077,799,000	1.5%
21	Connecticut	9,210,348,000	1.5%
46	Delaware	1,882,216,000	0.3%
5	Florida	26,663,155,000	4.4%
9	Georgia	18,247,880,000	3.0%
43	Hawaii	1,991,017,000	0.3%
44	Idaho	1,978,009,000	0.3%
7	Illinois	26,330,079,000	4.3%
19	Indiana	9,764,209,000	1.6%
29	Iowa	6,401,072,000	1.0%
31	Kansas	5,666,794,000	0.9%
27	Kentucky	6,907,042,000	1.1%
24	Louisiana	8,064,519,000	1.3%
41	Maine	2,411,179,000	0.4%
15	Maryland	12,742,631,000	2.1%
12	Massachusetts	15,543,891,000	2.5%
10	Michigan	16,730,543,000	2.7%
16	Minnesota	11,450,214,000	1.9%
33	Mississippi	4,569,305,000	0.7%
18	Missouri	10,149,884,000	1.7%
47	Montana	1,768,767,000	0.3%
35	Nebraska	4,177,012,000	0.7%
36	Nevada	4,010,110,000	0.7%
39	New Hampshire	2,855,092,000	0.5%
6	New Jersey	26,365,018,000	4.3%
37	New Mexico	3,771,782,000	0.6%
2	New York	63,748,645,000	10.4%
13	North Carolina	13,440,428,000	2.2%
48	North Dakota	1,724,102,000	0.3%
8	Ohio	22,462,382,000	3.7%
30	Oklahoma	5,943,244,000	1.0%
28	Oregon	6,650,721,000	1.1%
4	Pennsylvania	27,154,546,000	4.4%
42	Rhode Island	2,342,079,000	0.4%
23	South Carolina	8,354,694,000	1.4%
50	South Dakota	1,418,664,000	0.2%
20	Tennessee	9,220,804,000	1.5%
3	Texas	50,241,958,000	8.2%
34	Utah	4,427,409,000	0.7%
49	Vermont	1,595,844,000	0.3%
11	Virginia	16,329,081,000	2.7%
14	Washington	13,275,466,000	2.2%
38	West Virginia	3,149,841,000	0.5%
17	Wisconsin	10,898,889,000	1.8%
45	Wyoming	1,923,382,000	0.3%

RANK ORDER

RANK	STATE	EXPENDITURES	% of USA
1	California	$72,362,324,000	11.8%
2	New York	63,748,645,000	10.4%
3	Texas	50,241,958,000	8.2%
4	Pennsylvania	27,154,546,000	4.4%
5	Florida	26,663,155,000	4.4%
6	New Jersey	26,365,018,000	4.3%
7	Illinois	26,330,079,000	4.3%
8	Ohio	22,462,382,000	3.7%
9	Georgia	18,247,880,000	3.0%
10	Michigan	16,730,543,000	2.7%
11	Virginia	16,329,081,000	2.7%
12	Massachusetts	15,543,891,000	2.5%
13	North Carolina	13,440,428,000	2.2%
14	Washington	13,275,466,000	2.2%
15	Maryland	12,742,631,000	2.1%
16	Minnesota	11,450,214,000	1.9%
17	Wisconsin	10,898,889,000	1.8%
18	Missouri	10,149,884,000	1.7%
19	Indiana	9,764,209,000	1.6%
20	Tennessee	9,220,804,000	1.5%
21	Connecticut	9,210,348,000	1.5%
22	Colorado	9,077,799,000	1.5%
23	South Carolina	8,354,694,000	1.4%
24	Louisiana	8,064,519,000	1.3%
25	Arizona	7,732,726,000	1.3%
26	Alabama	7,508,621,000	1.2%
27	Kentucky	6,907,042,000	1.1%
28	Oregon	6,650,721,000	1.1%
29	Iowa	6,401,072,000	1.0%
30	Oklahoma	5,943,244,000	1.0%
31	Kansas	5,666,794,000	0.9%
32	Arkansas	5,021,308,000	0.8%
33	Mississippi	4,569,305,000	0.7%
34	Utah	4,427,409,000	0.7%
35	Nebraska	4,177,012,000	0.7%
36	Nevada	4,010,110,000	0.7%
37	New Mexico	3,771,782,000	0.6%
38	West Virginia	3,149,841,000	0.5%
39	New Hampshire	2,855,092,000	0.5%
40	Alaska	2,654,389,000	0.4%
41	Maine	2,411,179,000	0.4%
42	Rhode Island	2,342,079,000	0.4%
43	Hawaii	1,991,017,000	0.3%
44	Idaho	1,978,009,000	0.3%
45	Wyoming	1,923,382,000	0.3%
46	Delaware	1,882,216,000	0.3%
47	Montana	1,768,767,000	0.3%
48	North Dakota	1,724,102,000	0.3%
49	Vermont	1,595,844,000	0.3%
50	South Dakota	1,418,664,000	0.2%
	District of Columbia	2,546,206,000	0.4%

Source: U.S. Bureau of the Census, Governments Division
"2015 State and Local Government Finances" (http://www.census.gov/govs/local/)
*Direct general expenditures. Includes capital outlays.

Per Capita State and Local Government Expenditures for Elementary and Secondary Education in 2015
National Per Capita = $1,903*

ALPHA ORDER

RANK	STATE	PER CAPITA
39	Alabama	$1,548
1	Alaska	3,597
50	Arizona	1,137
32	Arkansas	1,687
23	California	1,854
35	Colorado	1,669
5	Connecticut	2,563
17	Delaware	1,994
48	Florida	1,315
27	Georgia	1,789
45	Hawaii	1,396
49	Idaho	1,199
16	Illinois	2,047
43	Indiana	1,477
15	Iowa	2,053
19	Kansas	1,950
38	Kentucky	1,562
28	Louisiana	1,726
25	Maine	1,816
12	Maryland	2,124
7	Massachusetts	2,288
32	Michigan	1,687
14	Minnesota	2,088
40	Mississippi	1,531
34	Missouri	1,671
29	Montana	1,720
10	Nebraska	2,206
46	Nevada	1,391
11	New Hampshire	2,146
4	New Jersey	2,943
26	New Mexico	1,811
3	New York	3,216
47	North Carolina	1,338
8	North Dakota	2,284
20	Ohio	1,935
41	Oklahoma	1,522
37	Oregon	1,656
13	Pennsylvania	2,123
9	Rhode Island	2,218
31	South Carolina	1,708
36	South Dakota	1,661
44	Tennessee	1,399
24	Texas	1,830
42	Utah	1,483
6	Vermont	2,556
18	Virginia	1,952
22	Washington	1,856
30	West Virginia	1,712
21	Wisconsin	1,892
2	Wyoming	3,282

RANK ORDER

RANK	STATE	PER CAPITA
1	Alaska	$3,597
2	Wyoming	3,282
3	New York	3,216
4	New Jersey	2,943
5	Connecticut	2,563
6	Vermont	2,556
7	Massachusetts	2,288
8	North Dakota	2,284
9	Rhode Island	2,218
10	Nebraska	2,206
11	New Hampshire	2,146
12	Maryland	2,124
13	Pennsylvania	2,123
14	Minnesota	2,088
15	Iowa	2,053
16	Illinois	2,047
17	Delaware	1,994
18	Virginia	1,952
19	Kansas	1,950
20	Ohio	1,935
21	Wisconsin	1,892
22	Washington	1,856
23	California	1,854
24	Texas	1,830
25	Maine	1,816
26	New Mexico	1,811
27	Georgia	1,789
28	Louisiana	1,726
29	Montana	1,720
30	West Virginia	1,712
31	South Carolina	1,708
32	Arkansas	1,687
32	Michigan	1,687
34	Missouri	1,671
35	Colorado	1,669
36	South Dakota	1,661
37	Oregon	1,656
38	Kentucky	1,562
39	Alabama	1,548
40	Mississippi	1,531
41	Oklahoma	1,522
42	Utah	1,483
43	Indiana	1,477
44	Tennessee	1,399
45	Hawaii	1,396
46	Nevada	1,391
47	North Carolina	1,338
48	Florida	1,315
49	Idaho	1,199
50	Arizona	1,137

| | District of Columbia | 3,785 |

Source: CQ Press using data from U.S. Bureau of the Census, Governments Division
"2015 State and Local Government Finances" (http://www.census.gov/govs/local/)
*Direct general expenditures. Includes capital outlays.

Expenditures for Elementary and Secondary Education as a Percent of All State and Local Government Expenditures in 2015
National Percent = 21.5%*

ALPHA ORDER

RANK	STATE	PERCENT
30	Alabama	20.3
44	Alaska	18.0
49	Arizona	17.2
22	Arkansas	21.5
48	California	17.6
38	Colorado	19.2
6	Connecticut	24.6
37	Delaware	19.4
40	Florida	18.7
3	Georgia	27.0
50	Hawaii	14.7
40	Idaho	18.7
14	Illinois	23.0
34	Indiana	19.9
25	Iowa	21.2
13	Kansas	23.1
42	Kentucky	18.5
34	Louisiana	19.9
18	Maine	21.7
17	Maryland	22.1
18	Massachusetts	21.7
27	Michigan	20.9
18	Minnesota	21.7
43	Mississippi	18.1
11	Missouri	23.2
30	Montana	20.3
4	Nebraska	25.1
34	Nevada	19.9
2	New Hampshire	27.3
1	New Jersey	29.2
44	New Mexico	18.0
5	New York	24.8
44	North Carolina	18.0
39	North Dakota	19.0
10	Ohio	23.6
28	Oklahoma	20.7
47	Oregon	17.7
8	Pennsylvania	24.0
11	Rhode Island	23.2
23	South Carolina	21.4
18	South Dakota	21.7
26	Tennessee	21.0
7	Texas	24.3
30	Utah	20.3
14	Vermont	23.0
9	Virginia	23.7
33	Washington	20.0
28	West Virginia	20.7
24	Wisconsin	21.3
16	Wyoming	22.9

RANK ORDER

RANK	STATE	PERCENT
1	New Jersey	29.2
2	New Hampshire	27.3
3	Georgia	27.0
4	Nebraska	25.1
5	New York	24.8
6	Connecticut	24.6
7	Texas	24.3
8	Pennsylvania	24.0
9	Virginia	23.7
10	Ohio	23.6
11	Missouri	23.2
11	Rhode Island	23.2
13	Kansas	23.1
14	Illinois	23.0
14	Vermont	23.0
16	Wyoming	22.9
17	Maryland	22.1
18	Maine	21.7
18	Massachusetts	21.7
18	Minnesota	21.7
18	South Dakota	21.7
22	Arkansas	21.5
23	South Carolina	21.4
24	Wisconsin	21.3
25	Iowa	21.2
26	Tennessee	21.0
27	Michigan	20.9
28	Oklahoma	20.7
28	West Virginia	20.7
30	Alabama	20.3
30	Montana	20.3
30	Utah	20.3
33	Washington	20.0
34	Indiana	19.9
34	Louisiana	19.9
34	Nevada	19.9
37	Delaware	19.4
38	Colorado	19.2
39	North Dakota	19.0
40	Florida	18.7
40	Idaho	18.7
42	Kentucky	18.5
43	Mississippi	18.1
44	Alaska	18.0
44	New Mexico	18.0
44	North Carolina	18.0
47	Oregon	17.7
48	California	17.6
49	Arizona	17.2
50	Hawaii	14.7

	District of Columbia	20.5

Source: CQ Press using data from U.S. Bureau of the Census, Governments Division
"2015 State and Local Government Finances" (http://www.census.gov/govs/local/)
*Direct general expenditures as a percent of all direct general expenditures. Includes capital outlays.

Estimated Per Pupil Public Elementary and Secondary School Current Expenditures in 2017
National Per Pupil = $11,984*

ALPHA ORDER

RANK	STATE	PER PUPIL
37	Alabama	$9,255
3	Alaska	21,261
47	Arizona	7,501
34	Arkansas	9,749
20	California	11,743
24	Colorado	11,169
4	Connecticut	20,861
13	Delaware	14,462
36	Florida	9,277
39	Georgia	9,013
19	Hawaii	11,964
50	Idaho	6,515
14	Illinois	13,875
48	Indiana	7,267
27	Iowa	10,891
32	Kansas	10,204
16	Kentucky	12,257
22	Louisiana	11,495
41	Maine	8,956
12	Maryland	14,768
6	Massachusetts	18,072
10	Michigan	15,981
15	Minnesota	12,522
43	Mississippi	8,361
28	Missouri	10,828
23	Montana	11,195
30	Nebraska	10,367
44	Nevada	8,165
9	New Hampshire	16,200
5	New Jersey	20,556
29	New Mexico	10,785
2	New York	22,659
42	North Carolina	8,940
46	North Dakota	8,077
31	Ohio	10,333
45	Oklahoma	8,164
17	Oregon	12,161
11	Pennsylvania	15,139
8	Rhode Island	16,401
26	South Carolina	11,039
40	South Dakota	8,961
38	Tennessee	9,148
35	Texas	9,336
49	Utah	6,906
1	Vermont	24,421
25	Virginia	11,141
33	Washington	10,119
18	West Virginia	12,127
21	Wisconsin	11,533
7	Wyoming	17,052

RANK ORDER

RANK	STATE	PER PUPIL
1	Vermont	$24,421
2	New York	22,659
3	Alaska	21,261
4	Connecticut	20,861
5	New Jersey	20,556
6	Massachusetts	18,072
7	Wyoming	17,052
8	Rhode Island	16,401
9	New Hampshire	16,200
10	Michigan	15,981
11	Pennsylvania	15,139
12	Maryland	14,768
13	Delaware	14,462
14	Illinois	13,875
15	Minnesota	12,522
16	Kentucky	12,257
17	Oregon	12,161
18	West Virginia	12,127
19	Hawaii	11,964
20	California	11,743
21	Wisconsin	11,533
22	Louisiana	11,495
23	Montana	11,195
24	Colorado	11,169
25	Virginia	11,141
26	South Carolina	11,039
27	Iowa	10,891
28	Missouri	10,828
29	New Mexico	10,785
30	Nebraska	10,367
31	Ohio	10,333
32	Kansas	10,204
33	Washington	10,119
34	Arkansas	9,749
35	Texas	9,336
36	Florida	9,277
37	Alabama	9,255
38	Tennessee	9,148
39	Georgia	9,013
40	South Dakota	8,961
41	Maine	8,956
42	North Carolina	8,940
43	Mississippi	8,361
44	Nevada	8,165
45	Oklahoma	8,164
46	North Dakota	8,077
47	Arizona	7,501
48	Indiana	7,267
49	Utah	6,906
50	Idaho	6,515
	District of Columbia	20,640

Source: National Education Association, Washington, D.C.
"Rankings and Estimates" (Copyright © 2017, NEA, http://www.nea.org/home/44479.htm)
*Estimates for school year 2016-2017. Based on student membership.

Higher Education Expenditures by State and Local Governments in 2015

National Total = $273,931,616,000*

ALPHA ORDER

RANK	STATE	EXPENDITURES	% of USA
20	Alabama	$4,863,337,000	1.8%
44	Alaska	865,372,000	0.3%
17	Arizona	5,467,525,000	2.0%
35	Arkansas	2,561,814,000	0.9%
1	California	37,209,474,000	13.6%
18	Colorado	5,366,103,000	2.0%
31	Connecticut	3,122,267,000	1.1%
39	Delaware	1,282,998,000	0.5%
5	Florida	10,304,869,000	3.8%
16	Georgia	5,852,180,000	2.1%
41	Hawaii	1,082,318,000	0.4%
42	Idaho	1,046,240,000	0.4%
6	Illinois	9,668,060,000	3.5%
15	Indiana	5,862,727,000	2.1%
26	Iowa	3,945,339,000	1.4%
30	Kansas	3,251,234,000	1.2%
25	Kentucky	3,990,766,000	1.5%
32	Louisiana	3,121,847,000	1.1%
47	Maine	788,044,000	0.3%
14	Maryland	5,948,712,000	2.2%
19	Massachusetts	5,199,902,000	1.9%
4	Michigan	10,982,299,000	4.0%
21	Minnesota	4,692,019,000	1.7%
33	Mississippi	2,844,525,000	1.0%
24	Missouri	4,056,634,000	1.5%
45	Montana	861,813,000	0.3%
36	Nebraska	2,166,617,000	0.8%
38	Nevada	1,475,390,000	0.5%
43	New Hampshire	902,074,000	0.3%
12	New Jersey	6,414,401,000	2.3%
34	New Mexico	2,570,081,000	0.9%
3	New York	13,634,408,000	5.0%
7	North Carolina	9,662,971,000	3.5%
40	North Dakota	1,103,481,000	0.4%
9	Ohio	9,452,711,000	3.5%
29	Oklahoma	3,600,445,000	1.3%
22	Oregon	4,293,411,000	1.6%
8	Pennsylvania	9,572,394,000	3.5%
50	Rhode Island	647,146,000	0.2%
23	South Carolina	4,058,964,000	1.5%
49	South Dakota	696,364,000	0.3%
27	Tennessee	3,921,348,000	1.4%
2	Texas	27,854,037,000	10.2%
28	Utah	3,850,800,000	1.4%
48	Vermont	761,518,000	0.3%
10	Virginia	7,792,375,000	2.8%
11	Washington	6,571,340,000	2.4%
37	West Virginia	1,661,232,000	0.6%
13	Wisconsin	6,020,021,000	2.2%
46	Wyoming	793,630,000	0.3%

RANK ORDER

RANK	STATE	EXPENDITURES	% of USA
1	California	$37,209,474,000	13.6%
2	Texas	27,854,037,000	10.2%
3	New York	13,634,408,000	5.0%
4	Michigan	10,982,299,000	4.0%
5	Florida	10,304,869,000	3.8%
6	Illinois	9,668,060,000	3.5%
7	North Carolina	9,662,971,000	3.5%
8	Pennsylvania	9,572,394,000	3.5%
9	Ohio	9,452,711,000	3.5%
10	Virginia	7,792,375,000	2.8%
11	Washington	6,571,340,000	2.4%
12	New Jersey	6,414,401,000	2.3%
13	Wisconsin	6,020,021,000	2.2%
14	Maryland	5,948,712,000	2.2%
15	Indiana	5,862,727,000	2.1%
16	Georgia	5,852,180,000	2.1%
17	Arizona	5,467,525,000	2.0%
18	Colorado	5,366,103,000	2.0%
19	Massachusetts	5,199,902,000	1.9%
20	Alabama	4,863,337,000	1.8%
21	Minnesota	4,692,019,000	1.7%
22	Oregon	4,293,411,000	1.6%
23	South Carolina	4,058,964,000	1.5%
24	Missouri	4,056,634,000	1.5%
25	Kentucky	3,990,766,000	1.5%
26	Iowa	3,945,339,000	1.4%
27	Tennessee	3,921,348,000	1.4%
28	Utah	3,850,800,000	1.4%
29	Oklahoma	3,600,445,000	1.3%
30	Kansas	3,251,234,000	1.2%
31	Connecticut	3,122,267,000	1.1%
32	Louisiana	3,121,847,000	1.1%
33	Mississippi	2,844,525,000	1.0%
34	New Mexico	2,570,081,000	0.9%
35	Arkansas	2,561,814,000	0.9%
36	Nebraska	2,166,617,000	0.8%
37	West Virginia	1,661,232,000	0.6%
38	Nevada	1,475,390,000	0.5%
39	Delaware	1,282,998,000	0.5%
40	North Dakota	1,103,481,000	0.4%
41	Hawaii	1,082,318,000	0.4%
42	Idaho	1,046,240,000	0.4%
43	New Hampshire	902,074,000	0.3%
44	Alaska	865,372,000	0.3%
45	Montana	861,813,000	0.3%
46	Wyoming	793,630,000	0.3%
47	Maine	788,044,000	0.3%
48	Vermont	761,518,000	0.3%
49	South Dakota	696,364,000	0.3%
50	Rhode Island	647,146,000	0.2%
	District of Columbia	216,039,000	0.1%

Source: U.S. Bureau of the Census, Governments Division
"2015 State and Local Government Finances" (http://www.census.gov/govs/local/)
*Direct general expenditures. Includes capital outlays.

Per Capita State and Local Government Expenditures for Higher Education in 2015
National Per Capita = $853*

ALPHA ORDER

RANK	STATE	PER CAPITA
15	Alabama	$1,003
8	Alaska	1,173
34	Arizona	804
28	Arkansas	861
19	California	953
17	Colorado	986
27	Connecticut	869
2	Delaware	1,359
50	Florida	508
48	Georgia	574
36	Hawaii	759
44	Idaho	634
37	Illinois	752
26	Indiana	887
5	Iowa	1,265
10	Kansas	1,119
25	Kentucky	902
42	Louisiana	668
47	Maine	594
16	Maryland	991
35	Massachusetts	765
11	Michigan	1,107
29	Minnesota	856
19	Mississippi	953
42	Missouri	668
30	Montana	838
9	Nebraska	1,144
49	Nevada	512
41	New Hampshire	678
39	New Jersey	716
6	New Mexico	1,234
40	New York	688
18	North Carolina	962
1	North Dakota	1,462
33	Ohio	814
22	Oklahoma	922
12	Oregon	1,069
38	Pennsylvania	748
45	Rhode Island	613
31	South Carolina	830
32	South Dakota	815
46	Tennessee	595
14	Texas	1,015
4	Utah	1,290
7	Vermont	1,219
21	Virginia	931
23	Washington	919
24	West Virginia	903
13	Wisconsin	1,045
3	Wyoming	1,354

RANK ORDER

RANK	STATE	PER CAPITA
1	North Dakota	$1,462
2	Delaware	1,359
3	Wyoming	1,354
4	Utah	1,290
5	Iowa	1,265
6	New Mexico	1,234
7	Vermont	1,219
8	Alaska	1,173
9	Nebraska	1,144
10	Kansas	1,119
11	Michigan	1,107
12	Oregon	1,069
13	Wisconsin	1,045
14	Texas	1,015
15	Alabama	1,003
16	Maryland	991
17	Colorado	986
18	North Carolina	962
19	California	953
19	Mississippi	953
21	Virginia	931
22	Oklahoma	922
23	Washington	919
24	West Virginia	903
25	Kentucky	902
26	Indiana	887
27	Connecticut	869
28	Arkansas	861
29	Minnesota	856
30	Montana	838
31	South Carolina	830
32	South Dakota	815
33	Ohio	814
34	Arizona	804
35	Massachusetts	765
36	Hawaii	759
37	Illinois	752
38	Pennsylvania	748
39	New Jersey	716
40	New York	688
41	New Hampshire	678
42	Louisiana	668
42	Missouri	668
44	Idaho	634
45	Rhode Island	613
46	Tennessee	595
47	Maine	594
48	Georgia	574
49	Nevada	512
50	Florida	508
	District of Columbia	321

Source: CQ Press using data from U.S. Bureau of the Census, Governments Division
"2015 State and Local Government Finances" (http://www.census.gov/govs/local/)
*Direct general expenditures. Includes capital outlays.

Expenditures for Higher Education as a Percent
of All State and Local Government Expenditures in 2015
National Percent = 9.7%*

ALPHA ORDER

RANK	STATE	PERCENT
6	Alabama	13.1
49	Alaska	5.9
12	Arizona	12.2
20	Arkansas	11.0
33	California	9.1
16	Colorado	11.4
40	Connecticut	8.3
4	Delaware	13.3
44	Florida	7.2
36	Georgia	8.6
41	Hawaii	8.0
27	Idaho	9.9
38	Illinois	8.4
14	Indiana	11.9
6	Iowa	13.1
4	Kansas	13.3
23	Kentucky	10.7
42	Louisiana	7.7
46	Maine	7.1
26	Maryland	10.3
44	Massachusetts	7.2
2	Michigan	13.7
34	Minnesota	8.9
18	Mississippi	11.3
32	Missouri	9.3
27	Montana	9.9
8	Nebraska	13.0
43	Nevada	7.3
36	New Hampshire	8.6
46	New Jersey	7.1
11	New Mexico	12.3
50	New York	5.3
8	North Carolina	13.0
12	North Dakota	12.2
27	Ohio	9.9
10	Oklahoma	12.6
16	Oregon	11.4
38	Pennsylvania	8.4
48	Rhode Island	6.4
25	South Carolina	10.4
24	South Dakota	10.6
34	Tennessee	8.9
3	Texas	13.5
1	Utah	17.6
20	Vermont	11.0
18	Virginia	11.3
27	Washington	9.9
22	West Virginia	10.9
15	Wisconsin	11.8
31	Wyoming	9.5

RANK ORDER

RANK	STATE	PERCENT
1	Utah	17.6
2	Michigan	13.7
3	Texas	13.5
4	Delaware	13.3
4	Kansas	13.3
6	Alabama	13.1
6	Iowa	13.1
8	Nebraska	13.0
8	North Carolina	13.0
10	Oklahoma	12.6
11	New Mexico	12.3
12	Arizona	12.2
12	North Dakota	12.2
14	Indiana	11.9
15	Wisconsin	11.8
16	Colorado	11.4
16	Oregon	11.4
18	Mississippi	11.3
18	Virginia	11.3
20	Arkansas	11.0
20	Vermont	11.0
22	West Virginia	10.9
23	Kentucky	10.7
24	South Dakota	10.6
25	South Carolina	10.4
26	Maryland	10.3
27	Idaho	9.9
27	Montana	9.9
27	Ohio	9.9
27	Washington	9.9
31	Wyoming	9.5
32	Missouri	9.3
33	California	9.1
34	Minnesota	8.9
34	Tennessee	8.9
36	Georgia	8.6
36	New Hampshire	8.6
38	Illinois	8.4
38	Pennsylvania	8.4
40	Connecticut	8.3
41	Hawaii	8.0
42	Louisiana	7.7
43	Nevada	7.3
44	Florida	7.2
44	Massachusetts	7.2
46	Maine	7.1
46	New Jersey	7.1
48	Rhode Island	6.4
49	Alaska	5.9
50	New York	5.3
	District of Columbia	1.7

Source: CQ Press using data from U.S. Bureau of the Census, Governments Division
"2015 State and Local Government Finances" (http://www.census.gov/govs/local/)
*Direct general expenditures for higher education as a percent of all direct general expenditures. Includes capital outlays.

Average Faculty Salary at Institutions of Higher Education in 2016

National Average = $82,101*

ALPHA ORDER

RANK	STATE	AVERAGE SALARY
37	Alabama	$69,672
18	Alaska	78,853
14	Arizona	82,147
49	Arkansas	59,482
4	California	96,892
16	Colorado	79,658
3	Connecticut	101,923
5	Delaware	95,888
21	Florida	76,970
31	Georgia	74,162
12	Hawaii	85,460
47	Idaho	63,174
11	Illinois	86,567
17	Indiana	79,557
28	Iowa	74,829
39	Kansas	67,141
43	Kentucky	65,271
42	Louisiana	66,043
25	Maine	76,236
15	Maryland	80,400
1	Massachusetts	106,159
9	Michigan	86,714
20	Minnesota	77,871
50	Mississippi	59,297
34	Missouri	73,404
46	Montana	63,243
35	Nebraska	73,350
13	Nevada	82,818
8	New Hampshire	91,165
2	New Jersey	102,961
41	New Mexico	66,453
7	New York	93,704
30	North Carolina	74,168
44	North Dakota	64,027
26	Ohio	75,918
38	Oklahoma	67,941
27	Oregon	75,592
10	Pennsylvania	86,672
6	Rhode Island	95,719
40	South Carolina	66,610
48	South Dakota	62,895
36	Tennessee	73,154
22	Texas	76,968
29	Utah	74,732
19	Vermont	78,447
23	Virginia	76,674
24	Washington	76,287
45	West Virginia	63,853
32	Wisconsin	74,109
33	Wyoming	73,581

RANK ORDER

RANK	STATE	AVERAGE SALARY
1	Massachusetts	$106,159
2	New Jersey	102,961
3	Connecticut	101,923
4	California	96,892
5	Delaware	95,888
6	Rhode Island	95,719
7	New York	93,704
8	New Hampshire	91,165
9	Michigan	86,714
10	Pennsylvania	86,672
11	Illinois	86,567
12	Hawaii	85,460
13	Nevada	82,818
14	Arizona	82,147
15	Maryland	80,400
16	Colorado	79,658
17	Indiana	79,557
18	Alaska	78,853
19	Vermont	78,447
20	Minnesota	77,871
21	Florida	76,970
22	Texas	76,968
23	Virginia	76,674
24	Washington	76,287
25	Maine	76,236
26	Ohio	75,918
27	Oregon	75,592
28	Iowa	74,829
29	Utah	74,732
30	North Carolina	74,168
31	Georgia	74,162
32	Wisconsin	74,109
33	Wyoming	73,581
34	Missouri	73,404
35	Nebraska	73,350
36	Tennessee	73,154
37	Alabama	69,672
38	Oklahoma	67,941
39	Kansas	67,141
40	South Carolina	66,610
41	New Mexico	66,453
42	Louisiana	66,043
43	Kentucky	65,271
44	North Dakota	64,027
45	West Virginia	63,853
46	Montana	63,243
47	Idaho	63,174
48	South Dakota	62,895
49	Arkansas	59,482
50	Mississippi	59,297
	District of Columbia	96,496

Source: U.S. Department of Education, National Center for Education Statistics
"Digest of Education Statistics" (http://nces.ed.gov/programs/digest/index.asp)
*For 2015-2016 school year. For full-time instructional faculty on 9-month contracts at four-year and two-year public and private degree-granting institutions.

Average Student Costs at Public Institutions of Higher Education in 2016

National Average = $19,189*

ALPHA ORDER

RANK	STATE	AVERAGE COSTS
26	Alabama	$18,509
35	Alaska	16,701
16	Arizona	20,621
41	Arkansas	15,976
10	California	22,151
17	Colorado	20,594
8	Connecticut	23,351
6	Delaware	23,566
47	Florida	14,457
30	Georgia	17,292
19	Hawaii	20,098
48	Idaho	14,211
5	Illinois	24,098
23	Indiana	18,712
34	Iowa	16,748
32	Kansas	16,783
24	Kentucky	18,702
31	Louisiana	17,287
22	Maine	18,767
20	Maryland	20,076
7	Massachusetts	23,389
13	Michigan	21,380
21	Minnesota	19,266
36	Mississippi	16,434
28	Missouri	17,418
44	Montana	14,853
33	Nebraska	16,761
42	Nevada	15,570
1	New Hampshire	26,008
3	New Jersey	25,544
43	New Mexico	15,029
12	New York	21,489
38	North Carolina	16,364
45	North Dakota	14,847
15	Ohio	20,931
46	Oklahoma	14,677
18	Oregon	20,516
4	Pennsylvania	24,236
9	Rhode Island	22,722
14	South Carolina	21,150
40	South Dakota	16,108
27	Tennessee	17,735
29	Texas	17,395
50	Utah	13,344
2	Vermont	25,910
11	Virginia	21,889
25	Washington	18,665
37	West Virginia	16,426
39	Wisconsin	16,194
49	Wyoming	13,942

RANK ORDER

RANK	STATE	AVERAGE COSTS
1	New Hampshire	$26,008
2	Vermont	25,910
3	New Jersey	25,544
4	Pennsylvania	24,236
5	Illinois	24,098
6	Delaware	23,566
7	Massachusetts	23,389
8	Connecticut	23,351
9	Rhode Island	22,722
10	California	22,151
11	Virginia	21,889
12	New York	21,489
13	Michigan	21,380
14	South Carolina	21,150
15	Ohio	20,931
16	Arizona	20,621
17	Colorado	20,594
18	Oregon	20,516
19	Hawaii	20,098
20	Maryland	20,076
21	Minnesota	19,266
22	Maine	18,767
23	Indiana	18,712
24	Kentucky	18,702
25	Washington	18,665
26	Alabama	18,509
27	Tennessee	17,735
28	Missouri	17,418
29	Texas	17,395
30	Georgia	17,292
31	Louisiana	17,287
32	Kansas	16,783
33	Nebraska	16,761
34	Iowa	16,748
35	Alaska	16,701
36	Mississippi	16,434
37	West Virginia	16,426
38	North Carolina	16,364
39	Wisconsin	16,194
40	South Dakota	16,108
41	Arkansas	15,976
42	Nevada	15,570
43	New Mexico	15,029
44	Montana	14,853
45	North Dakota	14,847
46	Oklahoma	14,677
47	Florida	14,457
48	Idaho	14,211
49	Wyoming	13,942
50	Utah	13,344

District of Columbia** — NA

Source: U.S. Department of Education, National Center for Education Statistics
"Digest of Education Statistics" (http://nces.ed.gov/programs/digest/index.asp)
*Data for 2015-2016 school year. Based on average in-state tuition, room and board, and fees for full-time students in public four-year institutions for an entire academic year.
**Not available.

Average Student Costs at Private Institutions of Higher Education in 2016

National Average = $39,529*

ALPHA ORDER				RANK ORDER		
RANK	STATE	AVERAGE COSTS		RANK	STATE	AVERAGE COSTS
43	Alabama	$24,648		1	Massachusetts	$55,024
40	Alaska	26,388		2	Maryland	52,013
45	Arizona	22,245		3	Vermont	51,862
38	Arkansas	28,827		4	Connecticut	51,570
15	California	41,182		5	Rhode Island	51,053
26	Colorado	33,651		6	New York	50,295
4	Connecticut	51,570		7	Pennsylvania	49,895
42	Delaware	25,511		8	New Jersey	46,835
25	Florida	33,973		9	Maine	46,578
22	Georgia	37,464		10	Oregon	46,262
39	Hawaii	27,895		11	Washington	45,470
49	Idaho	13,069		12	New Hampshire	44,945
14	Illinois	41,331		13	Louisiana	44,652
16	Indiana	41,030		14	Illinois	41,331
24	Iowa	34,144		15	California	41,182
41	Kansas	26,114		16	Indiana	41,030
27	Kentucky	32,996		17	North Carolina	40,532
13	Louisiana	44,652		18	Texas	39,613
9	Maine	46,578		19	Ohio	39,449
2	Maryland	52,013		20	Wisconsin	39,363
1	Massachusetts	55,024		21	Minnesota	39,131
33	Michigan	30,954		22	Georgia	37,464
21	Minnesota	39,131		23	Tennessee	34,621
44	Mississippi	24,034		24	Iowa	34,144
31	Missouri	31,692		25	Florida	33,973
32	Montana	31,239		26	Colorado	33,651
36	Nebraska	29,873		27	Kentucky	32,996
29	Nevada	32,302		28	Oklahoma	32,303
12	New Hampshire	44,945		29	Nevada	32,302
8	New Jersey	46,835		30	South Carolina	32,109
35	New Mexico	30,395		31	Missouri	31,692
6	New York	50,295		32	Montana	31,239
17	North Carolina	40,532		33	Michigan	30,954
47	North Dakota	20,103		34	Virginia	30,916
19	Ohio	39,449		35	New Mexico	30,395
28	Oklahoma	32,303		36	Nebraska	29,873
10	Oregon	46,262		37	South Dakota	29,775
7	Pennsylvania	49,895		38	Arkansas	28,827
5	Rhode Island	51,053		39	Hawaii	27,895
30	South Carolina	32,109		40	Alaska	26,388
37	South Dakota	29,775		41	Kansas	26,114
23	Tennessee	34,621		42	Delaware	25,511
18	Texas	39,613		43	Alabama	24,648
48	Utah	15,221		44	Mississippi	24,034
3	Vermont	51,862		45	Arizona	22,245
34	Virginia	30,916		46	West Virginia	20,186
11	Washington	45,470		47	North Dakota	20,103
46	West Virginia	20,186		48	Utah	15,221
20	Wisconsin	39,363		49	Idaho	13,069
NA	Wyoming**	NA		NA	Wyoming**	NA
					District of Columbia	53,572

Source: U.S. Department of Education, National Center for Education Statistics
  "Digest of Education Statistics" (http://nces.ed.gov/programs/digest/index.asp)
*Data for 2015-2016 school year. Based on average in-state tuition, room and board, and fees for full-time students in private four-year institutions for an entire academic year.
**Not available.

Average College Graduate Debt: Class of 2015

National Average Debt = $30,100*

ALPHA ORDER

RANK	STATE	AVERAGE DEBT
19	Alabama	$29,153
35	Alaska	26,171
42	Arizona	23,780
37	Arkansas	26,082
47	California	22,191
38	Colorado	25,840
3	Connecticut	34,773
4	Delaware	33,849
45	Florida	23,379
23	Georgia	27,754
44	Hawaii	23,456
28	Idaho	27,639
18	Illinois	29,305
20	Indiana	29,022
14	Iowa	29,547
22	Kansas	28,008
31	Kentucky	27,225
32	Louisiana	26,865
13	Maine	29,644
27	Maryland	27,672
7	Massachusetts	31,466
11	Michigan	30,045
6	Minnesota	31,526
12	Mississippi	29,942
29	Missouri	27,480
33	Montana	26,280
34	Nebraska	26,235
43	Nevada	23,462
1	New Hampshire	36,101
10	New Jersey	30,104
48	New Mexico	20,193
17	New York	29,320
39	North Carolina	25,645
NA	North Dakota**	NA
9	Ohio	30,239
40	Oklahoma	24,849
26	Oregon	27,697
2	Pennsylvania	34,798
5	Rhode Island	32,920
8	South Carolina	30,564
16	South Dakota	29,364
36	Tennessee	26,083
30	Texas	27,324
49	Utah	18,873
21	Vermont	28,283
24	Virginia	27,717
41	Washington	24,600
25	West Virginia	27,713
15	Wisconsin	29,460
46	Wyoming	22,683

RANK ORDER

RANK	STATE	AVERAGE DEBT
1	New Hampshire	$36,101
2	Pennsylvania	34,798
3	Connecticut	34,773
4	Delaware	33,849
5	Rhode Island	32,920
6	Minnesota	31,526
7	Massachusetts	31,466
8	South Carolina	30,564
9	Ohio	30,239
10	New Jersey	30,104
11	Michigan	30,045
12	Mississippi	29,942
13	Maine	29,644
14	Iowa	29,547
15	Wisconsin	29,460
16	South Dakota	29,364
17	New York	29,320
18	Illinois	29,305
19	Alabama	29,153
20	Indiana	29,022
21	Vermont	28,283
22	Kansas	28,008
23	Georgia	27,754
24	Virginia	27,717
25	West Virginia	27,713
26	Oregon	27,697
27	Maryland	27,672
28	Idaho	27,639
29	Missouri	27,480
30	Texas	27,324
31	Kentucky	27,225
32	Louisiana	26,865
33	Montana	26,280
34	Nebraska	26,235
35	Alaska	26,171
36	Tennessee	26,083
37	Arkansas	26,082
38	Colorado	25,840
39	North Carolina	25,645
40	Oklahoma	24,849
41	Washington	24,600
42	Arizona	23,780
43	Nevada	23,462
44	Hawaii	23,456
45	Florida	23,379
46	Wyoming	22,683
47	California	22,191
48	New Mexico	20,193
49	Utah	18,873
NA	North Dakota**	NA

| | District of Columbia | 31,452 |

Source: The Project on Student Debt
    "Student Debt and The Class of 2015" (October 2016, http://ticas.org/posd/map-state-data)
*For students receiving a bachelor's degree in 2015.
**Not available.

Percent of College Graduates with Debt: Class of 2015

National Percent = 68%*

<table>
<tr><td colspan="3">ALPHA ORDER</td><td colspan="3">RANK ORDER</td></tr>
<tr><td>RANK</td><td>STATE</td><td>PERCENT</td><td>RANK</td><td>STATE</td><td>PERCENT</td></tr>
<tr><td>43</td><td>Alabama</td><td>52</td><td>1</td><td>New Hampshire</td><td>76</td></tr>
<tr><td>40</td><td>Alaska</td><td>55</td><td>2</td><td>South Dakota</td><td>73</td></tr>
<tr><td>36</td><td>Arizona</td><td>56</td><td>3</td><td>Idaho</td><td>71</td></tr>
<tr><td>34</td><td>Arkansas</td><td>57</td><td>3</td><td>Pennsylvania</td><td>71</td></tr>
<tr><td>41</td><td>California</td><td>54</td><td>5</td><td>Minnesota</td><td>70</td></tr>
<tr><td>36</td><td>Colorado</td><td>56</td><td>5</td><td>Wisconsin</td><td>70</td></tr>
<tr><td>14</td><td>Connecticut</td><td>64</td><td>7</td><td>West Virginia</td><td>68</td></tr>
<tr><td>13</td><td>Delaware</td><td>65</td><td>8</td><td>Illinois</td><td>66</td></tr>
<tr><td>42</td><td>Florida</td><td>53</td><td>8</td><td>Iowa</td><td>66</td></tr>
<tr><td>23</td><td>Georgia</td><td>61</td><td>8</td><td>Massachusetts</td><td>66</td></tr>
<tr><td>46</td><td>Hawaii</td><td>50</td><td>8</td><td>New Jersey</td><td>66</td></tr>
<tr><td>3</td><td>Idaho</td><td>71</td><td>8</td><td>Ohio</td><td>66</td></tr>
<tr><td>8</td><td>Illinois</td><td>66</td><td>13</td><td>Delaware</td><td>65</td></tr>
<tr><td>23</td><td>Indiana</td><td>61</td><td>14</td><td>Connecticut</td><td>64</td></tr>
<tr><td>8</td><td>Iowa</td><td>66</td><td>14</td><td>Kentucky</td><td>64</td></tr>
<tr><td>17</td><td>Kansas</td><td>63</td><td>14</td><td>Rhode Island</td><td>64</td></tr>
<tr><td>14</td><td>Kentucky</td><td>64</td><td>17</td><td>Kansas</td><td>63</td></tr>
<tr><td>45</td><td>Louisiana</td><td>51</td><td>17</td><td>Maine</td><td>63</td></tr>
<tr><td>17</td><td>Maine</td><td>63</td><td>17</td><td>Michigan</td><td>63</td></tr>
<tr><td>36</td><td>Maryland</td><td>56</td><td>17</td><td>Oregon</td><td>63</td></tr>
<tr><td>8</td><td>Massachusetts</td><td>66</td><td>21</td><td>Mississippi</td><td>62</td></tr>
<tr><td>17</td><td>Michigan</td><td>63</td><td>21</td><td>Vermont</td><td>62</td></tr>
<tr><td>5</td><td>Minnesota</td><td>70</td><td>23</td><td>Georgia</td><td>61</td></tr>
<tr><td>21</td><td>Mississippi</td><td>62</td><td>23</td><td>Indiana</td><td>61</td></tr>
<tr><td>23</td><td>Missouri</td><td>61</td><td>23</td><td>Missouri</td><td>61</td></tr>
<tr><td>27</td><td>Montana</td><td>60</td><td>23</td><td>North Carolina</td><td>61</td></tr>
<tr><td>27</td><td>Nebraska</td><td>60</td><td>27</td><td>Montana</td><td>60</td></tr>
<tr><td>47</td><td>Nevada</td><td>47</td><td>27</td><td>Nebraska</td><td>60</td></tr>
<tr><td>1</td><td>New Hampshire</td><td>76</td><td>27</td><td>South Carolina</td><td>60</td></tr>
<tr><td>8</td><td>New Jersey</td><td>66</td><td>27</td><td>Tennessee</td><td>60</td></tr>
<tr><td>33</td><td>New Mexico</td><td>58</td><td>31</td><td>New York</td><td>59</td></tr>
<tr><td>31</td><td>New York</td><td>59</td><td>31</td><td>Virginia</td><td>59</td></tr>
<tr><td>23</td><td>North Carolina</td><td>61</td><td>33</td><td>New Mexico</td><td>58</td></tr>
<tr><td>NA</td><td>North Dakota**</td><td>NA</td><td>34</td><td>Arkansas</td><td>57</td></tr>
<tr><td>8</td><td>Ohio</td><td>66</td><td>34</td><td>Washington</td><td>57</td></tr>
<tr><td>43</td><td>Oklahoma</td><td>52</td><td>36</td><td>Arizona</td><td>56</td></tr>
<tr><td>17</td><td>Oregon</td><td>63</td><td>36</td><td>Colorado</td><td>56</td></tr>
<tr><td>3</td><td>Pennsylvania</td><td>71</td><td>36</td><td>Maryland</td><td>56</td></tr>
<tr><td>14</td><td>Rhode Island</td><td>64</td><td>36</td><td>Texas</td><td>56</td></tr>
<tr><td>27</td><td>South Carolina</td><td>60</td><td>40</td><td>Alaska</td><td>55</td></tr>
<tr><td>2</td><td>South Dakota</td><td>73</td><td>41</td><td>California</td><td>54</td></tr>
<tr><td>27</td><td>Tennessee</td><td>60</td><td>42</td><td>Florida</td><td>53</td></tr>
<tr><td>36</td><td>Texas</td><td>56</td><td>43</td><td>Alabama</td><td>52</td></tr>
<tr><td>49</td><td>Utah</td><td>41</td><td>43</td><td>Oklahoma</td><td>52</td></tr>
<tr><td>21</td><td>Vermont</td><td>62</td><td>45</td><td>Louisiana</td><td>51</td></tr>
<tr><td>31</td><td>Virginia</td><td>59</td><td>46</td><td>Hawaii</td><td>50</td></tr>
<tr><td>34</td><td>Washington</td><td>57</td><td>47</td><td>Nevada</td><td>47</td></tr>
<tr><td>7</td><td>West Virginia</td><td>68</td><td>48</td><td>Wyoming</td><td>46</td></tr>
<tr><td>5</td><td>Wisconsin</td><td>70</td><td>49</td><td>Utah</td><td>41</td></tr>
<tr><td>48</td><td>Wyoming</td><td>46</td><td>NA</td><td>North Dakota**</td><td>NA</td></tr>
<tr><td></td><td></td><td></td><td></td><td>District of Columbia</td><td>55</td></tr>
</table>

Source: The Project on Student Debt
"Student Debt and The Class of 2015" (October 2016, http://ticas.org/posd/map-state-data)
*For students receiving a bachelor's degree in 2015.
**Not available.

Institutions of Higher Education in 2016

National Total = 4,583 Institutions*

ALPHA ORDER			
RANK	STATE	INSTITUTIONS	% of USA
21	Alabama	77	1.7%
49	Alaska	9	0.2%
17	Arizona	86	1.9%
31	Arkansas	53	1.2%
1	California	448	9.8%
16	Colorado	87	1.9%
33	Connecticut	43	0.9%
49	Delaware	9	0.2%
5	Florida	229	5.0%
10	Georgia	130	2.8%
44	Hawaii	20	0.4%
46	Idaho	19	0.4%
7	Illinois	185	4.0%
19	Indiana	84	1.8%
27	Iowa	64	1.4%
23	Kansas	75	1.6%
24	Kentucky	72	1.6%
27	Louisiana	64	1.4%
38	Maine	31	0.7%
30	Maryland	58	1.3%
12	Massachusetts	124	2.7%
15	Michigan	103	2.2%
13	Minnesota	115	2.5%
36	Mississippi	41	0.9%
11	Missouri	125	2.7%
43	Montana	22	0.5%
35	Nebraska	42	0.9%
40	Nevada	26	0.6%
39	New Hampshire	27	0.6%
24	New Jersey	72	1.6%
33	New Mexico	43	0.9%
2	New York	304	6.6%
8	North Carolina	150	3.3%
44	North Dakota	20	0.4%
6	Ohio	208	4.5%
26	Oklahoma	67	1.5%
29	Oregon	63	1.4%
4	Pennsylvania	256	5.6%
47	Rhode Island	13	0.3%
21	South Carolina	77	1.7%
41	South Dakota	25	0.5%
14	Tennessee	105	2.3%
3	Texas	272	5.9%
37	Utah	36	0.8%
42	Vermont	24	0.5%
9	Virginia	131	2.9%
17	Washington	86	1.9%
32	West Virginia	44	1.0%
19	Wisconsin	84	1.8%
48	Wyoming	10	0.2%

RANK ORDER			
RANK	STATE	INSTITUTIONS	% of USA
1	California	448	9.8%
2	New York	304	6.6%
3	Texas	272	5.9%
4	Pennsylvania	256	5.6%
5	Florida	229	5.0%
6	Ohio	208	4.5%
7	Illinois	185	4.0%
8	North Carolina	150	3.3%
9	Virginia	131	2.9%
10	Georgia	130	2.8%
11	Missouri	125	2.7%
12	Massachusetts	124	2.7%
13	Minnesota	115	2.5%
14	Tennessee	105	2.3%
15	Michigan	103	2.2%
16	Colorado	87	1.9%
17	Arizona	86	1.9%
17	Washington	86	1.9%
19	Indiana	84	1.8%
19	Wisconsin	84	1.8%
21	Alabama	77	1.7%
21	South Carolina	77	1.7%
23	Kansas	75	1.6%
24	Kentucky	72	1.6%
24	New Jersey	72	1.6%
26	Oklahoma	67	1.5%
27	Iowa	64	1.4%
27	Louisiana	64	1.4%
29	Oregon	63	1.4%
30	Maryland	58	1.3%
31	Arkansas	53	1.2%
32	West Virginia	44	1.0%
33	Connecticut	43	0.9%
33	New Mexico	43	0.9%
35	Nebraska	42	0.9%
36	Mississippi	41	0.9%
37	Utah	36	0.8%
38	Maine	31	0.7%
39	New Hampshire	27	0.6%
40	Nevada	26	0.6%
41	South Dakota	25	0.5%
42	Vermont	24	0.5%
43	Montana	22	0.5%
44	Hawaii	20	0.4%
44	North Dakota	20	0.4%
46	Idaho	19	0.4%
47	Rhode Island	13	0.3%
48	Wyoming	10	0.2%
49	Alaska	9	0.2%
49	Delaware	9	0.2%
	District of Columbia	20	0.4%

Source: U.S. Department of Education, National Center for Education Statistics
"Digest of Education Statistics" (http://nces.ed.gov/programs/digest/index.asp)
*For 2015-2016 school year. Consists of 3,004 four-year and 1,579 two-year public and private (profit and not-for-profit)
degree-granting institutions. Includes five U.S. Service Schools not shown by state.

Enrollment in Institutions of Higher Education in 2015

National Total = 19,977,270 Students*

ALPHA ORDER

RANK	STATE	STUDENTS	% of USA
23	Alabama	302,959	1.5%
50	Alaska	31,331	0.2%
8	Arizona	649,732	3.3%
34	Arkansas	168,402	0.8%
1	California	2,688,355	13.5%
21	Colorado	348,098	1.7%
32	Connecticut	199,666	1.0%
44	Delaware	60,392	0.3%
4	Florida	1,083,262	5.4%
12	Georgia	531,299	2.7%
43	Hawaii	69,331	0.3%
39	Idaho	121,108	0.6%
5	Illinois	802,243	4.0%
15	Indiana	426,363	2.1%
25	Iowa	275,106	1.4%
30	Kansas	220,222	1.1%
26	Kentucky	255,722	1.3%
28	Louisiana	244,660	1.2%
42	Maine	71,715	0.4%
19	Maryland	363,931	1.8%
13	Massachusetts	510,396	2.6%
9	Michigan	600,203	3.0%
14	Minnesota	427,757	2.1%
33	Mississippi	172,136	0.9%
17	Missouri	409,996	2.1%
47	Montana	50,798	0.3%
37	Nebraska	136,087	0.7%
40	Nevada	116,097	0.6%
38	New Hampshire	123,966	0.6%
16	New Jersey	423,779	2.1%
36	New Mexico	138,189	0.7%
3	New York	1,285,420	6.4%
11	North Carolina	562,442	2.8%
45	North Dakota	53,840	0.3%
7	Ohio	667,760	3.3%
31	Oklahoma	210,904	1.1%
29	Oregon	240,646	1.2%
6	Pennsylvania	736,670	3.7%
41	Rhode Island	82,292	0.4%
27	South Carolina	249,654	1.2%
46	South Dakota	53,664	0.3%
22	Tennessee	323,499	1.6%
2	Texas	1,570,614	7.9%
24	Utah	293,527	1.5%
48	Vermont	43,863	0.2%
10	Virginia	569,759	2.9%
18	Washington	365,412	1.8%
35	West Virginia	150,743	0.8%
20	Wisconsin	350,248	1.8%
49	Wyoming	34,205	0.2%

RANK ORDER

RANK	STATE	STUDENTS	% of USA
1	California	2,688,355	13.5%
2	Texas	1,570,614	7.9%
3	New York	1,285,420	6.4%
4	Florida	1,083,262	5.4%
5	Illinois	802,243	4.0%
6	Pennsylvania	736,670	3.7%
7	Ohio	667,760	3.3%
8	Arizona	649,732	3.3%
9	Michigan	600,203	3.0%
10	Virginia	569,759	2.9%
11	North Carolina	562,442	2.8%
12	Georgia	531,299	2.7%
13	Massachusetts	510,396	2.6%
14	Minnesota	427,757	2.1%
15	Indiana	426,363	2.1%
16	New Jersey	423,779	2.1%
17	Missouri	409,996	2.1%
18	Washington	365,412	1.8%
19	Maryland	363,931	1.8%
20	Wisconsin	350,248	1.8%
21	Colorado	348,098	1.7%
22	Tennessee	323,499	1.6%
23	Alabama	302,959	1.5%
24	Utah	293,527	1.5%
25	Iowa	275,106	1.4%
26	Kentucky	255,722	1.3%
27	South Carolina	249,654	1.2%
28	Louisiana	244,660	1.2%
29	Oregon	240,646	1.2%
30	Kansas	220,222	1.1%
31	Oklahoma	210,904	1.1%
32	Connecticut	199,666	1.0%
33	Mississippi	172,136	0.9%
34	Arkansas	168,402	0.8%
35	West Virginia	150,743	0.8%
36	New Mexico	138,189	0.7%
37	Nebraska	136,087	0.7%
38	New Hampshire	123,966	0.6%
39	Idaho	121,108	0.6%
40	Nevada	116,097	0.6%
41	Rhode Island	82,292	0.4%
42	Maine	71,715	0.4%
43	Hawaii	69,331	0.3%
44	Delaware	60,392	0.3%
45	North Dakota	53,840	0.3%
46	South Dakota	53,664	0.3%
47	Montana	50,798	0.3%
48	Vermont	43,863	0.2%
49	Wyoming	34,205	0.2%
50	Alaska	31,331	0.2%
	District of Columbia	93,995	0.5%

Source: U.S. Department of Education, National Center for Education Statistics
"Digest of Education Statistics" (http://nces.ed.gov/programs/digest/index.asp)
*Fall 2015 enrollment. Includes full-time and part-time students at Title IV eligible, degree-granting four-year and two-year institutions. National total includes 14,812 students at U.S. Service Schools not shown by state.

Enrollment Rate in Institutions of Higher Education in 2015

National Rate = 640 Students per 1,000 Population 18 to 24 Years Old*

ALPHA ORDER

RANK ORDER

RANK	STATE	RATE	RANK	STATE	RATE
23	Alabama	646	1	Arizona	966
50	Alaska	389	2	New Hampshire	961
1	Arizona	966	3	West Virginia	910
34	Arkansas	593	4	Utah	862
15	California	683	5	Iowa	854
20	Colorado	655	6	Minnesota	845
36	Connecticut	567	7	Idaho	777
14	Delaware	687	8	Massachusetts	728
28	Florida	616	9	Kansas	724
45	Georgia	522	10	Rhode Island	716
47	Hawaii	509	11	Nebraska	706
7	Idaho	777	12	Missouri	698
21	Illinois	649	13	Virginia	692
25	Indiana	640	14	Delaware	687
5	Iowa	854	15	California	683
9	Kansas	724	16	New Mexico	675
33	Kentucky	603	17	New York	662
42	Louisiana	537	17	Oregon	662
22	Maine	648	19	Maryland	657
19	Maryland	657	20	Colorado	655
8	Massachusetts	728	21	Illinois	649
31	Michigan	608	22	Maine	648
6	Minnesota	845	23	Alabama	646
36	Mississippi	567	23	Vermont	646
12	Missouri	698	25	Indiana	640
48	Montana	504	26	South Dakota	634
11	Nebraska	706	27	Wisconsin	622
49	Nevada	460	28	Florida	616
2	New Hampshire	961	29	Ohio	615
43	New Jersey	535	30	Pennsylvania	612
16	New Mexico	675	31	Michigan	608
17	New York	662	32	Wyoming	605
35	North Carolina	569	33	Kentucky	603
39	North Dakota	564	34	Arkansas	593
29	Ohio	615	35	North Carolina	569
41	Oklahoma	541	36	Connecticut	567
17	Oregon	662	36	Mississippi	567
30	Pennsylvania	612	36	Texas	567
10	Rhode Island	716	39	North Dakota	564
44	South Carolina	523	40	Washington	548
26	South Dakota	634	41	Oklahoma	541
46	Tennessee	516	42	Louisiana	537
36	Texas	567	43	New Jersey	535
4	Utah	862	44	South Carolina	523
23	Vermont	646	45	Georgia	522
13	Virginia	692	46	Tennessee	516
40	Washington	548	47	Hawaii	509
3	West Virginia	910	48	Montana	504
27	Wisconsin	622	49	Nevada	460
32	Wyoming	605	50	Alaska	389

District of Columbia   1,151

Source: CQ Press using data from U.S. Department of Education, National Center for Education Statistics
"Digest of Education Statistics" (http://nces.ed.gov/programs/digest/index.asp)

*Based on fall 2015 enrollment and population. National rate includes U.S. Service Schools. Includes students at four-year and two-year public and private degree-granting institutions. Enrollment based on location of institution. Population based on residence.

Enrollment in Public Institutions of Higher Education in 2015

National Total = 14,568,103 Students*

ALPHA ORDER

RANK	STATE	STUDENTS	% of USA
21	Alabama	247,451	1.7%
49	Alaska	28,393	0.2%
12	Arizona	360,976	2.5%
33	Arkansas	150,165	1.0%
1	California	2,203,094	15.1%
18	Colorado	265,828	1.8%
35	Connecticut	119,766	0.8%
47	Delaware	40,611	0.3%
3	Florida	794,390	5.5%
9	Georgia	418,453	2.9%
40	Hawaii	55,756	0.4%
39	Idaho	72,339	0.5%
5	Illinois	509,104	3.5%
14	Indiana	321,500	2.2%
31	Iowa	171,005	1.2%
28	Kansas	179,760	1.2%
25	Kentucky	205,908	1.4%
24	Louisiana	211,334	1.5%
42	Maine	47,404	0.3%
16	Maryland	303,554	2.1%
23	Massachusetts	222,243	1.5%
7	Michigan	502,281	3.4%
19	Minnesota	256,187	1.8%
32	Mississippi	153,300	1.1%
20	Missouri	248,516	1.7%
43	Montana	45,934	0.3%
37	Nebraska	100,030	0.7%
36	Nevada	104,418	0.7%
45	New Hampshire	42,866	0.3%
13	New Jersey	339,743	2.3%
34	New Mexico	131,287	0.9%
4	New York	709,143	4.9%
8	North Carolina	448,055	3.1%
41	North Dakota	48,197	0.3%
6	Ohio	504,815	3.5%
29	Oklahoma	179,008	1.2%
27	Oregon	197,948	1.4%
10	Pennsylvania	409,054	2.8%
46	Rhode Island	41,320	0.3%
26	South Carolina	202,487	1.4%
44	South Dakota	44,254	0.3%
22	Tennessee	223,411	1.5%
2	Texas	1,379,276	9.5%
30	Utah	171,225	1.2%
50	Vermont	25,383	0.2%
11	Virginia	394,210	2.7%
15	Washington	314,506	2.2%
38	West Virginia	86,342	0.6%
17	Wisconsin	282,250	1.9%
48	Wyoming	33,693	0.2%

RANK ORDER

RANK	STATE	STUDENTS	% of USA
1	California	2,203,094	15.1%
2	Texas	1,379,276	9.5%
3	Florida	794,390	5.5%
4	New York	709,143	4.9%
5	Illinois	509,104	3.5%
6	Ohio	504,815	3.5%
7	Michigan	502,281	3.4%
8	North Carolina	448,055	3.1%
9	Georgia	418,453	2.9%
10	Pennsylvania	409,054	2.8%
11	Virginia	394,210	2.7%
12	Arizona	360,976	2.5%
13	New Jersey	339,743	2.3%
14	Indiana	321,500	2.2%
15	Washington	314,506	2.2%
16	Maryland	303,554	2.1%
17	Wisconsin	282,250	1.9%
18	Colorado	265,828	1.8%
19	Minnesota	256,187	1.8%
20	Missouri	248,516	1.7%
21	Alabama	247,451	1.7%
22	Tennessee	223,411	1.5%
23	Massachusetts	222,243	1.5%
24	Louisiana	211,334	1.5%
25	Kentucky	205,908	1.4%
26	South Carolina	202,487	1.4%
27	Oregon	197,948	1.4%
28	Kansas	179,760	1.2%
29	Oklahoma	179,008	1.2%
30	Utah	171,225	1.2%
31	Iowa	171,005	1.2%
32	Mississippi	153,300	1.1%
33	Arkansas	150,165	1.0%
34	New Mexico	131,287	0.9%
35	Connecticut	119,766	0.8%
36	Nevada	104,418	0.7%
37	Nebraska	100,030	0.7%
38	West Virginia	86,342	0.6%
39	Idaho	72,339	0.5%
40	Hawaii	55,756	0.4%
41	North Dakota	48,197	0.3%
42	Maine	47,404	0.3%
43	Montana	45,934	0.3%
44	South Dakota	44,254	0.3%
45	New Hampshire	42,866	0.3%
46	Rhode Island	41,320	0.3%
47	Delaware	40,611	0.3%
48	Wyoming	33,693	0.2%
49	Alaska	28,393	0.2%
50	Vermont	25,383	0.2%
	District of Columbia	5,118	0.0%

Source: U.S. Department of Education, National Center for Education Statistics
"Digest of Education Statistics" (http://nces.ed.gov/programs/digest/index.asp)
*Fall 2015 enrollment. Includes full-time and part-time students at Title IV eligible, degree-granting four-year and two-year institutions. National total includes 14,812 students at U.S. Service Schools not shown by state.

Enrollment in Private Institutions of Higher Education in 2015

National Total = 5,409,167 Students*

ALPHA ORDER

RANK	STATE	STUDENTS	% of USA
27	Alabama	55,508	1.0%
49	Alaska	2,938	0.1%
6	Arizona	288,756	5.3%
42	Arkansas	18,237	0.3%
2	California	485,261	9.0%
21	Colorado	82,270	1.5%
23	Connecticut	79,900	1.5%
39	Delaware	19,781	0.4%
5	Florida	288,872	5.3%
15	Georgia	112,846	2.1%
43	Hawaii	13,575	0.3%
30	Idaho	48,769	0.9%
4	Illinois	293,139	5.4%
16	Indiana	104,863	1.9%
17	Iowa	104,101	1.9%
34	Kansas	40,462	0.7%
29	Kentucky	49,814	0.9%
36	Louisiana	33,326	0.6%
38	Maine	24,311	0.4%
26	Maryland	60,377	1.1%
7	Massachusetts	288,153	5.3%
19	Michigan	97,922	1.8%
10	Minnesota	171,570	3.2%
40	Mississippi	18,836	0.3%
12	Missouri	161,480	3.0%
48	Montana	4,864	0.1%
35	Nebraska	36,057	0.7%
44	Nevada	11,679	0.2%
22	New Hampshire	81,100	1.5%
20	New Jersey	84,036	1.6%
46	New Mexico	6,902	0.1%
1	New York	576,277	10.7%
14	North Carolina	114,387	2.1%
47	North Dakota	5,643	0.1%
11	Ohio	162,945	3.0%
37	Oklahoma	31,896	0.6%
32	Oregon	42,698	0.8%
3	Pennsylvania	327,616	6.1%
33	Rhode Island	40,972	0.8%
31	South Carolina	47,167	0.9%
45	South Dakota	9,410	0.2%
18	Tennessee	100,088	1.9%
8	Texas	191,338	3.5%
13	Utah	122,302	2.3%
41	Vermont	18,480	0.3%
9	Virginia	175,549	3.2%
28	Washington	50,906	0.9%
25	West Virginia	64,401	1.2%
24	Wisconsin	67,998	1.3%
50	Wyoming	512	0.0%

RANK ORDER

RANK	STATE	STUDENTS	% of USA
1	New York	576,277	10.7%
2	California	485,261	9.0%
3	Pennsylvania	327,616	6.1%
4	Illinois	293,139	5.4%
5	Florida	288,872	5.3%
6	Arizona	288,756	5.3%
7	Massachusetts	288,153	5.3%
8	Texas	191,338	3.5%
9	Virginia	175,549	3.2%
10	Minnesota	171,570	3.2%
11	Ohio	162,945	3.0%
12	Missouri	161,480	3.0%
13	Utah	122,302	2.3%
14	North Carolina	114,387	2.1%
15	Georgia	112,846	2.1%
16	Indiana	104,863	1.9%
17	Iowa	104,101	1.9%
18	Tennessee	100,088	1.9%
19	Michigan	97,922	1.8%
20	New Jersey	84,036	1.6%
21	Colorado	82,270	1.5%
22	New Hampshire	81,100	1.5%
23	Connecticut	79,900	1.5%
24	Wisconsin	67,998	1.3%
25	West Virginia	64,401	1.2%
26	Maryland	60,377	1.1%
27	Alabama	55,508	1.0%
28	Washington	50,906	0.9%
29	Kentucky	49,814	0.9%
30	Idaho	48,769	0.9%
31	South Carolina	47,167	0.9%
32	Oregon	42,698	0.8%
33	Rhode Island	40,972	0.8%
34	Kansas	40,462	0.7%
35	Nebraska	36,057	0.7%
36	Louisiana	33,326	0.6%
37	Oklahoma	31,896	0.6%
38	Maine	24,311	0.4%
39	Delaware	19,781	0.4%
40	Mississippi	18,836	0.3%
41	Vermont	18,480	0.3%
42	Arkansas	18,237	0.3%
43	Hawaii	13,575	0.3%
44	Nevada	11,679	0.2%
45	South Dakota	9,410	0.2%
46	New Mexico	6,902	0.1%
47	North Dakota	5,643	0.1%
48	Montana	4,864	0.1%
49	Alaska	2,938	0.1%
50	Wyoming	512	0.0%
	District of Columbia	88,877	1.6%

Source: U.S. Department of Education, National Center for Education Statistics
   "Digest of Education Statistics" (http://nces.ed.gov/programs/digest/index.asp)
*Fall 2015 enrollment. Includes full-time and part-time students at Title IV eligible, degree-granting four-year and two-year institutions.

Percent of Population with a Bachelor's Degree or More in 2016

National Percent = 31.3%*

ALPHA ORDER

RANK	STATE	PERCENT
44	Alabama	24.7
26	Alaska	29.6
29	Arizona	28.9
48	Arkansas	22.4
14	California	32.9
2	Colorado	39.9
4	Connecticut	38.6
20	Delaware	31.0
32	Florida	28.6
23	Georgia	30.5
18	Hawaii	31.9
36	Idaho	27.6
13	Illinois	34.0
42	Indiana	25.6
34	Iowa	28.4
15	Kansas	32.8
46	Kentucky	23.4
46	Louisiana	23.4
25	Maine	30.1
3	Maryland	39.3
1	Massachusetts	42.7
35	Michigan	28.3
11	Minnesota	34.8
49	Mississippi	21.8
33	Missouri	28.5
20	Montana	31.0
19	Nebraska	31.4
45	Nevada	23.5
7	New Hampshire	36.6
4	New Jersey	38.6
38	New Mexico	27.2
9	New York	35.7
24	North Carolina	30.4
26	North Dakota	29.6
37	Ohio	27.5
43	Oklahoma	25.2
16	Oregon	32.7
22	Pennsylvania	30.8
12	Rhode Island	34.1
38	South Carolina	27.2
29	South Dakota	28.9
41	Tennessee	26.1
29	Texas	28.9
17	Utah	32.6
8	Vermont	36.4
6	Virginia	38.1
10	Washington	35.1
50	West Virginia	20.8
28	Wisconsin	29.5
40	Wyoming	27.1

RANK ORDER

RANK	STATE	PERCENT
1	Massachusetts	42.7
2	Colorado	39.9
3	Maryland	39.3
4	Connecticut	38.6
4	New Jersey	38.6
6	Virginia	38.1
7	New Hampshire	36.6
8	Vermont	36.4
9	New York	35.7
10	Washington	35.1
11	Minnesota	34.8
12	Rhode Island	34.1
13	Illinois	34.0
14	California	32.9
15	Kansas	32.8
16	Oregon	32.7
17	Utah	32.6
18	Hawaii	31.9
19	Nebraska	31.4
20	Delaware	31.0
20	Montana	31.0
22	Pennsylvania	30.8
23	Georgia	30.5
24	North Carolina	30.4
25	Maine	30.1
26	Alaska	29.6
26	North Dakota	29.6
28	Wisconsin	29.5
29	Arizona	28.9
29	South Dakota	28.9
29	Texas	28.9
32	Florida	28.6
33	Missouri	28.5
34	Iowa	28.4
35	Michigan	28.3
36	Idaho	27.6
37	Ohio	27.5
38	New Mexico	27.2
38	South Carolina	27.2
40	Wyoming	27.1
41	Tennessee	26.1
42	Indiana	25.6
43	Oklahoma	25.2
44	Alabama	24.7
45	Nevada	23.5
46	Kentucky	23.4
46	Louisiana	23.4
48	Arkansas	22.4
49	Mississippi	21.8
50	West Virginia	20.8

District of Columbia 56.8

Source: U.S. Bureau of the Census
"2016 American Community Survey-Table S1501" (http://www.census.gov/programs-surveys/acs/)
*Persons age 25 and older.

Percent of Population Who Have Completed an Advanced Degree in 2016

National Percent = 11.9%*

ALPHA ORDER

RANK	STATE	PERCENT
38	Alabama	9.4
27	Alaska	10.6
24	Arizona	10.8
45	Arkansas	8.2
15	California	12.3
7	Colorado	14.9
3	Connecticut	16.7
14	Delaware	12.6
29	Florida	10.4
18	Georgia	11.7
27	Hawaii	10.6
43	Idaho	8.9
12	Illinois	13.0
40	Indiana	9.3
40	Iowa	9.3
16	Kansas	12.2
37	Kentucky	9.5
45	Louisiana	8.2
21	Maine	11.3
2	Maryland	18.5
1	Massachusetts	19.0
23	Michigan	11.1
18	Minnesota	11.7
45	Mississippi	8.2
24	Missouri	10.8
33	Montana	10.1
29	Nebraska	10.4
49	Nevada	8.1
9	New Hampshire	14.1
7	New Jersey	14.9
18	New Mexico	11.7
5	New York	15.5
24	North Carolina	10.8
50	North Dakota	7.8
31	Ohio	10.3
44	Oklahoma	8.4
13	Oregon	12.7
17	Pennsylvania	12.0
10	Rhode Island	13.5
35	South Carolina	9.8
42	South Dakota	9.2
38	Tennessee	9.4
34	Texas	10.0
22	Utah	11.2
6	Vermont	15.2
4	Virginia	16.4
11	Washington	13.2
45	West Virginia	8.2
32	Wisconsin	10.2
36	Wyoming	9.7

RANK ORDER

RANK	STATE	PERCENT
1	Massachusetts	19.0
2	Maryland	18.5
3	Connecticut	16.7
4	Virginia	16.4
5	New York	15.5
6	Vermont	15.2
7	Colorado	14.9
7	New Jersey	14.9
9	New Hampshire	14.1
10	Rhode Island	13.5
11	Washington	13.2
12	Illinois	13.0
13	Oregon	12.7
14	Delaware	12.6
15	California	12.3
16	Kansas	12.2
17	Pennsylvania	12.0
18	Georgia	11.7
18	Minnesota	11.7
18	New Mexico	11.7
21	Maine	11.3
22	Utah	11.2
23	Michigan	11.1
24	Arizona	10.8
24	Missouri	10.8
24	North Carolina	10.8
27	Alaska	10.6
27	Hawaii	10.6
29	Florida	10.4
29	Nebraska	10.4
31	Ohio	10.3
32	Wisconsin	10.2
33	Montana	10.1
34	Texas	10.0
35	South Carolina	9.8
36	Wyoming	9.7
37	Kentucky	9.5
38	Alabama	9.4
38	Tennessee	9.4
40	Indiana	9.3
40	Iowa	9.3
42	South Dakota	9.2
43	Idaho	8.9
44	Oklahoma	8.4
45	Arkansas	8.2
45	Louisiana	8.2
45	Mississippi	8.2
45	West Virginia	8.2
49	Nevada	8.1
50	North Dakota	7.8

| District of Columbia | | 32.9 |

Source: U.S. Bureau of the Census
"2016 American Community Survey-Table S1501" (http://www.census.gov/programs-surveys/acs/)
*Persons age 25 and older who have earned a master's degree or higher.

Public Libraries and Branches in 2015

National Total = 16,560 Libraries and Branches*

ALPHA ORDER

RANK	STATE	LIBRARIES	% of USA
22	Alabama	291	1.8%
44	Alaska	96	0.6%
32	Arizona	221	1.3%
28	Arkansas	233	1.4%
1	California	1,115	6.7%
25	Colorado	258	1.6%
29	Connecticut	229	1.4%
50	Delaware	32	0.2%
9	Florida	535	3.2%
14	Georgia	400	2.4%
49	Hawaii	50	0.3%
39	Idaho	144	0.9%
4	Illinois	779	4.7%
12	Indiana	427	2.6%
8	Iowa	558	3.4%
16	Kansas	367	2.2%
34	Kentucky	205	1.2%
21	Louisiana	340	2.1%
27	Maine	234	1.4%
36	Maryland	188	1.1%
10	Massachusetts	462	2.8%
6	Michigan	640	3.9%
19	Minnesota	355	2.1%
26	Mississippi	236	1.4%
17	Missouri	361	2.2%
43	Montana	114	0.7%
24	Nebraska	266	1.6%
45	Nevada	85	0.5%
30	New Hampshire	224	1.4%
13	New Jersey	425	2.6%
42	New Mexico	116	0.7%
2	New York	1,063	6.4%
15	North Carolina	385	2.3%
46	North Dakota	75	0.5%
5	Ohio	713	4.3%
33	Oklahoma	214	1.3%
31	Oregon	223	1.3%
7	Pennsylvania	621	3.8%
48	Rhode Island	70	0.4%
35	South Carolina	192	1.2%
40	South Dakota	143	0.9%
23	Tennessee	284	1.7%
3	Texas	869	5.2%
41	Utah	125	0.8%
38	Vermont	161	1.0%
18	Virginia	357	2.2%
20	Washington	345	2.1%
37	West Virginia	173	1.0%
11	Wisconsin	460	2.8%
46	Wyoming	75	0.5%

RANK ORDER

RANK	STATE	LIBRARIES	% of USA
1	California	1,115	6.7%
2	New York	1,063	6.4%
3	Texas	869	5.2%
4	Illinois	779	4.7%
5	Ohio	713	4.3%
6	Michigan	640	3.9%
7	Pennsylvania	621	3.8%
8	Iowa	558	3.4%
9	Florida	535	3.2%
10	Massachusetts	462	2.8%
11	Wisconsin	460	2.8%
12	Indiana	427	2.6%
13	New Jersey	425	2.6%
14	Georgia	400	2.4%
15	North Carolina	385	2.3%
16	Kansas	367	2.2%
17	Missouri	361	2.2%
18	Virginia	357	2.2%
19	Minnesota	355	2.1%
20	Washington	345	2.1%
21	Louisiana	340	2.1%
22	Alabama	291	1.8%
23	Tennessee	284	1.7%
24	Nebraska	266	1.6%
25	Colorado	258	1.6%
26	Mississippi	236	1.4%
27	Maine	234	1.4%
28	Arkansas	233	1.4%
29	Connecticut	229	1.4%
30	New Hampshire	224	1.4%
31	Oregon	223	1.3%
32	Arizona	221	1.3%
33	Oklahoma	214	1.3%
34	Kentucky	205	1.2%
35	South Carolina	192	1.2%
36	Maryland	188	1.1%
37	West Virginia	173	1.0%
38	Vermont	161	1.0%
39	Idaho	144	0.9%
40	South Dakota	143	0.9%
41	Utah	125	0.8%
42	New Mexico	116	0.7%
43	Montana	114	0.7%
44	Alaska	96	0.6%
45	Nevada	85	0.5%
46	North Dakota	75	0.5%
46	Wyoming	75	0.5%
48	Rhode Island	70	0.4%
49	Hawaii	50	0.3%
50	Delaware	32	0.2%
	District of Columbia	26	0.2%

Source: Institute of Museum and Library Services
"Public Library Survey Fiscal Year 2015" (http://www.imls.gov/research/default.aspx)
*For fiscal year 2015. Total of central and branch outlets. Does not include bookmobiles. There are 9,068 public libraries.

Rate of Public Libraries and Branches in 2015

National Average = 19,386 Population per Library*

ALPHA ORDER				RANK ORDER		
RANK	STATE	RATE		RANK	STATE	RATE
25	Alabama	16,670		1	Florida	37,885
44	Alaska	7,687		2	California	35,007
6	Arizona	30,779		3	Nevada	33,918
35	Arkansas	12,771		4	Maryland	31,918
2	California	35,007		5	Texas	31,594
16	Colorado	21,087		6	Arizona	30,779
28	Connecticut	15,694		7	Delaware	29,503
7	Delaware	29,503		8	Hawaii	28,526
1	Florida	37,885		9	North Carolina	26,083
10	Georgia	25,499		10	Georgia	25,499
8	Hawaii	28,526		11	South Carolina	25,481
38	Idaho	11,454		12	Utah	23,879
26	Illinois	16,511		13	Virginia	23,436
30	Indiana	15,481		14	Tennessee	23,207
49	Iowa	5,589		15	Kentucky	21,571
42	Kansas	7,918		16	Colorado	21,087
15	Kentucky	21,571		17	New Jersey	21,082
34	Louisiana	13,739		18	Washington	20,733
48	Maine	5,674		19	Pennsylvania	20,598
4	Maryland	31,918		20	New York	18,645
33	Massachusetts	14,706		21	Oklahoma	18,245
29	Michigan	15,497		22	Oregon	18,011
31	Minnesota	15,446		23	New Mexico	17,951
36	Mississippi	12,650		24	Missouri	16,822
24	Missouri	16,822		25	Alabama	16,670
41	Montana	9,020		26	Illinois	16,511
45	Nebraska	7,119		27	Ohio	16,278
3	Nevada	33,918		28	Connecticut	15,694
47	New Hampshire	5,938		29	Michigan	15,497
17	New Jersey	21,082		30	Indiana	15,481
23	New Mexico	17,951		31	Minnesota	15,446
20	New York	18,645		32	Rhode Island	15,085
9	North Carolina	26,083		33	Massachusetts	14,706
40	North Dakota	10,065		34	Louisiana	13,739
27	Ohio	16,278		35	Arkansas	12,771
21	Oklahoma	18,245		36	Mississippi	12,650
22	Oregon	18,011		37	Wisconsin	12,521
19	Pennsylvania	20,598		38	Idaho	11,454
32	Rhode Island	15,085		39	West Virginia	10,634
11	South Carolina	25,481		40	North Dakota	10,065
46	South Dakota	5,972		41	Montana	9,020
14	Tennessee	23,207		42	Kansas	7,918
5	Texas	31,594		43	Wyoming	7,815
12	Utah	23,879		44	Alaska	7,687
50	Vermont	3,879		45	Nebraska	7,119
13	Virginia	23,436		46	South Dakota	5,972
18	Washington	20,733		47	New Hampshire	5,938
39	West Virginia	10,634		48	Maine	5,674
37	Wisconsin	12,521		49	Iowa	5,589
43	Wyoming	7,815		50	Vermont	3,879
					District of Columbia	25,874

Source: CQ Press using data from Institute of Museum and Library Services
  "Public Library Survey Fiscal Year 2015" (http://www.imls.gov/research/default.aspx)
*For fiscal year 2015. Based on total of central and branch outlets. Does not include bookmobiles.

Rate of Books in Public Libraries in 2015

National Rate = 2,337 Books per 1,000 Population*

ALPHA ORDER

RANK	STATE	RATE
37	Alabama	1,902
16	Alaska	3,190
50	Arizona	1,205
30	Arkansas	2,141
44	California	1,631
40	Colorado	1,828
8	Connecticut	3,778
43	Delaware	1,743
47	Florida	1,519
45	Georgia	1,620
28	Hawaii	2,241
23	Idaho	2,633
12	Illinois	3,294
10	Indiana	3,511
7	Iowa	3,827
17	Kansas	3,136
31	Kentucky	2,074
26	Louisiana	2,533
2	Maine	4,504
34	Maryland	1,987
1	Massachusetts	4,542
15	Michigan	3,208
24	Minnesota	2,619
36	Mississippi	1,911
22	Missouri	2,682
25	Montana	2,550
19	Nebraska	3,028
49	Nevada	1,428
4	New Hampshire	4,374
18	New Jersey	3,033
33	New Mexico	2,032
11	New York	3,497
46	North Carolina	1,595
20	North Dakota	2,879
9	Ohio	3,535
41	Oklahoma	1,817
27	Oregon	2,441
35	Pennsylvania	1,978
6	Rhode Island	4,016
38	South Carolina	1,862
14	South Dakota	3,241
42	Tennessee	1,779
48	Texas	1,445
29	Utah	2,220
3	Vermont	4,469
32	Virginia	2,057
39	Washington	1,854
21	West Virginia	2,720
13	Wisconsin	3,261
5	Wyoming	4,068

RANK ORDER

RANK	STATE	RATE
1	Massachusetts	4,542
2	Maine	4,504
3	Vermont	4,469
4	New Hampshire	4,374
5	Wyoming	4,068
6	Rhode Island	4,016
7	Iowa	3,827
8	Connecticut	3,778
9	Ohio	3,535
10	Indiana	3,511
11	New York	3,497
12	Illinois	3,294
13	Wisconsin	3,261
14	South Dakota	3,241
15	Michigan	3,208
16	Alaska	3,190
17	Kansas	3,136
18	New Jersey	3,033
19	Nebraska	3,028
20	North Dakota	2,879
21	West Virginia	2,720
22	Missouri	2,682
23	Idaho	2,633
24	Minnesota	2,619
25	Montana	2,550
26	Louisiana	2,533
27	Oregon	2,441
28	Hawaii	2,241
29	Utah	2,220
30	Arkansas	2,141
31	Kentucky	2,074
32	Virginia	2,057
33	New Mexico	2,032
34	Maryland	1,987
35	Pennsylvania	1,978
36	Mississippi	1,911
37	Alabama	1,902
38	South Carolina	1,862
39	Washington	1,854
40	Colorado	1,828
41	Oklahoma	1,817
42	Tennessee	1,779
43	Delaware	1,743
44	California	1,631
45	Georgia	1,620
46	North Carolina	1,595
47	Florida	1,519
48	Texas	1,445
49	Nevada	1,428
50	Arizona	1,205

District of Columbia 2,769

Source: CQ Press using data from Institute of Museum and Library Services
"Public Library Survey Fiscal Year 2015" (http://www.imls.gov/research/default.aspx)
*For fiscal year 2015. Includes serial back files in print.

Rate of Electronic Books in Public Libraries in 2015

National Rate = 1,024 Electronic Books per 1,000 Population*

ALPHA ORDER

RANK	STATE	RATE
22	Alabama	690
23	Alaska	681
39	Arizona	250
40	Arkansas	199
43	California	143
35	Colorado	314
30	Connecticut	431
27	Delaware	577
44	Florida	120
49	Georgia	40
50	Hawaii	27
38	Idaho	256
17	Illinois	926
19	Indiana	792
8	Iowa	2,065
1	Kansas	14,445
9	Kentucky	2,044
37	Louisiana	269
14	Maine	1,125
29	Maryland	456
6	Massachusetts	2,385
33	Michigan	359
20	Minnesota	727
48	Mississippi	51
36	Missouri	308
16	Montana	935
10	Nebraska	1,810
47	Nevada	93
5	New Hampshire	2,805
31	New Jersey	406
46	New Mexico	117
18	New York	839
11	North Carolina	1,648
25	North Dakota	625
3	Ohio	4,081
26	Oklahoma	612
15	Oregon	967
24	Pennsylvania	647
12	Rhode Island	1,585
45	South Carolina	119
13	South Dakota	1,363
4	Tennessee	3,270
41	Texas	165
32	Utah	383
42	Vermont	149
28	Virginia	551
34	Washington	355
7	West Virginia	2,204
2	Wisconsin	9,315
21	Wyoming	695

RANK ORDER

RANK	STATE	RATE
1	Kansas	14,445
2	Wisconsin	9,315
3	Ohio	4,081
4	Tennessee	3,270
5	New Hampshire	2,805
6	Massachusetts	2,385
7	West Virginia	2,204
8	Iowa	2,065
9	Kentucky	2,044
10	Nebraska	1,810
11	North Carolina	1,648
12	Rhode Island	1,585
13	South Dakota	1,363
14	Maine	1,125
15	Oregon	967
16	Montana	935
17	Illinois	926
18	New York	839
19	Indiana	792
20	Minnesota	727
21	Wyoming	695
22	Alabama	690
23	Alaska	681
24	Pennsylvania	647
25	North Dakota	625
26	Oklahoma	612
27	Delaware	577
28	Virginia	551
29	Maryland	456
30	Connecticut	431
31	New Jersey	406
32	Utah	383
33	Michigan	359
34	Washington	355
35	Colorado	314
36	Missouri	308
37	Louisiana	269
38	Idaho	256
39	Arizona	250
40	Arkansas	199
41	Texas	165
42	Vermont	149
43	California	143
44	Florida	120
45	South Carolina	119
46	New Mexico	117
47	Nevada	93
48	Mississippi	51
49	Georgia	40
50	Hawaii	27

District of Columbia	363

Source: CQ Press using data from Institute of Museum and Library Services
"Public Library Survey Fiscal Year 2015" (http://www.imls.gov/research/default.aspx)
*For fiscal year 2015.

Internet Terminals in Public Libraries in 2015

National Total = 294,319 Terminals*

ALPHA ORDER					RANK ORDER			
RANK	STATE	TERMINALS	% of USA		RANK	STATE	TERMINALS	% of USA
21	Alabama	5,516	1.9%		1	California	22,251	7.6%
47	Alaska	1,040	0.4%		2	New York	20,585	7.0%
13	Arizona	7,630	2.6%		3	Texas	19,820	6.7%
34	Arkansas	2,718	0.9%		4	Florida	16,852	5.7%
1	California	22,251	7.6%		5	Illinois	16,526	5.6%
16	Colorado	6,475	2.2%		6	Ohio	13,421	4.6%
28	Connecticut	4,262	1.4%		7	Michigan	11,954	4.1%
45	Delaware	1,076	0.4%		8	Georgia	8,892	3.0%
4	Florida	16,852	5.7%		9	Indiana	8,681	2.9%
8	Georgia	8,892	3.0%		10	Pennsylvania	8,028	2.7%
50	Hawaii	532	0.2%		11	New Jersey	7,998	2.7%
36	Idaho	1,861	0.6%		12	North Carolina	7,899	2.7%
5	Illinois	16,526	5.6%		13	Arizona	7,630	2.6%
9	Indiana	8,681	2.9%		14	Virginia	7,084	2.4%
26	Iowa	4,831	1.6%		15	Massachusetts	6,521	2.2%
29	Kansas	3,711	1.3%		16	Colorado	6,475	2.2%
25	Kentucky	4,893	1.7%		17	Washington	6,374	2.2%
20	Louisiana	5,569	1.9%		18	Wisconsin	6,327	2.1%
37	Maine	1,845	0.6%		19	Minnesota	5,730	1.9%
23	Maryland	5,157	1.8%		20	Louisiana	5,569	1.9%
15	Massachusetts	6,521	2.2%		21	Alabama	5,516	1.9%
7	Michigan	11,954	4.1%		22	Tennessee	5,308	1.8%
19	Minnesota	5,730	1.9%		23	Maryland	5,157	1.8%
33	Mississippi	2,742	0.9%		24	Missouri	5,077	1.7%
24	Missouri	5,077	1.7%		25	Kentucky	4,893	1.7%
42	Montana	1,288	0.4%		26	Iowa	4,831	1.6%
32	Nebraska	2,871	1.0%		27	South Carolina	4,263	1.4%
43	Nevada	1,268	0.4%		28	Connecticut	4,262	1.4%
39	New Hampshire	1,478	0.5%		29	Kansas	3,711	1.3%
11	New Jersey	7,998	2.7%		30	Oklahoma	3,252	1.1%
38	New Mexico	1,694	0.6%		31	Oregon	3,177	1.1%
2	New York	20,585	7.0%		32	Nebraska	2,871	1.0%
12	North Carolina	7,899	2.7%		33	Mississippi	2,742	0.9%
49	North Dakota	818	0.3%		34	Arkansas	2,718	0.9%
6	Ohio	13,421	4.6%		35	Utah	2,101	0.7%
30	Oklahoma	3,252	1.1%		36	Idaho	1,861	0.6%
31	Oregon	3,177	1.1%		37	Maine	1,845	0.6%
10	Pennsylvania	8,028	2.7%		38	New Mexico	1,694	0.6%
41	Rhode Island	1,405	0.5%		39	New Hampshire	1,478	0.5%
27	South Carolina	4,263	1.4%		40	West Virginia	1,469	0.5%
44	South Dakota	1,099	0.4%		41	Rhode Island	1,405	0.5%
22	Tennessee	5,308	1.8%		42	Montana	1,288	0.4%
3	Texas	19,820	6.7%		43	Nevada	1,268	0.4%
35	Utah	2,101	0.7%		44	South Dakota	1,099	0.4%
46	Vermont	1,069	0.4%		45	Delaware	1,076	0.4%
14	Virginia	7,084	2.4%		46	Vermont	1,069	0.4%
17	Washington	6,374	2.2%		47	Alaska	1,040	0.4%
40	West Virginia	1,469	0.5%		48	Wyoming	881	0.3%
18	Wisconsin	6,327	2.1%		49	North Dakota	818	0.3%
48	Wyoming	881	0.3%		50	Hawaii	532	0.2%
						District of Columbia	1,000	0.3%

Source: Institute of Museum and Library Services
   "Public Library Survey Fiscal Year 2015" (http://www.imls.gov/research/default.aspx)
*For fiscal year 2015. Total of public-use Internet terminals in central and branch outlets.

Rate of Internet Terminals in Public Libraries in 2015

National Rate = 17.8 Terminals per Library*

ALPHA ORDER				RANK ORDER		
RANK	STATE	RATE		RANK	STATE	RATE
17	Alabama	19.0		1	Arizona	34.5
41	Alaska	10.8		2	Delaware	33.6
1	Arizona	34.5		3	Florida	31.5
36	Arkansas	11.7		4	Maryland	27.4
14	California	20.0		5	Colorado	25.1
5	Colorado	25.1		6	Kentucky	23.9
22	Connecticut	18.6		7	Texas	22.8
2	Delaware	33.6		8	Georgia	22.2
3	Florida	31.5		8	South Carolina	22.2
8	Georgia	22.2		10	Illinois	21.2
43	Hawaii	10.6		11	North Carolina	20.5
34	Idaho	12.9		12	Indiana	20.3
10	Illinois	21.2		13	Rhode Island	20.1
12	Indiana	20.3		14	California	20.0
45	Iowa	8.7		15	Virginia	19.8
44	Kansas	10.1		16	New York	19.4
6	Kentucky	23.9		17	Alabama	19.0
25	Louisiana	16.4		18	New Jersey	18.8
47	Maine	7.9		18	Ohio	18.8
4	Maryland	27.4		20	Michigan	18.7
31	Massachusetts	14.1		20	Tennessee	18.7
20	Michigan	18.7		22	Connecticut	18.6
26	Minnesota	16.1		23	Washington	18.5
38	Mississippi	11.6		24	Utah	16.8
31	Missouri	14.1		25	Louisiana	16.4
39	Montana	11.3		26	Minnesota	16.1
41	Nebraska	10.8		27	Oklahoma	15.2
28	Nevada	14.9		28	Nevada	14.9
49	New Hampshire	6.6		29	New Mexico	14.6
18	New Jersey	18.8		30	Oregon	14.2
29	New Mexico	14.6		31	Massachusetts	14.1
16	New York	19.4		31	Missouri	14.1
11	North Carolina	20.5		33	Wisconsin	13.8
40	North Dakota	10.9		34	Idaho	12.9
18	Ohio	18.8		34	Pennsylvania	12.9
27	Oklahoma	15.2		36	Arkansas	11.7
30	Oregon	14.2		36	Wyoming	11.7
34	Pennsylvania	12.9		38	Mississippi	11.6
13	Rhode Island	20.1		39	Montana	11.3
8	South Carolina	22.2		40	North Dakota	10.9
48	South Dakota	7.7		41	Alaska	10.8
20	Tennessee	18.7		41	Nebraska	10.8
7	Texas	22.8		43	Hawaii	10.6
24	Utah	16.8		44	Kansas	10.1
49	Vermont	6.6		45	Iowa	8.7
15	Virginia	19.8		46	West Virginia	8.5
23	Washington	18.5		47	Maine	7.9
46	West Virginia	8.5		48	South Dakota	7.7
33	Wisconsin	13.8		49	New Hampshire	6.6
36	Wyoming	11.7		49	Vermont	6.6
					District of Columbia	38.5

Source: CQ Press using data from Institute of Museum and Library Services
"Public Library Survey Fiscal Year 2015" (http://www.imls.gov/research/default.aspx)
*For fiscal year 2015. Total of public-use Internet terminals in central and branch outlets divided by the number of outlets.

Per Capita State Art Agencies' Legislative Appropriations in 2018

National Per Capita = $1.05*

ALPHA ORDER				RANK ORDER		
RANK	STATE	PER CAPITA		RANK	STATE	PER CAPITA
20	Alabama	$0.99		1	Minnesota	$6.29
21	Alaska	0.94		2	Hawaii	4.64
46	Arizona	0.21		3	Delaware	3.35
23	Arkansas	0.84		4	Maryland	2.99
38	California	0.46		5	Rhode Island	2.16
43	Colorado	0.36		6	New York	2.07
12	Connecticut	1.43		7	Massachusetts	2.03
3	Delaware	3.35		8	Missouri	1.93
11	Florida	1.53		9	New Jersey	1.82
49	Georgia	0.11		10	Wyoming	1.79
2	Hawaii	4.64		11	Florida	1.53
37	Idaho	0.47		12	Connecticut	1.43
22	Illinois	0.85		13	Ohio	1.25
32	Indiana	0.60		14	South Dakota	1.08
42	Iowa	0.39		15	Vermont	1.08
50	Kansas	0.06		16	Tennessee	1.05
33	Kentucky	0.59		17	North Dakota	1.04
39	Louisiana	0.45		18	Utah	1.02
28	Maine	0.71		19	Michigan	1.00
4	Maryland	2.99		20	Alabama	0.99
7	Massachusetts	2.03		21	Alaska	0.94
19	Michigan	1.00		22	Illinois	0.85
1	Minnesota	6.29		23	Arkansas	0.84
34	Mississippi	0.53		24	Nebraska	0.80
8	Missouri	1.93		25	Pennsylvania	0.75
36	Montana	0.49		26	North Carolina	0.72
24	Nebraska	0.80		27	Oklahoma	0.71
31	Nevada	0.60		28	Maine	0.71
44	New Hampshire	0.30		29	South Carolina	0.67
9	New Jersey	1.82		30	New Mexico	0.63
30	New Mexico	0.63		31	Nevada	0.60
6	New York	2.07		32	Indiana	0.60
26	North Carolina	0.72		33	Kentucky	0.59
17	North Dakota	1.04		34	Mississippi	0.53
13	Ohio	1.25		35	West Virginia	0.51
27	Oklahoma	0.71		36	Montana	0.49
40	Oregon	0.45		37	Idaho	0.47
25	Pennsylvania	0.75		38	California	0.46
5	Rhode Island	2.16		39	Louisiana	0.45
29	South Carolina	0.67		40	Oregon	0.45
14	South Dakota	1.08		41	Virginia	0.41
16	Tennessee	1.05		42	Iowa	0.39
47	Texas	0.19		43	Colorado	0.36
18	Utah	1.02		44	New Hampshire	0.30
15	Vermont	1.08		45	Washington	0.22
41	Virginia	0.41		46	Arizona	0.21
45	Washington	0.22		47	Texas	0.19
35	West Virginia	0.51		48	Wisconsin	0.14
48	Wisconsin	0.14		49	Georgia	0.11
10	Wyoming	1.79		50	Kansas	0.06

District of Columbia   28.93

Source: National Assembly of State Arts Agencies
"State Arts Agency Legislative Appropriations Preview Fiscal Year 2018" (http://www.nasaa-arts.org/Research/Funding/)
*Projected figures for fiscal year 2018. Includes line item appropriations. Line items are legislative appropriations that are not controlled by the state art agencies but are passed through their budgets directly to another entity. Calculated using 2017 Census population estimates.

Federal Allocations for Head Start Program in 2016

National Total = $9,168,095,000*

<table>
<tr><td colspan="4"><u>ALPHA ORDER</u></td><td colspan="4"><u>RANK ORDER</u></td></tr>
<tr><th>RANK</th><th>STATE</th><th>EXPENDITURES</th><th>% of USA</th><th>RANK</th><th>STATE</th><th>EXPENDITURES</th><th>% of USA</th></tr>
<tr><td>17</td><td>Alabama</td><td>$140,702,210</td><td>1.5%</td><td>1</td><td>California</td><td>$1,094,230,167</td><td>11.9%</td></tr>
<tr><td>50</td><td>Alaska</td><td>14,954,571</td><td>0.2%</td><td>2</td><td>Texas</td><td>635,572,228</td><td>6.9%</td></tr>
<tr><td>18</td><td>Arizona</td><td>139,932,479</td><td>1.5%</td><td>3</td><td>New York</td><td>547,552,882</td><td>6.0%</td></tr>
<tr><td>29</td><td>Arkansas</td><td>89,109,613</td><td>1.0%</td><td>4</td><td>Florida</td><td>366,094,539</td><td>4.0%</td></tr>
<tr><td>1</td><td>California</td><td>1,094,230,167</td><td>11.9%</td><td>5</td><td>Illinois</td><td>355,108,783</td><td>3.9%</td></tr>
<tr><td>28</td><td>Colorado</td><td>93,033,219</td><td>1.0%</td><td>6</td><td>Ohio</td><td>324,549,262</td><td>3.5%</td></tr>
<tr><td>32</td><td>Connecticut</td><td>66,043,700</td><td>0.7%</td><td>7</td><td>Pennsylvania</td><td>298,262,784</td><td>3.3%</td></tr>
<tr><td>47</td><td>Delaware</td><td>17,431,814</td><td>0.2%</td><td>8</td><td>Michigan</td><td>297,675,414</td><td>3.2%</td></tr>
<tr><td>4</td><td>Florida</td><td>366,094,539</td><td>4.0%</td><td>9</td><td>Georgia</td><td>232,819,337</td><td>2.5%</td></tr>
<tr><td>9</td><td>Georgia</td><td>232,819,337</td><td>2.5%</td><td>10</td><td>North Carolina</td><td>211,750,756</td><td>2.3%</td></tr>
<tr><td>43</td><td>Hawaii</td><td>28,461,325</td><td>0.3%</td><td>11</td><td>Mississippi</td><td>197,454,022</td><td>2.2%</td></tr>
<tr><td>40</td><td>Idaho</td><td>30,018,417</td><td>0.3%</td><td>12</td><td>Louisiana</td><td>180,767,741</td><td>2.0%</td></tr>
<tr><td>5</td><td>Illinois</td><td>355,108,783</td><td>3.9%</td><td>13</td><td>New Jersey</td><td>172,509,276</td><td>1.9%</td></tr>
<tr><td>22</td><td>Indiana</td><td>126,877,245</td><td>1.4%</td><td>14</td><td>Tennessee</td><td>158,249,996</td><td>1.7%</td></tr>
<tr><td>35</td><td>Iowa</td><td>64,847,595</td><td>0.7%</td><td>15</td><td>Missouri</td><td>156,662,621</td><td>1.7%</td></tr>
<tr><td>33</td><td>Kansas</td><td>65,531,577</td><td>0.7%</td><td>16</td><td>Kentucky</td><td>143,589,046</td><td>1.6%</td></tr>
<tr><td>16</td><td>Kentucky</td><td>143,589,046</td><td>1.6%</td><td>17</td><td>Alabama</td><td>140,702,210</td><td>1.5%</td></tr>
<tr><td>12</td><td>Louisiana</td><td>180,767,741</td><td>2.0%</td><td>18</td><td>Arizona</td><td>139,932,479</td><td>1.5%</td></tr>
<tr><td>39</td><td>Maine</td><td>35,452,428</td><td>0.4%</td><td>19</td><td>Massachusetts</td><td>135,372,279</td><td>1.5%</td></tr>
<tr><td>26</td><td>Maryland</td><td>98,558,454</td><td>1.1%</td><td>20</td><td>Washington</td><td>135,155,100</td><td>1.5%</td></tr>
<tr><td>19</td><td>Massachusetts</td><td>135,372,279</td><td>1.5%</td><td>21</td><td>Virginia</td><td>133,172,846</td><td>1.5%</td></tr>
<tr><td>8</td><td>Michigan</td><td>297,675,414</td><td>3.2%</td><td>22</td><td>Indiana</td><td>126,877,245</td><td>1.4%</td></tr>
<tr><td>27</td><td>Minnesota</td><td>96,666,494</td><td>1.1%</td><td>23</td><td>Wisconsin</td><td>122,149,024</td><td>1.3%</td></tr>
<tr><td>11</td><td>Mississippi</td><td>197,454,022</td><td>2.2%</td><td>24</td><td>Oklahoma</td><td>116,906,721</td><td>1.3%</td></tr>
<tr><td>15</td><td>Missouri</td><td>156,662,621</td><td>1.7%</td><td>25</td><td>South Carolina</td><td>114,169,321</td><td>1.2%</td></tr>
<tr><td>41</td><td>Montana</td><td>29,181,554</td><td>0.3%</td><td>26</td><td>Maryland</td><td>98,558,454</td><td>1.1%</td></tr>
<tr><td>37</td><td>Nebraska</td><td>49,167,835</td><td>0.5%</td><td>27</td><td>Minnesota</td><td>96,666,494</td><td>1.1%</td></tr>
<tr><td>38</td><td>Nevada</td><td>37,717,203</td><td>0.4%</td><td>28</td><td>Colorado</td><td>93,033,219</td><td>1.0%</td></tr>
<tr><td>48</td><td>New Hampshire</td><td>17,283,202</td><td>0.2%</td><td>29</td><td>Arkansas</td><td>89,109,613</td><td>1.0%</td></tr>
<tr><td>13</td><td>New Jersey</td><td>172,509,276</td><td>1.9%</td><td>30</td><td>Oregon</td><td>83,621,349</td><td>0.9%</td></tr>
<tr><td>31</td><td>New Mexico</td><td>67,755,179</td><td>0.7%</td><td>31</td><td>New Mexico</td><td>67,755,179</td><td>0.7%</td></tr>
<tr><td>3</td><td>New York</td><td>547,552,882</td><td>6.0%</td><td>32</td><td>Connecticut</td><td>66,043,700</td><td>0.7%</td></tr>
<tr><td>10</td><td>North Carolina</td><td>211,750,756</td><td>2.3%</td><td>33</td><td>Kansas</td><td>65,531,577</td><td>0.7%</td></tr>
<tr><td>45</td><td>North Dakota</td><td>21,272,786</td><td>0.2%</td><td>34</td><td>West Virginia</td><td>65,259,418</td><td>0.7%</td></tr>
<tr><td>6</td><td>Ohio</td><td>324,549,262</td><td>3.5%</td><td>35</td><td>Iowa</td><td>64,847,595</td><td>0.7%</td></tr>
<tr><td>24</td><td>Oklahoma</td><td>116,906,721</td><td>1.3%</td><td>36</td><td>Utah</td><td>53,586,801</td><td>0.6%</td></tr>
<tr><td>30</td><td>Oregon</td><td>83,621,349</td><td>0.9%</td><td>37</td><td>Nebraska</td><td>49,167,835</td><td>0.5%</td></tr>
<tr><td>7</td><td>Pennsylvania</td><td>298,262,784</td><td>3.3%</td><td>38</td><td>Nevada</td><td>37,717,203</td><td>0.4%</td></tr>
<tr><td>42</td><td>Rhode Island</td><td>28,884,499</td><td>0.3%</td><td>39</td><td>Maine</td><td>35,452,428</td><td>0.4%</td></tr>
<tr><td>25</td><td>South Carolina</td><td>114,169,321</td><td>1.2%</td><td>40</td><td>Idaho</td><td>30,018,417</td><td>0.3%</td></tr>
<tr><td>44</td><td>South Dakota</td><td>23,683,258</td><td>0.3%</td><td>41</td><td>Montana</td><td>29,181,554</td><td>0.3%</td></tr>
<tr><td>14</td><td>Tennessee</td><td>158,249,996</td><td>1.7%</td><td>42</td><td>Rhode Island</td><td>28,884,499</td><td>0.3%</td></tr>
<tr><td>2</td><td>Texas</td><td>635,572,228</td><td>6.9%</td><td>43</td><td>Hawaii</td><td>28,461,325</td><td>0.3%</td></tr>
<tr><td>36</td><td>Utah</td><td>53,586,801</td><td>0.6%</td><td>44</td><td>South Dakota</td><td>23,683,258</td><td>0.3%</td></tr>
<tr><td>46</td><td>Vermont</td><td>18,194,079</td><td>0.2%</td><td>45</td><td>North Dakota</td><td>21,272,786</td><td>0.2%</td></tr>
<tr><td>21</td><td>Virginia</td><td>133,172,846</td><td>1.5%</td><td>46</td><td>Vermont</td><td>18,194,079</td><td>0.2%</td></tr>
<tr><td>20</td><td>Washington</td><td>135,155,100</td><td>1.5%</td><td>47</td><td>Delaware</td><td>17,431,814</td><td>0.2%</td></tr>
<tr><td>34</td><td>West Virginia</td><td>65,259,418</td><td>0.7%</td><td>48</td><td>New Hampshire</td><td>17,283,202</td><td>0.2%</td></tr>
<tr><td>23</td><td>Wisconsin</td><td>122,149,024</td><td>1.3%</td><td>49</td><td>Wyoming</td><td>15,377,527</td><td>0.2%</td></tr>
<tr><td>49</td><td>Wyoming</td><td>15,377,527</td><td>0.2%</td><td>50</td><td>Alaska</td><td>14,954,571</td><td>0.2%</td></tr>
<tr><td></td><td></td><td></td><td></td><td></td><td>District of Columbia</td><td>29,329,416</td><td>0.3%</td></tr>
</table>

Source: U.S. Department of Health and Human Services, Administration for Children and Families
"Head Start Fact Sheet Fiscal Year 2016" (https://eclkc.ohs.acf.hhs.gov/about-us/article/office-head-start-ohs)
*For fiscal year 2016. National total includes $627,211,569 to Migrant and Native American programs not included in state totals, $322,278,329 to U.S. territories, $605,941,418 in "support activities" expenditures, and $650,000,000 to expand access to high-quality early learning and development opportunities for infants and toddlers through Early Head Start-Child Care Partnerships.

Head Start Program Enrollment in 2016

National Total = 915,603 Children*

ALPHA ORDER

RANK ORDER

RANK	STATE	ENROLLMENT	% of USA		RANK	STATE	ENROLLMENT	% of USA
14	Alabama	16,414	1.8%		1	California	96,258	10.5%
49	Alaska	1,494	0.2%		2	Texas	72,657	7.9%
22	Arizona	13,678	1.5%		3	New York	50,748	5.5%
30	Arkansas	9,838	1.1%		4	Illinois	40,399	4.4%
1	California	96,258	10.5%		5	Florida	39,249	4.3%
28	Colorado	10,379	1.1%		6	Ohio	36,145	3.9%
35	Connecticut	6,383	0.7%		7	Pennsylvania	36,013	3.9%
45	Delaware	2,242	0.2%		8	Michigan	30,379	3.3%
5	Florida	39,249	4.3%		9	Georgia	25,033	2.7%
9	Georgia	25,033	2.7%		10	Mississippi	24,255	2.6%
42	Hawaii	3,040	0.3%		11	North Carolina	21,408	2.3%
41	Idaho	3,053	0.3%		12	Louisiana	21,187	2.3%
4	Illinois	40,399	4.4%		13	Tennessee	17,430	1.9%
18	Indiana	14,733	1.6%		14	Alabama	16,414	1.8%
33	Iowa	7,449	0.8%		15	Kentucky	16,097	1.8%
34	Kansas	7,437	0.8%		16	New Jersey	16,053	1.8%
15	Kentucky	16,097	1.8%		17	Missouri	15,021	1.6%
12	Louisiana	21,187	2.3%		18	Indiana	14,733	1.6%
38	Maine	3,137	0.3%		19	Virginia	14,397	1.6%
29	Maryland	10,120	1.1%		20	Oklahoma	14,396	1.6%
25	Massachusetts	12,284	1.3%		21	Wisconsin	13,954	1.5%
8	Michigan	30,379	3.3%		22	Arizona	13,678	1.5%
27	Minnesota	11,364	1.2%		23	Oregon	13,045	1.4%
10	Mississippi	24,255	2.6%		24	South Carolina	12,549	1.4%
17	Missouri	15,021	1.6%		25	Massachusetts	12,284	1.3%
40	Montana	3,059	0.3%		26	Washington	11,952	1.3%
37	Nebraska	4,826	0.5%		27	Minnesota	11,364	1.2%
39	Nevada	3,072	0.3%		28	Colorado	10,379	1.1%
47	New Hampshire	1,640	0.2%		29	Maryland	10,120	1.1%
16	New Jersey	16,053	1.8%		30	Arkansas	9,838	1.1%
32	New Mexico	7,512	0.8%		31	West Virginia	8,078	0.9%
3	New York	50,748	5.5%		32	New Mexico	7,512	0.8%
11	North Carolina	21,408	2.3%		33	Iowa	7,449	0.8%
46	North Dakota	2,147	0.2%		34	Kansas	7,437	0.8%
6	Ohio	36,145	3.9%		35	Connecticut	6,383	0.7%
20	Oklahoma	14,396	1.6%		36	Utah	5,978	0.7%
23	Oregon	13,045	1.4%		37	Nebraska	4,826	0.5%
7	Pennsylvania	36,013	3.9%		38	Maine	3,137	0.3%
44	Rhode Island	2,803	0.3%		39	Nevada	3,072	0.3%
24	South Carolina	12,549	1.4%		40	Montana	3,059	0.3%
43	South Dakota	2,874	0.3%		41	Idaho	3,053	0.3%
13	Tennessee	17,430	1.9%		42	Hawaii	3,040	0.3%
2	Texas	72,657	7.9%		43	South Dakota	2,874	0.3%
36	Utah	5,978	0.7%		44	Rhode Island	2,803	0.3%
50	Vermont	1,425	0.2%		45	Delaware	2,242	0.2%
19	Virginia	14,397	1.6%		46	North Dakota	2,147	0.2%
26	Washington	11,952	1.3%		47	New Hampshire	1,640	0.2%
31	West Virginia	8,078	0.9%		48	Wyoming	1,607	0.2%
21	Wisconsin	13,954	1.5%		49	Alaska	1,494	0.2%
48	Wyoming	1,607	0.2%		50	Vermont	1,425	0.2%
						District of Columbia	3,289	0.4%

Source: U.S. Department of Health and Human Services, Administration for Children and Families
    "Head Start Fact Sheet Fiscal Year 2016" (https://eclkc.ohs.acf.hhs.gov/about-us/article/office-head-start-ohs)
*For fiscal year 2016. National total includes 32,087 enrollees not included in state totals enrolled in Migrant and Native American programs and 22,600 enrollees in U.S. territories.

VI. Employment and Labor

Average Annual Pay in 2016

National Average = $53,621*

ALPHA ORDER			RANK ORDER		
RANK	STATE	ANNUAL PAY	RANK	STATE	ANNUAL PAY
36	Alabama	$44,832	1	New York	$67,940
14	Alaska	53,605	2	Massachusetts	67,432
22	Arizona	48,523	3	Connecticut	65,870
46	Arkansas	41,571	4	California	62,964
4	California	62,964	5	New Jersey	62,777
10	Colorado	54,664	6	Washington	59,024
3	Connecticut	65,870	7	Maryland	58,106
13	Delaware	53,765	8	Illinois	56,447
28	Florida	47,035	9	Virginia	54,836
19	Georgia	50,676	10	Colorado	54,664
23	Hawaii	48,178	11	Texas	54,333
49	Idaho	39,637	12	Minnesota	54,297
8	Illinois	56,447	13	Delaware	53,765
37	Indiana	44,590	14	Alaska	53,605
35	Iowa	44,910	15	New Hampshire	53,563
38	Kansas	44,142	16	Pennsylvania	52,460
39	Kentucky	44,099	17	Rhode Island	51,453
31	Louisiana	45,622	18	Michigan	50,943
44	Maine	42,596	19	Georgia	50,676
7	Maryland	58,106	20	Oregon	49,474
2	Massachusetts	67,432	21	North Dakota	48,873
18	Michigan	50,943	22	Arizona	48,523
12	Minnesota	54,297	23	Hawaii	48,178
50	Mississippi	38,144	24	Ohio	47,700
29	Missouri	46,122	25	Tennessee	47,403
48	Montana	40,716	26	North Carolina	47,269
41	Nebraska	43,597	27	Nevada	47,114
27	Nevada	47,114	28	Florida	47,035
15	New Hampshire	53,563	29	Missouri	46,122
5	New Jersey	62,777	30	Wisconsin	46,008
43	New Mexico	42,599	31	Louisiana	45,622
1	New York	67,940	32	Utah	45,255
26	North Carolina	47,269	33	Vermont	45,030
21	North Dakota	48,873	34	Wyoming	44,974
24	Ohio	47,700	35	Iowa	44,910
40	Oklahoma	43,906	36	Alabama	44,832
20	Oregon	49,474	37	Indiana	44,590
16	Pennsylvania	52,460	38	Kansas	44,142
17	Rhode Island	51,453	39	Kentucky	44,099
42	South Carolina	42,881	40	Oklahoma	43,906
47	South Dakota	41,178	41	Nebraska	43,597
25	Tennessee	47,403	42	South Carolina	42,881
11	Texas	54,333	43	New Mexico	42,599
32	Utah	45,255	44	Maine	42,596
33	Vermont	45,030	45	West Virginia	41,665
9	Virginia	54,836	46	Arkansas	41,571
6	Washington	59,024	47	South Dakota	41,178
45	West Virginia	41,665	48	Montana	40,716
30	Wisconsin	46,008	49	Idaho	39,637
34	Wyoming	44,974	50	Mississippi	38,144
				District of Columbia	89,481

Source: U.S. Department of Labor, Bureau of Labor Statistics
"Quarterly Census of Employment and Wages" (http://www.bls.gov/cew/data.htm)
*Computed by dividing total annual wages of employees covered by unemployment insurance programs by the average monthly number of these employees. Includes bonuses, cash value of meals and lodging, tips and, in many states, employer contributions to certain deferred compensation plans such as 401(k) plans.

Percent Change in Average Annual Pay: 2015 to 2016

National Percent Change = 1.3% Increase*

ALPHA ORDER

RANK	STATE	PERCENT CHANGE
28	Alabama	1.3
48	Alaska	(2.1)
30	Arizona	1.2
16	Arkansas	1.7
7	California	2.1
35	Colorado	0.9
40	Connecticut	0.5
45	Delaware	(0.4)
16	Florida	1.7
6	Georgia	2.3
3	Hawaii	2.7
10	Idaho	2.0
36	Illinois	0.8
20	Indiana	1.6
13	Iowa	1.8
38	Kansas	0.6
16	Kentucky	1.7
46	Louisiana	(0.7)
11	Maine	1.9
20	Maryland	1.6
33	Massachusetts	1.1
13	Michigan	1.8
25	Minnesota	1.4
28	Mississippi	1.3
30	Missouri	1.2
20	Montana	1.6
16	Nebraska	1.7
2	Nevada	3.0
11	New Hampshire	1.9
37	New Jersey	0.7
42	New Mexico	0.1
38	New York	0.6
20	North Carolina	1.6
50	North Dakota	(3.6)
30	Ohio	1.2
47	Oklahoma	(0.9)
5	Oregon	2.4
40	Pennsylvania	0.5
20	Rhode Island	1.6
7	South Carolina	2.1
4	South Dakota	2.5
25	Tennessee	1.4
42	Texas	0.1
7	Utah	2.1
13	Vermont	1.8
34	Virginia	1.0
1	Washington	4.2
44	West Virginia	(0.1)
25	Wisconsin	1.4
49	Wyoming	(2.9)

RANK ORDER

RANK	STATE	PERCENT CHANGE
1	Washington	4.2
2	Nevada	3.0
3	Hawaii	2.7
4	South Dakota	2.5
5	Oregon	2.4
6	Georgia	2.3
7	California	2.1
7	South Carolina	2.1
7	Utah	2.1
10	Idaho	2.0
11	Maine	1.9
11	New Hampshire	1.9
13	Iowa	1.8
13	Michigan	1.8
13	Vermont	1.8
16	Arkansas	1.7
16	Florida	1.7
16	Kentucky	1.7
16	Nebraska	1.7
20	Indiana	1.6
20	Maryland	1.6
20	Montana	1.6
20	North Carolina	1.6
20	Rhode Island	1.6
25	Minnesota	1.4
25	Tennessee	1.4
25	Wisconsin	1.4
28	Alabama	1.3
28	Mississippi	1.3
30	Arizona	1.2
30	Missouri	1.2
30	Ohio	1.2
33	Massachusetts	1.1
34	Virginia	1.0
35	Colorado	0.9
36	Illinois	0.8
37	New Jersey	0.7
38	Kansas	0.6
38	New York	0.6
40	Connecticut	0.5
40	Pennsylvania	0.5
42	New Mexico	0.1
42	Texas	0.1
44	West Virginia	(0.1)
45	Delaware	(0.4)
46	Louisiana	(0.7)
47	Oklahoma	(0.9)
48	Alaska	(2.1)
49	Wyoming	(2.9)
50	North Dakota	(3.6)

District of Columbia — 1.5

Source: CQ Press using data from U.S. Department of Labor, Bureau of Labor Statistics
"Quarterly Census of Employment and Wages" (http://www.bls.gov/cew/data.htm)
*Includes bonuses, cash value of meals and lodging, tips and, in many states, employer contributions to certain deferred compensation plans such as 401(k) plans.

Median Earnings of Male Full-Time Workers in 2016

National Median = $50,586

ALPHA ORDER

RANK	STATE	EARNINGS
33	Alabama	$47,034
6	Alaska	56,422
37	Arizona	46,386
50	Arkansas	41,156
15	California	51,417
16	Colorado	51,264
1	Connecticut	64,220
19	Delaware	50,924
49	Florida	41,586
34	Georgia	46,712
26	Hawaii	49,373
43	Idaho	45,305
12	Illinois	53,111
27	Indiana	49,157
25	Iowa	49,385
28	Kansas	47,891
40	Kentucky	45,521
24	Louisiana	50,031
29	Maine	47,890
4	Maryland	61,321
2	Massachusetts	62,868
20	Michigan	50,869
10	Minnesota	53,200
48	Mississippi	42,146
36	Missouri	46,543
35	Montana	46,545
31	Nebraska	47,352
42	Nevada	45,326
8	New Hampshire	53,581
3	New Jersey	62,311
47	New Mexico	42,297
11	New York	53,124
44	North Carolina	45,180
13	North Dakota	51,789
23	Ohio	50,227
39	Oklahoma	46,027
21	Oregon	50,676
14	Pennsylvania	51,780
9	Rhode Island	53,400
45	South Carolina	45,038
41	South Dakota	45,384
46	Tennessee	43,661
32	Texas	47,351
18	Utah	51,099
30	Vermont	47,840
7	Virginia	55,817
5	Washington	58,864
38	West Virginia	46,029
22	Wisconsin	50,399
17	Wyoming	51,234

RANK ORDER

RANK	STATE	EARNINGS
1	Connecticut	$64,220
2	Massachusetts	62,868
3	New Jersey	62,311
4	Maryland	61,321
5	Washington	58,864
6	Alaska	56,422
7	Virginia	55,817
8	New Hampshire	53,581
9	Rhode Island	53,400
10	Minnesota	53,200
11	New York	53,124
12	Illinois	53,111
13	North Dakota	51,789
14	Pennsylvania	51,780
15	California	51,417
16	Colorado	51,264
17	Wyoming	51,234
18	Utah	51,099
19	Delaware	50,924
20	Michigan	50,869
21	Oregon	50,676
22	Wisconsin	50,399
23	Ohio	50,227
24	Louisiana	50,031
25	Iowa	49,385
26	Hawaii	49,373
27	Indiana	49,157
28	Kansas	47,891
29	Maine	47,890
30	Vermont	47,840
31	Nebraska	47,352
32	Texas	47,351
33	Alabama	47,034
34	Georgia	46,712
35	Montana	46,545
36	Missouri	46,543
37	Arizona	46,386
38	West Virginia	46,029
39	Oklahoma	46,027
40	Kentucky	45,521
41	South Dakota	45,384
42	Nevada	45,326
43	Idaho	45,305
44	North Carolina	45,180
45	South Carolina	45,038
46	Tennessee	43,661
47	New Mexico	42,297
48	Mississippi	42,146
49	Florida	41,586
50	Arkansas	41,156
	District of Columbia	75,343

Source: U.S. Bureau of the Census
"2016 American Community Survey-Table S2001" (http://www.census.gov/programs-surveys/acs/)

Median Earnings of Female Full-Time Workers in 2016

National Median = $40,626

ALPHA ORDER

ALPHA ORDER

RANK	STATE	EARNINGS
42	Alabama	$35,012
5	Alaska	47,518
27	Arizona	37,966
49	Arkansas	32,242
7	California	45,489
13	Colorado	43,206
3	Connecticut	50,991
15	Delaware	41,771
37	Florida	36,112
26	Georgia	38,278
16	Hawaii	41,224
45	Idaho	34,403
14	Illinois	42,108
35	Indiana	36,440
28	Iowa	37,791
30	Kansas	37,091
36	Kentucky	36,259
43	Louisiana	34,793
19	Maine	40,240
2	Maryland	51,247
1	Massachusetts	51,666
21	Michigan	39,825
11	Minnesota	44,132
50	Mississippi	31,757
34	Missouri	36,514
46	Montana	34,028
32	Nebraska	36,699
33	Nevada	36,681
10	New Hampshire	44,550
4	New Jersey	50,574
44	New Mexico	34,668
6	New York	47,358
31	North Carolina	36,987
25	North Dakota	38,407
24	Ohio	38,750
47	Oklahoma	33,972
20	Oregon	40,193
18	Pennsylvania	41,047
12	Rhode Island	43,541
41	South Carolina	35,043
40	South Dakota	35,436
39	Tennessee	35,916
29	Texas	37,576
38	Utah	36,022
17	Vermont	41,122
9	Virginia	44,798
8	Washington	45,056
48	West Virginia	33,228
22	Wisconsin	39,440
23	Wyoming	39,338

RANK ORDER

RANK	STATE	EARNINGS
1	Massachusetts	$51,666
2	Maryland	51,247
3	Connecticut	50,991
4	New Jersey	50,574
5	Alaska	47,518
6	New York	47,358
7	California	45,489
8	Washington	45,056
9	Virginia	44,798
10	New Hampshire	44,550
11	Minnesota	44,132
12	Rhode Island	43,541
13	Colorado	43,206
14	Illinois	42,108
15	Delaware	41,771
16	Hawaii	41,224
17	Vermont	41,122
18	Pennsylvania	41,047
19	Maine	40,240
20	Oregon	40,193
21	Michigan	39,825
22	Wisconsin	39,440
23	Wyoming	39,338
24	Ohio	38,750
25	North Dakota	38,407
26	Georgia	38,278
27	Arizona	37,966
28	Iowa	37,791
29	Texas	37,576
30	Kansas	37,091
31	North Carolina	36,987
32	Nebraska	36,699
33	Nevada	36,681
34	Missouri	36,514
35	Indiana	36,440
36	Kentucky	36,259
37	Florida	36,112
38	Utah	36,022
39	Tennessee	35,916
40	South Dakota	35,436
41	South Carolina	35,043
42	Alabama	35,012
43	Louisiana	34,793
44	New Mexico	34,668
45	Idaho	34,403
46	Montana	34,028
47	Oklahoma	33,972
48	West Virginia	33,228
49	Arkansas	32,242
50	Mississippi	31,757
	District of Columbia	64,908

Source: U.S. Bureau of the Census
"2016 American Community Survey-Table S2001" (http://www.census.gov/programs-surveys/acs/)

State Minimum Wage Rates in 2018

National Rate = $7.25 per Hour*

ALPHA ORDER

RANK	STATE	MINIMUM WAGE
NA	Alabama**	NA
13	Alaska	9.84
4	Arizona	10.50
21	Arkansas	8.50
2	California	11.00
8	Colorado	10.20
9	Connecticut	10.10
24	Delaware	8.25
24	Florida	8.25
44	Georgia	5.15
9	Hawaii	10.10
30	Idaho	7.25
24	Illinois	8.25
30	Indiana	7.25
30	Iowa	7.25
30	Kansas	7.25
30	Kentucky	7.25
NA	Louisiana**	NA
12	Maine	10.00
15	Maryland	9.25
2	Massachusetts	11.00
15	Michigan	9.25
14	Minnesota	9.65
NA	Mississippi**	NA
28	Missouri	7.85
22	Montana	8.30
17	Nebraska	9.00
24	Nevada	8.25
30	New Hampshire	7.25
20	New Jersey	8.60
29	New Mexico	7.50
6	New York	10.40
30	North Carolina	7.25
30	North Dakota	7.25
22	Ohio	8.30
30	Oklahoma	7.25
7	Oregon	10.25
30	Pennsylvania	7.25
9	Rhode Island	10.10
NA	South Carolina**	NA
18	South Dakota	8.85
NA	Tennessee**	NA
30	Texas	7.25
30	Utah	7.25
4	Vermont	10.50
30	Virginia	7.25
1	Washington	11.50
19	West Virginia	8.75
30	Wisconsin	7.25
44	Wyoming	5.15

RANK ORDER

RANK	STATE	MINIMUM WAGE
1	Washington	$11.50
2	California	11.00
2	Massachusetts	11.00
4	Arizona	10.50
4	Vermont	10.50
6	New York	10.40
7	Oregon	10.25
8	Colorado	10.20
9	Connecticut	10.10
9	Hawaii	10.10
9	Rhode Island	10.10
12	Maine	10.00
13	Alaska	9.84
14	Minnesota	9.65
15	Maryland	9.25
15	Michigan	9.25
17	Nebraska	9.00
18	South Dakota	8.85
19	West Virginia	8.75
20	New Jersey	8.60
21	Arkansas	8.50
22	Montana	8.30
22	Ohio	8.30
24	Delaware	8.25
24	Florida	8.25
24	Illinois	8.25
24	Nevada	8.25
28	Missouri	7.85
29	New Mexico	7.50
30	Idaho	7.25
30	Indiana	7.25
30	Iowa	7.25
30	Kansas	7.25
30	Kentucky	7.25
30	New Hampshire	7.25
30	North Carolina	7.25
30	North Dakota	7.25
30	Oklahoma	7.25
30	Pennsylvania	7.25
30	Texas	7.25
30	Utah	7.25
30	Virginia	7.25
30	Wisconsin	7.25
44	Georgia	5.15
44	Wyoming	5.15
NA	Alabama**	NA
NA	Louisiana**	NA
NA	Mississippi**	NA
NA	South Carolina**	NA
NA	Tennessee**	NA

District of Columbia — 12.50

Source: U.S. Department of Labor, Employment Standards Administration
"Minimum Wage Laws in the States" (http://www.dol.gov/whd/minwage/america.htm)
*As of January 1, 2018. State minimum wage rates are for those employers and jobs not covered by the federal program.
**No separate state program.

Average Hourly Earnings of Production Workers
on Manufacturing Payrolls in 2017
National Average = $26.74*

ALPHA ORDER

RANK	STATE	HOURLY EARNINGS
32	Alabama	$19.99
1	Alaska	31.79
48	Arizona	17.66
50	Arkansas	16.18
6	California	23.42
3	Colorado	27.27
4	Connecticut	24.50
40	Delaware	19.24
19	Florida	21.27
44	Georgia	18.64
30	Hawaii	20.15
46	Idaho	18.37
24	Illinois	20.76
25	Indiana	20.73
37	Iowa	19.73
35	Kansas	19.80
29	Kentucky	20.24
11	Louisiana	22.27
10	Maine	22.33
15	Maryland	21.68
5	Massachusetts	24.24
20	Michigan	21.02
16	Minnesota	21.59
28	Mississippi	20.27
9	Missouri	22.47
33	Montana	19.94
34	Nebraska	19.81
43	Nevada	18.74
13	New Hampshire	21.75
12	New Jersey	21.88
49	New Mexico	17.60
18	New York	21.41
47	North Carolina	18.06
31	North Dakota	20.08
14	Ohio	21.69
38	Oklahoma	19.42
22	Oregon	21.00
26	Pennsylvania	20.68
41	Rhode Island	19.14
42	South Carolina	18.88
45	South Dakota	18.60
36	Tennessee	19.78
7	Texas	23.32
20	Utah	21.02
23	Vermont	20.92
39	Virginia	19.31
2	Washington	28.59
17	West Virginia	21.46
27	Wisconsin	20.43
8	Wyoming	22.92

RANK ORDER

RANK	STATE	HOURLY EARNINGS
1	Alaska	$31.79
2	Washington	28.59
3	Colorado	27.27
4	Connecticut	24.50
5	Massachusetts	24.24
6	California	23.42
7	Texas	23.32
8	Wyoming	22.92
9	Missouri	22.47
10	Maine	22.33
11	Louisiana	22.27
12	New Jersey	21.88
13	New Hampshire	21.75
14	Ohio	21.69
15	Maryland	21.68
16	Minnesota	21.59
17	West Virginia	21.46
18	New York	21.41
19	Florida	21.27
20	Michigan	21.02
20	Utah	21.02
22	Oregon	21.00
23	Vermont	20.92
24	Illinois	20.76
25	Indiana	20.73
26	Pennsylvania	20.68
27	Wisconsin	20.43
28	Mississippi	20.27
29	Kentucky	20.24
30	Hawaii	20.15
31	North Dakota	20.08
32	Alabama	19.99
33	Montana	19.94
34	Nebraska	19.81
35	Kansas	19.80
36	Tennessee	19.78
37	Iowa	19.73
38	Oklahoma	19.42
39	Virginia	19.31
40	Delaware	19.24
41	Rhode Island	19.14
42	South Carolina	18.88
43	Nevada	18.74
44	Georgia	18.64
45	South Dakota	18.60
46	Idaho	18.37
47	North Carolina	18.06
48	Arizona	17.66
49	New Mexico	17.60
50	Arkansas	16.18
	District of Columbia**	NA

Source: U.S. Department of Labor, Bureau of Labor Statistics
   "State and Metro Area Employment, Hours and Earnings" (http://www.bls.gov/sae/home.htm)
*Preliminary data for December 2017. Not seasonally adjusted except for national figure.
**Not available.

Average Weekly Earnings of Production Workers on Manufacturing Payrolls in 2017
National Average = $1,090.99*

<table>
<tr><td colspan="3"><u>ALPHA ORDER</u></td><td colspan="3"><u>RANK ORDER</u></td></tr>
<tr><td>RANK</td><td>STATE</td><td>WEEKLY EARNINGS</td><td>RANK</td><td>STATE</td><td>WEEKLY EARNINGS</td></tr>
<tr><td>18</td><td>Alabama</td><td>$891.55</td><td>1</td><td>Washington</td><td>$1,212.22</td></tr>
<tr><td>32</td><td>Alaska</td><td>839.26</td><td>2</td><td>Colorado</td><td>1,101.71</td></tr>
<tr><td>48</td><td>Arizona</td><td>729.36</td><td>3</td><td>Massachusetts</td><td>1,022.93</td></tr>
<tr><td>50</td><td>Arkansas</td><td>658.53</td><td>4</td><td>Connecticut</td><td>1,006.95</td></tr>
<tr><td>8</td><td>California</td><td>962.56</td><td>5</td><td>Texas</td><td>1,002.76</td></tr>
<tr><td>2</td><td>Colorado</td><td>1,101.71</td><td>6</td><td>Maryland</td><td>988.61</td></tr>
<tr><td>4</td><td>Connecticut</td><td>1,006.95</td><td>7</td><td>Wyoming</td><td>969.52</td></tr>
<tr><td>39</td><td>Delaware</td><td>790.76</td><td>8</td><td>California</td><td>962.56</td></tr>
<tr><td>9</td><td>Florida</td><td>957.15</td><td>9</td><td>Florida</td><td>957.15</td></tr>
<tr><td>37</td><td>Georgia</td><td>820.16</td><td>10</td><td>Missouri</td><td>954.98</td></tr>
<tr><td>44</td><td>Hawaii</td><td>765.70</td><td>11</td><td>Louisiana</td><td>944.25</td></tr>
<tr><td>42</td><td>Idaho</td><td>769.70</td><td>12</td><td>New Hampshire</td><td>941.78</td></tr>
<tr><td>16</td><td>Illinois</td><td>900.98</td><td>13</td><td>Michigan</td><td>939.59</td></tr>
<tr><td>21</td><td>Indiana</td><td>885.17</td><td>14</td><td>Ohio</td><td>930.50</td></tr>
<tr><td>34</td><td>Iowa</td><td>834.58</td><td>15</td><td>Maine</td><td>920.00</td></tr>
<tr><td>23</td><td>Kansas</td><td>879.12</td><td>16</td><td>Illinois</td><td>900.98</td></tr>
<tr><td>28</td><td>Kentucky</td><td>846.03</td><td>17</td><td>Minnesota</td><td>895.99</td></tr>
<tr><td>11</td><td>Louisiana</td><td>944.25</td><td>18</td><td>Alabama</td><td>891.55</td></tr>
<tr><td>15</td><td>Maine</td><td>920.00</td><td>19</td><td>New Jersey</td><td>888.33</td></tr>
<tr><td>6</td><td>Maryland</td><td>988.61</td><td>20</td><td>West Virginia</td><td>886.30</td></tr>
<tr><td>3</td><td>Massachusetts</td><td>1,022.93</td><td>21</td><td>Indiana</td><td>885.17</td></tr>
<tr><td>13</td><td>Michigan</td><td>939.59</td><td>22</td><td>New York</td><td>879.95</td></tr>
<tr><td>17</td><td>Minnesota</td><td>895.99</td><td>23</td><td>Kansas</td><td>879.12</td></tr>
<tr><td>27</td><td>Mississippi</td><td>853.37</td><td>24</td><td>Tennessee</td><td>864.39</td></tr>
<tr><td>10</td><td>Missouri</td><td>954.98</td><td>25</td><td>Pennsylvania</td><td>856.15</td></tr>
<tr><td>45</td><td>Montana</td><td>759.71</td><td>26</td><td>Wisconsin</td><td>856.02</td></tr>
<tr><td>36</td><td>Nebraska</td><td>822.12</td><td>27</td><td>Mississippi</td><td>853.37</td></tr>
<tr><td>41</td><td>Nevada</td><td>777.71</td><td>28</td><td>Kentucky</td><td>846.03</td></tr>
<tr><td>12</td><td>New Hampshire</td><td>941.78</td><td>29</td><td>South Carolina</td><td>845.82</td></tr>
<tr><td>19</td><td>New Jersey</td><td>888.33</td><td>30</td><td>Vermont</td><td>843.08</td></tr>
<tr><td>49</td><td>New Mexico</td><td>718.08</td><td>31</td><td>Oregon</td><td>840.00</td></tr>
<tr><td>22</td><td>New York</td><td>879.95</td><td>32</td><td>Alaska</td><td>839.26</td></tr>
<tr><td>46</td><td>North Carolina</td><td>758.52</td><td>33</td><td>Utah</td><td>838.70</td></tr>
<tr><td>47</td><td>North Dakota</td><td>757.02</td><td>34</td><td>Iowa</td><td>834.58</td></tr>
<tr><td>14</td><td>Ohio</td><td>930.50</td><td>35</td><td>Oklahoma</td><td>829.23</td></tr>
<tr><td>35</td><td>Oklahoma</td><td>829.23</td><td>36</td><td>Nebraska</td><td>822.12</td></tr>
<tr><td>31</td><td>Oregon</td><td>840.00</td><td>37</td><td>Georgia</td><td>820.16</td></tr>
<tr><td>25</td><td>Pennsylvania</td><td>856.15</td><td>38</td><td>Rhode Island</td><td>817.28</td></tr>
<tr><td>38</td><td>Rhode Island</td><td>817.28</td><td>39</td><td>Delaware</td><td>790.76</td></tr>
<tr><td>29</td><td>South Carolina</td><td>845.82</td><td>40</td><td>Virginia</td><td>783.99</td></tr>
<tr><td>43</td><td>South Dakota</td><td>766.32</td><td>41</td><td>Nevada</td><td>777.71</td></tr>
<tr><td>24</td><td>Tennessee</td><td>864.39</td><td>42</td><td>Idaho</td><td>769.70</td></tr>
<tr><td>5</td><td>Texas</td><td>1,002.76</td><td>43</td><td>South Dakota</td><td>766.32</td></tr>
<tr><td>33</td><td>Utah</td><td>838.70</td><td>44</td><td>Hawaii</td><td>765.70</td></tr>
<tr><td>30</td><td>Vermont</td><td>843.08</td><td>45</td><td>Montana</td><td>759.71</td></tr>
<tr><td>40</td><td>Virginia</td><td>783.99</td><td>46</td><td>North Carolina</td><td>758.52</td></tr>
<tr><td>1</td><td>Washington</td><td>1,212.22</td><td>47</td><td>North Dakota</td><td>757.02</td></tr>
<tr><td>20</td><td>West Virginia</td><td>886.30</td><td>48</td><td>Arizona</td><td>729.36</td></tr>
<tr><td>26</td><td>Wisconsin</td><td>856.02</td><td>49</td><td>New Mexico</td><td>718.08</td></tr>
<tr><td>7</td><td>Wyoming</td><td>969.52</td><td>50</td><td>Arkansas</td><td>658.53</td></tr>
<tr><td></td><td></td><td></td><td></td><td>District of Columbia**</td><td>NA</td></tr>
</table>

Source: U.S. Department of Labor, Bureau of Labor Statistics
"State and Metro Area Employment, Hours and Earnings" (http://www.bls.gov/sae/home.htm)
*Preliminary data for December 2017. Not seasonally adjusted except for national figure.
**Not available.

Average Work Week of Production Workers
on Manufacturing Payrolls in 2017
National Average = 40.8 Hours per Week*

ALPHA ORDER

RANK	STATE	WEEKLY HOURS
5	Alabama	44.6
50	Alaska	26.4
31	Arizona	41.3
40	Arkansas	40.7
35	California	41.1
43	Colorado	40.4
35	Connecticut	41.1
35	Delaware	41.1
2	Florida	45.0
7	Georgia	44.0
48	Hawaii	38.0
24	Idaho	41.9
9	Illinois	43.4
13	Indiana	42.7
19	Iowa	42.3
6	Kansas	44.4
26	Kentucky	41.8
17	Louisiana	42.4
33	Maine	41.2
1	Maryland	45.6
21	Massachusetts	42.2
4	Michigan	44.7
27	Minnesota	41.5
22	Mississippi	42.1
16	Missouri	42.5
47	Montana	38.1
27	Nebraska	41.5
27	Nevada	41.5
10	New Hampshire	43.3
41	New Jersey	40.6
39	New Mexico	40.8
35	New York	41.1
23	North Carolina	42.0
49	North Dakota	37.7
12	Ohio	42.9
13	Oklahoma	42.7
45	Oregon	40.0
30	Pennsylvania	41.4
13	Rhode Island	42.7
3	South Carolina	44.8
33	South Dakota	41.2
8	Tennessee	43.7
11	Texas	43.0
46	Utah	39.9
44	Vermont	40.3
41	Virginia	40.6
17	Washington	42.4
31	West Virginia	41.3
24	Wisconsin	41.9
19	Wyoming	42.3

RANK ORDER

RANK	STATE	WEEKLY HOURS
1	Maryland	45.6
2	Florida	45.0
3	South Carolina	44.8
4	Michigan	44.7
5	Alabama	44.6
6	Kansas	44.4
7	Georgia	44.0
8	Tennessee	43.7
9	Illinois	43.4
10	New Hampshire	43.3
11	Texas	43.0
12	Ohio	42.9
13	Indiana	42.7
13	Oklahoma	42.7
13	Rhode Island	42.7
16	Missouri	42.5
17	Louisiana	42.4
17	Washington	42.4
19	Iowa	42.3
19	Wyoming	42.3
21	Massachusetts	42.2
22	Mississippi	42.1
23	North Carolina	42.0
24	Idaho	41.9
24	Wisconsin	41.9
26	Kentucky	41.8
27	Minnesota	41.5
27	Nebraska	41.5
27	Nevada	41.5
30	Pennsylvania	41.4
31	Arizona	41.3
31	West Virginia	41.3
33	Maine	41.2
33	South Dakota	41.2
35	California	41.1
35	Connecticut	41.1
35	Delaware	41.1
35	New York	41.1
39	New Mexico	40.8
40	Arkansas	40.7
41	New Jersey	40.6
41	Virginia	40.6
43	Colorado	40.4
44	Vermont	40.3
45	Oregon	40.0
46	Utah	39.9
47	Montana	38.1
48	Hawaii	38.0
49	North Dakota	37.7
50	Alaska	26.4

| District of Columbia** | | NA |

Source: U.S. Department of Labor, Bureau of Labor Statistics
   "State and Metro Area Employment, Hours and Earnings" (http://www.bls.gov/sae/home.htm)
*Preliminary data for December 2017. Not seasonally adjusted except for national figure.
**Not available.

Average Weekly Unemployment Benefit in 2017

National Average = $350.79 a Week

RANK	STATE	BENEFIT
48	Alabama	$221.16
39	Alaska	273.17
47	Arizona	227.95
40	Arkansas	267.72
29	California	324.65
7	Colorado	421.85
10	Connecticut	391.09
41	Delaware	261.06
45	Florida	244.00
36	Georgia	287.95
3	Hawaii	495.49
32	Idaho	316.13
16	Illinois	374.37
38	Indiana	281.94
11	Iowa	390.57
14	Kansas	380.03
28	Kentucky	326.93
49	Louisiana	213.28
30	Maine	323.91
21	Maryland	341.93
1	Massachusetts	508.13
35	Michigan	306.44
5	Minnesota	446.59
50	Mississippi	206.30
42	Missouri	260.74
24	Montana	338.41
27	Nebraska	327.10
22	Nevada	339.10
26	New Hampshire	328.40
6	New Jersey	440.40
25	New Mexico	330.36
23	New York	338.80
44	North Carolina	257.34
4	North Dakota	476.96
18	Ohio	362.18
17	Oklahoma	362.78
12	Oregon	384.46
13	Pennsylvania	381.07
19	Rhode Island	354.68
43	South Carolina	257.36
31	South Dakota	321.09
46	Tennessee	236.69
8	Texas	399.36
9	Utah	392.44
20	Vermont	351.71
34	Virginia	308.72
2	Washington	496.24
37	West Virginia	283.88
33	Wisconsin	314.97
15	Wyoming	379.69

RANK	STATE	BENEFIT
1	Massachusetts	$508.13
2	Washington	496.24
3	Hawaii	495.49
4	North Dakota	476.96
5	Minnesota	446.59
6	New Jersey	440.40
7	Colorado	421.85
8	Texas	399.36
9	Utah	392.44
10	Connecticut	391.09
11	Iowa	390.57
12	Oregon	384.46
13	Pennsylvania	381.07
14	Kansas	380.03
15	Wyoming	379.69
16	Illinois	374.37
17	Oklahoma	362.78
18	Ohio	362.18
19	Rhode Island	354.68
20	Vermont	351.71
21	Maryland	341.93
22	Nevada	339.10
23	New York	338.80
24	Montana	338.41
25	New Mexico	330.36
26	New Hampshire	328.40
27	Nebraska	327.10
28	Kentucky	326.93
29	California	324.65
30	Maine	323.91
31	South Dakota	321.09
32	Idaho	316.13
33	Wisconsin	314.97
34	Virginia	308.72
35	Michigan	306.44
36	Georgia	287.95
37	West Virginia	283.88
38	Indiana	281.94
39	Alaska	273.17
40	Arkansas	267.72
41	Delaware	261.06
42	Missouri	260.74
43	South Carolina	257.36
44	North Carolina	257.34
45	Florida	244.00
46	Tennessee	236.69
47	Arizona	227.95
48	Alabama	221.16
49	Louisiana	213.28
50	Mississippi	206.30
	District of Columbia	343.52

Source: CQ Press using data from U.S. Department of Labor, Bureau of Labor Statistics
"Unemployment Insurance Data Summary" (https://workforcesecurity.doleta.gov/unemploy/DataDashboard.asp)

Workers' Compensation Benefit Payments in 2015

National Total = $61,856,542,000*

ALPHA ORDER

RANK	STATE	PAYMENTS	% of USA
28	Alabama	$617,622,000	1.0%
43	Alaska	228,034,000	0.4%
23	Arizona	740,783,000	1.2%
45	Arkansas	217,190,000	0.4%
1	California	12,065,579,000	19.5%
21	Colorado	835,265,000	1.4%
18	Connecticut	908,069,000	1.5%
42	Delaware	228,240,000	0.4%
3	Florida	3,051,390,000	4.9%
10	Georgia	1,362,480,000	2.2%
37	Hawaii	298,237,000	0.5%
39	Idaho	262,674,000	0.4%
5	Illinois	2,420,417,000	3.9%
30	Indiana	567,536,000	0.9%
29	Iowa	617,375,000	1.0%
32	Kansas	361,558,000	0.6%
26	Kentucky	684,422,000	1.1%
22	Louisiana	755,714,000	1.2%
41	Maine	232,464,000	0.4%
16	Maryland	966,069,000	1.6%
13	Massachusetts	1,129,393,000	1.8%
14	Michigan	1,077,947,000	1.7%
15	Minnesota	1,035,657,000	1.7%
34	Mississippi	331,683,000	0.5%
20	Missouri	888,004,000	1.4%
40	Montana	253,017,000	0.4%
35	Nebraska	307,034,000	0.5%
33	Nevada	344,604,000	0.6%
44	New Hampshire	222,064,000	0.4%
7	New Jersey	2,285,378,000	3.7%
36	New Mexico	304,077,000	0.5%
2	New York	5,803,753,000	9.4%
11	North Carolina	1,246,968,000	2.0%
46	North Dakota	180,401,000	0.3%
8	Ohio	1,929,262,000	3.1%
24	Oklahoma	732,542,000	1.2%
27	Oregon	631,907,000	1.0%
4	Pennsylvania	2,971,644,000	4.8%
48	Rhode Island	161,460,000	0.3%
19	South Carolina	889,428,000	1.4%
50	South Dakota	106,594,000	0.2%
25	Tennessee	687,595,000	1.1%
9	Texas	1,553,497,000	2.5%
38	Utah	280,124,000	0.5%
49	Vermont	151,544,000	0.2%
17	Virginia	936,322,000	1.5%
6	Washington	2,404,364,000	3.9%
31	West Virginia	414,958,000	0.7%
12	Wisconsin	1,169,754,000	1.9%
47	Wyoming	178,444,000	0.3%

RANK ORDER

RANK	STATE	PAYMENTS	% of USA
1	California	$12,065,579,000	19.5%
2	New York	5,803,753,000	9.4%
3	Florida	3,051,390,000	4.9%
4	Pennsylvania	2,971,644,000	4.8%
5	Illinois	2,420,417,000	3.9%
6	Washington	2,404,364,000	3.9%
7	New Jersey	2,285,378,000	3.7%
8	Ohio	1,929,262,000	3.1%
9	Texas	1,553,497,000	2.5%
10	Georgia	1,362,480,000	2.2%
11	North Carolina	1,246,968,000	2.0%
12	Wisconsin	1,169,754,000	1.9%
13	Massachusetts	1,129,393,000	1.8%
14	Michigan	1,077,947,000	1.7%
15	Minnesota	1,035,657,000	1.7%
16	Maryland	966,069,000	1.6%
17	Virginia	936,322,000	1.5%
18	Connecticut	908,069,000	1.5%
19	South Carolina	889,428,000	1.4%
20	Missouri	888,004,000	1.4%
21	Colorado	835,265,000	1.4%
22	Louisiana	755,714,000	1.2%
23	Arizona	740,783,000	1.2%
24	Oklahoma	732,542,000	1.2%
25	Tennessee	687,595,000	1.1%
26	Kentucky	684,422,000	1.1%
27	Oregon	631,907,000	1.0%
28	Alabama	617,622,000	1.0%
29	Iowa	617,375,000	1.0%
30	Indiana	567,536,000	0.9%
31	West Virginia	414,958,000	0.7%
32	Kansas	361,558,000	0.6%
33	Nevada	344,604,000	0.6%
34	Mississippi	331,683,000	0.5%
35	Nebraska	307,034,000	0.5%
36	New Mexico	304,077,000	0.5%
37	Hawaii	298,237,000	0.5%
38	Utah	280,124,000	0.5%
39	Idaho	262,674,000	0.4%
40	Montana	253,017,000	0.4%
41	Maine	232,464,000	0.4%
42	Delaware	228,240,000	0.4%
43	Alaska	228,034,000	0.4%
44	New Hampshire	222,064,000	0.4%
45	Arkansas	217,190,000	0.4%
46	North Dakota	180,401,000	0.3%
47	Wyoming	178,444,000	0.3%
48	Rhode Island	161,460,000	0.3%
49	Vermont	151,544,000	0.2%
50	South Dakota	106,594,000	0.2%
	District of Columbia	120,154,000	0.2%

Source: National Academy of Social Insurance (Washington, DC)
"Workers' Compensation: Benefits, Coverage, and Costs, 2015" (http://www.nasi.org)
*Estimated payments from private insurance, state and federal funds, and self insurance. National total includes payments for federal civilian employee program, Black Lung Program, and other federal programs.

Workers' Compensation Benefit Payment per Covered Worker in 2015

National Average = $456*

ALPHA ORDER

RANK	STATE	AVERAGE
30	Alabama	$354
3	Alaska	719
40	Arizona	290
49	Arkansas	193
2	California	752
35	Colorado	344
9	Connecticut	552
10	Delaware	535
20	Florida	406
34	Georgia	345
14	Hawaii	493
22	Idaho	403
18	Illinois	421
48	Indiana	196
19	Iowa	412
42	Kansas	271
26	Kentucky	382
24	Louisiana	399
23	Maine	402
25	Maryland	395
36	Massachusetts	334
43	Michigan	269
27	Minnesota	380
38	Mississippi	322
31	Missouri	353
8	Montana	586
37	Nebraska	330
41	Nevada	282
31	New Hampshire	353
7	New Jersey	595
21	New Mexico	404
4	New York	654
39	North Carolina	313
17	North Dakota	425
28	Ohio	372
13	Oklahoma	502
29	Oregon	359
11	Pennsylvania	533
33	Rhode Island	352
15	South Carolina	482
45	South Dakota	266
46	Tennessee	259
50	Texas	168
47	Utah	215
12	Vermont	509
43	Virginia	269
1	Washington	789
6	West Virginia	631
16	Wisconsin	435
5	Wyoming	649

RANK ORDER

RANK	STATE	AVERAGE
1	Washington	$789
2	California	752
3	Alaska	719
4	New York	654
5	Wyoming	649
6	West Virginia	631
7	New Jersey	595
8	Montana	586
9	Connecticut	552
10	Delaware	535
11	Pennsylvania	533
12	Vermont	509
13	Oklahoma	502
14	Hawaii	493
15	South Carolina	482
16	Wisconsin	435
17	North Dakota	425
18	Illinois	421
19	Iowa	412
20	Florida	406
21	New Mexico	404
22	Idaho	403
23	Maine	402
24	Louisiana	399
25	Maryland	395
26	Kentucky	382
27	Minnesota	380
28	Ohio	372
29	Oregon	359
30	Alabama	354
31	Missouri	353
31	New Hampshire	353
33	Rhode Island	352
34	Georgia	345
35	Colorado	344
36	Massachusetts	334
37	Nebraska	330
38	Mississippi	322
39	North Carolina	313
40	Arizona	290
41	Nevada	282
42	Kansas	271
43	Michigan	269
43	Virginia	269
45	South Dakota	266
46	Tennessee	259
47	Utah	215
48	Indiana	196
49	Arkansas	193
50	Texas	168
	District of Columbia	220

Source: CQ Press using data from National Academy of Social Insurance (Washington, DC)
"Workers' Compensation: Benefits, Coverage, and Costs, 2015" (http://www.nasi.org)
*Estimated payments from private insurance, state and federal funds, and self insurance. National rate includes payments for federal civilian employee program, Black Lung Program, and other federal programs. Total divided by number of workers covered by workers' compensation.

Percent Change in Workers' Compensation Benefit Payments: 2014 to 2015

National Percent Change = 1.3% Decrease*

ALPHA ORDER

RANK	STATE	PERCENT CHANGE
32	Alabama	(3.0)
28	Alaska	(2.5)
13	Arizona	0.8
44	Arkansas	(4.8)
18	California	(0.3)
4	Colorado	5.9
17	Connecticut	(0.1)
49	Delaware	(8.5)
45	Florida	(4.9)
25	Georgia	(1.7)
1	Hawaii	10.2
8	Idaho	3.4
50	Illinois	(11.7)
38	Indiana	(3.8)
41	Iowa	(4.1)
39	Kansas	(3.9)
5	Kentucky	5.4
42	Louisiana	(4.3)
48	Maine	(7.8)
22	Maryland	(1.4)
26	Massachusetts	(1.9)
30	Michigan	(2.8)
40	Minnesota	(4.0)
23	Mississippi	(1.5)
7	Missouri	4.6
10	Montana	2.9
43	Nebraska	(4.5)
32	Nevada	(3.0)
6	New Hampshire	4.7
29	New Jersey	(2.7)
12	New Mexico	1.6
11	New York	1.9
34	North Carolina	(3.1)
47	North Dakota	(6.2)
46	Ohio	(5.4)
36	Oklahoma	(3.5)
37	Oregon	(3.7)
20	Pennsylvania	(0.9)
27	Rhode Island	(2.1)
19	South Carolina	(0.7)
2	South Dakota	9.2
24	Tennessee	(1.6)
9	Texas	3.3
3	Utah	7.7
15	Vermont	0.5
13	Virginia	0.8
15	Washington	0.5
21	West Virginia	(1.1)
30	Wisconsin	(2.8)
35	Wyoming	(3.2)

RANK ORDER

RANK	STATE	PERCENT CHANGE
1	Hawaii	10.2
2	South Dakota	9.2
3	Utah	7.7
4	Colorado	5.9
5	Kentucky	5.4
6	New Hampshire	4.7
7	Missouri	4.6
8	Idaho	3.4
9	Texas	3.3
10	Montana	2.9
11	New York	1.9
12	New Mexico	1.6
13	Arizona	0.8
13	Virginia	0.8
15	Vermont	0.5
15	Washington	0.5
17	Connecticut	(0.1)
18	California	(0.3)
19	South Carolina	(0.7)
20	Pennsylvania	(0.9)
21	West Virginia	(1.1)
22	Maryland	(1.4)
23	Mississippi	(1.5)
24	Tennessee	(1.6)
25	Georgia	(1.7)
26	Massachusetts	(1.9)
27	Rhode Island	(2.1)
28	Alaska	(2.5)
29	New Jersey	(2.7)
30	Michigan	(2.8)
30	Wisconsin	(2.8)
32	Alabama	(3.0)
32	Nevada	(3.0)
34	North Carolina	(3.1)
35	Wyoming	(3.2)
36	Oklahoma	(3.5)
37	Oregon	(3.7)
38	Indiana	(3.8)
39	Kansas	(3.9)
40	Minnesota	(4.0)
41	Iowa	(4.1)
42	Louisiana	(4.3)
43	Nebraska	(4.5)
44	Arkansas	(4.8)
45	Florida	(4.9)
46	Ohio	(5.4)
47	North Dakota	(6.2)
48	Maine	(7.8)
49	Delaware	(8.5)
50	Illinois	(11.7)

District of Columbia	1.6

Source: CQ Press using data from National Academy of Social Insurance (Washington, DC)
   "Workers' Compensation: Benefits, Coverage, and Costs, 2015" (http://www.nasi.org)
*Estimated payments from private insurance, state and federal funds, and self insurance. National rate includes payments for federal civilian employee program, Black Lung Program, and other federal programs.

Civilian Labor Force in 2017

National Total = 160,597,000 Workers*

ALPHA ORDER

RANK	STATE	LABOR FORCE	% of USA
24	Alabama	2,168,761	1.4%
48	Alaska	363,230	0.2%
15	Arizona	3,340,127	2.1%
34	Arkansas	1,362,173	0.8%
1	California	19,386,306	12.1%
21	Colorado	3,050,118	1.9%
28	Connecticut	1,901,529	1.2%
45	Delaware	475,543	0.3%
3	Florida	10,127,020	6.3%
8	Georgia	5,095,939	3.2%
42	Hawaii	682,184	0.4%
38	Idaho	842,429	0.5%
5	Illinois	6,464,449	4.0%
16	Indiana	3,301,415	2.1%
30	Iowa	1,684,799	1.0%
32	Kansas	1,482,444	0.9%
27	Kentucky	2,063,106	1.3%
26	Louisiana	2,116,924	1.3%
41	Maine	699,973	0.4%
18	Maryland	3,230,359	2.0%
14	Massachusetts	3,646,947	2.3%
10	Michigan	4,887,450	3.0%
20	Minnesota	3,081,549	1.9%
35	Mississippi	1,271,691	0.8%
22	Missouri	3,028,178	1.9%
44	Montana	526,002	0.3%
36	Nebraska	1,010,518	0.6%
33	Nevada	1,473,867	0.9%
40	New Hampshire	744,038	0.5%
11	New Jersey	4,489,655	2.8%
37	New Mexico	935,651	0.6%
4	New York	9,685,002	6.0%
9	North Carolina	4,949,223	3.1%
47	North Dakota	416,393	0.3%
7	Ohio	5,774,214	3.6%
29	Oklahoma	1,847,899	1.2%
25	Oregon	2,143,455	1.3%
6	Pennsylvania	6,391,884	4.0%
43	Rhode Island	554,893	0.3%
23	South Carolina	2,323,976	1.4%
46	South Dakota	459,771	0.3%
17	Tennessee	3,230,761	2.0%
2	Texas	13,547,022	8.4%
31	Utah	1,580,966	1.0%
49	Vermont	345,756	0.2%
12	Virginia	4,308,950	2.7%
13	Washington	3,763,136	2.3%
39	West Virginia	783,036	0.5%
19	Wisconsin	3,170,646	2.0%
50	Wyoming	292,303	0.2%

RANK ORDER

RANK	STATE	LABOR FORCE	% of USA
1	California	19,386,306	12.1%
2	Texas	13,547,022	8.4%
3	Florida	10,127,020	6.3%
4	New York	9,685,002	6.0%
5	Illinois	6,464,449	4.0%
6	Pennsylvania	6,391,884	4.0%
7	Ohio	5,774,214	3.6%
8	Georgia	5,095,939	3.2%
9	North Carolina	4,949,223	3.1%
10	Michigan	4,887,450	3.0%
11	New Jersey	4,489,655	2.8%
12	Virginia	4,308,950	2.7%
13	Washington	3,763,136	2.3%
14	Massachusetts	3,646,947	2.3%
15	Arizona	3,340,127	2.1%
16	Indiana	3,301,415	2.1%
17	Tennessee	3,230,761	2.0%
18	Maryland	3,230,359	2.0%
19	Wisconsin	3,170,646	2.0%
20	Minnesota	3,081,549	1.9%
21	Colorado	3,050,118	1.9%
22	Missouri	3,028,178	1.9%
23	South Carolina	2,323,976	1.4%
24	Alabama	2,168,761	1.4%
25	Oregon	2,143,455	1.3%
26	Louisiana	2,116,924	1.3%
27	Kentucky	2,063,106	1.3%
28	Connecticut	1,901,529	1.2%
29	Oklahoma	1,847,899	1.2%
30	Iowa	1,684,799	1.0%
31	Utah	1,580,966	1.0%
32	Kansas	1,482,444	0.9%
33	Nevada	1,473,867	0.9%
34	Arkansas	1,362,173	0.8%
35	Mississippi	1,271,691	0.8%
36	Nebraska	1,010,518	0.6%
37	New Mexico	935,651	0.6%
38	Idaho	842,429	0.5%
39	West Virginia	783,036	0.5%
40	New Hampshire	744,038	0.5%
41	Maine	699,973	0.4%
42	Hawaii	682,184	0.4%
43	Rhode Island	554,893	0.3%
44	Montana	526,002	0.3%
45	Delaware	475,543	0.3%
46	South Dakota	459,771	0.3%
47	North Dakota	416,393	0.3%
48	Alaska	363,230	0.2%
49	Vermont	345,756	0.2%
50	Wyoming	292,303	0.2%
	District of Columbia	401,047	0.2%

Source: U.S. Department of Labor, Bureau of Labor Statistics
"State Employment and Unemployment" (press release, January 23, 2018, www.bls.gov/bls/newsrels.htm)
*Seasonally adjusted preliminary data as of December 2017. National total calculated through a different formula.

Employed Civilian Labor Force in 2017

National Total = 154,021,000 Employed Workers*

ALPHA ORDER

RANK	STATE	EMPLOYED	% of USA
24	Alabama	2,093,063	1.4%
48	Alaska	336,869	0.2%
15	Arizona	3,190,571	2.1%
34	Arkansas	1,311,977	0.9%
1	California	18,547,566	12.0%
21	Colorado	2,957,032	1.9%
28	Connecticut	1,814,489	1.2%
45	Delaware	453,710	0.3%
3	Florida	9,752,649	6.3%
8	Georgia	4,871,108	3.2%
42	Hawaii	668,623	0.4%
38	Idaho	817,734	0.5%
5	Illinois	6,155,287	4.0%
16	Indiana	3,188,884	2.1%
30	Iowa	1,637,789	1.1%
32	Kansas	1,431,994	0.9%
27	Kentucky	1,972,150	1.3%
26	Louisiana	2,019,587	1.3%
41	Maine	679,271	0.4%
18	Maryland	3,100,112	2.0%
14	Massachusetts	3,518,905	2.3%
10	Michigan	4,656,087	3.0%
20	Minnesota	2,987,322	1.9%
35	Mississippi	1,213,640	0.8%
22	Missouri	2,923,490	1.9%
44	Montana	504,660	0.3%
36	Nebraska	982,851	0.6%
33	Nevada	1,400,542	0.9%
40	New Hampshire	724,511	0.5%
11	New Jersey	4,265,463	2.8%
37	New Mexico	879,838	0.6%
4	New York	9,235,241	6.0%
9	North Carolina	4,727,107	3.1%
47	North Dakota	405,555	0.3%
7	Ohio	5,504,122	3.6%
29	Oklahoma	1,771,895	1.2%
25	Oregon	2,054,821	1.3%
6	Pennsylvania	6,092,931	4.0%
43	Rhode Island	530,346	0.3%
23	South Carolina	2,227,542	1.4%
46	South Dakota	443,694	0.3%
17	Tennessee	3,128,707	2.0%
2	Texas	13,024,811	8.5%
31	Utah	1,531,239	1.0%
49	Vermont	335,906	0.2%
12	Virginia	4,151,484	2.7%
13	Washington	3,593,588	2.3%
39	West Virginia	739,907	0.5%
19	Wisconsin	3,074,995	2.0%
50	Wyoming	279,958	0.2%

RANK ORDER

RANK	STATE	EMPLOYED	% of USA
1	California	18,547,566	12.0%
2	Texas	13,024,811	8.5%
3	Florida	9,752,649	6.3%
4	New York	9,235,241	6.0%
5	Illinois	6,155,287	4.0%
6	Pennsylvania	6,092,931	4.0%
7	Ohio	5,504,122	3.6%
8	Georgia	4,871,108	3.2%
9	North Carolina	4,727,107	3.1%
10	Michigan	4,656,087	3.0%
11	New Jersey	4,265,463	2.8%
12	Virginia	4,151,484	2.7%
13	Washington	3,593,588	2.3%
14	Massachusetts	3,518,905	2.3%
15	Arizona	3,190,571	2.1%
16	Indiana	3,188,884	2.1%
17	Tennessee	3,128,707	2.0%
18	Maryland	3,100,112	2.0%
19	Wisconsin	3,074,995	2.0%
20	Minnesota	2,987,322	1.9%
21	Colorado	2,957,032	1.9%
22	Missouri	2,923,490	1.9%
23	South Carolina	2,227,542	1.4%
24	Alabama	2,093,063	1.4%
25	Oregon	2,054,821	1.3%
26	Louisiana	2,019,587	1.3%
27	Kentucky	1,972,150	1.3%
28	Connecticut	1,814,489	1.2%
29	Oklahoma	1,771,895	1.2%
30	Iowa	1,637,789	1.1%
31	Utah	1,531,239	1.0%
32	Kansas	1,431,994	0.9%
33	Nevada	1,400,542	0.9%
34	Arkansas	1,311,977	0.9%
35	Mississippi	1,213,640	0.8%
36	Nebraska	982,851	0.6%
37	New Mexico	879,838	0.6%
38	Idaho	817,734	0.5%
39	West Virginia	739,907	0.5%
40	New Hampshire	724,511	0.5%
41	Maine	679,271	0.4%
42	Hawaii	668,623	0.4%
43	Rhode Island	530,346	0.3%
44	Montana	504,660	0.3%
45	Delaware	453,710	0.3%
46	South Dakota	443,694	0.3%
47	North Dakota	405,555	0.3%
48	Alaska	336,869	0.2%
49	Vermont	335,906	0.2%
50	Wyoming	279,958	0.2%
	District of Columbia	376,956	0.2%

Source: U.S. Department of Labor, Bureau of Labor Statistics
"State Employment and Unemployment" (press release, January 23, 2018, www.bls.gov/bls/newsrels.htm)
*Seasonally adjusted preliminary data as of December 2017. National total calculated through a different formula.

Employment to Population Ratio in 2017

National Percent = 59.7% of Population 16 Years and Older Employed*

ALPHA ORDER

RANK	STATE	PERCENT
47	Alabama	53.7
34	Alaska	58.6
37	Arizona	58.2
45	Arkansas	55.5
29	California	59.5
4	Colorado	66.9
15	Connecticut	62.1
32	Delaware	58.8
41	Florida	57.5
24	Georgia	60.2
39	Hawaii	58.0
12	Idaho	63.1
24	Illinois	60.2
21	Indiana	60.8
7	Iowa	65.9
13	Kansas	63.0
44	Kentucky	55.7
46	Louisiana	54.7
19	Maine	61.3
11	Maryland	64.3
14	Massachusetts	62.8
37	Michigan	58.2
2	Minnesota	68.3
49	Mississippi	51.6
26	Missouri	60.1
26	Montana	60.1
5	Nebraska	66.2
28	Nevada	59.9
9	New Hampshire	65.4
30	New Jersey	59.3
48	New Mexico	53.4
41	New York	57.5
36	North Carolina	58.3
3	North Dakota	67.7
31	Ohio	59.1
40	Oklahoma	57.8
16	Oregon	61.8
35	Pennsylvania	58.4
22	Rhode Island	60.7
43	South Carolina	55.8
8	South Dakota	65.8
32	Tennessee	58.8
20	Texas	60.9
1	Utah	68.7
10	Vermont	64.5
17	Virginia	61.5
17	Washington	61.5
50	West Virginia	49.3
5	Wisconsin	66.2
22	Wyoming	60.7

RANK ORDER

RANK	STATE	PERCENT
1	Utah	68.7
2	Minnesota	68.3
3	North Dakota	67.7
4	Colorado	66.9
5	Nebraska	66.2
5	Wisconsin	66.2
7	Iowa	65.9
8	South Dakota	65.8
9	New Hampshire	65.4
10	Vermont	64.5
11	Maryland	64.3
12	Idaho	63.1
13	Kansas	63.0
14	Massachusetts	62.8
15	Connecticut	62.1
16	Oregon	61.8
17	Virginia	61.5
17	Washington	61.5
19	Maine	61.3
20	Texas	60.9
21	Indiana	60.8
22	Rhode Island	60.7
22	Wyoming	60.7
24	Georgia	60.2
24	Illinois	60.2
26	Missouri	60.1
26	Montana	60.1
28	Nevada	59.9
29	California	59.5
30	New Jersey	59.3
31	Ohio	59.1
32	Delaware	58.8
32	Tennessee	58.8
34	Alaska	58.6
35	Pennsylvania	58.4
36	North Carolina	58.3
37	Arizona	58.2
37	Michigan	58.2
39	Hawaii	58.0
40	Oklahoma	57.8
41	Florida	57.5
41	New York	57.5
43	South Carolina	55.8
44	Kentucky	55.7
45	Arkansas	55.5
46	Louisiana	54.7
47	Alabama	53.7
48	New Mexico	53.4
49	Mississippi	51.6
50	West Virginia	49.3

	District of Columbia	66.0

Source: CQ Press using data from U.S. Department of Labor, Bureau of Labor Statistics
"State Employment and Unemployment" (press release, January 23, 2018, www.bls.gov/bls/newsrels.htm)
*Seasonally adjusted preliminary data as of December 2017. Calculated with 2016 population data.

Unemployed Civilian Labor Force in 2017

National Total = 6,576,000 Unemployed Workers*

ALPHA ORDER

RANK	STATE	UNEMPLOYED	% of USA
29	Alabama	75,698	1.2%
39	Alaska	26,361	0.4%
14	Arizona	149,556	2.3%
34	Arkansas	50,196	0.8%
1	California	838,740	12.8%
24	Colorado	93,086	1.4%
27	Connecticut	87,040	1.3%
42	Delaware	21,833	0.3%
4	Florida	374,371	5.7%
9	Georgia	224,831	3.4%
47	Hawaii	13,561	0.2%
40	Idaho	24,695	0.4%
5	Illinois	309,162	4.7%
17	Indiana	112,531	1.7%
36	Iowa	47,010	0.7%
33	Kansas	50,450	0.8%
25	Kentucky	90,956	1.4%
20	Louisiana	97,337	1.5%
44	Maine	20,702	0.3%
15	Maryland	130,247	2.0%
16	Massachusetts	128,042	1.9%
8	Michigan	231,363	3.5%
23	Minnesota	94,227	1.4%
31	Mississippi	58,051	0.9%
18	Missouri	104,688	1.6%
43	Montana	21,342	0.3%
38	Nebraska	27,667	0.4%
30	Nevada	73,325	1.1%
45	New Hampshire	19,527	0.3%
10	New Jersey	224,192	3.4%
32	New Mexico	55,813	0.8%
3	New York	449,761	6.8%
11	North Carolina	222,116	3.4%
49	North Dakota	10,838	0.2%
7	Ohio	270,092	4.1%
28	Oklahoma	76,004	1.2%
26	Oregon	88,634	1.3%
6	Pennsylvania	298,953	4.5%
41	Rhode Island	24,547	0.4%
21	South Carolina	96,434	1.5%
46	South Dakota	16,077	0.2%
19	Tennessee	102,054	1.6%
2	Texas	522,211	7.9%
35	Utah	49,727	0.8%
50	Vermont	9,850	0.1%
13	Virginia	157,466	2.4%
12	Washington	169,548	2.6%
37	West Virginia	43,129	0.7%
22	Wisconsin	95,651	1.5%
48	Wyoming	12,345	0.2%

RANK ORDER

RANK	STATE	UNEMPLOYED	% of USA
1	California	838,740	12.8%
2	Texas	522,211	7.9%
3	New York	449,761	6.8%
4	Florida	374,371	5.7%
5	Illinois	309,162	4.7%
6	Pennsylvania	298,953	4.5%
7	Ohio	270,092	4.1%
8	Michigan	231,363	3.5%
9	Georgia	224,831	3.4%
10	New Jersey	224,192	3.4%
11	North Carolina	222,116	3.4%
12	Washington	169,548	2.6%
13	Virginia	157,466	2.4%
14	Arizona	149,556	2.3%
15	Maryland	130,247	2.0%
16	Massachusetts	128,042	1.9%
17	Indiana	112,531	1.7%
18	Missouri	104,688	1.6%
19	Tennessee	102,054	1.6%
20	Louisiana	97,337	1.5%
21	South Carolina	96,434	1.5%
22	Wisconsin	95,651	1.5%
23	Minnesota	94,227	1.4%
24	Colorado	93,086	1.4%
25	Kentucky	90,956	1.4%
26	Oregon	88,634	1.3%
27	Connecticut	87,040	1.3%
28	Oklahoma	76,004	1.2%
29	Alabama	75,698	1.2%
30	Nevada	73,325	1.1%
31	Mississippi	58,051	0.9%
32	New Mexico	55,813	0.8%
33	Kansas	50,450	0.8%
34	Arkansas	50,196	0.8%
35	Utah	49,727	0.8%
36	Iowa	47,010	0.7%
37	West Virginia	43,129	0.7%
38	Nebraska	27,667	0.4%
39	Alaska	26,361	0.4%
40	Idaho	24,695	0.4%
41	Rhode Island	24,547	0.4%
42	Delaware	21,833	0.3%
43	Montana	21,342	0.3%
44	Maine	20,702	0.3%
45	New Hampshire	19,527	0.3%
46	South Dakota	16,077	0.2%
47	Hawaii	13,561	0.2%
48	Wyoming	12,345	0.2%
49	North Dakota	10,838	0.2%
50	Vermont	9,850	0.1%
	District of Columbia	24,091	0.4%

Source: U.S. Department of Labor, Bureau of Labor Statistics
   "State Employment and Unemployment" (press release, January 23, 2018, www.bls.gov/bls/newsrels.htm)
*Seasonally adjusted preliminary data as of December 2017. National total calculated through a different formula.

Unemployment Rate in 2017

National Rate = 4.1% of Labor Force Unemployed*

ALPHA ORDER

RANK	STATE	PERCENT
32	Alabama	3.5
1	Alaska	7.3
15	Arizona	4.5
29	Arkansas	3.7
21	California	4.3
39	Colorado	3.1
10	Connecticut	4.6
10	Delaware	4.6
29	Florida	3.7
18	Georgia	4.4
50	Hawaii	2.0
44	Idaho	2.9
6	Illinois	4.8
36	Indiana	3.4
45	Iowa	2.8
36	Kansas	3.4
18	Kentucky	4.4
10	Louisiana	4.6
42	Maine	3.0
27	Maryland	4.0
32	Massachusetts	3.5
7	Michigan	4.7
39	Minnesota	3.1
10	Mississippi	4.6
32	Missouri	3.5
23	Montana	4.1
47	Nebraska	2.7
4	Nevada	5.0
48	New Hampshire	2.6
4	New Jersey	5.0
2	New Mexico	6.0
10	New York	4.6
15	North Carolina	4.5
48	North Dakota	2.6
7	Ohio	4.7
23	Oklahoma	4.1
23	Oregon	4.1
7	Pennsylvania	4.7
18	Rhode Island	4.4
23	South Carolina	4.1
32	South Dakota	3.5
38	Tennessee	3.2
28	Texas	3.9
39	Utah	3.1
45	Vermont	2.8
29	Virginia	3.7
15	Washington	4.5
3	West Virginia	5.5
42	Wisconsin	3.0
22	Wyoming	4.2

RANK ORDER

RANK	STATE	PERCENT
1	Alaska	7.3
2	New Mexico	6.0
3	West Virginia	5.5
4	Nevada	5.0
4	New Jersey	5.0
6	Illinois	4.8
7	Michigan	4.7
7	Ohio	4.7
7	Pennsylvania	4.7
10	Connecticut	4.6
10	Delaware	4.6
10	Louisiana	4.6
10	Mississippi	4.6
10	New York	4.6
15	Arizona	4.5
15	North Carolina	4.5
15	Washington	4.5
18	Georgia	4.4
18	Kentucky	4.4
18	Rhode Island	4.4
21	California	4.3
22	Wyoming	4.2
23	Montana	4.1
23	Oklahoma	4.1
23	Oregon	4.1
23	South Carolina	4.1
27	Maryland	4.0
28	Texas	3.9
29	Arkansas	3.7
29	Florida	3.7
29	Virginia	3.7
32	Alabama	3.5
32	Massachusetts	3.5
32	Missouri	3.5
32	South Dakota	3.5
36	Indiana	3.4
36	Kansas	3.4
38	Tennessee	3.2
39	Colorado	3.1
39	Minnesota	3.1
39	Utah	3.1
42	Maine	3.0
42	Wisconsin	3.0
44	Idaho	2.9
45	Iowa	2.8
45	Vermont	2.8
47	Nebraska	2.7
48	New Hampshire	2.6
48	North Dakota	2.6
50	Hawaii	2.0
	District of Columbia	6.0

Source: U.S. Department of Labor, Bureau of Labor Statistics
"State Employment and Unemployment" (press release, January 23, 2018, www.bls.gov/bls/newsrels.htm)
*Seasonally adjusted preliminary data as of December 2017. National figure calculated through a different formula.

Women in Civilian Labor Force in 2016

National Total = 74,432,000 Women*

ALPHA ORDER				RANK ORDER			
RANK	STATE	WOMEN	% of USA	RANK	STATE	WOMEN	% of USA
25	Alabama	1,022,000	1.4%	1	California	8,560,000	11.5%
49	Alaska	166,000	0.2%	2	Texas	5,915,000	7.9%
19	Arizona	1,477,000	2.0%	3	Florida	4,634,000	6.2%
33	Arkansas	633,000	0.9%	4	New York	4,573,000	6.1%
1	California	8,560,000	11.5%	5	Pennsylvania	3,108,000	4.2%
22	Colorado	1,303,000	1.8%	6	Illinois	3,085,000	4.1%
28	Connecticut	915,000	1.2%	7	Ohio	2,717,000	3.7%
45	Delaware	231,000	0.3%	8	Georgia	2,363,000	3.2%
3	Florida	4,634,000	6.2%	9	North Carolina	2,323,000	3.1%
8	Georgia	2,363,000	3.2%	10	Michigan	2,285,000	3.1%
42	Hawaii	324,000	0.4%	11	New Jersey	2,096,000	2.8%
38	Idaho	368,000	0.5%	12	Virginia	1,987,000	2.7%
6	Illinois	3,085,000	4.1%	13	Massachusetts	1,727,000	2.3%
15	Indiana	1,580,000	2.1%	14	Washington	1,714,000	2.3%
30	Iowa	812,000	1.1%	15	Indiana	1,580,000	2.1%
31	Kansas	691,000	0.9%	16	Maryland	1,550,000	2.1%
27	Kentucky	947,000	1.3%	17	Missouri	1,497,000	2.0%
24	Louisiana	1,033,000	1.4%	18	Wisconsin	1,495,000	2.0%
41	Maine	329,000	0.4%	19	Arizona	1,477,000	2.0%
16	Maryland	1,550,000	2.1%	20	Tennessee	1,466,000	2.0%
13	Massachusetts	1,727,000	2.3%	21	Minnesota	1,413,000	1.9%
10	Michigan	2,285,000	3.1%	22	Colorado	1,303,000	1.8%
21	Minnesota	1,413,000	1.9%	23	South Carolina	1,130,000	1.5%
35	Mississippi	626,000	0.8%	24	Louisiana	1,033,000	1.4%
17	Missouri	1,497,000	2.0%	25	Alabama	1,022,000	1.4%
44	Montana	245,000	0.3%	26	Oregon	971,000	1.3%
36	Nebraska	479,000	0.6%	27	Kentucky	947,000	1.3%
34	Nevada	629,000	0.8%	28	Connecticut	915,000	1.2%
40	New Hampshire	354,000	0.5%	29	Oklahoma	825,000	1.1%
11	New Jersey	2,096,000	2.8%	30	Iowa	812,000	1.1%
37	New Mexico	437,000	0.6%	31	Kansas	691,000	0.9%
4	New York	4,573,000	6.1%	32	Utah	656,000	0.9%
9	North Carolina	2,323,000	3.1%	33	Arkansas	633,000	0.9%
47	North Dakota	190,000	0.3%	34	Nevada	629,000	0.8%
7	Ohio	2,717,000	3.7%	35	Mississippi	626,000	0.8%
29	Oklahoma	825,000	1.1%	36	Nebraska	479,000	0.6%
26	Oregon	971,000	1.3%	37	New Mexico	437,000	0.6%
5	Pennsylvania	3,108,000	4.2%	38	Idaho	368,000	0.5%
43	Rhode Island	269,000	0.4%	39	West Virginia	364,000	0.5%
23	South Carolina	1,130,000	1.5%	40	New Hampshire	354,000	0.5%
46	South Dakota	210,000	0.3%	41	Maine	329,000	0.4%
20	Tennessee	1,466,000	2.0%	42	Hawaii	324,000	0.4%
2	Texas	5,915,000	7.9%	43	Rhode Island	269,000	0.4%
32	Utah	656,000	0.9%	44	Montana	245,000	0.3%
48	Vermont	167,000	0.2%	45	Delaware	231,000	0.3%
12	Virginia	1,987,000	2.7%	46	South Dakota	210,000	0.3%
14	Washington	1,714,000	2.3%	47	North Dakota	190,000	0.3%
39	West Virginia	364,000	0.5%	48	Vermont	167,000	0.2%
18	Wisconsin	1,495,000	2.0%	49	Alaska	166,000	0.2%
50	Wyoming	135,000	0.2%	50	Wyoming	135,000	0.2%
					District of Columbia	200,000	0.3%

Source: U.S. Department of Labor, Bureau of Labor Statistics
    "Geographic Profiles of Employment and Unemployment, 2016" (http://www.bls.gov/gps/)
*Annual averages.

Percent of Women in the Civilian Labor Force in 2016

National Percent = 56.8% of Women*

ALPHA ORDER

RANK	STATE	PERCENT
49	Alabama	50.8
9	Alaska	62.6
42	Arizona	53.5
46	Arkansas	52.8
39	California	54.6
17	Colorado	59.7
11	Connecticut	61.3
26	Delaware	58.0
42	Florida	53.5
31	Georgia	56.9
26	Hawaii	58.0
30	Idaho	57.2
19	Illinois	59.5
18	Indiana	59.6
2	Iowa	65.5
11	Kansas	61.3
45	Kentucky	52.9
38	Louisiana	54.8
25	Maine	58.3
10	Maryland	62.2
15	Massachusetts	60.0
33	Michigan	56.1
4	Minnesota	64.7
48	Mississippi	51.7
13	Missouri	60.8
20	Montana	59.3
3	Nebraska	65.0
40	Nevada	54.1
6	New Hampshire	63.9
31	New Jersey	56.9
47	New Mexico	52.7
35	New York	55.3
34	North Carolina	55.9
1	North Dakota	66.7
29	Ohio	57.4
42	Oklahoma	53.5
28	Oregon	57.8
23	Pennsylvania	58.6
15	Rhode Island	60.0
37	South Carolina	55.1
7	South Dakota	63.6
41	Tennessee	53.8
36	Texas	55.2
21	Utah	59.2
8	Vermont	63.2
24	Virginia	58.4
22	Washington	59.0
50	West Virginia	48.1
5	Wisconsin	64.3
14	Wyoming	60.6

RANK ORDER

RANK	STATE	PERCENT
1	North Dakota	66.7
2	Iowa	65.5
3	Nebraska	65.0
4	Minnesota	64.7
5	Wisconsin	64.3
6	New Hampshire	63.9
7	South Dakota	63.6
8	Vermont	63.2
9	Alaska	62.6
10	Maryland	62.2
11	Connecticut	61.3
11	Kansas	61.3
13	Missouri	60.8
14	Wyoming	60.6
15	Massachusetts	60.0
15	Rhode Island	60.0
17	Colorado	59.7
18	Indiana	59.6
19	Illinois	59.5
20	Montana	59.3
21	Utah	59.2
22	Washington	59.0
23	Pennsylvania	58.6
24	Virginia	58.4
25	Maine	58.3
26	Delaware	58.0
26	Hawaii	58.0
28	Oregon	57.8
29	Ohio	57.4
30	Idaho	57.2
31	Georgia	56.9
31	New Jersey	56.9
33	Michigan	56.1
34	North Carolina	55.9
35	New York	55.3
36	Texas	55.2
37	South Carolina	55.1
38	Louisiana	54.8
39	California	54.6
40	Nevada	54.1
41	Tennessee	53.8
42	Arizona	53.5
42	Florida	53.5
42	Oklahoma	53.5
45	Kentucky	52.9
46	Arkansas	52.8
47	New Mexico	52.7
48	Mississippi	51.7
49	Alabama	50.8
50	West Virginia	48.1
	District of Columbia	66.5

Source: U.S. Department of Labor, Bureau of Labor Statistics
   "Geographic Profiles of Employment and Unemployment, 2016" (http://www.bls.gov/gps/)
*Annual averages. Women 16 years and older.

Percent of Civilian Labor Force Comprised of Women in 2016

National Percent = 46.8% of Civilian Labor Force*

ALPHA ORDER

RANK	STATE	PERCENT
24	Alabama	47.2
40	Alaska	46.2
41	Arizona	45.5
30	Arkansas	47.0
45	California	44.9
45	Colorado	44.9
7	Connecticut	48.3
4	Delaware	48.8
16	Florida	47.5
11	Georgia	47.9
24	Hawaii	47.2
43	Idaho	45.2
27	Illinois	47.1
22	Indiana	47.3
16	Iowa	47.5
35	Kansas	46.6
22	Kentucky	47.3
6	Louisiana	48.6
19	Maine	47.4
1	Maryland	48.9
9	Massachusetts	48.1
27	Michigan	47.1
19	Minnesota	47.4
1	Mississippi	48.9
12	Missouri	47.8
34	Montana	46.8
19	Nebraska	47.4
49	Nevada	44.4
27	New Hampshire	47.1
39	New Jersey	46.3
33	New Mexico	46.9
12	New York	47.8
15	North Carolina	47.7
41	North Dakota	45.5
16	Ohio	47.5
43	Oklahoma	45.2
30	Oregon	47.0
10	Pennsylvania	48.0
1	Rhode Island	48.9
5	South Carolina	48.7
38	South Dakota	46.4
35	Tennessee	46.6
48	Texas	44.5
50	Utah	43.4
7	Vermont	48.3
24	Virginia	47.2
30	Washington	47.0
37	West Virginia	46.5
12	Wisconsin	47.8
47	Wyoming	44.7

RANK ORDER

RANK	STATE	PERCENT
1	Maryland	48.9
1	Mississippi	48.9
1	Rhode Island	48.9
4	Delaware	48.8
5	South Carolina	48.7
6	Louisiana	48.6
7	Connecticut	48.3
7	Vermont	48.3
9	Massachusetts	48.1
10	Pennsylvania	48.0
11	Georgia	47.9
12	Missouri	47.8
12	New York	47.8
12	Wisconsin	47.8
15	North Carolina	47.7
16	Florida	47.5
16	Iowa	47.5
16	Ohio	47.5
19	Maine	47.4
19	Minnesota	47.4
19	Nebraska	47.4
22	Indiana	47.3
22	Kentucky	47.3
24	Alabama	47.2
24	Hawaii	47.2
24	Virginia	47.2
27	Illinois	47.1
27	Michigan	47.1
27	New Hampshire	47.1
30	Arkansas	47.0
30	Oregon	47.0
30	Washington	47.0
33	New Mexico	46.9
34	Montana	46.8
35	Kansas	46.6
35	Tennessee	46.6
37	West Virginia	46.5
38	South Dakota	46.4
39	New Jersey	46.3
40	Alaska	46.2
41	Arizona	45.5
41	North Dakota	45.5
43	Idaho	45.2
43	Oklahoma	45.2
45	California	44.9
45	Colorado	44.9
47	Wyoming	44.7
48	Texas	44.5
49	Nevada	44.4
50	Utah	43.4

| | District of Columbia | 51.0 |

Source: CQ Press using data from U.S. Department of Labor, Bureau of Labor Statistics
"Geographic Profiles of Employment and Unemployment, 2016" (http://www.bls.gov/gps/)
*Annual averages.

Job Growth: 2016 to 2017

National Percent Change = 1.4% Increase*

ALPHA ORDER

RANK	STATE	PERCENT CHANGE
15	Alabama	1.7
50	Alaska	(0.7)
19	Arizona	1.3
32	Arkansas	0.9
7	California	2.1
10	Colorado	2.0
42	Connecticut	0.5
49	Delaware	(0.1)
4	Florida	2.5
11	Georgia	1.9
26	Hawaii	1.1
7	Idaho	2.1
42	Illinois	0.5
32	Indiana	0.9
12	Iowa	1.8
44	Kansas	0.4
26	Kentucky	1.1
47	Louisiana	0.3
35	Maine	0.8
26	Maryland	1.1
12	Massachusetts	1.8
19	Michigan	1.3
19	Minnesota	1.3
17	Mississippi	1.6
35	Missouri	0.8
12	Montana	1.8
26	Nebraska	1.1
1	Nevada	3.3
35	New Hampshire	0.8
41	New Jersey	0.6
23	New Mexico	1.2
30	New York	1.0
15	North Carolina	1.7
44	North Dakota	0.4
40	Ohio	0.7
23	Oklahoma	1.2
2	Oregon	2.7
19	Pennsylvania	1.3
23	Rhode Island	1.2
6	South Carolina	2.2
32	South Dakota	0.9
30	Tennessee	1.0
4	Texas	2.5
3	Utah	2.6
35	Vermont	0.8
35	Virginia	0.8
7	Washington	2.1
48	West Virginia	0.2
18	Wisconsin	1.4
44	Wyoming	0.4

RANK ORDER

RANK	STATE	PERCENT CHANGE
1	Nevada	3.3
2	Oregon	2.7
3	Utah	2.6
4	Florida	2.5
4	Texas	2.5
6	South Carolina	2.2
7	California	2.1
7	Idaho	2.1
7	Washington	2.1
10	Colorado	2.0
11	Georgia	1.9
12	Iowa	1.8
12	Massachusetts	1.8
12	Montana	1.8
15	Alabama	1.7
15	North Carolina	1.7
17	Mississippi	1.6
18	Wisconsin	1.4
19	Arizona	1.3
19	Michigan	1.3
19	Minnesota	1.3
19	Pennsylvania	1.3
23	New Mexico	1.2
23	Oklahoma	1.2
23	Rhode Island	1.2
26	Hawaii	1.1
26	Kentucky	1.1
26	Maryland	1.1
26	Nebraska	1.1
30	New York	1.0
30	Tennessee	1.0
32	Arkansas	0.9
32	Indiana	0.9
32	South Dakota	0.9
35	Maine	0.8
35	Missouri	0.8
35	New Hampshire	0.8
35	Vermont	0.8
35	Virginia	0.8
40	Ohio	0.7
41	New Jersey	0.6
42	Connecticut	0.5
42	Illinois	0.5
44	Kansas	0.4
44	North Dakota	0.4
44	Wyoming	0.4
47	Louisiana	0.3
48	West Virginia	0.2
49	Delaware	(0.1)
50	Alaska	(0.7)

| | District of Columbia | 1.0 |

Source: CQ Press using data from U.S. Department of Labor, Bureau of Labor Statistics
"State Employment and Unemployment" (press release, January 23, 2018, www.bls.gov/bls/newsrels.htm)
*Nonfarm jobs. December 2016 to December 2017, seasonally adjusted. National figure based on nonfarm employment from a different survey.

Employees on Nonfarm Payrolls in 2017

National Total = 147,360,000 Employees*

ALPHA ORDER

RANK	STATE	EMPLOYEES	% of USA
24	Alabama	2,017,800	1.4%
48	Alaska	327,200	0.2%
20	Arizona	2,770,400	1.9%
34	Arkansas	1,248,600	0.8%
1	California	16,980,400	11.5%
22	Colorado	2,671,500	1.8%
28	Connecticut	1,685,200	1.1%
45	Delaware	453,800	0.3%
4	Florida	8,705,900	5.9%
8	Georgia	4,518,900	3.1%
41	Hawaii	659,100	0.4%
39	Idaho	722,600	0.5%
5	Illinois	6,050,900	4.1%
15	Indiana	3,136,200	2.1%
30	Iowa	1,600,100	1.1%
32	Kansas	1,416,800	1.0%
26	Kentucky	1,952,500	1.3%
25	Louisiana	1,974,500	1.3%
42	Maine	622,600	0.4%
21	Maryland	2,762,200	1.9%
13	Massachusetts	3,649,400	2.5%
10	Michigan	4,426,000	3.0%
18	Minnesota	2,958,700	2.0%
35	Mississippi	1,162,800	0.8%
19	Missouri	2,894,500	2.0%
44	Montana	480,000	0.3%
36	Nebraska	1,032,800	0.7%
33	Nevada	1,365,100	0.9%
40	New Hampshire	678,900	0.5%
11	New Jersey	4,126,600	2.8%
37	New Mexico	846,800	0.6%
3	New York	9,556,600	6.5%
9	North Carolina	4,457,700	3.0%
47	North Dakota	435,600	0.3%
7	Ohio	5,542,200	3.8%
29	Oklahoma	1,670,600	1.1%
27	Oregon	1,901,800	1.3%
6	Pennsylvania	5,994,700	4.1%
43	Rhode Island	497,300	0.3%
23	South Carolina	2,117,200	1.4%
46	South Dakota	439,400	0.3%
16	Tennessee	3,022,800	2.1%
2	Texas	12,444,700	8.4%
31	Utah	1,487,300	1.0%
49	Vermont	316,400	0.2%
12	Virginia	3,966,500	2.7%
14	Washington	3,360,000	2.3%
38	West Virginia	748,100	0.5%
17	Wisconsin	2,974,500	2.0%
50	Wyoming	277,900	0.2%

RANK ORDER

RANK	STATE	EMPLOYEES	% of USA
1	California	16,980,400	11.5%
2	Texas	12,444,700	8.4%
3	New York	9,556,600	6.5%
4	Florida	8,705,900	5.9%
5	Illinois	6,050,900	4.1%
6	Pennsylvania	5,994,700	4.1%
7	Ohio	5,542,200	3.8%
8	Georgia	4,518,900	3.1%
9	North Carolina	4,457,700	3.0%
10	Michigan	4,426,000	3.0%
11	New Jersey	4,126,600	2.8%
12	Virginia	3,966,500	2.7%
13	Massachusetts	3,649,400	2.5%
14	Washington	3,360,000	2.3%
15	Indiana	3,136,200	2.1%
16	Tennessee	3,022,800	2.1%
17	Wisconsin	2,974,500	2.0%
18	Minnesota	2,958,700	2.0%
19	Missouri	2,894,500	2.0%
20	Arizona	2,770,400	1.9%
21	Maryland	2,762,200	1.9%
22	Colorado	2,671,500	1.8%
23	South Carolina	2,117,200	1.4%
24	Alabama	2,017,800	1.4%
25	Louisiana	1,974,500	1.3%
26	Kentucky	1,952,500	1.3%
27	Oregon	1,901,800	1.3%
28	Connecticut	1,685,200	1.1%
29	Oklahoma	1,670,600	1.1%
30	Iowa	1,600,100	1.1%
31	Utah	1,487,300	1.0%
32	Kansas	1,416,800	1.0%
33	Nevada	1,365,100	0.9%
34	Arkansas	1,248,600	0.8%
35	Mississippi	1,162,800	0.8%
36	Nebraska	1,032,800	0.7%
37	New Mexico	846,800	0.6%
38	West Virginia	748,100	0.5%
39	Idaho	722,600	0.5%
40	New Hampshire	678,900	0.5%
41	Hawaii	659,100	0.4%
42	Maine	622,600	0.4%
43	Rhode Island	497,300	0.3%
44	Montana	480,000	0.3%
45	Delaware	453,800	0.3%
46	South Dakota	439,400	0.3%
47	North Dakota	435,600	0.3%
48	Alaska	327,200	0.2%
49	Vermont	316,400	0.2%
50	Wyoming	277,900	0.2%
	District of Columbia	795,600	0.5%

Source: U.S. Department of Labor, Bureau of Labor Statistics
   "State Employment and Unemployment" (press release, January 23, 2018, www.bls.gov/bls/newsrels.htm)
*Seasonally adjusted preliminary data as of December 2017. National total calculated through a different formula.

Employees in Construction in 2017

National Total = 6,993,000 Employees*

RANK	STATE	EMPLOYEES	% of USA
28	Alabama	89,800	1.3%
49	Alaska	17,000	0.2%
18	Arizona	143,400	2.1%
34	Arkansas	52,600	0.8%
1	California	839,900	12.0%
13	Colorado	164,900	2.4%
33	Connecticut	56,100	0.8%
46	Delaware**	21,100	0.3%
3	Florida	528,400	7.6%
11	Georgia	183,500	2.6%
39	Hawaii**	38,800	0.6%
37	Idaho	44,200	0.6%
6	Illinois	216,200	3.1%
19	Indiana	139,700	2.0%
31	Iowa	73,600	1.1%
32	Kansas	63,900	0.9%
30	Kentucky	80,900	1.2%
17	Louisiana	153,000	2.2%
43	Maine	27,900	0.4%
12	Maryland**	168,300	2.4%
15	Massachusetts	156,400	2.2%
13	Michigan	164,900	2.4%
20	Minnesota	127,300	1.8%
38	Mississippi	44,100	0.6%
22	Missouri	114,200	1.6%
42	Montana	28,700	0.4%
35	Nebraska**	51,500	0.7%
27	Nevada	91,700	1.3%
44	New Hampshire	27,700	0.4%
16	New Jersey	154,300	2.2%
36	New Mexico	46,700	0.7%
4	New York	380,200	5.4%
9	North Carolina	201,900	2.9%
41	North Dakota	30,700	0.4%
7	Ohio	210,200	3.0%
29	Oklahoma	84,700	1.2%
24	Oregon	104,800	1.5%
5	Pennsylvania	254,000	3.6%
48	Rhode Island	20,700	0.3%
25	South Carolina	100,900	1.4%
45	South Dakota**	24,000	0.3%
21	Tennessee**	126,100	1.8%
2	Texas	732,800	10.5%
26	Utah	98,700	1.4%
50	Vermont	15,300	0.2%
10	Virginia	194,600	2.8%
8	Washington	203,600	2.9%
40	West Virginia	33,100	0.5%
23	Wisconsin	112,900	1.6%
47	Wyoming	20,800	0.3%

RANK	STATE	EMPLOYEES	% of USA
1	California	839,900	12.0%
2	Texas	732,800	10.5%
3	Florida	528,400	7.6%
4	New York	380,200	5.4%
5	Pennsylvania	254,000	3.6%
6	Illinois	216,200	3.1%
7	Ohio	210,200	3.0%
8	Washington	203,600	2.9%
9	North Carolina	201,900	2.9%
10	Virginia	194,600	2.8%
11	Georgia	183,500	2.6%
12	Maryland**	168,300	2.4%
13	Colorado	164,900	2.4%
13	Michigan	164,900	2.4%
15	Massachusetts	156,400	2.2%
16	New Jersey	154,300	2.2%
17	Louisiana	153,000	2.2%
18	Arizona	143,400	2.1%
19	Indiana	139,700	2.0%
20	Minnesota	127,300	1.8%
21	Tennessee**	126,100	1.8%
22	Missouri	114,200	1.6%
23	Wisconsin	112,900	1.6%
24	Oregon	104,800	1.5%
25	South Carolina	100,900	1.4%
26	Utah	98,700	1.4%
27	Nevada	91,700	1.3%
28	Alabama	89,800	1.3%
29	Oklahoma	84,700	1.2%
30	Kentucky	80,900	1.2%
31	Iowa	73,600	1.1%
32	Kansas	63,900	0.9%
33	Connecticut	56,100	0.8%
34	Arkansas	52,600	0.8%
35	Nebraska**	51,500	0.7%
36	New Mexico	46,700	0.7%
37	Idaho	44,200	0.6%
38	Mississippi	44,100	0.6%
39	Hawaii**	38,800	0.6%
40	West Virginia	33,100	0.5%
41	North Dakota	30,700	0.4%
42	Montana	28,700	0.4%
43	Maine	27,900	0.4%
44	New Hampshire	27,700	0.4%
45	South Dakota**	24,000	0.3%
46	Delaware**	21,100	0.3%
47	Wyoming	20,800	0.3%
48	Rhode Island	20,700	0.3%
49	Alaska	17,000	0.2%
50	Vermont	15,300	0.2%
	District of Columbia**	14,700	0.2%

Source: U.S. Department of Labor, Bureau of Labor Statistics
"State Employment and Unemployment" (press release, January 23, 2018, www.bls.gov/bls/newsrels.htm)
*Seasonally adjusted preliminary data as of December 2017. National total calculated through a different formula.
**Figures for these states include employees in mining and logging.

Percent of Nonfarm Employees in Construction in 2017

National Percent = 4.7% of Employees*

ALPHA ORDER

RANK	STATE	PERCENT
27	Alabama	4.5
17	Alaska	5.2
17	Arizona	5.2
35	Arkansas	4.2
21	California	4.9
6	Colorado	6.2
50	Connecticut	3.3
25	Delaware**	4.6
7	Florida	6.1
39	Georgia	4.1
12	Hawaii**	5.9
7	Idaho	6.1
49	Illinois	3.6
27	Indiana	4.5
25	Iowa	4.6
27	Kansas	4.5
39	Kentucky	4.1
1	Louisiana	7.7
27	Maine	4.5
7	Maryland**	6.1
33	Massachusetts	4.3
47	Michigan	3.7
33	Minnesota	4.3
44	Mississippi	3.8
43	Missouri	3.9
11	Montana	6.0
20	Nebraska**	5.0
4	Nevada	6.7
39	New Hampshire	4.1
47	New Jersey	3.7
14	New Mexico	5.5
42	New York	4.0
27	North Carolina	4.5
3	North Dakota	7.0
44	Ohio	3.8
19	Oklahoma	5.1
14	Oregon	5.5
35	Pennsylvania	4.2
35	Rhode Island	4.2
23	South Carolina	4.8
14	South Dakota**	5.5
35	Tennessee**	4.2
12	Texas	5.9
5	Utah	6.6
23	Vermont	4.8
21	Virginia	4.9
7	Washington	6.1
32	West Virginia	4.4
44	Wisconsin	3.8
2	Wyoming	7.5

RANK ORDER

RANK	STATE	PERCENT
1	Louisiana	7.7
2	Wyoming	7.5
3	North Dakota	7.0
4	Nevada	6.7
5	Utah	6.6
6	Colorado	6.2
7	Florida	6.1
7	Idaho	6.1
7	Maryland**	6.1
7	Washington	6.1
11	Montana	6.0
12	Hawaii**	5.9
12	Texas	5.9
14	New Mexico	5.5
14	Oregon	5.5
14	South Dakota**	5.5
17	Alaska	5.2
17	Arizona	5.2
19	Oklahoma	5.1
20	Nebraska**	5.0
21	California	4.9
21	Virginia	4.9
23	South Carolina	4.8
23	Vermont	4.8
25	Delaware**	4.6
25	Iowa	4.6
27	Alabama	4.5
27	Indiana	4.5
27	Kansas	4.5
27	Maine	4.5
27	North Carolina	4.5
32	West Virginia	4.4
33	Massachusetts	4.3
33	Minnesota	4.3
35	Arkansas	4.2
35	Pennsylvania	4.2
35	Rhode Island	4.2
35	Tennessee**	4.2
39	Georgia	4.1
39	Kentucky	4.1
39	New Hampshire	4.1
42	New York	4.0
43	Missouri	3.9
44	Mississippi	3.8
44	Ohio	3.8
44	Wisconsin	3.8
47	Michigan	3.7
47	New Jersey	3.7
49	Illinois	3.6
50	Connecticut	3.3

District of Columbia**   1.8

Source: CQ Press using data from U.S. Department of Labor, Bureau of Labor Statistics
"State Employment and Unemployment" (press release, January 23, 2018, www.bls.gov/bls/newsrels.htm)
*Seasonally adjusted preliminary data as of December 2017. National figure calculated through a different formula.
**Figures for these states include employees in mining and logging.

Employees in Education and Health Services in 2017

National Total = 23,309,000 Employees*

RANK	STATE	EMPLOYEES	% of USA
28	Alabama	240,700	1.0%
49	Alaska	49,000	0.2%
21	Arizona	424,700	1.8%
33	Arkansas	190,400	0.8%
1	California	2,650,500	11.4%
22	Colorado	338,800	1.5%
23	Connecticut	334,900	1.4%
44	Delaware	79,700	0.3%
4	Florida	1,285,000	5.5%
12	Georgia	589,300	2.5%
43	Hawaii	86,100	0.4%
42	Idaho	107,200	0.5%
7	Illinois	924,700	4.0%
16	Indiana	478,800	2.1%
30	Iowa	235,100	1.0%
32	Kansas	198,300	0.9%
26	Kentucky	274,300	1.2%
24	Louisiana	316,200	1.4%
39	Maine	128,300	0.6%
17	Maryland	475,600	2.0%
8	Massachusetts	805,400	3.5%
10	Michigan	674,600	2.9%
14	Minnesota	543,100	2.3%
35	Mississippi	145,700	0.6%
18	Missouri	467,600	2.0%
45	Montana	77,100	0.3%
34	Nebraska	155,400	0.7%
37	Nevada	136,600	0.6%
40	New Hampshire	125,000	0.5%
9	New Jersey	696,700	3.0%
36	New Mexico	143,300	0.6%
2	New York	2,019,400	8.7%
11	North Carolina	605,400	2.6%
48	North Dakota	63,300	0.3%
6	Ohio	946,800	4.1%
29	Oklahoma	240,100	1.0%
25	Oregon	280,300	1.2%
5	Pennsylvania	1,268,100	5.4%
41	Rhode Island	108,100	0.5%
27	South Carolina	252,500	1.1%
46	South Dakota	72,300	0.3%
20	Tennessee	435,600	1.9%
3	Texas	1,689,300	7.2%
31	Utah	201,700	0.9%
47	Vermont	65,600	0.3%
13	Virginia	552,500	2.4%
15	Washington	482,100	2.1%
38	West Virginia	134,200	0.6%
19	Wisconsin	452,500	1.9%
50	Wyoming	27,600	0.1%

RANK	STATE	EMPLOYEES	% of USA
1	California	2,650,500	11.4%
2	New York	2,019,400	8.7%
3	Texas	1,689,300	7.2%
4	Florida	1,285,000	5.5%
5	Pennsylvania	1,268,100	5.4%
6	Ohio	946,800	4.1%
7	Illinois	924,700	4.0%
8	Massachusetts	805,400	3.5%
9	New Jersey	696,700	3.0%
10	Michigan	674,600	2.9%
11	North Carolina	605,400	2.6%
12	Georgia	589,300	2.5%
13	Virginia	552,500	2.4%
14	Minnesota	543,100	2.3%
15	Washington	482,100	2.1%
16	Indiana	478,800	2.1%
17	Maryland	475,600	2.0%
18	Missouri	467,600	2.0%
19	Wisconsin	452,500	1.9%
20	Tennessee	435,600	1.9%
21	Arizona	424,700	1.8%
22	Colorado	338,800	1.5%
23	Connecticut	334,900	1.4%
24	Louisiana	316,200	1.4%
25	Oregon	280,300	1.2%
26	Kentucky	274,300	1.2%
27	South Carolina	252,500	1.1%
28	Alabama	240,700	1.0%
29	Oklahoma	240,100	1.0%
30	Iowa	235,100	1.0%
31	Utah	201,700	0.9%
32	Kansas	198,300	0.9%
33	Arkansas	190,400	0.8%
34	Nebraska	155,400	0.7%
35	Mississippi	145,700	0.6%
36	New Mexico	143,300	0.6%
37	Nevada	136,600	0.6%
38	West Virginia	134,200	0.6%
39	Maine	128,300	0.6%
40	New Hampshire	125,000	0.5%
41	Rhode Island	108,100	0.5%
42	Idaho	107,200	0.5%
43	Hawaii	86,100	0.4%
44	Delaware	79,700	0.3%
45	Montana	77,100	0.3%
46	South Dakota	72,300	0.3%
47	Vermont	65,600	0.3%
48	North Dakota	63,300	0.3%
49	Alaska	49,000	0.2%
50	Wyoming	27,600	0.1%
	District of Columbia	138,600	0.6%

Source: U.S. Department of Labor, Bureau of Labor Statistics
"State Employment and Unemployment" (press release, January 23, 2018, www.bls.gov/bls/newsrels.htm)
*Seasonally adjusted preliminary data as of December 2017. National total calculated through a different formula.

Percent of Nonfarm Employees in Education and Health Services in 2017

National Percent = 15.8% of Employees*

ALPHA ORDER

RANK	STATE	PERCENT
47	Alabama	11.9
27	Alaska	15.0
21	Arizona	15.3
24	Arkansas	15.2
20	California	15.6
45	Colorado	12.7
7	Connecticut	19.9
11	Delaware	17.6
29	Florida	14.8
44	Georgia	13.0
43	Hawaii	13.1
29	Idaho	14.8
21	Illinois	15.3
21	Indiana	15.3
31	Iowa	14.7
37	Kansas	14.0
37	Kentucky	14.0
19	Louisiana	16.0
6	Maine	20.6
12	Maryland	17.2
1	Massachusetts	22.1
24	Michigan	15.2
8	Minnesota	18.4
46	Mississippi	12.5
17	Missouri	16.2
18	Montana	16.1
27	Nebraska	15.0
49	Nevada	10.0
8	New Hampshire	18.4
14	New Jersey	16.9
14	New Mexico	16.9
4	New York	21.1
40	North Carolina	13.6
33	North Dakota	14.5
13	Ohio	17.1
34	Oklahoma	14.4
31	Oregon	14.7
3	Pennsylvania	21.2
2	Rhode Island	21.7
47	South Carolina	11.9
16	South Dakota	16.5
34	Tennessee	14.4
40	Texas	13.6
40	Utah	13.6
5	Vermont	20.7
39	Virginia	13.9
36	Washington	14.3
10	West Virginia	17.9
24	Wisconsin	15.2
50	Wyoming	9.9

RANK ORDER

RANK	STATE	PERCENT
1	Massachusetts	22.1
2	Rhode Island	21.7
3	Pennsylvania	21.2
4	New York	21.1
5	Vermont	20.7
6	Maine	20.6
7	Connecticut	19.9
8	Minnesota	18.4
8	New Hampshire	18.4
10	West Virginia	17.9
11	Delaware	17.6
12	Maryland	17.2
13	Ohio	17.1
14	New Jersey	16.9
14	New Mexico	16.9
16	South Dakota	16.5
17	Missouri	16.2
18	Montana	16.1
19	Louisiana	16.0
20	California	15.6
21	Arizona	15.3
21	Illinois	15.3
21	Indiana	15.3
24	Arkansas	15.2
24	Michigan	15.2
24	Wisconsin	15.2
27	Alaska	15.0
27	Nebraska	15.0
29	Florida	14.8
29	Idaho	14.8
31	Iowa	14.7
31	Oregon	14.7
33	North Dakota	14.5
34	Oklahoma	14.4
34	Tennessee	14.4
36	Washington	14.3
37	Kansas	14.0
37	Kentucky	14.0
39	Virginia	13.9
40	North Carolina	13.6
40	Texas	13.6
40	Utah	13.6
43	Hawaii	13.1
44	Georgia	13.0
45	Colorado	12.7
46	Mississippi	12.5
47	Alabama	11.9
47	South Carolina	11.9
49	Nevada	10.0
50	Wyoming	9.9
	District of Columbia	17.4

Source: CQ Press using data from U.S. Department of Labor, Bureau of Labor Statistics

"State Employment and Unemployment" (press release, January 23, 2018, www.bls.gov/bls/newsrels.htm)

*Seasonally adjusted preliminary data as of December 2017. National figure calculated through a different formula.

Employees in Financial Activities in 2017

National Total = 8,498,000 Employees*

ALPHA ORDER

RANK	STATE	EMPLOYEES	% of USA
27	Alabama	97,800	1.2%
49	Alaska	11,700	0.1%
13	Arizona	210,600	2.5%
35	Arkansas	51,500	0.6%
1	California	844,900	9.9%
17	Colorado	164,800	1.9%
23	Connecticut	132,400	1.6%
36	Delaware	48,000	0.6%
4	Florida	568,300	6.7%
9	Georgia	244,800	2.9%
44	Hawaii	28,100	0.3%
39	Idaho	35,700	0.4%
5	Illinois	393,800	4.6%
22	Indiana	137,900	1.6%
24	Iowa	114,600	1.3%
30	Kansas	86,300	1.0%
28	Kentucky	95,200	1.1%
29	Louisiana	92,800	1.1%
42	Maine	30,800	0.4%
21	Maryland	149,100	1.8%
11	Massachusetts	227,400	2.7%
12	Michigan	219,000	2.6%
15	Minnesota	176,100	2.1%
37	Mississippi	44,600	0.5%
16	Missouri	175,400	2.1%
46	Montana	25,200	0.3%
33	Nebraska	74,500	0.9%
34	Nevada	63,700	0.7%
38	New Hampshire	39,000	0.5%
8	New Jersey	249,000	2.9%
40	New Mexico	34,900	0.4%
3	New York	715,800	8.4%
10	North Carolina	230,900	2.7%
47	North Dakota	24,600	0.3%
7	Ohio	310,200	3.7%
32	Oklahoma	80,700	0.9%
26	Oregon	98,500	1.2%
6	Pennsylvania	319,400	3.8%
41	Rhode Island	33,600	0.4%
25	South Carolina	100,700	1.2%
43	South Dakota	30,100	0.4%
19	Tennessee	155,600	1.8%
2	Texas	765,200	9.0%
31	Utah	82,600	1.0%
48	Vermont	12,100	0.1%
14	Virginia	207,100	2.4%
18	Washington	158,900	1.9%
45	West Virginia	27,500	0.3%
20	Wisconsin	150,600	1.8%
50	Wyoming	11,000	0.1%

RANK ORDER

RANK	STATE	EMPLOYEES	% of USA
1	California	844,900	9.9%
2	Texas	765,200	9.0%
3	New York	715,800	8.4%
4	Florida	568,300	6.7%
5	Illinois	393,800	4.6%
6	Pennsylvania	319,400	3.8%
7	Ohio	310,200	3.7%
8	New Jersey	249,000	2.9%
9	Georgia	244,800	2.9%
10	North Carolina	230,900	2.7%
11	Massachusetts	227,400	2.7%
12	Michigan	219,000	2.6%
13	Arizona	210,600	2.5%
14	Virginia	207,100	2.4%
15	Minnesota	176,100	2.1%
16	Missouri	175,400	2.1%
17	Colorado	164,800	1.9%
18	Washington	158,900	1.9%
19	Tennessee	155,600	1.8%
20	Wisconsin	150,600	1.8%
21	Maryland	149,100	1.8%
22	Indiana	137,900	1.6%
23	Connecticut	132,400	1.6%
24	Iowa	114,600	1.3%
25	South Carolina	100,700	1.2%
26	Oregon	98,500	1.2%
27	Alabama	97,800	1.2%
28	Kentucky	95,200	1.1%
29	Louisiana	92,800	1.1%
30	Kansas	86,300	1.0%
31	Utah	82,600	1.0%
32	Oklahoma	80,700	0.9%
33	Nebraska	74,500	0.9%
34	Nevada	63,700	0.7%
35	Arkansas	51,500	0.6%
36	Delaware	48,000	0.6%
37	Mississippi	44,600	0.5%
38	New Hampshire	39,000	0.5%
39	Idaho	35,700	0.4%
40	New Mexico	34,900	0.4%
41	Rhode Island	33,600	0.4%
42	Maine	30,800	0.4%
43	South Dakota	30,100	0.4%
44	Hawaii	28,100	0.3%
45	West Virginia	27,500	0.3%
46	Montana	25,200	0.3%
47	North Dakota	24,600	0.3%
48	Vermont	12,100	0.1%
49	Alaska	11,700	0.1%
50	Wyoming	11,000	0.1%
	District of Columbia	29,700	0.3%

Source: U.S. Department of Labor, Bureau of Labor Statistics
"State Employment and Unemployment" (press release, January 23, 2018, www.bls.gov/bls/newsrels.htm)
*Seasonally adjusted preliminary data as of December 2017. National total calculated through a different formula. Financial activities include insurance and real estate.

Percent of Nonfarm Employees in Financial Activities in 2017

National Percent = 5.8% of Employees*

RANK	STATE	PERCENT
36	Alabama	4.8
50	Alaska	3.6
3	Arizona	7.6
44	Arkansas	4.1
31	California	5.0
11	Colorado	6.2
2	Connecticut	7.9
1	Delaware	10.6
9	Florida	6.5
22	Georgia	5.4
43	Hawaii	4.3
32	Idaho	4.9
9	Illinois	6.5
42	Indiana	4.4
5	Iowa	7.2
13	Kansas	6.1
32	Kentucky	4.9
39	Louisiana	4.7
32	Maine	4.9
22	Maryland	5.4
11	Massachusetts	6.2
32	Michigan	4.9
16	Minnesota	6.0
47	Mississippi	3.8
13	Missouri	6.1
24	Montana	5.3
5	Nebraska	7.2
39	Nevada	4.7
18	New Hampshire	5.7
16	New Jersey	6.0
44	New Mexico	4.1
4	New York	7.5
26	North Carolina	5.2
19	North Dakota	5.6
19	Ohio	5.6
36	Oklahoma	4.8
26	Oregon	5.2
24	Pennsylvania	5.3
8	Rhode Island	6.8
36	South Carolina	4.8
7	South Dakota	6.9
29	Tennessee	5.1
13	Texas	6.1
19	Utah	5.6
47	Vermont	3.8
26	Virginia	5.2
39	Washington	4.7
49	West Virginia	3.7
29	Wisconsin	5.1
46	Wyoming	4.0

RANK	STATE	PERCENT
1	Delaware	10.6
2	Connecticut	7.9
3	Arizona	7.6
4	New York	7.5
5	Iowa	7.2
5	Nebraska	7.2
7	South Dakota	6.9
8	Rhode Island	6.8
9	Florida	6.5
9	Illinois	6.5
11	Colorado	6.2
11	Massachusetts	6.2
13	Kansas	6.1
13	Missouri	6.1
13	Texas	6.1
16	Minnesota	6.0
16	New Jersey	6.0
18	New Hampshire	5.7
19	North Dakota	5.6
19	Ohio	5.6
19	Utah	5.6
22	Georgia	5.4
22	Maryland	5.4
24	Montana	5.3
24	Pennsylvania	5.3
26	North Carolina	5.2
26	Oregon	5.2
26	Virginia	5.2
29	Tennessee	5.1
29	Wisconsin	5.1
31	California	5.0
32	Idaho	4.9
32	Kentucky	4.9
32	Maine	4.9
32	Michigan	4.9
36	Alabama	4.8
36	Oklahoma	4.8
36	South Carolina	4.8
39	Louisiana	4.7
39	Nevada	4.7
39	Washington	4.7
42	Indiana	4.4
43	Hawaii	4.3
44	Arkansas	4.1
44	New Mexico	4.1
46	Wyoming	4.0
47	Mississippi	3.8
47	Vermont	3.8
49	West Virginia	3.7
50	Alaska	3.6

	District of Columbia	3.7

Source: CQ Press using data from U.S. Department of Labor, Bureau of Labor Statistics
  "State Employment and Unemployment" (press release, January 23, 2018, www.bls.gov/bls/newsrels.htm)
*Seasonally adjusted preliminary data as of December 2017. National figure calculated through a different formula. Financial activities include insurance and real estate.

Employees in Government in 2017

National Total = 22,341,000 Employees*

ALPHA ORDER

RANK	STATE	EMPLOYEES	% of USA
23	Alabama	384,700	1.7%
45	Alaska	80,700	0.4%
22	Arizona	413,100	1.8%
34	Arkansas	210,200	0.9%
1	California	2,593,900	11.6%
20	Colorado	428,800	1.9%
33	Connecticut	230,800	1.0%
48	Delaware	65,300	0.3%
4	Florida	1,108,900	5.0%
9	Georgia	698,100	3.1%
40	Hawaii	125,200	0.6%
39	Idaho	126,500	0.6%
5	Illinois	827,500	3.7%
16	Indiana	438,500	2.0%
29	Iowa	259,500	1.2%
30	Kansas	255,600	1.1%
27	Kentucky	316,800	1.4%
26	Louisiana	318,100	1.4%
41	Maine	99,300	0.4%
14	Maryland	512,600	2.3%
15	Massachusetts	459,100	2.1%
11	Michigan	615,100	2.8%
19	Minnesota	430,700	1.9%
32	Mississippi	243,800	1.1%
17	Missouri	433,300	1.9%
42	Montana	92,500	0.4%
36	Nebraska	172,100	0.8%
37	Nevada	165,700	0.7%
43	New Hampshire	89,900	0.4%
12	New Jersey	607,600	2.7%
35	New Mexico	190,700	0.9%
3	New York	1,453,900	6.5%
7	North Carolina	739,700	3.3%
44	North Dakota	83,600	0.4%
6	Ohio	766,900	3.4%
25	Oklahoma	353,900	1.6%
28	Oregon	310,900	1.4%
10	Pennsylvania	697,500	3.1%
49	Rhode Island	60,500	0.3%
24	South Carolina	368,400	1.6%
45	South Dakota	80,700	0.4%
17	Tennessee	433,300	1.9%
2	Texas	1,977,800	8.9%
31	Utah	245,700	1.1%
50	Vermont	55,700	0.2%
8	Virginia	713,100	3.2%
13	Washington	591,400	2.6%
38	West Virginia	154,500	0.7%
21	Wisconsin	414,900	1.9%
47	Wyoming	69,200	0.3%

RANK ORDER

RANK	STATE	EMPLOYEES	% of USA
1	California	2,593,900	11.6%
2	Texas	1,977,800	8.9%
3	New York	1,453,900	6.5%
4	Florida	1,108,900	5.0%
5	Illinois	827,500	3.7%
6	Ohio	766,900	3.4%
7	North Carolina	739,700	3.3%
8	Virginia	713,100	3.2%
9	Georgia	698,100	3.1%
10	Pennsylvania	697,500	3.1%
11	Michigan	615,100	2.8%
12	New Jersey	607,600	2.7%
13	Washington	591,400	2.6%
14	Maryland	512,600	2.3%
15	Massachusetts	459,100	2.1%
16	Indiana	438,500	2.0%
17	Missouri	433,300	1.9%
17	Tennessee	433,300	1.9%
19	Minnesota	430,700	1.9%
20	Colorado	428,800	1.9%
21	Wisconsin	414,900	1.9%
22	Arizona	413,100	1.8%
23	Alabama	384,700	1.7%
24	South Carolina	368,400	1.6%
25	Oklahoma	353,900	1.6%
26	Louisiana	318,100	1.4%
27	Kentucky	316,800	1.4%
28	Oregon	310,900	1.4%
29	Iowa	259,500	1.2%
30	Kansas	255,600	1.1%
31	Utah	245,700	1.1%
32	Mississippi	243,800	1.1%
33	Connecticut	230,800	1.0%
34	Arkansas	210,200	0.9%
35	New Mexico	190,700	0.9%
36	Nebraska	172,100	0.8%
37	Nevada	165,700	0.7%
38	West Virginia	154,500	0.7%
39	Idaho	126,500	0.6%
40	Hawaii	125,200	0.6%
41	Maine	99,300	0.4%
42	Montana	92,500	0.4%
43	New Hampshire	89,900	0.4%
44	North Dakota	83,600	0.4%
45	Alaska	80,700	0.4%
45	South Dakota	80,700	0.4%
47	Wyoming	69,200	0.3%
48	Delaware	65,300	0.3%
49	Rhode Island	60,500	0.3%
50	Vermont	55,700	0.2%
	District of Columbia	238,000	1.1%

Source: U.S. Department of Labor, Bureau of Labor Statistics
"State Employment and Unemployment" (press release, January 23, 2018, www.bls.gov/bls/newsrels.htm)
*Seasonally adjusted preliminary data as of December 2017. National total calculated through a different formula.

Percent of Nonfarm Employees in Government in 2017

National Percent = 15.2% of Employees*

RANK	STATE	PERCENT
9	Alabama	19.1
2	Alaska	24.7
34	Arizona	14.9
19	Arkansas	16.8
31	California	15.3
26	Colorado	16.1
43	Connecticut	13.7
37	Delaware	14.4
46	Florida	12.7
30	Georgia	15.4
10	Hawaii	19.0
17	Idaho	17.5
43	Illinois	13.7
39	Indiana	14.0
24	Iowa	16.2
13	Kansas	18.0
24	Kentucky	16.2
26	Louisiana	16.1
28	Maine	15.9
11	Maryland	18.6
47	Massachusetts	12.6
40	Michigan	13.9
36	Minnesota	14.6
5	Mississippi	21.0
33	Missouri	15.0
7	Montana	19.3
20	Nebraska	16.7
49	Nevada	12.1
45	New Hampshire	13.2
35	New Jersey	14.7
3	New Mexico	22.5
32	New York	15.2
21	North Carolina	16.6
8	North Dakota	19.2
42	Ohio	13.8
4	Oklahoma	21.2
23	Oregon	16.3
50	Pennsylvania	11.6
48	Rhode Island	12.2
18	South Carolina	17.4
12	South Dakota	18.4
38	Tennessee	14.3
28	Texas	15.9
22	Utah	16.5
15	Vermont	17.6
13	Virginia	18.0
15	Washington	17.6
6	West Virginia	20.7
40	Wisconsin	13.9
1	Wyoming	24.9

RANK	STATE	PERCENT
1	Wyoming	24.9
2	Alaska	24.7
3	New Mexico	22.5
4	Oklahoma	21.2
5	Mississippi	21.0
6	West Virginia	20.7
7	Montana	19.3
8	North Dakota	19.2
9	Alabama	19.1
10	Hawaii	19.0
11	Maryland	18.6
12	South Dakota	18.4
13	Kansas	18.0
13	Virginia	18.0
15	Vermont	17.6
15	Washington	17.6
17	Idaho	17.5
18	South Carolina	17.4
19	Arkansas	16.8
20	Nebraska	16.7
21	North Carolina	16.6
22	Utah	16.5
23	Oregon	16.3
24	Iowa	16.2
24	Kentucky	16.2
26	Colorado	16.1
26	Louisiana	16.1
28	Maine	15.9
28	Texas	15.9
30	Georgia	15.4
31	California	15.3
32	New York	15.2
33	Missouri	15.0
34	Arizona	14.9
35	New Jersey	14.7
36	Minnesota	14.6
37	Delaware	14.4
38	Tennessee	14.3
39	Indiana	14.0
40	Michigan	13.9
40	Wisconsin	13.9
42	Ohio	13.8
43	Connecticut	13.7
43	Illinois	13.7
45	New Hampshire	13.2
46	Florida	12.7
47	Massachusetts	12.6
48	Rhode Island	12.2
49	Nevada	12.1
50	Pennsylvania	11.6

District of Columbia   29.9

Source: CQ Press using data from U.S. Department of Labor, Bureau of Labor Statistics
"State Employment and Unemployment" (press release, January 23, 2018, www.bls.gov/bls/newsrels.htm)
*Seasonally adjusted preliminary data as of December 2017. National figure calculated through a different formula.

Employees in Leisure and Hospitality in 2017

National Total = 16,050,000 Employees*

ALPHA ORDER

RANK	STATE	EMPLOYEES	% of USA
27	Alabama	208,300	1.3%
49	Alaska	36,300	0.2%
18	Arizona	327,200	2.0%
36	Arkansas	116,500	0.7%
1	California	1,985,300	12.4%
16	Colorado	335,700	2.1%
30	Connecticut	153,300	1.0%
45	Delaware	50,300	0.3%
3	Florida	1,203,100	7.5%
8	Georgia	495,900	3.1%
35	Hawaii	122,400	0.8%
40	Idaho	73,300	0.5%
5	Illinois	595,500	3.7%
20	Indiana	307,700	1.9%
31	Iowa	149,300	0.9%
34	Kansas	128,300	0.8%
28	Kentucky	196,100	1.2%
25	Louisiana	235,800	1.5%
43	Maine	65,600	0.4%
22	Maryland	273,400	1.7%
13	Massachusetts	372,800	2.3%
10	Michigan	443,100	2.8%
23	Minnesota	262,900	1.6%
33	Mississippi	137,500	0.9%
19	Missouri	317,800	2.0%
42	Montana	67,600	0.4%
38	Nebraska	96,700	0.6%
14	Nevada	350,900	2.2%
41	New Hampshire	72,300	0.5%
12	New Jersey	389,000	2.4%
37	New Mexico	101,000	0.6%
4	New York	943,600	5.9%
9	North Carolina	492,800	3.1%
48	North Dakota	37,000	0.2%
7	Ohio	570,800	3.6%
29	Oklahoma	168,800	1.1%
26	Oregon	208,900	1.3%
6	Pennsylvania	588,100	3.7%
44	Rhode Island	59,200	0.4%
24	South Carolina	253,800	1.6%
46	South Dakota	48,200	0.3%
17	Tennessee	333,100	2.1%
2	Texas	1,355,000	8.4%
31	Utah	149,300	0.9%
47	Vermont	38,900	0.2%
11	Virginia	401,800	2.5%
15	Washington	338,700	2.1%
39	West Virginia	75,600	0.5%
21	Wisconsin	286,800	1.8%
50	Wyoming	35,200	0.2%

RANK ORDER

RANK	STATE	EMPLOYEES	% of USA
1	California	1,985,300	12.4%
2	Texas	1,355,000	8.4%
3	Florida	1,203,100	7.5%
4	New York	943,600	5.9%
5	Illinois	595,500	3.7%
6	Pennsylvania	588,100	3.7%
7	Ohio	570,800	3.6%
8	Georgia	495,900	3.1%
9	North Carolina	492,800	3.1%
10	Michigan	443,100	2.8%
11	Virginia	401,800	2.5%
12	New Jersey	389,000	2.4%
13	Massachusetts	372,800	2.3%
14	Nevada	350,900	2.2%
15	Washington	338,700	2.1%
16	Colorado	335,700	2.1%
17	Tennessee	333,100	2.1%
18	Arizona	327,200	2.0%
19	Missouri	317,800	2.0%
20	Indiana	307,700	1.9%
21	Wisconsin	286,800	1.8%
22	Maryland	273,400	1.7%
23	Minnesota	262,900	1.6%
24	South Carolina	253,800	1.6%
25	Louisiana	235,800	1.5%
26	Oregon	208,900	1.3%
27	Alabama	208,300	1.3%
28	Kentucky	196,100	1.2%
29	Oklahoma	168,800	1.1%
30	Connecticut	153,300	1.0%
31	Iowa	149,300	0.9%
31	Utah	149,300	0.9%
33	Mississippi	137,500	0.9%
34	Kansas	128,300	0.8%
35	Hawaii	122,400	0.8%
36	Arkansas	116,500	0.7%
37	New Mexico	101,000	0.6%
38	Nebraska	96,700	0.6%
39	West Virginia	75,600	0.5%
40	Idaho	73,300	0.5%
41	New Hampshire	72,300	0.5%
42	Montana	67,600	0.4%
43	Maine	65,600	0.4%
44	Rhode Island	59,200	0.4%
45	Delaware	50,300	0.3%
46	South Dakota	48,200	0.3%
47	Vermont	38,900	0.2%
48	North Dakota	37,000	0.2%
49	Alaska	36,300	0.2%
50	Wyoming	35,200	0.2%
	District of Columbia	80,900	0.5%

Source: U.S. Department of Labor, Bureau of Labor Statistics
"State Employment and Unemployment" (press release, January 23, 2018, www.bls.gov/bls/newsrels.htm)
*Seasonally adjusted preliminary data as of December 2017. National total calculated through a different formula.

Percent of Nonfarm Employees in Leisure and Hospitality in 2017

National Percent = 10.9% of Employees*

ALPHA ORDER

RANK	STATE	PERCENT
26	Alabama	10.3
15	Alaska	11.1
12	Arizona	11.8
45	Arkansas	9.3
14	California	11.7
6	Colorado	12.6
47	Connecticut	9.1
15	Delaware	11.1
4	Florida	13.8
18	Georgia	11.0
2	Hawaii	18.6
29	Idaho	10.1
39	Illinois	9.8
39	Indiana	9.8
45	Iowa	9.3
47	Kansas	9.1
34	Kentucky	10.0
9	Louisiana	11.9
25	Maine	10.5
37	Maryland	9.9
28	Massachusetts	10.2
34	Michigan	10.0
49	Minnesota	8.9
12	Mississippi	11.8
18	Missouri	11.0
3	Montana	14.1
43	Nebraska	9.4
1	Nevada	25.7
24	New Hampshire	10.6
43	New Jersey	9.4
9	New Mexico	11.9
37	New York	9.9
15	North Carolina	11.1
50	North Dakota	8.5
26	Ohio	10.3
29	Oklahoma	10.1
18	Oregon	11.0
39	Pennsylvania	9.8
9	Rhode Island	11.9
8	South Carolina	12.0
18	South Dakota	11.0
18	Tennessee	11.0
23	Texas	10.9
34	Utah	10.0
7	Vermont	12.3
29	Virginia	10.1
29	Washington	10.1
29	West Virginia	10.1
42	Wisconsin	9.6
5	Wyoming	12.7

RANK ORDER

RANK	STATE	PERCENT
1	Nevada	25.7
2	Hawaii	18.6
3	Montana	14.1
4	Florida	13.8
5	Wyoming	12.7
6	Colorado	12.6
7	Vermont	12.3
8	South Carolina	12.0
9	Louisiana	11.9
9	New Mexico	11.9
9	Rhode Island	11.9
12	Arizona	11.8
12	Mississippi	11.8
14	California	11.7
15	Alaska	11.1
15	Delaware	11.1
15	North Carolina	11.1
18	Georgia	11.0
18	Missouri	11.0
18	Oregon	11.0
18	South Dakota	11.0
18	Tennessee	11.0
23	Texas	10.9
24	New Hampshire	10.6
25	Maine	10.5
26	Alabama	10.3
26	Ohio	10.3
28	Massachusetts	10.2
29	Idaho	10.1
29	Oklahoma	10.1
29	Virginia	10.1
29	Washington	10.1
29	West Virginia	10.1
34	Kentucky	10.0
34	Michigan	10.0
34	Utah	10.0
37	Maryland	9.9
37	New York	9.9
39	Illinois	9.8
39	Indiana	9.8
39	Pennsylvania	9.8
42	Wisconsin	9.6
43	Nebraska	9.4
43	New Jersey	9.4
45	Arkansas	9.3
45	Iowa	9.3
47	Connecticut	9.1
47	Kansas	9.1
49	Minnesota	8.9
50	North Dakota	8.5

District of Columbia   10.2

Source: CQ Press using data from U.S. Department of Labor, Bureau of Labor Statistics
"State Employment and Unemployment" (press release, January 23, 2018, www.bls.gov/bls/newsrels.htm)
*Seasonally adjusted preliminary data as of December 2017. National figure calculated through a different formula.

Employees in Manufacturing in 2017

National Total = 12,539,000 Employees*

ALPHA ORDER

RANK	STATE	EMPLOYEES	% of USA
17	Alabama	269,200	2.1%
50	Alaska	9,100	0.1%
25	Arizona	167,100	1.3%
26	Arkansas	160,800	1.3%
1	California	1,302,300	10.4%
30	Colorado	143,200	1.1%
27	Connecticut	160,300	1.3%
45	Delaware	26,000	0.2%
12	Florida	373,900	3.0%
11	Georgia	387,100	3.1%
48	Hawaii	13,800	0.1%
37	Idaho	67,700	0.5%
5	Illinois	577,600	4.6%
7	Indiana	534,500	4.3%
23	Iowa	222,600	1.8%
28	Kansas	158,600	1.3%
18	Kentucky	252,200	2.0%
31	Louisiana	134,300	1.1%
38	Maine	50,900	0.4%
34	Maryland	104,400	0.8%
21	Massachusetts	247,300	2.0%
4	Michigan	607,100	4.8%
14	Minnesota	321,200	2.6%
29	Mississippi	144,500	1.2%
16	Missouri	269,700	2.2%
47	Montana	19,800	0.2%
35	Nebraska	98,400	0.8%
39	Nevada	46,100	0.4%
36	New Hampshire	69,300	0.6%
20	New Jersey	248,500	2.0%
44	New Mexico	26,400	0.2%
10	New York	435,300	3.5%
9	North Carolina	467,500	3.7%
46	North Dakota	24,100	0.2%
3	Ohio	698,900	5.6%
33	Oklahoma	130,500	1.0%
24	Oregon	195,300	1.6%
6	Pennsylvania	553,000	4.4%
42	Rhode Island	42,000	0.3%
19	South Carolina	250,900	2.0%
41	South Dakota	42,900	0.3%
13	Tennessee	346,400	2.8%
2	Texas	878,200	7.0%
32	Utah	131,600	1.0%
43	Vermont	28,700	0.2%
22	Virginia	235,500	1.9%
15	Washington	286,900	2.3%
40	West Virginia	46,000	0.4%
8	Wisconsin	479,900	3.8%
49	Wyoming	9,400	0.1%

RANK ORDER

RANK	STATE	EMPLOYEES	% of USA
1	California	1,302,300	10.4%
2	Texas	878,200	7.0%
3	Ohio	698,900	5.6%
4	Michigan	607,100	4.8%
5	Illinois	577,600	4.6%
6	Pennsylvania	553,000	4.4%
7	Indiana	534,500	4.3%
8	Wisconsin	479,900	3.8%
9	North Carolina	467,500	3.7%
10	New York	435,300	3.5%
11	Georgia	387,100	3.1%
12	Florida	373,900	3.0%
13	Tennessee	346,400	2.8%
14	Minnesota	321,200	2.6%
15	Washington	286,900	2.3%
16	Missouri	269,700	2.2%
17	Alabama	269,200	2.1%
18	Kentucky	252,200	2.0%
19	South Carolina	250,900	2.0%
20	New Jersey	248,500	2.0%
21	Massachusetts	247,300	2.0%
22	Virginia	235,500	1.9%
23	Iowa	222,600	1.8%
24	Oregon	195,300	1.6%
25	Arizona	167,100	1.3%
26	Arkansas	160,800	1.3%
27	Connecticut	160,300	1.3%
28	Kansas	158,600	1.3%
29	Mississippi	144,500	1.2%
30	Colorado	143,200	1.1%
31	Louisiana	134,300	1.1%
32	Utah	131,600	1.0%
33	Oklahoma	130,500	1.0%
34	Maryland	104,400	0.8%
35	Nebraska	98,400	0.8%
36	New Hampshire	69,300	0.6%
37	Idaho	67,700	0.5%
38	Maine	50,900	0.4%
39	Nevada	46,100	0.4%
40	West Virginia	46,000	0.4%
41	South Dakota	42,900	0.3%
42	Rhode Island	42,000	0.3%
43	Vermont	28,700	0.2%
44	New Mexico	26,400	0.2%
45	Delaware	26,000	0.2%
46	North Dakota	24,100	0.2%
47	Montana	19,800	0.2%
48	Hawaii	13,800	0.1%
49	Wyoming	9,400	0.1%
50	Alaska	9,100	0.1%
	District of Columbia**	NA	NA

Source: U.S. Department of Labor, Bureau of Labor Statistics
   "State Employment and Unemployment" (press release, January 23, 2018, www.bls.gov/bls/newsrels.htm)
*Seasonally adjusted preliminary data as of December 2017. National total calculated through a different formula.
**The Bureau of Labor Statistics does not publish seasonally adjusted figures in this category for these states.

Percent of Nonfarm Employees in Manufacturing in 2017

National Percent = 8.5% of Employees*

ALPHA ORDER

RANK	STATE	PERCENT
5	Alabama	13.3
49	Alaska	2.8
36	Arizona	6.0
6	Arkansas	12.9
31	California	7.7
41	Colorado	5.4
18	Connecticut	9.5
39	Delaware	5.7
43	Florida	4.3
26	Georgia	8.6
50	Hawaii	2.1
21	Idaho	9.4
18	Illinois	9.5
1	Indiana	17.0
3	Iowa	13.9
12	Kansas	11.2
6	Kentucky	12.9
33	Louisiana	6.8
29	Maine	8.2
45	Maryland	3.8
33	Massachusetts	6.8
4	Michigan	13.7
13	Minnesota	10.9
9	Mississippi	12.4
22	Missouri	9.3
44	Montana	4.1
18	Nebraska	9.5
46	Nevada	3.4
16	New Hampshire	10.2
36	New Jersey	6.0
48	New Mexico	3.1
42	New York	4.6
14	North Carolina	10.5
40	North Dakota	5.5
8	Ohio	12.6
30	Oklahoma	7.8
15	Oregon	10.3
23	Pennsylvania	9.2
28	Rhode Island	8.4
10	South Carolina	11.9
17	South Dakota	9.8
11	Tennessee	11.5
32	Texas	7.1
25	Utah	8.8
24	Vermont	9.1
38	Virginia	5.9
27	Washington	8.5
35	West Virginia	6.1
2	Wisconsin	16.1
46	Wyoming	3.4

RANK ORDER

RANK	STATE	PERCENT
1	Indiana	17.0
2	Wisconsin	16.1
3	Iowa	13.9
4	Michigan	13.7
5	Alabama	13.3
6	Arkansas	12.9
6	Kentucky	12.9
8	Ohio	12.6
9	Mississippi	12.4
10	South Carolina	11.9
11	Tennessee	11.5
12	Kansas	11.2
13	Minnesota	10.9
14	North Carolina	10.5
15	Oregon	10.3
16	New Hampshire	10.2
17	South Dakota	9.8
18	Connecticut	9.5
18	Illinois	9.5
18	Nebraska	9.5
21	Idaho	9.4
22	Missouri	9.3
23	Pennsylvania	9.2
24	Vermont	9.1
25	Utah	8.8
26	Georgia	8.6
27	Washington	8.5
28	Rhode Island	8.4
29	Maine	8.2
30	Oklahoma	7.8
31	California	7.7
32	Texas	7.1
33	Louisiana	6.8
33	Massachusetts	6.8
35	West Virginia	6.1
36	Arizona	6.0
36	New Jersey	6.0
38	Virginia	5.9
39	Delaware	5.7
40	North Dakota	5.5
41	Colorado	5.4
42	New York	4.6
43	Florida	4.3
44	Montana	4.1
45	Maryland	3.8
46	Nevada	3.4
46	Wyoming	3.4
48	New Mexico	3.1
49	Alaska	2.8
50	Hawaii	2.1
	District of Columbia**	NA

Source: CQ Press using data from U.S. Department of Labor, Bureau of Labor Statistics
  "State Employment and Unemployment" (press release, January 23, 2018, www.bls.gov/bls/newsrels.htm)
*Seasonally adjusted preliminary data as of December 2017. National figure calculated through a different formula.
**The Bureau of Labor Statistics does not publish seasonally adjusted figures in this category for these states.

Employees in Mining and Logging in 2017

National Total = 730,000 Employees*

ALPHA ORDER

RANK	STATE	EMPLOYEES	% of USA
16	Alabama	9,600	1.3%
12	Alaska	13,000	1.8%
13	Arizona	11,200	1.5%
29	Arkansas	6,000	0.8%
5	California	22,300	3.1%
7	Colorado	21,700	3.0%
47	Connecticut	600	0.1%
NA	Delaware**	NA	NA
31	Florida	5,700	0.8%
14	Georgia	10,700	1.5%
NA	Hawaii**	NA	NA
37	Idaho	3,600	0.5%
18	Illinois	8,000	1.1%
28	Indiana	6,400	0.9%
39	Iowa	2,500	0.3%
22	Kansas	7,300	1.0%
17	Kentucky	9,500	1.3%
3	Louisiana	35,600	4.9%
38	Maine	2,600	0.4%
40	Maryland	1,300	0.2%
42	Massachusetts	1,100	0.2%
22	Michigan	7,300	1.0%
25	Minnesota	6,900	0.9%
26	Mississippi	6,800	0.9%
33	Missouri	4,400	0.6%
22	Montana	7,300	1.0%
43	Nebraska	1,000	0.1%
11	Nevada	14,200	1.9%
43	New Hampshire	1,000	0.1%
40	New Jersey	1,300	0.2%
10	New Mexico	18,000	2.5%
32	New York	5,100	0.7%
30	North Carolina	5,900	0.8%
9	North Dakota	19,100	2.6%
15	Ohio	10,400	1.4%
2	Oklahoma	48,900	6.7%
19	Oregon	7,900	1.1%
4	Pennsylvania	23,600	3.2%
48	Rhode Island	200	0.0%
35	South Carolina	4,200	0.6%
43	South Dakota	1,000	0.1%
34	Tennessee	4,300	0.6%
1	Texas	249,400	34.2%
21	Utah	7,600	1.0%
46	Vermont	800	0.1%
19	Virginia	7,900	1.1%
27	Washington	6,600	0.9%
6	West Virginia	21,900	3.0%
36	Wisconsin	3,800	0.5%
8	Wyoming	20,700	2.8%

RANK ORDER

RANK	STATE	EMPLOYEES	% of USA
1	Texas	249,400	34.2%
2	Oklahoma	48,900	6.7%
3	Louisiana	35,600	4.9%
4	Pennsylvania	23,600	3.2%
5	California	22,300	3.1%
6	West Virginia	21,900	3.0%
7	Colorado	21,700	3.0%
8	Wyoming	20,700	2.8%
9	North Dakota	19,100	2.6%
10	New Mexico	18,000	2.5%
11	Nevada	14,200	1.9%
12	Alaska	13,000	1.8%
13	Arizona	11,200	1.5%
14	Georgia	10,700	1.5%
15	Ohio	10,400	1.4%
16	Alabama	9,600	1.3%
17	Kentucky	9,500	1.3%
18	Illinois	8,000	1.1%
19	Oregon	7,900	1.1%
19	Virginia	7,900	1.1%
21	Utah	7,600	1.0%
22	Kansas	7,300	1.0%
22	Michigan	7,300	1.0%
22	Montana	7,300	1.0%
25	Minnesota	6,900	0.9%
26	Mississippi	6,800	0.9%
27	Washington	6,600	0.9%
28	Indiana	6,400	0.9%
29	Arkansas	6,000	0.8%
30	North Carolina	5,900	0.8%
31	Florida	5,700	0.8%
32	New York	5,100	0.7%
33	Missouri	4,400	0.6%
34	Tennessee	4,300	0.6%
35	South Carolina	4,200	0.6%
36	Wisconsin	3,800	0.5%
37	Idaho	3,600	0.5%
38	Maine	2,600	0.4%
39	Iowa	2,500	0.3%
40	Maryland	1,300	0.2%
40	New Jersey	1,300	0.2%
42	Massachusetts	1,100	0.2%
43	Nebraska	1,000	0.1%
43	New Hampshire	1,000	0.1%
43	South Dakota	1,000	0.1%
46	Vermont	800	0.1%
47	Connecticut	600	0.1%
48	Rhode Island	200	0.0%
NA	Delaware**	NA	NA
NA	Hawaii**	NA	NA
	District of Columbia**	NA	NA

Source: U.S. Department of Labor, Bureau of Labor Statistics
"State Employment and Unemployment" (press release, January 23, 2018, www.bls.gov/bls/newsrels.htm)
*Not seasonally adjusted preliminary data as of December 2017. National total calculated through a different formula.
**The Bureau of Labor Statistics does not publish figures in this category for these states.

Percent of Nonfarm Employees in Mining and Logging in 2017

National Percent = 0.5% of Employees*

ALPHA ORDER

RANK	STATE	PERCENT
13	Alabama	0.5
3	Alaska	4.1
19	Arizona	0.4
13	Arkansas	0.5
35	California	0.1
11	Colorado	0.8
44	Connecticut	0.0
NA	Delaware**	NA
35	Florida	0.1
23	Georgia	0.2
NA	Hawaii**	NA
13	Idaho	0.5
35	Illinois	0.1
23	Indiana	0.2
23	Iowa	0.2
13	Kansas	0.5
13	Kentucky	0.5
8	Louisiana	1.8
19	Maine	0.4
44	Maryland	0.0
44	Massachusetts	0.0
23	Michigan	0.2
23	Minnesota	0.2
12	Mississippi	0.6
23	Missouri	0.2
9	Montana	1.5
35	Nebraska	0.1
10	Nevada	1.0
35	New Hampshire	0.1
44	New Jersey	0.0
6	New Mexico	2.1
35	New York	0.1
35	North Carolina	0.1
2	North Dakota	4.4
23	Ohio	0.2
4	Oklahoma	2.9
19	Oregon	0.4
19	Pennsylvania	0.4
44	Rhode Island	0.0
23	South Carolina	0.2
23	South Dakota	0.2
35	Tennessee	0.1
7	Texas	2.0
13	Utah	0.5
23	Vermont	0.2
23	Virginia	0.2
23	Washington	0.2
4	West Virginia	2.9
35	Wisconsin	0.1
1	Wyoming	7.5

RANK ORDER

RANK	STATE	PERCENT
1	Wyoming	7.5
2	North Dakota	4.4
3	Alaska	4.1
4	Oklahoma	2.9
4	West Virginia	2.9
6	New Mexico	2.1
7	Texas	2.0
8	Louisiana	1.8
9	Montana	1.5
10	Nevada	1.0
11	Colorado	0.8
12	Mississippi	0.6
13	Alabama	0.5
13	Arkansas	0.5
13	Idaho	0.5
13	Kansas	0.5
13	Kentucky	0.5
13	Utah	0.5
19	Arizona	0.4
19	Maine	0.4
19	Oregon	0.4
19	Pennsylvania	0.4
23	Georgia	0.2
23	Indiana	0.2
23	Iowa	0.2
23	Michigan	0.2
23	Minnesota	0.2
23	Missouri	0.2
23	Ohio	0.2
23	South Carolina	0.2
23	South Dakota	0.2
23	Vermont	0.2
23	Virginia	0.2
23	Washington	0.2
35	California	0.1
35	Florida	0.1
35	Illinois	0.1
35	Nebraska	0.1
35	New Hampshire	0.1
35	New York	0.1
35	North Carolina	0.1
35	Tennessee	0.1
35	Wisconsin	0.1
44	Connecticut	0.0
44	Maryland	0.0
44	Massachusetts	0.0
44	New Jersey	0.0
44	Rhode Island	0.0
NA	Delaware**	NA
NA	Hawaii**	NA
	District of Columbia**	NA

Source: CQ Press using data from U.S. Department of Labor, Bureau of Labor Statistics
"State Employment and Unemployment" (press release, January 23, 2018, www.bls.gov/bls/newsrels.htm)
*Not seasonally adjusted preliminary data as of December 2017. National figure calculated through a different formula.
**The Bureau of Labor Statistics does not publish seasonally adjusted figures in this category for these states.

Employees in Professional and Business Services in 2017

National Total = 20,943,000 Employees*

ALPHA ORDER

RANK	STATE	EMPLOYEES	% of USA
25	Alabama	240,500	1.1%
49	Alaska	27,900	0.1%
15	Arizona	427,500	2.0%
33	Arkansas	147,000	0.7%
1	California	2,577,400	12.3%
16	Colorado	425,300	2.0%
27	Connecticut	219,000	1.0%
44	Delaware	60,600	0.3%
3	Florida	1,350,200	6.4%
9	Georgia	691,600	3.3%
39	Hawaii	86,600	0.4%
38	Idaho	87,200	0.4%
5	Illinois	951,500	4.5%
21	Indiana	335,200	1.6%
34	Iowa	142,500	0.7%
31	Kansas	183,400	0.9%
26	Kentucky	230,700	1.1%
28	Louisiana	213,400	1.0%
41	Maine	67,700	0.3%
14	Maryland	458,700	2.2%
13	Massachusetts	572,800	2.7%
10	Michigan	677,300	3.2%
20	Minnesota	380,000	1.8%
36	Mississippi	110,200	0.5%
19	Missouri	398,000	1.9%
45	Montana	43,300	0.2%
35	Nebraska	124,100	0.6%
30	Nevada	191,300	0.9%
40	New Hampshire	78,600	0.4%
11	New Jersey	669,200	3.2%
37	New Mexico	103,400	0.5%
4	New York	1,348,500	6.4%
12	North Carolina	655,200	3.1%
46	North Dakota	36,100	0.2%
8	Ohio	723,100	3.5%
32	Oklahoma	180,400	0.9%
24	Oregon	248,900	1.2%
6	Pennsylvania	820,500	3.9%
42	Rhode Island	65,600	0.3%
23	South Carolina	280,000	1.3%
47	South Dakota	31,800	0.2%
18	Tennessee	412,200	2.0%
2	Texas	1,699,800	8.1%
29	Utah	211,800	1.0%
48	Vermont	28,400	0.1%
7	Virginia	725,300	3.5%
17	Washington	415,300	2.0%
43	West Virginia	64,600	0.3%
22	Wisconsin	329,100	1.6%
50	Wyoming	17,700	0.1%

RANK ORDER

RANK	STATE	EMPLOYEES	% of USA
1	California	2,577,400	12.3%
2	Texas	1,699,800	8.1%
3	Florida	1,350,200	6.4%
4	New York	1,348,500	6.4%
5	Illinois	951,500	4.5%
6	Pennsylvania	820,500	3.9%
7	Virginia	725,300	3.5%
8	Ohio	723,100	3.5%
9	Georgia	691,600	3.3%
10	Michigan	677,300	3.2%
11	New Jersey	669,200	3.2%
12	North Carolina	655,200	3.1%
13	Massachusetts	572,800	2.7%
14	Maryland	458,700	2.2%
15	Arizona	427,500	2.0%
16	Colorado	425,300	2.0%
17	Washington	415,300	2.0%
18	Tennessee	412,200	2.0%
19	Missouri	398,000	1.9%
20	Minnesota	380,000	1.8%
21	Indiana	335,200	1.6%
22	Wisconsin	329,100	1.6%
23	South Carolina	280,000	1.3%
24	Oregon	248,900	1.2%
25	Alabama	240,500	1.1%
26	Kentucky	230,700	1.1%
27	Connecticut	219,000	1.0%
28	Louisiana	213,400	1.0%
29	Utah	211,800	1.0%
30	Nevada	191,300	0.9%
31	Kansas	183,400	0.9%
32	Oklahoma	180,400	0.9%
33	Arkansas	147,000	0.7%
34	Iowa	142,500	0.7%
35	Nebraska	124,100	0.6%
36	Mississippi	110,200	0.5%
37	New Mexico	103,400	0.5%
38	Idaho	87,200	0.4%
39	Hawaii	86,600	0.4%
40	New Hampshire	78,600	0.4%
41	Maine	67,700	0.3%
42	Rhode Island	65,600	0.3%
43	West Virginia	64,600	0.3%
44	Delaware	60,600	0.3%
45	Montana	43,300	0.2%
46	North Dakota	36,100	0.2%
47	South Dakota	31,800	0.2%
48	Vermont	28,400	0.1%
49	Alaska	27,900	0.1%
50	Wyoming	17,700	0.1%
	District of Columbia	169,600	0.8%

Source: U.S. Department of Labor, Bureau of Labor Statistics
    "State Employment and Unemployment" (press release, January 23, 2018, www.bls.gov/bls/newsrels.htm)
*Seasonally adjusted preliminary data as of December 2017. National total calculated through a different formula.

Percent of Nonfarm Employees in Professional and Business Services in 2017

National Percent = 14.2% of Employees*

ALPHA ORDER

RANK	STATE	PERCENT
33	Alabama	11.9
47	Alaska	8.5
8	Arizona	15.4
34	Arkansas	11.8
11	California	15.2
4	Colorado	15.9
25	Connecticut	13.0
20	Delaware	13.4
7	Florida	15.5
9	Georgia	15.3
23	Hawaii	13.1
31	Idaho	12.1
5	Illinois	15.7
41	Indiana	10.7
45	Iowa	8.9
27	Kansas	12.9
34	Kentucky	11.8
39	Louisiana	10.8
38	Maine	10.9
2	Maryland	16.6
5	Massachusetts	15.7
9	Michigan	15.3
28	Minnesota	12.8
42	Mississippi	9.5
16	Missouri	13.8
43	Montana	9.0
32	Nebraska	12.0
15	Nevada	14.0
36	New Hampshire	11.6
3	New Jersey	16.2
30	New Mexico	12.2
14	New York	14.1
12	North Carolina	14.7
48	North Dakota	8.3
25	Ohio	13.0
39	Oklahoma	10.8
23	Oregon	13.1
17	Pennsylvania	13.7
21	Rhode Island	13.2
21	South Carolina	13.2
49	South Dakota	7.2
19	Tennessee	13.6
17	Texas	13.7
13	Utah	14.2
43	Vermont	9.0
1	Virginia	18.3
29	Washington	12.4
46	West Virginia	8.6
37	Wisconsin	11.1
50	Wyoming	6.4

RANK ORDER

RANK	STATE	PERCENT
1	Virginia	18.3
2	Maryland	16.6
3	New Jersey	16.2
4	Colorado	15.9
5	Illinois	15.7
5	Massachusetts	15.7
7	Florida	15.5
8	Arizona	15.4
9	Georgia	15.3
9	Michigan	15.3
11	California	15.2
12	North Carolina	14.7
13	Utah	14.2
14	New York	14.1
15	Nevada	14.0
16	Missouri	13.8
17	Pennsylvania	13.7
17	Texas	13.7
19	Tennessee	13.6
20	Delaware	13.4
21	Rhode Island	13.2
21	South Carolina	13.2
23	Hawaii	13.1
23	Oregon	13.1
25	Connecticut	13.0
25	Ohio	13.0
27	Kansas	12.9
28	Minnesota	12.8
29	Washington	12.4
30	New Mexico	12.2
31	Idaho	12.1
32	Nebraska	12.0
33	Alabama	11.9
34	Arkansas	11.8
34	Kentucky	11.8
36	New Hampshire	11.6
37	Wisconsin	11.1
38	Maine	10.9
39	Louisiana	10.8
39	Oklahoma	10.8
41	Indiana	10.7
42	Mississippi	9.5
43	Montana	9.0
43	Vermont	9.0
45	Iowa	8.9
46	West Virginia	8.6
47	Alaska	8.5
48	North Dakota	8.3
49	South Dakota	7.2
50	Wyoming	6.4

District of Columbia — 21.3

Source: CQ Press using data from U.S. Department of Labor, Bureau of Labor Statistics
"State Employment and Unemployment" (press release, January 23, 2018, www.bls.gov/bls/newsrels.htm)
*Seasonally adjusted preliminary data as of December 2017. National figure calculated through a different formula.

Employees in Trade, Transportation, and Public Utilities in 2017

National Total = 27,448,000 Employees*

ALPHA ORDER

RANK	STATE	EMPLOYEES	% of USA
26	Alabama	373,900	1.4%
48	Alaska	64,500	0.2%
20	Arizona	514,600	1.9%
33	Arkansas	251,100	0.9%
1	California	3,037,000	11.1%
22	Colorado	465,400	1.7%
30	Connecticut	300,300	1.1%
46	Delaware	79,700	0.3%
3	Florida	1,771,400	6.5%
8	Georgia	942,300	3.4%
41	Hawaii	121,800	0.4%
37	Idaho	142,300	0.5%
5	Illinois	1,206,600	4.4%
15	Indiana	596,800	2.2%
28	Iowa	320,700	1.2%
32	Kansas	265,100	1.0%
24	Kentucky	402,900	1.5%
25	Louisiana	376,700	1.4%
42	Maine	120,800	0.4%
21	Maryland	468,900	1.7%
16	Massachusetts	577,700	2.1%
11	Michigan	783,300	2.9%
19	Minnesota	542,200	2.0%
35	Mississippi	233,800	0.9%
17	Missouri	546,300	2.0%
44	Montana	94,100	0.3%
36	Nebraska	203,300	0.7%
34	Nevada	248,800	0.9%
39	New Hampshire	139,000	0.5%
9	New Jersey	870,000	3.2%
38	New Mexico	140,900	0.5%
4	New York	1,574,300	5.7%
10	North Carolina	829,000	3.0%
43	North Dakota	95,200	0.3%
7	Ohio	1,016,900	3.7%
29	Oklahoma	302,500	1.1%
27	Oregon	346,200	1.3%
6	Pennsylvania	1,127,600	4.1%
47	Rhode Island	76,200	0.3%
23	South Carolina	404,000	1.5%
45	South Dakota	87,400	0.3%
14	Tennessee	623,200	2.3%
2	Texas	2,460,000	9.0%
31	Utah	280,200	1.0%
49	Vermont	55,500	0.2%
12	Virginia	659,200	2.4%
13	Washington	627,700	2.3%
40	West Virginia	128,200	0.5%
18	Wisconsin	545,400	2.0%
50	Wyoming	52,200	0.2%

RANK ORDER

RANK	STATE	EMPLOYEES	% of USA
1	California	3,037,000	11.1%
2	Texas	2,460,000	9.0%
3	Florida	1,771,400	6.5%
4	New York	1,574,300	5.7%
5	Illinois	1,206,600	4.4%
6	Pennsylvania	1,127,600	4.1%
7	Ohio	1,016,900	3.7%
8	Georgia	942,300	3.4%
9	New Jersey	870,000	3.2%
10	North Carolina	829,000	3.0%
11	Michigan	783,300	2.9%
12	Virginia	659,200	2.4%
13	Washington	627,700	2.3%
14	Tennessee	623,200	2.3%
15	Indiana	596,800	2.2%
16	Massachusetts	577,700	2.1%
17	Missouri	546,300	2.0%
18	Wisconsin	545,400	2.0%
19	Minnesota	542,200	2.0%
20	Arizona	514,600	1.9%
21	Maryland	468,900	1.7%
22	Colorado	465,400	1.7%
23	South Carolina	404,000	1.5%
24	Kentucky	402,900	1.5%
25	Louisiana	376,700	1.4%
26	Alabama	373,900	1.4%
27	Oregon	346,200	1.3%
28	Iowa	320,700	1.2%
29	Oklahoma	302,500	1.1%
30	Connecticut	300,300	1.1%
31	Utah	280,200	1.0%
32	Kansas	265,100	1.0%
33	Arkansas	251,100	0.9%
34	Nevada	248,800	0.9%
35	Mississippi	233,800	0.9%
36	Nebraska	203,300	0.7%
37	Idaho	142,300	0.5%
38	New Mexico	140,900	0.5%
39	New Hampshire	139,000	0.5%
40	West Virginia	128,200	0.5%
41	Hawaii	121,800	0.4%
42	Maine	120,800	0.4%
43	North Dakota	95,200	0.3%
44	Montana	94,100	0.3%
45	South Dakota	87,400	0.3%
46	Delaware	79,700	0.3%
47	Rhode Island	76,200	0.3%
48	Alaska	64,500	0.2%
49	Vermont	55,500	0.2%
50	Wyoming	52,200	0.2%
	District of Columbia	32,300	0.1%

Source: U.S. Department of Labor, Bureau of Labor Statistics
"State Employment and Unemployment" (press release, January 23, 2018, www.bls.gov/bls/newsrels.htm)
*Seasonally adjusted preliminary data as of December 2017. National total calculated through a different formula.

Percent of Nonfarm Employees in
Trade, Transportation, and Public Utilities in 2017
National Percent = 18.6% of Employees*

ALPHA ORDER

RANK ORDER

RANK	STATE	PERCENT		RANK	STATE	PERCENT
30	Alabama	18.5		1	North Dakota	21.9
14	Alaska	19.7		2	New Jersey	21.1
28	Arizona	18.6		3	Georgia	20.9
8	Arkansas	20.1		4	Kentucky	20.6
38	California	17.9		4	Tennessee	20.6
43	Colorado	17.4		6	New Hampshire	20.5
39	Connecticut	17.8		7	Florida	20.3
41	Delaware	17.6		8	Arkansas	20.1
7	Florida	20.3		8	Mississippi	20.1
3	Georgia	20.9		10	Iowa	20.0
30	Hawaii	18.5		11	Illinois	19.9
14	Idaho	19.7		11	South Dakota	19.9
11	Illinois	19.9		13	Texas	19.8
21	Indiana	19.0		14	Alaska	19.7
10	Iowa	20.0		14	Idaho	19.7
26	Kansas	18.7		14	Nebraska	19.7
4	Kentucky	20.6		17	Montana	19.6
19	Louisiana	19.1		18	Maine	19.4
18	Maine	19.4		19	Louisiana	19.1
45	Maryland	17.0		19	South Carolina	19.1
49	Massachusetts	15.8		21	Indiana	19.0
40	Michigan	17.7		22	Missouri	18.9
32	Minnesota	18.3		23	Pennsylvania	18.8
8	Mississippi	20.1		23	Utah	18.8
22	Missouri	18.9		23	Wyoming	18.8
17	Montana	19.6		26	Kansas	18.7
14	Nebraska	19.7		26	Washington	18.7
35	Nevada	18.2		28	Arizona	18.6
6	New Hampshire	20.5		28	North Carolina	18.6
2	New Jersey	21.1		30	Alabama	18.5
46	New Mexico	16.6		30	Hawaii	18.5
48	New York	16.5		32	Minnesota	18.3
28	North Carolina	18.6		32	Ohio	18.3
1	North Dakota	21.9		32	Wisconsin	18.3
32	Ohio	18.3		35	Nevada	18.2
37	Oklahoma	18.1		35	Oregon	18.2
35	Oregon	18.2		37	Oklahoma	18.1
23	Pennsylvania	18.8		38	California	17.9
50	Rhode Island	15.3		39	Connecticut	17.8
19	South Carolina	19.1		40	Michigan	17.7
11	South Dakota	19.9		41	Delaware	17.6
4	Tennessee	20.6		42	Vermont	17.5
13	Texas	19.8		43	Colorado	17.4
23	Utah	18.8		44	West Virginia	17.1
42	Vermont	17.5		45	Maryland	17.0
46	Virginia	16.6		46	New Mexico	16.6
26	Washington	18.7		46	Virginia	16.6
44	West Virginia	17.1		48	New York	16.5
32	Wisconsin	18.3		49	Massachusetts	15.8
23	Wyoming	18.8		50	Rhode Island	15.3

District of Columbia   4.1

Source: CQ Press using data from U.S. Department of Labor, Bureau of Labor Statistics
"State Employment and Unemployment" (press release, January 23, 2018, www.bls.gov/bls/newsrels.htm)
*Seasonally adjusted preliminary data as of December 2017. National figure calculated through a different formula.

VII. Energy and Environment

Energy Consumption in 2015

National Total = 97,251,000,000,000,000 BTUs*

ALPHA ORDER

RANK	STATE	BTUs	% of USA
17	Alabama	1,909,600,000,000,000	2.0%
39	Alaska	619,900,000,000,000	0.6%
27	Arizona	1,439,900,000,000,000	1.5%
31	Arkansas	1,055,500,000,000,000	1.1%
2	California	7,676,300,000,000,000	7.9%
25	Colorado	1,480,200,000,000,000	1.5%
36	Connecticut	751,600,000,000,000	0.8%
48	Delaware	278,000,000,000,000	0.3%
4	Florida	4,241,700,000,000,000	4.4%
9	Georgia	2,851,200,000,000,000	2.9%
47	Hawaii	282,400,000,000,000	0.3%
41	Idaho	524,400,000,000,000	0.5%
5	Illinois	3,942,700,000,000,000	4.1%
10	Indiana	2,846,400,000,000,000	2.9%
24	Iowa	1,494,800,000,000,000	1.5%
30	Kansas	1,082,600,000,000,000	1.1%
21	Kentucky	1,725,500,000,000,000	1.8%
3	Louisiana	4,258,900,000,000,000	4.4%
43	Maine	405,600,000,000,000	0.4%
28	Maryland	1,399,500,000,000,000	1.4%
26	Massachusetts	1,444,900,000,000,000	1.5%
11	Michigan	2,767,300,000,000,000	2.8%
20	Minnesota	1,769,900,000,000,000	1.8%
29	Mississippi	1,132,700,000,000,000	1.2%
18	Missouri	1,826,800,000,000,000	1.9%
44	Montana	391,400,000,000,000	0.4%
33	Nebraska	853,100,000,000,000	0.9%
38	Nevada	649,500,000,000,000	0.7%
46	New Hampshire	305,200,000,000,000	0.3%
14	New Jersey	2,287,700,000,000,000	2.4%
37	New Mexico	675,600,000,000,000	0.7%
8	New York	3,724,500,000,000,000	3.8%
12	North Carolina	2,523,700,000,000,000	2.6%
40	North Dakota	607,600,000,000,000	0.6%
7	Ohio	3,740,800,000,000,000	3.8%
23	Oklahoma	1,630,900,000,000,000	1.7%
32	Oregon	956,700,000,000,000	1.0%
6	Pennsylvania	3,881,400,000,000,000	4.0%
49	Rhode Island	202,700,000,000,000	0.2%
22	South Carolina	1,648,500,000,000,000	1.7%
45	South Dakota	383,500,000,000,000	0.4%
15	Tennessee	2,167,500,000,000,000	2.2%
1	Texas	12,897,600,000,000,000	13.3%
34	Utah	791,000,000,000,000	0.8%
50	Vermont	132,000,000,000,000	0.1%
13	Virginia	2,367,700,000,000,000	2.4%
16	Washington	1,988,400,000,000,000	2.0%
35	West Virginia	774,900,000,000,000	0.8%
19	Wisconsin	1,776,200,000,000,000	1.8%
42	Wyoming	523,800,000,000,000	0.5%

RANK ORDER

RANK	STATE	BTUs	% of USA
1	Texas	12,897,600,000,000,000	13.3%
2	California	7,676,300,000,000,000	7.9%
3	Louisiana	4,258,900,000,000,000	4.4%
4	Florida	4,241,700,000,000,000	4.4%
5	Illinois	3,942,700,000,000,000	4.1%
6	Pennsylvania	3,881,400,000,000,000	4.0%
7	Ohio	3,740,800,000,000,000	3.8%
8	New York	3,724,500,000,000,000	3.8%
9	Georgia	2,851,200,000,000,000	2.9%
10	Indiana	2,846,400,000,000,000	2.9%
11	Michigan	2,767,300,000,000,000	2.8%
12	North Carolina	2,523,700,000,000,000	2.6%
13	Virginia	2,367,700,000,000,000	2.4%
14	New Jersey	2,287,700,000,000,000	2.4%
15	Tennessee	2,167,500,000,000,000	2.2%
16	Washington	1,988,400,000,000,000	2.0%
17	Alabama	1,909,600,000,000,000	2.0%
18	Missouri	1,826,800,000,000,000	1.9%
19	Wisconsin	1,776,200,000,000,000	1.8%
20	Minnesota	1,769,900,000,000,000	1.8%
21	Kentucky	1,725,500,000,000,000	1.8%
22	South Carolina	1,648,500,000,000,000	1.7%
23	Oklahoma	1,630,900,000,000,000	1.7%
24	Iowa	1,494,800,000,000,000	1.5%
25	Colorado	1,480,200,000,000,000	1.5%
26	Massachusetts	1,444,900,000,000,000	1.5%
27	Arizona	1,439,900,000,000,000	1.5%
28	Maryland	1,399,500,000,000,000	1.4%
29	Mississippi	1,132,700,000,000,000	1.2%
30	Kansas	1,082,600,000,000,000	1.1%
31	Arkansas	1,055,500,000,000,000	1.1%
32	Oregon	956,700,000,000,000	1.0%
33	Nebraska	853,100,000,000,000	0.9%
34	Utah	791,000,000,000,000	0.8%
35	West Virginia	774,900,000,000,000	0.8%
36	Connecticut	751,600,000,000,000	0.8%
37	New Mexico	675,600,000,000,000	0.7%
38	Nevada	649,500,000,000,000	0.7%
39	Alaska	619,900,000,000,000	0.6%
40	North Dakota	607,600,000,000,000	0.6%
41	Idaho	524,400,000,000,000	0.5%
42	Wyoming	523,800,000,000,000	0.5%
43	Maine	405,600,000,000,000	0.4%
44	Montana	391,400,000,000,000	0.4%
45	South Dakota	383,500,000,000,000	0.4%
46	New Hampshire	305,200,000,000,000	0.3%
47	Hawaii	282,400,000,000,000	0.3%
48	Delaware	278,000,000,000,000	0.3%
49	Rhode Island	202,700,000,000,000	0.2%
50	Vermont	132,000,000,000,000	0.1%
	District of Columbia	178,800,000,000,000	0.2%

Source: U.S. Department of Energy, Energy Information Administration
"State Energy Data 2015: Consumption" (http://www.eia.gov/state/seds/)
*British Thermal Units: The amount of heat required to raise the temperature of one pound of water one degree. National total includes 17.8 trillion Btu of net imports of coal coke that are not allocated to the states.

Per Capita Energy Consumption in 2015

National Per Capita = 302,925,021 BTUs*

ALPHA ORDER

RANK	STATE	PER CAPITA
12	Alabama	393,662,317
3	Alaska	839,996,802
43	Arizona	211,679,585
17	Arkansas	354,715,277
48	California	196,664,600
34	Colorado	272,073,332
46	Connecticut	209,134,352
29	Delaware	294,458,149
45	Florida	209,274,785
31	Georgia	279,542,210
47	Hawaii	197,992,035
23	Idaho	317,948,444
25	Illinois	306,537,425
9	Indiana	430,581,448
5	Iowa	479,337,163
16	Kansas	372,566,625
13	Kentucky	390,203,021
1	Louisiana	911,733,595
26	Maine	305,470,682
39	Maryland	233,228,193
42	Massachusetts	212,672,884
32	Michigan	279,013,165
21	Minnesota	322,783,727
15	Mississippi	379,426,235
28	Missouri	300,824,683
14	Montana	380,621,929
7	Nebraska	450,526,098
41	Nevada	225,281,706
40	New Hampshire	229,450,567
36	New Jersey	255,323,632
20	New Mexico	324,454,536
50	New York	187,922,438
37	North Carolina	251,320,260
4	North Dakota	804,918,534
22	Ohio	322,315,294
11	Oklahoma	417,713,255
38	Oregon	238,190,262
27	Pennsylvania	303,444,795
49	Rhode Island	191,966,028
18	South Carolina	336,949,606
8	South Dakota	449,044,303
19	Tennessee	328,871,205
6	Texas	469,774,408
35	Utah	264,998,993
44	Vermont	211,384,327
30	Virginia	282,988,638
33	Washington	277,988,340
10	West Virginia	421,194,640
24	Wisconsin	308,381,761
2	Wyoming	893,701,096

RANK ORDER

RANK	STATE	PER CAPITA
1	Louisiana	911,733,595
2	Wyoming	893,701,096
3	Alaska	839,996,802
4	North Dakota	804,918,534
5	Iowa	479,337,163
6	Texas	469,774,408
7	Nebraska	450,526,098
8	South Dakota	449,044,303
9	Indiana	430,581,448
10	West Virginia	421,194,640
11	Oklahoma	417,713,255
12	Alabama	393,662,317
13	Kentucky	390,203,021
14	Montana	380,621,929
15	Mississippi	379,426,235
16	Kansas	372,566,625
17	Arkansas	354,715,277
18	South Carolina	336,949,606
19	Tennessee	328,871,205
20	New Mexico	324,454,536
21	Minnesota	322,783,727
22	Ohio	322,315,294
23	Idaho	317,948,444
24	Wisconsin	308,381,761
25	Illinois	306,537,425
26	Maine	305,470,682
27	Pennsylvania	303,444,795
28	Missouri	300,824,683
29	Delaware	294,458,149
30	Virginia	282,988,638
31	Georgia	279,542,210
32	Michigan	279,013,165
33	Washington	277,988,340
34	Colorado	272,073,332
35	Utah	264,998,993
36	New Jersey	255,323,632
37	North Carolina	251,320,260
38	Oregon	238,190,262
39	Maryland	233,228,193
40	New Hampshire	229,450,567
41	Nevada	225,281,706
42	Massachusetts	212,672,884
43	Arizona	211,679,585
44	Vermont	211,384,327
45	Florida	209,274,785
46	Connecticut	209,134,352
47	Hawaii	197,992,035
48	California	196,664,600
49	Rhode Island	191,966,028
50	New York	187,922,438

District of Columbia 265,780,336

Source: CQ Press using data from U.S. Department of Energy, Energy Information Administration
"State Energy Data 2015: Consumption" (http://www.eia.gov/state/seds/)
*British Thermal Units: The amount of heat required to raise the temperature of one pound of water one degree. National figure includes 17.8 trillion Btu of net imports of coal coke that are not allocated to the states.

Energy Prices in 2015

National Rate = $17.31 per Million BTUs*

RANK	STATE	RATE
43	Alabama	$15.69
16	Alaska	18.63
6	Arizona	22.43
42	Arkansas	15.92
8	California	21.87
30	Colorado	17.08
2	Connecticut	23.37
12	Delaware	20.16
10	Florida	20.36
27	Georgia	17.38
1	Hawaii	28.35
33	Idaho	16.89
41	Illinois	15.99
45	Indiana	15.02
47	Iowa	14.49
25	Kansas	17.55
36	Kentucky	16.65
50	Louisiana	10.31
20	Maine	18.49
9	Maryland	21.34
5	Massachusetts	22.53
34	Michigan	16.81
39	Minnesota	16.34
37	Mississippi	16.56
19	Missouri	18.53
23	Montana	17.84
44	Nebraska	15.62
13	Nevada	20.02
3	New Hampshire	23.11
16	New Jersey	18.63
18	New Mexico	18.58
11	New York	20.21
14	North Carolina	19.23
48	North Dakota	13.62
35	Ohio	16.68
40	Oklahoma	16.02
15	Oregon	19.08
22	Pennsylvania	17.97
4	Rhode Island	22.68
21	South Carolina	18.00
38	South Dakota	16.50
26	Tennessee	17.49
49	Texas	13.34
31	Utah	17.04
7	Vermont	22.12
23	Virginia	17.84
28	Washington	17.34
32	West Virginia	16.96
29	Wisconsin	17.13
46	Wyoming	14.74

RANK	STATE	RATE
1	Hawaii	$28.35
2	Connecticut	23.37
3	New Hampshire	23.11
4	Rhode Island	22.68
5	Massachusetts	22.53
6	Arizona	22.43
7	Vermont	22.12
8	California	21.87
9	Maryland	21.34
10	Florida	20.36
11	New York	20.21
12	Delaware	20.16
13	Nevada	20.02
14	North Carolina	19.23
15	Oregon	19.08
16	Alaska	18.63
16	New Jersey	18.63
18	New Mexico	18.58
19	Missouri	18.53
20	Maine	18.49
21	South Carolina	18.00
22	Pennsylvania	17.97
23	Montana	17.84
23	Virginia	17.84
25	Kansas	17.55
26	Tennessee	17.49
27	Georgia	17.38
28	Washington	17.34
29	Wisconsin	17.13
30	Colorado	17.08
31	Utah	17.04
32	West Virginia	16.96
33	Idaho	16.89
34	Michigan	16.81
35	Ohio	16.68
36	Kentucky	16.65
37	Mississippi	16.56
38	South Dakota	16.50
39	Minnesota	16.34
40	Oklahoma	16.02
41	Illinois	15.99
42	Arkansas	15.92
43	Alabama	15.69
44	Nebraska	15.62
45	Indiana	15.02
46	Wyoming	14.74
47	Iowa	14.49
48	North Dakota	13.62
49	Texas	13.34
50	Louisiana	10.31

District of Columbia   23.18

Source: U.S. Department of Energy, Energy Information Administration
    "State Energy Data 2015: Prices and Expenditures" (http://www.eia.gov/state/seds/)
*British Thermal Units: The amount of heat required to raise the temperature of one pound of water one degree.

Energy Expenditures in 2015

National Total = $1,127,132,400,000*

ALPHA ORDER

RANK	STATE	EXPENDITURES	% of USA
20	Alabama	$20,094,900,000	1.8%
42	Alaska	5,523,000,000	0.5%
21	Arizona	20,022,200,000	1.8%
33	Arkansas	11,172,300,000	1.0%
1	California	121,894,300,000	10.8%
27	Colorado	15,939,100,000	1.4%
29	Connecticut	13,109,400,000	1.2%
49	Delaware	3,422,300,000	0.3%
3	Florida	56,605,500,000	5.0%
8	Georgia	33,378,700,000	3.0%
41	Hawaii	5,701,600,000	0.5%
40	Idaho	5,981,100,000	0.5%
6	Illinois	42,226,500,000	3.7%
13	Indiana	27,831,600,000	2.5%
28	Iowa	13,939,000,000	1.2%
32	Kansas	11,298,600,000	1.0%
25	Kentucky	17,725,800,000	1.6%
12	Louisiana	30,536,000,000	2.7%
39	Maine	6,069,400,000	0.5%
23	Maryland	19,430,900,000	1.7%
16	Massachusetts	23,840,200,000	2.1%
9	Michigan	33,224,900,000	2.9%
22	Minnesota	19,479,200,000	1.7%
31	Mississippi	12,645,700,000	1.1%
17	Missouri	21,844,400,000	1.9%
46	Montana	4,337,000,000	0.4%
36	Nebraska	8,192,200,000	0.7%
34	Nevada	9,003,600,000	0.8%
44	New Hampshire	5,232,800,000	0.5%
10	New Jersey	31,137,400,000	2.8%
38	New Mexico	7,139,000,000	0.6%
4	New York	55,849,300,000	5.0%
11	North Carolina	30,840,800,000	2.7%
43	North Dakota	5,485,300,000	0.5%
7	Ohio	41,822,300,000	3.7%
26	Oklahoma	16,033,100,000	1.4%
30	Oregon	12,652,400,000	1.1%
5	Pennsylvania	45,466,700,000	4.0%
48	Rhode Island	3,595,500,000	0.3%
24	South Carolina	18,420,900,000	1.6%
47	South Dakota	3,859,600,000	0.3%
15	Tennessee	23,877,600,000	2.1%
2	Texas	116,141,900,000	10.3%
35	Utah	8,734,400,000	0.8%
50	Vermont	2,675,300,000	0.2%
14	Virginia	27,514,700,000	2.4%
18	Washington	21,797,700,000	1.9%
37	West Virginia	7,286,600,000	0.6%
19	Wisconsin	20,732,200,000	1.8%
45	Wyoming	4,380,100,000	0.4%

RANK ORDER

RANK	STATE	EXPENDITURES	% of USA
1	California	$121,894,300,000	10.8%
2	Texas	116,141,900,000	10.3%
3	Florida	56,605,500,000	5.0%
4	New York	55,849,300,000	5.0%
5	Pennsylvania	45,466,700,000	4.0%
6	Illinois	42,226,500,000	3.7%
7	Ohio	41,822,300,000	3.7%
8	Georgia	33,378,700,000	3.0%
9	Michigan	33,224,900,000	2.9%
10	New Jersey	31,137,400,000	2.8%
11	North Carolina	30,840,800,000	2.7%
12	Louisiana	30,536,000,000	2.7%
13	Indiana	27,831,600,000	2.5%
14	Virginia	27,514,700,000	2.4%
15	Tennessee	23,877,600,000	2.1%
16	Massachusetts	23,840,200,000	2.1%
17	Missouri	21,844,400,000	1.9%
18	Washington	21,797,700,000	1.9%
19	Wisconsin	20,732,200,000	1.8%
20	Alabama	20,094,900,000	1.8%
21	Arizona	20,022,200,000	1.8%
22	Minnesota	19,479,200,000	1.7%
23	Maryland	19,430,900,000	1.7%
24	South Carolina	18,420,900,000	1.6%
25	Kentucky	17,725,800,000	1.6%
26	Oklahoma	16,033,100,000	1.4%
27	Colorado	15,939,100,000	1.4%
28	Iowa	13,939,000,000	1.2%
29	Connecticut	13,109,400,000	1.2%
30	Oregon	12,652,400,000	1.1%
31	Mississippi	12,645,700,000	1.1%
32	Kansas	11,298,600,000	1.0%
33	Arkansas	11,172,300,000	1.0%
34	Nevada	9,003,600,000	0.8%
35	Utah	8,734,400,000	0.8%
36	Nebraska	8,192,200,000	0.7%
37	West Virginia	7,286,600,000	0.6%
38	New Mexico	7,139,000,000	0.6%
39	Maine	6,069,400,000	0.5%
40	Idaho	5,981,100,000	0.5%
41	Hawaii	5,701,600,000	0.5%
42	Alaska	5,523,000,000	0.5%
43	North Dakota	5,485,300,000	0.5%
44	New Hampshire	5,232,800,000	0.5%
45	Wyoming	4,380,100,000	0.4%
46	Montana	4,337,000,000	0.4%
47	South Dakota	3,859,600,000	0.3%
48	Rhode Island	3,595,500,000	0.3%
49	Delaware	3,422,300,000	0.3%
50	Vermont	2,675,300,000	0.2%
	District of Columbia	2,163,800,000	0.2%

Source: U.S. Department of Energy, Energy Information Administration
"State Energy Data 2015: Prices and Expenditures" (http://www.eia.gov/state/seds/)
*The national total includes a negative $177 million for coal coke net imports, which is not allocated to the states.

Per Capita Energy Expenditures in 2015

National Per Capita = $3,511

ALPHA ORDER

RANK	STATE	PER CAPITA
14	Alabama	$4,143
1	Alaska	7,484
46	Arizona	2,943
22	Arkansas	3,755
42	California	3,123
47	Colorado	2,930
23	Connecticut	3,648
25	Delaware	3,625
50	Florida	2,793
39	Georgia	3,273
17	Hawaii	3,997
24	Idaho	3,626
38	Illinois	3,283
13	Indiana	4,210
7	Iowa	4,470
20	Kansas	3,888
16	Kentucky	4,008
4	Louisiana	6,537
5	Maine	4,571
40	Maryland	3,238
32	Massachusetts	3,509
36	Michigan	3,350
31	Minnesota	3,552
10	Mississippi	4,236
29	Missouri	3,597
12	Montana	4,218
8	Nebraska	4,326
42	Nevada	3,123
19	New Hampshire	3,934
33	New Jersey	3,475
34	New Mexico	3,428
49	New York	2,818
44	North Carolina	3,071
3	North Dakota	7,267
27	Ohio	3,603
15	Oklahoma	4,106
41	Oregon	3,150
30	Pennsylvania	3,555
35	Rhode Island	3,405
21	South Carolina	3,765
6	South Dakota	4,519
26	Tennessee	3,623
11	Texas	4,230
48	Utah	2,926
9	Vermont	4,284
37	Virginia	3,289
45	Washington	3,047
18	West Virginia	3,961
28	Wisconsin	3,600
2	Wyoming	7,473

RANK ORDER

RANK	STATE	PER CAPITA
1	Alaska	$7,484
2	Wyoming	7,473
3	North Dakota	7,267
4	Louisiana	6,537
5	Maine	4,571
6	South Dakota	4,519
7	Iowa	4,470
8	Nebraska	4,326
9	Vermont	4,284
10	Mississippi	4,236
11	Texas	4,230
12	Montana	4,218
13	Indiana	4,210
14	Alabama	4,143
15	Oklahoma	4,106
16	Kentucky	4,008
17	Hawaii	3,997
18	West Virginia	3,961
19	New Hampshire	3,934
20	Kansas	3,888
21	South Carolina	3,765
22	Arkansas	3,755
23	Connecticut	3,648
24	Idaho	3,626
25	Delaware	3,625
26	Tennessee	3,623
27	Ohio	3,603
28	Wisconsin	3,600
29	Missouri	3,597
30	Pennsylvania	3,555
31	Minnesota	3,552
32	Massachusetts	3,509
33	New Jersey	3,475
34	New Mexico	3,428
35	Rhode Island	3,405
36	Michigan	3,350
37	Virginia	3,289
38	Illinois	3,283
39	Georgia	3,273
40	Maryland	3,238
41	Oregon	3,150
42	California	3,123
42	Nevada	3,123
44	North Carolina	3,071
45	Washington	3,047
46	Arizona	2,943
47	Colorado	2,930
48	Utah	2,926
49	New York	2,818
50	Florida	2,793

District of Columbia   3,216

Source: CQ Press using data from U.S. Department of Energy, Energy Information Administration
"State Energy Data 2015: Prices and Expenditures" (http://www.eia.gov/state/seds/)

Average Monthly Electric Bill for Industrial Customers in 2016

National Average = $6,570 per Month

ALPHA ORDER

RANK	STATE	MONTHLY BILL
9	Alabama	$22,550
18	Alaska	13,081
21	Arizona	9,314
47	Arkansas	2,256
42	California	3,409
32	Colorado	5,693
22	Connecticut	8,162
12	Delaware	17,505
35	Florida	5,074
25	Georgia	7,211
2	Hawaii	80,143
49	Idaho	1,688
4	Illinois	39,088
14	Indiana	14,919
16	Iowa	14,386
44	Kansas	3,001
10	Kentucky	18,246
23	Louisiana	7,896
26	Maine	7,093
45	Maryland	2,847
29	Massachusetts	6,119
6	Michigan	28,775
15	Minnesota	14,483
27	Mississippi	6,919
24	Missouri	7,886
48	Montana	1,896
50	Nebraska	1,160
11	Nevada	18,121
28	New Hampshire	6,328
34	New Jersey	5,177
40	New Mexico	3,961
19	New York	11,638
17	North Carolina	14,305
31	North Dakota	5,726
13	Ohio	15,312
41	Oklahoma	3,949
46	Oregon	2,600
20	Pennsylvania	11,632
38	Rhode Island	4,716
5	South Carolina	33,347
39	South Dakota	4,608
1	Tennessee	93,413
37	Texas	4,770
36	Utah	5,061
3	Vermont	53,578
8	Virginia	26,000
43	Washington	3,270
30	West Virginia	6,022
7	Wisconsin	27,115
33	Wyoming	5,437

RANK ORDER

RANK	STATE	MONTHLY BILL
1	Tennessee	$93,413
2	Hawaii	80,143
3	Vermont	53,578
4	Illinois	39,088
5	South Carolina	33,347
6	Michigan	28,775
7	Wisconsin	27,115
8	Virginia	26,000
9	Alabama	22,550
10	Kentucky	18,246
11	Nevada	18,121
12	Delaware	17,505
13	Ohio	15,312
14	Indiana	14,919
15	Minnesota	14,483
16	Iowa	14,386
17	North Carolina	14,305
18	Alaska	13,081
19	New York	11,638
20	Pennsylvania	11,632
21	Arizona	9,314
22	Connecticut	8,162
23	Louisiana	7,896
24	Missouri	7,886
25	Georgia	7,211
26	Maine	7,093
27	Mississippi	6,919
28	New Hampshire	6,328
29	Massachusetts	6,119
30	West Virginia	6,022
31	North Dakota	5,726
32	Colorado	5,693
33	Wyoming	5,437
34	New Jersey	5,177
35	Florida	5,074
36	Utah	5,061
37	Texas	4,770
38	Rhode Island	4,716
39	South Dakota	4,608
40	New Mexico	3,961
41	Oklahoma	3,949
42	California	3,409
43	Washington	3,270
44	Kansas	3,001
45	Maryland	2,847
46	Oregon	2,600
47	Arkansas	2,256
48	Montana	1,896
49	Idaho	1,688
50	Nebraska	1,160

District of Columbia   1,411,917

Source: U.S. Department of Energy, Energy Information Administration
"Electric Sales, Revenue and Average Price 2016" (http://www.eia.gov/electricity/sales_revenue_price/index.cfm)

Average Monthly Electric Bill for Commercial Customers in 2016

National Average = $655 per Month

ALPHA ORDER

RANK	STATE	MONTHLY BILL
25	Alabama	$596
10	Alaska	757
7	Arizona	806
43	Arkansas	439
4	California	867
42	Colorado	453
1	Connecticut	1,095
14	Delaware	666
27	Florida	591
12	Georgia	688
3	Hawaii	1,050
50	Idaho	377
20	Illinois	630
28	Indiana	576
48	Iowa	398
26	Kansas	595
31	Kentucky	528
23	Louisiana	615
46	Maine	410
2	Maryland	1,083
6	Massachusetts	837
18	Michigan	642
15	Minnesota	662
38	Mississippi	498
20	Missouri	630
49	Montana	387
41	Nebraska	456
47	Nevada	406
37	New Hampshire	503
8	New Jersey	768
36	New Mexico	505
5	New York	859
32	North Carolina	519
17	North Dakota	657
19	Ohio	636
40	Oklahoma	475
34	Oregon	515
39	Pennsylvania	481
8	Rhode Island	768
33	South Carolina	516
30	South Dakota	530
22	Tennessee	627
16	Texas	661
13	Utah	677
43	Vermont	439
11	Virginia	756
29	Washington	554
45	West Virginia	427
24	Wisconsin	614
35	Wyoming	513

RANK ORDER

RANK	STATE	MONTHLY BILL
1	Connecticut	$1,095
2	Maryland	1,083
3	Hawaii	1,050
4	California	867
5	New York	859
6	Massachusetts	837
7	Arizona	806
8	New Jersey	768
8	Rhode Island	768
10	Alaska	757
11	Virginia	756
12	Georgia	688
13	Utah	677
14	Delaware	666
15	Minnesota	662
16	Texas	661
17	North Dakota	657
18	Michigan	642
19	Ohio	636
20	Illinois	630
20	Missouri	630
22	Tennessee	627
23	Louisiana	615
24	Wisconsin	614
25	Alabama	596
26	Kansas	595
27	Florida	591
28	Indiana	576
29	Washington	554
30	South Dakota	530
31	Kentucky	528
32	North Carolina	519
33	South Carolina	516
34	Oregon	515
35	Wyoming	513
36	New Mexico	505
37	New Hampshire	503
38	Mississippi	498
39	Pennsylvania	481
40	Oklahoma	475
41	Nebraska	456
42	Colorado	453
43	Arkansas	439
43	Vermont	439
45	West Virginia	427
46	Maine	410
47	Nevada	406
48	Iowa	398
49	Montana	387
50	Idaho	377
	District of Columbia	3,152

Source: U.S. Department of Energy, Energy Information Administration
"Electric Sales, Revenue and Average Price 2016" (http://www.eia.gov/electricity/sales_revenue_price/index.cfm)

Average Monthly Electric Bill for Residential Customers in 2016

National Average = $113 per Month

ALPHA ORDER

RANK	STATE	MONTHLY BILL
1	Alabama	$146
16	Alaska	120
13	Arizona	125
30	Arkansas	107
40	California	95
48	Colorado	84
3	Connecticut	142
8	Delaware	127
14	Florida	123
6	Georgia	131
5	Hawaii	139
40	Idaho	95
44	Illinois	92
22	Indiana	115
35	Iowa	103
18	Kansas	117
17	Kentucky	118
21	Louisiana	116
47	Maine	86
3	Maryland	142
23	Massachusetts	114
36	Michigan	102
37	Minnesota	97
11	Mississippi	126
18	Missouri	117
46	Montana	89
32	Nebraska	105
32	Nevada	105
25	New Hampshire	111
28	New Jersey	109
50	New Mexico	76
32	New York	105
15	North Carolina	121
31	North Dakota	106
25	Ohio	111
25	Oklahoma	111
37	Oregon	97
18	Pennsylvania	117
28	Rhode Island	109
1	South Carolina	146
24	South Dakota	113
7	Tennessee	129
8	Texas	127
49	Utah	83
40	Vermont	95
8	Virginia	127
45	Washington	91
11	West Virginia	126
39	Wisconsin	96
40	Wyoming	95

RANK ORDER

RANK	STATE	MONTHLY BILL
1	Alabama	$146
1	South Carolina	146
3	Connecticut	142
3	Maryland	142
5	Hawaii	139
6	Georgia	131
7	Tennessee	129
8	Delaware	127
8	Texas	127
8	Virginia	127
11	Mississippi	126
11	West Virginia	126
13	Arizona	125
14	Florida	123
15	North Carolina	121
16	Alaska	120
17	Kentucky	118
18	Kansas	117
18	Missouri	117
18	Pennsylvania	117
21	Louisiana	116
22	Indiana	115
23	Massachusetts	114
24	South Dakota	113
25	New Hampshire	111
25	Ohio	111
25	Oklahoma	111
28	New Jersey	109
28	Rhode Island	109
30	Arkansas	107
31	North Dakota	106
32	Nebraska	105
32	Nevada	105
32	New York	105
35	Iowa	103
36	Michigan	102
37	Minnesota	97
37	Oregon	97
39	Wisconsin	96
40	California	95
40	Idaho	95
40	Vermont	95
40	Wyoming	95
44	Illinois	92
45	Washington	91
46	Montana	89
47	Maine	86
48	Colorado	84
49	Utah	83
50	New Mexico	76
	District of Columbia	99

Source: U.S. Department of Energy, Energy Information Administration
"Electric Sales, Revenue and Average Price 2016" (http://www.eia.gov/electricity/sales_revenue_price/index.cfm)

Electricity Generated through Renewable Sources in 2016

National Total = 609,445,101,000 Kilowatthours*

ALPHA ORDER

RANK	STATE	KWH	% of USA
16	Alabama	10,351,310,000	1.7%
44	Alaska	1,871,470,000	0.3%
13	Arizona	11,689,548,000	1.9%
30	Arkansas	4,965,956,000	0.8%
2	California	78,654,385,000	12.9%
12	Colorado	12,024,189,000	2.0%
48	Connecticut	1,117,475,000	0.2%
50	Delaware	124,394,000	0.0%
29	Florida	5,041,672,000	0.8%
18	Georgia	8,827,016,000	1.4%
47	Hawaii	1,438,055,000	0.2%
10	Idaho	12,245,056,000	2.0%
14	Illinois	11,312,090,000	1.9%
25	Indiana	5,984,370,000	1.0%
7	Iowa	21,240,654,000	3.5%
8	Kansas	14,202,353,000	2.3%
35	Kentucky	3,954,557,000	0.6%
34	Louisiana	3,979,296,000	0.7%
24	Maine	7,454,962,000	1.2%
40	Maryland	2,673,640,000	0.4%
39	Massachusetts	2,742,072,000	0.4%
19	Michigan	8,764,458,000	1.4%
9	Minnesota	13,044,114,000	2.1%
46	Mississippi	1,524,200,000	0.3%
41	Missouri	2,561,679,000	0.4%
11	Montana	12,242,870,000	2.0%
31	Nebraska	4,756,593,000	0.8%
20	Nevada	8,665,807,000	1.4%
36	New Hampshire	3,267,078,000	0.5%
45	New Jersey	1,847,976,000	0.3%
33	New Mexico	4,537,260,000	0.7%
5	New York	33,211,534,000	5.4%
15	North Carolina	10,400,457,000	1.7%
17	North Dakota	10,089,533,000	1.7%
42	Ohio	2,533,315,000	0.4%
6	Oklahoma	23,010,355,000	3.8%
4	Oregon	42,931,682,000	7.0%
22	Pennsylvania	8,317,002,000	1.4%
49	Rhode Island	248,099,000	0.0%
32	South Carolina	4,607,399,000	0.8%
21	South Dakota	8,520,149,000	1.4%
23	Tennessee	7,823,792,000	1.3%
3	Texas	61,286,294,000	10.1%
37	Utah	3,204,663,000	0.5%
43	Vermont	1,905,225,000	0.3%
27	Virginia	5,584,116,000	0.9%
1	Washington	88,395,945,000	14.5%
38	West Virginia	3,070,401,000	0.5%
26	Wisconsin	5,782,990,000	0.9%
28	Wyoming	5,362,826,000	0.9%

RANK ORDER

RANK	STATE	KWH	% of USA
1	Washington	88,395,945,000	14.5%
2	California	78,654,385,000	12.9%
3	Texas	61,286,294,000	10.1%
4	Oregon	42,931,682,000	7.0%
5	New York	33,211,534,000	5.4%
6	Oklahoma	23,010,355,000	3.8%
7	Iowa	21,240,654,000	3.5%
8	Kansas	14,202,353,000	2.3%
9	Minnesota	13,044,114,000	2.1%
10	Idaho	12,245,056,000	2.0%
11	Montana	12,242,870,000	2.0%
12	Colorado	12,024,189,000	2.0%
13	Arizona	11,689,548,000	1.9%
14	Illinois	11,312,090,000	1.9%
15	North Carolina	10,400,457,000	1.7%
16	Alabama	10,351,310,000	1.7%
17	North Dakota	10,089,533,000	1.7%
18	Georgia	8,827,016,000	1.4%
19	Michigan	8,764,458,000	1.4%
20	Nevada	8,665,807,000	1.4%
21	South Dakota	8,520,149,000	1.4%
22	Pennsylvania	8,317,002,000	1.4%
23	Tennessee	7,823,792,000	1.3%
24	Maine	7,454,962,000	1.2%
25	Indiana	5,984,370,000	1.0%
26	Wisconsin	5,782,990,000	0.9%
27	Virginia	5,584,116,000	0.9%
28	Wyoming	5,362,826,000	0.9%
29	Florida	5,041,672,000	0.8%
30	Arkansas	4,965,956,000	0.8%
31	Nebraska	4,756,593,000	0.8%
32	South Carolina	4,607,399,000	0.8%
33	New Mexico	4,537,260,000	0.7%
34	Louisiana	3,979,296,000	0.7%
35	Kentucky	3,954,557,000	0.6%
36	New Hampshire	3,267,078,000	0.5%
37	Utah	3,204,663,000	0.5%
38	West Virginia	3,070,401,000	0.5%
39	Massachusetts	2,742,072,000	0.4%
40	Maryland	2,673,640,000	0.4%
41	Missouri	2,561,679,000	0.4%
42	Ohio	2,533,315,000	0.4%
43	Vermont	1,905,225,000	0.3%
44	Alaska	1,871,470,000	0.3%
45	New Jersey	1,847,976,000	0.3%
46	Mississippi	1,524,200,000	0.3%
47	Hawaii	1,438,055,000	0.2%
48	Connecticut	1,117,475,000	0.2%
49	Rhode Island	248,099,000	0.0%
50	Delaware	124,394,000	0.0%
	District of Columbia	52,771,000	0.0%

Source: U.S. Department of Energy, Energy Information Administration
    "Electricity" (http://www.eia.gov/electricity/data/state/)
*Includes hydroelectric, geothermal, solar thermal and photovoltaic, wind, wood and wood-derived fuels, and other biomass.

Percent of Electricity Generated through Renewable Sources in 2016

National Percent = 14.9%*

<table>
<tr><td colspan="3">ALPHA ORDER</td><td colspan="3">RANK ORDER</td></tr>
<tr><th>RANK</th><th>STATE</th><th>PERCENT</th><th>RANK</th><th>STATE</th><th>PERCENT</th></tr>
<tr><td>32</td><td>Alabama</td><td>7.3</td><td>1</td><td>Vermont</td><td>99.7</td></tr>
<tr><td>11</td><td>Alaska</td><td>29.5</td><td>2</td><td>Idaho</td><td>78.2</td></tr>
<tr><td>24</td><td>Arizona</td><td>10.7</td><td>3</td><td>Washington</td><td>77.5</td></tr>
<tr><td>29</td><td>Arkansas</td><td>8.2</td><td>4</td><td>South Dakota</td><td>73.9</td></tr>
<tr><td>8</td><td>California</td><td>39.9</td><td>5</td><td>Oregon</td><td>71.3</td></tr>
<tr><td>15</td><td>Colorado</td><td>22.1</td><td>6</td><td>Maine</td><td>64.7</td></tr>
<tr><td>45</td><td>Connecticut</td><td>3.1</td><td>7</td><td>Montana</td><td>44.1</td></tr>
<tr><td>50</td><td>Delaware</td><td>1.4</td><td>8</td><td>California</td><td>39.9</td></tr>
<tr><td>48</td><td>Florida</td><td>2.1</td><td>9</td><td>Iowa</td><td>39.1</td></tr>
<tr><td>34</td><td>Georgia</td><td>6.6</td><td>10</td><td>Kansas</td><td>29.8</td></tr>
<tr><td>19</td><td>Hawaii</td><td>14.5</td><td>11</td><td>Alaska</td><td>29.5</td></tr>
<tr><td>2</td><td>Idaho</td><td>78.2</td><td>12</td><td>Oklahoma</td><td>29.3</td></tr>
<tr><td>35</td><td>Illinois</td><td>6.0</td><td>13</td><td>North Dakota</td><td>26.7</td></tr>
<tr><td>37</td><td>Indiana</td><td>5.9</td><td>14</td><td>New York</td><td>24.7</td></tr>
<tr><td>9</td><td>Iowa</td><td>39.1</td><td>15</td><td>Colorado</td><td>22.1</td></tr>
<tr><td>10</td><td>Kansas</td><td>29.8</td><td>16</td><td>Minnesota</td><td>21.9</td></tr>
<tr><td>38</td><td>Kentucky</td><td>4.9</td><td>17</td><td>Nevada</td><td>21.8</td></tr>
<tr><td>43</td><td>Louisiana</td><td>3.7</td><td>18</td><td>New Hampshire</td><td>16.9</td></tr>
<tr><td>6</td><td>Maine</td><td>64.7</td><td>19</td><td>Hawaii</td><td>14.5</td></tr>
<tr><td>33</td><td>Maryland</td><td>7.2</td><td>20</td><td>New Mexico</td><td>13.8</td></tr>
<tr><td>27</td><td>Massachusetts</td><td>8.6</td><td>21</td><td>Texas</td><td>13.5</td></tr>
<tr><td>31</td><td>Michigan</td><td>7.8</td><td>22</td><td>Nebraska</td><td>13.0</td></tr>
<tr><td>16</td><td>Minnesota</td><td>21.9</td><td>23</td><td>Wyoming</td><td>11.5</td></tr>
<tr><td>46</td><td>Mississippi</td><td>2.4</td><td>24</td><td>Arizona</td><td>10.7</td></tr>
<tr><td>44</td><td>Missouri</td><td>3.3</td><td>25</td><td>Tennessee</td><td>9.9</td></tr>
<tr><td>7</td><td>Montana</td><td>44.1</td><td>26</td><td>Wisconsin</td><td>8.9</td></tr>
<tr><td>22</td><td>Nebraska</td><td>13.0</td><td>27</td><td>Massachusetts</td><td>8.6</td></tr>
<tr><td>17</td><td>Nevada</td><td>21.8</td><td>28</td><td>Utah</td><td>8.4</td></tr>
<tr><td>18</td><td>New Hampshire</td><td>16.9</td><td>29</td><td>Arkansas</td><td>8.2</td></tr>
<tr><td>46</td><td>New Jersey</td><td>2.4</td><td>30</td><td>North Carolina</td><td>8.0</td></tr>
<tr><td>20</td><td>New Mexico</td><td>13.8</td><td>31</td><td>Michigan</td><td>7.8</td></tr>
<tr><td>14</td><td>New York</td><td>24.7</td><td>32</td><td>Alabama</td><td>7.3</td></tr>
<tr><td>30</td><td>North Carolina</td><td>8.0</td><td>33</td><td>Maryland</td><td>7.2</td></tr>
<tr><td>13</td><td>North Dakota</td><td>26.7</td><td>34</td><td>Georgia</td><td>6.6</td></tr>
<tr><td>48</td><td>Ohio</td><td>2.1</td><td>35</td><td>Illinois</td><td>6.0</td></tr>
<tr><td>12</td><td>Oklahoma</td><td>29.3</td><td>35</td><td>Virginia</td><td>6.0</td></tr>
<tr><td>5</td><td>Oregon</td><td>71.3</td><td>37</td><td>Indiana</td><td>5.9</td></tr>
<tr><td>41</td><td>Pennsylvania</td><td>3.9</td><td>38</td><td>Kentucky</td><td>4.9</td></tr>
<tr><td>42</td><td>Rhode Island</td><td>3.8</td><td>39</td><td>South Carolina</td><td>4.8</td></tr>
<tr><td>39</td><td>South Carolina</td><td>4.8</td><td>40</td><td>West Virginia</td><td>4.0</td></tr>
<tr><td>4</td><td>South Dakota</td><td>73.9</td><td>41</td><td>Pennsylvania</td><td>3.9</td></tr>
<tr><td>25</td><td>Tennessee</td><td>9.9</td><td>42</td><td>Rhode Island</td><td>3.8</td></tr>
<tr><td>21</td><td>Texas</td><td>13.5</td><td>43</td><td>Louisiana</td><td>3.7</td></tr>
<tr><td>28</td><td>Utah</td><td>8.4</td><td>44</td><td>Missouri</td><td>3.3</td></tr>
<tr><td>1</td><td>Vermont</td><td>99.7</td><td>45</td><td>Connecticut</td><td>3.1</td></tr>
<tr><td>35</td><td>Virginia</td><td>6.0</td><td>46</td><td>Mississippi</td><td>2.4</td></tr>
<tr><td>3</td><td>Washington</td><td>77.5</td><td>46</td><td>New Jersey</td><td>2.4</td></tr>
<tr><td>40</td><td>West Virginia</td><td>4.0</td><td>48</td><td>Florida</td><td>2.1</td></tr>
<tr><td>26</td><td>Wisconsin</td><td>8.9</td><td>48</td><td>Ohio</td><td>2.1</td></tr>
<tr><td>23</td><td>Wyoming</td><td>11.5</td><td>50</td><td>Delaware</td><td>1.4</td></tr>
<tr><td></td><td></td><td></td><td></td><td>District of Columbia</td><td>69.0</td></tr>
</table>

Source: CQ Press using data from U.S. Department of Energy, Energy Information Administration
"Electricity" (http://www.eia.gov/electricity/data/state/)
*Includes hydroelectric, geothermal, solar thermal and photovoltaic, wind, wood and wood-derived fuels, and other biomass.

Average Price of Natural Gas Delivered to Industrial Customers in 2016

National Average = $3.52 per Thousand Cubic Feet

ALPHA ORDER

RANK	STATE	RATE
44	Alabama	$3.79
27	Alaska	5.06
17	Arizona	5.79
18	Arkansas	5.78
11	California	6.79
31	Colorado	4.89
14	Connecticut	6.07
2	Delaware	9.02
19	Florida	5.77
41	Georgia	4.10
1	Hawaii	15.70
26	Idaho	5.19
29	Illinois	5.03
30	Indiana	4.99
34	Iowa	4.70
46	Kansas	3.69
45	Kentucky	3.77
47	Louisiana	3.11
7	Maine	7.68
3	Maryland	8.80
9	Massachusetts	7.40
20	Michigan	5.75
39	Minnesota	4.19
37	Mississippi	4.35
13	Missouri	6.29
22	Montana	5.68
42	Nebraska	4.04
16	Nevada	5.90
5	New Hampshire	8.59
12	New Jersey	6.59
40	New Mexico	4.18
15	New York	5.92
24	North Carolina	5.43
49	North Dakota	2.62
32	Ohio	4.81
6	Oklahoma	8.04
21	Oregon	5.73
9	Pennsylvania	7.40
4	Rhode Island	8.70
38	South Carolina	4.20
33	South Dakota	4.78
35	Tennessee	4.44
48	Texas	2.65
23	Utah	5.52
25	Vermont	5.20
36	Virginia	4.42
8	Washington	7.47
50	West Virginia	2.43
28	Wisconsin	5.05
43	Wyoming	3.96

RANK ORDER

RANK	STATE	RATE
1	Hawaii	$15.70
2	Delaware	9.02
3	Maryland	8.80
4	Rhode Island	8.70
5	New Hampshire	8.59
6	Oklahoma	8.04
7	Maine	7.68
8	Washington	7.47
9	Massachusetts	7.40
9	Pennsylvania	7.40
11	California	6.79
12	New Jersey	6.59
13	Missouri	6.29
14	Connecticut	6.07
15	New York	5.92
16	Nevada	5.90
17	Arizona	5.79
18	Arkansas	5.78
19	Florida	5.77
20	Michigan	5.75
21	Oregon	5.73
22	Montana	5.68
23	Utah	5.52
24	North Carolina	5.43
25	Vermont	5.20
26	Idaho	5.19
27	Alaska	5.06
28	Wisconsin	5.05
29	Illinois	5.03
30	Indiana	4.99
31	Colorado	4.89
32	Ohio	4.81
33	South Dakota	4.78
34	Iowa	4.70
35	Tennessee	4.44
36	Virginia	4.42
37	Mississippi	4.35
38	South Carolina	4.20
39	Minnesota	4.19
40	New Mexico	4.18
41	Georgia	4.10
42	Nebraska	4.04
43	Wyoming	3.96
44	Alabama	3.79
45	Kentucky	3.77
46	Kansas	3.69
47	Louisiana	3.11
48	Texas	2.65
49	North Dakota	2.62
50	West Virginia	2.43
	District of Columbia*	NA

Source: U.S. Department of Energy, Energy Information Administration
   "Natural Gas" (http://www.eia.gov/naturalgas/annual/)
*Not available.

Average Price of Natural Gas Delivered to Commercial Customers in 2016

National Average = $7.28 per Thousand Cubic Feet

ALPHA ORDER

RANK	STATE	RATE
4	Alabama	$10.65
17	Alaska	8.34
11	Arizona	8.83
31	Arkansas	7.14
14	California	8.42
42	Colorado	6.42
12	Connecticut	8.79
7	Delaware	9.58
6	Florida	10.42
20	Georgia	7.92
1	Hawaii	27.02
34	Idaho	7.12
31	Illinois	7.14
39	Indiana	6.55
45	Iowa	5.99
16	Kansas	8.41
22	Kentucky	7.89
20	Louisiana	7.92
5	Maine	10.63
10	Maryland	8.94
8	Massachusetts	9.48
35	Michigan	6.90
41	Minnesota	6.44
24	Mississippi	7.80
22	Missouri	7.89
33	Montana	7.13
49	Nebraska	5.45
37	Nevada	6.84
2	New Hampshire	11.36
19	New Jersey	7.93
47	New Mexico	5.68
44	New York	6.18
28	North Carolina	7.71
49	North Dakota	5.45
46	Ohio	5.74
27	Oklahoma	7.72
9	Oregon	9.30
18	Pennsylvania	8.15
3	Rhode Island	11.16
14	South Carolina	8.42
48	South Dakota	5.64
24	Tennessee	7.80
36	Texas	6.89
29	Utah	7.43
38	Vermont	6.63
30	Virginia	7.23
13	Washington	8.49
26	West Virginia	7.75
43	Wisconsin	6.29
40	Wyoming	6.54

RANK ORDER

RANK	STATE	RATE
1	Hawaii	$27.02
2	New Hampshire	11.36
3	Rhode Island	11.16
4	Alabama	10.65
5	Maine	10.63
6	Florida	10.42
7	Delaware	9.58
8	Massachusetts	9.48
9	Oregon	9.30
10	Maryland	8.94
11	Arizona	8.83
12	Connecticut	8.79
13	Washington	8.49
14	California	8.42
14	South Carolina	8.42
16	Kansas	8.41
17	Alaska	8.34
18	Pennsylvania	8.15
19	New Jersey	7.93
20	Georgia	7.92
20	Louisiana	7.92
22	Kentucky	7.89
22	Missouri	7.89
24	Mississippi	7.80
24	Tennessee	7.80
26	West Virginia	7.75
27	Oklahoma	7.72
28	North Carolina	7.71
29	Utah	7.43
30	Virginia	7.23
31	Arkansas	7.14
31	Illinois	7.14
33	Montana	7.13
34	Idaho	7.12
35	Michigan	6.90
36	Texas	6.89
37	Nevada	6.84
38	Vermont	6.63
39	Indiana	6.55
40	Wyoming	6.54
41	Minnesota	6.44
42	Colorado	6.42
43	Wisconsin	6.29
44	New York	6.18
45	Iowa	5.99
46	Ohio	5.74
47	New Mexico	5.68
48	South Dakota	5.64
49	Nebraska	5.45
49	North Dakota	5.45

District of Columbia	9.88

Source: U.S. Department of Energy, Energy Information Administration
"Natural Gas" (http://www.eia.gov/naturalgas/annual/)

Average Price of Natural Gas Delivered to Residential Customers in 2016

National Average = $10.05 per Thousand Cubic Feet

<table>
<tr><td colspan="3">ALPHA ORDER</td><td colspan="3">RANK ORDER</td></tr>
<tr><td>RANK</td><td>STATE</td><td>RATE</td><td>RANK</td><td>STATE</td><td>RATE</td></tr>
<tr><td>7</td><td>Alabama</td><td>$14.05</td><td>1</td><td>Hawaii</td><td>$36.48</td></tr>
<tr><td>31</td><td>Alaska</td><td>9.81</td><td>2</td><td>Florida</td><td>20.27</td></tr>
<tr><td>3</td><td>Arizona</td><td>15.28</td><td>3</td><td>Arizona</td><td>15.28</td></tr>
<tr><td>20</td><td>Arkansas</td><td>11.17</td><td>4</td><td>Georgia</td><td>14.56</td></tr>
<tr><td>14</td><td>California</td><td>11.84</td><td>5</td><td>New Hampshire</td><td>14.25</td></tr>
<tr><td>48</td><td>Colorado</td><td>7.35</td><td>6</td><td>Vermont</td><td>14.15</td></tr>
<tr><td>10</td><td>Connecticut</td><td>12.91</td><td>7</td><td>Alabama</td><td>14.05</td></tr>
<tr><td>13</td><td>Delaware</td><td>11.88</td><td>8</td><td>Maine</td><td>13.82</td></tr>
<tr><td>2</td><td>Florida</td><td>20.27</td><td>9</td><td>Rhode Island</td><td>13.80</td></tr>
<tr><td>4</td><td>Georgia</td><td>14.56</td><td>10</td><td>Connecticut</td><td>12.91</td></tr>
<tr><td>1</td><td>Hawaii</td><td>36.48</td><td>11</td><td>South Carolina</td><td>12.62</td></tr>
<tr><td>39</td><td>Idaho</td><td>8.14</td><td>12</td><td>Massachusetts</td><td>12.46</td></tr>
<tr><td>46</td><td>Illinois</td><td>7.88</td><td>13</td><td>Delaware</td><td>11.88</td></tr>
<tr><td>45</td><td>Indiana</td><td>7.92</td><td>14</td><td>California</td><td>11.84</td></tr>
<tr><td>40</td><td>Iowa</td><td>8.13</td><td>15</td><td>Texas</td><td>11.73</td></tr>
<tr><td>30</td><td>Kansas</td><td>9.85</td><td>16</td><td>Oregon</td><td>11.67</td></tr>
<tr><td>28</td><td>Kentucky</td><td>10.14</td><td>17</td><td>Maryland</td><td>11.53</td></tr>
<tr><td>18</td><td>Louisiana</td><td>11.32</td><td>18</td><td>Louisiana</td><td>11.32</td></tr>
<tr><td>8</td><td>Maine</td><td>13.82</td><td>19</td><td>North Carolina</td><td>11.31</td></tr>
<tr><td>17</td><td>Maryland</td><td>11.53</td><td>20</td><td>Arkansas</td><td>11.17</td></tr>
<tr><td>12</td><td>Massachusetts</td><td>12.46</td><td>21</td><td>Missouri</td><td>10.94</td></tr>
<tr><td>38</td><td>Michigan</td><td>8.21</td><td>22</td><td>Virginia</td><td>10.88</td></tr>
<tr><td>43</td><td>Minnesota</td><td>8.01</td><td>23</td><td>New York</td><td>10.84</td></tr>
<tr><td>29</td><td>Mississippi</td><td>10.06</td><td>24</td><td>Washington</td><td>10.78</td></tr>
<tr><td>21</td><td>Missouri</td><td>10.94</td><td>25</td><td>Oklahoma</td><td>10.57</td></tr>
<tr><td>49</td><td>Montana</td><td>7.27</td><td>26</td><td>Nevada</td><td>10.23</td></tr>
<tr><td>43</td><td>Nebraska</td><td>8.01</td><td>27</td><td>Pennsylvania</td><td>10.18</td></tr>
<tr><td>26</td><td>Nevada</td><td>10.23</td><td>28</td><td>Kentucky</td><td>10.14</td></tr>
<tr><td>5</td><td>New Hampshire</td><td>14.25</td><td>29</td><td>Mississippi</td><td>10.06</td></tr>
<tr><td>37</td><td>New Jersey</td><td>8.30</td><td>30</td><td>Kansas</td><td>9.85</td></tr>
<tr><td>42</td><td>New Mexico</td><td>8.05</td><td>31</td><td>Alaska</td><td>9.81</td></tr>
<tr><td>23</td><td>New York</td><td>10.84</td><td>32</td><td>West Virginia</td><td>9.26</td></tr>
<tr><td>19</td><td>North Carolina</td><td>11.31</td><td>33</td><td>Tennessee</td><td>9.21</td></tr>
<tr><td>50</td><td>North Dakota</td><td>7.21</td><td>34</td><td>Utah</td><td>9.12</td></tr>
<tr><td>35</td><td>Ohio</td><td>9.03</td><td>35</td><td>Ohio</td><td>9.03</td></tr>
<tr><td>25</td><td>Oklahoma</td><td>10.57</td><td>36</td><td>Wyoming</td><td>8.51</td></tr>
<tr><td>16</td><td>Oregon</td><td>11.67</td><td>37</td><td>New Jersey</td><td>8.30</td></tr>
<tr><td>27</td><td>Pennsylvania</td><td>10.18</td><td>38</td><td>Michigan</td><td>8.21</td></tr>
<tr><td>9</td><td>Rhode Island</td><td>13.80</td><td>39</td><td>Idaho</td><td>8.14</td></tr>
<tr><td>11</td><td>South Carolina</td><td>12.62</td><td>40</td><td>Iowa</td><td>8.13</td></tr>
<tr><td>47</td><td>South Dakota</td><td>7.60</td><td>41</td><td>Wisconsin</td><td>8.07</td></tr>
<tr><td>33</td><td>Tennessee</td><td>9.21</td><td>42</td><td>New Mexico</td><td>8.05</td></tr>
<tr><td>15</td><td>Texas</td><td>11.73</td><td>43</td><td>Minnesota</td><td>8.01</td></tr>
<tr><td>34</td><td>Utah</td><td>9.12</td><td>43</td><td>Nebraska</td><td>8.01</td></tr>
<tr><td>6</td><td>Vermont</td><td>14.15</td><td>45</td><td>Indiana</td><td>7.92</td></tr>
<tr><td>22</td><td>Virginia</td><td>10.88</td><td>46</td><td>Illinois</td><td>7.88</td></tr>
<tr><td>24</td><td>Washington</td><td>10.78</td><td>47</td><td>South Dakota</td><td>7.60</td></tr>
<tr><td>32</td><td>West Virginia</td><td>9.26</td><td>48</td><td>Colorado</td><td>7.35</td></tr>
<tr><td>41</td><td>Wisconsin</td><td>8.07</td><td>49</td><td>Montana</td><td>7.27</td></tr>
<tr><td>36</td><td>Wyoming</td><td>8.51</td><td>50</td><td>North Dakota</td><td>7.21</td></tr>
<tr><td></td><td></td><td></td><td></td><td>District of Columbia</td><td>10.90</td></tr>
</table>

Source: U.S. Department of Energy, Energy Information Administration
"Natural Gas" (http://www.eia.gov/naturalgas/annual/)

Natural Gas Consumption in 2016

National Total = 27,485,517,000,000 Cubic Feet*

ALPHA ORDER

ALPHA ORDER

RANK	STATE	CUBIC FEET	% of USA
14	Alabama	697,763,000,000	2.5%
25	Alaska	324,579,000,000	1.2%
22	Arizona	358,355,000,000	1.3%
26	Arkansas	310,828,000,000	1.1%
2	California	2,177,467,000,000	7.9%
19	Colorado	473,751,000,000	1.7%
34	Connecticut	247,175,000,000	0.9%
41	Delaware	108,333,000,000	0.4%
4	Florida	1,381,502,000,000	5.0%
12	Georgia	707,299,000,000	2.6%
50	Hawaii	3,040,000,000	0.0%
42	Idaho	106,970,000,000	0.4%
7	Illinois	1,024,788,000,000	3.7%
11	Indiana	738,142,000,000	2.7%
23	Iowa	329,505,000,000	1.2%
31	Kansas	268,917,000,000	1.0%
29	Kentucky	276,415,000,000	1.0%
3	Louisiana	1,571,640,000,000	5.7%
48	Maine	53,177,000,000	0.2%
37	Maryland	218,683,000,000	0.8%
21	Massachusetts	433,439,000,000	1.6%
9	Michigan	891,798,000,000	3.2%
20	Minnesota	450,276,000,000	1.6%
15	Mississippi	546,870,000,000	2.0%
32	Missouri	265,866,000,000	1.0%
46	Montana	76,957,000,000	0.3%
39	Nebraska	163,909,000,000	0.6%
28	Nevada	303,221,000,000	1.1%
47	New Hampshire	57,817,000,000	0.2%
10	New Jersey	764,699,000,000	2.8%
33	New Mexico	249,841,000,000	0.9%
6	New York	1,300,377,000,000	4.7%
17	North Carolina	522,349,000,000	1.9%
43	North Dakota	100,555,000,000	0.4%
8	Ohio	930,253,000,000	3.4%
13	Oklahoma	701,366,000,000	2.6%
36	Oregon	235,980,000,000	0.9%
5	Pennsylvania	1,309,598,000,000	4.8%
44	Rhode Island	86,429,000,000	0.3%
30	South Carolina	275,392,000,000	1.0%
45	South Dakota	81,223,000,000	0.3%
24	Tennessee	329,380,000,000	1.2%
1	Texas	4,029,949,000,000	14.7%
35	Utah	239,101,000,000	0.9%
49	Vermont	12,093,000,000	0.0%
16	Virginia	541,620,000,000	2.0%
27	Washington	305,071,000,000	1.1%
38	West Virginia	171,100,000,000	0.6%
18	Wisconsin	481,987,000,000	1.8%
40	Wyoming	124,122,000,000	0.5%

RANK ORDER

RANK	STATE	CUBIC FEET	% of USA
1	Texas	4,029,949,000,000	14.7%
2	California	2,177,467,000,000	7.9%
3	Louisiana	1,571,640,000,000	5.7%
4	Florida	1,381,502,000,000	5.0%
5	Pennsylvania	1,309,598,000,000	4.8%
6	New York	1,300,377,000,000	4.7%
7	Illinois	1,024,788,000,000	3.7%
8	Ohio	930,253,000,000	3.4%
9	Michigan	891,798,000,000	3.2%
10	New Jersey	764,699,000,000	2.8%
11	Indiana	738,142,000,000	2.7%
12	Georgia	707,299,000,000	2.6%
13	Oklahoma	701,366,000,000	2.6%
14	Alabama	697,763,000,000	2.5%
15	Mississippi	546,870,000,000	2.0%
16	Virginia	541,620,000,000	2.0%
17	North Carolina	522,349,000,000	1.9%
18	Wisconsin	481,987,000,000	1.8%
19	Colorado	473,751,000,000	1.7%
20	Minnesota	450,276,000,000	1.6%
21	Massachusetts	433,439,000,000	1.6%
22	Arizona	358,355,000,000	1.3%
23	Iowa	329,505,000,000	1.2%
24	Tennessee	329,380,000,000	1.2%
25	Alaska	324,579,000,000	1.2%
26	Arkansas	310,828,000,000	1.1%
27	Washington	305,071,000,000	1.1%
28	Nevada	303,221,000,000	1.1%
29	Kentucky	276,415,000,000	1.0%
30	South Carolina	275,392,000,000	1.0%
31	Kansas	268,917,000,000	1.0%
32	Missouri	265,866,000,000	1.0%
33	New Mexico	249,841,000,000	0.9%
34	Connecticut	247,175,000,000	0.9%
35	Utah	239,101,000,000	0.9%
36	Oregon	235,980,000,000	0.9%
37	Maryland	218,683,000,000	0.8%
38	West Virginia	171,100,000,000	0.6%
39	Nebraska	163,909,000,000	0.6%
40	Wyoming	124,122,000,000	0.5%
41	Delaware	108,333,000,000	0.4%
42	Idaho	106,970,000,000	0.4%
43	North Dakota	100,555,000,000	0.4%
44	Rhode Island	86,429,000,000	0.3%
45	South Dakota	81,223,000,000	0.3%
46	Montana	76,957,000,000	0.3%
47	New Hampshire	57,817,000,000	0.2%
48	Maine	53,177,000,000	0.2%
49	Vermont	12,093,000,000	0.0%
50	Hawaii	3,040,000,000	0.0%
	District of Columbia	28,792,000,000	0.1%

Source: U.S. Department of Energy, Energy Information Administration
"Natural Gas" (http://www.eia.gov/naturalgas/annual/)
*National total includes 95,757,000,000 cubic feet of consumption in the Gulf of Mexico not shown by state.

Coal Mines in 2016

National Total = 710 Mines*

ALPHA ORDER

ALPHA ORDER

RANK	STATE	MINES	% of USA
5	Alabama	30	4.2%
22	Alaska	1	0.1%
22	Arizona	1	0.1%
18	Arkansas	3	0.4%
NA	California**	NA	NA
12	Colorado	8	1.1%
NA	Connecticut**	NA	NA
NA	Delaware**	NA	NA
NA	Florida**	NA	NA
NA	Georgia**	NA	NA
NA	Hawaii**	NA	NA
NA	Idaho**	NA	NA
6	Illinois	21	3.0%
7	Indiana	20	2.8%
NA	Iowa**	NA	NA
22	Kansas	1	0.1%
2	Kentucky	158	22.3%
20	Louisiana	2	0.3%
NA	Maine**	NA	NA
9	Maryland	17	2.4%
NA	Massachusetts**	NA	NA
NA	Michigan**	NA	NA
NA	Minnesota**	NA	NA
20	Mississippi	2	0.3%
22	Missouri	1	0.1%
14	Montana	6	0.8%
NA	Nebraska**	NA	NA
NA	Nevada**	NA	NA
NA	New Hampshire**	NA	NA
NA	New Jersey**	NA	NA
18	New Mexico	3	0.4%
NA	New York**	NA	NA
NA	North Carolina**	NA	NA
16	North Dakota	5	0.7%
8	Ohio	19	2.7%
17	Oklahoma	4	0.6%
NA	Oregon**	NA	NA
1	Pennsylvania	172	24.2%
NA	Rhode Island**	NA	NA
NA	South Carolina**	NA	NA
NA	South Dakota**	NA	NA
14	Tennessee	6	0.8%
11	Texas	14	2.0%
12	Utah	8	1.1%
NA	Vermont**	NA	NA
4	Virginia	54	7.6%
NA	Washington**	NA	NA
3	West Virginia	123	17.3%
NA	Wisconsin**	NA	NA
10	Wyoming	16	2.3%

RANK ORDER

RANK	STATE	MINES	% of USA
1	Pennsylvania	172	24.2%
2	Kentucky	158	22.3%
3	West Virginia	123	17.3%
4	Virginia	54	7.6%
5	Alabama	30	4.2%
6	Illinois	21	3.0%
7	Indiana	20	2.8%
8	Ohio	19	2.7%
9	Maryland	17	2.4%
10	Wyoming	16	2.3%
11	Texas	14	2.0%
12	Colorado	8	1.1%
12	Utah	8	1.1%
14	Montana	6	0.8%
14	Tennessee	6	0.8%
16	North Dakota	5	0.7%
17	Oklahoma	4	0.6%
18	Arkansas	3	0.4%
18	New Mexico	3	0.4%
20	Louisiana	2	0.3%
20	Mississippi	2	0.3%
22	Alaska	1	0.1%
22	Arizona	1	0.1%
22	Kansas	1	0.1%
22	Missouri	1	0.1%
NA	California**	NA	NA
NA	Connecticut**	NA	NA
NA	Delaware**	NA	NA
NA	Florida**	NA	NA
NA	Georgia**	NA	NA
NA	Hawaii**	NA	NA
NA	Idaho**	NA	NA
NA	Iowa**	NA	NA
NA	Maine**	NA	NA
NA	Massachusetts**	NA	NA
NA	Michigan**	NA	NA
NA	Minnesota**	NA	NA
NA	Nebraska**	NA	NA
NA	Nevada**	NA	NA
NA	New Hampshire**	NA	NA
NA	New Jersey**	NA	NA
NA	New York**	NA	NA
NA	North Carolina**	NA	NA
NA	Oregon**	NA	NA
NA	Rhode Island**	NA	NA
NA	South Carolina**	NA	NA
NA	South Dakota**	NA	NA
NA	Vermont**	NA	NA
NA	Washington**	NA	NA
NA	Wisconsin**	NA	NA
	District of Columbia**	NA	NA

Source: U.S. Department of Energy, Energy Information Administration
    "Annual Coal Report" (http://www.eia.gov/coal/annual/)
*National total includes 15 coal mines in refuse recovery not shown by state.
**Not available or no mines.

Coal Production in 2016

National Total = 728,364,000 Short Tons*

ALPHA ORDER

RANK	STATE	SHORT TONS	% of USA
15	Alabama	9,643,000	1.3%
20	Alaska	932,000	0.1%
16	Arizona	5,423,000	0.7%
24	Arkansas	49,000	0.0%
NA	California**	NA	NA
13	Colorado	12,634,000	1.7%
NA	Connecticut**	NA	NA
NA	Delaware**	NA	NA
NA	Florida**	NA	NA
NA	Georgia**	NA	NA
NA	Hawaii**	NA	NA
NA	Idaho**	NA	NA
4	Illinois	43,422,000	6.0%
8	Indiana	28,767,000	3.9%
NA	Iowa**	NA	NA
25	Kansas	27,000	0.0%
5	Kentucky	42,868,000	5.9%
18	Louisiana	2,798,000	0.4%
NA	Maine**	NA	NA
19	Maryland	1,616,000	0.2%
NA	Massachusetts**	NA	NA
NA	Michigan**	NA	NA
NA	Minnesota**	NA	NA
17	Mississippi	2,870,000	0.4%
23	Missouri	234,000	0.0%
7	Montana	32,336,000	4.4%
NA	Nebraska**	NA	NA
NA	Nevada**	NA	NA
NA	New Hampshire**	NA	NA
NA	New Jersey**	NA	NA
11	New Mexico	13,341,000	1.8%
NA	New York**	NA	NA
NA	North Carolina**	NA	NA
9	North Dakota	28,121,000	3.9%
14	Ohio	12,564,000	1.7%
21	Oklahoma	654,000	0.1%
NA	Oregon**	NA	NA
3	Pennsylvania	45,720,000	6.3%
NA	Rhode Island**	NA	NA
NA	South Carolina**	NA	NA
NA	South Dakota**	NA	NA
22	Tennessee	644,000	0.1%
6	Texas	39,001,000	5.4%
10	Utah	13,966,000	1.9%
NA	Vermont**	NA	NA
12	Virginia	12,910,000	1.8%
NA	Washington**	NA	NA
2	West Virginia	79,757,000	11.0%
NA	Wisconsin**	NA	NA
1	Wyoming	297,218,000	40.8%

RANK ORDER

RANK	STATE	SHORT TONS	% of USA
1	Wyoming	297,218,000	40.8%
2	West Virginia	79,757,000	11.0%
3	Pennsylvania	45,720,000	6.3%
4	Illinois	43,422,000	6.0%
5	Kentucky	42,868,000	5.9%
6	Texas	39,001,000	5.4%
7	Montana	32,336,000	4.4%
8	Indiana	28,767,000	3.9%
9	North Dakota	28,121,000	3.9%
10	Utah	13,966,000	1.9%
11	New Mexico	13,341,000	1.8%
12	Virginia	12,910,000	1.8%
13	Colorado	12,634,000	1.7%
14	Ohio	12,564,000	1.7%
15	Alabama	9,643,000	1.3%
16	Arizona	5,423,000	0.7%
17	Mississippi	2,870,000	0.4%
18	Louisiana	2,798,000	0.4%
19	Maryland	1,616,000	0.2%
20	Alaska	932,000	0.1%
21	Oklahoma	654,000	0.1%
22	Tennessee	644,000	0.1%
23	Missouri	234,000	0.0%
24	Arkansas	49,000	0.0%
25	Kansas	27,000	0.0%
NA	California**	NA	NA
NA	Connecticut**	NA	NA
NA	Delaware**	NA	NA
NA	Florida**	NA	NA
NA	Georgia**	NA	NA
NA	Hawaii**	NA	NA
NA	Idaho**	NA	NA
NA	Iowa**	NA	NA
NA	Maine**	NA	NA
NA	Massachusetts**	NA	NA
NA	Michigan**	NA	NA
NA	Minnesota**	NA	NA
NA	Nebraska**	NA	NA
NA	Nevada**	NA	NA
NA	New Hampshire**	NA	NA
NA	New Jersey**	NA	NA
NA	New York**	NA	NA
NA	North Carolina**	NA	NA
NA	Oregon**	NA	NA
NA	Rhode Island**	NA	NA
NA	South Carolina**	NA	NA
NA	South Dakota**	NA	NA
NA	Vermont**	NA	NA
NA	Washington**	NA	NA
NA	Wisconsin**	NA	NA
	District of Columbia**	NA	NA

Source: U.S. Department of Energy, Energy Information Administration
"Annual Coal Report" (http://www.eia.gov/coal/annual/)
*National total includes 851,000 short tons from refuse recovery not shown by state.
**Not available or no production.

Gasoline Used in 2015

National Total = 141,223,831,000 Gallons*

ALPHA ORDER					RANK ORDER			
RANK	STATE	GALLONS	% of USA		RANK	STATE	GALLONS	% of USA
21	Alabama	2,693,621,000	1.9%		1	California	15,119,963,000	10.7%
50	Alaska	292,676,000	0.2%		2	Texas	13,879,235,000	9.8%
17	Arizona	2,817,171,000	2.0%		3	Florida	8,801,605,000	6.2%
32	Arkansas	1,449,145,000	1.0%		4	New York	5,476,920,000	3.9%
1	California	15,119,963,000	10.7%		5	Illinois	5,107,398,000	3.6%
25	Colorado	2,267,717,000	1.6%		6	Ohio	5,099,848,000	3.6%
31	Connecticut	1,483,597,000	1.1%		7	Georgia	4,958,128,000	3.5%
45	Delaware	469,581,000	0.3%		8	Pennsylvania	4,910,701,000	3.5%
3	Florida	8,801,605,000	6.2%		9	Michigan	4,697,295,000	3.3%
7	Georgia	4,958,128,000	3.5%		10	North Carolina	4,520,357,000	3.2%
46	Hawaii	461,423,000	0.3%		11	New Jersey	4,116,723,000	2.9%
40	Idaho	750,158,000	0.5%		12	Virginia	4,024,639,000	2.8%
5	Illinois	5,107,398,000	3.6%		13	Tennessee	3,258,699,000	2.3%
14	Indiana	3,155,186,000	2.2%		14	Indiana	3,155,186,000	2.2%
29	Iowa	1,665,151,000	1.2%		15	Missouri	3,139,992,000	2.2%
33	Kansas	1,284,413,000	0.9%		16	Maryland	2,842,601,000	2.0%
26	Kentucky	2,184,747,000	1.5%		17	Arizona	2,817,171,000	2.0%
24	Louisiana	2,340,903,000	1.7%		18	South Carolina	2,816,907,000	2.0%
39	Maine	784,443,000	0.6%		19	Washington	2,798,481,000	2.0%
16	Maryland	2,842,601,000	2.0%		20	Massachusetts	2,797,063,000	2.0%
20	Massachusetts	2,797,063,000	2.0%		21	Alabama	2,693,621,000	1.9%
9	Michigan	4,697,295,000	3.3%		22	Wisconsin	2,602,085,000	1.8%
23	Minnesota	2,563,490,000	1.8%		23	Minnesota	2,563,490,000	1.8%
28	Mississippi	1,693,817,000	1.2%		24	Louisiana	2,340,903,000	1.7%
15	Missouri	3,139,992,000	2.2%		25	Colorado	2,267,717,000	1.6%
42	Montana	539,982,000	0.4%		26	Kentucky	2,184,747,000	1.5%
37	Nebraska	891,405,000	0.6%		27	Oklahoma	1,956,297,000	1.4%
34	Nevada	1,153,966,000	0.8%		28	Mississippi	1,693,817,000	1.2%
41	New Hampshire	716,055,000	0.5%		29	Iowa	1,665,151,000	1.2%
11	New Jersey	4,116,723,000	2.9%		30	Oregon	1,556,347,000	1.1%
36	New Mexico	981,607,000	0.7%		31	Connecticut	1,483,597,000	1.1%
4	New York	5,476,920,000	3.9%		32	Arkansas	1,449,145,000	1.0%
10	North Carolina	4,520,357,000	3.2%		33	Kansas	1,284,413,000	0.9%
43	North Dakota	471,451,000	0.3%		34	Nevada	1,153,966,000	0.8%
6	Ohio	5,099,848,000	3.6%		35	Utah	1,117,474,000	0.8%
27	Oklahoma	1,956,297,000	1.4%		36	New Mexico	981,607,000	0.7%
30	Oregon	1,556,347,000	1.1%		37	Nebraska	891,405,000	0.6%
8	Pennsylvania	4,910,701,000	3.5%		38	West Virginia	865,036,000	0.6%
47	Rhode Island	380,918,000	0.3%		39	Maine	784,443,000	0.6%
18	South Carolina	2,816,907,000	2.0%		40	Idaho	750,158,000	0.5%
44	South Dakota	471,443,000	0.3%		41	New Hampshire	716,055,000	0.5%
13	Tennessee	3,258,699,000	2.3%		42	Montana	539,982,000	0.4%
2	Texas	13,879,235,000	9.8%		43	North Dakota	471,451,000	0.3%
35	Utah	1,117,474,000	0.8%		44	South Dakota	471,443,000	0.3%
49	Vermont	312,937,000	0.2%		45	Delaware	469,581,000	0.3%
12	Virginia	4,024,639,000	2.8%		46	Hawaii	461,423,000	0.3%
19	Washington	2,798,481,000	2.0%		47	Rhode Island	380,918,000	0.3%
38	West Virginia	865,036,000	0.6%		48	Wyoming	369,150,000	0.3%
22	Wisconsin	2,602,085,000	1.8%		49	Vermont	312,937,000	0.2%
48	Wyoming	369,150,000	0.3%		50	Alaska	292,676,000	0.2%
						District of Columbia	113,884,000	0.1%

Source: U.S. Department of Transportation, Federal Highway Administration
"Highway Statistics 2015" (Table MF-21, http://www.fhwa.dot.gov/policyinformation/statistics/2015/)
*Includes gasoline for highway and nonhighway uses as well as for losses allowed for evaporation and handling. "Gasoline"
includes gasohol but excludes "special fuels" such as diesel.

Per Capita Gasoline Used in 2015

National Per Capita = 440 Gallons*

<table>
<tr><th colspan="3">ALPHA ORDER</th><th colspan="3">RANK ORDER</th></tr>
<tr><th>RANK</th><th>STATE</th><th>PER CAPITA</th><th>RANK</th><th>STATE</th><th>PER CAPITA</th></tr>
<tr><td>6</td><td>Alabama</td><td>555</td><td>1</td><td>Wyoming</td><td>629</td></tr>
<tr><td>42</td><td>Alaska</td><td>397</td><td>2</td><td>North Dakota</td><td>623</td></tr>
<tr><td>38</td><td>Arizona</td><td>413</td><td>3</td><td>Maine</td><td>590</td></tr>
<tr><td>19</td><td>Arkansas</td><td>487</td><td>4</td><td>South Carolina</td><td>575</td></tr>
<tr><td>44</td><td>California</td><td>388</td><td>5</td><td>Mississippi</td><td>567</td></tr>
<tr><td>36</td><td>Colorado</td><td>416</td><td>6</td><td>Alabama</td><td>555</td></tr>
<tr><td>37</td><td>Connecticut</td><td>414</td><td>7</td><td>South Dakota</td><td>550</td></tr>
<tr><td>16</td><td>Delaware</td><td>497</td><td>8</td><td>New Hampshire</td><td>538</td></tr>
<tr><td>35</td><td>Florida</td><td>435</td><td>9</td><td>Iowa</td><td>533</td></tr>
<tr><td>20</td><td>Georgia</td><td>486</td><td>10</td><td>Montana</td><td>523</td></tr>
<tr><td>49</td><td>Hawaii</td><td>324</td><td>11</td><td>Missouri</td><td>517</td></tr>
<tr><td>30</td><td>Idaho</td><td>454</td><td>12</td><td>Texas</td><td>506</td></tr>
<tr><td>41</td><td>Illinois</td><td>398</td><td>13</td><td>Louisiana</td><td>501</td></tr>
<tr><td>22</td><td>Indiana</td><td>477</td><td>13</td><td>Oklahoma</td><td>501</td></tr>
<tr><td>9</td><td>Iowa</td><td>533</td><td>15</td><td>Vermont</td><td>500</td></tr>
<tr><td>33</td><td>Kansas</td><td>442</td><td>16</td><td>Delaware</td><td>497</td></tr>
<tr><td>17</td><td>Kentucky</td><td>494</td><td>17</td><td>Kentucky</td><td>494</td></tr>
<tr><td>13</td><td>Louisiana</td><td>501</td><td>17</td><td>Tennessee</td><td>494</td></tr>
<tr><td>3</td><td>Maine</td><td>590</td><td>19</td><td>Arkansas</td><td>487</td></tr>
<tr><td>23</td><td>Maryland</td><td>474</td><td>20</td><td>Georgia</td><td>486</td></tr>
<tr><td>39</td><td>Massachusetts</td><td>412</td><td>21</td><td>Virginia</td><td>481</td></tr>
<tr><td>23</td><td>Michigan</td><td>474</td><td>22</td><td>Indiana</td><td>477</td></tr>
<tr><td>28</td><td>Minnesota</td><td>468</td><td>23</td><td>Maryland</td><td>474</td></tr>
<tr><td>5</td><td>Mississippi</td><td>567</td><td>23</td><td>Michigan</td><td>474</td></tr>
<tr><td>11</td><td>Missouri</td><td>517</td><td>25</td><td>New Mexico</td><td>472</td></tr>
<tr><td>10</td><td>Montana</td><td>523</td><td>26</td><td>Nebraska</td><td>471</td></tr>
<tr><td>26</td><td>Nebraska</td><td>471</td><td>27</td><td>West Virginia</td><td>470</td></tr>
<tr><td>40</td><td>Nevada</td><td>400</td><td>28</td><td>Minnesota</td><td>468</td></tr>
<tr><td>8</td><td>New Hampshire</td><td>538</td><td>29</td><td>New Jersey</td><td>461</td></tr>
<tr><td>29</td><td>New Jersey</td><td>461</td><td>30</td><td>Idaho</td><td>454</td></tr>
<tr><td>25</td><td>New Mexico</td><td>472</td><td>31</td><td>Wisconsin</td><td>451</td></tr>
<tr><td>50</td><td>New York</td><td>277</td><td>32</td><td>North Carolina</td><td>450</td></tr>
<tr><td>32</td><td>North Carolina</td><td>450</td><td>33</td><td>Kansas</td><td>442</td></tr>
<tr><td>2</td><td>North Dakota</td><td>623</td><td>34</td><td>Ohio</td><td>439</td></tr>
<tr><td>34</td><td>Ohio</td><td>439</td><td>35</td><td>Florida</td><td>435</td></tr>
<tr><td>13</td><td>Oklahoma</td><td>501</td><td>36</td><td>Colorado</td><td>416</td></tr>
<tr><td>45</td><td>Oregon</td><td>387</td><td>37</td><td>Connecticut</td><td>414</td></tr>
<tr><td>46</td><td>Pennsylvania</td><td>384</td><td>38</td><td>Arizona</td><td>413</td></tr>
<tr><td>48</td><td>Rhode Island</td><td>361</td><td>39</td><td>Massachusetts</td><td>412</td></tr>
<tr><td>4</td><td>South Carolina</td><td>575</td><td>40</td><td>Nevada</td><td>400</td></tr>
<tr><td>7</td><td>South Dakota</td><td>550</td><td>41</td><td>Illinois</td><td>398</td></tr>
<tr><td>17</td><td>Tennessee</td><td>494</td><td>42</td><td>Alaska</td><td>397</td></tr>
<tr><td>12</td><td>Texas</td><td>506</td><td>43</td><td>Washington</td><td>391</td></tr>
<tr><td>47</td><td>Utah</td><td>374</td><td>44</td><td>California</td><td>388</td></tr>
<tr><td>15</td><td>Vermont</td><td>500</td><td>45</td><td>Oregon</td><td>387</td></tr>
<tr><td>21</td><td>Virginia</td><td>481</td><td>46</td><td>Pennsylvania</td><td>384</td></tr>
<tr><td>43</td><td>Washington</td><td>391</td><td>47</td><td>Utah</td><td>374</td></tr>
<tr><td>27</td><td>West Virginia</td><td>470</td><td>48</td><td>Rhode Island</td><td>361</td></tr>
<tr><td>31</td><td>Wisconsin</td><td>451</td><td>49</td><td>Hawaii</td><td>324</td></tr>
<tr><td>1</td><td>Wyoming</td><td>629</td><td>50</td><td>New York</td><td>277</td></tr>
<tr><td></td><td></td><td></td><td></td><td>District of Columbia</td><td>170</td></tr>
</table>

Source: CQ Press using data from U.S. Department of Transportation, Federal Highway Administration
"Highway Statistics 2015" (Table MF-21, http://www.fhwa.dot.gov/policyinformation/statistics/2015/)
*Includes gasoline for highway and nonhighway uses as well as for losses allowed for evaporation and handling. "Gasoline" includes gasohol but excludes "special fuels" such as diesel.

Daily Production of Crude Oil in 2016

National Total = 8,856,806 Barrels a Day*

ALPHA ORDER

RANK	STATE	BARRELS	% of USA
16	Alabama	22,150	0.3%
4	Alaska	489,533	5.5%
31	Arizona	22	0.0%
20	Arkansas	14,937	0.2%
3	California	508,413	5.7%
7	Colorado	316,658	3.6%
NA	Connecticut**	NA	NA
NA	Delaware**	NA	NA
23	Florida	5,284	0.1%
NA	Georgia**	NA	NA
NA	Hawaii**	NA	NA
29	Idaho	587	0.0%
15	Illinois	23,604	0.3%
24	Indiana	4,964	0.1%
NA	Iowa**	NA	NA
10	Kansas	103,970	1.2%
21	Kentucky	7,090	0.1%
9	Louisiana	154,186	1.7%
NA	Maine**	NA	NA
NA	Maryland**	NA	NA
NA	Massachusetts**	NA	NA
19	Michigan	15,344	0.2%
NA	Minnesota**	NA	NA
14	Mississippi	55,697	0.6%
30	Missouri	336	0.0%
12	Montana	63,352	0.7%
22	Nebraska	6,169	0.1%
26	Nevada	757	0.0%
NA	New Hampshire**	NA	NA
NA	New Jersey**	NA	NA
6	New Mexico	398,978	4.5%
28	New York	607	0.0%
NA	North Carolina**	NA	NA
2	North Dakota	1,032,699	11.7%
13	Ohio	60,137	0.7%
5	Oklahoma	419,817	4.7%
NA	Oregon**	NA	NA
18	Pennsylvania	17,230	0.2%
NA	Rhode Island**	NA	NA
NA	South Carolina**	NA	NA
25	South Dakota	3,844	0.0%
27	Tennessee	702	0.0%
1	Texas	3,213,227	36.3%
11	Utah	83,393	0.9%
NA	Vermont**	NA	NA
32	Virginia	19	0.0%
NA	Washington**	NA	NA
17	West Virginia	20,454	0.2%
NA	Wisconsin**	NA	NA
8	Wyoming	198,208	2.2%

RANK ORDER

RANK	STATE	BARRELS	% of USA
1	Texas	3,213,227	36.3%
2	North Dakota	1,032,699	11.7%
3	California	508,413	5.7%
4	Alaska	489,533	5.5%
5	Oklahoma	419,817	4.7%
6	New Mexico	398,978	4.5%
7	Colorado	316,658	3.6%
8	Wyoming	198,208	2.2%
9	Louisiana	154,186	1.7%
10	Kansas	103,970	1.2%
11	Utah	83,393	0.9%
12	Montana	63,352	0.7%
13	Ohio	60,137	0.7%
14	Mississippi	55,697	0.6%
15	Illinois	23,604	0.3%
16	Alabama	22,150	0.3%
17	West Virginia	20,454	0.2%
18	Pennsylvania	17,230	0.2%
19	Michigan	15,344	0.2%
20	Arkansas	14,937	0.2%
21	Kentucky	7,090	0.1%
22	Nebraska	6,169	0.1%
23	Florida	5,284	0.1%
24	Indiana	4,964	0.1%
25	South Dakota	3,844	0.0%
26	Nevada	757	0.0%
27	Tennessee	702	0.0%
28	New York	607	0.0%
29	Idaho	587	0.0%
30	Missouri	336	0.0%
31	Arizona	22	0.0%
32	Virginia	19	0.0%
NA	Connecticut**	NA	NA
NA	Delaware**	NA	NA
NA	Georgia**	NA	NA
NA	Hawaii**	NA	NA
NA	Iowa**	NA	NA
NA	Maine**	NA	NA
NA	Maryland**	NA	NA
NA	Massachusetts**	NA	NA
NA	Minnesota**	NA	NA
NA	New Hampshire**	NA	NA
NA	New Jersey**	NA	NA
NA	North Carolina**	NA	NA
NA	Oregon**	NA	NA
NA	Rhode Island**	NA	NA
NA	South Carolina**	NA	NA
NA	Vermont**	NA	NA
NA	Washington**	NA	NA
NA	Wisconsin**	NA	NA
	District of Columbia**	NA	NA

Source: CQ Press using data from U.S. Department of Energy, Energy Information Administration
  "Petroleum Supply Annual 2016, Volume 1" (http://tonto.eia.doe.gov/dnav/pet/pet_crd_crpdn_adc_mbbl_m.htm)
*National total includes 1,614,437 barrels a day in federal offshore production. Figures for Alaska, California, Louisiana, and Texas include state offshore production.
**No reported production.

Fossil Fuel Emissions in 2015

National Total = 5,049,800,000 Metric Tons of Carbon Dioxide (CO2)*

<table>
<tr><td colspan="4">ALPHA ORDER</td><td colspan="4">RANK ORDER</td></tr>
<tr><th>RANK</th><th>STATE</th><th>TONS OF CO2</th><th>% of USA</th><th>RANK</th><th>STATE</th><th>TONS OF CO2</th><th>% of USA</th></tr>
<tr><td>15</td><td>Alabama</td><td>118,330,000</td><td>2.3%</td><td>1</td><td>Texas</td><td>698,850,000</td><td>13.8%</td></tr>
<tr><td>40</td><td>Alaska</td><td>35,920,000</td><td>0.7%</td><td>2</td><td>California</td><td>364,760,000</td><td>7.2%</td></tr>
<tr><td>22</td><td>Arizona</td><td>90,560,000</td><td>1.8%</td><td>3</td><td>Pennsylvania</td><td>230,710,000</td><td>4.6%</td></tr>
<tr><td>34</td><td>Arkansas</td><td>58,880,000</td><td>1.2%</td><td>4</td><td>Florida</td><td>230,380,000</td><td>4.6%</td></tr>
<tr><td>2</td><td>California</td><td>364,760,000</td><td>7.2%</td><td>5</td><td>Illinois</td><td>219,540,000</td><td>4.3%</td></tr>
<tr><td>23</td><td>Colorado</td><td>89,470,000</td><td>1.8%</td><td>6</td><td>Ohio</td><td>212,410,000</td><td>4.2%</td></tr>
<tr><td>39</td><td>Connecticut</td><td>36,520,000</td><td>0.7%</td><td>7</td><td>Louisiana</td><td>209,670,000</td><td>4.2%</td></tr>
<tr><td>48</td><td>Delaware</td><td>13,480,000</td><td>0.3%</td><td>8</td><td>Indiana</td><td>185,470,000</td><td>3.7%</td></tr>
<tr><td>4</td><td>Florida</td><td>230,380,000</td><td>4.6%</td><td>9</td><td>New York</td><td>168,790,000</td><td>3.3%</td></tr>
<tr><td>11</td><td>Georgia</td><td>136,250,000</td><td>2.7%</td><td>10</td><td>Michigan</td><td>161,630,000</td><td>3.2%</td></tr>
<tr><td>43</td><td>Hawaii</td><td>18,430,000</td><td>0.4%</td><td>11</td><td>Georgia</td><td>136,250,000</td><td>2.7%</td></tr>
<tr><td>44</td><td>Idaho</td><td>17,820,000</td><td>0.4%</td><td>12</td><td>Kentucky</td><td>129,290,000</td><td>2.6%</td></tr>
<tr><td>5</td><td>Illinois</td><td>219,540,000</td><td>4.3%</td><td>13</td><td>Missouri</td><td>122,760,000</td><td>2.4%</td></tr>
<tr><td>8</td><td>Indiana</td><td>185,470,000</td><td>3.7%</td><td>14</td><td>North Carolina</td><td>119,450,000</td><td>2.4%</td></tr>
<tr><td>25</td><td>Iowa</td><td>77,460,000</td><td>1.5%</td><td>15</td><td>Alabama</td><td>118,330,000</td><td>2.3%</td></tr>
<tr><td>31</td><td>Kansas</td><td>63,030,000</td><td>1.2%</td><td>16</td><td>New Jersey</td><td>112,600,000</td><td>2.2%</td></tr>
<tr><td>12</td><td>Kentucky</td><td>129,290,000</td><td>2.6%</td><td>17</td><td>Virginia</td><td>102,460,000</td><td>2.0%</td></tr>
<tr><td>7</td><td>Louisiana</td><td>209,670,000</td><td>4.2%</td><td>18</td><td>Oklahoma</td><td>100,880,000</td><td>2.0%</td></tr>
<tr><td>45</td><td>Maine</td><td>16,810,000</td><td>0.3%</td><td>19</td><td>Tennessee</td><td>99,140,000</td><td>2.0%</td></tr>
<tr><td>33</td><td>Maryland</td><td>60,090,000</td><td>1.2%</td><td>20</td><td>Wisconsin</td><td>99,060,000</td><td>2.0%</td></tr>
<tr><td>28</td><td>Massachusetts</td><td>65,770,000</td><td>1.3%</td><td>21</td><td>West Virginia</td><td>90,850,000</td><td>1.8%</td></tr>
<tr><td>10</td><td>Michigan</td><td>161,630,000</td><td>3.2%</td><td>22</td><td>Arizona</td><td>90,560,000</td><td>1.8%</td></tr>
<tr><td>24</td><td>Minnesota</td><td>87,110,000</td><td>1.7%</td><td>23</td><td>Colorado</td><td>89,470,000</td><td>1.8%</td></tr>
<tr><td>29</td><td>Mississippi</td><td>64,810,000</td><td>1.3%</td><td>24</td><td>Minnesota</td><td>87,110,000</td><td>1.7%</td></tr>
<tr><td>13</td><td>Missouri</td><td>122,760,000</td><td>2.4%</td><td>25</td><td>Iowa</td><td>77,460,000</td><td>1.5%</td></tr>
<tr><td>42</td><td>Montana</td><td>32,130,000</td><td>0.6%</td><td>26</td><td>Washington</td><td>76,120,000</td><td>1.5%</td></tr>
<tr><td>36</td><td>Nebraska</td><td>50,370,000</td><td>1.0%</td><td>27</td><td>South Carolina</td><td>73,150,000</td><td>1.4%</td></tr>
<tr><td>41</td><td>Nevada</td><td>35,160,000</td><td>0.7%</td><td>28</td><td>Massachusetts</td><td>65,770,000</td><td>1.3%</td></tr>
<tr><td>46</td><td>New Hampshire</td><td>15,100,000</td><td>0.3%</td><td>29</td><td>Mississippi</td><td>64,810,000</td><td>1.3%</td></tr>
<tr><td>16</td><td>New Jersey</td><td>112,600,000</td><td>2.2%</td><td>30</td><td>Wyoming</td><td>64,360,000</td><td>1.3%</td></tr>
<tr><td>37</td><td>New Mexico</td><td>50,360,000</td><td>1.0%</td><td>31</td><td>Kansas</td><td>63,030,000</td><td>1.2%</td></tr>
<tr><td>9</td><td>New York</td><td>168,790,000</td><td>3.3%</td><td>32</td><td>Utah</td><td>62,350,000</td><td>1.2%</td></tr>
<tr><td>14</td><td>North Carolina</td><td>119,450,000</td><td>2.4%</td><td>33</td><td>Maryland</td><td>60,090,000</td><td>1.2%</td></tr>
<tr><td>35</td><td>North Dakota</td><td>53,810,000</td><td>1.1%</td><td>34</td><td>Arkansas</td><td>58,880,000</td><td>1.2%</td></tr>
<tr><td>6</td><td>Ohio</td><td>212,410,000</td><td>4.2%</td><td>35</td><td>North Dakota</td><td>53,810,000</td><td>1.1%</td></tr>
<tr><td>18</td><td>Oklahoma</td><td>100,880,000</td><td>2.0%</td><td>36</td><td>Nebraska</td><td>50,370,000</td><td>1.0%</td></tr>
<tr><td>38</td><td>Oregon</td><td>38,030,000</td><td>0.8%</td><td>37</td><td>New Mexico</td><td>50,360,000</td><td>1.0%</td></tr>
<tr><td>3</td><td>Pennsylvania</td><td>230,710,000</td><td>4.6%</td><td>38</td><td>Oregon</td><td>38,030,000</td><td>0.8%</td></tr>
<tr><td>49</td><td>Rhode Island</td><td>10,920,000</td><td>0.2%</td><td>39</td><td>Connecticut</td><td>36,520,000</td><td>0.7%</td></tr>
<tr><td>27</td><td>South Carolina</td><td>73,150,000</td><td>1.4%</td><td>40</td><td>Alaska</td><td>35,920,000</td><td>0.7%</td></tr>
<tr><td>47</td><td>South Dakota</td><td>14,090,000</td><td>0.3%</td><td>41</td><td>Nevada</td><td>35,160,000</td><td>0.7%</td></tr>
<tr><td>19</td><td>Tennessee</td><td>99,140,000</td><td>2.0%</td><td>42</td><td>Montana</td><td>32,130,000</td><td>0.6%</td></tr>
<tr><td>1</td><td>Texas</td><td>698,850,000</td><td>13.8%</td><td>43</td><td>Hawaii</td><td>18,430,000</td><td>0.4%</td></tr>
<tr><td>32</td><td>Utah</td><td>62,350,000</td><td>1.2%</td><td>44</td><td>Idaho</td><td>17,820,000</td><td>0.4%</td></tr>
<tr><td>50</td><td>Vermont</td><td>6,140,000</td><td>0.1%</td><td>45</td><td>Maine</td><td>16,810,000</td><td>0.3%</td></tr>
<tr><td>17</td><td>Virginia</td><td>102,460,000</td><td>2.0%</td><td>46</td><td>New Hampshire</td><td>15,100,000</td><td>0.3%</td></tr>
<tr><td>26</td><td>Washington</td><td>76,120,000</td><td>1.5%</td><td>47</td><td>South Dakota</td><td>14,090,000</td><td>0.3%</td></tr>
<tr><td>21</td><td>West Virginia</td><td>90,850,000</td><td>1.8%</td><td>48</td><td>Delaware</td><td>13,480,000</td><td>0.3%</td></tr>
<tr><td>20</td><td>Wisconsin</td><td>99,060,000</td><td>2.0%</td><td>49</td><td>Rhode Island</td><td>10,920,000</td><td>0.2%</td></tr>
<tr><td>30</td><td>Wyoming</td><td>64,360,000</td><td>1.3%</td><td>50</td><td>Vermont</td><td>6,140,000</td><td>0.1%</td></tr>
<tr><td></td><td></td><td></td><td></td><td></td><td>District of Columbia</td><td>3,010,000</td><td>0.1%</td></tr>
</table>

Source: U.S. Environmental Protection Agency
   "Energy CO2 Emissions by State" (https://www.epa.gov/statelocalclimate/state-energy-co2-emissions)
*Carbon dioxide (CO2) emissions from fossil fuel combustion. This represents the largest source (93%) of total CO2 emissions from all emission sources. Emissions are based on the location where fossil fuels are used. Fuels can be used in one state to generate electricity consumed in another. National figure does not include non-energy use of fuels.

Per Capita Fossil Fuel Emissions in 2015

National Per Capita = 15.7 Metric Tons of Carbon Dioxide (CO2)*

ALPHA ORDER

RANK	STATE	PER CAPITA
13	Alabama	24.4
4	Alaska	48.7
32	Arizona	13.3
19	Arkansas	19.8
49	California	9.3
25	Colorado	16.4
44	Connecticut	10.2
30	Delaware	14.3
39	Florida	11.4
31	Georgia	13.4
33	Hawaii	12.9
41	Idaho	10.8
23	Illinois	17.1
8	Indiana	28.1
12	Iowa	24.8
15	Kansas	21.7
7	Kentucky	29.2
5	Louisiana	44.9
34	Maine	12.7
45	Maryland	10.0
47	Massachusetts	9.7
26	Michigan	16.3
27	Minnesota	15.9
15	Mississippi	21.7
18	Missouri	20.2
6	Montana	31.2
9	Nebraska	26.6
36	Nevada	12.2
39	New Hampshire	11.4
35	New Jersey	12.6
14	New Mexico	24.2
50	New York	8.5
38	North Carolina	11.9
2	North Dakota	71.3
20	Ohio	18.3
10	Oklahoma	25.8
48	Oregon	9.5
21	Pennsylvania	18.0
43	Rhode Island	10.3
28	South Carolina	15.0
24	South Dakota	16.5
28	Tennessee	15.0
11	Texas	25.5
17	Utah	20.9
46	Vermont	9.8
36	Virginia	12.2
42	Washington	10.6
3	West Virginia	49.4
22	Wisconsin	17.2
1	Wyoming	109.8

RANK ORDER

RANK	STATE	PER CAPITA
1	Wyoming	109.8
2	North Dakota	71.3
3	West Virginia	49.4
4	Alaska	48.7
5	Louisiana	44.9
6	Montana	31.2
7	Kentucky	29.2
8	Indiana	28.1
9	Nebraska	26.6
10	Oklahoma	25.8
11	Texas	25.5
12	Iowa	24.8
13	Alabama	24.4
14	New Mexico	24.2
15	Kansas	21.7
15	Mississippi	21.7
17	Utah	20.9
18	Missouri	20.2
19	Arkansas	19.8
20	Ohio	18.3
21	Pennsylvania	18.0
22	Wisconsin	17.2
23	Illinois	17.1
24	South Dakota	16.5
25	Colorado	16.4
26	Michigan	16.3
27	Minnesota	15.9
28	South Carolina	15.0
28	Tennessee	15.0
30	Delaware	14.3
31	Georgia	13.4
32	Arizona	13.3
33	Hawaii	12.9
34	Maine	12.7
35	New Jersey	12.6
36	Nevada	12.2
36	Virginia	12.2
38	North Carolina	11.9
39	Florida	11.4
39	New Hampshire	11.4
41	Idaho	10.8
42	Washington	10.6
43	Rhode Island	10.3
44	Connecticut	10.2
45	Maryland	10.0
46	Vermont	9.8
47	Massachusetts	9.7
48	Oregon	9.5
49	California	9.3
50	New York	8.5
	District of Columbia	4.5

Source: CQ Press using data from U.S. Environmental Protection Agency
"Energy CO2 Emissions by State" (https://www.epa.gov/statelocalclimate/state-energy-co2-emissions)
*Carbon dioxide (CO2) emissions from fossil fuel combustion. This represents the largest source (93%) of total CO2 emissions from all emission sources. Emissions are based on the location where fossil fuels are used. Fuels can be used in one state to generate electricity consumed in another. National figure doe not include non-energy use of fuels.

Percent Change in Fossil Fuel Emissions: 2011 to 2015

National Percent Change = 3.4% Decrease*

ALPHA ORDER				RANK ORDER		
RANK	STATE	PERCENT CHANGE		RANK	STATE	PERCENT CHANGE
40	Alabama	(7.6)		1	Idaho	12.7
32	Alaska	(5.9)		2	Washington	8.1
22	Arizona	(2.6)		3	North Dakota	7.3
48	Arkansas	(12.1)		4	Mississippi	7.1
10	California	3.3		5	Vermont	5.3
20	Colorado	(1.8)		6	Connecticut	4.5
6	Connecticut	4.5		7	Nevada	4.2
9	Delaware	3.6		8	Texas	4.0
16	Florida	1.2		9	Delaware	3.6
49	Georgia	(12.3)		10	California	3.3
29	Hawaii	(4.4)		10	Virginia	3.3
1	Idaho	12.7		12	Oregon	2.3
28	Illinois	(4.3)		13	New York	2.2
45	Indiana	(10.5)		14	Wisconsin	1.9
46	Iowa	(10.7)		15	Michigan	1.5
47	Kansas	(10.8)		16	Florida	1.2
50	Kentucky	(12.4)		16	Montana	1.2
37	Louisiana	(6.4)		18	Wyoming	1.0
27	Maine	(4.2)		19	Rhode Island	(1.3)
39	Maryland	(7.4)		20	Colorado	(1.8)
26	Massachusetts	(3.5)		21	Utah	(2.0)
15	Michigan	1.5		22	Arizona	(2.6)
30	Minnesota	(5.0)		23	Nebraska	(3.0)
4	Mississippi	7.1		24	New Jersey	(3.3)
42	Missouri	(8.7)		25	South Dakota	(3.4)
16	Montana	1.2		26	Massachusetts	(3.5)
23	Nebraska	(3.0)		27	Maine	(4.2)
7	Nevada	4.2		28	Illinois	(4.3)
38	New Hampshire	(6.5)		29	Hawaii	(4.4)
24	New Jersey	(3.3)		30	Minnesota	(5.0)
43	New Mexico	(9.6)		31	West Virginia	(5.1)
13	New York	2.2		32	Alaska	(5.9)
32	North Carolina	(5.9)		32	North Carolina	(5.9)
3	North Dakota	7.3		32	Pennsylvania	(5.9)
44	Ohio	(9.7)		35	Tennessee	(6.0)
36	Oklahoma	(6.1)		36	Oklahoma	(6.1)
12	Oregon	2.3		37	Louisiana	(6.4)
32	Pennsylvania	(5.9)		38	New Hampshire	(6.5)
19	Rhode Island	(1.3)		39	Maryland	(7.4)
41	South Carolina	(8.1)		40	Alabama	(7.6)
25	South Dakota	(3.4)		41	South Carolina	(8.1)
35	Tennessee	(6.0)		42	Missouri	(8.7)
8	Texas	4.0		43	New Mexico	(9.6)
21	Utah	(2.0)		44	Ohio	(9.7)
5	Vermont	5.3		45	Indiana	(10.5)
10	Virginia	3.3		46	Iowa	(10.7)
2	Washington	8.1		47	Kansas	(10.8)
31	West Virginia	(5.1)		48	Arkansas	(12.1)
14	Wisconsin	1.9		49	Georgia	(12.3)
18	Wyoming	1.0		50	Kentucky	(12.4)
				District of Columbia		(2.9)

Source: CQ Press using data from U.S. Environmental Protection Agency
"Energy CO2 Emissions by State" (https://www.epa.gov/statelocalclimate/state-energy-co2-emissions)
*Based on metric tons of carbon dioxide (CO2).

Toxic Releases: Total Pollution Released in 2016

National Total = 3,441,783,851 Pounds*

ALPHA ORDER				RANK ORDER			
RANK	STATE	POUNDS	% of USA	RANK	STATE	POUNDS	% of USA
10	Alabama	82,464,289	2.4%	1	Alaska	833,848,953	24.2%
1	Alaska	833,848,953	24.2%	2	Nevada	316,820,585	9.2%
9	Arizona	85,055,785	2.5%	3	Utah	271,384,698	7.9%
29	Arkansas	30,607,200	0.9%	4	Texas	201,224,890	5.8%
23	California	35,086,590	1.0%	5	Louisiana	142,811,333	4.1%
27	Colorado	32,394,491	0.9%	6	Indiana	129,990,697	3.8%
47	Connecticut	1,724,056	0.1%	7	Illinois	109,549,325	3.2%
44	Delaware	3,880,208	0.1%	8	Ohio	96,491,263	2.8%
14	Florida	63,962,536	1.9%	9	Arizona	85,055,785	2.5%
18	Georgia	54,029,047	1.6%	10	Alabama	82,464,289	2.4%
45	Hawaii	2,942,128	0.1%	11	Tennessee	81,149,369	2.4%
20	Idaho	46,248,562	1.3%	12	Michigan	70,207,570	2.0%
7	Illinois	109,549,325	3.2%	13	Missouri	66,940,874	1.9%
6	Indiana	129,990,697	3.8%	14	Florida	63,962,536	1.9%
31	Iowa	29,697,337	0.9%	15	Mississippi	56,695,967	1.6%
36	Kansas	18,215,203	0.5%	16	Pennsylvania	55,505,416	1.6%
19	Kentucky	53,385,563	1.6%	17	North Carolina	54,950,313	1.6%
5	Louisiana	142,811,333	4.1%	18	Georgia	54,029,047	1.6%
41	Maine	9,494,899	0.3%	19	Kentucky	53,385,563	1.6%
43	Maryland	5,682,676	0.2%	20	Idaho	46,248,562	1.3%
46	Massachusetts	2,648,318	0.1%	21	Virginia	39,074,597	1.1%
12	Michigan	70,207,570	2.0%	22	North Dakota	36,159,333	1.1%
33	Minnesota	24,038,858	0.7%	23	California	35,086,590	1.0%
15	Mississippi	56,695,967	1.6%	24	Montana	34,406,446	1.0%
13	Missouri	66,940,874	1.9%	25	Washington	33,942,548	1.0%
24	Montana	34,406,446	1.0%	26	South Carolina	33,742,354	1.0%
37	Nebraska	17,864,708	0.5%	27	Colorado	32,394,491	0.9%
2	Nevada	316,820,585	9.2%	28	West Virginia	32,131,407	0.9%
50	New Hampshire	261,343	0.0%	29	Arkansas	30,607,200	0.9%
40	New Jersey	10,515,407	0.3%	30	Oklahoma	29,818,486	0.9%
34	New Mexico	19,333,815	0.6%	31	Iowa	29,697,337	0.9%
39	New York	14,027,856	0.4%	32	Wisconsin	29,406,987	0.9%
17	North Carolina	54,950,313	1.6%	33	Minnesota	24,038,858	0.7%
22	North Dakota	36,159,333	1.1%	34	New Mexico	19,333,815	0.6%
8	Ohio	96,491,263	2.8%	35	Wyoming	18,276,888	0.5%
30	Oklahoma	29,818,486	0.9%	36	Kansas	18,215,203	0.5%
38	Oregon	16,757,818	0.5%	37	Nebraska	17,864,708	0.5%
16	Pennsylvania	55,505,416	1.6%	38	Oregon	16,757,818	0.5%
49	Rhode Island	295,082	0.0%	39	New York	14,027,856	0.4%
26	South Carolina	33,742,354	1.0%	40	New Jersey	10,515,407	0.3%
42	South Dakota	6,213,442	0.2%	41	Maine	9,494,899	0.3%
11	Tennessee	81,149,369	2.4%	42	South Dakota	6,213,442	0.2%
4	Texas	201,224,890	5.8%	43	Maryland	5,682,676	0.2%
3	Utah	271,384,698	7.9%	44	Delaware	3,880,208	0.1%
48	Vermont	398,575	0.0%	45	Hawaii	2,942,128	0.1%
21	Virginia	39,074,597	1.1%	46	Massachusetts	2,648,318	0.1%
25	Washington	33,942,548	1.0%	47	Connecticut	1,724,056	0.1%
28	West Virginia	32,131,407	0.9%	48	Vermont	398,575	0.0%
32	Wisconsin	29,406,987	0.9%	49	Rhode Island	295,082	0.0%
35	Wyoming	18,276,888	0.5%	50	New Hampshire	261,343	0.0%
					District of Columbia	27,760	0.0%

Source: U.S. Environmental Protection Agency, Office of Pollution Prevention and Toxics Information Management
"2016 Toxics Release Inventory" (http://www.epa.gov/triexplorer/)
*National total does not include 2,420,596 pounds of toxins in U.S. territories. Includes discharges to air, surface water, underground injection, and surface land. Includes both original (or manufacturing) industries and those added by EPA since it began tracking releases.

Toxic Releases: Total Air Emissions in 2016

National Total = 607,894,693 Pounds*

ALPHA ORDER					RANK ORDER			
RANK	STATE	POUNDS	% of USA		RANK	STATE	POUNDS	% of USA
5	Alabama	29,770,292	4.9%		1	Louisiana	56,085,018	9.2%
47	Alaska	353,782	0.1%		2	Texas	52,701,402	8.7%
36	Arizona	2,323,602	0.4%		3	Georgia	34,081,849	5.6%
18	Arkansas	14,897,451	2.5%		4	Ohio	32,659,148	5.4%
27	California	7,667,484	1.3%		5	Alabama	29,770,292	4.9%
35	Colorado	2,493,674	0.4%		6	Indiana	26,957,622	4.4%
45	Connecticut	758,694	0.1%		7	Tennessee	26,090,960	4.3%
46	Delaware	546,310	0.1%		8	Illinois	23,332,320	3.8%
12	Florida	19,442,390	3.2%		9	Kentucky	22,160,011	3.6%
3	Georgia	34,081,849	5.6%		10	North Carolina	21,698,794	3.6%
38	Hawaii	1,840,694	0.3%		11	South Carolina	20,585,740	3.4%
32	Idaho	4,660,775	0.8%		12	Florida	19,442,390	3.2%
8	Illinois	23,332,320	3.8%		13	Virginia	19,059,847	3.1%
6	Indiana	26,957,622	4.4%		14	Mississippi	16,440,495	2.7%
16	Iowa	15,691,032	2.6%		15	Oklahoma	16,246,331	2.7%
23	Kansas	9,114,818	1.5%		16	Iowa	15,691,032	2.6%
9	Kentucky	22,160,011	3.6%		17	Pennsylvania	15,678,724	2.6%
1	Louisiana	56,085,018	9.2%		18	Arkansas	14,897,451	2.5%
34	Maine	3,102,745	0.5%		19	North Dakota	13,501,251	2.2%
33	Maryland	4,269,604	0.7%		20	West Virginia	13,167,735	2.2%
43	Massachusetts	1,247,155	0.2%		21	Michigan	11,744,609	1.9%
21	Michigan	11,744,609	1.9%		22	Wisconsin	10,069,680	1.7%
24	Minnesota	8,745,770	1.4%		23	Kansas	9,114,818	1.5%
14	Mississippi	16,440,495	2.7%		24	Minnesota	8,745,770	1.4%
25	Missouri	7,859,618	1.3%		25	Missouri	7,859,618	1.3%
39	Montana	1,839,185	0.3%		26	Washington	7,813,148	1.3%
30	Nebraska	5,339,694	0.9%		27	California	7,667,484	1.3%
41	Nevada	1,657,232	0.3%		28	Utah	6,746,319	1.1%
48	New Hampshire	169,829	0.0%		29	Oregon	6,243,479	1.0%
40	New Jersey	1,804,827	0.3%		30	Nebraska	5,339,694	0.9%
44	New Mexico	925,108	0.2%		31	New York	4,695,566	0.8%
31	New York	4,695,566	0.8%		32	Idaho	4,660,775	0.8%
10	North Carolina	21,698,794	3.6%		33	Maryland	4,269,604	0.7%
19	North Dakota	13,501,251	2.2%		34	Maine	3,102,745	0.5%
4	Ohio	32,659,148	5.4%		35	Colorado	2,493,674	0.4%
15	Oklahoma	16,246,331	2.7%		36	Arizona	2,323,602	0.4%
29	Oregon	6,243,479	1.0%		37	Wyoming	2,097,540	0.3%
17	Pennsylvania	15,678,724	2.6%		38	Hawaii	1,840,694	0.3%
49	Rhode Island	158,796	0.0%		39	Montana	1,839,185	0.3%
11	South Carolina	20,585,740	3.4%		40	New Jersey	1,804,827	0.3%
42	South Dakota	1,320,850	0.2%		41	Nevada	1,657,232	0.3%
7	Tennessee	26,090,960	4.3%		42	South Dakota	1,320,850	0.2%
2	Texas	52,701,402	8.7%		43	Massachusetts	1,247,155	0.2%
28	Utah	6,746,319	1.1%		44	New Mexico	925,108	0.2%
50	Vermont	35,260	0.0%		45	Connecticut	758,694	0.1%
13	Virginia	19,059,847	3.1%		46	Delaware	546,310	0.1%
26	Washington	7,813,148	1.3%		47	Alaska	353,782	0.1%
20	West Virginia	13,167,735	2.2%		48	New Hampshire	169,829	0.0%
22	Wisconsin	10,069,680	1.7%		49	Rhode Island	158,796	0.0%
37	Wyoming	2,097,540	0.3%		50	Vermont	35,260	0.0%
						District of Columbia	434	0.0%

Source: U.S. Environmental Protection Agency, Office of Pollution Prevention and Toxics Information Management
    "2016 Toxics Release Inventory" (http://www.epa.gov/triexplorer/)
*Includes fugitive and point source air emissions. National total does not include 1,945,874 pounds of emissions in U.S. territories. Includes both original (or manufacturing) industries and those added by EPA since it began tracking releases.

Toxic Releases: Total Surface Water Discharges in 2016

National Total = 190,432,643 Pounds*

ALPHA ORDER				RANK ORDER			
RANK	STATE	POUNDS	% of USA	RANK	STATE	POUNDS	% of USA
5	Alabama	11,327,288	5.9%	1	Indiana	18,552,187	9.7%
37	Alaska	420,953	0.2%	2	Texas	13,612,540	7.1%
48	Arizona	888	0.0%	3	Virginia	13,571,326	7.1%
17	Arkansas	4,309,762	2.3%	4	Louisiana	11,581,592	6.1%
20	California	4,118,074	2.2%	5	Alabama	11,327,288	5.9%
34	Colorado	923,236	0.5%	6	Georgia	9,943,420	5.2%
43	Connecticut	63,958	0.0%	7	North Carolina	7,988,963	4.2%
25	Delaware	2,812,016	1.5%	8	Kentucky	7,385,824	3.9%
31	Florida	1,655,211	0.9%	9	Ohio	6,984,328	3.7%
6	Georgia	9,943,420	5.2%	10	Illinois	6,808,518	3.6%
36	Hawaii	522,258	0.3%	11	Mississippi	5,993,714	3.1%
24	Idaho	2,857,840	1.5%	12	Pennsylvania	5,950,590	3.1%
10	Illinois	6,808,518	3.6%	13	New York	5,879,491	3.1%
1	Indiana	18,552,187	9.7%	14	Nebraska	4,849,222	2.5%
18	Iowa	4,260,680	2.2%	15	South Carolina	4,433,957	2.3%
33	Kansas	988,493	0.5%	16	Tennessee	4,432,666	2.3%
8	Kentucky	7,385,824	3.9%	17	Arkansas	4,309,762	2.3%
4	Louisiana	11,581,592	6.1%	18	Iowa	4,260,680	2.2%
27	Maine	2,415,748	1.3%	19	New Jersey	4,130,820	2.2%
39	Maryland	119,997	0.1%	20	California	4,118,074	2.2%
46	Massachusetts	8,390	0.0%	21	Oklahoma	3,605,039	1.9%
22	Michigan	3,051,299	1.6%	22	Michigan	3,051,299	1.6%
30	Minnesota	1,909,410	1.0%	23	Wisconsin	2,989,573	1.6%
11	Mississippi	5,993,714	3.1%	24	Idaho	2,857,840	1.5%
29	Missouri	1,990,350	1.0%	25	Delaware	2,812,016	1.5%
41	Montana	115,122	0.1%	26	South Dakota	2,720,247	1.4%
14	Nebraska	4,849,222	2.5%	27	Maine	2,415,748	1.3%
45	Nevada	11,475	0.0%	28	Washington	2,209,488	1.2%
50	New Hampshire	391	0.0%	29	Missouri	1,990,350	1.0%
19	New Jersey	4,130,820	2.2%	30	Minnesota	1,909,410	1.0%
44	New Mexico	36,452	0.0%	31	Florida	1,655,211	0.9%
13	New York	5,879,491	3.1%	32	West Virginia	1,634,346	0.9%
7	North Carolina	7,988,963	4.2%	33	Kansas	988,493	0.5%
42	North Dakota	110,795	0.1%	34	Colorado	923,236	0.5%
9	Ohio	6,984,328	3.7%	35	Oregon	888,035	0.5%
21	Oklahoma	3,605,039	1.9%	36	Hawaii	522,258	0.3%
35	Oregon	888,035	0.5%	37	Alaska	420,953	0.2%
12	Pennsylvania	5,950,590	3.1%	38	Vermont	132,247	0.1%
49	Rhode Island	698	0.0%	39	Maryland	119,997	0.1%
15	South Carolina	4,433,957	2.3%	40	Utah	116,148	0.1%
26	South Dakota	2,720,247	1.4%	41	Montana	115,122	0.1%
16	Tennessee	4,432,666	2.3%	42	North Dakota	110,795	0.1%
2	Texas	13,612,540	7.1%	43	Connecticut	63,958	0.0%
40	Utah	116,148	0.1%	44	New Mexico	36,452	0.0%
38	Vermont	132,247	0.1%	45	Nevada	11,475	0.0%
3	Virginia	13,571,326	7.1%	46	Massachusetts	8,390	0.0%
28	Washington	2,209,488	1.2%	47	Wyoming	6,287	0.0%
32	West Virginia	1,634,346	0.9%	48	Arizona	888	0.0%
23	Wisconsin	2,989,573	1.6%	49	Rhode Island	698	0.0%
47	Wyoming	6,287	0.0%	50	New Hampshire	391	0.0%
					District of Columbia	1,291	0.0%

Source: U.S. Environmental Protection Agency, Office of Pollution Prevention and Toxics Information Management
   "2016 Toxics Release Inventory" (http://www.epa.gov/triexplorer/)
*National total does not include 289,746 pounds of discharges in U.S. territories. Includes both original (or manufacturing)
industries and those added by EPA since it began tracking releases.

Hazardous Waste Sites on the National Priority List in 2018

National Total = 1,400 Sites*

ALPHA ORDER

RANK	STATE	SITES	% of USA
31	Alabama	14	1.0%
45	Alaska	6	0.4%
41	Arizona	9	0.6%
41	Arkansas	9	0.6%
2	California	100	7.1%
19	Colorado	21	1.5%
30	Connecticut	15	1.1%
27	Delaware	16	1.1%
7	Florida	55	3.9%
25	Georgia	17	1.2%
46	Hawaii	3	0.2%
41	Idaho	9	0.6%
9	Illinois	49	3.5%
11	Indiana	42	3.0%
33	Iowa	13	0.9%
33	Kansas	13	0.9%
33	Kentucky	13	0.9%
27	Louisiana	16	1.1%
33	Maine	13	0.9%
19	Maryland	21	1.5%
14	Massachusetts	33	2.4%
5	Michigan	67	4.8%
18	Minnesota	25	1.8%
39	Mississippi	11	0.8%
14	Missouri	33	2.4%
23	Montana	18	1.3%
25	Nebraska	17	1.2%
47	Nevada	2	0.1%
19	New Hampshire	21	1.5%
1	New Jersey	115	8.2%
27	New Mexico	16	1.1%
4	New York	87	6.2%
12	North Carolina	39	2.8%
50	North Dakota	0	0.0%
10	Ohio	43	3.1%
41	Oklahoma	9	0.6%
31	Oregon	14	1.0%
3	Pennsylvania	97	6.9%
37	Rhode Island	12	0.9%
17	South Carolina	26	1.9%
47	South Dakota	2	0.1%
22	Tennessee	19	1.4%
6	Texas	56	4.0%
23	Utah	18	1.3%
37	Vermont	12	0.9%
16	Virginia	31	2.2%
8	Washington	51	3.6%
40	West Virginia	10	0.7%
13	Wisconsin	38	2.7%
47	Wyoming	2	0.1%

RANK ORDER

RANK	STATE	SITES	% of USA
1	New Jersey	115	8.2%
2	California	100	7.1%
3	Pennsylvania	97	6.9%
4	New York	87	6.2%
5	Michigan	67	4.8%
6	Texas	56	4.0%
7	Florida	55	3.9%
8	Washington	51	3.6%
9	Illinois	49	3.5%
10	Ohio	43	3.1%
11	Indiana	42	3.0%
12	North Carolina	39	2.8%
13	Wisconsin	38	2.7%
14	Massachusetts	33	2.4%
14	Missouri	33	2.4%
16	Virginia	31	2.2%
17	South Carolina	26	1.9%
18	Minnesota	25	1.8%
19	Colorado	21	1.5%
19	Maryland	21	1.5%
19	New Hampshire	21	1.5%
22	Tennessee	19	1.4%
23	Montana	18	1.3%
23	Utah	18	1.3%
25	Georgia	17	1.2%
25	Nebraska	17	1.2%
27	Delaware	16	1.1%
27	Louisiana	16	1.1%
27	New Mexico	16	1.1%
30	Connecticut	15	1.1%
31	Alabama	14	1.0%
31	Oregon	14	1.0%
33	Iowa	13	0.9%
33	Kansas	13	0.9%
33	Kentucky	13	0.9%
33	Maine	13	0.9%
37	Rhode Island	12	0.9%
37	Vermont	12	0.9%
39	Mississippi	11	0.8%
40	West Virginia	10	0.7%
41	Arizona	9	0.6%
41	Arkansas	9	0.6%
41	Idaho	9	0.6%
41	Oklahoma	9	0.6%
45	Alaska	6	0.4%
46	Hawaii	3	0.2%
47	Nevada	2	0.1%
47	South Dakota	2	0.1%
47	Wyoming	2	0.1%
50	North Dakota	0	0.0%
	District of Columbia	1	0.1%

Source: U.S. Environmental Protection Agency
"National Priorities List (NPL) Sites in the United States" (http://www.epa.gov/superfund/sites/npl/)
*As of January 18, 2018. Includes final and proposed General Superfund and Federal Facilities Sites. National total includes 18 sites in Puerto Rico, two in Guam, and one in the U.S. Virgin Islands.

Hazardous Waste Sites on the National Priority List
per 10,000 Square Miles in 2018
National Rate = 3.6 Sites per 10,000 Square Miles*

ALPHA ORDER

RANK	STATE	RATE
30	Alabama	2.7
49	Alaska	0.1
45	Arizona	0.8
38	Arkansas	1.7
20	California	6.1
37	Colorado	2.0
5	Connecticut	27.1
3	Delaware	64.3
14	Florida	8.4
28	Georgia	2.9
30	Hawaii	2.7
44	Idaho	1.1
13	Illinois	8.5
11	Indiana	11.5
32	Iowa	2.3
39	Kansas	1.6
26	Kentucky	3.2
27	Louisiana	3.1
25	Maine	3.7
8	Maryland	16.9
4	Massachusetts	31.3
19	Michigan	6.9
28	Minnesota	2.9
32	Mississippi	2.3
22	Missouri	4.7
43	Montana	1.2
34	Nebraska	2.2
47	Nevada	0.2
6	New Hampshire	22.5
1	New Jersey	131.8
41	New Mexico	1.3
9	New York	15.9
16	North Carolina	7.2
50	North Dakota	0.0
12	Ohio	9.6
41	Oklahoma	1.3
40	Oregon	1.4
7	Pennsylvania	21.1
2	Rhode Island	77.7
15	South Carolina	8.1
46	South Dakota	0.3
23	Tennessee	4.5
35	Texas	2.1
35	Utah	2.1
10	Vermont	12.5
16	Virginia	7.2
16	Washington	7.2
24	West Virginia	4.1
21	Wisconsin	5.8
47	Wyoming	0.2

RANK ORDER

RANK	STATE	RATE
1	New Jersey	131.8
2	Rhode Island	77.7
3	Delaware	64.3
4	Massachusetts	31.3
5	Connecticut	27.1
6	New Hampshire	22.5
7	Pennsylvania	21.1
8	Maryland	16.9
9	New York	15.9
10	Vermont	12.5
11	Indiana	11.5
12	Ohio	9.6
13	Illinois	8.5
14	Florida	8.4
15	South Carolina	8.1
16	North Carolina	7.2
16	Virginia	7.2
16	Washington	7.2
19	Michigan	6.9
20	California	6.1
21	Wisconsin	5.8
22	Missouri	4.7
23	Tennessee	4.5
24	West Virginia	4.1
25	Maine	3.7
26	Kentucky	3.2
27	Louisiana	3.1
28	Georgia	2.9
28	Minnesota	2.9
30	Alabama	2.7
30	Hawaii	2.7
32	Iowa	2.3
32	Mississippi	2.3
34	Nebraska	2.2
35	Texas	2.1
35	Utah	2.1
37	Colorado	2.0
38	Arkansas	1.7
39	Kansas	1.6
40	Oregon	1.4
41	New Mexico	1.3
41	Oklahoma	1.3
43	Montana	1.2
44	Idaho	1.1
45	Arizona	0.8
46	South Dakota	0.3
47	Nevada	0.2
47	Wyoming	0.2
49	Alaska	0.1
50	North Dakota	0.0

District of Columbia**   NA

Source: CQ Press using data from U.S. Environmental Protection Agency
   "National Priorities List (NPL) Sites in the United States" (http://www.epa.gov/superfund/sites/npl/)
*As of January 18, 2018. Includes final and proposed General Superfund and Federal Facilities Sites. National rate excludes
sites and square miles in Puerto Rico, Guam and the Virgin Islands. Based on land and water area of states.
**The District of Columbia has one site in its 68 square miles.

Hazardous Waste Sites Deleted from the National Priorities List as of 2018

National Total = 395 Sites*

<u>ALPHA ORDER</u>

RANK	STATE	SITES	% of USA
31	Alabama	3	0.8%
31	Alaska	3	0.8%
31	Arizona	3	0.8%
13	Arkansas	8	2.0%
8	California	13	3.3%
31	Colorado	3	0.8%
31	Connecticut	3	0.8%
14	Delaware	7	1.8%
4	Florida	26	6.6%
24	Georgia	5	1.3%
44	Hawaii	1	0.3%
31	Idaho	3	0.8%
20	Illinois	6	1.5%
11	Indiana	10	2.5%
11	Iowa	10	2.5%
24	Kansas	5	1.3%
14	Kentucky	7	1.8%
9	Louisiana	12	3.0%
31	Maine	3	0.8%
28	Maryland	4	1.0%
14	Massachusetts	7	1.8%
6	Michigan	20	5.1%
5	Minnesota	22	5.6%
31	Mississippi	3	0.8%
24	Missouri	5	1.3%
49	Montana	0	0.0%
44	Nebraska	1	0.3%
49	Nevada	0	0.0%
44	New Hampshire	1	0.3%
1	New Jersey	35	8.9%
28	New Mexico	4	1.0%
2	New York	32	8.1%
31	North Carolina	3	0.8%
40	North Dakota	2	0.5%
14	Ohio	7	1.8%
14	Oklahoma	7	1.8%
24	Oregon	5	1.3%
3	Pennsylvania	30	7.6%
44	Rhode Island	1	0.3%
20	South Carolina	6	1.5%
40	South Dakota	2	0.5%
20	Tennessee	6	1.5%
9	Texas	12	3.0%
20	Utah	6	1.5%
40	Vermont	2	0.5%
28	Virginia	4	1.0%
7	Washington	17	4.3%
40	West Virginia	2	0.5%
14	Wisconsin	7	1.8%
44	Wyoming	1	0.3%

<u>RANK ORDER</u>

RANK	STATE	SITES	% of USA
1	New Jersey	35	8.9%
2	New York	32	8.1%
3	Pennsylvania	30	7.6%
4	Florida	26	6.6%
5	Minnesota	22	5.6%
6	Michigan	20	5.1%
7	Washington	17	4.3%
8	California	13	3.3%
9	Louisiana	12	3.0%
9	Texas	12	3.0%
11	Indiana	10	2.5%
11	Iowa	10	2.5%
13	Arkansas	8	2.0%
14	Delaware	7	1.8%
14	Kentucky	7	1.8%
14	Massachusetts	7	1.8%
14	Ohio	7	1.8%
14	Oklahoma	7	1.8%
14	Wisconsin	7	1.8%
20	Illinois	6	1.5%
20	South Carolina	6	1.5%
20	Tennessee	6	1.5%
20	Utah	6	1.5%
24	Georgia	5	1.3%
24	Kansas	5	1.3%
24	Missouri	5	1.3%
24	Oregon	5	1.3%
28	Maryland	4	1.0%
28	New Mexico	4	1.0%
28	Virginia	4	1.0%
31	Alabama	3	0.8%
31	Alaska	3	0.8%
31	Arizona	3	0.8%
31	Colorado	3	0.8%
31	Connecticut	3	0.8%
31	Idaho	3	0.8%
31	Maine	3	0.8%
31	Mississippi	3	0.8%
31	North Carolina	3	0.8%
40	North Dakota	2	0.5%
40	South Dakota	2	0.5%
40	Vermont	2	0.5%
40	West Virginia	2	0.5%
44	Hawaii	1	0.3%
44	Nebraska	1	0.3%
44	New Hampshire	1	0.3%
44	Rhode Island	1	0.3%
44	Wyoming	1	0.3%
49	Montana	0	0.0%
49	Nevada	0	0.0%
	District of Columbia	0	0.0%

Source: U.S. Environmental Protection Agency
"National Priorities List (NPL) Sites in the United States" (http://www.epa.gov/superfund/sites/npl/)
*Cumulative total as of January 18, 2018. National total includes six sites in Puerto Rico and four in other U.S. territories.

VIII. Geography

Total Area of States in Square Miles in 2010

National Total = 3,796,742 Square Miles*

ALPHA ORDER

RANK	STATE	MILES	% of USA
30	Alabama	52,420	1.4%
1	Alaska	665,384	17.5%
6	Arizona	113,990	3.0%
29	Arkansas	53,179	1.4%
3	California	163,695	4.3%
8	Colorado	104,094	2.7%
48	Connecticut	5,543	0.1%
49	Delaware	2,489	0.1%
22	Florida	65,758	1.7%
24	Georgia	59,425	1.6%
43	Hawaii	10,932	0.3%
14	Idaho	83,569	2.2%
25	Illinois	57,914	1.5%
38	Indiana	36,420	1.0%
26	Iowa	56,273	1.5%
15	Kansas	82,278	2.2%
37	Kentucky	40,408	1.1%
31	Louisiana	52,378	1.4%
39	Maine	35,380	0.9%
42	Maryland	12,406	0.3%
44	Massachusetts	10,554	0.3%
11	Michigan	96,714	2.5%
12	Minnesota	86,936	2.3%
32	Mississippi	48,432	1.3%
21	Missouri	69,707	1.8%
4	Montana	147,040	3.9%
16	Nebraska	77,348	2.0%
7	Nevada	110,572	2.9%
46	New Hampshire	9,349	0.2%
47	New Jersey	8,723	0.2%
5	New Mexico	121,590	3.2%
27	New York	54,555	1.4%
28	North Carolina	53,819	1.4%
19	North Dakota	70,698	1.9%
34	Ohio	44,826	1.2%
20	Oklahoma	69,899	1.8%
9	Oregon	98,379	2.6%
33	Pennsylvania	46,054	1.2%
50	Rhode Island	1,545	0.0%
40	South Carolina	32,020	0.8%
17	South Dakota	77,116	2.0%
36	Tennessee	42,144	1.1%
2	Texas	268,596	7.1%
13	Utah	84,897	2.2%
45	Vermont	9,616	0.3%
35	Virginia	42,775	1.1%
18	Washington	71,298	1.9%
41	West Virginia	24,230	0.6%
23	Wisconsin	65,496	1.7%
10	Wyoming	97,813	2.6%

RANK ORDER

RANK	STATE	MILES	% of USA
1	Alaska	665,384	17.5%
2	Texas	268,596	7.1%
3	California	163,695	4.3%
4	Montana	147,040	3.9%
5	New Mexico	121,590	3.2%
6	Arizona	113,990	3.0%
7	Nevada	110,572	2.9%
8	Colorado	104,094	2.7%
9	Oregon	98,379	2.6%
10	Wyoming	97,813	2.6%
11	Michigan	96,714	2.5%
12	Minnesota	86,936	2.3%
13	Utah	84,897	2.2%
14	Idaho	83,569	2.2%
15	Kansas	82,278	2.2%
16	Nebraska	77,348	2.0%
17	South Dakota	77,116	2.0%
18	Washington	71,298	1.9%
19	North Dakota	70,698	1.9%
20	Oklahoma	69,899	1.8%
21	Missouri	69,707	1.8%
22	Florida	65,758	1.7%
23	Wisconsin	65,496	1.7%
24	Georgia	59,425	1.6%
25	Illinois	57,914	1.5%
26	Iowa	56,273	1.5%
27	New York	54,555	1.4%
28	North Carolina	53,819	1.4%
29	Arkansas	53,179	1.4%
30	Alabama	52,420	1.4%
31	Louisiana	52,378	1.4%
32	Mississippi	48,432	1.3%
33	Pennsylvania	46,054	1.2%
34	Ohio	44,826	1.2%
35	Virginia	42,775	1.1%
36	Tennessee	42,144	1.1%
37	Kentucky	40,408	1.1%
38	Indiana	36,420	1.0%
39	Maine	35,380	0.9%
40	South Carolina	32,020	0.8%
41	West Virginia	24,230	0.6%
42	Maryland	12,406	0.3%
43	Hawaii	10,932	0.3%
44	Massachusetts	10,554	0.3%
45	Vermont	9,616	0.3%
46	New Hampshire	9,349	0.2%
47	New Jersey	8,723	0.2%
48	Connecticut	5,543	0.1%
49	Delaware	2,489	0.1%
50	Rhode Island	1,545	0.0%
	District of Columbia	68	0.0%

Source: U.S. Bureau of the Census
  "State Area Measurements" (http://www.census.gov/geo/reference/state-area.html)
*Total of land and water area. Revised figures as of January 1, 2010

Land Area of States in Square Miles in 2010

National Total = 3,531,905 Square Miles of Land Area*

ALPHA ORDER

RANK	STATE	MILES	% of USA
28	Alabama	50,645	1.4%
1	Alaska	570,641	16.2%
6	Arizona	113,594	3.2%
27	Arkansas	52,035	1.5%
3	California	155,779	4.4%
8	Colorado	103,642	2.9%
48	Connecticut	4,842	0.1%
49	Delaware	1,949	0.1%
26	Florida	53,625	1.5%
21	Georgia	57,513	1.6%
47	Hawaii	6,423	0.2%
11	Idaho	82,643	2.3%
24	Illinois	55,519	1.6%
38	Indiana	35,826	1.0%
23	Iowa	55,857	1.6%
13	Kansas	81,759	2.3%
37	Kentucky	39,486	1.1%
33	Louisiana	43,204	1.2%
39	Maine	30,843	0.9%
42	Maryland	9,707	0.3%
45	Massachusetts	7,800	0.2%
22	Michigan	56,539	1.6%
14	Minnesota	79,627	2.3%
31	Mississippi	46,923	1.3%
18	Missouri	68,742	1.9%
4	Montana	145,546	4.1%
15	Nebraska	76,824	2.2%
7	Nevada	109,781	3.1%
44	New Hampshire	8,953	0.3%
46	New Jersey	7,354	0.2%
5	New Mexico	121,298	3.4%
30	New York	47,126	1.3%
29	North Carolina	48,618	1.4%
17	North Dakota	69,001	2.0%
35	Ohio	40,861	1.2%
19	Oklahoma	68,595	1.9%
10	Oregon	95,988	2.7%
32	Pennsylvania	44,743	1.3%
50	Rhode Island	1,034	0.0%
40	South Carolina	30,061	0.9%
16	South Dakota	75,811	2.1%
34	Tennessee	41,235	1.2%
2	Texas	261,232	7.4%
12	Utah	82,170	2.3%
43	Vermont	9,217	0.3%
36	Virginia	39,490	1.1%
20	Washington	66,456	1.9%
41	West Virginia	24,038	0.7%
25	Wisconsin	54,158	1.5%
9	Wyoming	97,093	2.7%

RANK ORDER

RANK	STATE	MILES	% of USA
1	Alaska	570,641	16.2%
2	Texas	261,232	7.4%
3	California	155,779	4.4%
4	Montana	145,546	4.1%
5	New Mexico	121,298	3.4%
6	Arizona	113,594	3.2%
7	Nevada	109,781	3.1%
8	Colorado	103,642	2.9%
9	Wyoming	97,093	2.7%
10	Oregon	95,988	2.7%
11	Idaho	82,643	2.3%
12	Utah	82,170	2.3%
13	Kansas	81,759	2.3%
14	Minnesota	79,627	2.3%
15	Nebraska	76,824	2.2%
16	South Dakota	75,811	2.1%
17	North Dakota	69,001	2.0%
18	Missouri	68,742	1.9%
19	Oklahoma	68,595	1.9%
20	Washington	66,456	1.9%
21	Georgia	57,513	1.6%
22	Michigan	56,539	1.6%
23	Iowa	55,857	1.6%
24	Illinois	55,519	1.6%
25	Wisconsin	54,158	1.5%
26	Florida	53,625	1.5%
27	Arkansas	52,035	1.5%
28	Alabama	50,645	1.4%
29	North Carolina	48,618	1.4%
30	New York	47,126	1.3%
31	Mississippi	46,923	1.3%
32	Pennsylvania	44,743	1.3%
33	Louisiana	43,204	1.2%
34	Tennessee	41,235	1.2%
35	Ohio	40,861	1.2%
36	Virginia	39,490	1.1%
37	Kentucky	39,486	1.1%
38	Indiana	35,826	1.0%
39	Maine	30,843	0.9%
40	South Carolina	30,061	0.9%
41	West Virginia	24,038	0.7%
42	Maryland	9,707	0.3%
43	Vermont	9,217	0.3%
44	New Hampshire	8,953	0.3%
45	Massachusetts	7,800	0.2%
46	New Jersey	7,354	0.2%
47	Hawaii	6,423	0.2%
48	Connecticut	4,842	0.1%
49	Delaware	1,949	0.1%
50	Rhode Island	1,034	0.0%
	District of Columbia	61	0.0%

Source: U.S. Bureau of the Census
"State Area Measurements" (http://www.census.gov/geo/reference/state-area.html)
*Includes dry land temporarily or partially covered by water, such as marshland, swamps, etc.; streams and canals under one-eighth mile wide; and lakes, reservoirs, and ponds under 40 acres. Revised figures as of August 2010.

Water Area of States in Square Miles in 2010

National Total = 264,837 Square Miles of Water*

RANK	STATE	MILES	% of USA		RANK	STATE	MILES	% of USA
23	Alabama	1,775	0.7%		1	Alaska	94,743	35.8%
1	Alaska	94,743	35.8%		2	Michigan	40,175	15.2%
48	Arizona	396	0.1%		3	Florida	12,133	4.6%
31	Arkansas	1,143	0.4%		4	Wisconsin	11,339	4.3%
6	California	7,916	3.0%		5	Louisiana	9,174	3.5%
44	Colorado	452	0.2%		6	California	7,916	3.0%
38	Connecticut	701	0.3%		7	New York	7,429	2.8%
40	Delaware	540	0.2%		8	Texas	7,365	2.8%
3	Florida	12,133	4.6%		9	Minnesota	7,309	2.8%
22	Georgia	1,912	0.7%		10	North Carolina	5,201	2.0%
13	Hawaii	4,509	1.7%		11	Washington	4,842	1.8%
33	Idaho	926	0.3%		12	Maine	4,537	1.7%
19	Illinois	2,395	0.9%		13	Hawaii	4,509	1.7%
39	Indiana	593	0.2%		14	Ohio	3,965	1.5%
45	Iowa	416	0.2%		15	Virginia	3,285	1.2%
42	Kansas	520	0.2%		16	Massachusetts	2,754	1.0%
34	Kentucky	921	0.3%		17	Utah	2,727	1.0%
5	Louisiana	9,174	3.5%		18	Maryland	2,699	1.0%
12	Maine	4,537	1.7%		19	Illinois	2,395	0.9%
18	Maryland	2,699	1.0%		20	Oregon	2,391	0.9%
16	Massachusetts	2,754	1.0%		21	South Carolina	1,960	0.7%
2	Michigan	40,175	15.2%		22	Georgia	1,912	0.7%
9	Minnesota	7,309	2.8%		23	Alabama	1,775	0.7%
25	Mississippi	1,509	0.6%		24	North Dakota	1,698	0.6%
32	Missouri	965	0.4%		25	Mississippi	1,509	0.6%
26	Montana	1,494	0.6%		26	Montana	1,494	0.6%
41	Nebraska	524	0.2%		27	New Jersey	1,368	0.5%
36	Nevada	791	0.3%		28	Pennsylvania	1,312	0.5%
47	New Hampshire	397	0.1%		29	South Dakota	1,305	0.5%
27	New Jersey	1,368	0.5%		30	Oklahoma	1,304	0.5%
49	New Mexico	292	0.1%		31	Arkansas	1,143	0.4%
7	New York	7,429	2.8%		32	Missouri	965	0.4%
10	North Carolina	5,201	2.0%		33	Idaho	926	0.3%
24	North Dakota	1,698	0.6%		34	Kentucky	921	0.3%
14	Ohio	3,965	1.5%		35	Tennessee	909	0.3%
30	Oklahoma	1,304	0.5%		36	Nevada	791	0.3%
20	Oregon	2,391	0.9%		37	Wyoming	720	0.3%
28	Pennsylvania	1,312	0.5%		38	Connecticut	701	0.3%
43	Rhode Island	511	0.2%		39	Indiana	593	0.2%
21	South Carolina	1,960	0.7%		40	Delaware	540	0.2%
29	South Dakota	1,305	0.5%		41	Nebraska	524	0.2%
35	Tennessee	909	0.3%		42	Kansas	520	0.2%
8	Texas	7,365	2.8%		43	Rhode Island	511	0.2%
17	Utah	2,727	1.0%		44	Colorado	452	0.2%
46	Vermont	400	0.2%		45	Iowa	416	0.2%
15	Virginia	3,285	1.2%		46	Vermont	400	0.2%
11	Washington	4,842	1.8%		47	New Hampshire	397	0.1%
50	West Virginia	192	0.1%		48	Arizona	396	0.1%
4	Wisconsin	11,339	4.3%		49	New Mexico	292	0.1%
37	Wyoming	720	0.3%		50	West Virginia	192	0.1%
						District of Columbia	7	0.0%

ALPHA ORDER

RANK ORDER

Source: U.S. Bureau of the Census
   "State Area Measurements" (http://www.census.gov/geo/reference/state-area.html)
*Includes permanent inland water surface, such as lakes, reservoirs, and ponds having an area of 40 acres or more, canals one-eighth mile or more in width; coastal waters behind or sheltered by headlands or islands separated by less than 1 nautical mile of water, and islands under 40 acres in area. Excludes areas of oceans, bays, etc., lying within U.S. jurisdiction but not defined as inland water. Revised figures as of August 2010.

Highest Point of Elevation in Feet

National High Point = 20,320 Feet Above Sea Level (Mt. McKinley, Alaska)

ALPHA ORDER			RANK ORDER		
RANK	STATE	HIGHEST POINT	RANK	STATE	HIGHEST POINT
35	Alabama	2,407	1	Alaska	20,320
1	Alaska	20,320	2	California	14,494
12	Arizona	12,633	3	Colorado	14,433
34	Arkansas	2,753	4	Washington	14,411
2	California	14,494	5	Wyoming	13,804
3	Colorado	14,433	6	Hawaii	13,796
36	Connecticut	2,380	7	Utah	13,528
49	Delaware	448	8	New Mexico	13,161
50	Florida	345	9	Nevada	13,140
25	Georgia	4,784	10	Montana	12,799
6	Hawaii	13,796	11	Idaho	12,662
11	Idaho	12,662	12	Arizona	12,633
45	Illinois	1,235	13	Oregon	11,239
44	Indiana	1,257	14	Texas	8,749
42	Iowa	1,670	15	South Dakota	7,242
28	Kansas	4,039	16	North Carolina	6,684
27	Kentucky	4,145	17	Tennessee	6,643
48	Louisiana	535	18	New Hampshire	6,288
22	Maine	5,268	19	Virginia	5,729
32	Maryland	3,360	20	Nebraska	5,424
31	Massachusetts	3,491	21	New York	5,344
38	Michigan	1,979	22	Maine	5,268
37	Minnesota	2,301	23	Oklahoma	4,973
47	Mississippi	806	24	West Virginia	4,863
41	Missouri	1,772	25	Georgia	4,784
10	Montana	12,799	26	Vermont	4,393
20	Nebraska	5,424	27	Kentucky	4,145
9	Nevada	13,140	28	Kansas	4,039
18	New Hampshire	6,288	29	South Carolina	3,560
40	New Jersey	1,803	30	North Dakota	3,506
8	New Mexico	13,161	31	Massachusetts	3,491
21	New York	5,344	32	Maryland	3,360
16	North Carolina	6,684	33	Pennsylvania	3,213
30	North Dakota	3,506	34	Arkansas	2,753
43	Ohio	1,550	35	Alabama	2,407
23	Oklahoma	4,973	36	Connecticut	2,380
13	Oregon	11,239	37	Minnesota	2,301
33	Pennsylvania	3,213	38	Michigan	1,979
46	Rhode Island	812	39	Wisconsin	1,951
29	South Carolina	3,560	40	New Jersey	1,803
15	South Dakota	7,242	41	Missouri	1,772
17	Tennessee	6,643	42	Iowa	1,670
14	Texas	8,749	43	Ohio	1,550
7	Utah	13,528	44	Indiana	1,257
26	Vermont	4,393	45	Illinois	1,235
19	Virginia	5,729	46	Rhode Island	812
4	Washington	14,411	47	Mississippi	806
24	West Virginia	4,863	48	Louisiana	535
39	Wisconsin	1,951	49	Delaware	448
5	Wyoming	13,804	50	Florida	345
				District of Columbia	410

Source: U.S. Department of Interior, U.S. Geological Survey
"Elevations and Distances in the United States" (https://pubs.usgs.gov/gip/Elevations-Distances/elvadist.html)

Lowest Point of Elevation in Feet

National Low Point = 282 Feet Below Sea Level (Death Valley, California)*

ALPHA ORDER

RANK	STATE	LOWEST POINT
3	Alabama	0
3	Alaska	0
26	Arizona	70
25	Arkansas	55
1	California	(282)
50	Colorado	3,315
3	Connecticut	0
3	Delaware	0
3	Florida	0
3	Georgia	0
3	Hawaii	0
42	Idaho	710
32	Illinois	279
34	Indiana	320
37	Iowa	480
41	Kansas	679
31	Kentucky	257
2	Louisiana	(8)
3	Maine	0
3	Maryland	0
3	Massachusetts	0
38	Michigan	571
40	Minnesota	601
3	Mississippi	0
29	Missouri	230
46	Montana	1,800
44	Nebraska	840
36	Nevada	479
3	New Hampshire	0
3	New Jersey	0
48	New Mexico	2,842
3	New York	0
3	North Carolina	0
43	North Dakota	750
35	Ohio	455
33	Oklahoma	289
3	Oregon	0
3	Pennsylvania	0
3	Rhode Island	0
3	South Carolina	0
45	South Dakota	966
28	Tennessee	178
3	Texas	0
47	Utah	2,000
27	Vermont	95
3	Virginia	0
3	Washington	0
30	West Virginia	240
39	Wisconsin	579
49	Wyoming	3,099

RANK ORDER

RANK	STATE	LOWEST POINT
1	California	(282)
2	Louisiana	(8)
3	Alabama*	0
3	Alaska	0
3	Connecticut	0
3	Delaware	0
3	Florida	0
3	Georgia	0
3	Hawaii	0
3	Maine	0
3	Maryland	0
3	Massachusetts	0
3	Mississippi	0
3	New Hampshire	0
3	New Jersey	0
3	New York	0
3	North Carolina	0
3	Oregon	0
3	Pennsylvania	0
3	Rhode Island	0
3	South Carolina	0
3	Texas	0
3	Virginia	0
3	Washington	0
25	Arkansas	55
26	Arizona	70
27	Vermont	95
28	Tennessee	178
29	Missouri	230
30	West Virginia	240
31	Kentucky	257
32	Illinois	279
33	Oklahoma	289
34	Indiana	320
35	Ohio	455
36	Nevada	479
37	Iowa	480
38	Michigan	571
39	Wisconsin	579
40	Minnesota	601
41	Kansas	679
42	Idaho	710
43	North Dakota	750
44	Nebraska	840
45	South Dakota	966
46	Montana	1,800
47	Utah	2,000
48	New Mexico	2,842
49	Wyoming	3,099
50	Colorado	3,315
	District of Columbia	1

Source: U.S. Department of Interior, U.S. Geological Survey
"Elevations and Distances in the United States" (https://pubs.usgs.gov/gip/Elevations-Distances/elvadist.html)
*States with "0" have sea level as lowest point.

Approximate Mean Elevation in Feet

Approximate National Mean Elevation = 2,500 Feet Above Sea Level

ALPHA ORDER

RANK	STATE	MEAN ELEVATION
40	Alabama	500
15	Alaska	1,900
7	Arizona	4,100
36	Arkansas	650
11	California	2,900
1	Colorado	6,800
40	Connecticut	500
50	Delaware	60
48	Florida	100
37	Georgia	600
10	Hawaii	3,030
6	Idaho	5,000
37	Illinois	600
34	Indiana	700
22	Iowa	1,100
14	Kansas	2,000
33	Kentucky	750
48	Louisiana	100
37	Maine	600
43	Maryland	350
40	Massachusetts	500
29	Michigan	900
21	Minnesota	1,200
45	Mississippi	300
32	Missouri	800
8	Montana	3,400
12	Nebraska	2,600
5	Nevada	5,500
25	New Hampshire	1,000
46	New Jersey	250
4	New Mexico	5,700
25	New York	1,000
34	North Carolina	700
15	North Dakota	1,900
31	Ohio	850
20	Oklahoma	1,300
9	Oregon	3,300
22	Pennsylvania	1,100
47	Rhode Island	200
43	South Carolina	350
13	South Dakota	2,200
29	Tennessee	900
17	Texas	1,700
3	Utah	6,100
25	Vermont	1,000
28	Virginia	950
17	Washington	1,700
19	West Virginia	1,500
24	Wisconsin	1,050
2	Wyoming	6,700

RANK ORDER

RANK	STATE	MEAN ELEVATION
1	Colorado	6,800
2	Wyoming	6,700
3	Utah	6,100
4	New Mexico	5,700
5	Nevada	5,500
6	Idaho	5,000
7	Arizona	4,100
8	Montana	3,400
9	Oregon	3,300
10	Hawaii	3,030
11	California	2,900
12	Nebraska	2,600
13	South Dakota	2,200
14	Kansas	2,000
15	Alaska	1,900
15	North Dakota	1,900
17	Texas	1,700
17	Washington	1,700
19	West Virginia	1,500
20	Oklahoma	1,300
21	Minnesota	1,200
22	Iowa	1,100
22	Pennsylvania	1,100
24	Wisconsin	1,050
25	New Hampshire	1,000
25	New York	1,000
25	Vermont	1,000
28	Virginia	950
29	Michigan	900
29	Tennessee	900
31	Ohio	850
32	Missouri	800
33	Kentucky	750
34	Indiana	700
34	North Carolina	700
36	Arkansas	650
37	Georgia	600
37	Illinois	600
37	Maine	600
40	Alabama	500
40	Connecticut	500
40	Massachusetts	500
43	Maryland	350
43	South Carolina	350
45	Mississippi	300
46	New Jersey	250
47	Rhode Island	200
48	Florida	100
48	Louisiana	100
50	Delaware	60

District of Columbia	150

Source: U.S. Department of Interior, U.S. Geological Survey
"Elevations and Distances in the United States" (http://erg.usgs.gov/isb/pubs/booklets/elvadist/elvadist.html)

Normal Daily Mean Temperature*

ALPHA ORDER			RANK ORDER		
RANK	**STATE**	**MEAN TEMPERATURE**	**RANK**	**STATE**	**MEAN TEMPERATURE**
7	Alabama	63.7	1	Hawaii	75.7
50	Alaska	31.9	2	Florida	72.0
6	Arizona	63.9	3	Louisiana	67.4
10	Arkansas	62.0	4	Texas	66.8
12	California	60.3	5	South Carolina	64.0
38	Colorado	48.4	6	Arizona	63.9
27	Connecticut	51.2	7	Alabama	63.7
20	Delaware**	54.4	8	Georgia	63.6
2	Florida	72.0	9	Mississippi	63.4
8	Georgia	63.6	10	Arkansas	62.0
1	Hawaii	75.7	11	Oklahoma	60.5
31	Idaho	50.3	12	California	60.3
33	Illinois	50.1	13	North Carolina	60.1
24	Indiana	52.0	14	Tennessee	58.7
39	Iowa	48.1	15	Virginia	57.2
22	Kansas	54.0	16	New Mexico	57.0
17	Kentucky	55.8	17	Kentucky	55.8
3	Louisiana	67.4	18	Missouri	55.2
47	Maine	42.5	19	Maryland**	54.6
19	Maryland**	54.6	20	Delaware**	54.4
37	Massachusetts	49.3	20	New Jersey	54.4
45	Michigan	44.7	22	Kansas	54.0
48	Minnesota	41.4	23	West Virginia	52.7
9	Mississippi	63.4	24	Indiana	52.0
18	Missouri	55.2	24	Nevada	52.0
46	Montana	44.0	26	Pennsylvania	51.6
36	Nebraska	49.4	27	Connecticut	51.2
24	Nevada	52.0	28	Oregon	51.1
41	New Hampshire**	45.9	28	Rhode Island**	51.1
20	New Jersey	54.4	28	Utah	51.1
16	New Mexico	57.0	31	Idaho	50.3
32	New York	50.2	32	New York	50.2
13	North Carolina	60.1	33	Illinois	50.1
49	North Dakota	41.3	34	Ohio	50.0
34	Ohio	50.0	34	Washington	50.0
11	Oklahoma	60.5	36	Nebraska	49.4
28	Oregon	51.1	37	Massachusetts	49.3
26	Pennsylvania	51.6	38	Colorado	48.4
28	Rhode Island**	51.1	39	Iowa	48.1
5	South Carolina	64.0	40	Wisconsin	46.3
42	South Dakota	45.2	41	New Hampshire**	45.9
14	Tennessee	58.7	42	South Dakota	45.2
4	Texas	66.8	42	Vermont**	45.2
28	Utah	51.1	44	Wyoming	44.8
42	Vermont**	45.2	45	Michigan	44.7
15	Virginia	57.2	46	Montana	44.0
34	Washington	50.0	47	Maine	42.5
23	West Virginia	52.7	48	Minnesota	41.4
40	Wisconsin	46.3	49	North Dakota	41.3
44	Wyoming	44.8	50	Alaska	31.9
				District of Columbia	55.9

Source: CQ Press using data from U.S. Department of Commerce, National Oceanic and Atmospheric Administration
  "Comparative Climatic Data Through 2012" (ftp://ftp.ncdc.noaa.gov/pub/data/ccd-data/CCD-2012.pdf)
*Based on 30-year averages, 1971-2000.
**Temperatures from these states are from a single location. All other states are from two or more reporting cities within each
state, which were averaged to determine each state's average.

Percent of Days That Are Sunny*

ALPHA ORDER

RANK	STATE	PERCENT OF DAYS SUNNY
26	Alabama	58
50	Alaska	38
1	Arizona	85
8	Arkansas	66
4	California	72
4	Colorado	72
34	Connecticut**	56
36	Delaware**	55
7	Florida	67
16	Georgia	63
8	Hawaii	66
14	Idaho	64
31	Illinois	57
26	Indiana	58
22	Iowa	60
8	Kansas	66
36	Kentucky	55
14	Louisiana	64
31	Maine**	57
31	Maryland**	57
36	Massachusetts	55
44	Michigan	49
36	Minnesota	55
16	Mississippi	63
26	Missouri	58
24	Montana	59
16	Nebraska	63
2	Nevada	76
48	New Hampshire	44
34	New Jersey**	56
3	New Mexico	75
42	New York	51
22	North Carolina	60
24	North Dakota	59
42	Ohio	51
12	Oklahoma	65
46	Oregon**	48
41	Pennsylvania	53
26	Rhode Island**	58
20	South Carolina	62
16	South Dakota	63
26	Tennessee	58
12	Texas	65
6	Utah	68
44	Vermont**	49
21	Virginia	61
47	Washington	45
49	West Virginia**	40
40	Wisconsin	54
8	Wyoming	66

RANK ORDER

RANK	STATE	PERCENT OF DAYS SUNNY
1	Arizona	85
2	Nevada	76
3	New Mexico	75
4	California	72
4	Colorado	72
6	Utah	68
7	Florida	67
8	Arkansas	66
8	Hawaii	66
8	Kansas	66
8	Wyoming	66
12	Oklahoma	65
12	Texas	65
14	Idaho	64
14	Louisiana	64
16	Georgia	63
16	Mississippi	63
16	Nebraska	63
16	South Dakota	63
20	South Carolina	62
21	Virginia	61
22	Iowa	60
22	North Carolina	60
24	Montana	59
24	North Dakota	59
26	Alabama	58
26	Indiana	58
26	Missouri	58
26	Rhode Island**	58
26	Tennessee	58
31	Illinois	57
31	Maine**	57
31	Maryland**	57
34	Connecticut**	56
34	New Jersey**	56
36	Delaware**	55
36	Kentucky	55
36	Massachusetts	55
36	Minnesota	55
40	Wisconsin	54
41	Pennsylvania	53
42	New York	51
42	Ohio	51
44	Michigan	49
44	Vermont**	49
46	Oregon**	48
47	Washington	45
48	New Hampshire	44
49	West Virginia**	40
50	Alaska	38

District of Columbia**	56

Source: CQ Press using data from U.S. Department of Commerce, National Oceanic and Atmospheric Administration
   "Comparative Climatic Data Through 2012" (ftp://ftp.ncdc.noaa.gov/pub/data/ccd-data/CCD-2012.pdf)
*As a percent of possible sunshine updated through 2012.
**Percentages from these states are from a single location. All other states are from two or more reporting cities within each state, which were averaged to determine each state's average.

Average Wind Speed (MPH)*

<table>
<thead>
<tr><th colspan="3">ALPHA ORDER</th><th colspan="3">RANK ORDER</th></tr>
<tr><th>RANK</th><th>STATE</th><th>MILES PER HOUR</th><th>RANK</th><th>STATE</th><th>MILES PER HOUR</th></tr>
</thead>
<tbody>
<tr><td>41</td><td>Alabama</td><td>7.6</td><td>1</td><td>Massachusetts</td><td>12.5</td></tr>
<tr><td>24</td><td>Alaska</td><td>9.3</td><td>2</td><td>Kansas</td><td>12.0</td></tr>
<tr><td>42</td><td>Arizona</td><td>7.5</td><td>3</td><td>Oklahoma</td><td>11.2</td></tr>
<tr><td>40</td><td>Arkansas</td><td>7.7</td><td>4</td><td>South Dakota</td><td>11.1</td></tr>
<tr><td>46</td><td>California</td><td>6.9</td><td>5</td><td>Hawaii</td><td>10.9</td></tr>
<tr><td>32</td><td>Colorado</td><td>8.5</td><td>6</td><td>Iowa</td><td>10.7</td></tr>
<tr><td>19</td><td>Connecticut</td><td>9.6</td><td>7</td><td>North Dakota</td><td>10.6</td></tr>
<tr><td>26</td><td>Delaware**</td><td>9.0</td><td>8</td><td>Rhode Island</td><td>10.5</td></tr>
<tr><td>33</td><td>Florida</td><td>8.3</td><td>9</td><td>Nebraska</td><td>10.3</td></tr>
<tr><td>45</td><td>Georgia</td><td>7.4</td><td>9</td><td>Texas</td><td>10.3</td></tr>
<tr><td>5</td><td>Hawaii</td><td>10.9</td><td>11</td><td>Minnesota</td><td>10.2</td></tr>
<tr><td>22</td><td>Idaho</td><td>9.4</td><td>11</td><td>New York</td><td>10.2</td></tr>
<tr><td>18</td><td>Illinois</td><td>9.8</td><td>13</td><td>Missouri</td><td>10.1</td></tr>
<tr><td>22</td><td>Indiana</td><td>9.4</td><td>13</td><td>Wyoming</td><td>10.1</td></tr>
<tr><td>6</td><td>Iowa</td><td>10.7</td><td>15</td><td>New Jersey</td><td>10.0</td></tr>
<tr><td>2</td><td>Kansas</td><td>12.0</td><td>16</td><td>New Mexico</td><td>9.9</td></tr>
<tr><td>39</td><td>Kentucky</td><td>7.8</td><td>16</td><td>Wisconsin</td><td>9.9</td></tr>
<tr><td>36</td><td>Louisiana</td><td>8.1</td><td>18</td><td>Illinois</td><td>9.8</td></tr>
<tr><td>27</td><td>Maine</td><td>8.9</td><td>19</td><td>Connecticut</td><td>9.6</td></tr>
<tr><td>30</td><td>Maryland**</td><td>8.6</td><td>19</td><td>Ohio</td><td>9.6</td></tr>
<tr><td>1</td><td>Massachusetts</td><td>12.5</td><td>21</td><td>Michigan</td><td>9.5</td></tr>
<tr><td>21</td><td>Michigan</td><td>9.5</td><td>22</td><td>Idaho</td><td>9.4</td></tr>
<tr><td>11</td><td>Minnesota</td><td>10.2</td><td>22</td><td>Indiana</td><td>9.4</td></tr>
<tr><td>48</td><td>Mississippi</td><td>6.5</td><td>24</td><td>Alaska</td><td>9.3</td></tr>
<tr><td>13</td><td>Missouri</td><td>10.1</td><td>25</td><td>Montana</td><td>9.2</td></tr>
<tr><td>25</td><td>Montana</td><td>9.2</td><td>26</td><td>Delaware**</td><td>9.0</td></tr>
<tr><td>9</td><td>Nebraska</td><td>10.3</td><td>27</td><td>Maine</td><td>8.9</td></tr>
<tr><td>37</td><td>Nevada</td><td>8.0</td><td>27</td><td>Vermont**</td><td>8.9</td></tr>
<tr><td>47</td><td>New Hampshire**</td><td>6.7</td><td>29</td><td>Utah**</td><td>8.8</td></tr>
<tr><td>15</td><td>New Jersey</td><td>10.0</td><td>30</td><td>Maryland**</td><td>8.6</td></tr>
<tr><td>16</td><td>New Mexico</td><td>9.9</td><td>30</td><td>Pennsylvania</td><td>8.6</td></tr>
<tr><td>11</td><td>New York</td><td>10.2</td><td>32</td><td>Colorado</td><td>8.5</td></tr>
<tr><td>34</td><td>North Carolina</td><td>8.2</td><td>33</td><td>Florida</td><td>8.3</td></tr>
<tr><td>7</td><td>North Dakota</td><td>10.6</td><td>34</td><td>North Carolina</td><td>8.2</td></tr>
<tr><td>19</td><td>Ohio</td><td>9.6</td><td>34</td><td>Virginia</td><td>8.2</td></tr>
<tr><td>3</td><td>Oklahoma</td><td>11.2</td><td>36</td><td>Louisiana</td><td>8.1</td></tr>
<tr><td>38</td><td>Oregon</td><td>7.9</td><td>37</td><td>Nevada</td><td>8.0</td></tr>
<tr><td>30</td><td>Pennsylvania</td><td>8.6</td><td>38</td><td>Oregon</td><td>7.9</td></tr>
<tr><td>8</td><td>Rhode Island</td><td>10.5</td><td>39</td><td>Kentucky</td><td>7.8</td></tr>
<tr><td>42</td><td>South Carolina</td><td>7.5</td><td>40</td><td>Arkansas</td><td>7.7</td></tr>
<tr><td>4</td><td>South Dakota</td><td>11.1</td><td>41</td><td>Alabama</td><td>7.6</td></tr>
<tr><td>48</td><td>Tennessee</td><td>6.5</td><td>42</td><td>Arizona</td><td>7.5</td></tr>
<tr><td>9</td><td>Texas</td><td>10.3</td><td>42</td><td>South Carolina</td><td>7.5</td></tr>
<tr><td>29</td><td>Utah**</td><td>8.8</td><td>42</td><td>Washington</td><td>7.5</td></tr>
<tr><td>27</td><td>Vermont**</td><td>8.9</td><td>45</td><td>Georgia</td><td>7.4</td></tr>
<tr><td>34</td><td>Virginia</td><td>8.2</td><td>46</td><td>California</td><td>6.9</td></tr>
<tr><td>42</td><td>Washington</td><td>7.5</td><td>47</td><td>New Hampshire**</td><td>6.7</td></tr>
<tr><td>48</td><td>West Virginia</td><td>6.5</td><td>48</td><td>Mississippi</td><td>6.5</td></tr>
<tr><td>16</td><td>Wisconsin</td><td>9.9</td><td>48</td><td>Tennessee</td><td>6.5</td></tr>
<tr><td>13</td><td>Wyoming</td><td>10.1</td><td>48</td><td>West Virginia</td><td>6.5</td></tr>
</tbody>
</table>

District of Columbia   8.4

Source: CQ Press using data from U.S. Department of Commerce, National Oceanic and Atmospheric Administration
"Comparative Climatic Data Through 2012" (ftp://ftp.ncdc.noaa.gov/pub/data/ccd-data/CCD-2012.pdf)
*Updated through 2012.
**Averages from these states are from a single location. All other states are from two or more reporting cities within each state, which were averaged to determine each state's average.

Hazardous Weather Fatalities in 2016

National Total = 442 Fatalities*

ALPHA ORDER

RANK	STATE	FATALITIES	% of USA
16	Alabama	7	1.6%
25	Alaska	4	0.9%
10	Arizona	11	2.5%
36	Arkansas	2	0.5%
6	California	22	5.0%
21	Colorado	5	1.1%
45	Connecticut	0	0.0%
45	Delaware	0	0.0%
4	Florida	31	7.0%
10	Georgia	11	2.5%
32	Hawaii	3	0.7%
39	Idaho	1	0.2%
14	Illinois	9	2.0%
21	Indiana	5	1.1%
36	Iowa	2	0.5%
21	Kansas	5	1.1%
32	Kentucky	3	0.7%
7	Louisiana	21	4.8%
45	Maine	0	0.0%
25	Maryland	4	0.9%
25	Massachusetts	4	0.9%
36	Michigan	2	0.5%
14	Minnesota	9	2.0%
25	Mississippi	4	0.9%
16	Missouri	7	1.6%
32	Montana	3	0.7%
45	Nebraska	0	0.0%
2	Nevada	53	12.0%
39	New Hampshire	1	0.2%
25	New Jersey	4	0.9%
32	New Mexico	3	0.7%
16	New York	7	1.6%
3	North Carolina	38	8.6%
45	North Dakota	0	0.0%
39	Ohio	1	0.2%
9	Oklahoma	13	2.9%
39	Oregon	1	0.2%
19	Pennsylvania	6	1.4%
45	Rhode Island	0	0.0%
25	South Carolina	4	0.9%
39	South Dakota	1	0.2%
10	Tennessee	11	2.5%
1	Texas	54	12.2%
25	Utah	4	0.9%
39	Vermont	1	0.2%
13	Virginia	10	2.3%
21	Washington	5	1.1%
5	West Virginia	24	5.4%
8	Wisconsin	20	4.5%
19	Wyoming	6	1.4%

RANK ORDER

RANK	STATE	FATALITIES	% of USA
1	Texas	54	12.2%
2	Nevada	53	12.0%
3	North Carolina	38	8.6%
4	Florida	31	7.0%
5	West Virginia	24	5.4%
6	California	22	5.0%
7	Louisiana	21	4.8%
8	Wisconsin	20	4.5%
9	Oklahoma	13	2.9%
10	Arizona	11	2.5%
10	Georgia	11	2.5%
10	Tennessee	11	2.5%
13	Virginia	10	2.3%
14	Illinois	9	2.0%
14	Minnesota	9	2.0%
16	Alabama	7	1.6%
16	Missouri	7	1.6%
16	New York	7	1.6%
19	Pennsylvania	6	1.4%
19	Wyoming	6	1.4%
21	Colorado	5	1.1%
21	Indiana	5	1.1%
21	Kansas	5	1.1%
21	Washington	5	1.1%
25	Alaska	4	0.9%
25	Maryland	4	0.9%
25	Massachusetts	4	0.9%
25	Mississippi	4	0.9%
25	New Jersey	4	0.9%
25	South Carolina	4	0.9%
25	Utah	4	0.9%
32	Hawaii	3	0.7%
32	Kentucky	3	0.7%
32	Montana	3	0.7%
32	New Mexico	3	0.7%
36	Arkansas	2	0.5%
36	Iowa	2	0.5%
36	Michigan	2	0.5%
39	Idaho	1	0.2%
39	New Hampshire	1	0.2%
39	Ohio	1	0.2%
39	Oregon	1	0.2%
39	South Dakota	1	0.2%
39	Vermont	1	0.2%
45	Connecticut	0	0.0%
45	Delaware	0	0.0%
45	Maine	0	0.0%
45	Nebraska	0	0.0%
45	North Dakota	0	0.0%
45	Rhode Island	0	0.0%
	District of Columbia	0	0.0%

Source: National Weather Service, Water and Weather Services
"2016 Summary of Hazardous Weather Fatalities" (http://www.nws.noaa.gov/om/hazstats.shtml)
*Includes lightning, tornado, thunderstorm, extreme temperature, flood, coastal storm, rip current, hurricane, winter storm, fog, avalanche, and other weather events. National total does not include 16 fatalities in U.S. waters or territories.

Tornadoes in 2017

National Total = 1,522 Tornadoes*

ALPHA ORDER

RANK	STATE	TORNADOES	% of USA
7	Alabama	65	4.3%
43	Alaska	0	0.0%
34	Arizona	3	0.2%
22	Arkansas	26	1.7%
37	California	2	0.1%
26	Colorado	20	1.3%
43	Connecticut	0	0.0%
41	Delaware	1	0.1%
13	Florida	41	2.7%
2	Georgia	131	8.6%
43	Hawaii	0	0.0%
41	Idaho	1	0.1%
7	Illinois	65	4.3%
17	Indiana	36	2.4%
10	Iowa	57	3.7%
6	Kansas	74	4.9%
20	Kentucky	29	1.9%
4	Louisiana	88	5.8%
31	Maine	10	0.7%
33	Maryland	4	0.3%
37	Massachusetts	2	0.1%
29	Michigan	11	0.7%
13	Minnesota	41	2.7%
5	Mississippi	81	5.3%
3	Missouri	102	6.7%
37	Montana	2	0.1%
16	Nebraska	38	2.5%
43	Nevada	0	0.0%
43	New Hampshire	0	0.0%
37	New Jersey	2	0.1%
29	New Mexico	11	0.7%
28	New York	12	0.8%
19	North Carolina	34	2.2%
13	North Dakota	41	2.7%
12	Ohio	43	2.8%
9	Oklahoma	62	4.1%
34	Oregon	3	0.2%
22	Pennsylvania	26	1.7%
43	Rhode Island	0	0.0%
11	South Carolina	51	3.4%
25	South Dakota	21	1.4%
18	Tennessee	35	2.3%
1	Texas	176	11.6%
43	Utah	0	0.0%
43	Vermont	0	0.0%
24	Virginia	23	1.5%
34	Washington	3	0.2%
32	West Virginia	5	0.3%
21	Wisconsin	28	1.8%
27	Wyoming	15	1.0%

RANK ORDER

RANK	STATE	TORNADOES	% of USA
1	Texas	176	11.6%
2	Georgia	131	8.6%
3	Missouri	102	6.7%
4	Louisiana	88	5.8%
5	Mississippi	81	5.3%
6	Kansas	74	4.9%
7	Alabama	65	4.3%
7	Illinois	65	4.3%
9	Oklahoma	62	4.1%
10	Iowa	57	3.7%
11	South Carolina	51	3.4%
12	Ohio	43	2.8%
13	Florida	41	2.7%
13	Minnesota	41	2.7%
13	North Dakota	41	2.7%
16	Nebraska	38	2.5%
17	Indiana	36	2.4%
18	Tennessee	35	2.3%
19	North Carolina	34	2.2%
20	Kentucky	29	1.9%
21	Wisconsin	28	1.8%
22	Arkansas	26	1.7%
22	Pennsylvania	26	1.7%
24	Virginia	23	1.5%
25	South Dakota	21	1.4%
26	Colorado	20	1.3%
27	Wyoming	15	1.0%
28	New York	12	0.8%
29	Michigan	11	0.7%
29	New Mexico	11	0.7%
31	Maine	10	0.7%
32	West Virginia	5	0.3%
33	Maryland	4	0.3%
34	Arizona	3	0.2%
34	Oregon	3	0.2%
34	Washington	3	0.2%
37	California	2	0.1%
37	Massachusetts	2	0.1%
37	Montana	2	0.1%
37	New Jersey	2	0.1%
41	Delaware	1	0.1%
41	Idaho	1	0.1%
43	Alaska	0	0.0%
43	Connecticut	0	0.0%
43	Hawaii	0	0.0%
43	Nevada	0	0.0%
43	New Hampshire	0	0.0%
43	Rhode Island	0	0.0%
43	Utah	0	0.0%
43	Vermont	0	0.0%
	District of Columbia	1	0.1%

Source: National Weather Service, Storm Prediction Center
"Annual Severe Weather Report Summary - 2017" (http://www.spc.noaa.gov/climo/online/monthly/newm.html)
*Preliminary figures. Tornadoes striking more than one state are counted in each state.

Fatalities Caused by Tornadoes: 2008 to 2017

National Total = 1,003 Fatalities

RANK	STATE	FATALITIES	% of USA
1	Alabama	260	25.9%
31	Alaska	0	0.0%
31	Arizona	0	0.0%
6	Arkansas	63	6.3%
31	California	0	0.0%
26	Colorado	1	0.1%
31	Connecticut	0	0.0%
31	Delaware	0	0.0%
20	Florida	4	0.4%
7	Georgia	39	3.9%
31	Hawaii	0	0.0%
31	Idaho	0	0.0%
11	Illinois	23	2.3%
12	Indiana	17	1.7%
13	Iowa	16	1.6%
17	Kansas	8	0.8%
8	Kentucky	31	3.1%
16	Louisiana	9	0.9%
31	Maine	0	0.0%
31	Maryland	0	0.0%
22	Massachusetts	3	0.3%
26	Michigan	1	0.1%
18	Minnesota	5	0.5%
3	Mississippi	81	8.1%
2	Missouri	192	19.1%
23	Montana	2	0.2%
23	Nebraska	2	0.2%
31	Nevada	0	0.0%
26	New Hampshire	1	0.1%
31	New Jersey	0	0.0%
31	New Mexico	0	0.0%
18	New York	5	0.5%
9	North Carolina	30	3.0%
26	North Dakota	1	0.1%
14	Ohio	11	1.1%
4	Oklahoma	77	7.7%
31	Oregon	0	0.0%
31	Pennsylvania	0	0.0%
31	Rhode Island	0	0.0%
20	South Carolina	4	0.4%
31	South Dakota	0	0.0%
5	Tennessee	75	7.5%
10	Texas	29	2.9%
31	Utah	0	0.0%
31	Vermont	0	0.0%
15	Virginia	10	1.0%
31	Washington	0	0.0%
26	West Virginia	1	0.1%
23	Wisconsin	2	0.2%
31	Wyoming	0	0.0%

RANK	STATE	FATALITIES	% of USA
1	Alabama	260	25.9%
2	Missouri	192	19.1%
3	Mississippi	81	8.1%
4	Oklahoma	77	7.7%
5	Tennessee	75	7.5%
6	Arkansas	63	6.3%
7	Georgia	39	3.9%
8	Kentucky	31	3.1%
9	North Carolina	30	3.0%
10	Texas	29	2.9%
11	Illinois	23	2.3%
12	Indiana	17	1.7%
13	Iowa	16	1.6%
14	Ohio	11	1.1%
15	Virginia	10	1.0%
16	Louisiana	9	0.9%
17	Kansas	8	0.8%
18	Minnesota	5	0.5%
18	New York	5	0.5%
20	Florida	4	0.4%
20	South Carolina	4	0.4%
22	Massachusetts	3	0.3%
23	Montana	2	0.2%
23	Nebraska	2	0.2%
23	Wisconsin	2	0.2%
26	Colorado	1	0.1%
26	Michigan	1	0.1%
26	New Hampshire	1	0.1%
26	North Dakota	1	0.1%
26	West Virginia	1	0.1%
31	Alaska	0	0.0%
31	Arizona	0	0.0%
31	California	0	0.0%
31	Connecticut	0	0.0%
31	Delaware	0	0.0%
31	Hawaii	0	0.0%
31	Idaho	0	0.0%
31	Maine	0	0.0%
31	Maryland	0	0.0%
31	Nevada	0	0.0%
31	New Jersey	0	0.0%
31	New Mexico	0	0.0%
31	Oregon	0	0.0%
31	Pennsylvania	0	0.0%
31	Rhode Island	0	0.0%
31	South Dakota	0	0.0%
31	Utah	0	0.0%
31	Vermont	0	0.0%
31	Washington	0	0.0%
31	Wyoming	0	0.0%
	District of Columbia	0	0.0%

Source: CQ Press using data from National Weather Service, Storm Prediction Center
"Annual U.S. Killer Tornado Statistics" (http://www.spc.noaa.gov/climo/torn/fatalmap.php)

Cost of Damage from Hazardous Weather in 2016

National Total = $18,436,480,000*

ALPHA ORDER

RANK	STATE	DAMAGE	% of USA
38	Alabama	$4,310,000	0.0%
48	Alaska	200,000	0.0%
32	Arizona	10,930,000	0.1%
30	Arkansas	13,580,000	0.1%
11	California	74,380,000	0.4%
45	Colorado	900,000	0.0%
43	Connecticut	1,750,000	0.0%
49	Delaware	40,000	0.0%
3	Florida	3,116,320,000	16.9%
17	Georgia	38,250,000	0.2%
50	Hawaii	0	0.0%
44	Idaho	1,140,000	0.0%
21	Illinois	24,270,000	0.1%
28	Indiana	15,420,000	0.1%
16	Iowa	40,600,000	0.2%
10	Kansas	79,890,000	0.4%
24	Kentucky	19,610,000	0.1%
1	Louisiana	9,203,830,000	49.9%
42	Maine	1,930,000	0.0%
20	Maryland	24,450,000	0.1%
36	Massachusetts	7,020,000	0.0%
14	Michigan	50,630,000	0.3%
26	Minnesota	18,950,000	0.1%
15	Mississippi	41,630,000	0.2%
29	Missouri	14,800,000	0.1%
37	Montana	5,010,000	0.0%
13	Nebraska	53,740,000	0.3%
9	Nevada	81,090,000	0.4%
47	New Hampshire	270,000	0.0%
40	New Jersey	3,890,000	0.0%
25	New Mexico	19,440,000	0.1%
27	New York	17,020,000	0.1%
4	North Carolina	1,005,580,000	5.5%
8	North Dakota	93,400,000	0.5%
22	Ohio	21,330,000	0.1%
23	Oklahoma	20,320,000	0.1%
35	Oregon	7,260,000	0.0%
12	Pennsylvania	61,320,000	0.3%
45	Rhode Island	900,000	0.0%
5	South Carolina	254,580,000	1.4%
33	South Dakota	10,550,000	0.1%
19	Tennessee	26,220,000	0.1%
2	Texas	3,611,890,000	19.6%
31	Utah	13,440,000	0.1%
39	Vermont	3,940,000	0.0%
7	Virginia	98,440,000	0.5%
34	Washington	8,430,000	0.0%
6	West Virginia	172,540,000	0.9%
18	Wisconsin	37,950,000	0.2%
41	Wyoming	3,100,000	0.0%

RANK ORDER

RANK	STATE	DAMAGE	% of USA
1	Louisiana	$9,203,830,000	49.9%
2	Texas	3,611,890,000	19.6%
3	Florida	3,116,320,000	16.9%
4	North Carolina	1,005,580,000	5.5%
5	South Carolina	254,580,000	1.4%
6	West Virginia	172,540,000	0.9%
7	Virginia	98,440,000	0.5%
8	North Dakota	93,400,000	0.5%
9	Nevada	81,090,000	0.4%
10	Kansas	79,890,000	0.4%
11	California	74,380,000	0.4%
12	Pennsylvania	61,320,000	0.3%
13	Nebraska	53,740,000	0.3%
14	Michigan	50,630,000	0.3%
15	Mississippi	41,630,000	0.2%
16	Iowa	40,600,000	0.2%
17	Georgia	38,250,000	0.2%
18	Wisconsin	37,950,000	0.2%
19	Tennessee	26,220,000	0.1%
20	Maryland	24,450,000	0.1%
21	Illinois	24,270,000	0.1%
22	Ohio	21,330,000	0.1%
23	Oklahoma	20,320,000	0.1%
24	Kentucky	19,610,000	0.1%
25	New Mexico	19,440,000	0.1%
26	Minnesota	18,950,000	0.1%
27	New York	17,020,000	0.1%
28	Indiana	15,420,000	0.1%
29	Missouri	14,800,000	0.1%
30	Arkansas	13,580,000	0.1%
31	Utah	13,440,000	0.1%
32	Arizona	10,930,000	0.1%
33	South Dakota	10,550,000	0.1%
34	Washington	8,430,000	0.0%
35	Oregon	7,260,000	0.0%
36	Massachusetts	7,020,000	0.0%
37	Montana	5,010,000	0.0%
38	Alabama	4,310,000	0.0%
39	Vermont	3,940,000	0.0%
40	New Jersey	3,890,000	0.0%
41	Wyoming	3,100,000	0.0%
42	Maine	1,930,000	0.0%
43	Connecticut	1,750,000	0.0%
44	Idaho	1,140,000	0.0%
45	Colorado	900,000	0.0%
45	Rhode Island	900,000	0.0%
47	New Hampshire	270,000	0.0%
48	Alaska	200,000	0.0%
49	Delaware	40,000	0.0%
50	Hawaii	0	0.0%

| | District of Columbia | 0 | 0.0% |

Source: National Weather Service, Water and Weather Services
   "2016 Summary of Hazardous Weather Fatalities" (http://www.nws.noaa.gov/om/hazstats.shtml)
*Includes property and crop damage from lightning, tornado, thunderstorm, extreme temperature, flood, coastal storm, rip current, hurricane, winter storm, fog, avalanche, and other weather events. National total does not include damage costs in U.S. territories.

National Park Service Land in 2014

National Total = 84,479,064 Acres*

ALPHA ORDER

RANK	STATE	ACRES	% of USA
41	Alabama	22,737	0.0%
1	Alaska	54,654,154	64.7%
3	Arizona	2,947,312	3.5%
25	Arkansas	104,977	0.1%
2	California	8,144,518	9.6%
11	Colorado	737,812	0.9%
46	Connecticut	7,782	0.0%
48	Delaware	900	0.0%
4	Florida	2,638,658	3.1%
34	Georgia	63,338	0.1%
17	Hawaii	369,166	0.4%
13	Idaho	518,224	0.6%
49	Illinois	115	0.0%
43	Indiana	15,540	0.0%
47	Iowa	2,713	0.0%
44	Kansas	11,636	0.0%
27	Kentucky	95,942	0.1%
39	Louisiana	23,545	0.0%
29	Maine	91,826	0.1%
31	Maryland	73,893	0.1%
35	Massachusetts	57,962	0.1%
12	Michigan	718,148	0.9%
20	Minnesota	301,330	0.4%
24	Mississippi	118,587	0.1%
30	Missouri	83,476	0.1%
8	Montana	1,274,364	1.5%
36	Nebraska	45,735	0.1%
10	Nevada	778,512	0.9%
42	New Hampshire	21,015	0.0%
26	New Jersey	99,313	0.1%
15	New Mexico	391,078	0.5%
32	New York	72,992	0.1%
14	North Carolina	407,225	0.5%
33	North Dakota	72,568	0.1%
37	Ohio	34,544	0.0%
45	Oklahoma	10,241	0.0%
21	Oregon	199,319	0.2%
22	Pennsylvania	138,683	0.2%
50	Rhode Island	5	0.0%
38	South Carolina	32,348	0.0%
19	South Dakota	302,998	0.4%
16	Tennessee	384,978	0.5%
9	Texas	1,247,918	1.5%
6	Utah	2,117,683	2.5%
40	Vermont	23,265	0.0%
18	Virginia	364,371	0.4%
7	Washington	1,967,532	2.3%
28	West Virginia	92,721	0.1%
23	Wisconsin	133,755	0.2%
5	Wyoming	2,396,424	2.8%

RANK ORDER

RANK	STATE	ACRES	% of USA
1	Alaska	54,654,154	64.7%
2	California	8,144,518	9.6%
3	Arizona	2,947,312	3.5%
4	Florida	2,638,658	3.1%
5	Wyoming	2,396,424	2.8%
6	Utah	2,117,683	2.5%
7	Washington	1,967,532	2.3%
8	Montana	1,274,364	1.5%
9	Texas	1,247,918	1.5%
10	Nevada	778,512	0.9%
11	Colorado	737,812	0.9%
12	Michigan	718,148	0.9%
13	Idaho	518,224	0.6%
14	North Carolina	407,225	0.5%
15	New Mexico	391,078	0.5%
16	Tennessee	384,978	0.5%
17	Hawaii	369,166	0.4%
18	Virginia	364,371	0.4%
19	South Dakota	302,998	0.4%
20	Minnesota	301,330	0.4%
21	Oregon	199,319	0.2%
22	Pennsylvania	138,683	0.2%
23	Wisconsin	133,755	0.2%
24	Mississippi	118,587	0.1%
25	Arkansas	104,977	0.1%
26	New Jersey	99,313	0.1%
27	Kentucky	95,942	0.1%
28	West Virginia	92,721	0.1%
29	Maine	91,826	0.1%
30	Missouri	83,476	0.1%
31	Maryland	73,893	0.1%
32	New York	72,992	0.1%
33	North Dakota	72,568	0.1%
34	Georgia	63,338	0.1%
35	Massachusetts	57,962	0.1%
36	Nebraska	45,735	0.1%
37	Ohio	34,544	0.0%
38	South Carolina	32,348	0.0%
39	Louisiana	23,545	0.0%
40	Vermont	23,265	0.0%
41	Alabama	22,737	0.0%
42	New Hampshire	21,015	0.0%
43	Indiana	15,540	0.0%
44	Kansas	11,636	0.0%
45	Oklahoma	10,241	0.0%
46	Connecticut	7,782	0.0%
47	Iowa	2,713	0.0%
48	Delaware	900	0.0%
49	Illinois	115	0.0%
50	Rhode Island	5	0.0%
	District of Columbia	7,131	0.0%

Source: National Park Service
  "Listing of Acreage by State" (unpublished data)
*As of December 31, 2014. Includes federal and nonfederal land in national parks, monuments, historic sites, recreation areas, preserves, battlefields, grasslands, seashores, parkways, trails, and rivers. Does not include land in national forest or wildlife areas. Includes 58,057 acres in U.S. territories.

Recreation Visits to National Park Service Areas in 2014

National Total = 292,800,082 Visits*

ALPHA ORDER					RANK ORDER			
RANK	STATE	VISITS	% of USA		RANK	STATE	VISITS	% of USA
37	Alabama	753,178	0.3%		1	California	37,363,392	12.8%
25	Alaska	2,684,693	0.9%		2	Virginia	22,870,531	7.8%
5	Arizona	10,747,219	3.7%		3	North Carolina	16,710,759	5.7%
24	Arkansas	3,132,898	1.1%		4	New York	16,141,397	5.5%
1	California	37,363,392	12.8%		5	Arizona	10,747,219	3.7%
16	Colorado	6,031,874	2.1%		6	Florida	10,667,459	3.6%
49	Connecticut	34,082	0.0%		7	Utah	10,551,040	3.6%
50	Delaware	0	0.0%		8	Massachusetts	9,850,586	3.4%
6	Florida	10,667,459	3.6%		9	Pennsylvania	9,005,244	3.1%
12	Georgia	7,491,109	2.6%		10	Tennessee	8,470,460	2.9%
18	Hawaii	5,213,817	1.8%		11	Washington	7,652,073	2.6%
40	Idaho	553,739	0.2%		12	Georgia	7,491,109	2.6%
43	Illinois	218,132	0.1%		13	Maryland	6,815,195	2.3%
30	Indiana	1,778,385	0.6%		14	Mississippi	6,557,120	2.2%
44	Iowa	216,898	0.1%		15	Wyoming	6,387,455	2.2%
45	Kansas	98,591	0.0%		16	Colorado	6,031,874	2.1%
29	Kentucky	1,828,192	0.6%		17	Nevada	5,314,681	1.8%
41	Louisiana	510,522	0.2%		18	Hawaii	5,213,817	1.8%
26	Maine	2,574,717	0.9%		19	Texas	4,680,387	1.6%
13	Maryland	6,815,195	2.3%		20	Montana	4,590,398	1.6%
8	Massachusetts	9,850,586	3.4%		21	New Jersey	4,389,637	1.5%
28	Michigan	1,993,139	0.7%		22	South Dakota	3,861,090	1.3%
36	Minnesota	811,616	0.3%		23	Missouri	3,385,772	1.2%
14	Mississippi	6,557,120	2.2%		24	Arkansas	3,132,898	1.1%
23	Missouri	3,385,772	1.2%		25	Alaska	2,684,693	0.9%
20	Montana	4,590,398	1.6%		26	Maine	2,574,717	0.9%
42	Nebraska	254,198	0.1%		27	Ohio	2,470,177	0.8%
17	Nevada	5,314,681	1.8%		28	Michigan	1,993,139	0.7%
48	New Hampshire	37,785	0.0%		29	Kentucky	1,828,192	0.6%
21	New Jersey	4,389,637	1.5%		30	Indiana	1,778,385	0.6%
31	New Mexico	1,602,114	0.5%		31	New Mexico	1,602,114	0.5%
4	New York	16,141,397	5.5%		32	West Virginia	1,541,805	0.5%
3	North Carolina	16,710,759	5.7%		33	South Carolina	1,519,746	0.5%
39	North Dakota	581,851	0.2%		34	Oklahoma	1,165,269	0.4%
27	Ohio	2,470,177	0.8%		35	Oregon	1,033,254	0.4%
34	Oklahoma	1,165,269	0.4%		36	Minnesota	811,616	0.3%
35	Oregon	1,033,254	0.4%		37	Alabama	753,178	0.3%
9	Pennsylvania	9,005,244	3.1%		38	Wisconsin	625,850	0.2%
46	Rhode Island	51,523	0.0%		39	North Dakota	581,851	0.2%
33	South Carolina	1,519,746	0.5%		40	Idaho	553,739	0.2%
22	South Dakota	3,861,090	1.3%		41	Louisiana	510,522	0.2%
10	Tennessee	8,470,460	2.9%		42	Nebraska	254,198	0.1%
19	Texas	4,680,387	1.6%		43	Illinois	218,132	0.1%
7	Utah	10,551,040	3.6%		44	Iowa	216,898	0.1%
47	Vermont	39,086	0.0%		45	Kansas	98,591	0.0%
2	Virginia	22,870,531	7.8%		46	Rhode Island	51,523	0.0%
11	Washington	7,652,073	2.6%		47	Vermont	39,086	0.0%
32	West Virginia	1,541,805	0.5%		48	New Hampshire	37,785	0.0%
38	Wisconsin	625,850	0.2%		49	Connecticut	34,082	0.0%
15	Wyoming	6,387,455	2.2%		50	Delaware	0	0.0%
						District of Columbia	37,701,216	12.9%

Source: National Park Service, Public Use Statistics Office
"National Park Service Statistical Abstract 2014" (https://irma.nps.gov/Stats/Reports/AbstractsandForecasts)
*National total includes 2,238,731 visits in U.S. territories.

Percent Change in National Park Service Recreation Visits: 2013 to 2014

National Percent Change = 7.0% Increase*

ALPHA ORDER

RANK	STATE	PERCENT CHANGE
37	Alabama	0.4
28	Alaska	3.8
17	Arizona	6.4
10	Arkansas	12.9
24	California	5.0
11	Colorado	11.8
2	Connecticut	49.1
NA	Delaware**	NA
30	Florida	3.7
19	Georgia	6.3
17	Hawaii	6.4
46	Idaho	(9.9)
26	Illinois	4.2
45	Indiana	(8.1)
13	Iowa	8.5
14	Kansas	7.3
8	Kentucky	13.9
49	Louisiana	(18.2)
9	Maine	13.6
32	Maryland	3.0
35	Massachusetts	1.8
38	Michigan	0.2
5	Minnesota	23.3
44	Mississippi	(3.4)
48	Missouri	(12.9)
15	Montana	7.2
41	Nebraska	(1.4)
12	Nevada	9.6
40	New Hampshire	(0.1)
47	New Jersey	(12.7)
20	New Mexico	5.9
3	New York	46.9
31	North Carolina	3.6
36	North Dakota	1.6
34	Ohio	2.7
22	Oklahoma	5.2
16	Oregon	6.6
43	Pennsylvania	(1.5)
20	Rhode Island	5.9
38	South Carolina	0.2
41	South Dakota	(1.4)
25	Tennessee	4.7
4	Texas	34.4
6	Utah	17.5
7	Vermont	14.6
28	Virginia	3.8
26	Washington	4.2
33	West Virginia	2.9
1	Wisconsin	95.6
23	Wyoming	5.1

RANK ORDER

RANK	STATE	PERCENT CHANGE
1	Wisconsin	95.6
2	Connecticut	49.1
3	New York	46.9
4	Texas	34.4
5	Minnesota	23.3
6	Utah	17.5
7	Vermont	14.6
8	Kentucky	13.9
9	Maine	13.6
10	Arkansas	12.9
11	Colorado	11.8
12	Nevada	9.6
13	Iowa	8.5
14	Kansas	7.3
15	Montana	7.2
16	Oregon	6.6
17	Arizona	6.4
17	Hawaii	6.4
19	Georgia	6.3
20	New Mexico	5.9
20	Rhode Island	5.9
22	Oklahoma	5.2
23	Wyoming	5.1
24	California	5.0
25	Tennessee	4.7
26	Illinois	4.2
26	Washington	4.2
28	Alaska	3.8
28	Virginia	3.8
30	Florida	3.7
31	North Carolina	3.6
32	Maryland	3.0
33	West Virginia	2.9
34	Ohio	2.7
35	Massachusetts	1.8
36	North Dakota	1.6
37	Alabama	0.4
38	Michigan	0.2
38	South Carolina	0.2
40	New Hampshire	(0.1)
41	Nebraska	(1.4)
41	South Dakota	(1.4)
43	Pennsylvania	(1.5)
44	Mississippi	(3.4)
45	Indiana	(8.1)
46	Idaho	(9.9)
47	New Jersey	(12.7)
48	Missouri	(12.9)
49	Louisiana	(18.2)
NA	Delaware**	NA

District of Columbia 10.2

Source: National Park Service, Public Use Statistics Office
    "National Park Service Statistical Abstract 2014" (https://irma.nps.gov/Stats/Reports/AbstractsandForecasts)
*National percent change includes visits in U.S. territories.
**Not applicable.

IX. Government Finances: Federal

Internal Revenue Service Gross Collections in 2016

National Total = $3,333,449,083,000*

ALPHA ORDER

RANK	STATE	COLLECTIONS	% of USA
29	Alabama	$25,769,798,000	0.8%
48	Alaska	5,585,614,000	0.2%
23	Arizona	42,036,980,000	1.3%
26	Arkansas	32,041,729,000	1.0%
1	California	422,679,255,000	12.7%
21	Colorado	54,750,471,000	1.6%
19	Connecticut	62,910,820,000	1.9%
35	Delaware	19,970,924,000	0.6%
4	Florida	188,417,969,000	5.7%
11	Georgia	90,808,049,000	2.7%
41	Hawaii	8,811,882,000	0.3%
40	Idaho	10,083,241,000	0.3%
5	Illinois	161,938,790,000	4.9%
20	Indiana	57,138,639,000	1.7%
33	Iowa	23,946,703,000	0.7%
31	Kansas	25,291,646,000	0.8%
25	Kentucky	34,250,551,000	1.0%
24	Louisiana	41,543,677,000	1.2%
43	Maine	7,851,996,000	0.2%
16	Maryland	67,700,772,000	2.0%
9	Massachusetts	108,818,811,000	3.3%
14	Michigan	81,235,365,000	2.4%
10	Minnesota	103,696,439,000	3.1%
38	Mississippi	12,585,739,000	0.4%
17	Missouri	66,485,775,000	2.0%
47	Montana	5,972,785,000	0.2%
32	Nebraska	25,179,346,000	0.8%
36	Nevada	19,911,272,000	0.6%
39	New Hampshire	11,477,991,000	0.3%
6	New Jersey	143,011,905,000	4.3%
42	New Mexico	8,738,963,000	0.3%
2	New York	265,989,543,000	8.0%
12	North Carolina	83,714,348,000	2.5%
45	North Dakota	6,925,658,000	0.2%
7	Ohio	141,113,704,000	4.2%
28	Oklahoma	27,953,499,000	0.8%
27	Oregon	31,955,480,000	1.0%
8	Pennsylvania	135,924,018,000	4.1%
37	Rhode Island	14,607,467,000	0.4%
30	South Carolina	25,486,880,000	0.8%
44	South Dakota	7,779,688,000	0.2%
18	Tennessee	65,002,725,000	2.0%
3	Texas	261,128,693,000	7.8%
34	Utah	21,129,551,000	0.6%
50	Vermont	4,460,846,000	0.1%
13	Virginia	83,616,961,000	2.5%
15	Washington	77,083,460,000	2.3%
46	West Virginia	6,915,238,000	0.2%
22	Wisconsin	52,468,187,000	1.6%
49	Wyoming	4,475,631,000	0.1%

RANK ORDER

RANK	STATE	COLLECTIONS	% of USA
1	California	$422,679,255,000	12.7%
2	New York	265,989,543,000	8.0%
3	Texas	261,128,693,000	7.8%
4	Florida	188,417,969,000	5.7%
5	Illinois	161,938,790,000	4.9%
6	New Jersey	143,011,905,000	4.3%
7	Ohio	141,113,704,000	4.2%
8	Pennsylvania	135,924,018,000	4.1%
9	Massachusetts	108,818,811,000	3.3%
10	Minnesota	103,696,439,000	3.1%
11	Georgia	90,808,049,000	2.7%
12	North Carolina	83,714,348,000	2.5%
13	Virginia	83,616,961,000	2.5%
14	Michigan	81,235,365,000	2.4%
15	Washington	77,083,460,000	2.3%
16	Maryland	67,700,772,000	2.0%
17	Missouri	66,485,775,000	2.0%
18	Tennessee	65,002,725,000	2.0%
19	Connecticut	62,910,820,000	1.9%
20	Indiana	57,138,639,000	1.7%
21	Colorado	54,750,471,000	1.6%
22	Wisconsin	52,468,187,000	1.6%
23	Arizona	42,036,980,000	1.3%
24	Louisiana	41,543,677,000	1.2%
25	Kentucky	34,250,551,000	1.0%
26	Arkansas	32,041,729,000	1.0%
27	Oregon	31,955,480,000	1.0%
28	Oklahoma	27,953,499,000	0.8%
29	Alabama	25,769,798,000	0.8%
30	South Carolina	25,486,880,000	0.8%
31	Kansas	25,291,646,000	0.8%
32	Nebraska	25,179,346,000	0.8%
33	Iowa	23,946,703,000	0.7%
34	Utah	21,129,551,000	0.6%
35	Delaware	19,970,924,000	0.6%
36	Nevada	19,911,272,000	0.6%
37	Rhode Island	14,607,467,000	0.4%
38	Mississippi	12,585,739,000	0.4%
39	New Hampshire	11,477,991,000	0.3%
40	Idaho	10,083,241,000	0.3%
41	Hawaii	8,811,882,000	0.3%
42	New Mexico	8,738,963,000	0.3%
43	Maine	7,851,996,000	0.2%
44	South Dakota	7,779,688,000	0.2%
45	North Dakota	6,925,658,000	0.2%
46	West Virginia	6,915,238,000	0.2%
47	Montana	5,972,785,000	0.2%
48	Alaska	5,585,614,000	0.2%
49	Wyoming	4,475,631,000	0.1%
50	Vermont	4,460,846,000	0.1%
	District of Columbia	27,255,713,000	0.8%

Source: U.S. Department of the Treasury, Internal Revenue Service
"Fiscal Year 2016 IRS Data Book" (http://www.irs.gov/uac/SOI-Tax-Stats-IRS-Data-Book)
*Total includes $17,817,895,000 from U.S. citizens abroad and other miscellaneous returns not shown separately.

Per Capita Internal Revenue Service Gross Collections in 2016

National Per Capita = $10,252*

ALPHA ORDER

ALPHA ORDER

RANK	STATE	PER CAPITA
46	Alabama	$5,302
36	Alaska	7,533
42	Arizona	6,085
14	Arkansas	10,723
13	California	10,756
18	Colorado	9,900
3	Connecticut	17,535
1	Delaware	20,962
22	Florida	9,121
26	Georgia	8,805
41	Hawaii	6,168
43	Idaho	6,002
9	Illinois	12,616
28	Indiana	8,613
35	Iowa	7,649
27	Kansas	8,698
33	Kentucky	7,721
25	Louisiana	8,865
44	Maine	5,903
11	Maryland	11,237
4	Massachusetts	15,947
31	Michigan	8,178
2	Minnesota	18,768
48	Mississippi	4,216
12	Missouri	10,915
45	Montana	5,750
8	Nebraska	13,199
40	Nevada	6,774
29	New Hampshire	8,598
5	New Jersey	15,928
49	New Mexico	4,190
7	New York	13,409
30	North Carolina	8,242
21	North Dakota	9,166
10	Ohio	12,141
38	Oklahoma	7,129
32	Oregon	7,821
15	Pennsylvania	10,630
6	Rhode Island	13,812
47	South Carolina	5,139
24	South Dakota	9,030
19	Tennessee	9,776
20	Texas	9,358
39	Utah	6,941
37	Vermont	7,156
17	Virginia	9,937
16	Washington	10,587
50	West Virginia	3,782
23	Wisconsin	9,089
34	Wyoming	7,652

RANK ORDER

RANK	STATE	PER CAPITA
1	Delaware	$20,962
2	Minnesota	18,768
3	Connecticut	17,535
4	Massachusetts	15,947
5	New Jersey	15,928
6	Rhode Island	13,812
7	New York	13,409
8	Nebraska	13,199
9	Illinois	12,616
10	Ohio	12,141
11	Maryland	11,237
12	Missouri	10,915
13	California	10,756
14	Arkansas	10,723
15	Pennsylvania	10,630
16	Washington	10,587
17	Virginia	9,937
18	Colorado	9,900
19	Tennessee	9,776
20	Texas	9,358
21	North Dakota	9,166
22	Florida	9,121
23	Wisconsin	9,089
24	South Dakota	9,030
25	Louisiana	8,865
26	Georgia	8,805
27	Kansas	8,698
28	Indiana	8,613
29	New Hampshire	8,598
30	North Carolina	8,242
31	Michigan	8,178
32	Oregon	7,821
33	Kentucky	7,721
34	Wyoming	7,652
35	Iowa	7,649
36	Alaska	7,533
37	Vermont	7,156
38	Oklahoma	7,129
39	Utah	6,941
40	Nevada	6,774
41	Hawaii	6,168
42	Arizona	6,085
43	Idaho	6,002
44	Maine	5,903
45	Montana	5,750
46	Alabama	5,302
47	South Carolina	5,139
48	Mississippi	4,216
49	New Mexico	4,190
50	West Virginia	3,782

District of Columbia   39,828

Source: CQ Press using data from U.S. Department of the Treasury, Internal Revenue Service
"Fiscal Year 2016 IRS Data Book" (http://www.irs.gov/uac/SOI-Tax-Stats-IRS-Data-Book)
*National per capita does not include collections from U.S. citizens abroad and other miscellaneous returns not shown separately.

Federal Individual Income Tax Collections in 2016

National Total = $2,889,726,850,000*

ALPHA ORDER

RANK	STATE	COLLECTIONS	% of USA
28	Alabama	$23,701,732,000	0.8%
48	Alaska	5,320,151,000	0.2%
24	Arizona	37,748,900,000	1.3%
27	Arkansas	24,855,286,000	0.9%
1	California	365,225,572,000	12.6%
20	Colorado	50,033,278,000	1.7%
21	Connecticut	49,258,145,000	1.7%
36	Delaware	15,540,053,000	0.5%
4	Florida	172,450,572,000	6.0%
11	Georgia	74,344,840,000	2.6%
42	Hawaii	7,864,419,000	0.3%
40	Idaho	9,710,649,000	0.3%
5	Illinois	138,434,275,000	4.8%
19	Indiana	51,035,537,000	1.8%
32	Iowa	22,025,777,000	0.8%
31	Kansas	22,315,786,000	0.8%
25	Kentucky	30,386,590,000	1.1%
23	Louisiana	39,746,817,000	1.4%
44	Maine	7,232,445,000	0.3%
16	Maryland	62,904,457,000	2.2%
9	Massachusetts	98,880,648,000	3.4%
12	Michigan	73,520,578,000	2.5%
10	Minnesota	80,723,820,000	2.8%
37	Mississippi	11,657,976,000	0.4%
18	Missouri	54,754,718,000	1.9%
47	Montana	5,738,218,000	0.2%
35	Nebraska	18,243,763,000	0.6%
34	Nevada	18,734,870,000	0.6%
38	New Hampshire	10,917,982,000	0.4%
8	New Jersey	114,953,108,000	4.0%
41	New Mexico	8,390,557,000	0.3%
2	New York	232,171,654,000	8.0%
13	North Carolina	72,377,782,000	2.5%
46	North Dakota	6,534,589,000	0.2%
6	Ohio	124,675,836,000	4.3%
30	Oklahoma	22,768,650,000	0.8%
26	Oregon	29,749,545,000	1.0%
7	Pennsylvania	117,342,049,000	4.1%
39	Rhode Island	10,897,975,000	0.4%
29	South Carolina	23,241,146,000	0.8%
43	South Dakota	7,268,145,000	0.3%
17	Tennessee	56,406,412,000	2.0%
3	Texas	218,950,277,000	7.6%
33	Utah	19,194,605,000	0.7%
49	Vermont	4,202,276,000	0.1%
15	Virginia	70,011,653,000	2.4%
14	Washington	70,468,914,000	2.4%
45	West Virginia	6,620,799,000	0.2%
22	Wisconsin	46,893,577,000	1.6%
50	Wyoming	4,173,281,000	0.1%

RANK ORDER

RANK	STATE	COLLECTIONS	% of USA
1	California	$365,225,572,000	12.6%
2	New York	232,171,654,000	8.0%
3	Texas	218,950,277,000	7.6%
4	Florida	172,450,572,000	6.0%
5	Illinois	138,434,275,000	4.8%
6	Ohio	124,675,836,000	4.3%
7	Pennsylvania	117,342,049,000	4.1%
8	New Jersey	114,953,108,000	4.0%
9	Massachusetts	98,880,648,000	3.4%
10	Minnesota	80,723,820,000	2.8%
11	Georgia	74,344,840,000	2.6%
12	Michigan	73,520,578,000	2.5%
13	North Carolina	72,377,782,000	2.5%
14	Washington	70,468,914,000	2.4%
15	Virginia	70,011,653,000	2.4%
16	Maryland	62,904,457,000	2.2%
17	Tennessee	56,406,412,000	2.0%
18	Missouri	54,754,718,000	1.9%
19	Indiana	51,035,537,000	1.8%
20	Colorado	50,033,278,000	1.7%
21	Connecticut	49,258,145,000	1.7%
22	Wisconsin	46,893,577,000	1.6%
23	Louisiana	39,746,817,000	1.4%
24	Arizona	37,748,900,000	1.3%
25	Kentucky	30,386,590,000	1.1%
26	Oregon	29,749,545,000	1.0%
27	Arkansas	24,855,286,000	0.9%
28	Alabama	23,701,732,000	0.8%
29	South Carolina	23,241,146,000	0.8%
30	Oklahoma	22,768,650,000	0.8%
31	Kansas	22,315,786,000	0.8%
32	Iowa	22,025,777,000	0.8%
33	Utah	19,194,605,000	0.7%
34	Nevada	18,734,870,000	0.6%
35	Nebraska	18,243,763,000	0.6%
36	Delaware	15,540,053,000	0.5%
37	Mississippi	11,657,976,000	0.4%
38	New Hampshire	10,917,982,000	0.4%
39	Rhode Island	10,897,975,000	0.4%
40	Idaho	9,710,649,000	0.3%
41	New Mexico	8,390,557,000	0.3%
42	Hawaii	7,864,419,000	0.3%
43	South Dakota	7,268,145,000	0.3%
44	Maine	7,232,445,000	0.3%
45	West Virginia	6,620,799,000	0.2%
46	North Dakota	6,534,589,000	0.2%
47	Montana	5,738,218,000	0.2%
48	Alaska	5,320,151,000	0.2%
49	Vermont	4,202,276,000	0.1%
50	Wyoming	4,173,281,000	0.1%
	District of Columbia	24,909,535,000	0.9%

Source: U.S. Department of the Treasury, Internal Revenue Service
"Fiscal Year 2016 IRS Data Book" (http://www.irs.gov/uac/SOI-Tax-Stats-IRS-Data-Book)
*Total includes $14,216,631,000 from U.S. citizens abroad and other miscellaneous returns not shown separately.

Average Revenue Collection per Federal Individual Income Tax Return in 2016

National Average = $19,174 per Return*

ALPHA ORDER

RANK	STATE	PER RETURN
43	Alabama	$11,548
37	Alaska	14,873
41	Arizona	13,006
14	Arkansas	20,234
11	California	20,596
17	Colorado	19,149
4	Connecticut	27,952
1	Delaware	34,378
21	Florida	17,945
25	Georgia	16,759
45	Hawaii	11,436
40	Idaho	13,489
7	Illinois	22,473
28	Indiana	16,429
35	Iowa	15,169
26	Kansas	16,656
30	Kentucky	15,889
15	Louisiana	19,826
46	Maine	11,202
9	Maryland	21,259
3	Massachusetts	29,112
33	Michigan	15,597
2	Minnesota	29,632
48	Mississippi	9,365
16	Missouri	19,650
44	Montana	11,507
13	Nebraska	20,247
38	Nevada	13,894
32	New Hampshire	15,760
5	New Jersey	26,220
49	New Mexico	9,149
6	New York	24,150
29	North Carolina	16,239
23	North Dakota	17,639
8	Ohio	22,292
39	Oklahoma	13,856
31	Oregon	15,868
19	Pennsylvania	18,915
10	Rhode Island	20,630
47	South Carolina	10,749
24	South Dakota	17,478
18	Tennessee	19,013
20	Texas	18,069
34	Utah	15,214
42	Vermont	12,889
22	Virginia	17,925
12	Washington	20,585
50	West Virginia	8,472
27	Wisconsin	16,518
36	Wyoming	14,963

RANK ORDER

RANK	STATE	PER RETURN
1	Delaware	$34,378
2	Minnesota	29,632
3	Massachusetts	29,112
4	Connecticut	27,952
5	New Jersey	26,220
6	New York	24,150
7	Illinois	22,473
8	Ohio	22,292
9	Maryland	21,259
10	Rhode Island	20,630
11	California	20,596
12	Washington	20,585
13	Nebraska	20,247
14	Arkansas	20,234
15	Louisiana	19,826
16	Missouri	19,650
17	Colorado	19,149
18	Tennessee	19,013
19	Pennsylvania	18,915
20	Texas	18,069
21	Florida	17,945
22	Virginia	17,925
23	North Dakota	17,639
24	South Dakota	17,478
25	Georgia	16,759
26	Kansas	16,656
27	Wisconsin	16,518
28	Indiana	16,429
29	North Carolina	16,239
30	Kentucky	15,889
31	Oregon	15,868
32	New Hampshire	15,760
33	Michigan	15,597
34	Utah	15,214
35	Iowa	15,169
36	Wyoming	14,963
37	Alaska	14,873
38	Nevada	13,894
39	Oklahoma	13,856
40	Idaho	13,489
41	Arizona	13,006
42	Vermont	12,889
43	Alabama	11,548
44	Montana	11,507
45	Hawaii	11,436
46	Maine	11,202
47	South Carolina	10,749
48	Mississippi	9,365
49	New Mexico	9,149
50	West Virginia	8,472

District of Columbia   72,426

Source: CQ Press using data from U.S. Department of the Treasury, Internal Revenue Service
"Fiscal Year 2016 IRS Data Book" (http://www.irs.gov/uac/SOI-Tax-Stats-IRS-Data-Book)
*National Rate includes collections and returns from U.S. citizens abroad and other miscellaneous returns not shown separately.

Adjusted Gross Income in 2015

National Total = $10,149,347,083,000*

ALPHA ORDER

RANK	STATE	A.G.I.	% of USA
27	Alabama	$111,842,765,000	1.1%
48	Alaska	25,060,929,000	0.2%
20	Arizona	171,481,193,000	1.7%
34	Arkansas	66,570,126,000	0.7%
1	California	1,381,946,567,000	13.6%
17	Colorado	188,898,999,000	1.9%
22	Connecticut	167,477,008,000	1.7%
44	Delaware	28,796,094,000	0.3%
4	Florida	613,537,254,000	6.0%
12	Georgia	266,462,788,000	2.6%
39	Hawaii	41,845,278,000	0.4%
41	Idaho	39,165,046,000	0.4%
5	Illinois	441,641,632,000	4.4%
19	Indiana	173,427,367,000	1.7%
30	Iowa	88,048,301,000	0.9%
31	Kansas	83,668,519,000	0.8%
28	Kentucky	102,643,311,000	1.0%
26	Louisiana	112,187,963,000	1.1%
42	Maine	35,558,513,000	0.4%
15	Maryland	222,248,974,000	2.2%
9	Massachusetts	298,525,491,000	2.9%
11	Michigan	277,631,440,000	2.7%
16	Minnesota	193,029,363,000	1.9%
35	Mississippi	59,014,792,000	0.6%
23	Missouri	162,877,435,000	1.6%
45	Montana	27,848,271,000	0.3%
36	Nebraska	55,306,997,000	0.5%
32	Nevada	82,483,628,000	0.8%
37	New Hampshire	49,675,622,000	0.5%
7	New Jersey	366,858,387,000	3.6%
38	New Mexico	46,682,483,000	0.5%
3	New York	782,600,743,000	7.7%
13	North Carolina	262,136,593,000	2.6%
47	North Dakota	25,516,373,000	0.3%
8	Ohio	323,081,301,000	3.2%
29	Oklahoma	96,748,174,000	1.0%
25	Oregon	118,011,231,000	1.2%
6	Pennsylvania	405,142,214,000	4.0%
43	Rhode Island	33,254,020,000	0.3%
24	South Carolina	119,053,942,000	1.2%
46	South Dakota	25,538,550,000	0.3%
21	Tennessee	168,594,874,000	1.7%
2	Texas	813,802,449,000	8.0%
33	Utah	79,253,592,000	0.8%
50	Vermont	19,007,885,000	0.2%
10	Virginia	289,309,508,000	2.9%
14	Washington	261,164,063,000	2.6%
40	West Virginia	39,661,833,000	0.4%
18	Wisconsin	174,432,708,000	1.7%
49	Wyoming	20,837,862,000	0.2%

RANK ORDER

RANK	STATE	A.G.I.	% of USA
1	California	$1,381,946,567,000	13.6%
2	Texas	813,802,449,000	8.0%
3	New York	782,600,743,000	7.7%
4	Florida	613,537,254,000	6.0%
5	Illinois	441,641,632,000	4.4%
6	Pennsylvania	405,142,214,000	4.0%
7	New Jersey	366,858,387,000	3.6%
8	Ohio	323,081,301,000	3.2%
9	Massachusetts	298,525,491,000	2.9%
10	Virginia	289,309,508,000	2.9%
11	Michigan	277,631,440,000	2.7%
12	Georgia	266,462,788,000	2.6%
13	North Carolina	262,136,593,000	2.6%
14	Washington	261,164,063,000	2.6%
15	Maryland	222,248,974,000	2.2%
16	Minnesota	193,029,363,000	1.9%
17	Colorado	188,898,999,000	1.9%
18	Wisconsin	174,432,708,000	1.7%
19	Indiana	173,427,367,000	1.7%
20	Arizona	171,481,193,000	1.7%
21	Tennessee	168,594,874,000	1.7%
22	Connecticut	167,477,008,000	1.7%
23	Missouri	162,877,435,000	1.6%
24	South Carolina	119,053,942,000	1.2%
25	Oregon	118,011,231,000	1.2%
26	Louisiana	112,187,963,000	1.1%
27	Alabama	111,842,765,000	1.1%
28	Kentucky	102,643,311,000	1.0%
29	Oklahoma	96,748,174,000	1.0%
30	Iowa	88,048,301,000	0.9%
31	Kansas	83,668,519,000	0.8%
32	Nevada	82,483,628,000	0.8%
33	Utah	79,253,592,000	0.8%
34	Arkansas	66,570,126,000	0.7%
35	Mississippi	59,014,792,000	0.6%
36	Nebraska	55,306,997,000	0.5%
37	New Hampshire	49,675,622,000	0.5%
38	New Mexico	46,682,483,000	0.5%
39	Hawaii	41,845,278,000	0.4%
40	West Virginia	39,661,833,000	0.4%
41	Idaho	39,165,046,000	0.4%
42	Maine	35,558,513,000	0.4%
43	Rhode Island	33,254,020,000	0.3%
44	Delaware	28,796,094,000	0.3%
45	Montana	27,848,271,000	0.3%
46	South Dakota	25,538,550,000	0.3%
47	North Dakota	25,516,373,000	0.3%
48	Alaska	25,060,929,000	0.2%
49	Wyoming	20,837,862,000	0.2%
50	Vermont	19,007,885,000	0.2%
	District of Columbia	32,135,120,000	0.3%

Source: U.S. Department of the Treasury, Internal Revenue Service
"Individual Tax Statistics, State Income" (http://www.irs.gov/taxstats/index.html)
*Total includes $77,621,512,000 from U.S. citizens abroad and other miscellaneous returns not shown separately.

Per Capita Adjusted Gross Income in 2015

National Per Capita = $31,372*

ALPHA ORDER

RANK	STATE	PER CAPITA
46	Alabama	$23,056
14	Alaska	33,959
40	Arizona	25,209
48	Arkansas	22,372
9	California	35,405
11	Colorado	34,721
1	Connecticut	46,601
18	Delaware	30,501
21	Florida	30,270
37	Georgia	26,125
25	Hawaii	29,338
44	Idaho	23,746
13	Illinois	34,337
36	Indiana	26,235
29	Iowa	28,234
27	Kansas	28,794
45	Kentucky	23,212
43	Louisiana	24,017
34	Maine	26,780
6	Maryland	37,038
2	Massachusetts	43,940
30	Michigan	27,992
10	Minnesota	35,204
50	Mississippi	19,768
33	Missouri	26,822
32	Montana	27,081
26	Nebraska	29,208
28	Nevada	28,610
5	New Hampshire	37,346
3	New Jersey	40,944
47	New Mexico	22,419
4	New York	39,487
38	North Carolina	26,105
15	North Dakota	33,803
31	Ohio	27,837
41	Oklahoma	24,780
24	Oregon	29,381
16	Pennsylvania	31,674
17	Rhode Island	31,493
42	South Carolina	24,334
22	South Dakota	29,903
39	Tennessee	25,581
23	Texas	29,641
35	Utah	26,551
19	Vermont	30,439
12	Virginia	34,578
7	Washington	36,512
49	West Virginia	21,558
20	Wisconsin	30,285
8	Wyoming	35,553

RANK ORDER

RANK	STATE	PER CAPITA
1	Connecticut	$46,601
2	Massachusetts	43,940
3	New Jersey	40,944
4	New York	39,487
5	New Hampshire	37,346
6	Maryland	37,038
7	Washington	36,512
8	Wyoming	35,553
9	California	35,405
10	Minnesota	35,204
11	Colorado	34,721
12	Virginia	34,578
13	Illinois	34,337
14	Alaska	33,959
15	North Dakota	33,803
16	Pennsylvania	31,674
17	Rhode Island	31,493
18	Delaware	30,501
19	Vermont	30,439
20	Wisconsin	30,285
21	Florida	30,270
22	South Dakota	29,903
23	Texas	29,641
24	Oregon	29,381
25	Hawaii	29,338
26	Nebraska	29,208
27	Kansas	28,794
28	Nevada	28,610
29	Iowa	28,234
30	Michigan	27,992
31	Ohio	27,837
32	Montana	27,081
33	Missouri	26,822
34	Maine	26,780
35	Utah	26,551
36	Indiana	26,235
37	Georgia	26,125
38	North Carolina	26,105
39	Tennessee	25,581
40	Arizona	25,209
41	Oklahoma	24,780
42	South Carolina	24,334
43	Louisiana	24,017
44	Idaho	23,746
45	Kentucky	23,212
46	Alabama	23,056
47	New Mexico	22,419
48	Arkansas	22,372
49	West Virginia	21,558
50	Mississippi	19,768
	District of Columbia	47,768

Source: CQ Press using data from U.S. Department of the Treasury, Internal Revenue Service
"Individual Tax Statistics, State Income" (http://www.irs.gov/taxstats/index.html)
*National per capita does not include income from U.S. citizens abroad and other miscellaneous returns not shown separately.

Federal Business Income Tax Collections in 2016

National Total = $345,552,427,000*

ALPHA ORDER

RANK	STATE	COLLECTIONS	% of USA
30	Alabama	$1,571,713,000	0.5%
48	Alaska	187,371,000	0.1%
27	Arizona	2,563,871,000	0.7%
19	Arkansas	6,346,477,000	1.8%
1	California	48,416,393,000	14.0%
25	Colorado	3,595,318,000	1.0%
10	Connecticut	11,877,254,000	3.4%
23	Delaware	4,111,383,000	1.2%
11	Florida	11,773,302,000	3.4%
9	Georgia	12,567,697,000	3.6%
39	Hawaii	581,689,000	0.2%
43	Idaho	278,643,000	0.1%
5	Illinois	19,034,595,000	5.5%
22	Indiana	4,245,518,000	1.2%
31	Iowa	1,540,230,000	0.4%
33	Kansas	1,283,159,000	0.4%
28	Kentucky	2,482,345,000	0.7%
35	Louisiana	1,239,176,000	0.4%
41	Maine	393,879,000	0.1%
24	Maryland	4,040,984,000	1.2%
15	Massachusetts	8,117,082,000	2.3%
18	Michigan	6,539,155,000	1.9%
4	Minnesota	19,774,489,000	5.7%
38	Mississippi	659,542,000	0.2%
14	Missouri	9,975,985,000	2.9%
49	Montana	181,397,000	0.1%
17	Nebraska	6,722,660,000	1.9%
37	Nevada	767,939,000	0.2%
44	New Hampshire	236,307,000	0.1%
3	New Jersey	25,566,668,000	7.4%
46	New Mexico	200,103,000	0.1%
2	New York	28,810,484,000	8.3%
13	North Carolina	10,574,820,000	3.1%
42	North Dakota	285,640,000	0.1%
12	Ohio	11,673,464,000	3.4%
32	Oklahoma	1,379,289,000	0.4%
36	Oregon	1,074,218,000	0.3%
7	Pennsylvania	14,231,262,000	4.1%
26	Rhode Island	3,462,554,000	1.0%
29	South Carolina	1,708,414,000	0.5%
40	South Dakota	434,630,000	0.1%
16	Tennessee	6,940,458,000	2.0%
6	Texas	19,021,716,000	5.5%
34	Utah	1,252,583,000	0.4%
47	Vermont	200,000,000	0.1%
8	Virginia	12,845,576,000	3.7%
20	Washington	5,250,717,000	1.5%
45	West Virginia	220,567,000	0.1%
21	Wisconsin	4,749,321,000	1.4%
50	Wyoming	152,712,000	0.0%

RANK ORDER

RANK	STATE	COLLECTIONS	% of USA
1	California	$48,416,393,000	14.0%
2	New York	28,810,484,000	8.3%
3	New Jersey	25,566,668,000	7.4%
4	Minnesota	19,774,489,000	5.7%
5	Illinois	19,034,595,000	5.5%
6	Texas	19,021,716,000	5.5%
7	Pennsylvania	14,231,262,000	4.1%
8	Virginia	12,845,576,000	3.7%
9	Georgia	12,567,697,000	3.6%
10	Connecticut	11,877,254,000	3.4%
11	Florida	11,773,302,000	3.4%
12	Ohio	11,673,464,000	3.4%
13	North Carolina	10,574,820,000	3.1%
14	Missouri	9,975,985,000	2.9%
15	Massachusetts	8,117,082,000	2.3%
16	Tennessee	6,940,458,000	2.0%
17	Nebraska	6,722,660,000	1.9%
18	Michigan	6,539,155,000	1.9%
19	Arkansas	6,346,477,000	1.8%
20	Washington	5,250,717,000	1.5%
21	Wisconsin	4,749,321,000	1.4%
22	Indiana	4,245,518,000	1.2%
23	Delaware	4,111,383,000	1.2%
24	Maryland	4,040,984,000	1.2%
25	Colorado	3,595,318,000	1.0%
26	Rhode Island	3,462,554,000	1.0%
27	Arizona	2,563,871,000	0.7%
28	Kentucky	2,482,345,000	0.7%
29	South Carolina	1,708,414,000	0.5%
30	Alabama	1,571,713,000	0.5%
31	Iowa	1,540,230,000	0.4%
32	Oklahoma	1,379,289,000	0.4%
33	Kansas	1,283,159,000	0.4%
34	Utah	1,252,583,000	0.4%
35	Louisiana	1,239,176,000	0.4%
36	Oregon	1,074,218,000	0.3%
37	Nevada	767,939,000	0.2%
38	Mississippi	659,542,000	0.2%
39	Hawaii	581,689,000	0.2%
40	South Dakota	434,630,000	0.1%
41	Maine	393,879,000	0.1%
42	North Dakota	285,640,000	0.1%
43	Idaho	278,643,000	0.1%
44	New Hampshire	236,307,000	0.1%
45	West Virginia	220,567,000	0.1%
46	New Mexico	200,103,000	0.1%
47	Vermont	200,000,000	0.1%
48	Alaska	187,371,000	0.1%
49	Montana	181,397,000	0.1%
50	Wyoming	152,712,000	0.0%
	District of Columbia	2,251,996,000	0.7%

Source: U.S. Department of the Treasury, Internal Revenue Service
"Fiscal Year 2016 IRS Data Book" (http://www.irs.gov/uac/SOI-Tax-Stats-IRS-Data-Book)
*Total includes collections and returns from international sources and others not distributed by state. Includes taxes on corporation income (Form 1120 series) and unrelated business income from tax-exempt organizations.

Average Revenue Collection per Federal Business Income Tax Return in 2016

National Average = $49,149 per Return*

ALPHA ORDER

RANK	STATE	PER RETURN
28	Alabama	$23,127
39	Alaska	14,468
31	Arizona	21,291
7	Arkansas	119,272
13	California	58,210
29	Colorado	22,746
1	Connecticut	227,555
2	Delaware	162,319
41	Florida	13,863
14	Georgia	56,074
32	Hawaii	21,212
48	Idaho	7,759
17	Illinois	53,433
21	Indiana	37,662
27	Iowa	24,784
26	Kansas	24,947
22	Kentucky	37,550
38	Louisiana	15,281
42	Maine	13,117
25	Maryland	31,123
15	Massachusetts	54,894
24	Michigan	33,902
3	Minnesota	158,032
37	Mississippi	16,332
9	Missouri	101,760
50	Montana	5,144
4	Nebraska	150,301
46	Nevada	10,863
45	New Hampshire	10,963
6	New Jersey	136,816
49	New Mexico	6,814
19	New York	42,794
16	North Carolina	53,484
35	North Dakota	17,256
11	Ohio	66,706
34	Oklahoma	18,564
40	Oregon	14,103
12	Pennsylvania	65,449
5	Rhode Island	147,449
33	South Carolina	20,052
30	South Dakota	22,740
8	Tennessee	105,623
20	Texas	40,119
36	Utah	16,539
43	Vermont	12,719
10	Virginia	76,561
23	Washington	37,518
44	West Virginia	11,130
18	Wisconsin	51,782
47	Wyoming	8,110

RANK ORDER

RANK	STATE	PER RETURN
1	Connecticut	$227,555
2	Delaware	162,319
3	Minnesota	158,032
4	Nebraska	150,301
5	Rhode Island	147,449
6	New Jersey	136,816
7	Arkansas	119,272
8	Tennessee	105,623
9	Missouri	101,760
10	Virginia	76,561
11	Ohio	66,706
12	Pennsylvania	65,449
13	California	58,210
14	Georgia	56,074
15	Massachusetts	54,894
16	North Carolina	53,484
17	Illinois	53,433
18	Wisconsin	51,782
19	New York	42,794
20	Texas	40,119
21	Indiana	37,662
22	Kentucky	37,550
23	Washington	37,518
24	Michigan	33,902
25	Maryland	31,123
26	Kansas	24,947
27	Iowa	24,784
28	Alabama	23,127
29	Colorado	22,746
30	South Dakota	22,740
31	Arizona	21,291
32	Hawaii	21,212
33	South Carolina	20,052
34	Oklahoma	18,564
35	North Dakota	17,256
36	Utah	16,539
37	Mississippi	16,332
38	Louisiana	15,281
39	Alaska	14,468
40	Oregon	14,103
41	Florida	13,863
42	Maine	13,117
43	Vermont	12,719
44	West Virginia	11,130
45	New Hampshire	10,963
46	Nevada	10,863
47	Wyoming	8,110
48	Idaho	7,759
49	New Mexico	6,814
50	Montana	5,144

District of Columbia   123,702

Source: CQ Press using data from U.S. Department of the Treasury, Internal Revenue Service
"Fiscal Year 2016 IRS Data Book" (http://www.irs.gov/uac/SOI-Tax-Stats-IRS-Data-Book)
*National average does not include income from U.S. citizens abroad and other miscellaneous returns not shown separately.
Includes taxes on corporation income (Form 1120 series) and unrelated business income from tax-exempt organizations.

Federal Tax Returns Filed in 2016

National Total = 244,246,247 Returns*

ALPHA ORDER

RANK	STATE	RETURNS	% of USA
26	Alabama	3,078,691	1.3%
48	Alaska	586,036	0.2%
17	Arizona	4,599,450	1.9%
34	Arkansas	1,944,135	0.8%
1	California	29,554,578	12.1%
18	Colorado	4,585,326	1.9%
27	Connecticut	2,940,039	1.2%
45	Delaware	792,140	0.3%
3	Florida	16,958,612	6.9%
10	Georgia	6,971,889	2.9%
40	Hawaii	1,123,282	0.5%
38	Idaho	1,225,081	0.5%
5	Illinois	10,050,937	4.1%
16	Indiana	4,650,580	1.9%
30	Iowa	2,407,329	1.0%
31	Kansas	2,204,710	0.9%
28	Kentucky	2,889,684	1.2%
25	Louisiana	3,168,474	1.3%
42	Maine	1,099,588	0.5%
15	Maryland	4,694,897	1.9%
14	Massachusetts	5,628,620	2.3%
9	Michigan	7,293,461	3.0%
20	Minnesota	4,472,052	1.8%
35	Mississippi	1,843,989	0.8%
19	Missouri	4,520,600	1.9%
43	Montana	955,406	0.4%
36	Nebraska	1,512,300	0.6%
33	Nevada	2,125,508	0.9%
41	New Hampshire	1,120,145	0.5%
8	New Jersey	7,380,820	3.0%
37	New Mexico	1,410,953	0.6%
4	New York	16,067,203	6.6%
11	North Carolina	6,932,683	2.8%
47	North Dakota	672,091	0.3%
7	Ohio	8,430,915	3.5%
29	Oklahoma	2,709,215	1.1%
24	Oregon	3,217,893	1.3%
6	Pennsylvania	9,748,492	4.0%
44	Rhode Island	859,976	0.4%
23	South Carolina	3,299,524	1.4%
46	South Dakota	751,265	0.3%
22	Tennessee	4,356,222	1.8%
2	Texas	19,124,036	7.8%
32	Utah	2,141,999	0.9%
49	Vermont	575,771	0.2%
12	Virginia	6,189,463	2.5%
13	Washington	5,671,823	2.3%
39	West Virginia	1,142,352	0.5%
21	Wisconsin	4,461,990	1.8%
50	Wyoming	527,373	0.2%

RANK ORDER

RANK	STATE	RETURNS	% of USA
1	California	29,554,578	12.1%
2	Texas	19,124,036	7.8%
3	Florida	16,958,612	6.9%
4	New York	16,067,203	6.6%
5	Illinois	10,050,937	4.1%
6	Pennsylvania	9,748,492	4.0%
7	Ohio	8,430,915	3.5%
8	New Jersey	7,380,820	3.0%
9	Michigan	7,293,461	3.0%
10	Georgia	6,971,889	2.9%
11	North Carolina	6,932,683	2.8%
12	Virginia	6,189,463	2.5%
13	Washington	5,671,823	2.3%
14	Massachusetts	5,628,620	2.3%
15	Maryland	4,694,897	1.9%
16	Indiana	4,650,580	1.9%
17	Arizona	4,599,450	1.9%
18	Colorado	4,585,326	1.9%
19	Missouri	4,520,600	1.9%
20	Minnesota	4,472,052	1.8%
21	Wisconsin	4,461,990	1.8%
22	Tennessee	4,356,222	1.8%
23	South Carolina	3,299,524	1.4%
24	Oregon	3,217,893	1.3%
25	Louisiana	3,168,474	1.3%
26	Alabama	3,078,691	1.3%
27	Connecticut	2,940,039	1.2%
28	Kentucky	2,889,684	1.2%
29	Oklahoma	2,709,215	1.1%
30	Iowa	2,407,329	1.0%
31	Kansas	2,204,710	0.9%
32	Utah	2,141,999	0.9%
33	Nevada	2,125,508	0.9%
34	Arkansas	1,944,135	0.8%
35	Mississippi	1,843,989	0.8%
36	Nebraska	1,512,300	0.6%
37	New Mexico	1,410,953	0.6%
38	Idaho	1,225,081	0.5%
39	West Virginia	1,142,352	0.5%
40	Hawaii	1,123,282	0.5%
41	New Hampshire	1,120,145	0.5%
42	Maine	1,099,588	0.5%
43	Montana	955,406	0.4%
44	Rhode Island	859,976	0.4%
45	Delaware	792,140	0.3%
46	South Dakota	751,265	0.3%
47	North Dakota	672,091	0.3%
48	Alaska	586,036	0.2%
49	Vermont	575,771	0.2%
50	Wyoming	527,373	0.2%
	District of Columbia	599,570	0.2%

Source: U.S. Department of the Treasury, Internal Revenue Service
    "Fiscal Year 2016 IRS Data Book" (http://www.irs.gov/uac/SOI-Tax-Stats-IRS-Data-Book)
*Total includes returns from international sources and other miscellaneous returns not shown separately.

Percent of Federal Returns Filed Electronically in 2016

National Percent = 69.1%*

<table>
<tr><td colspan="3">ALPHA ORDER</td><td colspan="3">RANK ORDER</td></tr>
<tr><th>RANK</th><th>STATE</th><th>PERCENT</th><th>RANK</th><th>STATE</th><th>PERCENT</th></tr>
<tr><td>7</td><td>Alabama</td><td>71.7</td><td>1</td><td>New York</td><td>74.3</td></tr>
<tr><td>43</td><td>Alaska</td><td>66.0</td><td>2</td><td>Georgia</td><td>72.9</td></tr>
<tr><td>23</td><td>Arizona</td><td>69.2</td><td>3</td><td>Rhode Island</td><td>72.6</td></tr>
<tr><td>17</td><td>Arkansas</td><td>70.1</td><td>4</td><td>Utah</td><td>72.2</td></tr>
<tr><td>21</td><td>California</td><td>69.3</td><td>5</td><td>Tennessee</td><td>72.0</td></tr>
<tr><td>41</td><td>Colorado</td><td>66.4</td><td>6</td><td>Mississippi</td><td>71.8</td></tr>
<tr><td>26</td><td>Connecticut</td><td>68.9</td><td>7</td><td>Alabama</td><td>71.7</td></tr>
<tr><td>35</td><td>Delaware</td><td>67.6</td><td>8</td><td>Massachusetts</td><td>71.4</td></tr>
<tr><td>32</td><td>Florida</td><td>68.0</td><td>8</td><td>Nevada</td><td>71.4</td></tr>
<tr><td>2</td><td>Georgia</td><td>72.9</td><td>10</td><td>Ohio</td><td>71.3</td></tr>
<tr><td>50</td><td>Hawaii</td><td>60.9</td><td>11</td><td>South Carolina</td><td>71.1</td></tr>
<tr><td>42</td><td>Idaho</td><td>66.3</td><td>12</td><td>Indiana</td><td>70.9</td></tr>
<tr><td>28</td><td>Illinois</td><td>68.4</td><td>13</td><td>Kentucky</td><td>70.7</td></tr>
<tr><td>12</td><td>Indiana</td><td>70.9</td><td>14</td><td>Texas</td><td>70.5</td></tr>
<tr><td>36</td><td>Iowa</td><td>67.2</td><td>15</td><td>Louisiana</td><td>70.4</td></tr>
<tr><td>21</td><td>Kansas</td><td>69.3</td><td>16</td><td>New Jersey</td><td>70.3</td></tr>
<tr><td>13</td><td>Kentucky</td><td>70.7</td><td>17</td><td>Arkansas</td><td>70.1</td></tr>
<tr><td>15</td><td>Louisiana</td><td>70.4</td><td>18</td><td>Michigan</td><td>70.0</td></tr>
<tr><td>44</td><td>Maine</td><td>65.4</td><td>19</td><td>North Carolina</td><td>69.4</td></tr>
<tr><td>39</td><td>Maryland</td><td>66.8</td><td>19</td><td>Wisconsin</td><td>69.4</td></tr>
<tr><td>8</td><td>Massachusetts</td><td>71.4</td><td>21</td><td>California</td><td>69.3</td></tr>
<tr><td>18</td><td>Michigan</td><td>70.0</td><td>21</td><td>Kansas</td><td>69.3</td></tr>
<tr><td>27</td><td>Minnesota</td><td>68.7</td><td>23</td><td>Arizona</td><td>69.2</td></tr>
<tr><td>6</td><td>Mississippi</td><td>71.8</td><td>23</td><td>Oklahoma</td><td>69.2</td></tr>
<tr><td>30</td><td>Missouri</td><td>68.3</td><td>25</td><td>Virginia</td><td>69.1</td></tr>
<tr><td>48</td><td>Montana</td><td>63.0</td><td>26</td><td>Connecticut</td><td>68.9</td></tr>
<tr><td>31</td><td>Nebraska</td><td>68.1</td><td>27</td><td>Minnesota</td><td>68.7</td></tr>
<tr><td>8</td><td>Nevada</td><td>71.4</td><td>28</td><td>Illinois</td><td>68.4</td></tr>
<tr><td>36</td><td>New Hampshire</td><td>67.2</td><td>28</td><td>Pennsylvania</td><td>68.4</td></tr>
<tr><td>16</td><td>New Jersey</td><td>70.3</td><td>30</td><td>Missouri</td><td>68.3</td></tr>
<tr><td>34</td><td>New Mexico</td><td>67.8</td><td>31</td><td>Nebraska</td><td>68.1</td></tr>
<tr><td>1</td><td>New York</td><td>74.3</td><td>32</td><td>Florida</td><td>68.0</td></tr>
<tr><td>19</td><td>North Carolina</td><td>69.4</td><td>33</td><td>West Virginia</td><td>67.9</td></tr>
<tr><td>49</td><td>North Dakota</td><td>61.9</td><td>34</td><td>New Mexico</td><td>67.8</td></tr>
<tr><td>10</td><td>Ohio</td><td>71.3</td><td>35</td><td>Delaware</td><td>67.6</td></tr>
<tr><td>23</td><td>Oklahoma</td><td>69.2</td><td>36</td><td>Iowa</td><td>67.2</td></tr>
<tr><td>39</td><td>Oregon</td><td>66.8</td><td>36</td><td>New Hampshire</td><td>67.2</td></tr>
<tr><td>28</td><td>Pennsylvania</td><td>68.4</td><td>38</td><td>Washington</td><td>66.9</td></tr>
<tr><td>3</td><td>Rhode Island</td><td>72.6</td><td>39</td><td>Maryland</td><td>66.8</td></tr>
<tr><td>11</td><td>South Carolina</td><td>71.1</td><td>39</td><td>Oregon</td><td>66.8</td></tr>
<tr><td>46</td><td>South Dakota</td><td>63.8</td><td>41</td><td>Colorado</td><td>66.4</td></tr>
<tr><td>5</td><td>Tennessee</td><td>72.0</td><td>42</td><td>Idaho</td><td>66.3</td></tr>
<tr><td>14</td><td>Texas</td><td>70.5</td><td>43</td><td>Alaska</td><td>66.0</td></tr>
<tr><td>4</td><td>Utah</td><td>72.2</td><td>44</td><td>Maine</td><td>65.4</td></tr>
<tr><td>47</td><td>Vermont</td><td>63.6</td><td>45</td><td>Wyoming</td><td>63.9</td></tr>
<tr><td>25</td><td>Virginia</td><td>69.1</td><td>46</td><td>South Dakota</td><td>63.8</td></tr>
<tr><td>38</td><td>Washington</td><td>66.9</td><td>47</td><td>Vermont</td><td>63.6</td></tr>
<tr><td>33</td><td>West Virginia</td><td>67.9</td><td>48</td><td>Montana</td><td>63.0</td></tr>
<tr><td>19</td><td>Wisconsin</td><td>69.4</td><td>49</td><td>North Dakota</td><td>61.9</td></tr>
<tr><td>45</td><td>Wyoming</td><td>63.9</td><td>50</td><td>Hawaii</td><td>60.9</td></tr>
<tr><td colspan="3"></td><td colspan="2">District of Columbia</td><td>67.4</td></tr>
</table>

Source: CQ Press using data from U.S. Department of the Treasury, Internal Revenue Service
   "Fiscal Year 2016 IRS Data Book" (http://www.irs.gov/uac/SOI-Tax-Stats-IRS-Data-Book)
*Total includes returns from international sources and other miscellaneous returns. Includes corporate, individual, partnership, estate, employment and other returns. Excludes returns that cannot be filed electronically including informational returns.

Federal Individual Income Tax Returns Filed in 2016

National Total = 150,711,378 Returns*

ALPHA ORDER

RANK	STATE	RETURNS	% of USA
24	Alabama	2,052,504	1.4%
48	Alaska	357,694	0.2%
18	Arizona	2,902,462	1.9%
35	Arkansas	1,228,367	0.8%
1	California	17,732,788	11.8%
22	Colorado	2,612,861	1.7%
28	Connecticut	1,762,244	1.2%
45	Delaware	452,036	0.3%
4	Florida	9,609,762	6.4%
10	Georgia	4,436,031	2.9%
41	Hawaii	687,716	0.5%
39	Idaho	719,886	0.5%
6	Illinois	6,159,898	4.1%
15	Indiana	3,106,353	2.1%
30	Iowa	1,451,989	1.0%
32	Kansas	1,339,801	0.9%
26	Kentucky	1,912,397	1.3%
25	Louisiana	2,004,800	1.3%
42	Maine	645,613	0.4%
17	Maryland	2,959,007	2.0%
14	Massachusetts	3,396,548	2.3%
8	Michigan	4,713,811	3.1%
21	Minnesota	2,724,229	1.8%
34	Mississippi	1,244,900	0.8%
20	Missouri	2,786,539	1.8%
44	Montana	498,689	0.3%
37	Nebraska	901,056	0.6%
31	Nevada	1,348,434	0.9%
40	New Hampshire	692,769	0.5%
11	New Jersey	4,384,240	2.9%
36	New Mexico	917,077	0.6%
3	New York	9,613,550	6.4%
9	North Carolina	4,456,900	3.0%
47	North Dakota	370,463	0.2%
7	Ohio	5,592,772	3.7%
29	Oklahoma	1,643,206	1.1%
27	Oregon	1,874,761	1.2%
5	Pennsylvania	6,203,714	4.1%
43	Rhode Island	528,266	0.4%
23	South Carolina	2,162,243	1.4%
46	South Dakota	415,835	0.3%
16	Tennessee	2,966,799	2.0%
2	Texas	12,117,250	8.0%
33	Utah	1,261,678	0.8%
49	Vermont	326,024	0.2%
12	Virginia	3,905,827	2.6%
13	Washington	3,423,368	2.3%
38	West Virginia	781,526	0.5%
19	Wisconsin	2,838,902	1.9%
50	Wyoming	278,904	0.2%

RANK ORDER

RANK	STATE	RETURNS	% of USA
1	California	17,732,788	11.8%
2	Texas	12,117,250	8.0%
3	New York	9,613,550	6.4%
4	Florida	9,609,762	6.4%
5	Pennsylvania	6,203,714	4.1%
6	Illinois	6,159,898	4.1%
7	Ohio	5,592,772	3.7%
8	Michigan	4,713,811	3.1%
9	North Carolina	4,456,900	3.0%
10	Georgia	4,436,031	2.9%
11	New Jersey	4,384,240	2.9%
12	Virginia	3,905,827	2.6%
13	Washington	3,423,368	2.3%
14	Massachusetts	3,396,548	2.3%
15	Indiana	3,106,353	2.1%
16	Tennessee	2,966,799	2.0%
17	Maryland	2,959,007	2.0%
18	Arizona	2,902,462	1.9%
19	Wisconsin	2,838,902	1.9%
20	Missouri	2,786,539	1.8%
21	Minnesota	2,724,229	1.8%
22	Colorado	2,612,861	1.7%
23	South Carolina	2,162,243	1.4%
24	Alabama	2,052,504	1.4%
25	Louisiana	2,004,800	1.3%
26	Kentucky	1,912,397	1.3%
27	Oregon	1,874,761	1.2%
28	Connecticut	1,762,244	1.2%
29	Oklahoma	1,643,206	1.1%
30	Iowa	1,451,989	1.0%
31	Nevada	1,348,434	0.9%
32	Kansas	1,339,801	0.9%
33	Utah	1,261,678	0.8%
34	Mississippi	1,244,900	0.8%
35	Arkansas	1,228,367	0.8%
36	New Mexico	917,077	0.6%
37	Nebraska	901,056	0.6%
38	West Virginia	781,526	0.5%
39	Idaho	719,886	0.5%
40	New Hampshire	692,769	0.5%
41	Hawaii	687,716	0.5%
42	Maine	645,613	0.4%
43	Rhode Island	528,266	0.4%
44	Montana	498,689	0.3%
45	Delaware	452,036	0.3%
46	South Dakota	415,835	0.3%
47	North Dakota	370,463	0.2%
48	Alaska	357,694	0.2%
49	Vermont	326,024	0.2%
50	Wyoming	278,904	0.2%
	District of Columbia	343,931	0.2%

Source: U.S. Department of the Treasury, Internal Revenue Service
  "Fiscal Year 2016 IRS Data Book" (http://www.irs.gov/uac/SOI-Tax-Stats-IRS-Data-Book)
*Total includes returns from international sources and other miscellaneous returns not shown separately.

Percent of Federal Individual Income Tax Returns Filed Electronically in 2016

National Percent = 87.0%*

ALPHA ORDER

RANK	STATE	PERCENT
20	Alabama	89.0
47	Alaska	85.9
44	Arizona	86.2
9	Arkansas	89.7
44	California	86.2
39	Colorado	86.7
31	Connecticut	87.2
40	Delaware	86.5
46	Florida	86.0
21	Georgia	88.6
50	Hawaii	82.1
13	Idaho	89.3
35	Illinois	87.0
8	Indiana	90.0
1	Iowa	92.6
3	Kansas	91.3
7	Kentucky	90.2
28	Louisiana	87.7
47	Maine	85.9
49	Maryland	83.0
32	Massachusetts	87.1
26	Michigan	88.1
13	Minnesota	89.3
11	Mississippi	89.5
25	Missouri	88.3
10	Montana	89.6
2	Nebraska	92.0
40	Nevada	86.5
37	New Hampshire	86.8
32	New Jersey	87.1
37	New Mexico	86.8
5	New York	90.8
22	North Carolina	88.5
6	North Dakota	90.3
22	Ohio	88.5
11	Oklahoma	89.5
30	Oregon	87.3
40	Pennsylvania	86.5
24	Rhode Island	88.4
19	South Carolina	89.1
4	South Dakota	91.0
13	Tennessee	89.3
43	Texas	86.3
13	Utah	89.3
29	Vermont	87.6
35	Virginia	87.0
32	Washington	87.1
27	West Virginia	87.9
17	Wisconsin	89.2
17	Wyoming	89.2

RANK ORDER

RANK	STATE	PERCENT
1	Iowa	92.6
2	Nebraska	92.0
3	Kansas	91.3
4	South Dakota	91.0
5	New York	90.8
6	North Dakota	90.3
7	Kentucky	90.2
8	Indiana	90.0
9	Arkansas	89.7
10	Montana	89.6
11	Mississippi	89.5
11	Oklahoma	89.5
13	Idaho	89.3
13	Minnesota	89.3
13	Tennessee	89.3
13	Utah	89.3
17	Wisconsin	89.2
17	Wyoming	89.2
19	South Carolina	89.1
20	Alabama	89.0
21	Georgia	88.6
22	North Carolina	88.5
22	Ohio	88.5
24	Rhode Island	88.4
25	Missouri	88.3
26	Michigan	88.1
27	West Virginia	87.9
28	Louisiana	87.7
29	Vermont	87.6
30	Oregon	87.3
31	Connecticut	87.2
32	Massachusetts	87.1
32	New Jersey	87.1
32	Washington	87.1
35	Illinois	87.0
35	Virginia	87.0
37	New Hampshire	86.8
37	New Mexico	86.8
39	Colorado	86.7
40	Delaware	86.5
40	Nevada	86.5
40	Pennsylvania	86.5
43	Texas	86.3
44	Arizona	86.2
44	California	86.2
46	Florida	86.0
47	Alaska	85.9
47	Maine	85.9
49	Maryland	83.0
50	Hawaii	82.1

| | District of Columbia | 83.8 |

Source: CQ Press using data from U.S. Department of the Treasury, Internal Revenue Service
   "Fiscal Year 2016 IRS Data Book" (http://www.irs.gov/uac/SOI-Tax-Stats-IRS-Data-Book)
*Total includes returns from international sources and other miscellaneous returns. Includes returns filed electronically by practitioners.

Federal Business Income Tax Returns Filed in 2016

National Total = 7,039,311 Returns*

ALPHA ORDER

RANK	STATE	RETURNS	% of USA
28	Alabama	67,960	1.0%
50	Alaska	12,951	0.2%
18	Arizona	120,420	1.7%
32	Arkansas	53,210	0.8%
2	California	831,761	11.8%
13	Colorado	158,062	2.2%
33	Connecticut	52,195	0.7%
42	Delaware	25,329	0.4%
1	Florida	849,276	12.1%
6	Georgia	224,126	3.2%
41	Hawaii	27,423	0.4%
37	Idaho	35,913	0.5%
5	Illinois	356,230	5.1%
19	Indiana	112,727	1.6%
31	Iowa	62,146	0.9%
34	Kansas	51,435	0.7%
29	Kentucky	66,108	0.9%
23	Louisiana	81,095	1.2%
39	Maine	30,028	0.4%
16	Maryland	129,838	1.8%
14	Massachusetts	147,868	2.1%
9	Michigan	192,883	2.7%
17	Minnesota	125,130	1.8%
36	Mississippi	40,383	0.6%
20	Missouri	98,034	1.4%
38	Montana	35,262	0.5%
35	Nebraska	44,728	0.6%
27	Nevada	70,691	1.0%
44	New Hampshire	21,555	0.3%
10	New Jersey	186,869	2.7%
40	New Mexico	29,368	0.4%
3	New York	673,242	9.6%
8	North Carolina	197,719	2.8%
48	North Dakota	16,553	0.2%
11	Ohio	174,998	2.5%
26	Oklahoma	74,298	1.1%
24	Oregon	76,167	1.1%
7	Pennsylvania	217,439	3.1%
43	Rhode Island	23,483	0.3%
22	South Carolina	85,200	1.2%
46	South Dakota	19,113	0.3%
30	Tennessee	65,710	0.9%
4	Texas	474,129	6.7%
25	Utah	75,735	1.1%
49	Vermont	15,725	0.2%
12	Virginia	167,783	2.4%
15	Washington	139,952	2.0%
45	West Virginia	19,817	0.3%
21	Wisconsin	91,717	1.3%
47	Wyoming	18,831	0.3%

RANK ORDER

RANK	STATE	RETURNS	% of USA
1	Florida	849,276	12.1%
2	California	831,761	11.8%
3	New York	673,242	9.6%
4	Texas	474,129	6.7%
5	Illinois	356,230	5.1%
6	Georgia	224,126	3.2%
7	Pennsylvania	217,439	3.1%
8	North Carolina	197,719	2.8%
9	Michigan	192,883	2.7%
10	New Jersey	186,869	2.7%
11	Ohio	174,998	2.5%
12	Virginia	167,783	2.4%
13	Colorado	158,062	2.2%
14	Massachusetts	147,868	2.1%
15	Washington	139,952	2.0%
16	Maryland	129,838	1.8%
17	Minnesota	125,130	1.8%
18	Arizona	120,420	1.7%
19	Indiana	112,727	1.6%
20	Missouri	98,034	1.4%
21	Wisconsin	91,717	1.3%
22	South Carolina	85,200	1.2%
23	Louisiana	81,095	1.2%
24	Oregon	76,167	1.1%
25	Utah	75,735	1.1%
26	Oklahoma	74,298	1.1%
27	Nevada	70,691	1.0%
28	Alabama	67,960	1.0%
29	Kentucky	66,108	0.9%
30	Tennessee	65,710	0.9%
31	Iowa	62,146	0.9%
32	Arkansas	53,210	0.8%
33	Connecticut	52,195	0.7%
34	Kansas	51,435	0.7%
35	Nebraska	44,728	0.6%
36	Mississippi	40,383	0.6%
37	Idaho	35,913	0.5%
38	Montana	35,262	0.5%
39	Maine	30,028	0.4%
40	New Mexico	29,368	0.4%
41	Hawaii	27,423	0.4%
42	Delaware	25,329	0.4%
43	Rhode Island	23,483	0.3%
44	New Hampshire	21,555	0.3%
45	West Virginia	19,817	0.3%
46	South Dakota	19,113	0.3%
47	Wyoming	18,831	0.3%
48	North Dakota	16,553	0.2%
49	Vermont	15,725	0.2%
50	Alaska	12,951	0.2%
	District of Columbia	18,205	0.3%

Source: U.S. Department of the Treasury, Internal Revenue Service
"Fiscal Year 2016 IRS Data Book" (http://www.irs.gov/uac/SOI-Tax-Stats-IRS-Data-Book)
*Total includes returns from international sources and other miscellaneous returns not shown separately.

Federal Tax Refunds in 2016

National Total = 122,310,753 Refunds*

ALPHA ORDER

RANK	STATE	REFUNDS	% of USA
24	Alabama	1,708,165	1.4%
48	Alaska	281,523	0.2%
19	Arizona	2,275,224	1.9%
35	Arkansas	1,019,783	0.8%
1	California	13,899,411	11.4%
22	Colorado	2,034,716	1.7%
28	Connecticut	1,423,779	1.2%
45	Delaware	375,169	0.3%
3	Florida	7,943,801	6.5%
9	Georgia	3,703,399	3.0%
41	Hawaii	546,574	0.4%
39	Idaho	567,403	0.5%
6	Illinois	5,119,125	4.2%
15	Indiana	2,631,591	2.2%
30	Iowa	1,166,709	1.0%
32	Kansas	1,073,416	0.9%
26	Kentucky	1,623,585	1.3%
25	Louisiana	1,681,679	1.4%
42	Maine	520,104	0.4%
17	Maryland	2,371,294	1.9%
14	Massachusetts	2,740,859	2.2%
8	Michigan	3,845,391	3.1%
21	Minnesota	2,125,229	1.7%
33	Mississippi	1,056,702	0.9%
18	Missouri	2,277,259	1.9%
44	Montana	381,873	0.3%
37	Nebraska	726,691	0.6%
31	Nevada	1,123,309	0.9%
40	New Hampshire	565,609	0.5%
11	New Jersey	3,552,086	2.9%
36	New Mexico	747,683	0.6%
4	New York	7,886,277	6.4%
10	North Carolina	3,629,594	3.0%
47	North Dakota	290,239	0.2%
7	Ohio	4,656,235	3.8%
29	Oklahoma	1,347,983	1.1%
27	Oregon	1,449,206	1.2%
5	Pennsylvania	5,137,920	4.2%
43	Rhode Island	445,813	0.4%
23	South Carolina	1,739,985	1.4%
46	South Dakota	329,825	0.3%
16	Tennessee	2,508,227	2.1%
2	Texas	10,350,571	8.5%
34	Utah	1,038,676	0.8%
49	Vermont	260,257	0.2%
12	Virginia	3,184,073	2.6%
13	Washington	2,770,080	2.3%
38	West Virginia	671,961	0.5%
20	Wisconsin	2,268,727	1.9%
50	Wyoming	228,380	0.2%

RANK ORDER

RANK	STATE	REFUNDS	% of USA
1	California	13,899,411	11.4%
2	Texas	10,350,571	8.5%
3	Florida	7,943,801	6.5%
4	New York	7,886,277	6.4%
5	Pennsylvania	5,137,920	4.2%
6	Illinois	5,119,125	4.2%
7	Ohio	4,656,235	3.8%
8	Michigan	3,845,391	3.1%
9	Georgia	3,703,399	3.0%
10	North Carolina	3,629,594	3.0%
11	New Jersey	3,552,086	2.9%
12	Virginia	3,184,073	2.6%
13	Washington	2,770,080	2.3%
14	Massachusetts	2,740,859	2.2%
15	Indiana	2,631,591	2.2%
16	Tennessee	2,508,227	2.1%
17	Maryland	2,371,294	1.9%
18	Missouri	2,277,259	1.9%
19	Arizona	2,275,224	1.9%
20	Wisconsin	2,268,727	1.9%
21	Minnesota	2,125,229	1.7%
22	Colorado	2,034,716	1.7%
23	South Carolina	1,739,985	1.4%
24	Alabama	1,708,165	1.4%
25	Louisiana	1,681,679	1.4%
26	Kentucky	1,623,585	1.3%
27	Oregon	1,449,206	1.2%
28	Connecticut	1,423,779	1.2%
29	Oklahoma	1,347,983	1.1%
30	Iowa	1,166,709	1.0%
31	Nevada	1,123,309	0.9%
32	Kansas	1,073,416	0.9%
33	Mississippi	1,056,702	0.9%
34	Utah	1,038,676	0.8%
35	Arkansas	1,019,783	0.8%
36	New Mexico	747,683	0.6%
37	Nebraska	726,691	0.6%
38	West Virginia	671,961	0.5%
39	Idaho	567,403	0.5%
40	New Hampshire	565,609	0.5%
41	Hawaii	546,574	0.4%
42	Maine	520,104	0.4%
43	Rhode Island	445,813	0.4%
44	Montana	381,873	0.3%
45	Delaware	375,169	0.3%
46	South Dakota	329,825	0.3%
47	North Dakota	290,239	0.2%
48	Alaska	281,523	0.2%
49	Vermont	260,257	0.2%
50	Wyoming	228,380	0.2%
	District of Columbia	280,455	0.2%

Source: U.S. Department of the Treasury, Internal Revenue Service
"Fiscal Year 2016 IRS Data Book" (http://www.irs.gov/uac/SOI-Tax-Stats-IRS-Data-Book)
*Total includes refunds to international sources and other miscellaneous refunds not shown separately.

Value of Federal Tax Refunds in 2016

National Total = $426,146,066,000*

ALPHA ORDER

RANK	STATE	REFUNDS	% of USA
26	Alabama	$4,953,015,000	1.2%
48	Alaska	787,403,000	0.2%
20	Arizona	6,293,831,000	1.5%
35	Arkansas	2,882,064,000	0.7%
1	California	44,282,181,000	10.4%
22	Colorado	6,154,327,000	1.4%
24	Connecticut	5,816,058,000	1.4%
41	Delaware	1,472,710,000	0.3%
4	Florida	24,014,820,000	5.6%
9	Georgia	11,576,727,000	2.7%
40	Hawaii	1,512,841,000	0.4%
42	Idaho	1,434,948,000	0.3%
6	Illinois	17,597,830,000	4.1%
18	Indiana	7,144,209,000	1.7%
29	Iowa	3,831,977,000	0.9%
32	Kansas	3,326,539,000	0.8%
28	Kentucky	4,489,379,000	1.1%
25	Louisiana	5,402,709,000	1.3%
43	Maine	1,284,673,000	0.3%
19	Maryland	6,808,979,000	1.6%
13	Massachusetts	8,513,954,000	2.0%
12	Michigan	10,216,191,000	2.4%
17	Minnesota	7,165,698,000	1.7%
33	Mississippi	3,266,076,000	0.8%
16	Missouri	7,182,010,000	1.7%
46	Montana	934,663,000	0.2%
36	Nebraska	2,343,408,000	0.5%
31	Nevada	3,409,652,000	0.8%
39	New Hampshire	1,563,756,000	0.4%
7	New Jersey	14,015,289,000	3.3%
37	New Mexico	1,981,121,000	0.5%
3	New York	27,766,185,000	6.5%
10	North Carolina	10,427,875,000	2.4%
45	North Dakota	944,930,000	0.2%
8	Ohio	12,556,839,000	2.9%
23	Oklahoma	5,958,904,000	1.4%
30	Oregon	3,593,757,000	0.8%
5	Pennsylvania	17,832,559,000	4.2%
44	Rhode Island	1,170,643,000	0.3%
27	South Carolina	4,591,295,000	1.1%
47	South Dakota	898,253,000	0.2%
15	Tennessee	7,644,675,000	1.8%
2	Texas	40,430,512,000	9.5%
34	Utah	3,179,568,000	0.7%
50	Vermont	633,267,000	0.1%
11	Virginia	10,281,798,000	2.4%
14	Washington	7,926,332,000	1.9%
38	West Virginia	1,759,823,000	0.4%
21	Wisconsin	6,201,713,000	1.5%
49	Wyoming	696,388,000	0.2%

RANK ORDER

RANK	STATE	REFUNDS	% of USA
1	California	$44,282,181,000	10.4%
2	Texas	40,430,512,000	9.5%
3	New York	27,766,185,000	6.5%
4	Florida	24,014,820,000	5.6%
5	Pennsylvania	17,832,559,000	4.2%
6	Illinois	17,597,830,000	4.1%
7	New Jersey	14,015,289,000	3.3%
8	Ohio	12,556,839,000	2.9%
9	Georgia	11,576,727,000	2.7%
10	North Carolina	10,427,875,000	2.4%
11	Virginia	10,281,798,000	2.4%
12	Michigan	10,216,191,000	2.4%
13	Massachusetts	8,513,954,000	2.0%
14	Washington	7,926,332,000	1.9%
15	Tennessee	7,644,675,000	1.8%
16	Missouri	7,182,010,000	1.7%
17	Minnesota	7,165,698,000	1.7%
18	Indiana	7,144,209,000	1.7%
19	Maryland	6,808,979,000	1.6%
20	Arizona	6,293,831,000	1.5%
21	Wisconsin	6,201,713,000	1.5%
22	Colorado	6,154,327,000	1.4%
23	Oklahoma	5,958,904,000	1.4%
24	Connecticut	5,816,058,000	1.4%
25	Louisiana	5,402,709,000	1.3%
26	Alabama	4,953,015,000	1.2%
27	South Carolina	4,591,295,000	1.1%
28	Kentucky	4,489,379,000	1.1%
29	Iowa	3,831,977,000	0.9%
30	Oregon	3,593,757,000	0.8%
31	Nevada	3,409,652,000	0.8%
32	Kansas	3,326,539,000	0.8%
33	Mississippi	3,266,076,000	0.8%
34	Utah	3,179,568,000	0.7%
35	Arkansas	2,882,064,000	0.7%
36	Nebraska	2,343,408,000	0.5%
37	New Mexico	1,981,121,000	0.5%
38	West Virginia	1,759,823,000	0.4%
39	New Hampshire	1,563,756,000	0.4%
40	Hawaii	1,512,841,000	0.4%
41	Delaware	1,472,710,000	0.3%
42	Idaho	1,434,948,000	0.3%
43	Maine	1,284,673,000	0.3%
44	Rhode Island	1,170,643,000	0.3%
45	North Dakota	944,930,000	0.2%
46	Montana	934,663,000	0.2%
47	South Dakota	898,253,000	0.2%
48	Alaska	787,403,000	0.2%
49	Wyoming	696,388,000	0.2%
50	Vermont	633,267,000	0.1%
	District of Columbia	1,012,996,000	0.2%

Source: U.S. Department of the Treasury, Internal Revenue Service
"Fiscal Year 2016 IRS Data Book" (http://www.irs.gov/uac/SOI-Tax-Stats-IRS-Data-Book)
*Total includes refunds to international sources and other miscellaneous refunds not shown separately.

Average Value of Federal Tax Refunds in 2016

National Average = $3,484*

ALPHA ORDER

RANK	STATE	AVERAGE REFUND	RANK	STATE	AVERAGE REFUND
27	Alabama	$2,900	1	Oklahoma	$4,421
32	Alaska	2,797	2	Connecticut	4,085
34	Arizona	2,766	3	New Jersey	3,946
31	Arkansas	2,826	4	Delaware	3,925
15	California	3,186	5	Texas	3,906
25	Colorado	3,025	6	New York	3,521
2	Connecticut	4,085	7	Pennsylvania	3,471
4	Delaware	3,925	8	Illinois	3,438
26	Florida	3,023	9	Minnesota	3,372
17	Georgia	3,126	10	Iowa	3,284
33	Hawaii	2,768	11	North Dakota	3,256
46	Idaho	2,529	12	Virginia	3,229
8	Illinois	3,438	13	Nebraska	3,225
39	Indiana	2,715	14	Louisiana	3,213
10	Iowa	3,284	15	California	3,186
19	Kansas	3,099	16	Missouri	3,154
35	Kentucky	2,765	17	Georgia	3,126
14	Louisiana	3,213	18	Massachusetts	3,106
48	Maine	2,470	19	Kansas	3,099
29	Maryland	2,871	20	Mississippi	3,091
18	Massachusetts	3,106	21	Utah	3,061
41	Michigan	2,657	22	Wyoming	3,049
9	Minnesota	3,372	23	Tennessee	3,048
20	Mississippi	3,091	24	Nevada	3,035
16	Missouri	3,154	25	Colorado	3,025
49	Montana	2,448	26	Florida	3,023
13	Nebraska	3,225	27	Alabama	2,900
24	Nevada	3,035	28	North Carolina	2,873
35	New Hampshire	2,765	29	Maryland	2,871
3	New Jersey	3,946	30	Washington	2,861
42	New Mexico	2,650	31	Arkansas	2,826
6	New York	3,521	32	Alaska	2,797
28	North Carolina	2,873	33	Hawaii	2,768
11	North Dakota	3,256	34	Arizona	2,766
40	Ohio	2,697	35	Kentucky	2,765
1	Oklahoma	4,421	35	New Hampshire	2,765
47	Oregon	2,480	37	Wisconsin	2,734
7	Pennsylvania	3,471	38	South Dakota	2,723
44	Rhode Island	2,626	39	Indiana	2,715
43	South Carolina	2,639	40	Ohio	2,697
38	South Dakota	2,723	41	Michigan	2,657
23	Tennessee	3,048	42	New Mexico	2,650
5	Texas	3,906	43	South Carolina	2,639
21	Utah	3,061	44	Rhode Island	2,626
50	Vermont	2,433	45	West Virginia	2,619
12	Virginia	3,229	46	Idaho	2,529
30	Washington	2,861	47	Oregon	2,480
45	West Virginia	2,619	48	Maine	2,470
37	Wisconsin	2,734	49	Montana	2,448
22	Wyoming	3,049	50	Vermont	2,433
				District of Columbia	3,612

Source: CQ Press using data from U.S. Department of the Treasury, Internal Revenue Service
"Fiscal Year 2016 IRS Data Book" (http://www.irs.gov/uac/SOI-Tax-Stats-IRS-Data-Book)
*National average includes refunds to international sources and other miscellaneous refunds not shown separately.

Value of Federal Individual Income Tax Refunds in 2016

National Total = $366,645,533,000*

RANK	STATE	REFUNDS	% of USA
24	Alabama	$4,688,126,000	1.3%
48	Alaska	733,712,000	0.2%
18	Arizona	5,878,302,000	1.6%
34	Arkansas	2,693,464,000	0.7%
1	California	38,371,233,000	10.5%
21	Colorado	5,120,458,000	1.4%
27	Connecticut	4,135,754,000	1.1%
44	Delaware	926,767,000	0.3%
4	Florida	22,424,195,000	6.1%
9	Georgia	10,189,362,000	2.8%
40	Hawaii	1,389,355,000	0.4%
41	Idaho	1,349,784,000	0.4%
5	Illinois	14,143,032,000	3.9%
15	Indiana	6,649,467,000	1.8%
32	Iowa	2,961,496,000	0.8%
33	Kansas	2,745,110,000	0.7%
26	Kentucky	4,158,268,000	1.1%
23	Louisiana	5,074,121,000	1.4%
42	Maine	1,175,875,000	0.3%
17	Maryland	6,474,993,000	1.8%
13	Massachusetts	7,360,408,000	2.0%
10	Michigan	9,419,601,000	2.6%
22	Minnesota	5,076,006,000	1.4%
30	Mississippi	3,069,017,000	0.8%
19	Missouri	5,709,194,000	1.6%
45	Montana	877,341,000	0.2%
37	Nebraska	1,799,572,000	0.5%
31	Nevada	3,047,313,000	0.8%
39	New Hampshire	1,402,402,000	0.4%
8	New Jersey	10,258,318,000	2.8%
36	New Mexico	1,925,136,000	0.5%
3	New York	23,081,246,000	6.3%
11	North Carolina	9,210,080,000	2.5%
47	North Dakota	817,849,000	0.2%
7	Ohio	11,420,757,000	3.1%
28	Oklahoma	4,081,642,000	1.1%
29	Oregon	3,330,183,000	0.9%
6	Pennsylvania	13,096,265,000	3.6%
43	Rhode Island	1,115,929,000	0.3%
25	South Carolina	4,340,271,000	1.2%
46	South Dakota	818,109,000	0.2%
16	Tennessee	6,634,605,000	1.8%
2	Texas	31,800,055,000	8.7%
35	Utah	2,691,774,000	0.7%
50	Vermont	597,739,000	0.2%
12	Virginia	8,450,015,000	2.3%
14	Washington	7,112,093,000	1.9%
38	West Virginia	1,715,726,000	0.5%
20	Wisconsin	5,242,369,000	1.4%
49	Wyoming	631,780,000	0.2%

RANK	STATE	REFUNDS	% of USA
1	California	$38,371,233,000	10.5%
2	Texas	31,800,055,000	8.7%
3	New York	23,081,246,000	6.3%
4	Florida	22,424,195,000	6.1%
5	Illinois	14,143,032,000	3.9%
6	Pennsylvania	13,096,265,000	3.6%
7	Ohio	11,420,757,000	3.1%
8	New Jersey	10,258,318,000	2.8%
9	Georgia	10,189,362,000	2.8%
10	Michigan	9,419,601,000	2.6%
11	North Carolina	9,210,080,000	2.5%
12	Virginia	8,450,015,000	2.3%
13	Massachusetts	7,360,408,000	2.0%
14	Washington	7,112,093,000	1.9%
15	Indiana	6,649,467,000	1.8%
16	Tennessee	6,634,605,000	1.8%
17	Maryland	6,474,993,000	1.8%
18	Arizona	5,878,302,000	1.6%
19	Missouri	5,709,194,000	1.6%
20	Wisconsin	5,242,369,000	1.4%
21	Colorado	5,120,458,000	1.4%
22	Minnesota	5,076,006,000	1.4%
23	Louisiana	5,074,121,000	1.4%
24	Alabama	4,688,126,000	1.3%
25	South Carolina	4,340,271,000	1.2%
26	Kentucky	4,158,268,000	1.1%
27	Connecticut	4,135,754,000	1.1%
28	Oklahoma	4,081,642,000	1.1%
29	Oregon	3,330,183,000	0.9%
30	Mississippi	3,069,017,000	0.8%
31	Nevada	3,047,313,000	0.8%
32	Iowa	2,961,496,000	0.8%
33	Kansas	2,745,110,000	0.7%
34	Arkansas	2,693,464,000	0.7%
35	Utah	2,691,774,000	0.7%
36	New Mexico	1,925,136,000	0.5%
37	Nebraska	1,799,572,000	0.5%
38	West Virginia	1,715,726,000	0.5%
39	New Hampshire	1,402,402,000	0.4%
40	Hawaii	1,389,355,000	0.4%
41	Idaho	1,349,784,000	0.4%
42	Maine	1,175,875,000	0.3%
43	Rhode Island	1,115,929,000	0.3%
44	Delaware	926,767,000	0.3%
45	Montana	877,341,000	0.2%
46	South Dakota	818,109,000	0.2%
47	North Dakota	817,849,000	0.2%
48	Alaska	733,712,000	0.2%
49	Wyoming	631,780,000	0.2%
50	Vermont	597,739,000	0.2%
	District of Columbia	797,719,000	0.2%

Source: U.S. Department of the Treasury, Internal Revenue Service
"Fiscal Year 2016 IRS Data Book" (http://www.irs.gov/uac/SOI-Tax-Stats-IRS-Data-Book)
*Total includes refunds to international sources and other miscellaneous refunds not shown separately.

Average Value of Federal Individual Income Tax Refunds in 2016

National Average = $3,052*

ALPHA ORDER

RANK	STATE	AVERAGE REFUND
14	Alabama	$2,787
21	Alaska	2,672
23	Arizona	2,622
19	Arkansas	2,692
12	California	2,811
34	Colorado	2,565
5	Connecticut	2,958
38	Delaware	2,543
9	Florida	2,877
13	Georgia	2,793
31	Hawaii	2,587
44	Idaho	2,433
11	Illinois	2,815
33	Indiana	2,569
29	Iowa	2,589
26	Kansas	2,611
27	Kentucky	2,601
3	Louisiana	3,073
50	Maine	2,302
15	Maryland	2,771
17	Massachusetts	2,734
42	Michigan	2,491
45	Minnesota	2,432
6	Mississippi	2,953
35	Missouri	2,555
46	Montana	2,367
39	Nebraska	2,534
16	Nevada	2,755
41	New Hampshire	2,527
7	New Jersey	2,943
25	New Mexico	2,618
4	New York	2,986
32	North Carolina	2,581
8	North Dakota	2,896
43	Ohio	2,489
2	Oklahoma	3,088
49	Oregon	2,342
30	Pennsylvania	2,588
36	Rhode Island	2,554
40	South Carolina	2,530
37	South Dakota	2,552
20	Tennessee	2,688
1	Texas	3,133
22	Utah	2,639
48	Vermont	2,348
18	Virginia	2,696
24	Washington	2,621
28	West Virginia	2,592
47	Wisconsin	2,353
10	Wyoming	2,853

RANK ORDER

RANK	STATE	AVERAGE REFUND
1	Texas	$3,133
2	Oklahoma	3,088
3	Louisiana	3,073
4	New York	2,986
5	Connecticut	2,958
6	Mississippi	2,953
7	New Jersey	2,943
8	North Dakota	2,896
9	Florida	2,877
10	Wyoming	2,853
11	Illinois	2,815
12	California	2,811
13	Georgia	2,793
14	Alabama	2,787
15	Maryland	2,771
16	Nevada	2,755
17	Massachusetts	2,734
18	Virginia	2,696
19	Arkansas	2,692
20	Tennessee	2,688
21	Alaska	2,672
22	Utah	2,639
23	Arizona	2,622
24	Washington	2,621
25	New Mexico	2,618
26	Kansas	2,611
27	Kentucky	2,601
28	West Virginia	2,592
29	Iowa	2,589
30	Pennsylvania	2,588
31	Hawaii	2,587
32	North Carolina	2,581
33	Indiana	2,569
34	Colorado	2,565
35	Missouri	2,555
36	Rhode Island	2,554
37	South Dakota	2,552
38	Delaware	2,543
39	Nebraska	2,534
40	South Carolina	2,530
41	New Hampshire	2,527
42	Michigan	2,491
43	Ohio	2,489
44	Idaho	2,433
45	Minnesota	2,432
46	Montana	2,367
47	Wisconsin	2,353
48	Vermont	2,348
49	Oregon	2,342
50	Maine	2,302

District of Columbia 2,904

Source: CQ Press using data from U.S. Department of the Treasury, Internal Revenue Service
"Fiscal Year 2016 IRS Data Book" (http://www.irs.gov/uac/SOI-Tax-Stats-IRS-Data-Book)
*National average includes refunds to international sources and other miscellaneous refunds not shown separately.

Value of Federal Business Income Tax Refunds in 2016

National Total = $51,281,426,000*

ALPHA ORDER

RANK	STATE	REFUNDS	% of USA
32	Alabama	$220,724,000	0.4%
44	Alaska	37,127,000	0.1%
28	Arizona	326,065,000	0.6%
37	Arkansas	158,622,000	0.3%
2	California	5,028,703,000	9.8%
16	Colorado	926,897,000	1.8%
10	Connecticut	1,501,516,000	2.9%
25	Delaware	436,788,000	0.9%
13	Florida	1,103,141,000	2.2%
12	Georgia	1,161,649,000	2.3%
40	Hawaii	107,204,000	0.2%
42	Idaho	61,698,000	0.1%
6	Illinois	2,986,699,000	5.8%
27	Indiana	360,547,000	0.7%
20	Iowa	819,650,000	1.6%
23	Kansas	532,723,000	1.0%
29	Kentucky	262,124,000	0.5%
30	Louisiana	246,330,000	0.5%
41	Maine	90,872,000	0.2%
31	Maryland	239,044,000	0.5%
15	Massachusetts	928,375,000	1.8%
22	Michigan	638,453,000	1.2%
7	Minnesota	1,956,586,000	3.8%
36	Mississippi	169,726,000	0.3%
11	Missouri	1,339,593,000	2.6%
47	Montana	28,904,000	0.1%
24	Nebraska	508,234,000	1.0%
35	Nevada	184,882,000	0.4%
38	New Hampshire	131,636,000	0.3%
5	New Jersey	3,505,031,000	6.8%
45	New Mexico	36,066,000	0.1%
4	New York	3,872,287,000	7.6%
14	North Carolina	1,087,441,000	2.1%
39	North Dakota	112,280,000	0.2%
17	Ohio	884,868,000	1.7%
8	Oklahoma	1,756,015,000	3.4%
33	Oregon	204,799,000	0.4%
3	Pennsylvania	4,487,608,000	8.8%
49	Rhode Island	24,380,000	0.0%
34	South Carolina	191,539,000	0.4%
43	South Dakota	42,400,000	0.1%
18	Tennessee	854,459,000	1.7%
1	Texas	7,596,513,000	14.8%
26	Utah	428,004,000	0.8%
50	Vermont	23,019,000	0.0%
9	Virginia	1,685,011,000	3.3%
21	Washington	663,828,000	1.3%
46	West Virginia	31,065,000	0.1%
19	Wisconsin	824,698,000	1.6%
48	Wyoming	24,910,000	0.0%

RANK ORDER

RANK	STATE	REFUNDS	% of USA
1	Texas	$7,596,513,000	14.8%
2	California	5,028,703,000	9.8%
3	Pennsylvania	4,487,608,000	8.8%
4	New York	3,872,287,000	7.6%
5	New Jersey	3,505,031,000	6.8%
6	Illinois	2,986,699,000	5.8%
7	Minnesota	1,956,586,000	3.8%
8	Oklahoma	1,756,015,000	3.4%
9	Virginia	1,685,011,000	3.3%
10	Connecticut	1,501,516,000	2.9%
11	Missouri	1,339,593,000	2.6%
12	Georgia	1,161,649,000	2.3%
13	Florida	1,103,141,000	2.2%
14	North Carolina	1,087,441,000	2.1%
15	Massachusetts	928,375,000	1.8%
16	Colorado	926,897,000	1.8%
17	Ohio	884,868,000	1.7%
18	Tennessee	854,459,000	1.7%
19	Wisconsin	824,698,000	1.6%
20	Iowa	819,650,000	1.6%
21	Washington	663,828,000	1.3%
22	Michigan	638,453,000	1.2%
23	Kansas	532,723,000	1.0%
24	Nebraska	508,234,000	1.0%
25	Delaware	436,788,000	0.9%
26	Utah	428,004,000	0.8%
27	Indiana	360,547,000	0.7%
28	Arizona	326,065,000	0.6%
29	Kentucky	262,124,000	0.5%
30	Louisiana	246,330,000	0.5%
31	Maryland	239,044,000	0.5%
32	Alabama	220,724,000	0.4%
33	Oregon	204,799,000	0.4%
34	South Carolina	191,539,000	0.4%
35	Nevada	184,882,000	0.4%
36	Mississippi	169,726,000	0.3%
37	Arkansas	158,622,000	0.3%
38	New Hampshire	131,636,000	0.3%
39	North Dakota	112,280,000	0.2%
40	Hawaii	107,204,000	0.2%
41	Maine	90,872,000	0.2%
42	Idaho	61,698,000	0.1%
43	South Dakota	42,400,000	0.1%
44	Alaska	37,127,000	0.1%
45	New Mexico	36,066,000	0.1%
46	West Virginia	31,065,000	0.1%
47	Montana	28,904,000	0.1%
48	Wyoming	24,910,000	0.0%
49	Rhode Island	24,380,000	0.0%
50	Vermont	23,019,000	0.0%
	District of Columbia	186,538,000	0.4%

Source: U.S. Department of the Treasury, Internal Revenue Service
    "Fiscal Year 2016 IRS Data Book" (http://www.irs.gov/uac/SOI-Tax-Stats-IRS-Data-Book)
*Total includes refunds to international sources and other miscellaneous refunds not shown separately. Includes taxes on corporation income (Form 1120 series) and unrelated business income from tax-exempt organizations.

Average Value of Federal Business Income Tax Refunds in 2016

National Average = $144,401*

ALPHA ORDER

RANK	STATE	AVERAGE REFUND
31	Alabama	$64,183
41	Alaska	43,171
28	Arizona	67,258
32	Arkansas	62,132
21	California	114,061
12	Colorado	163,416
1	Connecticut	412,391
5	Delaware	262,651
39	Florida	48,371
16	Georgia	134,357
37	Hawaii	54,920
43	Idaho	38,298
9	Illinois	204,919
29	Indiana	66,892
17	Iowa	130,830
20	Kansas	115,935
23	Kentucky	88,257
36	Louisiana	55,058
38	Maine	49,200
42	Maryland	42,226
18	Massachusetts	130,481
34	Michigan	55,537
7	Minnesota	243,205
30	Mississippi	66,585
10	Missouri	201,231
50	Montana	9,811
14	Nebraska	156,235
33	Nevada	56,042
25	New Hampshire	79,683
4	New Jersey	284,292
48	New Mexico	20,969
13	New York	160,237
19	North Carolina	123,601
27	North Dakota	70,483
26	Ohio	78,746
2	Oklahoma	407,239
40	Oregon	44,290
3	Pennsylvania	395,210
44	Rhode Island	26,821
35	South Carolina	55,278
45	South Dakota	23,006
11	Tennessee	170,415
6	Texas	249,565
15	Utah	154,069
46	Vermont	22,028
8	Virginia	206,572
24	Washington	84,039
47	West Virginia	21,573
22	Wisconsin	108,086
49	Wyoming	18,857

RANK ORDER

RANK	STATE	AVERAGE REFUND
1	Connecticut	$412,391
2	Oklahoma	407,239
3	Pennsylvania	395,210
4	New Jersey	284,292
5	Delaware	262,651
6	Texas	249,565
7	Minnesota	243,205
8	Virginia	206,572
9	Illinois	204,919
10	Missouri	201,231
11	Tennessee	170,415
12	Colorado	163,416
13	New York	160,237
14	Nebraska	156,235
15	Utah	154,069
16	Georgia	134,357
17	Iowa	130,830
18	Massachusetts	130,481
19	North Carolina	123,601
20	Kansas	115,935
21	California	114,061
22	Wisconsin	108,086
23	Kentucky	88,257
24	Washington	84,039
25	New Hampshire	79,683
26	Ohio	78,746
27	North Dakota	70,483
28	Arizona	67,258
29	Indiana	66,892
30	Mississippi	66,585
31	Alabama	64,183
32	Arkansas	62,132
33	Nevada	56,042
34	Michigan	55,537
35	South Carolina	55,278
36	Louisiana	55,058
37	Hawaii	54,920
38	Maine	49,200
39	Florida	48,371
40	Oregon	44,290
41	Alaska	43,171
42	Maryland	42,226
43	Idaho	38,298
44	Rhode Island	26,821
45	South Dakota	23,006
46	Vermont	22,028
47	West Virginia	21,573
48	New Mexico	20,969
49	Wyoming	18,857
50	Montana	9,811
	District of Columbia	179,709

Source: CQ Press using data from U.S. Department of the Treasury, Internal Revenue Service
"Fiscal Year 2016 IRS Data Book" (http://www.irs.gov/uac/SOI-Tax-Stats-IRS-Data-Book)
*National average includes refunds to international sources and other miscellaneous refunds not shown separately.

Federal Government Expenditures in 2016

National Total = $3,070,911,835,000*

ALPHA ORDER

RANK	STATE	EXPENDITURES	% of USA
19	Alabama	$66,905,396,454	2.2%
46	Alaska	7,988,794,136	0.3%
17	Arizona	71,716,060,266	2.3%
33	Arkansas	22,916,825,538	0.7%
1	California	289,906,001,150	9.4%
27	Colorado	39,503,488,964	1.3%
15	Connecticut	74,566,355,002	2.4%
48	Delaware	6,623,282,899	0.2%
3	Florida	170,930,415,295	5.5%
20	Georgia	65,125,282,549	2.1%
42	Hawaii	11,143,397,423	0.4%
39	Idaho	12,347,632,185	0.4%
11	Illinois	80,484,543,377	2.6%
6	Indiana	128,479,516,092	4.2%
32	Iowa	23,233,563,544	0.8%
36	Kansas	16,230,438,273	0.5%
8	Kentucky	89,350,644,054	2.9%
28	Louisiana	35,379,086,151	1.1%
41	Maine	11,676,642,139	0.4%
18	Maryland	66,930,108,551	2.2%
23	Massachusetts	62,275,579,959	2.0%
13	Michigan	77,419,893,893	2.5%
10	Minnesota	81,541,932,792	2.6%
31	Mississippi	24,510,955,972	0.8%
26	Missouri	52,921,761,250	1.7%
45	Montana	8,344,393,113	0.3%
40	Nebraska	12,302,857,615	0.4%
35	Nevada	17,777,453,540	0.6%
43	New Hampshire	9,695,691,786	0.3%
24	New Jersey	60,855,085,669	2.0%
34	New Mexico	22,829,600,877	0.7%
5	New York	158,593,098,950	5.1%
21	North Carolina	63,965,875,087	2.1%
22	North Dakota	62,598,781,139	2.0%
14	Ohio	76,121,678,221	2.5%
30	Oklahoma	28,207,147,827	0.9%
29	Oregon	32,010,847,969	1.0%
2	Pennsylvania	193,557,462,424	6.3%
44	Rhode Island	8,955,224,152	0.3%
12	South Carolina	77,734,372,433	2.5%
47	South Dakota	6,763,252,911	0.2%
16	Tennessee	73,875,092,624	2.4%
4	Texas	169,537,149,536	5.5%
38	Utah	14,534,864,156	0.5%
49	Vermont	5,482,828,443	0.2%
7	Virginia	94,755,289,501	3.1%
25	Washington	58,150,899,022	1.9%
37	West Virginia	15,262,409,794	0.5%
9	Wisconsin	84,166,564,963	2.7%
50	Wyoming	4,147,619,639	0.1%

RANK ORDER

RANK	STATE	EXPENDITURES	% of USA
1	California	$289,906,001,150	9.4%
2	Pennsylvania	193,557,462,424	6.3%
3	Florida	170,930,415,295	5.5%
4	Texas	169,537,149,536	5.5%
5	New York	158,593,098,950	5.1%
6	Indiana	128,479,516,092	4.2%
7	Virginia	94,755,289,501	3.1%
8	Kentucky	89,350,644,054	2.9%
9	Wisconsin	84,166,564,963	2.7%
10	Minnesota	81,541,932,792	2.6%
11	Illinois	80,484,543,377	2.6%
12	South Carolina	77,734,372,433	2.5%
13	Michigan	77,419,893,893	2.5%
14	Ohio	76,121,678,221	2.5%
15	Connecticut	74,566,355,002	2.4%
16	Tennessee	73,875,092,624	2.4%
17	Arizona	71,716,060,266	2.3%
18	Maryland	66,930,108,551	2.2%
19	Alabama	66,905,396,454	2.2%
20	Georgia	65,125,282,549	2.1%
21	North Carolina	63,965,875,087	2.1%
22	North Dakota	62,598,781,139	2.0%
23	Massachusetts	62,275,579,959	2.0%
24	New Jersey	60,855,085,669	2.0%
25	Washington	58,150,899,022	1.9%
26	Missouri	52,921,761,250	1.7%
27	Colorado	39,503,488,964	1.3%
28	Louisiana	35,379,086,151	1.1%
29	Oregon	32,010,847,969	1.0%
30	Oklahoma	28,207,147,827	0.9%
31	Mississippi	24,510,955,972	0.8%
32	Iowa	23,233,563,544	0.8%
33	Arkansas	22,916,825,538	0.7%
34	New Mexico	22,829,600,877	0.7%
35	Nevada	17,777,453,540	0.6%
36	Kansas	16,230,438,273	0.5%
37	West Virginia	15,262,409,794	0.5%
38	Utah	14,534,864,156	0.5%
39	Idaho	12,347,632,185	0.4%
40	Nebraska	12,302,857,615	0.4%
41	Maine	11,676,642,139	0.4%
42	Hawaii	11,143,397,423	0.4%
43	New Hampshire	9,695,691,786	0.3%
44	Rhode Island	8,955,224,152	0.3%
45	Montana	8,344,393,113	0.3%
46	Alaska	7,988,794,136	0.3%
47	South Dakota	6,763,252,911	0.2%
48	Delaware	6,623,282,899	0.2%
49	Vermont	5,482,828,443	0.2%
50	Wyoming	4,147,619,639	0.1%
	District of Columbia	31,089,311,296	1.0%

Source: U.S. Office of Management and Budget, USAspending.gov
   "Prime Award Spending Data Summary" (https://www.usaspending.gov/, as of January 26, 2018)
*Total includes $89,489,384,000 in U.S. territories and internationally as well as expenditures not distributed by state.
Expenditures allocated based on place of performance of a contract. Includes Contracts, Grants, Loans, and "Other Financial Assistance."

Per Capita Federal Government Expenditures in 2016

National Per Capita = $9,219*

ALPHA ORDER

ALPHA ORDER

RANK ORDER

RANK	STATE	PER CAPITA		RANK	STATE	PER CAPITA
9	Alabama	$13,765		1	North Dakota	$82,852
14	Alaska	10,774		2	Connecticut	20,784
15	Arizona	10,381		3	Kentucky	20,142
31	Arkansas	7,669		4	Indiana	19,367
34	California	7,377		5	South Carolina	15,881
38	Colorado	7,143		6	Pennsylvania	15,131
2	Connecticut	20,784		7	Minnesota	14,759
40	Delaware	6,952		8	Wisconsin	14,592
22	Florida	8,275		9	Alabama	13,765
44	Georgia	6,314		10	Virginia	11,324
29	Hawaii	7,800		11	Tennessee	11,202
35	Idaho	7,350		12	Maryland	11,109
46	Illinois	6,270		13	New Mexico	10,947
4	Indiana	19,367		14	Alaska	10,774
33	Iowa	7,421		15	Arizona	10,381
49	Kansas	5,582		16	Massachusetts	9,126
3	Kentucky	20,142		17	Maine	8,778
32	Louisiana	7,550		18	Vermont	8,757
17	Maine	8,778		19	Missouri	8,688
12	Maryland	11,109		20	Rhode Island	8,483
16	Massachusetts	9,126		21	West Virginia	8,290
30	Michigan	7,794		22	Florida	8,275
7	Minnesota	14,759		23	Mississippi	8,210
23	Mississippi	8,210		24	Washington	8,121
19	Missouri	8,688		25	Montana	8,034
25	Montana	8,034		26	New York	7,995
43	Nebraska	6,449		27	Oregon	7,954
48	Nevada	6,048		28	South Dakota	7,883
36	New Hampshire	7,263		29	Hawaii	7,800
41	New Jersey	6,778		30	Michigan	7,794
13	New Mexico	10,947		31	Arkansas	7,669
26	New York	7,995		32	Louisiana	7,550
45	North Carolina	6,298		33	Iowa	7,421
1	North Dakota	82,852		34	California	7,377
42	Ohio	6,549		35	Idaho	7,350
37	Oklahoma	7,193		36	New Hampshire	7,263
27	Oregon	7,954		37	Oklahoma	7,193
6	Pennsylvania	15,131		38	Colorado	7,143
20	Rhode Island	8,483		39	Wyoming	7,071
5	South Carolina	15,881		40	Delaware	6,952
28	South Dakota	7,883		41	New Jersey	6,778
11	Tennessee	11,202		42	Ohio	6,549
47	Texas	6,181		43	Nebraska	6,449
50	Utah	4,860		44	Georgia	6,314
18	Vermont	8,757		45	North Carolina	6,298
10	Virginia	11,324		46	Illinois	6,270
24	Washington	8,121		47	Texas	6,181
21	West Virginia	8,290		48	Nevada	6,048
8	Wisconsin	14,592		49	Kansas	5,582
39	Wyoming	7,071		50	Utah	4,860
					District of Columbia	45,430

Source: CQ Press using data from U.S. Office of Management and Budget, USAspending.gov
"Prime Award Spending Data Summary" (https://www.usaspending.gov/, as of January 26, 2018)
*National per capita excludes expenditures and population for territories and undistributed amounts. Expenditures allocated based on place of performance of a contract. Includes Contracts, Grants, Loans, and "Other Financial Assistance."

Federal Government Contract Awards in 2016

National Total = $473,955,518,000*

ALPHA ORDER

RANK	STATE	EXPENDITURES	% of USA
13	Alabama	$10,868,712,672	2.3%
37	Alaska	1,659,834,306	0.4%
12	Arizona	11,797,602,231	2.5%
43	Arkansas	901,341,705	0.2%
1	California	51,901,993,858	11.0%
14	Colorado	9,702,336,528	2.0%
7	Connecticut	14,492,244,971	3.1%
50	Delaware	253,213,593	0.1%
5	Florida	17,815,617,299	3.8%
11	Georgia	11,925,783,079	2.5%
33	Hawaii	2,193,655,931	0.5%
31	Idaho	2,599,403,716	0.5%
16	Illinois	8,740,882,341	1.8%
27	Indiana	3,946,383,677	0.8%
36	Iowa	1,661,890,047	0.4%
41	Kansas	1,152,923,485	0.2%
19	Kentucky	6,570,187,775	1.4%
30	Louisiana	2,838,173,444	0.6%
35	Maine	1,818,604,203	0.4%
4	Maryland	30,353,875,589	6.4%
9	Massachusetts	12,933,090,546	2.7%
23	Michigan	5,236,529,649	1.1%
24	Minnesota	4,842,358,641	1.0%
26	Mississippi	4,437,654,914	0.9%
10	Missouri	12,280,432,158	2.6%
48	Montana	523,156,523	0.1%
42	Nebraska	960,847,855	0.2%
32	Nevada	2,407,644,289	0.5%
38	New Hampshire	1,401,198,274	0.3%
18	New Jersey	7,222,026,999	1.5%
17	New Mexico	7,994,679,466	1.7%
15	New York	9,127,327,108	1.9%
25	North Carolina	4,636,612,802	1.0%
45	North Dakota	610,114,979	0.1%
21	Ohio	5,436,821,278	1.1%
28	Oklahoma	3,852,754,577	0.8%
40	Oregon	1,322,164,466	0.3%
6	Pennsylvania	15,413,011,555	3.3%
44	Rhode Island	756,487,243	0.2%
22	South Carolina	5,272,423,379	1.1%
46	South Dakota	540,702,710	0.1%
20	Tennessee	5,755,644,374	1.2%
3	Texas	33,003,412,756	7.0%
34	Utah	1,910,704,207	0.4%
47	Vermont	523,974,536	0.1%
2	Virginia	50,592,344,291	10.7%
8	Washington	14,190,612,655	3.0%
39	West Virginia	1,388,890,486	0.3%
29	Wisconsin	3,316,021,479	0.7%
49	Wyoming	317,939,354	0.1%

RANK ORDER

RANK	STATE	EXPENDITURES	% of USA
1	California	$51,901,993,858	11.0%
2	Virginia	50,592,344,291	10.7%
3	Texas	33,003,412,756	7.0%
4	Maryland	30,353,875,589	6.4%
5	Florida	17,815,617,299	3.8%
6	Pennsylvania	15,413,011,555	3.3%
7	Connecticut	14,492,244,971	3.1%
8	Washington	14,190,612,655	3.0%
9	Massachusetts	12,933,090,546	2.7%
10	Missouri	12,280,432,158	2.6%
11	Georgia	11,925,783,079	2.5%
12	Arizona	11,797,602,231	2.5%
13	Alabama	10,868,712,672	2.3%
14	Colorado	9,702,336,528	2.0%
15	New York	9,127,327,108	1.9%
16	Illinois	8,740,882,341	1.8%
17	New Mexico	7,994,679,466	1.7%
18	New Jersey	7,222,026,999	1.5%
19	Kentucky	6,570,187,775	1.4%
20	Tennessee	5,755,644,374	1.2%
21	Ohio	5,436,821,278	1.1%
22	South Carolina	5,272,423,379	1.1%
23	Michigan	5,236,529,649	1.1%
24	Minnesota	4,842,358,641	1.0%
25	North Carolina	4,636,612,802	1.0%
26	Mississippi	4,437,654,914	0.9%
27	Indiana	3,946,383,677	0.8%
28	Oklahoma	3,852,754,577	0.8%
29	Wisconsin	3,316,021,479	0.7%
30	Louisiana	2,838,173,444	0.6%
31	Idaho	2,599,403,716	0.5%
32	Nevada	2,407,644,289	0.5%
33	Hawaii	2,193,655,931	0.5%
34	Utah	1,910,704,207	0.4%
35	Maine	1,818,604,203	0.4%
36	Iowa	1,661,890,047	0.4%
37	Alaska	1,659,834,306	0.4%
38	New Hampshire	1,401,198,274	0.3%
39	West Virginia	1,388,890,486	0.3%
40	Oregon	1,322,164,466	0.3%
41	Kansas	1,152,923,485	0.2%
42	Nebraska	960,847,855	0.2%
43	Arkansas	901,341,705	0.2%
44	Rhode Island	756,487,243	0.2%
45	North Dakota	610,114,979	0.1%
46	South Dakota	540,702,710	0.1%
47	Vermont	523,974,536	0.1%
48	Montana	523,156,523	0.1%
49	Wyoming	317,939,354	0.1%
50	Delaware	253,213,593	0.1%
	District of Columbia	21,130,924,849	4.5%

Source: U.S. Office of Management and Budget, USAspending.gov
"Prime Award Spending Data Summary" (https://www.usaspending.gov/, as of January 26, 2018)
*Total includes $41,422,349,000 in U.S. territories and internationally as well as expenditures not distributed by state.
Expenditures allocated based on place of performance of a contract. Does not include grants, co-operative agreements, or contracts under grants.

Per Capita Expenditures for Federal Government Contract Awards in 2016
National Per Capita = $1,337*

ALPHA ORDER

RANK	STATE	PER CAPITA
6	Alabama	$2,236
5	Alaska	2,238
11	Arizona	1,708
49	Arkansas	302
17	California	1,321
10	Colorado	1,754
3	Connecticut	4,039
50	Delaware	266
26	Florida	862
20	Georgia	1,156
13	Hawaii	1,535
12	Idaho	1,547
33	Illinois	681
37	Indiana	595
40	Iowa	531
47	Kansas	397
15	Kentucky	1,481
36	Louisiana	606
16	Maine	1,367
2	Maryland	5,038
9	Massachusetts	1,895
41	Michigan	527
24	Minnesota	876
14	Mississippi	1,486
7	Missouri	2,016
42	Montana	504
42	Nebraska	504
28	Nevada	819
22	New Hampshire	1,050
30	New Jersey	804
4	New Mexico	3,834
45	New York	460
46	North Carolina	457
29	North Dakota	808
44	Ohio	468
23	Oklahoma	983
48	Oregon	329
18	Pennsylvania	1,205
32	Rhode Island	717
21	South Carolina	1,077
35	South Dakota	630
25	Tennessee	873
19	Texas	1,203
34	Utah	639
27	Vermont	837
1	Virginia	6,046
8	Washington	1,982
31	West Virginia	754
38	Wisconsin	575
39	Wyoming	542

RANK ORDER

RANK	STATE	PER CAPITA
1	Virginia	$6,046
2	Maryland	5,038
3	Connecticut	4,039
4	New Mexico	3,834
5	Alaska	2,238
6	Alabama	2,236
7	Missouri	2,016
8	Washington	1,982
9	Massachusetts	1,895
10	Colorado	1,754
11	Arizona	1,708
12	Idaho	1,547
13	Hawaii	1,535
14	Mississippi	1,486
15	Kentucky	1,481
16	Maine	1,367
17	California	1,321
18	Pennsylvania	1,205
19	Texas	1,203
20	Georgia	1,156
21	South Carolina	1,077
22	New Hampshire	1,050
23	Oklahoma	983
24	Minnesota	876
25	Tennessee	873
26	Florida	862
27	Vermont	837
28	Nevada	819
29	North Dakota	808
30	New Jersey	804
31	West Virginia	754
32	Rhode Island	717
33	Illinois	681
34	Utah	639
35	South Dakota	630
36	Louisiana	606
37	Indiana	595
38	Wisconsin	575
39	Wyoming	542
40	Iowa	531
41	Michigan	527
42	Montana	504
42	Nebraska	504
44	Ohio	468
45	New York	460
46	North Carolina	457
47	Kansas	397
48	Oregon	329
49	Arkansas	302
50	Delaware	266

| | District of Columbia | 30,878 |

Source: CQ Press using data from U.S. Office of Management and Budget, USAspending.gov
"Prime Award Spending Data Summary" (https://www.usaspending.gov/, as of January 26, 2018)
*National per capita excludes expenditures and population for territories and undistributed amounts. Expenditures allocated based on place of performance of a contract. Does not include grants, co-operative agreements, or contracts under grants.

Federal Government Assistance in 2016

National Total = $2,596,956,318,000*

ALPHA ORDER

RANK	STATE	EXPENDITURES	% of USA
19	Alabama	$56,036,683,782	2.2%
47	Alaska	6,328,959,830	0.2%
17	Arizona	59,918,458,035	2.3%
31	Arkansas	22,015,483,833	0.8%
1	California	238,004,007,292	9.2%
29	Colorado	29,801,152,436	1.1%
16	Connecticut	60,074,110,031	2.3%
46	Delaware	6,370,069,306	0.2%
3	Florida	153,114,797,996	5.9%
21	Georgia	53,199,499,470	2.0%
42	Hawaii	8,949,741,492	0.3%
41	Idaho	9,748,228,469	0.4%
12	Illinois	71,743,661,036	2.8%
6	Indiana	124,533,132,415	4.8%
32	Iowa	21,571,673,497	0.8%
35	Kansas	15,077,514,788	0.6%
7	Kentucky	82,780,456,279	3.2%
27	Louisiana	32,540,912,707	1.3%
40	Maine	9,858,037,936	0.4%
26	Maryland	36,576,232,962	1.4%
22	Massachusetts	49,342,489,413	1.9%
11	Michigan	72,183,364,244	2.8%
9	Minnesota	76,699,574,151	3.0%
33	Mississippi	20,073,301,058	0.8%
25	Missouri	40,641,329,092	1.6%
45	Montana	7,821,236,590	0.3%
39	Nebraska	11,342,009,760	0.4%
34	Nevada	15,369,809,251	0.6%
43	New Hampshire	8,294,493,512	0.3%
20	New Jersey	53,633,058,670	2.1%
36	New Mexico	14,834,921,411	0.6%
4	New York	149,465,771,842	5.8%
18	North Carolina	59,329,262,285	2.3%
15	North Dakota	61,988,666,160	2.4%
13	Ohio	70,684,856,943	2.7%
30	Oklahoma	24,354,393,250	0.9%
28	Oregon	30,688,683,503	1.2%
2	Pennsylvania	178,144,450,869	6.9%
44	Rhode Island	8,198,736,909	0.3%
10	South Carolina	72,461,949,054	2.8%
48	South Dakota	6,222,550,201	0.2%
14	Tennessee	68,119,448,250	2.6%
5	Texas	136,533,736,780	5.3%
38	Utah	12,624,159,949	0.5%
49	Vermont	4,958,853,907	0.2%
23	Virginia	44,162,945,210	1.7%
24	Washington	43,960,286,367	1.7%
37	West Virginia	13,873,519,308	0.5%
8	Wisconsin	80,850,543,484	3.1%
50	Wyoming	3,829,680,285	0.1%

RANK ORDER

RANK	STATE	EXPENDITURES	% of USA
1	California	$238,004,007,292	9.2%
2	Pennsylvania	178,144,450,869	6.9%
3	Florida	153,114,797,996	5.9%
4	New York	149,465,771,842	5.8%
5	Texas	136,533,736,780	5.3%
6	Indiana	124,533,132,415	4.8%
7	Kentucky	82,780,456,279	3.2%
8	Wisconsin	80,850,543,484	3.1%
9	Minnesota	76,699,574,151	3.0%
10	South Carolina	72,461,949,054	2.8%
11	Michigan	72,183,364,244	2.8%
12	Illinois	71,743,661,036	2.8%
13	Ohio	70,684,856,943	2.7%
14	Tennessee	68,119,448,250	2.6%
15	North Dakota	61,988,666,160	2.4%
16	Connecticut	60,074,110,031	2.3%
17	Arizona	59,918,458,035	2.3%
18	North Carolina	59,329,262,285	2.3%
19	Alabama	56,036,683,782	2.2%
20	New Jersey	53,633,058,670	2.1%
21	Georgia	53,199,499,470	2.0%
22	Massachusetts	49,342,489,413	1.9%
23	Virginia	44,162,945,210	1.7%
24	Washington	43,960,286,367	1.7%
25	Missouri	40,641,329,092	1.6%
26	Maryland	36,576,232,962	1.4%
27	Louisiana	32,540,912,707	1.3%
28	Oregon	30,688,683,503	1.2%
29	Colorado	29,801,152,436	1.1%
30	Oklahoma	24,354,393,250	0.9%
31	Arkansas	22,015,483,833	0.8%
32	Iowa	21,571,673,497	0.8%
33	Mississippi	20,073,301,058	0.8%
34	Nevada	15,369,809,251	0.6%
35	Kansas	15,077,514,788	0.6%
36	New Mexico	14,834,921,411	0.6%
37	West Virginia	13,873,519,308	0.5%
38	Utah	12,624,159,949	0.5%
39	Nebraska	11,342,009,760	0.4%
40	Maine	9,858,037,936	0.4%
41	Idaho	9,748,228,469	0.4%
42	Hawaii	8,949,741,492	0.3%
43	New Hampshire	8,294,493,512	0.3%
44	Rhode Island	8,198,736,909	0.3%
45	Montana	7,821,236,590	0.3%
46	Delaware	6,370,069,306	0.2%
47	Alaska	6,328,959,830	0.2%
48	South Dakota	6,222,550,201	0.2%
49	Vermont	4,958,853,907	0.2%
50	Wyoming	3,829,680,285	0.1%
	District of Columbia	9,958,386,447	0.4%

Source: CQ Press using data from U.S. Office of Management and Budget, USAspending.gov
"Prime Award Spending Data Summary" (https://www.usaspending.gov/, as of January 26, 2018)
*Total includes $48,067,036,000 in U.S. territories and internationally as well as expenditures not distributed by state.
Expenditures allocated based on place of performance of a contract. Includes grants, loans, and other financial assistance.

Per Capita Federal Government Assistance in 2016

National Per Capita = $7,881*

ALPHA ORDER				RANK ORDER		
RANK	STATE	PER CAPITA		RANK	STATE	PER CAPITA
9	Alabama	$11,529		1	North Dakota	$82,045
12	Alaska	8,535		2	Indiana	18,772
11	Arizona	8,673		3	Kentucky	18,661
21	Arkansas	7,367		4	Connecticut	16,745
38	California	6,057		5	South Carolina	14,804
44	Colorado	5,389		6	Wisconsin	14,017
4	Connecticut	16,745		7	Pennsylvania	13,926
29	Delaware	6,686		8	Minnesota	13,882
19	Florida	7,412		9	Alabama	11,529
48	Georgia	5,158		10	Tennessee	10,329
32	Hawaii	6,264		11	Arizona	8,673
42	Idaho	5,802		12	Alaska	8,535
43	Illinois	5,589		13	Vermont	7,920
2	Indiana	18,772		14	Rhode Island	7,767
27	Iowa	6,890		15	Oregon	7,625
47	Kansas	5,185		16	West Virginia	7,536
3	Kentucky	18,661		17	New York	7,535
26	Louisiana	6,944		18	Montana	7,530
20	Maine	7,411		19	Florida	7,412
37	Maryland	6,071		20	Maine	7,411
24	Massachusetts	7,231		21	Arkansas	7,367
22	Michigan	7,267		22	Michigan	7,267
8	Minnesota	13,882		23	South Dakota	7,253
28	Mississippi	6,724		24	Massachusetts	7,231
30	Missouri	6,672		25	New Mexico	7,114
18	Montana	7,530		26	Louisiana	6,944
40	Nebraska	5,946		27	Iowa	6,890
46	Nevada	5,229		28	Mississippi	6,724
33	New Hampshire	6,213		29	Delaware	6,686
39	New Jersey	5,974		30	Missouri	6,672
25	New Mexico	7,114		31	Wyoming	6,529
17	New York	7,535		32	Hawaii	6,264
41	North Carolina	5,841		33	New Hampshire	6,213
1	North Dakota	82,045		34	Oklahoma	6,211
36	Ohio	6,082		35	Washington	6,139
34	Oklahoma	6,211		36	Ohio	6,082
15	Oregon	7,625		37	Maryland	6,071
7	Pennsylvania	13,926		38	California	6,057
14	Rhode Island	7,767		39	New Jersey	5,974
5	South Carolina	14,804		40	Nebraska	5,946
23	South Dakota	7,253		41	North Carolina	5,841
10	Tennessee	10,329		42	Idaho	5,802
49	Texas	4,978		43	Illinois	5,589
50	Utah	4,221		44	Colorado	5,389
13	Vermont	7,920		45	Virginia	5,278
45	Virginia	5,278		46	Nevada	5,229
35	Washington	6,139		47	Kansas	5,185
16	West Virginia	7,536		48	Georgia	5,158
6	Wisconsin	14,017		49	Texas	4,978
31	Wyoming	6,529		50	Utah	4,221
					District of Columbia	14,552

Source: CQ Press using data from U.S. Office of Management and Budget, USAspending.gov
"Prime Award Spending Data Summary" (https://www.usaspending.gov/, as of January 26, 2018)
*National per capita excludes expenditures and population for territories and undistributed amounts. Expenditures allocated based on place of performance of a contract. Includes grants, loans and other financial assistance.

Federal Government Grants in 2016

National Total = $668,199,244,000*

RANK	STATE	EXPENDITURES	% of USA		RANK	STATE	EXPENDITURES	% of USA
26	Alabama	$8,447,657,744	1.3%		1	California	$94,149,533,851	14.1%
37	Alaska	3,397,723,535	0.5%		2	New York	61,800,418,784	9.2%
14	Arizona	14,249,468,152	2.1%		3	Texas	44,676,692,941	6.7%
29	Arkansas	7,336,826,829	1.1%		4	Florida	25,904,994,486	3.9%
1	California	94,149,533,851	14.1%		5	Pennsylvania	24,810,004,284	3.7%
22	Colorado	10,251,186,230	1.5%		6	Illinois	22,604,379,016	3.4%
27	Connecticut	8,404,060,852	1.3%		7	Michigan	21,975,743,949	3.3%
45	Delaware	2,286,979,015	0.3%		8	Ohio	20,923,713,441	3.1%
4	Florida	25,904,994,486	3.9%		9	Massachusetts	19,646,683,882	2.9%
12	Georgia	14,992,551,113	2.2%		10	New Jersey	16,992,879,747	2.5%
41	Hawaii	2,953,474,766	0.4%		11	North Carolina	16,679,391,260	2.5%
44	Idaho	2,604,148,220	0.4%		12	Georgia	14,992,551,113	2.2%
6	Illinois	22,604,379,016	3.4%		13	Washington	14,597,827,353	2.2%
15	Indiana	13,128,912,203	2.0%		14	Arizona	14,249,468,152	2.1%
32	Iowa	5,906,064,612	0.9%		15	Indiana	13,128,912,203	2.0%
38	Kansas	3,302,509,590	0.5%		16	Maryland	13,036,921,038	2.0%
18	Kentucky	11,794,841,777	1.8%		17	Louisiana	12,132,807,870	1.8%
17	Louisiana	12,132,807,870	1.8%		18	Kentucky	11,794,841,777	1.8%
39	Maine	3,085,371,399	0.5%		19	Missouri	11,746,210,228	1.8%
16	Maryland	13,036,921,038	2.0%		20	Minnesota	11,036,974,343	1.7%
9	Massachusetts	19,646,683,882	2.9%		21	Tennessee	10,977,643,998	1.6%
7	Michigan	21,975,743,949	3.3%		22	Colorado	10,251,186,230	1.5%
20	Minnesota	11,036,974,343	1.7%		23	Virginia	9,352,443,333	1.4%
31	Mississippi	6,933,952,027	1.0%		24	Oregon	9,170,080,309	1.4%
19	Missouri	11,746,210,228	1.8%		25	Wisconsin	8,595,613,468	1.3%
43	Montana	2,775,046,780	0.4%		26	Alabama	8,447,657,744	1.3%
42	Nebraska	2,835,516,838	0.4%		27	Connecticut	8,404,060,852	1.3%
34	Nevada	4,713,949,854	0.7%		28	South Carolina	7,982,142,953	1.2%
46	New Hampshire	2,240,382,525	0.3%		29	Arkansas	7,336,826,829	1.1%
10	New Jersey	16,992,879,747	2.5%		30	Oklahoma	6,993,952,011	1.0%
33	New Mexico	5,630,141,953	0.8%		31	Mississippi	6,933,952,027	1.0%
2	New York	61,800,418,784	9.2%		32	Iowa	5,906,064,612	0.9%
11	North Carolina	16,679,391,260	2.5%		33	New Mexico	5,630,141,953	0.8%
48	North Dakota	2,004,904,822	0.3%		34	Nevada	4,713,949,854	0.7%
8	Ohio	20,923,713,441	3.1%		35	West Virginia	4,150,901,078	0.6%
30	Oklahoma	6,993,952,011	1.0%		36	Utah	4,061,946,764	0.6%
24	Oregon	9,170,080,309	1.4%		37	Alaska	3,397,723,535	0.5%
5	Pennsylvania	24,810,004,284	3.7%		38	Kansas	3,302,509,590	0.5%
40	Rhode Island	3,032,563,000	0.5%		39	Maine	3,085,371,399	0.5%
28	South Carolina	7,982,142,953	1.2%		40	Rhode Island	3,032,563,000	0.5%
49	South Dakota	1,702,366,285	0.3%		41	Hawaii	2,953,474,766	0.4%
21	Tennessee	10,977,643,998	1.6%		42	Nebraska	2,835,516,838	0.4%
3	Texas	44,676,692,941	6.7%		43	Montana	2,775,046,780	0.4%
36	Utah	4,061,946,764	0.6%		44	Idaho	2,604,148,220	0.4%
47	Vermont	2,137,508,075	0.3%		45	Delaware	2,286,979,015	0.3%
23	Virginia	9,352,443,333	1.4%		46	New Hampshire	2,240,382,525	0.3%
13	Washington	14,597,827,353	2.2%		47	Vermont	2,137,508,075	0.3%
35	West Virginia	4,150,901,078	0.6%		48	North Dakota	2,004,904,822	0.3%
25	Wisconsin	8,595,613,468	1.3%		49	South Dakota	1,702,366,285	0.3%
50	Wyoming	1,460,303,748	0.2%		50	Wyoming	1,460,303,748	0.2%
						District of Columbia	7,389,235,998	1.1%

ALPHA ORDER

RANK ORDER

Source: U.S. Office of Management and Budget, USAspending.gov
"Prime Award Spending Data Summary" (https://www.usaspending.gov/, as of January 26, 2018)
*Total includes $19,201,695,000 in U.S. territories and internationally as well as expenditures not distributed by state.
Expenditures allocated based on place of performance of a contract. Includes funds awarded to a non-federal entity for a defined
public or private purpose in which services are not rendered to the federal government.

Per Capita Expenditures for Federal Government Grants in 2016

National Per Capita = $2,007*

ALPHA ORDER

RANK	STATE	PER CAPITA	RANK	STATE	PER CAPITA
36	Alabama	$1,738	1	Alaska	$4,582
1	Alaska	4,582	2	Vermont	3,414
23	Arizona	2,063	3	New York	3,116
12	Arkansas	2,455	4	Massachusetts	2,879
14	California	2,396	5	Rhode Island	2,873
32	Colorado	1,854	6	New Mexico	2,700
15	Connecticut	2,342	7	Montana	2,672
13	Delaware	2,401	8	Kentucky	2,659
48	Florida	1,254	9	North Dakota	2,654
46	Georgia	1,454	10	Louisiana	2,589
22	Hawaii	2,067	11	Wyoming	2,490
43	Idaho	1,550	12	Arkansas	2,455
35	Illinois	1,761	13	Delaware	2,401
27	Indiana	1,979	14	California	2,396
31	Iowa	1,886	15	Connecticut	2,342
49	Kansas	1,136	16	Mississippi	2,323
8	Kentucky	2,659	17	Maine	2,319
10	Louisiana	2,589	18	Oregon	2,278
17	Maine	2,319	19	West Virginia	2,255
21	Maryland	2,164	20	Michigan	2,212
4	Massachusetts	2,879	21	Maryland	2,164
20	Michigan	2,212	22	Hawaii	2,067
25	Minnesota	1,998	23	Arizona	2,063
16	Mississippi	2,323	24	Washington	2,039
29	Missouri	1,928	25	Minnesota	1,998
7	Montana	2,672	26	South Dakota	1,984
45	Nebraska	1,486	27	Indiana	1,979
42	Nevada	1,604	28	Pennsylvania	1,940
37	New Hampshire	1,678	29	Missouri	1,928
30	New Jersey	1,893	30	New Jersey	1,893
6	New Mexico	2,700	31	Iowa	1,886
3	New York	3,116	32	Colorado	1,854
39	North Carolina	1,642	33	Ohio	1,800
9	North Dakota	2,654	34	Oklahoma	1,784
33	Ohio	1,800	35	Illinois	1,761
34	Oklahoma	1,784	36	Alabama	1,738
18	Oregon	2,278	37	New Hampshire	1,678
28	Pennsylvania	1,940	38	Tennessee	1,665
5	Rhode Island	2,873	39	North Carolina	1,642
40	South Carolina	1,631	40	South Carolina	1,631
26	South Dakota	1,984	41	Texas	1,629
38	Tennessee	1,665	42	Nevada	1,604
41	Texas	1,629	43	Idaho	1,550
47	Utah	1,358	44	Wisconsin	1,490
2	Vermont	3,414	45	Nebraska	1,486
50	Virginia	1,118	46	Georgia	1,454
24	Washington	2,039	47	Utah	1,358
19	West Virginia	2,255	48	Florida	1,254
44	Wisconsin	1,490	49	Kansas	1,136
11	Wyoming	2,490	50	Virginia	1,118
				District of Columbia	10,798

Source: CQ Press using data from U.S. Office of Management and Budget, USAspending.gov
"Prime Award Spending Data Summary" (https://www.usaspending.gov/, as of January 26, 2018)
*National per capita excludes expenditures and population for territories and undistributed amounts. Expenditures allocated based on place of performance of a contract. Includes funds awarded to a non-federal entity for a defined public or private purpose in which services are not rendered to the federal government.

Federal Government Loans in 2016

National Total = $2,431,709,000*

<table>
<tr><td colspan="4">ALPHA ORDER</td><td colspan="4">RANK ORDER</td></tr>
<tr><td>RANK</td><td>STATE</td><td>EXPENDITURES</td><td>% of USA</td><td>RANK</td><td>STATE</td><td>EXPENDITURES</td><td>% of USA</td></tr>
<tr><td>26</td><td>Alabama</td><td>$16,053,720</td><td>0.7%</td><td>1</td><td>Maryland</td><td>$894,813,400</td><td>36.8%</td></tr>
<tr><td>46</td><td>Alaska</td><td>4,893,006</td><td>0.2%</td><td>2</td><td>Texas</td><td>413,045,539</td><td>17.0%</td></tr>
<tr><td>21</td><td>Arizona</td><td>20,014,079</td><td>0.8%</td><td>3</td><td>Illinois</td><td>272,999,146</td><td>11.2%</td></tr>
<tr><td>36</td><td>Arkansas</td><td>10,497,467</td><td>0.4%</td><td>4</td><td>New Hampshire</td><td>207,722,155</td><td>8.5%</td></tr>
<tr><td>5</td><td>California</td><td>101,428,699</td><td>4.2%</td><td>5</td><td>California</td><td>101,428,699</td><td>4.2%</td></tr>
<tr><td>16</td><td>Colorado</td><td>25,016,006</td><td>1.0%</td><td>6</td><td>New York</td><td>63,712,700</td><td>2.6%</td></tr>
<tr><td>37</td><td>Connecticut</td><td>10,398,730</td><td>0.4%</td><td>7</td><td>Georgia</td><td>63,510,872</td><td>2.6%</td></tr>
<tr><td>48</td><td>Delaware</td><td>3,133,065</td><td>0.1%</td><td>8</td><td>North Carolina</td><td>57,704,384</td><td>2.4%</td></tr>
<tr><td>9</td><td>Florida</td><td>53,984,234</td><td>2.2%</td><td>9</td><td>Florida</td><td>53,984,234</td><td>2.2%</td></tr>
<tr><td>7</td><td>Georgia</td><td>63,510,872</td><td>2.6%</td><td>10</td><td>Virginia</td><td>49,033,433</td><td>2.0%</td></tr>
<tr><td>38</td><td>Hawaii</td><td>10,151,385</td><td>0.4%</td><td>11</td><td>South Carolina</td><td>41,670,986</td><td>1.7%</td></tr>
<tr><td>43</td><td>Idaho</td><td>6,572,069</td><td>0.3%</td><td>12</td><td>Kentucky</td><td>33,907,071</td><td>1.4%</td></tr>
<tr><td>3</td><td>Illinois</td><td>272,999,146</td><td>11.2%</td><td>13</td><td>New Jersey</td><td>32,835,076</td><td>1.4%</td></tr>
<tr><td>39</td><td>Indiana</td><td>10,124,677</td><td>0.4%</td><td>14</td><td>Washington</td><td>27,930,534</td><td>1.1%</td></tr>
<tr><td>15</td><td>Iowa</td><td>27,075,948</td><td>1.1%</td><td>15</td><td>Iowa</td><td>27,075,948</td><td>1.1%</td></tr>
<tr><td>27</td><td>Kansas</td><td>15,501,011</td><td>0.6%</td><td>16</td><td>Colorado</td><td>25,016,006</td><td>1.0%</td></tr>
<tr><td>12</td><td>Kentucky</td><td>33,907,071</td><td>1.4%</td><td>17</td><td>Louisiana</td><td>23,767,518</td><td>1.0%</td></tr>
<tr><td>17</td><td>Louisiana</td><td>23,767,518</td><td>1.0%</td><td>18</td><td>Michigan</td><td>23,429,032</td><td>1.0%</td></tr>
<tr><td>44</td><td>Maine</td><td>5,605,749</td><td>0.2%</td><td>19</td><td>Ohio</td><td>22,904,227</td><td>0.9%</td></tr>
<tr><td>1</td><td>Maryland</td><td>894,813,400</td><td>36.8%</td><td>20</td><td>Missouri</td><td>21,355,244</td><td>0.9%</td></tr>
<tr><td>40</td><td>Massachusetts</td><td>7,504,139</td><td>0.3%</td><td>21</td><td>Arizona</td><td>20,014,079</td><td>0.8%</td></tr>
<tr><td>18</td><td>Michigan</td><td>23,429,032</td><td>1.0%</td><td>22</td><td>Tennessee</td><td>19,487,457</td><td>0.8%</td></tr>
<tr><td>28</td><td>Minnesota</td><td>15,429,125</td><td>0.6%</td><td>23</td><td>South Dakota</td><td>18,965,522</td><td>0.8%</td></tr>
<tr><td>25</td><td>Mississippi</td><td>16,640,858</td><td>0.7%</td><td>24</td><td>Oregon</td><td>17,243,354</td><td>0.7%</td></tr>
<tr><td>20</td><td>Missouri</td><td>21,355,244</td><td>0.9%</td><td>25</td><td>Mississippi</td><td>16,640,858</td><td>0.7%</td></tr>
<tr><td>41</td><td>Montana</td><td>7,094,312</td><td>0.3%</td><td>26</td><td>Alabama</td><td>16,053,720</td><td>0.7%</td></tr>
<tr><td>34</td><td>Nebraska</td><td>10,850,456</td><td>0.4%</td><td>27</td><td>Kansas</td><td>15,501,011</td><td>0.6%</td></tr>
<tr><td>33</td><td>Nevada</td><td>11,782,172</td><td>0.5%</td><td>28</td><td>Minnesota</td><td>15,429,125</td><td>0.6%</td></tr>
<tr><td>4</td><td>New Hampshire</td><td>207,722,155</td><td>8.5%</td><td>29</td><td>Wisconsin</td><td>15,278,908</td><td>0.6%</td></tr>
<tr><td>13</td><td>New Jersey</td><td>32,835,076</td><td>1.4%</td><td>30</td><td>Oklahoma</td><td>14,542,263</td><td>0.6%</td></tr>
<tr><td>47</td><td>New Mexico</td><td>4,643,607</td><td>0.2%</td><td>31</td><td>North Dakota</td><td>13,805,565</td><td>0.6%</td></tr>
<tr><td>6</td><td>New York</td><td>63,712,700</td><td>2.6%</td><td>32</td><td>Pennsylvania</td><td>13,280,077</td><td>0.5%</td></tr>
<tr><td>8</td><td>North Carolina</td><td>57,704,384</td><td>2.4%</td><td>33</td><td>Nevada</td><td>11,782,172</td><td>0.5%</td></tr>
<tr><td>31</td><td>North Dakota</td><td>13,805,565</td><td>0.6%</td><td>34</td><td>Nebraska</td><td>10,850,456</td><td>0.4%</td></tr>
<tr><td>19</td><td>Ohio</td><td>22,904,227</td><td>0.9%</td><td>35</td><td>Utah</td><td>10,705,188</td><td>0.4%</td></tr>
<tr><td>30</td><td>Oklahoma</td><td>14,542,263</td><td>0.6%</td><td>36</td><td>Arkansas</td><td>10,497,467</td><td>0.4%</td></tr>
<tr><td>24</td><td>Oregon</td><td>17,243,354</td><td>0.7%</td><td>37</td><td>Connecticut</td><td>10,398,730</td><td>0.4%</td></tr>
<tr><td>32</td><td>Pennsylvania</td><td>13,280,077</td><td>0.5%</td><td>38</td><td>Hawaii</td><td>10,151,385</td><td>0.4%</td></tr>
<tr><td>50</td><td>Rhode Island</td><td>1,675,540</td><td>0.1%</td><td>39</td><td>Indiana</td><td>10,124,677</td><td>0.4%</td></tr>
<tr><td>11</td><td>South Carolina</td><td>41,670,986</td><td>1.7%</td><td>40</td><td>Massachusetts</td><td>7,504,139</td><td>0.3%</td></tr>
<tr><td>23</td><td>South Dakota</td><td>18,965,522</td><td>0.8%</td><td>41</td><td>Montana</td><td>7,094,312</td><td>0.3%</td></tr>
<tr><td>22</td><td>Tennessee</td><td>19,487,457</td><td>0.8%</td><td>42</td><td>Vermont</td><td>6,785,676</td><td>0.3%</td></tr>
<tr><td>2</td><td>Texas</td><td>413,045,539</td><td>17.0%</td><td>43</td><td>Idaho</td><td>6,572,069</td><td>0.3%</td></tr>
<tr><td>35</td><td>Utah</td><td>10,705,188</td><td>0.4%</td><td>44</td><td>Maine</td><td>5,605,749</td><td>0.2%</td></tr>
<tr><td>42</td><td>Vermont</td><td>6,785,676</td><td>0.3%</td><td>45</td><td>West Virginia</td><td>5,412,554</td><td>0.2%</td></tr>
<tr><td>10</td><td>Virginia</td><td>49,033,433</td><td>2.0%</td><td>46</td><td>Alaska</td><td>4,893,006</td><td>0.2%</td></tr>
<tr><td>14</td><td>Washington</td><td>27,930,534</td><td>1.1%</td><td>47</td><td>New Mexico</td><td>4,643,607</td><td>0.2%</td></tr>
<tr><td>45</td><td>West Virginia</td><td>5,412,554</td><td>0.2%</td><td>48</td><td>Delaware</td><td>3,133,065</td><td>0.1%</td></tr>
<tr><td>29</td><td>Wisconsin</td><td>15,278,908</td><td>0.6%</td><td>49</td><td>Wyoming</td><td>3,048,182</td><td>0.1%</td></tr>
<tr><td>49</td><td>Wyoming</td><td>3,048,182</td><td>0.1%</td><td>50</td><td>Rhode Island</td><td>1,675,540</td><td>0.1%</td></tr>
<tr><td></td><td></td><td></td><td></td><td></td><td>District of Columbia</td><td>1,495,068</td><td>0.1%</td></tr>
</table>

Source: U.S. Office of Management and Budget, USAspending.gov
"Prime Award Spending Data Summary" (https://www.usaspending.gov/, as of January 26, 2018)
*Total includes a negative $354,753,000 in U.S. territories and internationally as well as expenditures not distributed by state. Expenditures allocated based on place of performance of a contract. Includes federal awards that the borrowers will eventually pay back to the government. Guaranteed loans require the federal government to pay the bank and take over the loan if the borrower defaults.

Per Capita Federal Government Loans in 2016

National Per Capita = $8.62*

ALPHA ORDER

RANK	STATE	PER CAPITA
33	Alabama	$3.30
13	Alaska	6.60
38	Arizona	2.90
31	Arkansas	3.51
43	California	2.58
22	Colorado	4.52
38	Connecticut	2.90
34	Delaware	3.29
42	Florida	2.61
14	Georgia	6.16
11	Hawaii	7.11
26	Idaho	3.91
4	Illinois	21.27
48	Indiana	1.53
8	Iowa	8.65
19	Kansas	5.33
10	Kentucky	7.64
21	Louisiana	5.07
24	Maine	4.21
2	Maryland	148.52
49	Massachusetts	1.10
44	Michigan	2.36
40	Minnesota	2.79
18	Mississippi	5.57
31	Missouri	3.51
12	Montana	6.83
16	Nebraska	5.69
25	Nevada	4.01
1	New Hampshire	155.60
29	New Jersey	3.66
45	New Mexico	2.23
35	New York	3.21
17	North Carolina	5.68
5	North Dakota	18.27
46	Ohio	1.97
28	Oklahoma	3.71
23	Oregon	4.28
50	Pennsylvania	1.04
47	Rhode Island	1.59
9	South Carolina	8.51
3	South Dakota	22.11
36	Tennessee	2.95
6	Texas	15.06
30	Utah	3.58
7	Vermont	10.84
15	Virginia	5.86
27	Washington	3.90
37	West Virginia	2.94
41	Wisconsin	2.65
20	Wyoming	5.20

RANK ORDER

RANK	STATE	PER CAPITA
1	New Hampshire	$155.60
2	Maryland	148.52
3	South Dakota	22.11
4	Illinois	21.27
5	North Dakota	18.27
6	Texas	15.06
7	Vermont	10.84
8	Iowa	8.65
9	South Carolina	8.51
10	Kentucky	7.64
11	Hawaii	7.11
12	Montana	6.83
13	Alaska	6.60
14	Georgia	6.16
15	Virginia	5.86
16	Nebraska	5.69
17	North Carolina	5.68
18	Mississippi	5.57
19	Kansas	5.33
20	Wyoming	5.20
21	Louisiana	5.07
22	Colorado	4.52
23	Oregon	4.28
24	Maine	4.21
25	Nevada	4.01
26	Idaho	3.91
27	Washington	3.90
28	Oklahoma	3.71
29	New Jersey	3.66
30	Utah	3.58
31	Arkansas	3.51
31	Missouri	3.51
33	Alabama	3.30
34	Delaware	3.29
35	New York	3.21
36	Tennessee	2.95
37	West Virginia	2.94
38	Arizona	2.90
38	Connecticut	2.90
40	Minnesota	2.79
41	Wisconsin	2.65
42	Florida	2.61
43	California	2.58
44	Michigan	2.36
45	New Mexico	2.23
46	Ohio	1.97
47	Rhode Island	1.59
48	Indiana	1.53
49	Massachusetts	1.10
50	Pennsylvania	1.04

District of Columbia 2.18

Source: CQ Press using data from U.S. Office of Management and Budget, USAspending.gov
"Prime Award Spending Data Summary" (https://www.usaspending.gov/, as of January 26, 2018)
*National per capita excludes expenditures and population for territories and undistributed amounts. Expenditures allocated based on place of performance of a contract. Includes Federal awards that the borrowers will eventually pay back to the government. Guaranteed loans require the federal government to pay the bank and take over the loan if the borrower defaults.

Federal Government "Other Financial Assistance" in 2016

National Total = $1,926,325,366,000*

ALPHA ORDER

RANK	STATE	EXPENDITURES	% of USA
17	Alabama	$47,572,972,318	2.5%
48	Alaska	2,926,343,289	0.2%
18	Arizona	45,648,975,804	2.4%
32	Arkansas	14,668,159,537	0.8%
2	California	143,753,044,742	7.5%
29	Colorado	19,524,950,200	1.0%
13	Connecticut	51,659,650,449	2.7%
47	Delaware	4,079,957,226	0.2%
3	Florida	127,155,819,276	6.6%
20	Georgia	38,143,437,485	2.0%
42	Hawaii	5,986,115,341	0.3%
40	Idaho	7,137,508,180	0.4%
16	Illinois	48,866,282,874	2.5%
4	Indiana	111,394,095,535	5.8%
31	Iowa	15,638,532,937	0.8%
34	Kansas	11,759,504,187	0.6%
8	Kentucky	70,951,707,431	3.7%
28	Louisiana	20,384,337,319	1.1%
41	Maine	6,767,060,788	0.4%
26	Maryland	22,644,498,524	1.2%
23	Massachusetts	29,688,301,392	1.5%
14	Michigan	50,184,191,263	2.6%
9	Minnesota	65,647,170,683	3.4%
33	Mississippi	13,122,708,173	0.7%
25	Missouri	28,873,763,620	1.5%
45	Montana	5,039,095,498	0.3%
39	Nebraska	8,495,642,466	0.4%
35	Nevada	10,644,077,225	0.6%
43	New Hampshire	5,846,388,832	0.3%
21	New Jersey	36,607,343,847	1.9%
37	New Mexico	9,200,135,851	0.5%
6	New York	87,601,640,358	4.5%
19	North Carolina	42,592,166,641	2.2%
11	North Dakota	59,969,955,773	3.1%
15	Ohio	49,738,239,275	2.6%
30	Oklahoma	17,345,898,976	0.9%
27	Oregon	21,501,359,840	1.1%
1	Pennsylvania	153,321,166,508	8.0%
44	Rhode Island	5,164,498,369	0.3%
10	South Carolina	64,438,135,115	3.3%
46	South Dakota	4,501,218,394	0.2%
12	Tennessee	57,122,316,795	3.0%
5	Texas	91,443,998,300	4.7%
38	Utah	8,551,507,997	0.4%
49	Vermont	2,814,560,156	0.1%
22	Virginia	34,761,468,444	1.8%
24	Washington	29,334,528,480	1.5%
36	West Virginia	9,717,205,676	0.5%
7	Wisconsin	72,239,651,108	3.8%
50	Wyoming	2,366,328,355	0.1%

RANK ORDER

RANK	STATE	EXPENDITURES	% of USA
1	Pennsylvania	$153,321,166,508	8.0%
2	California	143,753,044,742	7.5%
3	Florida	127,155,819,276	6.6%
4	Indiana	111,394,095,535	5.8%
5	Texas	91,443,998,300	4.7%
6	New York	87,601,640,358	4.5%
7	Wisconsin	72,239,651,108	3.8%
8	Kentucky	70,951,707,431	3.7%
9	Minnesota	65,647,170,683	3.4%
10	South Carolina	64,438,135,115	3.3%
11	North Dakota	59,969,955,773	3.1%
12	Tennessee	57,122,316,795	3.0%
13	Connecticut	51,659,650,449	2.7%
14	Michigan	50,184,191,263	2.6%
15	Ohio	49,738,239,275	2.6%
16	Illinois	48,866,282,874	2.5%
17	Alabama	47,572,972,318	2.5%
18	Arizona	45,648,975,804	2.4%
19	North Carolina	42,592,166,641	2.2%
20	Georgia	38,143,437,485	2.0%
21	New Jersey	36,607,343,847	1.9%
22	Virginia	34,761,468,444	1.8%
23	Massachusetts	29,688,301,392	1.5%
24	Washington	29,334,528,480	1.5%
25	Missouri	28,873,763,620	1.5%
26	Maryland	22,644,498,524	1.2%
27	Oregon	21,501,359,840	1.1%
28	Louisiana	20,384,337,319	1.1%
29	Colorado	19,524,950,200	1.0%
30	Oklahoma	17,345,898,976	0.9%
31	Iowa	15,638,532,937	0.8%
32	Arkansas	14,668,159,537	0.8%
33	Mississippi	13,122,708,173	0.7%
34	Kansas	11,759,504,187	0.6%
35	Nevada	10,644,077,225	0.6%
36	West Virginia	9,717,205,676	0.5%
37	New Mexico	9,200,135,851	0.5%
38	Utah	8,551,507,997	0.4%
39	Nebraska	8,495,642,466	0.4%
40	Idaho	7,137,508,180	0.4%
41	Maine	6,767,060,788	0.4%
42	Hawaii	5,986,115,341	0.3%
43	New Hampshire	5,846,388,832	0.3%
44	Rhode Island	5,164,498,369	0.3%
45	Montana	5,039,095,498	0.3%
46	South Dakota	4,501,218,394	0.2%
47	Delaware	4,079,957,226	0.2%
48	Alaska	2,926,343,289	0.2%
49	Vermont	2,814,560,156	0.1%
50	Wyoming	2,366,328,355	0.1%
	District of Columbia	2,567,655,381	0.1%

Source: CQ Press using data from U.S. Office of Management and Budget, USAspending.gov
"Prime Award Spending Data Summary" (https://www.usaspending.gov/, as of January 26, 2018)
*Total includes $29,220,093,000 in U.S. territories and internationally as well as expenditures not distributed by state.
Expenditures allocated based on place of performance of a contract. Includes direct payments to individuals (such as Medicare and food stamps), insurance payments (such as, unemployment benefits, flood insurance), and other types of assistance payments (such as, reimbursements for prescriptions for veterans).

Per Capita Federal Government "Other Financial Assistance" in 2016

National Per Capita = $5,866*

RANK	STATE	PER CAPITA
9	Alabama	$9,788
42	Alaska	3,946
11	Arizona	6,608
19	Arkansas	4,909
46	California	3,658
48	Colorado	3,531
4	Connecticut	14,399
32	Delaware	4,283
12	Florida	6,156
45	Georgia	3,698
36	Hawaii	4,190
34	Idaho	4,248
43	Illinois	3,807
2	Indiana	16,791
18	Iowa	4,995
40	Kansas	4,044
3	Kentucky	15,994
31	Louisiana	4,350
16	Maine	5,087
44	Maryland	3,759
30	Massachusetts	4,351
17	Michigan	5,052
8	Minnesota	11,882
28	Mississippi	4,396
22	Missouri	4,740
21	Montana	4,852
24	Nebraska	4,454
47	Nevada	3,621
29	New Hampshire	4,379
39	New Jersey	4,077
27	New Mexico	4,412
26	New York	4,416
35	North Carolina	4,194
1	North Dakota	79,373
33	Ohio	4,279
25	Oklahoma	4,424
13	Oregon	5,342
7	Pennsylvania	11,986
20	Rhode Island	4,892
5	South Carolina	13,165
15	South Dakota	5,247
10	Tennessee	8,661
49	Texas	3,334
50	Utah	2,859
23	Vermont	4,495
37	Virginia	4,154
38	Washington	4,097
14	West Virginia	5,278
6	Wisconsin	12,524
41	Wyoming	4,034

RANK	STATE	PER CAPITA
1	North Dakota	$79,373
2	Indiana	16,791
3	Kentucky	15,994
4	Connecticut	14,399
5	South Carolina	13,165
6	Wisconsin	12,524
7	Pennsylvania	11,986
8	Minnesota	11,882
9	Alabama	9,788
10	Tennessee	8,661
11	Arizona	6,608
12	Florida	6,156
13	Oregon	5,342
14	West Virginia	5,278
15	South Dakota	5,247
16	Maine	5,087
17	Michigan	5,052
18	Iowa	4,995
19	Arkansas	4,909
20	Rhode Island	4,892
21	Montana	4,852
22	Missouri	4,740
23	Vermont	4,495
24	Nebraska	4,454
25	Oklahoma	4,424
26	New York	4,416
27	New Mexico	4,412
28	Mississippi	4,396
29	New Hampshire	4,379
30	Massachusetts	4,351
31	Louisiana	4,350
32	Delaware	4,283
33	Ohio	4,279
34	Idaho	4,248
35	North Carolina	4,194
36	Hawaii	4,190
37	Virginia	4,154
38	Washington	4,097
39	New Jersey	4,077
40	Kansas	4,044
41	Wyoming	4,034
42	Alaska	3,946
43	Illinois	3,807
44	Maryland	3,759
45	Georgia	3,698
46	California	3,658
47	Nevada	3,621
48	Colorado	3,531
49	Texas	3,334
50	Utah	2,859
	District of Columbia	3,752

Source: CQ Press using data from U.S. Office of Management and Budget, USAspending.gov
"Prime Award Spending Data Summary" (https://www.usaspending.gov/, as of January 26, 2018)
*National per capita excludes expenditures and population for territories and undistributed amounts. Expenditures allocated based on place of performance of a contract. Includes direct payments to individuals (such as Medicare and food stamps), insurance payments (such as, unemployment benefits, flood insurance), and other types of assistance payments (such as, reimbursements for prescriptions for veterans).

Federal Civilian Employees in 2016

National Total = 1,868,027 Employees*

ALPHA ORDER

RANK	STATE	EMPLOYEES	% of USA
13	Alabama	37,717	2.0%
38	Alaska	10,410	0.6%
14	Arizona	37,458	2.0%
35	Arkansas	12,662	0.7%
1	California	152,534	8.2%
16	Colorado	36,917	2.0%
41	Connecticut	7,972	0.4%
50	Delaware	2,934	0.2%
5	Florida	88,764	4.8%
6	Georgia	71,622	3.8%
23	Hawaii	23,173	1.2%
44	Idaho	7,421	0.4%
11	Illinois	45,040	2.4%
25	Indiana	22,235	1.2%
42	Iowa	7,944	0.4%
33	Kansas	15,559	0.8%
24	Kentucky	22,407	1.2%
28	Louisiana	19,161	1.0%
37	Maine	11,109	0.6%
4	Maryland	120,828	6.5%
21	Massachusetts	25,044	1.3%
18	Michigan	27,456	1.5%
32	Minnesota	16,493	0.9%
30	Mississippi	17,399	0.9%
17	Missouri	33,504	1.8%
40	Montana	8,545	0.5%
39	Nebraska	10,272	0.5%
36	Nevada	11,947	0.6%
49	New Hampshire	4,391	0.2%
22	New Jersey	24,776	1.3%
26	New Mexico	21,925	1.2%
8	New York	61,383	3.3%
12	North Carolina	42,333	2.3%
46	North Dakota	5,499	0.3%
10	Ohio	49,214	2.6%
15	Oklahoma	37,431	2.0%
31	Oregon	17,305	0.9%
7	Pennsylvania	62,410	3.3%
45	Rhode Island	6,749	0.4%
27	South Carolina	20,725	1.1%
43	South Dakota	7,435	0.4%
20	Tennessee	25,228	1.4%
3	Texas	132,617	7.1%
19	Utah	26,544	1.4%
48	Vermont	4,756	0.3%
2	Virginia	144,777	7.8%
9	Washington	53,002	2.8%
29	West Virginia	18,464	1.0%
34	Wisconsin	14,110	0.8%
47	Wyoming	4,853	0.3%

RANK ORDER

RANK	STATE	EMPLOYEES	% of USA
1	California	152,534	8.2%
2	Virginia	144,777	7.8%
3	Texas	132,617	7.1%
4	Maryland	120,828	6.5%
5	Florida	88,764	4.8%
6	Georgia	71,622	3.8%
7	Pennsylvania	62,410	3.3%
8	New York	61,383	3.3%
9	Washington	53,002	2.8%
10	Ohio	49,214	2.6%
11	Illinois	45,040	2.4%
12	North Carolina	42,333	2.3%
13	Alabama	37,717	2.0%
14	Arizona	37,458	2.0%
15	Oklahoma	37,431	2.0%
16	Colorado	36,917	2.0%
17	Missouri	33,504	1.8%
18	Michigan	27,456	1.5%
19	Utah	26,544	1.4%
20	Tennessee	25,228	1.4%
21	Massachusetts	25,044	1.3%
22	New Jersey	24,776	1.3%
23	Hawaii	23,173	1.2%
24	Kentucky	22,407	1.2%
25	Indiana	22,235	1.2%
26	New Mexico	21,925	1.2%
27	South Carolina	20,725	1.1%
28	Louisiana	19,161	1.0%
29	West Virginia	18,464	1.0%
30	Mississippi	17,399	0.9%
31	Oregon	17,305	0.9%
32	Minnesota	16,493	0.9%
33	Kansas	15,559	0.8%
34	Wisconsin	14,110	0.8%
35	Arkansas	12,662	0.7%
36	Nevada	11,947	0.6%
37	Maine	11,109	0.6%
38	Alaska	10,410	0.6%
39	Nebraska	10,272	0.5%
40	Montana	8,545	0.5%
41	Connecticut	7,972	0.4%
42	Iowa	7,944	0.4%
43	South Dakota	7,435	0.4%
44	Idaho	7,421	0.4%
45	Rhode Island	6,749	0.4%
46	North Dakota	5,499	0.3%
47	Wyoming	4,853	0.3%
48	Vermont	4,756	0.3%
49	New Hampshire	4,391	0.2%
50	Delaware	2,934	0.2%
	District of Columbia	142,218	7.6%

Source: U.S. Office of Personnel Management
"Common Characteristics of the Government" (http://www.opm.gov/feddata/)
*Non-seasonal, full-time, permanent employees as of September. Head count based on place of employment. There were an estimated 2,097,038 federal civilian employees including seasonal and non permanent employees. Total includes 35,355 employees either outside the U.S. or unspecified. Excludes Central Intelligence Agency, Defense Intelligence Agency, and National Security Agency.

Rate of Federal Civilian Employees in 2016

National Rate = 57 Employees per 10,000 Population*

ALPHA ORDER

RANK	STATE	RATE
13	Alabama	78
4	Alaska	140
22	Arizona	54
30	Arkansas	42
37	California	39
18	Colorado	67
50	Connecticut	22
43	Delaware	31
29	Florida	43
17	Georgia	69
3	Hawaii	162
28	Idaho	44
40	Illinois	35
41	Indiana	34
48	Iowa	25
22	Kansas	54
25	Kentucky	51
35	Louisiana	41
10	Maine	84
1	Maryland	201
39	Massachusetts	37
46	Michigan	28
45	Minnesota	30
20	Mississippi	58
21	Missouri	55
12	Montana	82
22	Nebraska	54
35	Nevada	41
42	New Hampshire	33
46	New Jersey	28
5	New Mexico	105
43	New York	31
30	North Carolina	42
15	North Dakota	73
30	Ohio	42
7	Oklahoma	95
30	Oregon	42
26	Pennsylvania	49
19	Rhode Island	64
30	South Carolina	42
9	South Dakota	86
38	Tennessee	38
27	Texas	48
8	Utah	87
14	Vermont	76
2	Virginia	172
15	Washington	73
6	West Virginia	101
49	Wisconsin	24
11	Wyoming	83

RANK ORDER

RANK	STATE	RATE
1	Maryland	201
2	Virginia	172
3	Hawaii	162
4	Alaska	140
5	New Mexico	105
6	West Virginia	101
7	Oklahoma	95
8	Utah	87
9	South Dakota	86
10	Maine	84
11	Wyoming	83
12	Montana	82
13	Alabama	78
14	Vermont	76
15	North Dakota	73
15	Washington	73
17	Georgia	69
18	Colorado	67
19	Rhode Island	64
20	Mississippi	58
21	Missouri	55
22	Arizona	54
22	Kansas	54
22	Nebraska	54
25	Kentucky	51
26	Pennsylvania	49
27	Texas	48
28	Idaho	44
29	Florida	43
30	Arkansas	42
30	North Carolina	42
30	Ohio	42
30	Oregon	42
30	South Carolina	42
35	Louisiana	41
35	Nevada	41
37	California	39
38	Tennessee	38
39	Massachusetts	37
40	Illinois	35
41	Indiana	34
42	New Hampshire	33
43	Delaware	31
43	New York	31
45	Minnesota	30
46	Michigan	28
46	New Jersey	28
48	Iowa	25
49	Wisconsin	24
50	Connecticut	22

District of Columbia   2,078

Source: CQ Press using data from U.S. Office of Personnel Management
"Common Characteristics of the Government" (http://www.opm.gov/feddata/)
*Non-seasonal, full-time, permanent employees as of September. Head count based on place of employment. There were an estimated 2,097,038 federal civilian employees including seasonal and non permanent employees. National rate excludes employees either outside the U.S. or unspecified. Excludes Central Intelligence Agency, Defense Intelligence Agency, and National Security Agency.

X. Government Finances: State and Local

(Continued)

(Continued)

State and Local Government Total Revenue in 2015

National Total = $3,418,803,448,000*

ALPHA ORDER

RANK	STATE	REVENUE	% of USA
27	Alabama	$42,032,097,000	1.2%
45	Alaska	11,469,386,000	0.3%
21	Arizona	56,076,635,000	1.6%
34	Arkansas	26,847,632,000	0.8%
1	California	510,788,639,000	14.9%
18	Colorado	58,812,977,000	1.7%
26	Connecticut	43,064,501,000	1.3%
47	Delaware	10,307,082,000	0.3%
4	Florida	166,537,857,000	4.9%
13	Georgia	78,835,025,000	2.3%
39	Hawaii	16,817,069,000	0.5%
40	Idaho	12,907,955,000	0.4%
5	Illinois	136,793,053,000	4.0%
19	Indiana	57,629,439,000	1.7%
29	Iowa	34,855,616,000	1.0%
32	Kansas	27,717,356,000	0.8%
28	Kentucky	40,194,753,000	1.2%
25	Louisiana	43,320,991,000	1.3%
41	Maine	12,453,344,000	0.4%
16	Maryland	64,933,970,000	1.9%
11	Massachusetts	84,176,972,000	2.5%
9	Michigan	95,518,460,000	2.8%
15	Minnesota	66,206,652,000	1.9%
31	Mississippi	29,287,105,000	0.9%
22	Missouri	53,232,929,000	1.6%
48	Montana	10,033,775,000	0.3%
37	Nebraska	23,101,535,000	0.7%
35	Nevada	25,432,620,000	0.7%
43	New Hampshire	12,267,126,000	0.4%
8	New Jersey	105,737,607,000	3.1%
36	New Mexico	24,166,084,000	0.7%
2	New York	338,419,732,000	9.9%
10	North Carolina	88,736,272,000	2.6%
42	North Dakota	12,361,163,000	0.4%
7	Ohio	123,716,578,000	3.6%
30	Oklahoma	34,848,767,000	1.0%
23	Oregon	48,779,267,000	1.4%
6	Pennsylvania	132,104,450,000	3.9%
44	Rhode Island	11,739,473,000	0.3%
24	South Carolina	45,731,049,000	1.3%
49	South Dakota	7,630,002,000	0.2%
20	Tennessee	56,562,407,000	1.7%
3	Texas	238,487,074,000	7.0%
33	Utah	27,444,001,000	0.8%
50	Vermont	7,541,188,000	0.2%
14	Virginia	78,233,157,000	2.3%
12	Washington	82,373,541,000	2.4%
38	West Virginia	17,946,648,000	0.5%
17	Wisconsin	59,092,939,000	1.7%
46	Wyoming	10,456,716,000	0.3%

RANK ORDER

RANK	STATE	REVENUE	% of USA
1	California	$510,788,639,000	14.9%
2	New York	338,419,732,000	9.9%
3	Texas	238,487,074,000	7.0%
4	Florida	166,537,857,000	4.9%
5	Illinois	136,793,053,000	4.0%
6	Pennsylvania	132,104,450,000	3.9%
7	Ohio	123,716,578,000	3.6%
8	New Jersey	105,737,607,000	3.1%
9	Michigan	95,518,460,000	2.8%
10	North Carolina	88,736,272,000	2.6%
11	Massachusetts	84,176,972,000	2.5%
12	Washington	82,373,541,000	2.4%
13	Georgia	78,835,025,000	2.3%
14	Virginia	78,233,157,000	2.3%
15	Minnesota	66,206,652,000	1.9%
16	Maryland	64,933,970,000	1.9%
17	Wisconsin	59,092,939,000	1.7%
18	Colorado	58,812,977,000	1.7%
19	Indiana	57,629,439,000	1.7%
20	Tennessee	56,562,407,000	1.7%
21	Arizona	56,076,635,000	1.6%
22	Missouri	53,232,929,000	1.6%
23	Oregon	48,779,267,000	1.4%
24	South Carolina	45,731,049,000	1.3%
25	Louisiana	43,320,991,000	1.3%
26	Connecticut	43,064,501,000	1.3%
27	Alabama	42,032,097,000	1.2%
28	Kentucky	40,194,753,000	1.2%
29	Iowa	34,855,616,000	1.0%
30	Oklahoma	34,848,767,000	1.0%
31	Mississippi	29,287,105,000	0.9%
32	Kansas	27,717,356,000	0.8%
33	Utah	27,444,001,000	0.8%
34	Arkansas	26,847,632,000	0.8%
35	Nevada	25,432,620,000	0.7%
36	New Mexico	24,166,084,000	0.7%
37	Nebraska	23,101,535,000	0.7%
38	West Virginia	17,946,648,000	0.5%
39	Hawaii	16,817,069,000	0.5%
40	Idaho	12,907,955,000	0.4%
41	Maine	12,453,344,000	0.4%
42	North Dakota	12,361,163,000	0.4%
43	New Hampshire	12,267,126,000	0.4%
44	Rhode Island	11,739,473,000	0.3%
45	Alaska	11,469,386,000	0.3%
46	Wyoming	10,456,716,000	0.3%
47	Delaware	10,307,082,000	0.3%
48	Montana	10,033,775,000	0.3%
49	South Dakota	7,630,002,000	0.2%
50	Vermont	7,541,188,000	0.2%
	District of Columbia	15,042,782,000	0.4%

Source: U.S. Bureau of the Census, Governments Division
"2015 State and Local Government Finances" (http://www.census.gov/govs/local/)
*Total revenue includes all money received from external sources. This includes taxes, intergovernmental transfers and insurance trust revenue, and revenue from government owned utilities and other commercial or auxiliary enterprise.

Per Capita State and Local Government Revenue in 2015

National Per Capita = $10,649*

ALPHA ORDER

RANK	STATE	PER CAPITA
45	Alabama	$8,665
4	Alaska	15,542
47	Arizona	8,244
37	Arkansas	9,023
5	California	13,086
20	Colorado	10,810
11	Connecticut	11,983
18	Delaware	10,917
48	Florida	8,217
50	Georgia	7,729
13	Hawaii	11,791
49	Idaho	7,826
22	Illinois	10,635
43	Indiana	8,718
16	Iowa	11,177
29	Kansas	9,539
36	Kentucky	9,090
33	Louisiana	9,274
30	Maine	9,379
19	Maryland	10,821
6	Massachusetts	12,390
28	Michigan	9,631
10	Minnesota	12,074
25	Mississippi	9,810
42	Missouri	8,766
26	Montana	9,757
7	Nebraska	12,200
41	Nevada	8,821
34	New Hampshire	9,222
12	New Jersey	11,801
14	New Mexico	11,606
2	New York	17,075
40	North Carolina	8,837
3	North Dakota	16,375
21	Ohio	10,660
39	Oklahoma	8,926
8	Oregon	12,145
23	Pennsylvania	10,328
17	Rhode Island	11,118
32	South Carolina	9,347
38	South Dakota	8,934
46	Tennessee	8,582
44	Texas	8,687
35	Utah	9,194
9	Vermont	12,076
31	Virginia	9,350
15	Washington	11,516
27	West Virginia	9,755
24	Wisconsin	10,260
1	Wyoming	17,841

RANK ORDER

RANK	STATE	PER CAPITA
1	Wyoming	$17,841
2	New York	17,075
3	North Dakota	16,375
4	Alaska	15,542
5	California	13,086
6	Massachusetts	12,390
7	Nebraska	12,200
8	Oregon	12,145
9	Vermont	12,076
10	Minnesota	12,074
11	Connecticut	11,983
12	New Jersey	11,801
13	Hawaii	11,791
14	New Mexico	11,606
15	Washington	11,516
16	Iowa	11,177
17	Rhode Island	11,118
18	Delaware	10,917
19	Maryland	10,821
20	Colorado	10,810
21	Ohio	10,660
22	Illinois	10,635
23	Pennsylvania	10,328
24	Wisconsin	10,260
25	Mississippi	9,810
26	Montana	9,757
27	West Virginia	9,755
28	Michigan	9,631
29	Kansas	9,539
30	Maine	9,379
31	Virginia	9,350
32	South Carolina	9,347
33	Louisiana	9,274
34	New Hampshire	9,222
35	Utah	9,194
36	Kentucky	9,090
37	Arkansas	9,023
38	South Dakota	8,934
39	Oklahoma	8,926
40	North Carolina	8,837
41	Nevada	8,821
42	Missouri	8,766
43	Indiana	8,718
44	Texas	8,687
45	Alabama	8,665
46	Tennessee	8,582
47	Arizona	8,244
48	Florida	8,217
49	Idaho	7,826
50	Georgia	7,729

District of Columbia   22,361

Source: CQ Press using data from U.S. Bureau of the Census, Governments Division
"2015 State and Local Government Finances" (http://www.census.gov/govs/local/)
*Total revenue includes all money received from external sources. This includes taxes, intergovernmental transfers and insurance trust revenue, and revenue from government owned utilities and other commercial or auxiliary enterprise.

State and Local Government Revenue from the Federal Government in 2015

National Total = $657,676,745,000

ALPHA ORDER

RANK	STATE	REVENUE	% of USA
25	Alabama	$9,558,956,000	1.5%
40	Alaska	2,932,543,000	0.4%
14	Arizona	13,337,326,000	2.0%
31	Arkansas	7,256,732,000	1.1%
1	California	93,347,567,000	14.2%
26	Colorado	8,992,172,000	1.4%
30	Connecticut	7,452,018,000	1.1%
48	Delaware	1,970,667,000	0.3%
4	Florida	29,906,622,000	4.5%
12	Georgia	14,695,785,000	2.2%
39	Hawaii	3,041,158,000	0.5%
42	Idaho	2,709,174,000	0.4%
7	Illinois	22,489,644,000	3.4%
16	Indiana	11,971,213,000	1.8%
33	Iowa	7,023,091,000	1.1%
37	Kansas	4,151,882,000	0.6%
22	Kentucky	11,046,254,000	1.7%
23	Louisiana	10,756,569,000	1.6%
41	Maine	2,884,819,000	0.4%
15	Maryland	13,214,056,000	2.0%
11	Massachusetts	15,896,691,000	2.4%
8	Michigan	22,033,858,000	3.4%
17	Minnesota	11,889,051,000	1.8%
28	Mississippi	8,180,255,000	1.2%
21	Missouri	11,232,016,000	1.7%
43	Montana	2,678,414,000	0.4%
38	Nebraska	3,347,552,000	0.5%
36	Nevada	4,533,415,000	0.7%
47	New Hampshire	2,139,529,000	0.3%
9	New Jersey	18,387,432,000	2.8%
32	New Mexico	7,189,320,000	1.1%
2	New York	58,385,148,000	8.9%
10	North Carolina	18,198,301,000	2.8%
49	North Dakota	1,877,794,000	0.3%
5	Ohio	25,513,768,000	3.9%
29	Oklahoma	7,467,081,000	1.1%
18	Oregon	11,879,291,000	1.8%
6	Pennsylvania	25,230,423,000	3.8%
44	Rhode Island	2,565,046,000	0.4%
27	South Carolina	8,328,564,000	1.3%
50	South Dakota	1,665,269,000	0.3%
20	Tennessee	11,234,333,000	1.7%
3	Texas	45,420,520,000	6.9%
35	Utah	4,671,786,000	0.7%
45	Vermont	2,171,971,000	0.3%
19	Virginia	11,323,409,000	1.7%
13	Washington	14,582,935,000	2.2%
34	West Virginia	4,771,416,000	0.7%
24	Wisconsin	9,780,755,000	1.5%
46	Wyoming	2,155,501,000	0.3%

RANK ORDER

RANK	STATE	REVENUE	% of USA
1	California	$93,347,567,000	14.2%
2	New York	58,385,148,000	8.9%
3	Texas	45,420,520,000	6.9%
4	Florida	29,906,622,000	4.5%
5	Ohio	25,513,768,000	3.9%
6	Pennsylvania	25,230,423,000	3.8%
7	Illinois	22,489,644,000	3.4%
8	Michigan	22,033,858,000	3.4%
9	New Jersey	18,387,432,000	2.8%
10	North Carolina	18,198,301,000	2.8%
11	Massachusetts	15,896,691,000	2.4%
12	Georgia	14,695,785,000	2.2%
13	Washington	14,582,935,000	2.2%
14	Arizona	13,337,326,000	2.0%
15	Maryland	13,214,056,000	2.0%
16	Indiana	11,971,213,000	1.8%
17	Minnesota	11,889,051,000	1.8%
18	Oregon	11,879,291,000	1.8%
19	Virginia	11,323,409,000	1.7%
20	Tennessee	11,234,333,000	1.7%
21	Missouri	11,232,016,000	1.7%
22	Kentucky	11,046,254,000	1.7%
23	Louisiana	10,756,569,000	1.6%
24	Wisconsin	9,780,755,000	1.5%
25	Alabama	9,558,956,000	1.5%
26	Colorado	8,992,172,000	1.4%
27	South Carolina	8,328,564,000	1.3%
28	Mississippi	8,180,255,000	1.2%
29	Oklahoma	7,467,081,000	1.1%
30	Connecticut	7,452,018,000	1.1%
31	Arkansas	7,256,732,000	1.1%
32	New Mexico	7,189,320,000	1.1%
33	Iowa	7,023,091,000	1.1%
34	West Virginia	4,771,416,000	0.7%
35	Utah	4,671,786,000	0.7%
36	Nevada	4,533,415,000	0.7%
37	Kansas	4,151,882,000	0.6%
38	Nebraska	3,347,552,000	0.5%
39	Hawaii	3,041,158,000	0.5%
40	Alaska	2,932,543,000	0.4%
41	Maine	2,884,819,000	0.4%
42	Idaho	2,709,174,000	0.4%
43	Montana	2,678,414,000	0.4%
44	Rhode Island	2,565,046,000	0.4%
45	Vermont	2,171,971,000	0.3%
46	Wyoming	2,155,501,000	0.3%
47	New Hampshire	2,139,529,000	0.3%
48	Delaware	1,970,667,000	0.3%
49	North Dakota	1,877,794,000	0.3%
50	South Dakota	1,665,269,000	0.3%
	District of Columbia	4,207,653,000	0.6%

Source: U.S. Bureau of the Census, Governments Division
"2015 State and Local Government Finances" (http://www.census.gov/govs/local/)

Per Capita State and Local Government Revenue from the Federal Government in 2015
National Per Capita = $2,049

RANK	STATE	PER CAPITA
29	Alabama	$1,971
1	Alaska	3,974
30	Arizona	1,961
12	Arkansas	2,439
14	California	2,392
42	Colorado	1,653
25	Connecticut	2,074
24	Delaware	2,087
47	Florida	1,476
48	Georgia	1,441
23	Hawaii	2,132
43	Idaho	1,643
37	Illinois	1,749
35	Indiana	1,811
17	Iowa	2,252
49	Kansas	1,429
10	Kentucky	2,498
16	Louisiana	2,303
21	Maine	2,173
19	Maryland	2,202
15	Massachusetts	2,340
18	Michigan	2,222
22	Minnesota	2,168
7	Mississippi	2,740
33	Missouri	1,850
8	Montana	2,605
36	Nebraska	1,768
45	Nevada	1,572
44	New Hampshire	1,609
26	New Jersey	2,052
4	New Mexico	3,453
6	New York	2,946
34	North Carolina	1,812
11	North Dakota	2,488
20	Ohio	2,198
32	Oklahoma	1,913
5	Oregon	2,958
28	Pennsylvania	1,972
13	Rhode Island	2,429
39	South Carolina	1,702
31	South Dakota	1,950
38	Tennessee	1,705
41	Texas	1,654
46	Utah	1,565
3	Vermont	3,478
50	Virginia	1,353
27	Washington	2,039
9	West Virginia	2,593
40	Wisconsin	1,698
2	Wyoming	3,678

RANK	STATE	PER CAPITA
1	Alaska	$3,974
2	Wyoming	3,678
3	Vermont	3,478
4	New Mexico	3,453
5	Oregon	2,958
6	New York	2,946
7	Mississippi	2,740
8	Montana	2,605
9	West Virginia	2,593
10	Kentucky	2,498
11	North Dakota	2,488
12	Arkansas	2,439
13	Rhode Island	2,429
14	California	2,392
15	Massachusetts	2,340
16	Louisiana	2,303
17	Iowa	2,252
18	Michigan	2,222
19	Maryland	2,202
20	Ohio	2,198
21	Maine	2,173
22	Minnesota	2,168
23	Hawaii	2,132
24	Delaware	2,087
25	Connecticut	2,074
26	New Jersey	2,052
27	Washington	2,039
28	Pennsylvania	1,972
29	Alabama	1,971
30	Arizona	1,961
31	South Dakota	1,950
32	Oklahoma	1,913
33	Missouri	1,850
34	North Carolina	1,812
35	Indiana	1,811
36	Nebraska	1,768
37	Illinois	1,749
38	Tennessee	1,705
39	South Carolina	1,702
40	Wisconsin	1,698
41	Texas	1,654
42	Colorado	1,653
43	Idaho	1,643
44	New Hampshire	1,609
45	Nevada	1,572
46	Utah	1,565
47	Florida	1,476
48	Georgia	1,441
49	Kansas	1,429
50	Virginia	1,353

District of Columbia   6,255

Source: CQ Press using data from U.S. Bureau of the Census, Governments Division
"2015 State and Local Government Finances" (http://www.census.gov/govs/local/)

Percent of State and Local Government Revenue
from the Federal Government in 2015
National Percent = 19.2%*

ALPHA ORDER

RANK	STATE	PERCENT
14	Alabama	22.7
8	Alaska	25.6
11	Arizona	23.8
5	Arkansas	27.0
32	California	18.3
46	Colorado	15.3
41	Connecticut	17.3
27	Delaware	19.1
35	Florida	18.0
31	Georgia	18.6
34	Hawaii	18.1
19	Idaho	21.0
45	Illinois	16.4
20	Indiana	20.8
25	Iowa	20.1
48	Kansas	15.0
4	Kentucky	27.5
9	Louisiana	24.8
12	Maine	23.2
24	Maryland	20.3
30	Massachusetts	18.9
13	Michigan	23.1
35	Minnesota	18.0
3	Mississippi	27.9
18	Missouri	21.1
6	Montana	26.7
49	Nebraska	14.5
37	Nevada	17.8
39	New Hampshire	17.4
39	New Jersey	17.4
1	New Mexico	29.7
41	New York	17.3
23	North Carolina	20.5
47	North Dakota	15.2
21	Ohio	20.6
17	Oklahoma	21.4
10	Oregon	24.4
27	Pennsylvania	19.1
15	Rhode Island	21.8
33	South Carolina	18.2
15	South Dakota	21.8
26	Tennessee	19.9
29	Texas	19.0
43	Utah	17.0
2	Vermont	28.8
49	Virginia	14.5
38	Washington	17.7
7	West Virginia	26.6
44	Wisconsin	16.6
21	Wyoming	20.6

RANK ORDER

RANK	STATE	PERCENT
1	New Mexico	29.7
2	Vermont	28.8
3	Mississippi	27.9
4	Kentucky	27.5
5	Arkansas	27.0
6	Montana	26.7
7	West Virginia	26.6
8	Alaska	25.6
9	Louisiana	24.8
10	Oregon	24.4
11	Arizona	23.8
12	Maine	23.2
13	Michigan	23.1
14	Alabama	22.7
15	Rhode Island	21.8
15	South Dakota	21.8
17	Oklahoma	21.4
18	Missouri	21.1
19	Idaho	21.0
20	Indiana	20.8
21	Ohio	20.6
21	Wyoming	20.6
23	North Carolina	20.5
24	Maryland	20.3
25	Iowa	20.1
26	Tennessee	19.9
27	Delaware	19.1
27	Pennsylvania	19.1
29	Texas	19.0
30	Massachusetts	18.9
31	Georgia	18.6
32	California	18.3
33	South Carolina	18.2
34	Hawaii	18.1
35	Florida	18.0
35	Minnesota	18.0
37	Nevada	17.8
38	Washington	17.7
39	New Hampshire	17.4
39	New Jersey	17.4
41	Connecticut	17.3
41	New York	17.3
43	Utah	17.0
44	Wisconsin	16.6
45	Illinois	16.4
46	Colorado	15.3
47	North Dakota	15.2
48	Kansas	15.0
49	Nebraska	14.5
49	Virginia	14.5

District of Columbia — 28.0

Source: CQ Press using data from U.S. Bureau of the Census, Governments Division
"2015 State and Local Government Finances" (http://www.census.gov/govs/local/)
*As a percent of total revenue.

State and Local Government Own Source Revenue in 2015

National Total = $2,262,447,997,000*

ALPHA ORDER

RANK	STATE	REVENUE	% of USA
26	Alabama	$27,139,157,000	1.2%
45	Alaska	7,404,982,000	0.3%
20	Arizona	33,260,878,000	1.5%
35	Arkansas	16,373,183,000	0.7%
1	California	325,667,559,000	14.4%
17	Colorado	40,777,190,000	1.8%
23	Connecticut	31,789,031,000	1.4%
46	Delaware	7,192,928,000	0.3%
4	Florida	114,046,343,000	5.0%
13	Georgia	52,505,519,000	2.3%
38	Hawaii	12,106,506,000	0.5%
42	Idaho	8,548,657,000	0.4%
5	Illinois	94,660,162,000	4.2%
18	Indiana	39,795,804,000	1.8%
29	Iowa	23,528,766,000	1.0%
31	Kansas	20,265,894,000	0.9%
28	Kentucky	24,113,479,000	1.1%
27	Louisiana	27,109,795,000	1.2%
41	Maine	8,654,763,000	0.4%
15	Maryland	46,099,981,000	2.0%
12	Massachusetts	56,735,729,000	2.5%
9	Michigan	61,905,733,000	2.7%
16	Minnesota	44,714,721,000	2.0%
33	Mississippi	17,555,948,000	0.8%
21	Missouri	33,218,807,000	1.5%
48	Montana	6,022,679,000	0.3%
37	Nebraska	13,826,992,000	0.6%
34	Nevada	16,376,514,000	0.7%
43	New Hampshire	8,521,615,000	0.4%
7	New Jersey	77,214,285,000	3.4%
36	New Mexico	14,356,415,000	0.6%
2	New York	227,925,197,000	10.1%
10	North Carolina	59,702,566,000	2.6%
40	North Dakota	9,199,370,000	0.4%
8	Ohio	75,391,157,000	3.3%
30	Oklahoma	22,742,137,000	1.0%
25	Oregon	28,417,216,000	1.3%
6	Pennsylvania	88,932,592,000	3.9%
44	Rhode Island	7,976,226,000	0.4%
24	South Carolina	30,780,375,000	1.4%
49	South Dakota	4,896,753,000	0.2%
22	Tennessee	32,787,056,000	1.4%
3	Texas	164,321,848,000	7.3%
32	Utah	17,760,236,000	0.8%
50	Vermont	4,824,809,000	0.2%
11	Virginia	57,261,877,000	2.5%
14	Washington	52,157,470,000	2.3%
39	West Virginia	11,635,145,000	0.5%
19	Wisconsin	38,472,110,000	1.7%
47	Wyoming	6,860,025,000	0.3%

RANK ORDER

RANK	STATE	REVENUE	% of USA
1	California	$325,667,559,000	14.4%
2	New York	227,925,197,000	10.1%
3	Texas	164,321,848,000	7.3%
4	Florida	114,046,343,000	5.0%
5	Illinois	94,660,162,000	4.2%
6	Pennsylvania	88,932,592,000	3.9%
7	New Jersey	77,214,285,000	3.4%
8	Ohio	75,391,157,000	3.3%
9	Michigan	61,905,733,000	2.7%
10	North Carolina	59,702,566,000	2.6%
11	Virginia	57,261,877,000	2.5%
12	Massachusetts	56,735,729,000	2.5%
13	Georgia	52,505,519,000	2.3%
14	Washington	52,157,470,000	2.3%
15	Maryland	46,099,981,000	2.0%
16	Minnesota	44,714,721,000	2.0%
17	Colorado	40,777,190,000	1.8%
18	Indiana	39,795,804,000	1.8%
19	Wisconsin	38,472,110,000	1.7%
20	Arizona	33,260,878,000	1.5%
21	Missouri	33,218,807,000	1.5%
22	Tennessee	32,787,056,000	1.4%
23	Connecticut	31,789,031,000	1.4%
24	South Carolina	30,780,375,000	1.4%
25	Oregon	28,417,216,000	1.3%
26	Alabama	27,139,157,000	1.2%
27	Louisiana	27,109,795,000	1.2%
28	Kentucky	24,113,479,000	1.1%
29	Iowa	23,528,766,000	1.0%
30	Oklahoma	22,742,137,000	1.0%
31	Kansas	20,265,894,000	0.9%
32	Utah	17,760,236,000	0.8%
33	Mississippi	17,555,948,000	0.8%
34	Nevada	16,376,514,000	0.7%
35	Arkansas	16,373,183,000	0.7%
36	New Mexico	14,356,415,000	0.6%
37	Nebraska	13,826,992,000	0.6%
38	Hawaii	12,106,506,000	0.5%
39	West Virginia	11,635,145,000	0.5%
40	North Dakota	9,199,370,000	0.4%
41	Maine	8,654,763,000	0.4%
42	Idaho	8,548,657,000	0.4%
43	New Hampshire	8,521,615,000	0.4%
44	Rhode Island	7,976,226,000	0.4%
45	Alaska	7,404,982,000	0.3%
46	Delaware	7,192,928,000	0.3%
47	Wyoming	6,860,025,000	0.3%
48	Montana	6,022,679,000	0.3%
49	South Dakota	4,896,753,000	0.2%
50	Vermont	4,824,809,000	0.2%
	District of Columbia	8,913,817,000	0.4%

Source: U.S. Bureau of the Census, Governments Division
"2015 State and Local Government Finances" (http://www.census.gov/govs/local/)
*Own source revenue includes taxes, current charges, and miscellaneous general revenue. Excluded are intergovernmental transfers, insurance trust revenue, and revenue from government owned utilities and other commercial or auxiliary enterprise.

Per Capita State and Local Government Own Source Revenue in 2015

National Per Capita = $7,047*

ALPHA ORDER

RANK	STATE	PER CAPITA
43	Alabama	$5,595
4	Alaska	10,034
50	Arizona	4,890
44	Arkansas	5,502
9	California	8,344
16	Colorado	7,495
5	Connecticut	8,845
13	Delaware	7,619
42	Florida	5,627
48	Georgia	5,148
7	Hawaii	8,488
47	Idaho	5,183
17	Illinois	7,360
32	Indiana	6,020
15	Iowa	7,545
21	Kansas	6,974
46	Kentucky	5,453
39	Louisiana	5,804
26	Maine	6,518
12	Maryland	7,683
8	Massachusetts	8,351
31	Michigan	6,242
10	Minnesota	8,155
36	Mississippi	5,881
45	Missouri	5,470
37	Montana	5,857
18	Nebraska	7,302
41	Nevada	5,680
28	New Hampshire	6,407
6	New Jersey	8,618
23	New Mexico	6,895
3	New York	11,500
35	North Carolina	5,945
1	North Dakota	12,187
27	Ohio	6,496
38	Oklahoma	5,825
20	Oregon	7,075
22	Pennsylvania	6,953
14	Rhode Island	7,554
30	South Carolina	6,291
40	South Dakota	5,734
49	Tennessee	4,975
33	Texas	5,985
34	Utah	5,950
11	Vermont	7,726
24	Virginia	6,844
19	Washington	7,292
29	West Virginia	6,324
25	Wisconsin	6,679
2	Wyoming	11,704

RANK ORDER

RANK	STATE	PER CAPITA
1	North Dakota	$12,187
2	Wyoming	11,704
3	New York	11,500
4	Alaska	10,034
5	Connecticut	8,845
6	New Jersey	8,618
7	Hawaii	8,488
8	Massachusetts	8,351
9	California	8,344
10	Minnesota	8,155
11	Vermont	7,726
12	Maryland	7,683
13	Delaware	7,619
14	Rhode Island	7,554
15	Iowa	7,545
16	Colorado	7,495
17	Illinois	7,360
18	Nebraska	7,302
19	Washington	7,292
20	Oregon	7,075
21	Kansas	6,974
22	Pennsylvania	6,953
23	New Mexico	6,895
24	Virginia	6,844
25	Wisconsin	6,679
26	Maine	6,518
27	Ohio	6,496
28	New Hampshire	6,407
29	West Virginia	6,324
30	South Carolina	6,291
31	Michigan	6,242
32	Indiana	6,020
33	Texas	5,985
34	Utah	5,950
35	North Carolina	5,945
36	Mississippi	5,881
37	Montana	5,857
38	Oklahoma	5,825
39	Louisiana	5,804
40	South Dakota	5,734
41	Nevada	5,680
42	Florida	5,627
43	Alabama	5,595
44	Arkansas	5,502
45	Missouri	5,470
46	Kentucky	5,453
47	Idaho	5,183
48	Georgia	5,148
49	Tennessee	4,975
50	Arizona	4,890

District of Columbia   13,250

Source: CQ Press using data from U.S. Bureau of the Census, Governments Division
"2015 State and Local Government Finances" (http://www.census.gov/govs/local/)
*Own source revenue includes taxes, current charges, and miscellaneous general revenue. Excluded are intergovernmental transfers, insurance trust revenue, and revenue from government owned utilities and other commercial or auxiliary enterprise.

State and Local Government Tax Revenue in 2015

National Total = $1,567,019,904,000

ALPHA ORDER

RANK	STATE	REVENUE	% of USA
28	Alabama	$15,262,651,000	1.0%
50	Alaska	2,585,053,000	0.2%
21	Arizona	23,761,491,000	1.5%
33	Arkansas	11,519,786,000	0.7%
1	California	228,664,512,000	14.6%
20	Colorado	25,057,723,000	1.6%
18	Connecticut	26,607,123,000	1.7%
45	Delaware	4,502,253,000	0.3%
5	Florida	69,901,214,000	4.5%
13	Georgia	35,902,719,000	2.3%
37	Hawaii	8,709,528,000	0.6%
44	Idaho	5,680,588,000	0.4%
4	Illinois	73,838,240,000	4.7%
19	Indiana	25,388,748,000	1.6%
29	Iowa	14,858,540,000	0.9%
31	Kansas	12,769,988,000	0.8%
27	Kentucky	16,735,691,000	1.1%
24	Louisiana	18,448,039,000	1.2%
41	Maine	6,787,296,000	0.4%
14	Maryland	35,113,989,000	2.2%
9	Massachusetts	43,071,679,000	2.7%
10	Michigan	39,765,875,000	2.5%
16	Minnesota	32,640,248,000	2.1%
34	Mississippi	10,979,601,000	0.7%
22	Missouri	22,169,258,000	1.4%
46	Montana	4,175,329,000	0.3%
36	Nebraska	9,576,940,000	0.6%
32	Nevada	11,850,297,000	0.8%
42	New Hampshire	6,183,717,000	0.4%
7	New Jersey	59,693,019,000	3.8%
38	New Mexico	8,655,484,000	0.6%
2	New York	172,649,265,000	11.0%
11	North Carolina	38,043,256,000	2.4%
40	North Dakota	6,949,844,000	0.4%
8	Ohio	51,256,816,000	3.3%
30	Oklahoma	14,459,593,000	0.9%
25	Oregon	17,567,570,000	1.1%
6	Pennsylvania	63,366,215,000	4.0%
43	Rhode Island	5,722,972,000	0.4%
26	South Carolina	16,768,878,000	1.1%
49	South Dakota	3,292,526,000	0.2%
23	Tennessee	21,567,563,000	1.4%
3	Texas	113,185,942,000	7.2%
35	Utah	10,850,561,000	0.7%
48	Vermont	3,631,382,000	0.2%
12	Virginia	37,366,321,000	2.4%
15	Washington	34,168,995,000	2.2%
39	West Virginia	7,557,021,000	0.5%
17	Wisconsin	26,901,975,000	1.7%
47	Wyoming	3,747,354,000	0.2%

RANK ORDER

RANK	STATE	REVENUE	% of USA
1	California	$228,664,512,000	14.6%
2	New York	172,649,265,000	11.0%
3	Texas	113,185,942,000	7.2%
4	Illinois	73,838,240,000	4.7%
5	Florida	69,901,214,000	4.5%
6	Pennsylvania	63,366,215,000	4.0%
7	New Jersey	59,693,019,000	3.8%
8	Ohio	51,256,816,000	3.3%
9	Massachusetts	43,071,679,000	2.7%
10	Michigan	39,765,875,000	2.5%
11	North Carolina	38,043,256,000	2.4%
12	Virginia	37,366,321,000	2.4%
13	Georgia	35,902,719,000	2.3%
14	Maryland	35,113,989,000	2.2%
15	Washington	34,168,995,000	2.2%
16	Minnesota	32,640,248,000	2.1%
17	Wisconsin	26,901,975,000	1.7%
18	Connecticut	26,607,123,000	1.7%
19	Indiana	25,388,748,000	1.6%
20	Colorado	25,057,723,000	1.6%
21	Arizona	23,761,491,000	1.5%
22	Missouri	22,169,258,000	1.4%
23	Tennessee	21,567,563,000	1.4%
24	Louisiana	18,448,039,000	1.2%
25	Oregon	17,567,570,000	1.1%
26	South Carolina	16,768,878,000	1.1%
27	Kentucky	16,735,691,000	1.1%
28	Alabama	15,262,651,000	1.0%
29	Iowa	14,858,540,000	0.9%
30	Oklahoma	14,459,593,000	0.9%
31	Kansas	12,769,988,000	0.8%
32	Nevada	11,850,297,000	0.8%
33	Arkansas	11,519,786,000	0.7%
34	Mississippi	10,979,601,000	0.7%
35	Utah	10,850,561,000	0.7%
36	Nebraska	9,576,940,000	0.6%
37	Hawaii	8,709,528,000	0.6%
38	New Mexico	8,655,484,000	0.6%
39	West Virginia	7,557,021,000	0.5%
40	North Dakota	6,949,844,000	0.4%
41	Maine	6,787,296,000	0.4%
42	New Hampshire	6,183,717,000	0.4%
43	Rhode Island	5,722,972,000	0.4%
44	Idaho	5,680,588,000	0.4%
45	Delaware	4,502,253,000	0.3%
46	Montana	4,175,329,000	0.3%
47	Wyoming	3,747,354,000	0.2%
48	Vermont	3,631,382,000	0.2%
49	South Dakota	3,292,526,000	0.2%
50	Alaska	2,585,053,000	0.2%
	District of Columbia	7,109,236,000	0.5%

Source: U.S. Bureau of the Census, Governments Division
   "2015 State and Local Government Finances" (http://www.census.gov/govs/local/)

Per Capita State and Local Government Tax Revenue in 2015

National Per Capita = $4,881

ALPHA ORDER

RANK	STATE	PER CAPITA
50	Alabama	$3,146
44	Alaska	3,503
45	Arizona	3,493
34	Arkansas	3,871
9	California	5,858
22	Colorado	4,606
3	Connecticut	7,403
18	Delaware	4,769
46	Florida	3,449
43	Georgia	3,520
7	Hawaii	6,106
47	Idaho	3,444
12	Illinois	5,741
36	Indiana	3,841
19	Iowa	4,765
25	Kansas	4,395
38	Kentucky	3,785
33	Louisiana	3,949
14	Maine	5,112
10	Maryland	5,852
6	Massachusetts	6,340
32	Michigan	4,009
8	Minnesota	5,953
40	Mississippi	3,678
41	Missouri	3,651
31	Montana	4,060
15	Nebraska	5,058
29	Nevada	4,110
21	New Hampshire	4,649
4	New Jersey	6,662
27	New Mexico	4,157
2	New York	8,711
37	North Carolina	3,789
1	North Dakota	9,207
24	Ohio	4,416
39	Oklahoma	3,703
26	Oregon	4,374
16	Pennsylvania	4,954
13	Rhode Island	5,420
48	South Carolina	3,428
35	South Dakota	3,855
49	Tennessee	3,272
28	Texas	4,123
42	Utah	3,635
11	Vermont	5,815
23	Virginia	4,466
17	Washington	4,777
30	West Virginia	4,108
20	Wisconsin	4,671
5	Wyoming	6,394

RANK ORDER

RANK	STATE	PER CAPITA
1	North Dakota	$9,207
2	New York	8,711
3	Connecticut	7,403
4	New Jersey	6,662
5	Wyoming	6,394
6	Massachusetts	6,340
7	Hawaii	6,106
8	Minnesota	5,953
9	California	5,858
10	Maryland	5,852
11	Vermont	5,815
12	Illinois	5,741
13	Rhode Island	5,420
14	Maine	5,112
15	Nebraska	5,058
16	Pennsylvania	4,954
17	Washington	4,777
18	Delaware	4,769
19	Iowa	4,765
20	Wisconsin	4,671
21	New Hampshire	4,649
22	Colorado	4,606
23	Virginia	4,466
24	Ohio	4,416
25	Kansas	4,395
26	Oregon	4,374
27	New Mexico	4,157
28	Texas	4,123
29	Nevada	4,110
30	West Virginia	4,108
31	Montana	4,060
32	Michigan	4,009
33	Louisiana	3,949
34	Arkansas	3,871
35	South Dakota	3,855
36	Indiana	3,841
37	North Carolina	3,789
38	Kentucky	3,785
39	Oklahoma	3,703
40	Mississippi	3,678
41	Missouri	3,651
42	Utah	3,635
43	Georgia	3,520
44	Alaska	3,503
45	Arizona	3,493
46	Florida	3,449
47	Idaho	3,444
48	South Carolina	3,428
49	Tennessee	3,272
50	Alabama	3,146

District of Columbia   10,568

Source: CQ Press using data from U.S. Bureau of the Census, Governments Division
"2015 State and Local Government Finances" (http://www.census.gov/govs/local/)

Percent of State and Local Government Revenue from Taxes in 2015

National Percent = 45.8%

RANK	STATE	PERCENT
46	Alabama	36.3
50	Alaska	22.5
31	Arizona	42.4
26	Arkansas	42.9
21	California	44.8
28	Colorado	42.6
1	Connecticut	61.8
24	Delaware	43.7
33	Florida	42.0
19	Georgia	45.5
7	Hawaii	51.8
23	Idaho	44.0
6	Illinois	54.0
22	Indiana	44.1
28	Iowa	42.6
18	Kansas	46.1
34	Kentucky	41.6
28	Louisiana	42.6
4	Maine	54.5
5	Maryland	54.1
8	Massachusetts	51.2
34	Michigan	41.6
11	Minnesota	49.3
44	Mississippi	37.5
34	Missouri	41.6
34	Montana	41.6
38	Nebraska	41.5
17	Nevada	46.6
10	New Hampshire	50.4
2	New Jersey	56.5
48	New Mexico	35.8
9	New York	51.0
26	North Carolina	42.9
3	North Dakota	56.2
41	Ohio	41.4
38	Oklahoma	41.5
47	Oregon	36.0
14	Pennsylvania	48.0
12	Rhode Island	48.7
45	South Carolina	36.7
25	South Dakota	43.2
43	Tennessee	38.1
16	Texas	47.5
42	Utah	39.5
13	Vermont	48.2
15	Virginia	47.8
38	Washington	41.5
32	West Virginia	42.1
19	Wisconsin	45.5
48	Wyoming	35.8

RANK	STATE	PERCENT
1	Connecticut	61.8
2	New Jersey	56.5
3	North Dakota	56.2
4	Maine	54.5
5	Maryland	54.1
6	Illinois	54.0
7	Hawaii	51.8
8	Massachusetts	51.2
9	New York	51.0
10	New Hampshire	50.4
11	Minnesota	49.3
12	Rhode Island	48.7
13	Vermont	48.2
14	Pennsylvania	48.0
15	Virginia	47.8
16	Texas	47.5
17	Nevada	46.6
18	Kansas	46.1
19	Georgia	45.5
19	Wisconsin	45.5
21	California	44.8
22	Indiana	44.1
23	Idaho	44.0
24	Delaware	43.7
25	South Dakota	43.2
26	Arkansas	42.9
26	North Carolina	42.9
28	Colorado	42.6
28	Iowa	42.6
28	Louisiana	42.6
31	Arizona	42.4
32	West Virginia	42.1
33	Florida	42.0
34	Kentucky	41.6
34	Michigan	41.6
34	Missouri	41.6
34	Montana	41.6
38	Nebraska	41.5
38	Oklahoma	41.5
38	Washington	41.5
41	Ohio	41.4
42	Utah	39.5
43	Tennessee	38.1
44	Mississippi	37.5
45	South Carolina	36.7
46	Alabama	36.3
47	Oregon	36.0
48	New Mexico	35.8
48	Wyoming	35.8
50	Alaska	22.5

District of Columbia		47.3

Source: CQ Press using data from U.S. Bureau of the Census, Governments Division
"2015 State and Local Government Finances" (http://www.census.gov/govs/local/)

State and Local Government Tax Revenue
as a Percent of Personal Income in 2015
National Percent = 10.1% of Personal Income*

ALPHA ORDER

RANK	STATE	PERCENT
46	Alabama	8.2
50	Alaska	6.2
37	Arizona	8.8
23	Arkansas	9.9
14	California	10.7
36	Colorado	8.9
12	Connecticut	10.9
19	Delaware	10.1
49	Florida	7.6
41	Georgia	8.6
3	Hawaii	12.5
37	Idaho	8.8
8	Illinois	11.3
31	Indiana	9.2
16	Iowa	10.4
29	Kansas	9.3
25	Kentucky	9.8
31	Louisiana	9.2
4	Maine	11.9
16	Maryland	10.4
19	Massachusetts	10.1
29	Michigan	9.3
6	Minnesota	11.6
15	Mississippi	10.6
41	Missouri	8.6
27	Montana	9.5
18	Nebraska	10.2
27	Nevada	9.5
44	New Hampshire	8.5
10	New Jersey	11.1
11	New Mexico	11.0
2	New York	14.9
31	North Carolina	9.2
1	North Dakota	16.5
19	Ohio	10.1
45	Oklahoma	8.4
25	Oregon	9.8
23	Pennsylvania	9.9
12	Rhode Island	10.9
37	South Carolina	8.8
47	South Dakota	8.1
48	Tennessee	7.8
37	Texas	8.8
34	Utah	9.1
4	Vermont	11.9
41	Virginia	8.6
35	Washington	9.0
9	West Virginia	11.2
19	Wisconsin	10.1
7	Wyoming	11.4

RANK ORDER

RANK	STATE	PERCENT
1	North Dakota	16.5
2	New York	14.9
3	Hawaii	12.5
4	Maine	11.9
4	Vermont	11.9
6	Minnesota	11.6
7	Wyoming	11.4
8	Illinois	11.3
9	West Virginia	11.2
10	New Jersey	11.1
11	New Mexico	11.0
12	Connecticut	10.9
12	Rhode Island	10.9
14	California	10.7
15	Mississippi	10.6
16	Iowa	10.4
16	Maryland	10.4
18	Nebraska	10.2
19	Delaware	10.1
19	Massachusetts	10.1
19	Ohio	10.1
19	Wisconsin	10.1
23	Arkansas	9.9
23	Pennsylvania	9.9
25	Kentucky	9.8
25	Oregon	9.8
27	Montana	9.5
27	Nevada	9.5
29	Kansas	9.3
29	Michigan	9.3
31	Indiana	9.2
31	Louisiana	9.2
31	North Carolina	9.2
34	Utah	9.1
35	Washington	9.0
36	Colorado	8.9
37	Arizona	8.8
37	Idaho	8.8
37	South Carolina	8.8
37	Texas	8.8
41	Georgia	8.6
41	Missouri	8.6
41	Virginia	8.6
44	New Hampshire	8.5
45	Oklahoma	8.4
46	Alabama	8.2
47	South Dakota	8.1
48	Tennessee	7.8
49	Florida	7.6
50	Alaska	6.2
	District of Columbia	14.3

Source: CQ Press using data from U.S. Bureau of the Census, Governments Division
"Annual State Personal Income" (http://www.bea.gov/iTable/index_regional.cfm) and
"2015 State and Local Government Finances" (http://www.census.gov/govs/local/)
*The personal income total used for this table is the sum of state estimates. This total differs from the national income and
product accounts (NIPA) estimate of personal income because it omits the earnings of federal civilian and military personnel
stationed abroad and of U.S. residents employed abroad temporarily by private U.S. firms.

State and Local Government General Sales Tax Revenue in 2015

National Total = $368,189,271,000*

ALPHA ORDER

RANK	STATE	REVENUE	% of USA
25	Alabama	$4,558,496,000	1.2%
46	Alaska	231,195,000	0.1%
10	Arizona	9,279,253,000	2.5%
27	Arkansas	4,266,502,000	1.2%
1	California	49,944,511,000	13.6%
17	Colorado	6,592,409,000	1.8%
28	Connecticut	4,082,787,000	1.1%
47	Delaware	0	0.0%
4	Florida	23,888,830,000	6.5%
12	Georgia	9,190,403,000	2.5%
35	Hawaii	3,216,373,000	0.9%
39	Idaho	1,464,881,000	0.4%
7	Illinois	13,057,747,000	3.5%
15	Indiana	7,279,604,000	2.0%
32	Iowa	3,357,874,000	0.9%
30	Kansas	4,020,993,000	1.1%
33	Kentucky	3,267,331,000	0.9%
16	Louisiana	7,103,677,000	1.9%
42	Maine	1,283,420,000	0.3%
26	Maryland	4,409,919,000	1.2%
19	Massachusetts	5,803,934,000	1.6%
11	Michigan	9,211,783,000	2.5%
20	Minnesota	5,634,980,000	1.5%
31	Mississippi	3,422,774,000	0.9%
18	Missouri	5,873,898,000	1.6%
47	Montana	0	0.0%
37	Nebraska	2,160,113,000	0.6%
24	Nevada	4,708,528,000	1.3%
47	New Hampshire	0	0.0%
13	New Jersey	9,146,025,000	2.5%
34	New Mexico	3,239,273,000	0.9%
3	New York	28,833,461,000	7.8%
9	North Carolina	9,456,459,000	2.6%
38	North Dakota	1,611,320,000	0.4%
6	Ohio	14,160,592,000	3.8%
23	Oklahoma	4,774,924,000	1.3%
47	Oregon	0	0.0%
8	Pennsylvania	10,723,197,000	2.9%
44	Rhode Island	959,513,000	0.3%
29	South Carolina	4,037,109,000	1.1%
40	South Dakota	1,333,628,000	0.4%
14	Tennessee	8,775,743,000	2.4%
2	Texas	41,067,648,000	11.2%
36	Utah	2,636,633,000	0.7%
45	Vermont	378,654,000	0.1%
22	Virginia	5,104,162,000	1.4%
5	Washington	15,680,951,000	4.3%
41	West Virginia	1,309,244,000	0.4%
21	Wisconsin	5,283,074,000	1.4%
43	Wyoming	1,049,521,000	0.3%

RANK ORDER

RANK	STATE	REVENUE	% of USA
1	California	$49,944,511,000	13.6%
2	Texas	41,067,648,000	11.2%
3	New York	28,833,461,000	7.8%
4	Florida	23,888,830,000	6.5%
5	Washington	15,680,951,000	4.3%
6	Ohio	14,160,592,000	3.8%
7	Illinois	13,057,747,000	3.5%
8	Pennsylvania	10,723,197,000	2.9%
9	North Carolina	9,456,459,000	2.6%
10	Arizona	9,279,253,000	2.5%
11	Michigan	9,211,783,000	2.5%
12	Georgia	9,190,403,000	2.5%
13	New Jersey	9,146,025,000	2.5%
14	Tennessee	8,775,743,000	2.4%
15	Indiana	7,279,604,000	2.0%
16	Louisiana	7,103,677,000	1.9%
17	Colorado	6,592,409,000	1.8%
18	Missouri	5,873,898,000	1.6%
19	Massachusetts	5,803,934,000	1.6%
20	Minnesota	5,634,980,000	1.5%
21	Wisconsin	5,283,074,000	1.4%
22	Virginia	5,104,162,000	1.4%
23	Oklahoma	4,774,924,000	1.3%
24	Nevada	4,708,528,000	1.3%
25	Alabama	4,558,496,000	1.2%
26	Maryland	4,409,919,000	1.2%
27	Arkansas	4,266,502,000	1.2%
28	Connecticut	4,082,787,000	1.1%
29	South Carolina	4,037,109,000	1.1%
30	Kansas	4,020,993,000	1.1%
31	Mississippi	3,422,774,000	0.9%
32	Iowa	3,357,874,000	0.9%
33	Kentucky	3,267,331,000	0.9%
34	New Mexico	3,239,273,000	0.9%
35	Hawaii	3,216,373,000	0.9%
36	Utah	2,636,633,000	0.7%
37	Nebraska	2,160,113,000	0.6%
38	North Dakota	1,611,320,000	0.4%
39	Idaho	1,464,881,000	0.4%
40	South Dakota	1,333,628,000	0.4%
41	West Virginia	1,309,244,000	0.4%
42	Maine	1,283,420,000	0.3%
43	Wyoming	1,049,521,000	0.3%
44	Rhode Island	959,513,000	0.3%
45	Vermont	378,654,000	0.1%
46	Alaska	231,195,000	0.1%
47	Delaware	0	0.0%
47	Montana	0	0.0%
47	New Hampshire	0	0.0%
47	Oregon	0	0.0%
	District of Columbia	1,315,925,000	0.4%

Source: U.S. Bureau of the Census, Governments Division
"2015 State and Local Government Finances" (http://www.census.gov/govs/local/)
*Does not include special sales taxes such as those on sale of alcohol, gasoline, or tobacco.

Per Capita State and Local Government General Sales Tax Revenue in 2015

National Per Capita = $1,147*

ALPHA ORDER				RANK ORDER		
RANK	STATE	PER CAPITA		RANK	STATE	PER CAPITA
31	Alabama	$940		1	Hawaii	$2,255
46	Alaska	313		2	Washington	2,192
13	Arizona	1,364		3	North Dakota	2,135
11	Arkansas	1,434		4	Wyoming	1,791
15	California	1,280		5	Nevada	1,633
18	Colorado	1,212		6	South Dakota	1,562
22	Connecticut	1,136		7	New Mexico	1,556
47	Delaware	0		8	Louisiana	1,521
19	Florida	1,179		9	Texas	1,496
35	Georgia	901		10	New York	1,455
1	Hawaii	2,255		11	Arkansas	1,434
36	Idaho	888		12	Kansas	1,384
27	Illinois	1,015		13	Arizona	1,364
23	Indiana	1,101		14	Tennessee	1,332
24	Iowa	1,077		15	California	1,280
12	Kansas	1,384		16	Oklahoma	1,223
41	Kentucky	739		17	Ohio	1,220
8	Louisiana	1,521		18	Colorado	1,212
28	Maine	967		19	Florida	1,179
42	Maryland	735		20	Mississippi	1,147
38	Massachusetts	854		21	Nebraska	1,141
32	Michigan	929		22	Connecticut	1,136
25	Minnesota	1,028		23	Indiana	1,101
20	Mississippi	1,147		24	Iowa	1,077
28	Missouri	967		25	Minnesota	1,028
47	Montana	0		26	New Jersey	1,021
21	Nebraska	1,141		27	Illinois	1,015
5	Nevada	1,633		28	Maine	967
47	New Hampshire	0		28	Missouri	967
26	New Jersey	1,021		30	North Carolina	942
7	New Mexico	1,556		31	Alabama	940
10	New York	1,455		32	Michigan	929
30	North Carolina	942		33	Wisconsin	917
3	North Dakota	2,135		34	Rhode Island	909
17	Ohio	1,220		35	Georgia	901
16	Oklahoma	1,223		36	Idaho	888
47	Oregon	0		37	Utah	883
39	Pennsylvania	838		38	Massachusetts	854
34	Rhode Island	909		39	Pennsylvania	838
40	South Carolina	825		40	South Carolina	825
6	South Dakota	1,562		41	Kentucky	739
14	Tennessee	1,332		42	Maryland	735
9	Texas	1,496		43	West Virginia	712
37	Utah	883		44	Virginia	610
45	Vermont	606		45	Vermont	606
44	Virginia	610		46	Alaska	313
2	Washington	2,192		47	Delaware	0
43	West Virginia	712		47	Montana	0
33	Wisconsin	917		47	New Hampshire	0
4	Wyoming	1,791		47	Oregon	0
					District of Columbia	1,956

Source: CQ Press using data from U.S. Bureau of the Census, Governments Division
"2015 State and Local Government Finances" (http://www.census.gov/govs/local/)
*Does not include special sales taxes such as those on sale of alcohol, gasoline, or tobacco.

State and Local Government General Retail Sales Tax Rates in 2017

National Median = 6.85 Percent*

ALPHA ORDER

RANK	STATE	PERCENT
4	Alabama	9.01
46	Alaska	1.76
10	Arizona	8.25
3	Arkansas	9.30
10	California	8.25
16	Colorado	7.50
32	Connecticut	6.35
47	Delaware	0.00
27	Florida	6.80
21	Georgia	7.00
45	Hawaii	4.35
37	Idaho	6.03
7	Illinois	8.64
21	Indiana	7.00
27	Iowa	6.80
8	Kansas	8.62
38	Kentucky	6.00
1	Louisiana	9.98
42	Maine	5.50
38	Maryland	6.00
35	Massachusetts	6.25
38	Michigan	6.00
17	Minnesota	7.30
20	Mississippi	7.07
14	Missouri	7.89
47	Montana	0.00
25	Nebraska	6.89
13	Nevada	7.98
47	New Hampshire	0.00
26	New Jersey	6.85
15	New Mexico	7.55
9	New York	8.49
24	North Carolina	6.90
29	North Dakota	6.78
19	Ohio	7.14
6	Oklahoma	8.86
47	Oregon	0.00
33	Pennsylvania	6.34
21	Rhode Island	7.00
18	South Carolina	7.22
31	South Dakota	6.39
2	Tennessee	9.46
12	Texas	8.19
30	Utah	6.76
36	Vermont	6.18
41	Virginia	5.63
5	Washington	8.92
34	West Virginia	6.29
43	Wisconsin	5.42
44	Wyoming	5.40

RANK ORDER

RANK	STATE	PERCENT
1	Louisiana	9.98
2	Tennessee	9.46
3	Arkansas	9.30
4	Alabama	9.01
5	Washington	8.92
6	Oklahoma	8.86
7	Illinois	8.64
8	Kansas	8.62
9	New York	8.49
10	Arizona	8.25
10	California	8.25
12	Texas	8.19
13	Nevada	7.98
14	Missouri	7.89
15	New Mexico	7.55
16	Colorado	7.50
17	Minnesota	7.30
18	South Carolina	7.22
19	Ohio	7.14
20	Mississippi	7.07
21	Georgia	7.00
21	Indiana	7.00
21	Rhode Island	7.00
24	North Carolina	6.90
25	Nebraska	6.89
26	New Jersey	6.85
27	Florida	6.80
27	Iowa	6.80
29	North Dakota	6.78
30	Utah	6.76
31	South Dakota	6.39
32	Connecticut	6.35
33	Pennsylvania	6.34
34	West Virginia	6.29
35	Massachusetts	6.25
36	Vermont	6.18
37	Idaho	6.03
38	Kentucky	6.00
38	Maryland	6.00
38	Michigan	6.00
41	Virginia	5.63
42	Maine	5.50
43	Wisconsin	5.42
44	Wyoming	5.40
45	Hawaii	4.35
46	Alaska	1.76
47	Delaware	0.00
47	Montana	0.00
47	New Hampshire	0.00
47	Oregon	0.00
	District of Columbia	5.75

Source: The Tax Foundation
    "State and Local Sales Tax Rates in 2017" (https://taxfoundation.org/state-and-local-sales-tax-rates-in-2017/)
*As of January 1, 2017. There are great differences on what states exempt from sales taxes. These rates are based on average local rates where local governments can set different tax rates.

State and Local Government Property Tax Revenue in 2015

National Total = $488,045,336,000

ALPHA ORDER

RANK	STATE	REVENUE	% of USA
37	Alabama	$2,622,704,000	0.5%
46	Alaska	1,477,921,000	0.3%
20	Arizona	7,076,779,000	1.5%
39	Arkansas	2,080,578,000	0.4%
1	California	56,795,529,000	11.6%
19	Colorado	7,540,549,000	1.5%
13	Connecticut	10,221,482,000	2.1%
50	Delaware	809,046,000	0.2%
6	Florida	24,979,562,000	5.1%
12	Georgia	11,489,725,000	2.4%
45	Hawaii	1,531,270,000	0.3%
42	Idaho	1,595,084,000	0.3%
5	Illinois	26,844,471,000	5.5%
21	Indiana	6,453,335,000	1.3%
26	Iowa	4,902,086,000	1.0%
27	Kansas	4,193,502,000	0.9%
31	Kentucky	3,456,161,000	0.7%
29	Louisiana	4,057,782,000	0.8%
35	Maine	2,731,768,000	0.6%
16	Maryland	9,342,202,000	1.9%
8	Massachusetts	15,343,269,000	3.1%
10	Michigan	13,713,979,000	2.8%
18	Minnesota	8,418,388,000	1.7%
33	Mississippi	2,907,429,000	0.6%
22	Missouri	6,025,519,000	1.2%
44	Montana	1,558,275,000	0.3%
30	Nebraska	3,593,646,000	0.7%
34	Nevada	2,773,062,000	0.6%
28	New Hampshire	4,064,071,000	0.8%
4	New Jersey	27,540,789,000	5.6%
41	New Mexico	1,606,477,000	0.3%
2	New York	53,387,177,000	10.9%
15	North Carolina	9,565,377,000	2.0%
49	North Dakota	924,591,000	0.2%
9	Ohio	14,765,897,000	3.0%
36	Oklahoma	2,652,405,000	0.5%
24	Oregon	5,657,313,000	1.2%
7	Pennsylvania	18,958,870,000	3.9%
38	Rhode Island	2,471,043,000	0.5%
25	South Carolina	5,530,717,000	1.1%
48	South Dakota	1,185,469,000	0.2%
23	Tennessee	5,693,601,000	1.2%
3	Texas	47,559,117,000	9.7%
32	Utah	2,923,895,000	0.6%
43	Vermont	1,591,224,000	0.3%
11	Virginia	12,742,202,000	2.6%
14	Washington	10,100,425,000	2.1%
40	West Virginia	1,637,562,000	0.3%
17	Wisconsin	9,324,786,000	1.9%
47	Wyoming	1,375,501,000	0.3%

RANK ORDER

RANK	STATE	REVENUE	% of USA
1	California	$56,795,529,000	11.6%
2	New York	53,387,177,000	10.9%
3	Texas	47,559,117,000	9.7%
4	New Jersey	27,540,789,000	5.6%
5	Illinois	26,844,471,000	5.5%
6	Florida	24,979,562,000	5.1%
7	Pennsylvania	18,958,870,000	3.9%
8	Massachusetts	15,343,269,000	3.1%
9	Ohio	14,765,897,000	3.0%
10	Michigan	13,713,979,000	2.8%
11	Virginia	12,742,202,000	2.6%
12	Georgia	11,489,725,000	2.4%
13	Connecticut	10,221,482,000	2.1%
14	Washington	10,100,425,000	2.1%
15	North Carolina	9,565,377,000	2.0%
16	Maryland	9,342,202,000	1.9%
17	Wisconsin	9,324,786,000	1.9%
18	Minnesota	8,418,388,000	1.7%
19	Colorado	7,540,549,000	1.5%
20	Arizona	7,076,779,000	1.5%
21	Indiana	6,453,335,000	1.3%
22	Missouri	6,025,519,000	1.2%
23	Tennessee	5,693,601,000	1.2%
24	Oregon	5,657,313,000	1.2%
25	South Carolina	5,530,717,000	1.1%
26	Iowa	4,902,086,000	1.0%
27	Kansas	4,193,502,000	0.9%
28	New Hampshire	4,064,071,000	0.8%
29	Louisiana	4,057,782,000	0.8%
30	Nebraska	3,593,646,000	0.7%
31	Kentucky	3,456,161,000	0.7%
32	Utah	2,923,895,000	0.6%
33	Mississippi	2,907,429,000	0.6%
34	Nevada	2,773,062,000	0.6%
35	Maine	2,731,768,000	0.6%
36	Oklahoma	2,652,405,000	0.5%
37	Alabama	2,622,704,000	0.5%
38	Rhode Island	2,471,043,000	0.5%
39	Arkansas	2,080,578,000	0.4%
40	West Virginia	1,637,562,000	0.3%
41	New Mexico	1,606,477,000	0.3%
42	Idaho	1,595,084,000	0.3%
43	Vermont	1,591,224,000	0.3%
44	Montana	1,558,275,000	0.3%
45	Hawaii	1,531,270,000	0.3%
46	Alaska	1,477,921,000	0.3%
47	Wyoming	1,375,501,000	0.3%
48	South Dakota	1,185,469,000	0.2%
49	North Dakota	924,591,000	0.2%
50	Delaware	809,046,000	0.2%
	District of Columbia	2,251,724,000	0.5%

Source: U.S. Bureau of the Census, Governments Division
"2015 State and Local Government Finances" (http://www.census.gov/govs/local/)

Per Capita State and Local Government Property Tax Revenue in 2015

National Per Capita = $1,520

ALPHA ORDER

RANK	STATE	PER CAPITA
50	Alabama	$541
11	Alaska	2,003
34	Arizona	1,040
48	Arkansas	699
21	California	1,455
26	Colorado	1,386
3	Connecticut	2,844
45	Delaware	857
29	Florida	1,232
32	Georgia	1,126
33	Hawaii	1,074
39	Idaho	967
9	Illinois	2,087
37	Indiana	976
15	Iowa	1,572
22	Kansas	1,443
46	Kentucky	782
43	Louisiana	869
10	Maine	2,057
16	Maryland	1,557
8	Massachusetts	2,258
27	Michigan	1,383
17	Minnesota	1,535
38	Mississippi	974
35	Missouri	992
19	Montana	1,515
12	Nebraska	1,898
40	Nevada	962
2	New Hampshire	3,055
1	New Jersey	3,074
47	New Mexico	772
4	New York	2,694
41	North Carolina	953
30	North Dakota	1,225
28	Ohio	1,272
49	Oklahoma	679
24	Oregon	1,409
20	Pennsylvania	1,482
7	Rhode Island	2,340
31	South Carolina	1,130
25	South Dakota	1,388
44	Tennessee	864
13	Texas	1,732
36	Utah	980
5	Vermont	2,548
18	Virginia	1,523
23	Washington	1,412
42	West Virginia	890
14	Wisconsin	1,619
6	Wyoming	2,347

RANK ORDER

RANK	STATE	PER CAPITA
1	New Jersey	$3,074
2	New Hampshire	3,055
3	Connecticut	2,844
4	New York	2,694
5	Vermont	2,548
6	Wyoming	2,347
7	Rhode Island	2,340
8	Massachusetts	2,258
9	Illinois	2,087
10	Maine	2,057
11	Alaska	2,003
12	Nebraska	1,898
13	Texas	1,732
14	Wisconsin	1,619
15	Iowa	1,572
16	Maryland	1,557
17	Minnesota	1,535
18	Virginia	1,523
19	Montana	1,515
20	Pennsylvania	1,482
21	California	1,455
22	Kansas	1,443
23	Washington	1,412
24	Oregon	1,409
25	South Dakota	1,388
26	Colorado	1,386
27	Michigan	1,383
28	Ohio	1,272
29	Florida	1,232
30	North Dakota	1,225
31	South Carolina	1,130
32	Georgia	1,126
33	Hawaii	1,074
34	Arizona	1,040
35	Missouri	992
36	Utah	980
37	Indiana	976
38	Mississippi	974
39	Idaho	967
40	Nevada	962
41	North Carolina	953
42	West Virginia	890
43	Louisiana	869
44	Tennessee	864
45	Delaware	857
46	Kentucky	782
47	New Mexico	772
48	Arkansas	699
49	Oklahoma	679
50	Alabama	541

District of Columbia   3,347

Source: CQ Press using data from U.S. Bureau of the Census, Governments Division
"2015 State and Local Government Finances" (http://www.census.gov/govs/local/)

State and Local Government Property Tax as a Percent of State and Local Government Total Revenue in 2015
National Percent = 14.3%

ALPHA ORDER

RANK	STATE	PERCENT
50	Alabama	6.2
24	Alaska	12.9
27	Arizona	12.6
46	Arkansas	7.7
35	California	11.1
25	Colorado	12.8
3	Connecticut	23.7
45	Delaware	7.8
17	Florida	15.0
18	Georgia	14.6
42	Hawaii	9.1
28	Idaho	12.4
8	Illinois	19.6
34	Indiana	11.2
22	Iowa	14.1
16	Kansas	15.1
44	Kentucky	8.6
41	Louisiana	9.4
4	Maine	21.9
19	Maryland	14.4
9	Massachusetts	18.2
19	Michigan	14.4
26	Minnesota	12.7
40	Mississippi	9.9
33	Missouri	11.3
14	Montana	15.5
13	Nebraska	15.6
36	Nevada	10.9
1	New Hampshire	33.1
2	New Jersey	26.0
49	New Mexico	6.6
11	New York	15.8
37	North Carolina	10.8
48	North Dakota	7.5
31	Ohio	11.9
47	Oklahoma	7.6
32	Oregon	11.6
19	Pennsylvania	14.4
6	Rhode Island	21.0
30	South Carolina	12.1
14	South Dakota	15.5
39	Tennessee	10.1
7	Texas	19.9
38	Utah	10.7
5	Vermont	21.1
10	Virginia	16.3
29	Washington	12.3
42	West Virginia	9.1
11	Wisconsin	15.8
23	Wyoming	13.2

RANK ORDER

RANK	STATE	PERCENT
1	New Hampshire	33.1
2	New Jersey	26.0
3	Connecticut	23.7
4	Maine	21.9
5	Vermont	21.1
6	Rhode Island	21.0
7	Texas	19.9
8	Illinois	19.6
9	Massachusetts	18.2
10	Virginia	16.3
11	New York	15.8
11	Wisconsin	15.8
13	Nebraska	15.6
14	Montana	15.5
14	South Dakota	15.5
16	Kansas	15.1
17	Florida	15.0
18	Georgia	14.6
19	Maryland	14.4
19	Michigan	14.4
19	Pennsylvania	14.4
22	Iowa	14.1
23	Wyoming	13.2
24	Alaska	12.9
25	Colorado	12.8
26	Minnesota	12.7
27	Arizona	12.6
28	Idaho	12.4
29	Washington	12.3
30	South Carolina	12.1
31	Ohio	11.9
32	Oregon	11.6
33	Missouri	11.3
34	Indiana	11.2
35	California	11.1
36	Nevada	10.9
37	North Carolina	10.8
38	Utah	10.7
39	Tennessee	10.1
40	Mississippi	9.9
41	Louisiana	9.4
42	Hawaii	9.1
42	West Virginia	9.1
44	Kentucky	8.6
45	Delaware	7.8
46	Arkansas	7.7
47	Oklahoma	7.6
48	North Dakota	7.5
49	New Mexico	6.6
50	Alabama	6.2
	District of Columbia	15.0

Source: CQ Press using data from U.S. Bureau of the Census, Governments Division
"2015 State and Local Government Finances" (http://www.census.gov/govs/local/)

State and Local Government Property Tax Revenue as a Percent of State and Local Government Own Source Revenue in 2015
National Percent = 21.6%*

ALPHA ORDER

RANK	STATE	PERCENT
50	Alabama	9.7
25	Alaska	20.0
19	Arizona	21.3
44	Arkansas	12.7
34	California	17.4
31	Colorado	18.5
4	Connecticut	32.2
47	Delaware	11.2
17	Florida	21.9
17	Georgia	21.9
45	Hawaii	12.6
30	Idaho	18.7
8	Illinois	28.4
39	Indiana	16.2
21	Iowa	20.8
22	Kansas	20.7
42	Kentucky	14.3
41	Louisiana	15.0
5	Maine	31.6
23	Maryland	20.3
9	Massachusetts	27.0
16	Michigan	22.2
29	Minnesota	18.8
37	Mississippi	16.6
32	Missouri	18.1
11	Montana	25.9
10	Nebraska	26.0
36	Nevada	16.9
1	New Hampshire	47.7
2	New Jersey	35.7
47	New Mexico	11.2
14	New York	23.4
40	North Carolina	16.0
49	North Dakota	10.1
27	Ohio	19.6
46	Oklahoma	11.7
26	Oregon	19.9
19	Pennsylvania	21.3
6	Rhode Island	31.0
33	South Carolina	18.0
12	South Dakota	24.2
34	Tennessee	17.4
7	Texas	28.9
38	Utah	16.5
3	Vermont	33.0
15	Virginia	22.3
28	Washington	19.4
43	West Virginia	14.1
12	Wisconsin	24.2
24	Wyoming	20.1

RANK ORDER

RANK	STATE	PERCENT
1	New Hampshire	47.7
2	New Jersey	35.7
3	Vermont	33.0
4	Connecticut	32.2
5	Maine	31.6
6	Rhode Island	31.0
7	Texas	28.9
8	Illinois	28.4
9	Massachusetts	27.0
10	Nebraska	26.0
11	Montana	25.9
12	South Dakota	24.2
12	Wisconsin	24.2
14	New York	23.4
15	Virginia	22.3
16	Michigan	22.2
17	Florida	21.9
17	Georgia	21.9
19	Arizona	21.3
19	Pennsylvania	21.3
21	Iowa	20.8
22	Kansas	20.7
23	Maryland	20.3
24	Wyoming	20.1
25	Alaska	20.0
26	Oregon	19.9
27	Ohio	19.6
28	Washington	19.4
29	Minnesota	18.8
30	Idaho	18.7
31	Colorado	18.5
32	Missouri	18.1
33	South Carolina	18.0
34	California	17.4
34	Tennessee	17.4
36	Nevada	16.9
37	Mississippi	16.6
38	Utah	16.5
39	Indiana	16.2
40	North Carolina	16.0
41	Louisiana	15.0
42	Kentucky	14.3
43	West Virginia	14.1
44	Arkansas	12.7
45	Hawaii	12.6
46	Oklahoma	11.7
47	Delaware	11.2
47	New Mexico	11.2
49	North Dakota	10.1
50	Alabama	9.7

District of Columbia	25.3

Source: CQ Press using data from U.S. Bureau of the Census, Governments Division
"2015 State and Local Government Finances" (http://www.census.gov/govs/local/)
*Own source revenue includes taxes, current charges, and miscellaneous general revenue. Excluded are intergovernmental transfers, insurance trust revenue, and revenue from government owned utilities and other commercial or auxiliary enterprise.

State and Local Tax Burden as a Percent of Income in 2015

National Percent = 9.0% of Income*

ALPHA ORDER				RANK ORDER		
RANK	**STATE**	**PERCENT**		**RANK**	**STATE**	**PERCENT**
43	Alabama	7.3		1	New York	13.0
50	Alaska	4.9		2	Hawaii	11.6
31	Arizona	8.2		3	Maine	11.0
18	Arkansas	9.0		4	Vermont	10.9
10	California	9.7		5	Minnesota	10.4
31	Colorado	8.2		6	Connecticut	10.2
6	Connecticut	10.2		7	Rhode Island	10.1
49	Delaware	5.7		8	Illinois	10.0
47	Florida	6.6		8	New Jersey	10.0
37	Georgia	8.0		10	California	9.7
2	Hawaii	11.6		11	Maryland	9.5
38	Idaho	7.9		11	Ohio	9.5
8	Illinois	10.0		13	West Virginia	9.4
25	Indiana	8.5		14	Iowa	9.3
14	Iowa	9.3		14	Mississippi	9.3
24	Kansas	8.6		14	Wisconsin	9.3
21	Kentucky	8.8		17	Nebraska	9.2
27	Louisiana	8.4		18	Arkansas	9.0
3	Maine	11.0		18	Massachusetts	9.0
11	Maryland	9.5		20	New Mexico	8.9
18	Massachusetts	9.0		21	Kentucky	8.8
25	Michigan	8.5		22	North Dakota	8.7
5	Minnesota	10.4		22	Pennsylvania	8.7
14	Mississippi	9.3		24	Kansas	8.6
38	Missouri	7.9		25	Indiana	8.5
41	Montana	7.7		25	Michigan	8.5
17	Nebraska	9.2		27	Louisiana	8.4
31	Nevada	8.2		27	Oregon	8.4
46	New Hampshire	7.0		27	Utah	8.4
8	New Jersey	10.0		30	North Carolina	8.3
20	New Mexico	8.9		31	Arizona	8.2
1	New York	13.0		31	Colorado	8.2
30	North Carolina	8.3		31	Nevada	8.2
22	North Dakota	8.7		31	Texas	8.2
11	Ohio	9.5		31	Washington	8.2
45	Oklahoma	7.1		36	Wyoming	8.1
27	Oregon	8.4		37	Georgia	8.0
22	Pennsylvania	8.7		38	Idaho	7.9
7	Rhode Island	10.1		38	Missouri	7.9
38	South Carolina	7.9		38	South Carolina	7.9
44	South Dakota	7.2		41	Montana	7.7
48	Tennessee	6.4		41	Virginia	7.7
31	Texas	8.2		43	Alabama	7.3
27	Utah	8.4		44	South Dakota	7.2
4	Vermont	10.9		45	Oklahoma	7.1
41	Virginia	7.7		46	New Hampshire	7.0
31	Washington	8.2		47	Florida	6.6
13	West Virginia	9.4		48	Tennessee	6.4
14	Wisconsin	9.3		49	Delaware	5.7
36	Wyoming	8.1		50	Alaska	4.9
					District of Columbia	11.8

Source: CQ Press using data from U.S. Bureau of the Census, Governments Division
  "Annual State Personal Income" (http://www.bea.gov/iTable/index_regional.cfm) and
  "2015 State and Local Government Finances" (http://www.census.gov/govs/local/)
*Calculated using property taxes, personal income taxes, and sales and gross receipts taxes.

State and Local Government Total Expenditures in 2015

National Total = $3,400,879,711,000*

ALPHA ORDER

RANK	STATE	EXPENDITURES	% of USA
26	Alabama	$44,192,672,000	1.3%
39	Alaska	16,803,591,000	0.5%
20	Arizona	55,374,633,000	1.6%
33	Arkansas	26,304,029,000	0.8%
1	California	515,033,207,000	15.1%
18	Colorado	57,361,876,000	1.7%
27	Connecticut	44,096,922,000	1.3%
45	Delaware	10,974,987,000	0.3%
4	Florida	164,784,005,000	4.8%
13	Georgia	81,192,105,000	2.4%
40	Hawaii	16,027,481,000	0.5%
42	Idaho	11,994,623,000	0.4%
5	Illinois	141,989,878,000	4.2%
21	Indiana	54,844,712,000	1.6%
29	Iowa	34,069,718,000	1.0%
32	Kansas	27,994,632,000	0.8%
28	Kentucky	43,739,732,000	1.3%
23	Louisiana	46,841,739,000	1.4%
41	Maine	12,347,821,000	0.4%
15	Maryland	65,931,260,000	1.9%
10	Massachusetts	86,749,764,000	2.6%
9	Michigan	93,749,760,000	2.8%
16	Minnesota	61,185,746,000	1.8%
31	Mississippi	28,990,546,000	0.9%
22	Missouri	51,662,681,000	1.5%
47	Montana	9,942,077,000	0.3%
37	Nebraska	22,128,033,000	0.7%
36	Nevada	23,894,054,000	0.7%
44	New Hampshire	11,860,767,000	0.3%
8	New Jersey	106,988,395,000	3.1%
35	New Mexico	23,916,225,000	0.7%
2	New York	321,690,180,000	9.5%
11	North Carolina	86,356,301,000	2.5%
46	North Dakota	10,111,210,000	0.3%
7	Ohio	116,550,419,000	3.4%
30	Oklahoma	33,538,310,000	1.0%
25	Oregon	45,583,464,000	1.3%
6	Pennsylvania	134,141,610,000	3.9%
43	Rhode Island	11,932,815,000	0.4%
24	South Carolina	45,907,608,000	1.3%
50	South Dakota	7,463,126,000	0.2%
19	Tennessee	56,798,034,000	1.7%
3	Texas	242,370,360,000	7.1%
34	Utah	26,013,474,000	0.8%
49	Vermont	7,659,888,000	0.2%
14	Virginia	77,746,415,000	2.3%
12	Washington	82,304,492,000	2.4%
38	West Virginia	17,068,849,000	0.5%
17	Wisconsin	59,350,338,000	1.7%
48	Wyoming	9,583,145,000	0.3%

RANK ORDER

RANK	STATE	EXPENDITURES	% of USA
1	California	$515,033,207,000	15.1%
2	New York	321,690,180,000	9.5%
3	Texas	242,370,360,000	7.1%
4	Florida	164,784,005,000	4.8%
5	Illinois	141,989,878,000	4.2%
6	Pennsylvania	134,141,610,000	3.9%
7	Ohio	116,550,419,000	3.4%
8	New Jersey	106,988,395,000	3.1%
9	Michigan	93,749,760,000	2.8%
10	Massachusetts	86,749,764,000	2.6%
11	North Carolina	86,356,301,000	2.5%
12	Washington	82,304,492,000	2.4%
13	Georgia	81,192,105,000	2.4%
14	Virginia	77,746,415,000	2.3%
15	Maryland	65,931,260,000	1.9%
16	Minnesota	61,185,746,000	1.8%
17	Wisconsin	59,350,338,000	1.7%
18	Colorado	57,361,876,000	1.7%
19	Tennessee	56,798,034,000	1.7%
20	Arizona	55,374,633,000	1.6%
21	Indiana	54,844,712,000	1.6%
22	Missouri	51,662,681,000	1.5%
23	Louisiana	46,841,739,000	1.4%
24	South Carolina	45,907,608,000	1.3%
25	Oregon	45,583,464,000	1.3%
26	Alabama	44,192,672,000	1.3%
27	Connecticut	44,096,922,000	1.3%
28	Kentucky	43,739,732,000	1.3%
29	Iowa	34,069,718,000	1.0%
30	Oklahoma	33,538,310,000	1.0%
31	Mississippi	28,990,546,000	0.9%
32	Kansas	27,994,632,000	0.8%
33	Arkansas	26,304,029,000	0.8%
34	Utah	26,013,474,000	0.8%
35	New Mexico	23,916,225,000	0.7%
36	Nevada	23,894,054,000	0.7%
37	Nebraska	22,128,033,000	0.7%
38	West Virginia	17,068,849,000	0.5%
39	Alaska	16,803,591,000	0.5%
40	Hawaii	16,027,481,000	0.5%
41	Maine	12,347,821,000	0.4%
42	Idaho	11,994,623,000	0.4%
43	Rhode Island	11,932,815,000	0.4%
44	New Hampshire	11,860,767,000	0.3%
45	Delaware	10,974,987,000	0.3%
46	North Dakota	10,111,210,000	0.3%
47	Montana	9,942,077,000	0.3%
48	Wyoming	9,583,145,000	0.3%
49	Vermont	7,659,888,000	0.2%
50	South Dakota	7,463,126,000	0.2%
	District of Columbia	15,742,002,000	0.5%

Source: U.S. Bureau of the Census, Governments Division
   "2015 State and Local Government Finances" (http://www.census.gov/govs/local/)
*Total expenditures includes all money paid other than for retirement of debt and extension of loans. Includes payments from all sources of funds including current revenues and proceeds from borrowing and prior year fund balances. Includes intergovernmental transfers and expenditures for government owned utilities and other commercial or auxiliary enterprise, and insurance trust expenditures.

Per Capita State and Local Government Total Expenditures in 2015

National Per Capita = $10,593*

<table>
<tr><td colspan="3">ALPHA ORDER</td><td colspan="3">RANK ORDER</td></tr>
<tr><th>RANK</th><th>STATE</th><th>PER CAPITA</th><th>RANK</th><th>STATE</th><th>PER CAPITA</th></tr>
<tr><td>35</td><td>Alabama</td><td>$9,110</td><td>1</td><td>Alaska</td><td>$22,770</td></tr>
<tr><td>1</td><td>Alaska</td><td>22,770</td><td>2</td><td>Wyoming</td><td>16,351</td></tr>
<tr><td>47</td><td>Arizona</td><td>8,141</td><td>3</td><td>New York</td><td>16,231</td></tr>
<tr><td>37</td><td>Arkansas</td><td>8,840</td><td>4</td><td>North Dakota</td><td>13,395</td></tr>
<tr><td>5</td><td>California</td><td>13,195</td><td>5</td><td>California</td><td>13,195</td></tr>
<tr><td>21</td><td>Colorado</td><td>10,544</td><td>6</td><td>Massachusetts</td><td>12,769</td></tr>
<tr><td>7</td><td>Connecticut</td><td>12,270</td><td>7</td><td>Connecticut</td><td>12,270</td></tr>
<tr><td>11</td><td>Delaware</td><td>11,625</td><td>8</td><td>Vermont</td><td>12,267</td></tr>
<tr><td>48</td><td>Florida</td><td>8,130</td><td>9</td><td>New Jersey</td><td>11,941</td></tr>
<tr><td>49</td><td>Georgia</td><td>7,960</td><td>10</td><td>Nebraska</td><td>11,686</td></tr>
<tr><td>16</td><td>Hawaii</td><td>11,237</td><td>11</td><td>Delaware</td><td>11,625</td></tr>
<tr><td>50</td><td>Idaho</td><td>7,272</td><td>12</td><td>Washington</td><td>11,507</td></tr>
<tr><td>18</td><td>Illinois</td><td>11,039</td><td>13</td><td>New Mexico</td><td>11,486</td></tr>
<tr><td>45</td><td>Indiana</td><td>8,296</td><td>14</td><td>Oregon</td><td>11,349</td></tr>
<tr><td>20</td><td>Iowa</td><td>10,925</td><td>15</td><td>Rhode Island</td><td>11,301</td></tr>
<tr><td>29</td><td>Kansas</td><td>9,634</td><td>16</td><td>Hawaii</td><td>11,237</td></tr>
<tr><td>26</td><td>Kentucky</td><td>9,891</td><td>17</td><td>Minnesota</td><td>11,159</td></tr>
<tr><td>25</td><td>Louisiana</td><td>10,028</td><td>18</td><td>Illinois</td><td>11,039</td></tr>
<tr><td>32</td><td>Maine</td><td>9,300</td><td>19</td><td>Maryland</td><td>10,988</td></tr>
<tr><td>19</td><td>Maryland</td><td>10,988</td><td>20</td><td>Iowa</td><td>10,925</td></tr>
<tr><td>6</td><td>Massachusetts</td><td>12,769</td><td>21</td><td>Colorado</td><td>10,544</td></tr>
<tr><td>30</td><td>Michigan</td><td>9,452</td><td>22</td><td>Pennsylvania</td><td>10,487</td></tr>
<tr><td>17</td><td>Minnesota</td><td>11,159</td><td>23</td><td>Wisconsin</td><td>10,304</td></tr>
<tr><td>27</td><td>Mississippi</td><td>9,711</td><td>24</td><td>Ohio</td><td>10,042</td></tr>
<tr><td>44</td><td>Missouri</td><td>8,507</td><td>25</td><td>Louisiana</td><td>10,028</td></tr>
<tr><td>28</td><td>Montana</td><td>9,668</td><td>26</td><td>Kentucky</td><td>9,891</td></tr>
<tr><td>10</td><td>Nebraska</td><td>11,686</td><td>27</td><td>Mississippi</td><td>9,711</td></tr>
<tr><td>46</td><td>Nevada</td><td>8,288</td><td>28</td><td>Montana</td><td>9,668</td></tr>
<tr><td>36</td><td>New Hampshire</td><td>8,917</td><td>29</td><td>Kansas</td><td>9,634</td></tr>
<tr><td>9</td><td>New Jersey</td><td>11,941</td><td>30</td><td>Michigan</td><td>9,452</td></tr>
<tr><td>13</td><td>New Mexico</td><td>11,486</td><td>31</td><td>South Carolina</td><td>9,383</td></tr>
<tr><td>3</td><td>New York</td><td>16,231</td><td>32</td><td>Maine</td><td>9,300</td></tr>
<tr><td>42</td><td>North Carolina</td><td>8,600</td><td>33</td><td>Virginia</td><td>9,292</td></tr>
<tr><td>4</td><td>North Dakota</td><td>13,395</td><td>34</td><td>West Virginia</td><td>9,278</td></tr>
<tr><td>24</td><td>Ohio</td><td>10,042</td><td>35</td><td>Alabama</td><td>9,110</td></tr>
<tr><td>43</td><td>Oklahoma</td><td>8,590</td><td>36</td><td>New Hampshire</td><td>8,917</td></tr>
<tr><td>14</td><td>Oregon</td><td>11,349</td><td>37</td><td>Arkansas</td><td>8,840</td></tr>
<tr><td>22</td><td>Pennsylvania</td><td>10,487</td><td>38</td><td>Texas</td><td>8,828</td></tr>
<tr><td>15</td><td>Rhode Island</td><td>11,301</td><td>39</td><td>South Dakota</td><td>8,739</td></tr>
<tr><td>31</td><td>South Carolina</td><td>9,383</td><td>40</td><td>Utah</td><td>8,715</td></tr>
<tr><td>39</td><td>South Dakota</td><td>8,739</td><td>41</td><td>Tennessee</td><td>8,618</td></tr>
<tr><td>41</td><td>Tennessee</td><td>8,618</td><td>42</td><td>North Carolina</td><td>8,600</td></tr>
<tr><td>38</td><td>Texas</td><td>8,828</td><td>43</td><td>Oklahoma</td><td>8,590</td></tr>
<tr><td>40</td><td>Utah</td><td>8,715</td><td>44</td><td>Missouri</td><td>8,507</td></tr>
<tr><td>8</td><td>Vermont</td><td>12,267</td><td>45</td><td>Indiana</td><td>8,296</td></tr>
<tr><td>33</td><td>Virginia</td><td>9,292</td><td>46</td><td>Nevada</td><td>8,288</td></tr>
<tr><td>12</td><td>Washington</td><td>11,507</td><td>47</td><td>Arizona</td><td>8,141</td></tr>
<tr><td>34</td><td>West Virginia</td><td>9,278</td><td>48</td><td>Florida</td><td>8,130</td></tr>
<tr><td>23</td><td>Wisconsin</td><td>10,304</td><td>49</td><td>Georgia</td><td>7,960</td></tr>
<tr><td>2</td><td>Wyoming</td><td>16,351</td><td>50</td><td>Idaho</td><td>7,272</td></tr>
<tr><td></td><td></td><td></td><td></td><td>District of Columbia</td><td>23,400</td></tr>
</table>

Source: CQ Press using data from U.S. Bureau of the Census, Governments Division
"2015 State and Local Government Finances" (http://www.census.gov/govs/local/)
*Total expenditures includes all money paid other than for retirement of debt and extension of loans. Includes payments from all sources of funds including current revenues and proceeds from borrowing and prior year fund balances. Includes intergovernmental transfers and expenditures for government owned utilities and other commercial or auxiliary enterprise, and insurance trust expenditures.

State and Local Government Direct General Expenditures in 2015

National Total = $2,838,366,097,000*

RANK	STATE	EXPENDITURES	% of USA
28	Alabama	$37,028,870,000	1.3%
39	Alaska	14,728,643,000	0.5%
20	Arizona	44,999,217,000	1.6%
33	Arkansas	23,380,028,000	0.8%
1	California	409,988,825,000	14.4%
19	Colorado	47,231,288,000	1.7%
26	Connecticut	37,484,540,000	1.3%
45	Delaware	9,680,694,000	0.3%
4	Florida	142,935,819,000	5.0%
13	Georgia	67,695,803,000	2.4%
40	Hawaii	13,523,799,000	0.5%
42	Idaho	10,589,088,000	0.4%
5	Illinois	114,650,365,000	4.0%
18	Indiana	49,141,974,000	1.7%
29	Iowa	30,202,570,000	1.1%
32	Kansas	24,505,099,000	0.9%
27	Kentucky	37,281,594,000	1.3%
23	Louisiana	40,602,968,000	1.4%
41	Maine	11,101,096,000	0.4%
15	Maryland	57,621,667,000	2.0%
11	Massachusetts	71,789,943,000	2.5%
9	Michigan	79,943,853,000	2.8%
16	Minnesota	52,705,362,000	1.9%
31	Mississippi	25,237,430,000	0.9%
22	Missouri	43,791,854,000	1.5%
47	Montana	8,730,521,000	0.3%
37	Nebraska	16,629,791,000	0.6%
36	Nevada	20,158,672,000	0.7%
43	New Hampshire	10,455,049,000	0.4%
8	New Jersey	90,358,410,000	3.2%
35	New Mexico	20,977,014,000	0.7%
2	New York	257,360,094,000	9.1%
10	North Carolina	74,588,643,000	2.6%
46	North Dakota	9,063,834,000	0.3%
7	Ohio	95,269,653,000	3.4%
30	Oklahoma	28,658,804,000	1.0%
25	Oregon	37,637,413,000	1.3%
6	Pennsylvania	113,370,256,000	4.0%
44	Rhode Island	10,080,433,000	0.4%
24	South Carolina	39,060,939,000	1.4%
50	South Dakota	6,550,483,000	0.2%
21	Tennessee	43,996,022,000	1.6%
3	Texas	206,337,274,000	7.3%
34	Utah	21,855,170,000	0.8%
49	Vermont	6,927,631,000	0.2%
12	Virginia	68,831,862,000	2.4%
14	Washington	66,491,321,000	2.3%
38	West Virginia	15,182,162,000	0.5%
17	Wisconsin	51,134,800,000	1.8%
48	Wyoming	8,392,796,000	0.3%

RANK	STATE	EXPENDITURES	% of USA
1	California	$409,988,825,000	14.4%
2	New York	257,360,094,000	9.1%
3	Texas	206,337,274,000	7.3%
4	Florida	142,935,819,000	5.0%
5	Illinois	114,650,365,000	4.0%
6	Pennsylvania	113,370,256,000	4.0%
7	Ohio	95,269,653,000	3.4%
8	New Jersey	90,358,410,000	3.2%
9	Michigan	79,943,853,000	2.8%
10	North Carolina	74,588,643,000	2.6%
11	Massachusetts	71,789,943,000	2.5%
12	Virginia	68,831,862,000	2.4%
13	Georgia	67,695,803,000	2.4%
14	Washington	66,491,321,000	2.3%
15	Maryland	57,621,667,000	2.0%
16	Minnesota	52,705,362,000	1.9%
17	Wisconsin	51,134,800,000	1.8%
18	Indiana	49,141,974,000	1.7%
19	Colorado	47,231,288,000	1.7%
20	Arizona	44,999,217,000	1.6%
21	Tennessee	43,996,022,000	1.6%
22	Missouri	43,791,854,000	1.5%
23	Louisiana	40,602,968,000	1.4%
24	South Carolina	39,060,939,000	1.4%
25	Oregon	37,637,413,000	1.3%
26	Connecticut	37,484,540,000	1.3%
27	Kentucky	37,281,594,000	1.3%
28	Alabama	37,028,870,000	1.3%
29	Iowa	30,202,570,000	1.1%
30	Oklahoma	28,658,804,000	1.0%
31	Mississippi	25,237,430,000	0.9%
32	Kansas	24,505,099,000	0.9%
33	Arkansas	23,380,028,000	0.8%
34	Utah	21,855,170,000	0.8%
35	New Mexico	20,977,014,000	0.7%
36	Nevada	20,158,672,000	0.7%
37	Nebraska	16,629,791,000	0.6%
38	West Virginia	15,182,162,000	0.5%
39	Alaska	14,728,643,000	0.5%
40	Hawaii	13,523,799,000	0.5%
41	Maine	11,101,096,000	0.4%
42	Idaho	10,589,088,000	0.4%
43	New Hampshire	10,455,049,000	0.4%
44	Rhode Island	10,080,433,000	0.4%
45	Delaware	9,680,694,000	0.3%
46	North Dakota	9,063,834,000	0.3%
47	Montana	8,730,521,000	0.3%
48	Wyoming	8,392,796,000	0.3%
49	Vermont	6,927,631,000	0.2%
50	South Dakota	6,550,483,000	0.2%
	District of Columbia	12,424,661,000	0.4%

Source: U.S. Bureau of the Census, Governments Division
"2015 State and Local Government Finances" (http://www.census.gov/govs/local/)
*Direct general expenditures include expenditures for current operations, assistance and subsidies, interest on debt, and capital outlay. Excludes intergovernmental transfers, expenditures for government owned utilities and other commercial or auxiliary enterprise, and insurance trust expenditures.

Per Capita State and Local Government Direct General Expenditures in 2015

National Per Capita = $8,841*

ALPHA ORDER

RANK	STATE	PER CAPITA
38	Alabama	$7,633
1	Alaska	19,958
49	Arizona	6,615
36	Arkansas	7,857
7	California	10,504
24	Colorado	8,682
8	Connecticut	10,430
9	Delaware	10,254
45	Florida	7,052
48	Georgia	6,637
16	Hawaii	9,482
50	Idaho	6,420
19	Illinois	8,914
40	Indiana	7,434
12	Iowa	9,685
27	Kansas	8,433
28	Kentucky	8,431
23	Louisiana	8,692
29	Maine	8,361
14	Maryland	9,603
6	Massachusetts	10,567
33	Michigan	8,060
13	Minnesota	9,612
26	Mississippi	8,454
44	Missouri	7,211
25	Montana	8,490
22	Nebraska	8,782
46	Nevada	6,992
35	New Hampshire	7,860
10	New Jersey	10,085
11	New Mexico	10,074
3	New York	12,985
41	North Carolina	7,428
4	North Dakota	12,007
32	Ohio	8,209
42	Oklahoma	7,340
17	Oregon	9,371
21	Pennsylvania	8,863
15	Rhode Island	9,547
34	South Carolina	7,984
37	South Dakota	7,670
47	Tennessee	6,675
39	Texas	7,516
43	Utah	7,322
5	Vermont	11,094
31	Virginia	8,227
18	Washington	9,296
30	West Virginia	8,252
20	Wisconsin	8,878
2	Wyoming	14,320

RANK ORDER

RANK	STATE	PER CAPITA
1	Alaska	$19,958
2	Wyoming	14,320
3	New York	12,985
4	North Dakota	12,007
5	Vermont	11,094
6	Massachusetts	10,567
7	California	10,504
8	Connecticut	10,430
9	Delaware	10,254
10	New Jersey	10,085
11	New Mexico	10,074
12	Iowa	9,685
13	Minnesota	9,612
14	Maryland	9,603
15	Rhode Island	9,547
16	Hawaii	9,482
17	Oregon	9,371
18	Washington	9,296
19	Illinois	8,914
20	Wisconsin	8,878
21	Pennsylvania	8,863
22	Nebraska	8,782
23	Louisiana	8,692
24	Colorado	8,682
25	Montana	8,490
26	Mississippi	8,454
27	Kansas	8,433
28	Kentucky	8,431
29	Maine	8,361
30	West Virginia	8,252
31	Virginia	8,227
32	Ohio	8,209
33	Michigan	8,060
34	South Carolina	7,984
35	New Hampshire	7,860
36	Arkansas	7,857
37	South Dakota	7,670
38	Alabama	7,633
39	Texas	7,516
40	Indiana	7,434
41	North Carolina	7,428
42	Oklahoma	7,340
43	Utah	7,322
44	Missouri	7,211
45	Florida	7,052
46	Nevada	6,992
47	Tennessee	6,675
48	Georgia	6,637
49	Arizona	6,615
50	Idaho	6,420

District of Columbia   18,469

Source: CQ Press using data from U.S. Bureau of the Census, Governments Division
"2015 State and Local Government Finances" (http://www.census.gov/govs/local/)
*Direct general expenditures include expenditures for current operations, assistance and subsidies, interest on debt, and capital outlay. Excludes intergovernmental transfers, expenditures for government owned utilities and other commercial or auxiliary enterprise, and insurance trust expenditures.

State and Local Government Debt Outstanding in 2015

National Total = $2,997,765,483,000*

ALPHA ORDER

RANK ORDER

RANK	STATE	DEBT	% of USA	RANK	STATE	DEBT	% of USA
28	Alabama	$30,114,358,000	1.0%	1	California	$420,979,308,000	14.0%
42	Alaska	9,056,630,000	0.3%	2	New York	346,127,656,000	11.5%
19	Arizona	47,902,910,000	1.6%	3	Texas	277,646,648,000	9.3%
34	Arkansas	16,621,427,000	0.6%	4	Florida	148,661,533,000	5.0%
1	California	420,979,308,000	14.0%	5	Illinois	148,532,543,000	5.0%
14	Colorado	56,149,682,000	1.9%	6	Pennsylvania	127,130,314,000	4.2%
20	Connecticut	46,937,948,000	1.6%	7	New Jersey	100,106,273,000	3.3%
44	Delaware	7,625,280,000	0.3%	8	Massachusetts	93,169,108,000	3.1%
4	Florida	148,661,533,000	5.0%	9	Ohio	85,736,583,000	2.9%
13	Georgia	56,154,523,000	1.9%	10	Washington	81,449,756,000	2.7%
37	Hawaii	14,823,819,000	0.5%	11	Michigan	76,462,015,000	2.6%
45	Idaho	6,341,047,000	0.2%	12	Virginia	65,093,695,000	2.2%
5	Illinois	148,532,543,000	5.0%	13	Georgia	56,154,523,000	1.9%
17	Indiana	50,828,145,000	1.7%	14	Colorado	56,149,682,000	1.9%
33	Iowa	18,499,920,000	0.6%	15	Minnesota	51,414,232,000	1.7%
30	Kansas	28,330,319,000	0.9%	16	Maryland	51,070,274,000	1.7%
25	Kentucky	40,017,067,000	1.3%	17	Indiana	50,828,145,000	1.7%
26	Louisiana	39,444,427,000	1.3%	18	North Carolina	50,140,461,000	1.7%
43	Maine	7,904,941,000	0.3%	19	Arizona	47,902,910,000	1.6%
16	Maryland	51,070,274,000	1.7%	20	Connecticut	46,937,948,000	1.6%
8	Massachusetts	93,169,108,000	3.1%	21	Missouri	46,931,718,000	1.6%
11	Michigan	76,462,015,000	2.6%	22	Tennessee	44,777,912,000	1.5%
15	Minnesota	51,414,232,000	1.7%	23	Wisconsin	43,902,381,000	1.5%
38	Mississippi	14,177,299,000	0.5%	24	South Carolina	43,411,833,000	1.4%
21	Missouri	46,931,718,000	1.6%	25	Kentucky	40,017,067,000	1.3%
48	Montana	5,151,898,000	0.2%	26	Louisiana	39,444,427,000	1.3%
36	Nebraska	15,497,965,000	0.5%	27	Oregon	34,889,977,000	1.2%
29	Nevada	28,668,571,000	1.0%	28	Alabama	30,114,358,000	1.0%
40	New Hampshire	10,796,326,000	0.4%	29	Nevada	28,668,571,000	1.0%
7	New Jersey	100,106,273,000	3.3%	30	Kansas	28,330,319,000	0.9%
35	New Mexico	15,518,137,000	0.5%	31	Utah	20,256,685,000	0.7%
2	New York	346,127,656,000	11.5%	32	Oklahoma	18,914,993,000	0.6%
18	North Carolina	50,140,461,000	1.7%	33	Iowa	18,499,920,000	0.6%
46	North Dakota	6,023,159,000	0.2%	34	Arkansas	16,621,427,000	0.6%
9	Ohio	85,736,583,000	2.9%	35	New Mexico	15,518,137,000	0.5%
32	Oklahoma	18,914,993,000	0.6%	36	Nebraska	15,497,965,000	0.5%
27	Oregon	34,889,977,000	1.2%	37	Hawaii	14,823,819,000	0.5%
6	Pennsylvania	127,130,314,000	4.2%	38	Mississippi	14,177,299,000	0.5%
39	Rhode Island	11,610,070,000	0.4%	39	Rhode Island	11,610,070,000	0.4%
24	South Carolina	43,411,833,000	1.4%	40	New Hampshire	10,796,326,000	0.4%
47	South Dakota	5,814,391,000	0.2%	41	West Virginia	10,468,682,000	0.3%
22	Tennessee	44,777,912,000	1.5%	42	Alaska	9,056,630,000	0.3%
3	Texas	277,646,648,000	9.3%	43	Maine	7,904,941,000	0.3%
31	Utah	20,256,685,000	0.7%	44	Delaware	7,625,280,000	0.3%
49	Vermont	4,575,963,000	0.2%	45	Idaho	6,341,047,000	0.2%
12	Virginia	65,093,695,000	2.2%	46	North Dakota	6,023,159,000	0.2%
10	Washington	81,449,756,000	2.7%	47	South Dakota	5,814,391,000	0.2%
41	West Virginia	10,468,682,000	0.3%	48	Montana	5,151,898,000	0.2%
23	Wisconsin	43,902,381,000	1.5%	49	Vermont	4,575,963,000	0.2%
50	Wyoming	1,980,437,000	0.1%	50	Wyoming	1,980,437,000	0.1%
					District of Columbia	13,924,244,000	0.5%

Source: U.S. Bureau of the Census, Governments Division
   "2015 State and Local Government Finances" (http://www.census.gov/govs/local/)
*Includes short-term, long-term, full faith and credit, nonguaranteed, and public debt for private purposes.

Per Capita State and Local Government Debt Outstanding in 2015

National Per Capita = $9,338*

ALPHA ORDER

RANK	STATE	PER CAPITA
39	Alabama	$6,208
4	Alaska	12,272
35	Arizona	7,042
43	Arkansas	5,586
9	California	10,785
11	Colorado	10,321
3	Connecticut	13,061
24	Delaware	8,077
33	Florida	7,335
44	Georgia	5,506
10	Hawaii	10,393
49	Idaho	3,845
5	Illinois	11,548
29	Indiana	7,689
41	Iowa	5,932
15	Kansas	9,750
17	Kentucky	9,049
21	Louisiana	8,444
40	Maine	5,953
20	Maryland	8,511
2	Massachusetts	13,713
28	Michigan	7,709
16	Minnesota	9,377
48	Mississippi	4,749
27	Missouri	7,728
45	Montana	5,010
22	Nebraska	8,185
13	Nevada	9,944
23	New Hampshire	8,117
7	New Jersey	11,173
31	New Mexico	7,453
1	New York	17,464
46	North Carolina	4,993
25	North Dakota	7,979
32	Ohio	7,387
47	Oklahoma	4,845
19	Oregon	8,687
14	Pennsylvania	9,939
8	Rhode Island	10,995
18	South Carolina	8,873
36	South Dakota	6,808
37	Tennessee	6,794
12	Texas	10,113
38	Utah	6,786
34	Vermont	7,328
26	Virginia	7,780
6	Washington	11,387
42	West Virginia	5,690
30	Wisconsin	7,622
50	Wyoming	3,379

RANK ORDER

RANK	STATE	PER CAPITA
1	New York	$17,464
2	Massachusetts	13,713
3	Connecticut	13,061
4	Alaska	12,272
5	Illinois	11,548
6	Washington	11,387
7	New Jersey	11,173
8	Rhode Island	10,995
9	California	10,785
10	Hawaii	10,393
11	Colorado	10,321
12	Texas	10,113
13	Nevada	9,944
14	Pennsylvania	9,939
15	Kansas	9,750
16	Minnesota	9,377
17	Kentucky	9,049
18	South Carolina	8,873
19	Oregon	8,687
20	Maryland	8,511
21	Louisiana	8,444
22	Nebraska	8,185
23	New Hampshire	8,117
24	Delaware	8,077
25	North Dakota	7,979
26	Virginia	7,780
27	Missouri	7,728
28	Michigan	7,709
29	Indiana	7,689
30	Wisconsin	7,622
31	New Mexico	7,453
32	Ohio	7,387
33	Florida	7,335
34	Vermont	7,328
35	Arizona	7,042
36	South Dakota	6,808
37	Tennessee	6,794
38	Utah	6,786
39	Alabama	6,208
40	Maine	5,953
41	Iowa	5,932
42	West Virginia	5,690
43	Arkansas	5,586
44	Georgia	5,506
45	Montana	5,010
46	North Carolina	4,993
47	Oklahoma	4,845
48	Mississippi	4,749
49	Idaho	3,845
50	Wyoming	3,379

District of Columbia   20,698

Source: CQ Press using data from U.S. Bureau of the Census, Governments Division
   "2015 State and Local Government Finances" (http://www.census.gov/govs/local/)
*Includes short-term, long-term, full faith and credit, nonguaranteed, and public debt for private purposes.

State and Local Government Full-Time Equivalent Employees in 2016

National Total = 16,435,105 FTE Employees*

ALPHA ORDER

RANK	STATE	EMPLOYEES	% of USA
23	Alabama	280,681	1.7%
44	Alaska	52,704	0.3%
22	Arizona	281,548	1.7%
33	Arkansas	170,174	1.0%
1	California	1,814,756	11.0%
19	Colorado	293,546	1.8%
30	Connecticut	193,152	1.2%
46	Delaware	49,282	0.3%
4	Florida	885,649	5.4%
9	Georgia	513,462	3.1%
40	Hawaii	75,694	0.5%
39	Idaho	82,134	0.5%
5	Illinois	630,595	3.8%
16	Indiana	321,390	2.0%
32	Iowa	184,309	1.1%
28	Kansas	198,259	1.2%
26	Kentucky	244,888	1.5%
25	Louisiana	258,291	1.6%
42	Maine	69,428	0.4%
18	Maryland	304,023	1.8%
14	Massachusetts	336,065	2.0%
12	Michigan	438,841	2.7%
20	Minnesota	291,552	1.8%
31	Mississippi	190,903	1.2%
17	Missouri	315,244	1.9%
43	Montana	57,691	0.4%
36	Nebraska	119,484	0.7%
37	Nevada	113,355	0.7%
41	New Hampshire	70,473	0.4%
10	New Jersey	478,391	2.9%
35	New Mexico	125,978	0.8%
3	New York	1,183,581	7.2%
8	North Carolina	548,795	3.3%
48	North Dakota	48,023	0.3%
6	Ohio	588,550	3.6%
27	Oklahoma	215,986	1.3%
29	Oregon	197,696	1.2%
7	Pennsylvania	562,276	3.4%
47	Rhode Island	48,206	0.3%
24	South Carolina	262,417	1.6%
49	South Dakota	46,338	0.3%
15	Tennessee	329,029	2.0%
2	Texas	1,486,219	9.0%
34	Utah	147,135	0.9%
50	Vermont	40,130	0.2%
11	Virginia	447,546	2.7%
13	Washington	352,641	2.1%
38	West Virginia	104,609	0.6%
21	Wisconsin	285,316	1.7%
45	Wyoming	50,972	0.3%

RANK ORDER

RANK	STATE	EMPLOYEES	% of USA
1	California	1,814,756	11.0%
2	Texas	1,486,219	9.0%
3	New York	1,183,581	7.2%
4	Florida	885,649	5.4%
5	Illinois	630,595	3.8%
6	Ohio	588,550	3.6%
7	Pennsylvania	562,276	3.4%
8	North Carolina	548,795	3.3%
9	Georgia	513,462	3.1%
10	New Jersey	478,391	2.9%
11	Virginia	447,546	2.7%
12	Michigan	438,841	2.7%
13	Washington	352,641	2.1%
14	Massachusetts	336,065	2.0%
15	Tennessee	329,029	2.0%
16	Indiana	321,390	2.0%
17	Missouri	315,244	1.9%
18	Maryland	304,023	1.8%
19	Colorado	293,546	1.8%
20	Minnesota	291,552	1.8%
21	Wisconsin	285,316	1.7%
22	Arizona	281,548	1.7%
23	Alabama	280,681	1.7%
24	South Carolina	262,417	1.6%
25	Louisiana	258,291	1.6%
26	Kentucky	244,888	1.5%
27	Oklahoma	215,986	1.3%
28	Kansas	198,259	1.2%
29	Oregon	197,696	1.2%
30	Connecticut	193,152	1.2%
31	Mississippi	190,903	1.2%
32	Iowa	184,309	1.1%
33	Arkansas	170,174	1.0%
34	Utah	147,135	0.9%
35	New Mexico	125,978	0.8%
36	Nebraska	119,484	0.7%
37	Nevada	113,355	0.7%
38	West Virginia	104,609	0.6%
39	Idaho	82,134	0.5%
40	Hawaii	75,694	0.5%
41	New Hampshire	70,473	0.4%
42	Maine	69,428	0.4%
43	Montana	57,691	0.4%
44	Alaska	52,704	0.3%
45	Wyoming	50,972	0.3%
46	Delaware	49,282	0.3%
47	Rhode Island	48,206	0.3%
48	North Dakota	48,023	0.3%
49	South Dakota	46,338	0.3%
50	Vermont	40,130	0.2%
	District of Columbia	47,698	0.3%

Source: U.S. Bureau of the Census, Governments Division
   "Annual Survey of Public Employment and Payroll" (https://www.census.gov/data/datasets.html)
*Full-time equivalent as of March 2016.

Rate of State and Local Government Full-Time Equivalent Employees in 2016

National Rate = 508 FTE Employees per 10,000 Population*

ALPHA ORDER

RANK	STATE	RATE
11	Alabama	577
2	Alaska	711
49	Arizona	408
13	Arkansas	569
44	California	462
24	Colorado	531
19	Connecticut	538
31	Delaware	517
48	Florida	429
34	Georgia	498
25	Hawaii	530
39	Idaho	489
38	Illinois	491
40	Indiana	484
10	Iowa	589
3	Kansas	682
15	Kentucky	552
16	Louisiana	551
29	Maine	522
33	Maryland	505
37	Massachusetts	492
46	Michigan	442
27	Minnesota	528
5	Mississippi	639
30	Missouri	518
14	Montana	555
7	Nebraska	626
50	Nevada	386
27	New Hampshire	528
21	New Jersey	533
8	New Mexico	604
9	New York	597
18	North Carolina	540
6	North Dakota	636
32	Ohio	506
16	Oklahoma	551
40	Oregon	484
47	Pennsylvania	440
45	Rhode Island	456
26	South Carolina	529
19	South Dakota	538
35	Tennessee	495
21	Texas	533
43	Utah	483
4	Vermont	644
23	Virginia	532
40	Washington	484
12	West Virginia	572
36	Wisconsin	494
1	Wyoming	871

RANK ORDER

RANK	STATE	RATE
1	Wyoming	871
2	Alaska	711
3	Kansas	682
4	Vermont	644
5	Mississippi	639
6	North Dakota	636
7	Nebraska	626
8	New Mexico	604
9	New York	597
10	Iowa	589
11	Alabama	577
12	West Virginia	572
13	Arkansas	569
14	Montana	555
15	Kentucky	552
16	Louisiana	551
16	Oklahoma	551
18	North Carolina	540
19	Connecticut	538
19	South Dakota	538
21	New Jersey	533
21	Texas	533
23	Virginia	532
24	Colorado	531
25	Hawaii	530
26	South Carolina	529
27	Minnesota	528
27	New Hampshire	528
29	Maine	522
30	Missouri	518
31	Delaware	517
32	Ohio	506
33	Maryland	505
34	Georgia	498
35	Tennessee	495
36	Wisconsin	494
37	Massachusetts	492
38	Illinois	491
39	Idaho	489
40	Indiana	484
40	Oregon	484
40	Washington	484
43	Utah	483
44	California	462
45	Rhode Island	456
46	Michigan	442
47	Pennsylvania	440
48	Florida	429
49	Arizona	408
50	Nevada	386

District of Columbia 697

Source: CQ Press using data from U.S. Bureau of the Census, Governments Division
"Annual Survey of Public Employment and Payroll" (https://www.census.gov/data/datasets.html)
*Full-time equivalent as of March 2016.

Average Annual Earnings of Full-Time State and Local Government Employees in 2016
National Average = $58,677*

ALPHA ORDER

RANK	STATE	SALARY
40	Alabama	$46,765
6	Alaska	68,268
26	Arizona	54,430
49	Arkansas	42,731
1	California	80,370
15	Colorado	60,053
5	Connecticut	68,835
19	Delaware	57,622
31	Florida	50,985
41	Georgia	46,341
17	Hawaii	58,730
36	Idaho	48,233
10	Illinois	64,134
37	Indiana	47,892
18	Iowa	58,272
38	Kansas	47,415
45	Kentucky	45,720
42	Louisiana	46,288
35	Maine	48,690
9	Maryland	65,180
8	Massachusetts	66,251
14	Michigan	60,763
12	Minnesota	61,633
50	Mississippi	41,862
46	Missouri	44,954
32	Montana	50,427
29	Nebraska	53,021
11	Nevada	63,762
22	New Hampshire	55,688
2	New Jersey	73,625
34	New Mexico	49,300
3	New York	72,426
33	North Carolina	49,815
27	North Dakota	54,389
25	Ohio	54,440
47	Oklahoma	43,793
13	Oregon	61,089
16	Pennsylvania	59,577
7	Rhode Island	67,209
39	South Carolina	47,002
43	South Dakota	46,201
44	Tennessee	45,936
30	Texas	51,028
24	Utah	54,506
23	Vermont	54,619
28	Virginia	54,316
4	Washington	70,897
48	West Virginia	43,239
20	Wisconsin	57,471
21	Wyoming	56,149

RANK ORDER

RANK	STATE	SALARY
1	California	$80,370
2	New Jersey	73,625
3	New York	72,426
4	Washington	70,897
5	Connecticut	68,835
6	Alaska	68,268
7	Rhode Island	67,209
8	Massachusetts	66,251
9	Maryland	65,180
10	Illinois	64,134
11	Nevada	63,762
12	Minnesota	61,633
13	Oregon	61,089
14	Michigan	60,763
15	Colorado	60,053
16	Pennsylvania	59,577
17	Hawaii	58,730
18	Iowa	58,272
19	Delaware	57,622
20	Wisconsin	57,471
21	Wyoming	56,149
22	New Hampshire	55,688
23	Vermont	54,619
24	Utah	54,506
25	Ohio	54,440
26	Arizona	54,430
27	North Dakota	54,389
28	Virginia	54,316
29	Nebraska	53,021
30	Texas	51,028
31	Florida	50,985
32	Montana	50,427
33	North Carolina	49,815
34	New Mexico	49,300
35	Maine	48,690
36	Idaho	48,233
37	Indiana	47,892
38	Kansas	47,415
39	South Carolina	47,002
40	Alabama	46,765
41	Georgia	46,341
42	Louisiana	46,288
43	South Dakota	46,201
44	Tennessee	45,936
45	Kentucky	45,720
46	Missouri	44,954
47	Oklahoma	43,793
48	West Virginia	43,239
49	Arkansas	42,731
50	Mississippi	41,862
	District of Columbia	84,633

Source: CQ Press using data from U.S. Bureau of the Census, Governments Division
"Annual Survey of Public Employment and Payroll" (https://www.census.gov/data/datasets.html)
*March 2016 full-time payroll (multiplied by 12) divided by full-time employees.

State Government Total Revenue in 2015

National Total = $2,159,747,677,000*

ALPHA ORDER

RANK	STATE	REVENUE	% of USA
28	Alabama	$26,639,654,000	1.2%
46	Alaska	7,867,783,000	0.4%
19	Arizona	35,657,797,000	1.7%
31	Arkansas	21,586,590,000	1.0%
1	California	319,289,874,000	14.8%
21	Colorado	34,753,867,000	1.6%
26	Connecticut	29,360,781,000	1.4%
44	Delaware	8,175,923,000	0.4%
4	Florida	89,038,806,000	4.1%
15	Georgia	45,293,832,000	2.1%
38	Hawaii	13,065,465,000	0.6%
41	Idaho	9,337,188,000	0.4%
7	Illinois	81,011,629,000	3.8%
18	Indiana	37,987,476,000	1.8%
30	Iowa	23,450,709,000	1.1%
35	Kansas	17,823,727,000	0.8%
24	Kentucky	29,783,118,000	1.4%
27	Louisiana	27,498,054,000	1.3%
42	Maine	8,792,906,000	0.4%
16	Maryland	42,398,723,000	2.0%
10	Massachusetts	58,427,432,000	2.7%
9	Michigan	66,961,892,000	3.1%
14	Minnesota	47,213,269,000	2.2%
32	Mississippi	21,139,337,000	1.0%
22	Missouri	33,619,314,000	1.6%
47	Montana	7,477,942,000	0.3%
39	Nebraska	10,998,007,000	0.5%
36	Nevada	16,439,338,000	0.8%
45	New Hampshire	7,873,147,000	0.4%
8	New Jersey	69,719,299,000	3.2%
33	New Mexico	19,352,371,000	0.9%
2	New York	195,537,845,000	9.1%
11	North Carolina	54,737,894,000	2.5%
40	North Dakota	9,803,028,000	0.5%
6	Ohio	85,069,587,000	3.9%
29	Oklahoma	24,952,770,000	1.2%
20	Oregon	35,058,351,000	1.6%
5	Pennsylvania	87,588,117,000	4.1%
43	Rhode Island	8,261,089,000	0.4%
25	South Carolina	29,544,397,000	1.4%
50	South Dakota	4,848,683,000	0.2%
23	Tennessee	30,257,750,000	1.4%
3	Texas	136,923,517,000	6.3%
34	Utah	18,619,387,000	0.9%
49	Vermont	6,287,836,000	0.3%
12	Virginia	51,138,267,000	2.4%
13	Washington	49,889,305,000	2.3%
37	West Virginia	14,298,734,000	0.7%
17	Wisconsin	41,633,946,000	1.9%
48	Wyoming	7,261,924,000	0.3%

RANK ORDER

RANK	STATE	REVENUE	% of USA
1	California	$319,289,874,000	14.8%
2	New York	195,537,845,000	9.1%
3	Texas	136,923,517,000	6.3%
4	Florida	89,038,806,000	4.1%
5	Pennsylvania	87,588,117,000	4.1%
6	Ohio	85,069,587,000	3.9%
7	Illinois	81,011,629,000	3.8%
8	New Jersey	69,719,299,000	3.2%
9	Michigan	66,961,892,000	3.1%
10	Massachusetts	58,427,432,000	2.7%
11	North Carolina	54,737,894,000	2.5%
12	Virginia	51,138,267,000	2.4%
13	Washington	49,889,305,000	2.3%
14	Minnesota	47,213,269,000	2.2%
15	Georgia	45,293,832,000	2.1%
16	Maryland	42,398,723,000	2.0%
17	Wisconsin	41,633,946,000	1.9%
18	Indiana	37,987,476,000	1.8%
19	Arizona	35,657,797,000	1.7%
20	Oregon	35,058,351,000	1.6%
21	Colorado	34,753,867,000	1.6%
22	Missouri	33,619,314,000	1.6%
23	Tennessee	30,257,750,000	1.4%
24	Kentucky	29,783,118,000	1.4%
25	South Carolina	29,544,397,000	1.4%
26	Connecticut	29,360,781,000	1.4%
27	Louisiana	27,498,054,000	1.3%
28	Alabama	26,639,654,000	1.2%
29	Oklahoma	24,952,770,000	1.2%
30	Iowa	23,450,709,000	1.1%
31	Arkansas	21,586,590,000	1.0%
32	Mississippi	21,139,337,000	1.0%
33	New Mexico	19,352,371,000	0.9%
34	Utah	18,619,387,000	0.9%
35	Kansas	17,823,727,000	0.8%
36	Nevada	16,439,338,000	0.8%
37	West Virginia	14,298,734,000	0.7%
38	Hawaii	13,065,465,000	0.6%
39	Nebraska	10,998,007,000	0.5%
40	North Dakota	9,803,028,000	0.5%
41	Idaho	9,337,188,000	0.4%
42	Maine	8,792,906,000	0.4%
43	Rhode Island	8,261,089,000	0.4%
44	Delaware	8,175,923,000	0.4%
45	New Hampshire	7,873,147,000	0.4%
46	Alaska	7,867,783,000	0.4%
47	Montana	7,477,942,000	0.3%
48	Wyoming	7,261,924,000	0.3%
49	Vermont	6,287,836,000	0.3%
50	South Dakota	4,848,683,000	0.2%
	District of Columbia**	NA	NA

Source: U.S. Bureau of the Census, Governments Division
  "2015 State and Local Government Finances" (http://www.census.gov/govs/local/)
*Total revenue includes all money received from external sources. This includes taxes, intergovernmental transfers and
insurance trust revenue, and revenue from government owned utilities and other commercial or auxiliary enterprise.
**Not applicable.

Per Capita State Government Total Revenue in 2015

National Per Capita = $6,741*

ALPHA ORDER

RANK	STATE	PER CAPITA
44	Alabama	$5,492
3	Alaska	10,661
46	Arizona	5,242
20	Arkansas	7,254
12	California	8,180
30	Colorado	6,388
13	Connecticut	8,170
9	Delaware	8,660
50	Florida	4,393
49	Georgia	4,441
7	Hawaii	9,160
42	Idaho	5,661
31	Illinois	6,299
39	Indiana	5,746
17	Iowa	7,520
33	Kansas	6,134
27	Kentucky	6,735
37	Louisiana	5,887
28	Maine	6,622
23	Maryland	7,066
11	Massachusetts	8,600
26	Michigan	6,751
10	Minnesota	8,610
22	Mississippi	7,081
43	Missouri	5,536
19	Montana	7,272
38	Nebraska	5,808
40	Nevada	5,702
36	New Hampshire	5,919
15	New Jersey	7,781
6	New Mexico	9,294
5	New York	9,866
45	North Carolina	5,451
1	North Dakota	12,987
18	Ohio	7,330
29	Oklahoma	6,391
8	Oregon	8,729
25	Pennsylvania	6,848
14	Rhode Island	7,824
35	South Carolina	6,039
41	South Dakota	5,677
48	Tennessee	4,591
47	Texas	4,987
32	Utah	6,238
4	Vermont	10,069
34	Virginia	6,112
24	Washington	6,975
16	West Virginia	7,772
21	Wisconsin	7,228
2	Wyoming	12,390

RANK ORDER

RANK	STATE	PER CAPITA
1	North Dakota	$12,987
2	Wyoming	12,390
3	Alaska	10,661
4	Vermont	10,069
5	New York	9,866
6	New Mexico	9,294
7	Hawaii	9,160
8	Oregon	8,729
9	Delaware	8,660
10	Minnesota	8,610
11	Massachusetts	8,600
12	California	8,180
13	Connecticut	8,170
14	Rhode Island	7,824
15	New Jersey	7,781
16	West Virginia	7,772
17	Iowa	7,520
18	Ohio	7,330
19	Montana	7,272
20	Arkansas	7,254
21	Wisconsin	7,228
22	Mississippi	7,081
23	Maryland	7,066
24	Washington	6,975
25	Pennsylvania	6,848
26	Michigan	6,751
27	Kentucky	6,735
28	Maine	6,622
29	Oklahoma	6,391
30	Colorado	6,388
31	Illinois	6,299
32	Utah	6,238
33	Kansas	6,134
34	Virginia	6,112
35	South Carolina	6,039
36	New Hampshire	5,919
37	Louisiana	5,887
38	Nebraska	5,808
39	Indiana	5,746
40	Nevada	5,702
41	South Dakota	5,677
42	Idaho	5,661
43	Missouri	5,536
44	Alabama	5,492
45	North Carolina	5,451
46	Arizona	5,242
47	Texas	4,987
48	Tennessee	4,591
49	Georgia	4,441
50	Florida	4,393

District of Columbia**　　　　　　　　NA

Source: CQ Press using data from U.S. Bureau of the Census, Governments Division
  "2015 State and Local Government Finances" (http://www.census.gov/govs/local/)
*Total revenue includes all money received from external sources. This includes taxes, intergovernmental transfers and insurance trust revenue, and revenue from government owned utilities and other commercial or auxiliary enterprise.
**Not applicable.

State Government Intergovernmental Revenue in 2015

National Total = $604,818,048,000*

ALPHA ORDER

RANK	STATE	REVENUE	% of USA
25	Alabama	$8,838,667,000	1.5%
41	Alaska	2,642,995,000	0.4%
14	Arizona	12,752,207,000	2.1%
31	Arkansas	7,002,577,000	1.2%
1	California	82,907,118,000	13.7%
28	Colorado	7,866,964,000	1.3%
32	Connecticut	6,898,669,000	1.1%
48	Delaware	1,974,674,000	0.3%
4	Florida	26,270,941,000	4.3%
12	Georgia	13,837,168,000	2.3%
40	Hawaii	2,697,519,000	0.4%
42	Idaho	2,590,690,000	0.4%
8	Illinois	19,732,875,000	3.3%
16	Indiana	11,689,694,000	1.9%
33	Iowa	6,548,007,000	1.1%
37	Kansas	3,948,181,000	0.7%
21	Kentucky	10,559,736,000	1.7%
23	Louisiana	9,910,427,000	1.6%
39	Maine	2,784,359,000	0.5%
15	Maryland	12,342,856,000	2.0%
11	Massachusetts	15,060,943,000	2.5%
7	Michigan	20,487,351,000	3.4%
17	Minnesota	11,253,891,000	1.9%
27	Mississippi	7,944,619,000	1.3%
19	Missouri	10,736,241,000	1.8%
43	Montana	2,468,165,000	0.4%
38	Nebraska	3,033,641,000	0.5%
36	Nevada	4,147,557,000	0.7%
45	New Hampshire	2,266,476,000	0.4%
9	New Jersey	18,015,768,000	3.0%
30	New Mexico	7,014,832,000	1.2%
2	New York	52,693,323,000	8.7%
10	North Carolina	16,021,314,000	2.6%
49	North Dakota	1,677,677,000	0.3%
5	Ohio	24,008,999,000	4.0%
29	Oklahoma	7,169,356,000	1.2%
18	Oregon	11,033,172,000	1.8%
6	Pennsylvania	23,065,920,000	3.8%
44	Rhode Island	2,466,598,000	0.4%
26	South Carolina	8,443,093,000	1.4%
50	South Dakota	1,498,716,000	0.2%
20	Tennessee	10,568,128,000	1.7%
3	Texas	43,863,312,000	7.3%
35	Utah	4,207,318,000	0.7%
47	Vermont	2,107,303,000	0.3%
22	Virginia	10,135,321,000	1.7%
13	Washington	13,333,590,000	2.2%
34	West Virginia	4,654,167,000	0.8%
24	Wisconsin	9,440,463,000	1.6%
46	Wyoming	2,204,470,000	0.4%

RANK ORDER

RANK	STATE	REVENUE	% of USA
1	California	$82,907,118,000	13.7%
2	New York	52,693,323,000	8.7%
3	Texas	43,863,312,000	7.3%
4	Florida	26,270,941,000	4.3%
5	Ohio	24,008,999,000	4.0%
6	Pennsylvania	23,065,920,000	3.8%
7	Michigan	20,487,351,000	3.4%
8	Illinois	19,732,875,000	3.3%
9	New Jersey	18,015,768,000	3.0%
10	North Carolina	16,021,314,000	2.6%
11	Massachusetts	15,060,943,000	2.5%
12	Georgia	13,837,168,000	2.3%
13	Washington	13,333,590,000	2.2%
14	Arizona	12,752,207,000	2.1%
15	Maryland	12,342,856,000	2.0%
16	Indiana	11,689,694,000	1.9%
17	Minnesota	11,253,891,000	1.9%
18	Oregon	11,033,172,000	1.8%
19	Missouri	10,736,241,000	1.8%
20	Tennessee	10,568,128,000	1.7%
21	Kentucky	10,559,736,000	1.7%
22	Virginia	10,135,321,000	1.7%
23	Louisiana	9,910,427,000	1.6%
24	Wisconsin	9,440,463,000	1.6%
25	Alabama	8,838,667,000	1.5%
26	South Carolina	8,443,093,000	1.4%
27	Mississippi	7,944,619,000	1.3%
28	Colorado	7,866,964,000	1.3%
29	Oklahoma	7,169,356,000	1.2%
30	New Mexico	7,014,832,000	1.2%
31	Arkansas	7,002,577,000	1.2%
32	Connecticut	6,898,669,000	1.1%
33	Iowa	6,548,007,000	1.1%
34	West Virginia	4,654,167,000	0.8%
35	Utah	4,207,318,000	0.7%
36	Nevada	4,147,557,000	0.7%
37	Kansas	3,948,181,000	0.7%
38	Nebraska	3,033,641,000	0.5%
39	Maine	2,784,359,000	0.5%
40	Hawaii	2,697,519,000	0.4%
41	Alaska	2,642,995,000	0.4%
42	Idaho	2,590,690,000	0.4%
43	Montana	2,468,165,000	0.4%
44	Rhode Island	2,466,598,000	0.4%
45	New Hampshire	2,266,476,000	0.4%
46	Wyoming	2,204,470,000	0.4%
47	Vermont	2,107,303,000	0.3%
48	Delaware	1,974,674,000	0.3%
49	North Dakota	1,677,677,000	0.3%
50	South Dakota	1,498,716,000	0.2%
	District of Columbia**	NA	NA

Source: U.S. Bureau of the Census, Governments Division
"2015 State and Local Government Finances" (http://www.census.gov/govs/local/)
*Includes revenue from federal and local government sources.
**Not applicable.

Per Capita State Government Intergovernmental Revenue in 2015

National Per Capita = $1,888*

<table>
<tr><td colspan="3">ALPHA ORDER</td><td colspan="3">RANK ORDER</td></tr>
<tr><td>RANK</td><td>STATE</td><td>PER CAPITA</td><td>RANK</td><td>STATE</td><td>PER CAPITA</td></tr>
<tr><td>30</td><td>Alabama</td><td>$1,822</td><td>1</td><td>Wyoming</td><td>$3,761</td></tr>
<tr><td>2</td><td>Alaska</td><td>3,581</td><td>2</td><td>Alaska</td><td>3,581</td></tr>
<tr><td>27</td><td>Arizona</td><td>1,875</td><td>3</td><td>Vermont</td><td>3,375</td></tr>
<tr><td>11</td><td>Arkansas</td><td>2,353</td><td>4</td><td>New Mexico</td><td>3,369</td></tr>
<tr><td>15</td><td>California</td><td>2,124</td><td>5</td><td>Oregon</td><td>2,747</td></tr>
<tr><td>44</td><td>Colorado</td><td>1,446</td><td>6</td><td>Mississippi</td><td>2,661</td></tr>
<tr><td>25</td><td>Connecticut</td><td>1,920</td><td>7</td><td>New York</td><td>2,659</td></tr>
<tr><td>19</td><td>Delaware</td><td>2,092</td><td>8</td><td>West Virginia</td><td>2,530</td></tr>
<tr><td>49</td><td>Florida</td><td>1,296</td><td>9</td><td>Montana</td><td>2,400</td></tr>
<tr><td>48</td><td>Georgia</td><td>1,357</td><td>10</td><td>Kentucky</td><td>2,388</td></tr>
<tr><td>26</td><td>Hawaii</td><td>1,891</td><td>11</td><td>Arkansas</td><td>2,353</td></tr>
<tr><td>42</td><td>Idaho</td><td>1,571</td><td>12</td><td>Rhode Island</td><td>2,336</td></tr>
<tr><td>43</td><td>Illinois</td><td>1,534</td><td>13</td><td>North Dakota</td><td>2,223</td></tr>
<tr><td>32</td><td>Indiana</td><td>1,768</td><td>14</td><td>Massachusetts</td><td>2,217</td></tr>
<tr><td>17</td><td>Iowa</td><td>2,100</td><td>15</td><td>California</td><td>2,124</td></tr>
<tr><td>47</td><td>Kansas</td><td>1,359</td><td>16</td><td>Louisiana</td><td>2,122</td></tr>
<tr><td>10</td><td>Kentucky</td><td>2,388</td><td>17</td><td>Iowa</td><td>2,100</td></tr>
<tr><td>16</td><td>Louisiana</td><td>2,122</td><td>18</td><td>Maine</td><td>2,097</td></tr>
<tr><td>18</td><td>Maine</td><td>2,097</td><td>19</td><td>Delaware</td><td>2,092</td></tr>
<tr><td>22</td><td>Maryland</td><td>2,057</td><td>20</td><td>Ohio</td><td>2,069</td></tr>
<tr><td>14</td><td>Massachusetts</td><td>2,217</td><td>21</td><td>Michigan</td><td>2,066</td></tr>
<tr><td>21</td><td>Michigan</td><td>2,066</td><td>22</td><td>Maryland</td><td>2,057</td></tr>
<tr><td>23</td><td>Minnesota</td><td>2,052</td><td>23</td><td>Minnesota</td><td>2,052</td></tr>
<tr><td>6</td><td>Mississippi</td><td>2,661</td><td>24</td><td>New Jersey</td><td>2,011</td></tr>
<tr><td>32</td><td>Missouri</td><td>1,768</td><td>25</td><td>Connecticut</td><td>1,920</td></tr>
<tr><td>9</td><td>Montana</td><td>2,400</td><td>26</td><td>Hawaii</td><td>1,891</td></tr>
<tr><td>39</td><td>Nebraska</td><td>1,602</td><td>27</td><td>Arizona</td><td>1,875</td></tr>
<tr><td>45</td><td>Nevada</td><td>1,439</td><td>28</td><td>Washington</td><td>1,864</td></tr>
<tr><td>36</td><td>New Hampshire</td><td>1,704</td><td>29</td><td>Oklahoma</td><td>1,836</td></tr>
<tr><td>24</td><td>New Jersey</td><td>2,011</td><td>30</td><td>Alabama</td><td>1,822</td></tr>
<tr><td>4</td><td>New Mexico</td><td>3,369</td><td>31</td><td>Pennsylvania</td><td>1,803</td></tr>
<tr><td>7</td><td>New York</td><td>2,659</td><td>32</td><td>Indiana</td><td>1,768</td></tr>
<tr><td>41</td><td>North Carolina</td><td>1,595</td><td>32</td><td>Missouri</td><td>1,768</td></tr>
<tr><td>13</td><td>North Dakota</td><td>2,223</td><td>34</td><td>South Dakota</td><td>1,755</td></tr>
<tr><td>20</td><td>Ohio</td><td>2,069</td><td>35</td><td>South Carolina</td><td>1,726</td></tr>
<tr><td>29</td><td>Oklahoma</td><td>1,836</td><td>36</td><td>New Hampshire</td><td>1,704</td></tr>
<tr><td>5</td><td>Oregon</td><td>2,747</td><td>37</td><td>Wisconsin</td><td>1,639</td></tr>
<tr><td>31</td><td>Pennsylvania</td><td>1,803</td><td>38</td><td>Tennessee</td><td>1,603</td></tr>
<tr><td>12</td><td>Rhode Island</td><td>2,336</td><td>39</td><td>Nebraska</td><td>1,602</td></tr>
<tr><td>35</td><td>South Carolina</td><td>1,726</td><td>40</td><td>Texas</td><td>1,598</td></tr>
<tr><td>34</td><td>South Dakota</td><td>1,755</td><td>41</td><td>North Carolina</td><td>1,595</td></tr>
<tr><td>38</td><td>Tennessee</td><td>1,603</td><td>42</td><td>Idaho</td><td>1,571</td></tr>
<tr><td>40</td><td>Texas</td><td>1,598</td><td>43</td><td>Illinois</td><td>1,534</td></tr>
<tr><td>46</td><td>Utah</td><td>1,410</td><td>44</td><td>Colorado</td><td>1,446</td></tr>
<tr><td>3</td><td>Vermont</td><td>3,375</td><td>45</td><td>Nevada</td><td>1,439</td></tr>
<tr><td>50</td><td>Virginia</td><td>1,211</td><td>46</td><td>Utah</td><td>1,410</td></tr>
<tr><td>28</td><td>Washington</td><td>1,864</td><td>47</td><td>Kansas</td><td>1,359</td></tr>
<tr><td>8</td><td>West Virginia</td><td>2,530</td><td>48</td><td>Georgia</td><td>1,357</td></tr>
<tr><td>37</td><td>Wisconsin</td><td>1,639</td><td>49</td><td>Florida</td><td>1,296</td></tr>
<tr><td>1</td><td>Wyoming</td><td>3,761</td><td>50</td><td>Virginia</td><td>1,211</td></tr>
<tr><td></td><td></td><td></td><td></td><td>District of Columbia**</td><td>NA</td></tr>
</table>

Source: CQ Press using data from U.S. Bureau of the Census, Governments Division
"2015 State and Local Government Finances" (http://www.census.gov/govs/local/)
*Includes revenue from federal and local government sources.
**Not applicable.

State Government Own Source Revenue in 2015

National Total = $1,248,082,251,000*

ALPHA ORDER

RANK	STATE	REVENUE	% of USA
27	Alabama	$15,785,973,000	1.3%
45	Alaska	4,519,454,000	0.4%
21	Arizona	18,460,659,000	1.5%
31	Arkansas	12,377,185,000	1.0%
1	California	182,530,202,000	14.6%
19	Colorado	20,986,234,000	1.7%
20	Connecticut	19,737,125,000	1.6%
41	Delaware	5,598,783,000	0.4%
4	Florida	53,216,612,000	4.3%
16	Georgia	25,664,582,000	2.1%
36	Hawaii	9,116,199,000	0.7%
42	Idaho	5,333,936,000	0.4%
6	Illinois	50,258,307,000	4.0%
18	Indiana	23,140,438,000	1.9%
29	Iowa	13,771,735,000	1.1%
32	Kansas	12,174,612,000	1.0%
26	Kentucky	16,073,794,000	1.3%
30	Louisiana	13,510,617,000	1.1%
43	Maine	5,224,391,000	0.4%
15	Maryland	26,458,584,000	2.1%
10	Massachusetts	36,729,999,000	2.9%
9	Michigan	39,240,287,000	3.1%
13	Minnesota	29,175,578,000	2.3%
34	Mississippi	10,551,550,000	0.8%
22	Missouri	17,302,704,000	1.4%
49	Montana	3,808,447,000	0.3%
40	Nebraska	6,924,800,000	0.6%
37	Nevada	8,923,098,000	0.7%
46	New Hampshire	4,139,626,000	0.3%
7	New Jersey	42,652,767,000	3.4%
35	New Mexico	10,325,610,000	0.8%
2	New York	104,110,477,000	8.3%
12	North Carolina	33,674,707,000	2.7%
39	North Dakota	7,126,666,000	0.6%
8	Ohio	41,372,405,000	3.3%
28	Oklahoma	14,506,612,000	1.2%
23	Oregon	17,128,827,000	1.4%
5	Pennsylvania	51,665,634,000	4.1%
44	Rhode Island	4,897,787,000	0.4%
25	South Carolina	16,265,275,000	1.3%
50	South Dakota	2,671,211,000	0.2%
24	Tennessee	17,064,219,000	1.4%
3	Texas	80,175,982,000	6.4%
33	Utah	11,462,669,000	0.9%
47	Vermont	3,901,434,000	0.3%
11	Virginia	33,941,061,000	2.7%
14	Washington	28,105,893,000	2.3%
38	West Virginia	8,421,508,000	0.7%
17	Wisconsin	24,035,311,000	1.9%
48	Wyoming	3,840,685,000	0.3%

RANK ORDER

RANK	STATE	REVENUE	% of USA
1	California	$182,530,202,000	14.6%
2	New York	104,110,477,000	8.3%
3	Texas	80,175,982,000	6.4%
4	Florida	53,216,612,000	4.3%
5	Pennsylvania	51,665,634,000	4.1%
6	Illinois	50,258,307,000	4.0%
7	New Jersey	42,652,767,000	3.4%
8	Ohio	41,372,405,000	3.3%
9	Michigan	39,240,287,000	3.1%
10	Massachusetts	36,729,999,000	2.9%
11	Virginia	33,941,061,000	2.7%
12	North Carolina	33,674,707,000	2.7%
13	Minnesota	29,175,578,000	2.3%
14	Washington	28,105,893,000	2.3%
15	Maryland	26,458,584,000	2.1%
16	Georgia	25,664,582,000	2.1%
17	Wisconsin	24,035,311,000	1.9%
18	Indiana	23,140,438,000	1.9%
19	Colorado	20,986,234,000	1.7%
20	Connecticut	19,737,125,000	1.6%
21	Arizona	18,460,659,000	1.5%
22	Missouri	17,302,704,000	1.4%
23	Oregon	17,128,827,000	1.4%
24	Tennessee	17,064,219,000	1.4%
25	South Carolina	16,265,275,000	1.3%
26	Kentucky	16,073,794,000	1.3%
27	Alabama	15,785,973,000	1.3%
28	Oklahoma	14,506,612,000	1.2%
29	Iowa	13,771,735,000	1.1%
30	Louisiana	13,510,617,000	1.1%
31	Arkansas	12,377,185,000	1.0%
32	Kansas	12,174,612,000	1.0%
33	Utah	11,462,669,000	0.9%
34	Mississippi	10,551,550,000	0.8%
35	New Mexico	10,325,610,000	0.8%
36	Hawaii	9,116,199,000	0.7%
37	Nevada	8,923,098,000	0.7%
38	West Virginia	8,421,508,000	0.7%
39	North Dakota	7,126,666,000	0.6%
40	Nebraska	6,924,800,000	0.6%
41	Delaware	5,598,783,000	0.4%
42	Idaho	5,333,936,000	0.4%
43	Maine	5,224,391,000	0.4%
44	Rhode Island	4,897,787,000	0.4%
45	Alaska	4,519,454,000	0.4%
46	New Hampshire	4,139,626,000	0.3%
47	Vermont	3,901,434,000	0.3%
48	Wyoming	3,840,685,000	0.3%
49	Montana	3,808,447,000	0.3%
50	South Dakota	2,671,211,000	0.2%

District of Columbia**	NA	NA

Source: U.S. Bureau of the Census, Governments Division
"2015 State and Local Government Finances" (http://www.census.gov/govs/local/)
*Own source revenue includes taxes, current charges, and miscellaneous general revenue. Excluded are intergovernmental transfers, insurance trust revenue, and revenue from government owned utilities and other commercial or auxiliary enterprise.
**Not applicable.

Per Capita State Government Own Source Revenue in 2015

National Per Capita = $3,896*

ALPHA ORDER			RANK ORDER		
RANK	STATE	PER CAPITA	RANK	STATE	PER CAPITA
39	Alabama	$3,254	1	North Dakota	$9,441
5	Alaska	6,124	2	Wyoming	6,553
47	Arizona	2,714	3	Hawaii	6,391
21	Arkansas	4,160	4	Vermont	6,248
13	California	4,676	5	Alaska	6,124
28	Colorado	3,857	6	Delaware	5,930
7	Connecticut	5,492	7	Connecticut	5,492
6	Delaware	5,930	8	Massachusetts	5,406
48	Florida	2,626	9	Minnesota	5,321
50	Georgia	2,516	10	New York	5,253
3	Hawaii	6,391	11	New Mexico	4,959
40	Idaho	3,234	12	New Jersey	4,760
27	Illinois	3,907	13	California	4,676
36	Indiana	3,501	14	Rhode Island	4,638
16	Iowa	4,416	15	West Virginia	4,577
19	Kansas	4,190	16	Iowa	4,416
33	Kentucky	3,635	17	Maryland	4,409
45	Louisiana	2,892	18	Oregon	4,265
25	Maine	3,935	19	Kansas	4,190
17	Maryland	4,409	20	Wisconsin	4,173
8	Massachusetts	5,406	21	Arkansas	4,160
24	Michigan	3,956	22	Virginia	4,057
9	Minnesota	5,321	23	Pennsylvania	4,039
35	Mississippi	3,535	24	Michigan	3,956
46	Missouri	2,849	25	Maine	3,935
31	Montana	3,704	26	Washington	3,929
32	Nebraska	3,657	27	Illinois	3,907
43	Nevada	3,095	28	Colorado	3,857
42	New Hampshire	3,112	29	Utah	3,840
12	New Jersey	4,760	30	Oklahoma	3,715
11	New Mexico	4,959	31	Montana	3,704
10	New York	5,253	32	Nebraska	3,657
37	North Carolina	3,353	33	Kentucky	3,635
1	North Dakota	9,441	34	Ohio	3,565
34	Ohio	3,565	35	Mississippi	3,535
30	Oklahoma	3,715	36	Indiana	3,501
18	Oregon	4,265	37	North Carolina	3,353
23	Pennsylvania	4,039	38	South Carolina	3,325
14	Rhode Island	4,638	39	Alabama	3,254
38	South Carolina	3,325	40	Idaho	3,234
41	South Dakota	3,128	41	South Dakota	3,128
49	Tennessee	2,589	42	New Hampshire	3,112
44	Texas	2,920	43	Nevada	3,095
29	Utah	3,840	44	Texas	2,920
4	Vermont	6,248	45	Louisiana	2,892
22	Virginia	4,057	46	Missouri	2,849
26	Washington	3,929	47	Arizona	2,714
15	West Virginia	4,577	48	Florida	2,626
20	Wisconsin	4,173	49	Tennessee	2,589
2	Wyoming	6,553	50	Georgia	2,516

District of Columbia**   NA

Source: CQ Press using data from U.S. Bureau of the Census, Governments Division
"2015 State and Local Government Finances" (http://www.census.gov/govs/local/)
*Own source revenue includes taxes, current charges, and miscellaneous general revenue. Excluded are intergovernmental transfers, insurance trust revenue, and revenue from government owned utilities and other commercial or auxiliary enterprise.
**Not applicable.

Projected vs. Actual State Tax Collections in 2017

National Percent = 98.2% of Projected Taxes*

ALPHA ORDER			RANK ORDER		
RANK	STATE	PERCENT	RANK	STATE	PERCENT
12	Alabama	100.9	1	Alaska	194.6
1	Alaska	194.6	2	New Hampshire	111.1
17	Arizona	99.8	3	Tennessee	106.7
14	Arkansas	100.2	4	Oregon	104.6
25	California	98.1	5	Texas	103.8
37	Colorado	96.3	6	Washington	103.6
34	Connecticut	96.8	7	Idaho	102.3
29	Delaware	97.5	8	Maine	101.8
17	Florida	99.8	9	Georgia	101.5
9	Georgia	101.5	10	Kansas	101.4
20	Hawaii	98.6	11	North Carolina	101.1
7	Idaho	102.3	12	Alabama	100.9
19	Illinois	99.0	13	Utah	100.8
21	Indiana	98.5	14	Arkansas	100.2
35	Iowa	96.4	14	Michigan	100.2
10	Kansas	101.4	16	South Carolina	100.0
24	Kentucky	98.2	17	Arizona	99.8
41	Louisiana	95.5	17	Florida	99.8
8	Maine	101.8	19	Illinois	99.0
30	Maryland	97.4	20	Hawaii	98.6
21	Massachusetts	98.5	21	Indiana	98.5
14	Michigan	100.2	21	Massachusetts	98.5
25	Minnesota	98.1	21	Virginia	98.5
35	Mississippi	96.4	24	Kentucky	98.2
39	Missouri	95.8	25	California	98.1
47	Montana	92.1	25	Minnesota	98.1
46	Nebraska	92.9	27	Wisconsin	98.0
28	Nevada	97.8	28	Nevada	97.8
2	New Hampshire	111.1	29	Delaware	97.5
31	New Jersey	97.2	30	Maryland	97.4
48	New Mexico	87.5	31	New Jersey	97.2
39	New York	95.8	32	Rhode Island	97.1
11	North Carolina	101.1	33	Pennsylvania	96.9
50	North Dakota	56.8	34	Connecticut	96.8
42	Ohio	95.3	35	Iowa	96.4
45	Oklahoma	93.8	35	Mississippi	96.4
4	Oregon	104.6	37	Colorado	96.3
33	Pennsylvania	96.9	38	Vermont	96.2
32	Rhode Island	97.1	39	Missouri	95.8
16	South Carolina	100.0	39	New York	95.8
44	South Dakota	94.4	41	Louisiana	95.5
3	Tennessee	106.7	42	Ohio	95.3
5	Texas	103.8	43	West Virginia	94.7
13	Utah	100.8	44	South Dakota	94.4
38	Vermont	96.2	45	Oklahoma	93.8
21	Virginia	98.5	46	Nebraska	92.9
6	Washington	103.6	47	Montana	92.1
43	West Virginia	94.7	48	New Mexico	87.5
27	Wisconsin	98.0	49	Wyoming	86.0
49	Wyoming	86.0	50	North Dakota	56.8
				District of Columbia**	NA

Source: CQ Press using data from National Association of State Budget Officers
"The Fiscal Survey of States" (Fall 2017, http://www.nasbo.org)
*For fiscal year 2017. This table compares sales, personal, and corporate income tax collections projected in adopting budgets with the amount collected.
**Not available.

State Government Tax Revenue in 2016

National Total = $930,263,745,000

ALPHA ORDER

RANK	STATE	REVENUE	% of USA
26	Alabama	$9,919,794,000	1.1%
50	Alaska	1,042,164,000	0.1%
20	Arizona	14,676,375,000	1.6%
29	Arkansas	9,452,883,000	1.0%
1	California	155,231,252,000	16.7%
22	Colorado	12,795,318,000	1.4%
19	Connecticut	15,244,947,000	1.6%
43	Delaware	3,522,301,000	0.4%
5	Florida	37,640,420,000	4.0%
14	Georgia	21,454,446,000	2.3%
36	Hawaii	6,919,035,000	0.7%
40	Idaho	4,209,514,000	0.5%
4	Illinois	38,907,220,000	4.2%
18	Indiana	17,587,958,000	1.9%
27	Iowa	9,558,563,000	1.0%
32	Kansas	8,058,949,000	0.9%
24	Kentucky	11,778,866,000	1.3%
30	Louisiana	9,309,673,000	1.0%
41	Maine	4,130,242,000	0.4%
16	Maryland	20,894,199,000	2.2%
10	Massachusetts	27,283,005,000	2.9%
9	Michigan	27,436,607,000	2.9%
12	Minnesota	25,189,128,000	2.7%
34	Mississippi	7,660,391,000	0.8%
23	Missouri	12,245,169,000	1.3%
47	Montana	2,627,943,000	0.3%
39	Nebraska	5,117,133,000	0.6%
33	Nevada	8,025,046,000	0.9%
46	New Hampshire	2,641,946,000	0.3%
7	New Jersey	31,546,720,000	3.4%
37	New Mexico	5,462,107,000	0.6%
2	New York	81,353,963,000	8.7%
11	North Carolina	26,201,576,000	2.8%
42	North Dakota	3,709,105,000	0.4%
8	Ohio	28,694,883,000	3.1%
31	Oklahoma	8,491,187,000	0.9%
25	Oregon	11,043,311,000	1.2%
6	Pennsylvania	37,394,589,000	4.0%
44	Rhode Island	3,265,727,000	0.4%
28	South Carolina	9,551,052,000	1.0%
49	South Dakota	1,747,550,000	0.2%
21	Tennessee	13,386,169,000	1.4%
3	Texas	52,132,817,000	5.6%
35	Utah	7,082,961,000	0.8%
45	Vermont	3,085,865,000	0.3%
15	Virginia	21,219,757,000	2.3%
13	Washington	22,280,088,000	2.4%
38	West Virginia	5,127,970,000	0.6%
17	Wisconsin	17,607,733,000	1.9%
48	Wyoming	1,913,607,000	0.2%

RANK ORDER

RANK	STATE	REVENUE	% of USA
1	California	$155,231,252,000	16.7%
2	New York	81,353,963,000	8.7%
3	Texas	52,132,817,000	5.6%
4	Illinois	38,907,220,000	4.2%
5	Florida	37,640,420,000	4.0%
6	Pennsylvania	37,394,589,000	4.0%
7	New Jersey	31,546,720,000	3.4%
8	Ohio	28,694,883,000	3.1%
9	Michigan	27,436,607,000	2.9%
10	Massachusetts	27,283,005,000	2.9%
11	North Carolina	26,201,576,000	2.8%
12	Minnesota	25,189,128,000	2.7%
13	Washington	22,280,088,000	2.4%
14	Georgia	21,454,446,000	2.3%
15	Virginia	21,219,757,000	2.3%
16	Maryland	20,894,199,000	2.2%
17	Wisconsin	17,607,733,000	1.9%
18	Indiana	17,587,958,000	1.9%
19	Connecticut	15,244,947,000	1.6%
20	Arizona	14,676,375,000	1.6%
21	Tennessee	13,386,169,000	1.4%
22	Colorado	12,795,318,000	1.4%
23	Missouri	12,245,169,000	1.3%
24	Kentucky	11,778,866,000	1.3%
25	Oregon	11,043,311,000	1.2%
26	Alabama	9,919,794,000	1.1%
27	Iowa	9,558,563,000	1.0%
28	South Carolina	9,551,052,000	1.0%
29	Arkansas	9,452,883,000	1.0%
30	Louisiana	9,309,673,000	1.0%
31	Oklahoma	8,491,187,000	0.9%
32	Kansas	8,058,949,000	0.9%
33	Nevada	8,025,046,000	0.9%
34	Mississippi	7,660,391,000	0.8%
35	Utah	7,082,961,000	0.8%
36	Hawaii	6,919,035,000	0.7%
37	New Mexico	5,462,107,000	0.6%
38	West Virginia	5,127,970,000	0.6%
39	Nebraska	5,117,133,000	0.6%
40	Idaho	4,209,514,000	0.5%
41	Maine	4,130,242,000	0.4%
42	North Dakota	3,709,105,000	0.4%
43	Delaware	3,522,301,000	0.4%
44	Rhode Island	3,265,727,000	0.4%
45	Vermont	3,085,865,000	0.3%
46	New Hampshire	2,641,946,000	0.3%
47	Montana	2,627,943,000	0.3%
48	Wyoming	1,913,607,000	0.2%
49	South Dakota	1,747,550,000	0.2%
50	Alaska	1,042,164,000	0.1%
	District of Columbia	7,404,521,000	0.8%

Source: U.S. Bureau of the Census, Governments Division
"2016 State Government Tax Collections" (http://www.census.gov/govs/statetax/)

Per Capita State Government Tax Revenue in 2016

National Per Capita = $2,876

ALPHA ORDER				RANK ORDER		
RANK	STATE	PER CAPITA		RANK	STATE	PER CAPITA
41	Alabama	$2,041		1	Vermont	$4,950
50	Alaska	1,405		2	North Dakota	4,909
39	Arizona	2,124		3	Hawaii	4,843
13	Arkansas	3,163		4	Minnesota	4,559
8	California	3,950		5	Connecticut	4,249
37	Colorado	2,314		6	New York	4,101
5	Connecticut	4,249		7	Massachusetts	3,998
9	Delaware	3,697		8	California	3,950
49	Florida	1,822		9	Delaware	3,697
40	Georgia	2,080		10	New Jersey	3,514
3	Hawaii	4,843		11	Maryland	3,468
34	Idaho	2,506		12	Wyoming	3,272
19	Illinois	3,031		13	Arkansas	3,163
28	Indiana	2,651		14	Maine	3,105
17	Iowa	3,053		15	Rhode Island	3,088
22	Kansas	2,772		16	Washington	3,060
27	Kentucky	2,655		17	Iowa	3,053
45	Louisiana	1,987		18	Wisconsin	3,050
14	Maine	3,105		19	Illinois	3,031
11	Maryland	3,468		20	Pennsylvania	2,924
7	Massachusetts	3,998		21	West Virginia	2,804
23	Michigan	2,762		22	Kansas	2,772
4	Minnesota	4,559		23	Michigan	2,762
31	Mississippi	2,566		24	Nevada	2,730
44	Missouri	2,010		25	Oregon	2,703
32	Montana	2,530		26	Nebraska	2,682
26	Nebraska	2,682		27	Kentucky	2,655
24	Nevada	2,730		28	Indiana	2,651
46	New Hampshire	1,979		29	New Mexico	2,619
10	New Jersey	3,514		30	North Carolina	2,580
29	New Mexico	2,619		31	Mississippi	2,566
6	New York	4,101		32	Montana	2,530
30	North Carolina	2,580		33	Virginia	2,522
2	North Dakota	4,909		34	Idaho	2,506
35	Ohio	2,469		35	Ohio	2,469
38	Oklahoma	2,165		36	Utah	2,327
25	Oregon	2,703		37	Colorado	2,314
20	Pennsylvania	2,924		38	Oklahoma	2,165
15	Rhode Island	3,088		39	Arizona	2,124
47	South Carolina	1,926		40	Georgia	2,080
42	South Dakota	2,028		41	Alabama	2,041
43	Tennessee	2,013		42	South Dakota	2,028
48	Texas	1,868		43	Tennessee	2,013
36	Utah	2,327		44	Missouri	2,010
1	Vermont	4,950		45	Louisiana	1,987
33	Virginia	2,522		46	New Hampshire	1,979
16	Washington	3,060		47	South Carolina	1,926
21	West Virginia	2,804		48	Texas	1,868
18	Wisconsin	3,050		49	Florida	1,822
12	Wyoming	3,272		50	Alaska	1,405
					District of Columbia	10,820

Source: CQ Press using data from U.S. Bureau of the Census, Governments Division
"2016 State Government Tax Collections" (http://www.census.gov/govs/statetax/)

State Government Tax Revenue as a Percent of Personal Income in 2016

National Percent = 5.8% of Personal Income

ALPHA ORDER				RANK ORDER		
RANK	**STATE**	**PERCENT**		**RANK**	**STATE**	**PERCENT**
36	Alabama	5.2		1	Vermont	9.9
50	Alaska	2.5		2	Hawaii	9.6
36	Arizona	5.2		3	North Dakota	9.0
5	Arkansas	8.0		4	Minnesota	8.8
9	California	7.0		5	Arkansas	8.0
45	Colorado	4.4		6	Delaware	7.7
21	Connecticut	6.1		7	West Virginia	7.6
6	Delaware	7.7		8	Mississippi	7.2
47	Florida	4.0		9	California	7.0
39	Georgia	4.9		9	Maine	7.0
2	Hawaii	9.6		11	New York	6.9
16	Idaho	6.3		12	Kentucky	6.8
25	Illinois	5.9		12	New Mexico	6.8
18	Indiana	6.2		14	Iowa	6.6
14	Iowa	6.6		15	Wisconsin	6.5
25	Kansas	5.9		16	Idaho	6.3
12	Kentucky	6.8		16	Nevada	6.3
42	Louisiana	4.7		18	Indiana	6.2
9	Maine	7.0		18	Massachusetts	6.2
24	Maryland	6.0		18	Michigan	6.2
18	Massachusetts	6.2		21	Connecticut	6.1
18	Michigan	6.2		21	North Carolina	6.1
4	Minnesota	8.8		21	Rhode Island	6.1
8	Mississippi	7.2		24	Maryland	6.0
42	Missouri	4.7		25	Illinois	5.9
25	Montana	5.9		25	Kansas	5.9
35	Nebraska	5.4		25	Montana	5.9
16	Nevada	6.3		25	Oregon	5.9
49	New Hampshire	3.5		25	Wyoming	5.9
31	New Jersey	5.7		30	Pennsylvania	5.8
12	New Mexico	6.8		31	New Jersey	5.7
11	New York	6.9		31	Utah	5.7
21	North Carolina	6.1		33	Washington	5.6
3	North Dakota	9.0		34	Ohio	5.5
34	Ohio	5.5		35	Nebraska	5.4
38	Oklahoma	5.1		36	Alabama	5.2
25	Oregon	5.9		36	Arizona	5.2
30	Pennsylvania	5.8		38	Oklahoma	5.1
21	Rhode Island	6.1		39	Georgia	4.9
39	South Carolina	4.9		39	South Carolina	4.9
46	South Dakota	4.2		41	Virginia	4.8
44	Tennessee	4.6		42	Louisiana	4.7
47	Texas	4.0		42	Missouri	4.7
31	Utah	5.7		44	Tennessee	4.6
1	Vermont	9.9		45	Colorado	4.4
41	Virginia	4.8		46	South Dakota	4.2
33	Washington	5.6		47	Florida	4.0
7	West Virginia	7.6		47	Texas	4.0
15	Wisconsin	6.5		49	New Hampshire	3.5
25	Wyoming	5.9		50	Alaska	2.5
					District of Columbia	14.3

Source: CQ Press using data from U.S. Bureau of the Census, Governments Division
"2016 State Government Tax Collections" (http://www.census.gov/govs/statetax/)
U.S. Department of Commerce, Bureau of Economic Analysis
"Annual State Personal Income" (http://www.bea.gov/iTable/index_regional.cfm)

State Government Individual Income Tax Revenue in 2016

National Total = $345,528,601,000

ALPHA ORDER

RANK	STATE	REVENUE	% of USA
24	Alabama	$3,492,904,000	1.0%
44	Alaska	0	0.0%
21	Arizona	3,967,924,000	1.1%
28	Arkansas	2,781,458,000	0.8%
1	California	80,753,345,000	23.4%
17	Colorado	6,485,602,000	1.9%
15	Connecticut	7,557,153,000	2.2%
39	Delaware	1,112,368,000	0.3%
44	Florida	0	0.0%
10	Georgia	10,439,534,000	3.0%
31	Hawaii	2,116,130,000	0.6%
35	Idaho	1,521,238,000	0.4%
4	Illinois	13,806,525,000	4.0%
19	Indiana	5,218,166,000	1.5%
23	Iowa	3,553,325,000	1.0%
30	Kansas	2,231,902,000	0.6%
20	Kentucky	4,282,080,000	1.2%
27	Louisiana	2,866,456,000	0.8%
34	Maine	1,551,637,000	0.4%
12	Maryland	8,517,529,000	2.5%
3	Massachusetts	14,430,331,000	4.2%
11	Michigan	9,303,847,000	2.7%
9	Minnesota	10,732,570,000	3.1%
33	Mississippi	1,800,053,000	0.5%
18	Missouri	6,023,701,000	1.7%
38	Montana	1,181,042,000	0.3%
29	Nebraska	2,244,719,000	0.6%
44	Nevada	0	0.0%
43	New Hampshire	87,973,000	0.0%
5	New Jersey	13,355,992,000	3.9%
36	New Mexico	1,409,811,000	0.4%
2	New York	46,508,632,000	13.5%
7	North Carolina	12,042,957,000	3.5%
41	North Dakota	351,125,000	0.1%
13	Ohio	8,169,197,000	2.4%
26	Oklahoma	2,996,870,000	0.9%
14	Oregon	7,690,019,000	2.2%
8	Pennsylvania	11,932,232,000	3.5%
37	Rhode Island	1,236,194,000	0.4%
22	South Carolina	3,869,342,000	1.1%
44	South Dakota	0	0.0%
42	Tennessee	323,952,000	0.1%
44	Texas	0	0.0%
25	Utah	3,374,535,000	1.0%
40	Vermont	729,986,000	0.2%
6	Virginia	12,237,996,000	3.5%
44	Washington	0	0.0%
32	West Virginia	1,845,711,000	0.5%
16	Wisconsin	7,486,676,000	2.2%
44	Wyoming	0	0.0%

RANK ORDER

RANK	STATE	REVENUE	% of USA
1	California	$80,753,345,000	23.4%
2	New York	46,508,632,000	13.5%
3	Massachusetts	14,430,331,000	4.2%
4	Illinois	13,806,525,000	4.0%
5	New Jersey	13,355,992,000	3.9%
6	Virginia	12,237,996,000	3.5%
7	North Carolina	12,042,957,000	3.5%
8	Pennsylvania	11,932,232,000	3.5%
9	Minnesota	10,732,570,000	3.1%
10	Georgia	10,439,534,000	3.0%
11	Michigan	9,303,847,000	2.7%
12	Maryland	8,517,529,000	2.5%
13	Ohio	8,169,197,000	2.4%
14	Oregon	7,690,019,000	2.2%
15	Connecticut	7,557,153,000	2.2%
16	Wisconsin	7,486,676,000	2.2%
17	Colorado	6,485,602,000	1.9%
18	Missouri	6,023,701,000	1.7%
19	Indiana	5,218,166,000	1.5%
20	Kentucky	4,282,080,000	1.2%
21	Arizona	3,967,924,000	1.1%
22	South Carolina	3,869,342,000	1.1%
23	Iowa	3,553,325,000	1.0%
24	Alabama	3,492,904,000	1.0%
25	Utah	3,374,535,000	1.0%
26	Oklahoma	2,996,870,000	0.9%
27	Louisiana	2,866,456,000	0.8%
28	Arkansas	2,781,458,000	0.8%
29	Nebraska	2,244,719,000	0.6%
30	Kansas	2,231,902,000	0.6%
31	Hawaii	2,116,130,000	0.6%
32	West Virginia	1,845,711,000	0.5%
33	Mississippi	1,800,053,000	0.5%
34	Maine	1,551,637,000	0.4%
35	Idaho	1,521,238,000	0.4%
36	New Mexico	1,409,811,000	0.4%
37	Rhode Island	1,236,194,000	0.4%
38	Montana	1,181,042,000	0.3%
39	Delaware	1,112,368,000	0.3%
40	Vermont	729,986,000	0.2%
41	North Dakota	351,125,000	0.1%
42	Tennessee	323,952,000	0.1%
43	New Hampshire	87,973,000	0.0%
44	Alaska	0	0.0%
44	Florida	0	0.0%
44	Nevada	0	0.0%
44	South Dakota	0	0.0%
44	Texas	0	0.0%
44	Washington	0	0.0%
44	Wyoming	0	0.0%
	District of Columbia	1,907,862,000	0.6%

Source: U.S. Bureau of the Census, Governments Division
"2016 State Government Tax Collections" (http://www.census.gov/govs/statetax/)

Per Capita State Government Individual Income Tax Revenue in 2016

National Per Capita = $1,068

<table>
<tr><td colspan="3">ALPHA ORDER</td><td colspan="3">RANK ORDER</td></tr>
<tr><td>RANK</td><td>STATE</td><td>PER CAPITA</td><td>RANK</td><td>STATE</td><td>PER CAPITA</td></tr>
<tr><td>35</td><td>Alabama</td><td>$719</td><td>1</td><td>New York</td><td>$2,345</td></tr>
<tr><td>44</td><td>Alaska</td><td>0</td><td>2</td><td>Massachusetts</td><td>2,115</td></tr>
<tr><td>40</td><td>Arizona</td><td>574</td><td>3</td><td>Connecticut</td><td>2,106</td></tr>
<tr><td>29</td><td>Arkansas</td><td>931</td><td>4</td><td>California</td><td>2,055</td></tr>
<tr><td>4</td><td>California</td><td>2,055</td><td>5</td><td>Minnesota</td><td>1,943</td></tr>
<tr><td>14</td><td>Colorado</td><td>1,173</td><td>6</td><td>Oregon</td><td>1,882</td></tr>
<tr><td>3</td><td>Connecticut</td><td>2,106</td><td>7</td><td>New Jersey</td><td>1,488</td></tr>
<tr><td>17</td><td>Delaware</td><td>1,168</td><td>8</td><td>Hawaii</td><td>1,481</td></tr>
<tr><td>44</td><td>Florida</td><td>0</td><td>9</td><td>Virginia</td><td>1,454</td></tr>
<tr><td>23</td><td>Georgia</td><td>1,012</td><td>10</td><td>Maryland</td><td>1,414</td></tr>
<tr><td>8</td><td>Hawaii</td><td>1,481</td><td>11</td><td>Wisconsin</td><td>1,297</td></tr>
<tr><td>30</td><td>Idaho</td><td>905</td><td>12</td><td>North Carolina</td><td>1,186</td></tr>
<tr><td>22</td><td>Illinois</td><td>1,076</td><td>13</td><td>Nebraska</td><td>1,177</td></tr>
<tr><td>31</td><td>Indiana</td><td>787</td><td>14</td><td>Colorado</td><td>1,173</td></tr>
<tr><td>20</td><td>Iowa</td><td>1,135</td><td>15</td><td>Vermont</td><td>1,171</td></tr>
<tr><td>33</td><td>Kansas</td><td>768</td><td>16</td><td>Rhode Island</td><td>1,169</td></tr>
<tr><td>26</td><td>Kentucky</td><td>965</td><td>17</td><td>Delaware</td><td>1,168</td></tr>
<tr><td>38</td><td>Louisiana</td><td>612</td><td>18</td><td>Maine</td><td>1,166</td></tr>
<tr><td>18</td><td>Maine</td><td>1,166</td><td>19</td><td>Montana</td><td>1,137</td></tr>
<tr><td>10</td><td>Maryland</td><td>1,414</td><td>20</td><td>Iowa</td><td>1,135</td></tr>
<tr><td>2</td><td>Massachusetts</td><td>2,115</td><td>21</td><td>Utah</td><td>1,108</td></tr>
<tr><td>27</td><td>Michigan</td><td>937</td><td>22</td><td>Illinois</td><td>1,076</td></tr>
<tr><td>5</td><td>Minnesota</td><td>1,943</td><td>23</td><td>Georgia</td><td>1,012</td></tr>
<tr><td>39</td><td>Mississippi</td><td>603</td><td>24</td><td>West Virginia</td><td>1,009</td></tr>
<tr><td>25</td><td>Missouri</td><td>989</td><td>25</td><td>Missouri</td><td>989</td></tr>
<tr><td>19</td><td>Montana</td><td>1,137</td><td>26</td><td>Kentucky</td><td>965</td></tr>
<tr><td>13</td><td>Nebraska</td><td>1,177</td><td>27</td><td>Michigan</td><td>937</td></tr>
<tr><td>44</td><td>Nevada</td><td>0</td><td>28</td><td>Pennsylvania</td><td>933</td></tr>
<tr><td>42</td><td>New Hampshire</td><td>66</td><td>29</td><td>Arkansas</td><td>931</td></tr>
<tr><td>7</td><td>New Jersey</td><td>1,488</td><td>30</td><td>Idaho</td><td>905</td></tr>
<tr><td>37</td><td>New Mexico</td><td>676</td><td>31</td><td>Indiana</td><td>787</td></tr>
<tr><td>1</td><td>New York</td><td>2,345</td><td>32</td><td>South Carolina</td><td>780</td></tr>
<tr><td>12</td><td>North Carolina</td><td>1,186</td><td>33</td><td>Kansas</td><td>768</td></tr>
<tr><td>41</td><td>North Dakota</td><td>465</td><td>34</td><td>Oklahoma</td><td>764</td></tr>
<tr><td>36</td><td>Ohio</td><td>703</td><td>35</td><td>Alabama</td><td>719</td></tr>
<tr><td>34</td><td>Oklahoma</td><td>764</td><td>36</td><td>Ohio</td><td>703</td></tr>
<tr><td>6</td><td>Oregon</td><td>1,882</td><td>37</td><td>New Mexico</td><td>676</td></tr>
<tr><td>28</td><td>Pennsylvania</td><td>933</td><td>38</td><td>Louisiana</td><td>612</td></tr>
<tr><td>16</td><td>Rhode Island</td><td>1,169</td><td>39</td><td>Mississippi</td><td>603</td></tr>
<tr><td>32</td><td>South Carolina</td><td>780</td><td>40</td><td>Arizona</td><td>574</td></tr>
<tr><td>44</td><td>South Dakota</td><td>0</td><td>41</td><td>North Dakota</td><td>465</td></tr>
<tr><td>43</td><td>Tennessee</td><td>49</td><td>42</td><td>New Hampshire</td><td>66</td></tr>
<tr><td>44</td><td>Texas</td><td>0</td><td>43</td><td>Tennessee</td><td>49</td></tr>
<tr><td>21</td><td>Utah</td><td>1,108</td><td>44</td><td>Alaska</td><td>0</td></tr>
<tr><td>15</td><td>Vermont</td><td>1,171</td><td>44</td><td>Florida</td><td>0</td></tr>
<tr><td>9</td><td>Virginia</td><td>1,454</td><td>44</td><td>Nevada</td><td>0</td></tr>
<tr><td>44</td><td>Washington</td><td>0</td><td>44</td><td>South Dakota</td><td>0</td></tr>
<tr><td>24</td><td>West Virginia</td><td>1,009</td><td>44</td><td>Texas</td><td>0</td></tr>
<tr><td>11</td><td>Wisconsin</td><td>1,297</td><td>44</td><td>Washington</td><td>0</td></tr>
<tr><td>44</td><td>Wyoming</td><td>0</td><td>44</td><td>Wyoming</td><td>0</td></tr>
<tr><td></td><td></td><td></td><td></td><td>District of Columbia</td><td>2,788</td></tr>
</table>

Source: CQ Press using data from U.S. Bureau of the Census, Governments Division
  "2016 State Government Tax Collections" (http://www.census.gov/govs/statetax/)

State Government Corporation Net Income Tax Revenue in 2016

National Total = $46,758,309,000

ALPHA ORDER

RANK	STATE	REVENUE	% of USA
28	Alabama	$376,680,000	0.8%
34	Alaska	212,252,000	0.5%
22	Arizona	570,548,000	1.2%
24	Arkansas	450,159,000	1.0%
1	California	9,902,185,000	21.2%
19	Colorado	626,109,000	1.3%
17	Connecticut	719,467,000	1.5%
32	Delaware	318,152,000	0.7%
6	Florida	2,272,230,000	4.9%
14	Georgia	981,002,000	2.1%
42	Hawaii	108,169,000	0.2%
35	Idaho	188,996,000	0.4%
3	Illinois	3,367,461,000	7.2%
12	Indiana	1,034,367,000	2.2%
27	Iowa	376,865,000	0.8%
26	Kansas	391,877,000	0.8%
21	Kentucky	606,840,000	1.3%
36	Louisiana	171,579,000	0.4%
39	Maine	137,492,000	0.3%
10	Maryland	1,129,008,000	2.4%
5	Massachusetts	2,333,892,000	5.0%
15	Michigan	898,213,000	1.9%
9	Minnesota	1,515,697,000	3.2%
23	Mississippi	463,111,000	1.0%
30	Missouri	328,736,000	0.7%
40	Montana	118,969,000	0.3%
33	Nebraska	307,672,000	0.7%
47	Nevada	0	0.0%
18	New Hampshire	700,237,000	1.5%
7	New Jersey	2,229,487,000	4.8%
41	New Mexico	113,942,000	0.2%
2	New York	4,181,811,000	8.9%
11	North Carolina	1,066,511,000	2.3%
43	North Dakota	103,069,000	0.2%
45	Ohio	33,235,000	0.1%
31	Oklahoma	327,783,000	0.7%
20	Oregon	609,868,000	1.3%
4	Pennsylvania	2,456,231,000	5.3%
38	Rhode Island	144,269,000	0.3%
25	South Carolina	440,489,000	0.9%
46	South Dakota	32,684,000	0.1%
8	Tennessee	1,538,649,000	3.3%
47	Texas	0	0.0%
29	Utah	333,358,000	0.7%
44	Vermont	98,336,000	0.2%
16	Virginia	752,689,000	1.6%
47	Washington	0	0.0%
37	West Virginia	144,680,000	0.3%
13	Wisconsin	986,785,000	2.1%
47	Wyoming	0	0.0%

RANK ORDER

RANK	STATE	REVENUE	% of USA
1	California	$9,902,185,000	21.2%
2	New York	4,181,811,000	8.9%
3	Illinois	3,367,461,000	7.2%
4	Pennsylvania	2,456,231,000	5.3%
5	Massachusetts	2,333,892,000	5.0%
6	Florida	2,272,230,000	4.9%
7	New Jersey	2,229,487,000	4.8%
8	Tennessee	1,538,649,000	3.3%
9	Minnesota	1,515,697,000	3.2%
10	Maryland	1,129,008,000	2.4%
11	North Carolina	1,066,511,000	2.3%
12	Indiana	1,034,367,000	2.2%
13	Wisconsin	986,785,000	2.1%
14	Georgia	981,002,000	2.1%
15	Michigan	898,213,000	1.9%
16	Virginia	752,689,000	1.6%
17	Connecticut	719,467,000	1.5%
18	New Hampshire	700,237,000	1.5%
19	Colorado	626,109,000	1.3%
20	Oregon	609,868,000	1.3%
21	Kentucky	606,840,000	1.3%
22	Arizona	570,548,000	1.2%
23	Mississippi	463,111,000	1.0%
24	Arkansas	450,159,000	1.0%
25	South Carolina	440,489,000	0.9%
26	Kansas	391,877,000	0.8%
27	Iowa	376,865,000	0.8%
28	Alabama	376,680,000	0.8%
29	Utah	333,358,000	0.7%
30	Missouri	328,736,000	0.7%
31	Oklahoma	327,783,000	0.7%
32	Delaware	318,152,000	0.7%
33	Nebraska	307,672,000	0.7%
34	Alaska	212,252,000	0.5%
35	Idaho	188,996,000	0.4%
36	Louisiana	171,579,000	0.4%
37	West Virginia	144,680,000	0.3%
38	Rhode Island	144,269,000	0.3%
39	Maine	137,492,000	0.3%
40	Montana	118,969,000	0.3%
41	New Mexico	113,942,000	0.2%
42	Hawaii	108,169,000	0.2%
43	North Dakota	103,069,000	0.2%
44	Vermont	98,336,000	0.2%
45	Ohio	33,235,000	0.1%
46	South Dakota	32,684,000	0.1%
47	Nevada	0	0.0%
47	Texas	0	0.0%
47	Washington	0	0.0%
47	Wyoming	0	0.0%
	District of Columbia	556,468,000	1.2%

Source: U.S. Bureau of the Census, Governments Division
"2016 State Government Tax Collections" (http://www.census.gov/govs/statetax/)

Per Capita State Government Corporation Net Income Tax Revenue in 2016

National Per Capita = $145

RANK	STATE	PER CAPITA
40	Alabama	$77
4	Alaska	286
38	Arizona	83
19	Arkansas	151
7	California	252
27	Colorado	113
11	Connecticut	201
3	Delaware	334
29	Florida	110
33	Georgia	95
41	Hawaii	76
28	Idaho	112
6	Illinois	262
17	Indiana	156
25	Iowa	120
24	Kansas	135
21	Kentucky	137
45	Louisiana	37
32	Maine	103
13	Maryland	187
2	Massachusetts	342
34	Michigan	90
5	Minnesota	274
18	Mississippi	155
43	Missouri	54
26	Montana	115
15	Nebraska	161
47	Nevada	0
1	New Hampshire	525
8	New Jersey	248
42	New Mexico	55
10	New York	211
31	North Carolina	105
22	North Dakota	136
46	Ohio	3
37	Oklahoma	84
20	Oregon	149
12	Pennsylvania	192
22	Rhode Island	136
35	South Carolina	89
44	South Dakota	38
9	Tennessee	231
47	Texas	0
29	Utah	110
16	Vermont	158
35	Virginia	89
47	Washington	0
39	West Virginia	79
14	Wisconsin	171
47	Wyoming	0

RANK	STATE	PER CAPITA
1	New Hampshire	$525
2	Massachusetts	342
3	Delaware	334
4	Alaska	286
5	Minnesota	274
6	Illinois	262
7	California	252
8	New Jersey	248
9	Tennessee	231
10	New York	211
11	Connecticut	201
12	Pennsylvania	192
13	Maryland	187
14	Wisconsin	171
15	Nebraska	161
16	Vermont	158
17	Indiana	156
18	Mississippi	155
19	Arkansas	151
20	Oregon	149
21	Kentucky	137
22	North Dakota	136
22	Rhode Island	136
24	Kansas	135
25	Iowa	120
26	Montana	115
27	Colorado	113
28	Idaho	112
29	Florida	110
29	Utah	110
31	North Carolina	105
32	Maine	103
33	Georgia	95
34	Michigan	90
35	South Carolina	89
35	Virginia	89
37	Oklahoma	84
38	Arizona	83
39	West Virginia	79
40	Alabama	77
41	Hawaii	76
42	New Mexico	55
43	Missouri	54
44	South Dakota	38
45	Louisiana	37
46	Ohio	3
47	Nevada	0
47	Texas	0
47	Washington	0
47	Wyoming	0

District of Columbia	813

Source: CQ Press using data from U.S. Bureau of the Census, Governments Division
"2016 State Government Tax Collections" (http://www.census.gov/govs/statetax/)

State Government General Sales Tax Revenue in 2016

National Total = $292,815,900,000*

ALPHA ORDER

RANK	STATE	REVENUE	% of USA
33	Alabama	$2,596,223,000	0.9%
46	Alaska	0	0.0%
14	Arizona	6,660,817,000	2.3%
25	Arkansas	3,314,363,000	1.1%
1	California	39,189,007,000	13.4%
32	Colorado	2,840,173,000	1.0%
22	Connecticut	3,752,793,000	1.3%
46	Delaware	0	0.0%
3	Florida	22,291,157,000	7.6%
17	Georgia	5,480,196,000	1.9%
29	Hawaii	3,206,154,000	1.1%
38	Idaho	1,559,332,000	0.5%
7	Illinois	11,344,480,000	3.9%
11	Indiana	7,306,331,000	2.5%
31	Iowa	3,162,854,000	1.1%
28	Kansas	3,240,354,000	1.1%
24	Kentucky	3,462,704,000	1.2%
30	Louisiana	3,186,614,000	1.1%
39	Maine	1,359,190,000	0.5%
19	Maryland	4,504,242,000	1.5%
15	Massachusetts	6,089,860,000	2.1%
10	Michigan	9,163,542,000	3.1%
16	Minnesota	5,583,910,000	1.9%
26	Mississippi	3,297,760,000	1.1%
23	Missouri	3,536,396,000	1.2%
46	Montana	0	0.0%
37	Nebraska	1,783,498,000	0.6%
20	Nevada	4,266,267,000	1.5%
46	New Hampshire	0	0.0%
9	New Jersey	9,267,703,000	3.2%
35	New Mexico	2,085,366,000	0.7%
5	New York	13,534,170,000	4.6%
12	North Carolina	7,187,844,000	2.5%
41	North Dakota	1,017,269,000	0.3%
6	Ohio	12,226,504,000	4.2%
34	Oklahoma	2,471,242,000	0.8%
46	Oregon	0	0.0%
8	Pennsylvania	10,221,593,000	3.5%
42	Rhode Island	973,585,000	0.3%
27	South Carolina	3,268,415,000	1.1%
43	South Dakota	968,787,000	0.3%
13	Tennessee	7,006,376,000	2.4%
2	Texas	32,131,385,000	11.0%
36	Utah	2,083,671,000	0.7%
45	Vermont	371,365,000	0.1%
21	Virginia	3,931,717,000	1.3%
4	Washington	13,560,382,000	4.6%
40	West Virginia	1,286,833,000	0.4%
18	Wisconsin	5,058,789,000	1.7%
44	Wyoming	641,495,000	0.2%

RANK ORDER

RANK	STATE	REVENUE	% of USA
1	California	$39,189,007,000	13.4%
2	Texas	32,131,385,000	11.0%
3	Florida	22,291,157,000	7.6%
4	Washington	13,560,382,000	4.6%
5	New York	13,534,170,000	4.6%
6	Ohio	12,226,504,000	4.2%
7	Illinois	11,344,480,000	3.9%
8	Pennsylvania	10,221,593,000	3.5%
9	New Jersey	9,267,703,000	3.2%
10	Michigan	9,163,542,000	3.1%
11	Indiana	7,306,331,000	2.5%
12	North Carolina	7,187,844,000	2.5%
13	Tennessee	7,006,376,000	2.4%
14	Arizona	6,660,817,000	2.3%
15	Massachusetts	6,089,860,000	2.1%
16	Minnesota	5,583,910,000	1.9%
17	Georgia	5,480,196,000	1.9%
18	Wisconsin	5,058,789,000	1.7%
19	Maryland	4,504,242,000	1.5%
20	Nevada	4,266,267,000	1.5%
21	Virginia	3,931,717,000	1.3%
22	Connecticut	3,752,793,000	1.3%
23	Missouri	3,536,396,000	1.2%
24	Kentucky	3,462,704,000	1.2%
25	Arkansas	3,314,363,000	1.1%
26	Mississippi	3,297,760,000	1.1%
27	South Carolina	3,268,415,000	1.1%
28	Kansas	3,240,354,000	1.1%
29	Hawaii	3,206,154,000	1.1%
30	Louisiana	3,186,614,000	1.1%
31	Iowa	3,162,854,000	1.1%
32	Colorado	2,840,173,000	1.0%
33	Alabama	2,596,223,000	0.9%
34	Oklahoma	2,471,242,000	0.8%
35	New Mexico	2,085,366,000	0.7%
36	Utah	2,083,671,000	0.7%
37	Nebraska	1,783,498,000	0.6%
38	Idaho	1,559,332,000	0.5%
39	Maine	1,359,190,000	0.5%
40	West Virginia	1,286,833,000	0.4%
41	North Dakota	1,017,269,000	0.3%
42	Rhode Island	973,585,000	0.3%
43	South Dakota	968,787,000	0.3%
44	Wyoming	641,495,000	0.2%
45	Vermont	371,365,000	0.1%
46	Alaska	0	0.0%
46	Delaware	0	0.0%
46	Montana	0	0.0%
46	New Hampshire	0	0.0%
46	Oregon	0	0.0%
	District of Columbia	1,343,192,000	0.5%

Source: U.S. Bureau of the Census, Governments Division
 "2016 State Government Tax Collections" (http://www.census.gov/govs/statetax/)
*Does not include special sales taxes such as those on sale of alcohol, gasoline, or tobacco.

Per Capita State Government General Sales Tax Revenue in 2016

National Per Capita = $905*

<table>
<tr><td colspan="3">ALPHA ORDER</td><td colspan="3">RANK ORDER</td></tr>
<tr><th>RANK</th><th>STATE</th><th>PER CAPITA</th><th>RANK</th><th>STATE</th><th>PER CAPITA</th></tr>
<tr><td>42</td><td>Alabama</td><td>$534</td><td>1</td><td>Hawaii</td><td>$2,244</td></tr>
<tr><td>46</td><td>Alaska</td><td>0</td><td>2</td><td>Washington</td><td>1,862</td></tr>
<tr><td>22</td><td>Arizona</td><td>964</td><td>3</td><td>Nevada</td><td>1,451</td></tr>
<tr><td>8</td><td>Arkansas</td><td>1,109</td><td>4</td><td>North Dakota</td><td>1,346</td></tr>
<tr><td>21</td><td>California</td><td>997</td><td>5</td><td>Texas</td><td>1,151</td></tr>
<tr><td>44</td><td>Colorado</td><td>514</td><td>6</td><td>South Dakota</td><td>1,124</td></tr>
<tr><td>15</td><td>Connecticut</td><td>1,046</td><td>7</td><td>Kansas</td><td>1,114</td></tr>
<tr><td>46</td><td>Delaware</td><td>0</td><td>8</td><td>Arkansas</td><td>1,109</td></tr>
<tr><td>12</td><td>Florida</td><td>1,079</td><td>9</td><td>Mississippi</td><td>1,105</td></tr>
<tr><td>43</td><td>Georgia</td><td>531</td><td>10</td><td>Indiana</td><td>1,101</td></tr>
<tr><td>1</td><td>Hawaii</td><td>2,244</td><td>11</td><td>Wyoming</td><td>1,097</td></tr>
<tr><td>24</td><td>Idaho</td><td>928</td><td>12</td><td>Florida</td><td>1,079</td></tr>
<tr><td>28</td><td>Illinois</td><td>884</td><td>13</td><td>Tennessee</td><td>1,054</td></tr>
<tr><td>10</td><td>Indiana</td><td>1,101</td><td>14</td><td>Ohio</td><td>1,052</td></tr>
<tr><td>19</td><td>Iowa</td><td>1,010</td><td>15</td><td>Connecticut</td><td>1,046</td></tr>
<tr><td>7</td><td>Kansas</td><td>1,114</td><td>16</td><td>New Jersey</td><td>1,032</td></tr>
<tr><td>31</td><td>Kentucky</td><td>781</td><td>17</td><td>Maine</td><td>1,022</td></tr>
<tr><td>37</td><td>Louisiana</td><td>680</td><td>18</td><td>Minnesota</td><td>1,011</td></tr>
<tr><td>17</td><td>Maine</td><td>1,022</td><td>19</td><td>Iowa</td><td>1,010</td></tr>
<tr><td>32</td><td>Maryland</td><td>748</td><td>20</td><td>New Mexico</td><td>1,000</td></tr>
<tr><td>27</td><td>Massachusetts</td><td>892</td><td>21</td><td>California</td><td>997</td></tr>
<tr><td>25</td><td>Michigan</td><td>922</td><td>22</td><td>Arizona</td><td>964</td></tr>
<tr><td>18</td><td>Minnesota</td><td>1,011</td><td>23</td><td>Nebraska</td><td>935</td></tr>
<tr><td>9</td><td>Mississippi</td><td>1,105</td><td>24</td><td>Idaho</td><td>928</td></tr>
<tr><td>41</td><td>Missouri</td><td>581</td><td>25</td><td>Michigan</td><td>922</td></tr>
<tr><td>46</td><td>Montana</td><td>0</td><td>26</td><td>Rhode Island</td><td>921</td></tr>
<tr><td>23</td><td>Nebraska</td><td>935</td><td>27</td><td>Massachusetts</td><td>892</td></tr>
<tr><td>3</td><td>Nevada</td><td>1,451</td><td>28</td><td>Illinois</td><td>884</td></tr>
<tr><td>46</td><td>New Hampshire</td><td>0</td><td>29</td><td>Wisconsin</td><td>876</td></tr>
<tr><td>16</td><td>New Jersey</td><td>1,032</td><td>30</td><td>Pennsylvania</td><td>799</td></tr>
<tr><td>20</td><td>New Mexico</td><td>1,000</td><td>31</td><td>Kentucky</td><td>781</td></tr>
<tr><td>36</td><td>New York</td><td>682</td><td>32</td><td>Maryland</td><td>748</td></tr>
<tr><td>33</td><td>North Carolina</td><td>708</td><td>33</td><td>North Carolina</td><td>708</td></tr>
<tr><td>4</td><td>North Dakota</td><td>1,346</td><td>34</td><td>West Virginia</td><td>704</td></tr>
<tr><td>14</td><td>Ohio</td><td>1,052</td><td>35</td><td>Utah</td><td>684</td></tr>
<tr><td>39</td><td>Oklahoma</td><td>630</td><td>36</td><td>New York</td><td>682</td></tr>
<tr><td>46</td><td>Oregon</td><td>0</td><td>37</td><td>Louisiana</td><td>680</td></tr>
<tr><td>30</td><td>Pennsylvania</td><td>799</td><td>38</td><td>South Carolina</td><td>659</td></tr>
<tr><td>26</td><td>Rhode Island</td><td>921</td><td>39</td><td>Oklahoma</td><td>630</td></tr>
<tr><td>38</td><td>South Carolina</td><td>659</td><td>40</td><td>Vermont</td><td>596</td></tr>
<tr><td>6</td><td>South Dakota</td><td>1,124</td><td>41</td><td>Missouri</td><td>581</td></tr>
<tr><td>13</td><td>Tennessee</td><td>1,054</td><td>42</td><td>Alabama</td><td>534</td></tr>
<tr><td>5</td><td>Texas</td><td>1,151</td><td>43</td><td>Georgia</td><td>531</td></tr>
<tr><td>35</td><td>Utah</td><td>684</td><td>44</td><td>Colorado</td><td>514</td></tr>
<tr><td>40</td><td>Vermont</td><td>596</td><td>45</td><td>Virginia</td><td>467</td></tr>
<tr><td>45</td><td>Virginia</td><td>467</td><td>46</td><td>Alaska</td><td>0</td></tr>
<tr><td>2</td><td>Washington</td><td>1,862</td><td>46</td><td>Delaware</td><td>0</td></tr>
<tr><td>34</td><td>West Virginia</td><td>704</td><td>46</td><td>Montana</td><td>0</td></tr>
<tr><td>29</td><td>Wisconsin</td><td>876</td><td>46</td><td>New Hampshire</td><td>0</td></tr>
<tr><td>11</td><td>Wyoming</td><td>1,097</td><td>46</td><td>Oregon</td><td>0</td></tr>
<tr><td></td><td></td><td></td><td></td><td>District of Columbia</td><td>1,963</td></tr>
</table>

Source: CQ Press using data from U.S. Bureau of the Census, Governments Division
"2016 State Government Tax Collections" (http://www.census.gov/govs/statetax/)
*Does not include special sales taxes such as those on sale of alcohol, gasoline, or tobacco.

State Government Motor Fuels Sales Tax Revenue in 2016

National Total = $43,757,220,000

ALPHA ORDER

RANK	STATE	REVENUE	% of USA
27	Alabama	$526,763,000	1.2%
50	Alaska	48,773,000	0.1%
15	Arizona	898,234,000	2.1%
29	Arkansas	479,879,000	1.1%
1	California	5,000,539,000	11.4%
23	Colorado	667,037,000	1.5%
30	Connecticut	467,749,000	1.1%
45	Delaware	125,453,000	0.3%
4	Florida	2,611,492,000	6.0%
7	Georgia	1,655,028,000	3.8%
47	Hawaii	92,591,000	0.2%
37	Idaho	337,335,000	0.8%
10	Illinois	1,354,039,000	3.1%
18	Indiana	845,384,000	1.9%
22	Iowa	689,693,000	1.6%
32	Kansas	450,633,000	1.0%
20	Kentucky	750,034,000	1.7%
24	Louisiana	622,234,000	1.4%
40	Maine	245,053,000	0.6%
13	Maryland	1,017,769,000	2.3%
19	Massachusetts	766,553,000	1.8%
12	Michigan	1,028,780,000	2.4%
14	Minnesota	901,156,000	2.1%
33	Mississippi	443,578,000	1.0%
21	Missouri	717,178,000	1.6%
43	Montana	186,083,000	0.4%
36	Nebraska	342,004,000	0.8%
38	Nevada	315,897,000	0.7%
44	New Hampshire	144,930,000	0.3%
26	New Jersey	554,473,000	1.3%
39	New Mexico	245,447,000	0.6%
8	New York	1,612,425,000	3.7%
5	North Carolina	1,936,102,000	4.4%
41	North Dakota	196,837,000	0.4%
6	Ohio	1,855,699,000	4.2%
31	Oklahoma	463,962,000	1.1%
28	Oregon	517,757,000	1.2%
3	Pennsylvania	2,971,950,000	6.8%
48	Rhode Island	90,032,000	0.2%
25	South Carolina	565,405,000	1.3%
42	South Dakota	186,990,000	0.4%
16	Tennessee	897,608,000	2.1%
2	Texas	3,500,210,000	8.0%
34	Utah	419,727,000	1.0%
49	Vermont	77,404,000	0.2%
17	Virginia	895,589,000	2.0%
9	Washington	1,457,933,000	3.3%
35	West Virginia	396,010,000	0.9%
11	Wisconsin	1,043,282,000	2.4%
46	Wyoming	115,175,000	0.3%

RANK ORDER

RANK	STATE	REVENUE	% of USA
1	California	$5,000,539,000	11.4%
2	Texas	3,500,210,000	8.0%
3	Pennsylvania	2,971,950,000	6.8%
4	Florida	2,611,492,000	6.0%
5	North Carolina	1,936,102,000	4.4%
6	Ohio	1,855,699,000	4.2%
7	Georgia	1,655,028,000	3.8%
8	New York	1,612,425,000	3.7%
9	Washington	1,457,933,000	3.3%
10	Illinois	1,354,039,000	3.1%
11	Wisconsin	1,043,282,000	2.4%
12	Michigan	1,028,780,000	2.4%
13	Maryland	1,017,769,000	2.3%
14	Minnesota	901,156,000	2.1%
15	Arizona	898,234,000	2.1%
16	Tennessee	897,608,000	2.1%
17	Virginia	895,589,000	2.0%
18	Indiana	845,384,000	1.9%
19	Massachusetts	766,553,000	1.8%
20	Kentucky	750,034,000	1.7%
21	Missouri	717,178,000	1.6%
22	Iowa	689,693,000	1.6%
23	Colorado	667,037,000	1.5%
24	Louisiana	622,234,000	1.4%
25	South Carolina	565,405,000	1.3%
26	New Jersey	554,473,000	1.3%
27	Alabama	526,763,000	1.2%
28	Oregon	517,757,000	1.2%
29	Arkansas	479,879,000	1.1%
30	Connecticut	467,749,000	1.1%
31	Oklahoma	463,962,000	1.1%
32	Kansas	450,633,000	1.0%
33	Mississippi	443,578,000	1.0%
34	Utah	419,727,000	1.0%
35	West Virginia	396,010,000	0.9%
36	Nebraska	342,004,000	0.8%
37	Idaho	337,335,000	0.8%
38	Nevada	315,897,000	0.7%
39	New Mexico	245,447,000	0.6%
40	Maine	245,053,000	0.6%
41	North Dakota	196,837,000	0.4%
42	South Dakota	186,990,000	0.4%
43	Montana	186,083,000	0.4%
44	New Hampshire	144,930,000	0.3%
45	Delaware	125,453,000	0.3%
46	Wyoming	115,175,000	0.3%
47	Hawaii	92,591,000	0.2%
48	Rhode Island	90,032,000	0.2%
49	Vermont	77,404,000	0.2%
50	Alaska	48,773,000	0.1%
	District of Columbia	25,332,000	0.1%

Source: U.S. Bureau of the Census, Governments Division
"2016 State Government Tax Collections" (http://www.census.gov/govs/statetax/)

Per Capita State Government Motor Fuel Sales Tax Revenue in 2016

National Per Capita = $135

<table>
<tr><td colspan="3">ALPHA ORDER</td><td colspan="3">RANK ORDER</td></tr>
<tr><td>RANK</td><td>STATE</td><td>PER CAPITA</td><td>RANK</td><td>STATE</td><td>PER CAPITA</td></tr>
<tr><td>41</td><td>Alabama</td><td>$108</td><td>1</td><td>North Dakota</td><td>$261</td></tr>
<tr><td>48</td><td>Alaska</td><td>66</td><td>2</td><td>Pennsylvania</td><td>232</td></tr>
<tr><td>26</td><td>Arizona</td><td>130</td><td>3</td><td>Iowa</td><td>220</td></tr>
<tr><td>17</td><td>Arkansas</td><td>161</td><td>4</td><td>South Dakota</td><td>217</td></tr>
<tr><td>28</td><td>California</td><td>127</td><td>4</td><td>West Virginia</td><td>217</td></tr>
<tr><td>34</td><td>Colorado</td><td>121</td><td>6</td><td>Idaho</td><td>201</td></tr>
<tr><td>26</td><td>Connecticut</td><td>130</td><td>7</td><td>Washington</td><td>200</td></tr>
<tr><td>25</td><td>Delaware</td><td>132</td><td>8</td><td>Wyoming</td><td>197</td></tr>
<tr><td>31</td><td>Florida</td><td>126</td><td>9</td><td>North Carolina</td><td>191</td></tr>
<tr><td>18</td><td>Georgia</td><td>160</td><td>10</td><td>Maine</td><td>184</td></tr>
<tr><td>49</td><td>Hawaii</td><td>65</td><td>11</td><td>Wisconsin</td><td>181</td></tr>
<tr><td>6</td><td>Idaho</td><td>201</td><td>12</td><td>Montana</td><td>179</td></tr>
<tr><td>44</td><td>Illinois</td><td>105</td><td>12</td><td>Nebraska</td><td>179</td></tr>
<tr><td>28</td><td>Indiana</td><td>127</td><td>14</td><td>Kentucky</td><td>169</td></tr>
<tr><td>3</td><td>Iowa</td><td>220</td><td>14</td><td>Maryland</td><td>169</td></tr>
<tr><td>20</td><td>Kansas</td><td>155</td><td>16</td><td>Minnesota</td><td>163</td></tr>
<tr><td>14</td><td>Kentucky</td><td>169</td><td>17</td><td>Arkansas</td><td>161</td></tr>
<tr><td>24</td><td>Louisiana</td><td>133</td><td>18</td><td>Georgia</td><td>160</td></tr>
<tr><td>10</td><td>Maine</td><td>184</td><td>18</td><td>Ohio</td><td>160</td></tr>
<tr><td>14</td><td>Maryland</td><td>169</td><td>20</td><td>Kansas</td><td>155</td></tr>
<tr><td>39</td><td>Massachusetts</td><td>112</td><td>21</td><td>Mississippi</td><td>149</td></tr>
<tr><td>45</td><td>Michigan</td><td>104</td><td>22</td><td>Utah</td><td>138</td></tr>
<tr><td>16</td><td>Minnesota</td><td>163</td><td>23</td><td>Tennessee</td><td>135</td></tr>
<tr><td>21</td><td>Mississippi</td><td>149</td><td>24</td><td>Louisiana</td><td>133</td></tr>
<tr><td>35</td><td>Missouri</td><td>118</td><td>25</td><td>Delaware</td><td>132</td></tr>
<tr><td>12</td><td>Montana</td><td>179</td><td>26</td><td>Arizona</td><td>130</td></tr>
<tr><td>12</td><td>Nebraska</td><td>179</td><td>26</td><td>Connecticut</td><td>130</td></tr>
<tr><td>42</td><td>Nevada</td><td>107</td><td>28</td><td>California</td><td>127</td></tr>
<tr><td>40</td><td>New Hampshire</td><td>109</td><td>28</td><td>Indiana</td><td>127</td></tr>
<tr><td>50</td><td>New Jersey</td><td>62</td><td>28</td><td>Oregon</td><td>127</td></tr>
<tr><td>35</td><td>New Mexico</td><td>118</td><td>31</td><td>Florida</td><td>126</td></tr>
<tr><td>47</td><td>New York</td><td>81</td><td>32</td><td>Texas</td><td>125</td></tr>
<tr><td>9</td><td>North Carolina</td><td>191</td><td>33</td><td>Vermont</td><td>124</td></tr>
<tr><td>1</td><td>North Dakota</td><td>261</td><td>34</td><td>Colorado</td><td>121</td></tr>
<tr><td>18</td><td>Ohio</td><td>160</td><td>35</td><td>Missouri</td><td>118</td></tr>
<tr><td>35</td><td>Oklahoma</td><td>118</td><td>35</td><td>New Mexico</td><td>118</td></tr>
<tr><td>28</td><td>Oregon</td><td>127</td><td>35</td><td>Oklahoma</td><td>118</td></tr>
<tr><td>2</td><td>Pennsylvania</td><td>232</td><td>38</td><td>South Carolina</td><td>114</td></tr>
<tr><td>46</td><td>Rhode Island</td><td>85</td><td>39</td><td>Massachusetts</td><td>112</td></tr>
<tr><td>38</td><td>South Carolina</td><td>114</td><td>40</td><td>New Hampshire</td><td>109</td></tr>
<tr><td>4</td><td>South Dakota</td><td>217</td><td>41</td><td>Alabama</td><td>108</td></tr>
<tr><td>23</td><td>Tennessee</td><td>135</td><td>42</td><td>Nevada</td><td>107</td></tr>
<tr><td>32</td><td>Texas</td><td>125</td><td>43</td><td>Virginia</td><td>106</td></tr>
<tr><td>22</td><td>Utah</td><td>138</td><td>44</td><td>Illinois</td><td>105</td></tr>
<tr><td>33</td><td>Vermont</td><td>124</td><td>45</td><td>Michigan</td><td>104</td></tr>
<tr><td>43</td><td>Virginia</td><td>106</td><td>46</td><td>Rhode Island</td><td>85</td></tr>
<tr><td>7</td><td>Washington</td><td>200</td><td>47</td><td>New York</td><td>81</td></tr>
<tr><td>4</td><td>West Virginia</td><td>217</td><td>48</td><td>Alaska</td><td>66</td></tr>
<tr><td>11</td><td>Wisconsin</td><td>181</td><td>49</td><td>Hawaii</td><td>65</td></tr>
<tr><td>8</td><td>Wyoming</td><td>197</td><td>50</td><td>New Jersey</td><td>62</td></tr>
<tr><td></td><td></td><td></td><td></td><td>District of Columbia</td><td>37</td></tr>
</table>

Source: CQ Press using data from U.S. Bureau of the Census, Governments Division
"2016 State Government Tax Collections" (http://www.census.gov/govs/statetax/)

State Tax Rates on Gasoline in 2018

National Median = 25.40 Cents per Gallon*

ALPHA ORDER

RANK	STATE	CENTS PER GALLON
44	Alabama	18.00
50	Alaska	8.95
41	Arizona	19.00
37	Arkansas	21.80
3	California	46.70
36	Colorado	22.00
28	Connecticut	25.00
34	Delaware	23.00
13	Florida	31.43
23	Georgia	26.80
49	Hawaii	16.00
10	Idaho	33.00
39	Illinois	20.10
21	Indiana	28.00
15	Iowa	30.50
27	Kansas	25.03
25	Kentucky	26.00
38	Louisiana	20.13
16	Maine	30.00
9	Maryland	33.80
30	Massachusetts	24.00
24	Michigan	26.30
20	Minnesota	28.60
43	Mississippi	18.40
45	Missouri	17.30
12	Montana	31.50
19	Nebraska	29.30
33	Nevada	23.81
32	New Hampshire	23.83
4	New Jersey	37.10
42	New Mexico	18.88
29	New York	24.90
6	North Carolina	35.35
34	North Dakota	23.00
21	Ohio	28.00
46	Oklahoma	17.00
7	Oregon	34.00
1	Pennsylvania	57.60
7	Rhode Island	34.00
47	South Carolina	16.75
16	South Dakota	30.00
26	Tennessee	25.40
40	Texas	20.00
18	Utah	29.40
14	Vermont	30.72
48	Virginia	16.20
2	Washington	49.40
5	West Virginia	35.70
11	Wisconsin	32.90
30	Wyoming	24.00

RANK ORDER

RANK	STATE	CENTS PER GALLON
1	Pennsylvania	57.60
2	Washington	49.40
3	California	46.70
4	New Jersey	37.10
5	West Virginia	35.70
6	North Carolina	35.35
7	Oregon	34.00
7	Rhode Island	34.00
9	Maryland	33.80
10	Idaho	33.00
11	Wisconsin	32.90
12	Montana	31.50
13	Florida	31.43
14	Vermont	30.72
15	Iowa	30.50
16	Maine	30.00
16	South Dakota	30.00
18	Utah	29.40
19	Nebraska	29.30
20	Minnesota	28.60
21	Indiana	28.00
21	Ohio	28.00
23	Georgia	26.80
24	Michigan	26.30
25	Kentucky	26.00
26	Tennessee	25.40
27	Kansas	25.03
28	Connecticut	25.00
29	New York	24.90
30	Massachusetts	24.00
30	Wyoming	24.00
32	New Hampshire	23.83
33	Nevada	23.81
34	Delaware	23.00
34	North Dakota	23.00
36	Colorado	22.00
37	Arkansas	21.80
38	Louisiana	20.13
39	Illinois	20.10
40	Texas	20.00
41	Arizona	19.00
42	New Mexico	18.88
43	Mississippi	18.40
44	Alabama	18.00
45	Missouri	17.30
46	Oklahoma	17.00
47	South Carolina	16.75
48	Virginia	16.20
49	Hawaii	16.00
50	Alaska	8.95

District of Columbia		23.50

Source: Federation of Tax Administrators
"Motor Fuel Excise Tax Rates" (http://www.taxadmin.org/current-tax-rates)
*As of January 1, 2018. Federal gasoline tax rate is an additional 18.4 cents per gallon. Many states also allow additional local option taxes on gasoline.

State Government Motor Vehicle and Operators' License Tax Revenue in 2016

National Total = $28,201,006,000

ALPHA ORDER

RANK	STATE	REVENUE	% of USA
28	Alabama	$247,514,000	0.9%
50	Alaska	38,000,000	0.1%
26	Arizona	260,343,000	0.9%
36	Arkansas	184,848,000	0.7%
1	California	4,292,249,000	15.2%
17	Colorado	540,761,000	1.9%
25	Connecticut	273,006,000	1.0%
48	Delaware	61,025,000	0.2%
4	Florida	1,669,397,000	5.9%
22	Georgia	475,372,000	1.7%
35	Hawaii	187,091,000	0.7%
34	Idaho	188,447,000	0.7%
3	Illinois	1,812,156,000	6.4%
19	Indiana	531,538,000	1.9%
14	Iowa	627,512,000	2.2%
30	Kansas	239,652,000	0.8%
32	Kentucky	224,453,000	0.8%
39	Louisiana	147,639,000	0.5%
42	Maine	119,780,000	0.4%
20	Maryland	529,350,000	1.9%
16	Massachusetts	563,479,000	2.0%
6	Michigan	1,130,026,000	4.0%
10	Minnesota	789,390,000	2.8%
37	Mississippi	173,301,000	0.6%
24	Missouri	306,480,000	1.1%
38	Montana	153,546,000	0.5%
43	Nebraska	115,125,000	0.4%
31	Nevada	227,469,000	0.8%
41	New Hampshire	121,976,000	0.4%
13	New Jersey	698,410,000	2.5%
29	New Mexico	247,131,000	0.9%
5	New York	1,516,114,000	5.4%
8	North Carolina	848,899,000	3.0%
40	North Dakota	123,699,000	0.4%
9	Ohio	847,906,000	3.0%
11	Oklahoma	746,481,000	2.6%
15	Oregon	577,447,000	2.0%
7	Pennsylvania	971,892,000	3.4%
49	Rhode Island	50,270,000	0.2%
27	South Carolina	249,237,000	0.9%
45	South Dakota	94,391,000	0.3%
23	Tennessee	357,698,000	1.3%
2	Texas	2,365,368,000	8.4%
33	Utah	199,492,000	0.7%
46	Vermont	81,176,000	0.3%
21	Virginia	517,684,000	1.8%
12	Washington	723,190,000	2.6%
44	West Virginia	99,609,000	0.4%
18	Wisconsin	533,406,000	1.9%
47	Wyoming	78,751,000	0.3%

RANK ORDER

RANK	STATE	REVENUE	% of USA
1	California	$4,292,249,000	15.2%
2	Texas	2,365,368,000	8.4%
3	Illinois	1,812,156,000	6.4%
4	Florida	1,669,397,000	5.9%
5	New York	1,516,114,000	5.4%
6	Michigan	1,130,026,000	4.0%
7	Pennsylvania	971,892,000	3.4%
8	North Carolina	848,899,000	3.0%
9	Ohio	847,906,000	3.0%
10	Minnesota	789,390,000	2.8%
11	Oklahoma	746,481,000	2.6%
12	Washington	723,190,000	2.6%
13	New Jersey	698,410,000	2.5%
14	Iowa	627,512,000	2.2%
15	Oregon	577,447,000	2.0%
16	Massachusetts	563,479,000	2.0%
17	Colorado	540,761,000	1.9%
18	Wisconsin	533,406,000	1.9%
19	Indiana	531,538,000	1.9%
20	Maryland	529,350,000	1.9%
21	Virginia	517,684,000	1.8%
22	Georgia	475,372,000	1.7%
23	Tennessee	357,698,000	1.3%
24	Missouri	306,480,000	1.1%
25	Connecticut	273,006,000	1.0%
26	Arizona	260,343,000	0.9%
27	South Carolina	249,237,000	0.9%
28	Alabama	247,514,000	0.9%
29	New Mexico	247,131,000	0.9%
30	Kansas	239,652,000	0.8%
31	Nevada	227,469,000	0.8%
32	Kentucky	224,453,000	0.8%
33	Utah	199,492,000	0.7%
34	Idaho	188,447,000	0.7%
35	Hawaii	187,091,000	0.7%
36	Arkansas	184,848,000	0.7%
37	Mississippi	173,301,000	0.6%
38	Montana	153,546,000	0.5%
39	Louisiana	147,639,000	0.5%
40	North Dakota	123,699,000	0.4%
41	New Hampshire	121,976,000	0.4%
42	Maine	119,780,000	0.4%
43	Nebraska	115,125,000	0.4%
44	West Virginia	99,609,000	0.4%
45	South Dakota	94,391,000	0.3%
46	Vermont	81,176,000	0.3%
47	Wyoming	78,751,000	0.3%
48	Delaware	61,025,000	0.2%
49	Rhode Island	50,270,000	0.2%
50	Alaska	38,000,000	0.1%
	District of Columbia	41,830,000	0.1%

Source: U.S. Bureau of the Census, Governments Division
"2016 State Government Tax Collections" (http://www.census.gov/govs/statetax/)

Per Capita State Government Motor Vehicle and Operators' License Tax Revenue in 2016
National Per Capita = $87

RANK	STATE	PER CAPITA
42	Alabama	$51
42	Alaska	51
49	Arizona	38
36	Arkansas	62
15	California	109
17	Colorado	98
30	Connecticut	76
35	Delaware	64
26	Florida	81
48	Georgia	46
9	Hawaii	131
13	Idaho	112
6	Illinois	141
27	Indiana	80
1	Iowa	200
25	Kansas	82
42	Kentucky	51
50	Louisiana	32
20	Maine	90
21	Maryland	88
24	Massachusetts	83
12	Michigan	114
5	Minnesota	143
39	Mississippi	58
45	Missouri	50
4	Montana	148
38	Nebraska	60
29	Nevada	77
19	New Hampshire	91
28	New Jersey	78
11	New Mexico	119
30	New York	76
23	North Carolina	84
3	North Dakota	164
33	Ohio	73
2	Oklahoma	190
6	Oregon	141
30	Pennsylvania	76
47	Rhode Island	48
45	South Carolina	50
14	South Dakota	110
40	Tennessee	54
22	Texas	85
34	Utah	66
10	Vermont	130
36	Virginia	62
16	Washington	99
40	West Virginia	54
18	Wisconsin	92
8	Wyoming	135

RANK	STATE	PER CAPITA
1	Iowa	$200
2	Oklahoma	190
3	North Dakota	164
4	Montana	148
5	Minnesota	143
6	Illinois	141
6	Oregon	141
8	Wyoming	135
9	Hawaii	131
10	Vermont	130
11	New Mexico	119
12	Michigan	114
13	Idaho	112
14	South Dakota	110
15	California	109
16	Washington	99
17	Colorado	98
18	Wisconsin	92
19	New Hampshire	91
20	Maine	90
21	Maryland	88
22	Texas	85
23	North Carolina	84
24	Massachusetts	83
25	Kansas	82
26	Florida	81
27	Indiana	80
28	New Jersey	78
29	Nevada	77
30	Connecticut	76
30	New York	76
30	Pennsylvania	76
33	Ohio	73
34	Utah	66
35	Delaware	64
36	Arkansas	62
36	Virginia	62
38	Nebraska	60
39	Mississippi	58
40	Tennessee	54
40	West Virginia	54
42	Alabama	51
42	Alaska	51
42	Kentucky	51
45	Missouri	50
45	South Carolina	50
47	Rhode Island	48
48	Georgia	46
49	Arizona	38
50	Louisiana	32
	District of Columbia	61

Source: CQ Press using data from U.S. Bureau of the Census, Governments Division
"2016 State Government Tax Collections" (http://www.census.gov/govs/statetax/)

State Government Tobacco Product Sales Tax Revenue in 2016

National Total = $18,011,700,000

ALPHA ORDER

RANK	STATE	REVENUE	% of USA
28	Alabama	$180,301,000	1.0%
44	Alaska	67,918,000	0.4%
17	Arizona	317,331,000	1.8%
23	Arkansas	230,527,000	1.3%
8	California	840,034,000	4.7%
27	Colorado	201,187,000	1.1%
16	Connecticut	350,723,000	1.9%
38	Delaware	111,762,000	0.6%
3	Florida	1,223,029,000	6.8%
26	Georgia	219,870,000	1.2%
35	Hawaii	124,890,000	0.7%
47	Idaho	50,574,000	0.3%
7	Illinois	844,928,000	4.7%
14	Indiana	443,210,000	2.5%
24	Iowa	227,901,000	1.3%
31	Kansas	146,552,000	0.8%
22	Kentucky	245,581,000	1.4%
36	Louisiana	121,200,000	0.7%
34	Maine	141,464,000	0.8%
15	Maryland	395,266,000	2.2%
12	Massachusetts	640,839,000	3.6%
6	Michigan	947,194,000	5.3%
10	Minnesota	650,042,000	3.6%
32	Mississippi	145,931,000	0.8%
39	Missouri	101,944,000	0.6%
41	Montana	86,289,000	0.5%
46	Nebraska	61,258,000	0.3%
30	Nevada	174,663,000	1.0%
25	New Hampshire	226,482,000	1.3%
9	New Jersey	677,216,000	3.8%
42	New Mexico	82,826,000	0.5%
2	New York	1,247,078,000	6.9%
19	North Carolina	286,286,000	1.6%
48	North Dakota	30,757,000	0.2%
4	Ohio	1,008,798,000	5.6%
18	Oklahoma	316,471,000	1.8%
20	Oregon	268,808,000	1.5%
5	Pennsylvania	962,110,000	5.3%
33	Rhode Island	144,403,000	0.8%
49	South Carolina	27,264,000	0.2%
45	South Dakota	63,082,000	0.4%
21	Tennessee	263,739,000	1.5%
1	Texas	1,479,863,000	8.2%
37	Utah	119,717,000	0.7%
43	Vermont	80,418,000	0.4%
29	Virginia	178,847,000	1.0%
13	Washington	450,805,000	2.5%
40	West Virginia	100,273,000	0.6%
11	Wisconsin	649,538,000	3.6%
50	Wyoming	24,060,000	0.1%

RANK ORDER

RANK	STATE	REVENUE	% of USA
1	Texas	$1,479,863,000	8.2%
2	New York	1,247,078,000	6.9%
3	Florida	1,223,029,000	6.8%
4	Ohio	1,008,798,000	5.6%
5	Pennsylvania	962,110,000	5.3%
6	Michigan	947,194,000	5.3%
7	Illinois	844,928,000	4.7%
8	California	840,034,000	4.7%
9	New Jersey	677,216,000	3.8%
10	Minnesota	650,042,000	3.6%
11	Wisconsin	649,538,000	3.6%
12	Massachusetts	640,839,000	3.6%
13	Washington	450,805,000	2.5%
14	Indiana	443,210,000	2.5%
15	Maryland	395,266,000	2.2%
16	Connecticut	350,723,000	1.9%
17	Arizona	317,331,000	1.8%
18	Oklahoma	316,471,000	1.8%
19	North Carolina	286,286,000	1.6%
20	Oregon	268,808,000	1.5%
21	Tennessee	263,739,000	1.5%
22	Kentucky	245,581,000	1.4%
23	Arkansas	230,527,000	1.3%
24	Iowa	227,901,000	1.3%
25	New Hampshire	226,482,000	1.3%
26	Georgia	219,870,000	1.2%
27	Colorado	201,187,000	1.1%
28	Alabama	180,301,000	1.0%
29	Virginia	178,847,000	1.0%
30	Nevada	174,663,000	1.0%
31	Kansas	146,552,000	0.8%
32	Mississippi	145,931,000	0.8%
33	Rhode Island	144,403,000	0.8%
34	Maine	141,464,000	0.8%
35	Hawaii	124,890,000	0.7%
36	Louisiana	121,200,000	0.7%
37	Utah	119,717,000	0.7%
38	Delaware	111,762,000	0.6%
39	Missouri	101,944,000	0.6%
40	West Virginia	100,273,000	0.6%
41	Montana	86,289,000	0.5%
42	New Mexico	82,826,000	0.5%
43	Vermont	80,418,000	0.4%
44	Alaska	67,918,000	0.4%
45	South Dakota	63,082,000	0.4%
46	Nebraska	61,258,000	0.3%
47	Idaho	50,574,000	0.3%
48	North Dakota	30,757,000	0.2%
49	South Carolina	27,264,000	0.2%
50	Wyoming	24,060,000	0.1%
	District of Columbia	30,451,000	0.2%

Source: U.S. Bureau of the Census, Governments Division
"2016 State Government Tax Collections" (http://www.census.gov/govs/statetax/)

Per Capita State Government Tobacco Sales Tax Revenue in 2016

National Per Capita = $56

ALPHA ORDER

ALPHA ORDER

RANK	STATE	PER CAPITA
40	Alabama	$37
11	Alaska	92
34	Arizona	46
16	Arkansas	77
46	California	21
41	Colorado	36
8	Connecticut	98
5	Delaware	117
27	Florida	59
46	Georgia	21
12	Hawaii	87
43	Idaho	30
22	Illinois	66
21	Indiana	67
19	Iowa	73
32	Kansas	50
29	Kentucky	55
45	Louisiana	26
7	Maine	106
22	Maryland	66
10	Massachusetts	94
9	Michigan	95
4	Minnesota	118
33	Mississippi	49
49	Missouri	17
14	Montana	83
42	Nebraska	32
27	Nevada	59
1	New Hampshire	170
17	New Jersey	75
37	New Mexico	40
25	New York	63
44	North Carolina	28
35	North Dakota	41
12	Ohio	87
15	Oklahoma	81
22	Oregon	66
17	Pennsylvania	75
2	Rhode Island	137
50	South Carolina	5
19	South Dakota	73
37	Tennessee	40
31	Texas	53
39	Utah	39
3	Vermont	129
46	Virginia	21
26	Washington	62
29	West Virginia	55
6	Wisconsin	113
35	Wyoming	41

RANK ORDER

RANK	STATE	PER CAPITA
1	New Hampshire	$170
2	Rhode Island	137
3	Vermont	129
4	Minnesota	118
5	Delaware	117
6	Wisconsin	113
7	Maine	106
8	Connecticut	98
9	Michigan	95
10	Massachusetts	94
11	Alaska	92
12	Hawaii	87
12	Ohio	87
14	Montana	83
15	Oklahoma	81
16	Arkansas	77
17	New Jersey	75
17	Pennsylvania	75
19	Iowa	73
19	South Dakota	73
21	Indiana	67
22	Illinois	66
22	Maryland	66
22	Oregon	66
25	New York	63
26	Washington	62
27	Florida	59
27	Nevada	59
29	Kentucky	55
29	West Virginia	55
31	Texas	53
32	Kansas	50
33	Mississippi	49
34	Arizona	46
35	North Dakota	41
35	Wyoming	41
37	New Mexico	40
37	Tennessee	40
39	Utah	39
40	Alabama	37
41	Colorado	36
42	Nebraska	32
43	Idaho	30
44	North Carolina	28
45	Louisiana	26
46	California	21
46	Georgia	21
46	Virginia	21
49	Missouri	17
50	South Carolina	5

District of Columbia	44

Source: CQ Press using data from U.S. Bureau of the Census, Governments Division
"2016 State Government Tax Collections" (http://www.census.gov/govs/statetax/)

State Tax on a Pack of Cigarettes in 2018

National Median = $1.60 per Pack*

<table>
<tr><td colspan="3">ALPHA ORDER</td><td colspan="3">RANK ORDER</td></tr>
<tr><td>RANK</td><td>STATE</td><td>TAX PER PACK</td><td>RANK</td><td>STATE</td><td>TAX PER PACK</td></tr>
<tr><td>38</td><td>Alabama</td><td>$0.68</td><td>1</td><td>Connecticut</td><td>$4.35</td></tr>
<tr><td>14</td><td>Alaska</td><td>2.00</td><td>1</td><td>New York</td><td>4.35</td></tr>
<tr><td>14</td><td>Arizona</td><td>2.00</td><td>3</td><td>Rhode Island</td><td>4.25</td></tr>
<tr><td>33</td><td>Arkansas</td><td>1.15</td><td>4</td><td>Massachusetts</td><td>3.51</td></tr>
<tr><td>9</td><td>California</td><td>2.87</td><td>5</td><td>Hawaii</td><td>3.20</td></tr>
<tr><td>37</td><td>Colorado</td><td>0.84</td><td>6</td><td>Vermont</td><td>3.08</td></tr>
<tr><td>1</td><td>Connecticut</td><td>4.35</td><td>7</td><td>Minnesota</td><td>3.04</td></tr>
<tr><td>13</td><td>Delaware</td><td>2.10</td><td>8</td><td>Washington</td><td>3.03</td></tr>
<tr><td>29</td><td>Florida</td><td>1.34</td><td>9</td><td>California</td><td>2.87</td></tr>
<tr><td>48</td><td>Georgia</td><td>0.37</td><td>10</td><td>New Jersey</td><td>2.70</td></tr>
<tr><td>5</td><td>Hawaii</td><td>3.20</td><td>11</td><td>Pennsylvania</td><td>2.60</td></tr>
<tr><td>44</td><td>Idaho</td><td>0.57</td><td>12</td><td>Wisconsin</td><td>2.52</td></tr>
<tr><td>19</td><td>Illinois</td><td>1.98</td><td>13</td><td>Delaware</td><td>2.10</td></tr>
<tr><td>36</td><td>Indiana</td><td>1.00</td><td>14</td><td>Alaska</td><td>2.00</td></tr>
<tr><td>28</td><td>Iowa</td><td>1.36</td><td>14</td><td>Arizona</td><td>2.00</td></tr>
<tr><td>31</td><td>Kansas</td><td>1.29</td><td>14</td><td>Maine</td><td>2.00</td></tr>
<tr><td>42</td><td>Kentucky</td><td>0.60</td><td>14</td><td>Maryland</td><td>2.00</td></tr>
<tr><td>34</td><td>Louisiana</td><td>1.08</td><td>14</td><td>Michigan</td><td>2.00</td></tr>
<tr><td>14</td><td>Maine</td><td>2.00</td><td>19</td><td>Illinois</td><td>1.98</td></tr>
<tr><td>14</td><td>Maryland</td><td>2.00</td><td>20</td><td>Nevada</td><td>1.80</td></tr>
<tr><td>4</td><td>Massachusetts</td><td>3.51</td><td>21</td><td>New Hampshire</td><td>1.78</td></tr>
<tr><td>14</td><td>Michigan</td><td>2.00</td><td>22</td><td>Montana</td><td>1.70</td></tr>
<tr><td>7</td><td>Minnesota</td><td>3.04</td><td>22</td><td>Utah</td><td>1.70</td></tr>
<tr><td>38</td><td>Mississippi</td><td>0.68</td><td>24</td><td>New Mexico</td><td>1.66</td></tr>
<tr><td>50</td><td>Missouri</td><td>0.17</td><td>25</td><td>Ohio</td><td>1.60</td></tr>
<tr><td>22</td><td>Montana</td><td>1.70</td><td>26</td><td>South Dakota</td><td>1.53</td></tr>
<tr><td>40</td><td>Nebraska</td><td>0.64</td><td>27</td><td>Texas</td><td>1.41</td></tr>
<tr><td>20</td><td>Nevada</td><td>1.80</td><td>28</td><td>Iowa</td><td>1.36</td></tr>
<tr><td>21</td><td>New Hampshire</td><td>1.78</td><td>29</td><td>Florida</td><td>1.34</td></tr>
<tr><td>10</td><td>New Jersey</td><td>2.70</td><td>30</td><td>Oregon</td><td>1.33</td></tr>
<tr><td>24</td><td>New Mexico</td><td>1.66</td><td>31</td><td>Kansas</td><td>1.29</td></tr>
<tr><td>1</td><td>New York</td><td>4.35</td><td>32</td><td>West Virginia</td><td>1.20</td></tr>
<tr><td>46</td><td>North Carolina</td><td>0.45</td><td>33</td><td>Arkansas</td><td>1.15</td></tr>
<tr><td>47</td><td>North Dakota</td><td>0.44</td><td>34</td><td>Louisiana</td><td>1.08</td></tr>
<tr><td>25</td><td>Ohio</td><td>1.60</td><td>35</td><td>Oklahoma</td><td>1.03</td></tr>
<tr><td>35</td><td>Oklahoma</td><td>1.03</td><td>36</td><td>Indiana</td><td>1.00</td></tr>
<tr><td>30</td><td>Oregon</td><td>1.33</td><td>37</td><td>Colorado</td><td>0.84</td></tr>
<tr><td>11</td><td>Pennsylvania</td><td>2.60</td><td>38</td><td>Alabama</td><td>0.68</td></tr>
<tr><td>3</td><td>Rhode Island</td><td>4.25</td><td>38</td><td>Mississippi</td><td>0.68</td></tr>
<tr><td>44</td><td>South Carolina</td><td>0.57</td><td>40</td><td>Nebraska</td><td>0.64</td></tr>
<tr><td>26</td><td>South Dakota</td><td>1.53</td><td>41</td><td>Tennessee</td><td>0.62</td></tr>
<tr><td>41</td><td>Tennessee</td><td>0.62</td><td>42</td><td>Kentucky</td><td>0.60</td></tr>
<tr><td>27</td><td>Texas</td><td>1.41</td><td>42</td><td>Wyoming</td><td>0.60</td></tr>
<tr><td>22</td><td>Utah</td><td>1.70</td><td>44</td><td>Idaho</td><td>0.57</td></tr>
<tr><td>6</td><td>Vermont</td><td>3.08</td><td>44</td><td>South Carolina</td><td>0.57</td></tr>
<tr><td>49</td><td>Virginia</td><td>0.30</td><td>46</td><td>North Carolina</td><td>0.45</td></tr>
<tr><td>8</td><td>Washington</td><td>3.03</td><td>47</td><td>North Dakota</td><td>0.44</td></tr>
<tr><td>32</td><td>West Virginia</td><td>1.20</td><td>48</td><td>Georgia</td><td>0.37</td></tr>
<tr><td>12</td><td>Wisconsin</td><td>2.52</td><td>49</td><td>Virginia</td><td>0.30</td></tr>
<tr><td>42</td><td>Wyoming</td><td>0.60</td><td>50</td><td>Missouri</td><td>0.17</td></tr>
<tr><td></td><td></td><td></td><td></td><td>District of Columbia</td><td>2.50</td></tr>
</table>

Source: Federation of Tax Administrators
    "State Excise Tax Rates on Cigarettes" (http://www.taxadmin.org/current-tax-rates)
*As of January 1, 2018. Many states also allow additional local option taxes on cigarettes.

State Government Alcoholic Beverage Sales Tax Revenue in 2016

National Total = $6,620,096,000

ALPHA ORDER

RANK	STATE	REVENUE	% of USA
10	Alabama	$210,535,000	3.2%
32	Alaska	42,430,000	0.6%
22	Arizona	72,281,000	1.1%
26	Arkansas	55,164,000	0.8%
5	California	368,699,000	5.6%
31	Colorado	43,407,000	0.7%
25	Connecticut	56,345,000	0.9%
42	Delaware	20,274,000	0.3%
2	Florida	396,418,000	6.0%
11	Georgia	190,536,000	2.9%
28	Hawaii	50,590,000	0.8%
48	Idaho	9,235,000	0.1%
8	Illinois	287,865,000	4.3%
29	Indiana	48,310,000	0.7%
40	Iowa	22,423,000	0.3%
17	Kansas	133,709,000	2.0%
15	Kentucky	139,248,000	2.1%
23	Louisiana	63,356,000	1.0%
43	Maine	18,741,000	0.3%
37	Maryland	31,627,000	0.5%
21	Massachusetts	83,395,000	1.3%
14	Michigan	157,242,000	2.4%
20	Minnesota	88,352,000	1.3%
33	Mississippi	42,352,000	0.6%
35	Missouri	36,849,000	0.6%
36	Montana	31,907,000	0.5%
38	Nebraska	30,520,000	0.5%
30	Nevada	45,098,000	0.7%
47	New Hampshire	12,850,000	0.2%
16	New Jersey	138,799,000	2.1%
34	New Mexico	37,084,000	0.6%
7	New York	299,931,000	4.5%
3	North Carolina	378,744,000	5.7%
49	North Dakota	9,026,000	0.1%
19	Ohio	100,712,000	1.5%
18	Oklahoma	120,099,000	1.8%
44	Oregon	18,375,000	0.3%
4	Pennsylvania	373,004,000	5.6%
41	Rhode Island	20,399,000	0.3%
13	South Carolina	173,138,000	2.6%
46	South Dakota	16,656,000	0.3%
12	Tennessee	174,340,000	2.6%
1	Texas	1,191,961,000	18.0%
27	Utah	51,563,000	0.8%
39	Vermont	25,025,000	0.4%
9	Virginia	268,547,000	4.1%
6	Washington	347,642,000	5.3%
45	West Virginia	17,936,000	0.3%
24	Wisconsin	58,970,000	0.9%
50	Wyoming	1,919,000	0.0%

RANK ORDER

RANK	STATE	REVENUE	% of USA
1	Texas	$1,191,961,000	18.0%
2	Florida	396,418,000	6.0%
3	North Carolina	378,744,000	5.7%
4	Pennsylvania	373,004,000	5.6%
5	California	368,699,000	5.6%
6	Washington	347,642,000	5.3%
7	New York	299,931,000	4.5%
8	Illinois	287,865,000	4.3%
9	Virginia	268,547,000	4.1%
10	Alabama	210,535,000	3.2%
11	Georgia	190,536,000	2.9%
12	Tennessee	174,340,000	2.6%
13	South Carolina	173,138,000	2.6%
14	Michigan	157,242,000	2.4%
15	Kentucky	139,248,000	2.1%
16	New Jersey	138,799,000	2.1%
17	Kansas	133,709,000	2.0%
18	Oklahoma	120,099,000	1.8%
19	Ohio	100,712,000	1.5%
20	Minnesota	88,352,000	1.3%
21	Massachusetts	83,395,000	1.3%
22	Arizona	72,281,000	1.1%
23	Louisiana	63,356,000	1.0%
24	Wisconsin	58,970,000	0.9%
25	Connecticut	56,345,000	0.9%
26	Arkansas	55,164,000	0.8%
27	Utah	51,563,000	0.8%
28	Hawaii	50,590,000	0.8%
29	Indiana	48,310,000	0.7%
30	Nevada	45,098,000	0.7%
31	Colorado	43,407,000	0.7%
32	Alaska	42,430,000	0.6%
33	Mississippi	42,352,000	0.6%
34	New Mexico	37,084,000	0.6%
35	Missouri	36,849,000	0.6%
36	Montana	31,907,000	0.5%
37	Maryland	31,627,000	0.5%
38	Nebraska	30,520,000	0.5%
39	Vermont	25,025,000	0.4%
40	Iowa	22,423,000	0.3%
41	Rhode Island	20,399,000	0.3%
42	Delaware	20,274,000	0.3%
43	Maine	18,741,000	0.3%
44	Oregon	18,375,000	0.3%
45	West Virginia	17,936,000	0.3%
46	South Dakota	16,656,000	0.3%
47	New Hampshire	12,850,000	0.2%
48	Idaho	9,235,000	0.1%
49	North Dakota	9,026,000	0.1%
50	Wyoming	1,919,000	0.0%
	District of Columbia	6,468,000	0.1%

Source: U.S. Bureau of the Census, Governments Division
"2016 State Government Tax Collections" (http://www.census.gov/govs/statetax/)

Per Capita State Government Alcoholic Beverage Sales Tax Revenue in 2016

National Per Capita = $20

ALPHA ORDER

RANK	STATE	PER CAPITA
4	Alabama	$43
1	Alaska	57
37	Arizona	10
21	Arkansas	18
41	California	9
43	Colorado	8
25	Connecticut	16
17	Delaware	21
18	Florida	19
21	Georgia	18
8	Hawaii	35
47	Idaho	5
16	Illinois	22
44	Indiana	7
44	Iowa	7
3	Kansas	46
11	Kentucky	31
32	Louisiana	14
32	Maine	14
47	Maryland	5
35	Massachusetts	12
25	Michigan	16
25	Minnesota	16
32	Mississippi	14
46	Missouri	6
11	Montana	31
25	Nebraska	16
29	Nevada	15
37	New Hampshire	10
29	New Jersey	15
21	New Mexico	18
29	New York	15
7	North Carolina	37
35	North Dakota	12
41	Ohio	9
11	Oklahoma	31
49	Oregon	4
14	Pennsylvania	29
18	Rhode Island	19
8	South Carolina	35
18	South Dakota	19
15	Tennessee	26
4	Texas	43
24	Utah	17
6	Vermont	40
10	Virginia	32
2	Washington	48
37	West Virginia	10
37	Wisconsin	10
50	Wyoming	3

RANK ORDER

RANK	STATE	PER CAPITA
1	Alaska	$57
2	Washington	48
3	Kansas	46
4	Alabama	43
4	Texas	43
6	Vermont	40
7	North Carolina	37
8	Hawaii	35
8	South Carolina	35
10	Virginia	32
11	Kentucky	31
11	Montana	31
11	Oklahoma	31
14	Pennsylvania	29
15	Tennessee	26
16	Illinois	22
17	Delaware	21
18	Florida	19
18	Rhode Island	19
18	South Dakota	19
21	Arkansas	18
21	Georgia	18
21	New Mexico	18
24	Utah	17
25	Connecticut	16
25	Michigan	16
25	Minnesota	16
25	Nebraska	16
29	Nevada	15
29	New Jersey	15
29	New York	15
32	Louisiana	14
32	Maine	14
32	Mississippi	14
35	Massachusetts	12
35	North Dakota	12
37	Arizona	10
37	New Hampshire	10
37	West Virginia	10
37	Wisconsin	10
41	California	9
41	Ohio	9
43	Colorado	8
44	Indiana	7
44	Iowa	7
46	Missouri	6
47	Idaho	5
47	Maryland	5
49	Oregon	4
50	Wyoming	3

District of Columbia   9

Source: CQ Press using data from U.S. Bureau of the Census, Governments Division
"2016 State Government Tax Collections" (http://www.census.gov/govs/statetax/)

State Government Total Expenditures in 2015

National Total = $2,149,513,004,000*

ALPHA ORDER

RANK	STATE	EXPENDITURES	% of USA
28	Alabama	$29,188,623,000	1.4%
38	Alaska	13,006,529,000	0.6%
19	Arizona	35,336,024,000	1.6%
31	Arkansas	21,367,613,000	1.0%
1	California	320,579,900,000	14.9%
20	Colorado	34,434,767,000	1.6%
26	Connecticut	30,891,450,000	1.4%
41	Delaware	8,994,764,000	0.4%
5	Florida	86,281,014,000	4.0%
14	Georgia	46,520,754,000	2.2%
39	Hawaii	12,414,891,000	0.6%
42	Idaho	8,872,137,000	0.4%
6	Illinois	82,299,829,000	3.8%
18	Indiana	37,485,428,000	1.7%
30	Iowa	22,764,494,000	1.1%
34	Kansas	17,930,704,000	0.8%
21	Kentucky	33,319,167,000	1.6%
25	Louisiana	30,986,030,000	1.4%
43	Maine	8,841,802,000	0.4%
16	Maryland	43,183,962,000	2.0%
10	Massachusetts	61,382,626,000	2.9%
9	Michigan	67,661,561,000	3.1%
15	Minnesota	43,233,851,000	2.0%
32	Mississippi	21,110,405,000	1.0%
23	Missouri	31,772,450,000	1.5%
46	Montana	7,447,633,000	0.3%
40	Nebraska	10,449,394,000	0.5%
36	Nevada	14,720,817,000	0.7%
47	New Hampshire	7,077,949,000	0.3%
8	New Jersey	71,434,624,000	3.3%
33	New Mexico	20,044,781,000	0.9%
2	New York	185,604,816,000	8.6%
11	North Carolina	52,700,019,000	2.5%
45	North Dakota	8,223,497,000	0.4%
7	Ohio	79,016,517,000	3.7%
29	Oklahoma	23,984,220,000	1.1%
22	Oregon	32,060,817,000	1.5%
4	Pennsylvania	88,945,260,000	4.1%
44	Rhode Island	8,577,940,000	0.4%
27	South Carolina	30,563,749,000	1.4%
50	South Dakota	4,676,769,000	0.2%
24	Tennessee	31,281,022,000	1.5%
3	Texas	136,927,357,000	6.4%
35	Utah	17,906,781,000	0.8%
48	Vermont	6,454,902,000	0.3%
12	Virginia	51,013,501,000	2.4%
13	Washington	50,865,802,000	2.4%
37	West Virginia	13,489,726,000	0.6%
17	Wisconsin	39,778,003,000	1.9%
49	Wyoming	6,406,333,000	0.3%

RANK ORDER

RANK	STATE	EXPENDITURES	% of USA
1	California	$320,579,900,000	14.9%
2	New York	185,604,816,000	8.6%
3	Texas	136,927,357,000	6.4%
4	Pennsylvania	88,945,260,000	4.1%
5	Florida	86,281,014,000	4.0%
6	Illinois	82,299,829,000	3.8%
7	Ohio	79,016,517,000	3.7%
8	New Jersey	71,434,624,000	3.3%
9	Michigan	67,661,561,000	3.1%
10	Massachusetts	61,382,626,000	2.9%
11	North Carolina	52,700,019,000	2.5%
12	Virginia	51,013,501,000	2.4%
13	Washington	50,865,802,000	2.4%
14	Georgia	46,520,754,000	2.2%
15	Minnesota	43,233,851,000	2.0%
16	Maryland	43,183,962,000	2.0%
17	Wisconsin	39,778,003,000	1.9%
18	Indiana	37,485,428,000	1.7%
19	Arizona	35,336,024,000	1.6%
20	Colorado	34,434,767,000	1.6%
21	Kentucky	33,319,167,000	1.6%
22	Oregon	32,060,817,000	1.5%
23	Missouri	31,772,450,000	1.5%
24	Tennessee	31,281,022,000	1.5%
25	Louisiana	30,986,030,000	1.4%
26	Connecticut	30,891,450,000	1.4%
27	South Carolina	30,563,749,000	1.4%
28	Alabama	29,188,623,000	1.4%
29	Oklahoma	23,984,220,000	1.1%
30	Iowa	22,764,494,000	1.1%
31	Arkansas	21,367,613,000	1.0%
32	Mississippi	21,110,405,000	1.0%
33	New Mexico	20,044,781,000	0.9%
34	Kansas	17,930,704,000	0.8%
35	Utah	17,906,781,000	0.8%
36	Nevada	14,720,817,000	0.7%
37	West Virginia	13,489,726,000	0.6%
38	Alaska	13,006,529,000	0.6%
39	Hawaii	12,414,891,000	0.6%
40	Nebraska	10,449,394,000	0.5%
41	Delaware	8,994,764,000	0.4%
42	Idaho	8,872,137,000	0.4%
43	Maine	8,841,802,000	0.4%
44	Rhode Island	8,577,940,000	0.4%
45	North Dakota	8,223,497,000	0.4%
46	Montana	7,447,633,000	0.3%
47	New Hampshire	7,077,949,000	0.3%
48	Vermont	6,454,902,000	0.3%
49	Wyoming	6,406,333,000	0.3%
50	South Dakota	4,676,769,000	0.2%

District of Columbia**   NA   NA

Source: U.S. Bureau of the Census, Governments Division
"2015 State and Local Government Finances" (http://www.census.gov/govs/local/)
*Total expenditures includes all money paid other than for retirement of debt and extension of loans. Includes payments from all sources of funds including current revenues and proceeds from borrowing and prior year fund balances. Includes intergovernmental transfers and expenditures for government owned utilities and other commercial or auxiliary enterprise, and insurance trust expenditures. **Not applicable.

Per Capita State Government Total Expenditures in 2015

National Per Capita = $6,710*

ALPHA ORDER

ALPHA ORDER

RANK	STATE	PER CAPITA
36	Alabama	$6,017
1	Alaska	17,625
45	Arizona	5,195
21	Arkansas	7,181
11	California	8,213
31	Colorado	6,329
10	Connecticut	8,596
6	Delaware	9,527
50	Florida	4,257
49	Georgia	4,561
9	Hawaii	8,704
41	Idaho	5,379
30	Illinois	6,399
38	Indiana	5,671
18	Iowa	7,300
33	Kansas	6,171
16	Kentucky	7,535
29	Louisiana	6,633
28	Maine	6,659
20	Maryland	7,197
8	Massachusetts	9,035
26	Michigan	6,822
15	Minnesota	7,885
23	Mississippi	7,071
44	Missouri	5,232
19	Montana	7,243
39	Nebraska	5,518
46	Nevada	5,106
42	New Hampshire	5,321
14	New Jersey	7,973
5	New Mexico	9,626
7	New York	9,365
43	North Carolina	5,248
3	North Dakota	10,894
27	Ohio	6,808
34	Oklahoma	6,143
13	Oregon	7,982
24	Pennsylvania	6,954
12	Rhode Island	8,124
32	South Carolina	6,247
40	South Dakota	5,476
48	Tennessee	4,746
47	Texas	4,987
37	Utah	5,999
4	Vermont	10,337
35	Virginia	6,097
22	Washington	7,111
17	West Virginia	7,332
25	Wisconsin	6,906
2	Wyoming	10,930

RANK ORDER

RANK	STATE	PER CAPITA
1	Alaska	$17,625
2	Wyoming	10,930
3	North Dakota	10,894
4	Vermont	10,337
5	New Mexico	9,626
6	Delaware	9,527
7	New York	9,365
8	Massachusetts	9,035
9	Hawaii	8,704
10	Connecticut	8,596
11	California	8,213
12	Rhode Island	8,124
13	Oregon	7,982
14	New Jersey	7,973
15	Minnesota	7,885
16	Kentucky	7,535
17	West Virginia	7,332
18	Iowa	7,300
19	Montana	7,243
20	Maryland	7,197
21	Arkansas	7,181
22	Washington	7,111
23	Mississippi	7,071
24	Pennsylvania	6,954
25	Wisconsin	6,906
26	Michigan	6,822
27	Ohio	6,808
28	Maine	6,659
29	Louisiana	6,633
30	Illinois	6,399
31	Colorado	6,329
32	South Carolina	6,247
33	Kansas	6,171
34	Oklahoma	6,143
35	Virginia	6,097
36	Alabama	6,017
37	Utah	5,999
38	Indiana	5,671
39	Nebraska	5,518
40	South Dakota	5,476
41	Idaho	5,379
42	New Hampshire	5,321
43	North Carolina	5,248
44	Missouri	5,232
45	Arizona	5,195
46	Nevada	5,106
47	Texas	4,987
48	Tennessee	4,746
49	Georgia	4,561
50	Florida	4,257

District of Columbia** NA

Source: CQ Press using data from U.S. Bureau of the Census, Governments Division
"2015 State and Local Government Finances" (http://www.census.gov/govs/local/)
*Total expenditures includes all money paid other than for retirement of debt and extension of loans. Includes payments from all sources of funds including current revenues and proceeds from borrowing and prior year fund balances. Includes intergovernmental transfers and expenditures for government owned utilities and other commercial or auxiliary enterprise, and insurance trust expenditures. **Not applicable.

State Government Direct General Expenditures in 2015

National Total = $1,324,135,840,000*

RANK	STATE	EXPENDITURES	% of USA
28	Alabama	$18,823,989,000	1.4%
38	Alaska	9,544,964,000	0.7%
20	Arizona	23,340,524,000	1.8%
31	Arkansas	14,255,962,000	1.1%
1	California	172,096,061,000	13.0%
21	Colorado	21,669,014,000	1.6%
26	Connecticut	20,411,584,000	1.5%
41	Delaware	6,744,689,000	0.5%
4	Florida	58,478,233,000	4.4%
14	Georgia	29,148,501,000	2.2%
36	Hawaii	10,779,913,000	0.8%
44	Idaho	5,557,675,000	0.4%
6	Illinois	50,133,233,000	3.8%
16	Indiana	25,001,453,000	1.9%
30	Iowa	14,955,596,000	1.1%
35	Kansas	11,220,395,000	0.8%
18	Kentucky	24,403,674,000	1.8%
24	Louisiana	20,799,701,000	1.6%
42	Maine	6,533,302,000	0.5%
15	Maryland	28,654,732,000	2.2%
9	Massachusetts	41,828,417,000	3.2%
10	Michigan	38,597,749,000	2.9%
17	Minnesota	24,907,271,000	1.9%
32	Mississippi	13,186,420,000	1.0%
23	Missouri	21,368,734,000	1.6%
46	Montana	5,011,887,000	0.4%
40	Nebraska	7,434,335,000	0.6%
39	Nevada	7,966,968,000	0.6%
45	New Hampshire	5,258,085,000	0.4%
8	New Jersey	43,476,729,000	3.3%
33	New Mexico	12,977,664,000	1.0%
2	New York	92,950,365,000	7.0%
11	North Carolina	33,819,163,000	2.6%
47	North Dakota	4,982,865,000	0.4%
7	Ohio	43,729,459,000	3.3%
29	Oklahoma	16,164,126,000	1.2%
25	Oregon	20,456,150,000	1.5%
5	Pennsylvania	55,956,657,000	4.2%
43	Rhode Island	5,945,110,000	0.4%
27	South Carolina	19,465,453,000	1.5%
50	South Dakota	3,394,622,000	0.3%
22	Tennessee	21,546,789,000	1.6%
3	Texas	90,773,512,000	6.9%
34	Utah	12,639,364,000	1.0%
48	Vermont	4,421,824,000	0.3%
12	Virginia	33,132,742,000	2.5%
13	Washington	32,916,625,000	2.5%
37	West Virginia	9,690,300,000	0.7%
19	Wisconsin	24,133,948,000	1.8%
49	Wyoming	3,449,312,000	0.3%

RANK	STATE	EXPENDITURES	% of USA
1	California	$172,096,061,000	13.0%
2	New York	92,950,365,000	7.0%
3	Texas	90,773,512,000	6.9%
4	Florida	58,478,233,000	4.4%
5	Pennsylvania	55,956,657,000	4.2%
6	Illinois	50,133,233,000	3.8%
7	Ohio	43,729,459,000	3.3%
8	New Jersey	43,476,729,000	3.3%
9	Massachusetts	41,828,417,000	3.2%
10	Michigan	38,597,749,000	2.9%
11	North Carolina	33,819,163,000	2.6%
12	Virginia	33,132,742,000	2.5%
13	Washington	32,916,625,000	2.5%
14	Georgia	29,148,501,000	2.2%
15	Maryland	28,654,732,000	2.2%
16	Indiana	25,001,453,000	1.9%
17	Minnesota	24,907,271,000	1.9%
18	Kentucky	24,403,674,000	1.8%
19	Wisconsin	24,133,948,000	1.8%
20	Arizona	23,340,524,000	1.8%
21	Colorado	21,669,014,000	1.6%
22	Tennessee	21,546,789,000	1.6%
23	Missouri	21,368,734,000	1.6%
24	Louisiana	20,799,701,000	1.6%
25	Oregon	20,456,150,000	1.5%
26	Connecticut	20,411,584,000	1.5%
27	South Carolina	19,465,453,000	1.5%
28	Alabama	18,823,989,000	1.4%
29	Oklahoma	16,164,126,000	1.2%
30	Iowa	14,955,596,000	1.1%
31	Arkansas	14,255,962,000	1.1%
32	Mississippi	13,186,420,000	1.0%
33	New Mexico	12,977,664,000	1.0%
34	Utah	12,639,364,000	1.0%
35	Kansas	11,220,395,000	0.8%
36	Hawaii	10,779,913,000	0.8%
37	West Virginia	9,690,300,000	0.7%
38	Alaska	9,544,964,000	0.7%
39	Nevada	7,966,968,000	0.6%
40	Nebraska	7,434,335,000	0.6%
41	Delaware	6,744,689,000	0.5%
42	Maine	6,533,302,000	0.5%
43	Rhode Island	5,945,110,000	0.4%
44	Idaho	5,557,675,000	0.4%
45	New Hampshire	5,258,085,000	0.4%
46	Montana	5,011,887,000	0.4%
47	North Dakota	4,982,865,000	0.4%
48	Vermont	4,421,824,000	0.3%
49	Wyoming	3,449,312,000	0.3%
50	South Dakota	3,394,622,000	0.3%
	District of Columbia**	NA	NA

Source: U.S. Bureau of the Census, Governments Division
  "2015 State and Local Government Finances" (http://www.census.gov/govs/local/)
*Direct general expenditures include expenditures for current operations, assistance and subsidies, interest on debt, and capital outlay. Excludes intergovernmental transfers, expenditures for government owned utilities and other commercial or auxiliary enterprise, and insurance trust expenditures.
**Not applicable.

Per Capita State Government Direct General Expenditures in 2015

National Per Capita = $4,133*

ALPHA ORDER

RANK	STATE	PER CAPITA
38	Alabama	$3,881
1	Alaska	12,934
43	Arizona	3,431
18	Arkansas	4,791
25	California	4,409
30	Colorado	3,983
9	Connecticut	5,680
3	Delaware	7,144
48	Florida	2,885
49	Georgia	2,858
2	Hawaii	7,558
44	Idaho	3,370
36	Illinois	3,898
40	Indiana	3,782
17	Iowa	4,796
39	Kansas	3,861
11	Kentucky	5,519
23	Louisiana	4,453
14	Maine	4,920
19	Maryland	4,775
7	Massachusetts	6,157
37	Michigan	3,892
22	Minnesota	4,542
24	Mississippi	4,417
42	Missouri	3,519
15	Montana	4,874
35	Nebraska	3,926
50	Nevada	2,763
34	New Hampshire	3,953
16	New Jersey	4,852
6	New Mexico	6,232
20	New York	4,690
45	North Carolina	3,368
5	North Dakota	6,601
41	Ohio	3,768
29	Oklahoma	4,140
13	Oregon	5,093
26	Pennsylvania	4,375
10	Rhode Island	5,630
31	South Carolina	3,979
32	South Dakota	3,975
47	Tennessee	3,269
46	Texas	3,306
27	Utah	4,234
4	Vermont	7,081
33	Virginia	3,960
21	Washington	4,602
12	West Virginia	5,267
28	Wisconsin	4,190
8	Wyoming	5,885

RANK ORDER

RANK	STATE	PER CAPITA
1	Alaska	$12,934
2	Hawaii	7,558
3	Delaware	7,144
4	Vermont	7,081
5	North Dakota	6,601
6	New Mexico	6,232
7	Massachusetts	6,157
8	Wyoming	5,885
9	Connecticut	5,680
10	Rhode Island	5,630
11	Kentucky	5,519
12	West Virginia	5,267
13	Oregon	5,093
14	Maine	4,920
15	Montana	4,874
16	New Jersey	4,852
17	Iowa	4,796
18	Arkansas	4,791
19	Maryland	4,775
20	New York	4,690
21	Washington	4,602
22	Minnesota	4,542
23	Louisiana	4,453
24	Mississippi	4,417
25	California	4,409
26	Pennsylvania	4,375
27	Utah	4,234
28	Wisconsin	4,190
29	Oklahoma	4,140
30	Colorado	3,983
31	South Carolina	3,979
32	South Dakota	3,975
33	Virginia	3,960
34	New Hampshire	3,953
35	Nebraska	3,926
36	Illinois	3,898
37	Michigan	3,892
38	Alabama	3,881
39	Kansas	3,861
40	Indiana	3,782
41	Ohio	3,768
42	Missouri	3,519
43	Arizona	3,431
44	Idaho	3,370
45	North Carolina	3,368
46	Texas	3,306
47	Tennessee	3,269
48	Florida	2,885
49	Georgia	2,858
50	Nevada	2,763

District of Columbia**　　　　　　　　NA

Source: CQ Press using data from U.S. Bureau of the Census, Governments Division
"2015 State and Local Government Finances" (http://www.census.gov/govs/local/)
*Direct general expenditures include expenditures for current operations, assistance and subsidies, interest on debt, and capital outlay. Excludes intergovernmental transfers, expenditures for government owned utilities and other commercial or auxiliary enterprise, and insurance trust expenditures.
**Not applicable.

State Government Debt Outstanding in 2015

National Total = $1,149,926,081,000*

ALPHA ORDER

RANK	STATE	DEBT	% of USA
28	Alabama	$8,969,350,000	0.8%
39	Alaska	5,727,891,000	0.5%
23	Arizona	14,243,659,000	1.2%
41	Arkansas	4,985,140,000	0.4%
1	California	151,715,007,000	13.2%
20	Colorado	17,200,428,000	1.5%
8	Connecticut	35,351,526,000	3.1%
42	Delaware	4,964,915,000	0.4%
9	Florida	33,315,277,000	2.9%
25	Georgia	13,247,675,000	1.2%
30	Hawaii	8,757,730,000	0.8%
43	Idaho	3,685,377,000	0.3%
5	Illinois	64,221,381,000	5.6%
15	Indiana	22,463,710,000	2.0%
37	Iowa	6,120,464,000	0.5%
32	Kansas	7,581,462,000	0.7%
24	Kentucky	13,784,882,000	1.2%
18	Louisiana	17,593,764,000	1.5%
40	Maine	5,011,671,000	0.4%
14	Maryland	26,592,571,000	2.3%
3	Massachusetts	75,307,661,000	6.5%
10	Michigan	33,245,109,000	2.9%
21	Minnesota	16,755,784,000	1.5%
34	Mississippi	7,470,450,000	0.6%
17	Missouri	19,350,325,000	1.7%
47	Montana	3,206,612,000	0.3%
49	Nebraska	1,809,126,000	0.2%
44	Nevada	3,351,972,000	0.3%
31	New Hampshire	8,210,346,000	0.7%
4	New Jersey	66,923,327,000	5.8%
36	New Mexico	6,738,313,000	0.6%
2	New York	137,369,089,000	11.9%
19	North Carolina	17,463,787,000	1.5%
48	North Dakota	2,063,788,000	0.2%
11	Ohio	33,108,954,000	2.9%
29	Oklahoma	8,899,021,000	0.8%
26	Oregon	13,061,182,000	1.1%
7	Pennsylvania	47,052,095,000	4.1%
27	Rhode Island	9,004,835,000	0.8%
22	South Carolina	15,122,266,000	1.3%
46	South Dakota	3,286,231,000	0.3%
38	Tennessee	6,025,074,000	0.5%
6	Texas	48,237,511,000	4.2%
33	Utah	7,479,978,000	0.7%
45	Vermont	3,340,624,000	0.3%
13	Virginia	28,231,613,000	2.5%
12	Washington	32,231,967,000	2.8%
35	West Virginia	7,123,763,000	0.6%
16	Wisconsin	22,086,615,000	1.9%
50	Wyoming	834,783,000	0.1%

RANK ORDER

RANK	STATE	DEBT	% of USA
1	California	$151,715,007,000	13.2%
2	New York	137,369,089,000	11.9%
3	Massachusetts	75,307,661,000	6.5%
4	New Jersey	66,923,327,000	5.8%
5	Illinois	64,221,381,000	5.6%
6	Texas	48,237,511,000	4.2%
7	Pennsylvania	47,052,095,000	4.1%
8	Connecticut	35,351,526,000	3.1%
9	Florida	33,315,277,000	2.9%
10	Michigan	33,245,109,000	2.9%
11	Ohio	33,108,954,000	2.9%
12	Washington	32,231,967,000	2.8%
13	Virginia	28,231,613,000	2.5%
14	Maryland	26,592,571,000	2.3%
15	Indiana	22,463,710,000	2.0%
16	Wisconsin	22,086,615,000	1.9%
17	Missouri	19,350,325,000	1.7%
18	Louisiana	17,593,764,000	1.5%
19	North Carolina	17,463,787,000	1.5%
20	Colorado	17,200,428,000	1.5%
21	Minnesota	16,755,784,000	1.5%
22	South Carolina	15,122,266,000	1.3%
23	Arizona	14,243,659,000	1.2%
24	Kentucky	13,784,882,000	1.2%
25	Georgia	13,247,675,000	1.2%
26	Oregon	13,061,182,000	1.1%
27	Rhode Island	9,004,835,000	0.8%
28	Alabama	8,969,350,000	0.8%
29	Oklahoma	8,899,021,000	0.8%
30	Hawaii	8,757,730,000	0.8%
31	New Hampshire	8,210,346,000	0.7%
32	Kansas	7,581,462,000	0.7%
33	Utah	7,479,978,000	0.7%
34	Mississippi	7,470,450,000	0.6%
35	West Virginia	7,123,763,000	0.6%
36	New Mexico	6,738,313,000	0.6%
37	Iowa	6,120,464,000	0.5%
38	Tennessee	6,025,074,000	0.5%
39	Alaska	5,727,891,000	0.5%
40	Maine	5,011,671,000	0.4%
41	Arkansas	4,985,140,000	0.4%
42	Delaware	4,964,915,000	0.4%
43	Idaho	3,685,377,000	0.3%
44	Nevada	3,351,972,000	0.3%
45	Vermont	3,340,624,000	0.3%
46	South Dakota	3,286,231,000	0.3%
47	Montana	3,206,612,000	0.3%
48	North Dakota	2,063,788,000	0.2%
49	Nebraska	1,809,126,000	0.2%
50	Wyoming	834,783,000	0.1%
	District of Columbia**	NA	NA

Source: U.S. Bureau of the Census, Governments Division
"2015 State and Local Government Finances" (http://www.census.gov/govs/local/)
*Includes short-term, long-term, full faith and credit, nonguaranteed, and public debt for private purposes.
**Not applicable.

Per Capita State Government Debt Outstanding in 2015

National Per Capita = $3,589*

ALPHA ORDER			RANK ORDER		
RANK	STATE	PER CAPITA	RANK	STATE	PER CAPITA
41	Alabama	$1,849	1	Massachusetts	$11,084
4	Alaska	7,762	2	Connecticut	9,837
39	Arizona	2,094	3	Rhode Island	8,528
44	Arkansas	1,675	4	Alaska	7,762
14	California	3,887	5	New Jersey	7,469
27	Colorado	3,162	6	New York	6,931
2	Connecticut	9,837	7	New Hampshire	6,173
10	Delaware	5,259	8	Hawaii	6,140
45	Florida	1,644	9	Vermont	5,350
47	Georgia	1,299	10	Delaware	5,259
8	Hawaii	6,140	11	Illinois	4,993
38	Idaho	2,234	12	Washington	4,506
11	Illinois	4,993	13	Maryland	4,432
21	Indiana	3,398	14	California	3,887
40	Iowa	1,963	15	West Virginia	3,872
34	Kansas	2,609	16	South Dakota	3,848
29	Kentucky	3,117	17	Wisconsin	3,835
19	Louisiana	3,766	18	Maine	3,774
18	Maine	3,774	19	Louisiana	3,766
13	Maryland	4,432	20	Pennsylvania	3,678
1	Massachusetts	11,084	21	Indiana	3,398
23	Michigan	3,352	22	Virginia	3,374
31	Minnesota	3,056	23	Michigan	3,352
36	Mississippi	2,502	24	Oregon	3,252
26	Missouri	3,186	25	New Mexico	3,236
28	Montana	3,118	26	Missouri	3,186
49	Nebraska	955	27	Colorado	3,162
48	Nevada	1,163	28	Montana	3,118
7	New Hampshire	6,173	29	Kentucky	3,117
5	New Jersey	7,469	30	South Carolina	3,091
25	New Mexico	3,236	31	Minnesota	3,056
6	New York	6,931	32	Ohio	2,853
43	North Carolina	1,739	33	North Dakota	2,734
33	North Dakota	2,734	34	Kansas	2,609
32	Ohio	2,853	35	Utah	2,506
37	Oklahoma	2,279	36	Mississippi	2,502
24	Oregon	3,252	37	Oklahoma	2,279
20	Pennsylvania	3,678	38	Idaho	2,234
3	Rhode Island	8,528	39	Arizona	2,094
30	South Carolina	3,091	40	Iowa	1,963
16	South Dakota	3,848	41	Alabama	1,849
50	Tennessee	914	42	Texas	1,757
42	Texas	1,757	43	North Carolina	1,739
35	Utah	2,506	44	Arkansas	1,675
9	Vermont	5,350	45	Florida	1,644
22	Virginia	3,374	46	Wyoming	1,424
12	Washington	4,506	47	Georgia	1,299
15	West Virginia	3,872	48	Nevada	1,163
17	Wisconsin	3,835	49	Nebraska	955
46	Wyoming	1,424	50	Tennessee	914
				District of Columbia**	NA

Source: CQ Press using data from U.S. Bureau of the Census, Governments Division
   "2015 State and Local Government Finances" (http://www.census.gov/govs/local/)
*Includes short-term, long-term, full faith and credit, nonguaranteed, and public debt for private purposes.
**Not applicable.

State Government Full-Time Equivalent Employees in 2016

National Total = 4,360,635 FTE Employees*

ALPHA ORDER

RANK	STATE	EMPLOYEES	% of USA
15	Alabama	90,141	2.1%
41	Alaska	25,073	0.6%
26	Arizona	72,316	1.7%
30	Arkansas	62,476	1.4%
1	California	414,679	9.5%
17	Colorado	87,844	2.0%
29	Connecticut	62,863	1.4%
40	Delaware	25,881	0.6%
4	Florida	178,571	4.1%
10	Georgia	128,151	2.9%
31	Hawaii	58,777	1.3%
42	Idaho	24,025	0.6%
13	Illinois	123,611	2.8%
16	Indiana	89,278	2.0%
35	Iowa	51,005	1.2%
34	Kansas	52,118	1.2%
20	Kentucky	85,606	2.0%
24	Louisiana	73,796	1.7%
43	Maine	20,647	0.5%
19	Maryland	85,928	2.0%
14	Massachusetts	99,315	2.3%
6	Michigan	144,350	3.3%
21	Minnesota	82,697	1.9%
33	Mississippi	56,841	1.3%
18	Missouri	87,140	2.0%
44	Montana	20,392	0.5%
38	Nebraska	31,924	0.7%
39	Nevada	28,314	0.6%
46	New Hampshire	19,092	0.4%
8	New Jersey	139,043	3.2%
36	New Mexico	45,775	1.0%
3	New York	242,184	5.6%
7	North Carolina	140,047	3.2%
45	North Dakota	19,321	0.4%
9	Ohio	137,846	3.2%
27	Oklahoma	68,649	1.6%
28	Oregon	68,128	1.6%
5	Pennsylvania	162,573	3.7%
47	Rhode Island	18,302	0.4%
22	South Carolina	79,917	1.8%
49	South Dakota	14,106	0.3%
23	Tennessee	78,599	1.8%
2	Texas	309,862	7.1%
32	Utah	57,733	1.3%
48	Vermont	14,388	0.3%
12	Virginia	126,741	2.9%
11	Washington	126,970	2.9%
37	West Virginia	41,422	0.9%
25	Wisconsin	72,676	1.7%
50	Wyoming	13,502	0.3%

RANK ORDER

RANK	STATE	EMPLOYEES	% of USA
1	California	414,679	9.5%
2	Texas	309,862	7.1%
3	New York	242,184	5.6%
4	Florida	178,571	4.1%
5	Pennsylvania	162,573	3.7%
6	Michigan	144,350	3.3%
7	North Carolina	140,047	3.2%
8	New Jersey	139,043	3.2%
9	Ohio	137,846	3.2%
10	Georgia	128,151	2.9%
11	Washington	126,970	2.9%
12	Virginia	126,741	2.9%
13	Illinois	123,611	2.8%
14	Massachusetts	99,315	2.3%
15	Alabama	90,141	2.1%
16	Indiana	89,278	2.0%
17	Colorado	87,844	2.0%
18	Missouri	87,140	2.0%
19	Maryland	85,928	2.0%
20	Kentucky	85,606	2.0%
21	Minnesota	82,697	1.9%
22	South Carolina	79,917	1.8%
23	Tennessee	78,599	1.8%
24	Louisiana	73,796	1.7%
25	Wisconsin	72,676	1.7%
26	Arizona	72,316	1.7%
27	Oklahoma	68,649	1.6%
28	Oregon	68,128	1.6%
29	Connecticut	62,863	1.4%
30	Arkansas	62,476	1.4%
31	Hawaii	58,777	1.3%
32	Utah	57,733	1.3%
33	Mississippi	56,841	1.3%
34	Kansas	52,118	1.2%
35	Iowa	51,005	1.2%
36	New Mexico	45,775	1.0%
37	West Virginia	41,422	0.9%
38	Nebraska	31,924	0.7%
39	Nevada	28,314	0.6%
40	Delaware	25,881	0.6%
41	Alaska	25,073	0.6%
42	Idaho	24,025	0.6%
43	Maine	20,647	0.5%
44	Montana	20,392	0.5%
45	North Dakota	19,321	0.4%
46	New Hampshire	19,092	0.4%
47	Rhode Island	18,302	0.4%
48	Vermont	14,388	0.3%
49	South Dakota	14,106	0.3%
50	Wyoming	13,502	0.3%
	District of Columbia**	NA	NA

Source: U.S. Bureau of the Census, Governments Division
"Annual Survey of Public Employment and Payroll" (https://www.census.gov/data/datasets.html)
*Full-time equivalent as of March 2016.
**Not applicable.

Rate of State Government Full-Time Equivalent Employees in 2016

National Rate = 135 FTE Employees per 10,000 Population*

ALPHA ORDER

RANK	STATE	RATE
14	Alabama	185
2	Alaska	338
47	Arizona	105
9	Arkansas	209
46	California	106
25	Colorado	159
16	Connecticut	175
3	Delaware	272
50	Florida	86
41	Georgia	124
1	Hawaii	411
33	Idaho	143
48	Illinois	96
38	Indiana	135
23	Iowa	163
15	Kansas	179
11	Kentucky	193
26	Louisiana	157
27	Maine	155
33	Maryland	143
31	Massachusetts	146
32	Michigan	145
30	Minnesota	150
12	Mississippi	190
33	Missouri	143
10	Montana	196
20	Nebraska	167
48	Nevada	96
33	New Hampshire	143
27	New Jersey	155
8	New Mexico	219
42	New York	122
37	North Carolina	138
4	North Dakota	256
43	Ohio	119
16	Oklahoma	175
20	Oregon	167
39	Pennsylvania	127
19	Rhode Island	173
24	South Carolina	161
22	South Dakota	164
44	Tennessee	118
45	Texas	111
12	Utah	190
5	Vermont	231
29	Virginia	151
18	Washington	174
7	West Virginia	227
40	Wisconsin	126
5	Wyoming	231

RANK ORDER

RANK	STATE	RATE
1	Hawaii	411
2	Alaska	338
3	Delaware	272
4	North Dakota	256
5	Vermont	231
5	Wyoming	231
7	West Virginia	227
8	New Mexico	219
9	Arkansas	209
10	Montana	196
11	Kentucky	193
12	Mississippi	190
12	Utah	190
14	Alabama	185
15	Kansas	179
16	Connecticut	175
16	Oklahoma	175
18	Washington	174
19	Rhode Island	173
20	Nebraska	167
20	Oregon	167
22	South Dakota	164
23	Iowa	163
24	South Carolina	161
25	Colorado	159
26	Louisiana	157
27	Maine	155
27	New Jersey	155
29	Virginia	151
30	Minnesota	150
31	Massachusetts	146
32	Michigan	145
33	Idaho	143
33	Maryland	143
33	Missouri	143
33	New Hampshire	143
37	North Carolina	138
38	Indiana	135
39	Pennsylvania	127
40	Wisconsin	126
41	Georgia	124
42	New York	122
43	Ohio	119
44	Tennessee	118
45	Texas	111
46	California	106
47	Arizona	105
48	Illinois	96
48	Nevada	96
50	Florida	86

District of Columbia**   NA

Source: CQ Press using data from U.S. Bureau of the Census, Governments Division
   "Annual Survey of Public Employment and Payroll" (https://www.census.gov/data/datasets.html)
*Full-time equivalent as of March 2016.
**Not applicable.

Average Annual Earnings of Full-Time State Government Employees in 2016

National Average = $63,290*

RANK	STATE	SALARY
36	Alabama	$55,195
8	Alaska	70,606
26	Arizona	58,882
47	Arkansas	49,841
1	California	84,513
12	Colorado	68,598
2	Connecticut	76,262
33	Delaware	55,745
40	Florida	52,553
44	Georgia	51,119
29	Hawaii	56,838
19	Idaho	62,010
10	Illinois	69,944
39	Indiana	52,892
3	Iowa	75,889
31	Kansas	56,066
38	Kentucky	53,677
28	Louisiana	56,914
42	Maine	52,394
17	Maryland	63,060
7	Massachusetts	70,966
11	Michigan	69,854
9	Minnesota	70,159
48	Mississippi	46,888
49	Missouri	46,770
34	Montana	55,638
41	Nebraska	52,473
25	Nevada	59,571
16	New Hampshire	63,177
4	New Jersey	75,017
30	New Mexico	56,094
5	New York	74,666
32	North Carolina	56,021
27	North Dakota	58,383
13	Ohio	64,716
44	Oklahoma	51,119
21	Oregon	61,577
22	Pennsylvania	61,253
6	Rhode Island	71,547
46	South Carolina	50,939
37	South Dakota	55,092
43	Tennessee	52,362
20	Texas	61,746
24	Utah	60,260
18	Vermont	62,446
23	Virginia	60,906
14	Washington	64,708
50	West Virginia	45,546
15	Wisconsin	63,937
35	Wyoming	55,490

RANK	STATE	SALARY
1	California	$84,513
2	Connecticut	76,262
3	Iowa	75,889
4	New Jersey	75,017
5	New York	74,666
6	Rhode Island	71,547
7	Massachusetts	70,966
8	Alaska	70,606
9	Minnesota	70,159
10	Illinois	69,944
11	Michigan	69,854
12	Colorado	68,598
13	Ohio	64,716
14	Washington	64,708
15	Wisconsin	63,937
16	New Hampshire	63,177
17	Maryland	63,060
18	Vermont	62,446
19	Idaho	62,010
20	Texas	61,746
21	Oregon	61,577
22	Pennsylvania	61,253
23	Virginia	60,906
24	Utah	60,260
25	Nevada	59,571
26	Arizona	58,882
27	North Dakota	58,383
28	Louisiana	56,914
29	Hawaii	56,838
30	New Mexico	56,094
31	Kansas	56,066
32	North Carolina	56,021
33	Delaware	55,745
34	Montana	55,638
35	Wyoming	55,490
36	Alabama	55,195
37	South Dakota	55,092
38	Kentucky	53,677
39	Indiana	52,892
40	Florida	52,553
41	Nebraska	52,473
42	Maine	52,394
43	Tennessee	52,362
44	Georgia	51,119
44	Oklahoma	51,119
46	South Carolina	50,939
47	Arkansas	49,841
48	Mississippi	46,888
49	Missouri	46,770
50	West Virginia	45,546

District of Columbia**   NA

Source: CQ Press using data from U.S. Bureau of the Census, Governments Division
"Annual Survey of Public Employment and Payroll" (https://www.census.gov/data/datasets.html)
*March 2016 full-time payroll (multiplied by 12) divided by full-time employees.
**Not applicable.

Local Government Total Revenue in 2015

National Total = $1,777,150,241,000*

ALPHA ORDER

RANK	STATE	REVENUE	% of USA
25	Alabama	$21,361,885,000	1.2%
39	Alaska	5,773,814,000	0.3%
21	Arizona	28,639,085,000	1.6%
36	Arkansas	10,226,680,000	0.6%
1	California	292,936,194,000	16.5%
17	Colorado	30,842,258,000	1.7%
27	Connecticut	18,497,121,000	1.0%
49	Delaware	3,542,629,000	0.2%
4	Florida	97,362,136,000	5.5%
11	Georgia	44,923,646,000	2.5%
46	Hawaii	3,978,687,000	0.2%
40	Idaho	5,690,112,000	0.3%
5	Illinois	75,053,318,000	4.2%
19	Indiana	29,653,077,000	1.7%
28	Iowa	16,742,905,000	0.9%
30	Kansas	14,723,990,000	0.8%
29	Kentucky	15,014,473,000	0.8%
24	Louisiana	21,722,761,000	1.2%
43	Maine	4,997,639,000	0.3%
18	Maryland	30,611,946,000	1.7%
14	Massachusetts	35,213,855,000	2.0%
10	Michigan	47,400,489,000	2.7%
16	Minnesota	30,927,429,000	1.7%
34	Mississippi	12,749,774,000	0.7%
22	Missouri	26,100,971,000	1.5%
47	Montana	3,907,926,000	0.2%
31	Nebraska	14,494,774,000	0.8%
32	Nevada	13,984,958,000	0.8%
38	New Hampshire	6,081,885,000	0.3%
8	New Jersey	48,981,215,000	2.8%
37	New Mexico	8,911,093,000	0.5%
2	New York	195,030,929,000	11.0%
9	North Carolina	47,596,159,000	2.7%
45	North Dakota	4,551,933,000	0.3%
7	Ohio	56,898,874,000	3.2%
33	Oklahoma	13,978,099,000	0.8%
26	Oregon	20,078,031,000	1.1%
6	Pennsylvania	65,416,463,000	3.7%
44	Rhode Island	4,691,124,000	0.3%
23	South Carolina	22,119,332,000	1.2%
48	South Dakota	3,561,894,000	0.2%
15	Tennessee	33,468,387,000	1.9%
3	Texas	134,886,402,000	7.6%
35	Utah	12,116,492,000	0.7%
50	Vermont	2,964,378,000	0.2%
13	Virginia	39,349,309,000	2.2%
12	Washington	44,541,498,000	2.5%
41	West Virginia	5,542,791,000	0.3%
20	Wisconsin	28,861,399,000	1.6%
42	Wyoming	5,310,670,000	0.3%

RANK ORDER

RANK	STATE	REVENUE	% of USA
1	California	$292,936,194,000	16.5%
2	New York	195,030,929,000	11.0%
3	Texas	134,886,402,000	7.6%
4	Florida	97,362,136,000	5.5%
5	Illinois	75,053,318,000	4.2%
6	Pennsylvania	65,416,463,000	3.7%
7	Ohio	56,898,874,000	3.2%
8	New Jersey	48,981,215,000	2.8%
9	North Carolina	47,596,159,000	2.7%
10	Michigan	47,400,489,000	2.7%
11	Georgia	44,923,646,000	2.5%
12	Washington	44,541,498,000	2.5%
13	Virginia	39,349,309,000	2.2%
14	Massachusetts	35,213,855,000	2.0%
15	Tennessee	33,468,387,000	1.9%
16	Minnesota	30,927,429,000	1.7%
17	Colorado	30,842,258,000	1.7%
18	Maryland	30,611,946,000	1.7%
19	Indiana	29,653,077,000	1.7%
20	Wisconsin	28,861,399,000	1.6%
21	Arizona	28,639,085,000	1.6%
22	Missouri	26,100,971,000	1.5%
23	South Carolina	22,119,332,000	1.2%
24	Louisiana	21,722,761,000	1.2%
25	Alabama	21,361,885,000	1.2%
26	Oregon	20,078,031,000	1.1%
27	Connecticut	18,497,121,000	1.0%
28	Iowa	16,742,905,000	0.9%
29	Kentucky	15,014,473,000	0.8%
30	Kansas	14,723,990,000	0.8%
31	Nebraska	14,494,774,000	0.8%
32	Nevada	13,984,958,000	0.8%
33	Oklahoma	13,978,099,000	0.8%
34	Mississippi	12,749,774,000	0.7%
35	Utah	12,116,492,000	0.7%
36	Arkansas	10,226,680,000	0.6%
37	New Mexico	8,911,093,000	0.5%
38	New Hampshire	6,081,885,000	0.3%
39	Alaska	5,773,814,000	0.3%
40	Idaho	5,690,112,000	0.3%
41	West Virginia	5,542,791,000	0.3%
42	Wyoming	5,310,670,000	0.3%
43	Maine	4,997,639,000	0.3%
44	Rhode Island	4,691,124,000	0.3%
45	North Dakota	4,551,933,000	0.3%
46	Hawaii	3,978,687,000	0.2%
47	Montana	3,907,926,000	0.2%
48	South Dakota	3,561,894,000	0.2%
49	Delaware	3,542,629,000	0.2%
50	Vermont	2,964,378,000	0.2%
	District of Columbia	15,137,352,000	0.9%

Source: U.S. Bureau of the Census, Governments Division
"2015 State and Local Government Finances" (http://www.census.gov/govs/local/)
*Total revenue includes all money received from external sources. This includes taxes, intergovernmental transfers and insurance trust revenue, and revenue from government owned utilities and other commercial or auxiliary enterprise.

Per Capita Local Government Total Revenue in 2015

National Per Capita = $5,536*

<table>
<tr><th colspan="3">ALPHA ORDER</th><th colspan="3">RANK ORDER</th></tr>
<tr><th>RANK</th><th>STATE</th><th>PER CAPITA</th><th>RANK</th><th>STATE</th><th>PER CAPITA</th></tr>
<tr><td>34</td><td>Alabama</td><td>$4,404</td><td>1</td><td>New York</td><td>$9,840</td></tr>
<tr><td>3</td><td>Alaska</td><td>7,824</td><td>2</td><td>Wyoming</td><td>9,061</td></tr>
<tr><td>39</td><td>Arizona</td><td>4,210</td><td>3</td><td>Alaska</td><td>7,824</td></tr>
<tr><td>47</td><td>Arkansas</td><td>3,437</td><td>4</td><td>Nebraska</td><td>7,655</td></tr>
<tr><td>5</td><td>California</td><td>7,505</td><td>5</td><td>California</td><td>7,505</td></tr>
<tr><td>9</td><td>Colorado</td><td>5,669</td><td>6</td><td>Washington</td><td>6,227</td></tr>
<tr><td>14</td><td>Connecticut</td><td>5,147</td><td>7</td><td>North Dakota</td><td>6,030</td></tr>
<tr><td>44</td><td>Delaware</td><td>3,752</td><td>8</td><td>Illinois</td><td>5,835</td></tr>
<tr><td>24</td><td>Florida</td><td>4,804</td><td>9</td><td>Colorado</td><td>5,669</td></tr>
<tr><td>34</td><td>Georgia</td><td>4,404</td><td>10</td><td>Minnesota</td><td>5,640</td></tr>
<tr><td>50</td><td>Hawaii</td><td>2,789</td><td>11</td><td>New Jersey</td><td>5,467</td></tr>
<tr><td>46</td><td>Idaho</td><td>3,450</td><td>12</td><td>Iowa</td><td>5,369</td></tr>
<tr><td>8</td><td>Illinois</td><td>5,835</td><td>13</td><td>Massachusetts</td><td>5,183</td></tr>
<tr><td>32</td><td>Indiana</td><td>4,486</td><td>14</td><td>Connecticut</td><td>5,147</td></tr>
<tr><td>12</td><td>Iowa</td><td>5,369</td><td>15</td><td>Pennsylvania</td><td>5,114</td></tr>
<tr><td>18</td><td>Kansas</td><td>5,067</td><td>16</td><td>Maryland</td><td>5,102</td></tr>
<tr><td>48</td><td>Kentucky</td><td>3,395</td><td>17</td><td>Tennessee</td><td>5,078</td></tr>
<tr><td>29</td><td>Louisiana</td><td>4,650</td><td>18</td><td>Kansas</td><td>5,067</td></tr>
<tr><td>43</td><td>Maine</td><td>3,764</td><td>19</td><td>Wisconsin</td><td>5,011</td></tr>
<tr><td>16</td><td>Maryland</td><td>5,102</td><td>20</td><td>Oregon</td><td>4,999</td></tr>
<tr><td>13</td><td>Massachusetts</td><td>5,183</td><td>21</td><td>Texas</td><td>4,913</td></tr>
<tr><td>25</td><td>Michigan</td><td>4,779</td><td>22</td><td>Ohio</td><td>4,903</td></tr>
<tr><td>10</td><td>Minnesota</td><td>5,640</td><td>23</td><td>Nevada</td><td>4,851</td></tr>
<tr><td>38</td><td>Mississippi</td><td>4,271</td><td>24</td><td>Florida</td><td>4,804</td></tr>
<tr><td>36</td><td>Missouri</td><td>4,298</td><td>25</td><td>Michigan</td><td>4,779</td></tr>
<tr><td>42</td><td>Montana</td><td>3,800</td><td>26</td><td>Vermont</td><td>4,747</td></tr>
<tr><td>4</td><td>Nebraska</td><td>7,655</td><td>27</td><td>North Carolina</td><td>4,740</td></tr>
<tr><td>23</td><td>Nevada</td><td>4,851</td><td>28</td><td>Virginia</td><td>4,703</td></tr>
<tr><td>30</td><td>New Hampshire</td><td>4,572</td><td>29</td><td>Louisiana</td><td>4,650</td></tr>
<tr><td>11</td><td>New Jersey</td><td>5,467</td><td>30</td><td>New Hampshire</td><td>4,572</td></tr>
<tr><td>37</td><td>New Mexico</td><td>4,280</td><td>31</td><td>South Carolina</td><td>4,521</td></tr>
<tr><td>1</td><td>New York</td><td>9,840</td><td>32</td><td>Indiana</td><td>4,486</td></tr>
<tr><td>27</td><td>North Carolina</td><td>4,740</td><td>33</td><td>Rhode Island</td><td>4,443</td></tr>
<tr><td>7</td><td>North Dakota</td><td>6,030</td><td>34</td><td>Alabama</td><td>4,404</td></tr>
<tr><td>22</td><td>Ohio</td><td>4,903</td><td>34</td><td>Georgia</td><td>4,404</td></tr>
<tr><td>45</td><td>Oklahoma</td><td>3,580</td><td>36</td><td>Missouri</td><td>4,298</td></tr>
<tr><td>20</td><td>Oregon</td><td>4,999</td><td>37</td><td>New Mexico</td><td>4,280</td></tr>
<tr><td>15</td><td>Pennsylvania</td><td>5,114</td><td>38</td><td>Mississippi</td><td>4,271</td></tr>
<tr><td>33</td><td>Rhode Island</td><td>4,443</td><td>39</td><td>Arizona</td><td>4,210</td></tr>
<tr><td>31</td><td>South Carolina</td><td>4,521</td><td>40</td><td>South Dakota</td><td>4,171</td></tr>
<tr><td>40</td><td>South Dakota</td><td>4,171</td><td>41</td><td>Utah</td><td>4,059</td></tr>
<tr><td>17</td><td>Tennessee</td><td>5,078</td><td>42</td><td>Montana</td><td>3,800</td></tr>
<tr><td>21</td><td>Texas</td><td>4,913</td><td>43</td><td>Maine</td><td>3,764</td></tr>
<tr><td>41</td><td>Utah</td><td>4,059</td><td>44</td><td>Delaware</td><td>3,752</td></tr>
<tr><td>26</td><td>Vermont</td><td>4,747</td><td>45</td><td>Oklahoma</td><td>3,580</td></tr>
<tr><td>28</td><td>Virginia</td><td>4,703</td><td>46</td><td>Idaho</td><td>3,450</td></tr>
<tr><td>6</td><td>Washington</td><td>6,227</td><td>47</td><td>Arkansas</td><td>3,437</td></tr>
<tr><td>49</td><td>West Virginia</td><td>3,013</td><td>48</td><td>Kentucky</td><td>3,395</td></tr>
<tr><td>19</td><td>Wisconsin</td><td>5,011</td><td>49</td><td>West Virginia</td><td>3,013</td></tr>
<tr><td>2</td><td>Wyoming</td><td>9,061</td><td>50</td><td>Hawaii</td><td>2,789</td></tr>
<tr><td></td><td></td><td></td><td></td><td>District of Columbia</td><td>22,501</td></tr>
</table>

Source: U.S. Bureau of the Census, Governments Division
"2015 State and Local Government Finances" (http://www.census.gov/govs/local/)
*Total revenue includes all money received from external sources. This includes taxes, intergovernmental transfers and insurance trust revenue, and revenue from government owned utilities and other commercial or auxiliary enterprise.

Local Government Revenue from the Federal Government in 2015

National Total = $67,103,128,000

ALPHA ORDER

RANK	STATE	REVENUE	% of USA
17	Alabama	$906,492,000	1.4%
38	Alaska	296,211,000	0.4%
18	Arizona	903,668,000	1.3%
37	Arkansas	296,941,000	0.4%
1	California	12,693,167,000	18.9%
14	Colorado	1,205,886,000	1.8%
25	Connecticut	568,328,000	0.8%
50	Delaware	64,191,000	0.1%
4	Florida	3,949,694,000	5.9%
15	Georgia	1,135,909,000	1.7%
36	Hawaii	350,445,000	0.5%
46	Idaho	134,326,000	0.2%
5	Illinois	3,192,155,000	4.8%
34	Indiana	374,794,000	0.6%
28	Iowa	512,674,000	0.8%
39	Kansas	266,069,000	0.4%
27	Kentucky	524,586,000	0.8%
20	Louisiana	874,194,000	1.3%
45	Maine	137,253,000	0.2%
13	Maryland	1,260,229,000	1.9%
12	Massachusetts	1,396,616,000	2.1%
10	Michigan	1,706,512,000	2.5%
19	Minnesota	875,247,000	1.3%
32	Mississippi	398,929,000	0.6%
23	Missouri	731,097,000	1.1%
41	Montana	221,381,000	0.3%
33	Nebraska	381,038,000	0.6%
26	Nevada	568,065,000	0.8%
48	New Hampshire	109,273,000	0.2%
16	New Jersey	1,045,237,000	1.6%
35	New Mexico	371,722,000	0.6%
2	New York	6,516,154,000	9.7%
6	North Carolina	2,401,376,000	3.6%
40	North Dakota	258,745,000	0.4%
8	Ohio	2,144,519,000	3.2%
31	Oklahoma	423,748,000	0.6%
21	Oregon	864,922,000	1.3%
7	Pennsylvania	2,377,560,000	3.5%
44	Rhode Island	145,546,000	0.2%
30	South Carolina	428,914,000	0.6%
42	South Dakota	202,427,000	0.3%
22	Tennessee	744,504,000	1.1%
3	Texas	3,978,554,000	5.9%
29	Utah	468,891,000	0.7%
49	Vermont	66,679,000	0.1%
9	Virginia	1,837,837,000	2.7%
11	Washington	1,672,689,000	2.5%
43	West Virginia	199,587,000	0.3%
24	Wisconsin	581,555,000	0.9%
47	Wyoming	128,939,000	0.2%

RANK ORDER

RANK	STATE	REVENUE	% of USA
1	California	$12,693,167,000	18.9%
2	New York	6,516,154,000	9.7%
3	Texas	3,978,554,000	5.9%
4	Florida	3,949,694,000	5.9%
5	Illinois	3,192,155,000	4.8%
6	North Carolina	2,401,376,000	3.6%
7	Pennsylvania	2,377,560,000	3.5%
8	Ohio	2,144,519,000	3.2%
9	Virginia	1,837,837,000	2.7%
10	Michigan	1,706,512,000	2.5%
11	Washington	1,672,689,000	2.5%
12	Massachusetts	1,396,616,000	2.1%
13	Maryland	1,260,229,000	1.9%
14	Colorado	1,205,886,000	1.8%
15	Georgia	1,135,909,000	1.7%
16	New Jersey	1,045,237,000	1.6%
17	Alabama	906,492,000	1.4%
18	Arizona	903,668,000	1.3%
19	Minnesota	875,247,000	1.3%
20	Louisiana	874,194,000	1.3%
21	Oregon	864,922,000	1.3%
22	Tennessee	744,504,000	1.1%
23	Missouri	731,097,000	1.1%
24	Wisconsin	581,555,000	0.9%
25	Connecticut	568,328,000	0.8%
26	Nevada	568,065,000	0.8%
27	Kentucky	524,586,000	0.8%
28	Iowa	512,674,000	0.8%
29	Utah	468,891,000	0.7%
30	South Carolina	428,914,000	0.6%
31	Oklahoma	423,748,000	0.6%
32	Mississippi	398,929,000	0.6%
33	Nebraska	381,038,000	0.6%
34	Indiana	374,794,000	0.6%
35	New Mexico	371,722,000	0.6%
36	Hawaii	350,445,000	0.5%
37	Arkansas	296,941,000	0.4%
38	Alaska	296,211,000	0.4%
39	Kansas	266,069,000	0.4%
40	North Dakota	258,745,000	0.4%
41	Montana	221,381,000	0.3%
42	South Dakota	202,427,000	0.3%
43	West Virginia	199,587,000	0.3%
44	Rhode Island	145,546,000	0.2%
45	Maine	137,253,000	0.2%
46	Idaho	134,326,000	0.2%
47	Wyoming	128,939,000	0.2%
48	New Hampshire	109,273,000	0.2%
49	Vermont	66,679,000	0.1%
50	Delaware	64,191,000	0.1%
	District of Columbia	4,207,653,000	6.3%

Source: U.S. Bureau of the Census, Governments Division
"2015 State and Local Government Finances" (http://www.census.gov/govs/local/)

Per Capita Local Government Revenue from the Federal Government in 2015

National Per Capita = $209

ALPHA ORDER

RANK	STATE	PER CAPITA
20	Alabama	$187
1	Alaska	401
33	Arizona	133
44	Arkansas	100
4	California	325
10	Colorado	222
28	Connecticut	158
49	Delaware	68
19	Florida	195
38	Georgia	111
6	Hawaii	246
48	Idaho	81
5	Illinois	248
50	Indiana	57
26	Iowa	164
45	Kansas	92
35	Kentucky	119
20	Louisiana	187
42	Maine	103
15	Maryland	210
16	Massachusetts	206
25	Michigan	172
27	Minnesota	160
32	Mississippi	134
34	Missouri	120
13	Montana	215
17	Nebraska	201
18	Nevada	197
47	New Hampshire	82
36	New Jersey	117
24	New Mexico	179
3	New York	329
7	North Carolina	239
2	North Dakota	343
23	Ohio	185
39	Oklahoma	109
13	Oregon	215
22	Pennsylvania	186
31	Rhode Island	138
46	South Carolina	88
8	South Dakota	237
37	Tennessee	113
30	Texas	145
29	Utah	157
41	Vermont	107
11	Virginia	220
9	Washington	234
40	West Virginia	108
43	Wisconsin	101
11	Wyoming	220

RANK ORDER

RANK	STATE	PER CAPITA
1	Alaska	$401
2	North Dakota	343
3	New York	329
4	California	325
5	Illinois	248
6	Hawaii	246
7	North Carolina	239
8	South Dakota	237
9	Washington	234
10	Colorado	222
11	Virginia	220
11	Wyoming	220
13	Montana	215
13	Oregon	215
15	Maryland	210
16	Massachusetts	206
17	Nebraska	201
18	Nevada	197
19	Florida	195
20	Alabama	187
20	Louisiana	187
22	Pennsylvania	186
23	Ohio	185
24	New Mexico	179
25	Michigan	172
26	Iowa	164
27	Minnesota	160
28	Connecticut	158
29	Utah	157
30	Texas	145
31	Rhode Island	138
32	Mississippi	134
33	Arizona	133
34	Missouri	120
35	Kentucky	119
36	New Jersey	117
37	Tennessee	113
38	Georgia	111
39	Oklahoma	109
40	West Virginia	108
41	Vermont	107
42	Maine	103
43	Wisconsin	101
44	Arkansas	100
45	Kansas	92
46	South Carolina	88
47	New Hampshire	82
48	Idaho	81
49	Delaware	68
50	Indiana	57

District of Columbia	6,255

Source: CQ Press using data from U.S. Bureau of the Census, Governments Division
"2015 State and Local Government Finances" (http://www.census.gov/govs/local/)

Local Government Own Source Revenue in 2015

National Total = $1,014,365,746,000*

ALPHA ORDER

ALPHA ORDER

RANK	STATE	REVENUE	% of USA
26	Alabama	$11,353,184,000	1.1%
45	Alaska	2,885,528,000	0.3%
21	Arizona	14,800,219,000	1.5%
38	Arkansas	3,995,998,000	0.4%
1	California	143,137,357,000	14.1%
15	Colorado	19,790,956,000	2.0%
25	Connecticut	12,051,906,000	1.2%
49	Delaware	1,594,145,000	0.2%
4	Florida	60,829,731,000	6.0%
9	Georgia	26,840,937,000	2.6%
44	Hawaii	2,990,307,000	0.3%
40	Idaho	3,214,721,000	0.3%
5	Illinois	44,401,855,000	4.4%
17	Indiana	16,655,366,000	1.6%
28	Iowa	9,757,031,000	1.0%
30	Kansas	8,091,282,000	0.8%
31	Kentucky	8,039,685,000	0.8%
24	Louisiana	13,599,178,000	1.3%
39	Maine	3,430,372,000	0.3%
16	Maryland	19,641,397,000	1.9%
14	Massachusetts	20,005,730,000	2.0%
13	Michigan	22,665,446,000	2.2%
20	Minnesota	15,539,143,000	1.5%
33	Mississippi	7,004,398,000	0.7%
18	Missouri	15,916,103,000	1.6%
47	Montana	2,214,232,000	0.2%
34	Nebraska	6,902,192,000	0.7%
32	Nevada	7,453,416,000	0.7%
36	New Hampshire	4,381,989,000	0.4%
7	New Jersey	34,561,518,000	3.4%
37	New Mexico	4,030,805,000	0.4%
2	New York	123,814,720,000	12.2%
10	North Carolina	26,027,859,000	2.6%
48	North Dakota	2,072,704,000	0.2%
8	Ohio	34,018,752,000	3.4%
29	Oklahoma	8,235,525,000	0.8%
27	Oregon	11,288,389,000	1.1%
6	Pennsylvania	37,266,958,000	3.7%
42	Rhode Island	3,078,439,000	0.3%
22	South Carolina	14,515,100,000	1.4%
46	South Dakota	2,225,542,000	0.2%
19	Tennessee	15,722,837,000	1.6%
3	Texas	84,145,866,000	8.3%
35	Utah	6,297,567,000	0.6%
50	Vermont	923,375,000	0.1%
12	Virginia	23,320,816,000	2.3%
11	Washington	24,051,577,000	2.4%
41	West Virginia	3,213,637,000	0.3%
23	Wisconsin	14,436,799,000	1.4%
43	Wyoming	3,019,340,000	0.3%

RANK ORDER

RANK	STATE	REVENUE	% of USA
1	California	$143,137,357,000	14.1%
2	New York	123,814,720,000	12.2%
3	Texas	84,145,866,000	8.3%
4	Florida	60,829,731,000	6.0%
5	Illinois	44,401,855,000	4.4%
6	Pennsylvania	37,266,958,000	3.7%
7	New Jersey	34,561,518,000	3.4%
8	Ohio	34,018,752,000	3.4%
9	Georgia	26,840,937,000	2.6%
10	North Carolina	26,027,859,000	2.6%
11	Washington	24,051,577,000	2.4%
12	Virginia	23,320,816,000	2.3%
13	Michigan	22,665,446,000	2.2%
14	Massachusetts	20,005,730,000	2.0%
15	Colorado	19,790,956,000	2.0%
16	Maryland	19,641,397,000	1.9%
17	Indiana	16,655,366,000	1.6%
18	Missouri	15,916,103,000	1.6%
19	Tennessee	15,722,837,000	1.6%
20	Minnesota	15,539,143,000	1.5%
21	Arizona	14,800,219,000	1.5%
22	South Carolina	14,515,100,000	1.4%
23	Wisconsin	14,436,799,000	1.4%
24	Louisiana	13,599,178,000	1.3%
25	Connecticut	12,051,906,000	1.2%
26	Alabama	11,353,184,000	1.1%
27	Oregon	11,288,389,000	1.1%
28	Iowa	9,757,031,000	1.0%
29	Oklahoma	8,235,525,000	0.8%
30	Kansas	8,091,282,000	0.8%
31	Kentucky	8,039,685,000	0.8%
32	Nevada	7,453,416,000	0.7%
33	Mississippi	7,004,398,000	0.7%
34	Nebraska	6,902,192,000	0.7%
35	Utah	6,297,567,000	0.6%
36	New Hampshire	4,381,989,000	0.4%
37	New Mexico	4,030,805,000	0.4%
38	Arkansas	3,995,998,000	0.4%
39	Maine	3,430,372,000	0.3%
40	Idaho	3,214,721,000	0.3%
41	West Virginia	3,213,637,000	0.3%
42	Rhode Island	3,078,439,000	0.3%
43	Wyoming	3,019,340,000	0.3%
44	Hawaii	2,990,307,000	0.3%
45	Alaska	2,885,528,000	0.3%
46	South Dakota	2,225,542,000	0.2%
47	Montana	2,214,232,000	0.2%
48	North Dakota	2,072,704,000	0.2%
49	Delaware	1,594,145,000	0.2%
50	Vermont	923,375,000	0.1%
	District of Columbia	8,913,817,000	0.9%

Source: U.S. Bureau of the Census, Governments Division
"2015 State and Local Government Finances" (http://www.census.gov/govs/local/)
*Own source revenue includes taxes, current charges, and miscellaneous general revenue. Excluded are intergovernmental transfers, insurance trust revenue, and revenue from government owned utilities and other commercial or auxiliary enterprise.

Per Capita Local Government Own Source Revenue in 2015

National Per Capita = $3,160*

<table>
<tr><td colspan="3">ALPHA ORDER</td><td colspan="3">RANK ORDER</td></tr>
<tr><td>RANK</td><td>STATE</td><td>PER CAPITA</td><td>RANK</td><td>STATE</td><td>PER CAPITA</td></tr>
<tr><td>37</td><td>Alabama</td><td>$2,340</td><td>1</td><td>New York</td><td>$6,247</td></tr>
<tr><td>3</td><td>Alaska</td><td>3,910</td><td>2</td><td>Wyoming</td><td>5,152</td></tr>
<tr><td>39</td><td>Arizona</td><td>2,176</td><td>3</td><td>Alaska</td><td>3,910</td></tr>
<tr><td>50</td><td>Arkansas</td><td>1,343</td><td>4</td><td>New Jersey</td><td>3,857</td></tr>
<tr><td>5</td><td>California</td><td>3,667</td><td>5</td><td>California</td><td>3,667</td></tr>
<tr><td>7</td><td>Colorado</td><td>3,638</td><td>6</td><td>Nebraska</td><td>3,645</td></tr>
<tr><td>10</td><td>Connecticut</td><td>3,353</td><td>7</td><td>Colorado</td><td>3,638</td></tr>
<tr><td>48</td><td>Delaware</td><td>1,689</td><td>8</td><td>Illinois</td><td>3,452</td></tr>
<tr><td>15</td><td>Florida</td><td>3,001</td><td>9</td><td>Washington</td><td>3,363</td></tr>
<tr><td>27</td><td>Georgia</td><td>2,632</td><td>10</td><td>Connecticut</td><td>3,353</td></tr>
<tr><td>43</td><td>Hawaii</td><td>2,097</td><td>11</td><td>New Hampshire</td><td>3,294</td></tr>
<tr><td>44</td><td>Idaho</td><td>1,949</td><td>12</td><td>Maryland</td><td>3,273</td></tr>
<tr><td>8</td><td>Illinois</td><td>3,452</td><td>13</td><td>Iowa</td><td>3,129</td></tr>
<tr><td>33</td><td>Indiana</td><td>2,519</td><td>14</td><td>Texas</td><td>3,065</td></tr>
<tr><td>13</td><td>Iowa</td><td>3,129</td><td>15</td><td>Florida</td><td>3,001</td></tr>
<tr><td>25</td><td>Kansas</td><td>2,785</td><td>16</td><td>South Carolina</td><td>2,967</td></tr>
<tr><td>46</td><td>Kentucky</td><td>1,818</td><td>17</td><td>Massachusetts</td><td>2,945</td></tr>
<tr><td>21</td><td>Louisiana</td><td>2,911</td><td>18</td><td>Ohio</td><td>2,931</td></tr>
<tr><td>32</td><td>Maine</td><td>2,584</td><td>19</td><td>Rhode Island</td><td>2,915</td></tr>
<tr><td>12</td><td>Maryland</td><td>3,273</td><td>20</td><td>Pennsylvania</td><td>2,914</td></tr>
<tr><td>17</td><td>Massachusetts</td><td>2,945</td><td>21</td><td>Louisiana</td><td>2,911</td></tr>
<tr><td>38</td><td>Michigan</td><td>2,285</td><td>22</td><td>Minnesota</td><td>2,834</td></tr>
<tr><td>22</td><td>Minnesota</td><td>2,834</td><td>23</td><td>Oregon</td><td>2,810</td></tr>
<tr><td>36</td><td>Mississippi</td><td>2,346</td><td>24</td><td>Virginia</td><td>2,787</td></tr>
<tr><td>28</td><td>Missouri</td><td>2,621</td><td>25</td><td>Kansas</td><td>2,785</td></tr>
<tr><td>40</td><td>Montana</td><td>2,153</td><td>26</td><td>North Dakota</td><td>2,746</td></tr>
<tr><td>6</td><td>Nebraska</td><td>3,645</td><td>27</td><td>Georgia</td><td>2,632</td></tr>
<tr><td>31</td><td>Nevada</td><td>2,585</td><td>28</td><td>Missouri</td><td>2,621</td></tr>
<tr><td>11</td><td>New Hampshire</td><td>3,294</td><td>29</td><td>South Dakota</td><td>2,606</td></tr>
<tr><td>4</td><td>New Jersey</td><td>3,857</td><td>30</td><td>North Carolina</td><td>2,592</td></tr>
<tr><td>45</td><td>New Mexico</td><td>1,936</td><td>31</td><td>Nevada</td><td>2,585</td></tr>
<tr><td>1</td><td>New York</td><td>6,247</td><td>32</td><td>Maine</td><td>2,584</td></tr>
<tr><td>30</td><td>North Carolina</td><td>2,592</td><td>33</td><td>Indiana</td><td>2,519</td></tr>
<tr><td>26</td><td>North Dakota</td><td>2,746</td><td>34</td><td>Wisconsin</td><td>2,507</td></tr>
<tr><td>18</td><td>Ohio</td><td>2,931</td><td>35</td><td>Tennessee</td><td>2,386</td></tr>
<tr><td>42</td><td>Oklahoma</td><td>2,109</td><td>36</td><td>Mississippi</td><td>2,346</td></tr>
<tr><td>23</td><td>Oregon</td><td>2,810</td><td>37</td><td>Alabama</td><td>2,340</td></tr>
<tr><td>20</td><td>Pennsylvania</td><td>2,914</td><td>38</td><td>Michigan</td><td>2,285</td></tr>
<tr><td>19</td><td>Rhode Island</td><td>2,915</td><td>39</td><td>Arizona</td><td>2,176</td></tr>
<tr><td>16</td><td>South Carolina</td><td>2,967</td><td>40</td><td>Montana</td><td>2,153</td></tr>
<tr><td>29</td><td>South Dakota</td><td>2,606</td><td>41</td><td>Utah</td><td>2,110</td></tr>
<tr><td>35</td><td>Tennessee</td><td>2,386</td><td>42</td><td>Oklahoma</td><td>2,109</td></tr>
<tr><td>14</td><td>Texas</td><td>3,065</td><td>43</td><td>Hawaii</td><td>2,097</td></tr>
<tr><td>41</td><td>Utah</td><td>2,110</td><td>44</td><td>Idaho</td><td>1,949</td></tr>
<tr><td>49</td><td>Vermont</td><td>1,479</td><td>45</td><td>New Mexico</td><td>1,936</td></tr>
<tr><td>24</td><td>Virginia</td><td>2,787</td><td>46</td><td>Kentucky</td><td>1,818</td></tr>
<tr><td>9</td><td>Washington</td><td>3,363</td><td>47</td><td>West Virginia</td><td>1,747</td></tr>
<tr><td>47</td><td>West Virginia</td><td>1,747</td><td>48</td><td>Delaware</td><td>1,689</td></tr>
<tr><td>34</td><td>Wisconsin</td><td>2,507</td><td>49</td><td>Vermont</td><td>1,479</td></tr>
<tr><td>2</td><td>Wyoming</td><td>5,152</td><td>50</td><td>Arkansas</td><td>1,343</td></tr>
<tr><td></td><td></td><td></td><td></td><td>District of Columbia</td><td>13,250</td></tr>
</table>

Source: CQ Press using data from U.S. Bureau of the Census, Governments Division
"2015 State and Local Government Finances" (http://www.census.gov/govs/local/)
*Own source revenue includes taxes, current charges, and miscellaneous general revenue. Excluded are intergovernmental
transfers, insurance trust revenue, and revenue from government owned utilities and other commercial or auxiliary enterprise.

Local Government Tax Revenue in 2015

National Total = $655,977,117,000

ALPHA ORDER

RANK	STATE	REVENUE	% of USA
28	Alabama	$5,507,212,000	0.8%
43	Alaska	1,721,330,000	0.3%
20	Arizona	9,679,391,000	1.5%
40	Arkansas	2,329,574,000	0.4%
2	California	77,491,869,000	11.8%
16	Colorado	12,247,091,000	1.9%
17	Connecticut	10,382,427,000	1.6%
49	Delaware	988,337,000	0.2%
5	Florida	32,683,455,000	5.0%
10	Georgia	16,178,989,000	2.5%
41	Hawaii	2,223,965,000	0.3%
44	Idaho	1,705,143,000	0.3%
4	Illinois	33,016,855,000	5.0%
24	Indiana	7,989,098,000	1.2%
27	Iowa	5,669,285,000	0.9%
31	Kansas	4,885,897,000	0.7%
29	Kentucky	5,137,708,000	0.8%
22	Louisiana	8,751,309,000	1.3%
37	Maine	2,723,221,000	0.4%
12	Maryland	15,112,685,000	2.3%
11	Massachusetts	16,059,473,000	2.4%
15	Michigan	12,808,538,000	2.0%
23	Minnesota	8,200,995,000	1.3%
36	Mississippi	3,076,716,000	0.5%
18	Missouri	10,213,115,000	1.6%
47	Montana	1,331,864,000	0.2%
32	Nebraska	4,490,181,000	0.7%
33	Nevada	4,317,308,000	0.7%
35	New Hampshire	3,695,980,000	0.6%
6	New Jersey	28,125,365,000	4.3%
38	New Mexico	2,646,041,000	0.4%
1	New York	94,443,860,000	14.4%
14	North Carolina	12,959,983,000	2.0%
48	North Dakota	1,210,001,000	0.2%
8	Ohio	22,959,660,000	3.5%
30	Oklahoma	5,052,200,000	0.8%
26	Oregon	6,992,405,000	1.1%
7	Pennsylvania	27,255,904,000	4.2%
39	Rhode Island	2,526,299,000	0.4%
25	South Carolina	7,135,847,000	1.1%
45	South Dakota	1,618,418,000	0.2%
21	Tennessee	8,869,067,000	1.4%
3	Texas	58,099,504,000	8.9%
34	Utah	4,147,205,000	0.6%
50	Vermont	588,230,000	0.1%
9	Virginia	16,829,436,000	2.6%
13	Washington	13,524,541,000	2.1%
42	West Virginia	1,991,037,000	0.3%
19	Wisconsin	9,882,836,000	1.5%
46	Wyoming	1,391,031,000	0.2%

RANK ORDER

RANK	STATE	REVENUE	% of USA
1	New York	$94,443,860,000	14.4%
2	California	77,491,869,000	11.8%
3	Texas	58,099,504,000	8.9%
4	Illinois	33,016,855,000	5.0%
5	Florida	32,683,455,000	5.0%
6	New Jersey	28,125,365,000	4.3%
7	Pennsylvania	27,255,904,000	4.2%
8	Ohio	22,959,660,000	3.5%
9	Virginia	16,829,436,000	2.6%
10	Georgia	16,178,989,000	2.5%
11	Massachusetts	16,059,473,000	2.4%
12	Maryland	15,112,685,000	2.3%
13	Washington	13,524,541,000	2.1%
14	North Carolina	12,959,983,000	2.0%
15	Michigan	12,808,538,000	2.0%
16	Colorado	12,247,091,000	1.9%
17	Connecticut	10,382,427,000	1.6%
18	Missouri	10,213,115,000	1.6%
19	Wisconsin	9,882,836,000	1.5%
20	Arizona	9,679,391,000	1.5%
21	Tennessee	8,869,067,000	1.4%
22	Louisiana	8,751,309,000	1.3%
23	Minnesota	8,200,995,000	1.3%
24	Indiana	7,989,098,000	1.2%
25	South Carolina	7,135,847,000	1.1%
26	Oregon	6,992,405,000	1.1%
27	Iowa	5,669,285,000	0.9%
28	Alabama	5,507,212,000	0.8%
29	Kentucky	5,137,708,000	0.8%
30	Oklahoma	5,052,200,000	0.8%
31	Kansas	4,885,897,000	0.7%
32	Nebraska	4,490,181,000	0.7%
33	Nevada	4,317,308,000	0.7%
34	Utah	4,147,205,000	0.6%
35	New Hampshire	3,695,980,000	0.6%
36	Mississippi	3,076,716,000	0.5%
37	Maine	2,723,221,000	0.4%
38	New Mexico	2,646,041,000	0.4%
39	Rhode Island	2,526,299,000	0.4%
40	Arkansas	2,329,574,000	0.4%
41	Hawaii	2,223,965,000	0.3%
42	West Virginia	1,991,037,000	0.3%
43	Alaska	1,721,330,000	0.3%
44	Idaho	1,705,143,000	0.3%
45	South Dakota	1,618,418,000	0.2%
46	Wyoming	1,391,031,000	0.2%
47	Montana	1,331,864,000	0.2%
48	North Dakota	1,210,001,000	0.2%
49	Delaware	988,337,000	0.2%
50	Vermont	588,230,000	0.1%
	District of Columbia	7,109,236,000	1.1%

Source: U.S. Bureau of the Census, Governments Division
"2015 State and Local Government Finances" (http://www.census.gov/govs/local/)

Per Capita Local Government Tax Revenue in 2015

National Per Capita = $2,043

ALPHA ORDER				RANK ORDER		
RANK	STATE	PER CAPITA		RANK	STATE	PER CAPITA
44	Alabama	$1,135		1	New York	$4,765
11	Alaska	2,332		2	New Jersey	3,139
34	Arizona	1,423		3	Connecticut	2,889
50	Arkansas	783		4	New Hampshire	2,779
17	California	1,985		5	Illinois	2,567
12	Colorado	2,251		6	Maryland	2,519
3	Connecticut	2,889		7	Rhode Island	2,393
46	Delaware	1,047		8	Wyoming	2,373
27	Florida	1,613		9	Nebraska	2,371
29	Georgia	1,586		10	Massachusetts	2,364
30	Hawaii	1,559		11	Alaska	2,332
47	Idaho	1,034		12	Colorado	2,251
5	Illinois	2,567		13	Pennsylvania	2,131
42	Indiana	1,209		14	Texas	2,116
22	Iowa	1,818		15	Maine	2,051
26	Kansas	1,681		16	Virginia	2,011
43	Kentucky	1,162		17	California	1,985
21	Louisiana	1,873		18	Ohio	1,978
15	Maine	2,051		19	South Dakota	1,895
6	Maryland	2,519		20	Washington	1,891
10	Massachusetts	2,364		21	Louisiana	1,873
39	Michigan	1,291		22	Iowa	1,818
32	Minnesota	1,496		23	Oregon	1,741
48	Mississippi	1,031		24	Wisconsin	1,716
25	Missouri	1,682		25	Missouri	1,682
37	Montana	1,295		26	Kansas	1,681
9	Nebraska	2,371		27	Florida	1,613
31	Nevada	1,497		28	North Dakota	1,603
4	New Hampshire	2,779		29	Georgia	1,586
2	New Jersey	3,139		30	Hawaii	1,559
41	New Mexico	1,271		31	Nevada	1,497
1	New York	4,765		32	Minnesota	1,496
39	North Carolina	1,291		33	South Carolina	1,459
28	North Dakota	1,603		34	Arizona	1,423
18	Ohio	1,978		35	Utah	1,389
38	Oklahoma	1,294		36	Tennessee	1,346
23	Oregon	1,741		37	Montana	1,295
13	Pennsylvania	2,131		38	Oklahoma	1,294
7	Rhode Island	2,393		39	Michigan	1,291
33	South Carolina	1,459		39	North Carolina	1,291
19	South Dakota	1,895		41	New Mexico	1,271
36	Tennessee	1,346		42	Indiana	1,209
14	Texas	2,116		43	Kentucky	1,162
35	Utah	1,389		44	Alabama	1,135
49	Vermont	942		45	West Virginia	1,082
16	Virginia	2,011		46	Delaware	1,047
20	Washington	1,891		47	Idaho	1,034
45	West Virginia	1,082		48	Mississippi	1,031
24	Wisconsin	1,716		49	Vermont	942
8	Wyoming	2,373		50	Arkansas	783

District of Columbia — 10,568

Source: CQ Press using data from U.S. Bureau of the Census, Governments Division
"2015 State and Local Government Finances" (http://www.census.gov/govs/local/)

Local Government Total Expenditures in 2015

National Total = $1,779,704,490,000*

RANK	STATE	EXPENDITURES	% of USA		RANK	STATE	EXPENDITURES	% of USA
23	Alabama	$21,639,531,000	1.2%		1	California	$290,019,882,000	16.3%
39	Alaska	5,833,648,000	0.3%		2	New York	205,371,248,000	11.5%
20	Arizona	28,011,913,000	1.6%		3	Texas	136,955,201,000	7.7%
36	Arkansas	10,169,298,000	0.6%		4	Florida	97,948,817,000	5.5%
1	California	290,019,882,000	16.3%		5	Illinois	78,240,009,000	4.4%
18	Colorado	30,420,480,000	1.7%		6	Pennsylvania	64,486,609,000	3.6%
27	Connecticut	18,550,220,000	1.0%		7	Ohio	55,870,143,000	3.1%
49	Delaware	3,437,308,000	0.2%		8	New Jersey	48,460,958,000	2.7%
4	Florida	97,948,817,000	5.5%		9	North Carolina	46,853,356,000	2.6%
11	Georgia	45,797,300,000	2.6%		10	Michigan	46,825,946,000	2.6%
47	Hawaii	3,880,071,000	0.2%		11	Georgia	45,797,300,000	2.6%
41	Idaho	5,280,206,000	0.3%		12	Washington	42,517,596,000	2.4%
5	Illinois	78,240,009,000	4.4%		13	Virginia	39,336,219,000	2.2%
21	Indiana	26,911,498,000	1.5%		14	Massachusetts	35,334,036,000	2.0%
28	Iowa	16,581,643,000	0.9%		15	Tennessee	32,751,193,000	1.8%
30	Kansas	14,885,510,000	0.8%		16	Maryland	31,912,542,000	1.8%
29	Kentucky	15,139,796,000	0.9%		17	Minnesota	30,842,125,000	1.7%
24	Louisiana	21,610,060,000	1.2%		18	Colorado	30,420,480,000	1.7%
43	Maine	4,755,094,000	0.3%		19	Wisconsin	30,002,200,000	1.7%
16	Maryland	31,912,542,000	1.8%		20	Arizona	28,011,913,000	1.6%
14	Massachusetts	35,334,036,000	2.0%		21	Indiana	26,911,498,000	1.5%
10	Michigan	46,825,946,000	2.6%		22	Missouri	25,824,853,000	1.5%
17	Minnesota	30,842,125,000	1.7%		23	Alabama	21,639,531,000	1.2%
34	Mississippi	13,020,038,000	0.7%		24	Louisiana	21,610,060,000	1.2%
22	Missouri	25,824,853,000	1.5%		25	South Carolina	21,319,744,000	1.2%
46	Montana	3,890,006,000	0.2%		26	Oregon	19,736,242,000	1.1%
31	Nebraska	13,944,255,000	0.8%		27	Connecticut	18,550,220,000	1.0%
33	Nevada	13,519,652,000	0.8%		28	Iowa	16,581,643,000	0.9%
40	New Hampshire	5,421,893,000	0.3%		29	Kentucky	15,139,796,000	0.9%
8	New Jersey	48,460,958,000	2.7%		30	Kansas	14,885,510,000	0.8%
37	New Mexico	8,760,954,000	0.5%		31	Nebraska	13,944,255,000	0.8%
2	New York	205,371,248,000	11.5%		32	Oklahoma	13,838,983,000	0.8%
9	North Carolina	46,853,356,000	2.6%		33	Nevada	13,519,652,000	0.8%
45	North Dakota	4,457,291,000	0.3%		34	Mississippi	13,020,038,000	0.7%
7	Ohio	55,870,143,000	3.1%		35	Utah	11,459,031,000	0.6%
32	Oklahoma	13,838,983,000	0.8%		36	Arkansas	10,169,298,000	0.6%
26	Oregon	19,736,242,000	1.1%		37	New Mexico	8,760,954,000	0.5%
6	Pennsylvania	64,486,609,000	3.6%		38	West Virginia	5,927,945,000	0.3%
44	Rhode Island	4,563,419,000	0.3%		39	Alaska	5,833,648,000	0.3%
25	South Carolina	21,319,744,000	1.2%		40	New Hampshire	5,421,893,000	0.3%
48	South Dakota	3,558,821,000	0.2%		41	Idaho	5,280,206,000	0.3%
15	Tennessee	32,751,193,000	1.8%		42	Wyoming	5,267,393,000	0.3%
3	Texas	136,955,201,000	7.7%		43	Maine	4,755,094,000	0.3%
35	Utah	11,459,031,000	0.6%		44	Rhode Island	4,563,419,000	0.3%
50	Vermont	2,820,312,000	0.2%		45	North Dakota	4,457,291,000	0.3%
13	Virginia	39,336,219,000	2.2%		46	Montana	3,890,006,000	0.2%
12	Washington	42,517,596,000	2.4%		47	Hawaii	3,880,071,000	0.2%
38	West Virginia	5,927,945,000	0.3%		48	South Dakota	3,558,821,000	0.2%
19	Wisconsin	30,002,200,000	1.7%		49	Delaware	3,437,308,000	0.2%
42	Wyoming	5,267,393,000	0.3%		50	Vermont	2,820,312,000	0.2%
						District of Columbia	15,742,002,000	0.9%

ALPHA ORDER — RANK ORDER

Source: U.S. Bureau of the Census, Governments Division
   "2015 State and Local Government Finances" (http://www.census.gov/govs/local/)
*Total expenditures includes all money paid other than for retirement of debt and extension of loans. Includes payments from all sources of funds including current revenues and proceeds from borrowing and prior year fund balances. Includes intergovernmental transfers and expenditures for government owned utilities and other commercial or auxiliary enterprise and insurance trust expenditures.

Per Capita Local Government Total Expenditures in 2015

National Per Capita = $5,544*

ALPHA ORDER

RANK	STATE	PER CAPITA
31	Alabama	$4,461
3	Alaska	7,905
38	Arizona	4,118
47	Arkansas	3,418
4	California	7,430
10	Colorado	5,592
16	Connecticut	5,162
43	Delaware	3,641
22	Florida	4,833
30	Georgia	4,490
50	Hawaii	2,720
49	Idaho	3,201
6	Illinois	6,083
40	Indiana	4,071
13	Iowa	5,317
17	Kansas	5,123
46	Kentucky	3,424
28	Louisiana	4,626
44	Maine	3,581
12	Maryland	5,318
15	Massachusetts	5,201
24	Michigan	4,721
9	Minnesota	5,625
32	Mississippi	4,361
35	Missouri	4,253
42	Montana	3,783
5	Nebraska	7,364
26	Nevada	4,689
39	New Hampshire	4,076
11	New Jersey	5,409
36	New Mexico	4,207
1	New York	10,362
27	North Carolina	4,666
8	North Dakota	5,905
23	Ohio	4,814
45	Oklahoma	3,545
21	Oregon	4,914
18	Pennsylvania	5,042
34	Rhode Island	4,322
33	South Carolina	4,358
37	South Dakota	4,167
20	Tennessee	4,969
19	Texas	4,988
41	Utah	3,839
29	Vermont	4,516
25	Virginia	4,701
7	Washington	5,944
48	West Virginia	3,222
14	Wisconsin	5,209
2	Wyoming	8,987

RANK ORDER

RANK	STATE	PER CAPITA
1	New York	$10,362
2	Wyoming	8,987
3	Alaska	7,905
4	California	7,430
5	Nebraska	7,364
6	Illinois	6,083
7	Washington	5,944
8	North Dakota	5,905
9	Minnesota	5,625
10	Colorado	5,592
11	New Jersey	5,409
12	Maryland	5,318
13	Iowa	5,317
14	Wisconsin	5,209
15	Massachusetts	5,201
16	Connecticut	5,162
17	Kansas	5,123
18	Pennsylvania	5,042
19	Texas	4,988
20	Tennessee	4,969
21	Oregon	4,914
22	Florida	4,833
23	Ohio	4,814
24	Michigan	4,721
25	Virginia	4,701
26	Nevada	4,689
27	North Carolina	4,666
28	Louisiana	4,626
29	Vermont	4,516
30	Georgia	4,490
31	Alabama	4,461
32	Mississippi	4,361
33	South Carolina	4,358
34	Rhode Island	4,322
35	Missouri	4,253
36	New Mexico	4,207
37	South Dakota	4,167
38	Arizona	4,118
39	New Hampshire	4,076
40	Indiana	4,071
41	Utah	3,839
42	Montana	3,783
43	Delaware	3,641
44	Maine	3,581
45	Oklahoma	3,545
46	Kentucky	3,424
47	Arkansas	3,418
48	West Virginia	3,222
49	Idaho	3,201
50	Hawaii	2,720

District of Columbia   23,400

Source: CQ Press using data from U.S. Bureau of the Census, Governments Division
"2015 State and Local Government Finances" (http://www.census.gov/govs/local/)
*Total expenditures includes all money paid other than for retirement of debt and extension of loans. Includes payments from all sources of funds including current revenues and proceeds from borrowing and prior year fund balances. Includes intergovernmental transfers and expenditures for government owned utilities and other commercial or auxiliary enterprise and insurance trust expenditures.

Local Government Direct General Expenditures in 2015

National Total = $1,514,230,257,000*

ALPHA ORDER

ALPHA ORDER

RANK	STATE	EXPENDITURES	% of USA
25	Alabama	$18,204,881,000	1.2%
40	Alaska	5,183,679,000	0.3%
22	Arizona	21,658,693,000	1.4%
36	Arkansas	9,124,066,000	0.6%
1	California	237,892,764,000	15.7%
18	Colorado	25,562,274,000	1.7%
27	Connecticut	17,072,956,000	1.1%
48	Delaware	2,936,005,000	0.2%
4	Florida	84,457,586,000	5.6%
11	Georgia	38,547,302,000	2.5%
49	Hawaii	2,743,886,000	0.2%
41	Idaho	5,031,413,000	0.3%
5	Illinois	64,517,132,000	4.3%
19	Indiana	24,140,521,000	1.6%
28	Iowa	15,246,974,000	1.0%
29	Kansas	13,284,704,000	0.9%
30	Kentucky	12,877,920,000	0.9%
23	Louisiana	19,803,267,000	1.3%
43	Maine	4,567,794,000	0.3%
15	Maryland	28,966,935,000	1.9%
14	Massachusetts	29,961,526,000	2.0%
9	Michigan	41,346,104,000	2.7%
16	Minnesota	27,798,091,000	1.8%
33	Mississippi	12,051,010,000	0.8%
21	Missouri	22,423,120,000	1.5%
46	Montana	3,718,634,000	0.2%
35	Nebraska	9,195,456,000	0.6%
32	Nevada	12,191,704,000	0.8%
39	New Hampshire	5,196,964,000	0.3%
8	New Jersey	46,881,681,000	3.1%
37	New Mexico	7,999,350,000	0.5%
2	New York	164,409,729,000	10.9%
10	North Carolina	40,769,480,000	2.7%
45	North Dakota	4,080,969,000	0.3%
7	Ohio	51,540,194,000	3.4%
31	Oklahoma	12,494,678,000	0.8%
26	Oregon	17,181,263,000	1.1%
6	Pennsylvania	57,413,599,000	3.8%
44	Rhode Island	4,135,323,000	0.3%
24	South Carolina	19,595,486,000	1.3%
47	South Dakota	3,155,861,000	0.2%
20	Tennessee	22,449,233,000	1.5%
3	Texas	115,563,762,000	7.6%
34	Utah	9,215,806,000	0.6%
50	Vermont	2,505,807,000	0.2%
12	Virginia	35,699,120,000	2.4%
13	Washington	33,574,696,000	2.2%
38	West Virginia	5,491,862,000	0.4%
17	Wisconsin	27,000,852,000	1.8%
42	Wyoming	4,943,484,000	0.3%

RANK ORDER

RANK	STATE	EXPENDITURES	% of USA
1	California	$237,892,764,000	15.7%
2	New York	164,409,729,000	10.9%
3	Texas	115,563,762,000	7.6%
4	Florida	84,457,586,000	5.6%
5	Illinois	64,517,132,000	4.3%
6	Pennsylvania	57,413,599,000	3.8%
7	Ohio	51,540,194,000	3.4%
8	New Jersey	46,881,681,000	3.1%
9	Michigan	41,346,104,000	2.7%
10	North Carolina	40,769,480,000	2.7%
11	Georgia	38,547,302,000	2.5%
12	Virginia	35,699,120,000	2.4%
13	Washington	33,574,696,000	2.2%
14	Massachusetts	29,961,526,000	2.0%
15	Maryland	28,966,935,000	1.9%
16	Minnesota	27,798,091,000	1.8%
17	Wisconsin	27,000,852,000	1.8%
18	Colorado	25,562,274,000	1.7%
19	Indiana	24,140,521,000	1.6%
20	Tennessee	22,449,233,000	1.5%
21	Missouri	22,423,120,000	1.5%
22	Arizona	21,658,693,000	1.4%
23	Louisiana	19,803,267,000	1.3%
24	South Carolina	19,595,486,000	1.3%
25	Alabama	18,204,881,000	1.2%
26	Oregon	17,181,263,000	1.1%
27	Connecticut	17,072,956,000	1.1%
28	Iowa	15,246,974,000	1.0%
29	Kansas	13,284,704,000	0.9%
30	Kentucky	12,877,920,000	0.9%
31	Oklahoma	12,494,678,000	0.8%
32	Nevada	12,191,704,000	0.8%
33	Mississippi	12,051,010,000	0.8%
34	Utah	9,215,806,000	0.6%
35	Nebraska	9,195,456,000	0.6%
36	Arkansas	9,124,066,000	0.6%
37	New Mexico	7,999,350,000	0.5%
38	West Virginia	5,491,862,000	0.4%
39	New Hampshire	5,196,964,000	0.3%
40	Alaska	5,183,679,000	0.3%
41	Idaho	5,031,413,000	0.3%
42	Wyoming	4,943,484,000	0.3%
43	Maine	4,567,794,000	0.3%
44	Rhode Island	4,135,323,000	0.3%
45	North Dakota	4,080,969,000	0.3%
46	Montana	3,718,634,000	0.2%
47	South Dakota	3,155,861,000	0.2%
48	Delaware	2,936,005,000	0.2%
49	Hawaii	2,743,886,000	0.2%
50	Vermont	2,505,807,000	0.2%
	District of Columbia	12,424,661,000	0.8%

Source: U.S. Bureau of the Census, Governments Division
"2015 State and Local Government Finances" (http://www.census.gov/govs/local/)
*Direct general expenditures include expenditures for current operations, assistance and subsidies, interest on debt, and capital outlay. Excludes intergovernmental transfers, expenditures for government owned utilities and other commercial or auxiliary enterprise, and insurance trust expenditures.

Per Capita Local Government Direct General Expenditures in 2015

National Per Capita = $4,717*

ALPHA ORDER

RANK	STATE	PER CAPITA
35	Alabama	$3,753
3	Alaska	7,024
43	Arizona	3,184
46	Arkansas	3,066
4	California	6,095
13	Colorado	4,699
12	Connecticut	4,751
44	Delaware	3,110
26	Florida	4,167
34	Georgia	3,779
50	Hawaii	1,924
47	Idaho	3,051
8	Illinois	5,016
38	Indiana	3,652
9	Iowa	4,889
16	Kansas	4,572
49	Kentucky	2,912
22	Louisiana	4,239
40	Maine	3,440
11	Maryland	4,827
19	Massachusetts	4,410
25	Michigan	4,169
7	Minnesota	5,070
28	Mississippi	4,037
37	Missouri	3,692
39	Montana	3,616
10	Nebraska	4,856
23	Nevada	4,229
32	New Hampshire	3,907
6	New Jersey	5,232
33	New Mexico	3,842
2	New York	8,295
27	North Carolina	4,060
5	North Dakota	5,406
18	Ohio	4,441
42	Oklahoma	3,200
20	Oregon	4,278
17	Pennsylvania	4,489
31	Rhode Island	3,916
30	South Carolina	4,005
36	South Dakota	3,695
41	Tennessee	3,406
24	Texas	4,209
45	Utah	3,087
29	Vermont	4,013
21	Virginia	4,267
14	Washington	4,694
48	West Virginia	2,985
15	Wisconsin	4,688
1	Wyoming	8,435

RANK ORDER

RANK	STATE	PER CAPITA
1	Wyoming	$8,435
2	New York	8,295
3	Alaska	7,024
4	California	6,095
5	North Dakota	5,406
6	New Jersey	5,232
7	Minnesota	5,070
8	Illinois	5,016
9	Iowa	4,889
10	Nebraska	4,856
11	Maryland	4,827
12	Connecticut	4,751
13	Colorado	4,699
14	Washington	4,694
15	Wisconsin	4,688
16	Kansas	4,572
17	Pennsylvania	4,489
18	Ohio	4,441
19	Massachusetts	4,410
20	Oregon	4,278
21	Virginia	4,267
22	Louisiana	4,239
23	Nevada	4,229
24	Texas	4,209
25	Michigan	4,169
26	Florida	4,167
27	North Carolina	4,060
28	Mississippi	4,037
29	Vermont	4,013
30	South Carolina	4,005
31	Rhode Island	3,916
32	New Hampshire	3,907
33	New Mexico	3,842
34	Georgia	3,779
35	Alabama	3,753
36	South Dakota	3,695
37	Missouri	3,692
38	Indiana	3,652
39	Montana	3,616
40	Maine	3,440
41	Tennessee	3,406
42	Oklahoma	3,200
43	Arizona	3,184
44	Delaware	3,110
45	Utah	3,087
46	Arkansas	3,066
47	Idaho	3,051
48	West Virginia	2,985
49	Kentucky	2,912
50	Hawaii	1,924

District of Columbia   18,469

Source: CQ Press using data from U.S. Bureau of the Census, Governments Division
"2015 State and Local Government Finances" (http://www.census.gov/govs/local/)
*Direct general expenditures include expenditures for current operations, assistance and subsidies, interest on debt, and capital outlay. Excludes intergovernmental transfers, expenditures for government owned utilities and other commercial or auxiliary enterprise, and insurance trust expenditures.

Local Government Debt Outstanding in 2015

National Total = $1,847,839,402,000*

ALPHA ORDER

RANK	STATE	DEBT	% of USA
27	Alabama	$21,145,008,000	1.1%
41	Alaska	3,328,739,000	0.2%
15	Arizona	33,659,251,000	1.8%
33	Arkansas	11,636,287,000	0.6%
1	California	269,264,301,000	14.6%
11	Colorado	38,949,254,000	2.1%
34	Connecticut	11,586,422,000	0.6%
43	Delaware	2,660,365,000	0.1%
4	Florida	115,346,256,000	6.2%
10	Georgia	42,906,848,000	2.3%
38	Hawaii	6,066,089,000	0.3%
44	Idaho	2,655,670,000	0.1%
5	Illinois	84,311,162,000	4.6%
18	Indiana	28,364,435,000	1.5%
32	Iowa	12,379,456,000	0.7%
28	Kansas	20,748,857,000	1.1%
21	Kentucky	26,232,185,000	1.4%
24	Louisiana	21,850,663,000	1.2%
42	Maine	2,893,270,000	0.2%
23	Maryland	24,477,703,000	1.3%
29	Massachusetts	17,861,447,000	1.0%
9	Michigan	43,216,906,000	2.3%
14	Minnesota	34,658,448,000	1.9%
37	Mississippi	6,706,849,000	0.4%
20	Missouri	27,581,393,000	1.5%
48	Montana	1,945,286,000	0.1%
30	Nebraska	13,688,839,000	0.7%
22	Nevada	25,316,599,000	1.4%
46	New Hampshire	2,585,980,000	0.1%
16	New Jersey	33,182,946,000	1.8%
36	New Mexico	8,779,824,000	0.5%
3	New York	208,758,567,000	11.3%
17	North Carolina	32,676,674,000	1.8%
39	North Dakota	3,959,371,000	0.2%
7	Ohio	52,627,629,000	2.8%
35	Oklahoma	10,015,972,000	0.5%
25	Oregon	21,828,795,000	1.2%
6	Pennsylvania	80,078,219,000	4.3%
45	Rhode Island	2,605,235,000	0.1%
19	South Carolina	28,289,567,000	1.5%
47	South Dakota	2,528,160,000	0.1%
12	Tennessee	38,752,838,000	2.1%
2	Texas	229,409,137,000	12.4%
31	Utah	12,776,707,000	0.7%
49	Vermont	1,235,339,000	0.1%
13	Virginia	36,862,082,000	2.0%
8	Washington	49,217,789,000	2.7%
40	West Virginia	3,344,919,000	0.2%
26	Wisconsin	21,815,766,000	1.2%
50	Wyoming	1,145,654,000	0.1%

RANK ORDER

RANK	STATE	DEBT	% of USA
1	California	$269,264,301,000	14.6%
2	Texas	229,409,137,000	12.4%
3	New York	208,758,567,000	11.3%
4	Florida	115,346,256,000	6.2%
5	Illinois	84,311,162,000	4.6%
6	Pennsylvania	80,078,219,000	4.3%
7	Ohio	52,627,629,000	2.8%
8	Washington	49,217,789,000	2.7%
9	Michigan	43,216,906,000	2.3%
10	Georgia	42,906,848,000	2.3%
11	Colorado	38,949,254,000	2.1%
12	Tennessee	38,752,838,000	2.1%
13	Virginia	36,862,082,000	2.0%
14	Minnesota	34,658,448,000	1.9%
15	Arizona	33,659,251,000	1.8%
16	New Jersey	33,182,946,000	1.8%
17	North Carolina	32,676,674,000	1.8%
18	Indiana	28,364,435,000	1.5%
19	South Carolina	28,289,567,000	1.5%
20	Missouri	27,581,393,000	1.5%
21	Kentucky	26,232,185,000	1.4%
22	Nevada	25,316,599,000	1.4%
23	Maryland	24,477,703,000	1.3%
24	Louisiana	21,850,663,000	1.2%
25	Oregon	21,828,795,000	1.2%
26	Wisconsin	21,815,766,000	1.2%
27	Alabama	21,145,008,000	1.1%
28	Kansas	20,748,857,000	1.1%
29	Massachusetts	17,861,447,000	1.0%
30	Nebraska	13,688,839,000	0.7%
31	Utah	12,776,707,000	0.7%
32	Iowa	12,379,456,000	0.7%
33	Arkansas	11,636,287,000	0.6%
34	Connecticut	11,586,422,000	0.6%
35	Oklahoma	10,015,972,000	0.5%
36	New Mexico	8,779,824,000	0.5%
37	Mississippi	6,706,849,000	0.4%
38	Hawaii	6,066,089,000	0.3%
39	North Dakota	3,959,371,000	0.2%
40	West Virginia	3,344,919,000	0.2%
41	Alaska	3,328,739,000	0.2%
42	Maine	2,893,270,000	0.2%
43	Delaware	2,660,365,000	0.1%
44	Idaho	2,655,670,000	0.1%
45	Rhode Island	2,605,235,000	0.1%
46	New Hampshire	2,585,980,000	0.1%
47	South Dakota	2,528,160,000	0.1%
48	Montana	1,945,286,000	0.1%
49	Vermont	1,235,339,000	0.1%
50	Wyoming	1,145,654,000	0.1%
	District of Columbia	13,924,244,000	0.8%

Source: U.S. Bureau of the Census, Governments Division
"2015 State and Local Government Finances" (http://www.census.gov/govs/local/)
*Includes short-term, long-term, full faith and credit, nonguaranteed, and public debt for private purposes.

Per Capita Local Government Debt Outstanding in 2015

National Per Capita = $5,756*

ALPHA ORDER

RANK	STATE	PER CAPITA
24	Alabama	$4,359
22	Alaska	4,511
18	Arizona	4,948
33	Arkansas	3,911
7	California	6,898
5	Colorado	7,159
37	Connecticut	3,224
39	Delaware	2,818
15	Florida	5,691
30	Georgia	4,207
28	Hawaii	4,253
50	Idaho	1,610
9	Illinois	6,555
26	Indiana	4,291
32	Iowa	3,970
6	Kansas	7,141
12	Kentucky	5,932
19	Louisiana	4,678
44	Maine	2,179
31	Maryland	4,079
40	Massachusetts	2,629
25	Michigan	4,357
10	Minnesota	6,321
43	Mississippi	2,247
20	Missouri	4,542
48	Montana	1,892
4	Nebraska	7,229
2	Nevada	8,781
47	New Hampshire	1,944
35	New Jersey	3,703
29	New Mexico	4,216
1	New York	10,533
36	North Carolina	3,254
17	North Dakota	5,245
21	Ohio	4,535
41	Oklahoma	2,565
16	Oregon	5,435
11	Pennsylvania	6,260
42	Rhode Island	2,467
14	South Carolina	5,782
38	South Dakota	2,960
13	Tennessee	5,880
3	Texas	8,356
27	Utah	4,280
45	Vermont	1,978
23	Virginia	4,406
8	Washington	6,881
49	West Virginia	1,818
34	Wisconsin	3,788
46	Wyoming	1,955

RANK ORDER

RANK	STATE	PER CAPITA
1	New York	$10,533
2	Nevada	8,781
3	Texas	8,356
4	Nebraska	7,229
5	Colorado	7,159
6	Kansas	7,141
7	California	6,898
8	Washington	6,881
9	Illinois	6,555
10	Minnesota	6,321
11	Pennsylvania	6,260
12	Kentucky	5,932
13	Tennessee	5,880
14	South Carolina	5,782
15	Florida	5,691
16	Oregon	5,435
17	North Dakota	5,245
18	Arizona	4,948
19	Louisiana	4,678
20	Missouri	4,542
21	Ohio	4,535
22	Alaska	4,511
23	Virginia	4,406
24	Alabama	4,359
25	Michigan	4,357
26	Indiana	4,291
27	Utah	4,280
28	Hawaii	4,253
29	New Mexico	4,216
30	Georgia	4,207
31	Maryland	4,079
32	Iowa	3,970
33	Arkansas	3,911
34	Wisconsin	3,788
35	New Jersey	3,703
36	North Carolina	3,254
37	Connecticut	3,224
38	South Dakota	2,960
39	Delaware	2,818
40	Massachusetts	2,629
41	Oklahoma	2,565
42	Rhode Island	2,467
43	Mississippi	2,247
44	Maine	2,179
45	Vermont	1,978
46	Wyoming	1,955
47	New Hampshire	1,944
48	Montana	1,892
49	West Virginia	1,818
50	Idaho	1,610

District of Columbia   20,698

Source: CQ Press using data from U.S. Bureau of the Census, Governments Division
"2015 State and Local Government Finances" (http://www.census.gov/govs/local/)
*Includes short-term, long-term, full faith and credit, nonguaranteed, and public debt for private purposes.

Local Government Full-Time Equivalent Employees in 2016

National Total = 12,074,470 FTE Employees*

ALPHA ORDER

RANK	STATE	EMPLOYEES	% of USA
23	Alabama	190,540	1.6%
47	Alaska	27,631	0.2%
20	Arizona	209,232	1.7%
33	Arkansas	107,698	0.9%
1	California	1,400,077	11.6%
22	Colorado	205,702	1.7%
31	Connecticut	130,289	1.1%
49	Delaware	23,401	0.2%
4	Florida	707,078	5.9%
9	Georgia	385,311	3.2%
50	Hawaii	16,917	0.1%
39	Idaho	58,109	0.5%
5	Illinois	506,984	4.2%
15	Indiana	232,112	1.9%
30	Iowa	133,304	1.1%
28	Kansas	146,141	1.2%
26	Kentucky	159,282	1.3%
24	Louisiana	184,495	1.5%
41	Maine	48,781	0.4%
18	Maryland	218,095	1.8%
14	Massachusetts	236,750	2.0%
12	Michigan	294,491	2.4%
21	Minnesota	208,855	1.7%
29	Mississippi	134,062	1.1%
16	Missouri	228,104	1.9%
43	Montana	37,299	0.3%
35	Nebraska	87,560	0.7%
36	Nevada	85,041	0.7%
40	New Hampshire	51,381	0.4%
10	New Jersey	339,348	2.8%
37	New Mexico	80,203	0.7%
3	New York	941,397	7.8%
7	North Carolina	408,748	3.4%
46	North Dakota	28,702	0.2%
6	Ohio	450,704	3.7%
27	Oklahoma	147,337	1.2%
32	Oregon	129,568	1.1%
8	Pennsylvania	399,703	3.3%
45	Rhode Island	29,904	0.2%
25	South Carolina	182,500	1.5%
44	South Dakota	32,232	0.3%
13	Tennessee	250,430	2.1%
2	Texas	1,176,357	9.7%
34	Utah	89,402	0.7%
48	Vermont	25,742	0.2%
11	Virginia	320,805	2.7%
17	Washington	225,671	1.9%
38	West Virginia	63,187	0.5%
19	Wisconsin	212,640	1.8%
42	Wyoming	37,470	0.3%

RANK ORDER

RANK	STATE	EMPLOYEES	% of USA
1	California	1,400,077	11.6%
2	Texas	1,176,357	9.7%
3	New York	941,397	7.8%
4	Florida	707,078	5.9%
5	Illinois	506,984	4.2%
6	Ohio	450,704	3.7%
7	North Carolina	408,748	3.4%
8	Pennsylvania	399,703	3.3%
9	Georgia	385,311	3.2%
10	New Jersey	339,348	2.8%
11	Virginia	320,805	2.7%
12	Michigan	294,491	2.4%
13	Tennessee	250,430	2.1%
14	Massachusetts	236,750	2.0%
15	Indiana	232,112	1.9%
16	Missouri	228,104	1.9%
17	Washington	225,671	1.9%
18	Maryland	218,095	1.8%
19	Wisconsin	212,640	1.8%
20	Arizona	209,232	1.7%
21	Minnesota	208,855	1.7%
22	Colorado	205,702	1.7%
23	Alabama	190,540	1.6%
24	Louisiana	184,495	1.5%
25	South Carolina	182,500	1.5%
26	Kentucky	159,282	1.3%
27	Oklahoma	147,337	1.2%
28	Kansas	146,141	1.2%
29	Mississippi	134,062	1.1%
30	Iowa	133,304	1.1%
31	Connecticut	130,289	1.1%
32	Oregon	129,568	1.1%
33	Arkansas	107,698	0.9%
34	Utah	89,402	0.7%
35	Nebraska	87,560	0.7%
36	Nevada	85,041	0.7%
37	New Mexico	80,203	0.7%
38	West Virginia	63,187	0.5%
39	Idaho	58,109	0.5%
40	New Hampshire	51,381	0.4%
41	Maine	48,781	0.4%
42	Wyoming	37,470	0.3%
43	Montana	37,299	0.3%
44	South Dakota	32,232	0.3%
45	Rhode Island	29,904	0.2%
46	North Dakota	28,702	0.2%
47	Alaska	27,631	0.2%
48	Vermont	25,742	0.2%
49	Delaware	23,401	0.2%
50	Hawaii	16,917	0.1%
	District of Columbia	47,698	0.4%

Source: U.S. Bureau of the Census, Governments Division
    "Annual Survey of Public Employment and Payroll" (https://www.census.gov/data/datasets.html)
*As of March 2016.

Rate of Local Government Full-Time Equivalent Employees in 2016

National Rate = 373 FTE Employees per 10,000 Population*

ALPHA ORDER

RANK	STATE	RATE
12	Alabama	392
25	Alaska	373
44	Arizona	303
32	Arkansas	360
35	California	356
26	Colorado	372
30	Connecticut	363
49	Delaware	246
40	Florida	342
22	Georgia	374
50	Hawaii	118
38	Idaho	346
10	Illinois	395
36	Indiana	350
6	Iowa	426
2	Kansas	503
33	Kentucky	359
11	Louisiana	394
29	Maine	367
31	Maryland	362
37	Massachusetts	347
45	Michigan	296
18	Minnesota	378
5	Mississippi	449
22	Missouri	374
33	Montana	359
4	Nebraska	459
47	Nevada	289
14	New Hampshire	385
18	New Jersey	378
14	New Mexico	385
3	New York	475
9	North Carolina	402
17	North Dakota	380
13	Ohio	388
21	Oklahoma	376
41	Oregon	317
42	Pennsylvania	313
48	Rhode Island	283
27	South Carolina	368
22	South Dakota	374
20	Tennessee	377
7	Texas	422
46	Utah	294
8	Vermont	413
16	Virginia	381
43	Washington	310
38	West Virginia	346
27	Wisconsin	368
1	Wyoming	641

RANK ORDER

RANK	STATE	RATE
1	Wyoming	641
2	Kansas	503
3	New York	475
4	Nebraska	459
5	Mississippi	449
6	Iowa	426
7	Texas	422
8	Vermont	413
9	North Carolina	402
10	Illinois	395
11	Louisiana	394
12	Alabama	392
13	Ohio	388
14	New Hampshire	385
14	New Mexico	385
16	Virginia	381
17	North Dakota	380
18	Minnesota	378
18	New Jersey	378
20	Tennessee	377
21	Oklahoma	376
22	Georgia	374
22	Missouri	374
22	South Dakota	374
25	Alaska	373
26	Colorado	372
27	South Carolina	368
27	Wisconsin	368
29	Maine	367
30	Connecticut	363
31	Maryland	362
32	Arkansas	360
33	Kentucky	359
33	Montana	359
35	California	356
36	Indiana	350
37	Massachusetts	347
38	Idaho	346
38	West Virginia	346
40	Florida	342
41	Oregon	317
42	Pennsylvania	313
43	Washington	310
44	Arizona	303
45	Michigan	296
46	Utah	294
47	Nevada	289
48	Rhode Island	283
49	Delaware	246
50	Hawaii	118

District of Columbia — 697

Source: CQ Press using data from U.S. Bureau of the Census, Governments Division
"Annual Survey of Public Employment and Payroll" (https://www.census.gov/data/datasets.html)
*Full-time equivalent as of March 2016.

Average Annual Earnings of Full-Time Local Government Employees in 2016

National Average = $57,065*

ALPHA ORDER

RANK	STATE	SALARY
42	Alabama	$43,066
5	Alaska	66,090
23	Arizona	52,973
50	Arkansas	38,753
1	California	79,155
17	Colorado	57,156
7	Connecticut	65,399
14	Delaware	59,680
28	Florida	50,602
38	Georgia	44,842
9	Hawaii	64,714
43	Idaho	42,697
12	Illinois	62,795
35	Indiana	46,022
25	Iowa	51,766
39	Kansas	44,344
47	Kentucky	41,699
45	Louisiana	42,170
34	Maine	47,097
6	Maryland	66,038
11	Massachusetts	64,300
18	Michigan	56,489
16	Minnesota	58,236
49	Mississippi	39,801
40	Missouri	44,279
33	Montana	47,598
21	Nebraska	53,209
8	Nevada	65,215
22	New Hampshire	53,081
3	New Jersey	73,044
36	New Mexico	45,576
4	New York	71,841
32	North Carolina	47,752
26	North Dakota	51,706
27	Ohio	51,657
48	Oklahoma	40,612
13	Oregon	60,816
15	Pennsylvania	58,906
10	Rhode Island	64,546
37	South Carolina	45,347
44	South Dakota	42,339
41	Tennessee	43,987
31	Texas	48,362
29	Utah	50,538
30	Vermont	49,910
24	Virginia	51,893
2	Washington	74,555
46	West Virginia	41,756
20	Wisconsin	55,393
19	Wyoming	56,403

RANK ORDER

RANK	STATE	SALARY
1	California	$79,155
2	Washington	74,555
3	New Jersey	73,044
4	New York	71,841
5	Alaska	66,090
6	Maryland	66,038
7	Connecticut	65,399
8	Nevada	65,215
9	Hawaii	64,714
10	Rhode Island	64,546
11	Massachusetts	64,300
12	Illinois	62,795
13	Oregon	60,816
14	Delaware	59,680
15	Pennsylvania	58,906
16	Minnesota	58,236
17	Colorado	57,156
18	Michigan	56,489
19	Wyoming	56,403
20	Wisconsin	55,393
21	Nebraska	53,209
22	New Hampshire	53,081
23	Arizona	52,973
24	Virginia	51,893
25	Iowa	51,766
26	North Dakota	51,706
27	Ohio	51,657
28	Florida	50,602
29	Utah	50,538
30	Vermont	49,910
31	Texas	48,362
32	North Carolina	47,752
33	Montana	47,598
34	Maine	47,097
35	Indiana	46,022
36	New Mexico	45,576
37	South Carolina	45,347
38	Georgia	44,842
39	Kansas	44,344
40	Missouri	44,279
41	Tennessee	43,987
42	Alabama	43,066
43	Idaho	42,697
44	South Dakota	42,339
45	Louisiana	42,170
46	West Virginia	41,756
47	Kentucky	41,699
48	Oklahoma	40,612
49	Mississippi	39,801
50	Arkansas	38,753
	District of Columbia	84,633

Source: CQ Press using data from U.S. Bureau of the Census, Governments Division
  "Annual Survey of Public Employment and Payroll" (https://www.census.gov/data/datasets.html)
*March 2016 full-time payroll (multiplied by 12) divided by full-time employees.

XI. Health

Average Annual Single Coverage Health Insurance Premium per Enrolled Employee in 2016
National Average = $6,101*

ALPHA ORDER				RANK ORDER		
RANK	STATE	PREMIUM		RANK	STATE	PREMIUM
48	Alabama	$5,536		1	Alaska	$7,886
1	Alaska	7,886		2	Rhode Island	6,665
29	Arizona	6,046		3	New Hampshire	6,637
50	Arkansas	5,341		4	Massachusetts	6,621
28	California	6,054		5	New York	6,614
32	Colorado	5,972		6	Connecticut	6,545
6	Connecticut	6,545		7	Delaware	6,522
7	Delaware	6,522		8	Wyoming	6,509
17	Florida	6,260		9	New Jersey	6,492
27	Georgia	6,055		10	Montana	6,442
38	Hawaii	5,863		11	Washington	6,433
46	Idaho	5,594		12	Wisconsin	6,386
16	Illinois	6,268		13	West Virginia	6,340
24	Indiana	6,130		14	Vermont	6,338
34	Iowa	5,893		15	Ohio	6,291
39	Kansas	5,844		16	Illinois	6,268
42	Kentucky	5,758		17	Florida	6,260
43	Louisiana	5,735		18	New Mexico	6,240
19	Maine	6,212		19	Maine	6,212
22	Maryland	6,158		20	Pennsylvania	6,201
4	Massachusetts	6,621		21	Virginia	6,180
33	Michigan	5,906		22	Maryland	6,158
30	Minnesota	6,030		23	North Dakota	6,155
45	Mississippi	5,642		24	Indiana	6,130
35	Missouri	5,881		25	Utah	6,117
10	Montana	6,442		26	Nebraska	6,088
26	Nebraska	6,088		27	Georgia	6,055
49	Nevada	5,490		28	California	6,054
3	New Hampshire	6,637		29	Arizona	6,046
9	New Jersey	6,492		30	Minnesota	6,030
18	New Mexico	6,240		31	Oregon	5,974
5	New York	6,614		32	Colorado	5,972
44	North Carolina	5,717		33	Michigan	5,906
23	North Dakota	6,155		34	Iowa	5,893
15	Ohio	6,291		35	Missouri	5,881
41	Oklahoma	5,784		35	South Dakota	5,881
31	Oregon	5,974		37	Texas	5,869
20	Pennsylvania	6,201		38	Hawaii	5,863
2	Rhode Island	6,665		39	Kansas	5,844
40	South Carolina	5,797		40	South Carolina	5,797
35	South Dakota	5,881		41	Oklahoma	5,784
47	Tennessee	5,543		42	Kentucky	5,758
37	Texas	5,869		43	Louisiana	5,735
25	Utah	6,117		44	North Carolina	5,717
14	Vermont	6,338		45	Mississippi	5,642
21	Virginia	6,180		46	Idaho	5,594
11	Washington	6,433		47	Tennessee	5,543
13	West Virginia	6,340		48	Alabama	5,536
12	Wisconsin	6,386		49	Nevada	5,490
8	Wyoming	6,509		50	Arkansas	5,341
					District of Columbia	6,504

Source: U.S. Department of Health and Human Services, Agency for Healthcare Research and Quality
"Private-Sector Data by Firm Size and State" (Table II Series, Medical Expenditures Panel Survey)
(http://www.meps.ahrq.gov/mepsweb/survey_comp/Insurance.jsp)
*Enrolled employees at private-sector establishments that offer health insurance coverage.

Average Annual Family Coverage Health Insurance Premium per Enrolled Employee in 2016
National Average = $17,710*

ALPHA ORDER

RANK	STATE	PREMIUM
48	Alabama	$16,098
1	Alaska	22,490
26	Arizona	17,484
50	Arkansas	14,929
29	California	17,458
28	Colorado	17,459
7	Connecticut	18,637
6	Delaware	18,648
15	Florida	17,989
11	Georgia	18,252
45	Hawaii	16,362
25	Idaho	17,499
9	Illinois	18,510
14	Indiana	17,996
47	Iowa	16,123
39	Kansas	16,784
41	Kentucky	16,678
30	Louisiana	17,330
16	Maine	17,987
8	Maryland	18,519
5	Massachusetts	18,955
34	Michigan	17,113
22	Minnesota	17,545
49	Mississippi	15,765
43	Missouri	16,638
19	Montana	17,835
44	Nebraska	16,617
46	Nevada	16,133
4	New Hampshire	19,066
12	New Jersey	18,242
37	New Mexico	16,954
3	New York	19,375
36	North Carolina	16,986
38	North Dakota	16,804
24	Ohio	17,523
42	Oklahoma	16,646
32	Oregon	17,127
18	Pennsylvania	17,900
13	Rhode Island	18,010
21	South Carolina	17,673
33	South Dakota	17,117
40	Tennessee	16,721
23	Texas	17,529
35	Utah	17,025
20	Vermont	17,795
17	Virginia	17,945
10	Washington	18,301
31	West Virginia	17,260
27	Wisconsin	17,477
2	Wyoming	19,617

RANK ORDER

RANK	STATE	PREMIUM
1	Alaska	$22,490
2	Wyoming	19,617
3	New York	19,375
4	New Hampshire	19,066
5	Massachusetts	18,955
6	Delaware	18,648
7	Connecticut	18,637
8	Maryland	18,519
9	Illinois	18,510
10	Washington	18,301
11	Georgia	18,252
12	New Jersey	18,242
13	Rhode Island	18,010
14	Indiana	17,996
15	Florida	17,989
16	Maine	17,987
17	Virginia	17,945
18	Pennsylvania	17,900
19	Montana	17,835
20	Vermont	17,795
21	South Carolina	17,673
22	Minnesota	17,545
23	Texas	17,529
24	Ohio	17,523
25	Idaho	17,499
26	Arizona	17,484
27	Wisconsin	17,477
28	Colorado	17,459
29	California	17,458
30	Louisiana	17,330
31	West Virginia	17,260
32	Oregon	17,127
33	South Dakota	17,117
34	Michigan	17,113
35	Utah	17,025
36	North Carolina	16,986
37	New Mexico	16,954
38	North Dakota	16,804
39	Kansas	16,784
40	Tennessee	16,721
41	Kentucky	16,678
42	Oklahoma	16,646
43	Missouri	16,638
44	Nebraska	16,617
45	Hawaii	16,362
46	Nevada	16,133
47	Iowa	16,123
48	Alabama	16,098
49	Mississippi	15,765
50	Arkansas	14,929

| | District of Columbia | 18,864 |

Source: U.S. Department of Health and Human Services, Agency for Healthcare Research and Quality
   "Private-Sector Data by Firm Size and State" (Table II Series, Medical Expenditures Panel Survey)
   (http://www.meps.ahrq.gov/mepsweb/survey_comp/Insurance.jsp)
*Enrolled employees at private-sector establishments that offer health insurance coverage.

Percent of Private-Sector Establishments That Offer Health Insurance: 2016

National Percent = 45.3%

ALPHA ORDER			RANK ORDER		
RANK	STATE	PERCENT	RANK	STATE	PERCENT
12	Alabama	50.7	1	Hawaii	78.1
46	Alaska	37.8	2	Massachusetts	56.9
44	Arizona	38.4	3	Ohio	54.8
41	Arkansas	39.4	4	Nevada	54.6
26	California	44.4	5	Rhode Island	52.8
25	Colorado	44.8	6	Connecticut	52.6
6	Connecticut	52.6	7	New Hampshire	51.6
36	Delaware	42.0	7	Oklahoma	51.6
48	Florida	37.2	9	North Dakota	51.4
42	Georgia	39.1	10	New Jersey	51.2
1	Hawaii	78.1	11	Mississippi	50.8
47	Idaho	37.7	12	Alabama	50.7
24	Illinois	44.9	13	Maryland	49.7
39	Indiana	41.3	14	Virginia	49.1
21	Iowa	45.8	15	Pennsylvania	48.5
18	Kansas	47.9	16	Louisiana	48.4
17	Kentucky	48.2	17	Kentucky	48.2
16	Louisiana	48.4	18	Kansas	47.9
30	Maine	43.2	19	Texas	47.6
13	Maryland	49.7	20	Tennessee	46.8
2	Massachusetts	56.9	21	Iowa	45.8
31	Michigan	42.8	22	Oregon	45.7
36	Minnesota	42.0	23	Wisconsin	45.6
11	Mississippi	50.8	24	Illinois	44.9
32	Missouri	42.5	25	Colorado	44.8
50	Montana	28.3	26	California	44.4
49	Nebraska	36.1	27	New York	44.3
4	Nevada	54.6	28	West Virginia	44.0
7	New Hampshire	51.6	29	Washington	43.7
10	New Jersey	51.2	30	Maine	43.2
33	New Mexico	42.4	31	Michigan	42.8
27	New York	44.3	32	Missouri	42.5
40	North Carolina	39.9	33	New Mexico	42.4
9	North Dakota	51.4	34	Utah	42.3
3	Ohio	54.8	35	Vermont	42.2
7	Oklahoma	51.6	36	Delaware	42.0
22	Oregon	45.7	36	Minnesota	42.0
15	Pennsylvania	48.5	38	South Carolina	41.7
5	Rhode Island	52.8	39	Indiana	41.3
38	South Carolina	41.7	40	North Carolina	39.9
42	South Dakota	39.1	41	Arkansas	39.4
20	Tennessee	46.8	42	Georgia	39.1
19	Texas	47.6	42	South Dakota	39.1
34	Utah	42.3	44	Arizona	38.4
35	Vermont	42.2	45	Wyoming	38.0
14	Virginia	49.1	46	Alaska	37.8
29	Washington	43.7	47	Idaho	37.7
28	West Virginia	44.0	48	Florida	37.2
23	Wisconsin	45.6	49	Nebraska	36.1
45	Wyoming	38.0	50	Montana	28.3
				District of Columbia	64.4

Source: U.S. Department of Health and Human Services, Agency for Healthcare Research and Quality
"Private-Sector Data by Firm Size and State" (Table II Series, Medical Expenditures Panel Survey)
(http://www.meps.ahrq.gov/mepsweb/survey_comp/Insurance.jsp)

Persons Not Covered by Health Insurance in 2016

National Total = 27,304,297 Uninsured

ALPHA ORDER					RANK ORDER			
RANK	STATE	UNINSURED	% of USA		RANK	STATE	UNINSURED	% of USA
20	Alabama	434,973	1.6%		1	Texas	4,545,380	16.6%
40	Alaska	100,628	0.4%		2	California	2,843,903	10.4%
11	Arizona	681,238	2.5%		3	Florida	2,544,247	9.3%
30	Arkansas	231,775	0.8%		4	Georgia	1,309,573	4.8%
2	California	2,843,903	10.4%		5	New York	1,182,694	4.3%
22	Colorado	409,743	1.5%		6	North Carolina	1,038,399	3.8%
34	Connecticut	172,214	0.6%		7	Illinois	816,602	3.0%
46	Delaware	53,139	0.2%		8	Virginia	714,884	2.6%
3	Florida	2,544,247	9.3%		9	Pennsylvania	708,477	2.6%
4	Georgia	1,309,573	4.8%		10	New Jersey	704,970	2.6%
48	Hawaii	48,673	0.2%		11	Arizona	681,238	2.5%
36	Idaho	168,110	0.6%		12	Ohio	643,728	2.4%
7	Illinois	816,602	3.0%		13	Tennessee	592,310	2.2%
15	Indiana	530,363	1.9%		14	Missouri	531,923	1.9%
38	Iowa	131,612	0.5%		15	Indiana	530,363	1.9%
29	Kansas	248,974	0.9%		16	Oklahoma	529,658	1.9%
32	Kentucky	223,350	0.8%		17	Michigan	526,990	1.9%
19	Louisiana	469,832	1.7%		18	South Carolina	485,906	1.8%
39	Maine	105,973	0.4%		19	Louisiana	469,832	1.7%
23	Maryland	363,179	1.3%		20	Alabama	434,973	1.6%
35	Massachusetts	171,059	0.6%		21	Washington	428,092	1.6%
17	Michigan	526,990	1.9%		22	Colorado	409,743	1.5%
31	Minnesota	224,946	0.8%		23	Maryland	363,179	1.3%
24	Mississippi	346,181	1.3%		24	Mississippi	346,181	1.3%
14	Missouri	531,923	1.9%		25	Nevada	330,418	1.2%
42	Montana	83,416	0.3%		26	Wisconsin	300,206	1.1%
37	Nebraska	160,563	0.6%		27	Utah	264,807	1.0%
25	Nevada	330,418	1.2%		28	Oregon	252,766	0.9%
43	New Hampshire	77,677	0.3%		29	Kansas	248,974	0.9%
10	New Jersey	704,970	2.6%		30	Arkansas	231,775	0.8%
33	New Mexico	187,689	0.7%		31	Minnesota	224,946	0.8%
5	New York	1,182,694	4.3%		32	Kentucky	223,350	0.8%
6	North Carolina	1,038,399	3.8%		33	New Mexico	187,689	0.7%
47	North Dakota	52,138	0.2%		34	Connecticut	172,214	0.6%
12	Ohio	643,728	2.4%		35	Massachusetts	171,059	0.6%
16	Oklahoma	529,658	1.9%		36	Idaho	168,110	0.6%
28	Oregon	252,766	0.9%		37	Nebraska	160,563	0.6%
9	Pennsylvania	708,477	2.6%		38	Iowa	131,612	0.5%
49	Rhode Island	44,966	0.2%		39	Maine	105,973	0.4%
18	South Carolina	485,906	1.8%		40	Alaska	100,628	0.4%
44	South Dakota	74,218	0.3%		41	West Virginia	95,882	0.4%
13	Tennessee	592,310	2.2%		42	Montana	83,416	0.3%
1	Texas	4,545,380	16.6%		43	New Hampshire	77,677	0.3%
27	Utah	264,807	1.0%		44	South Dakota	74,218	0.3%
50	Vermont	22,994	0.1%		45	Wyoming	66,513	0.2%
8	Virginia	714,884	2.6%		46	Delaware	53,139	0.2%
21	Washington	428,092	1.6%		47	North Dakota	52,138	0.2%
41	West Virginia	95,882	0.4%		48	Hawaii	48,673	0.2%
26	Wisconsin	300,206	1.1%		49	Rhode Island	44,966	0.2%
45	Wyoming	66,513	0.2%		50	Vermont	22,994	0.1%
						District of Columbia	26,346	0.1%

Source: U.S. Bureau of the Census
"2016 American Community Survey-Table S2701" (http://www.census.gov/programs-surveys/acs/)

Percent of Population Not Covered by Health Insurance in 2016

National Percent = 8.6% of Population*

ALPHA ORDER			RANK ORDER		
RANK	STATE	PERCENT	RANK	STATE	PERCENT
15	Alabama	9.1	1	Texas	16.6
2	Alaska	14.0	2	Alaska	14.0
12	Arizona	10.0	3	Oklahoma	13.8
27	Arkansas	7.9	4	Georgia	12.9
29	California	7.3	5	Florida	12.5
28	Colorado	7.5	6	Mississippi	11.8
44	Connecticut	4.9	7	Wyoming	11.5
37	Delaware	5.7	8	Nevada	11.4
5	Florida	12.5	9	North Carolina	10.4
4	Georgia	12.9	10	Louisiana	10.3
49	Hawaii	3.5	11	Idaho	10.1
11	Idaho	10.1	12	Arizona	10.0
31	Illinois	6.5	12	South Carolina	10.0
23	Indiana	8.1	14	New Mexico	9.2
45	Iowa	4.3	15	Alabama	9.1
19	Kansas	8.7	16	Tennessee	9.0
43	Kentucky	5.1	17	Missouri	8.9
10	Louisiana	10.3	18	Utah	8.8
25	Maine	8.0	19	Kansas	8.7
33	Maryland	6.1	19	South Dakota	8.7
50	Massachusetts	2.5	19	Virginia	8.7
40	Michigan	5.4	22	Nebraska	8.6
47	Minnesota	4.1	23	Indiana	8.1
6	Mississippi	11.8	23	Montana	8.1
17	Missouri	8.9	25	Maine	8.0
23	Montana	8.1	25	New Jersey	8.0
22	Nebraska	8.6	27	Arkansas	7.9
8	Nevada	11.4	28	Colorado	7.5
36	New Hampshire	5.9	29	California	7.3
25	New Jersey	8.0	30	North Dakota	7.0
14	New Mexico	9.2	31	Illinois	6.5
33	New York	6.1	32	Oregon	6.2
9	North Carolina	10.4	33	Maryland	6.1
30	North Dakota	7.0	33	New York	6.1
38	Ohio	5.6	35	Washington	6.0
3	Oklahoma	13.8	36	New Hampshire	5.9
32	Oregon	6.2	37	Delaware	5.7
38	Pennsylvania	5.6	38	Ohio	5.6
45	Rhode Island	4.3	38	Pennsylvania	5.6
12	South Carolina	10.0	40	Michigan	5.4
19	South Dakota	8.7	41	West Virginia	5.3
16	Tennessee	9.0	41	Wisconsin	5.3
1	Texas	16.6	43	Kentucky	5.1
18	Utah	8.8	44	Connecticut	4.9
48	Vermont	3.7	45	Iowa	4.3
19	Virginia	8.7	45	Rhode Island	4.3
35	Washington	6.0	47	Minnesota	4.1
41	West Virginia	5.3	48	Vermont	3.7
41	Wisconsin	5.3	49	Hawaii	3.5
7	Wyoming	11.5	50	Massachusetts	2.5
				District of Columbia	3.9

Source: U.S. Bureau of the Census
    "2016 American Community Survey-Table S2701" (http://www.census.gov/programs-surveys/acs/)
*This is a one-year figure. Census has discontinued three-year averages that had been used previously.

Percent of Population Lacking Access to Primary Care in 2018

National Percent = 12.7% of Population*

RANK	STATE	PERCENT
13	Alabama	16.7
26	Alaska	11.2
2	Arizona	37.3
36	Arkansas	8.2
27	California	10.9
25	Colorado	11.7
21	Connecticut	12.8
16	Delaware	16.5
6	Florida	22.3
11	Georgia	17.4
44	Hawaii	3.9
17	Idaho	16.0
21	Illinois	12.8
29	Indiana	10.6
34	Iowa	8.7
20	Kansas	13.4
31	Kentucky	9.8
10	Louisiana	18.5
46	Maine	3.7
30	Maryland	10.3
42	Massachusetts	4.8
33	Michigan	9.7
43	Minnesota	4.4
3	Mississippi	34.5
4	Missouri	31.4
8	Montana	19.4
49	Nebraska	0.6
7	Nevada	20.1
45	New Hampshire	3.8
50	New Jersey	0.1
1	New Mexico	38.7
12	New York	17.1
31	North Carolina	9.8
13	North Dakota	16.7
40	Ohio	5.4
18	Oklahoma	14.5
24	Oregon	11.8
47	Pennsylvania	2.5
41	Rhode Island	5.0
19	South Carolina	13.6
13	South Dakota	16.7
27	Tennessee	10.9
39	Texas	6.6
37	Utah	8.0
48	Vermont	0.9
38	Virginia	6.7
5	Washington	29.8
9	West Virginia	19.0
35	Wisconsin	8.3
23	Wyoming	12.1

RANK	STATE	PERCENT
1	New Mexico	38.7
2	Arizona	37.3
3	Mississippi	34.5
4	Missouri	31.4
5	Washington	29.8
6	Florida	22.3
7	Nevada	20.1
8	Montana	19.4
9	West Virginia	19.0
10	Louisiana	18.5
11	Georgia	17.4
12	New York	17.1
13	Alabama	16.7
13	North Dakota	16.7
13	South Dakota	16.7
16	Delaware	16.5
17	Idaho	16.0
18	Oklahoma	14.5
19	South Carolina	13.6
20	Kansas	13.4
21	Connecticut	12.8
21	Illinois	12.8
23	Wyoming	12.1
24	Oregon	11.8
25	Colorado	11.7
26	Alaska	11.2
27	California	10.9
27	Tennessee	10.9
29	Indiana	10.6
30	Maryland	10.3
31	Kentucky	9.8
31	North Carolina	9.8
33	Michigan	9.7
34	Iowa	8.7
35	Wisconsin	8.3
36	Arkansas	8.2
37	Utah	8.0
38	Virginia	6.7
39	Texas	6.6
40	Ohio	5.4
41	Rhode Island	5.0
42	Massachusetts	4.8
43	Minnesota	4.4
44	Hawaii	3.9
45	New Hampshire	3.8
46	Maine	3.7
47	Pennsylvania	2.5
48	Vermont	0.9
49	Nebraska	0.6
50	New Jersey	0.1

District of Columbia 26.1

Source: CQ Press using data from U.S. Department of Health and Human Services, Division of Shortage Designation
"State Population and HPSA Designation Population Statistics" (as of January 1, 2018)
(https://datawarehouse.hrsa.gov/tools/hdwreports/Reports.aspx)

*Percent of population considered under-served by primary medical practitioners (Family and General Practice doctors, Internists, Ob/Gyns, and Pediatricians). An under-served population does not have primary medical care within reasonable economic and geographic bounds.

Professionally Active Physicians in 2017

National Total = 951,061 Physicians*

ALPHA ORDER

RANK	STATE	PHYSICIANS	% of USA
26	Alabama	11,475	1.2%
49	Alaska	1,810	0.2%
19	Arizona	17,192	1.8%
32	Arkansas	6,813	0.7%
1	California	106,435	11.2%
23	Colorado	13,890	1.5%
22	Connecticut	14,621	1.5%
43	Delaware	2,951	0.3%
4	Florida	53,702	5.6%
12	Georgia	23,915	2.5%
42	Hawaii	3,524	0.4%
44	Idaho	2,865	0.3%
6	Illinois	40,915	4.3%
21	Indiana	16,132	1.7%
30	Iowa	8,101	0.9%
31	Kansas	7,571	0.8%
28	Kentucky	11,187	1.2%
24	Louisiana	13,020	1.4%
40	Maine	4,480	0.5%
13	Maryland	23,484	2.5%
9	Massachusetts	34,054	3.6%
8	Michigan	36,580	3.8%
18	Minnesota	17,224	1.8%
33	Mississippi	6,342	0.7%
16	Missouri	19,286	2.0%
45	Montana	2,257	0.2%
38	Nebraska	5,400	0.6%
35	Nevada	5,842	0.6%
41	New Hampshire	4,060	0.4%
10	New Jersey	28,826	3.0%
37	New Mexico	5,412	0.6%
2	New York	84,499	8.9%
11	North Carolina	26,907	2.8%
48	North Dakota	1,897	0.2%
7	Ohio	39,838	4.2%
29	Oklahoma	9,104	1.0%
27	Oregon	11,461	1.2%
5	Pennsylvania	47,731	5.0%
39	Rhode Island	4,750	0.5%
25	South Carolina	12,248	1.3%
47	South Dakota	1,924	0.2%
17	Tennessee	18,344	1.9%
3	Texas	61,797	6.5%
34	Utah	6,341	0.7%
46	Vermont	2,184	0.2%
14	Virginia	22,105	2.3%
15	Washington	20,553	2.2%
36	West Virginia	5,443	0.6%
20	Wisconsin	16,644	1.8%
50	Wyoming	1,144	0.1%

RANK ORDER

RANK	STATE	PHYSICIANS	% of USA
1	California	106,435	11.2%
2	New York	84,499	8.9%
3	Texas	61,797	6.5%
4	Florida	53,702	5.6%
5	Pennsylvania	47,731	5.0%
6	Illinois	40,915	4.3%
7	Ohio	39,838	4.2%
8	Michigan	36,580	3.8%
9	Massachusetts	34,054	3.6%
10	New Jersey	28,826	3.0%
11	North Carolina	26,907	2.8%
12	Georgia	23,915	2.5%
13	Maryland	23,484	2.5%
14	Virginia	22,105	2.3%
15	Washington	20,553	2.2%
16	Missouri	19,286	2.0%
17	Tennessee	18,344	1.9%
18	Minnesota	17,224	1.8%
19	Arizona	17,192	1.8%
20	Wisconsin	16,644	1.8%
21	Indiana	16,132	1.7%
22	Connecticut	14,621	1.5%
23	Colorado	13,890	1.5%
24	Louisiana	13,020	1.4%
25	South Carolina	12,248	1.3%
26	Alabama	11,475	1.2%
27	Oregon	11,461	1.2%
28	Kentucky	11,187	1.2%
29	Oklahoma	9,104	1.0%
30	Iowa	8,101	0.9%
31	Kansas	7,571	0.8%
32	Arkansas	6,813	0.7%
33	Mississippi	6,342	0.7%
34	Utah	6,341	0.7%
35	Nevada	5,842	0.6%
36	West Virginia	5,443	0.6%
37	New Mexico	5,412	0.6%
38	Nebraska	5,400	0.6%
39	Rhode Island	4,750	0.5%
40	Maine	4,480	0.5%
41	New Hampshire	4,060	0.4%
42	Hawaii	3,524	0.4%
43	Delaware	2,951	0.3%
44	Idaho	2,865	0.3%
45	Montana	2,257	0.2%
46	Vermont	2,184	0.2%
47	South Dakota	1,924	0.2%
48	North Dakota	1,897	0.2%
49	Alaska	1,810	0.2%
50	Wyoming	1,144	0.1%
	District of Columbia	6,781	0.7%

Source: The Henry J. Kaiser Family Foundation
"Professionally Active Dentists" (http://kff.org/other/state-indicator/total-active-physicians/)
*Includes MDs (medical doctors) and DOs (osteopathic physicians). Includes primary care physicians and specialist physicians.

Rate of Professionally Active Physicians in 2017

National Rate = 292 Physicians per 100,000 Population*

ALPHA ORDER

RANK	STATE	RATE
39	Alabama	235
35	Alaska	245
35	Arizona	245
42	Arkansas	227
24	California	269
33	Colorado	248
4	Connecticut	407
15	Delaware	307
30	Florida	256
41	Georgia	229
34	Hawaii	247
50	Idaho	167
11	Illinois	320
38	Indiana	242
29	Iowa	258
27	Kansas	260
31	Kentucky	251
20	Louisiana	278
10	Maine	335
5	Maryland	388
1	Massachusetts	496
7	Michigan	367
14	Minnesota	309
46	Mississippi	213
13	Missouri	315
45	Montana	215
19	Nebraska	281
49	Nevada	195
16	New Hampshire	302
11	New Jersey	320
28	New Mexico	259
3	New York	426
25	North Carolina	262
31	North Dakota	251
9	Ohio	342
40	Oklahoma	232
22	Oregon	277
6	Pennsylvania	373
2	Rhode Island	448
37	South Carolina	244
43	South Dakota	221
23	Tennessee	273
44	Texas	218
47	Utah	204
8	Vermont	350
26	Virginia	261
20	Washington	278
17	West Virginia	300
18	Wisconsin	287
48	Wyoming	197

RANK ORDER

RANK	STATE	RATE
1	Massachusetts	496
2	Rhode Island	448
3	New York	426
4	Connecticut	407
5	Maryland	388
6	Pennsylvania	373
7	Michigan	367
8	Vermont	350
9	Ohio	342
10	Maine	335
11	Illinois	320
11	New Jersey	320
13	Missouri	315
14	Minnesota	309
15	Delaware	307
16	New Hampshire	302
17	West Virginia	300
18	Wisconsin	287
19	Nebraska	281
20	Louisiana	278
20	Washington	278
22	Oregon	277
23	Tennessee	273
24	California	269
25	North Carolina	262
26	Virginia	261
27	Kansas	260
28	New Mexico	259
29	Iowa	258
30	Florida	256
31	Kentucky	251
31	North Dakota	251
33	Colorado	248
34	Hawaii	247
35	Alaska	245
35	Arizona	245
37	South Carolina	244
38	Indiana	242
39	Alabama	235
40	Oklahoma	232
41	Georgia	229
42	Arkansas	227
43	South Dakota	221
44	Texas	218
45	Montana	215
46	Mississippi	213
47	Utah	204
48	Wyoming	197
49	Nevada	195
50	Idaho	167
	District of Columbia	977

Source: CQ Press using data from The Henry J. Kaiser Family Foundation
"Professionally Active Dentists" (http://kff.org/other/state-indicator/total-active-physicians/)
*Includes MDs (medical doctors) and DOs (osteopathic physicians). Includes primary care physicians and specialist physicians.

Rate of Registered Nurses in 2016

National Rate = 884 Nurses per 100,000 Population*

ALPHA ORDER

RANK	STATE	RATE
17	Alabama	975
43	Alaska	751
40	Arizona	759
38	Arkansas	782
49	California	700
33	Colorado	859
27	Connecticut	921
3	Delaware	1,189
35	Florida	848
46	Georgia	711
37	Hawaii	791
45	Idaho	733
22	Illinois	950
18	Indiana	963
13	Iowa	1,033
25	Kansas	933
14	Kentucky	1,025
21	Louisiana	956
12	Maine	1,066
31	Maryland	886
2	Massachusetts	1,250
25	Michigan	933
7	Minnesota	1,120
20	Mississippi	957
8	Missouri	1,115
23	Montana	940
9	Nebraska	1,114
50	Nevada	689
15	New Hampshire	993
30	New Jersey	888
39	New Mexico	778
28	New York	915
16	North Carolina	976
5	North Dakota	1,149
10	Ohio	1,102
47	Oklahoma	705
32	Oregon	860
11	Pennsylvania	1,091
4	Rhode Island	1,150
36	South Carolina	843
1	South Dakota	1,402
29	Tennessee	903
44	Texas	746
48	Utah	704
24	Vermont	937
40	Virginia	759
40	Washington	759
6	West Virginia	1,140
19	Wisconsin	959
34	Wyoming	849

RANK ORDER

RANK	STATE	RATE
1	South Dakota	1,402
2	Massachusetts	1,250
3	Delaware	1,189
4	Rhode Island	1,150
5	North Dakota	1,149
6	West Virginia	1,140
7	Minnesota	1,120
8	Missouri	1,115
9	Nebraska	1,114
10	Ohio	1,102
11	Pennsylvania	1,091
12	Maine	1,066
13	Iowa	1,033
14	Kentucky	1,025
15	New Hampshire	993
16	North Carolina	976
17	Alabama	975
18	Indiana	963
19	Wisconsin	959
20	Mississippi	957
21	Louisiana	956
22	Illinois	950
23	Montana	940
24	Vermont	937
25	Kansas	933
25	Michigan	933
27	Connecticut	921
28	New York	915
29	Tennessee	903
30	New Jersey	888
31	Maryland	886
32	Oregon	860
33	Colorado	859
34	Wyoming	849
35	Florida	848
36	South Carolina	843
37	Hawaii	791
38	Arkansas	782
39	New Mexico	778
40	Arizona	759
40	Virginia	759
40	Washington	759
43	Alaska	751
44	Texas	746
45	Idaho	733
46	Georgia	711
47	Oklahoma	705
48	Utah	704
49	California	700
50	Nevada	689

| District of Columbia | | 1,515 |

Source: CQ Press using data from U.S. Department of Labor, Bureau of Labor Statistics
"Occupational Employment and Wages, 2016" (http://www.bls.gov/oes/)
*Does not include self-employed.

Rate of Dentists in 2017

National Rate = 58 Dentists per 100,000 Population*

ALPHA ORDER				RANK ORDER		
RANK	STATE	RATE		RANK	STATE	RATE
47	Alabama	42		1	Massachusetts	79
7	Alaska	68		2	New Jersey	78
23	Arizona	51		3	California	75
49	Arkansas	39		4	New York	73
3	California	75		5	Connecticut	71
9	Colorado	66		6	Hawaii	69
5	Connecticut	71		7	Alaska	68
48	Delaware	41		7	Maryland	68
24	Florida	50		9	Colorado	66
45	Georgia	44		9	Washington	66
6	Hawaii	69		11	Illinois	65
24	Idaho	50		12	Nebraska	61
11	Illinois	65		12	Virginia	61
42	Indiana	45		14	Pennsylvania	60
29	Iowa	49		15	Michigan	58
37	Kansas	47		15	Utah	58
19	Kentucky	56		17	New Hampshire	57
41	Louisiana	46		17	Vermont	57
37	Maine	47		19	Kentucky	56
7	Maryland	68		19	Montana	56
1	Massachusetts	79		21	Minnesota	54
15	Michigan	58		22	Wisconsin	53
21	Minnesota	54		23	Arizona	51
49	Mississippi	39		24	Florida	50
37	Missouri	47		24	Idaho	50
19	Montana	56		24	North Dakota	50
12	Nebraska	61		24	Ohio	50
29	Nevada	49		24	Texas	50
17	New Hampshire	57		29	Iowa	49
2	New Jersey	78		29	Nevada	49
29	New Mexico	49		29	New Mexico	49
4	New York	73		29	North Carolina	49
29	North Carolina	49		29	Rhode Island	49
24	North Dakota	50		29	Wyoming	49
24	Ohio	50		35	South Dakota	48
37	Oklahoma	47		35	Tennessee	48
46	Oregon	43		37	Kansas	47
14	Pennsylvania	60		37	Maine	47
29	Rhode Island	49		37	Missouri	47
42	South Carolina	45		37	Oklahoma	47
35	South Dakota	48		41	Louisiana	46
35	Tennessee	48		42	Indiana	45
24	Texas	50		42	South Carolina	45
15	Utah	58		42	West Virginia	45
17	Vermont	57		45	Georgia	44
12	Virginia	61		46	Oregon	43
9	Washington	66		47	Alabama	42
42	West Virginia	45		48	Delaware	41
22	Wisconsin	53		49	Arkansas	39
29	Wyoming	49		49	Mississippi	39
					District of Columbia	89

Source: CQ Press using data from American Dental Association as reported by The Henry J. Kaiser Family Foundation "Professionally Active Dentists" (http://kff.org/other/state-indicator/total-dentists/)
*Professionally active dentists. Rates calculated using 2017 Census population estimates.

Community Hospitals in 2015

National Total = 4,862 Hospitals*

ALPHA ORDER					RANK ORDER			
RANK	STATE	HOSPITALS	% of USA		RANK	STATE	HOSPITALS	% of USA
21	Alabama	95	2.0%		1	Texas	404	8.3%
47	Alaska	21	0.4%		2	California	342	7.0%
30	Arizona	71	1.5%		3	Florida	210	4.3%
27	Arkansas	80	1.6%		4	Illinois	188	3.9%
2	California	342	7.0%		5	Pennsylvania	186	3.8%
26	Colorado	81	1.7%		6	Ohio	179	3.7%
43	Connecticut	32	0.7%		7	New York	170	3.5%
50	Delaware	7	0.1%		8	Michigan	147	3.0%
3	Florida	210	4.3%		9	Georgia	141	2.9%
9	Georgia	141	2.9%		10	Kansas	131	2.7%
45	Hawaii	24	0.5%		11	Minnesota	130	2.7%
38	Idaho	40	0.8%		12	Wisconsin	127	2.6%
4	Illinois	188	3.9%		13	Missouri	121	2.5%
15	Indiana	120	2.5%		13	Tennessee	121	2.5%
17	Iowa	118	2.4%		15	Indiana	120	2.5%
10	Kansas	131	2.7%		15	Louisiana	120	2.5%
20	Kentucky	103	2.1%		17	Iowa	118	2.4%
15	Louisiana	120	2.5%		18	North Carolina	113	2.3%
42	Maine	34	0.7%		19	Oklahoma	110	2.3%
35	Maryland	50	1.0%		20	Kentucky	103	2.1%
28	Massachusetts	76	1.6%		21	Alabama	95	2.0%
8	Michigan	147	3.0%		21	Mississippi	95	2.0%
11	Minnesota	130	2.7%		23	Virginia	92	1.9%
21	Mississippi	95	2.0%		24	Washington	90	1.9%
13	Missouri	121	2.5%		25	Nebraska	88	1.8%
35	Montana	50	1.0%		26	Colorado	81	1.7%
25	Nebraska	88	1.8%		27	Arkansas	80	1.6%
40	Nevada	36	0.7%		28	Massachusetts	76	1.6%
44	New Hampshire	28	0.6%		29	New Jersey	75	1.5%
29	New Jersey	75	1.5%		30	Arizona	71	1.5%
40	New Mexico	36	0.7%		31	South Carolina	68	1.4%
7	New York	170	3.5%		32	Oregon	59	1.2%
18	North Carolina	113	2.3%		33	West Virginia	54	1.1%
38	North Dakota	40	0.8%		34	South Dakota	53	1.1%
6	Ohio	179	3.7%		35	Maryland	50	1.0%
19	Oklahoma	110	2.3%		35	Montana	50	1.0%
32	Oregon	59	1.2%		37	Utah	47	1.0%
5	Pennsylvania	186	3.8%		38	Idaho	40	0.8%
49	Rhode Island	11	0.2%		38	North Dakota	40	0.8%
31	South Carolina	68	1.4%		40	Nevada	36	0.7%
34	South Dakota	53	1.1%		40	New Mexico	36	0.7%
13	Tennessee	121	2.5%		42	Maine	34	0.7%
1	Texas	404	8.3%		43	Connecticut	32	0.7%
37	Utah	47	1.0%		44	New Hampshire	28	0.6%
48	Vermont	14	0.3%		45	Hawaii	24	0.5%
23	Virginia	92	1.9%		46	Wyoming	23	0.5%
24	Washington	90	1.9%		47	Alaska	21	0.4%
33	West Virginia	54	1.1%		48	Vermont	14	0.3%
12	Wisconsin	127	2.6%		49	Rhode Island	11	0.2%
46	Wyoming	23	0.5%		50	Delaware	7	0.1%
					District of Columbia		11	0.2%

Source: American Hospital Association (Chicago, IL)
  "Hospital Statistics" (2017 edition)

*Community hospitals are all nonfederal, short-term general, and special hospitals whose facilities and services are available to the public.

Rate of Community Hospitals in 2015

National Rate = 1.5 Community Hospitals per 100,000 Population*

ALPHA ORDER

RANK	STATE	RATE
21	Alabama	2.0
10	Alaska	2.8
42	Arizona	1.0
12	Arkansas	2.7
45	California	0.9
28	Colorado	1.5
45	Connecticut	0.9
50	Delaware	0.7
42	Florida	1.0
35	Georgia	1.4
25	Hawaii	1.7
15	Idaho	2.4
28	Illinois	1.5
23	Indiana	1.8
7	Iowa	3.8
5	Kansas	4.5
17	Kentucky	2.3
13	Louisiana	2.6
13	Maine	2.6
48	Maryland	0.8
39	Massachusetts	1.1
28	Michigan	1.5
15	Minnesota	2.4
8	Mississippi	3.2
21	Missouri	2.0
3	Montana	4.8
4	Nebraska	4.6
38	Nevada	1.2
20	New Hampshire	2.1
48	New Jersey	0.8
25	New Mexico	1.7
45	New York	0.9
39	North Carolina	1.1
2	North Dakota	5.3
28	Ohio	1.5
10	Oklahoma	2.8
28	Oregon	1.5
28	Pennsylvania	1.5
42	Rhode Island	1.0
35	South Carolina	1.4
1	South Dakota	6.2
23	Tennessee	1.8
28	Texas	1.5
27	Utah	1.6
18	Vermont	2.2
39	Virginia	1.1
37	Washington	1.3
9	West Virginia	2.9
18	Wisconsin	2.2
6	Wyoming	3.9

RANK ORDER

RANK	STATE	RATE
1	South Dakota	6.2
2	North Dakota	5.3
3	Montana	4.8
4	Nebraska	4.6
5	Kansas	4.5
6	Wyoming	3.9
7	Iowa	3.8
8	Mississippi	3.2
9	West Virginia	2.9
10	Alaska	2.8
10	Oklahoma	2.8
12	Arkansas	2.7
13	Louisiana	2.6
13	Maine	2.6
15	Idaho	2.4
15	Minnesota	2.4
17	Kentucky	2.3
18	Vermont	2.2
18	Wisconsin	2.2
20	New Hampshire	2.1
21	Alabama	2.0
21	Missouri	2.0
23	Indiana	1.8
23	Tennessee	1.8
25	Hawaii	1.7
25	New Mexico	1.7
27	Utah	1.6
28	Colorado	1.5
28	Illinois	1.5
28	Michigan	1.5
28	Ohio	1.5
28	Oregon	1.5
28	Pennsylvania	1.5
28	Texas	1.5
35	Georgia	1.4
35	South Carolina	1.4
37	Washington	1.3
38	Nevada	1.2
39	Massachusetts	1.1
39	North Carolina	1.1
39	Virginia	1.1
42	Arizona	1.0
42	Florida	1.0
42	Rhode Island	1.0
45	California	0.9
45	Connecticut	0.9
45	New York	0.9
48	Maryland	0.8
48	New Jersey	0.8
50	Delaware	0.7

| | District of Columbia | 1.6 |

Source: CQ Press using data from American Hospital Association (Chicago, IL)
   "Hospital Statistics" (2017 edition)
*Community hospitals are all nonfederal, short-term general, and special hospitals whose facilities and services are available to the public.

Births in 2016

National Total = 3,945,875 Live Births*

ALPHA ORDER					RANK ORDER			
RANK	STATE	BIRTHS	% of USA		RANK	STATE	BIRTHS	% of USA
24	Alabama	59,151	1.5%		1	California	488,827	12.4%
46	Alaska	11,209	0.3%		2	Texas	398,047	10.1%
14	Arizona	84,520	2.1%		3	New York	234,283	5.9%
31	Arkansas	38,274	1.0%		4	Florida	225,022	5.7%
1	California	488,827	12.4%		5	Illinois	154,445	3.9%
22	Colorado	66,613	1.7%		6	Pennsylvania	139,409	3.5%
35	Connecticut	36,015	0.9%		7	Ohio	138,085	3.5%
47	Delaware	10,992	0.3%		8	Georgia	130,042	3.3%
4	Florida	225,022	5.7%		9	North Carolina	120,779	3.1%
8	Georgia	130,042	3.3%		10	Michigan	113,315	2.9%
40	Hawaii	18,059	0.5%		11	New Jersey	102,647	2.6%
38	Idaho	22,482	0.6%		12	Virginia	102,460	2.6%
5	Illinois	154,445	3.9%		13	Washington	90,505	2.3%
15	Indiana	83,091	2.1%		14	Arizona	84,520	2.1%
30	Iowa	39,403	1.0%		15	Indiana	83,091	2.1%
32	Kansas	38,053	1.0%		16	Tennessee	80,807	2.0%
26	Kentucky	55,449	1.4%		17	Missouri	74,705	1.9%
23	Louisiana	63,178	1.6%		18	Maryland	73,136	1.9%
41	Maine	12,705	0.3%		19	Massachusetts	71,317	1.8%
18	Maryland	73,136	1.9%		20	Minnesota	69,749	1.8%
19	Massachusetts	71,317	1.8%		21	Wisconsin	66,615	1.7%
10	Michigan	113,315	2.9%		22	Colorado	66,613	1.7%
20	Minnesota	69,749	1.8%		23	Louisiana	63,178	1.6%
33	Mississippi	37,928	1.0%		24	Alabama	59,151	1.5%
17	Missouri	74,705	1.9%		25	South Carolina	57,342	1.5%
42	Montana	12,282	0.3%		26	Kentucky	55,449	1.4%
36	Nebraska	26,589	0.7%		27	Oklahoma	52,592	1.3%
34	Nevada	36,260	0.9%		28	Utah	50,464	1.3%
44	New Hampshire	12,267	0.3%		29	Oregon	45,535	1.2%
11	New Jersey	102,647	2.6%		30	Iowa	39,403	1.0%
37	New Mexico	24,692	0.6%		31	Arkansas	38,274	1.0%
3	New York	234,283	5.9%		32	Kansas	38,053	1.0%
9	North Carolina	120,779	3.1%		33	Mississippi	37,928	1.0%
45	North Dakota	11,383	0.3%		34	Nevada	36,260	0.9%
7	Ohio	138,085	3.5%		35	Connecticut	36,015	0.9%
27	Oklahoma	52,592	1.3%		36	Nebraska	26,589	0.7%
29	Oregon	45,535	1.2%		37	New Mexico	24,692	0.6%
6	Pennsylvania	139,409	3.5%		38	Idaho	22,482	0.6%
48	Rhode Island	10,798	0.3%		39	West Virginia	19,079	0.5%
25	South Carolina	57,342	1.5%		40	Hawaii	18,059	0.5%
43	South Dakota	12,275	0.3%		41	Maine	12,705	0.3%
16	Tennessee	80,807	2.0%		42	Montana	12,282	0.3%
2	Texas	398,047	10.1%		43	South Dakota	12,275	0.3%
28	Utah	50,464	1.3%		44	New Hampshire	12,267	0.3%
50	Vermont	5,756	0.1%		45	North Dakota	11,383	0.3%
12	Virginia	102,460	2.6%		46	Alaska	11,209	0.3%
13	Washington	90,505	2.3%		47	Delaware	10,992	0.3%
39	West Virginia	19,079	0.5%		48	Rhode Island	10,798	0.3%
21	Wisconsin	66,615	1.7%		49	Wyoming	7,386	0.2%
49	Wyoming	7,386	0.2%		50	Vermont	5,756	0.1%
						District of Columbia	9,858	0.2%

Source: U.S. Department of Health and Human Services, National Center for Health Statistics
   "National Vital Statistics Reports" (Vol. 67, No. 1, January 31, 2018, http://www.cdc.gov/nchs/births.htm)
*Final data by state of residence.

Birth Rate in 2016

National Rate = 12.2 Live Births per 1,000 Population*

ALPHA ORDER

RANK	STATE	RATE
24	Alabama	12.2
2	Alaska	15.1
24	Arizona	12.2
11	Arkansas	12.8
18	California	12.5
30	Colorado	12.0
47	Connecticut	10.1
37	Delaware	11.5
42	Florida	10.9
13	Georgia	12.6
13	Hawaii	12.6
8	Idaho	13.4
28	Illinois	12.1
18	Indiana	12.5
13	Iowa	12.6
10	Kansas	13.1
18	Kentucky	12.5
7	Louisiana	13.5
48	Maine	9.5
24	Maryland	12.2
44	Massachusetts	10.5
40	Michigan	11.4
13	Minnesota	12.6
12	Mississippi	12.7
22	Missouri	12.3
35	Montana	11.8
6	Nebraska	13.9
22	Nevada	12.3
49	New Hampshire	9.2
37	New Jersey	11.5
31	New Mexico	11.9
31	New York	11.9
31	North Carolina	11.9
3	North Dakota	15.0
31	Ohio	11.9
8	Oklahoma	13.4
41	Oregon	11.1
42	Pennsylvania	10.9
46	Rhode Island	10.2
36	South Carolina	11.6
5	South Dakota	14.2
28	Tennessee	12.1
4	Texas	14.3
1	Utah	16.5
49	Vermont	9.2
24	Virginia	12.2
21	Washington	12.4
45	West Virginia	10.4
37	Wisconsin	11.5
13	Wyoming	12.6

RANK ORDER

RANK	STATE	RATE
1	Utah	16.5
2	Alaska	15.1
3	North Dakota	15.0
4	Texas	14.3
5	South Dakota	14.2
6	Nebraska	13.9
7	Louisiana	13.5
8	Idaho	13.4
8	Oklahoma	13.4
10	Kansas	13.1
11	Arkansas	12.8
12	Mississippi	12.7
13	Georgia	12.6
13	Hawaii	12.6
13	Iowa	12.6
13	Minnesota	12.6
13	Wyoming	12.6
18	California	12.5
18	Indiana	12.5
18	Kentucky	12.5
21	Washington	12.4
22	Missouri	12.3
22	Nevada	12.3
24	Alabama	12.2
24	Arizona	12.2
24	Maryland	12.2
24	Virginia	12.2
28	Illinois	12.1
28	Tennessee	12.1
30	Colorado	12.0
31	New Mexico	11.9
31	New York	11.9
31	North Carolina	11.9
31	Ohio	11.9
35	Montana	11.8
36	South Carolina	11.6
37	Delaware	11.5
37	New Jersey	11.5
37	Wisconsin	11.5
40	Michigan	11.4
41	Oregon	11.1
42	Florida	10.9
42	Pennsylvania	10.9
44	Massachusetts	10.5
45	West Virginia	10.4
46	Rhode Island	10.2
47	Connecticut	10.1
48	Maine	9.5
49	New Hampshire	9.2
49	Vermont	9.2
	District of Columbia	14.5

Source: U.S. Department of Health and Human Services, National Center for Health Statistics
  "National Vital Statistics Reports" (Vol. 67, No. 1, January 31, 2018, http://www.cdc.gov/nchs/births.htm)
*Final data by state of residence.

Births of Low Birthweight as a Percent of All Births in 2016

National Percent = 8.2% of Live Births*

ALPHA ORDER

RANK	STATE	PERCENT
3	Alabama	10.3
50	Alaska	5.9
35	Arizona	7.3
13	Arkansas	8.8
42	California	6.8
10	Colorado	9.0
31	Connecticut	7.8
12	Delaware	8.9
14	Florida	8.7
4	Georgia	9.8
17	Hawaii	8.5
38	Idaho	7.0
22	Illinois	8.4
24	Indiana	8.2
42	Iowa	6.8
38	Kansas	7.0
9	Kentucky	9.1
2	Louisiana	10.6
37	Maine	7.1
17	Maryland	8.5
33	Massachusetts	7.5
17	Michigan	8.5
45	Minnesota	6.6
1	Mississippi	11.5
14	Missouri	8.7
29	Montana	7.9
38	Nebraska	7.0
17	Nevada	8.5
48	New Hampshire	6.4
26	New Jersey	8.1
10	New Mexico	9.0
29	New York	7.9
8	North Carolina	9.2
45	North Dakota	6.6
14	Ohio	8.7
31	Oklahoma	7.8
47	Oregon	6.5
24	Pennsylvania	8.2
28	Rhode Island	8.0
5	South Carolina	9.6
42	South Dakota	6.8
7	Tennessee	9.3
22	Texas	8.4
36	Utah	7.2
41	Vermont	6.9
26	Virginia	8.1
48	Washington	6.4
5	West Virginia	9.6
34	Wisconsin	7.4
17	Wyoming	8.5

RANK ORDER

RANK	STATE	PERCENT
1	Mississippi	11.5
2	Louisiana	10.6
3	Alabama	10.3
4	Georgia	9.8
5	South Carolina	9.6
5	West Virginia	9.6
7	Tennessee	9.3
8	North Carolina	9.2
9	Kentucky	9.1
10	Colorado	9.0
10	New Mexico	9.0
12	Delaware	8.9
13	Arkansas	8.8
14	Florida	8.7
14	Missouri	8.7
14	Ohio	8.7
17	Hawaii	8.5
17	Maryland	8.5
17	Michigan	8.5
17	Nevada	8.5
17	Wyoming	8.5
22	Illinois	8.4
22	Texas	8.4
24	Indiana	8.2
24	Pennsylvania	8.2
26	New Jersey	8.1
26	Virginia	8.1
28	Rhode Island	8.0
29	Montana	7.9
29	New York	7.9
31	Connecticut	7.8
31	Oklahoma	7.8
33	Massachusetts	7.5
34	Wisconsin	7.4
35	Arizona	7.3
36	Utah	7.2
37	Maine	7.1
38	Idaho	7.0
38	Kansas	7.0
38	Nebraska	7.0
41	Vermont	6.9
42	California	6.8
42	Iowa	6.8
42	South Dakota	6.8
45	Minnesota	6.6
45	North Dakota	6.6
47	Oregon	6.5
48	New Hampshire	6.4
48	Washington	6.4
50	Alaska	5.9

	District of Columbia	10.1

Source: U.S. Department of Health and Human Services, National Center for Health Statistics
   "National Vital Statistics Reports" (Vol. 67, No. 1, January 31, 2018, http://www.cdc.gov/nchs/births.htm)
*Final data by state of residence. Births of less than 2,500 grams (5 pounds 8 ounces).

Births to Teenage Mothers as a Percent of All Births in 2015

National Percent = 5.8% of Live Births*

ALPHA ORDER

RANK	STATE	PERCENT
8	Alabama	7.9
22	Alaska	5.9
11	Arizona	6.9
1	Arkansas	9.5
31	California	4.9
31	Colorado	4.9
47	Connecticut	3.5
34	Delaware	4.8
27	Florida	5.3
14	Georgia	6.7
41	Hawaii	4.3
24	Idaho	5.6
26	Illinois	5.5
11	Indiana	6.9
31	Iowa	4.9
18	Kansas	6.3
7	Kentucky	8.0
9	Louisiana	7.8
34	Maine	4.8
39	Maryland	4.4
50	Massachusetts	3.0
24	Michigan	5.6
48	Minnesota	3.4
2	Mississippi	9.2
17	Missouri	6.4
21	Montana	6.1
28	Nebraska	5.2
16	Nevada	6.5
45	New Hampshire	3.8
49	New Jersey	3.3
3	New Mexico	9.0
45	New York	3.8
18	North Carolina	6.3
37	North Dakota	4.7
18	Ohio	6.3
5	Oklahoma	8.3
30	Oregon	5.0
29	Pennsylvania	5.1
34	Rhode Island	4.8
11	South Carolina	6.9
23	South Dakota	5.8
10	Tennessee	7.7
6	Texas	8.1
44	Utah	4.0
42	Vermont	4.2
39	Virginia	4.4
42	Washington	4.2
4	West Virginia	8.7
38	Wisconsin	4.5
15	Wyoming	6.6

RANK ORDER

RANK	STATE	PERCENT
1	Arkansas	9.5
2	Mississippi	9.2
3	New Mexico	9.0
4	West Virginia	8.7
5	Oklahoma	8.3
6	Texas	8.1
7	Kentucky	8.0
8	Alabama	7.9
9	Louisiana	7.8
10	Tennessee	7.7
11	Arizona	6.9
11	Indiana	6.9
11	South Carolina	6.9
14	Georgia	6.7
15	Wyoming	6.6
16	Nevada	6.5
17	Missouri	6.4
18	Kansas	6.3
18	North Carolina	6.3
18	Ohio	6.3
21	Montana	6.1
22	Alaska	5.9
23	South Dakota	5.8
24	Idaho	5.6
24	Michigan	5.6
26	Illinois	5.5
27	Florida	5.3
28	Nebraska	5.2
29	Pennsylvania	5.1
30	Oregon	5.0
31	California	4.9
31	Colorado	4.9
31	Iowa	4.9
34	Delaware	4.8
34	Maine	4.8
34	Rhode Island	4.8
37	North Dakota	4.7
38	Wisconsin	4.5
39	Maryland	4.4
39	Virginia	4.4
41	Hawaii	4.3
42	Vermont	4.2
42	Washington	4.2
44	Utah	4.0
45	New Hampshire	3.8
45	New York	3.8
47	Connecticut	3.5
48	Minnesota	3.4
49	New Jersey	3.3
50	Massachusetts	3.0

District of Columbia	5.2

Source: CQ Press using data from U.S. Department of Health and Human Services, Centers for Disease Control and Prevention "CDC Wonder" (http://wonder.cdc.gov)

*Final data. Live births to women 15 to 19 years old by state of residence.

Births to Unmarried Women as a Percent of All Births in 2016

National Percent = 39.8% of Live Births*

ALPHA ORDER

RANK ORDER

RANK	STATE	PERCENT	RANK	STATE	PERCENT
12	Alabama	44.7	1	Mississippi	53.2
35	Alaska	36.1	2	Louisiana	52.0
8	Arizona	45.0	3	New Mexico	51.1
13	Arkansas	44.5	4	Nevada	47.8
29	California	38.2	5	Florida	46.9
49	Colorado	22.5	6	Delaware	45.8
32	Connecticut	36.9	7	South Carolina	45.3
6	Delaware	45.8	8	Arizona	45.0
5	Florida	46.9	8	West Virginia	45.0
10	Georgia	44.9	10	Georgia	44.9
31	Hawaii	37.0	10	Rhode Island	44.9
48	Idaho	27.6	12	Alabama	44.7
24	Illinois	39.7	13	Arkansas	44.5
16	Indiana	42.7	14	Tennessee	43.6
38	Iowa	35.0	15	Ohio	43.0
36	Kansas	36.0	16	Indiana	42.7
18	Kentucky	41.4	17	Oklahoma	42.3
2	Louisiana	52.0	18	Kentucky	41.4
24	Maine	39.7	19	Texas	41.3
24	Maryland	39.7	20	Michigan	41.0
42	Massachusetts	33.0	21	Pennsylvania	40.7
20	Michigan	41.0	22	North Carolina	40.4
45	Minnesota	32.2	23	Missouri	39.8
1	Mississippi	53.2	24	Illinois	39.7
23	Missouri	39.8	24	Maine	39.7
34	Montana	36.4	24	Maryland	39.7
44	Nebraska	32.3	27	Vermont	39.4
4	Nevada	47.8	28	New York	38.5
41	New Hampshire	33.7	29	California	38.2
39	New Jersey	34.6	30	Wisconsin	37.2
3	New Mexico	51.1	31	Hawaii	37.0
28	New York	38.5	32	Connecticut	36.9
22	North Carolina	40.4	32	South Dakota	36.9
47	North Dakota	31.6	34	Montana	36.4
15	Ohio	43.0	35	Alaska	36.1
17	Oklahoma	42.3	36	Kansas	36.0
37	Oregon	35.8	37	Oregon	35.8
21	Pennsylvania	40.7	38	Iowa	35.0
10	Rhode Island	44.9	39	New Jersey	34.6
7	South Carolina	45.3	40	Virginia	34.0
32	South Dakota	36.9	41	New Hampshire	33.7
14	Tennessee	43.6	42	Massachusetts	33.0
19	Texas	41.3	43	Wyoming	32.8
50	Utah	18.6	44	Nebraska	32.3
27	Vermont	39.4	45	Minnesota	32.2
40	Virginia	34.0	46	Washington	31.7
46	Washington	31.7	47	North Dakota	31.6
8	West Virginia	45.0	48	Idaho	27.6
30	Wisconsin	37.2	49	Colorado	22.5
43	Wyoming	32.8	50	Utah	18.6
				District of Columbia	48.4

Source: U.S. Department of Health and Human Services, National Center for Health Statistics
   "National Vital Statistics Reports" (Vol. 67, No. 1, January 31, 2018, http://www.cdc.gov/nchs/births.htm)
*Final data by state of residence.

Percent of Women Receiving Late or No Prenatal Care in 2015

National Percent = 6.0% of Women*

RANK	STATE	PERCENT
14	Alabama	6.6
23	Alaska	5.9
6	Arizona	8.1
2	Arkansas	9.8
41	California	3.7
8	Colorado	7.5
NA	Connecticut**	NA
10	Delaware	6.8
20	Florida	6.2
6	Georgia	8.1
18	Hawaii	6.5
34	Idaho	4.8
28	Illinois	5.3
25	Indiana	5.7
40	Iowa	3.8
44	Kansas	3.5
29	Kentucky	5.2
11	Louisiana	6.7
45	Maine	2.9
4	Maryland	8.3
36	Massachusetts	4.2
32	Michigan	4.9
41	Minnesota	3.7
35	Mississippi	4.7
30	Missouri	5.1
18	Montana	6.5
30	Nebraska	5.1
4	Nevada	8.3
41	New Hampshire	3.7
NA	New Jersey**	NA
1	New Mexico	9.9
32	New York	4.9
14	North Carolina	6.6
11	North Dakota	6.7
14	Ohio	6.6
11	Oklahoma	6.7
36	Oregon	4.2
14	Pennsylvania	6.6
48	Rhode Island	1.6
9	South Carolina	7.3
26	South Dakota	5.4
23	Tennessee	5.9
3	Texas	9.7
46	Utah	2.6
47	Vermont	2.1
36	Virginia	4.2
21	Washington	6.1
26	West Virginia	5.4
39	Wisconsin	3.9
22	Wyoming	6.0

RANK	STATE	PERCENT
1	New Mexico	9.9
2	Arkansas	9.8
3	Texas	9.7
4	Maryland	8.3
4	Nevada	8.3
6	Arizona	8.1
6	Georgia	8.1
8	Colorado	7.5
9	South Carolina	7.3
10	Delaware	6.8
11	Louisiana	6.7
11	North Dakota	6.7
11	Oklahoma	6.7
14	Alabama	6.6
14	North Carolina	6.6
14	Ohio	6.6
14	Pennsylvania	6.6
18	Hawaii	6.5
18	Montana	6.5
20	Florida	6.2
21	Washington	6.1
22	Wyoming	6.0
23	Alaska	5.9
23	Tennessee	5.9
25	Indiana	5.7
26	South Dakota	5.4
26	West Virginia	5.4
28	Illinois	5.3
29	Kentucky	5.2
30	Missouri	5.1
30	Nebraska	5.1
32	Michigan	4.9
32	New York	4.9
34	Idaho	4.8
35	Mississippi	4.7
36	Massachusetts	4.2
36	Oregon	4.2
36	Virginia	4.2
39	Wisconsin	3.9
40	Iowa	3.8
41	California	3.7
41	Minnesota	3.7
41	New Hampshire	3.7
44	Kansas	3.5
45	Maine	2.9
46	Utah	2.6
47	Vermont	2.1
48	Rhode Island	1.6
NA	Connecticut**	NA
NA	New Jersey**	NA

District of Columbia 9.3

Source: CQ Press using data from U.S. Department of Health and Human Services, Centers for Disease Control and Prevention
"CDC Wonder" (http://wonder.cdc.gov)

*Final data by state of residence. "Late" means care begun in third trimester. National figure is for reporting states only.

**Not available.

Reported Legal Abortions in 2014

Reporting States' Total = 652,639 Abortions*

ALPHA ORDER

RANK	STATE	ABORTIONS	% of USA
23	Alabama	8,080	1.2%
42	Alaska	1,518	0.2%
14	Arizona	12,900	2.0%
30	Arkansas	4,253	0.7%
NA	California**	NA	NA
16	Colorado	10,648	1.6%
17	Connecticut	10,611	1.6%
35	Delaware	2,937	0.5%
2	Florida	72,107	11.0%
6	Georgia	30,013	4.6%
38	Hawaii	2,147	0.3%
43	Idaho	1,353	0.2%
4	Illinois	38,472	5.9%
22	Indiana	8,118	1.2%
31	Iowa	4,020	0.6%
24	Kansas	7,219	1.1%
32	Kentucky	3,442	0.5%
18	Louisiana	10,322	1.6%
39	Maine	2,021	0.3%
NA	Maryland**	NA	NA
12	Massachusetts	19,354	3.0%
7	Michigan	27,629	4.2%
19	Minnesota	10,123	1.6%
36	Mississippi	2,303	0.4%
27	Missouri	5,060	0.8%
41	Montana	1,690	0.3%
37	Nebraska	2,270	0.3%
21	Nevada	8,132	1.2%
NA	New Hampshire**	NA	NA
9	New Jersey	24,181	3.7%
29	New Mexico	4,500	0.7%
1	New York	96,711	14.8%
8	North Carolina	24,605	3.8%
44	North Dakota	1,264	0.2%
10	Ohio	21,186	3.2%
28	Oklahoma	4,916	0.8%
20	Oregon	8,231	1.3%
5	Pennsylvania	32,126	4.9%
33	Rhode Island	2,990	0.5%
26	South Carolina	5,714	0.9%
46	South Dakota	551	0.1%
15	Tennessee	12,373	1.9%
3	Texas	54,148	8.3%
34	Utah	2,948	0.5%
45	Vermont	1,235	0.2%
11	Virginia	20,187	3.1%
13	Washington	17,710	2.7%
40	West Virginia	1,730	0.3%
25	Wisconsin	5,800	0.9%
NA	Wyoming**	NA	NA

RANK ORDER

RANK	STATE	ABORTIONS	% of USA
1	New York	96,711	14.8%
2	Florida	72,107	11.0%
3	Texas	54,148	8.3%
4	Illinois	38,472	5.9%
5	Pennsylvania	32,126	4.9%
6	Georgia	30,013	4.6%
7	Michigan	27,629	4.2%
8	North Carolina	24,605	3.8%
9	New Jersey	24,181	3.7%
10	Ohio	21,186	3.2%
11	Virginia	20,187	3.1%
12	Massachusetts	19,354	3.0%
13	Washington	17,710	2.7%
14	Arizona	12,900	2.0%
15	Tennessee	12,373	1.9%
16	Colorado	10,648	1.6%
17	Connecticut	10,611	1.6%
18	Louisiana	10,322	1.6%
19	Minnesota	10,123	1.6%
20	Oregon	8,231	1.3%
21	Nevada	8,132	1.2%
22	Indiana	8,118	1.2%
23	Alabama	8,080	1.2%
24	Kansas	7,219	1.1%
25	Wisconsin	5,800	0.9%
26	South Carolina	5,714	0.9%
27	Missouri	5,060	0.8%
28	Oklahoma	4,916	0.8%
29	New Mexico	4,500	0.7%
30	Arkansas	4,253	0.7%
31	Iowa	4,020	0.6%
32	Kentucky	3,442	0.5%
33	Rhode Island	2,990	0.5%
34	Utah	2,948	0.5%
35	Delaware	2,937	0.5%
36	Mississippi	2,303	0.4%
37	Nebraska	2,270	0.3%
38	Hawaii	2,147	0.3%
39	Maine	2,021	0.3%
40	West Virginia	1,730	0.3%
41	Montana	1,690	0.3%
42	Alaska	1,518	0.2%
43	Idaho	1,353	0.2%
44	North Dakota	1,264	0.2%
45	Vermont	1,235	0.2%
46	South Dakota	551	0.1%
NA	California**	NA	NA
NA	Maryland**	NA	NA
NA	New Hampshire**	NA	NA
NA	Wyoming**	NA	NA
	District of Columbia	2,790	0.4%

Source: U.S. Department of Health and Human Services, Centers for Disease Control and Prevention
"Abortion Surveillance-United States, 2014" (MMWR, Vol. 66, No. SS-24, 11/24/17, www.cdc.gov/mmwr/mmwr_ss/ss_pvol.html)
*By state of occurrence. Total is for reporting states only.
**Not reported.

Reported Legal Abortions per 1,000 Live Births in 2014

Reporting States' Ratio = 186 Abortions per 1,000 Live Births*

ALPHA ORDER

RANK	STATE	RATIO
27	Alabama	136
30	Alaska	133
25	Arizona	148
33	Arkansas	110
NA	California**	NA
20	Colorado	162
2	Connecticut	292
6	Delaware	268
1	Florida	328
10	Georgia	229
31	Hawaii	116
43	Idaho	59
7	Illinois	243
36	Indiana	97
34	Iowa	101
17	Kansas	184
42	Kentucky	61
21	Louisiana	160
22	Maine	159
NA	Maryland**	NA
5	Massachusetts	269
8	Michigan	242
26	Minnesota	145
43	Mississippi	59
41	Missouri	67
27	Montana	136
39	Nebraska	85
11	Nevada	227
NA	New Hampshire**	NA
9	New Jersey	234
19	New Mexico	173
4	New York	271
13	North Carolina	203
32	North Dakota	111
23	Ohio	152
37	Oklahoma	92
18	Oregon	181
12	Pennsylvania	226
3	Rhode Island	276
35	South Carolina	99
46	South Dakota	45
23	Tennessee	152
29	Texas	135
45	Utah	58
14	Vermont	201
16	Virginia	195
15	Washington	200
39	West Virginia	85
38	Wisconsin	86
NA	Wyoming**	NA

RANK ORDER

RANK	STATE	RATIO
1	Florida	328
2	Connecticut	292
3	Rhode Island	276
4	New York	271
5	Massachusetts	269
6	Delaware	268
7	Illinois	243
8	Michigan	242
9	New Jersey	234
10	Georgia	229
11	Nevada	227
12	Pennsylvania	226
13	North Carolina	203
14	Vermont	201
15	Washington	200
16	Virginia	195
17	Kansas	184
18	Oregon	181
19	New Mexico	173
20	Colorado	162
21	Louisiana	160
22	Maine	159
23	Ohio	152
23	Tennessee	152
25	Arizona	148
26	Minnesota	145
27	Alabama	136
27	Montana	136
29	Texas	135
30	Alaska	133
31	Hawaii	116
32	North Dakota	111
33	Arkansas	110
34	Iowa	101
35	South Carolina	99
36	Indiana	97
37	Oklahoma	92
38	Wisconsin	86
39	Nebraska	85
39	West Virginia	85
41	Missouri	67
42	Kentucky	61
43	Idaho	59
43	Mississippi	59
45	Utah	58
46	South Dakota	45
NA	California**	NA
NA	Maryland**	NA
NA	New Hampshire**	NA
NA	Wyoming**	NA
	District of Columbia	293

Source: U.S. Department of Health and Human Services, Centers for Disease Control and Prevention
   "Abortion Surveillance-United States, 2014" (MMWR, Vol. 66, No. SS-24, 11/24/17, www.cdc.gov/mmwr/mmwr_ss/ss_pvol.html)
*By state of occurrence. National figure is for reporting states only.
**Not reported.

Infant Deaths in 2015

National Total = 23,455 Infant Deaths*

ALPHA ORDER

RANK	STATE	DEATHS	% of USA
15	Alabama	495	2.1%
45	Alaska	78	0.3%
19	Arizona	469	2.0%
29	Arkansas	293	1.2%
2	California	2,169	9.2%
27	Colorado	309	1.3%
33	Connecticut	200	0.9%
41	Delaware	100	0.4%
3	Florida	1,400	6.0%
5	Georgia	1,024	4.4%
39	Hawaii	108	0.5%
40	Idaho	106	0.5%
7	Illinois	953	4.1%
12	Indiana	611	2.6%
35	Iowa	166	0.7%
31	Kansas	232	1.0%
24	Kentucky	375	1.6%
14	Louisiana	498	2.1%
43	Maine	83	0.4%
16	Maryland	490	2.1%
27	Massachusetts	309	1.3%
10	Michigan	744	3.2%
25	Minnesota	360	1.5%
26	Mississippi	356	1.5%
16	Missouri	490	2.1%
46	Montana	75	0.3%
36	Nebraska	153	0.7%
34	Nevada	190	0.8%
48	New Hampshire	52	0.2%
18	New Jersey	487	2.1%
38	New Mexico	131	0.6%
4	New York	1,087	4.6%
8	North Carolina	884	3.8%
44	North Dakota	81	0.3%
6	Ohio	1,005	4.3%
22	Oklahoma	386	1.6%
31	Oregon	232	1.0%
9	Pennsylvania	862	3.7%
47	Rhode Island	62	0.3%
21	South Carolina	405	1.7%
42	South Dakota	90	0.4%
13	Tennessee	570	2.4%
1	Texas	2,308	9.8%
30	Utah	257	1.1%
50	Vermont	27	0.1%
11	Virginia	612	2.6%
20	Washington	432	1.8%
37	West Virginia	142	0.6%
22	Wisconsin	386	1.6%
49	Wyoming	39	0.2%

RANK ORDER

RANK	STATE	DEATHS	% of USA
1	Texas	2,308	9.8%
2	California	2,169	9.2%
3	Florida	1,400	6.0%
4	New York	1,087	4.6%
5	Georgia	1,024	4.4%
6	Ohio	1,005	4.3%
7	Illinois	953	4.1%
8	North Carolina	884	3.8%
9	Pennsylvania	862	3.7%
10	Michigan	744	3.2%
11	Virginia	612	2.6%
12	Indiana	611	2.6%
13	Tennessee	570	2.4%
14	Louisiana	498	2.1%
15	Alabama	495	2.1%
16	Maryland	490	2.1%
16	Missouri	490	2.1%
18	New Jersey	487	2.1%
19	Arizona	469	2.0%
20	Washington	432	1.8%
21	South Carolina	405	1.7%
22	Oklahoma	386	1.6%
22	Wisconsin	386	1.6%
24	Kentucky	375	1.6%
25	Minnesota	360	1.5%
26	Mississippi	356	1.5%
27	Colorado	309	1.3%
27	Massachusetts	309	1.3%
29	Arkansas	293	1.2%
30	Utah	257	1.1%
31	Kansas	232	1.0%
31	Oregon	232	1.0%
33	Connecticut	200	0.9%
34	Nevada	190	0.8%
35	Iowa	166	0.7%
36	Nebraska	153	0.7%
37	West Virginia	142	0.6%
38	New Mexico	131	0.6%
39	Hawaii	108	0.5%
40	Idaho	106	0.5%
41	Delaware	100	0.4%
42	South Dakota	90	0.4%
43	Maine	83	0.4%
44	North Dakota	81	0.3%
45	Alaska	78	0.3%
46	Montana	75	0.3%
47	Rhode Island	62	0.3%
48	New Hampshire	52	0.2%
49	Wyoming	39	0.2%
50	Vermont	27	0.1%
	District of Columbia	82	0.3%

Source: U.S. Department of Health and Human Services, National Center for Health Statistics
"National Vital Statistics Reports" (Vol. 66, No. 6, 2017, http://www.cdc.gov/nchs/deaths.htm)
*Final data. Deaths of infants under 1 year old by state of residence.

Infant Mortality Rate in 2015

National Rate = 5.9 Infant Deaths per 1,000 Live Births*

ALPHA ORDER

ALPHA ORDER

RANK ORDER

RANK	STATE	RATE		RANK	STATE	RATE
3	Alabama	8.3		1	Mississippi	9.3
16	Alaska	6.9		2	Delaware	9.0
34	Arizona	5.5		3	Alabama	8.3
6	Arkansas	7.5		4	Georgia	7.8
47	California	4.4		5	Louisiana	7.7
43	Colorado	4.6		6	Arkansas	7.5
32	Connecticut	5.6		7	Indiana	7.3
2	Delaware	9.0		7	North Carolina	7.3
22	Florida	6.2		7	Oklahoma	7.3
4	Georgia	7.8		7	South Dakota	7.3
26	Hawaii	5.9		11	North Dakota	7.2
43	Idaho	4.6		11	Ohio	7.2
24	Illinois	6.0		11	West Virginia	7.2
7	Indiana	7.3		14	South Carolina	7.0
49	Iowa	4.2		14	Tennessee	7.0
26	Kansas	5.9		16	Alaska	6.9
17	Kentucky	6.7		17	Kentucky	6.7
5	Louisiana	7.7		17	Maryland	6.7
19	Maine	6.6		19	Maine	6.6
17	Maryland	6.7		19	Michigan	6.6
48	Massachusetts	4.3		21	Missouri	6.5
19	Michigan	6.6		22	Florida	6.2
35	Minnesota	5.2		23	Pennsylvania	6.1
1	Mississippi	9.3		24	Illinois	6.0
21	Missouri	6.5		24	Montana	6.0
24	Montana	6.0		26	Hawaii	5.9
30	Nebraska	5.7		26	Kansas	5.9
35	Nevada	5.2		26	Virginia	5.9
49	New Hampshire	4.2		29	Wisconsin	5.8
42	New Jersey	4.7		30	Nebraska	5.7
37	New Mexico	5.1		30	Texas	5.7
43	New York	4.6		32	Connecticut	5.6
7	North Carolina	7.3		32	Rhode Island	5.6
11	North Dakota	7.2		34	Arizona	5.5
11	Ohio	7.2		35	Minnesota	5.2
7	Oklahoma	7.3		35	Nevada	5.2
37	Oregon	5.1		37	New Mexico	5.1
23	Pennsylvania	6.1		37	Oregon	5.1
32	Rhode Island	5.6		37	Utah	5.1
14	South Carolina	7.0		40	Wyoming	5.0
7	South Dakota	7.3		41	Washington	4.9
14	Tennessee	7.0		42	New Jersey	4.7
30	Texas	5.7		43	Colorado	4.6
37	Utah	5.1		43	Idaho	4.6
43	Vermont	4.6		43	New York	4.6
26	Virginia	5.9		43	Vermont	4.6
41	Washington	4.9		47	California	4.4
11	West Virginia	7.2		48	Massachusetts	4.3
29	Wisconsin	5.8		49	Iowa	4.2
40	Wyoming	5.0		49	New Hampshire	4.2

District of Columbia   8.6

Source: U.S. Department of Health and Human Services, National Center for Health Statistics
   "National Vital Statistics Reports" (Vol. 66, No. 6, 2017, http://www.cdc.gov/nchs/deaths.htm)
*Final data. Deaths of infants under 1 year old by state of residence.

Deaths in 2015

National Total = 2,712,630 Deaths*

RANK	STATE	DEATHS	% of USA
19	Alabama	51,909	1.9%
50	Alaska	4,316	0.2%
18	Arizona	54,299	2.0%
30	Arkansas	31,617	1.2%
1	California	259,206	9.6%
27	Colorado	36,349	1.3%
31	Connecticut	30,535	1.1%
45	Delaware	8,582	0.3%
2	Florida	191,737	7.1%
10	Georgia	79,942	2.9%
42	Hawaii	11,053	0.4%
40	Idaho	13,026	0.5%
7	Illinois	106,872	3.9%
14	Indiana	62,713	2.3%
32	Iowa	29,600	1.1%
33	Kansas	26,664	1.0%
23	Kentucky	46,564	1.7%
24	Louisiana	43,716	1.6%
39	Maine	14,479	0.5%
21	Maryland	47,247	1.7%
16	Massachusetts	57,806	2.1%
8	Michigan	95,140	3.5%
25	Minnesota	42,800	1.6%
29	Mississippi	31,783	1.2%
15	Missouri	59,871	2.2%
44	Montana	9,942	0.4%
38	Nebraska	16,740	0.6%
34	Nevada	22,879	0.8%
41	New Hampshire	11,984	0.4%
11	New Jersey	72,271	2.7%
36	New Mexico	17,685	0.7%
4	New York	153,628	5.7%
9	North Carolina	89,133	3.3%
47	North Dakota	6,223	0.2%
6	Ohio	118,188	4.4%
26	Oklahoma	39,422	1.5%
28	Oregon	35,705	1.3%
5	Pennsylvania	132,598	4.9%
43	Rhode Island	10,163	0.4%
22	South Carolina	47,198	1.7%
46	South Dakota	7,731	0.3%
12	Tennessee	66,570	2.5%
3	Texas	189,654	7.0%
37	Utah	17,334	0.6%
48	Vermont	5,919	0.2%
13	Virginia	65,577	2.4%
17	Washington	54,595	2.0%
35	West Virginia	22,752	0.8%
20	Wisconsin	51,264	1.9%
49	Wyoming	4,778	0.2%

RANK	STATE	DEATHS	% of USA
1	California	259,206	9.6%
2	Florida	191,737	7.1%
3	Texas	189,654	7.0%
4	New York	153,628	5.7%
5	Pennsylvania	132,598	4.9%
6	Ohio	118,188	4.4%
7	Illinois	106,872	3.9%
8	Michigan	95,140	3.5%
9	North Carolina	89,133	3.3%
10	Georgia	79,942	2.9%
11	New Jersey	72,271	2.7%
12	Tennessee	66,570	2.5%
13	Virginia	65,577	2.4%
14	Indiana	62,713	2.3%
15	Missouri	59,871	2.2%
16	Massachusetts	57,806	2.1%
17	Washington	54,595	2.0%
18	Arizona	54,299	2.0%
19	Alabama	51,909	1.9%
20	Wisconsin	51,264	1.9%
21	Maryland	47,247	1.7%
22	South Carolina	47,198	1.7%
23	Kentucky	46,564	1.7%
24	Louisiana	43,716	1.6%
25	Minnesota	42,800	1.6%
26	Oklahoma	39,422	1.5%
27	Colorado	36,349	1.3%
28	Oregon	35,705	1.3%
29	Mississippi	31,783	1.2%
30	Arkansas	31,617	1.2%
31	Connecticut	30,535	1.1%
32	Iowa	29,600	1.1%
33	Kansas	26,664	1.0%
34	Nevada	22,879	0.8%
35	West Virginia	22,752	0.8%
36	New Mexico	17,685	0.7%
37	Utah	17,334	0.6%
38	Nebraska	16,740	0.6%
39	Maine	14,479	0.5%
40	Idaho	13,026	0.5%
41	New Hampshire	11,984	0.4%
42	Hawaii	11,053	0.4%
43	Rhode Island	10,163	0.4%
44	Montana	9,942	0.4%
45	Delaware	8,582	0.3%
46	South Dakota	7,731	0.3%
47	North Dakota	6,223	0.2%
48	Vermont	5,919	0.2%
49	Wyoming	4,778	0.2%
50	Alaska	4,316	0.2%
	District of Columbia	4,871	0.2%

Source: U.S. Department of Health and Human Services, National Center for Health Statistics
   "National Vital Statistics Reports" (Vol. 66, No. 6, 2017, http://www.cdc.gov/nchs/deaths.htm)
*Final data by state of residence.

Age-Adjusted Death Rate in 2015

National Rate = 733.1 Deaths per 100,000 Population*

ALPHA ORDER

RANK	STATE	RATE
4	Alabama	924.5
22	Alaska	747.4
42	Arizona	671.8
6	Arkansas	901.8
49	California	621.6
44	Colorado	665.0
46	Connecticut	656.1
24	Delaware	741.5
45	Florida	662.9
13	Georgia	808.1
50	Hawaii	588.2
28	Idaho	727.8
27	Illinois	728.3
10	Indiana	833.9
29	Iowa	724.6
17	Kansas	774.1
3	Kentucky	924.7
8	Louisiana	874.2
16	Maine	783.5
38	Maryland	705.7
41	Massachusetts	684.8
15	Michigan	784.4
47	Minnesota	653.8
1	Mississippi	963.7
12	Missouri	816.9
19	Montana	762.7
26	Nebraska	739.2
20	Nevada	757.2
33	New Hampshire	720.6
43	New Jersey	666.0
24	New Mexico	741.5
48	New York	644.0
14	North Carolina	789.9
39	North Dakota	696.8
11	Ohio	828.4
5	Oklahoma	904.3
30	Oregon	722.3
18	Pennsylvania	768.3
31	Rhode Island	721.9
9	South Carolina	840.0
35	South Dakota	715.4
7	Tennessee	886.4
23	Texas	745.0
37	Utah	712.1
36	Vermont	714.7
32	Virginia	721.6
40	Washington	687.4
2	West Virginia	943.4
34	Wisconsin	715.9
21	Wyoming	748.3

RANK ORDER

RANK	STATE	RATE
1	Mississippi	963.7
2	West Virginia	943.4
3	Kentucky	924.7
4	Alabama	924.5
5	Oklahoma	904.3
6	Arkansas	901.8
7	Tennessee	886.4
8	Louisiana	874.2
9	South Carolina	840.0
10	Indiana	833.9
11	Ohio	828.4
12	Missouri	816.9
13	Georgia	808.1
14	North Carolina	789.9
15	Michigan	784.4
16	Maine	783.5
17	Kansas	774.1
18	Pennsylvania	768.3
19	Montana	762.7
20	Nevada	757.2
21	Wyoming	748.3
22	Alaska	747.4
23	Texas	745.0
24	Delaware	741.5
24	New Mexico	741.5
26	Nebraska	739.2
27	Illinois	728.3
28	Idaho	727.8
29	Iowa	724.6
30	Oregon	722.3
31	Rhode Island	721.9
32	Virginia	721.6
33	New Hampshire	720.6
34	Wisconsin	715.9
35	South Dakota	715.4
36	Vermont	714.7
37	Utah	712.1
38	Maryland	705.7
39	North Dakota	696.8
40	Washington	687.4
41	Massachusetts	684.8
42	Arizona	671.8
43	New Jersey	666.0
44	Colorado	665.0
45	Florida	662.9
46	Connecticut	656.1
47	Minnesota	653.8
48	New York	644.0
49	California	621.6
50	Hawaii	588.2

District of Columbia	748.6

Source: U.S. Department of Health and Human Services, National Center for Health Statistics
"National Vital Statistics Reports" (Vol. 66, No. 6, 2017, http://www.cdc.gov/nchs/deaths.htm)
*Final data by state of residence. Age-adjusted rates eliminate the distorting effects of the aging of the population. Rates based on the year 2000 standard population.

Estimated Deaths by Cancer in 2018

National Estimated Total = 609,640 Deaths

ALPHA ORDER					RANK ORDER			
RANK	STATE	DEATHS	% of USA		RANK	STATE	DEATHS	% of USA
21	Alabama	10,720	1.8%		1	California	60,650	9.9%
49	Alaska	1,120	0.2%		2	Florida	45,030	7.4%
18	Arizona	12,390	2.0%		3	Texas	41,030	6.7%
29	Arkansas	6,910	1.1%		4	New York	35,350	5.8%
1	California	60,650	9.9%		5	Pennsylvania	28,620	4.7%
28	Colorado	8,000	1.3%		6	Ohio	25,740	4.2%
31	Connecticut	6,590	1.1%		7	Illinois	24,670	4.0%
45	Delaware	2,080	0.3%		8	Michigan	21,380	3.5%
2	Florida	45,030	7.4%		9	North Carolina	20,380	3.3%
10	Georgia	17,730	2.9%		10	Georgia	17,730	2.9%
42	Hawaii	2,580	0.4%		11	New Jersey	16,040	2.6%
40	Idaho	3,020	0.5%		12	Virginia	15,260	2.5%
7	Illinois	24,670	4.0%		13	Tennessee	14,900	2.4%
14	Indiana	13,820	2.3%		14	Indiana	13,820	2.3%
32	Iowa	6,570	1.1%		15	Missouri	13,280	2.2%
33	Kansas	5,600	0.9%		16	Washington	13,030	2.1%
23	Kentucky	10,590	1.7%		17	Massachusetts	12,610	2.1%
25	Louisiana	9,370	1.5%		18	Arizona	12,390	2.0%
38	Maine	3,360	0.6%		19	Wisconsin	11,840	1.9%
20	Maryland	10,780	1.8%		20	Maryland	10,780	1.8%
17	Massachusetts	12,610	2.1%		21	Alabama	10,720	1.8%
8	Michigan	21,380	3.5%		22	South Carolina	10,630	1.7%
24	Minnesota	10,080	1.7%		23	Kentucky	10,590	1.7%
30	Mississippi	6,750	1.1%		24	Minnesota	10,080	1.7%
15	Missouri	13,280	2.2%		25	Louisiana	9,370	1.5%
44	Montana	2,110	0.3%		26	Oklahoma	8,470	1.4%
37	Nebraska	3,550	0.6%		27	Oregon	8,310	1.4%
34	Nevada	5,330	0.9%		28	Colorado	8,000	1.3%
41	New Hampshire	2,810	0.5%		29	Arkansas	6,910	1.1%
11	New Jersey	16,040	2.6%		30	Mississippi	6,750	1.1%
36	New Mexico	3,750	0.6%		31	Connecticut	6,590	1.1%
4	New York	35,350	5.8%		32	Iowa	6,570	1.1%
9	North Carolina	20,380	3.3%		33	Kansas	5,600	0.9%
48	North Dakota	1,290	0.2%		34	Nevada	5,330	0.9%
6	Ohio	25,740	4.2%		35	West Virginia	4,900	0.8%
26	Oklahoma	8,470	1.4%		36	New Mexico	3,750	0.6%
27	Oregon	8,310	1.4%		37	Nebraska	3,550	0.6%
5	Pennsylvania	28,620	4.7%		38	Maine	3,360	0.6%
43	Rhode Island	2,180	0.4%		39	Utah	3,270	0.5%
22	South Carolina	10,630	1.7%		40	Idaho	3,020	0.5%
46	South Dakota	1,680	0.3%		41	New Hampshire	2,810	0.5%
13	Tennessee	14,900	2.4%		42	Hawaii	2,580	0.4%
3	Texas	41,030	6.7%		43	Rhode Island	2,180	0.4%
39	Utah	3,270	0.5%		44	Montana	2,110	0.3%
47	Vermont	1,450	0.2%		45	Delaware	2,080	0.3%
12	Virginia	15,260	2.5%		46	South Dakota	1,680	0.3%
16	Washington	13,030	2.1%		47	Vermont	1,450	0.2%
35	West Virginia	4,900	0.8%		48	North Dakota	1,290	0.2%
19	Wisconsin	11,840	1.9%		49	Alaska	1,120	0.2%
50	Wyoming	980	0.2%		50	Wyoming	980	0.2%
						District of Columbia	1,030	0.2%

Source: American Cancer Society
"Cancer Facts & Figures 2018" (Copyright 2018, American Cancer Society, www.cancer.org/research/cancer-facts-statistics.html)

Estimated Death Rate by Cancer in 2018

National Estimated Rate = 187.2 Deaths per 100,000 Population*

ALPHA ORDER

RANK	STATE	RATE
10	Alabama	219.9
47	Alaska	151.4
40	Arizona	176.6
5	Arkansas	230.0
46	California	153.4
49	Colorado	142.7
31	Connecticut	183.7
12	Delaware	216.2
14	Florida	214.6
44	Georgia	170.0
33	Hawaii	180.7
41	Idaho	175.9
27	Illinois	192.7
19	Indiana	207.3
18	Iowa	208.9
28	Kansas	192.2
3	Kentucky	237.8
24	Louisiana	200.0
2	Maine	251.5
36	Maryland	178.1
30	Massachusetts	183.8
14	Michigan	214.6
32	Minnesota	180.8
6	Mississippi	226.2
11	Missouri	217.2
22	Montana	200.9
29	Nebraska	184.9
39	Nevada	177.8
17	New Hampshire	209.3
36	New Jersey	178.1
35	New Mexico	179.6
36	New York	178.1
25	North Carolina	198.4
43	North Dakota	170.8
9	Ohio	220.8
13	Oklahoma	215.5
23	Oregon	200.6
7	Pennsylvania	223.5
20	Rhode Island	205.7
16	South Carolina	211.6
26	South Dakota	193.2
8	Tennessee	221.9
48	Texas	145.0
50	Utah	105.4
4	Vermont	232.5
34	Virginia	180.2
41	Washington	175.9
1	West Virginia	269.8
21	Wisconsin	204.3
45	Wyoming	169.2

RANK ORDER

RANK	STATE	RATE
1	West Virginia	269.8
2	Maine	251.5
3	Kentucky	237.8
4	Vermont	232.5
5	Arkansas	230.0
6	Mississippi	226.2
7	Pennsylvania	223.5
8	Tennessee	221.9
9	Ohio	220.8
10	Alabama	219.9
11	Missouri	217.2
12	Delaware	216.2
13	Oklahoma	215.5
14	Florida	214.6
14	Michigan	214.6
16	South Carolina	211.6
17	New Hampshire	209.3
18	Iowa	208.9
19	Indiana	207.3
20	Rhode Island	205.7
21	Wisconsin	204.3
22	Montana	200.9
23	Oregon	200.6
24	Louisiana	200.0
25	North Carolina	198.4
26	South Dakota	193.2
27	Illinois	192.7
28	Kansas	192.2
29	Nebraska	184.9
30	Massachusetts	183.8
31	Connecticut	183.7
32	Minnesota	180.8
33	Hawaii	180.7
34	Virginia	180.2
35	New Mexico	179.6
36	Maryland	178.1
36	New Jersey	178.1
36	New York	178.1
39	Nevada	177.8
40	Arizona	176.6
41	Idaho	175.9
41	Washington	175.9
43	North Dakota	170.8
44	Georgia	170.0
45	Wyoming	169.2
46	California	153.4
47	Alaska	151.4
48	Texas	145.0
49	Colorado	142.7
50	Utah	105.4

District of Columbia	148.4

Source: CQ Press using data from American Cancer Society
"Cancer Facts & Figures 2018" (Copyright 2018, American Cancer Society, www.cancer.org/research/cancer-facts-statistics.html)
*Rates calculated using 2017 Census resident population estimates. Not age-adjusted.

Estimated New Cancer Cases in 2018

National Estimated Total = 1,735,350 New Cases*

ALPHA ORDER

RANK	STATE	CASES	% of USA
23	Alabama	27,830	1.6%
49	Alaska	3,550	0.2%
18	Arizona	34,740	2.0%
32	Arkansas	16,130	0.9%
1	California	178,130	10.3%
25	Colorado	25,570	1.5%
28	Connecticut	21,240	1.2%
43	Delaware	6,110	0.4%
2	Florida	135,170	7.8%
8	Georgia	56,920	3.3%
42	Hawaii	6,280	0.4%
40	Idaho	8,450	0.5%
7	Illinois	66,330	3.8%
13	Indiana	37,250	2.1%
31	Iowa	17,630	1.0%
33	Kansas	15,400	0.9%
24	Kentucky	25,990	1.5%
26	Louisiana	25,080	1.4%
39	Maine	8,600	0.5%
19	Maryland	33,810	1.9%
14	Massachusetts	37,130	2.1%
9	Michigan	56,590	3.3%
21	Minnesota	31,270	1.8%
30	Mississippi	18,130	1.0%
17	Missouri	35,520	2.0%
44	Montana	6,080	0.4%
37	Nebraska	10,320	0.6%
34	Nevada	14,060	0.8%
41	New Hampshire	8,080	0.5%
11	New Jersey	53,260	3.1%
38	New Mexico	9,730	0.6%
4	New York	110,800	6.4%
10	North Carolina	55,130	3.2%
47	North Dakota	4,110	0.2%
6	Ohio	68,470	3.9%
29	Oklahoma	19,030	1.1%
27	Oregon	21,520	1.2%
5	Pennsylvania	80,960	4.7%
45	Rhode Island	5,920	0.3%
22	South Carolina	30,450	1.8%
46	South Dakota	5,100	0.3%
15	Tennessee	36,760	2.1%
3	Texas	121,860	7.0%
36	Utah	10,950	0.6%
48	Vermont	3,840	0.2%
12	Virginia	42,420	2.4%
16	Washington	36,170	2.1%
35	West Virginia	12,110	0.7%
20	Wisconsin	33,340	1.9%
50	Wyoming	2,780	0.2%

RANK ORDER

RANK	STATE	CASES	% of USA
1	California	178,130	10.3%
2	Florida	135,170	7.8%
3	Texas	121,860	7.0%
4	New York	110,800	6.4%
5	Pennsylvania	80,960	4.7%
6	Ohio	68,470	3.9%
7	Illinois	66,330	3.8%
8	Georgia	56,920	3.3%
9	Michigan	56,590	3.3%
10	North Carolina	55,130	3.2%
11	New Jersey	53,260	3.1%
12	Virginia	42,420	2.4%
13	Indiana	37,250	2.1%
14	Massachusetts	37,130	2.1%
15	Tennessee	36,760	2.1%
16	Washington	36,170	2.1%
17	Missouri	35,520	2.0%
18	Arizona	34,740	2.0%
19	Maryland	33,810	1.9%
20	Wisconsin	33,340	1.9%
21	Minnesota	31,270	1.8%
22	South Carolina	30,450	1.8%
23	Alabama	27,830	1.6%
24	Kentucky	25,990	1.5%
25	Colorado	25,570	1.5%
26	Louisiana	25,080	1.4%
27	Oregon	21,520	1.2%
28	Connecticut	21,240	1.2%
29	Oklahoma	19,030	1.1%
30	Mississippi	18,130	1.0%
31	Iowa	17,630	1.0%
32	Arkansas	16,130	0.9%
33	Kansas	15,400	0.9%
34	Nevada	14,060	0.8%
35	West Virginia	12,110	0.7%
36	Utah	10,950	0.6%
37	Nebraska	10,320	0.6%
38	New Mexico	9,730	0.6%
39	Maine	8,600	0.5%
40	Idaho	8,450	0.5%
41	New Hampshire	8,080	0.5%
42	Hawaii	6,280	0.4%
43	Delaware	6,110	0.4%
44	Montana	6,080	0.4%
45	Rhode Island	5,920	0.3%
46	South Dakota	5,100	0.3%
47	North Dakota	4,110	0.2%
48	Vermont	3,840	0.2%
49	Alaska	3,550	0.2%
50	Wyoming	2,780	0.2%
	District of Columbia	3,260	0.2%

Source: American Cancer Society
"Cancer Facts & Figures 2018" (Copyright 2018, American Cancer Society, www.cancer.org/research/cancer-facts-statistics.html)
*These estimates are offered as a rough guide and should not be regarded as definitive. They are calculated by the American Cancer Society using a model based on 2000-2014 incidence data. Totals do not include basal and squamous cell skin cancers or in situ carcinomas except urinary bladder.

Estimated Rate of New Cancer Cases in 2018

National Estimated Rate = 532.8 New Cases per 100,000 Population*

ALPHA ORDER

RANK ORDER

RANK	STATE	RATE	RANK	STATE	RATE
18	Alabama	570.9	1	West Virginia	666.9
42	Alaska	479.9	2	Florida	644.1
38	Arizona	495.1	3	Maine	643.8
31	Arkansas	536.9	4	Delaware	635.2
47	California	450.5	5	Pennsylvania	632.2
46	Colorado	456.0	6	Vermont	615.7
10	Connecticut	591.9	7	Mississippi	607.6
4	Delaware	635.2	8	South Carolina	606.0
2	Florida	644.1	9	New Hampshire	601.7
27	Georgia	545.8	10	Connecticut	591.9
48	Hawaii	439.9	11	New Jersey	591.4
39	Idaho	492.2	12	Ohio	587.3
36	Illinois	518.1	13	South Dakota	586.4
22	Indiana	558.7	14	Kentucky	583.5
21	Iowa	560.4	15	Missouri	581.0
34	Kansas	528.6	16	Montana	578.8
14	Kentucky	583.5	17	Wisconsin	575.3
33	Louisiana	535.4	18	Alabama	570.9
3	Maine	643.8	19	Michigan	568.0
24	Maryland	558.6	20	Minnesota	560.7
29	Massachusetts	541.3	21	Iowa	560.4
19	Michigan	568.0	22	Indiana	558.7
20	Minnesota	560.7	22	Rhode Island	558.7
7	Mississippi	607.6	24	Maryland	558.6
15	Missouri	581.0	25	New York	558.2
16	Montana	578.8	26	Tennessee	547.4
30	Nebraska	537.5	27	Georgia	545.8
44	Nevada	469.0	28	North Dakota	544.1
9	New Hampshire	601.7	29	Massachusetts	541.3
11	New Jersey	591.4	30	Nebraska	537.5
45	New Mexico	466.0	31	Arkansas	536.9
25	New York	558.2	32	North Carolina	536.6
32	North Carolina	536.6	33	Louisiana	535.4
28	North Dakota	544.1	34	Kansas	528.6
12	Ohio	587.3	35	Oregon	519.5
41	Oklahoma	484.1	36	Illinois	518.1
35	Oregon	519.5	37	Virginia	500.8
5	Pennsylvania	632.2	38	Arizona	495.1
22	Rhode Island	558.7	39	Idaho	492.2
8	South Carolina	606.0	40	Washington	488.4
13	South Dakota	586.4	41	Oklahoma	484.1
26	Tennessee	547.4	42	Alaska	479.9
49	Texas	430.5	42	Wyoming	479.9
50	Utah	353.0	44	Nevada	469.0
6	Vermont	615.7	45	New Mexico	466.0
37	Virginia	500.8	46	Colorado	456.0
40	Washington	488.4	47	California	450.5
1	West Virginia	666.9	48	Hawaii	439.9
17	Wisconsin	575.3	49	Texas	430.5
42	Wyoming	479.9	50	Utah	353.0

District of Columbia 469.8

Source: CQ Press using data from American Cancer Society
"Cancer Facts & Figures 2018" (Copyright 2018, American Cancer Society, www.cancer.org/research/cancer-facts-statistics.html)
*These estimates are offered as a rough guide and should not be regarded as definitive. They are calculated by the American
Cancer Society using a model based on 2000-2014 incidence data. Totals do not include basal and squamous cell skin cancers
or in situ carcinomas except urinary bladder. Rates calculated using 2017 Census resident population estimates.

Deaths by Accidents in 2015

National Total = 146,571 Deaths*

ALPHA ORDER

RANK	STATE	DEATHS	% of USA
25	Alabama	2,552	1.7%
48	Alaska	388	0.3%
12	Arizona	3,539	2.4%
31	Arkansas	1,538	1.0%
1	California	12,544	8.6%
22	Colorado	2,725	1.9%
30	Connecticut	1,799	1.2%
46	Delaware	449	0.3%
2	Florida	10,578	7.2%
10	Georgia	4,344	3.0%
44	Hawaii	536	0.4%
41	Idaho	746	0.5%
8	Illinois	4,850	3.3%
15	Indiana	3,258	2.2%
32	Iowa	1,537	1.0%
34	Kansas	1,475	1.0%
20	Kentucky	2,962	2.0%
23	Louisiana	2,578	1.8%
39	Maine	802	0.5%
28	Maryland	1,903	1.3%
16	Massachusetts	3,229	2.2%
9	Michigan	4,647	3.2%
24	Minnesota	2,574	1.8%
29	Mississippi	1,814	1.2%
14	Missouri	3,309	2.3%
43	Montana	637	0.4%
40	Nebraska	799	0.5%
36	Nevada	1,340	0.9%
38	New Hampshire	815	0.6%
17	New Jersey	3,218	2.2%
35	New Mexico	1,430	1.0%
6	New York	6,515	4.4%
7	North Carolina	4,991	3.4%
49	North Dakota	368	0.3%
5	Ohio	6,756	4.6%
26	Oklahoma	2,422	1.7%
27	Oregon	1,999	1.4%
4	Pennsylvania	7,324	5.0%
42	Rhode Island	649	0.4%
21	South Carolina	2,737	1.9%
45	South Dakota	469	0.3%
11	Tennessee	3,873	2.6%
3	Texas	9,976	6.8%
37	Utah	1,223	0.8%
50	Vermont	346	0.2%
13	Virginia	3,429	2.3%
19	Washington	3,192	2.2%
33	West Virginia	1,516	1.0%
18	Wisconsin	3,206	2.2%
47	Wyoming	400	0.3%

RANK ORDER

RANK	STATE	DEATHS	% of USA
1	California	12,544	8.6%
2	Florida	10,578	7.2%
3	Texas	9,976	6.8%
4	Pennsylvania	7,324	5.0%
5	Ohio	6,756	4.6%
6	New York	6,515	4.4%
7	North Carolina	4,991	3.4%
8	Illinois	4,850	3.3%
9	Michigan	4,647	3.2%
10	Georgia	4,344	3.0%
11	Tennessee	3,873	2.6%
12	Arizona	3,539	2.4%
13	Virginia	3,429	2.3%
14	Missouri	3,309	2.3%
15	Indiana	3,258	2.2%
16	Massachusetts	3,229	2.2%
17	New Jersey	3,218	2.2%
18	Wisconsin	3,206	2.2%
19	Washington	3,192	2.2%
20	Kentucky	2,962	2.0%
21	South Carolina	2,737	1.9%
22	Colorado	2,725	1.9%
23	Louisiana	2,578	1.8%
24	Minnesota	2,574	1.8%
25	Alabama	2,552	1.7%
26	Oklahoma	2,422	1.7%
27	Oregon	1,999	1.4%
28	Maryland	1,903	1.3%
29	Mississippi	1,814	1.2%
30	Connecticut	1,799	1.2%
31	Arkansas	1,538	1.0%
32	Iowa	1,537	1.0%
33	West Virginia	1,516	1.0%
34	Kansas	1,475	1.0%
35	New Mexico	1,430	1.0%
36	Nevada	1,340	0.9%
37	Utah	1,223	0.8%
38	New Hampshire	815	0.6%
39	Maine	802	0.5%
40	Nebraska	799	0.5%
41	Idaho	746	0.5%
42	Rhode Island	649	0.4%
43	Montana	637	0.4%
44	Hawaii	536	0.4%
45	South Dakota	469	0.3%
46	Delaware	449	0.3%
47	Wyoming	400	0.3%
48	Alaska	388	0.3%
49	North Dakota	368	0.3%
50	Vermont	346	0.2%
	District of Columbia	265	0.2%

Source: U.S. Department of Health and Human Services, National Center for Health Statistics
"National Vital Statistics Reports" (Vol. 66, No. 6, 2017, http://www.cdc.gov/nchs/deaths.htm)
*Final data by state of residence. Includes motor vehicle deaths, poisoning, falls, drowning, and other accidents.

Age-Adjusted Death Rate by Accidents in 2015

National Rate = 43.2 Deaths per 100,000 Population*

ALPHA ORDER

RANK	STATE	RATE
17	Alabama	50.9
8	Alaska	57.9
23	Arizona	49.2
20	Arkansas	49.6
48	California	30.6
19	Colorado	49.7
32	Connecticut	44.8
29	Delaware	46.0
28	Florida	46.2
38	Georgia	43.2
47	Hawaii	32.2
33	Idaho	44.7
45	Illinois	35.8
26	Indiana	47.7
39	Iowa	42.1
27	Kansas	47.2
3	Kentucky	66.0
12	Louisiana	54.7
14	Maine	53.8
50	Maryland	29.7
36	Massachusetts	44.0
37	Michigan	43.9
40	Minnesota	42.0
6	Mississippi	59.8
17	Missouri	50.9
10	Montana	56.3
43	Nebraska	38.9
31	Nevada	45.4
7	New Hampshire	59.0
46	New Jersey	33.7
2	New Mexico	67.3
49	New York	30.2
25	North Carolina	47.9
35	North Dakota	44.1
11	Ohio	55.9
5	Oklahoma	60.1
34	Oregon	44.5
16	Pennsylvania	52.0
15	Rhode Island	53.1
13	South Carolina	54.0
21	South Dakota	49.5
9	Tennessee	56.4
44	Texas	37.4
30	Utah	45.6
24	Vermont	48.4
42	Virginia	39.6
41	Washington	41.9
1	West Virginia	77.9
22	Wisconsin	49.3
4	Wyoming	65.8

RANK ORDER

RANK	STATE	RATE
1	West Virginia	77.9
2	New Mexico	67.3
3	Kentucky	66.0
4	Wyoming	65.8
5	Oklahoma	60.1
6	Mississippi	59.8
7	New Hampshire	59.0
8	Alaska	57.9
9	Tennessee	56.4
10	Montana	56.3
11	Ohio	55.9
12	Louisiana	54.7
13	South Carolina	54.0
14	Maine	53.8
15	Rhode Island	53.1
16	Pennsylvania	52.0
17	Alabama	50.9
17	Missouri	50.9
19	Colorado	49.7
20	Arkansas	49.6
21	South Dakota	49.5
22	Wisconsin	49.3
23	Arizona	49.2
24	Vermont	48.4
25	North Carolina	47.9
26	Indiana	47.7
27	Kansas	47.2
28	Florida	46.2
29	Delaware	46.0
30	Utah	45.6
31	Nevada	45.4
32	Connecticut	44.8
33	Idaho	44.7
34	Oregon	44.5
35	North Dakota	44.1
36	Massachusetts	44.0
37	Michigan	43.9
38	Georgia	43.2
39	Iowa	42.1
40	Minnesota	42.0
41	Washington	41.9
42	Virginia	39.6
43	Nebraska	38.9
44	Texas	37.4
45	Illinois	35.8
46	New Jersey	33.7
47	Hawaii	32.2
48	California	30.6
49	New York	30.2
50	Maryland	29.7

District of Columbia 40.2

Source: U.S. Department of Health and Human Services, National Center for Health Statistics
"National Vital Statistics Reports" (Vol. 66, No. 6, 2017, http://www.cdc.gov/nchs/deaths.htm)
*Final data by state of residence. Includes motor vehicle deaths, poisoning, falls, drowning, and other accidents. Age-adjusted rates based on the year 2000 standard population.

Deaths by Cerebrovascular Diseases in 2015

National Total = 140,323 Deaths*

ALPHA ORDER

RANK	STATE	DEATHS	% of USA
16	Alabama	2,937	2.1%
50	Alaska	182	0.1%
21	Arizona	2,522	1.8%
30	Arkansas	1,653	1.2%
1	California	15,065	10.7%
28	Colorado	1,856	1.3%
32	Connecticut	1,388	1.0%
42	Delaware	466	0.3%
2	Florida	11,433	8.1%
10	Georgia	4,335	3.1%
39	Hawaii	735	0.5%
40	Idaho	641	0.5%
7	Illinois	5,709	4.1%
15	Indiana	2,959	2.1%
31	Iowa	1,418	1.0%
33	Kansas	1,364	1.0%
25	Kentucky	2,050	1.5%
23	Louisiana	2,280	1.6%
41	Maine	616	0.4%
20	Maryland	2,540	1.8%
22	Massachusetts	2,475	1.8%
9	Michigan	4,666	3.3%
24	Minnesota	2,238	1.6%
29	Mississippi	1,734	1.2%
14	Missouri	3,037	2.2%
43	Montana	458	0.3%
38	Nebraska	776	0.6%
35	Nevada	1,078	0.8%
44	New Hampshire	457	0.3%
12	New Jersey	3,413	2.4%
37	New Mexico	786	0.6%
5	New York	6,292	4.5%
8	North Carolina	5,033	3.6%
47	North Dakota	308	0.2%
6	Ohio	5,945	4.2%
26	Oklahoma	1,881	1.3%
27	Oregon	1,873	1.3%
4	Pennsylvania	6,987	5.0%
45	Rhode Island	394	0.3%
19	South Carolina	2,600	1.9%
46	South Dakota	383	0.3%
11	Tennessee	3,447	2.5%
3	Texas	10,485	7.5%
36	Utah	888	0.6%
48	Vermont	307	0.2%
13	Virginia	3,393	2.4%
17	Washington	2,703	1.9%
34	West Virginia	1,079	0.8%
18	Wisconsin	2,618	1.9%
49	Wyoming	198	0.1%

RANK ORDER

RANK	STATE	DEATHS	% of USA
1	California	15,065	10.7%
2	Florida	11,433	8.1%
3	Texas	10,485	7.5%
4	Pennsylvania	6,987	5.0%
5	New York	6,292	4.5%
6	Ohio	5,945	4.2%
7	Illinois	5,709	4.1%
8	North Carolina	5,033	3.6%
9	Michigan	4,666	3.3%
10	Georgia	4,335	3.1%
11	Tennessee	3,447	2.5%
12	New Jersey	3,413	2.4%
13	Virginia	3,393	2.4%
14	Missouri	3,037	2.2%
15	Indiana	2,959	2.1%
16	Alabama	2,937	2.1%
17	Washington	2,703	1.9%
18	Wisconsin	2,618	1.9%
19	South Carolina	2,600	1.9%
20	Maryland	2,540	1.8%
21	Arizona	2,522	1.8%
22	Massachusetts	2,475	1.8%
23	Louisiana	2,280	1.6%
24	Minnesota	2,238	1.6%
25	Kentucky	2,050	1.5%
26	Oklahoma	1,881	1.3%
27	Oregon	1,873	1.3%
28	Colorado	1,856	1.3%
29	Mississippi	1,734	1.2%
30	Arkansas	1,653	1.2%
31	Iowa	1,418	1.0%
32	Connecticut	1,388	1.0%
33	Kansas	1,364	1.0%
34	West Virginia	1,079	0.8%
35	Nevada	1,078	0.8%
36	Utah	888	0.6%
37	New Mexico	786	0.6%
38	Nebraska	776	0.6%
39	Hawaii	735	0.5%
40	Idaho	641	0.5%
41	Maine	616	0.4%
42	Delaware	466	0.3%
43	Montana	458	0.3%
44	New Hampshire	457	0.3%
45	Rhode Island	394	0.3%
46	South Dakota	383	0.3%
47	North Dakota	308	0.2%
48	Vermont	307	0.2%
49	Wyoming	198	0.1%
50	Alaska	182	0.1%
	District of Columbia	242	0.2%

Source: U.S. Department of Health and Human Services, National Center for Health Statistics
"National Vital Statistics Reports" (Vol. 66, No. 6, 2017, http://www.cdc.gov/nchs/deaths.htm)
*Final data by state of residence. Cerebrovascular diseases include stroke and other disorders of the blood vessels of the brain.

Age-Adjusted Death Rate by Cerebrovascular Diseases in 2015

National Rate = 37.6 Deaths per 100,000 Population*

ALPHA ORDER

RANK	STATE	RATE
2	Alabama	52.2
28	Alaska	36.8
45	Arizona	30.7
3	Arkansas	46.8
31	California	36.2
33	Colorado	34.9
46	Connecticut	28.5
15	Delaware	39.4
26	Florida	37.1
7	Georgia	45.3
21	Hawaii	38.2
30	Idaho	36.3
19	Illinois	38.4
16	Indiana	39.1
39	Iowa	33.2
18	Kansas	38.6
12	Kentucky	40.8
5	Louisiana	46.0
41	Maine	32.6
23	Maryland	37.8
47	Massachusetts	28.4
24	Michigan	37.6
36	Minnesota	33.5
1	Mississippi	52.6
12	Missouri	40.8
35	Montana	33.8
37	Nebraska	33.4
27	Nevada	37.0
49	New Hampshire	26.9
44	New Jersey	31.1
42	New Mexico	32.5
50	New York	26.0
8	North Carolina	44.7
37	North Dakota	33.4
14	Ohio	40.7
10	Oklahoma	43.0
25	Oregon	37.5
17	Pennsylvania	38.8
48	Rhode Island	27.1
4	South Carolina	46.7
39	South Dakota	33.2
5	Tennessee	46.0
11	Texas	42.7
19	Utah	38.4
29	Vermont	36.4
22	Virginia	38.0
34	Washington	34.2
9	West Virginia	43.8
32	Wisconsin	35.6
43	Wyoming	31.4

RANK ORDER

RANK	STATE	RATE
1	Mississippi	52.6
2	Alabama	52.2
3	Arkansas	46.8
4	South Carolina	46.7
5	Louisiana	46.0
5	Tennessee	46.0
7	Georgia	45.3
8	North Carolina	44.7
9	West Virginia	43.8
10	Oklahoma	43.0
11	Texas	42.7
12	Kentucky	40.8
12	Missouri	40.8
14	Ohio	40.7
15	Delaware	39.4
16	Indiana	39.1
17	Pennsylvania	38.8
18	Kansas	38.6
19	Illinois	38.4
19	Utah	38.4
21	Hawaii	38.2
22	Virginia	38.0
23	Maryland	37.8
24	Michigan	37.6
25	Oregon	37.5
26	Florida	37.1
27	Nevada	37.0
28	Alaska	36.8
29	Vermont	36.4
30	Idaho	36.3
31	California	36.2
32	Wisconsin	35.6
33	Colorado	34.9
34	Washington	34.2
35	Montana	33.8
36	Minnesota	33.5
37	Nebraska	33.4
37	North Dakota	33.4
39	Iowa	33.2
39	South Dakota	33.2
41	Maine	32.6
42	New Mexico	32.5
43	Wyoming	31.4
44	New Jersey	31.1
45	Arizona	30.7
46	Connecticut	28.5
47	Massachusetts	28.4
48	Rhode Island	27.1
49	New Hampshire	26.9
50	New York	26.0

	District of Columbia	38.3

Source: U.S. Department of Health and Human Services, National Center for Health Statistics
"National Vital Statistics Reports" (Vol. 66, No. 6, 2017, http://www.cdc.gov/nchs/deaths.htm)
*Final data by state of residence. Cerebrovascular diseases include stroke and other disorders of the blood vessels of the brain. Age-adjusted rates based on the year 2000 standard population.

Deaths by Diseases of the Heart in 2015

National Total = 633,842 Deaths*

ALPHA ORDER

ALPHA ORDER

RANK	STATE	DEATHS	% of USA
16	Alabama	12,981	2.0%
50	Alaska	846	0.1%
20	Arizona	11,458	1.8%
27	Arkansas	7,938	1.3%
1	California	61,289	9.7%
30	Colorado	7,009	1.1%
29	Connecticut	7,205	1.1%
45	Delaware	1,940	0.3%
2	Florida	45,441	7.2%
11	Georgia	17,769	2.8%
41	Hawaii	2,605	0.4%
40	Idaho	2,825	0.4%
7	Illinois	25,652	4.0%
15	Indiana	13,948	2.2%
32	Iowa	6,813	1.1%
34	Kansas	5,624	0.9%
25	Kentucky	10,077	1.6%
22	Louisiana	10,665	1.7%
39	Maine	3,009	0.5%
18	Maryland	11,481	1.8%
17	Massachusetts	12,130	1.9%
8	Michigan	24,794	3.9%
28	Minnesota	7,844	1.2%
26	Mississippi	7,969	1.3%
13	Missouri	14,808	2.3%
44	Montana	2,104	0.3%
37	Nebraska	3,591	0.6%
33	Nevada	6,114	1.0%
42	New Hampshire	2,571	0.4%
9	New Jersey	18,647	2.9%
38	New Mexico	3,508	0.6%
3	New York	44,450	7.0%
10	North Carolina	18,474	2.9%
47	North Dakota	1,323	0.2%
6	Ohio	28,069	4.4%
23	Oklahoma	10,310	1.6%
31	Oregon	6,859	1.1%
5	Pennsylvania	32,042	5.1%
43	Rhode Island	2,371	0.4%
24	South Carolina	10,092	1.6%
46	South Dakota	1,711	0.3%
12	Tennessee	15,730	2.5%
4	Texas	43,298	6.8%
36	Utah	3,598	0.6%
48	Vermont	1,311	0.2%
14	Virginia	14,077	2.2%
21	Washington	11,025	1.7%
35	West Virginia	4,727	0.7%
19	Wisconsin	11,473	1.8%
49	Wyoming	1,030	0.2%

RANK ORDER

RANK	STATE	DEATHS	% of USA
1	California	61,289	9.7%
2	Florida	45,441	7.2%
3	New York	44,450	7.0%
4	Texas	43,298	6.8%
5	Pennsylvania	32,042	5.1%
6	Ohio	28,069	4.4%
7	Illinois	25,652	4.0%
8	Michigan	24,794	3.9%
9	New Jersey	18,647	2.9%
10	North Carolina	18,474	2.9%
11	Georgia	17,769	2.8%
12	Tennessee	15,730	2.5%
13	Missouri	14,808	2.3%
14	Virginia	14,077	2.2%
15	Indiana	13,948	2.2%
16	Alabama	12,981	2.0%
17	Massachusetts	12,130	1.9%
18	Maryland	11,481	1.8%
19	Wisconsin	11,473	1.8%
20	Arizona	11,458	1.8%
21	Washington	11,025	1.7%
22	Louisiana	10,665	1.7%
23	Oklahoma	10,310	1.6%
24	South Carolina	10,092	1.6%
25	Kentucky	10,077	1.6%
26	Mississippi	7,969	1.3%
27	Arkansas	7,938	1.3%
28	Minnesota	7,844	1.2%
29	Connecticut	7,205	1.1%
30	Colorado	7,009	1.1%
31	Oregon	6,859	1.1%
32	Iowa	6,813	1.1%
33	Nevada	6,114	1.0%
34	Kansas	5,624	0.9%
35	West Virginia	4,727	0.7%
36	Utah	3,598	0.6%
37	Nebraska	3,591	0.6%
38	New Mexico	3,508	0.6%
39	Maine	3,009	0.5%
40	Idaho	2,825	0.4%
41	Hawaii	2,605	0.4%
42	New Hampshire	2,571	0.4%
43	Rhode Island	2,371	0.4%
44	Montana	2,104	0.3%
45	Delaware	1,940	0.3%
46	South Dakota	1,711	0.3%
47	North Dakota	1,323	0.2%
48	Vermont	1,311	0.2%
49	Wyoming	1,030	0.2%
50	Alaska	846	0.1%
	District of Columbia	1,217	0.2%

Source: U.S. Department of Health and Human Services, National Center for Health Statistics
"National Vital Statistics Reports" (Vol. 66, No. 6, 2017, http://www.cdc.gov/nchs/deaths.htm)
*Final data by state of residence.

Age-Adjusted Death Rate by Diseases of the Heart in 2015

National Rate = 168.5 Deaths per 100,000 Population*

ALPHA ORDER

RANK	STATE	RATE
3	Alabama	229.7
34	Alaska	154.1
44	Arizona	138.8
4	Arkansas	223.2
41	California	145.6
49	Colorado	128.4
40	Connecticut	147.8
22	Delaware	165.2
38	Florida	149.8
15	Georgia	180.2
48	Hawaii	135.6
29	Idaho	156.4
19	Illinois	171.5
13	Indiana	182.3
24	Iowa	160.9
27	Kansas	158.5
10	Kentucky	197.8
5	Louisiana	212.1
28	Maine	157.3
20	Maryland	169.3
45	Massachusetts	138.5
8	Michigan	198.9
50	Minnesota	116.6
1	Mississippi	240.5
9	Missouri	197.9
31	Montana	155.8
32	Nebraska	154.5
7	Nevada	200.9
39	New Hampshire	149.0
21	New Jersey	166.7
42	New Mexico	142.4
14	New York	181.6
23	North Carolina	162.4
42	North Dakota	142.4
11	Ohio	191.7
2	Oklahoma	234.0
47	Oregon	136.1
16	Pennsylvania	177.8
25	Rhode Island	160.4
16	South Carolina	177.8
37	South Dakota	150.9
6	Tennessee	207.3
18	Texas	171.6
35	Utah	152.9
36	Vermont	152.5
33	Virginia	154.2
46	Washington	137.6
12	West Virginia	191.3
30	Wisconsin	156.0
26	Wyoming	159.4

RANK ORDER

RANK	STATE	RATE
1	Mississippi	240.5
2	Oklahoma	234.0
3	Alabama	229.7
4	Arkansas	223.2
5	Louisiana	212.1
6	Tennessee	207.3
7	Nevada	200.9
8	Michigan	198.9
9	Missouri	197.9
10	Kentucky	197.8
11	Ohio	191.7
12	West Virginia	191.3
13	Indiana	182.3
14	New York	181.6
15	Georgia	180.2
16	Pennsylvania	177.8
16	South Carolina	177.8
18	Texas	171.6
19	Illinois	171.5
20	Maryland	169.3
21	New Jersey	166.7
22	Delaware	165.2
23	North Carolina	162.4
24	Iowa	160.9
25	Rhode Island	160.4
26	Wyoming	159.4
27	Kansas	158.5
28	Maine	157.3
29	Idaho	156.4
30	Wisconsin	156.0
31	Montana	155.8
32	Nebraska	154.5
33	Virginia	154.2
34	Alaska	154.1
35	Utah	152.9
36	Vermont	152.5
37	South Dakota	150.9
38	Florida	149.8
39	New Hampshire	149.0
40	Connecticut	147.8
41	California	145.6
42	New Mexico	142.4
42	North Dakota	142.4
44	Arizona	138.8
45	Massachusetts	138.5
46	Washington	137.6
47	Oregon	136.1
48	Hawaii	135.6
49	Colorado	128.4
50	Minnesota	116.6

District of Columbia	187.6

Source: U.S. Department of Health and Human Services, National Center for Health Statistics
"National Vital Statistics Reports" (Vol. 66, No. 6, 2017, http://www.cdc.gov/nchs/deaths.htm)
*Final data by state of residence. Age-adjusted rates based on the year 2000 standard population.

Deaths by Suicide in 2015

National Total = 44,193 Suicides*

ALPHA ORDER

RANK	STATE	DEATHS	% of USA
23	Alabama	750	1.7%
43	Alaska	201	0.5%
11	Arizona	1,276	2.9%
29	Arkansas	577	1.3%
1	California	4,167	9.4%
14	Colorado	1,093	2.5%
36	Connecticut	384	0.9%
49	Delaware	122	0.3%
3	Florida	3,205	7.3%
10	Georgia	1,317	3.0%
43	Hawaii	201	0.5%
37	Idaho	359	0.8%
9	Illinois	1,363	3.1%
17	Indiana	960	2.2%
34	Iowa	433	1.0%
33	Kansas	477	1.1%
21	Kentucky	776	1.8%
26	Louisiana	722	1.6%
40	Maine	235	0.5%
31	Maryland	553	1.3%
27	Massachusetts	642	1.5%
7	Michigan	1,410	3.2%
25	Minnesota	730	1.7%
35	Mississippi	431	1.0%
16	Missouri	1,052	2.4%
39	Montana	272	0.6%
42	Nebraska	223	0.5%
30	Nevada	558	1.3%
41	New Hampshire	228	0.5%
20	New Jersey	789	1.8%
32	New Mexico	500	1.1%
5	New York	1,652	3.7%
8	North Carolina	1,406	3.2%
48	North Dakota	124	0.3%
6	Ohio	1,650	3.7%
19	Oklahoma	790	1.8%
22	Oregon	762	1.7%
4	Pennsylvania	1,894	4.3%
47	Rhode Island	127	0.3%
24	South Carolina	742	1.7%
45	South Dakota	173	0.4%
15	Tennessee	1,068	2.4%
2	Texas	3,403	7.7%
28	Utah	630	1.4%
50	Vermont	103	0.2%
13	Virginia	1,118	2.5%
12	Washington	1,137	2.6%
38	West Virginia	340	0.8%
18	Wisconsin	877	2.0%
46	Wyoming	157	0.4%

RANK ORDER

RANK	STATE	DEATHS	% of USA
1	California	4,167	9.4%
2	Texas	3,403	7.7%
3	Florida	3,205	7.3%
4	Pennsylvania	1,894	4.3%
5	New York	1,652	3.7%
6	Ohio	1,650	3.7%
7	Michigan	1,410	3.2%
8	North Carolina	1,406	3.2%
9	Illinois	1,363	3.1%
10	Georgia	1,317	3.0%
11	Arizona	1,276	2.9%
12	Washington	1,137	2.6%
13	Virginia	1,118	2.5%
14	Colorado	1,093	2.5%
15	Tennessee	1,068	2.4%
16	Missouri	1,052	2.4%
17	Indiana	960	2.2%
18	Wisconsin	877	2.0%
19	Oklahoma	790	1.8%
20	New Jersey	789	1.8%
21	Kentucky	776	1.8%
22	Oregon	762	1.7%
23	Alabama	750	1.7%
24	South Carolina	742	1.7%
25	Minnesota	730	1.7%
26	Louisiana	722	1.6%
27	Massachusetts	642	1.5%
28	Utah	630	1.4%
29	Arkansas	577	1.3%
30	Nevada	558	1.3%
31	Maryland	553	1.3%
32	New Mexico	500	1.1%
33	Kansas	477	1.1%
34	Iowa	433	1.0%
35	Mississippi	431	1.0%
36	Connecticut	384	0.9%
37	Idaho	359	0.8%
38	West Virginia	340	0.8%
39	Montana	272	0.6%
40	Maine	235	0.5%
41	New Hampshire	228	0.5%
42	Nebraska	223	0.5%
43	Alaska	201	0.5%
43	Hawaii	201	0.5%
45	South Dakota	173	0.4%
46	Wyoming	157	0.4%
47	Rhode Island	127	0.3%
48	North Dakota	124	0.3%
49	Delaware	122	0.3%
50	Vermont	103	0.2%
	District of Columbia	34	0.1%

Source: U.S. Department of Health and Human Services, National Center for Health Statistics
"National Vital Statistics Reports" (Vol. 66, No. 6, 2017, http://www.cdc.gov/nchs/deaths.htm)
*Final data by state of residence. Also referred to as "Intentional self-harm."

Age-Adjusted Death Rate by Suicide in 2015

National Rate = 13.3 Deaths per 100,000 Population*

<u>ALPHA ORDER</u>

RANK	STATE	RATE
24	Alabama	14.9
2	Alaska	26.9
12	Arizona	18.2
10	Arkansas	19.1
44	California	10.3
9	Colorado	19.5
46	Connecticut	9.9
40	Delaware	12.6
28	Florida	14.4
38	Georgia	12.7
35	Hawaii	13.5
6	Idaho	22.1
44	Illinois	10.3
28	Indiana	14.4
32	Iowa	13.9
19	Kansas	16.3
16	Kentucky	17.1
23	Louisiana	15.2
20	Maine	16.0
48	Maryland	8.8
47	Massachusetts	8.9
34	Michigan	13.8
37	Minnesota	13.2
30	Mississippi	14.0
16	Missouri	17.1
3	Montana	25.3
42	Nebraska	11.7
11	Nevada	18.4
18	New Hampshire	16.5
49	New Jersey	8.3
4	New Mexico	23.7
50	New York	7.8
36	North Carolina	13.4
14	North Dakota	17.5
32	Ohio	13.9
8	Oklahoma	20.3
13	Oregon	17.8
30	Pennsylvania	14.0
43	Rhode Island	11.2
25	South Carolina	14.8
7	South Dakota	20.4
21	Tennessee	15.7
41	Texas	12.5
5	Utah	22.4
25	Vermont	14.8
38	Virginia	12.7
22	Washington	15.4
15	West Virginia	17.4
27	Wisconsin	14.7
1	Wyoming	28.0

<u>RANK ORDER</u>

RANK	STATE	RATE
1	Wyoming	28.0
2	Alaska	26.9
3	Montana	25.3
4	New Mexico	23.7
5	Utah	22.4
6	Idaho	22.1
7	South Dakota	20.4
8	Oklahoma	20.3
9	Colorado	19.5
10	Arkansas	19.1
11	Nevada	18.4
12	Arizona	18.2
13	Oregon	17.8
14	North Dakota	17.5
15	West Virginia	17.4
16	Kentucky	17.1
16	Missouri	17.1
18	New Hampshire	16.5
19	Kansas	16.3
20	Maine	16.0
21	Tennessee	15.7
22	Washington	15.4
23	Louisiana	15.2
24	Alabama	14.9
25	South Carolina	14.8
25	Vermont	14.8
27	Wisconsin	14.7
28	Florida	14.4
28	Indiana	14.4
30	Mississippi	14.0
30	Pennsylvania	14.0
32	Iowa	13.9
32	Ohio	13.9
34	Michigan	13.8
35	Hawaii	13.5
36	North Carolina	13.4
37	Minnesota	13.2
38	Georgia	12.7
38	Virginia	12.7
40	Delaware	12.6
41	Texas	12.5
42	Nebraska	11.7
43	Rhode Island	11.2
44	California	10.3
44	Illinois	10.3
46	Connecticut	9.9
47	Massachusetts	8.9
48	Maryland	8.8
49	New Jersey	8.3
50	New York	7.8
	District of Columbia	4.9

Source: U.S. Department of Health and Human Services, National Center for Health Statistics
   "National Vital Statistics Reports" (Vol. 66, No. 6, 2017, http://www.cdc.gov/nchs/deaths.htm)
*Final data by state of residence. Also referred to as "Intentional self-harm." Age-adjusted rates based on the year 2000 standard population.

Deaths by AIDS in 2015

National Total = 6,465 Deaths*

ALPHA ORDER

RANK	STATE	DEATHS	% of USA
14	Alabama	126	1.9%
47	Alaska	3	0.0%
17	Arizona	110	1.7%
26	Arkansas	54	0.8%
2	California	710	11.0%
25	Colorado	56	0.9%
22	Connecticut	69	1.1%
32	Delaware	31	0.5%
1	Florida	873	13.5%
5	Georgia	377	5.8%
38	Hawaii	13	0.2%
45	Idaho	4	0.1%
8	Illinois	224	3.5%
21	Indiana	78	1.2%
36	Iowa	17	0.3%
35	Kansas	28	0.4%
30	Kentucky	41	0.6%
9	Louisiana	213	3.3%
43	Maine	8	0.1%
10	Maryland	193	3.0%
20	Massachusetts	91	1.4%
18	Michigan	109	1.7%
33	Minnesota	30	0.5%
19	Mississippi	107	1.7%
28	Missouri	52	0.8%
44	Montana	6	0.1%
40	Nebraska	12	0.2%
27	Nevada	53	0.8%
42	New Hampshire	10	0.2%
6	New Jersey	255	3.9%
31	New Mexico	32	0.5%
4	New York	581	9.0%
7	North Carolina	234	3.6%
45	North Dakota	4	0.1%
16	Ohio	116	1.8%
23	Oklahoma	66	1.0%
29	Oregon	46	0.7%
11	Pennsylvania	177	2.7%
40	Rhode Island	12	0.2%
13	South Carolina	138	2.1%
48	South Dakota	2	0.0%
12	Tennessee	158	2.4%
3	Texas	637	9.9%
38	Utah	13	0.2%
50	Vermont	1	0.0%
15	Virginia	118	1.8%
24	Washington	61	0.9%
37	West Virginia	15	0.2%
34	Wisconsin	29	0.4%
48	Wyoming	2	0.0%

RANK ORDER

RANK	STATE	DEATHS	% of USA
1	Florida	873	13.5%
2	California	710	11.0%
3	Texas	637	9.9%
4	New York	581	9.0%
5	Georgia	377	5.8%
6	New Jersey	255	3.9%
7	North Carolina	234	3.6%
8	Illinois	224	3.5%
9	Louisiana	213	3.3%
10	Maryland	193	3.0%
11	Pennsylvania	177	2.7%
12	Tennessee	158	2.4%
13	South Carolina	138	2.1%
14	Alabama	126	1.9%
15	Virginia	118	1.8%
16	Ohio	116	1.8%
17	Arizona	110	1.7%
18	Michigan	109	1.7%
19	Mississippi	107	1.7%
20	Massachusetts	91	1.4%
21	Indiana	78	1.2%
22	Connecticut	69	1.1%
23	Oklahoma	66	1.0%
24	Washington	61	0.9%
25	Colorado	56	0.9%
26	Arkansas	54	0.8%
27	Nevada	53	0.8%
28	Missouri	52	0.8%
29	Oregon	46	0.7%
30	Kentucky	41	0.6%
31	New Mexico	32	0.5%
32	Delaware	31	0.5%
33	Minnesota	30	0.5%
34	Wisconsin	29	0.4%
35	Kansas	28	0.4%
36	Iowa	17	0.3%
37	West Virginia	15	0.2%
38	Hawaii	13	0.2%
38	Utah	13	0.2%
40	Nebraska	12	0.2%
40	Rhode Island	12	0.2%
42	New Hampshire	10	0.2%
43	Maine	8	0.1%
44	Montana	6	0.1%
45	Idaho	4	0.1%
45	North Dakota	4	0.1%
47	Alaska	3	0.0%
48	South Dakota	2	0.0%
48	Wyoming	2	0.0%
50	Vermont	1	0.0%
	District of Columbia	70	1.1%

Source: U.S. Department of Health and Human Services, National Center for Health Statistics
"National Vital Statistics Reports" (Vol. 66, No. 6, 2017, http://www.cdc.gov/nchs/deaths.htm)
*Final data by state of residence. AIDS is Acquired Immunodeficiency Syndrome. It is a specific group of diseases or conditions which are indicative of severe immunosuppression related to infection with the Human Immunodeficiency Virus (HIV).

Age-Adjusted Death Rate by AIDS in 2015

National Rate = 1.9 Deaths per 100,000 Population*

ALPHA ORDER				RANK ORDER		
RANK	STATE	RATE		RANK	STATE	RATE
9	Alabama	2.5		1	Louisiana	4.5
NA	Alaska**	NA		2	Florida	3.9
21	Arizona	1.5		3	Georgia	3.6
14	Arkansas	1.8		4	Mississippi	3.5
16	California	1.7		5	Maryland	2.9
26	Colorado	1.0		6	Delaware	2.8
18	Connecticut	1.6		7	South Carolina	2.7
6	Delaware	2.8		8	New York	2.6
2	Florida	3.9		9	Alabama	2.5
3	Georgia	3.6		9	New Jersey	2.5
NA	Hawaii**	NA		11	Tennessee	2.3
NA	Idaho**	NA		11	Texas	2.3
18	Illinois	1.6		13	North Carolina	2.2
23	Indiana	1.2		14	Arkansas	1.8
NA	Iowa**	NA		14	Nevada	1.8
29	Kansas	0.9		16	California	1.7
29	Kentucky	0.9		16	Oklahoma	1.7
1	Louisiana	4.5		18	Connecticut	1.6
NA	Maine**	NA		18	Illinois	1.6
5	Maryland	2.9		18	New Mexico	1.6
25	Massachusetts	1.1		21	Arizona	1.5
26	Michigan	1.0		22	Virginia	1.3
34	Minnesota	0.5		23	Indiana	1.2
4	Mississippi	3.5		23	Pennsylvania	1.2
32	Missouri	0.8		25	Massachusetts	1.1
NA	Montana**	NA		26	Colorado	1.0
NA	Nebraska**	NA		26	Michigan	1.0
14	Nevada	1.8		26	Oregon	1.0
NA	New Hampshire**	NA		29	Kansas	0.9
9	New Jersey	2.5		29	Kentucky	0.9
18	New Mexico	1.6		29	Ohio	0.9
8	New York	2.6		32	Missouri	0.8
13	North Carolina	2.2		32	Washington	0.8
NA	North Dakota**	NA		34	Minnesota	0.5
29	Ohio	0.9		35	Wisconsin	0.4
16	Oklahoma	1.7		NA	Alaska**	NA
26	Oregon	1.0		NA	Hawaii**	NA
23	Pennsylvania	1.2		NA	Idaho**	NA
NA	Rhode Island**	NA		NA	Iowa**	NA
7	South Carolina	2.7		NA	Maine**	NA
NA	South Dakota**	NA		NA	Montana**	NA
11	Tennessee	2.3		NA	Nebraska**	NA
11	Texas	2.3		NA	New Hampshire**	NA
NA	Utah**	NA		NA	North Dakota**	NA
NA	Vermont**	NA		NA	Rhode Island**	NA
22	Virginia	1.3		NA	South Dakota**	NA
32	Washington	0.8		NA	Utah**	NA
NA	West Virginia**	NA		NA	Vermont**	NA
35	Wisconsin	0.4		NA	West Virginia**	NA
NA	Wyoming**	NA		NA	Wyoming**	NA

District of Columbia	10.3

Source: U.S. Department of Health and Human Services, National Center for Health Statistics
"National Vital Statistics Reports" (Vol. 66, No. 6, 2017, http://www.cdc.gov/nchs/deaths.htm)
*Final data by state of residence. AIDS is Acquired Immunodeficiency Syndrome. It is a specific group of diseases or conditions which are indicative of severe immunosuppression related to infection with the Human Immunodeficiency Virus (HIV). Age-adjusted rates based on the year 2000 standard population.
**Insufficient data to determine a reliable rate.

Adult Per Capita Alcohol Consumption in 2015

National Per Capita = 2.6 Gallons Consumed per Adult 21 Years and Older*

ALPHA ORDER

RANK	STATE	PER CAPITA
41	Alabama	2.3
9	Alaska	3.2
22	Arizona	2.7
47	Arkansas	2.1
26	California	2.6
11	Colorado	3.1
22	Connecticut	2.7
2	Delaware	4.1
16	Florida	2.9
44	Georgia	2.2
16	Hawaii	2.9
8	Idaho	3.3
22	Illinois	2.7
36	Indiana	2.4
22	Iowa	2.7
44	Kansas	2.2
44	Kentucky	2.2
16	Louisiana	2.9
11	Maine	3.1
36	Maryland	2.4
19	Massachusetts	2.8
31	Michigan	2.5
11	Minnesota	3.1
31	Mississippi	2.5
19	Missouri	2.8
6	Montana	3.4
26	Nebraska	2.6
3	Nevada	3.7
1	New Hampshire	5.3
26	New Jersey	2.6
31	New Mexico	2.5
36	New York	2.4
36	North Carolina	2.4
3	North Dakota	3.7
41	Ohio	2.3
47	Oklahoma	2.1
15	Oregon	3.0
26	Pennsylvania	2.6
19	Rhode Island	2.8
31	South Carolina	2.5
9	South Dakota	3.2
41	Tennessee	2.3
26	Texas	2.6
50	Utah	1.6
5	Vermont	3.5
36	Virginia	2.4
31	Washington	2.5
49	West Virginia	1.9
6	Wisconsin	3.4
11	Wyoming	3.1

RANK ORDER

RANK	STATE	PER CAPITA
1	New Hampshire	5.3
2	Delaware	4.1
3	Nevada	3.7
3	North Dakota	3.7
5	Vermont	3.5
6	Montana	3.4
6	Wisconsin	3.4
8	Idaho	3.3
9	Alaska	3.2
9	South Dakota	3.2
11	Colorado	3.1
11	Maine	3.1
11	Minnesota	3.1
11	Wyoming	3.1
15	Oregon	3.0
16	Florida	2.9
16	Hawaii	2.9
16	Louisiana	2.9
19	Massachusetts	2.8
19	Missouri	2.8
19	Rhode Island	2.8
22	Arizona	2.7
22	Connecticut	2.7
22	Illinois	2.7
22	Iowa	2.7
26	California	2.6
26	Nebraska	2.6
26	New Jersey	2.6
26	Pennsylvania	2.6
26	Texas	2.6
31	Michigan	2.5
31	Mississippi	2.5
31	New Mexico	2.5
31	South Carolina	2.5
31	Washington	2.5
36	Indiana	2.4
36	Maryland	2.4
36	New York	2.4
36	North Carolina	2.4
36	Virginia	2.4
41	Alabama	2.3
41	Ohio	2.3
41	Tennessee	2.3
44	Georgia	2.2
44	Kansas	2.2
44	Kentucky	2.2
47	Arkansas	2.1
47	Oklahoma	2.1
49	West Virginia	1.9
50	Utah	1.6

| | District of Columbia | 4.2 |

Source: CQ Press using data from U.S. Dept of Health and Human Services, National Institute on Alcohol Abuse and Alcoholism "Apparent Per Capita Alcohol Consumption, 1977-2015" (https://pubs.niaaa.nih.gov/publications/surveillance.htm)
*This is apparent consumption of actual alcohol, not entire volume of an alcoholic beverage (for example, wine is roughly 11% absolute alcohol content). Apparent consumption is based on several sources which together approximate sales but do not actually measure consumption. Accordingly, figures for some states may be skewed by purchases by nonresidents.

Percent of Adults Who Smoke: 2016

National Median = 17.1% of Adults*

ALPHA ORDER

RANK	STATE	PERCENT
9	Alabama	21.5
16	Alaska	19.0
38	Arizona	14.7
3	Arkansas	23.6
49	California	11.0
34	Colorado	15.6
47	Connecticut	13.4
24	Delaware	17.7
35	Florida	15.5
22	Georgia	17.9
48	Hawaii	13.1
39	Idaho	14.5
33	Illinois	15.8
10	Indiana	21.1
29	Iowa	16.7
25	Kansas	17.2
2	Kentucky	24.5
4	Louisiana	22.8
13	Maine	19.8
45	Maryland	13.7
46	Massachusetts	13.6
11	Michigan	20.4
37	Minnesota	15.2
5	Mississippi	22.7
7	Missouri	22.1
18	Montana	18.5
27	Nebraska	17.0
31	Nevada	16.5
20	New Hampshire	18.0
43	New Jersey	14.0
30	New Mexico	16.6
42	New York	14.2
22	North Carolina	17.9
13	North Dakota	19.8
6	Ohio	22.5
15	Oklahoma	19.6
32	Oregon	16.2
20	Pennsylvania	18.0
40	Rhode Island	14.4
12	South Carolina	20.0
19	South Dakota	18.1
7	Tennessee	22.1
41	Texas	14.3
50	Utah	8.8
27	Vermont	17.0
36	Virginia	15.3
43	Washington	14.0
1	West Virginia	24.8
26	Wisconsin	17.1
16	Wyoming	19.0

RANK ORDER

RANK	STATE	PERCENT
1	West Virginia	24.8
2	Kentucky	24.5
3	Arkansas	23.6
4	Louisiana	22.8
5	Mississippi	22.7
6	Ohio	22.5
7	Missouri	22.1
7	Tennessee	22.1
9	Alabama	21.5
10	Indiana	21.1
11	Michigan	20.4
12	South Carolina	20.0
13	Maine	19.8
13	North Dakota	19.8
15	Oklahoma	19.6
16	Alaska	19.0
16	Wyoming	19.0
18	Montana	18.5
19	South Dakota	18.1
20	New Hampshire	18.0
20	Pennsylvania	18.0
22	Georgia	17.9
22	North Carolina	17.9
24	Delaware	17.7
25	Kansas	17.2
26	Wisconsin	17.1
27	Nebraska	17.0
27	Vermont	17.0
29	Iowa	16.7
30	New Mexico	16.6
31	Nevada	16.5
32	Oregon	16.2
33	Illinois	15.8
34	Colorado	15.6
35	Florida	15.5
36	Virginia	15.3
37	Minnesota	15.2
38	Arizona	14.7
39	Idaho	14.5
40	Rhode Island	14.4
41	Texas	14.3
42	New York	14.2
43	New Jersey	14.0
43	Washington	14.0
45	Maryland	13.7
46	Massachusetts	13.6
47	Connecticut	13.4
48	Hawaii	13.1
49	California	11.0
50	Utah	8.8
	District of Columbia	14.7

Source: U.S. Department of Health and Human Services, Centers for Disease Control and Prevention
"Behavioral Risk Factor Surveillance Summary Prevalence Data" (https://www.cdc.gov/brfss/brfssprevalence/index.html)
*Persons 18 and older who have smoked more than 100 cigarettes during their lifetime and who currently smoke every day or some days.

Percent of Adults Overweight or Obese: 2016

National Median = 65.2% of Adults*

RANK	STATE	PERCENT
3	Alabama	69.6
21	Alaska	66.7
38	Arizona	63.2
11	Arkansas	68.2
45	California	61.0
49	Colorado	58.1
43	Connecticut	61.9
13	Delaware	68.0
38	Florida	63.2
24	Georgia	65.8
50	Hawaii	57.6
32	Idaho	64.5
28	Illinois	65.0
17	Indiana	67.2
7	Iowa	68.7
19	Kansas	66.8
5	Kentucky	69.1
4	Louisiana	69.2
27	Maine	65.2
31	Maryland	64.6
48	Massachusetts	60.3
14	Michigan	67.5
30	Minnesota	64.8
1	Mississippi	71.3
16	Missouri	67.3
40	Montana	62.8
8	Nebraska	68.6
42	Nevada	62.3
36	New Hampshire	63.5
34	New Jersey	63.9
29	New Mexico	64.9
46	New York	60.8
19	North Carolina	66.8
12	North Dakota	68.1
22	Ohio	66.3
6	Oklahoma	68.8
41	Oregon	62.6
25	Pennsylvania	65.5
35	Rhode Island	63.7
15	South Carolina	67.4
18	South Dakota	66.9
8	Tennessee	68.6
10	Texas	68.5
47	Utah	60.4
44	Vermont	61.8
25	Virginia	65.5
36	Washington	63.5
2	West Virginia	71.0
23	Wisconsin	66.2
33	Wyoming	64.2

RANK	STATE	PERCENT
1	Mississippi	71.3
2	West Virginia	71.0
3	Alabama	69.6
4	Louisiana	69.2
5	Kentucky	69.1
6	Oklahoma	68.8
7	Iowa	68.7
8	Nebraska	68.6
8	Tennessee	68.6
10	Texas	68.5
11	Arkansas	68.2
12	North Dakota	68.1
13	Delaware	68.0
14	Michigan	67.5
15	South Carolina	67.4
16	Missouri	67.3
17	Indiana	67.2
18	South Dakota	66.9
19	Kansas	66.8
19	North Carolina	66.8
21	Alaska	66.7
22	Ohio	66.3
23	Wisconsin	66.2
24	Georgia	65.8
25	Pennsylvania	65.5
25	Virginia	65.5
27	Maine	65.2
28	Illinois	65.0
29	New Mexico	64.9
30	Minnesota	64.8
31	Maryland	64.6
32	Idaho	64.5
33	Wyoming	64.2
34	New Jersey	63.9
35	Rhode Island	63.7
36	New Hampshire	63.5
36	Washington	63.5
38	Arizona	63.2
38	Florida	63.2
40	Montana	62.8
41	Oregon	62.6
42	Nevada	62.3
43	Connecticut	61.9
44	Vermont	61.8
45	California	61.0
46	New York	60.8
47	Utah	60.4
48	Massachusetts	60.3
49	Colorado	58.1
50	Hawaii	57.6

| | District of Columbia | 53.4 |

Source: CQ Press using data from U.S. Department of Health and Human Services, Centers for Disease Control and Prevention
"Behavioral Risk Factor Surveillance Summary Prevalence Data" (https://www.cdc.gov/brfss/brfssprevalence/index.html)
*Persons 18 and older. Overweight is defined as a Body Mass Index (BMI) of 25.0 to 29.9 regardless of sex. Obese is a BMI of 30.0 or greater. BMI is a ratio of height to weight. As an example, a person 5' 8" and weighing 165 pounds has a BMI of 25. The same height at 197 pounds has a BMI of 30.

Percent of Children Aged 19 to 35 Months Fully Immunized in 2016

National Percent = 70.7%*

<table>
<tr><td colspan="3"><u>ALPHA ORDER</u></td><td colspan="3"><u>RANK ORDER</u></td></tr>
<tr><td>RANK</td><td>STATE</td><td>PERCENT</td><td>RANK</td><td>STATE</td><td>PERCENT</td></tr>
<tr><td>7</td><td>Alabama</td><td>77.3</td><td>1</td><td>Massachusetts</td><td>85.3</td></tr>
<tr><td>34</td><td>Alaska</td><td>68.8</td><td>2</td><td>Nebraska</td><td>80.6</td></tr>
<tr><td>31</td><td>Arizona</td><td>69.9</td><td>3</td><td>Wisconsin</td><td>79.4</td></tr>
<tr><td>39</td><td>Arkansas</td><td>67.8</td><td>4</td><td>Delaware</td><td>78.1</td></tr>
<tr><td>46</td><td>California</td><td>65.3</td><td>5</td><td>New Hampshire</td><td>78.0</td></tr>
<tr><td>10</td><td>Colorado</td><td>76.4</td><td>6</td><td>North Carolina</td><td>77.8</td></tr>
<tr><td>12</td><td>Connecticut</td><td>75.7</td><td>7</td><td>Alabama</td><td>77.3</td></tr>
<tr><td>4</td><td>Delaware</td><td>78.1</td><td>7</td><td>Georgia</td><td>77.3</td></tr>
<tr><td>41</td><td>Florida</td><td>67.1</td><td>9</td><td>Vermont</td><td>76.8</td></tr>
<tr><td>7</td><td>Georgia</td><td>77.3</td><td>10</td><td>Colorado</td><td>76.4</td></tr>
<tr><td>15</td><td>Hawaii</td><td>75.1</td><td>10</td><td>Kansas</td><td>76.4</td></tr>
<tr><td>18</td><td>Idaho</td><td>73.9</td><td>12</td><td>Connecticut</td><td>75.7</td></tr>
<tr><td>25</td><td>Illinois</td><td>71.5</td><td>12</td><td>Washington</td><td>75.7</td></tr>
<tr><td>34</td><td>Indiana</td><td>68.8</td><td>14</td><td>Rhode Island</td><td>75.5</td></tr>
<tr><td>21</td><td>Iowa</td><td>73.5</td><td>15</td><td>Hawaii</td><td>75.1</td></tr>
<tr><td>10</td><td>Kansas</td><td>76.4</td><td>16</td><td>Kentucky</td><td>74.5</td></tr>
<tr><td>16</td><td>Kentucky</td><td>74.5</td><td>17</td><td>Maryland</td><td>74.4</td></tr>
<tr><td>44</td><td>Louisiana</td><td>66.8</td><td>18</td><td>Idaho</td><td>73.9</td></tr>
<tr><td>26</td><td>Maine</td><td>70.6</td><td>19</td><td>Minnesota</td><td>73.8</td></tr>
<tr><td>17</td><td>Maryland</td><td>74.4</td><td>20</td><td>Pennsylvania</td><td>73.7</td></tr>
<tr><td>1</td><td>Massachusetts</td><td>85.3</td><td>21</td><td>Iowa</td><td>73.5</td></tr>
<tr><td>29</td><td>Michigan</td><td>70.2</td><td>22</td><td>New York</td><td>72.3</td></tr>
<tr><td>19</td><td>Minnesota</td><td>73.8</td><td>23</td><td>Utah</td><td>72.2</td></tr>
<tr><td>27</td><td>Mississippi</td><td>70.4</td><td>24</td><td>Nevada</td><td>71.9</td></tr>
<tr><td>43</td><td>Missouri</td><td>66.9</td><td>25</td><td>Illinois</td><td>71.5</td></tr>
<tr><td>48</td><td>Montana</td><td>63.6</td><td>26</td><td>Maine</td><td>70.6</td></tr>
<tr><td>2</td><td>Nebraska</td><td>80.6</td><td>27</td><td>Mississippi</td><td>70.4</td></tr>
<tr><td>24</td><td>Nevada</td><td>71.9</td><td>27</td><td>South Dakota</td><td>70.4</td></tr>
<tr><td>5</td><td>New Hampshire</td><td>78.0</td><td>29</td><td>Michigan</td><td>70.2</td></tr>
<tr><td>29</td><td>New Jersey</td><td>70.2</td><td>29</td><td>New Jersey</td><td>70.2</td></tr>
<tr><td>36</td><td>New Mexico</td><td>68.5</td><td>31</td><td>Arizona</td><td>69.9</td></tr>
<tr><td>22</td><td>New York</td><td>72.3</td><td>32</td><td>South Carolina</td><td>69.7</td></tr>
<tr><td>6</td><td>North Carolina</td><td>77.8</td><td>33</td><td>Texas</td><td>69.5</td></tr>
<tr><td>37</td><td>North Dakota</td><td>68.2</td><td>34</td><td>Alaska</td><td>68.8</td></tr>
<tr><td>38</td><td>Ohio</td><td>68.0</td><td>34</td><td>Indiana</td><td>68.8</td></tr>
<tr><td>42</td><td>Oklahoma</td><td>67.0</td><td>36</td><td>New Mexico</td><td>68.5</td></tr>
<tr><td>50</td><td>Oregon</td><td>58.1</td><td>37</td><td>North Dakota</td><td>68.2</td></tr>
<tr><td>20</td><td>Pennsylvania</td><td>73.7</td><td>38</td><td>Ohio</td><td>68.0</td></tr>
<tr><td>14</td><td>Rhode Island</td><td>75.5</td><td>39</td><td>Arkansas</td><td>67.8</td></tr>
<tr><td>32</td><td>South Carolina</td><td>69.7</td><td>40</td><td>Tennessee</td><td>67.4</td></tr>
<tr><td>27</td><td>South Dakota</td><td>70.4</td><td>41</td><td>Florida</td><td>67.1</td></tr>
<tr><td>40</td><td>Tennessee</td><td>67.4</td><td>42</td><td>Oklahoma</td><td>67.0</td></tr>
<tr><td>33</td><td>Texas</td><td>69.5</td><td>43</td><td>Missouri</td><td>66.9</td></tr>
<tr><td>23</td><td>Utah</td><td>72.2</td><td>44</td><td>Louisiana</td><td>66.8</td></tr>
<tr><td>9</td><td>Vermont</td><td>76.8</td><td>45</td><td>Virginia</td><td>65.9</td></tr>
<tr><td>45</td><td>Virginia</td><td>65.9</td><td>46</td><td>California</td><td>65.3</td></tr>
<tr><td>12</td><td>Washington</td><td>75.7</td><td>47</td><td>West Virginia</td><td>64.7</td></tr>
<tr><td>47</td><td>West Virginia</td><td>64.7</td><td>48</td><td>Montana</td><td>63.6</td></tr>
<tr><td>3</td><td>Wisconsin</td><td>79.4</td><td>49</td><td>Wyoming</td><td>62.8</td></tr>
<tr><td>49</td><td>Wyoming</td><td>62.8</td><td>50</td><td>Oregon</td><td>58.1</td></tr>
<tr><td></td><td></td><td></td><td></td><td>District of Columbia</td><td>68.2</td></tr>
</table>

Source: U.S. Department of Health and Human Services, Centers for Disease Control and Prevention

"Vaccination Coverage Among Children" (MMWR, Vol. 66, No. 43, November 3, 2017, http://www.cdc.gov/mmwr/)

*Fully immunized (4:3:1:3:3:1:4 series) children received four doses of DTaP (Diphtheria, Tetanus Toxoids, Pertussis [Whooping Cough]), three doses of Poliovirus Vaccine, one dose of MCV (Measles-Containing Vaccine), full series (3 or 4 doses depending on product type) of Hib (Haemophilus influenzae type b), three doses of Hepatitis B vaccine, one dose of Varicella (chickenpox) vaccine, and four doses of PCV (pneumococcal conjugate vaccine). This differs from previous "fully" immunized tables.

XII. Households and Housing

Households in 2016

National Total = 118,860,065 Households*

ALPHA ORDER

RANK	STATE	HOUSEHOLDS	% of USA
24	Alabama	1,852,518	1.6%
49	Alaska	248,468	0.2%
17	Arizona	2,519,052	2.1%
31	Arkansas	1,142,718	1.0%
1	California	12,944,178	10.9%
22	Colorado	2,108,992	1.8%
29	Connecticut	1,357,269	1.1%
45	Delaware	351,085	0.3%
3	Florida	7,573,456	6.4%
10	Georgia	3,686,135	3.1%
42	Hawaii	455,868	0.4%
39	Idaho	610,872	0.5%
6	Illinois	4,822,046	4.1%
16	Indiana	2,533,270	2.1%
30	Iowa	1,247,932	1.0%
32	Kansas	1,110,407	0.9%
26	Kentucky	1,717,706	1.4%
25	Louisiana	1,720,801	1.4%
40	Maine	531,660	0.4%
20	Maryland	2,194,657	1.8%
14	Massachusetts	2,579,398	2.2%
8	Michigan	3,884,153	3.3%
21	Minnesota	2,148,725	1.8%
33	Mississippi	1,091,245	0.9%
18	Missouri	2,372,190	2.0%
43	Montana	416,125	0.4%
37	Nebraska	747,562	0.6%
34	Nevada	1,055,158	0.9%
41	New Hampshire	520,643	0.4%
11	New Jersey	3,194,519	2.7%
36	New Mexico	758,364	0.6%
4	New York	7,209,054	6.1%
9	North Carolina	3,882,423	3.3%
47	North Dakota	315,134	0.3%
7	Ohio	4,624,669	3.9%
28	Oklahoma	1,469,342	1.2%
27	Oregon	1,571,678	1.3%
5	Pennsylvania	4,937,771	4.2%
44	Rhode Island	408,239	0.3%
23	South Carolina	1,877,887	1.6%
46	South Dakota	334,003	0.3%
15	Tennessee	2,556,332	2.2%
2	Texas	9,535,612	8.0%
35	Utah	943,147	0.8%
48	Vermont	254,851	0.2%
12	Virginia	3,120,692	2.6%
13	Washington	2,768,076	2.3%
38	West Virginia	722,125	0.6%
19	Wisconsin	2,326,998	2.0%
50	Wyoming	223,619	0.2%

RANK ORDER

RANK	STATE	HOUSEHOLDS	% of USA
1	California	12,944,178	10.9%
2	Texas	9,535,612	8.0%
3	Florida	7,573,456	6.4%
4	New York	7,209,054	6.1%
5	Pennsylvania	4,937,771	4.2%
6	Illinois	4,822,046	4.1%
7	Ohio	4,624,669	3.9%
8	Michigan	3,884,153	3.3%
9	North Carolina	3,882,423	3.3%
10	Georgia	3,686,135	3.1%
11	New Jersey	3,194,519	2.7%
12	Virginia	3,120,692	2.6%
13	Washington	2,768,076	2.3%
14	Massachusetts	2,579,398	2.2%
15	Tennessee	2,556,332	2.2%
16	Indiana	2,533,270	2.1%
17	Arizona	2,519,052	2.1%
18	Missouri	2,372,190	2.0%
19	Wisconsin	2,326,998	2.0%
20	Maryland	2,194,657	1.8%
21	Minnesota	2,148,725	1.8%
22	Colorado	2,108,992	1.8%
23	South Carolina	1,877,887	1.6%
24	Alabama	1,852,518	1.6%
25	Louisiana	1,720,801	1.4%
26	Kentucky	1,717,706	1.4%
27	Oregon	1,571,678	1.3%
28	Oklahoma	1,469,342	1.2%
29	Connecticut	1,357,269	1.1%
30	Iowa	1,247,932	1.0%
31	Arkansas	1,142,718	1.0%
32	Kansas	1,110,407	0.9%
33	Mississippi	1,091,245	0.9%
34	Nevada	1,055,158	0.9%
35	Utah	943,147	0.8%
36	New Mexico	758,364	0.6%
37	Nebraska	747,562	0.6%
38	West Virginia	722,125	0.6%
39	Idaho	610,872	0.5%
40	Maine	531,660	0.4%
41	New Hampshire	520,643	0.4%
42	Hawaii	455,868	0.4%
43	Montana	416,125	0.4%
44	Rhode Island	408,239	0.3%
45	Delaware	351,085	0.3%
46	South Dakota	334,003	0.3%
47	North Dakota	315,134	0.3%
48	Vermont	254,851	0.2%
49	Alaska	248,468	0.2%
50	Wyoming	223,619	0.2%
	District of Columbia	281,241	0.2%

Source: U.S. Bureau of the Census

"2016 American Community Survey-Table CP02" (http://www.census.gov/programs-surveys/acs/)

*A household includes all persons who occupy a housing unit. A household consists of a single family, one person living alone, two or more families living together, or any other group of related or unrelated persons who share living arrangements.

Persons per Household in 2016

National Rate = 2.65 Persons per Household*

ALPHA ORDER				RANK ORDER		
RANK	STATE	PERSONS		RANK	STATE	PERSONS
24	Alabama	2.56		1	Utah	3.19
4	Alaska	2.87		2	Hawaii	3.04
10	Arizona	2.69		3	California	2.97
30	Arkansas	2.54		4	Alaska	2.87
3	California	2.97		5	Texas	2.86
22	Colorado	2.57		6	Nevada	2.75
25	Connecticut	2.55		7	New Jersey	2.74
17	Delaware	2.64		8	Georgia	2.73
13	Florida	2.66		9	Idaho	2.71
8	Georgia	2.73		10	Arizona	2.69
2	Hawaii	3.04		10	New Mexico	2.69
9	Idaho	2.71		12	Maryland	2.68
20	Illinois	2.59		13	Florida	2.66
30	Indiana	2.54		13	New York	2.66
47	Iowa	2.43		15	Louisiana	2.65
25	Kansas	2.55		15	Mississippi	2.65
34	Kentucky	2.51		17	Delaware	2.64
15	Louisiana	2.65		18	Virginia	2.62
44	Maine	2.44		19	Oklahoma	2.60
12	Maryland	2.68		20	Illinois	2.59
30	Massachusetts	2.54		21	Washington	2.58
36	Michigan	2.50		22	Colorado	2.57
34	Minnesota	2.51		22	South Carolina	2.57
15	Mississippi	2.65		24	Alabama	2.56
38	Missouri	2.49		25	Connecticut	2.55
44	Montana	2.44		25	Kansas	2.55
40	Nebraska	2.48		25	North Carolina	2.55
6	Nevada	2.75		25	Oregon	2.55
40	New Hampshire	2.48		25	Wyoming	2.55
7	New Jersey	2.74		30	Arkansas	2.54
10	New Mexico	2.69		30	Indiana	2.54
13	New York	2.66		30	Massachusetts	2.54
25	North Carolina	2.55		30	Tennessee	2.54
50	North Dakota	2.32		34	Kentucky	2.51
44	Ohio	2.44		34	Minnesota	2.51
19	Oklahoma	2.60		36	Michigan	2.50
25	Oregon	2.55		36	Pennsylvania	2.50
36	Pennsylvania	2.50		38	Missouri	2.49
40	Rhode Island	2.48		38	South Dakota	2.49
22	South Carolina	2.57		40	Nebraska	2.48
38	South Dakota	2.49		40	New Hampshire	2.48
30	Tennessee	2.54		40	Rhode Island	2.48
5	Texas	2.86		43	West Virginia	2.47
1	Utah	3.19		44	Maine	2.44
49	Vermont	2.35		44	Montana	2.44
18	Virginia	2.62		44	Ohio	2.44
21	Washington	2.58		47	Iowa	2.43
43	West Virginia	2.47		48	Wisconsin	2.42
48	Wisconsin	2.42		49	Vermont	2.35
25	Wyoming	2.55		50	North Dakota	2.32
					District of Columbia	2.28

Source: U.S. Bureau of the Census
    "2016 American Community Survey-Table CP02" (http://www.census.gov/programs-surveys/acs/)
*A household includes all persons who occupy a housing unit. A household consists of a single family, one person living alone, two or more families living together, or any other group of related or unrelated persons who share living arrangements.

Percent of Households with One Person in 2016

National Percent = 28.0% of Households*

ALPHA ORDER

ALPHA ORDER

RANK	STATE	PERCENT
4	Alabama	30.7
47	Alaska	25.1
38	Arizona	27.3
20	Arkansas	29.3
49	California	23.9
38	Colorado	27.3
28	Connecticut	28.7
35	Delaware	27.6
25	Florida	28.8
41	Georgia	27.2
48	Hawaii	24.5
43	Idaho	26.6
17	Illinois	29.6
31	Indiana	28.6
19	Iowa	29.4
17	Kansas	29.6
25	Kentucky	28.8
8	Louisiana	30.2
10	Maine	30.0
38	Maryland	27.3
24	Massachusetts	28.9
15	Michigan	29.7
22	Minnesota	29.2
25	Mississippi	28.8
22	Missouri	29.2
4	Montana	30.7
12	Nebraska	29.9
31	Nevada	28.6
44	New Hampshire	26.4
45	New Jersey	26.3
6	New Mexico	30.4
12	New York	29.9
33	North Carolina	28.5
1	North Dakota	32.3
7	Ohio	30.3
28	Oklahoma	28.7
36	Oregon	27.4
10	Pennsylvania	30.0
1	Rhode Island	32.3
20	South Carolina	29.3
3	South Dakota	31.0
28	Tennessee	28.7
46	Texas	25.2
50	Utah	18.7
8	Vermont	30.2
36	Virginia	27.4
42	Washington	27.0
15	West Virginia	29.7
14	Wisconsin	29.8
34	Wyoming	27.7

RANK ORDER

RANK	STATE	PERCENT
1	North Dakota	32.3
1	Rhode Island	32.3
3	South Dakota	31.0
4	Alabama	30.7
4	Montana	30.7
6	New Mexico	30.4
7	Ohio	30.3
8	Louisiana	30.2
8	Vermont	30.2
10	Maine	30.0
10	Pennsylvania	30.0
12	Nebraska	29.9
12	New York	29.9
14	Wisconsin	29.8
15	Michigan	29.7
15	West Virginia	29.7
17	Illinois	29.6
17	Kansas	29.6
19	Iowa	29.4
20	Arkansas	29.3
20	South Carolina	29.3
22	Minnesota	29.2
22	Missouri	29.2
24	Massachusetts	28.9
25	Florida	28.8
25	Kentucky	28.8
25	Mississippi	28.8
28	Connecticut	28.7
28	Oklahoma	28.7
28	Tennessee	28.7
31	Indiana	28.6
31	Nevada	28.6
33	North Carolina	28.5
34	Wyoming	27.7
35	Delaware	27.6
36	Oregon	27.4
36	Virginia	27.4
38	Arizona	27.3
38	Colorado	27.3
38	Maryland	27.3
41	Georgia	27.2
42	Washington	27.0
43	Idaho	26.6
44	New Hampshire	26.4
45	New Jersey	26.3
46	Texas	25.2
47	Alaska	25.1
48	Hawaii	24.5
49	California	23.9
50	Utah	18.7
	District of Columbia	43.8

Source: U.S. Bureau of the Census
"2016 American Community Survey-Table CP02" (http://www.census.gov/programs-surveys/acs/)
*A household includes all persons who occupy a housing unit. A household consists of a single family, one person living alone, two or more families living together, or any other group of related or unrelated persons who share living arrangements.

Percent of Households Headed by Married Couples in 2016

National Percent = 47.9% of Households*

RANK	STATE	PERCENT
40	Alabama	46.7
18	Alaska	49.2
32	Arizona	47.4
24	Arkansas	48.1
15	California	49.5
11	Colorado	49.9
28	Connecticut	47.8
30	Delaware	47.7
41	Florida	46.4
32	Georgia	47.4
5	Hawaii	51.8
2	Idaho	53.8
38	Illinois	47.0
21	Indiana	48.4
7	Iowa	50.6
10	Kansas	50.1
36	Kentucky	47.3
49	Louisiana	42.7
23	Maine	48.2
32	Maryland	47.4
43	Massachusetts	46.3
39	Michigan	46.8
8	Minnesota	50.3
45	Mississippi	44.9
26	Missouri	48.0
11	Montana	49.9
16	Nebraska	49.4
46	Nevada	44.4
4	New Hampshire	52.1
6	New Jersey	50.8
47	New Mexico	44.1
48	New York	43.8
26	North Carolina	48.0
30	North Dakota	47.7
44	Ohio	45.9
22	Oklahoma	48.3
19	Oregon	48.7
32	Pennsylvania	47.4
50	Rhode Island	42.3
41	South Carolina	46.4
17	South Dakota	49.3
28	Tennessee	47.8
11	Texas	49.9
1	Utah	61.3
37	Vermont	47.2
11	Virginia	49.9
9	Washington	50.2
24	West Virginia	48.1
20	Wisconsin	48.5
3	Wyoming	52.3

RANK	STATE	PERCENT
1	Utah	61.3
2	Idaho	53.8
3	Wyoming	52.3
4	New Hampshire	52.1
5	Hawaii	51.8
6	New Jersey	50.8
7	Iowa	50.6
8	Minnesota	50.3
9	Washington	50.2
10	Kansas	50.1
11	Colorado	49.9
11	Montana	49.9
11	Texas	49.9
11	Virginia	49.9
15	California	49.5
16	Nebraska	49.4
17	South Dakota	49.3
18	Alaska	49.2
19	Oregon	48.7
20	Wisconsin	48.5
21	Indiana	48.4
22	Oklahoma	48.3
23	Maine	48.2
24	Arkansas	48.1
24	West Virginia	48.1
26	Missouri	48.0
26	North Carolina	48.0
28	Connecticut	47.8
28	Tennessee	47.8
30	Delaware	47.7
30	North Dakota	47.7
32	Arizona	47.4
32	Georgia	47.4
32	Maryland	47.4
32	Pennsylvania	47.4
36	Kentucky	47.3
37	Vermont	47.2
38	Illinois	47.0
39	Michigan	46.8
40	Alabama	46.7
41	Florida	46.4
41	South Carolina	46.4
43	Massachusetts	46.3
44	Ohio	45.9
45	Mississippi	44.9
46	Nevada	44.4
47	New Mexico	44.1
48	New York	43.8
49	Louisiana	42.7
50	Rhode Island	42.3
	District of Columbia	25.3

Source: U.S. Bureau of the Census
"2016 American Community Survey-Table CP02" (http://www.census.gov/programs-surveys/acs/)
*A household includes all persons who occupy a housing unit. A household consists of a single family, one person living alone, two or more families living together, or any other group of related or unrelated persons who share living arrangements. Includes married same-sex couple households.

Percent of Households Headed by Single Mothers in 2016

National Percent = 6.7% of Households*

ALPHA ORDER

RANK	STATE	PERCENT
9	Alabama	7.2
31	Alaska	6.1
18	Arizona	6.7
9	Arkansas	7.2
27	California	6.3
40	Colorado	5.4
20	Connecticut	6.6
9	Delaware	7.2
23	Florida	6.5
3	Georgia	8.3
49	Hawaii	4.4
42	Idaho	5.3
18	Illinois	6.7
17	Indiana	6.8
31	Iowa	6.1
31	Kansas	6.1
9	Kentucky	7.2
2	Louisiana	8.7
45	Maine	4.9
14	Maryland	6.9
27	Massachusetts	6.3
20	Michigan	6.6
38	Minnesota	5.6
1	Mississippi	9.3
23	Missouri	6.5
50	Montana	4.2
26	Nebraska	6.4
14	Nevada	6.9
45	New Hampshire	4.9
27	New Jersey	6.3
5	New Mexico	7.6
20	New York	6.6
7	North Carolina	7.3
48	North Dakota	4.7
13	Ohio	7.1
23	Oklahoma	6.5
40	Oregon	5.4
35	Pennsylvania	6.0
7	Rhode Island	7.3
6	South Carolina	7.4
37	South Dakota	5.7
14	Tennessee	6.9
4	Texas	8.0
42	Utah	5.3
39	Vermont	5.5
27	Virginia	6.3
44	Washington	5.2
31	West Virginia	6.1
36	Wisconsin	5.9
45	Wyoming	4.9

RANK ORDER

RANK	STATE	PERCENT
1	Mississippi	9.3
2	Louisiana	8.7
3	Georgia	8.3
4	Texas	8.0
5	New Mexico	7.6
6	South Carolina	7.4
7	North Carolina	7.3
7	Rhode Island	7.3
9	Alabama	7.2
9	Arkansas	7.2
9	Delaware	7.2
9	Kentucky	7.2
13	Ohio	7.1
14	Maryland	6.9
14	Nevada	6.9
14	Tennessee	6.9
17	Indiana	6.8
18	Arizona	6.7
18	Illinois	6.7
20	Connecticut	6.6
20	Michigan	6.6
20	New York	6.6
23	Florida	6.5
23	Missouri	6.5
23	Oklahoma	6.5
26	Nebraska	6.4
27	California	6.3
27	Massachusetts	6.3
27	New Jersey	6.3
27	Virginia	6.3
31	Alaska	6.1
31	Iowa	6.1
31	Kansas	6.1
31	West Virginia	6.1
35	Pennsylvania	6.0
36	Wisconsin	5.9
37	South Dakota	5.7
38	Minnesota	5.6
39	Vermont	5.5
40	Colorado	5.4
40	Oregon	5.4
42	Idaho	5.3
42	Utah	5.3
44	Washington	5.2
45	Maine	4.9
45	New Hampshire	4.9
45	Wyoming	4.9
48	North Dakota	4.7
49	Hawaii	4.4
50	Montana	4.2
	District of Columbia	7.6

Source: U.S. Bureau of the Census
"2016 American Community Survey-Table CP02" (http://www.census.gov/programs-surveys/acs/)
*No spouse present in household with children under 18 years old. A household includes all persons who occupy a housing unit.
A household consists of a single family, one person living alone, two or more families living together, or any other group of
related or unrelated persons who share living arrangements.

Percent of Households Headed by Single Fathers in 2016

National Percent = 2.3% of Households*

<table>
<tr><td colspan="3">ALPHA ORDER</td><td colspan="3">RANK ORDER</td></tr>
<tr><td>RANK</td><td>STATE</td><td>PERCENT</td><td>RANK</td><td>STATE</td><td>PERCENT</td></tr>
<tr><td>45</td><td>Alabama</td><td>1.9</td><td>1</td><td>Alaska</td><td>3.2</td></tr>
<tr><td>1</td><td>Alaska</td><td>3.2</td><td>2</td><td>Wyoming</td><td>3.1</td></tr>
<tr><td>16</td><td>Arizona</td><td>2.4</td><td>3</td><td>Nevada</td><td>2.9</td></tr>
<tr><td>35</td><td>Arkansas</td><td>2.1</td><td>4</td><td>Oklahoma</td><td>2.8</td></tr>
<tr><td>5</td><td>California</td><td>2.6</td><td>5</td><td>California</td><td>2.6</td></tr>
<tr><td>35</td><td>Colorado</td><td>2.1</td><td>5</td><td>Maine</td><td>2.6</td></tr>
<tr><td>49</td><td>Connecticut</td><td>1.7</td><td>5</td><td>South Dakota</td><td>2.6</td></tr>
<tr><td>49</td><td>Delaware</td><td>1.7</td><td>5</td><td>Wisconsin</td><td>2.6</td></tr>
<tr><td>35</td><td>Florida</td><td>2.1</td><td>9</td><td>Idaho</td><td>2.5</td></tr>
<tr><td>28</td><td>Georgia</td><td>2.2</td><td>9</td><td>Indiana</td><td>2.5</td></tr>
<tr><td>28</td><td>Hawaii</td><td>2.2</td><td>9</td><td>Kansas</td><td>2.5</td></tr>
<tr><td>9</td><td>Idaho</td><td>2.5</td><td>9</td><td>Minnesota</td><td>2.5</td></tr>
<tr><td>28</td><td>Illinois</td><td>2.2</td><td>9</td><td>New Mexico</td><td>2.5</td></tr>
<tr><td>9</td><td>Indiana</td><td>2.5</td><td>9</td><td>North Dakota</td><td>2.5</td></tr>
<tr><td>16</td><td>Iowa</td><td>2.4</td><td>9</td><td>Ohio</td><td>2.5</td></tr>
<tr><td>9</td><td>Kansas</td><td>2.5</td><td>16</td><td>Arizona</td><td>2.4</td></tr>
<tr><td>16</td><td>Kentucky</td><td>2.4</td><td>16</td><td>Iowa</td><td>2.4</td></tr>
<tr><td>16</td><td>Louisiana</td><td>2.4</td><td>16</td><td>Kentucky</td><td>2.4</td></tr>
<tr><td>5</td><td>Maine</td><td>2.6</td><td>16</td><td>Louisiana</td><td>2.4</td></tr>
<tr><td>16</td><td>Maryland</td><td>2.4</td><td>16</td><td>Maryland</td><td>2.4</td></tr>
<tr><td>45</td><td>Massachusetts</td><td>1.9</td><td>16</td><td>Missouri</td><td>2.4</td></tr>
<tr><td>28</td><td>Michigan</td><td>2.2</td><td>16</td><td>New Hampshire</td><td>2.4</td></tr>
<tr><td>9</td><td>Minnesota</td><td>2.5</td><td>16</td><td>Oregon</td><td>2.4</td></tr>
<tr><td>45</td><td>Mississippi</td><td>1.9</td><td>16</td><td>Texas</td><td>2.4</td></tr>
<tr><td>16</td><td>Missouri</td><td>2.4</td><td>25</td><td>Utah</td><td>2.3</td></tr>
<tr><td>35</td><td>Montana</td><td>2.1</td><td>25</td><td>Vermont</td><td>2.3</td></tr>
<tr><td>41</td><td>Nebraska</td><td>2.0</td><td>25</td><td>Washington</td><td>2.3</td></tr>
<tr><td>3</td><td>Nevada</td><td>2.9</td><td>28</td><td>Georgia</td><td>2.2</td></tr>
<tr><td>16</td><td>New Hampshire</td><td>2.4</td><td>28</td><td>Hawaii</td><td>2.2</td></tr>
<tr><td>41</td><td>New Jersey</td><td>2.0</td><td>28</td><td>Illinois</td><td>2.2</td></tr>
<tr><td>9</td><td>New Mexico</td><td>2.5</td><td>28</td><td>Michigan</td><td>2.2</td></tr>
<tr><td>45</td><td>New York</td><td>1.9</td><td>28</td><td>North Carolina</td><td>2.2</td></tr>
<tr><td>28</td><td>North Carolina</td><td>2.2</td><td>28</td><td>Tennessee</td><td>2.2</td></tr>
<tr><td>9</td><td>North Dakota</td><td>2.5</td><td>28</td><td>West Virginia</td><td>2.2</td></tr>
<tr><td>9</td><td>Ohio</td><td>2.5</td><td>35</td><td>Arkansas</td><td>2.1</td></tr>
<tr><td>4</td><td>Oklahoma</td><td>2.8</td><td>35</td><td>Colorado</td><td>2.1</td></tr>
<tr><td>16</td><td>Oregon</td><td>2.4</td><td>35</td><td>Florida</td><td>2.1</td></tr>
<tr><td>35</td><td>Pennsylvania</td><td>2.1</td><td>35</td><td>Montana</td><td>2.1</td></tr>
<tr><td>35</td><td>Rhode Island</td><td>2.1</td><td>35</td><td>Pennsylvania</td><td>2.1</td></tr>
<tr><td>41</td><td>South Carolina</td><td>2.0</td><td>35</td><td>Rhode Island</td><td>2.1</td></tr>
<tr><td>5</td><td>South Dakota</td><td>2.6</td><td>41</td><td>Nebraska</td><td>2.0</td></tr>
<tr><td>28</td><td>Tennessee</td><td>2.2</td><td>41</td><td>New Jersey</td><td>2.0</td></tr>
<tr><td>16</td><td>Texas</td><td>2.4</td><td>41</td><td>South Carolina</td><td>2.0</td></tr>
<tr><td>25</td><td>Utah</td><td>2.3</td><td>41</td><td>Virginia</td><td>2.0</td></tr>
<tr><td>25</td><td>Vermont</td><td>2.3</td><td>45</td><td>Alabama</td><td>1.9</td></tr>
<tr><td>41</td><td>Virginia</td><td>2.0</td><td>45</td><td>Massachusetts</td><td>1.9</td></tr>
<tr><td>25</td><td>Washington</td><td>2.3</td><td>45</td><td>Mississippi</td><td>1.9</td></tr>
<tr><td>28</td><td>West Virginia</td><td>2.2</td><td>45</td><td>New York</td><td>1.9</td></tr>
<tr><td>5</td><td>Wisconsin</td><td>2.6</td><td>49</td><td>Connecticut</td><td>1.7</td></tr>
<tr><td>2</td><td>Wyoming</td><td>3.1</td><td>49</td><td>Delaware</td><td>1.7</td></tr>
<tr><td></td><td></td><td></td><td></td><td>District of Columbia</td><td>1.2</td></tr>
</table>

Source: U.S. Bureau of the Census
"2016 American Community Survey-Table CP02" (http://www.census.gov/programs-surveys/acs/)
*No spouse present in household with children under 18 years old. A household includes all persons who occupy a housing unit.
A household consists of a single family, one person living alone, two or more families living together, or any other group of
related or unrelated persons who share living arrangements.

Same-Sex Couple Households in 2015

National Total = 858,896 Households*

ALPHA ORDER

RANK	STATE	HOUSEHOLDS	% of USA
29	Alabama	7,814	0.9%
47	Alaska	1,359	0.2%
14	Arizona	20,781	2.4%
36	Arkansas	5,501	0.6%
1	California	120,998	14.1%
16	Colorado	18,902	2.2%
26	Connecticut	9,513	1.1%
42	Delaware	3,799	0.4%
4	Florida	58,565	6.8%
11	Georgia	22,490	2.6%
37	Hawaii	4,568	0.5%
41	Idaho	3,834	0.4%
6	Illinois	31,322	3.6%
21	Indiana	14,602	1.7%
33	Iowa	6,207	0.7%
32	Kansas	6,322	0.7%
27	Kentucky	9,158	1.1%
25	Louisiana	9,539	1.1%
34	Maine	6,202	0.7%
17	Maryland	18,098	2.1%
7	Massachusetts	27,977	3.3%
15	Michigan	19,817	2.3%
22	Minnesota	13,999	1.6%
40	Mississippi	3,893	0.5%
19	Missouri	15,593	1.8%
46	Montana	1,571	0.2%
45	Nebraska	3,361	0.4%
28	Nevada	8,683	1.0%
39	New Hampshire	4,397	0.5%
12	New Jersey	21,376	2.5%
30	New Mexico	7,525	0.9%
2	New York	67,267	7.8%
10	North Carolina	23,915	2.8%
48	North Dakota	1,323	0.2%
8	Ohio	26,863	3.1%
24	Oklahoma	9,797	1.1%
18	Oregon	15,850	1.8%
5	Pennsylvania	31,412	3.7%
44	Rhode Island	3,456	0.4%
31	South Carolina	7,471	0.9%
49	South Dakota	1,144	0.1%
20	Tennessee	15,254	1.8%
3	Texas	66,546	7.7%
35	Utah	5,856	0.7%
43	Vermont	3,590	0.4%
13	Virginia	21,175	2.5%
9	Washington	26,184	3.0%
38	West Virginia	4,414	0.5%
23	Wisconsin	13,483	1.6%
50	Wyoming	784	0.1%

RANK ORDER

RANK	STATE	HOUSEHOLDS	% of USA
1	California	120,998	14.1%
2	New York	67,267	7.8%
3	Texas	66,546	7.7%
4	Florida	58,565	6.8%
5	Pennsylvania	31,412	3.7%
6	Illinois	31,322	3.6%
7	Massachusetts	27,977	3.3%
8	Ohio	26,863	3.1%
9	Washington	26,184	3.0%
10	North Carolina	23,915	2.8%
11	Georgia	22,490	2.6%
12	New Jersey	21,376	2.5%
13	Virginia	21,175	2.5%
14	Arizona	20,781	2.4%
15	Michigan	19,817	2.3%
16	Colorado	18,902	2.2%
17	Maryland	18,098	2.1%
18	Oregon	15,850	1.8%
19	Missouri	15,593	1.8%
20	Tennessee	15,254	1.8%
21	Indiana	14,602	1.7%
22	Minnesota	13,999	1.6%
23	Wisconsin	13,483	1.6%
24	Oklahoma	9,797	1.1%
25	Louisiana	9,539	1.1%
26	Connecticut	9,513	1.1%
27	Kentucky	9,158	1.1%
28	Nevada	8,683	1.0%
29	Alabama	7,814	0.9%
30	New Mexico	7,525	0.9%
31	South Carolina	7,471	0.9%
32	Kansas	6,322	0.7%
33	Iowa	6,207	0.7%
34	Maine	6,202	0.7%
35	Utah	5,856	0.7%
36	Arkansas	5,501	0.6%
37	Hawaii	4,568	0.5%
38	West Virginia	4,414	0.5%
39	New Hampshire	4,397	0.5%
40	Mississippi	3,893	0.5%
41	Idaho	3,834	0.4%
42	Delaware	3,799	0.4%
43	Vermont	3,590	0.4%
44	Rhode Island	3,456	0.4%
45	Nebraska	3,361	0.4%
46	Montana	1,571	0.2%
47	Alaska	1,359	0.2%
48	North Dakota	1,323	0.2%
49	South Dakota	1,144	0.1%
50	Wyoming	784	0.1%
	District of Columbia	5,346	0.6%

Source: U.S. Bureau of the Census
"Same Sex Couples Main" (https://www.census.gov/topics/families/same-sex-couples.html)
*The total is comprised of 425,357 married couples and 433,539 unmarried couples. Male couples are 412,001 of the households.
Female couples are 446,895 of the households.

Percent of Same-Sex Household Couples Who Are Married: 2015

National Percent = 49.5% of Same-Sex Households*

ALPHA ORDER				RANK ORDER		
RANK	STATE	PERCENT		RANK	STATE	PERCENT
16	Alabama	54.5		1	South Dakota	71.2
25	Alaska	51.1		2	Vermont	66.3
49	Arizona	35.4		3	New Hampshire	64.7
12	Arkansas	56.3		4	Connecticut	64.4
15	California	55.5		5	Delaware	61.2
18	Colorado	53.5		6	Massachusetts	59.0
4	Connecticut	64.4		7	Indiana	58.0
5	Delaware	61.2		8	Minnesota	57.9
42	Florida	42.1		9	Maryland	57.4
41	Georgia	42.7		10	Washington	57.1
30	Hawaii	49.8		11	Kansas	56.6
48	Idaho	35.7		12	Arkansas	56.3
33	Illinois	49.2		12	Wyoming	56.3
7	Indiana	58.0		14	Utah	55.8
27	Iowa	50.4		15	California	55.5
11	Kansas	56.6		16	Alabama	54.5
31	Kentucky	49.7		17	New York	53.6
40	Louisiana	42.9		18	Colorado	53.5
23	Maine	51.6		18	New Jersey	53.5
9	Maryland	57.4		20	Oregon	53.1
6	Massachusetts	59.0		21	Oklahoma	53.0
47	Michigan	36.2		22	Rhode Island	52.9
8	Minnesota	57.9		23	Maine	51.6
45	Mississippi	38.5		24	New Mexico	51.2
46	Missouri	37.5		25	Alaska	51.1
50	Montana	34.6		26	Virginia	50.6
28	Nebraska	50.2		27	Iowa	50.4
34	Nevada	48.6		28	Nebraska	50.2
3	New Hampshire	64.7		29	West Virginia	49.9
18	New Jersey	53.5		30	Hawaii	49.8
24	New Mexico	51.2		31	Kentucky	49.7
17	New York	53.6		31	North Dakota	49.7
38	North Carolina	45.6		33	Illinois	49.2
31	North Dakota	49.7		34	Nevada	48.6
43	Ohio	41.4		35	Pennsylvania	47.2
21	Oklahoma	53.0		36	South Carolina	45.8
20	Oregon	53.1		37	Wisconsin	45.7
35	Pennsylvania	47.2		38	North Carolina	45.6
22	Rhode Island	52.9		39	Tennessee	43.1
36	South Carolina	45.8		40	Louisiana	42.9
1	South Dakota	71.2		41	Georgia	42.7
39	Tennessee	43.1		42	Florida	42.1
44	Texas	40.9		43	Ohio	41.4
14	Utah	55.8		44	Texas	40.9
2	Vermont	66.3		45	Mississippi	38.5
26	Virginia	50.6		46	Missouri	37.5
10	Washington	57.1		47	Michigan	36.2
29	West Virginia	49.9		48	Idaho	35.7
37	Wisconsin	45.7		49	Arizona	35.4
12	Wyoming	56.3		50	Montana	34.6
					District of Columbia	46.5

Source: U.S. Bureau of the Census
"Same Sex Couples Main" (https://www.census.gov/topics/families/same-sex-couples.html)
*Male-couple households are 49 percent married. Female couple households are 50 percent married.

Housing Units in 2016

National Total = 135,702,775 Housing Units*

ALPHA ORDER

RANK	STATE	HOUSING UNITS	% of USA
24	Alabama	2,230,180	1.6%
49	Alaska	310,672	0.2%
14	Arizona	2,961,136	2.2%
31	Arkansas	1,354,801	1.0%
1	California	14,061,375	10.4%
22	Colorado	2,339,140	1.7%
29	Connecticut	1,499,145	1.1%
45	Delaware	426,154	0.3%
3	Florida	9,302,140	6.9%
10	Georgia	4,219,103	3.1%
42	Hawaii	537,170	0.4%
40	Idaho	700,829	0.5%
6	Illinois	5,327,165	3.9%
17	Indiana	2,854,595	2.1%
30	Iowa	1,380,087	1.0%
33	Kansas	1,259,870	0.9%
26	Kentucky	1,965,577	1.4%
25	Louisiana	2,037,067	1.5%
39	Maine	730,786	0.5%
20	Maryland	2,447,211	1.8%
16	Massachusetts	2,858,087	2.1%
8	Michigan	4,560,164	3.4%
21	Minnesota	2,409,701	1.8%
32	Mississippi	1,307,492	1.0%
18	Missouri	2,760,226	2.0%
43	Montana	497,749	0.4%
38	Nebraska	827,191	0.6%
34	Nevada	1,221,759	0.9%
41	New Hampshire	625,337	0.5%
11	New Jersey	3,604,688	2.7%
36	New Mexico	917,641	0.7%
4	New York	8,232,039	6.1%
9	North Carolina	4,540,697	3.3%
47	North Dakota	368,545	0.3%
7	Ohio	5,164,400	3.8%
28	Oklahoma	1,721,072	1.3%
27	Oregon	1,732,887	1.3%
5	Pennsylvania	5,611,995	4.1%
44	Rhode Island	462,598	0.3%
23	South Carolina	2,236,262	1.6%
46	South Dakota	383,827	0.3%
15	Tennessee	2,919,698	2.2%
2	Texas	10,754,268	7.9%
35	Utah	1,054,242	0.8%
48	Vermont	329,539	0.2%
12	Virginia	3,491,185	2.6%
13	Washington	3,025,802	2.2%
37	West Virginia	886,710	0.7%
19	Wisconsin	2,668,443	2.0%
50	Wyoming	270,625	0.2%

RANK ORDER

RANK	STATE	HOUSING UNITS	% of USA
1	California	14,061,375	10.4%
2	Texas	10,754,268	7.9%
3	Florida	9,302,140	6.9%
4	New York	8,232,039	6.1%
5	Pennsylvania	5,611,995	4.1%
6	Illinois	5,327,165	3.9%
7	Ohio	5,164,400	3.8%
8	Michigan	4,560,164	3.4%
9	North Carolina	4,540,697	3.3%
10	Georgia	4,219,103	3.1%
11	New Jersey	3,604,688	2.7%
12	Virginia	3,491,185	2.6%
13	Washington	3,025,802	2.2%
14	Arizona	2,961,136	2.2%
15	Tennessee	2,919,698	2.2%
16	Massachusetts	2,858,087	2.1%
17	Indiana	2,854,595	2.1%
18	Missouri	2,760,226	2.0%
19	Wisconsin	2,668,443	2.0%
20	Maryland	2,447,211	1.8%
21	Minnesota	2,409,701	1.8%
22	Colorado	2,339,140	1.7%
23	South Carolina	2,236,262	1.6%
24	Alabama	2,230,180	1.6%
25	Louisiana	2,037,067	1.5%
26	Kentucky	1,965,577	1.4%
27	Oregon	1,732,887	1.3%
28	Oklahoma	1,721,072	1.3%
29	Connecticut	1,499,145	1.1%
30	Iowa	1,380,087	1.0%
31	Arkansas	1,354,801	1.0%
32	Mississippi	1,307,492	1.0%
33	Kansas	1,259,870	0.9%
34	Nevada	1,221,759	0.9%
35	Utah	1,054,242	0.8%
36	New Mexico	917,641	0.7%
37	West Virginia	886,710	0.7%
38	Nebraska	827,191	0.6%
39	Maine	730,786	0.5%
40	Idaho	700,829	0.5%
41	New Hampshire	625,337	0.5%
42	Hawaii	537,170	0.4%
43	Montana	497,749	0.4%
44	Rhode Island	462,598	0.3%
45	Delaware	426,154	0.3%
46	South Dakota	383,827	0.3%
47	North Dakota	368,545	0.3%
48	Vermont	329,539	0.2%
49	Alaska	310,672	0.2%
50	Wyoming	270,625	0.2%
	District of Columbia	313,703	0.2%

Source: U.S. Bureau of the Census

"2016 American Community Survey-Table B25001" (http://www.census.gov/programs-surveys/acs/)

*A housing unit is a house, an apartment, a mobile home, a group of rooms, or a single room that is occupied (or if vacant, is intended for occupancy) as separate living quarters. Separate living quarters are those in which the occupants live and eat separately from any other persons in the building and which have direct access from the outside of the building or through a common hall.

Housing Units per Square Mile in 2016

National Average = 38.4 Housing Units*

ALPHA ORDER			RANK ORDER		
RANK	STATE	RATE	RANK	STATE	RATE
26	Alabama	43.9	1	New Jersey	486.0
50	Alaska	0.5	2	Rhode Island	442.7
33	Arizona	26.1	3	Massachusetts	364.6
34	Arkansas	26.0	4	Connecticut	309.4
13	California	90.2	5	Maryland	250.4
38	Colorado	22.6	6	Delaware	218.1
4	Connecticut	309.4	7	New York	174.4
6	Delaware	218.1	8	Florida	172.5
8	Florida	172.5	9	Ohio	126.1
19	Georgia	72.9	10	Pennsylvania	125.2
15	Hawaii	83.6	11	Illinois	95.8
44	Idaho	8.5	12	North Carolina	93.2
11	Illinois	95.8	13	California	90.2
17	Indiana	79.6	14	Virginia	88.2
36	Iowa	24.7	15	Hawaii	83.6
40	Kansas	15.4	16	Michigan	80.3
22	Kentucky	49.5	17	Indiana	79.6
24	Louisiana	46.8	18	South Carolina	74.3
37	Maine	23.7	19	Georgia	72.9
5	Maryland	250.4	20	Tennessee	70.8
3	Massachusetts	364.6	21	New Hampshire	69.7
16	Michigan	80.3	22	Kentucky	49.5
31	Minnesota	30.3	23	Wisconsin	49.1
32	Mississippi	27.9	24	Louisiana	46.8
28	Missouri	40.1	25	Washington	45.5
48	Montana	3.4	26	Alabama	43.9
43	Nebraska	10.8	27	Texas	41.1
42	Nevada	11.1	28	Missouri	40.1
21	New Hampshire	69.7	29	West Virginia	36.8
1	New Jersey	486.0	30	Vermont	35.6
45	New Mexico	7.6	31	Minnesota	30.3
7	New York	174.4	32	Mississippi	27.9
12	North Carolina	93.2	33	Arizona	26.1
46	North Dakota	5.3	34	Arkansas	26.0
9	Ohio	126.1	35	Oklahoma	25.1
35	Oklahoma	25.1	36	Iowa	24.7
39	Oregon	18.1	37	Maine	23.7
10	Pennsylvania	125.2	38	Colorado	22.6
2	Rhode Island	442.7	39	Oregon	18.1
18	South Carolina	74.3	40	Kansas	15.4
47	South Dakota	5.1	41	Utah	12.8
20	Tennessee	70.8	42	Nevada	11.1
27	Texas	41.1	43	Nebraska	10.8
41	Utah	12.8	44	Idaho	8.5
30	Vermont	35.6	45	New Mexico	7.6
14	Virginia	88.2	46	North Dakota	5.3
25	Washington	45.5	47	South Dakota	5.1
29	West Virginia	36.8	48	Montana	3.4
23	Wisconsin	49.1	49	Wyoming	2.8
49	Wyoming	2.8	50	Alaska	0.5
				District of Columbia	5,142.7

Source: CQ Press using data from U.S. Bureau of the Census
"2016 American Community Survey-Table B25001" (http://www.census.gov/programs-surveys/acs/)
*Based on land area. A housing unit is a house, an apartment, a mobile home, a group of rooms, or a single room that is occupied (or if vacant, is intended for occupancy) as separate living quarters. Separate living quarters are those in which the occupants live and eat separately from any other persons in the building and which have direct access from the outside of the building or through a common hall.

Percent of Housing Units That Are Owner-Occupied in 2016

National Percent = 63.1% of Housing Units*

ALPHA ORDER

RANK	STATE	PERCENT
12	Alabama	68.5
34	Alaska	64.5
38	Arizona	63.2
33	Arkansas	64.6
49	California	53.6
31	Colorado	64.8
31	Connecticut	64.8
8	Delaware	69.8
37	Florida	64.1
44	Georgia	61.5
47	Hawaii	57.2
12	Idaho	68.5
26	Illinois	65.3
15	Indiana	68.3
4	Iowa	70.6
24	Kansas	65.7
20	Kentucky	66.8
35	Louisiana	64.3
2	Maine	71.9
23	Maryland	65.9
42	Massachusetts	62.0
5	Michigan	70.3
3	Minnesota	71.3
18	Mississippi	67.3
22	Missouri	66.1
16	Montana	68.0
26	Nebraska	65.3
48	Nevada	54.9
6	New Hampshire	70.1
38	New Jersey	63.2
17	New Mexico	67.4
50	New York	53.3
36	North Carolina	64.2
38	North Dakota	63.2
25	Ohio	65.4
30	Oklahoma	64.9
43	Oregon	61.7
12	Pennsylvania	68.5
46	Rhode Island	58.0
11	South Carolina	68.6
19	South Dakota	67.2
29	Tennessee	65.1
45	Texas	61.1
7	Utah	69.9
8	Vermont	69.8
26	Virginia	65.3
41	Washington	62.5
1	West Virginia	72.4
21	Wisconsin	66.7
10	Wyoming	68.8

RANK ORDER

RANK	STATE	PERCENT
1	West Virginia	72.4
2	Maine	71.9
3	Minnesota	71.3
4	Iowa	70.6
5	Michigan	70.3
6	New Hampshire	70.1
7	Utah	69.9
8	Delaware	69.8
8	Vermont	69.8
10	Wyoming	68.8
11	South Carolina	68.6
12	Alabama	68.5
12	Idaho	68.5
12	Pennsylvania	68.5
15	Indiana	68.3
16	Montana	68.0
17	New Mexico	67.4
18	Mississippi	67.3
19	South Dakota	67.2
20	Kentucky	66.8
21	Wisconsin	66.7
22	Missouri	66.1
23	Maryland	65.9
24	Kansas	65.7
25	Ohio	65.4
26	Illinois	65.3
26	Nebraska	65.3
26	Virginia	65.3
29	Tennessee	65.1
30	Oklahoma	64.9
31	Colorado	64.8
31	Connecticut	64.8
33	Arkansas	64.6
34	Alaska	64.5
35	Louisiana	64.3
36	North Carolina	64.2
37	Florida	64.1
38	Arizona	63.2
38	New Jersey	63.2
38	North Dakota	63.2
41	Washington	62.5
42	Massachusetts	62.0
43	Oregon	61.7
44	Georgia	61.5
45	Texas	61.1
46	Rhode Island	58.0
47	Hawaii	57.2
48	Nevada	54.9
49	California	53.6
50	New York	53.3
	District of Columbia	39.2

Source: U.S. Bureau of the Census
   "2016 American Community Survey-Table CP04" (http://www.census.gov/programs-surveys/acs/)
*For occupied housing units.

New Housing Units Authorized in 2017

National Total = 1,264,051 Units*

ALPHA ORDER					RANK ORDER			
RANK	STATE		UNITS	% of USA	RANK	STATE	UNITS	% of USA
28	Alabama		14,497	1.1%	1	Texas	169,885	13.4%
49	Alaska		1,553	0.1%	2	Florida	118,548	9.4%
10	Arizona		37,981	3.0%	3	California	113,320	9.0%
33	Arkansas		11,021	0.9%	4	North Carolina	65,009	5.1%
3	California		113,320	9.0%	5	Georgia	49,591	3.9%
7	Colorado		41,911	3.3%	6	Washington	45,780	3.6%
41	Connecticut		4,606	0.4%	7	Colorado	41,911	3.3%
37	Delaware		6,735	0.5%	8	New York	40,772	3.2%
2	Florida		118,548	9.4%	9	Tennessee	38,470	3.0%
5	Georgia		49,591	3.9%	10	Arizona	37,981	3.0%
43	Hawaii		4,035	0.3%	11	South Carolina	34,730	2.7%
29	Idaho		13,348	1.1%	12	Virginia	33,417	2.6%
14	Illinois		25,313	2.0%	13	New Jersey	28,893	2.3%
20	Indiana		20,115	1.6%	14	Illinois	25,313	2.0%
30	Iowa		13,233	1.0%	15	Michigan	24,518	1.9%
35	Kansas		8,636	0.7%	16	Utah	24,386	1.9%
31	Kentucky		13,055	1.0%	17	Ohio	23,755	1.9%
27	Louisiana		15,232	1.2%	18	Minnesota	22,927	1.8%
40	Maine		4,607	0.4%	19	Pennsylvania	22,509	1.8%
26	Maryland		16,008	1.3%	20	Indiana	20,115	1.6%
25	Massachusetts		17,230	1.4%	21	Oregon	19,886	1.6%
15	Michigan		24,518	1.9%	22	Nevada	19,376	1.5%
18	Minnesota		22,927	1.8%	23	Wisconsin	18,511	1.5%
36	Mississippi		7,881	0.6%	24	Missouri	17,852	1.4%
24	Missouri		17,852	1.4%	25	Massachusetts	17,230	1.4%
42	Montana		4,424	0.3%	26	Maryland	16,008	1.3%
34	Nebraska		8,919	0.7%	27	Louisiana	15,232	1.2%
22	Nevada		19,376	1.5%	28	Alabama	14,497	1.1%
44	New Hampshire		3,395	0.3%	29	Idaho	13,348	1.1%
13	New Jersey		28,893	2.3%	30	Iowa	13,233	1.0%
39	New Mexico		4,755	0.4%	31	Kentucky	13,055	1.0%
8	New York		40,772	3.2%	32	Oklahoma	11,168	0.9%
4	North Carolina		65,009	5.1%	33	Arkansas	11,021	0.9%
45	North Dakota		3,375	0.3%	34	Nebraska	8,919	0.7%
17	Ohio		23,755	1.9%	35	Kansas	8,636	0.7%
32	Oklahoma		11,168	0.9%	36	Mississippi	7,881	0.6%
21	Oregon		19,886	1.6%	37	Delaware	6,735	0.5%
19	Pennsylvania		22,509	1.8%	38	South Dakota	5,364	0.4%
50	Rhode Island		1,156	0.1%	39	New Mexico	4,755	0.4%
11	South Carolina		34,730	2.7%	40	Maine	4,607	0.4%
38	South Dakota		5,364	0.4%	41	Connecticut	4,606	0.4%
9	Tennessee		38,470	3.0%	42	Montana	4,424	0.3%
1	Texas		169,885	13.4%	43	Hawaii	4,035	0.3%
16	Utah		24,386	1.9%	44	New Hampshire	3,395	0.3%
48	Vermont		1,727	0.1%	45	North Dakota	3,375	0.3%
12	Virginia		33,417	2.6%	46	West Virginia	2,700	0.2%
6	Washington		45,780	3.6%	47	Wyoming	1,899	0.2%
46	West Virginia		2,700	0.2%	48	Vermont	1,727	0.1%
23	Wisconsin		18,511	1.5%	49	Alaska	1,553	0.1%
47	Wyoming		1,899	0.2%	50	Rhode Island	1,156	0.1%
						District of Columbia	6,037	0.5%

Source: U.S. Bureau of the Census
  "Building Permits Survey" (https://www.census.gov/construction/bps/stateannual.html)
*Preliminary and unadjusted year-to-date monthly data as of December 2017. Includes single and multifamily privately owned units. All places issuing building permits for privately owned residential structures. More than 98 percent of all privately owned residential buildings constructed are in permit-issuing places.

Value of New Housing Units Authorized in 2017

National Total = $254,605,033,000*

ALPHA ORDER

RANK	STATE	VALUE	% of USA
28	Alabama	$2,728,080,000	1.1%
48	Alaska	401,752,000	0.2%
8	Arizona	8,322,680,000	3.3%
33	Arkansas	1,764,771,000	0.7%
2	California	27,048,354,000	10.6%
7	Colorado	9,255,053,000	3.6%
37	Connecticut	1,170,409,000	0.5%
43	Delaware	818,053,000	0.3%
3	Florida	26,888,015,000	10.6%
6	Georgia	9,730,898,000	3.8%
38	Hawaii	1,132,364,000	0.4%
29	Idaho	2,530,075,000	1.0%
17	Illinois	4,662,939,000	1.8%
19	Indiana	4,324,752,000	1.7%
30	Iowa	2,489,575,000	1.0%
34	Kansas	1,705,287,000	0.7%
32	Kentucky	2,134,515,000	0.8%
27	Louisiana	2,960,474,000	1.2%
41	Maine	853,578,000	0.3%
26	Maryland	3,236,665,000	1.3%
22	Massachusetts	3,943,824,000	1.5%
15	Michigan	5,036,259,000	2.0%
16	Minnesota	5,006,506,000	2.0%
36	Mississippi	1,334,565,000	0.5%
25	Missouri	3,267,283,000	1.3%
42	Montana	844,812,000	0.3%
35	Nebraska	1,489,682,000	0.6%
24	Nevada	3,310,283,000	1.3%
44	New Hampshire	693,077,000	0.3%
20	New Jersey	4,150,146,000	1.6%
39	New Mexico	945,003,000	0.4%
10	New York	7,094,816,000	2.8%
4	North Carolina	12,353,457,000	4.9%
45	North Dakota	606,088,000	0.2%
14	Ohio	5,059,703,000	2.0%
31	Oklahoma	2,199,267,000	0.9%
21	Oregon	4,125,989,000	1.6%
18	Pennsylvania	4,379,442,000	1.7%
50	Rhode Island	251,186,000	0.1%
9	South Carolina	7,763,489,000	3.0%
40	South Dakota	878,028,000	0.3%
11	Tennessee	7,066,820,000	2.8%
1	Texas	31,879,563,000	12.5%
13	Utah	5,312,600,000	2.1%
49	Vermont	394,976,000	0.2%
12	Virginia	5,721,333,000	2.2%
5	Washington	9,843,132,000	3.9%
47	West Virginia	457,261,000	0.2%
23	Wisconsin	3,822,509,000	1.5%
46	Wyoming	526,106,000	0.2%

RANK ORDER

RANK	STATE	VALUE	% of USA
1	Texas	$31,879,563,000	12.5%
2	California	27,048,354,000	10.6%
3	Florida	26,888,015,000	10.6%
4	North Carolina	12,353,457,000	4.9%
5	Washington	9,843,132,000	3.9%
6	Georgia	9,730,898,000	3.8%
7	Colorado	9,255,053,000	3.6%
8	Arizona	8,322,680,000	3.3%
9	South Carolina	7,763,489,000	3.0%
10	New York	7,094,816,000	2.8%
11	Tennessee	7,066,820,000	2.8%
12	Virginia	5,721,333,000	2.2%
13	Utah	5,312,600,000	2.1%
14	Ohio	5,059,703,000	2.0%
15	Michigan	5,036,259,000	2.0%
16	Minnesota	5,006,506,000	2.0%
17	Illinois	4,662,939,000	1.8%
18	Pennsylvania	4,379,442,000	1.7%
19	Indiana	4,324,752,000	1.7%
20	New Jersey	4,150,146,000	1.6%
21	Oregon	4,125,989,000	1.6%
22	Massachusetts	3,943,824,000	1.5%
23	Wisconsin	3,822,509,000	1.5%
24	Nevada	3,310,283,000	1.3%
25	Missouri	3,267,283,000	1.3%
26	Maryland	3,236,665,000	1.3%
27	Louisiana	2,960,474,000	1.2%
28	Alabama	2,728,080,000	1.1%
29	Idaho	2,530,075,000	1.0%
30	Iowa	2,489,575,000	1.0%
31	Oklahoma	2,199,267,000	0.9%
32	Kentucky	2,134,515,000	0.8%
33	Arkansas	1,764,771,000	0.7%
34	Kansas	1,705,287,000	0.7%
35	Nebraska	1,489,682,000	0.6%
36	Mississippi	1,334,565,000	0.5%
37	Connecticut	1,170,409,000	0.5%
38	Hawaii	1,132,364,000	0.4%
39	New Mexico	945,003,000	0.4%
40	South Dakota	878,028,000	0.3%
41	Maine	853,578,000	0.3%
42	Montana	844,812,000	0.3%
43	Delaware	818,053,000	0.3%
44	New Hampshire	693,077,000	0.3%
45	North Dakota	606,088,000	0.2%
46	Wyoming	526,106,000	0.2%
47	West Virginia	457,261,000	0.2%
48	Alaska	401,752,000	0.2%
49	Vermont	394,976,000	0.2%
50	Rhode Island	251,186,000	0.1%
	District of Columbia	689,537,000	0.3%

Source: U.S. Bureau of the Census
"Building Permits Survey" (https://www.census.gov/construction/bps/stateannual.html)
*Preliminary and unadjusted year-to-date monthly data as of December 2017. Includes single and multifamily privately owned units. All places issuing building permits for privately owned residential structures. More than 98 percent of all privately owned residential buildings constructed are in permit-issuing places.

Average Value of New Housing Units in 2017

National Average = $201,420 per Unit*

<table>
<tr><td colspan="3">ALPHA ORDER</td><td colspan="3">RANK ORDER</td></tr>
<tr><td>RANK</td><td>STATE</td><td>VALUE</td><td>RANK</td><td>STATE</td><td>VALUE</td></tr>
<tr><td>32</td><td>Alabama</td><td>$188,182</td><td>1</td><td>Hawaii</td><td>$280,635</td></tr>
<tr><td>3</td><td>Alaska</td><td>258,694</td><td>2</td><td>Wyoming</td><td>277,044</td></tr>
<tr><td>11</td><td>Arizona</td><td>219,127</td><td>3</td><td>Alaska</td><td>258,694</td></tr>
<tr><td>48</td><td>Arkansas</td><td>160,128</td><td>4</td><td>Connecticut</td><td>254,105</td></tr>
<tr><td>5</td><td>California</td><td>238,690</td><td>5</td><td>California</td><td>238,690</td></tr>
<tr><td>10</td><td>Colorado</td><td>220,826</td><td>6</td><td>Massachusetts</td><td>228,893</td></tr>
<tr><td>4</td><td>Connecticut</td><td>254,105</td><td>7</td><td>Vermont</td><td>228,706</td></tr>
<tr><td>50</td><td>Delaware</td><td>121,463</td><td>8</td><td>Florida</td><td>226,811</td></tr>
<tr><td>8</td><td>Florida</td><td>226,811</td><td>9</td><td>South Carolina</td><td>223,538</td></tr>
<tr><td>26</td><td>Georgia</td><td>196,223</td><td>10</td><td>Colorado</td><td>220,826</td></tr>
<tr><td>1</td><td>Hawaii</td><td>280,635</td><td>11</td><td>Arizona</td><td>219,127</td></tr>
<tr><td>31</td><td>Idaho</td><td>189,547</td><td>12</td><td>Minnesota</td><td>218,367</td></tr>
<tr><td>36</td><td>Illinois</td><td>184,211</td><td>13</td><td>Utah</td><td>217,855</td></tr>
<tr><td>16</td><td>Indiana</td><td>215,001</td><td>14</td><td>Rhode Island</td><td>217,289</td></tr>
<tr><td>33</td><td>Iowa</td><td>188,134</td><td>15</td><td>Washington</td><td>215,009</td></tr>
<tr><td>24</td><td>Kansas</td><td>197,463</td><td>16</td><td>Indiana</td><td>215,001</td></tr>
<tr><td>47</td><td>Kentucky</td><td>163,502</td><td>17</td><td>Ohio</td><td>212,995</td></tr>
<tr><td>28</td><td>Louisiana</td><td>194,359</td><td>18</td><td>Oregon</td><td>207,482</td></tr>
<tr><td>35</td><td>Maine</td><td>185,278</td><td>19</td><td>Wisconsin</td><td>206,499</td></tr>
<tr><td>22</td><td>Maryland</td><td>202,190</td><td>20</td><td>Michigan</td><td>205,411</td></tr>
<tr><td>6</td><td>Massachusetts</td><td>228,893</td><td>21</td><td>New Hampshire</td><td>204,146</td></tr>
<tr><td>20</td><td>Michigan</td><td>205,411</td><td>22</td><td>Maryland</td><td>202,190</td></tr>
<tr><td>12</td><td>Minnesota</td><td>218,367</td><td>23</td><td>New Mexico</td><td>198,739</td></tr>
<tr><td>44</td><td>Mississippi</td><td>169,340</td><td>24</td><td>Kansas</td><td>197,463</td></tr>
<tr><td>38</td><td>Missouri</td><td>183,021</td><td>25</td><td>Oklahoma</td><td>196,926</td></tr>
<tr><td>29</td><td>Montana</td><td>190,961</td><td>26</td><td>Georgia</td><td>196,223</td></tr>
<tr><td>45</td><td>Nebraska</td><td>167,023</td><td>27</td><td>Pennsylvania</td><td>194,564</td></tr>
<tr><td>42</td><td>Nevada</td><td>170,844</td><td>28</td><td>Louisiana</td><td>194,359</td></tr>
<tr><td>21</td><td>New Hampshire</td><td>204,146</td><td>29</td><td>Montana</td><td>190,961</td></tr>
<tr><td>49</td><td>New Jersey</td><td>143,638</td><td>30</td><td>North Carolina</td><td>190,027</td></tr>
<tr><td>23</td><td>New Mexico</td><td>198,739</td><td>31</td><td>Idaho</td><td>189,547</td></tr>
<tr><td>40</td><td>New York</td><td>174,012</td><td>32</td><td>Alabama</td><td>188,182</td></tr>
<tr><td>30</td><td>North Carolina</td><td>190,027</td><td>33</td><td>Iowa</td><td>188,134</td></tr>
<tr><td>39</td><td>North Dakota</td><td>179,582</td><td>34</td><td>Texas</td><td>187,654</td></tr>
<tr><td>17</td><td>Ohio</td><td>212,995</td><td>35</td><td>Maine</td><td>185,278</td></tr>
<tr><td>25</td><td>Oklahoma</td><td>196,926</td><td>36</td><td>Illinois</td><td>184,211</td></tr>
<tr><td>18</td><td>Oregon</td><td>207,482</td><td>37</td><td>Tennessee</td><td>183,697</td></tr>
<tr><td>27</td><td>Pennsylvania</td><td>194,564</td><td>38</td><td>Missouri</td><td>183,021</td></tr>
<tr><td>14</td><td>Rhode Island</td><td>217,289</td><td>39</td><td>North Dakota</td><td>179,582</td></tr>
<tr><td>9</td><td>South Carolina</td><td>223,538</td><td>40</td><td>New York</td><td>174,012</td></tr>
<tr><td>46</td><td>South Dakota</td><td>163,689</td><td>41</td><td>Virginia</td><td>171,210</td></tr>
<tr><td>37</td><td>Tennessee</td><td>183,697</td><td>42</td><td>Nevada</td><td>170,844</td></tr>
<tr><td>34</td><td>Texas</td><td>187,654</td><td>43</td><td>West Virginia</td><td>169,356</td></tr>
<tr><td>13</td><td>Utah</td><td>217,855</td><td>44</td><td>Mississippi</td><td>169,340</td></tr>
<tr><td>7</td><td>Vermont</td><td>228,706</td><td>45</td><td>Nebraska</td><td>167,023</td></tr>
<tr><td>41</td><td>Virginia</td><td>171,210</td><td>46</td><td>South Dakota</td><td>163,689</td></tr>
<tr><td>15</td><td>Washington</td><td>215,009</td><td>47</td><td>Kentucky</td><td>163,502</td></tr>
<tr><td>43</td><td>West Virginia</td><td>169,356</td><td>48</td><td>Arkansas</td><td>160,128</td></tr>
<tr><td>19</td><td>Wisconsin</td><td>206,499</td><td>49</td><td>New Jersey</td><td>143,638</td></tr>
<tr><td>2</td><td>Wyoming</td><td>277,044</td><td>50</td><td>Delaware</td><td>121,463</td></tr>
<tr><td></td><td></td><td></td><td></td><td>District of Columbia</td><td>114,218</td></tr>
</table>

Source: CQ Press using data from U.S. Bureau of the Census
"Building Permits Survey" (https://www.census.gov/construction/bps/stateannual.html)
*Preliminary and unadjusted year-to-date monthly data as of December 2017. Includes single and multifamily privately owned units. All places issuing building permits for privately owned residential structures. More than 98 percent of all privately owned residential buildings constructed are in permit-issuing places.

Median Value of Owner-Occupied Housing in 2016

National Median = $205,000*

ALPHA ORDER

RANK	STATE	MEDIAN
44	Alabama	$136,200
11	Alaska	267,800
22	Arizona	205,900
48	Arkansas	123,300
2	California	477,500
5	Colorado	314,200
10	Connecticut	274,600
16	Delaware	243,400
23	Florida	197,700
31	Georgia	166,800
1	Hawaii	592,000
24	Idaho	189,400
25	Illinois	186,500
46	Indiana	134,800
42	Iowa	142,300
41	Kansas	144,900
45	Kentucky	135,600
35	Louisiana	158,000
26	Maine	184,700
6	Maryland	306,900
3	Massachusetts	366,900
40	Michigan	147,100
20	Minnesota	211,800
50	Mississippi	113,900
38	Missouri	151,400
19	Montana	217,200
39	Nebraska	148,100
17	Nevada	239,500
13	New Hampshire	251,100
4	New Jersey	328,200
30	New Mexico	167,500
8	New York	302,400
32	North Carolina	165,400
27	North Dakota	184,100
43	Ohio	140,100
47	Oklahoma	132,200
9	Oregon	287,100
28	Pennsylvania	174,100
15	Rhode Island	247,700
37	South Carolina	153,900
34	South Dakota	160,700
36	Tennessee	157,700
33	Texas	161,500
14	Utah	250,300
18	Vermont	223,700
12	Virginia	264,000
7	Washington	306,400
49	West Virginia	117,900
29	Wisconsin	173,200
21	Wyoming	209,500

RANK ORDER

RANK	STATE	MEDIAN
1	Hawaii	$592,000
2	California	477,500
3	Massachusetts	366,900
4	New Jersey	328,200
5	Colorado	314,200
6	Maryland	306,900
7	Washington	306,400
8	New York	302,400
9	Oregon	287,100
10	Connecticut	274,600
11	Alaska	267,800
12	Virginia	264,000
13	New Hampshire	251,100
14	Utah	250,300
15	Rhode Island	247,700
16	Delaware	243,400
17	Nevada	239,500
18	Vermont	223,700
19	Montana	217,200
20	Minnesota	211,800
21	Wyoming	209,500
22	Arizona	205,900
23	Florida	197,700
24	Idaho	189,400
25	Illinois	186,500
26	Maine	184,700
27	North Dakota	184,100
28	Pennsylvania	174,100
29	Wisconsin	173,200
30	New Mexico	167,500
31	Georgia	166,800
32	North Carolina	165,400
33	Texas	161,500
34	South Dakota	160,700
35	Louisiana	158,000
36	Tennessee	157,700
37	South Carolina	153,900
38	Missouri	151,400
39	Nebraska	148,100
40	Michigan	147,100
41	Kansas	144,900
42	Iowa	142,300
43	Ohio	140,100
44	Alabama	136,200
45	Kentucky	135,600
46	Indiana	134,800
47	Oklahoma	132,200
48	Arkansas	123,300
49	West Virginia	117,900
50	Mississippi	113,900

District of Columbia — 576,100

Source: U.S. Bureau of the Census
"2016 American Community Survey-Table CP04" (http://www.census.gov/programs-surveys/acs/)
*Housing units with a mortgage.

Percent Change in House Prices: 2016 to 2017

National Percent Change = 6.5% Increase*

ALPHA ORDER			RANK ORDER		
RANK	STATE	PERCENT CHANGE	RANK	STATE	PERCENT CHANGE
36	Alabama	4.3	1	Washington	11.5
43	Alaska	3.1	2	Arizona	10.0
2	Arizona	10.0	2	Hawaii	10.0
36	Arkansas	4.3	4	Nevada	9.6
10	California	8.4	5	Idaho	9.2
9	Colorado	8.5	5	Utah	9.2
43	Connecticut	3.1	7	Oregon	8.8
46	Delaware	2.2	8	Tennessee	8.7
11	Florida	8.1	9	Colorado	8.5
13	Georgia	7.6	10	California	8.4
2	Hawaii	10.0	11	Florida	8.1
5	Idaho	9.2	12	Michigan	7.9
40	Illinois	3.9	13	Georgia	7.6
32	Indiana	5.0	14	Massachusetts	7.4
42	Iowa	3.6	15	Kentucky	7.3
33	Kansas	4.6	15	Rhode Island	7.3
15	Kentucky	7.3	17	Maine	7.2
35	Louisiana	4.4	17	South Carolina	7.2
17	Maine	7.2	19	Texas	7.1
27	Maryland	5.8	20	Wisconsin	6.8
14	Massachusetts	7.4	21	New Hampshire	6.6
12	Michigan	7.9	22	Montana	6.5
23	Minnesota	6.2	23	Minnesota	6.2
49	Mississippi	1.9	24	Nebraska	6.1
30	Missouri	5.6	25	North Carolina	6.0
22	Montana	6.5	26	Ohio	5.9
24	Nebraska	6.1	27	Maryland	5.8
4	Nevada	9.6	27	New York	5.8
21	New Hampshire	6.6	29	South Dakota	5.7
40	New Jersey	3.9	30	Missouri	5.6
31	New Mexico	5.4	31	New Mexico	5.4
27	New York	5.8	32	Indiana	5.0
25	North Carolina	6.0	33	Kansas	4.6
47	North Dakota	2.0	33	Virginia	4.6
26	Ohio	5.9	35	Louisiana	4.4
39	Oklahoma	4.0	36	Alabama	4.3
7	Oregon	8.8	36	Arkansas	4.3
36	Pennsylvania	4.3	36	Pennsylvania	4.3
15	Rhode Island	7.3	39	Oklahoma	4.0
17	South Carolina	7.2	40	Illinois	3.9
29	South Dakota	5.7	40	New Jersey	3.9
8	Tennessee	8.7	42	Iowa	3.6
19	Texas	7.1	43	Alaska	3.1
5	Utah	9.2	43	Connecticut	3.1
47	Vermont	2.0	45	Wyoming	2.3
33	Virginia	4.6	46	Delaware	2.2
1	Washington	11.5	47	North Dakota	2.0
50	West Virginia	1.1	47	Vermont	2.0
20	Wisconsin	6.8	49	Mississippi	1.9
45	Wyoming	2.3	50	West Virginia	1.1
				District of Columbia	11.6

Source: Federal Housing Finance Agency
  "State HPI Summary" (http://www.fhfa.gov/DataTools/Tools/Pages/House-Price-Index-%28HPI%29.aspx)
*Single-family house prices. As of September 30, 2017.

Percent Change in House Prices: 2013 to 2017

National Percent Change = 34.6% Increase*

ALPHA ORDER			RANK ORDER		
RANK	STATE	PERCENT CHANGE	RANK	STATE	PERCENT CHANGE
32	Alabama	20.8	1	Nevada	82.3
46	Alaska	13.5	2	California	63.6
7	Arizona	54.2	3	Colorado	58.2
41	Arkansas	16.0	4	Florida	58.1
2	California	63.6	5	Washington	57.0
3	Colorado	58.2	6	Oregon	55.6
50	Connecticut	6.5	7	Arizona	54.2
48	Delaware	11.7	8	Utah	46.5
4	Florida	58.1	9	Idaho	45.9
10	Georgia	45.7	10	Georgia	45.7
13	Hawaii	41.4	11	Michigan	43.7
9	Idaho	45.9	12	Texas	41.5
38	Illinois	19.7	13	Hawaii	41.4
29	Indiana	24.8	14	Tennessee	35.7
34	Iowa	20.3	15	South Carolina	33.4
31	Kansas	21.6	16	Minnesota	32.3
28	Kentucky	25.1	17	Massachusetts	30.3
33	Louisiana	20.7	18	Montana	29.9
30	Maine	23.8	19	North Carolina	29.7
36	Maryland	19.8	20	Nebraska	27.5
17	Massachusetts	30.3	21	Rhode Island	27.4
11	Michigan	43.7	22	New Hampshire	26.2
16	Minnesota	32.3	23	Ohio	26.1
45	Mississippi	13.6	24	South Dakota	26.0
25	Missouri	25.9	25	Missouri	25.9
18	Montana	29.9	26	North Dakota	25.8
20	Nebraska	27.5	27	Wisconsin	25.3
1	Nevada	82.3	28	Kentucky	25.1
22	New Hampshire	26.2	29	Indiana	24.8
43	New Jersey	15.1	30	Maine	23.8
42	New Mexico	15.3	31	Kansas	21.6
40	New York	17.6	32	Alabama	20.8
19	North Carolina	29.7	33	Louisiana	20.7
26	North Dakota	25.8	34	Iowa	20.3
23	Ohio	26.1	35	Oklahoma	20.2
35	Oklahoma	20.2	36	Maryland	19.8
6	Oregon	55.6	36	Virginia	19.8
39	Pennsylvania	18.3	38	Illinois	19.7
21	Rhode Island	27.4	39	Pennsylvania	18.3
15	South Carolina	33.4	40	New York	17.6
24	South Dakota	26.0	41	Arkansas	16.0
14	Tennessee	35.7	42	New Mexico	15.3
12	Texas	41.5	43	New Jersey	15.1
8	Utah	46.5	44	Wyoming	13.8
49	Vermont	9.2	45	Mississippi	13.6
36	Virginia	19.8	46	Alaska	13.5
5	Washington	57.0	47	West Virginia	12.5
47	West Virginia	12.5	48	Delaware	11.7
27	Wisconsin	25.3	49	Vermont	9.2
44	Wyoming	13.8	50	Connecticut	6.5
				District of Columbia	47.1

Source: Federal Housing Finance Agency
"State HPI Summary" (http://www.fhfa.gov/DataTools/Tools/Pages/House-Price-Index-%28HPI%29.aspx)
*Single-family house prices. As of September 30, 2017.

Percent of Owner-Occupied Housing Units with a Mortgage in 2016

National Percent = 63.0% with Mortgages

ALPHA ORDER

RANK	STATE	PERCENT
41	Alabama	56.6
26	Alaska	63.1
21	Arizona	64.1
46	Arkansas	54.4
3	California	71.1
2	Colorado	71.6
9	Connecticut	67.9
20	Delaware	64.2
39	Florida	57.1
17	Georgia	65.0
15	Hawaii	65.9
18	Idaho	64.5
23	Illinois	64.0
16	Indiana	65.5
31	Iowa	60.6
34	Kansas	59.8
36	Kentucky	58.7
48	Louisiana	52.4
27	Maine	62.0
1	Maryland	73.6
5	Massachusetts	69.6
30	Michigan	60.7
12	Minnesota	67.2
49	Mississippi	50.1
28	Missouri	61.9
41	Montana	56.6
32	Nebraska	60.4
8	Nevada	68.1
13	New Hampshire	66.5
10	New Jersey	67.5
45	New Mexico	54.8
29	New York	61.1
24	North Carolina	63.4
47	North Dakota	53.5
25	Ohio	63.2
44	Oklahoma	55.9
14	Oregon	66.3
33	Pennsylvania	60.3
11	Rhode Island	67.3
37	South Carolina	58.1
43	South Dakota	56.2
35	Tennessee	59.5
38	Texas	57.8
4	Utah	70.9
19	Vermont	64.3
6	Virginia	69.2
7	Washington	69.0
50	West Virginia	47.9
21	Wisconsin	64.1
40	Wyoming	56.8

RANK ORDER

RANK	STATE	PERCENT
1	Maryland	73.6
2	Colorado	71.6
3	California	71.1
4	Utah	70.9
5	Massachusetts	69.6
6	Virginia	69.2
7	Washington	69.0
8	Nevada	68.1
9	Connecticut	67.9
10	New Jersey	67.5
11	Rhode Island	67.3
12	Minnesota	67.2
13	New Hampshire	66.5
14	Oregon	66.3
15	Hawaii	65.9
16	Indiana	65.5
17	Georgia	65.0
18	Idaho	64.5
19	Vermont	64.3
20	Delaware	64.2
21	Arizona	64.1
21	Wisconsin	64.1
23	Illinois	64.0
24	North Carolina	63.4
25	Ohio	63.2
26	Alaska	63.1
27	Maine	62.0
28	Missouri	61.9
29	New York	61.1
30	Michigan	60.7
31	Iowa	60.6
32	Nebraska	60.4
33	Pennsylvania	60.3
34	Kansas	59.8
35	Tennessee	59.5
36	Kentucky	58.7
37	South Carolina	58.1
38	Texas	57.8
39	Florida	57.1
40	Wyoming	56.8
41	Alabama	56.6
41	Montana	56.6
43	South Dakota	56.2
44	Oklahoma	55.9
45	New Mexico	54.8
46	Arkansas	54.4
47	North Dakota	53.5
48	Louisiana	52.4
49	Mississippi	50.1
50	West Virginia	47.9
	District of Columbia	75.7

Source: CQ Press using data from U.S. Bureau of the Census
"2016 American Community Survey-Table CP04" (http://www.census.gov/programs-surveys/acs/)

Median Monthly Mortgage Payment in 2016

National Median = $1,486*

ALPHA ORDER

RANK	STATE	MEDIAN
45	Alabama	$1,126
8	Alaska	1,851
27	Arizona	1,328
49	Arkansas	1,017
3	California	2,188
13	Colorado	1,597
6	Connecticut	1,997
19	Delaware	1,463
22	Florida	1,410
26	Georgia	1,336
2	Hawaii	2,239
43	Idaho	1,168
14	Illinois	1,588
48	Indiana	1,070
40	Iowa	1,186
32	Kansas	1,264
46	Kentucky	1,111
36	Louisiana	1,214
27	Maine	1,328
7	Maryland	1,918
4	Massachusetts	2,069
35	Michigan	1,215
17	Minnesota	1,472
47	Mississippi	1,087
38	Missouri	1,210
29	Montana	1,327
31	Nebraska	1,290
23	Nevada	1,401
9	New Hampshire	1,821
1	New Jersey	2,343
38	New Mexico	1,210
5	New York	2,020
34	North Carolina	1,225
30	North Dakota	1,318
37	Ohio	1,211
43	Oklahoma	1,168
15	Oregon	1,572
21	Pennsylvania	1,416
10	Rhode Island	1,740
41	South Carolina	1,182
33	South Dakota	1,239
42	Tennessee	1,172
18	Texas	1,469
20	Utah	1,437
16	Vermont	1,507
12	Virginia	1,692
11	Washington	1,727
50	West Virginia	997
25	Wisconsin	1,348
24	Wyoming	1,367

RANK ORDER

RANK	STATE	MEDIAN
1	New Jersey	$2,343
2	Hawaii	2,239
3	California	2,188
4	Massachusetts	2,069
5	New York	2,020
6	Connecticut	1,997
7	Maryland	1,918
8	Alaska	1,851
9	New Hampshire	1,821
10	Rhode Island	1,740
11	Washington	1,727
12	Virginia	1,692
13	Colorado	1,597
14	Illinois	1,588
15	Oregon	1,572
16	Vermont	1,507
17	Minnesota	1,472
18	Texas	1,469
19	Delaware	1,463
20	Utah	1,437
21	Pennsylvania	1,416
22	Florida	1,410
23	Nevada	1,401
24	Wyoming	1,367
25	Wisconsin	1,348
26	Georgia	1,336
27	Arizona	1,328
27	Maine	1,328
29	Montana	1,327
30	North Dakota	1,318
31	Nebraska	1,290
32	Kansas	1,264
33	South Dakota	1,239
34	North Carolina	1,225
35	Michigan	1,215
36	Louisiana	1,214
37	Ohio	1,211
38	Missouri	1,210
38	New Mexico	1,210
40	Iowa	1,186
41	South Carolina	1,182
42	Tennessee	1,172
43	Idaho	1,168
43	Oklahoma	1,168
45	Alabama	1,126
46	Kentucky	1,111
47	Mississippi	1,087
48	Indiana	1,070
49	Arkansas	1,017
50	West Virginia	997
	District of Columbia	2,422

Source: U.S. Bureau of the Census
"2016 American Community Survey-Table CP04" (http://www.census.gov/programs-surveys/acs/)
*Monthly housing costs for owner-occupied housing.

Percent of Home Owners Spending 30% or More of Household Income on Housing Costs in 2016
National Percent = 28.1% of Home Owners*

ALPHA ORDER

RANK	STATE	PERCENT
31	Alabama	25.0
18	Alaska	28.1
16	Arizona	28.3
44	Arkansas	20.9
1	California	38.6
22	Colorado	27.0
9	Connecticut	30.7
21	Delaware	27.1
4	Florida	34.0
28	Georgia	25.7
2	Hawaii	37.9
33	Idaho	24.8
17	Illinois	28.2
49	Indiana	19.4
47	Iowa	19.8
44	Kansas	20.9
40	Kentucky	22.3
25	Louisiana	26.5
18	Maine	28.1
15	Maryland	28.8
12	Massachusetts	29.8
36	Michigan	23.3
40	Minnesota	22.3
26	Mississippi	26.4
39	Missouri	22.4
13	Montana	29.7
48	Nebraska	19.5
8	Nevada	31.2
20	New Hampshire	27.7
3	New Jersey	36.4
10	New Mexico	30.1
5	New York	33.8
28	North Carolina	25.7
50	North Dakota	17.9
42	Ohio	21.9
38	Oklahoma	22.6
10	Oregon	30.1
30	Pennsylvania	25.4
7	Rhode Island	31.6
23	South Carolina	26.6
43	South Dakota	21.2
32	Tennessee	24.9
26	Texas	26.4
37	Utah	23.0
6	Vermont	32.5
23	Virginia	26.6
14	Washington	29.2
46	West Virginia	20.7
35	Wisconsin	23.9
34	Wyoming	24.4

RANK ORDER

RANK	STATE	PERCENT
1	California	38.6
2	Hawaii	37.9
3	New Jersey	36.4
4	Florida	34.0
5	New York	33.8
6	Vermont	32.5
7	Rhode Island	31.6
8	Nevada	31.2
9	Connecticut	30.7
10	New Mexico	30.1
10	Oregon	30.1
12	Massachusetts	29.8
13	Montana	29.7
14	Washington	29.2
15	Maryland	28.8
16	Arizona	28.3
17	Illinois	28.2
18	Alaska	28.1
18	Maine	28.1
20	New Hampshire	27.7
21	Delaware	27.1
22	Colorado	27.0
23	South Carolina	26.6
23	Virginia	26.6
25	Louisiana	26.5
26	Mississippi	26.4
26	Texas	26.4
28	Georgia	25.7
28	North Carolina	25.7
30	Pennsylvania	25.4
31	Alabama	25.0
32	Tennessee	24.9
33	Idaho	24.8
34	Wyoming	24.4
35	Wisconsin	23.9
36	Michigan	23.3
37	Utah	23.0
38	Oklahoma	22.6
39	Missouri	22.4
40	Kentucky	22.3
40	Minnesota	22.3
42	Ohio	21.9
43	South Dakota	21.2
44	Arkansas	20.9
44	Kansas	20.9
46	West Virginia	20.7
47	Iowa	19.8
48	Nebraska	19.5
49	Indiana	19.4
50	North Dakota	17.9
	District of Columbia	25.8

Source: U.S. Bureau of the Census
"2016 American Community Survey-Table R2513" (http://www.census.gov/programs-surveys/acs/)
*For owner-occupied housing units with a mortgage.

Median Annual Real Estate Taxes in 2016

National Median = $2,340*

ALPHA ORDER

RANK	STATE	MEDIAN
50	Alabama	$562
12	Alaska	3,198
35	Arizona	1,426
48	Arkansas	777
9	California	3,565
31	Colorado	1,611
2	Connecticut	5,663
38	Delaware	1,364
27	Florida	1,793
33	Georgia	1,493
30	Hawaii	1,619
37	Idaho	1,397
6	Illinois	4,185
43	Indiana	1,152
21	Iowa	2,209
25	Kansas	1,999
42	Kentucky	1,155
47	Louisiana	861
18	Maine	2,495
10	Maryland	3,290
5	Massachusetts	4,445
20	Michigan	2,290
19	Minnesota	2,359
45	Mississippi	909
34	Missouri	1,454
26	Montana	1,804
17	Nebraska	2,571
32	Nevada	1,520
3	New Hampshire	5,488
1	New Jersey	7,986
39	New Mexico	1,334
4	New York	5,054
36	North Carolina	1,402
28	North Dakota	1,777
22	Ohio	2,152
41	Oklahoma	1,179
15	Oregon	2,832
16	Pennsylvania	2,763
8	Rhode Island	4,021
46	South Carolina	870
23	South Dakota	2,133
44	Tennessee	1,139
14	Texas	2,863
29	Utah	1,627
7	Vermont	4,146
24	Virginia	2,112
13	Washington	3,049
49	West Virginia	681
11	Wisconsin	3,268
40	Wyoming	1,281

RANK ORDER

RANK	STATE	MEDIAN
1	New Jersey	$7,986
2	Connecticut	5,663
3	New Hampshire	5,488
4	New York	5,054
5	Massachusetts	4,445
6	Illinois	4,185
7	Vermont	4,146
8	Rhode Island	4,021
9	California	3,565
10	Maryland	3,290
11	Wisconsin	3,268
12	Alaska	3,198
13	Washington	3,049
14	Texas	2,863
15	Oregon	2,832
16	Pennsylvania	2,763
17	Nebraska	2,571
18	Maine	2,495
19	Minnesota	2,359
20	Michigan	2,290
21	Iowa	2,209
22	Ohio	2,152
23	South Dakota	2,133
24	Virginia	2,112
25	Kansas	1,999
26	Montana	1,804
27	Florida	1,793
28	North Dakota	1,777
29	Utah	1,627
30	Hawaii	1,619
31	Colorado	1,611
32	Nevada	1,520
33	Georgia	1,493
34	Missouri	1,454
35	Arizona	1,426
36	North Carolina	1,402
37	Idaho	1,397
38	Delaware	1,364
39	New Mexico	1,334
40	Wyoming	1,281
41	Oklahoma	1,179
42	Kentucky	1,155
43	Indiana	1,152
44	Tennessee	1,139
45	Mississippi	909
46	South Carolina	870
47	Louisiana	861
48	Arkansas	777
49	West Virginia	681
50	Alabama	562

| District of Columbia | | 3,255 |

Source: U.S. Bureau of the Census
   "2016 American Community Survey-Table B25103" (http://www.census.gov/programs-surveys/acs/)
*For owner-occupied housing units with or without mortgages.

Homeownership Rate in 2016

National Rate = 63.4%*

ALPHA ORDER

RANK	STATE	PERCENT
13	Alabama	69.7
33	Alaska	65.2
41	Arizona	61.9
21	Arkansas	67.6
49	California	53.8
38	Colorado	62.4
35	Connecticut	64.2
2	Delaware	73.0
34	Florida	64.3
39	Georgia	62.3
46	Hawaii	57.7
10	Idaho	70.5
32	Illinois	65.3
9	Indiana	70.9
12	Iowa	70.0
23	Kansas	67.1
19	Kentucky	67.9
35	Louisiana	64.2
4	Maine	72.6
27	Maryland	66.5
45	Massachusetts	59.7
3	Michigan	72.8
5	Minnesota	72.4
13	Mississippi	69.7
26	Missouri	66.7
23	Montana	67.1
18	Nebraska	68.0
48	Nevada	54.5
6	New Hampshire	71.8
40	New Jersey	62.2
22	New Mexico	67.4
50	New York	51.5
31	North Carolina	65.7
44	North Dakota	61.4
30	Ohio	66.1
25	Oklahoma	66.8
37	Oregon	62.6
17	Pennsylvania	68.5
47	Rhode Island	56.3
16	South Carolina	68.9
15	South Dakota	69.4
28	Tennessee	66.4
43	Texas	61.5
7	Utah	71.3
7	Vermont	71.3
29	Virginia	66.3
42	Washington	61.6
1	West Virginia	74.8
20	Wisconsin	67.7
11	Wyoming	70.2

RANK ORDER

RANK	STATE	PERCENT
1	West Virginia	74.8
2	Delaware	73.0
3	Michigan	72.8
4	Maine	72.6
5	Minnesota	72.4
6	New Hampshire	71.8
7	Utah	71.3
7	Vermont	71.3
9	Indiana	70.9
10	Idaho	70.5
11	Wyoming	70.2
12	Iowa	70.0
13	Alabama	69.7
13	Mississippi	69.7
15	South Dakota	69.4
16	South Carolina	68.9
17	Pennsylvania	68.5
18	Nebraska	68.0
19	Kentucky	67.9
20	Wisconsin	67.7
21	Arkansas	67.6
22	New Mexico	67.4
23	Kansas	67.1
23	Montana	67.1
25	Oklahoma	66.8
26	Missouri	66.7
27	Maryland	66.5
28	Tennessee	66.4
29	Virginia	66.3
30	Ohio	66.1
31	North Carolina	65.7
32	Illinois	65.3
33	Alaska	65.2
34	Florida	64.3
35	Connecticut	64.2
35	Louisiana	64.2
37	Oregon	62.6
38	Colorado	62.4
39	Georgia	62.3
40	New Jersey	62.2
41	Arizona	61.9
42	Washington	61.6
43	Texas	61.5
44	North Dakota	61.4
45	Massachusetts	59.7
46	Hawaii	57.7
47	Rhode Island	56.3
48	Nevada	54.5
49	California	53.8
50	New York	51.5
	District of Columbia	40.8

Source: U.S. Bureau of the Census
   "Housing Vacancies and Homeownership, Annual Statistics: 2016" (https://www.census.gov/housing/hvs/index.html)
*Percent of households occupied by the owner.

Percent of Housing Units That Are Renter-Occupied in 2016

National Percent = 36.9% of Housing Units*

ALPHA ORDER

ALPHA ORDER

RANK	STATE	PERCENT
37	Alabama	31.5
17	Alaska	35.5
11	Arizona	36.8
18	Arkansas	35.4
2	California	46.4
19	Colorado	35.2
19	Connecticut	35.2
42	Delaware	30.2
14	Florida	35.9
7	Georgia	38.5
4	Hawaii	42.8
37	Idaho	31.5
23	Illinois	34.7
36	Indiana	31.7
47	Iowa	29.4
27	Kansas	34.3
31	Kentucky	33.2
16	Louisiana	35.7
49	Maine	28.1
28	Maryland	34.1
9	Massachusetts	38.0
46	Michigan	29.7
48	Minnesota	28.7
33	Mississippi	32.7
29	Missouri	33.9
35	Montana	32.0
23	Nebraska	34.7
3	Nevada	45.1
45	New Hampshire	29.9
11	New Jersey	36.8
34	New Mexico	32.6
1	New York	46.7
15	North Carolina	35.8
11	North Dakota	36.8
26	Ohio	34.6
21	Oklahoma	35.1
8	Oregon	38.3
37	Pennsylvania	31.5
5	Rhode Island	42.0
40	South Carolina	31.4
32	South Dakota	32.8
22	Tennessee	34.9
6	Texas	38.9
44	Utah	30.1
42	Vermont	30.2
23	Virginia	34.7
10	Washington	37.5
50	West Virginia	27.6
30	Wisconsin	33.3
41	Wyoming	31.2

RANK ORDER

RANK	STATE	PERCENT
1	New York	46.7
2	California	46.4
3	Nevada	45.1
4	Hawaii	42.8
5	Rhode Island	42.0
6	Texas	38.9
7	Georgia	38.5
8	Oregon	38.3
9	Massachusetts	38.0
10	Washington	37.5
11	Arizona	36.8
11	New Jersey	36.8
11	North Dakota	36.8
14	Florida	35.9
15	North Carolina	35.8
16	Louisiana	35.7
17	Alaska	35.5
18	Arkansas	35.4
19	Colorado	35.2
19	Connecticut	35.2
21	Oklahoma	35.1
22	Tennessee	34.9
23	Illinois	34.7
23	Nebraska	34.7
23	Virginia	34.7
26	Ohio	34.6
27	Kansas	34.3
28	Maryland	34.1
29	Missouri	33.9
30	Wisconsin	33.3
31	Kentucky	33.2
32	South Dakota	32.8
33	Mississippi	32.7
34	New Mexico	32.6
35	Montana	32.0
36	Indiana	31.7
37	Alabama	31.5
37	Idaho	31.5
37	Pennsylvania	31.5
40	South Carolina	31.4
41	Wyoming	31.2
42	Delaware	30.2
42	Vermont	30.2
44	Utah	30.1
45	New Hampshire	29.9
46	Michigan	29.7
47	Iowa	29.4
48	Minnesota	28.7
49	Maine	28.1
50	West Virginia	27.6

District of Columbia 60.8

Source: CQ Press using data from U.S. Bureau of the Census
   "2016 American Community Survey-Table R2512" (http://www.census.gov/programs-surveys/acs/)
*For occupied housing units.

Median Monthly Rental Payment in 2016

National Median = $981*

ALPHA ORDER

RANK	STATE	MEDIAN
43	Alabama	$743
5	Alaska	1,208
17	Arizona	976
49	Arkansas	701
2	California	1,375
8	Colorado	1,171
11	Connecticut	1,115
13	Delaware	1,048
12	Florida	1,086
22	Georgia	933
1	Hawaii	1,483
35	Idaho	790
20	Illinois	950
40	Indiana	768
44	Iowa	741
36	Kansas	789
47	Kentucky	707
30	Louisiana	808
34	Maine	797
3	Maryland	1,314
7	Massachusetts	1,179
29	Michigan	818
24	Minnesota	912
46	Mississippi	728
38	Missouri	771
44	Montana	741
39	Nebraska	769
16	Nevada	1,003
14	New Hampshire	1,026
4	New Jersey	1,244
32	New Mexico	804
6	New York	1,194
28	North Carolina	839
37	North Dakota	776
41	Ohio	759
42	Oklahoma	744
15	Oregon	1,015
25	Pennsylvania	881
21	Rhode Island	948
26	South Carolina	841
48	South Dakota	706
31	Tennessee	806
18	Texas	956
19	Utah	954
23	Vermont	925
9	Virginia	1,159
10	Washington	1,135
50	West Virginia	682
33	Wisconsin	802
27	Wyoming	840

RANK ORDER

RANK	STATE	MEDIAN
1	Hawaii	$1,483
2	California	1,375
3	Maryland	1,314
4	New Jersey	1,244
5	Alaska	1,208
6	New York	1,194
7	Massachusetts	1,179
8	Colorado	1,171
9	Virginia	1,159
10	Washington	1,135
11	Connecticut	1,115
12	Florida	1,086
13	Delaware	1,048
14	New Hampshire	1,026
15	Oregon	1,015
16	Nevada	1,003
17	Arizona	976
18	Texas	956
19	Utah	954
20	Illinois	950
21	Rhode Island	948
22	Georgia	933
23	Vermont	925
24	Minnesota	912
25	Pennsylvania	881
26	South Carolina	841
27	Wyoming	840
28	North Carolina	839
29	Michigan	818
30	Louisiana	808
31	Tennessee	806
32	New Mexico	804
33	Wisconsin	802
34	Maine	797
35	Idaho	790
36	Kansas	789
37	North Dakota	776
38	Missouri	771
39	Nebraska	769
40	Indiana	768
41	Ohio	759
42	Oklahoma	744
43	Alabama	743
44	Iowa	741
44	Montana	741
46	Mississippi	728
47	Kentucky	707
48	South Dakota	706
49	Arkansas	701
50	West Virginia	682
	District of Columbia	1,376

Source: U.S. Bureau of the Census
   "2016 American Community Survey-Table R2514" (http://www.census.gov/programs-surveys/acs/)
*Monthly housing costs for renter-occupied housing.

Percent of Renters Spending 30% or More of Household Income on Rent and Utilities in 2016
National Percent = 46.1% of Renters

ALPHA ORDER

RANK	STATE	PERCENT
33	Alabama	41.8
47	Alaska	38.2
21	Arizona	44.3
45	Arkansas	39.2
1	California	52.6
5	Colorado	49.7
8	Connecticut	48.1
16	Delaware	45.6
2	Florida	52.1
19	Georgia	45.0
3	Hawaii	51.5
36	Idaho	41.3
18	Illinois	45.3
30	Indiana	42.3
40	Iowa	40.5
39	Kansas	40.6
41	Kentucky	40.2
9	Louisiana	47.4
26	Maine	42.8
13	Maryland	46.3
11	Massachusetts	46.8
14	Michigan	45.8
23	Minnesota	43.3
37	Mississippi	40.8
41	Missouri	40.2
46	Montana	39.0
38	Nebraska	40.7
10	Nevada	47.3
33	New Hampshire	41.8
6	New Jersey	49.1
29	New Mexico	42.4
4	New York	49.8
27	North Carolina	42.6
50	North Dakota	36.3
32	Ohio	42.0
44	Oklahoma	39.4
7	Oregon	48.4
24	Pennsylvania	43.1
15	Rhode Island	45.7
24	South Carolina	43.1
49	South Dakota	37.2
31	Tennessee	42.2
22	Texas	43.9
28	Utah	42.5
12	Vermont	46.7
16	Virginia	45.6
20	Washington	44.9
43	West Virginia	40.0
33	Wisconsin	41.8
48	Wyoming	37.5

RANK ORDER

RANK	STATE	PERCENT
1	California	52.6
2	Florida	52.1
3	Hawaii	51.5
4	New York	49.8
5	Colorado	49.7
6	New Jersey	49.1
7	Oregon	48.4
8	Connecticut	48.1
9	Louisiana	47.4
10	Nevada	47.3
11	Massachusetts	46.8
12	Vermont	46.7
13	Maryland	46.3
14	Michigan	45.8
15	Rhode Island	45.7
16	Delaware	45.6
16	Virginia	45.6
18	Illinois	45.3
19	Georgia	45.0
20	Washington	44.9
21	Arizona	44.3
22	Texas	43.9
23	Minnesota	43.3
24	Pennsylvania	43.1
24	South Carolina	43.1
26	Maine	42.8
27	North Carolina	42.6
28	Utah	42.5
29	New Mexico	42.4
30	Indiana	42.3
31	Tennessee	42.2
32	Ohio	42.0
33	Alabama	41.8
33	New Hampshire	41.8
33	Wisconsin	41.8
36	Idaho	41.3
37	Mississippi	40.8
38	Nebraska	40.7
39	Kansas	40.6
40	Iowa	40.5
41	Kentucky	40.2
41	Missouri	40.2
43	West Virginia	40.0
44	Oklahoma	39.4
45	Arkansas	39.2
46	Montana	39.0
47	Alaska	38.2
48	Wyoming	37.5
49	South Dakota	37.2
50	North Dakota	36.3

| District of Columbia | | 45.5 |

Source: U.S. Bureau of the Census
"2016 American Community Survey-Table R2515" (http://www.census.gov/programs-surveys/acs/)

State and Local Government Expenditures
for Housing and Community Development in 2015
National Total = $49,860,800,000*

ALPHA ORDER

RANK	STATE	EXPENDITURES	% of USA
25	Alabama	$481,970,000	1.0%
29	Alaska	352,627,000	0.7%
24	Arizona	520,519,000	1.0%
40	Arkansas	193,480,000	0.4%
1	California	8,307,670,000	16.7%
20	Colorado	803,333,000	1.6%
15	Connecticut	1,098,541,000	2.2%
44	Delaware	143,336,000	0.3%
4	Florida	2,424,478,000	4.9%
13	Georgia	1,228,086,000	2.5%
35	Hawaii	270,523,000	0.5%
45	Idaho	131,357,000	0.3%
5	Illinois	2,173,243,000	4.4%
21	Indiana	792,401,000	1.6%
41	Iowa	160,519,000	0.3%
33	Kansas	301,966,000	0.6%
28	Kentucky	385,900,000	0.8%
19	Louisiana	828,853,000	1.7%
34	Maine	285,708,000	0.6%
10	Maryland	1,432,026,000	2.9%
3	Massachusetts	2,596,221,000	5.2%
14	Michigan	1,158,545,000	2.3%
17	Minnesota	940,173,000	1.9%
36	Mississippi	266,215,000	0.5%
23	Missouri	638,039,000	1.3%
47	Montana	124,951,000	0.3%
38	Nebraska	218,967,000	0.4%
32	Nevada	303,295,000	0.6%
39	New Hampshire	203,587,000	0.4%
11	New Jersey	1,380,527,000	2.8%
42	New Mexico	148,995,000	0.3%
2	New York	5,405,915,000	10.8%
9	North Carolina	1,538,960,000	3.1%
49	North Dakota	81,358,000	0.2%
6	Ohio	2,162,237,000	4.3%
27	Oklahoma	433,537,000	0.9%
22	Oregon	638,739,000	1.3%
8	Pennsylvania	1,725,263,000	3.5%
37	Rhode Island	239,804,000	0.5%
26	South Carolina	466,921,000	0.9%
48	South Dakota	94,631,000	0.2%
18	Tennessee	872,582,000	1.8%
7	Texas	2,021,282,000	4.1%
30	Utah	349,488,000	0.7%
43	Vermont	147,949,000	0.3%
16	Virginia	976,519,000	2.0%
12	Washington	1,354,228,000	2.7%
46	West Virginia	125,471,000	0.3%
31	Wisconsin	311,627,000	0.6%
50	Wyoming	15,241,000	0.0%

RANK ORDER

RANK	STATE	EXPENDITURES	% of USA
1	California	$8,307,670,000	16.7%
2	New York	5,405,915,000	10.8%
3	Massachusetts	2,596,221,000	5.2%
4	Florida	2,424,478,000	4.9%
5	Illinois	2,173,243,000	4.4%
6	Ohio	2,162,237,000	4.3%
7	Texas	2,021,282,000	4.1%
8	Pennsylvania	1,725,263,000	3.5%
9	North Carolina	1,538,960,000	3.1%
10	Maryland	1,432,026,000	2.9%
11	New Jersey	1,380,527,000	2.8%
12	Washington	1,354,228,000	2.7%
13	Georgia	1,228,086,000	2.5%
14	Michigan	1,158,545,000	2.3%
15	Connecticut	1,098,541,000	2.2%
16	Virginia	976,519,000	2.0%
17	Minnesota	940,173,000	1.9%
18	Tennessee	872,582,000	1.8%
19	Louisiana	828,853,000	1.7%
20	Colorado	803,333,000	1.6%
21	Indiana	792,401,000	1.6%
22	Oregon	638,739,000	1.3%
23	Missouri	638,039,000	1.3%
24	Arizona	520,519,000	1.0%
25	Alabama	481,970,000	1.0%
26	South Carolina	466,921,000	0.9%
27	Oklahoma	433,537,000	0.9%
28	Kentucky	385,900,000	0.8%
29	Alaska	352,627,000	0.7%
30	Utah	349,488,000	0.7%
31	Wisconsin	311,627,000	0.6%
32	Nevada	303,295,000	0.6%
33	Kansas	301,966,000	0.6%
34	Maine	285,708,000	0.6%
35	Hawaii	270,523,000	0.5%
36	Mississippi	266,215,000	0.5%
37	Rhode Island	239,804,000	0.5%
38	Nebraska	218,967,000	0.4%
39	New Hampshire	203,587,000	0.4%
40	Arkansas	193,480,000	0.4%
41	Iowa	160,519,000	0.3%
42	New Mexico	148,995,000	0.3%
43	Vermont	147,949,000	0.3%
44	Delaware	143,336,000	0.3%
45	Idaho	131,357,000	0.3%
46	West Virginia	125,471,000	0.3%
47	Montana	124,951,000	0.3%
48	South Dakota	94,631,000	0.2%
49	North Dakota	81,358,000	0.2%
50	Wyoming	15,241,000	0.0%
	District of Columbia	602,997,000	1.2%

Source: U.S. Bureau of the Census, Governments Division
"2015 State and Local Government Finances" (http://www.census.gov/govs/local/)
*Direct general expenditures.

Per Capita State and Local Government Expenditures
for Housing and Community Development in 2015
National Per Capita = $155*

ALPHA ORDER

RANK	STATE	PER CAPITA
38	Alabama	$99
1	Alaska	478
43	Arizona	77
47	Arkansas	65
9	California	213
21	Colorado	148
3	Connecticut	306
20	Delaware	152
25	Florida	120
25	Georgia	120
10	Hawaii	190
42	Idaho	80
15	Illinois	169
25	Indiana	120
49	Iowa	51
37	Kansas	104
41	Kentucky	87
13	Louisiana	177
8	Maine	215
5	Maryland	239
2	Massachusetts	382
28	Michigan	117
14	Minnesota	171
40	Mississippi	89
35	Missouri	105
24	Montana	122
31	Nebraska	116
35	Nevada	105
18	New Hampshire	153
17	New Jersey	154
45	New Mexico	72
4	New York	273
18	North Carolina	153
34	North Dakota	108
12	Ohio	186
32	Oklahoma	111
16	Oregon	159
22	Pennsylvania	135
7	Rhode Island	227
39	South Carolina	95
32	South Dakota	111
23	Tennessee	132
44	Texas	74
28	Utah	117
6	Vermont	237
28	Virginia	117
11	Washington	189
46	West Virginia	68
48	Wisconsin	54
50	Wyoming	26

RANK ORDER

RANK	STATE	PER CAPITA
1	Alaska	$478
2	Massachusetts	382
3	Connecticut	306
4	New York	273
5	Maryland	239
6	Vermont	237
7	Rhode Island	227
8	Maine	215
9	California	213
10	Hawaii	190
11	Washington	189
12	Ohio	186
13	Louisiana	177
14	Minnesota	171
15	Illinois	169
16	Oregon	159
17	New Jersey	154
18	New Hampshire	153
18	North Carolina	153
20	Delaware	152
21	Colorado	148
22	Pennsylvania	135
23	Tennessee	132
24	Montana	122
25	Florida	120
25	Georgia	120
25	Indiana	120
28	Michigan	117
28	Utah	117
28	Virginia	117
31	Nebraska	116
32	Oklahoma	111
32	South Dakota	111
34	North Dakota	108
35	Missouri	105
35	Nevada	105
37	Kansas	104
38	Alabama	99
39	South Carolina	95
40	Mississippi	89
41	Kentucky	87
42	Idaho	80
43	Arizona	77
44	Texas	74
45	New Mexico	72
46	West Virginia	68
47	Arkansas	65
48	Wisconsin	54
49	Iowa	51
50	Wyoming	26

District of Columbia — 896

Source: CQ Press using data from U.S. Bureau of the Census, Governments Division
"2015 State and Local Government Finances" (http://www.census.gov/govs/local/)
*Direct general expenditures.

State & Local Government Spending for Housing and Community Development as a Percent of All State and Local Government Expenditures in 2015
National Percent = 1.8%*

ALPHA ORDER

RANK	STATE	PERCENT
35	Alabama	1.3
5	Alaska	2.4
37	Arizona	1.2
45	Arkansas	0.8
11	California	2.0
20	Colorado	1.7
2	Connecticut	2.9
25	Delaware	1.5
20	Florida	1.7
18	Georgia	1.8
11	Hawaii	2.0
37	Idaho	1.2
16	Illinois	1.9
23	Indiana	1.6
49	Iowa	0.5
37	Kansas	1.2
42	Kentucky	1.0
11	Louisiana	2.0
3	Maine	2.6
4	Maryland	2.5
1	Massachusetts	3.6
31	Michigan	1.4
18	Minnesota	1.8
41	Mississippi	1.1
25	Missouri	1.5
31	Montana	1.4
35	Nebraska	1.3
25	Nevada	1.5
16	New Hampshire	1.9
25	New Jersey	1.5
47	New Mexico	0.7
8	New York	2.1
8	North Carolina	2.1
44	North Dakota	0.9
7	Ohio	2.3
25	Oklahoma	1.5
20	Oregon	1.7
25	Pennsylvania	1.5
5	Rhode Island	2.4
37	South Carolina	1.2
31	South Dakota	1.4
11	Tennessee	2.0
42	Texas	1.0
23	Utah	1.6
8	Vermont	2.1
31	Virginia	1.4
11	Washington	2.0
45	West Virginia	0.8
48	Wisconsin	0.6
50	Wyoming	0.2

RANK ORDER

RANK	STATE	PERCENT
1	Massachusetts	3.6
2	Connecticut	2.9
3	Maine	2.6
4	Maryland	2.5
5	Alaska	2.4
5	Rhode Island	2.4
7	Ohio	2.3
8	New York	2.1
8	North Carolina	2.1
8	Vermont	2.1
11	California	2.0
11	Hawaii	2.0
11	Louisiana	2.0
11	Tennessee	2.0
11	Washington	2.0
16	Illinois	1.9
16	New Hampshire	1.9
18	Georgia	1.8
18	Minnesota	1.8
20	Colorado	1.7
20	Florida	1.7
20	Oregon	1.7
23	Indiana	1.6
23	Utah	1.6
25	Delaware	1.5
25	Missouri	1.5
25	Nevada	1.5
25	New Jersey	1.5
25	Oklahoma	1.5
25	Pennsylvania	1.5
31	Michigan	1.4
31	Montana	1.4
31	South Dakota	1.4
31	Virginia	1.4
35	Alabama	1.3
35	Nebraska	1.3
37	Arizona	1.2
37	Idaho	1.2
37	Kansas	1.2
37	South Carolina	1.2
41	Mississippi	1.1
42	Kentucky	1.0
42	Texas	1.0
44	North Dakota	0.9
45	Arkansas	0.8
45	West Virginia	0.8
47	New Mexico	0.7
48	Wisconsin	0.6
49	Iowa	0.5
50	Wyoming	0.2

District of Columbia 4.9

Source: CQ Press using data from U.S. Bureau of the Census, Governments Division
"2015 State and Local Government Finances" (http://www.census.gov/govs/local/)
*As a percent of direct general expenditures.

XIII. Population

Population in 2017

National Total = 325,719,178*

ALPHA ORDER

RANK	STATE	POPULATION	% of USA
24	Alabama	4,874,747	1.5%
48	Alaska	739,795	0.2%
14	Arizona	7,016,270	2.2%
32	Arkansas	3,004,279	0.9%
1	California	39,536,653	12.1%
21	Colorado	5,607,154	1.7%
29	Connecticut	3,588,184	1.1%
45	Delaware	961,939	0.3%
3	Florida	20,984,400	6.4%
8	Georgia	10,429,379	3.2%
40	Hawaii	1,427,538	0.4%
39	Idaho	1,716,943	0.5%
6	Illinois	12,802,023	3.9%
17	Indiana	6,666,818	2.0%
30	Iowa	3,145,711	1.0%
35	Kansas	2,913,123	0.9%
26	Kentucky	4,454,189	1.4%
25	Louisiana	4,684,333	1.4%
42	Maine	1,335,907	0.4%
19	Maryland	6,052,177	1.9%
15	Massachusetts	6,859,819	2.1%
10	Michigan	9,962,311	3.1%
22	Minnesota	5,576,606	1.7%
34	Mississippi	2,984,100	0.9%
18	Missouri	6,113,532	1.9%
44	Montana	1,050,493	0.3%
37	Nebraska	1,920,076	0.6%
33	Nevada	2,998,039	0.9%
41	New Hampshire	1,342,795	0.4%
11	New Jersey	9,005,644	2.8%
36	New Mexico	2,088,070	0.6%
4	New York	19,849,399	6.1%
9	North Carolina	10,273,419	3.2%
47	North Dakota	755,393	0.2%
7	Ohio	11,658,609	3.6%
28	Oklahoma	3,930,864	1.2%
27	Oregon	4,142,776	1.3%
5	Pennsylvania	12,805,537	3.9%
43	Rhode Island	1,059,639	0.3%
23	South Carolina	5,024,369	1.5%
46	South Dakota	869,666	0.3%
16	Tennessee	6,715,984	2.1%
2	Texas	28,304,596	8.7%
31	Utah	3,101,833	1.0%
49	Vermont	623,657	0.2%
12	Virginia	8,470,020	2.6%
13	Washington	7,405,743	2.3%
38	West Virginia	1,815,857	0.6%
20	Wisconsin	5,795,483	1.8%
50	Wyoming	579,315	0.2%

RANK ORDER

RANK	STATE	POPULATION	% of USA
1	California	39,536,653	12.1%
2	Texas	28,304,596	8.7%
3	Florida	20,984,400	6.4%
4	New York	19,849,399	6.1%
5	Pennsylvania	12,805,537	3.9%
6	Illinois	12,802,023	3.9%
7	Ohio	11,658,609	3.6%
8	Georgia	10,429,379	3.2%
9	North Carolina	10,273,419	3.2%
10	Michigan	9,962,311	3.1%
11	New Jersey	9,005,644	2.8%
12	Virginia	8,470,020	2.6%
13	Washington	7,405,743	2.3%
14	Arizona	7,016,270	2.2%
15	Massachusetts	6,859,819	2.1%
16	Tennessee	6,715,984	2.1%
17	Indiana	6,666,818	2.0%
18	Missouri	6,113,532	1.9%
19	Maryland	6,052,177	1.9%
20	Wisconsin	5,795,483	1.8%
21	Colorado	5,607,154	1.7%
22	Minnesota	5,576,606	1.7%
23	South Carolina	5,024,369	1.5%
24	Alabama	4,874,747	1.5%
25	Louisiana	4,684,333	1.4%
26	Kentucky	4,454,189	1.4%
27	Oregon	4,142,776	1.3%
28	Oklahoma	3,930,864	1.2%
29	Connecticut	3,588,184	1.1%
30	Iowa	3,145,711	1.0%
31	Utah	3,101,833	1.0%
32	Arkansas	3,004,279	0.9%
33	Nevada	2,998,039	0.9%
34	Mississippi	2,984,100	0.9%
35	Kansas	2,913,123	0.9%
36	New Mexico	2,088,070	0.6%
37	Nebraska	1,920,076	0.6%
38	West Virginia	1,815,857	0.6%
39	Idaho	1,716,943	0.5%
40	Hawaii	1,427,538	0.4%
41	New Hampshire	1,342,795	0.4%
42	Maine	1,335,907	0.4%
43	Rhode Island	1,059,639	0.3%
44	Montana	1,050,493	0.3%
45	Delaware	961,939	0.3%
46	South Dakota	869,666	0.3%
47	North Dakota	755,393	0.2%
48	Alaska	739,795	0.2%
49	Vermont	623,657	0.2%
50	Wyoming	579,315	0.2%
	District of Columbia	693,972	0.2%

Source: U.S. Bureau of the Census
"Population Estimates" (December 2017, http://www.census.gov/programs-surveys/popest.html)
*Resident population estimate as of July 1, 2017.

Population in 2016

National Total = 323,405,935*

ALPHA ORDER

RANK	STATE	POPULATION	% of USA
24	Alabama	4,860,545	1.5%
48	Alaska	741,522	0.2%
14	Arizona	6,908,642	2.1%
32	Arkansas	2,988,231	0.9%
1	California	39,296,476	12.2%
21	Colorado	5,530,105	1.7%
29	Connecticut	3,587,685	1.1%
45	Delaware	952,698	0.3%
3	Florida	20,656,589	6.4%
8	Georgia	10,313,620	3.2%
40	Hawaii	1,428,683	0.4%
39	Idaho	1,680,026	0.5%
5	Illinois	12,835,726	4.0%
17	Indiana	6,634,007	2.1%
30	Iowa	3,130,869	1.0%
35	Kansas	2,907,731	0.9%
26	Kentucky	4,436,113	1.4%
25	Louisiana	4,686,157	1.4%
42	Maine	1,330,232	0.4%
19	Maryland	6,024,752	1.9%
15	Massachusetts	6,823,721	2.1%
10	Michigan	9,933,445	3.1%
22	Minnesota	5,525,050	1.7%
33	Mississippi	2,985,415	0.9%
18	Missouri	6,091,176	1.9%
44	Montana	1,038,656	0.3%
37	Nebraska	1,907,603	0.6%
34	Nevada	2,939,254	0.9%
41	New Hampshire	1,335,015	0.4%
11	New Jersey	8,978,416	2.8%
36	New Mexico	2,085,432	0.6%
4	New York	19,836,286	6.1%
9	North Carolina	10,156,689	3.1%
47	North Dakota	755,548	0.2%
7	Ohio	11,622,554	3.6%
28	Oklahoma	3,921,207	1.2%
27	Oregon	4,085,989	1.3%
6	Pennsylvania	12,787,085	4.0%
43	Rhode Island	1,057,566	0.3%
23	South Carolina	4,959,822	1.5%
46	South Dakota	861,542	0.3%
16	Tennessee	6,649,404	2.1%
2	Texas	27,904,862	8.6%
31	Utah	3,044,321	0.9%
49	Vermont	623,354	0.2%
12	Virginia	8,414,380	2.6%
13	Washington	7,280,934	2.3%
38	West Virginia	1,828,637	0.6%
20	Wisconsin	5,772,917	1.8%
50	Wyoming	584,910	0.2%

RANK ORDER

RANK	STATE	POPULATION	% of USA
1	California	39,296,476	12.2%
2	Texas	27,904,862	8.6%
3	Florida	20,656,589	6.4%
4	New York	19,836,286	6.1%
5	Illinois	12,835,726	4.0%
6	Pennsylvania	12,787,085	4.0%
7	Ohio	11,622,554	3.6%
8	Georgia	10,313,620	3.2%
9	North Carolina	10,156,689	3.1%
10	Michigan	9,933,445	3.1%
11	New Jersey	8,978,416	2.8%
12	Virginia	8,414,380	2.6%
13	Washington	7,280,934	2.3%
14	Arizona	6,908,642	2.1%
15	Massachusetts	6,823,721	2.1%
16	Tennessee	6,649,404	2.1%
17	Indiana	6,634,007	2.1%
18	Missouri	6,091,176	1.9%
19	Maryland	6,024,752	1.9%
20	Wisconsin	5,772,917	1.8%
21	Colorado	5,530,105	1.7%
22	Minnesota	5,525,050	1.7%
23	South Carolina	4,959,822	1.5%
24	Alabama	4,860,545	1.5%
25	Louisiana	4,686,157	1.4%
26	Kentucky	4,436,113	1.4%
27	Oregon	4,085,989	1.3%
28	Oklahoma	3,921,207	1.2%
29	Connecticut	3,587,685	1.1%
30	Iowa	3,130,869	1.0%
31	Utah	3,044,321	0.9%
32	Arkansas	2,988,231	0.9%
33	Mississippi	2,985,415	0.9%
34	Nevada	2,939,254	0.9%
35	Kansas	2,907,731	0.9%
36	New Mexico	2,085,432	0.6%
37	Nebraska	1,907,603	0.6%
38	West Virginia	1,828,637	0.6%
39	Idaho	1,680,026	0.5%
40	Hawaii	1,428,683	0.4%
41	New Hampshire	1,335,015	0.4%
42	Maine	1,330,232	0.4%
43	Rhode Island	1,057,566	0.3%
44	Montana	1,038,656	0.3%
45	Delaware	952,698	0.3%
46	South Dakota	861,542	0.3%
47	North Dakota	755,548	0.2%
48	Alaska	741,522	0.2%
49	Vermont	623,354	0.2%
50	Wyoming	584,910	0.2%
	District of Columbia	684,336	0.2%

Source: U.S. Bureau of the Census
  "Population Estimates" (December 2017, http://www.census.gov/programs-surveys/popest.html)
*Resident population. Revised estimates of July 1, 2017.

Numerical Population Change: 2016 to 2017

National Total = 2,313,243 Increase*

ALPHA ORDER

RANK	STATE	GAIN/LOSS
29	Alabama	14,202
46	Alaska	(1,727)
7	Arizona	107,628
27	Arkansas	16,048
3	California	240,177
8	Colorado	77,049
41	Connecticut	499
34	Delaware	9,241
2	Florida	327,811
6	Georgia	115,759
44	Hawaii	(1,145)
16	Idaho	36,917
50	Illinois	(33,703)
19	Indiana	32,811
28	Iowa	14,842
38	Kansas	5,392
26	Kentucky	18,076
47	Louisiana	(1,824)
37	Maine	5,675
21	Maryland	27,425
17	Massachusetts	36,098
20	Michigan	28,866
15	Minnesota	51,556
45	Mississippi	(1,315)
24	Missouri	22,356
32	Montana	11,837
31	Nebraska	12,473
11	Nevada	58,785
36	New Hampshire	7,780
22	New Jersey	27,228
39	New Mexico	2,638
30	New York	13,113
5	North Carolina	116,730
43	North Dakota	(155)
18	Ohio	36,055
33	Oklahoma	9,657
13	Oregon	56,787
25	Pennsylvania	18,452
40	Rhode Island	2,073
10	South Carolina	64,547
35	South Dakota	8,124
9	Tennessee	66,580
1	Texas	399,734
12	Utah	57,512
42	Vermont	303
14	Virginia	55,640
4	Washington	124,809
49	West Virginia	(12,780)
23	Wisconsin	22,566
48	Wyoming	(5,595)

RANK ORDER

RANK	STATE	GAIN/LOSS
1	Texas	399,734
2	Florida	327,811
3	California	240,177
4	Washington	124,809
5	North Carolina	116,730
6	Georgia	115,759
7	Arizona	107,628
8	Colorado	77,049
9	Tennessee	66,580
10	South Carolina	64,547
11	Nevada	58,785
12	Utah	57,512
13	Oregon	56,787
14	Virginia	55,640
15	Minnesota	51,556
16	Idaho	36,917
17	Massachusetts	36,098
18	Ohio	36,055
19	Indiana	32,811
20	Michigan	28,866
21	Maryland	27,425
22	New Jersey	27,228
23	Wisconsin	22,566
24	Missouri	22,356
25	Pennsylvania	18,452
26	Kentucky	18,076
27	Arkansas	16,048
28	Iowa	14,842
29	Alabama	14,202
30	New York	13,113
31	Nebraska	12,473
32	Montana	11,837
33	Oklahoma	9,657
34	Delaware	9,241
35	South Dakota	8,124
36	New Hampshire	7,780
37	Maine	5,675
38	Kansas	5,392
39	New Mexico	2,638
40	Rhode Island	2,073
41	Connecticut	499
42	Vermont	303
43	North Dakota	(155)
44	Hawaii	(1,145)
45	Mississippi	(1,315)
46	Alaska	(1,727)
47	Louisiana	(1,824)
48	Wyoming	(5,595)
49	West Virginia	(12,780)
50	Illinois	(33,703)
	District of Columbia	9,636

Source: CQ Press using data from U.S. Bureau of the Census
"Population Estimates" (December 2017, http://www.census.gov/programs-surveys/popest.html)
*Resident population from July 1, 2016 to July 1, 2017.

Percent Change in Population: 2016 to 2017

National Percent Change = 0.7% Increase*

ALPHA ORDER

RANK	STATE	PERCENT CHANGE
31	Alabama	0.3
47	Alaska	(0.2)
5	Arizona	1.6
22	Arkansas	0.5
20	California	0.6
7	Colorado	1.4
41	Connecticut	0.0
14	Delaware	1.0
5	Florida	1.6
11	Georgia	1.1
46	Hawaii	(0.1)
1	Idaho	2.2
48	Illinois	(0.3)
22	Indiana	0.5
22	Iowa	0.5
35	Kansas	0.2
27	Kentucky	0.4
41	Louisiana	0.0
27	Maine	0.4
22	Maryland	0.5
22	Massachusetts	0.5
31	Michigan	0.3
16	Minnesota	0.9
41	Mississippi	0.0
27	Missouri	0.4
11	Montana	1.1
18	Nebraska	0.7
2	Nevada	2.0
20	New Hampshire	0.6
31	New Jersey	0.3
38	New Mexico	0.1
38	New York	0.1
11	North Carolina	1.1
41	North Dakota	0.0
31	Ohio	0.3
35	Oklahoma	0.2
7	Oregon	1.4
38	Pennsylvania	0.1
35	Rhode Island	0.2
10	South Carolina	1.3
16	South Dakota	0.9
14	Tennessee	1.0
7	Texas	1.4
3	Utah	1.9
41	Vermont	0.0
18	Virginia	0.7
4	Washington	1.7
49	West Virginia	(0.7)
27	Wisconsin	0.4
50	Wyoming	(1.0)

RANK ORDER

RANK	STATE	PERCENT CHANGE
1	Idaho	2.2
2	Nevada	2.0
3	Utah	1.9
4	Washington	1.7
5	Arizona	1.6
5	Florida	1.6
7	Colorado	1.4
7	Oregon	1.4
7	Texas	1.4
10	South Carolina	1.3
11	Georgia	1.1
11	Montana	1.1
11	North Carolina	1.1
14	Delaware	1.0
14	Tennessee	1.0
16	Minnesota	0.9
16	South Dakota	0.9
18	Nebraska	0.7
18	Virginia	0.7
20	California	0.6
20	New Hampshire	0.6
22	Arkansas	0.5
22	Indiana	0.5
22	Iowa	0.5
22	Maryland	0.5
22	Massachusetts	0.5
27	Kentucky	0.4
27	Maine	0.4
27	Missouri	0.4
27	Wisconsin	0.4
31	Alabama	0.3
31	Michigan	0.3
31	New Jersey	0.3
31	Ohio	0.3
35	Kansas	0.2
35	Oklahoma	0.2
35	Rhode Island	0.2
38	New Mexico	0.1
38	New York	0.1
38	Pennsylvania	0.1
41	Connecticut	0.0
41	Louisiana	0.0
41	Mississippi	0.0
41	North Dakota	0.0
41	Vermont	0.0
46	Hawaii	(0.1)
47	Alaska	(0.2)
48	Illinois	(0.3)
49	West Virginia	(0.7)
50	Wyoming	(1.0)

District of Columbia	1.4

Source: CQ Press using data from U.S. Bureau of the Census
   "Population Estimates" (December 2017, http://www.census.gov/programs-surveys/popest.html)
*Resident population from July 1, 2016 to July 1, 2017.

Population per Square Mile in 2017

National Rate = 92.2 Persons per Square Mile*

ALPHA ORDER

RANK	STATE	RATE
27	Alabama	96.3
50	Alaska	1.3
33	Arizona	61.8
34	Arkansas	57.7
11	California	253.8
37	Colorado	54.1
4	Connecticut	741.1
6	Delaware	493.6
8	Florida	391.3
17	Georgia	181.3
13	Hawaii	222.3
44	Idaho	20.8
12	Illinois	230.6
16	Indiana	186.1
36	Iowa	56.3
41	Kansas	35.6
22	Kentucky	112.8
24	Louisiana	108.4
38	Maine	43.3
5	Maryland	623.5
3	Massachusetts	879.5
18	Michigan	176.2
30	Minnesota	70.0
32	Mississippi	63.6
28	Missouri	88.9
48	Montana	7.2
43	Nebraska	25.0
42	Nevada	27.3
21	New Hampshire	150.0
1	New Jersey	1,224.6
45	New Mexico	17.2
7	New York	421.2
15	North Carolina	211.3
47	North Dakota	10.9
10	Ohio	285.3
35	Oklahoma	57.3
39	Oregon	43.2
9	Pennsylvania	286.2
2	Rhode Island	1,024.8
19	South Carolina	167.1
46	South Dakota	11.5
20	Tennessee	162.9
24	Texas	108.4
40	Utah	37.7
31	Vermont	67.7
14	Virginia	214.5
23	Washington	111.4
29	West Virginia	75.5
26	Wisconsin	107.0
49	Wyoming	6.0

RANK ORDER

RANK	STATE	RATE
1	New Jersey	1,224.6
2	Rhode Island	1,024.8
3	Massachusetts	879.5
4	Connecticut	741.1
5	Maryland	623.5
6	Delaware	493.6
7	New York	421.2
8	Florida	391.3
9	Pennsylvania	286.2
10	Ohio	285.3
11	California	253.8
12	Illinois	230.6
13	Hawaii	222.3
14	Virginia	214.5
15	North Carolina	211.3
16	Indiana	186.1
17	Georgia	181.3
18	Michigan	176.2
19	South Carolina	167.1
20	Tennessee	162.9
21	New Hampshire	150.0
22	Kentucky	112.8
23	Washington	111.4
24	Louisiana	108.4
24	Texas	108.4
26	Wisconsin	107.0
27	Alabama	96.3
28	Missouri	88.9
29	West Virginia	75.5
30	Minnesota	70.0
31	Vermont	67.7
32	Mississippi	63.6
33	Arizona	61.8
34	Arkansas	57.7
35	Oklahoma	57.3
36	Iowa	56.3
37	Colorado	54.1
38	Maine	43.3
39	Oregon	43.2
40	Utah	37.7
41	Kansas	35.6
42	Nevada	27.3
43	Nebraska	25.0
44	Idaho	20.8
45	New Mexico	17.2
46	South Dakota	11.5
47	North Dakota	10.9
48	Montana	7.2
49	Wyoming	6.0
50	Alaska	1.3
	District of Columbia	11,376.6

Source: CQ Press using data from U.S. Bureau of the Census
"Population Estimates" (December 2017, http://www.census.gov/programs-surveys/popest.html)
*Resident population. Based on land area of states.

Male Population in 2016

National Total = 159,078,923 Males

ALPHA ORDER

RANK	STATE	MALES	% of USA
24	Alabama	2,355,586	1.5%
48	Alaska	388,132	0.2%
14	Arizona	3,442,895	2.2%
33	Arkansas	1,467,873	0.9%
1	California	19,493,361	12.3%
21	Colorado	2,785,818	1.8%
29	Connecticut	1,745,615	1.1%
45	Delaware	460,670	0.3%
3	Florida	10,070,151	6.3%
8	Georgia	5,020,465	3.2%
40	Hawaii	717,615	0.5%
39	Idaho	843,532	0.5%
5	Illinois	6,291,791	4.0%
16	Indiana	3,269,562	2.1%
30	Iowa	1,559,119	1.0%
35	Kansas	1,447,759	0.9%
26	Kentucky	2,186,553	1.4%
25	Louisiana	2,289,370	1.4%
42	Maine	652,585	0.4%
19	Maryland	2,914,466	1.8%
15	Massachusetts	3,305,651	2.1%
10	Michigan	4,884,746	3.1%
22	Minnesota	2,747,630	1.7%
34	Mississippi	1,448,792	0.9%
18	Missouri	2,992,035	1.9%
43	Montana	524,775	0.3%
37	Nebraska	950,671	0.6%
32	Nevada	1,473,997	0.9%
41	New Hampshire	660,860	0.4%
11	New Jersey	4,367,744	2.7%
36	New Mexico	1,030,663	0.6%
4	New York	9,587,365	6.0%
9	North Carolina	4,932,952	3.1%
47	North Dakota	388,974	0.2%
7	Ohio	5,691,694	3.6%
28	Oklahoma	1,943,903	1.2%
27	Oregon	2,027,010	1.3%
6	Pennsylvania	6,261,194	3.9%
44	Rhode Island	513,081	0.3%
23	South Carolina	2,407,934	1.5%
46	South Dakota	436,272	0.3%
17	Tennessee	3,242,515	2.0%
2	Texas	13,831,432	8.7%
31	Utah	1,535,894	1.0%
49	Vermont	308,466	0.2%
12	Virginia	4,136,814	2.6%
13	Washington	3,641,400	2.3%
38	West Virginia	905,943	0.6%
20	Wisconsin	2,873,426	1.8%
50	Wyoming	298,942	0.2%

RANK ORDER

RANK	STATE	MALES	% of USA
1	California	19,493,361	12.3%
2	Texas	13,831,432	8.7%
3	Florida	10,070,151	6.3%
4	New York	9,587,365	6.0%
5	Illinois	6,291,791	4.0%
6	Pennsylvania	6,261,194	3.9%
7	Ohio	5,691,694	3.6%
8	Georgia	5,020,465	3.2%
9	North Carolina	4,932,952	3.1%
10	Michigan	4,884,746	3.1%
11	New Jersey	4,367,744	2.7%
12	Virginia	4,136,814	2.6%
13	Washington	3,641,400	2.3%
14	Arizona	3,442,895	2.2%
15	Massachusetts	3,305,651	2.1%
16	Indiana	3,269,562	2.1%
17	Tennessee	3,242,515	2.0%
18	Missouri	2,992,035	1.9%
19	Maryland	2,914,466	1.8%
20	Wisconsin	2,873,426	1.8%
21	Colorado	2,785,818	1.8%
22	Minnesota	2,747,630	1.7%
23	South Carolina	2,407,934	1.5%
24	Alabama	2,355,586	1.5%
25	Louisiana	2,289,370	1.4%
26	Kentucky	2,186,553	1.4%
27	Oregon	2,027,010	1.3%
28	Oklahoma	1,943,903	1.2%
29	Connecticut	1,745,615	1.1%
30	Iowa	1,559,119	1.0%
31	Utah	1,535,894	1.0%
32	Nevada	1,473,997	0.9%
33	Arkansas	1,467,873	0.9%
34	Mississippi	1,448,792	0.9%
35	Kansas	1,447,759	0.9%
36	New Mexico	1,030,663	0.6%
37	Nebraska	950,671	0.6%
38	West Virginia	905,943	0.6%
39	Idaho	843,532	0.5%
40	Hawaii	717,615	0.5%
41	New Hampshire	660,860	0.4%
42	Maine	652,585	0.4%
43	Montana	524,775	0.3%
44	Rhode Island	513,081	0.3%
45	Delaware	460,670	0.3%
46	South Dakota	436,272	0.3%
47	North Dakota	388,974	0.2%
48	Alaska	388,132	0.2%
49	Vermont	308,466	0.2%
50	Wyoming	298,942	0.2%
	District of Columbia	323,230	0.2%

Source: U.S. Bureau of the Census
"State Characteristics: Vintage 2016" (http://www.census.gov/programs-surveys/popest/data/data-sets.html)

Female Population in 2016

National Total = 164,048,590 Females

ALPHA ORDER

ALPHA ORDER

RANK	STATE	FEMALES	% of USA
24	Alabama	2,507,714	1.5%
48	Alaska	353,762	0.2%
15	Arizona	3,488,176	2.1%
32	Arkansas	1,520,375	0.9%
1	California	19,756,656	12.0%
22	Colorado	2,754,727	1.7%
29	Connecticut	1,830,837	1.1%
45	Delaware	491,395	0.3%
3	Florida	10,542,288	6.4%
8	Georgia	5,289,906	3.2%
40	Hawaii	710,942	0.4%
39	Idaho	839,608	0.5%
6	Illinois	6,509,748	4.0%
17	Indiana	3,363,491	2.1%
30	Iowa	1,575,574	1.0%
35	Kansas	1,459,530	0.9%
26	Kentucky	2,250,421	1.4%
25	Louisiana	2,392,296	1.5%
41	Maine	678,894	0.4%
18	Maryland	3,101,981	1.9%
14	Massachusetts	3,506,128	2.1%
10	Michigan	5,043,554	3.1%
21	Minnesota	2,772,322	1.7%
31	Mississippi	1,539,934	0.9%
19	Missouri	3,100,965	1.9%
44	Montana	517,745	0.3%
37	Nebraska	956,445	0.6%
34	Nevada	1,466,061	0.9%
42	New Hampshire	673,935	0.4%
11	New Jersey	4,576,725	2.8%
36	New Mexico	1,050,352	0.6%
4	New York	10,157,924	6.2%
9	North Carolina	5,213,836	3.2%
47	North Dakota	368,978	0.2%
7	Ohio	5,922,679	3.6%
28	Oklahoma	1,979,658	1.2%
27	Oregon	2,066,455	1.3%
5	Pennsylvania	6,523,033	4.0%
43	Rhode Island	543,345	0.3%
23	South Carolina	2,553,185	1.6%
46	South Dakota	429,182	0.3%
16	Tennessee	3,408,679	2.1%
2	Texas	14,031,164	8.6%
33	Utah	1,515,323	0.9%
49	Vermont	316,128	0.2%
12	Virginia	4,274,994	2.6%
13	Washington	3,646,600	2.2%
38	West Virginia	925,159	0.6%
20	Wisconsin	2,905,282	1.8%
50	Wyoming	286,559	0.2%

RANK ORDER

RANK	STATE	FEMALES	% of USA
1	California	19,756,656	12.0%
2	Texas	14,031,164	8.6%
3	Florida	10,542,288	6.4%
4	New York	10,157,924	6.2%
5	Pennsylvania	6,523,033	4.0%
6	Illinois	6,509,748	4.0%
7	Ohio	5,922,679	3.6%
8	Georgia	5,289,906	3.2%
9	North Carolina	5,213,836	3.2%
10	Michigan	5,043,554	3.1%
11	New Jersey	4,576,725	2.8%
12	Virginia	4,274,994	2.6%
13	Washington	3,646,600	2.2%
14	Massachusetts	3,506,128	2.1%
15	Arizona	3,488,176	2.1%
16	Tennessee	3,408,679	2.1%
17	Indiana	3,363,491	2.1%
18	Maryland	3,101,981	1.9%
19	Missouri	3,100,965	1.9%
20	Wisconsin	2,905,282	1.8%
21	Minnesota	2,772,322	1.7%
22	Colorado	2,754,727	1.7%
23	South Carolina	2,553,185	1.6%
24	Alabama	2,507,714	1.5%
25	Louisiana	2,392,296	1.5%
26	Kentucky	2,250,421	1.4%
27	Oregon	2,066,455	1.3%
28	Oklahoma	1,979,658	1.2%
29	Connecticut	1,830,837	1.1%
30	Iowa	1,575,574	1.0%
31	Mississippi	1,539,934	0.9%
32	Arkansas	1,520,375	0.9%
33	Utah	1,515,323	0.9%
34	Nevada	1,466,061	0.9%
35	Kansas	1,459,530	0.9%
36	New Mexico	1,050,352	0.6%
37	Nebraska	956,445	0.6%
38	West Virginia	925,159	0.6%
39	Idaho	839,608	0.5%
40	Hawaii	710,942	0.4%
41	Maine	678,894	0.4%
42	New Hampshire	673,935	0.4%
43	Rhode Island	543,345	0.3%
44	Montana	517,745	0.3%
45	Delaware	491,395	0.3%
46	South Dakota	429,182	0.3%
47	North Dakota	368,978	0.2%
48	Alaska	353,762	0.2%
49	Vermont	316,128	0.2%
50	Wyoming	286,559	0.2%
	District of Columbia	357,940	0.2%

Source: U.S. Bureau of the Census
"State Characteristics: Vintage 2016" (http://www.census.gov/programs-surveys/popest/data/data-sets.html)

Male to Female Ratio in 2016

National Ratio = 97.0 Males per 100 Females

ALPHA ORDER

RANK	STATE	RATIO
49	Alabama	93.9
1	Alaska	109.7
17	Arizona	98.7
31	Arkansas	96.5
17	California	98.7
7	Colorado	101.1
39	Connecticut	95.3
50	Delaware	93.7
37	Florida	95.5
41	Georgia	94.9
8	Hawaii	100.9
9	Idaho	100.5
30	Illinois	96.7
26	Indiana	97.2
15	Iowa	99.0
13	Kansas	99.2
26	Kentucky	97.2
36	Louisiana	95.7
33	Maine	96.1
48	Maryland	94.0
45	Massachusetts	94.3
28	Michigan	96.9
14	Minnesota	99.1
47	Mississippi	94.1
31	Missouri	96.5
5	Montana	101.4
12	Nebraska	99.4
9	Nevada	100.5
21	New Hampshire	98.1
38	New Jersey	95.4
21	New Mexico	98.1
43	New York	94.4
42	North Carolina	94.6
2	North Dakota	105.4
33	Ohio	96.1
20	Oklahoma	98.2
21	Oregon	98.1
35	Pennsylvania	96.0
43	Rhode Island	94.4
45	South Carolina	94.3
4	South Dakota	101.7
40	Tennessee	95.1
19	Texas	98.6
5	Utah	101.4
25	Vermont	97.6
29	Virginia	96.8
11	Washington	99.9
24	West Virginia	97.9
16	Wisconsin	98.9
3	Wyoming	104.3

RANK ORDER

RANK	STATE	RATIO
1	Alaska	109.7
2	North Dakota	105.4
3	Wyoming	104.3
4	South Dakota	101.7
5	Montana	101.4
5	Utah	101.4
7	Colorado	101.1
8	Hawaii	100.9
9	Idaho	100.5
9	Nevada	100.5
11	Washington	99.9
12	Nebraska	99.4
13	Kansas	99.2
14	Minnesota	99.1
15	Iowa	99.0
16	Wisconsin	98.9
17	Arizona	98.7
17	California	98.7
19	Texas	98.6
20	Oklahoma	98.2
21	New Hampshire	98.1
21	New Mexico	98.1
21	Oregon	98.1
24	West Virginia	97.9
25	Vermont	97.6
26	Indiana	97.2
26	Kentucky	97.2
28	Michigan	96.9
29	Virginia	96.8
30	Illinois	96.7
31	Arkansas	96.5
31	Missouri	96.5
33	Maine	96.1
33	Ohio	96.1
35	Pennsylvania	96.0
36	Louisiana	95.7
37	Florida	95.5
38	New Jersey	95.4
39	Connecticut	95.3
40	Tennessee	95.1
41	Georgia	94.9
42	North Carolina	94.6
43	New York	94.4
43	Rhode Island	94.4
45	Massachusetts	94.3
45	South Carolina	94.3
47	Mississippi	94.1
48	Maryland	94.0
49	Alabama	93.9
50	Delaware	93.7
	District of Columbia	90.3

Source: CQ Press using data from U.S. Bureau of the Census
"State Characteristics: Vintage 2016" (http://www.census.gov/programs-surveys/popest/data/data-sets.html)

Median Age in 2016

National Median = 37.9 Years Old

<table>
<tr><td colspan="3">ALPHA ORDER</td><td colspan="3">RANK ORDER</td></tr>
<tr><th>RANK</th><th>STATE</th><th>MEDIAN AGE</th><th>RANK</th><th>STATE</th><th>MEDIAN AGE</th></tr>
<tr><td>18</td><td>Alabama</td><td>38.9</td><td>1</td><td>Maine</td><td>44.6</td></tr>
<tr><td>49</td><td>Alaska</td><td>33.9</td><td>2</td><td>New Hampshire</td><td>43.0</td></tr>
<tr><td>33</td><td>Arizona</td><td>37.6</td><td>3</td><td>Vermont</td><td>42.7</td></tr>
<tr><td>27</td><td>Arkansas</td><td>38.0</td><td>4</td><td>West Virginia</td><td>42.2</td></tr>
<tr><td>43</td><td>California</td><td>36.4</td><td>5</td><td>Florida</td><td>42.1</td></tr>
<tr><td>39</td><td>Colorado</td><td>36.6</td><td>6</td><td>Connecticut</td><td>40.7</td></tr>
<tr><td>6</td><td>Connecticut</td><td>40.7</td><td>6</td><td>Pennsylvania</td><td>40.7</td></tr>
<tr><td>8</td><td>Delaware</td><td>40.2</td><td>8</td><td>Delaware</td><td>40.2</td></tr>
<tr><td>5</td><td>Florida</td><td>42.1</td><td>9</td><td>Rhode Island</td><td>40.0</td></tr>
<tr><td>41</td><td>Georgia</td><td>36.5</td><td>10</td><td>Montana</td><td>39.8</td></tr>
<tr><td>22</td><td>Hawaii</td><td>38.6</td><td>11</td><td>Michigan</td><td>39.7</td></tr>
<tr><td>46</td><td>Idaho</td><td>36.2</td><td>11</td><td>New Jersey</td><td>39.7</td></tr>
<tr><td>30</td><td>Illinois</td><td>37.8</td><td>13</td><td>Massachusetts</td><td>39.4</td></tr>
<tr><td>33</td><td>Indiana</td><td>37.6</td><td>14</td><td>Ohio</td><td>39.3</td></tr>
<tr><td>27</td><td>Iowa</td><td>38.0</td><td>14</td><td>Oregon</td><td>39.3</td></tr>
<tr><td>41</td><td>Kansas</td><td>36.5</td><td>14</td><td>Wisconsin</td><td>39.3</td></tr>
<tr><td>19</td><td>Kentucky</td><td>38.7</td><td>17</td><td>South Carolina</td><td>39.2</td></tr>
<tr><td>39</td><td>Louisiana</td><td>36.6</td><td>18</td><td>Alabama</td><td>38.9</td></tr>
<tr><td>1</td><td>Maine</td><td>44.6</td><td>19</td><td>Kentucky</td><td>38.7</td></tr>
<tr><td>23</td><td>Maryland</td><td>38.5</td><td>19</td><td>North Carolina</td><td>38.7</td></tr>
<tr><td>13</td><td>Massachusetts</td><td>39.4</td><td>19</td><td>Tennessee</td><td>38.7</td></tr>
<tr><td>11</td><td>Michigan</td><td>39.7</td><td>22</td><td>Hawaii</td><td>38.6</td></tr>
<tr><td>29</td><td>Minnesota</td><td>37.9</td><td>23</td><td>Maryland</td><td>38.5</td></tr>
<tr><td>36</td><td>Mississippi</td><td>37.1</td><td>23</td><td>New York</td><td>38.5</td></tr>
<tr><td>25</td><td>Missouri</td><td>38.4</td><td>25</td><td>Missouri</td><td>38.4</td></tr>
<tr><td>10</td><td>Montana</td><td>39.8</td><td>26</td><td>Virginia</td><td>38.1</td></tr>
<tr><td>45</td><td>Nebraska</td><td>36.3</td><td>27</td><td>Arkansas</td><td>38.0</td></tr>
<tr><td>30</td><td>Nevada</td><td>37.8</td><td>27</td><td>Iowa</td><td>38.0</td></tr>
<tr><td>2</td><td>New Hampshire</td><td>43.0</td><td>29</td><td>Minnesota</td><td>37.9</td></tr>
<tr><td>11</td><td>New Jersey</td><td>39.7</td><td>30</td><td>Illinois</td><td>37.8</td></tr>
<tr><td>33</td><td>New Mexico</td><td>37.6</td><td>30</td><td>Nevada</td><td>37.8</td></tr>
<tr><td>23</td><td>New York</td><td>38.5</td><td>32</td><td>Washington</td><td>37.7</td></tr>
<tr><td>19</td><td>North Carolina</td><td>38.7</td><td>33</td><td>Arizona</td><td>37.6</td></tr>
<tr><td>47</td><td>North Dakota</td><td>34.8</td><td>33</td><td>Indiana</td><td>37.6</td></tr>
<tr><td>14</td><td>Ohio</td><td>39.3</td><td>33</td><td>New Mexico</td><td>37.6</td></tr>
<tr><td>43</td><td>Oklahoma</td><td>36.4</td><td>36</td><td>Mississippi</td><td>37.1</td></tr>
<tr><td>14</td><td>Oregon</td><td>39.3</td><td>36</td><td>Wyoming</td><td>37.1</td></tr>
<tr><td>6</td><td>Pennsylvania</td><td>40.7</td><td>38</td><td>South Dakota</td><td>37.0</td></tr>
<tr><td>9</td><td>Rhode Island</td><td>40.0</td><td>39</td><td>Colorado</td><td>36.6</td></tr>
<tr><td>17</td><td>South Carolina</td><td>39.2</td><td>39</td><td>Louisiana</td><td>36.6</td></tr>
<tr><td>38</td><td>South Dakota</td><td>37.0</td><td>41</td><td>Georgia</td><td>36.5</td></tr>
<tr><td>19</td><td>Tennessee</td><td>38.7</td><td>41</td><td>Kansas</td><td>36.5</td></tr>
<tr><td>48</td><td>Texas</td><td>34.5</td><td>43</td><td>California</td><td>36.4</td></tr>
<tr><td>50</td><td>Utah</td><td>30.8</td><td>43</td><td>Oklahoma</td><td>36.4</td></tr>
<tr><td>3</td><td>Vermont</td><td>42.7</td><td>45</td><td>Nebraska</td><td>36.3</td></tr>
<tr><td>26</td><td>Virginia</td><td>38.1</td><td>46</td><td>Idaho</td><td>36.2</td></tr>
<tr><td>32</td><td>Washington</td><td>37.7</td><td>47</td><td>North Dakota</td><td>34.8</td></tr>
<tr><td>4</td><td>West Virginia</td><td>42.2</td><td>48</td><td>Texas</td><td>34.5</td></tr>
<tr><td>14</td><td>Wisconsin</td><td>39.3</td><td>49</td><td>Alaska</td><td>33.9</td></tr>
<tr><td>36</td><td>Wyoming</td><td>37.1</td><td>50</td><td>Utah</td><td>30.8</td></tr>
<tr><td></td><td></td><td></td><td></td><td>District of Columbia</td><td>33.9</td></tr>
</table>

Source: U.S. Bureau of the Census
"State Characteristics: Vintage 2016" (http://www.census.gov/programs-surveys/popest/data/data-sets.html)

Male Median Age in 2016

National Median = 36.6 Years Old

RANK	STATE	MEDIAN AGE
18	Alabama	37.4
48	Alaska	33.5
35	Arizona	36.3
30	Arkansas	36.7
42	California	35.3
38	Colorado	35.7
7	Connecticut	38.9
9	Delaware	38.5
5	Florida	40.5
45	Georgia	35.2
24	Hawaii	37.0
40	Idaho	35.4
31	Illinois	36.6
33	Indiana	36.4
28	Iowa	36.8
42	Kansas	35.3
18	Kentucky	37.4
40	Louisiana	35.4
1	Maine	43.2
26	Maryland	36.9
15	Massachusetts	37.9
10	Michigan	38.2
24	Minnesota	37.0
38	Mississippi	35.7
23	Missouri	37.1
8	Montana	38.7
42	Nebraska	35.3
21	Nevada	37.2
2	New Hampshire	41.7
13	New Jersey	38.1
36	New Mexico	36.2
26	New York	36.9
21	North Carolina	37.2
47	North Dakota	33.9
15	Ohio	37.9
45	Oklahoma	35.2
10	Oregon	38.2
6	Pennsylvania	39.0
13	Rhode Island	38.1
17	South Carolina	37.7
37	South Dakota	36.0
18	Tennessee	37.4
48	Texas	33.5
50	Utah	30.2
3	Vermont	41.2
28	Virginia	36.8
31	Washington	36.6
4	West Virginia	40.9
10	Wisconsin	38.2
33	Wyoming	36.4

RANK	STATE	MEDIAN AGE
1	Maine	43.2
2	New Hampshire	41.7
3	Vermont	41.2
4	West Virginia	40.9
5	Florida	40.5
6	Pennsylvania	39.0
7	Connecticut	38.9
8	Montana	38.7
9	Delaware	38.5
10	Michigan	38.2
10	Oregon	38.2
10	Wisconsin	38.2
13	New Jersey	38.1
13	Rhode Island	38.1
15	Massachusetts	37.9
15	Ohio	37.9
17	South Carolina	37.7
18	Alabama	37.4
18	Kentucky	37.4
18	Tennessee	37.4
21	Nevada	37.2
21	North Carolina	37.2
23	Missouri	37.1
24	Hawaii	37.0
24	Minnesota	37.0
26	Maryland	36.9
26	New York	36.9
28	Iowa	36.8
28	Virginia	36.8
30	Arkansas	36.7
31	Illinois	36.6
31	Washington	36.6
33	Indiana	36.4
33	Wyoming	36.4
35	Arizona	36.3
36	New Mexico	36.2
37	South Dakota	36.0
38	Colorado	35.7
38	Mississippi	35.7
40	Idaho	35.4
40	Louisiana	35.4
42	California	35.3
42	Kansas	35.3
42	Nebraska	35.3
45	Georgia	35.2
45	Oklahoma	35.2
47	North Dakota	33.9
48	Alaska	33.5
48	Texas	33.5
50	Utah	30.2
	District of Columbia	33.7

Source: U.S. Bureau of the Census
"State Characteristics: Vintage 2016" (http://www.census.gov/programs-surveys/popest/data/data-sets.html)

Female Median Age in 2016

National Median = 39.2 Years Old

RANK	STATE	MEDIAN AGE
18	Alabama	40.3
49	Alaska	34.4
31	Arizona	38.9
27	Arkansas	39.3
42	California	37.6
42	Colorado	37.6
6	Connecticut	42.4
8	Delaware	41.9
4	Florida	43.7
39	Georgia	37.8
17	Hawaii	40.4
46	Idaho	37.0
30	Illinois	39.1
33	Indiana	38.8
27	Iowa	39.3
39	Kansas	37.8
20	Kentucky	40.1
38	Louisiana	37.9
1	Maine	45.8
22	Maryland	40.0
13	Massachusetts	40.9
11	Michigan	41.1
31	Minnesota	38.9
35	Mississippi	38.6
25	Missouri	39.9
12	Montana	41.0
45	Nebraska	37.4
36	Nevada	38.5
3	New Hampshire	44.1
10	New Jersey	41.2
29	New Mexico	39.2
22	New York	40.0
20	North Carolina	40.1
47	North Dakota	35.9
14	Ohio	40.8
42	Oklahoma	37.6
18	Oregon	40.3
6	Pennsylvania	42.4
9	Rhode Island	41.8
14	South Carolina	40.8
37	South Dakota	38.1
22	Tennessee	40.0
48	Texas	35.5
50	Utah	31.4
2	Vermont	44.2
26	Virginia	39.4
33	Washington	38.8
5	West Virginia	43.6
16	Wisconsin	40.5
39	Wyoming	37.8

RANK	STATE	MEDIAN AGE
1	Maine	45.8
2	Vermont	44.2
3	New Hampshire	44.1
4	Florida	43.7
5	West Virginia	43.6
6	Connecticut	42.4
6	Pennsylvania	42.4
8	Delaware	41.9
9	Rhode Island	41.8
10	New Jersey	41.2
11	Michigan	41.1
12	Montana	41.0
13	Massachusetts	40.9
14	Ohio	40.8
14	South Carolina	40.8
16	Wisconsin	40.5
17	Hawaii	40.4
18	Alabama	40.3
18	Oregon	40.3
20	Kentucky	40.1
20	North Carolina	40.1
22	Maryland	40.0
22	New York	40.0
22	Tennessee	40.0
25	Missouri	39.9
26	Virginia	39.4
27	Arkansas	39.3
27	Iowa	39.3
29	New Mexico	39.2
30	Illinois	39.1
31	Arizona	38.9
31	Minnesota	38.9
33	Indiana	38.8
33	Washington	38.8
35	Mississippi	38.6
36	Nevada	38.5
37	South Dakota	38.1
38	Louisiana	37.9
39	Georgia	37.8
39	Kansas	37.8
39	Wyoming	37.8
42	California	37.6
42	Colorado	37.6
42	Oklahoma	37.6
45	Nebraska	37.4
46	Idaho	37.0
47	North Dakota	35.9
48	Texas	35.5
49	Alaska	34.4
50	Utah	31.4
	District of Columbia	34.1

Source: U.S. Bureau of the Census
"State Characteristics: Vintage 2016" (http://www.census.gov/programs-surveys/popest/data/data-sets.html)

White Population in 2016

National Total = 248,502,532*

ALPHA ORDER

RANK	STATE	POPULATION	% of USA
26	Alabama	3,372,524	1.4%
49	Alaska	490,389	0.2%
14	Arizona	5,772,667	2.3%
33	Arkansas	2,373,726	1.0%
1	California	28,539,253	11.5%
20	Colorado	4,846,441	2.0%
29	Connecticut	2,882,093	1.2%
45	Delaware	667,809	0.3%
3	Florida	15,996,473	6.4%
11	Georgia	6,311,001	2.5%
50	Hawaii	369,064	0.1%
39	Idaho	1,571,098	0.6%
6	Illinois	9,885,382	4.0%
15	Indiana	5,678,630	2.3%
30	Iowa	2,864,884	1.2%
32	Kansas	2,518,720	1.0%
22	Kentucky	3,903,419	1.6%
27	Louisiana	2,956,505	1.2%
40	Maine	1,262,168	0.5%
24	Maryland	3,567,397	1.4%
16	Massachusetts	5,570,872	2.2%
8	Michigan	7,902,903	3.2%
21	Minnesota	4,691,265	1.9%
35	Mississippi	1,772,995	0.7%
18	Missouri	5,071,682	2.0%
42	Montana	929,802	0.4%
38	Nebraska	1,694,976	0.7%
34	Nevada	2,209,037	0.9%
41	New Hampshire	1,251,893	0.5%
10	New Jersey	6,473,721	2.6%
36	New Mexico	1,718,307	0.7%
4	New York	13,797,556	5.6%
9	North Carolina	7,206,071	2.9%
46	North Dakota	665,977	0.3%
7	Ohio	9,576,321	3.9%
28	Oklahoma	2,925,602	1.2%
23	Oregon	3,578,285	1.4%
5	Pennsylvania	10,531,113	4.2%
43	Rhode Island	892,045	0.4%
25	South Carolina	3,396,931	1.4%
44	South Dakota	737,070	0.3%
17	Tennessee	5,234,030	2.1%
2	Texas	22,135,668	8.9%
31	Utah	2,778,175	1.1%
47	Vermont	590,869	0.2%
12	Virginia	5,891,553	2.4%
13	Washington	5,830,144	2.3%
37	West Virginia	1,713,756	0.7%
19	Wisconsin	5,057,070	2.0%
48	Wyoming	543,387	0.2%

RANK ORDER

RANK	STATE	POPULATION	% of USA
1	California	28,539,253	11.5%
2	Texas	22,135,668	8.9%
3	Florida	15,996,473	6.4%
4	New York	13,797,556	5.6%
5	Pennsylvania	10,531,113	4.2%
6	Illinois	9,885,382	4.0%
7	Ohio	9,576,321	3.9%
8	Michigan	7,902,903	3.2%
9	North Carolina	7,206,071	2.9%
10	New Jersey	6,473,721	2.6%
11	Georgia	6,311,001	2.5%
12	Virginia	5,891,553	2.4%
13	Washington	5,830,144	2.3%
14	Arizona	5,772,667	2.3%
15	Indiana	5,678,630	2.3%
16	Massachusetts	5,570,872	2.2%
17	Tennessee	5,234,030	2.1%
18	Missouri	5,071,682	2.0%
19	Wisconsin	5,057,070	2.0%
20	Colorado	4,846,441	2.0%
21	Minnesota	4,691,265	1.9%
22	Kentucky	3,903,419	1.6%
23	Oregon	3,578,285	1.4%
24	Maryland	3,567,397	1.4%
25	South Carolina	3,396,931	1.4%
26	Alabama	3,372,524	1.4%
27	Louisiana	2,956,505	1.2%
28	Oklahoma	2,925,602	1.2%
29	Connecticut	2,882,093	1.2%
30	Iowa	2,864,884	1.2%
31	Utah	2,778,175	1.1%
32	Kansas	2,518,720	1.0%
33	Arkansas	2,373,726	1.0%
34	Nevada	2,209,037	0.9%
35	Mississippi	1,772,995	0.7%
36	New Mexico	1,718,307	0.7%
37	West Virginia	1,713,756	0.7%
38	Nebraska	1,694,976	0.7%
39	Idaho	1,571,098	0.6%
40	Maine	1,262,168	0.5%
41	New Hampshire	1,251,893	0.5%
42	Montana	929,802	0.4%
43	Rhode Island	892,045	0.4%
44	South Dakota	737,070	0.3%
45	Delaware	667,809	0.3%
46	North Dakota	665,977	0.3%
47	Vermont	590,869	0.2%
48	Wyoming	543,387	0.2%
49	Alaska	490,389	0.2%
50	Hawaii	369,064	0.1%
	District of Columbia	303,813	0.1%

Source: U.S. Bureau of the Census
"State Characteristics: Vintage 2016" (http://www.census.gov/programs-surveys/popest/data/data-sets.html)
*Those who identified themselves as one race. "White" is defined by Census as a person having origins in any of the original peoples of Europe, North Africa, or the Middle East. There are 197,969,608 non-Hispanic whites. Census states "Race is a self-identification data item in which respondents choose the race or races with which they most closely identify."

Percent of Population White in 2016

National Percent = 76.9%*

ALPHA ORDER

RANK	STATE	PERCENT
43	Alabama	69.3
45	Alaska	66.1
21	Arizona	83.3
30	Arkansas	79.4
37	California	72.7
13	Colorado	87.5
27	Connecticut	80.6
40	Delaware	70.1
33	Florida	77.6
47	Georgia	61.2
50	Hawaii	25.8
5	Idaho	93.3
34	Illinois	77.2
17	Indiana	85.6
7	Iowa	91.4
16	Kansas	86.6
11	Kentucky	88.0
46	Louisiana	63.2
1	Maine	94.8
48	Maryland	59.3
26	Massachusetts	81.8
29	Michigan	79.6
19	Minnesota	85.0
48	Mississippi	59.3
22	Missouri	83.2
9	Montana	89.2
10	Nebraska	88.9
35	Nevada	75.1
3	New Hampshire	93.8
38	New Jersey	72.4
23	New Mexico	82.6
42	New York	69.9
39	North Carolina	71.0
12	North Dakota	87.9
24	Ohio	82.5
36	Oklahoma	74.6
15	Oregon	87.4
25	Pennsylvania	82.4
20	Rhode Island	84.4
44	South Carolina	68.5
18	South Dakota	85.2
32	Tennessee	78.7
30	Texas	79.4
8	Utah	91.1
2	Vermont	94.6
41	Virginia	70.0
28	Washington	80.0
4	West Virginia	93.6
13	Wisconsin	87.5
6	Wyoming	92.8

RANK ORDER

RANK	STATE	PERCENT
1	Maine	94.8
2	Vermont	94.6
3	New Hampshire	93.8
4	West Virginia	93.6
5	Idaho	93.3
6	Wyoming	92.8
7	Iowa	91.4
8	Utah	91.1
9	Montana	89.2
10	Nebraska	88.9
11	Kentucky	88.0
12	North Dakota	87.9
13	Colorado	87.5
13	Wisconsin	87.5
15	Oregon	87.4
16	Kansas	86.6
17	Indiana	85.6
18	South Dakota	85.2
19	Minnesota	85.0
20	Rhode Island	84.4
21	Arizona	83.3
22	Missouri	83.2
23	New Mexico	82.6
24	Ohio	82.5
25	Pennsylvania	82.4
26	Massachusetts	81.8
27	Connecticut	80.6
28	Washington	80.0
29	Michigan	79.6
30	Arkansas	79.4
30	Texas	79.4
32	Tennessee	78.7
33	Florida	77.6
34	Illinois	77.2
35	Nevada	75.1
36	Oklahoma	74.6
37	California	72.7
38	New Jersey	72.4
39	North Carolina	71.0
40	Delaware	70.1
41	Virginia	70.0
42	New York	69.9
43	Alabama	69.3
44	South Carolina	68.5
45	Alaska	66.1
46	Louisiana	63.2
47	Georgia	61.2
48	Maryland	59.3
48	Mississippi	59.3
50	Hawaii	25.8

District of Columbia 44.6

Source: CQ Press using data from U.S. Bureau of the Census
"State Characteristics: Vintage 2016" (http://www.census.gov/programs-surveys/popest/data/data-sets.html)
*Those who identified themselves as one race. "White" is defined by Census as a person having origins in any of the original peoples of Europe, North Africa, or the Middle East. Non-Hispanic whites comprise 61.3% of the total population. Census states "Race is a self-identification data item in which respondents choose the race or races with which they most closely identify."

Black Population in 2016

National Total = 43,000,691*

RANK	STATE	POPULATION	% of USA
16	Alabama	1,303,516	3.0%
42	Alaska	27,898	0.1%
27	Arizona	339,472	0.8%
22	Arkansas	468,502	1.1%
5	California	2,547,480	5.9%
31	Colorado	248,833	0.6%
23	Connecticut	421,023	1.0%
32	Delaware	214,914	0.5%
3	Florida	3,471,950	8.1%
4	Georgia	3,301,809	7.7%
41	Hawaii	31,073	0.1%
47	Idaho	14,183	0.0%
7	Illinois	1,877,776	4.4%
20	Indiana	641,409	1.5%
34	Iowa	114,874	0.3%
33	Kansas	179,599	0.4%
25	Kentucky	367,591	0.9%
10	Louisiana	1,524,638	3.5%
45	Maine	20,025	0.0%
8	Maryland	1,845,613	4.3%
21	Massachusetts	587,417	1.4%
13	Michigan	1,406,212	3.3%
26	Minnesota	344,322	0.8%
18	Mississippi	1,127,116	2.6%
19	Missouri	720,905	1.7%
50	Montana	6,034	0.0%
35	Nebraska	94,620	0.2%
30	Nevada	281,224	0.7%
44	New Hampshire	20,266	0.0%
15	New Jersey	1,337,890	3.1%
39	New Mexico	52,133	0.1%
2	New York	3,488,119	8.1%
6	North Carolina	2,252,403	5.2%
43	North Dakota	22,356	0.1%
12	Ohio	1,487,040	3.5%
28	Oklahoma	304,465	0.7%
36	Oregon	86,539	0.2%
11	Pennsylvania	1,505,204	3.5%
37	Rhode Island	85,355	0.2%
14	South Carolina	1,362,579	3.2%
46	South Dakota	17,302	0.0%
17	Tennessee	1,137,075	2.6%
1	Texas	3,515,215	8.2%
40	Utah	41,418	0.1%
48	Vermont	8,147	0.0%
9	Virginia	1,664,523	3.9%
29	Washington	301,955	0.7%
38	West Virginia	65,929	0.2%
24	Wisconsin	381,807	0.9%
49	Wyoming	7,753	0.0%

RANK	STATE	POPULATION	% of USA
1	Texas	3,515,215	8.2%
2	New York	3,488,119	8.1%
3	Florida	3,471,950	8.1%
4	Georgia	3,301,809	7.7%
5	California	2,547,480	5.9%
6	North Carolina	2,252,403	5.2%
7	Illinois	1,877,776	4.4%
8	Maryland	1,845,613	4.3%
9	Virginia	1,664,523	3.9%
10	Louisiana	1,524,638	3.5%
11	Pennsylvania	1,505,204	3.5%
12	Ohio	1,487,040	3.5%
13	Michigan	1,406,212	3.3%
14	South Carolina	1,362,579	3.2%
15	New Jersey	1,337,890	3.1%
16	Alabama	1,303,516	3.0%
17	Tennessee	1,137,075	2.6%
18	Mississippi	1,127,116	2.6%
19	Missouri	720,905	1.7%
20	Indiana	641,409	1.5%
21	Massachusetts	587,417	1.4%
22	Arkansas	468,502	1.1%
23	Connecticut	421,023	1.0%
24	Wisconsin	381,807	0.9%
25	Kentucky	367,591	0.9%
26	Minnesota	344,322	0.8%
27	Arizona	339,472	0.8%
28	Oklahoma	304,465	0.7%
29	Washington	301,955	0.7%
30	Nevada	281,224	0.7%
31	Colorado	248,833	0.6%
32	Delaware	214,914	0.5%
33	Kansas	179,599	0.4%
34	Iowa	114,874	0.3%
35	Nebraska	94,620	0.2%
36	Oregon	86,539	0.2%
37	Rhode Island	85,355	0.2%
38	West Virginia	65,929	0.2%
39	New Mexico	52,133	0.1%
40	Utah	41,418	0.1%
41	Hawaii	31,073	0.1%
42	Alaska	27,898	0.1%
43	North Dakota	22,356	0.1%
44	New Hampshire	20,266	0.0%
45	Maine	20,025	0.0%
46	South Dakota	17,302	0.0%
47	Idaho	14,183	0.0%
48	Vermont	8,147	0.0%
49	Wyoming	7,753	0.0%
50	Montana	6,034	0.0%
	District of Columbia	325,190	0.8%

Source: U.S. Bureau of the Census
   "State Characteristics: Vintage 2016" (http://www.census.gov/programs-surveys/popest/data/data-sets.html)
*Those who identified themselves as one race. "Black" is defined by Census as a person having origins in any of the Black racial groups of Africa. Census states "Race is a self-identification data item in which respondents choose the race or races with which they most closely identify."

Percent of Population Black in 2016

National Percent = 13.3%*

ALPHA ORDER				RANK ORDER		
RANK	**STATE**	**PERCENT**		**RANK**	**STATE**	**PERCENT**
6	Alabama	26.8		1	Mississippi	37.7
36	Alaska	3.8		2	Louisiana	32.6
33	Arizona	4.9		3	Georgia	32.0
13	Arkansas	15.7		4	Maryland	30.7
29	California	6.5		5	South Carolina	27.5
34	Colorado	4.5		6	Alabama	26.8
19	Connecticut	11.8		7	Delaware	22.6
7	Delaware	22.6		8	North Carolina	22.2
12	Florida	16.8		9	Virginia	19.8
3	Georgia	32.0		10	New York	17.7
41	Hawaii	2.2		11	Tennessee	17.1
49	Idaho	0.8		12	Florida	16.8
15	Illinois	14.7		13	Arkansas	15.7
22	Indiana	9.7		14	New Jersey	15.0
37	Iowa	3.7		15	Illinois	14.7
30	Kansas	6.2		16	Michigan	14.2
25	Kentucky	8.3		17	Ohio	12.8
2	Louisiana	32.6		18	Texas	12.6
44	Maine	1.5		19	Connecticut	11.8
4	Maryland	30.7		19	Missouri	11.8
24	Massachusetts	8.6		19	Pennsylvania	11.8
16	Michigan	14.2		22	Indiana	9.7
30	Minnesota	6.2		23	Nevada	9.6
1	Mississippi	37.7		24	Massachusetts	8.6
19	Missouri	11.8		25	Kentucky	8.3
50	Montana	0.6		26	Rhode Island	8.1
32	Nebraska	5.0		27	Oklahoma	7.8
23	Nevada	9.6		28	Wisconsin	6.6
44	New Hampshire	1.5		29	California	6.5
14	New Jersey	15.0		30	Kansas	6.2
40	New Mexico	2.5		30	Minnesota	6.2
10	New York	17.7		32	Nebraska	5.0
8	North Carolina	22.2		33	Arizona	4.9
39	North Dakota	2.9		34	Colorado	4.5
17	Ohio	12.8		35	Washington	4.1
27	Oklahoma	7.8		36	Alaska	3.8
42	Oregon	2.1		37	Iowa	3.7
19	Pennsylvania	11.8		38	West Virginia	3.6
26	Rhode Island	8.1		39	North Dakota	2.9
5	South Carolina	27.5		40	New Mexico	2.5
43	South Dakota	2.0		41	Hawaii	2.2
11	Tennessee	17.1		42	Oregon	2.1
18	Texas	12.6		43	South Dakota	2.0
46	Utah	1.4		44	Maine	1.5
47	Vermont	1.3		44	New Hampshire	1.5
9	Virginia	19.8		46	Utah	1.4
35	Washington	4.1		47	Vermont	1.3
38	West Virginia	3.6		47	Wyoming	1.3
28	Wisconsin	6.6		49	Idaho	0.8
47	Wyoming	1.3		50	Montana	0.6
					District of Columbia	47.7

Source: CQ Press using data from U.S. Bureau of the Census
   "State Characteristics: Vintage 2016" (http://www.census.gov/programs-surveys/popest/data/data-sets.html)
*Those who identified themselves as one race. "Black" is defined by Census as a person having origins in any of the Black racial groups of Africa. Census states "Race is a self-identification data item in which respondents choose the race or races with which they most closely identify."

Hispanic Population in 2016

National Total = 57,470,287*

ALPHA ORDER

ALPHA ORDER

RANK	STATE	POPULATION	% of USA
34	Alabama	203,845	0.4%
43	Alaska	51,599	0.1%
6	Arizona	2,144,775	3.7%
32	Arkansas	218,561	0.4%
1	California	15,280,773	26.6%
8	Colorado	1,181,219	2.1%
18	Connecticut	562,348	1.0%
41	Delaware	87,152	0.2%
3	Florida	5,126,975	8.9%
10	Georgia	972,698	1.7%
39	Hawaii	148,148	0.3%
33	Idaho	207,743	0.4%
5	Illinois	2,181,439	3.8%
21	Indiana	449,871	0.8%
36	Iowa	182,606	0.3%
27	Kansas	338,481	0.6%
38	Kentucky	155,520	0.3%
31	Louisiana	236,152	0.4%
49	Maine	21,058	0.0%
17	Maryland	586,801	1.0%
15	Massachusetts	780,661	1.4%
20	Michigan	492,382	0.9%
28	Minnesota	289,422	0.5%
40	Mississippi	91,448	0.2%
30	Missouri	250,476	0.4%
45	Montana	37,840	0.1%
35	Nebraska	203,320	0.4%
14	Nevada	836,626	1.5%
44	New Hampshire	47,118	0.1%
7	New Jersey	1,786,668	3.1%
9	New Mexico	1,009,873	1.8%
4	New York	3,747,125	6.5%
11	North Carolina	932,221	1.6%
48	North Dakota	27,538	0.0%
22	Ohio	424,625	0.7%
24	Oklahoma	403,938	0.7%
19	Oregon	522,571	0.9%
13	Pennsylvania	900,814	1.6%
37	Rhode Island	157,352	0.3%
29	South Carolina	274,596	0.5%
46	South Dakota	32,169	0.1%
26	Tennessee	348,725	0.6%
2	Texas	10,881,124	18.9%
23	Utah	420,440	0.7%
50	Vermont	11,651	0.0%
16	Virginia	766,004	1.3%
12	Washington	907,000	1.6%
47	West Virginia	28,295	0.0%
25	Wisconsin	387,666	0.7%
42	Wyoming	58,413	0.1%

RANK ORDER

RANK	STATE	POPULATION	% of USA
1	California	15,280,773	26.6%
2	Texas	10,881,124	18.9%
3	Florida	5,126,975	8.9%
4	New York	3,747,125	6.5%
5	Illinois	2,181,439	3.8%
6	Arizona	2,144,775	3.7%
7	New Jersey	1,786,668	3.1%
8	Colorado	1,181,219	2.1%
9	New Mexico	1,009,873	1.8%
10	Georgia	972,698	1.7%
11	North Carolina	932,221	1.6%
12	Washington	907,000	1.6%
13	Pennsylvania	900,814	1.6%
14	Nevada	836,626	1.5%
15	Massachusetts	780,661	1.4%
16	Virginia	766,004	1.3%
17	Maryland	586,801	1.0%
18	Connecticut	562,348	1.0%
19	Oregon	522,571	0.9%
20	Michigan	492,382	0.9%
21	Indiana	449,871	0.8%
22	Ohio	424,625	0.7%
23	Utah	420,440	0.7%
24	Oklahoma	403,938	0.7%
25	Wisconsin	387,666	0.7%
26	Tennessee	348,725	0.6%
27	Kansas	338,481	0.6%
28	Minnesota	289,422	0.5%
29	South Carolina	274,596	0.5%
30	Missouri	250,476	0.4%
31	Louisiana	236,152	0.4%
32	Arkansas	218,561	0.4%
33	Idaho	207,743	0.4%
34	Alabama	203,845	0.4%
35	Nebraska	203,320	0.4%
36	Iowa	182,606	0.3%
37	Rhode Island	157,352	0.3%
38	Kentucky	155,520	0.3%
39	Hawaii	148,148	0.3%
40	Mississippi	91,448	0.2%
41	Delaware	87,152	0.2%
42	Wyoming	58,413	0.1%
43	Alaska	51,599	0.1%
44	New Hampshire	47,118	0.1%
45	Montana	37,840	0.1%
46	South Dakota	32,169	0.1%
47	West Virginia	28,295	0.0%
48	North Dakota	27,538	0.0%
49	Maine	21,058	0.0%
50	Vermont	11,651	0.0%
	District of Columbia	74,422	0.1%

Source: U.S. Bureau of the Census

"State Characteristics: Vintage 2016" (http://www.census.gov/programs-surveys/popest/data/data-sets.html)
*Persons of Hispanic origin may be of any race. Census states "Race is a self-identification data item in which respondents choose the race or races with which they most closely identify."

Percent of Population Hispanic in 2016

National Percent = 17.8%*

RANK	STATE	PERCENT
39	Alabama	4.2
29	Alaska	7.0
4	Arizona	30.9
28	Arkansas	7.3
3	California	38.9
7	Colorado	21.3
11	Connecticut	15.7
25	Delaware	9.2
6	Florida	24.9
24	Georgia	9.4
20	Hawaii	10.4
16	Idaho	12.3
10	Illinois	17.0
31	Indiana	6.8
33	Iowa	5.8
17	Kansas	11.6
45	Kentucky	3.5
37	Louisiana	5.0
49	Maine	1.6
23	Maryland	9.8
18	Massachusetts	11.5
37	Michigan	5.0
35	Minnesota	5.2
47	Mississippi	3.1
40	Missouri	4.1
43	Montana	3.6
19	Nebraska	10.7
5	Nevada	28.5
45	New Hampshire	3.5
8	New Jersey	20.0
1	New Mexico	48.5
9	New York	19.0
25	North Carolina	9.2
43	North Dakota	3.6
41	Ohio	3.7
21	Oklahoma	10.3
14	Oregon	12.8
29	Pennsylvania	7.0
12	Rhode Island	14.9
34	South Carolina	5.5
41	South Dakota	3.7
35	Tennessee	5.2
2	Texas	39.1
13	Utah	13.8
48	Vermont	1.9
27	Virginia	9.1
15	Washington	12.4
50	West Virginia	1.5
32	Wisconsin	6.7
22	Wyoming	10.0

RANK	STATE	PERCENT
1	New Mexico	48.5
2	Texas	39.1
3	California	38.9
4	Arizona	30.9
5	Nevada	28.5
6	Florida	24.9
7	Colorado	21.3
8	New Jersey	20.0
9	New York	19.0
10	Illinois	17.0
11	Connecticut	15.7
12	Rhode Island	14.9
13	Utah	13.8
14	Oregon	12.8
15	Washington	12.4
16	Idaho	12.3
17	Kansas	11.6
18	Massachusetts	11.5
19	Nebraska	10.7
20	Hawaii	10.4
21	Oklahoma	10.3
22	Wyoming	10.0
23	Maryland	9.8
24	Georgia	9.4
25	Delaware	9.2
25	North Carolina	9.2
27	Virginia	9.1
28	Arkansas	7.3
29	Alaska	7.0
29	Pennsylvania	7.0
31	Indiana	6.8
32	Wisconsin	6.7
33	Iowa	5.8
34	South Carolina	5.5
35	Minnesota	5.2
35	Tennessee	5.2
37	Louisiana	5.0
37	Michigan	5.0
39	Alabama	4.2
40	Missouri	4.1
41	Ohio	3.7
41	South Dakota	3.7
43	Montana	3.6
43	North Dakota	3.6
45	Kentucky	3.5
45	New Hampshire	3.5
47	Mississippi	3.1
48	Vermont	1.9
49	Maine	1.6
50	West Virginia	1.5

District of Columbia 10.9

Source: CQ Press using data from U.S. Bureau of the Census

"State Characteristics: Vintage 2016" (http://www.census.gov/programs-surveys/popest/data/data-sets.html)

*Persons of Hispanic origin may be of any race. Census states "Race is a self-identification data item in which respondents choose the race or races with which they most closely identify."

Asian Population in 2016

National Total = 18,318,522*

ALPHA ORDER

RANK	STATE	POPULATION	% of USA
33	Alabama	68,864	0.4%
37	Alaska	46,912	0.3%
19	Arizona	236,628	1.3%
35	Arkansas	47,326	0.3%
1	California	5,817,509	31.8%
21	Colorado	180,510	1.0%
22	Connecticut	167,870	0.9%
38	Delaware	37,846	0.2%
7	Florida	587,722	3.2%
12	Georgia	420,391	2.3%
9	Hawaii	539,050	2.9%
43	Idaho	24,815	0.1%
5	Illinois	708,794	3.9%
24	Indiana	149,209	0.8%
31	Iowa	78,735	0.4%
28	Kansas	86,448	0.5%
34	Kentucky	66,230	0.4%
29	Louisiana	85,006	0.5%
44	Maine	16,517	0.1%
13	Maryland	395,887	2.2%
10	Massachusetts	454,371	2.5%
14	Michigan	306,396	1.7%
16	Minnesota	272,170	1.5%
42	Mississippi	31,969	0.2%
25	Missouri	121,812	0.7%
49	Montana	8,486	0.0%
36	Nebraska	47,282	0.3%
18	Nevada	254,432	1.4%
40	New Hampshire	35,776	0.2%
4	New Jersey	877,077	4.8%
41	New Mexico	35,287	0.2%
2	New York	1,750,857	9.6%
15	North Carolina	296,542	1.6%
47	North Dakota	11,561	0.1%
17	Ohio	255,464	1.4%
27	Oklahoma	88,156	0.5%
20	Oregon	183,054	1.0%
11	Pennsylvania	442,652	2.4%
39	Rhode Island	37,629	0.2%
30	South Carolina	79,941	0.4%
46	South Dakota	12,767	0.1%
26	Tennessee	120,219	0.7%
3	Texas	1,350,474	7.4%
32	Utah	77,033	0.4%
48	Vermont	11,079	0.1%
8	Virginia	555,515	3.0%
6	Washington	625,138	3.4%
45	West Virginia	15,385	0.1%
23	Wisconsin	163,622	0.9%
50	Wyoming	5,856	0.0%

RANK ORDER

RANK	STATE	POPULATION	% of USA
1	California	5,817,509	31.8%
2	New York	1,750,857	9.6%
3	Texas	1,350,474	7.4%
4	New Jersey	877,077	4.8%
5	Illinois	708,794	3.9%
6	Washington	625,138	3.4%
7	Florida	587,722	3.2%
8	Virginia	555,515	3.0%
9	Hawaii	539,050	2.9%
10	Massachusetts	454,371	2.5%
11	Pennsylvania	442,652	2.4%
12	Georgia	420,391	2.3%
13	Maryland	395,887	2.2%
14	Michigan	306,396	1.7%
15	North Carolina	296,542	1.6%
16	Minnesota	272,170	1.5%
17	Ohio	255,464	1.4%
18	Nevada	254,432	1.4%
19	Arizona	236,628	1.3%
20	Oregon	183,054	1.0%
21	Colorado	180,510	1.0%
22	Connecticut	167,870	0.9%
23	Wisconsin	163,622	0.9%
24	Indiana	149,209	0.8%
25	Missouri	121,812	0.7%
26	Tennessee	120,219	0.7%
27	Oklahoma	88,156	0.5%
28	Kansas	86,448	0.5%
29	Louisiana	85,006	0.5%
30	South Carolina	79,941	0.4%
31	Iowa	78,735	0.4%
32	Utah	77,033	0.4%
33	Alabama	68,864	0.4%
34	Kentucky	66,230	0.4%
35	Arkansas	47,326	0.3%
36	Nebraska	47,282	0.3%
37	Alaska	46,912	0.3%
38	Delaware	37,846	0.2%
39	Rhode Island	37,629	0.2%
40	New Hampshire	35,776	0.2%
41	New Mexico	35,287	0.2%
42	Mississippi	31,969	0.2%
43	Idaho	24,815	0.1%
44	Maine	16,517	0.1%
45	West Virginia	15,385	0.1%
46	South Dakota	12,767	0.1%
47	North Dakota	11,561	0.1%
48	Vermont	11,079	0.1%
49	Montana	8,486	0.0%
50	Wyoming	5,856	0.0%
	District of Columbia	28,251	0.2%

Source: U.S. Bureau of the Census
   "State Characteristics: Vintage 2016" (http://www.census.gov/programs-surveys/popest/data/data-sets.html)
*Those who identified themselves as one race. Census states "Race is a self-identification data item in which respondents
choose the race or races with which they most closely identify."

Percent of Population Asian in 2016

National Percent = 5.7%*

ALPHA ORDER				RANK ORDER		
RANK	STATE	PERCENT		RANK	STATE	PERCENT
45	Alabama	1.4		1	Hawaii	37.7
10	Alaska	6.3		2	California	14.8
20	Arizona	3.4		3	New Jersey	9.8
39	Arkansas	1.6		4	New York	8.9
2	California	14.8		5	Nevada	8.7
21	Colorado	3.3		6	Washington	8.6
14	Connecticut	4.7		7	Massachusetts	6.7
17	Delaware	4.0		8	Maryland	6.6
24	Florida	2.9		8	Virginia	6.6
16	Georgia	4.1		10	Alaska	6.3
1	Hawaii	37.7		11	Illinois	5.5
41	Idaho	1.5		12	Minnesota	4.9
11	Illinois	5.5		13	Texas	4.8
31	Indiana	2.2		14	Connecticut	4.7
28	Iowa	2.5		15	Oregon	4.5
23	Kansas	3.0		16	Georgia	4.1
41	Kentucky	1.5		17	Delaware	4.0
35	Louisiana	1.8		18	Rhode Island	3.6
46	Maine	1.2		19	Pennsylvania	3.5
8	Maryland	6.6		20	Arizona	3.4
7	Massachusetts	6.7		21	Colorado	3.3
22	Michigan	3.1		22	Michigan	3.1
12	Minnesota	4.9		23	Kansas	3.0
47	Mississippi	1.1		24	Florida	2.9
34	Missouri	2.0		24	North Carolina	2.9
49	Montana	0.8		26	Wisconsin	2.8
28	Nebraska	2.5		27	New Hampshire	2.7
5	Nevada	8.7		28	Iowa	2.5
27	New Hampshire	2.7		28	Nebraska	2.5
3	New Jersey	9.8		28	Utah	2.5
38	New Mexico	1.7		31	Indiana	2.2
4	New York	8.9		31	Ohio	2.2
24	North Carolina	2.9		31	Oklahoma	2.2
41	North Dakota	1.5		34	Missouri	2.0
31	Ohio	2.2		35	Louisiana	1.8
31	Oklahoma	2.2		35	Tennessee	1.8
15	Oregon	4.5		35	Vermont	1.8
19	Pennsylvania	3.5		38	New Mexico	1.7
18	Rhode Island	3.6		39	Arkansas	1.6
39	South Carolina	1.6		39	South Carolina	1.6
41	South Dakota	1.5		41	Idaho	1.5
35	Tennessee	1.8		41	Kentucky	1.5
13	Texas	4.8		41	North Dakota	1.5
28	Utah	2.5		41	South Dakota	1.5
35	Vermont	1.8		45	Alabama	1.4
8	Virginia	6.6		46	Maine	1.2
6	Washington	8.6		47	Mississippi	1.1
49	West Virginia	0.8		48	Wyoming	1.0
26	Wisconsin	2.8		49	Montana	0.8
48	Wyoming	1.0		49	West Virginia	0.8
				District of Columbia		4.1

Source: CQ Press using data from U.S. Bureau of the Census
"State Characteristics: Vintage 2016" (http://www.census.gov/programs-surveys/popest/data/data-sets.html)
*Those who identified themselves as one race. Census states "Race is a self-identification data item in which respondents choose the race or races with which they most closely identify."

American Indian Population in 2016

National Total = 4,054,649*

ALPHA ORDER				RANK ORDER			
RANK	STATE	POPULATION	% of USA	RANK	STATE	POPULATION	% of USA
29	Alabama	33,932	0.8%	1	California	648,055	16.0%
9	Alaska	112,404	2.8%	2	Arizona	371,605	9.2%
2	Arizona	371,605	9.2%	3	Oklahoma	360,158	8.9%
35	Arkansas	29,049	0.7%	4	Texas	283,393	7.0%
1	California	648,055	16.0%	5	New Mexico	219,953	5.4%
11	Colorado	88,197	2.2%	6	New York	191,449	4.7%
39	Connecticut	19,140	0.5%	7	North Carolina	158,476	3.9%
46	Delaware	6,174	0.2%	8	Washington	138,489	3.4%
10	Florida	102,439	2.5%	9	Alaska	112,404	2.8%
20	Georgia	52,365	1.3%	10	Florida	102,439	2.5%
47	Hawaii	5,695	0.1%	11	Colorado	88,197	2.2%
34	Idaho	29,457	0.7%	12	South Dakota	77,711	1.9%
13	Illinois	75,564	1.9%	13	Illinois	75,564	1.9%
38	Indiana	26,875	0.7%	14	Minnesota	73,970	1.8%
41	Iowa	15,924	0.4%	15	Oregon	73,274	1.8%
27	Kansas	34,616	0.9%	16	Michigan	72,252	1.8%
43	Kentucky	13,297	0.3%	17	Montana	69,073	1.7%
26	Louisiana	35,976	0.9%	18	Wisconsin	65,597	1.6%
45	Maine	9,329	0.2%	19	New Jersey	53,976	1.3%
28	Maryland	34,380	0.8%	20	Georgia	52,365	1.3%
31	Massachusetts	32,988	0.8%	21	Nevada	48,305	1.2%
16	Michigan	72,252	1.8%	22	Utah	47,514	1.2%
14	Minnesota	73,970	1.8%	23	Pennsylvania	46,770	1.2%
40	Mississippi	17,985	0.4%	24	Virginia	45,510	1.1%
30	Missouri	33,877	0.8%	25	North Dakota	41,596	1.0%
17	Montana	69,073	1.7%	26	Louisiana	35,976	0.9%
36	Nebraska	27,318	0.7%	27	Kansas	34,616	0.9%
21	Nevada	48,305	1.2%	28	Maryland	34,380	0.8%
49	New Hampshire	3,926	0.1%	29	Alabama	33,932	0.8%
19	New Jersey	53,976	1.3%	30	Missouri	33,877	0.8%
5	New Mexico	219,953	5.4%	31	Massachusetts	32,988	0.8%
6	New York	191,449	4.7%	32	Ohio	32,364	0.8%
7	North Carolina	158,476	3.9%	33	Tennessee	29,866	0.7%
25	North Dakota	41,596	1.0%	34	Idaho	29,457	0.7%
32	Ohio	32,364	0.8%	35	Arkansas	29,049	0.7%
3	Oklahoma	360,158	8.9%	36	Nebraska	27,318	0.7%
15	Oregon	73,274	1.8%	37	South Carolina	26,923	0.7%
23	Pennsylvania	46,770	1.2%	38	Indiana	26,875	0.7%
44	Rhode Island	10,576	0.3%	39	Connecticut	19,140	0.5%
37	South Carolina	26,923	0.7%	40	Mississippi	17,985	0.4%
12	South Dakota	77,711	1.9%	41	Iowa	15,924	0.4%
33	Tennessee	29,866	0.7%	42	Wyoming	15,762	0.4%
4	Texas	283,393	7.0%	43	Kentucky	13,297	0.3%
22	Utah	47,514	1.2%	44	Rhode Island	10,576	0.3%
50	Vermont	2,426	0.1%	45	Maine	9,329	0.2%
24	Virginia	45,510	1.1%	46	Delaware	6,174	0.2%
8	Washington	138,489	3.4%	47	Hawaii	5,695	0.1%
48	West Virginia	4,503	0.1%	48	West Virginia	4,503	0.1%
18	Wisconsin	65,597	1.6%	49	New Hampshire	3,926	0.1%
42	Wyoming	15,762	0.4%	50	Vermont	2,426	0.1%
					District of Columbia	4,196	0.1%

Source: U.S. Bureau of the Census
   "State Characteristics: Vintage 2016" (http://www.census.gov/programs-surveys/popest/data/data-sets.html)
*Those who identified themselves as one race. Includes Alaska Native populations. Census states "Race is a self-identification
data item in which respondents choose the race or races with which they most closely identify."

Percent of Population American Indian in 2016

National Percent = 1.3%*

ALPHA ORDER

RANK	STATE	PERCENT
26	Alabama	0.7
1	Alaska	15.2
7	Arizona	5.4
21	Arkansas	1.0
12	California	1.7
13	Colorado	1.6
35	Connecticut	0.5
29	Delaware	0.6
35	Florida	0.5
35	Georgia	0.5
42	Hawaii	0.4
10	Idaho	1.8
29	Illinois	0.6
42	Indiana	0.4
35	Iowa	0.5
19	Kansas	1.2
47	Kentucky	0.3
25	Louisiana	0.8
26	Maine	0.7
29	Maryland	0.6
35	Massachusetts	0.5
26	Michigan	0.7
18	Minnesota	1.3
29	Mississippi	0.6
29	Missouri	0.6
5	Montana	6.6
17	Nebraska	1.4
13	Nevada	1.6
47	New Hampshire	0.3
29	New Jersey	0.6
2	New Mexico	10.6
21	New York	1.0
13	North Carolina	1.6
6	North Dakota	5.5
47	Ohio	0.3
3	Oklahoma	9.2
10	Oregon	1.8
42	Pennsylvania	0.4
21	Rhode Island	1.0
35	South Carolina	0.5
4	South Dakota	9.0
42	Tennessee	0.4
21	Texas	1.0
13	Utah	1.6
42	Vermont	0.4
35	Virginia	0.5
9	Washington	1.9
50	West Virginia	0.2
20	Wisconsin	1.1
8	Wyoming	2.7

RANK ORDER

RANK	STATE	PERCENT
1	Alaska	15.2
2	New Mexico	10.6
3	Oklahoma	9.2
4	South Dakota	9.0
5	Montana	6.6
6	North Dakota	5.5
7	Arizona	5.4
8	Wyoming	2.7
9	Washington	1.9
10	Idaho	1.8
10	Oregon	1.8
12	California	1.7
13	Colorado	1.6
13	Nevada	1.6
13	North Carolina	1.6
13	Utah	1.6
17	Nebraska	1.4
18	Minnesota	1.3
19	Kansas	1.2
20	Wisconsin	1.1
21	Arkansas	1.0
21	New York	1.0
21	Rhode Island	1.0
21	Texas	1.0
25	Louisiana	0.8
26	Alabama	0.7
26	Maine	0.7
26	Michigan	0.7
29	Delaware	0.6
29	Illinois	0.6
29	Maryland	0.6
29	Mississippi	0.6
29	Missouri	0.6
29	New Jersey	0.6
35	Connecticut	0.5
35	Florida	0.5
35	Georgia	0.5
35	Iowa	0.5
35	Massachusetts	0.5
35	South Carolina	0.5
35	Virginia	0.5
42	Hawaii	0.4
42	Indiana	0.4
42	Pennsylvania	0.4
42	Tennessee	0.4
42	Vermont	0.4
47	Kentucky	0.3
47	New Hampshire	0.3
47	Ohio	0.3
50	West Virginia	0.2
	District of Columbia	0.6

Source: CQ Press using data from U.S. Bureau of the Census

"State Characteristics: Vintage 2016" (http://www.census.gov/programs-surveys/popest/data/data-sets.html)

*Those who identified themselves as one race. Includes Alaska Native populations. Census states "Race is a self-identification data item in which respondents choose the race or races with which they most closely identify."

Native Hawaiian or Other Pacific Islander Population in 2016

National Total = 771,475*

ALPHA ORDER

ALPHA ORDER

RANK	STATE	POPULATION	% of USA
26	Alabama	5,068	0.7%
14	Alaska	9,870	1.3%
9	Arizona	18,423	2.4%
19	Arkansas	9,000	1.2%
1	California	196,944	25.5%
13	Colorado	10,602	1.4%
30	Connecticut	3,815	0.5%
43	Delaware	918	0.1%
7	Florida	23,107	3.0%
12	Georgia	11,942	1.5%
2	Hawaii	145,368	18.8%
34	Idaho	3,514	0.5%
20	Illinois	8,276	1.1%
28	Indiana	4,214	0.5%
33	Iowa	3,592	0.5%
36	Kansas	3,235	0.4%
32	Kentucky	3,675	0.5%
37	Louisiana	3,079	0.4%
49	Maine	500	0.1%
24	Maryland	6,460	0.8%
22	Massachusetts	6,975	0.9%
29	Michigan	3,948	0.5%
31	Minnesota	3,761	0.5%
41	Mississippi	1,810	0.2%
18	Missouri	9,117	1.2%
42	Montana	931	0.1%
39	Nebraska	2,425	0.3%
8	Nevada	22,654	2.9%
45	New Hampshire	670	0.1%
16	New Jersey	9,295	1.2%
35	New Mexico	3,293	0.4%
6	New York	26,489	3.4%
11	North Carolina	12,623	1.6%
48	North Dakota	566	0.1%
23	Ohio	6,639	0.9%
21	Oklahoma	7,102	0.9%
10	Oregon	18,249	2.4%
17	Pennsylvania	9,265	1.2%
40	Rhode Island	1,970	0.3%
27	South Carolina	4,698	0.6%
46	South Dakota	656	0.1%
25	Tennessee	6,432	0.8%
4	Texas	39,079	5.1%
5	Utah	31,502	4.1%
50	Vermont	260	0.0%
15	Virginia	9,407	1.2%
3	Washington	54,702	7.1%
47	West Virginia	591	0.1%
38	Wisconsin	3,050	0.4%
44	Wyoming	673	0.1%

RANK ORDER

RANK	STATE	POPULATION	% of USA
1	California	196,944	25.5%
2	Hawaii	145,368	18.8%
3	Washington	54,702	7.1%
4	Texas	39,079	5.1%
5	Utah	31,502	4.1%
6	New York	26,489	3.4%
7	Florida	23,107	3.0%
8	Nevada	22,654	2.9%
9	Arizona	18,423	2.4%
10	Oregon	18,249	2.4%
11	North Carolina	12,623	1.6%
12	Georgia	11,942	1.5%
13	Colorado	10,602	1.4%
14	Alaska	9,870	1.3%
15	Virginia	9,407	1.2%
16	New Jersey	9,295	1.2%
17	Pennsylvania	9,265	1.2%
18	Missouri	9,117	1.2%
19	Arkansas	9,000	1.2%
20	Illinois	8,276	1.1%
21	Oklahoma	7,102	0.9%
22	Massachusetts	6,975	0.9%
23	Ohio	6,639	0.9%
24	Maryland	6,460	0.8%
25	Tennessee	6,432	0.8%
26	Alabama	5,068	0.7%
27	South Carolina	4,698	0.6%
28	Indiana	4,214	0.5%
29	Michigan	3,948	0.5%
30	Connecticut	3,815	0.5%
31	Minnesota	3,761	0.5%
32	Kentucky	3,675	0.5%
33	Iowa	3,592	0.5%
34	Idaho	3,514	0.5%
35	New Mexico	3,293	0.4%
36	Kansas	3,235	0.4%
37	Louisiana	3,079	0.4%
38	Wisconsin	3,050	0.4%
39	Nebraska	2,425	0.3%
40	Rhode Island	1,970	0.3%
41	Mississippi	1,810	0.2%
42	Montana	931	0.1%
43	Delaware	918	0.1%
44	Wyoming	673	0.1%
45	New Hampshire	670	0.1%
46	South Dakota	656	0.1%
47	West Virginia	591	0.1%
48	North Dakota	566	0.1%
49	Maine	500	0.1%
50	Vermont	260	0.0%
	District of Columbia	1,041	0.1%

Source: U.S. Bureau of the Census
"State Characteristics: Vintage 2016" (http://www.census.gov/programs-surveys/popest/data/data-sets.html)
*Those who identified themselves as one race. Census states "Race is a self-identification data item in which respondents choose the race or races with which they most closely identify."

Percent of Population Native Hawaiian or Other Pacific Islander in 2016

National Percent = 0.2%*

ALPHA ORDER

RANK	STATE	PERCENT
15	Alabama	0.1
2	Alaska	1.3
8	Arizona	0.3
8	Arkansas	0.3
6	California	0.5
10	Colorado	0.2
15	Connecticut	0.1
15	Delaware	0.1
15	Florida	0.1
15	Georgia	0.1
1	Hawaii	10.2
10	Idaho	0.2
15	Illinois	0.1
15	Indiana	0.1
15	Iowa	0.1
15	Kansas	0.1
15	Kentucky	0.1
15	Louisiana	0.1
47	Maine	0.0
15	Maryland	0.1
15	Massachusetts	0.1
47	Michigan	0.0
15	Minnesota	0.1
15	Mississippi	0.1
15	Missouri	0.1
15	Montana	0.1
15	Nebraska	0.1
4	Nevada	0.8
15	New Hampshire	0.1
15	New Jersey	0.1
10	New Mexico	0.2
15	New York	0.1
15	North Carolina	0.1
15	North Dakota	0.1
15	Ohio	0.1
10	Oklahoma	0.2
7	Oregon	0.4
15	Pennsylvania	0.1
10	Rhode Island	0.2
15	South Carolina	0.1
15	South Dakota	0.1
15	Tennessee	0.1
15	Texas	0.1
3	Utah	1.0
47	Vermont	0.0
15	Virginia	0.1
4	Washington	0.8
47	West Virginia	0.0
15	Wisconsin	0.1
15	Wyoming	0.1

RANK ORDER

RANK	STATE	PERCENT
1	Hawaii	10.2
2	Alaska	1.3
3	Utah	1.0
4	Nevada	0.8
4	Washington	0.8
6	California	0.5
7	Oregon	0.4
8	Arizona	0.3
8	Arkansas	0.3
10	Colorado	0.2
10	Idaho	0.2
10	New Mexico	0.2
10	Oklahoma	0.2
10	Rhode Island	0.2
15	Alabama	0.1
15	Connecticut	0.1
15	Delaware	0.1
15	Florida	0.1
15	Georgia	0.1
15	Illinois	0.1
15	Indiana	0.1
15	Iowa	0.1
15	Kansas	0.1
15	Kentucky	0.1
15	Louisiana	0.1
15	Maryland	0.1
15	Massachusetts	0.1
15	Minnesota	0.1
15	Mississippi	0.1
15	Missouri	0.1
15	Montana	0.1
15	Nebraska	0.1
15	New Hampshire	0.1
15	New Jersey	0.1
15	New York	0.1
15	North Carolina	0.1
15	North Dakota	0.1
15	Ohio	0.1
15	Pennsylvania	0.1
15	South Carolina	0.1
15	South Dakota	0.1
15	Tennessee	0.1
15	Texas	0.1
15	Virginia	0.1
15	Wisconsin	0.1
15	Wyoming	0.1
47	Maine	0.0
47	Michigan	0.0
47	Vermont	0.0
47	West Virginia	0.0
	District of Columbia	0.2

Source: CQ Press using data from U.S. Bureau of the Census
"State Characteristics: Vintage 2016" (http://www.census.gov/programs-surveys/popest/data/data-sets.html)
*Those who identified themselves as one race. Census states "Race is a self-identification data item in which respondents choose the race or races with which they most closely identify."

Non-Hispanic White Population in 2016

National Total = 197,969,608*

ALPHA ORDER

RANK	STATE	POPULATION	% of USA
23	Alabama	3,201,937	1.6%
49	Alaska	453,915	0.2%
20	Arizona	3,844,532	1.9%
33	Arkansas	2,177,898	1.1%
1	California	14,802,979	7.5%
21	Colorado	3,802,465	1.9%
30	Connecticut	2,420,461	1.2%
46	Delaware	598,485	0.3%
3	Florida	11,314,909	5.7%
10	Georgia	5,503,895	2.8%
50	Hawaii	316,077	0.2%
38	Idaho	1,386,279	0.7%
7	Illinois	7,896,462	4.0%
11	Indiana	5,282,559	2.7%
28	Iowa	2,702,702	1.4%
32	Kansas	2,217,600	1.1%
22	Kentucky	3,770,240	1.9%
27	Louisiana	2,760,505	1.4%
39	Maine	1,244,762	0.6%
26	Maryland	3,099,419	1.6%
15	Massachusetts	4,972,277	2.5%
8	Michigan	7,486,890	3.8%
19	Minnesota	4,448,493	2.2%
34	Mississippi	1,700,036	0.9%
17	Missouri	4,857,925	2.5%
41	Montana	901,301	0.5%
36	Nebraska	1,517,526	0.8%
37	Nevada	1,468,421	0.7%
40	New Hampshire	1,212,634	0.6%
14	New Jersey	4,990,905	2.5%
42	New Mexico	792,167	0.4%
4	New York	11,009,263	5.6%
9	North Carolina	6,447,335	3.3%
45	North Dakota	644,127	0.3%
6	Ohio	9,230,244	4.7%
29	Oklahoma	2,596,769	1.3%
25	Oregon	3,126,217	1.6%
5	Pennsylvania	9,848,778	5.0%
43	Rhode Island	774,832	0.4%
24	South Carolina	3,169,878	1.6%
44	South Dakota	713,665	0.4%
16	Tennessee	4,937,280	2.5%
2	Texas	11,872,926	6.0%
31	Utah	2,404,802	1.2%
47	Vermont	581,225	0.3%
12	Virginia	5,252,972	2.7%
13	Washington	5,062,580	2.6%
35	West Virginia	1,689,821	0.9%
18	Wisconsin	4,719,824	2.4%
48	Wyoming	492,245	0.2%

RANK ORDER

RANK	STATE	POPULATION	% of USA
1	California	14,802,979	7.5%
2	Texas	11,872,926	6.0%
3	Florida	11,314,909	5.7%
4	New York	11,009,263	5.6%
5	Pennsylvania	9,848,778	5.0%
6	Ohio	9,230,244	4.7%
7	Illinois	7,896,462	4.0%
8	Michigan	7,486,890	3.8%
9	North Carolina	6,447,335	3.3%
10	Georgia	5,503,895	2.8%
11	Indiana	5,282,559	2.7%
12	Virginia	5,252,972	2.7%
13	Washington	5,062,580	2.6%
14	New Jersey	4,990,905	2.5%
15	Massachusetts	4,972,277	2.5%
16	Tennessee	4,937,280	2.5%
17	Missouri	4,857,925	2.5%
18	Wisconsin	4,719,824	2.4%
19	Minnesota	4,448,493	2.2%
20	Arizona	3,844,532	1.9%
21	Colorado	3,802,465	1.9%
22	Kentucky	3,770,240	1.9%
23	Alabama	3,201,937	1.6%
24	South Carolina	3,169,878	1.6%
25	Oregon	3,126,217	1.6%
26	Maryland	3,099,419	1.6%
27	Louisiana	2,760,505	1.4%
28	Iowa	2,702,702	1.4%
29	Oklahoma	2,596,769	1.3%
30	Connecticut	2,420,461	1.2%
31	Utah	2,404,802	1.2%
32	Kansas	2,217,600	1.1%
33	Arkansas	2,177,898	1.1%
34	Mississippi	1,700,036	0.9%
35	West Virginia	1,689,821	0.9%
36	Nebraska	1,517,526	0.8%
37	Nevada	1,468,421	0.7%
38	Idaho	1,386,279	0.7%
39	Maine	1,244,762	0.6%
40	New Hampshire	1,212,634	0.6%
41	Montana	901,301	0.5%
42	New Mexico	792,167	0.4%
43	Rhode Island	774,832	0.4%
44	South Dakota	713,665	0.4%
45	North Dakota	644,127	0.3%
46	Delaware	598,485	0.3%
47	Vermont	581,225	0.3%
48	Wyoming	492,245	0.2%
49	Alaska	453,915	0.2%
50	Hawaii	316,077	0.2%
	District of Columbia	248,169	0.1%

Source: U.S. Bureau of the Census
    "State Characteristics: Vintage 2016" (http://www.census.gov/programs-surveys/popest/data/data-sets.html)
*Those who identified themselves as one race. "White" is defined by Census as a person having origins in any of the original peoples of Europe, North Africa, or the Middle East. This is a subset of the 248,502,532 white population. Persons of Hispanic origin may be of any race. Census states "Race is a self-identification data item in which respondents choose the race or races with which they most closely identify."

Percent of Population Non-Hispanic White in 2016

National Percent = 61.3%*

RANK	STATE	PERCENT
31	Alabama	65.8
37	Alaska	61.2
42	Arizona	55.5
26	Arkansas	72.9
49	California	37.7
28	Colorado	68.6
29	Connecticut	67.7
34	Delaware	62.9
43	Florida	54.9
44	Georgia	53.4
50	Hawaii	22.1
11	Idaho	82.4
36	Illinois	61.7
15	Indiana	79.6
6	Iowa	86.2
21	Kansas	76.3
7	Kentucky	85.0
38	Louisiana	59.0
1	Maine	93.5
45	Maryland	51.5
25	Massachusetts	73.0
22	Michigan	75.4
13	Minnesota	80.6
39	Mississippi	56.9
14	Missouri	79.7
5	Montana	86.5
15	Nebraska	79.6
46	Nevada	49.9
4	New Hampshire	90.8
40	New Jersey	55.8
48	New Mexico	38.1
40	New York	55.8
33	North Carolina	63.5
7	North Dakota	85.0
17	Ohio	79.5
30	Oklahoma	66.2
20	Oregon	76.4
19	Pennsylvania	77.0
24	Rhode Island	73.3
32	South Carolina	63.9
10	South Dakota	82.5
23	Tennessee	74.2
47	Texas	42.6
18	Utah	78.8
2	Vermont	93.1
35	Virginia	62.4
27	Washington	69.5
3	West Virginia	92.3
12	Wisconsin	81.7
9	Wyoming	84.1

RANK	STATE	PERCENT
1	Maine	93.5
2	Vermont	93.1
3	West Virginia	92.3
4	New Hampshire	90.8
5	Montana	86.5
6	Iowa	86.2
7	Kentucky	85.0
7	North Dakota	85.0
9	Wyoming	84.1
10	South Dakota	82.5
11	Idaho	82.4
12	Wisconsin	81.7
13	Minnesota	80.6
14	Missouri	79.7
15	Indiana	79.6
15	Nebraska	79.6
17	Ohio	79.5
18	Utah	78.8
19	Pennsylvania	77.0
20	Oregon	76.4
21	Kansas	76.3
22	Michigan	75.4
23	Tennessee	74.2
24	Rhode Island	73.3
25	Massachusetts	73.0
26	Arkansas	72.9
27	Washington	69.5
28	Colorado	68.6
29	Connecticut	67.7
30	Oklahoma	66.2
31	Alabama	65.8
32	South Carolina	63.9
33	North Carolina	63.5
34	Delaware	62.9
35	Virginia	62.4
36	Illinois	61.7
37	Alaska	61.2
38	Louisiana	59.0
39	Mississippi	56.9
40	New Jersey	55.8
40	New York	55.8
42	Arizona	55.5
43	Florida	54.9
44	Georgia	53.4
45	Maryland	51.5
46	Nevada	49.9
47	Texas	42.6
48	New Mexico	38.1
49	California	37.7
50	Hawaii	22.1
	District of Columbia	36.4

Source: CQ Press using data from U.S. Bureau of the Census
   "State Characteristics: Vintage 2016" (http://www.census.gov/programs-surveys/popest/data/data-sets.html)
*Those who identified themselves as one race. "White" is defined by Census as a person having origins in any of the original peoples of Europe, North Africa, or the Middle East. This non-Hispanic white subset is 79.7% of the total white population. Persons of Hispanic origin may be of any race. Census states "Race is a self-identification data item in which respondents choose the race or races with which they most closely identify."

Multiple Race Population in 2016

National Total = 8,479,644*

ALPHA ORDER

ALPHA ORDER

RANK	STATE	POPULATION	% of USA
31	Alabama	79,396	0.9%
36	Alaska	54,421	0.6%
16	Arizona	192,276	2.3%
34	Arkansas	60,645	0.7%
1	California	1,500,776	17.7%
18	Colorado	165,962	2.0%
30	Connecticut	82,511	1.0%
44	Delaware	24,404	0.3%
4	Florida	430,748	5.1%
14	Georgia	212,863	2.5%
5	Hawaii	338,307	4.0%
39	Idaho	40,073	0.5%
9	Illinois	245,747	2.9%
23	Indiana	132,716	1.6%
35	Iowa	56,684	0.7%
28	Kansas	84,671	1.0%
29	Kentucky	82,762	1.0%
32	Louisiana	76,462	0.9%
45	Maine	22,940	0.3%
17	Maryland	166,710	2.0%
19	Massachusetts	159,156	1.9%
12	Michigan	236,589	2.8%
22	Minnesota	134,464	1.6%
40	Mississippi	36,851	0.4%
21	Missouri	135,607	1.6%
43	Montana	28,194	0.3%
38	Nebraska	40,495	0.5%
24	Nevada	124,406	1.5%
46	New Hampshire	22,264	0.3%
15	New Jersey	192,510	2.3%
37	New Mexico	52,042	0.6%
3	New York	490,819	5.8%
13	North Carolina	220,673	2.6%
48	North Dakota	15,896	0.2%
7	Ohio	256,545	3.0%
11	Oklahoma	238,078	2.8%
20	Oregon	154,064	1.8%
8	Pennsylvania	249,223	2.9%
42	Rhode Island	28,851	0.3%
27	South Carolina	90,047	1.1%
47	South Dakota	19,948	0.2%
25	Tennessee	123,572	1.5%
2	Texas	538,767	6.4%
33	Utah	75,575	0.9%
50	Vermont	11,813	0.1%
10	Virginia	245,300	2.9%
6	Washington	337,572	4.0%
41	West Virginia	30,938	0.4%
26	Wisconsin	107,562	1.3%
49	Wyoming	12,070	0.1%

RANK ORDER

RANK	STATE	POPULATION	% of USA
1	California	1,500,776	17.7%
2	Texas	538,767	6.4%
3	New York	490,819	5.8%
4	Florida	430,748	5.1%
5	Hawaii	338,307	4.0%
6	Washington	337,572	4.0%
7	Ohio	256,545	3.0%
8	Pennsylvania	249,223	2.9%
9	Illinois	245,747	2.9%
10	Virginia	245,300	2.9%
11	Oklahoma	238,078	2.8%
12	Michigan	236,589	2.8%
13	North Carolina	220,673	2.6%
14	Georgia	212,863	2.5%
15	New Jersey	192,510	2.3%
16	Arizona	192,276	2.3%
17	Maryland	166,710	2.0%
18	Colorado	165,962	2.0%
19	Massachusetts	159,156	1.9%
20	Oregon	154,064	1.8%
21	Missouri	135,607	1.6%
22	Minnesota	134,464	1.6%
23	Indiana	132,716	1.6%
24	Nevada	124,406	1.5%
25	Tennessee	123,572	1.5%
26	Wisconsin	107,562	1.3%
27	South Carolina	90,047	1.1%
28	Kansas	84,671	1.0%
29	Kentucky	82,762	1.0%
30	Connecticut	82,511	1.0%
31	Alabama	79,396	0.9%
32	Louisiana	76,462	0.9%
33	Utah	75,575	0.9%
34	Arkansas	60,645	0.7%
35	Iowa	56,684	0.7%
36	Alaska	54,421	0.6%
37	New Mexico	52,042	0.6%
38	Nebraska	40,495	0.5%
39	Idaho	40,073	0.5%
40	Mississippi	36,851	0.4%
41	West Virginia	30,938	0.4%
42	Rhode Island	28,851	0.3%
43	Montana	28,194	0.3%
44	Delaware	24,404	0.3%
45	Maine	22,940	0.3%
46	New Hampshire	22,264	0.3%
47	South Dakota	19,948	0.2%
48	North Dakota	15,896	0.2%
49	Wyoming	12,070	0.1%
50	Vermont	11,813	0.1%
	District of Columbia	18,679	0.2%

Source: U.S. Bureau of the Census

"State Characteristics: Vintage 2016" (http://www.census.gov/programs-surveys/popest/data/data-sets.html)

*This includes those who identified themselves as two or more races. This is the population who did not identify themselves as one race (White, Black, American Indian/Native Alaska Native, Asian, or Native Hawaiian or Other Pacific Islander) but as a member of multiple racial groups. Census states "Race is a self-identification data item in which respondents choose the race or races with which they most closely identify."

Percent of Population Multiple Races in 2016

National Percent = 2.6%*

RANK	STATE	PERCENT
48	Alabama	1.6
2	Alaska	7.3
11	Arizona	2.8
34	Arkansas	2.0
6	California	3.8
8	Colorado	3.0
22	Connecticut	2.3
15	Delaware	2.6
29	Florida	2.1
29	Georgia	2.1
1	Hawaii	23.7
19	Idaho	2.4
36	Illinois	1.9
34	Indiana	2.0
43	Iowa	1.8
9	Kansas	2.9
36	Kentucky	1.9
48	Louisiana	1.6
45	Maine	1.7
11	Maryland	2.8
22	Massachusetts	2.3
19	Michigan	2.4
19	Minnesota	2.4
50	Mississippi	1.2
25	Missouri	2.2
13	Montana	2.7
29	Nebraska	2.1
5	Nevada	4.2
45	New Hampshire	1.7
25	New Jersey	2.2
16	New Mexico	2.5
16	New York	2.5
25	North Carolina	2.2
29	North Dakota	2.1
25	Ohio	2.2
3	Oklahoma	6.1
6	Oregon	3.8
36	Pennsylvania	1.9
13	Rhode Island	2.7
43	South Carolina	1.8
22	South Dakota	2.3
36	Tennessee	1.9
36	Texas	1.9
16	Utah	2.5
36	Vermont	1.9
9	Virginia	2.9
4	Washington	4.6
45	West Virginia	1.7
36	Wisconsin	1.9
29	Wyoming	2.1

RANK	STATE	PERCENT
1	Hawaii	23.7
2	Alaska	7.3
3	Oklahoma	6.1
4	Washington	4.6
5	Nevada	4.2
6	California	3.8
6	Oregon	3.8
8	Colorado	3.0
9	Kansas	2.9
9	Virginia	2.9
11	Arizona	2.8
11	Maryland	2.8
13	Montana	2.7
13	Rhode Island	2.7
15	Delaware	2.6
16	New Mexico	2.5
16	New York	2.5
16	Utah	2.5
19	Idaho	2.4
19	Michigan	2.4
19	Minnesota	2.4
22	Connecticut	2.3
22	Massachusetts	2.3
22	South Dakota	2.3
25	Missouri	2.2
25	New Jersey	2.2
25	North Carolina	2.2
25	Ohio	2.2
29	Florida	2.1
29	Georgia	2.1
29	Nebraska	2.1
29	North Dakota	2.1
29	Wyoming	2.1
34	Arkansas	2.0
34	Indiana	2.0
36	Illinois	1.9
36	Kentucky	1.9
36	Pennsylvania	1.9
36	Tennessee	1.9
36	Texas	1.9
36	Vermont	1.9
36	Wisconsin	1.9
43	Iowa	1.8
43	South Carolina	1.8
45	Maine	1.7
45	New Hampshire	1.7
45	West Virginia	1.7
48	Alabama	1.6
48	Louisiana	1.6
50	Mississippi	1.2

	District of Columbia	2.7

Source: CQ Press using data from U.S. Bureau of the Census

"State Characteristics: Vintage 2016" (http://www.census.gov/programs-surveys/popest/data/data-sets.html)

*This includes those who identified themselves as two or more races. This is the population who did not identify themselves as one race (White, Black, American Indian/Native Alaska Native, Asian, or Native Hawaiian or Other Pacific Islander) but as a member of multiple racial groups. Census states "Race is a self-identification data item in which respondents choose the race or races with which they most closely identify."

Population under 5 Years Old in 2016

National Total = 19,927,037

ALPHA ORDER

RANK	STATE	POPULATION	% of USA
25	Alabama	292,565	1.5%
48	Alaska	54,115	0.3%
14	Arizona	439,319	2.2%
32	Arkansas	190,277	1.0%
1	California	2,487,372	12.5%
21	Colorado	337,464	1.7%
34	Connecticut	185,321	0.9%
46	Delaware	54,834	0.3%
4	Florida	1,126,136	5.7%
8	Georgia	660,839	3.3%
40	Hawaii	91,535	0.5%
38	Idaho	115,289	0.6%
5	Illinois	772,511	3.9%
15	Indiana	421,987	2.1%
30	Iowa	199,415	1.0%
31	Kansas	194,307	1.0%
26	Kentucky	275,753	1.4%
23	Louisiana	310,601	1.6%
41	Maine	65,068	0.3%
18	Maryland	367,095	1.8%
19	Massachusetts	361,376	1.8%
10	Michigan	574,423	2.9%
20	Minnesota	352,504	1.8%
33	Mississippi	188,701	0.9%
17	Missouri	373,958	1.9%
43	Montana	63,029	0.3%
36	Nebraska	132,809	0.7%
35	Nevada	184,462	0.9%
42	New Hampshire	64,200	0.3%
11	New Jersey	521,332	2.6%
37	New Mexico	128,950	0.6%
3	New York	1,160,057	5.8%
9	North Carolina	606,310	3.0%
45	North Dakota	55,236	0.3%
7	Ohio	697,923	3.5%
27	Oklahoma	266,910	1.3%
29	Oregon	235,800	1.2%
6	Pennsylvania	711,765	3.6%
47	Rhode Island	54,708	0.3%
24	South Carolina	293,134	1.5%
44	South Dakota	61,369	0.3%
16	Tennessee	407,599	2.0%
2	Texas	2,019,171	10.1%
28	Utah	253,450	1.3%
50	Vermont	30,641	0.2%
12	Virginia	510,501	2.6%
13	Washington	455,339	2.3%
39	West Virginia	101,019	0.5%
22	Wisconsin	336,906	1.7%
49	Wyoming	38,145	0.2%

RANK ORDER

RANK	STATE	POPULATION	% of USA
1	California	2,487,372	12.5%
2	Texas	2,019,171	10.1%
3	New York	1,160,057	5.8%
4	Florida	1,126,136	5.7%
5	Illinois	772,511	3.9%
6	Pennsylvania	711,765	3.6%
7	Ohio	697,923	3.5%
8	Georgia	660,839	3.3%
9	North Carolina	606,310	3.0%
10	Michigan	574,423	2.9%
11	New Jersey	521,332	2.6%
12	Virginia	510,501	2.6%
13	Washington	455,339	2.3%
14	Arizona	439,319	2.2%
15	Indiana	421,987	2.1%
16	Tennessee	407,599	2.0%
17	Missouri	373,958	1.9%
18	Maryland	367,095	1.8%
19	Massachusetts	361,376	1.8%
20	Minnesota	352,504	1.8%
21	Colorado	337,464	1.7%
22	Wisconsin	336,906	1.7%
23	Louisiana	310,601	1.6%
24	South Carolina	293,134	1.5%
25	Alabama	292,565	1.5%
26	Kentucky	275,753	1.4%
27	Oklahoma	266,910	1.3%
28	Utah	253,450	1.3%
29	Oregon	235,800	1.2%
30	Iowa	199,415	1.0%
31	Kansas	194,307	1.0%
32	Arkansas	190,277	1.0%
33	Mississippi	188,701	0.9%
34	Connecticut	185,321	0.9%
35	Nevada	184,462	0.9%
36	Nebraska	132,809	0.7%
37	New Mexico	128,950	0.6%
38	Idaho	115,289	0.6%
39	West Virginia	101,019	0.5%
40	Hawaii	91,535	0.5%
41	Maine	65,068	0.3%
42	New Hampshire	64,200	0.3%
43	Montana	63,029	0.3%
44	South Dakota	61,369	0.3%
45	North Dakota	55,236	0.3%
46	Delaware	54,834	0.3%
47	Rhode Island	54,708	0.3%
48	Alaska	54,115	0.3%
49	Wyoming	38,145	0.2%
50	Vermont	30,641	0.2%
	District of Columbia	43,507	0.2%

Source: U.S. Bureau of the Census
"State Characteristics: Vintage 2016" (http://www.census.gov/programs-surveys/popest/data/data-sets.html)

Percent of Population under 5 Years Old in 2016

National Percent = 6.2% of Population

ALPHA ORDER

RANK	STATE	PERCENT
30	Alabama	6.0
2	Alaska	7.3
18	Arizona	6.3
12	Arkansas	6.4
18	California	6.3
25	Colorado	6.1
46	Connecticut	5.2
37	Delaware	5.8
43	Florida	5.5
12	Georgia	6.4
12	Hawaii	6.4
7	Idaho	6.8
30	Illinois	6.0
12	Indiana	6.4
12	Iowa	6.4
9	Kansas	6.7
22	Kentucky	6.2
10	Louisiana	6.6
48	Maine	4.9
25	Maryland	6.1
45	Massachusetts	5.3
37	Michigan	5.8
12	Minnesota	6.4
18	Mississippi	6.3
25	Missouri	6.1
30	Montana	6.0
6	Nebraska	7.0
18	Nevada	6.3
50	New Hampshire	4.8
37	New Jersey	5.8
22	New Mexico	6.2
35	New York	5.9
30	North Carolina	6.0
2	North Dakota	7.3
30	Ohio	6.0
7	Oklahoma	6.8
37	Oregon	5.8
42	Pennsylvania	5.6
46	Rhode Island	5.2
35	South Carolina	5.9
5	South Dakota	7.1
25	Tennessee	6.1
4	Texas	7.2
1	Utah	8.3
48	Vermont	4.9
25	Virginia	6.1
22	Washington	6.2
43	West Virginia	5.5
37	Wisconsin	5.8
11	Wyoming	6.5

RANK ORDER

RANK	STATE	PERCENT
1	Utah	8.3
2	Alaska	7.3
2	North Dakota	7.3
4	Texas	7.2
5	South Dakota	7.1
6	Nebraska	7.0
7	Idaho	6.8
7	Oklahoma	6.8
9	Kansas	6.7
10	Louisiana	6.6
11	Wyoming	6.5
12	Arkansas	6.4
12	Georgia	6.4
12	Hawaii	6.4
12	Indiana	6.4
12	Iowa	6.4
12	Minnesota	6.4
18	Arizona	6.3
18	California	6.3
18	Mississippi	6.3
18	Nevada	6.3
22	Kentucky	6.2
22	New Mexico	6.2
22	Washington	6.2
25	Colorado	6.1
25	Maryland	6.1
25	Missouri	6.1
25	Tennessee	6.1
25	Virginia	6.1
30	Alabama	6.0
30	Illinois	6.0
30	Montana	6.0
30	North Carolina	6.0
30	Ohio	6.0
35	New York	5.9
35	South Carolina	5.9
37	Delaware	5.8
37	Michigan	5.8
37	New Jersey	5.8
37	Oregon	5.8
37	Wisconsin	5.8
42	Pennsylvania	5.6
43	Florida	5.5
43	West Virginia	5.5
45	Massachusetts	5.3
46	Connecticut	5.2
46	Rhode Island	5.2
48	Maine	4.9
48	Vermont	4.9
50	New Hampshire	4.8
	District of Columbia	6.4

Source: CQ Press using data from U.S. Bureau of the Census
"State Characteristics: Vintage 2016" (http://www.census.gov/programs-surveys/popest/data/data-sets.html)

Population 5 to 17 Years Old in 2016

National Total = 53,715,248

RANK	STATE	POPULATION	% of USA
24	Alabama	804,258	1.5%
47	Alaska	133,212	0.2%
13	Arizona	1,192,173	2.2%
34	Arkansas	514,776	1.0%
1	California	6,605,491	12.3%
22	Colorado	923,908	1.7%
30	Connecticut	567,973	1.1%
46	Delaware	149,440	0.3%
3	Florida	3,020,576	5.6%
8	Georgia	1,850,705	3.4%
40	Hawaii	216,481	0.4%
38	Idaho	321,884	0.6%
5	Illinois	2,153,598	4.0%
15	Indiana	1,153,465	2.1%
32	Iowa	531,316	1.0%
33	Kansas	520,644	1.0%
26	Kentucky	734,876	1.4%
25	Louisiana	803,348	1.5%
42	Maine	189,646	0.4%
19	Maryland	981,633	1.8%
17	Massachusetts	1,016,726	1.9%
10	Michigan	1,616,634	3.0%
21	Minnesota	935,829	1.7%
31	Mississippi	532,587	1.0%
18	Missouri	1,012,905	1.9%
43	Montana	164,582	0.3%
37	Nebraska	340,516	0.6%
35	Nevada	492,965	0.9%
41	New Hampshire	196,388	0.4%
11	New Jersey	1,463,420	2.7%
36	New Mexico	361,713	0.7%
4	New York	3,020,502	5.6%
9	North Carolina	1,692,410	3.2%
48	North Dakota	121,075	0.2%
7	Ohio	1,914,249	3.6%
27	Oklahoma	694,718	1.3%
29	Oregon	632,927	1.2%
6	Pennsylvania	1,963,040	3.7%
44	Rhode Island	153,673	0.3%
23	South Carolina	804,487	1.5%
45	South Dakota	151,918	0.3%
16	Tennessee	1,094,196	2.0%
2	Texas	5,275,416	9.8%
28	Utah	668,323	1.2%
50	Vermont	87,887	0.2%
12	Virginia	1,359,622	2.5%
14	Washington	1,174,159	2.2%
39	West Virginia	274,049	0.5%
20	Wisconsin	950,787	1.8%
49	Wyoming	100,756	0.2%

RANK	STATE	POPULATION	% of USA
1	California	6,605,491	12.3%
2	Texas	5,275,416	9.8%
3	Florida	3,020,576	5.6%
4	New York	3,020,502	5.6%
5	Illinois	2,153,598	4.0%
6	Pennsylvania	1,963,040	3.7%
7	Ohio	1,914,249	3.6%
8	Georgia	1,850,705	3.4%
9	North Carolina	1,692,410	3.2%
10	Michigan	1,616,634	3.0%
11	New Jersey	1,463,420	2.7%
12	Virginia	1,359,622	2.5%
13	Arizona	1,192,173	2.2%
14	Washington	1,174,159	2.2%
15	Indiana	1,153,465	2.1%
16	Tennessee	1,094,196	2.0%
17	Massachusetts	1,016,726	1.9%
18	Missouri	1,012,905	1.9%
19	Maryland	981,633	1.8%
20	Wisconsin	950,787	1.8%
21	Minnesota	935,829	1.7%
22	Colorado	923,908	1.7%
23	South Carolina	804,487	1.5%
24	Alabama	804,258	1.5%
25	Louisiana	803,348	1.5%
26	Kentucky	734,876	1.4%
27	Oklahoma	694,718	1.3%
28	Utah	668,323	1.2%
29	Oregon	632,927	1.2%
30	Connecticut	567,973	1.1%
31	Mississippi	532,587	1.0%
32	Iowa	531,316	1.0%
33	Kansas	520,644	1.0%
34	Arkansas	514,776	1.0%
35	Nevada	492,965	0.9%
36	New Mexico	361,713	0.7%
37	Nebraska	340,516	0.6%
38	Idaho	321,884	0.6%
39	West Virginia	274,049	0.5%
40	Hawaii	216,481	0.4%
41	New Hampshire	196,388	0.4%
42	Maine	189,646	0.4%
43	Montana	164,582	0.3%
44	Rhode Island	153,673	0.3%
45	South Dakota	151,918	0.3%
46	Delaware	149,440	0.3%
47	Alaska	133,212	0.2%
48	North Dakota	121,075	0.2%
49	Wyoming	100,756	0.2%
50	Vermont	87,887	0.2%
	District of Columbia	77,386	0.1%

Source: CQ Press using data from U.S. Bureau of the Census
"State Characteristics: Vintage 2016" (http://www.census.gov/programs-surveys/popest/data/data-sets.html)

Percent of Population 5 to 17 Years Old in 2016

National Percent = 16.6% of Population

ALPHA ORDER

RANK	STATE	PERCENT
26	Alabama	16.5
4	Alaska	18.0
13	Arizona	17.2
13	Arkansas	17.2
19	California	16.8
22	Colorado	16.7
37	Connecticut	15.9
39	Delaware	15.7
46	Florida	14.7
5	Georgia	17.9
43	Hawaii	15.2
2	Idaho	19.1
19	Illinois	16.8
11	Indiana	17.4
18	Iowa	16.9
5	Kansas	17.9
24	Kentucky	16.6
13	Louisiana	17.2
49	Maine	14.2
31	Maryland	16.3
45	Massachusetts	14.9
31	Michigan	16.3
17	Minnesota	17.0
8	Mississippi	17.8
24	Missouri	16.6
38	Montana	15.8
5	Nebraska	17.9
19	Nevada	16.8
46	New Hampshire	14.7
30	New Jersey	16.4
11	New Mexico	17.4
42	New York	15.3
22	North Carolina	16.7
36	North Dakota	16.0
26	Ohio	16.5
9	Oklahoma	17.7
40	Oregon	15.5
41	Pennsylvania	15.4
48	Rhode Island	14.5
33	South Carolina	16.2
10	South Dakota	17.6
26	Tennessee	16.5
3	Texas	18.9
1	Utah	21.9
50	Vermont	14.1
33	Virginia	16.2
35	Washington	16.1
44	West Virginia	15.0
26	Wisconsin	16.5
13	Wyoming	17.2

RANK ORDER

RANK	STATE	PERCENT
1	Utah	21.9
2	Idaho	19.1
3	Texas	18.9
4	Alaska	18.0
5	Georgia	17.9
5	Kansas	17.9
5	Nebraska	17.9
8	Mississippi	17.8
9	Oklahoma	17.7
10	South Dakota	17.6
11	Indiana	17.4
11	New Mexico	17.4
13	Arizona	17.2
13	Arkansas	17.2
13	Louisiana	17.2
13	Wyoming	17.2
17	Minnesota	17.0
18	Iowa	16.9
19	California	16.8
19	Illinois	16.8
19	Nevada	16.8
22	Colorado	16.7
22	North Carolina	16.7
24	Kentucky	16.6
24	Missouri	16.6
26	Alabama	16.5
26	Ohio	16.5
26	Tennessee	16.5
26	Wisconsin	16.5
30	New Jersey	16.4
31	Maryland	16.3
31	Michigan	16.3
33	South Carolina	16.2
33	Virginia	16.2
35	Washington	16.1
36	North Dakota	16.0
37	Connecticut	15.9
38	Montana	15.8
39	Delaware	15.7
40	Oregon	15.5
41	Pennsylvania	15.4
42	New York	15.3
43	Hawaii	15.2
44	West Virginia	15.0
45	Massachusetts	14.9
46	Florida	14.7
46	New Hampshire	14.7
48	Rhode Island	14.5
49	Maine	14.2
50	Vermont	14.1
	District of Columbia	11.4

Source: CQ Press using data from U.S. Bureau of the Census
"State Characteristics: Vintage 2016" (http://www.census.gov/programs-surveys/popest/data/data-sets.html)

Population 18 Years Old and Older in 2016

National Total = 249,485,228

<table>
<tr><td colspan="4">ALPHA ORDER</td><td colspan="4">RANK ORDER</td></tr>
<tr><td>RANK</td><td>STATE</td><td>POPULATION</td><td>% of USA</td><td>RANK</td><td>STATE</td><td>POPULATION</td><td>% of USA</td></tr>
<tr><td>24</td><td>Alabama</td><td>3,766,477</td><td>1.5%</td><td>1</td><td>California</td><td>30,157,154</td><td>12.1%</td></tr>
<tr><td>48</td><td>Alaska</td><td>554,567</td><td>0.2%</td><td>2</td><td>Texas</td><td>20,568,009</td><td>8.2%</td></tr>
<tr><td>15</td><td>Arizona</td><td>5,299,579</td><td>2.1%</td><td>3</td><td>Florida</td><td>16,465,727</td><td>6.6%</td></tr>
<tr><td>31</td><td>Arkansas</td><td>2,283,195</td><td>0.9%</td><td>4</td><td>New York</td><td>15,564,730</td><td>6.2%</td></tr>
<tr><td>1</td><td>California</td><td>30,157,154</td><td>12.1%</td><td>5</td><td>Pennsylvania</td><td>10,109,422</td><td>4.1%</td></tr>
<tr><td>21</td><td>Colorado</td><td>4,279,173</td><td>1.7%</td><td>6</td><td>Illinois</td><td>9,875,430</td><td>4.0%</td></tr>
<tr><td>29</td><td>Connecticut</td><td>2,823,158</td><td>1.1%</td><td>7</td><td>Ohio</td><td>9,002,201</td><td>3.6%</td></tr>
<tr><td>45</td><td>Delaware</td><td>747,791</td><td>0.3%</td><td>8</td><td>North Carolina</td><td>7,848,068</td><td>3.1%</td></tr>
<tr><td>3</td><td>Florida</td><td>16,465,727</td><td>6.6%</td><td>9</td><td>Georgia</td><td>7,798,827</td><td>3.1%</td></tr>
<tr><td>9</td><td>Georgia</td><td>7,798,827</td><td>3.1%</td><td>10</td><td>Michigan</td><td>7,737,243</td><td>3.1%</td></tr>
<tr><td>40</td><td>Hawaii</td><td>1,120,541</td><td>0.4%</td><td>11</td><td>New Jersey</td><td>6,959,717</td><td>2.8%</td></tr>
<tr><td>39</td><td>Idaho</td><td>1,245,967</td><td>0.5%</td><td>12</td><td>Virginia</td><td>6,541,685</td><td>2.6%</td></tr>
<tr><td>6</td><td>Illinois</td><td>9,875,430</td><td>4.0%</td><td>13</td><td>Washington</td><td>5,658,502</td><td>2.3%</td></tr>
<tr><td>17</td><td>Indiana</td><td>5,057,601</td><td>2.0%</td><td>14</td><td>Massachusetts</td><td>5,433,677</td><td>2.2%</td></tr>
<tr><td>30</td><td>Iowa</td><td>2,403,962</td><td>1.0%</td><td>15</td><td>Arizona</td><td>5,299,579</td><td>2.1%</td></tr>
<tr><td>34</td><td>Kansas</td><td>2,192,338</td><td>0.9%</td><td>16</td><td>Tennessee</td><td>5,149,399</td><td>2.1%</td></tr>
<tr><td>26</td><td>Kentucky</td><td>3,426,345</td><td>1.4%</td><td>17</td><td>Indiana</td><td>5,057,601</td><td>2.0%</td></tr>
<tr><td>25</td><td>Louisiana</td><td>3,567,717</td><td>1.4%</td><td>18</td><td>Missouri</td><td>4,706,137</td><td>1.9%</td></tr>
<tr><td>41</td><td>Maine</td><td>1,076,765</td><td>0.4%</td><td>19</td><td>Maryland</td><td>4,667,719</td><td>1.9%</td></tr>
<tr><td>19</td><td>Maryland</td><td>4,667,719</td><td>1.9%</td><td>20</td><td>Wisconsin</td><td>4,491,015</td><td>1.8%</td></tr>
<tr><td>14</td><td>Massachusetts</td><td>5,433,677</td><td>2.2%</td><td>21</td><td>Colorado</td><td>4,279,173</td><td>1.7%</td></tr>
<tr><td>10</td><td>Michigan</td><td>7,737,243</td><td>3.1%</td><td>22</td><td>Minnesota</td><td>4,231,619</td><td>1.7%</td></tr>
<tr><td>22</td><td>Minnesota</td><td>4,231,619</td><td>1.7%</td><td>23</td><td>South Carolina</td><td>3,863,498</td><td>1.5%</td></tr>
<tr><td>32</td><td>Mississippi</td><td>2,267,438</td><td>0.9%</td><td>24</td><td>Alabama</td><td>3,766,477</td><td>1.5%</td></tr>
<tr><td>18</td><td>Missouri</td><td>4,706,137</td><td>1.9%</td><td>25</td><td>Louisiana</td><td>3,567,717</td><td>1.4%</td></tr>
<tr><td>44</td><td>Montana</td><td>814,909</td><td>0.3%</td><td>26</td><td>Kentucky</td><td>3,426,345</td><td>1.4%</td></tr>
<tr><td>38</td><td>Nebraska</td><td>1,433,791</td><td>0.6%</td><td>27</td><td>Oregon</td><td>3,224,738</td><td>1.3%</td></tr>
<tr><td>33</td><td>Nevada</td><td>2,262,631</td><td>0.9%</td><td>28</td><td>Oklahoma</td><td>2,961,933</td><td>1.2%</td></tr>
<tr><td>42</td><td>New Hampshire</td><td>1,074,207</td><td>0.4%</td><td>29</td><td>Connecticut</td><td>2,823,158</td><td>1.1%</td></tr>
<tr><td>11</td><td>New Jersey</td><td>6,959,717</td><td>2.8%</td><td>30</td><td>Iowa</td><td>2,403,962</td><td>1.0%</td></tr>
<tr><td>36</td><td>New Mexico</td><td>1,590,352</td><td>0.6%</td><td>31</td><td>Arkansas</td><td>2,283,195</td><td>0.9%</td></tr>
<tr><td>4</td><td>New York</td><td>15,564,730</td><td>6.2%</td><td>32</td><td>Mississippi</td><td>2,267,438</td><td>0.9%</td></tr>
<tr><td>8</td><td>North Carolina</td><td>7,848,068</td><td>3.1%</td><td>33</td><td>Nevada</td><td>2,262,631</td><td>0.9%</td></tr>
<tr><td>47</td><td>North Dakota</td><td>581,641</td><td>0.2%</td><td>34</td><td>Kansas</td><td>2,192,338</td><td>0.9%</td></tr>
<tr><td>7</td><td>Ohio</td><td>9,002,201</td><td>3.6%</td><td>35</td><td>Utah</td><td>2,129,444</td><td>0.9%</td></tr>
<tr><td>28</td><td>Oklahoma</td><td>2,961,933</td><td>1.2%</td><td>36</td><td>New Mexico</td><td>1,590,352</td><td>0.6%</td></tr>
<tr><td>27</td><td>Oregon</td><td>3,224,738</td><td>1.3%</td><td>37</td><td>West Virginia</td><td>1,456,034</td><td>0.6%</td></tr>
<tr><td>5</td><td>Pennsylvania</td><td>10,109,422</td><td>4.1%</td><td>38</td><td>Nebraska</td><td>1,433,791</td><td>0.6%</td></tr>
<tr><td>43</td><td>Rhode Island</td><td>848,045</td><td>0.3%</td><td>39</td><td>Idaho</td><td>1,245,967</td><td>0.5%</td></tr>
<tr><td>23</td><td>South Carolina</td><td>3,863,498</td><td>1.5%</td><td>40</td><td>Hawaii</td><td>1,120,541</td><td>0.4%</td></tr>
<tr><td>46</td><td>South Dakota</td><td>652,167</td><td>0.3%</td><td>41</td><td>Maine</td><td>1,076,765</td><td>0.4%</td></tr>
<tr><td>16</td><td>Tennessee</td><td>5,149,399</td><td>2.1%</td><td>42</td><td>New Hampshire</td><td>1,074,207</td><td>0.4%</td></tr>
<tr><td>2</td><td>Texas</td><td>20,568,009</td><td>8.2%</td><td>43</td><td>Rhode Island</td><td>848,045</td><td>0.3%</td></tr>
<tr><td>35</td><td>Utah</td><td>2,129,444</td><td>0.9%</td><td>44</td><td>Montana</td><td>814,909</td><td>0.3%</td></tr>
<tr><td>49</td><td>Vermont</td><td>506,066</td><td>0.2%</td><td>45</td><td>Delaware</td><td>747,791</td><td>0.3%</td></tr>
<tr><td>12</td><td>Virginia</td><td>6,541,685</td><td>2.6%</td><td>46</td><td>South Dakota</td><td>652,167</td><td>0.3%</td></tr>
<tr><td>13</td><td>Washington</td><td>5,658,502</td><td>2.3%</td><td>47</td><td>North Dakota</td><td>581,641</td><td>0.2%</td></tr>
<tr><td>37</td><td>West Virginia</td><td>1,456,034</td><td>0.6%</td><td>48</td><td>Alaska</td><td>554,567</td><td>0.2%</td></tr>
<tr><td>20</td><td>Wisconsin</td><td>4,491,015</td><td>1.8%</td><td>49</td><td>Vermont</td><td>506,066</td><td>0.2%</td></tr>
<tr><td>50</td><td>Wyoming</td><td>446,600</td><td>0.2%</td><td>50</td><td>Wyoming</td><td>446,600</td><td>0.2%</td></tr>
<tr><td></td><td></td><td></td><td></td><td></td><td>District of Columbia</td><td>560,277</td><td>0.2%</td></tr>
</table>

Source: U.S. Bureau of the Census
"State Characteristics: Vintage 2016" (http://www.census.gov/programs-surveys/popest/data/data-sets.html)

Percent of Population 18 Years Old and Older in 2016

National Percent = 77.2% of Population

ALPHA ORDER

ALPHA ORDER

RANK	STATE	PERCENT
23	Alabama	77.4
47	Alaska	74.8
35	Arizona	76.5
36	Arkansas	76.4
31	California	76.8
26	Colorado	77.2
9	Connecticut	78.9
12	Delaware	78.5
5	Florida	79.9
42	Georgia	75.6
13	Hawaii	78.4
48	Idaho	74.0
29	Illinois	77.1
39	Indiana	76.2
32	Iowa	76.7
44	Kansas	75.4
26	Kentucky	77.2
39	Louisiana	76.2
2	Maine	80.9
20	Maryland	77.6
6	Massachusetts	79.8
15	Michigan	77.9
32	Minnesota	76.7
41	Mississippi	75.9
26	Missouri	77.2
14	Montana	78.2
46	Nebraska	75.2
30	Nevada	77.0
3	New Hampshire	80.5
17	New Jersey	77.8
36	New Mexico	76.4
10	New York	78.8
25	North Carolina	77.3
32	North Dakota	76.7
22	Ohio	77.5
43	Oklahoma	75.5
10	Oregon	78.8
8	Pennsylvania	79.1
4	Rhode Island	80.3
15	South Carolina	77.9
44	South Dakota	75.4
23	Tennessee	77.4
49	Texas	73.8
50	Utah	69.8
1	Vermont	81.0
17	Virginia	77.8
20	Washington	77.6
7	West Virginia	79.5
19	Wisconsin	77.7
38	Wyoming	76.3

RANK ORDER

RANK	STATE	PERCENT
1	Vermont	81.0
2	Maine	80.9
3	New Hampshire	80.5
4	Rhode Island	80.3
5	Florida	79.9
6	Massachusetts	79.8
7	West Virginia	79.5
8	Pennsylvania	79.1
9	Connecticut	78.9
10	New York	78.8
10	Oregon	78.8
12	Delaware	78.5
13	Hawaii	78.4
14	Montana	78.2
15	Michigan	77.9
15	South Carolina	77.9
17	New Jersey	77.8
17	Virginia	77.8
19	Wisconsin	77.7
20	Maryland	77.6
20	Washington	77.6
22	Ohio	77.5
23	Alabama	77.4
23	Tennessee	77.4
25	North Carolina	77.3
26	Colorado	77.2
26	Kentucky	77.2
26	Missouri	77.2
29	Illinois	77.1
30	Nevada	77.0
31	California	76.8
32	Iowa	76.7
32	Minnesota	76.7
32	North Dakota	76.7
35	Arizona	76.5
36	Arkansas	76.4
36	New Mexico	76.4
38	Wyoming	76.3
39	Indiana	76.2
39	Louisiana	76.2
41	Mississippi	75.9
42	Georgia	75.6
43	Oklahoma	75.5
44	Kansas	75.4
44	South Dakota	75.4
46	Nebraska	75.2
47	Alaska	74.8
48	Idaho	74.0
49	Texas	73.8
50	Utah	69.8

District of Columbia	82.3

Source: CQ Press using data from U.S. Bureau of the Census
  "State Characteristics: Vintage 2016" (http://www.census.gov/programs-surveys/popest/data/data-sets.html)

Population 18 to 24 Years Old in 2016

National Total = 30,843,811

ALPHA ORDER

ALPHA ORDER

RANK	STATE	POPULATION	% of USA
24	Alabama	459,616	1.5%
48	Alaska	75,274	0.2%
14	Arizona	672,268	2.2%
34	Arkansas	281,738	0.9%
1	California	3,848,787	12.5%
21	Colorado	534,131	1.7%
29	Connecticut	352,024	1.1%
46	Delaware	85,584	0.3%
4	Florida	1,739,623	5.6%
8	Georgia	1,005,386	3.3%
40	Hawaii	128,771	0.4%
39	Idaho	156,563	0.5%
5	Illinois	1,214,511	3.9%
15	Indiana	661,254	2.1%
31	Iowa	322,097	1.0%
32	Kansas	297,133	1.0%
26	Kentucky	419,965	1.4%
25	Louisiana	442,533	1.4%
43	Maine	110,283	0.4%
20	Maryland	546,861	1.8%
13	Massachusetts	704,251	2.3%
9	Michigan	975,645	3.2%
22	Minnesota	507,542	1.6%
33	Mississippi	295,917	1.0%
18	Missouri	578,691	1.9%
44	Montana	99,302	0.3%
37	Nebraska	192,718	0.6%
35	Nevada	250,225	0.8%
41	New Hampshire	127,516	0.4%
12	New Jersey	786,743	2.6%
36	New Mexico	200,362	0.6%
3	New York	1,905,051	6.2%
10	North Carolina	966,234	3.1%
45	North Dakota	91,112	0.3%
7	Ohio	1,075,485	3.5%
27	Oklahoma	383,081	1.2%
28	Oregon	365,578	1.2%
6	Pennsylvania	1,187,598	3.9%
42	Rhode Island	114,376	0.4%
23	South Carolina	468,536	1.5%
47	South Dakota	84,605	0.3%
17	Tennessee	617,867	2.0%
2	Texas	2,767,722	9.0%
30	Utah	343,283	1.1%
49	Vermont	67,743	0.2%
11	Virginia	812,207	2.6%
16	Washington	661,194	2.1%
38	West Virginia	161,635	0.5%
19	Wisconsin	561,861	1.8%
50	Wyoming	55,188	0.2%

RANK ORDER

RANK	STATE	POPULATION	% of USA
1	California	3,848,787	12.5%
2	Texas	2,767,722	9.0%
3	New York	1,905,051	6.2%
4	Florida	1,739,623	5.6%
5	Illinois	1,214,511	3.9%
6	Pennsylvania	1,187,598	3.9%
7	Ohio	1,075,485	3.5%
8	Georgia	1,005,386	3.3%
9	Michigan	975,645	3.2%
10	North Carolina	966,234	3.1%
11	Virginia	812,207	2.6%
12	New Jersey	786,743	2.6%
13	Massachusetts	704,251	2.3%
14	Arizona	672,268	2.2%
15	Indiana	661,254	2.1%
16	Washington	661,194	2.1%
17	Tennessee	617,867	2.0%
18	Missouri	578,691	1.9%
19	Wisconsin	561,861	1.8%
20	Maryland	546,861	1.8%
21	Colorado	534,131	1.7%
22	Minnesota	507,542	1.6%
23	South Carolina	468,536	1.5%
24	Alabama	459,616	1.5%
25	Louisiana	442,533	1.4%
26	Kentucky	419,965	1.4%
27	Oklahoma	383,081	1.2%
28	Oregon	365,578	1.2%
29	Connecticut	352,024	1.1%
30	Utah	343,283	1.1%
31	Iowa	322,097	1.0%
32	Kansas	297,133	1.0%
33	Mississippi	295,917	1.0%
34	Arkansas	281,738	0.9%
35	Nevada	250,225	0.8%
36	New Mexico	200,362	0.6%
37	Nebraska	192,718	0.6%
38	West Virginia	161,635	0.5%
39	Idaho	156,563	0.5%
40	Hawaii	128,771	0.4%
41	New Hampshire	127,516	0.4%
42	Rhode Island	114,376	0.4%
43	Maine	110,283	0.4%
44	Montana	99,302	0.3%
45	North Dakota	91,112	0.3%
46	Delaware	85,584	0.3%
47	South Dakota	84,605	0.3%
48	Alaska	75,274	0.2%
49	Vermont	67,743	0.2%
50	Wyoming	55,188	0.2%
	District of Columbia	80,141	0.3%

Source: U.S. Bureau of the Census
"State Characteristics: Vintage 2016" (http://www.census.gov/programs-surveys/popest/data/data-sets.html)

Percent of Population 18 to 24 Years Old in 2016

National Percent = 9.5% of Population

ALPHA ORDER

RANK	STATE	PERCENT
26	Alabama	9.5
8	Alaska	10.1
19	Arizona	9.7
33	Arkansas	9.4
13	California	9.8
22	Colorado	9.6
13	Connecticut	9.8
43	Delaware	9.0
49	Florida	8.4
13	Georgia	9.8
43	Hawaii	9.0
36	Idaho	9.3
26	Illinois	9.5
10	Indiana	10.0
5	Iowa	10.3
7	Kansas	10.2
26	Kentucky	9.5
26	Louisiana	9.5
50	Maine	8.3
41	Maryland	9.1
5	Massachusetts	10.3
13	Michigan	9.8
40	Minnesota	9.2
11	Mississippi	9.9
26	Missouri	9.5
26	Montana	9.5
8	Nebraska	10.1
48	Nevada	8.5
22	New Hampshire	9.6
46	New Jersey	8.8
22	New Mexico	9.6
22	New York	9.6
26	North Carolina	9.5
1	North Dakota	12.0
36	Ohio	9.3
13	Oklahoma	9.8
45	Oregon	8.9
36	Pennsylvania	9.3
3	Rhode Island	10.8
33	South Carolina	9.4
13	South Dakota	9.8
36	Tennessee	9.3
11	Texas	9.9
2	Utah	11.3
3	Vermont	10.8
19	Virginia	9.7
41	Washington	9.1
46	West Virginia	8.8
19	Wisconsin	9.7
33	Wyoming	9.4

RANK ORDER

RANK	STATE	PERCENT
1	North Dakota	12.0
2	Utah	11.3
3	Rhode Island	10.8
3	Vermont	10.8
5	Iowa	10.3
5	Massachusetts	10.3
7	Kansas	10.2
8	Alaska	10.1
8	Nebraska	10.1
10	Indiana	10.0
11	Mississippi	9.9
11	Texas	9.9
13	California	9.8
13	Connecticut	9.8
13	Georgia	9.8
13	Michigan	9.8
13	Oklahoma	9.8
13	South Dakota	9.8
19	Arizona	9.7
19	Virginia	9.7
19	Wisconsin	9.7
22	Colorado	9.6
22	New Hampshire	9.6
22	New Mexico	9.6
22	New York	9.6
26	Alabama	9.5
26	Illinois	9.5
26	Kentucky	9.5
26	Louisiana	9.5
26	Missouri	9.5
26	Montana	9.5
26	North Carolina	9.5
33	Arkansas	9.4
33	South Carolina	9.4
33	Wyoming	9.4
36	Idaho	9.3
36	Ohio	9.3
36	Pennsylvania	9.3
36	Tennessee	9.3
40	Minnesota	9.2
41	Maryland	9.1
41	Washington	9.1
43	Delaware	9.0
43	Hawaii	9.0
45	Oregon	8.9
46	New Jersey	8.8
46	West Virginia	8.8
48	Nevada	8.5
49	Florida	8.4
50	Maine	8.3

District of Columbia — 11.8

Source: CQ Press using data from U.S. Bureau of the Census
"State Characteristics: Vintage 2016" (http://www.census.gov/programs-surveys/popest/data/data-sets.html)

Population 25 to 44 Years Old in 2016

National Total = 85,147,399

RANK	STATE	POPULATION	% of USA
25	Alabama	1,233,200	1.4%
46	Alaska	212,598	0.2%
14	Arizona	1,778,348	2.1%
34	Arkansas	757,481	0.9%
1	California	11,077,717	13.0%
19	Colorado	1,584,485	1.9%
29	Connecticut	865,026	1.0%
45	Delaware	236,926	0.3%
4	Florida	5,147,714	6.0%
8	Georgia	2,785,270	3.3%
40	Hawaii	385,131	0.5%
39	Idaho	427,556	0.5%
5	Illinois	3,420,788	4.0%
17	Indiana	1,674,571	2.0%
32	Iowa	761,908	0.9%
35	Kansas	731,695	0.9%
26	Kentucky	1,128,341	1.3%
23	Louisiana	1,255,903	1.5%
42	Maine	307,761	0.4%
18	Maryland	1,595,834	1.9%
15	Massachusetts	1,777,342	2.1%
10	Michigan	2,408,971	2.8%
21	Minnesota	1,425,118	1.7%
33	Mississippi	759,788	0.9%
20	Missouri	1,543,906	1.8%
44	Montana	252,419	0.3%
37	Nebraska	483,474	0.6%
31	Nevada	815,885	1.0%
41	New Hampshire	312,785	0.4%
11	New Jersey	2,308,261	2.7%
36	New Mexico	522,592	0.6%
3	New York	5,353,334	6.3%
9	North Carolina	2,625,691	3.1%
48	North Dakota	199,967	0.2%
7	Ohio	2,887,030	3.4%
28	Oklahoma	1,024,244	1.2%
27	Oregon	1,106,741	1.3%
6	Pennsylvania	3,158,878	3.7%
43	Rhode Island	266,053	0.3%
24	South Carolina	1,254,441	1.5%
47	South Dakota	210,858	0.2%
16	Tennessee	1,723,338	2.0%
2	Texas	7,812,015	9.2%
30	Utah	859,778	1.0%
50	Vermont	142,213	0.2%
12	Virginia	2,257,985	2.7%
13	Washington	2,022,565	2.4%
38	West Virginia	441,833	0.5%
22	Wisconsin	1,414,479	1.7%
49	Wyoming	153,282	0.2%

RANK	STATE	POPULATION	% of USA
1	California	11,077,717	13.0%
2	Texas	7,812,015	9.2%
3	New York	5,353,334	6.3%
4	Florida	5,147,714	6.0%
5	Illinois	3,420,788	4.0%
6	Pennsylvania	3,158,878	3.7%
7	Ohio	2,887,030	3.4%
8	Georgia	2,785,270	3.3%
9	North Carolina	2,625,691	3.1%
10	Michigan	2,408,971	2.8%
11	New Jersey	2,308,261	2.7%
12	Virginia	2,257,985	2.7%
13	Washington	2,022,565	2.4%
14	Arizona	1,778,348	2.1%
15	Massachusetts	1,777,342	2.1%
16	Tennessee	1,723,338	2.0%
17	Indiana	1,674,571	2.0%
18	Maryland	1,595,834	1.9%
19	Colorado	1,584,485	1.9%
20	Missouri	1,543,906	1.8%
21	Minnesota	1,425,118	1.7%
22	Wisconsin	1,414,479	1.7%
23	Louisiana	1,255,903	1.5%
24	South Carolina	1,254,441	1.5%
25	Alabama	1,233,200	1.4%
26	Kentucky	1,128,341	1.3%
27	Oregon	1,106,741	1.3%
28	Oklahoma	1,024,244	1.2%
29	Connecticut	865,026	1.0%
30	Utah	859,778	1.0%
31	Nevada	815,885	1.0%
32	Iowa	761,908	0.9%
33	Mississippi	759,788	0.9%
34	Arkansas	757,481	0.9%
35	Kansas	731,695	0.9%
36	New Mexico	522,592	0.6%
37	Nebraska	483,474	0.6%
38	West Virginia	441,833	0.5%
39	Idaho	427,556	0.5%
40	Hawaii	385,131	0.5%
41	New Hampshire	312,785	0.4%
42	Maine	307,761	0.4%
43	Rhode Island	266,053	0.3%
44	Montana	252,419	0.3%
45	Delaware	236,926	0.3%
46	Alaska	212,598	0.2%
47	South Dakota	210,858	0.2%
48	North Dakota	199,967	0.2%
49	Wyoming	153,282	0.2%
50	Vermont	142,213	0.2%
	District of Columbia	253,880	0.3%

Source: U.S. Bureau of the Census
"State Characteristics: Vintage 2016" (http://www.census.gov/programs-surveys/popest/data/data-sets.html)

Percent of Population 25 to 44 Years Old in 2016

National Percent = 26.4% of Population

ALPHA ORDER

RANK	STATE	PERCENT
25	Alabama	25.4
1	Alaska	28.7
24	Arizona	25.7
30	Arkansas	25.3
3	California	28.2
2	Colorado	28.6
45	Connecticut	24.2
38	Delaware	24.9
37	Florida	25.0
9	Georgia	27.0
9	Hawaii	27.0
25	Idaho	25.4
14	Illinois	26.7
33	Indiana	25.2
43	Iowa	24.3
33	Kansas	25.2
25	Kentucky	25.4
12	Louisiana	26.8
49	Maine	23.1
15	Maryland	26.5
18	Massachusetts	26.1
43	Michigan	24.3
22	Minnesota	25.8
25	Mississippi	25.4
30	Missouri	25.3
45	Montana	24.2
25	Nebraska	25.4
6	Nevada	27.8
48	New Hampshire	23.4
22	New Jersey	25.8
36	New Mexico	25.1
8	New York	27.1
20	North Carolina	25.9
16	North Dakota	26.4
38	Ohio	24.9
18	Oklahoma	26.1
9	Oregon	27.0
40	Pennsylvania	24.7
33	Rhode Island	25.2
30	South Carolina	25.3
42	South Dakota	24.4
20	Tennessee	25.9
5	Texas	28.0
3	Utah	28.2
50	Vermont	22.8
12	Virginia	26.8
6	Washington	27.8
47	West Virginia	24.1
41	Wisconsin	24.5
17	Wyoming	26.2

RANK ORDER

RANK	STATE	PERCENT
1	Alaska	28.7
2	Colorado	28.6
3	California	28.2
3	Utah	28.2
5	Texas	28.0
6	Nevada	27.8
6	Washington	27.8
8	New York	27.1
9	Georgia	27.0
9	Hawaii	27.0
9	Oregon	27.0
12	Louisiana	26.8
12	Virginia	26.8
14	Illinois	26.7
15	Maryland	26.5
16	North Dakota	26.4
17	Wyoming	26.2
18	Massachusetts	26.1
18	Oklahoma	26.1
20	North Carolina	25.9
20	Tennessee	25.9
22	Minnesota	25.8
22	New Jersey	25.8
24	Arizona	25.7
25	Alabama	25.4
25	Idaho	25.4
25	Kentucky	25.4
25	Mississippi	25.4
25	Nebraska	25.4
30	Arkansas	25.3
30	Missouri	25.3
30	South Carolina	25.3
33	Indiana	25.2
33	Kansas	25.2
33	Rhode Island	25.2
36	New Mexico	25.1
37	Florida	25.0
38	Delaware	24.9
38	Ohio	24.9
40	Pennsylvania	24.7
41	Wisconsin	24.5
42	South Dakota	24.4
43	Iowa	24.3
43	Michigan	24.3
45	Connecticut	24.2
45	Montana	24.2
47	West Virginia	24.1
48	New Hampshire	23.4
49	Maine	23.1
50	Vermont	22.8

District of Columbia	37.3

Source: CQ Press using data from U.S. Bureau of the Census
"State Characteristics: Vintage 2016" (http://www.census.gov/programs-surveys/popest/data/data-sets.html)

Population 45 to 64 Years Old in 2016

National Total = 84,249,823

RANK	STATE	POPULATION	% of USA
24	Alabama	1,289,110	1.5%
47	Alaska	189,489	0.2%
17	Arizona	1,678,039	2.0%
32	Arkansas	757,242	0.9%
1	California	9,884,015	11.7%
22	Colorado	1,417,033	1.7%
28	Connecticut	1,028,705	1.2%
45	Delaware	258,331	0.3%
3	Florida	5,483,473	6.5%
10	Georgia	2,653,509	3.1%
42	Hawaii	362,677	0.4%
40	Idaho	406,859	0.5%
6	Illinois	3,368,867	4.0%
16	Indiana	1,730,213	2.1%
30	Iowa	805,742	1.0%
34	Kansas	726,517	0.9%
26	Kentucky	1,187,322	1.4%
25	Louisiana	1,194,838	1.4%
41	Maine	401,038	0.5%
18	Maryland	1,648,814	2.0%
14	Massachusetts	1,878,120	2.2%
8	Michigan	2,740,872	3.3%
21	Minnesota	1,466,731	1.7%
31	Mississippi	760,792	0.9%
19	Missouri	1,605,519	1.9%
44	Montana	278,148	0.3%
38	Nebraska	470,855	0.6%
33	Nevada	755,379	0.9%
39	New Hampshire	407,102	0.5%
11	New Jersey	2,492,101	3.0%
36	New Mexico	524,972	0.6%
4	New York	5,273,836	6.3%
9	North Carolina	2,686,678	3.2%
49	North Dakota	180,563	0.2%
7	Ohio	3,153,057	3.7%
29	Oklahoma	964,470	1.1%
27	Oregon	1,063,541	1.3%
5	Pennsylvania	3,539,225	4.2%
43	Rhode Island	293,652	0.3%
23	South Carolina	1,310,289	1.6%
46	South Dakota	217,899	0.3%
15	Tennessee	1,761,142	2.1%
2	Texas	6,635,032	7.9%
35	Utah	605,219	0.7%
48	Vermont	183,178	0.2%
12	Virginia	2,242,749	2.7%
13	Washington	1,893,680	2.2%
37	West Virginia	509,049	0.6%
20	Wisconsin	1,586,257	1.9%
50	Wyoming	150,318	0.2%

RANK	STATE	POPULATION	% of USA
1	California	9,884,015	11.7%
2	Texas	6,635,032	7.9%
3	Florida	5,483,473	6.5%
4	New York	5,273,836	6.3%
5	Pennsylvania	3,539,225	4.2%
6	Illinois	3,368,867	4.0%
7	Ohio	3,153,057	3.7%
8	Michigan	2,740,872	3.3%
9	North Carolina	2,686,678	3.2%
10	Georgia	2,653,509	3.1%
11	New Jersey	2,492,101	3.0%
12	Virginia	2,242,749	2.7%
13	Washington	1,893,680	2.2%
14	Massachusetts	1,878,120	2.2%
15	Tennessee	1,761,142	2.1%
16	Indiana	1,730,213	2.1%
17	Arizona	1,678,039	2.0%
18	Maryland	1,648,814	2.0%
19	Missouri	1,605,519	1.9%
20	Wisconsin	1,586,257	1.9%
21	Minnesota	1,466,731	1.7%
22	Colorado	1,417,033	1.7%
23	South Carolina	1,310,289	1.6%
24	Alabama	1,289,110	1.5%
25	Louisiana	1,194,838	1.4%
26	Kentucky	1,187,322	1.4%
27	Oregon	1,063,541	1.3%
28	Connecticut	1,028,705	1.2%
29	Oklahoma	964,470	1.1%
30	Iowa	805,742	1.0%
31	Mississippi	760,792	0.9%
32	Arkansas	757,242	0.9%
33	Nevada	755,379	0.9%
34	Kansas	726,517	0.9%
35	Utah	605,219	0.7%
36	New Mexico	524,972	0.6%
37	West Virginia	509,049	0.6%
38	Nebraska	470,855	0.6%
39	New Hampshire	407,102	0.5%
40	Idaho	406,859	0.5%
41	Maine	401,038	0.5%
42	Hawaii	362,677	0.4%
43	Rhode Island	293,652	0.3%
44	Montana	278,148	0.3%
45	Delaware	258,331	0.3%
46	South Dakota	217,899	0.3%
47	Alaska	189,489	0.2%
48	Vermont	183,178	0.2%
49	North Dakota	180,563	0.2%
50	Wyoming	150,318	0.2%
	District of Columbia	147,565	0.2%

Source: U.S. Bureau of the Census
"State Characteristics: Vintage 2016" (http://www.census.gov/programs-surveys/popest/data/data-sets.html)

Percent of Population 45 to 64 Years Old in 2016

National Percent = 26.1% of Population

ALPHA ORDER				RANK ORDER		
RANK	STATE	PERCENT		RANK	STATE	PERCENT
21	Alabama	26.5		1	New Hampshire	30.5
35	Alaska	25.5		2	Maine	30.1
46	Arizona	24.2		3	Vermont	29.3
39	Arkansas	25.3		4	Connecticut	28.8
40	California	25.2		5	New Jersey	27.9
34	Colorado	25.6		6	Rhode Island	27.8
4	Connecticut	28.8		6	West Virginia	27.8
13	Delaware	27.1		8	Pennsylvania	27.7
19	Florida	26.6		9	Massachusetts	27.6
30	Georgia	25.7		9	Michigan	27.6
38	Hawaii	25.4		11	Wisconsin	27.5
46	Idaho	24.2		12	Maryland	27.4
26	Illinois	26.3		13	Delaware	27.1
27	Indiana	26.1		13	Ohio	27.1
30	Iowa	25.7		15	Kentucky	26.8
43	Kansas	25.0		16	Montana	26.7
15	Kentucky	26.8		16	New York	26.7
35	Louisiana	25.5		16	Virginia	26.7
2	Maine	30.1		19	Florida	26.6
12	Maryland	27.4		19	Minnesota	26.6
9	Massachusetts	27.6		21	Alabama	26.5
9	Michigan	27.6		21	North Carolina	26.5
19	Minnesota	26.6		21	Tennessee	26.5
35	Mississippi	25.5		24	Missouri	26.4
24	Missouri	26.4		24	South Carolina	26.4
16	Montana	26.7		26	Illinois	26.3
44	Nebraska	24.7		27	Indiana	26.1
30	Nevada	25.7		28	Oregon	26.0
1	New Hampshire	30.5		28	Washington	26.0
5	New Jersey	27.9		30	Georgia	25.7
40	New Mexico	25.2		30	Iowa	25.7
16	New York	26.7		30	Nevada	25.7
21	North Carolina	26.5		30	Wyoming	25.7
48	North Dakota	23.8		34	Colorado	25.6
13	Ohio	27.1		35	Alaska	25.5
45	Oklahoma	24.6		35	Louisiana	25.5
28	Oregon	26.0		35	Mississippi	25.5
8	Pennsylvania	27.7		38	Hawaii	25.4
6	Rhode Island	27.8		39	Arkansas	25.3
24	South Carolina	26.4		40	California	25.2
40	South Dakota	25.2		40	New Mexico	25.2
21	Tennessee	26.5		40	South Dakota	25.2
48	Texas	23.8		43	Kansas	25.0
50	Utah	19.8		44	Nebraska	24.7
3	Vermont	29.3		45	Oklahoma	24.6
16	Virginia	26.7		46	Arizona	24.2
28	Washington	26.0		46	Idaho	24.2
6	West Virginia	27.8		48	North Dakota	23.8
11	Wisconsin	27.5		48	Texas	23.8
30	Wyoming	25.7		50	Utah	19.8
				District of Columbia		21.7

Source: CQ Press using data from U.S. Bureau of the Census
"State Characteristics: Vintage 2016" (http://www.census.gov/programs-surveys/popest/data/data-sets.html)

Population 65 Years Old and Older in 2016

National Total = 49,244,195

ALPHA ORDER

RANK	STATE	POPULATION	% of USA
23	Alabama	784,551	1.6%
50	Alaska	77,206	0.2%
13	Arizona	1,170,924	2.4%
31	Arkansas	486,734	1.0%
1	California	5,346,635	10.9%
24	Colorado	743,524	1.5%
29	Connecticut	577,403	1.2%
45	Delaware	166,950	0.3%
2	Florida	4,094,917	8.3%
11	Georgia	1,354,662	2.8%
41	Hawaii	243,962	0.5%
40	Idaho	254,989	0.5%
7	Illinois	1,871,264	3.8%
17	Indiana	991,563	2.0%
30	Iowa	514,215	1.0%
34	Kansas	436,993	0.9%
25	Kentucky	690,717	1.4%
27	Louisiana	674,443	1.4%
39	Maine	257,683	0.5%
20	Maryland	876,210	1.8%
15	Massachusetts	1,073,964	2.2%
8	Michigan	1,611,755	3.3%
21	Minnesota	832,228	1.7%
32	Mississippi	450,941	0.9%
18	Missouri	978,021	2.0%
43	Montana	185,040	0.4%
38	Nebraska	286,744	0.6%
33	Nevada	441,142	0.9%
42	New Hampshire	226,804	0.5%
10	New Jersey	1,372,612	2.8%
36	New Mexico	342,426	0.7%
4	New York	3,032,509	6.2%
9	North Carolina	1,569,465	3.2%
48	North Dakota	109,999	0.2%
6	Ohio	1,886,629	3.8%
28	Oklahoma	590,138	1.2%
26	Oregon	688,878	1.4%
5	Pennsylvania	2,223,721	4.5%
44	Rhode Island	173,964	0.4%
22	South Carolina	830,232	1.7%
46	South Dakota	138,805	0.3%
16	Tennessee	1,047,052	2.1%
3	Texas	3,353,240	6.8%
37	Utah	321,164	0.7%
47	Vermont	112,932	0.2%
12	Virginia	1,228,744	2.5%
14	Washington	1,081,063	2.2%
35	West Virginia	343,517	0.7%
19	Wisconsin	928,418	1.9%
49	Wyoming	87,812	0.2%

RANK ORDER

RANK	STATE	POPULATION	% of USA
1	California	5,346,635	10.9%
2	Florida	4,094,917	8.3%
3	Texas	3,353,240	6.8%
4	New York	3,032,509	6.2%
5	Pennsylvania	2,223,721	4.5%
6	Ohio	1,886,629	3.8%
7	Illinois	1,871,264	3.8%
8	Michigan	1,611,755	3.3%
9	North Carolina	1,569,465	3.2%
10	New Jersey	1,372,612	2.8%
11	Georgia	1,354,662	2.8%
12	Virginia	1,228,744	2.5%
13	Arizona	1,170,924	2.4%
14	Washington	1,081,063	2.2%
15	Massachusetts	1,073,964	2.2%
16	Tennessee	1,047,052	2.1%
17	Indiana	991,563	2.0%
18	Missouri	978,021	2.0%
19	Wisconsin	928,418	1.9%
20	Maryland	876,210	1.8%
21	Minnesota	832,228	1.7%
22	South Carolina	830,232	1.7%
23	Alabama	784,551	1.6%
24	Colorado	743,524	1.5%
25	Kentucky	690,717	1.4%
26	Oregon	688,878	1.4%
27	Louisiana	674,443	1.4%
28	Oklahoma	590,138	1.2%
29	Connecticut	577,403	1.2%
30	Iowa	514,215	1.0%
31	Arkansas	486,734	1.0%
32	Mississippi	450,941	0.9%
33	Nevada	441,142	0.9%
34	Kansas	436,993	0.9%
35	West Virginia	343,517	0.7%
36	New Mexico	342,426	0.7%
37	Utah	321,164	0.7%
38	Nebraska	286,744	0.6%
39	Maine	257,683	0.5%
40	Idaho	254,989	0.5%
41	Hawaii	243,962	0.5%
42	New Hampshire	226,804	0.5%
43	Montana	185,040	0.4%
44	Rhode Island	173,964	0.4%
45	Delaware	166,950	0.3%
46	South Dakota	138,805	0.3%
47	Vermont	112,932	0.2%
48	North Dakota	109,999	0.2%
49	Wyoming	87,812	0.2%
50	Alaska	77,206	0.2%
	District of Columbia	78,691	0.2%

Source: U.S. Bureau of the Census
"State Characteristics: Vintage 2016" (http://www.census.gov/programs-surveys/popest/data/data-sets.html)

Percent of Population 65 Years Old and Older in 2016

National Percent = 15.2% of Population

ALPHA ORDER

RANK	STATE	PERCENT
19	Alabama	16.1
50	Alaska	10.4
10	Arizona	16.9
16	Arkansas	16.3
45	California	13.6
46	Colorado	13.4
19	Connecticut	16.1
6	Delaware	17.5
1	Florida	19.9
47	Georgia	13.1
8	Hawaii	17.1
30	Idaho	15.1
40	Illinois	14.6
38	Indiana	14.9
15	Iowa	16.4
33	Kansas	15.0
26	Kentucky	15.6
44	Louisiana	14.4
2	Maine	19.4
40	Maryland	14.6
24	Massachusetts	15.8
17	Michigan	16.2
30	Minnesota	15.1
30	Mississippi	15.1
19	Missouri	16.1
5	Montana	17.7
33	Nebraska	15.0
33	Nevada	15.0
9	New Hampshire	17.0
29	New Jersey	15.3
13	New Mexico	16.5
28	New York	15.4
27	North Carolina	15.5
43	North Dakota	14.5
17	Ohio	16.2
33	Oklahoma	15.0
11	Oregon	16.8
7	Pennsylvania	17.4
13	Rhode Island	16.5
12	South Carolina	16.7
23	South Dakota	16.0
25	Tennessee	15.7
48	Texas	12.0
49	Utah	10.5
4	Vermont	18.1
40	Virginia	14.6
39	Washington	14.8
3	West Virginia	18.8
19	Wisconsin	16.1
33	Wyoming	15.0

RANK ORDER

RANK	STATE	PERCENT
1	Florida	19.9
2	Maine	19.4
3	West Virginia	18.8
4	Vermont	18.1
5	Montana	17.7
6	Delaware	17.5
7	Pennsylvania	17.4
8	Hawaii	17.1
9	New Hampshire	17.0
10	Arizona	16.9
11	Oregon	16.8
12	South Carolina	16.7
13	New Mexico	16.5
13	Rhode Island	16.5
15	Iowa	16.4
16	Arkansas	16.3
17	Michigan	16.2
17	Ohio	16.2
19	Alabama	16.1
19	Connecticut	16.1
19	Missouri	16.1
19	Wisconsin	16.1
23	South Dakota	16.0
24	Massachusetts	15.8
25	Tennessee	15.7
26	Kentucky	15.6
27	North Carolina	15.5
28	New York	15.4
29	New Jersey	15.3
30	Idaho	15.1
30	Minnesota	15.1
30	Mississippi	15.1
33	Kansas	15.0
33	Nebraska	15.0
33	Nevada	15.0
33	Oklahoma	15.0
33	Wyoming	15.0
38	Indiana	14.9
39	Washington	14.8
40	Illinois	14.6
40	Maryland	14.6
40	Virginia	14.6
43	North Dakota	14.5
44	Louisiana	14.4
45	California	13.6
46	Colorado	13.4
47	Georgia	13.1
48	Texas	12.0
49	Utah	10.5
50	Alaska	10.4

District of Columbia 11.6

Source: CQ Press using data from U.S. Bureau of the Census
"State Characteristics: Vintage 2016" (http://www.census.gov/programs-surveys/popest/data/data-sets.html)

Population 85 Years Old and Older in 2016

National Total = 6,380,331

ALPHA ORDER

ALPHA ORDER

RANK	STATE	POPULATION	% of USA
23	Alabama	86,753	1.4%
50	Alaska	6,420	0.1%
14	Arizona	136,834	2.1%
32	Arkansas	56,680	0.9%
1	California	722,333	11.3%
24	Colorado	85,771	1.3%
22	Connecticut	89,928	1.4%
46	Delaware	19,087	0.3%
2	Florida	555,979	8.7%
13	Georgia	138,135	2.2%
38	Hawaii	38,952	0.6%
42	Idaho	28,435	0.4%
6	Illinois	259,483	4.1%
17	Indiana	128,469	2.0%
27	Iowa	78,700	1.2%
31	Kansas	64,804	1.0%
28	Kentucky	78,089	1.2%
29	Louisiana	77,461	1.2%
40	Maine	32,290	0.5%
21	Maryland	114,931	1.8%
11	Massachusetts	158,806	2.5%
8	Michigan	213,289	3.3%
19	Minnesota	119,364	1.9%
33	Mississippi	50,964	0.8%
18	Missouri	128,297	2.0%
44	Montana	22,775	0.4%
34	Nebraska	42,822	0.7%
35	Nevada	41,537	0.7%
41	New Hampshire	29,316	0.5%
9	New Jersey	198,726	3.1%
36	New Mexico	39,596	0.6%
3	New York	438,400	6.9%
10	North Carolina	177,810	2.8%
47	North Dakota	18,147	0.3%
7	Ohio	254,147	4.0%
30	Oklahoma	70,570	1.1%
25	Oregon	85,254	1.3%
5	Pennsylvania	334,468	5.2%
43	Rhode Island	28,360	0.4%
26	South Carolina	84,148	1.3%
45	South Dakota	21,516	0.3%
20	Tennessee	115,707	1.8%
4	Texas	387,790	6.1%
39	Utah	36,378	0.6%
48	Vermont	14,283	0.2%
12	Virginia	145,327	2.3%
15	Washington	132,489	2.1%
37	West Virginia	39,322	0.6%
16	Wisconsin	129,284	2.0%
49	Wyoming	10,535	0.2%

RANK ORDER

RANK	STATE	POPULATION	% of USA
1	California	722,333	11.3%
2	Florida	555,979	8.7%
3	New York	438,400	6.9%
4	Texas	387,790	6.1%
5	Pennsylvania	334,468	5.2%
6	Illinois	259,483	4.1%
7	Ohio	254,147	4.0%
8	Michigan	213,289	3.3%
9	New Jersey	198,726	3.1%
10	North Carolina	177,810	2.8%
11	Massachusetts	158,806	2.5%
12	Virginia	145,327	2.3%
13	Georgia	138,135	2.2%
14	Arizona	136,834	2.1%
15	Washington	132,489	2.1%
16	Wisconsin	129,284	2.0%
17	Indiana	128,469	2.0%
18	Missouri	128,297	2.0%
19	Minnesota	119,364	1.9%
20	Tennessee	115,707	1.8%
21	Maryland	114,931	1.8%
22	Connecticut	89,928	1.4%
23	Alabama	86,753	1.4%
24	Colorado	85,771	1.3%
25	Oregon	85,254	1.3%
26	South Carolina	84,148	1.3%
27	Iowa	78,700	1.2%
28	Kentucky	78,089	1.2%
29	Louisiana	77,461	1.2%
30	Oklahoma	70,570	1.1%
31	Kansas	64,804	1.0%
32	Arkansas	56,680	0.9%
33	Mississippi	50,964	0.8%
34	Nebraska	42,822	0.7%
35	Nevada	41,537	0.7%
36	New Mexico	39,596	0.6%
37	West Virginia	39,322	0.6%
38	Hawaii	38,952	0.6%
39	Utah	36,378	0.6%
40	Maine	32,290	0.5%
41	New Hampshire	29,316	0.5%
42	Idaho	28,435	0.4%
43	Rhode Island	28,360	0.4%
44	Montana	22,775	0.4%
45	South Dakota	21,516	0.3%
46	Delaware	19,087	0.3%
47	North Dakota	18,147	0.3%
48	Vermont	14,283	0.2%
49	Wyoming	10,535	0.2%
50	Alaska	6,420	0.1%
	District of Columbia	11,370	0.2%

Source: U.S. Bureau of the Census

"State Characteristics: Vintage 2016" (http://www.census.gov/programs-surveys/popest/data/data-sets.html)

Percent of Population 85 Years Old and Older in 2016

National Percent = 2.0% of Population

ALPHA ORDER

RANK	STATE	PERCENT
32	Alabama	1.8
50	Alaska	0.9
25	Arizona	2.0
28	Arkansas	1.9
32	California	1.8
45	Colorado	1.5
5	Connecticut	2.5
25	Delaware	2.0
1	Florida	2.7
48	Georgia	1.3
1	Hawaii	2.7
39	Idaho	1.7
25	Illinois	2.0
28	Indiana	1.9
5	Iowa	2.5
12	Kansas	2.2
32	Kentucky	1.8
39	Louisiana	1.7
8	Maine	2.4
28	Maryland	1.9
10	Massachusetts	2.3
21	Michigan	2.1
12	Minnesota	2.2
39	Mississippi	1.7
21	Missouri	2.1
12	Montana	2.2
12	Nebraska	2.2
46	Nevada	1.4
12	New Hampshire	2.2
12	New Jersey	2.2
28	New Mexico	1.9
12	New York	2.2
32	North Carolina	1.8
8	North Dakota	2.4
12	Ohio	2.2
32	Oklahoma	1.8
21	Oregon	2.1
4	Pennsylvania	2.6
1	Rhode Island	2.7
39	South Carolina	1.7
5	South Dakota	2.5
39	Tennessee	1.7
46	Texas	1.4
49	Utah	1.2
10	Vermont	2.3
39	Virginia	1.7
32	Washington	1.8
21	West Virginia	2.1
12	Wisconsin	2.2
32	Wyoming	1.8

RANK ORDER

RANK	STATE	PERCENT
1	Florida	2.7
1	Hawaii	2.7
1	Rhode Island	2.7
4	Pennsylvania	2.6
5	Connecticut	2.5
5	Iowa	2.5
5	South Dakota	2.5
8	Maine	2.4
8	North Dakota	2.4
10	Massachusetts	2.3
10	Vermont	2.3
12	Kansas	2.2
12	Minnesota	2.2
12	Montana	2.2
12	Nebraska	2.2
12	New Hampshire	2.2
12	New Jersey	2.2
12	New York	2.2
12	Ohio	2.2
12	Wisconsin	2.2
21	Michigan	2.1
21	Missouri	2.1
21	Oregon	2.1
21	West Virginia	2.1
25	Arizona	2.0
25	Delaware	2.0
25	Illinois	2.0
28	Arkansas	1.9
28	Indiana	1.9
28	Maryland	1.9
28	New Mexico	1.9
32	Alabama	1.8
32	California	1.8
32	Kentucky	1.8
32	North Carolina	1.8
32	Oklahoma	1.8
32	Washington	1.8
32	Wyoming	1.8
39	Idaho	1.7
39	Louisiana	1.7
39	Mississippi	1.7
39	South Carolina	1.7
39	Tennessee	1.7
39	Virginia	1.7
45	Colorado	1.5
46	Nevada	1.4
46	Texas	1.4
48	Georgia	1.3
49	Utah	1.2
50	Alaska	0.9

| | District of Columbia | 1.7 |

Source: CQ Press using data from U.S. Bureau of the Census
"State Characteristics: Vintage 2016" (http://www.census.gov/programs-surveys/popest/data/data-sets.html)

Percent of Native Population Born in Their State of Residence in 2016

National Percent = 67.5%

ALPHA ORDER				RANK ORDER		
RANK	STATE	PERCENT		RANK	STATE	PERCENT
14	Alabama	71.9		1	Michigan	81.8
48	Alaska	44.1		2	Louisiana	81.5
45	Arizona	45.6		3	New York	81.4
30	Arkansas	64.2		4	Ohio	78.5
7	California	75.5		5	Illinois	78.0
44	Colorado	47.5		6	Pennsylvania	77.7
28	Connecticut	64.5		7	California	75.5
43	Delaware	49.6		8	Wisconsin	75.3
46	Florida	45.1		9	Iowa	74.3
33	Georgia	60.8		10	Minnesota	74.0
24	Hawaii	65.3		11	Massachusetts	73.0
41	Idaho	51.3		11	Mississippi	73.0
5	Illinois	78.0		13	Indiana	72.0
13	Indiana	72.0		14	Alabama	71.9
9	Iowa	74.3		14	Texas	71.9
31	Kansas	63.6		16	Kentucky	71.4
16	Kentucky	71.4		17	West Virginia	70.1
2	Louisiana	81.5		18	Nebraska	69.5
26	Maine	65.1		19	Missouri	69.1
36	Maryland	56.3		20	Utah	67.6
11	Massachusetts	73.0		21	New Jersey	67.4
1	Michigan	81.8		22	South Dakota	66.9
10	Minnesota	74.0		23	Rhode Island	65.6
11	Mississippi	73.0		24	Hawaii	65.3
19	Missouri	69.1		25	Oklahoma	65.2
38	Montana	55.9		26	Maine	65.1
18	Nebraska	69.5		27	North Dakota	64.6
50	Nevada	33.0		28	Connecticut	64.5
47	New Hampshire	44.2		29	Tennessee	64.3
21	New Jersey	67.4		30	Arkansas	64.2
35	New Mexico	58.5		31	Kansas	63.6
3	New York	81.4		32	North Carolina	61.6
32	North Carolina	61.6		33	Georgia	60.8
27	North Dakota	64.6		34	South Carolina	59.8
4	Ohio	78.5		35	New Mexico	58.5
25	Oklahoma	65.2		36	Maryland	56.3
42	Oregon	51.2		36	Virginia	56.3
6	Pennsylvania	77.7		38	Montana	55.9
23	Rhode Island	65.6		39	Washington	54.4
34	South Carolina	59.8		40	Vermont	52.6
22	South Dakota	66.9		41	Idaho	51.3
29	Tennessee	64.3		42	Oregon	51.2
14	Texas	71.9		43	Delaware	49.6
20	Utah	67.6		44	Colorado	47.5
40	Vermont	52.6		45	Arizona	45.6
36	Virginia	56.3		46	Florida	45.1
39	Washington	54.4		47	New Hampshire	44.2
17	West Virginia	70.1		48	Alaska	44.1
8	Wisconsin	75.3		48	Wyoming	44.1
48	Wyoming	44.1		50	Nevada	33.0
					District of Columbia	42.9

Source: U.S. Bureau of the Census

"2016 American Community Survey-Table R0601" (http://www.census.gov/programs-surveys/acs/)

Domestic Migration of Population: 2016 to 2017

National Net Migration = 0 People*

ALPHA ORDER			RANK ORDER		
RANK	**STATE**	**NET MIGRATION**	**RANK**	**STATE**	**NET MIGRATION**
20	Alabama	3,840	1	Florida	160,854
35	Alaska	(9,938)	2	Texas	79,163
5	Arizona	63,111	3	North Carolina	66,051
17	Arkansas	4,718	4	Washington	64,579
49	California	(138,195)	5	Arizona	63,111
11	Colorado	36,653	6	South Carolina	49,015
42	Connecticut	(22,270)	7	Georgia	41,107
19	Delaware	4,484	8	Tennessee	40,232
1	Florida	160,854	9	Nevada	38,227
7	Georgia	41,107	10	Oregon	37,975
40	Hawaii	(13,537)	11	Colorado	36,653
12	Idaho	24,597	12	Idaho	24,597
48	Illinois	(114,779)	13	Utah	17,568
24	Indiana	(976)	14	Montana	8,666
27	Iowa	(2,724)	15	Minnesota	7,941
41	Kansas	(14,150)	16	Maine	5,376
22	Kentucky	1,024	17	Arkansas	4,718
46	Louisiana	(27,515)	18	New Hampshire	4,687
16	Maine	5,376	19	Delaware	4,484
44	Maryland	(23,984)	20	Alabama	3,840
43	Massachusetts	(23,089)	21	South Dakota	1,976
39	Michigan	(12,698)	22	Kentucky	1,024
15	Minnesota	7,941	23	Vermont	(918)
34	Mississippi	(9,885)	24	Indiana	(976)
25	Missouri	(1,050)	25	Missouri	(1,050)
14	Montana	8,666	26	Wisconsin	(2,086)
28	Nebraska	(3,493)	27	Iowa	(2,724)
9	Nevada	38,227	28	Nebraska	(3,493)
18	New Hampshire	4,687	29	Rhode Island	(3,854)
47	New Jersey	(57,274)	30	North Dakota	(6,653)
31	New Mexico	(7,437)	31	New Mexico	(7,437)
50	New York	(190,508)	32	Ohio	(8,205)
3	North Carolina	66,051	33	Wyoming	(8,613)
30	North Dakota	(6,653)	34	Mississippi	(9,885)
32	Ohio	(8,205)	35	Alaska	(9,938)
36	Oklahoma	(10,470)	36	Oklahoma	(10,470)
10	Oregon	37,975	37	West Virginia	(10,507)
45	Pennsylvania	(25,793)	38	Virginia	(12,395)
29	Rhode Island	(3,854)	39	Michigan	(12,698)
6	South Carolina	49,015	40	Hawaii	(13,537)
21	South Dakota	1,976	41	Kansas	(14,150)
8	Tennessee	40,232	42	Connecticut	(22,270)
2	Texas	79,163	43	Massachusetts	(23,089)
13	Utah	17,568	44	Maryland	(23,984)
23	Vermont	(918)	45	Pennsylvania	(25,793)
38	Virginia	(12,395)	46	Louisiana	(27,515)
4	Washington	64,579	47	New Jersey	(57,274)
37	West Virginia	(10,507)	48	Illinois	(114,779)
26	Wisconsin	(2,086)	49	California	(138,195)
33	Wyoming	(8,613)	50	New York	(190,508)

District of Columbia	1,152

Source: U.S. Bureau of the Census

"State Population Totals Tables" (http://www.census.gov/programs-surveys/popest/data/data-sets.html)

*From July 1, 2016 to June 30, 2017. Includes armed forces residing in each state. Net Domestic Migration is the difference between domestic inmigration to an area and domestic outmigration from it during the period. Domestic inmigration and outmigration consist of moves where both the origins and destinations are within the United States (excluding Puerto Rico).

Net International Migration: 2016 to 2017

National Net = 1,111,283 Immigrants*

<table>
<tr><td colspan="4">ALPHA ORDER</td><td colspan="4">RANK ORDER</td></tr>
<tr><td>RANK</td><td>STATE</td><td>IMMIGRANTS</td><td>% of USA</td><td>RANK</td><td>STATE</td><td>IMMIGRANTS</td><td>% of USA</td></tr>
<tr><td>36</td><td>Alabama</td><td>4,475</td><td>0.4%</td><td>1</td><td>California</td><td>164,867</td><td>14.8%</td></tr>
<tr><td>44</td><td>Alaska</td><td>1,557</td><td>0.1%</td><td>2</td><td>Florida</td><td>144,165</td><td>13.0%</td></tr>
<tr><td>18</td><td>Arizona</td><td>16,205</td><td>1.5%</td><td>3</td><td>New York</td><td>130,411</td><td>11.7%</td></tr>
<tr><td>37</td><td>Arkansas</td><td>3,499</td><td>0.3%</td><td>4</td><td>Texas</td><td>110,417</td><td>9.9%</td></tr>
<tr><td>1</td><td>California</td><td>164,867</td><td>14.8%</td><td>5</td><td>New Jersey</td><td>56,942</td><td>5.1%</td></tr>
<tr><td>21</td><td>Colorado</td><td>9,973</td><td>0.9%</td><td>6</td><td>Massachusetts</td><td>45,298</td><td>4.1%</td></tr>
<tr><td>16</td><td>Connecticut</td><td>17,758</td><td>1.6%</td><td>7</td><td>Pennsylvania</td><td>37,389</td><td>3.4%</td></tr>
<tr><td>39</td><td>Delaware</td><td>2,722</td><td>0.2%</td><td>8</td><td>Illinois</td><td>33,699</td><td>3.0%</td></tr>
<tr><td>2</td><td>Florida</td><td>144,165</td><td>13.0%</td><td>9</td><td>Virginia</td><td>33,365</td><td>3.0%</td></tr>
<tr><td>12</td><td>Georgia</td><td>25,870</td><td>2.3%</td><td>10</td><td>Maryland</td><td>29,031</td><td>2.6%</td></tr>
<tr><td>30</td><td>Hawaii</td><td>6,703</td><td>0.6%</td><td>11</td><td>Washington</td><td>25,984</td><td>2.3%</td></tr>
<tr><td>42</td><td>Idaho</td><td>1,928</td><td>0.2%</td><td>12</td><td>Georgia</td><td>25,870</td><td>2.3%</td></tr>
<tr><td>8</td><td>Illinois</td><td>33,699</td><td>3.0%</td><td>13</td><td>Michigan</td><td>23,179</td><td>2.1%</td></tr>
<tr><td>19</td><td>Indiana</td><td>11,410</td><td>1.0%</td><td>14</td><td>Ohio</td><td>22,131</td><td>2.0%</td></tr>
<tr><td>29</td><td>Iowa</td><td>6,836</td><td>0.6%</td><td>15</td><td>North Carolina</td><td>20,162</td><td>1.8%</td></tr>
<tr><td>31</td><td>Kansas</td><td>6,198</td><td>0.6%</td><td>16</td><td>Connecticut</td><td>17,758</td><td>1.6%</td></tr>
<tr><td>28</td><td>Kentucky</td><td>7,014</td><td>0.6%</td><td>17</td><td>Minnesota</td><td>16,460</td><td>1.5%</td></tr>
<tr><td>26</td><td>Louisiana</td><td>7,696</td><td>0.7%</td><td>18</td><td>Arizona</td><td>16,205</td><td>1.5%</td></tr>
<tr><td>43</td><td>Maine</td><td>1,578</td><td>0.1%</td><td>19</td><td>Indiana</td><td>11,410</td><td>1.0%</td></tr>
<tr><td>10</td><td>Maryland</td><td>29,031</td><td>2.6%</td><td>20</td><td>Tennessee</td><td>10,469</td><td>0.9%</td></tr>
<tr><td>6</td><td>Massachusetts</td><td>45,298</td><td>4.1%</td><td>21</td><td>Colorado</td><td>9,973</td><td>0.9%</td></tr>
<tr><td>13</td><td>Michigan</td><td>23,179</td><td>2.1%</td><td>22</td><td>Wisconsin</td><td>8,268</td><td>0.7%</td></tr>
<tr><td>17</td><td>Minnesota</td><td>16,460</td><td>1.5%</td><td>23</td><td>Missouri</td><td>8,076</td><td>0.7%</td></tr>
<tr><td>41</td><td>Mississippi</td><td>2,087</td><td>0.2%</td><td>24</td><td>Nevada</td><td>7,957</td><td>0.7%</td></tr>
<tr><td>23</td><td>Missouri</td><td>8,076</td><td>0.7%</td><td>25</td><td>Oregon</td><td>7,712</td><td>0.7%</td></tr>
<tr><td>50</td><td>Montana</td><td>296</td><td>0.0%</td><td>26</td><td>Louisiana</td><td>7,696</td><td>0.7%</td></tr>
<tr><td>34</td><td>Nebraska</td><td>4,853</td><td>0.4%</td><td>27</td><td>Oklahoma</td><td>7,322</td><td>0.7%</td></tr>
<tr><td>24</td><td>Nevada</td><td>7,957</td><td>0.7%</td><td>28</td><td>Kentucky</td><td>7,014</td><td>0.6%</td></tr>
<tr><td>40</td><td>New Hampshire</td><td>2,236</td><td>0.2%</td><td>29</td><td>Iowa</td><td>6,836</td><td>0.6%</td></tr>
<tr><td>5</td><td>New Jersey</td><td>56,942</td><td>5.1%</td><td>30</td><td>Hawaii</td><td>6,703</td><td>0.6%</td></tr>
<tr><td>38</td><td>New Mexico</td><td>2,771</td><td>0.2%</td><td>31</td><td>Kansas</td><td>6,198</td><td>0.6%</td></tr>
<tr><td>3</td><td>New York</td><td>130,411</td><td>11.7%</td><td>32</td><td>South Carolina</td><td>5,447</td><td>0.5%</td></tr>
<tr><td>15</td><td>North Carolina</td><td>20,162</td><td>1.8%</td><td>33</td><td>Utah</td><td>5,019</td><td>0.5%</td></tr>
<tr><td>45</td><td>North Dakota</td><td>1,489</td><td>0.1%</td><td>34</td><td>Nebraska</td><td>4,853</td><td>0.4%</td></tr>
<tr><td>14</td><td>Ohio</td><td>22,131</td><td>2.0%</td><td>35</td><td>Rhode Island</td><td>4,798</td><td>0.4%</td></tr>
<tr><td>27</td><td>Oklahoma</td><td>7,322</td><td>0.7%</td><td>36</td><td>Alabama</td><td>4,475</td><td>0.4%</td></tr>
<tr><td>25</td><td>Oregon</td><td>7,712</td><td>0.7%</td><td>37</td><td>Arkansas</td><td>3,499</td><td>0.3%</td></tr>
<tr><td>7</td><td>Pennsylvania</td><td>37,389</td><td>3.4%</td><td>38</td><td>New Mexico</td><td>2,771</td><td>0.2%</td></tr>
<tr><td>35</td><td>Rhode Island</td><td>4,798</td><td>0.4%</td><td>39</td><td>Delaware</td><td>2,722</td><td>0.2%</td></tr>
<tr><td>32</td><td>South Carolina</td><td>5,447</td><td>0.5%</td><td>40</td><td>New Hampshire</td><td>2,236</td><td>0.2%</td></tr>
<tr><td>46</td><td>South Dakota</td><td>1,273</td><td>0.1%</td><td>41</td><td>Mississippi</td><td>2,087</td><td>0.2%</td></tr>
<tr><td>20</td><td>Tennessee</td><td>10,469</td><td>0.9%</td><td>42</td><td>Idaho</td><td>1,928</td><td>0.2%</td></tr>
<tr><td>4</td><td>Texas</td><td>110,417</td><td>9.9%</td><td>43</td><td>Maine</td><td>1,578</td><td>0.1%</td></tr>
<tr><td>33</td><td>Utah</td><td>5,019</td><td>0.5%</td><td>44</td><td>Alaska</td><td>1,557</td><td>0.1%</td></tr>
<tr><td>47</td><td>Vermont</td><td>933</td><td>0.1%</td><td>45</td><td>North Dakota</td><td>1,489</td><td>0.1%</td></tr>
<tr><td>9</td><td>Virginia</td><td>33,365</td><td>3.0%</td><td>46</td><td>South Dakota</td><td>1,273</td><td>0.1%</td></tr>
<tr><td>11</td><td>Washington</td><td>25,984</td><td>2.3%</td><td>47</td><td>Vermont</td><td>933</td><td>0.1%</td></tr>
<tr><td>48</td><td>West Virginia</td><td>867</td><td>0.1%</td><td>48</td><td>West Virginia</td><td>867</td><td>0.1%</td></tr>
<tr><td>22</td><td>Wisconsin</td><td>8,268</td><td>0.7%</td><td>49</td><td>Wyoming</td><td>328</td><td>0.0%</td></tr>
<tr><td>49</td><td>Wyoming</td><td>328</td><td>0.0%</td><td>50</td><td>Montana</td><td>296</td><td>0.0%</td></tr>
<tr><td></td><td></td><td></td><td></td><td></td><td>District of Columbia</td><td>4,160</td><td>0.4%</td></tr>
</table>

Source: U.S. Bureau of the Census
"State Population Totals Tables" (http://www.census.gov/programs-surveys/popest/data/data-sets.html)
*From July 1, 2016 to June 30, 2017. Net International Migration is the difference between migration to an area from outside the United States (immigration) and migration from the area to outside the United States (emigration) during the period. Includes legal immigration and estimates of undocumented immigration.

Percent of Population Foreign Born in 2016

National Percent = 13.5% of Population*

RANK	STATE	PERCENT
45	Alabama	3.4
24	Alaska	7.7
14	Arizona	13.5
37	Arkansas	4.6
1	California	27.2
17	Colorado	9.8
10	Connecticut	14.4
20	Delaware	9.4
4	Florida	20.6
16	Georgia	10.1
6	Hawaii	18.4
29	Idaho	5.8
13	Illinois	13.9
32	Indiana	5.3
33	Iowa	5.1
25	Kansas	7.1
44	Kentucky	3.5
40	Louisiana	4.1
42	Maine	3.8
9	Maryland	15.3
8	Massachusetts	16.5
28	Michigan	6.7
22	Minnesota	8.2
49	Mississippi	2.0
40	Missouri	4.1
48	Montana	2.1
26	Nebraska	7.0
5	Nevada	20.0
31	New Hampshire	5.7
3	New Jersey	22.5
19	New Mexico	9.5
2	New York	23.0
23	North Carolina	7.8
46	North Dakota	3.2
39	Ohio	4.4
29	Oklahoma	5.8
18	Oregon	9.6
27	Pennsylvania	6.8
11	Rhode Island	14.1
35	South Carolina	4.8
43	South Dakota	3.6
35	Tennessee	4.8
7	Texas	17.0
21	Utah	8.3
38	Vermont	4.5
15	Virginia	12.3
12	Washington	14.0
50	West Virginia	1.7
34	Wisconsin	5.0
46	Wyoming	3.2

RANK	STATE	PERCENT
1	California	27.2
2	New York	23.0
3	New Jersey	22.5
4	Florida	20.6
5	Nevada	20.0
6	Hawaii	18.4
7	Texas	17.0
8	Massachusetts	16.5
9	Maryland	15.3
10	Connecticut	14.4
11	Rhode Island	14.1
12	Washington	14.0
13	Illinois	13.9
14	Arizona	13.5
15	Virginia	12.3
16	Georgia	10.1
17	Colorado	9.8
18	Oregon	9.6
19	New Mexico	9.5
20	Delaware	9.4
21	Utah	8.3
22	Minnesota	8.2
23	North Carolina	7.8
24	Alaska	7.7
25	Kansas	7.1
26	Nebraska	7.0
27	Pennsylvania	6.8
28	Michigan	6.7
29	Idaho	5.8
29	Oklahoma	5.8
31	New Hampshire	5.7
32	Indiana	5.3
33	Iowa	5.1
34	Wisconsin	5.0
35	South Carolina	4.8
35	Tennessee	4.8
37	Arkansas	4.6
38	Vermont	4.5
39	Ohio	4.4
40	Louisiana	4.1
40	Missouri	4.1
42	Maine	3.8
43	South Dakota	3.6
44	Kentucky	3.5
45	Alabama	3.4
46	North Dakota	3.2
46	Wyoming	3.2
48	Montana	2.1
49	Mississippi	2.0
50	West Virginia	1.7

District of Columbia — 13.3

Source: U.S. Bureau of the Census

"2016 American Community Survey-Table R0501" (http://www.census.gov/programs-surveys/acs/)

*"Foreign born" are persons not born in the United States, Puerto Rico, a U.S. Island Area, or abroad of American parent or parents.

Percent of Population Speaking a Language Other Than English at Home in 2016
National Percent = 21.6%*

ALPHA ORDER

RANK	STATE	PERCENT
47	Alabama	5.1
17	Alaska	16.5
8	Arizona	27.1
37	Arkansas	7.3
1	California	44.6
16	Colorado	17.1
13	Connecticut	22.7
22	Delaware	12.9
7	Florida	28.8
21	Georgia	14.0
9	Hawaii	26.5
28	Idaho	10.8
11	Illinois	22.9
32	Indiana	8.7
34	Iowa	7.7
23	Kansas	11.7
45	Kentucky	5.2
33	Louisiana	8.1
43	Maine	6.2
15	Maryland	18.9
10	Massachusetts	23.7
30	Michigan	9.5
24	Minnesota	11.6
48	Mississippi	3.8
42	Missouri	6.3
49	Montana	3.7
25	Nebraska	11.5
6	Nevada	30.7
34	New Hampshire	7.7
4	New Jersey	31.7
3	New Mexico	34.5
5	New York	31.0
25	North Carolina	11.5
45	North Dakota	5.2
38	Ohio	7.0
29	Oklahoma	10.3
20	Oregon	15.2
27	Pennsylvania	11.3
12	Rhode Island	22.8
40	South Carolina	6.8
41	South Dakota	6.5
38	Tennessee	7.0
2	Texas	35.6
19	Utah	15.3
44	Vermont	5.5
18	Virginia	16.2
14	Washington	19.3
50	West Virginia	2.5
31	Wisconsin	8.8
36	Wyoming	7.6

RANK ORDER

RANK	STATE	PERCENT
1	California	44.6
2	Texas	35.6
3	New Mexico	34.5
4	New Jersey	31.7
5	New York	31.0
6	Nevada	30.7
7	Florida	28.8
8	Arizona	27.1
9	Hawaii	26.5
10	Massachusetts	23.7
11	Illinois	22.9
12	Rhode Island	22.8
13	Connecticut	22.7
14	Washington	19.3
15	Maryland	18.9
16	Colorado	17.1
17	Alaska	16.5
18	Virginia	16.2
19	Utah	15.3
20	Oregon	15.2
21	Georgia	14.0
22	Delaware	12.9
23	Kansas	11.7
24	Minnesota	11.6
25	Nebraska	11.5
25	North Carolina	11.5
27	Pennsylvania	11.3
28	Idaho	10.8
29	Oklahoma	10.3
30	Michigan	9.5
31	Wisconsin	8.8
32	Indiana	8.7
33	Louisiana	8.1
34	Iowa	7.7
34	New Hampshire	7.7
36	Wyoming	7.6
37	Arkansas	7.3
38	Ohio	7.0
38	Tennessee	7.0
40	South Carolina	6.8
41	South Dakota	6.5
42	Missouri	6.3
43	Maine	6.2
44	Vermont	5.5
45	Kentucky	5.2
45	North Dakota	5.2
47	Alabama	5.1
48	Mississippi	3.8
49	Montana	3.7
50	West Virginia	2.5

District of Columbia 17.1

Source: U.S. Bureau of the Census
"2016 American Community Survey-Table R1601" (http://www.census.gov/programs-surveys/acs/)
*Population five years old and older.

Percent of Population Speaking Spanish at Home in 2016

National Percent = 13.3%*

ALPHA ORDER

RANK	STATE	PERCENT
37	Alabama	3.2
36	Alaska	3.7
6	Arizona	20.4
26	Arkansas	5.2
2	California	29.0
10	Colorado	12.0
12	Connecticut	11.9
24	Delaware	7.1
5	Florida	21.3
19	Georgia	8.0
42	Hawaii	2.2
18	Idaho	8.1
9	Illinois	13.5
28	Indiana	4.9
33	Iowa	4.0
20	Kansas	7.8
39	Kentucky	2.6
35	Louisiana	3.8
49	Maine	0.9
17	Maryland	8.3
14	Massachusetts	9.0
38	Michigan	3.0
34	Minnesota	3.9
41	Mississippi	2.4
39	Missouri	2.6
47	Montana	1.2
21	Nebraska	7.7
4	Nevada	21.8
42	New Hampshire	2.2
7	New Jersey	16.5
3	New Mexico	26.8
8	New York	15.2
22	North Carolina	7.4
46	North Dakota	1.8
42	Ohio	2.2
25	Oklahoma	7.0
14	Oregon	9.0
28	Pennsylvania	4.9
10	Rhode Island	12.0
31	South Carolina	4.4
45	South Dakota	2.1
32	Tennessee	4.2
1	Texas	29.6
13	Utah	10.4
49	Vermont	0.9
23	Virginia	7.2
16	Washington	8.5
48	West Virginia	1.1
30	Wisconsin	4.6
27	Wyoming	5.0

RANK ORDER

RANK	STATE	PERCENT
1	Texas	29.6
2	California	29.0
3	New Mexico	26.8
4	Nevada	21.8
5	Florida	21.3
6	Arizona	20.4
7	New Jersey	16.5
8	New York	15.2
9	Illinois	13.5
10	Colorado	12.0
10	Rhode Island	12.0
12	Connecticut	11.9
13	Utah	10.4
14	Massachusetts	9.0
14	Oregon	9.0
16	Washington	8.5
17	Maryland	8.3
18	Idaho	8.1
19	Georgia	8.0
20	Kansas	7.8
21	Nebraska	7.7
22	North Carolina	7.4
23	Virginia	7.2
24	Delaware	7.1
25	Oklahoma	7.0
26	Arkansas	5.2
27	Wyoming	5.0
28	Indiana	4.9
28	Pennsylvania	4.9
30	Wisconsin	4.6
31	South Carolina	4.4
32	Tennessee	4.2
33	Iowa	4.0
34	Minnesota	3.9
35	Louisiana	3.8
36	Alaska	3.7
37	Alabama	3.2
38	Michigan	3.0
39	Kentucky	2.6
39	Missouri	2.6
41	Mississippi	2.4
42	Hawaii	2.2
42	New Hampshire	2.2
42	Ohio	2.2
45	South Dakota	2.1
46	North Dakota	1.8
47	Montana	1.2
48	West Virginia	1.1
49	Maine	0.9
49	Vermont	0.9
	District of Columbia	9.2

Source: U.S. Bureau of the Census
   "2016 American Community Survey-Table R1602" (http://www.census.gov/programs-surveys/acs/)
*Population five years old and older.

Marriage Rate for Men in 2016

National Rate = 18.2 Marriages per 1,000 Men*

ALPHA ORDER

RANK	STATE	RATE
33	Alabama	16.7
4	Alaska	22.5
35	Arizona	16.5
5	Arkansas	22.2
24	California	18.2
3	Colorado	22.6
41	Connecticut	15.9
47	Delaware	14.1
30	Florida	16.9
12	Georgia	20.3
7	Hawaii	21.4
16	Idaho	19.5
30	Illinois	16.9
15	Indiana	19.9
38	Iowa	16.2
14	Kansas	20.1
21	Kentucky	18.9
46	Louisiana	14.7
49	Maine	12.6
27	Maryland	17.6
34	Massachusetts	16.6
35	Michigan	16.5
28	Minnesota	17.3
6	Mississippi	21.9
28	Missouri	17.3
25	Montana	18.1
26	Nebraska	18.0
16	Nevada	19.5
38	New Hampshire	16.2
44	New Jersey	15.4
45	New Mexico	15.3
40	New York	16.1
22	North Carolina	18.4
11	North Dakota	20.7
30	Ohio	16.9
8	Oklahoma	21.1
22	Oregon	18.4
42	Pennsylvania	15.7
43	Rhode Island	15.5
18	South Carolina	19.4
20	South Dakota	19.1
10	Tennessee	21.0
8	Texas	21.1
1	Utah	27.0
50	Vermont	12.1
13	Virginia	20.2
19	Washington	19.3
48	West Virginia	13.5
35	Wisconsin	16.5
2	Wyoming	23.7

RANK ORDER

RANK	STATE	RATE
1	Utah	27.0
2	Wyoming	23.7
3	Colorado	22.6
4	Alaska	22.5
5	Arkansas	22.2
6	Mississippi	21.9
7	Hawaii	21.4
8	Oklahoma	21.1
8	Texas	21.1
10	Tennessee	21.0
11	North Dakota	20.7
12	Georgia	20.3
13	Virginia	20.2
14	Kansas	20.1
15	Indiana	19.9
16	Idaho	19.5
16	Nevada	19.5
18	South Carolina	19.4
19	Washington	19.3
20	South Dakota	19.1
21	Kentucky	18.9
22	North Carolina	18.4
22	Oregon	18.4
24	California	18.2
25	Montana	18.1
26	Nebraska	18.0
27	Maryland	17.6
28	Minnesota	17.3
28	Missouri	17.3
30	Florida	16.9
30	Illinois	16.9
30	Ohio	16.9
33	Alabama	16.7
34	Massachusetts	16.6
35	Arizona	16.5
35	Michigan	16.5
35	Wisconsin	16.5
38	Iowa	16.2
38	New Hampshire	16.2
40	New York	16.1
41	Connecticut	15.9
42	Pennsylvania	15.7
43	Rhode Island	15.5
44	New Jersey	15.4
45	New Mexico	15.3
46	Louisiana	14.7
47	Delaware	14.1
48	West Virginia	13.5
49	Maine	12.6
50	Vermont	12.1

District of Columbia		27.8

Source: U.S. Bureau of the Census
"2016 American Community Survey-Table GCT1252" (http://www.census.gov/programs-surveys/acs/)
*Men age 15 and older. Marriages in the last year.

Estimated Median Age of Men at First Marriage in 2016

National Median = 29.9 Years*

ALPHA ORDER

RANK	STATE	YEARS
43	Alabama	28.3
8	Alaska	30.6
19	Arizona	29.8
48	Arkansas	27.2
8	California	30.6
28	Colorado	29.3
1	Connecticut	31.6
8	Delaware	30.6
6	Florida	30.7
28	Georgia	29.3
31	Hawaii	28.9
49	Idaho	27.0
13	Illinois	30.4
31	Indiana	28.9
38	Iowa	28.6
47	Kansas	27.5
41	Kentucky	28.4
19	Louisiana	29.8
15	Maine	30.0
12	Maryland	30.5
2	Massachusetts	31.2
16	Michigan	29.9
24	Minnesota	29.6
38	Mississippi	28.6
36	Missouri	28.7
24	Montana	29.6
36	Nebraska	28.7
22	Nevada	29.7
8	New Hampshire	30.6
4	New Jersey	30.9
40	New Mexico	28.5
3	New York	31.0
30	North Carolina	29.2
44	North Dakota	28.1
26	Ohio	29.5
46	Oklahoma	27.7
22	Oregon	29.7
13	Pennsylvania	30.4
4	Rhode Island	30.9
16	South Carolina	29.9
45	South Dakota	28.0
41	Tennessee	28.4
31	Texas	28.9
50	Utah	26.3
6	Vermont	30.7
16	Virginia	29.9
26	Washington	29.5
34	West Virginia	28.8
19	Wisconsin	29.8
34	Wyoming	28.8

RANK ORDER

RANK	STATE	YEARS
1	Connecticut	31.6
2	Massachusetts	31.2
3	New York	31.0
4	New Jersey	30.9
4	Rhode Island	30.9
6	Florida	30.7
6	Vermont	30.7
8	Alaska	30.6
8	California	30.6
8	Delaware	30.6
8	New Hampshire	30.6
12	Maryland	30.5
13	Illinois	30.4
13	Pennsylvania	30.4
15	Maine	30.0
16	Michigan	29.9
16	South Carolina	29.9
16	Virginia	29.9
19	Arizona	29.8
19	Louisiana	29.8
19	Wisconsin	29.8
22	Nevada	29.7
22	Oregon	29.7
24	Minnesota	29.6
24	Montana	29.6
26	Ohio	29.5
26	Washington	29.5
28	Colorado	29.3
28	Georgia	29.3
30	North Carolina	29.2
31	Hawaii	28.9
31	Indiana	28.9
31	Texas	28.9
34	West Virginia	28.8
34	Wyoming	28.8
36	Missouri	28.7
36	Nebraska	28.7
38	Iowa	28.6
38	Mississippi	28.6
40	New Mexico	28.5
41	Kentucky	28.4
41	Tennessee	28.4
43	Alabama	28.3
44	North Dakota	28.1
45	South Dakota	28.0
46	Oklahoma	27.7
47	Kansas	27.5
48	Arkansas	27.2
49	Idaho	27.0
50	Utah	26.3

| | District of Columbia | 30.9 |

Source: U.S. Bureau of the Census
  "2016 American Community Survey-Table R1204" (http://www.census.gov/programs-surveys/acs/)
*The median age at first marriage is calculated indirectly by estimating the proportion of young people who will marry during their lifetime, calculating one-half of this proportion, and determining the age (at the time of the survey) of people at this half-way mark. It does not represent the actual median age of the population who married during the calendar year.

Marriage Rate for Women in 2016

National Rate = 17.0 Marriages per 1,000 Women*

ALPHA ORDER

RANK	STATE	RATE
34	Alabama	15.9
2	Alaska	25.7
27	Arizona	16.9
5	Arkansas	20.9
30	California	16.5
3	Colorado	23.5
34	Connecticut	15.9
49	Delaware	13.2
42	Florida	14.5
21	Georgia	17.7
9	Hawaii	19.9
6	Idaho	20.7
39	Illinois	15.2
8	Indiana	20.0
34	Iowa	15.9
13	Kansas	19.3
19	Kentucky	18.1
41	Louisiana	15.0
37	Maine	15.5
29	Maryland	16.7
40	Massachusetts	15.1
31	Michigan	16.4
26	Minnesota	17.2
11	Mississippi	19.7
28	Missouri	16.8
19	Montana	18.1
25	Nebraska	17.4
17	Nevada	18.3
37	New Hampshire	15.5
50	New Jersey	13.1
48	New Mexico	13.6
44	New York	14.2
21	North Carolina	17.7
15	North Dakota	18.7
33	Ohio	16.0
9	Oklahoma	19.9
24	Oregon	17.5
43	Pennsylvania	14.3
46	Rhode Island	14.0
21	South Carolina	17.7
15	South Dakota	18.7
12	Tennessee	19.5
7	Texas	20.6
1	Utah	26.7
44	Vermont	14.2
18	Virginia	18.2
14	Washington	19.0
47	West Virginia	13.9
31	Wisconsin	16.4
4	Wyoming	22.6

RANK ORDER

RANK	STATE	RATE
1	Utah	26.7
2	Alaska	25.7
3	Colorado	23.5
4	Wyoming	22.6
5	Arkansas	20.9
6	Idaho	20.7
7	Texas	20.6
8	Indiana	20.0
9	Hawaii	19.9
9	Oklahoma	19.9
11	Mississippi	19.7
12	Tennessee	19.5
13	Kansas	19.3
14	Washington	19.0
15	North Dakota	18.7
15	South Dakota	18.7
17	Nevada	18.3
18	Virginia	18.2
19	Kentucky	18.1
19	Montana	18.1
21	Georgia	17.7
21	North Carolina	17.7
21	South Carolina	17.7
24	Oregon	17.5
25	Nebraska	17.4
26	Minnesota	17.2
27	Arizona	16.9
28	Missouri	16.8
29	Maryland	16.7
30	California	16.5
31	Michigan	16.4
31	Wisconsin	16.4
33	Ohio	16.0
34	Alabama	15.9
34	Connecticut	15.9
34	Iowa	15.9
37	Maine	15.5
37	New Hampshire	15.5
39	Illinois	15.2
40	Massachusetts	15.1
41	Louisiana	15.0
42	Florida	14.5
43	Pennsylvania	14.3
44	New York	14.2
44	Vermont	14.2
46	Rhode Island	14.0
47	West Virginia	13.9
48	New Mexico	13.6
49	Delaware	13.2
50	New Jersey	13.1

District of Columbia	23.5

Source: U.S. Bureau of the Census
   "2016 American Community Survey-Table GCT1251" (http://www.census.gov/programs-surveys/acs/)
*Women age 15 and older. Marriages in the last year.

Estimated Median Age of Women at First Marriage in 2016

National Median = 27.9 Years*

ALPHA ORDER

RANK	STATE	YEARS
41	Alabama	26.3
34	Alaska	26.8
17	Arizona	28.0
48	Arkansas	25.6
10	California	28.7
26	Colorado	27.3
4	Connecticut	29.5
11	Delaware	28.6
6	Florida	29.0
28	Georgia	27.1
20	Hawaii	27.7
49	Idaho	25.1
9	Illinois	28.8
32	Indiana	26.9
34	Iowa	26.8
44	Kansas	26.0
41	Kentucky	26.3
24	Louisiana	27.5
29	Maine	27.0
7	Maryland	28.9
2	Massachusetts	29.8
18	Michigan	27.9
22	Minnesota	27.6
38	Mississippi	26.6
26	Missouri	27.3
40	Montana	26.4
43	Nebraska	26.2
15	Nevada	28.2
12	New Hampshire	28.4
5	New Jersey	29.3
34	New Mexico	26.8
2	New York	29.8
20	North Carolina	27.7
37	North Dakota	26.7
19	Ohio	27.8
47	Oklahoma	25.7
22	Oregon	27.6
7	Pennsylvania	28.9
1	Rhode Island	30.0
12	South Carolina	28.4
44	South Dakota	26.0
29	Tennessee	27.0
32	Texas	26.9
50	Utah	24.7
12	Vermont	28.4
25	Virginia	27.4
29	Washington	27.0
39	West Virginia	26.5
16	Wisconsin	28.1
44	Wyoming	26.0

RANK ORDER

RANK	STATE	YEARS
1	Rhode Island	30.0
2	Massachusetts	29.8
2	New York	29.8
4	Connecticut	29.5
5	New Jersey	29.3
6	Florida	29.0
7	Maryland	28.9
7	Pennsylvania	28.9
9	Illinois	28.8
10	California	28.7
11	Delaware	28.6
12	New Hampshire	28.4
12	South Carolina	28.4
12	Vermont	28.4
15	Nevada	28.2
16	Wisconsin	28.1
17	Arizona	28.0
18	Michigan	27.9
19	Ohio	27.8
20	Hawaii	27.7
20	North Carolina	27.7
22	Minnesota	27.6
22	Oregon	27.6
24	Louisiana	27.5
25	Virginia	27.4
26	Colorado	27.3
26	Missouri	27.3
28	Georgia	27.1
29	Maine	27.0
29	Tennessee	27.0
29	Washington	27.0
32	Indiana	26.9
32	Texas	26.9
34	Alaska	26.8
34	Iowa	26.8
34	New Mexico	26.8
37	North Dakota	26.7
38	Mississippi	26.6
39	West Virginia	26.5
40	Montana	26.4
41	Alabama	26.3
41	Kentucky	26.3
43	Nebraska	26.2
44	Kansas	26.0
44	South Dakota	26.0
44	Wyoming	26.0
47	Oklahoma	25.7
48	Arkansas	25.6
49	Idaho	25.1
50	Utah	24.7
	District of Columbia	30.3

Source: U.S. Bureau of the Census
   "2016 American Community Survey-Table R1205" (http://www.census.gov/programs-surveys/acs/)
*The median age at first marriage is calculated indirectly by estimating the proportion of young people who will marry during their lifetime, calculating one-half of this proportion, and determining the age (at the time of the survey) of people at this half-way mark. It does not represent the actual median age of the population who married during the calendar year.

Ratio of Unmarried Men to Unmarried Women in 2016

National Ratio = 110.9 Unmarried Men for Every 100 Unmarried Women*

ALPHA ORDER			RANK ORDER		
RANK	STATE	RATIO	RANK	STATE	RATIO
46	Alabama	105.8	1	Alaska	131.9
1	Alaska	131.9	2	North Dakota	130.4
14	Arizona	115.0	3	South Dakota	126.7
35	Arkansas	109.6	4	Hawaii	126.5
20	California	114.0	5	Montana	121.8
6	Colorado	121.2	6	Colorado	121.2
32	Connecticut	110.6	7	Kansas	119.0
40	Delaware	107.8	8	Washington	118.1
34	Florida	109.9	9	Utah	117.6
49	Georgia	104.8	10	Idaho	117.1
4	Hawaii	126.5	11	Nevada	115.6
10	Idaho	117.1	12	Minnesota	115.5
39	Illinois	108.2	13	New Mexico	115.2
30	Indiana	111.0	14	Arizona	115.0
18	Iowa	114.7	15	Nebraska	114.9
7	Kansas	119.0	15	New Hampshire	114.9
27	Kentucky	112.0	17	Oklahoma	114.8
42	Louisiana	106.1	18	Iowa	114.7
23	Maine	113.0	19	West Virginia	114.5
47	Maryland	105.4	20	California	114.0
43	Massachusetts	106.0	21	Wisconsin	113.8
36	Michigan	109.5	22	Wyoming	113.7
12	Minnesota	115.5	23	Maine	113.0
50	Mississippi	102.0	24	Oregon	112.5
29	Missouri	111.6	24	Virginia	112.5
5	Montana	121.8	26	Texas	112.4
15	Nebraska	114.9	27	Kentucky	112.0
11	Nevada	115.6	28	New Jersey	111.7
15	New Hampshire	114.9	29	Missouri	111.6
28	New Jersey	111.7	30	Indiana	111.0
13	New Mexico	115.2	30	Vermont	111.0
47	New York	105.4	32	Connecticut	110.6
45	North Carolina	105.9	33	Pennsylvania	110.1
2	North Dakota	130.4	34	Florida	109.9
37	Ohio	109.4	35	Arkansas	109.6
17	Oklahoma	114.8	36	Michigan	109.5
24	Oregon	112.5	37	Ohio	109.4
33	Pennsylvania	110.1	38	Tennessee	108.9
41	Rhode Island	107.4	39	Illinois	108.2
43	South Carolina	106.0	40	Delaware	107.8
3	South Dakota	126.7	41	Rhode Island	107.4
38	Tennessee	108.9	42	Louisiana	106.1
26	Texas	112.4	43	Massachusetts	106.0
9	Utah	117.6	43	South Carolina	106.0
30	Vermont	111.0	45	North Carolina	105.9
24	Virginia	112.5	46	Alabama	105.8
8	Washington	118.1	47	Maryland	105.4
19	West Virginia	114.5	47	New York	105.4
21	Wisconsin	113.8	49	Georgia	104.8
22	Wyoming	113.7	50	Mississippi	102.0
				District of Columbia	89.8

Source: U.S. Bureau of the Census
   "2016 American Community Survey-Table R1203" (http://www.census.gov/programs-surveys/acs/)
*Population 15 to 44 years old.

Divorce Rate for Men in 2016

National Rate = 7.8 Divorces per 1,000 Men*

ALPHA ORDER			RANK ORDER		
RANK	**STATE**	**RATE**	**RANK**	**STATE**	**RATE**
15	Alabama	8.7	1	Idaho	12.4
10	Alaska	9.2	2	Arkansas	11.3
36	Arizona	7.2	3	Kansas	10.5
2	Arkansas	11.3	3	West Virginia	10.5
45	California	6.6	5	Oklahoma	10.4
14	Colorado	8.8	6	Nevada	10.3
47	Connecticut	6.1	7	Montana	9.8
37	Delaware	7.1	8	Indiana	9.6
18	Florida	8.5	8	Missouri	9.6
21	Georgia	8.2	10	Alaska	9.2
50	Hawaii	5.6	10	Kentucky	9.2
1	Idaho	12.4	12	Tennessee	9.1
39	Illinois	6.9	13	Louisiana	8.9
8	Indiana	9.6	14	Colorado	8.8
34	Iowa	7.3	15	Alabama	8.7
3	Kansas	10.5	16	North Dakota	8.6
10	Kentucky	9.2	16	South Carolina	8.6
13	Louisiana	8.9	18	Florida	8.5
27	Maine	7.9	18	Washington	8.5
24	Maryland	8.1	20	Michigan	8.3
48	Massachusetts	6.0	21	Georgia	8.2
20	Michigan	8.3	21	New Hampshire	8.2
43	Minnesota	6.7	21	Virginia	8.2
32	Mississippi	7.5	24	Maryland	8.1
8	Missouri	9.6	24	Texas	8.1
7	Montana	9.8	26	Oregon	8.0
34	Nebraska	7.3	27	Maine	7.9
6	Nevada	10.3	28	North Carolina	7.8
21	New Hampshire	8.2	29	Ohio	7.7
40	New Jersey	6.8	30	New Mexico	7.6
30	New Mexico	7.6	30	Pennsylvania	7.6
49	New York	5.7	32	Mississippi	7.5
28	North Carolina	7.8	33	Wisconsin	7.4
16	North Dakota	8.6	34	Iowa	7.3
29	Ohio	7.7	34	Nebraska	7.3
5	Oklahoma	10.4	36	Arizona	7.2
26	Oregon	8.0	37	Delaware	7.1
30	Pennsylvania	7.6	37	Utah	7.1
46	Rhode Island	6.4	39	Illinois	6.9
16	South Carolina	8.6	40	New Jersey	6.8
43	South Dakota	6.7	40	Vermont	6.8
12	Tennessee	9.1	40	Wyoming	6.8
24	Texas	8.1	43	Minnesota	6.7
37	Utah	7.1	43	South Dakota	6.7
40	Vermont	6.8	45	California	6.6
21	Virginia	8.2	46	Rhode Island	6.4
18	Washington	8.5	47	Connecticut	6.1
3	West Virginia	10.5	48	Massachusetts	6.0
33	Wisconsin	7.4	49	New York	5.7
40	Wyoming	6.8	50	Hawaii	5.6
				District of Columbia	6.7

Source: U.S. Bureau of the Census
"2016 American Community Survey-Table GCT1254" (http://www.census.gov/programs-surveys/acs/)
*Men age 15 and older. Divorces in the last year.

Divorce Rate for Women in 2016

National Rate = 8.2 Divorces per 1,000 Women*

ALPHA ORDER				RANK ORDER		
RANK	STATE	RATE		RANK	STATE	RATE
14	Alabama	9.4		1	Wyoming	14.6
25	Alaska	8.6		2	Arkansas	13.0
11	Arizona	9.9		3	Idaho	11.1
2	Arkansas	13.0		3	Utah	11.1
39	California	7.3		5	Oklahoma	10.6
30	Colorado	8.1		6	Oregon	10.2
14	Connecticut	9.4		7	Montana	10.1
22	Delaware	8.8		8	Kentucky	10.0
27	Florida	8.5		8	Louisiana	10.0
11	Georgia	9.9		8	Tennessee	10.0
41	Hawaii	7.2		11	Arizona	9.9
3	Idaho	11.1		11	Georgia	9.9
45	Illinois	6.8		11	Indiana	9.9
11	Indiana	9.9		14	Alabama	9.4
34	Iowa	7.7		14	Connecticut	9.4
20	Kansas	9.1		14	Nevada	9.4
8	Kentucky	10.0		17	Maine	9.3
8	Louisiana	10.0		18	Texas	9.2
17	Maine	9.3		18	Washington	9.2
28	Maryland	8.2		20	Kansas	9.1
50	Massachusetts	5.6		21	West Virginia	9.0
34	Michigan	7.7		22	Delaware	8.8
45	Minnesota	6.8		22	North Dakota	8.8
24	Mississippi	8.7		24	Mississippi	8.7
28	Missouri	8.2		25	Alaska	8.6
7	Montana	10.1		25	South Carolina	8.6
32	Nebraska	7.9		27	Florida	8.5
14	Nevada	9.4		28	Maryland	8.2
39	New Hampshire	7.3		28	Missouri	8.2
49	New Jersey	6.1		30	Colorado	8.1
30	New Mexico	8.1		30	New Mexico	8.1
48	New York	6.2		32	Nebraska	7.9
32	North Carolina	7.9		32	North Carolina	7.9
22	North Dakota	8.8		34	Iowa	7.7
34	Ohio	7.7		34	Michigan	7.7
5	Oklahoma	10.6		34	Ohio	7.7
6	Oregon	10.2		37	Pennsylvania	7.6
37	Pennsylvania	7.6		38	Virginia	7.4
42	Rhode Island	7.0		39	California	7.3
25	South Carolina	8.6		39	New Hampshire	7.3
42	South Dakota	7.0		41	Hawaii	7.2
8	Tennessee	10.0		42	Rhode Island	7.0
18	Texas	9.2		42	South Dakota	7.0
3	Utah	11.1		42	Wisconsin	7.0
47	Vermont	6.5		45	Illinois	6.8
38	Virginia	7.4		45	Minnesota	6.8
18	Washington	9.2		47	Vermont	6.5
21	West Virginia	9.0		48	New York	6.2
42	Wisconsin	7.0		49	New Jersey	6.1
1	Wyoming	14.6		50	Massachusetts	5.6
					District of Columbia	5.8

Source: U.S. Bureau of the Census
   "2016 American Community Survey-Table GCT1253" (http://www.census.gov/programs-surveys/acs/)
*Women age 15 and older. Divorces in the last year.

Average Family Size in 2016

National Average = 3.27 Persons per Family

RANK	STATE	PERSONS
19	Alabama	3.23
5	Alaska	3.45
12	Arizona	3.30
27	Arkansas	3.15
3	California	3.55
27	Colorado	3.15
24	Connecticut	3.17
18	Delaware	3.25
12	Florida	3.30
9	Georgia	3.34
2	Hawaii	3.63
15	Idaho	3.29
17	Illinois	3.26
29	Indiana	3.14
46	Iowa	3.01
24	Kansas	3.17
41	Kentucky	3.08
11	Louisiana	3.33
45	Maine	3.02
16	Maryland	3.27
26	Massachusetts	3.16
36	Michigan	3.11
36	Minnesota	3.11
12	Mississippi	3.30
40	Missouri	3.09
42	Montana	3.05
38	Nebraska	3.10
6	Nevada	3.42
48	New Hampshire	2.98
9	New Jersey	3.34
7	New Mexico	3.41
8	New York	3.35
29	North Carolina	3.14
48	North Dakota	2.98
42	Ohio	3.05
20	Oklahoma	3.21
38	Oregon	3.10
34	Pennsylvania	3.13
23	Rhode Island	3.18
22	South Carolina	3.19
29	South Dakota	3.14
29	Tennessee	3.14
4	Texas	3.47
1	Utah	3.65
50	Vermont	2.92
21	Virginia	3.20
29	Washington	3.14
44	West Virginia	3.03
46	Wisconsin	3.01
35	Wyoming	3.12

RANK	STATE	PERSONS
1	Utah	3.65
2	Hawaii	3.63
3	California	3.55
4	Texas	3.47
5	Alaska	3.45
6	Nevada	3.42
7	New Mexico	3.41
8	New York	3.35
9	Georgia	3.34
9	New Jersey	3.34
11	Louisiana	3.33
12	Arizona	3.30
12	Florida	3.30
12	Mississippi	3.30
15	Idaho	3.29
16	Maryland	3.27
17	Illinois	3.26
18	Delaware	3.25
19	Alabama	3.23
20	Oklahoma	3.21
21	Virginia	3.20
22	South Carolina	3.19
23	Rhode Island	3.18
24	Connecticut	3.17
24	Kansas	3.17
26	Massachusetts	3.16
27	Arkansas	3.15
27	Colorado	3.15
29	Indiana	3.14
29	North Carolina	3.14
29	South Dakota	3.14
29	Tennessee	3.14
29	Washington	3.14
34	Pennsylvania	3.13
35	Wyoming	3.12
36	Michigan	3.11
36	Minnesota	3.11
38	Nebraska	3.10
38	Oregon	3.10
40	Missouri	3.09
41	Kentucky	3.08
42	Montana	3.05
42	Ohio	3.05
44	West Virginia	3.03
45	Maine	3.02
46	Iowa	3.01
46	Wisconsin	3.01
48	New Hampshire	2.98
48	North Dakota	2.98
50	Vermont	2.92

	District of Columbia	3.25

Source: U.S. Bureau of the Census
"2016 American Community Survey-Table DP02" (http://www.census.gov/programs-surveys/acs/)

Seats in the U.S. House of Representatives in 2018

National Total = 435 Seats*

ALPHA ORDER

RANK	STATE	SEATS	% of USA
22	Alabama	7	1.6%
44	Alaska	1	0.2%
14	Arizona	9	2.1%
30	Arkansas	4	0.9%
1	California	53	12.2%
22	Colorado	7	1.6%
27	Connecticut	5	1.1%
44	Delaware	1	0.2%
3	Florida	27	6.2%
8	Georgia	14	3.2%
39	Hawaii	2	0.5%
39	Idaho	2	0.5%
5	Illinois	18	4.1%
14	Indiana	9	2.1%
30	Iowa	4	0.9%
30	Kansas	4	0.9%
25	Kentucky	6	1.4%
25	Louisiana	6	1.4%
39	Maine	2	0.5%
18	Maryland	8	1.8%
14	Massachusetts	9	2.1%
8	Michigan	14	3.2%
18	Minnesota	8	1.8%
30	Mississippi	4	0.9%
18	Missouri	8	1.8%
44	Montana	1	0.2%
36	Nebraska	3	0.7%
30	Nevada	4	0.9%
39	New Hampshire	2	0.5%
11	New Jersey	12	2.8%
36	New Mexico	3	0.7%
3	New York	27	6.2%
10	North Carolina	13	3.0%
44	North Dakota	1	0.2%
7	Ohio	16	3.7%
27	Oklahoma	5	1.1%
27	Oregon	5	1.1%
5	Pennsylvania	18	4.1%
39	Rhode Island	2	0.5%
22	South Carolina	7	1.6%
44	South Dakota	1	0.2%
14	Tennessee	9	2.1%
2	Texas	36	8.3%
30	Utah	4	0.9%
44	Vermont	1	0.2%
12	Virginia	11	2.5%
13	Washington	10	2.3%
36	West Virginia	3	0.7%
18	Wisconsin	8	1.8%
44	Wyoming	1	0.2%

RANK ORDER

RANK	STATE	SEATS	% of USA
1	California	53	12.2%
2	Texas	36	8.3%
3	Florida	27	6.2%
3	New York	27	6.2%
5	Illinois	18	4.1%
5	Pennsylvania	18	4.1%
7	Ohio	16	3.7%
8	Georgia	14	3.2%
8	Michigan	14	3.2%
10	North Carolina	13	3.0%
11	New Jersey	12	2.8%
12	Virginia	11	2.5%
13	Washington	10	2.3%
14	Arizona	9	2.1%
14	Indiana	9	2.1%
14	Massachusetts	9	2.1%
14	Tennessee	9	2.1%
18	Maryland	8	1.8%
18	Minnesota	8	1.8%
18	Missouri	8	1.8%
18	Wisconsin	8	1.8%
22	Alabama	7	1.6%
22	Colorado	7	1.6%
22	South Carolina	7	1.6%
25	Kentucky	6	1.4%
25	Louisiana	6	1.4%
27	Connecticut	5	1.1%
27	Oklahoma	5	1.1%
27	Oregon	5	1.1%
30	Arkansas	4	0.9%
30	Iowa	4	0.9%
30	Kansas	4	0.9%
30	Mississippi	4	0.9%
30	Nevada	4	0.9%
30	Utah	4	0.9%
36	Nebraska	3	0.7%
36	New Mexico	3	0.7%
36	West Virginia	3	0.7%
39	Hawaii	2	0.5%
39	Idaho	2	0.5%
39	Maine	2	0.5%
39	New Hampshire	2	0.5%
39	Rhode Island	2	0.5%
44	Alaska	1	0.2%
44	Delaware	1	0.2%
44	Montana	1	0.2%
44	North Dakota	1	0.2%
44	South Dakota	1	0.2%
44	Vermont	1	0.2%
44	Wyoming	1	0.2%
	District of Columbia**	0	0.0%

Source: U.S. Bureau of the Census
    "Congressional Apportionment" (http://www.census.gov/topics/public-sector/congressional-apportionment.html)
*This table shows the number of seats after reapportionment of the 2010 Census. This apportionment became effective with the Congress elected in November 2012 and that took office in January 2013.
**The District of Columbia has one non-voting delegate. Each state has two members in the U.S. Senate.

Estimated Population per U.S. House Seat in 2018

National Rate = 747,184 Persons per House Member*

ALPHA ORDER

RANK	STATE	RATE
42	Alabama	696,392
30	Alaska	739,795
12	Arizona	779,586
20	Arkansas	751,070
25	California	745,975
6	Colorado	801,022
36	Connecticut	717,637
2	Delaware	961,939
13	Florida	777,200
26	Georgia	744,956
37	Hawaii	713,769
4	Idaho	858,472
40	Illinois	711,224
28	Indiana	740,758
8	Iowa	786,428
33	Kansas	728,281
27	Kentucky	742,365
11	Louisiana	780,722
45	Maine	667,954
18	Maryland	756,522
17	Massachusetts	762,202
38	Michigan	711,594
41	Minnesota	697,076
24	Mississippi	746,025
16	Missouri	764,192
1	Montana	1,050,493
46	Nebraska	640,025
22	Nevada	749,510
44	New Hampshire	671,398
21	New Jersey	750,470
43	New Mexico	696,023
31	New York	735,163
7	North Carolina	790,263
19	North Dakota	755,393
32	Ohio	728,663
10	Oklahoma	786,173
5	Oregon	828,555
39	Pennsylvania	711,419
50	Rhode Island	529,820
35	South Carolina	717,767
3	South Dakota	869,666
23	Tennessee	746,220
9	Texas	786,239
14	Utah	775,458
47	Vermont	623,657
15	Virginia	770,002
29	Washington	740,574
48	West Virginia	605,286
34	Wisconsin	724,435
49	Wyoming	579,315

RANK ORDER

RANK	STATE	RATE
1	Montana	1,050,493
2	Delaware	961,939
3	South Dakota	869,666
4	Idaho	858,472
5	Oregon	828,555
6	Colorado	801,022
7	North Carolina	790,263
8	Iowa	786,428
9	Texas	786,239
10	Oklahoma	786,173
11	Louisiana	780,722
12	Arizona	779,586
13	Florida	777,200
14	Utah	775,458
15	Virginia	770,002
16	Missouri	764,192
17	Massachusetts	762,202
18	Maryland	756,522
19	North Dakota	755,393
20	Arkansas	751,070
21	New Jersey	750,470
22	Nevada	749,510
23	Tennessee	746,220
24	Mississippi	746,025
25	California	745,975
26	Georgia	744,956
27	Kentucky	742,365
28	Indiana	740,758
29	Washington	740,574
30	Alaska	739,795
31	New York	735,163
32	Ohio	728,663
33	Kansas	728,281
34	Wisconsin	724,435
35	South Carolina	717,767
36	Connecticut	717,637
37	Hawaii	713,769
38	Michigan	711,594
39	Pennsylvania	711,419
40	Illinois	711,224
41	Minnesota	697,076
42	Alabama	696,392
43	New Mexico	696,023
44	New Hampshire	671,398
45	Maine	667,954
46	Nebraska	640,025
47	Vermont	623,657
48	West Virginia	605,286
49	Wyoming	579,315
50	Rhode Island	529,820

District of Columbia** NA

Source: CQ Press using data from U.S. Bureau of the Census
"Congressional Apportionment" (http://www.census.gov/population/apportionment/)
*Rates calculated using 2017 population estimates and do not include population of the District of Columbia. The District has one non-voting delegate. Each state has two members in the U.S. Senate. This table is based only on U.S. Representatives and not U.S. Senate members. This table reflects reapportionment resulting from the 2010 census and taking effect after the 2012 election. **Not applicable.

State Legislators in 2017

National Total = 7,383 Legislators*

ALPHA ORDER

RANK	STATE	LEGISLATORS	% of USA
27	Alabama	140	1.9%
49	Alaska	60	0.8%
43	Arizona	90	1.2%
30	Arkansas	135	1.8%
35	California	120	1.6%
42	Colorado	100	1.4%
9	Connecticut	187	2.5%
48	Delaware	62	0.8%
18	Florida	160	2.2%
3	Georgia	236	3.2%
46	Hawaii	76	1.0%
39	Idaho	105	1.4%
13	Illinois	177	2.4%
19	Indiana	150	2.0%
19	Iowa	150	2.0%
17	Kansas	165	2.2%
29	Kentucky	138	1.9%
25	Louisiana	144	2.0%
10	Maine	186	2.5%
8	Maryland	188	2.5%
6	Massachusetts	200	2.7%
23	Michigan	148	2.0%
5	Minnesota	201	2.7%
14	Mississippi	174	2.4%
7	Missouri	197	2.7%
19	Montana	150	2.0%
50	Nebraska	49	0.7%
47	Nevada	63	0.9%
1	New Hampshire	424	5.7%
35	New Jersey	120	1.6%
38	New Mexico	112	1.5%
4	New York	213	2.9%
15	North Carolina	170	2.3%
26	North Dakota	141	1.9%
32	Ohio	132	1.8%
22	Oklahoma	149	2.0%
43	Oregon	90	1.2%
2	Pennsylvania	253	3.4%
37	Rhode Island	113	1.5%
15	South Carolina	170	2.3%
39	South Dakota	105	1.4%
32	Tennessee	132	1.8%
11	Texas	181	2.5%
41	Utah	104	1.4%
12	Vermont	180	2.4%
27	Virginia	140	1.9%
24	Washington	147	2.0%
31	West Virginia	134	1.8%
32	Wisconsin	132	1.8%
43	Wyoming	90	1.2%

RANK ORDER

RANK	STATE	LEGISLATORS	% of USA
1	New Hampshire	424	5.7%
2	Pennsylvania	253	3.4%
3	Georgia	236	3.2%
4	New York	213	2.9%
5	Minnesota	201	2.7%
6	Massachusetts	200	2.7%
7	Missouri	197	2.7%
8	Maryland	188	2.5%
9	Connecticut	187	2.5%
10	Maine	186	2.5%
11	Texas	181	2.5%
12	Vermont	180	2.4%
13	Illinois	177	2.4%
14	Mississippi	174	2.4%
15	North Carolina	170	2.3%
15	South Carolina	170	2.3%
17	Kansas	165	2.2%
18	Florida	160	2.2%
19	Indiana	150	2.0%
19	Iowa	150	2.0%
19	Montana	150	2.0%
22	Oklahoma	149	2.0%
23	Michigan	148	2.0%
24	Washington	147	2.0%
25	Louisiana	144	2.0%
26	North Dakota	141	1.9%
27	Alabama	140	1.9%
27	Virginia	140	1.9%
29	Kentucky	138	1.9%
30	Arkansas	135	1.8%
31	West Virginia	134	1.8%
32	Ohio	132	1.8%
32	Tennessee	132	1.8%
32	Wisconsin	132	1.8%
35	California	120	1.6%
35	New Jersey	120	1.6%
37	Rhode Island	113	1.5%
38	New Mexico	112	1.5%
39	Idaho	105	1.4%
39	South Dakota	105	1.4%
41	Utah	104	1.4%
42	Colorado	100	1.4%
43	Arizona	90	1.2%
43	Oregon	90	1.2%
43	Wyoming	90	1.2%
46	Hawaii	76	1.0%
47	Nevada	63	0.9%
48	Delaware	62	0.8%
49	Alaska	60	0.8%
50	Nebraska	49	0.7%
	District of Columbia**	NA	NA

Source: National Conference of State Legislatures (Denver, CO)
   "2017 Partisan Composition" (http://www.ncsl.org/research/about-state-legislatures/partisan-composition.aspx)
*There are 1,972 state senators (including Nebraska's 49 unicameral seats) and 5,411 state house members.
**Not applicable.

Population per State Legislator in 2017

National Rate = 44,023 Population per Legislator*

ALPHA ORDER			RANK ORDER		
RANK	STATE	RATE	RANK	STATE	RATE
22	Alabama	34,820	1	California	329,472
42	Alaska	12,330	2	Texas	156,379
6	Arizona	77,959	3	Florida	131,153
32	Arkansas	22,254	4	New York	93,190
1	California	329,472	5	Ohio	88,323
12	Colorado	56,072	6	Arizona	77,959
34	Connecticut	19,188	7	New Jersey	75,047
40	Delaware	15,515	8	Illinois	72,328
3	Florida	131,153	9	Michigan	67,313
19	Georgia	44,192	10	Virginia	60,500
35	Hawaii	18,783	11	North Carolina	60,432
39	Idaho	16,352	12	Colorado	56,072
8	Illinois	72,328	13	Tennessee	50,879
18	Indiana	44,445	14	Pennsylvania	50,615
33	Iowa	20,971	15	Washington	50,379
37	Kansas	17,655	16	Nevada	47,588
25	Kentucky	32,277	17	Oregon	46,031
24	Louisiana	32,530	18	Indiana	44,445
45	Maine	7,182	19	Georgia	44,192
26	Maryland	32,192	20	Wisconsin	43,905
23	Massachusetts	34,299	21	Nebraska	39,185
9	Michigan	67,313	22	Alabama	34,820
30	Minnesota	27,744	23	Massachusetts	34,299
38	Mississippi	17,150	24	Louisiana	32,530
27	Missouri	31,033	25	Kentucky	32,277
46	Montana	7,003	26	Maryland	32,192
21	Nebraska	39,185	27	Missouri	31,033
16	Nevada	47,588	28	Utah	29,825
50	New Hampshire	3,167	29	South Carolina	29,555
7	New Jersey	75,047	30	Minnesota	27,744
36	New Mexico	18,643	31	Oklahoma	26,382
4	New York	93,190	32	Arkansas	22,254
11	North Carolina	60,432	33	Iowa	20,971
48	North Dakota	5,357	34	Connecticut	19,188
5	Ohio	88,323	35	Hawaii	18,783
31	Oklahoma	26,382	36	New Mexico	18,643
17	Oregon	46,031	37	Kansas	17,655
14	Pennsylvania	50,615	38	Mississippi	17,150
43	Rhode Island	9,377	39	Idaho	16,352
29	South Carolina	29,555	40	Delaware	15,515
44	South Dakota	8,283	41	West Virginia	13,551
13	Tennessee	50,879	42	Alaska	12,330
2	Texas	156,379	43	Rhode Island	9,377
28	Utah	29,825	44	South Dakota	8,283
49	Vermont	3,465	45	Maine	7,182
10	Virginia	60,500	46	Montana	7,003
15	Washington	50,379	47	Wyoming	6,437
41	West Virginia	13,551	48	North Dakota	5,357
20	Wisconsin	43,905	49	Vermont	3,465
47	Wyoming	6,437	50	New Hampshire	3,167
				District of Columbia**	NA

Source: CQ Press using data from National Conference of State Legislatures (Denver, CO)

"2017 Partisan Composition" (http://www.ncsl.org/research/about-state-legislatures/partisan-composition.aspx)

*There are 1,972 state senators (including Nebraska's 49 unicameral seats) and 5,411 state house members. National rate does not include population for the District of Columbia. Calculated using 2017 population estimates.

**Not applicable.

Registered Voters in 2016

National Total = 157,596,000

RANK	STATE	REGISTERED	% of USA
24	Alabama	2,526,000	1.6%
48	Alaska	358,000	0.2%
19	Arizona	3,145,000	2.0%
32	Arkansas	1,456,000	0.9%
1	California	16,096,000	10.2%
22	Colorado	2,893,000	1.8%
29	Connecticut	1,763,000	1.1%
45	Delaware	487,000	0.3%
3	Florida	9,604,000	6.1%
10	Georgia	4,892,000	3.1%
44	Hawaii	530,000	0.3%
40	Idaho	790,000	0.5%
6	Illinois	6,665,000	4.2%
17	Indiana	3,298,000	2.1%
31	Iowa	1,657,000	1.1%
33	Kansas	1,438,000	0.9%
26	Kentucky	2,253,000	1.4%
25	Louisiana	2,446,000	1.6%
39	Maine	830,000	0.5%
20	Maryland	3,114,000	2.0%
14	Massachusetts	3,660,000	2.3%
8	Michigan	5,434,000	3.4%
21	Minnesota	3,055,000	1.9%
30	Mississippi	1,725,000	1.1%
15	Missouri	3,333,000	2.1%
42	Montana	581,000	0.4%
36	Nebraska	1,008,000	0.6%
35	Nevada	1,371,000	0.9%
41	New Hampshire	763,000	0.5%
12	New Jersey	4,165,000	2.6%
37	New Mexico	916,000	0.6%
4	New York	9,142,000	5.8%
9	North Carolina	5,194,000	3.3%
47	North Dakota	424,000	0.3%
7	Ohio	6,128,000	3.9%
28	Oklahoma	1,861,000	1.2%
27	Oregon	2,147,000	1.4%
5	Pennsylvania	6,909,000	4.4%
43	Rhode Island	538,000	0.3%
23	South Carolina	2,575,000	1.6%
46	South Dakota	437,000	0.3%
18	Tennessee	3,251,000	2.1%
2	Texas	11,724,000	7.4%
34	Utah	1,398,000	0.9%
49	Vermont	351,000	0.2%
11	Virginia	4,399,000	2.8%
13	Washington	3,906,000	2.5%
38	West Virginia	913,000	0.6%
16	Wisconsin	3,323,000	2.1%
50	Wyoming	304,000	0.2%

RANK	STATE	REGISTERED	% of USA
1	California	16,096,000	10.2%
2	Texas	11,724,000	7.4%
3	Florida	9,604,000	6.1%
4	New York	9,142,000	5.8%
5	Pennsylvania	6,909,000	4.4%
6	Illinois	6,665,000	4.2%
7	Ohio	6,128,000	3.9%
8	Michigan	5,434,000	3.4%
9	North Carolina	5,194,000	3.3%
10	Georgia	4,892,000	3.1%
11	Virginia	4,399,000	2.8%
12	New Jersey	4,165,000	2.6%
13	Washington	3,906,000	2.5%
14	Massachusetts	3,660,000	2.3%
15	Missouri	3,333,000	2.1%
16	Wisconsin	3,323,000	2.1%
17	Indiana	3,298,000	2.1%
18	Tennessee	3,251,000	2.1%
19	Arizona	3,145,000	2.0%
20	Maryland	3,114,000	2.0%
21	Minnesota	3,055,000	1.9%
22	Colorado	2,893,000	1.8%
23	South Carolina	2,575,000	1.6%
24	Alabama	2,526,000	1.6%
25	Louisiana	2,446,000	1.6%
26	Kentucky	2,253,000	1.4%
27	Oregon	2,147,000	1.4%
28	Oklahoma	1,861,000	1.2%
29	Connecticut	1,763,000	1.1%
30	Mississippi	1,725,000	1.1%
31	Iowa	1,657,000	1.1%
32	Arkansas	1,456,000	0.9%
33	Kansas	1,438,000	0.9%
34	Utah	1,398,000	0.9%
35	Nevada	1,371,000	0.9%
36	Nebraska	1,008,000	0.6%
37	New Mexico	916,000	0.6%
38	West Virginia	913,000	0.6%
39	Maine	830,000	0.5%
40	Idaho	790,000	0.5%
41	New Hampshire	763,000	0.5%
42	Montana	581,000	0.4%
43	Rhode Island	538,000	0.3%
44	Hawaii	530,000	0.3%
45	Delaware	487,000	0.3%
46	South Dakota	437,000	0.3%
47	North Dakota	424,000	0.3%
48	Alaska	358,000	0.2%
49	Vermont	351,000	0.2%
50	Wyoming	304,000	0.2%
	District of Columbia	420,000	0.3%

Source: U.S. Bureau of the Census
   "Voting and Registration" (Table 4a, http://www.census.gov/topics/public-sector/voting.html)

Percent of Eligible Voters Reported Registered in 2016

National Percent = 70.3%*

ALPHA ORDER				RANK ORDER		
RANK	STATE	PERCENT		RANK	STATE	PERCENT
37	Alabama	69.2		1	Maine	80.0
27	Alaska	71.3		2	Mississippi	79.5
41	Arizona	68.6		3	Minnesota	76.7
38	Arkansas	68.8		4	Washington	76.5
48	California	64.7		5	Wisconsin	76.3
12	Colorado	74.3		6	Nebraska	75.5
29	Connecticut	71.0		6	Virginia	75.5
20	Delaware	72.8		8	New Hampshire	75.4
45	Florida	66.6		9	North Dakota	75.2
34	Georgia	69.4		10	Maryland	74.9
50	Hawaii	54.4		11	North Carolina	74.6
40	Idaho	68.7		12	Colorado	74.3
12	Illinois	74.3		12	Illinois	74.3
38	Indiana	68.8		12	Missouri	74.3
21	Iowa	72.3		15	Michigan	74.1
31	Kansas	70.9		16	Massachusetts	73.7
34	Kentucky	69.4		17	Montana	73.5
19	Louisiana	73.0		18	Oregon	73.3
1	Maine	80.0		19	Louisiana	73.0
10	Maryland	74.9		20	Delaware	72.8
16	Massachusetts	73.7		21	Iowa	72.3
15	Michigan	74.1		22	Ohio	72.1
3	Minnesota	76.7		23	Pennsylvania	72.0
2	Mississippi	79.5		24	Vermont	71.9
12	Missouri	74.3		25	South Carolina	71.6
17	Montana	73.5		26	South Dakota	71.4
6	Nebraska	75.5		27	Alaska	71.3
34	Nevada	69.4		28	Wyoming	71.1
8	New Hampshire	75.4		29	Connecticut	71.0
33	New Jersey	69.9		29	Utah	71.0
47	New Mexico	65.6		31	Kansas	70.9
46	New York	66.5		32	Rhode Island	70.3
11	North Carolina	74.6		33	New Jersey	69.9
9	North Dakota	75.2		34	Georgia	69.4
22	Ohio	72.1		34	Kentucky	69.4
42	Oklahoma	67.8		34	Nevada	69.4
18	Oregon	73.3		37	Alabama	69.2
23	Pennsylvania	72.0		38	Arkansas	68.8
32	Rhode Island	70.3		38	Indiana	68.8
25	South Carolina	71.6		40	Idaho	68.7
26	South Dakota	71.4		41	Arizona	68.6
44	Tennessee	66.7		42	Oklahoma	67.8
43	Texas	67.5		43	Texas	67.5
29	Utah	71.0		44	Tennessee	66.7
24	Vermont	71.9		45	Florida	66.6
6	Virginia	75.5		46	New York	66.5
4	Washington	76.5		47	New Mexico	65.6
49	West Virginia	64.1		48	California	64.7
5	Wisconsin	76.3		49	West Virginia	64.1
28	Wyoming	71.1		50	Hawaii	54.4
					District of Columbia	82.1

Source: U.S. Bureau of the Census
   "Voting and Registration" (Table 4a, http://www.census.gov/topics/public-sector/voting.html)
*As a percent of citizen population 18 and older.

Persons Voting in 2016

National Total = 137,537,000

ALPHA ORDER

RANK	STATE	VOTERS	% of USA
24	Alabama	2,095,000	1.5%
48	Alaska	308,000	0.2%
18	Arizona	2,769,000	2.0%
33	Arkansas	1,241,000	0.9%
1	California	14,416,000	10.5%
21	Colorado	2,707,000	2.0%
28	Connecticut	1,586,000	1.2%
45	Delaware	417,000	0.3%
3	Florida	8,578,000	6.2%
10	Georgia	4,246,000	3.1%
44	Hawaii	460,000	0.3%
40	Idaho	714,000	0.5%
6	Illinois	5,719,000	4.2%
17	Indiana	2,795,000	2.0%
31	Iowa	1,454,000	1.1%
32	Kansas	1,243,000	0.9%
27	Kentucky	1,850,000	1.3%
25	Louisiana	2,067,000	1.5%
38	Maine	754,000	0.5%
20	Maryland	2,737,000	2.0%
14	Massachusetts	3,315,000	2.4%
8	Michigan	4,713,000	3.4%
19	Minnesota	2,738,000	2.0%
30	Mississippi	1,470,000	1.1%
16	Missouri	2,906,000	2.1%
42	Montana	521,000	0.4%
36	Nebraska	893,000	0.6%
35	Nevada	1,195,000	0.9%
41	New Hampshire	698,000	0.5%
12	New Jersey	3,665,000	2.7%
37	New Mexico	765,000	0.6%
4	New York	7,869,000	5.7%
9	North Carolina	4,700,000	3.4%
46	North Dakota	362,000	0.3%
7	Ohio	5,408,000	3.9%
29	Oklahoma	1,555,000	1.1%
26	Oregon	1,942,000	1.4%
5	Pennsylvania	6,008,000	4.4%
43	Rhode Island	464,000	0.3%
23	South Carolina	2,233,000	1.6%
46	South Dakota	362,000	0.3%
22	Tennessee	2,630,000	1.9%
2	Texas	9,626,000	7.0%
34	Utah	1,234,000	0.9%
49	Vermont	305,000	0.2%
11	Virginia	3,973,000	2.9%
13	Washington	3,382,000	2.5%
39	West Virginia	723,000	0.5%
15	Wisconsin	3,068,000	2.2%
50	Wyoming	277,000	0.2%

RANK ORDER

RANK	STATE	VOTERS	% of USA
1	California	14,416,000	10.5%
2	Texas	9,626,000	7.0%
3	Florida	8,578,000	6.2%
4	New York	7,869,000	5.7%
5	Pennsylvania	6,008,000	4.4%
6	Illinois	5,719,000	4.2%
7	Ohio	5,408,000	3.9%
8	Michigan	4,713,000	3.4%
9	North Carolina	4,700,000	3.4%
10	Georgia	4,246,000	3.1%
11	Virginia	3,973,000	2.9%
12	New Jersey	3,665,000	2.7%
13	Washington	3,382,000	2.5%
14	Massachusetts	3,315,000	2.4%
15	Wisconsin	3,068,000	2.2%
16	Missouri	2,906,000	2.1%
17	Indiana	2,795,000	2.0%
18	Arizona	2,769,000	2.0%
19	Minnesota	2,738,000	2.0%
20	Maryland	2,737,000	2.0%
21	Colorado	2,707,000	2.0%
22	Tennessee	2,630,000	1.9%
23	South Carolina	2,233,000	1.6%
24	Alabama	2,095,000	1.5%
25	Louisiana	2,067,000	1.5%
26	Oregon	1,942,000	1.4%
27	Kentucky	1,850,000	1.3%
28	Connecticut	1,586,000	1.2%
29	Oklahoma	1,555,000	1.1%
30	Mississippi	1,470,000	1.1%
31	Iowa	1,454,000	1.1%
32	Kansas	1,243,000	0.9%
33	Arkansas	1,241,000	0.9%
34	Utah	1,234,000	0.9%
35	Nevada	1,195,000	0.9%
36	Nebraska	893,000	0.6%
37	New Mexico	765,000	0.6%
38	Maine	754,000	0.5%
39	West Virginia	723,000	0.5%
40	Idaho	714,000	0.5%
41	New Hampshire	698,000	0.5%
42	Montana	521,000	0.4%
43	Rhode Island	464,000	0.3%
44	Hawaii	460,000	0.3%
45	Delaware	417,000	0.3%
46	North Dakota	362,000	0.3%
46	South Dakota	362,000	0.3%
48	Alaska	308,000	0.2%
49	Vermont	305,000	0.2%
50	Wyoming	277,000	0.2%
	District of Columbia	380,000	0.3%

Source: U.S. Bureau of the Census
"Voting and Registration" (Table 4a, http://www.census.gov/topics/public-sector/voting.html)

Percent of Eligible Population Reported Voting in 2016

National Percent = 61.4%*

RANK STATE PERCENT

ALPHA ORDER			RANK ORDER		
RANK	STATE	PERCENT	RANK	STATE	PERCENT
42	Alabama	57.4	1	Maine	72.7
31	Alaska	61.3	2	Wisconsin	70.5
35	Arizona	60.4	3	Colorado	69.5
39	Arkansas	58.7	4	New Hampshire	69.0
41	California	57.9	5	Minnesota	68.7
3	Colorado	69.5	6	Virginia	68.2
19	Connecticut	63.9	7	Mississippi	67.7
26	Delaware	62.3	8	North Carolina	67.5
37	Florida	59.5	9	Nebraska	66.8
36	Georgia	60.2	10	Massachusetts	66.7
50	Hawaii	47.3	11	Oregon	66.3
27	Idaho	62.1	11	Washington	66.3
20	Illinois	63.8	13	Montana	65.9
40	Indiana	58.3	14	Maryland	65.8
22	Iowa	63.4	15	Missouri	64.8
31	Kansas	61.3	15	Wyoming	64.8
44	Kentucky	57.0	17	Michigan	64.3
29	Louisiana	61.6	18	North Dakota	64.2
1	Maine	72.7	19	Connecticut	63.9
14	Maryland	65.8	20	Illinois	63.8
10	Massachusetts	66.7	21	Ohio	63.6
17	Michigan	64.3	22	Iowa	63.4
5	Minnesota	68.7	23	Utah	62.7
7	Mississippi	67.7	24	Pennsylvania	62.6
15	Missouri	64.8	25	Vermont	62.5
13	Montana	65.9	26	Delaware	62.3
9	Nebraska	66.8	27	Idaho	62.1
34	Nevada	60.5	27	South Carolina	62.1
4	New Hampshire	69.0	29	Louisiana	61.6
30	New Jersey	61.5	30	New Jersey	61.5
47	New Mexico	54.8	31	Alaska	61.3
43	New York	57.2	31	Kansas	61.3
8	North Carolina	67.5	33	Rhode Island	60.6
18	North Dakota	64.2	34	Nevada	60.5
21	Ohio	63.6	35	Arizona	60.4
45	Oklahoma	56.6	36	Georgia	60.2
11	Oregon	66.3	37	Florida	59.5
24	Pennsylvania	62.6	38	South Dakota	59.1
33	Rhode Island	60.6	39	Arkansas	58.7
27	South Carolina	62.1	40	Indiana	58.3
38	South Dakota	59.1	41	California	57.9
48	Tennessee	54.0	42	Alabama	57.4
46	Texas	55.4	43	New York	57.2
23	Utah	62.7	44	Kentucky	57.0
25	Vermont	62.5	45	Oklahoma	56.6
6	Virginia	68.2	46	Texas	55.4
11	Washington	66.3	47	New Mexico	54.8
49	West Virginia	50.8	48	Tennessee	54.0
2	Wisconsin	70.5	49	West Virginia	50.8
15	Wyoming	64.8	50	Hawaii	47.3
				District of Columbia	74.3

Source: U.S. Bureau of the Census
  "Voting and Registration" (Table 4a, http://www.census.gov/topics/public-sector/voting.html)
*As a percent of citizen population 18 and older.

Percent of Registered Population Reported Voting in 2016

National Percent = 87.3%*

ALPHA ORDER

RANK	STATE	PERCENT
45	Alabama	82.9
35	Alaska	86.0
19	Arizona	88.0
39	Arkansas	85.2
13	California	89.6
1	Colorado	93.6
11	Connecticut	90.0
37	Delaware	85.6
15	Florida	89.3
27	Georgia	86.8
27	Hawaii	86.8
9	Idaho	90.4
36	Illinois	85.8
41	Indiana	84.7
22	Iowa	87.7
32	Kansas	86.4
47	Kentucky	82.1
42	Louisiana	84.5
5	Maine	90.8
21	Maryland	87.9
6	Massachusetts	90.6
29	Michigan	86.7
13	Minnesota	89.6
39	Mississippi	85.2
23	Missouri	87.2
12	Montana	89.7
16	Nebraska	88.6
23	Nevada	87.2
3	New Hampshire	91.5
19	New Jersey	88.0
44	New Mexico	83.5
34	New York	86.1
7	North Carolina	90.5
38	North Dakota	85.4
17	Ohio	88.3
43	Oklahoma	83.6
7	Oregon	90.5
25	Pennsylvania	87.0
33	Rhode Island	86.2
29	South Carolina	86.7
46	South Dakota	82.8
49	Tennessee	80.9
47	Texas	82.1
17	Utah	88.3
26	Vermont	86.9
10	Virginia	90.3
31	Washington	86.6
50	West Virginia	79.2
2	Wisconsin	92.3
4	Wyoming	91.1

RANK ORDER

RANK	STATE	PERCENT
1	Colorado	93.6
2	Wisconsin	92.3
3	New Hampshire	91.5
4	Wyoming	91.1
5	Maine	90.8
6	Massachusetts	90.6
7	North Carolina	90.5
7	Oregon	90.5
9	Idaho	90.4
10	Virginia	90.3
11	Connecticut	90.0
12	Montana	89.7
13	California	89.6
13	Minnesota	89.6
15	Florida	89.3
16	Nebraska	88.6
17	Ohio	88.3
17	Utah	88.3
19	Arizona	88.0
19	New Jersey	88.0
21	Maryland	87.9
22	Iowa	87.7
23	Missouri	87.2
23	Nevada	87.2
25	Pennsylvania	87.0
26	Vermont	86.9
27	Georgia	86.8
27	Hawaii	86.8
29	Michigan	86.7
29	South Carolina	86.7
31	Washington	86.6
32	Kansas	86.4
33	Rhode Island	86.2
34	New York	86.1
35	Alaska	86.0
36	Illinois	85.8
37	Delaware	85.6
38	North Dakota	85.4
39	Arkansas	85.2
39	Mississippi	85.2
41	Indiana	84.7
42	Louisiana	84.5
43	Oklahoma	83.6
44	New Mexico	83.5
45	Alabama	82.9
46	South Dakota	82.8
47	Kentucky	82.1
47	Texas	82.1
49	Tennessee	80.9
50	West Virginia	79.2

District of Columbia	90.5

Source: CQ Press using data from U.S. Bureau of the Census
"Voting and Registration" (Table 4a, http://www.census.gov/topics/public-sector/voting.html)
*As a percent of citizen population 18 and older registered to vote.

XIV. Social Welfare

Poverty Rate in 2016

National Rate = 14.0% of Population in Poverty*

<table>
<tr><td colspan="3">ALPHA ORDER</td><td colspan="3">RANK ORDER</td></tr>
<tr><td>RANK</td><td>STATE</td><td>PERCENT</td><td>RANK</td><td>STATE</td><td>PERCENT</td></tr>
<tr><td>7</td><td>Alabama</td><td>17.1</td><td>1</td><td>Mississippi</td><td>20.8</td></tr>
<tr><td>45</td><td>Alaska</td><td>9.9</td><td>2</td><td>Louisiana</td><td>20.2</td></tr>
<tr><td>8</td><td>Arizona</td><td>16.4</td><td>3</td><td>New Mexico</td><td>19.8</td></tr>
<tr><td>6</td><td>Arkansas</td><td>17.2</td><td>4</td><td>Kentucky</td><td>18.5</td></tr>
<tr><td>20</td><td>California</td><td>14.3</td><td>5</td><td>West Virginia</td><td>17.9</td></tr>
<tr><td>39</td><td>Colorado</td><td>11.0</td><td>6</td><td>Arkansas</td><td>17.2</td></tr>
<tr><td>47</td><td>Connecticut</td><td>9.8</td><td>7</td><td>Alabama</td><td>17.1</td></tr>
<tr><td>35</td><td>Delaware</td><td>11.7</td><td>8</td><td>Arizona</td><td>16.4</td></tr>
<tr><td>16</td><td>Florida</td><td>14.7</td><td>9</td><td>Oklahoma</td><td>16.3</td></tr>
<tr><td>10</td><td>Georgia</td><td>16.0</td><td>10</td><td>Georgia</td><td>16.0</td></tr>
<tr><td>49</td><td>Hawaii</td><td>9.3</td><td>11</td><td>Tennessee</td><td>15.8</td></tr>
<tr><td>19</td><td>Idaho</td><td>14.4</td><td>12</td><td>Texas</td><td>15.6</td></tr>
<tr><td>27</td><td>Illinois</td><td>13.0</td><td>13</td><td>North Carolina</td><td>15.4</td></tr>
<tr><td>21</td><td>Indiana</td><td>14.1</td><td>14</td><td>South Carolina</td><td>15.3</td></tr>
<tr><td>33</td><td>Iowa</td><td>11.8</td><td>15</td><td>Michigan</td><td>15.0</td></tr>
<tr><td>31</td><td>Kansas</td><td>12.1</td><td>16</td><td>Florida</td><td>14.7</td></tr>
<tr><td>4</td><td>Kentucky</td><td>18.5</td><td>16</td><td>New York</td><td>14.7</td></tr>
<tr><td>2</td><td>Louisiana</td><td>20.2</td><td>18</td><td>Ohio</td><td>14.6</td></tr>
<tr><td>30</td><td>Maine</td><td>12.5</td><td>19</td><td>Idaho</td><td>14.4</td></tr>
<tr><td>48</td><td>Maryland</td><td>9.7</td><td>20</td><td>California</td><td>14.3</td></tr>
<tr><td>42</td><td>Massachusetts</td><td>10.4</td><td>21</td><td>Indiana</td><td>14.1</td></tr>
<tr><td>15</td><td>Michigan</td><td>15.0</td><td>22</td><td>Missouri</td><td>14.0</td></tr>
<tr><td>45</td><td>Minnesota</td><td>9.9</td><td>23</td><td>Nevada</td><td>13.8</td></tr>
<tr><td>1</td><td>Mississippi</td><td>20.8</td><td>24</td><td>Montana</td><td>13.3</td></tr>
<tr><td>22</td><td>Missouri</td><td>14.0</td><td>24</td><td>Oregon</td><td>13.3</td></tr>
<tr><td>24</td><td>Montana</td><td>13.3</td><td>24</td><td>South Dakota</td><td>13.3</td></tr>
<tr><td>36</td><td>Nebraska</td><td>11.4</td><td>27</td><td>Illinois</td><td>13.0</td></tr>
<tr><td>23</td><td>Nevada</td><td>13.8</td><td>28</td><td>Pennsylvania</td><td>12.9</td></tr>
<tr><td>50</td><td>New Hampshire</td><td>7.3</td><td>29</td><td>Rhode Island</td><td>12.8</td></tr>
<tr><td>42</td><td>New Jersey</td><td>10.4</td><td>30</td><td>Maine</td><td>12.5</td></tr>
<tr><td>3</td><td>New Mexico</td><td>19.8</td><td>31</td><td>Kansas</td><td>12.1</td></tr>
<tr><td>16</td><td>New York</td><td>14.7</td><td>32</td><td>Vermont</td><td>11.9</td></tr>
<tr><td>13</td><td>North Carolina</td><td>15.4</td><td>33</td><td>Iowa</td><td>11.8</td></tr>
<tr><td>41</td><td>North Dakota</td><td>10.7</td><td>33</td><td>Wisconsin</td><td>11.8</td></tr>
<tr><td>18</td><td>Ohio</td><td>14.6</td><td>35</td><td>Delaware</td><td>11.7</td></tr>
<tr><td>9</td><td>Oklahoma</td><td>16.3</td><td>36</td><td>Nebraska</td><td>11.4</td></tr>
<tr><td>24</td><td>Oregon</td><td>13.3</td><td>37</td><td>Washington</td><td>11.3</td></tr>
<tr><td>28</td><td>Pennsylvania</td><td>12.9</td><td>37</td><td>Wyoming</td><td>11.3</td></tr>
<tr><td>29</td><td>Rhode Island</td><td>12.8</td><td>39</td><td>Colorado</td><td>11.0</td></tr>
<tr><td>14</td><td>South Carolina</td><td>15.3</td><td>39</td><td>Virginia</td><td>11.0</td></tr>
<tr><td>24</td><td>South Dakota</td><td>13.3</td><td>41</td><td>North Dakota</td><td>10.7</td></tr>
<tr><td>11</td><td>Tennessee</td><td>15.8</td><td>42</td><td>Massachusetts</td><td>10.4</td></tr>
<tr><td>12</td><td>Texas</td><td>15.6</td><td>42</td><td>New Jersey</td><td>10.4</td></tr>
<tr><td>44</td><td>Utah</td><td>10.2</td><td>44</td><td>Utah</td><td>10.2</td></tr>
<tr><td>32</td><td>Vermont</td><td>11.9</td><td>45</td><td>Alaska</td><td>9.9</td></tr>
<tr><td>39</td><td>Virginia</td><td>11.0</td><td>45</td><td>Minnesota</td><td>9.9</td></tr>
<tr><td>37</td><td>Washington</td><td>11.3</td><td>47</td><td>Connecticut</td><td>9.8</td></tr>
<tr><td>5</td><td>West Virginia</td><td>17.9</td><td>48</td><td>Maryland</td><td>9.7</td></tr>
<tr><td>33</td><td>Wisconsin</td><td>11.8</td><td>49</td><td>Hawaii</td><td>9.3</td></tr>
<tr><td>37</td><td>Wyoming</td><td>11.3</td><td>50</td><td>New Hampshire</td><td>7.3</td></tr>
<tr><td></td><td></td><td></td><td></td><td>District of Columbia</td><td>18.6</td></tr>
</table>

Source: U.S. Bureau of the Census

"2016 American Community Survey-Table CP02" (http://www.census.gov/programs-surveys/acs/)

*This is a one-year figure. Census has discontinued three-year averages that had been used previously. The poverty threshold for a family of four (two children) in 2016 was $24,300.

Percent of Senior Citizens Living in Poverty in 2016

National Percent = 9.2%*

ALPHA ORDER

RANK	STATE	PERCENT
12	Alabama	10.0
50	Alaska	4.2
19	Arizona	9.0
7	Arkansas	10.5
10	California	10.3
40	Colorado	7.6
48	Connecticut	6.5
45	Delaware	6.9
9	Florida	10.4
11	Georgia	10.1
20	Hawaii	8.9
12	Idaho	10.0
16	Illinois	9.2
39	Indiana	7.7
45	Iowa	6.9
34	Kansas	8.0
5	Kentucky	11.1
1	Louisiana	13.0
17	Maine	9.1
30	Maryland	8.2
27	Massachusetts	8.5
32	Michigan	8.1
44	Minnesota	7.2
2	Mississippi	12.3
30	Missouri	8.2
20	Montana	8.9
36	Nebraska	7.8
23	Nevada	8.7
49	New Hampshire	4.6
29	New Jersey	8.3
3	New Mexico	11.5
4	New York	11.4
15	North Carolina	9.4
35	North Dakota	7.9
32	Ohio	8.1
25	Oklahoma	8.6
43	Oregon	7.5
36	Pennsylvania	7.8
17	Rhode Island	9.1
25	South Carolina	8.6
6	South Dakota	10.9
20	Tennessee	8.9
7	Texas	10.5
47	Utah	6.7
23	Vermont	8.7
36	Virginia	7.8
40	Washington	7.6
14	West Virginia	9.5
40	Wisconsin	7.6
27	Wyoming	8.5

RANK ORDER

RANK	STATE	PERCENT
1	Louisiana	13.0
2	Mississippi	12.3
3	New Mexico	11.5
4	New York	11.4
5	Kentucky	11.1
6	South Dakota	10.9
7	Arkansas	10.5
7	Texas	10.5
9	Florida	10.4
10	California	10.3
11	Georgia	10.1
12	Alabama	10.0
12	Idaho	10.0
14	West Virginia	9.5
15	North Carolina	9.4
16	Illinois	9.2
17	Maine	9.1
17	Rhode Island	9.1
19	Arizona	9.0
20	Hawaii	8.9
20	Montana	8.9
20	Tennessee	8.9
23	Nevada	8.7
23	Vermont	8.7
25	Oklahoma	8.6
25	South Carolina	8.6
27	Massachusetts	8.5
27	Wyoming	8.5
29	New Jersey	8.3
30	Maryland	8.2
30	Missouri	8.2
32	Michigan	8.1
32	Ohio	8.1
34	Kansas	8.0
35	North Dakota	7.9
36	Nebraska	7.8
36	Pennsylvania	7.8
36	Virginia	7.8
39	Indiana	7.7
40	Colorado	7.6
40	Washington	7.6
40	Wisconsin	7.6
43	Oregon	7.5
44	Minnesota	7.2
45	Delaware	6.9
45	Iowa	6.9
47	Utah	6.7
48	Connecticut	6.5
49	New Hampshire	4.6
50	Alaska	4.2
	District of Columbia	13.4

Source: U.S. Bureau of the Census
"2016 American Community Survey-Table DP03" (http://www.census.gov/programs-surveys/acs/)
*People 65 years and older living with incomes below the poverty level.

Percent of Children Living in Poverty in 2016

National Percent = 19.5%*

ALPHA ORDER

RANK	STATE	PERCENT
5	Alabama	24.5
38	Alaska	14.1
8	Arizona	23.6
7	Arkansas	23.8
19	California	19.9
42	Colorado	13.4
43	Connecticut	12.9
26	Delaware	17.4
15	Florida	21.0
10	Georgia	22.9
49	Hawaii	10.1
24	Idaho	17.7
24	Illinois	17.7
20	Indiana	19.5
33	Iowa	14.8
38	Kansas	14.1
4	Kentucky	25.0
3	Louisiana	28.6
27	Maine	17.2
44	Maryland	12.7
41	Massachusetts	13.6
16	Michigan	20.7
44	Minnesota	12.7
2	Mississippi	29.7
21	Missouri	19.2
32	Montana	15.1
37	Nebraska	14.2
22	Nevada	19.1
50	New Hampshire	7.9
35	New Jersey	14.6
1	New Mexico	30.1
16	New York	20.7
14	North Carolina	21.7
46	North Dakota	12.4
18	Ohio	20.5
10	Oklahoma	22.9
28	Oregon	17.0
23	Pennsylvania	18.5
28	Rhode Island	17.0
9	South Carolina	23.0
30	South Dakota	16.9
12	Tennessee	22.6
13	Texas	22.4
47	Utah	11.1
33	Vermont	14.8
36	Virginia	14.3
40	Washington	13.7
6	West Virginia	24.0
31	Wisconsin	15.7
47	Wyoming	11.1

RANK ORDER

RANK	STATE	PERCENT
1	New Mexico	30.1
2	Mississippi	29.7
3	Louisiana	28.6
4	Kentucky	25.0
5	Alabama	24.5
6	West Virginia	24.0
7	Arkansas	23.8
8	Arizona	23.6
9	South Carolina	23.0
10	Georgia	22.9
10	Oklahoma	22.9
12	Tennessee	22.6
13	Texas	22.4
14	North Carolina	21.7
15	Florida	21.0
16	Michigan	20.7
16	New York	20.7
18	Ohio	20.5
19	California	19.9
20	Indiana	19.5
21	Missouri	19.2
22	Nevada	19.1
23	Pennsylvania	18.5
24	Idaho	17.7
24	Illinois	17.7
26	Delaware	17.4
27	Maine	17.2
28	Oregon	17.0
28	Rhode Island	17.0
30	South Dakota	16.9
31	Wisconsin	15.7
32	Montana	15.1
33	Iowa	14.8
33	Vermont	14.8
35	New Jersey	14.6
36	Virginia	14.3
37	Nebraska	14.2
38	Alaska	14.1
38	Kansas	14.1
40	Washington	13.7
41	Massachusetts	13.6
42	Colorado	13.4
43	Connecticut	12.9
44	Maryland	12.7
44	Minnesota	12.7
46	North Dakota	12.4
47	Utah	11.1
47	Wyoming	11.1
49	Hawaii	10.1
50	New Hampshire	7.9

District of Columbia 25.8

Source: U.S. Bureau of the Census
"2016 American Community Survey-Table DP03" (http://www.census.gov/programs-surveys/acs/)
*Children 17 and under living in families with incomes below the poverty level.

Percent of Families Living in Poverty in 2016

National Percent = 10.0%*

ALPHA ORDER

RANK	STATE	PERCENT
6	Alabama	12.7
44	Alaska	6.7
10	Arizona	11.9
7	Arkansas	12.4
16	California	10.5
42	Colorado	7.0
43	Connecticut	6.8
29	Delaware	8.1
16	Florida	10.5
8	Georgia	12.0
48	Hawaii	6.0
21	Idaho	10.0
24	Illinois	9.5
23	Indiana	9.6
34	Iowa	7.6
31	Kansas	7.9
4	Kentucky	14.0
2	Louisiana	15.4
34	Maine	7.6
46	Maryland	6.3
39	Massachusetts	7.3
19	Michigan	10.2
49	Minnesota	5.9
1	Mississippi	16.5
22	Missouri	9.8
30	Montana	8.0
38	Nebraska	7.4
19	Nevada	10.2
50	New Hampshire	4.0
34	New Jersey	7.6
3	New Mexico	15.3
14	New York	10.9
13	North Carolina	11.2
45	North Dakota	6.4
16	Ohio	10.5
12	Oklahoma	11.5
27	Oregon	8.5
26	Pennsylvania	8.6
25	Rhode Island	9.2
15	South Carolina	10.8
28	South Dakota	8.2
11	Tennessee	11.6
8	Texas	12.0
40	Utah	7.2
32	Vermont	7.7
34	Virginia	7.6
41	Washington	7.1
5	West Virginia	12.9
32	Wisconsin	7.7
46	Wyoming	6.3

RANK ORDER

RANK	STATE	PERCENT
1	Mississippi	16.5
2	Louisiana	15.4
3	New Mexico	15.3
4	Kentucky	14.0
5	West Virginia	12.9
6	Alabama	12.7
7	Arkansas	12.4
8	Georgia	12.0
8	Texas	12.0
10	Arizona	11.9
11	Tennessee	11.6
12	Oklahoma	11.5
13	North Carolina	11.2
14	New York	10.9
15	South Carolina	10.8
16	California	10.5
16	Florida	10.5
16	Ohio	10.5
19	Michigan	10.2
19	Nevada	10.2
21	Idaho	10.0
22	Missouri	9.8
23	Indiana	9.6
24	Illinois	9.5
25	Rhode Island	9.2
26	Pennsylvania	8.6
27	Oregon	8.5
28	South Dakota	8.2
29	Delaware	8.1
30	Montana	8.0
31	Kansas	7.9
32	Vermont	7.7
32	Wisconsin	7.7
34	Iowa	7.6
34	Maine	7.6
34	New Jersey	7.6
34	Virginia	7.6
38	Nebraska	7.4
39	Massachusetts	7.3
40	Utah	7.2
41	Washington	7.1
42	Colorado	7.0
43	Connecticut	6.8
44	Alaska	6.7
45	North Dakota	6.4
46	Maryland	6.3
46	Wyoming	6.3
48	Hawaii	6.0
49	Minnesota	5.9
50	New Hampshire	4.0

District of Columbia	13.7

Source: U.S. Bureau of the Census
   "2016 American Community Survey-Table DP03" (http://www.census.gov/programs-surveys/acs/)
*Families living with incomes below the poverty level.

Percent of Female-Headed Families with Children Living in Poverty in 2016

National Percent = 37.0%*

<table>
<tr><td colspan="3">ALPHA ORDER</td><td colspan="3">RANK ORDER</td></tr>
<tr><td>RANK</td><td>STATE</td><td>PERCENT</td><td>RANK</td><td>STATE</td><td>PERCENT</td></tr>
<tr><td>7</td><td>Alabama</td><td>45.0</td><td>1</td><td>Mississippi</td><td>50.1</td></tr>
<tr><td>47</td><td>Alaska</td><td>29.0</td><td>2</td><td>Louisiana</td><td>49.3</td></tr>
<tr><td>22</td><td>Arizona</td><td>36.9</td><td>3</td><td>New Mexico</td><td>48.2</td></tr>
<tr><td>9</td><td>Arkansas</td><td>42.2</td><td>4</td><td>Kentucky</td><td>47.4</td></tr>
<tr><td>31</td><td>California</td><td>34.9</td><td>5</td><td>West Virginia</td><td>46.7</td></tr>
<tr><td>45</td><td>Colorado</td><td>29.7</td><td>6</td><td>Oklahoma</td><td>45.1</td></tr>
<tr><td>46</td><td>Connecticut</td><td>29.5</td><td>7</td><td>Alabama</td><td>45.0</td></tr>
<tr><td>41</td><td>Delaware</td><td>31.1</td><td>8</td><td>Idaho</td><td>42.7</td></tr>
<tr><td>32</td><td>Florida</td><td>33.8</td><td>9</td><td>Arkansas</td><td>42.2</td></tr>
<tr><td>16</td><td>Georgia</td><td>38.9</td><td>10</td><td>Ohio</td><td>41.1</td></tr>
<tr><td>49</td><td>Hawaii</td><td>23.9</td><td>11</td><td>Tennessee</td><td>41.0</td></tr>
<tr><td>8</td><td>Idaho</td><td>42.7</td><td>12</td><td>North Carolina</td><td>40.4</td></tr>
<tr><td>28</td><td>Illinois</td><td>35.7</td><td>13</td><td>Michigan</td><td>39.8</td></tr>
<tr><td>15</td><td>Indiana</td><td>39.0</td><td>13</td><td>South Carolina</td><td>39.8</td></tr>
<tr><td>23</td><td>Iowa</td><td>36.6</td><td>15</td><td>Indiana</td><td>39.0</td></tr>
<tr><td>35</td><td>Kansas</td><td>33.2</td><td>16</td><td>Georgia</td><td>38.9</td></tr>
<tr><td>4</td><td>Kentucky</td><td>47.4</td><td>17</td><td>Texas</td><td>38.8</td></tr>
<tr><td>2</td><td>Louisiana</td><td>49.3</td><td>18</td><td>South Dakota</td><td>38.1</td></tr>
<tr><td>39</td><td>Maine</td><td>31.5</td><td>19</td><td>Missouri</td><td>37.6</td></tr>
<tr><td>48</td><td>Maryland</td><td>24.7</td><td>20</td><td>North Dakota</td><td>37.5</td></tr>
<tr><td>36</td><td>Massachusetts</td><td>32.7</td><td>21</td><td>Montana</td><td>37.4</td></tr>
<tr><td>13</td><td>Michigan</td><td>39.8</td><td>22</td><td>Arizona</td><td>36.9</td></tr>
<tr><td>44</td><td>Minnesota</td><td>30.1</td><td>23</td><td>Iowa</td><td>36.6</td></tr>
<tr><td>1</td><td>Mississippi</td><td>50.1</td><td>24</td><td>Oregon</td><td>36.0</td></tr>
<tr><td>19</td><td>Missouri</td><td>37.6</td><td>25</td><td>Wisconsin</td><td>35.9</td></tr>
<tr><td>21</td><td>Montana</td><td>37.4</td><td>26</td><td>Nevada</td><td>35.8</td></tr>
<tr><td>37</td><td>Nebraska</td><td>32.1</td><td>26</td><td>Pennsylvania</td><td>35.8</td></tr>
<tr><td>26</td><td>Nevada</td><td>35.8</td><td>28</td><td>Illinois</td><td>35.7</td></tr>
<tr><td>50</td><td>New Hampshire</td><td>20.6</td><td>28</td><td>New York</td><td>35.7</td></tr>
<tr><td>39</td><td>New Jersey</td><td>31.5</td><td>30</td><td>Vermont</td><td>35.6</td></tr>
<tr><td>3</td><td>New Mexico</td><td>48.2</td><td>31</td><td>California</td><td>34.9</td></tr>
<tr><td>28</td><td>New York</td><td>35.7</td><td>32</td><td>Florida</td><td>33.8</td></tr>
<tr><td>12</td><td>North Carolina</td><td>40.4</td><td>33</td><td>Utah</td><td>33.5</td></tr>
<tr><td>20</td><td>North Dakota</td><td>37.5</td><td>34</td><td>Rhode Island</td><td>33.3</td></tr>
<tr><td>10</td><td>Ohio</td><td>41.1</td><td>35</td><td>Kansas</td><td>33.2</td></tr>
<tr><td>6</td><td>Oklahoma</td><td>45.1</td><td>36</td><td>Massachusetts</td><td>32.7</td></tr>
<tr><td>24</td><td>Oregon</td><td>36.0</td><td>37</td><td>Nebraska</td><td>32.1</td></tr>
<tr><td>26</td><td>Pennsylvania</td><td>35.8</td><td>38</td><td>Virginia</td><td>31.8</td></tr>
<tr><td>34</td><td>Rhode Island</td><td>33.3</td><td>39</td><td>Maine</td><td>31.5</td></tr>
<tr><td>13</td><td>South Carolina</td><td>39.8</td><td>39</td><td>New Jersey</td><td>31.5</td></tr>
<tr><td>18</td><td>South Dakota</td><td>38.1</td><td>41</td><td>Delaware</td><td>31.1</td></tr>
<tr><td>11</td><td>Tennessee</td><td>41.0</td><td>42</td><td>Washington</td><td>30.6</td></tr>
<tr><td>17</td><td>Texas</td><td>38.8</td><td>42</td><td>Wyoming</td><td>30.6</td></tr>
<tr><td>33</td><td>Utah</td><td>33.5</td><td>44</td><td>Minnesota</td><td>30.1</td></tr>
<tr><td>30</td><td>Vermont</td><td>35.6</td><td>45</td><td>Colorado</td><td>29.7</td></tr>
<tr><td>38</td><td>Virginia</td><td>31.8</td><td>46</td><td>Connecticut</td><td>29.5</td></tr>
<tr><td>42</td><td>Washington</td><td>30.6</td><td>47</td><td>Alaska</td><td>29.0</td></tr>
<tr><td>5</td><td>West Virginia</td><td>46.7</td><td>48</td><td>Maryland</td><td>24.7</td></tr>
<tr><td>25</td><td>Wisconsin</td><td>35.9</td><td>49</td><td>Hawaii</td><td>23.9</td></tr>
<tr><td>42</td><td>Wyoming</td><td>30.6</td><td>50</td><td>New Hampshire</td><td>20.6</td></tr>
<tr><td></td><td></td><td></td><td></td><td>District of Columbia</td><td>42.1</td></tr>
</table>

Source: U.S. Bureau of the Census
  "2016 American Community Survey-Table DP03" (http://www.census.gov/programs-surveys/acs/)
*Households headed by females with own children under 18 years living with them with incomes below the poverty level as a percent of all such female-headed households.

State and Local Government Expenditures for Public Welfare Programs in 2015

National Total = $609,597,153,000*

ALPHA ORDER

RANK	STATE	EXPENDITURES	% of USA
28	Alabama	$6,760,901,000	1.1%
45	Alaska	2,011,101,000	0.3%
21	Arizona	10,194,775,000	1.7%
29	Arkansas	6,660,852,000	1.1%
1	California	102,842,797,000	16.9%
25	Colorado	7,838,843,000	1.3%
26	Connecticut	7,432,756,000	1.2%
43	Delaware	2,314,912,000	0.4%
4	Florida	27,151,813,000	4.5%
14	Georgia	12,001,789,000	2.0%
41	Hawaii	2,521,330,000	0.4%
42	Idaho	2,336,066,000	0.4%
6	Illinois	20,975,644,000	3.4%
17	Indiana	11,518,103,000	1.9%
31	Iowa	6,182,475,000	1.0%
35	Kansas	4,020,333,000	0.7%
19	Kentucky	10,842,548,000	1.8%
24	Louisiana	8,276,877,000	1.4%
38	Maine	2,956,176,000	0.5%
13	Maryland	12,286,904,000	2.0%
8	Massachusetts	18,585,384,000	3.0%
10	Michigan	16,368,404,000	2.7%
11	Minnesota	14,089,089,000	2.3%
32	Mississippi	5,846,931,000	1.0%
23	Missouri	8,532,141,000	1.4%
47	Montana	1,571,150,000	0.3%
39	Nebraska	2,692,618,000	0.4%
36	Nevada	3,993,466,000	0.7%
44	New Hampshire	2,158,510,000	0.4%
9	New Jersey	17,337,353,000	2.8%
33	New Mexico	5,722,732,000	0.9%
2	New York	61,412,770,000	10.1%
12	North Carolina	13,730,562,000	2.3%
48	North Dakota	1,399,177,000	0.2%
7	Ohio	20,072,728,000	3.3%
30	Oklahoma	6,484,041,000	1.1%
22	Oregon	9,561,574,000	1.6%
5	Pennsylvania	26,788,634,000	4.4%
40	Rhode Island	2,613,174,000	0.4%
27	South Carolina	7,341,659,000	1.2%
49	South Dakota	1,049,764,000	0.2%
20	Tennessee	10,690,711,000	1.8%
3	Texas	35,375,142,000	5.8%
37	Utah	3,395,586,000	0.6%
46	Vermont	1,730,959,000	0.3%
18	Virginia	11,506,892,000	1.9%
16	Washington	11,674,657,000	1.9%
34	West Virginia	4,380,295,000	0.7%
15	Wisconsin	11,987,223,000	2.0%
50	Wyoming	813,259,000	0.1%

RANK ORDER

RANK	STATE	EXPENDITURES	% of USA
1	California	$102,842,797,000	16.9%
2	New York	61,412,770,000	10.1%
3	Texas	35,375,142,000	5.8%
4	Florida	27,151,813,000	4.5%
5	Pennsylvania	26,788,634,000	4.4%
6	Illinois	20,975,644,000	3.4%
7	Ohio	20,072,728,000	3.3%
8	Massachusetts	18,585,384,000	3.0%
9	New Jersey	17,337,353,000	2.8%
10	Michigan	16,368,404,000	2.7%
11	Minnesota	14,089,089,000	2.3%
12	North Carolina	13,730,562,000	2.3%
13	Maryland	12,286,904,000	2.0%
14	Georgia	12,001,789,000	2.0%
15	Wisconsin	11,987,223,000	2.0%
16	Washington	11,674,657,000	1.9%
17	Indiana	11,518,103,000	1.9%
18	Virginia	11,506,892,000	1.9%
19	Kentucky	10,842,548,000	1.8%
20	Tennessee	10,690,711,000	1.8%
21	Arizona	10,194,775,000	1.7%
22	Oregon	9,561,574,000	1.6%
23	Missouri	8,532,141,000	1.4%
24	Louisiana	8,276,877,000	1.4%
25	Colorado	7,838,843,000	1.3%
26	Connecticut	7,432,756,000	1.2%
27	South Carolina	7,341,659,000	1.2%
28	Alabama	6,760,901,000	1.1%
29	Arkansas	6,660,852,000	1.1%
30	Oklahoma	6,484,041,000	1.1%
31	Iowa	6,182,475,000	1.0%
32	Mississippi	5,846,931,000	1.0%
33	New Mexico	5,722,732,000	0.9%
34	West Virginia	4,380,295,000	0.7%
35	Kansas	4,020,333,000	0.7%
36	Nevada	3,993,466,000	0.7%
37	Utah	3,395,586,000	0.6%
38	Maine	2,956,176,000	0.5%
39	Nebraska	2,692,618,000	0.4%
40	Rhode Island	2,613,174,000	0.4%
41	Hawaii	2,521,330,000	0.4%
42	Idaho	2,336,066,000	0.4%
43	Delaware	2,314,912,000	0.4%
44	New Hampshire	2,158,510,000	0.4%
45	Alaska	2,011,101,000	0.3%
46	Vermont	1,730,959,000	0.3%
47	Montana	1,571,150,000	0.3%
48	North Dakota	1,399,177,000	0.2%
49	South Dakota	1,049,764,000	0.2%
50	Wyoming	813,259,000	0.1%
	District of Columbia	3,563,573,000	0.6%

Source: U.S. Bureau of the Census, Governments Division
"2015 State and Local Government Finances" (http://www.census.gov/govs/local/)
*Direct general expenditures. Includes funds for cash assistance programs, medical and other vendor payments, welfare institutions, and other public welfare programs.

Per Capita State and Local Government Expenditures for Public Welfare Programs in 2015
National Per Capita = $1,899*

ALPHA ORDER

RANK	STATE	PER CAPITA
40	Alabama	$1,394
5	Alaska	2,725
35	Arizona	1,499
13	Arkansas	2,238
6	California	2,635
36	Colorado	1,441
17	Connecticut	2,068
9	Delaware	2,452
46	Florida	1,340
49	Georgia	1,177
24	Hawaii	1,768
38	Idaho	1,416
30	Illinois	1,631
25	Indiana	1,742
19	Iowa	1,983
43	Kansas	1,384
9	Kentucky	2,452
23	Louisiana	1,772
14	Maine	2,226
18	Maryland	2,048
4	Massachusetts	2,736
28	Michigan	1,650
7	Minnesota	2,569
20	Mississippi	1,959
39	Missouri	1,405
33	Montana	1,528
37	Nebraska	1,422
42	Nevada	1,385
31	New Hampshire	1,623
21	New Jersey	1,935
3	New Mexico	2,748
1	New York	3,099
45	North Carolina	1,367
22	North Dakota	1,854
26	Ohio	1,730
27	Oklahoma	1,661
11	Oregon	2,381
15	Pennsylvania	2,094
8	Rhode Island	2,475
34	South Carolina	1,501
48	South Dakota	1,229
32	Tennessee	1,622
47	Texas	1,288
50	Utah	1,138
2	Vermont	2,772
44	Virginia	1,375
29	Washington	1,632
11	West Virginia	2,381
16	Wisconsin	2,081
41	Wyoming	1,388

RANK ORDER

RANK	STATE	PER CAPITA
1	New York	$3,099
2	Vermont	2,772
3	New Mexico	2,748
4	Massachusetts	2,736
5	Alaska	2,725
6	California	2,635
7	Minnesota	2,569
8	Rhode Island	2,475
9	Delaware	2,452
9	Kentucky	2,452
11	Oregon	2,381
11	West Virginia	2,381
13	Arkansas	2,238
14	Maine	2,226
15	Pennsylvania	2,094
16	Wisconsin	2,081
17	Connecticut	2,068
18	Maryland	2,048
19	Iowa	1,983
20	Mississippi	1,959
21	New Jersey	1,935
22	North Dakota	1,854
23	Louisiana	1,772
24	Hawaii	1,768
25	Indiana	1,742
26	Ohio	1,730
27	Oklahoma	1,661
28	Michigan	1,650
29	Washington	1,632
30	Illinois	1,631
31	New Hampshire	1,623
32	Tennessee	1,622
33	Montana	1,528
34	South Carolina	1,501
35	Arizona	1,499
36	Colorado	1,441
37	Nebraska	1,422
38	Idaho	1,416
39	Missouri	1,405
40	Alabama	1,394
41	Wyoming	1,388
42	Nevada	1,385
43	Kansas	1,384
44	Virginia	1,375
45	North Carolina	1,367
46	Florida	1,340
47	Texas	1,288
48	South Dakota	1,229
49	Georgia	1,177
50	Utah	1,138
	District of Columbia	5,297

Source: CQ Press using data from U.S. Bureau of the Census, Governments Division
"2015 State and Local Government Finances" (http://www.census.gov/govs/local/)
*Direct general expenditures. Includes funds for cash assistance programs, medical and other vendor payments, welfare institutions, and other public welfare programs.

State and Local Government Spending for Public Welfare Programs as a Percent of All State and Local Government Expenditures in 2015
National Percent = 21.5%*

ALPHA ORDER

RANK	STATE	PERCENT
36	Alabama	18.3
49	Alaska	13.7
19	Arizona	22.7
3	Arkansas	28.5
10	California	25.1
43	Colorado	16.6
28	Connecticut	19.8
13	Delaware	23.9
32	Florida	19.0
39	Georgia	17.7
34	Hawaii	18.6
21	Idaho	22.1
36	Illinois	18.3
16	Indiana	23.4
25	Iowa	20.5
44	Kansas	16.4
1	Kentucky	29.1
27	Louisiana	20.4
6	Maine	26.6
22	Maryland	21.3
7	Massachusetts	25.9
25	Michigan	20.5
5	Minnesota	26.7
18	Mississippi	23.2
30	Missouri	19.5
38	Montana	18.0
45	Nebraska	16.2
28	Nevada	19.8
24	New Hampshire	20.6
31	New Jersey	19.2
4	New Mexico	27.3
13	New York	23.9
35	North Carolina	18.4
48	North Dakota	15.4
23	Ohio	21.1
20	Oklahoma	22.6
9	Oregon	25.4
15	Pennsylvania	23.6
7	Rhode Island	25.9
33	South Carolina	18.8
46	South Dakota	16.0
12	Tennessee	24.3
41	Texas	17.1
47	Utah	15.5
11	Vermont	25.0
42	Virginia	16.7
40	Washington	17.6
2	West Virginia	28.9
16	Wisconsin	23.4
50	Wyoming	9.7

RANK ORDER

RANK	STATE	PERCENT
1	Kentucky	29.1
2	West Virginia	28.9
3	Arkansas	28.5
4	New Mexico	27.3
5	Minnesota	26.7
6	Maine	26.6
7	Massachusetts	25.9
7	Rhode Island	25.9
9	Oregon	25.4
10	California	25.1
11	Vermont	25.0
12	Tennessee	24.3
13	Delaware	23.9
13	New York	23.9
15	Pennsylvania	23.6
16	Indiana	23.4
16	Wisconsin	23.4
18	Mississippi	23.2
19	Arizona	22.7
20	Oklahoma	22.6
21	Idaho	22.1
22	Maryland	21.3
23	Ohio	21.1
24	New Hampshire	20.6
25	Iowa	20.5
25	Michigan	20.5
27	Louisiana	20.4
28	Connecticut	19.8
28	Nevada	19.8
30	Missouri	19.5
31	New Jersey	19.2
32	Florida	19.0
33	South Carolina	18.8
34	Hawaii	18.6
35	North Carolina	18.4
36	Alabama	18.3
36	Illinois	18.3
38	Montana	18.0
39	Georgia	17.7
40	Washington	17.6
41	Texas	17.1
42	Virginia	16.7
43	Colorado	16.6
44	Kansas	16.4
45	Nebraska	16.2
46	South Dakota	16.0
47	Utah	15.5
48	North Dakota	15.4
49	Alaska	13.7
50	Wyoming	9.7

District of Columbia	28.7

Source: CQ Press using data from U.S. Bureau of the Census, Governments Division
"2015 State and Local Government Finances" (http://www.census.gov/govs/local/)
*As a percent of direct general expenditures. Includes funds for cash assistance programs, medical and other vendor payments, welfare institutions, and other public welfare programs.

Social Security (OASDI) Payments in 2015

National Total = $886,012,000,000*

ALPHA ORDER

RANK	STATE	PAYMENTS	% of USA
20	Alabama	$15,943,000,000	1.8%
50	Alaska	1,286,000,000	0.1%
16	Arizona	18,713,000,000	2.1%
30	Arkansas	9,461,000,000	1.1%
1	California	82,554,000,000	9.3%
26	Colorado	12,070,000,000	1.4%
29	Connecticut	10,792,000,000	1.2%
44	Delaware	3,134,000,000	0.4%
2	Florida	63,947,000,000	7.2%
11	Georgia	24,935,000,000	2.8%
42	Hawaii	3,790,000,000	0.4%
40	Idaho	4,529,000,000	0.5%
8	Illinois	33,340,000,000	3.8%
14	Indiana	20,116,000,000	2.3%
31	Iowa	9,323,000,000	1.1%
33	Kansas	8,053,000,000	0.9%
24	Kentucky	13,555,000,000	1.5%
27	Louisiana	11,994,000,000	1.4%
39	Maine	4,550,000,000	0.5%
23	Maryland	14,824,000,000	1.7%
17	Massachusetts	18,643,000,000	2.1%
7	Michigan	33,762,000,000	3.8%
22	Minnesota	14,974,000,000	1.7%
32	Mississippi	8,931,000,000	1.0%
18	Missouri	18,392,000,000	2.1%
45	Montana	3,073,000,000	0.3%
38	Nebraska	4,899,000,000	0.6%
34	Nevada	7,263,000,000	0.8%
41	New Hampshire	4,461,000,000	0.5%
10	New Jersey	26,098,000,000	2.9%
36	New Mexico	5,632,000,000	0.6%
4	New York	54,137,000,000	6.1%
9	North Carolina	29,302,000,000	3.3%
48	North Dakota	1,798,000,000	0.2%
6	Ohio	33,856,000,000	3.8%
28	Oklahoma	10,916,000,000	1.2%
25	Oregon	12,204,000,000	1.4%
5	Pennsylvania	42,299,000,000	4.8%
43	Rhode Island	3,264,000,000	0.4%
21	South Carolina	15,778,000,000	1.8%
46	South Dakota	2,374,000,000	0.3%
13	Tennessee	20,264,000,000	2.3%
3	Texas	56,285,000,000	6.4%
37	Utah	5,587,000,000	0.6%
47	Vermont	2,098,000,000	0.2%
12	Virginia	21,743,000,000	2.5%
15	Washington	19,395,000,000	2.2%
35	West Virginia	6,843,000,000	0.8%
19	Wisconsin	17,862,000,000	2.0%
49	Wyoming	1,560,000,000	0.2%

RANK ORDER

RANK	STATE	PAYMENTS	% of USA
1	California	$82,554,000,000	9.3%
2	Florida	63,947,000,000	7.2%
3	Texas	56,285,000,000	6.4%
4	New York	54,137,000,000	6.1%
5	Pennsylvania	42,299,000,000	4.8%
6	Ohio	33,856,000,000	3.8%
7	Michigan	33,762,000,000	3.8%
8	Illinois	33,340,000,000	3.8%
9	North Carolina	29,302,000,000	3.3%
10	New Jersey	26,098,000,000	2.9%
11	Georgia	24,935,000,000	2.8%
12	Virginia	21,743,000,000	2.5%
13	Tennessee	20,264,000,000	2.3%
14	Indiana	20,116,000,000	2.3%
15	Washington	19,395,000,000	2.2%
16	Arizona	18,713,000,000	2.1%
17	Massachusetts	18,643,000,000	2.1%
18	Missouri	18,392,000,000	2.1%
19	Wisconsin	17,862,000,000	2.0%
20	Alabama	15,943,000,000	1.8%
21	South Carolina	15,778,000,000	1.8%
22	Minnesota	14,974,000,000	1.7%
23	Maryland	14,824,000,000	1.7%
24	Kentucky	13,555,000,000	1.5%
25	Oregon	12,204,000,000	1.4%
26	Colorado	12,070,000,000	1.4%
27	Louisiana	11,994,000,000	1.4%
28	Oklahoma	10,916,000,000	1.2%
29	Connecticut	10,792,000,000	1.2%
30	Arkansas	9,461,000,000	1.1%
31	Iowa	9,323,000,000	1.1%
32	Mississippi	8,931,000,000	1.0%
33	Kansas	8,053,000,000	0.9%
34	Nevada	7,263,000,000	0.8%
35	West Virginia	6,843,000,000	0.8%
36	New Mexico	5,632,000,000	0.6%
37	Utah	5,587,000,000	0.6%
38	Nebraska	4,899,000,000	0.6%
39	Maine	4,550,000,000	0.5%
40	Idaho	4,529,000,000	0.5%
41	New Hampshire	4,461,000,000	0.5%
42	Hawaii	3,790,000,000	0.4%
43	Rhode Island	3,264,000,000	0.4%
44	Delaware	3,134,000,000	0.4%
45	Montana	3,073,000,000	0.3%
46	South Dakota	2,374,000,000	0.3%
47	Vermont	2,098,000,000	0.2%
48	North Dakota	1,798,000,000	0.2%
49	Wyoming	1,560,000,000	0.2%
50	Alaska	1,286,000,000	0.1%
	District of Columbia	1,108,000,000	0.1%

Source: U.S. Department of Health and Human Services, Social Security Administration
"Social Security Bulletin, Annual Statistical Supplement 2016" (https://www.ssa.gov/policy/docs/statcomps/supplement/)
*"OASDI" is Old Age, Survivors and Disability Insurance. National total includes $14,296,000,000 in payments to recipients in U.S. territories and foreign countries.

Per Capita Social Security (OASDI) Payments in 2015

National Per Capita = $2,715*

ALPHA ORDER				RANK ORDER		
RANK	STATE	PER CAPITA		RANK	STATE	PER CAPITA
8	Alabama	$3,287		1	West Virginia	$3,719
50	Alaska	1,743		2	Maine	3,427
29	Arizona	2,751		3	Michigan	3,404
10	Arkansas	3,179		4	Vermont	3,360
47	California	2,115		5	New Hampshire	3,354
46	Colorado	2,219		6	Delaware	3,320
19	Connecticut	3,003		7	Pennsylvania	3,307
6	Delaware	3,320		8	Alabama	3,287
11	Florida	3,155		9	South Carolina	3,225
44	Georgia	2,445		10	Arkansas	3,179
37	Hawaii	2,657		11	Florida	3,155
30	Idaho	2,746		12	Wisconsin	3,101
39	Illinois	2,592		13	Rhode Island	3,091
16	Indiana	3,043		14	Tennessee	3,075
21	Iowa	2,990		15	Kentucky	3,065
28	Kansas	2,771		16	Indiana	3,043
15	Kentucky	3,065		17	Oregon	3,038
41	Louisiana	2,568		18	Missouri	3,029
2	Maine	3,427		19	Connecticut	3,003
43	Maryland	2,470		20	Mississippi	2,992
31	Massachusetts	2,744		21	Iowa	2,990
3	Michigan	3,404		22	Montana	2,988
33	Minnesota	2,731		23	North Carolina	2,918
20	Mississippi	2,992		24	Ohio	2,917
18	Missouri	3,029		25	New Jersey	2,913
22	Montana	2,988		26	Oklahoma	2,796
40	Nebraska	2,587		27	South Dakota	2,780
42	Nevada	2,519		28	Kansas	2,771
5	New Hampshire	3,354		29	Arizona	2,751
25	New Jersey	2,913		30	Idaho	2,746
35	New Mexico	2,705		31	Massachusetts	2,744
32	New York	2,732		32	New York	2,732
23	North Carolina	2,918		33	Minnesota	2,731
45	North Dakota	2,382		34	Washington	2,712
24	Ohio	2,917		35	New Mexico	2,705
26	Oklahoma	2,796		36	Wyoming	2,662
17	Oregon	3,038		37	Hawaii	2,657
7	Pennsylvania	3,307		38	Virginia	2,599
13	Rhode Island	3,091		39	Illinois	2,592
9	South Carolina	3,225		40	Nebraska	2,587
27	South Dakota	2,780		41	Louisiana	2,568
14	Tennessee	3,075		42	Nevada	2,519
48	Texas	2,050		43	Maryland	2,470
49	Utah	1,872		44	Georgia	2,445
4	Vermont	3,360		45	North Dakota	2,382
38	Virginia	2,599		46	Colorado	2,219
34	Washington	2,712		47	California	2,115
1	West Virginia	3,719		48	Texas	2,050
12	Wisconsin	3,101		49	Utah	1,872
36	Wyoming	2,662		50	Alaska	1,743
					District of Columbia	1,647

Source: CQ Press using data from U.S. Department of Health and Human Services, Social Security Administration
   "Social Security Bulletin, Annual Statistical Supplement 2016" (https://www.ssa.gov/policy/docs/statcomps/supplement/)
*"OASDI" is Old Age, Survivors and Disability Insurance. National per capita does not include payments or population in U.S. territories and foreign countries.

Social Security (OASDI) Monthly Payments in 2015

National Total = $73,642,029,000*

ALPHA ORDER					RANK ORDER			
RANK	STATE	PAYMENTS	% of USA		RANK	STATE	PAYMENTS	% of USA
21	Alabama	$1,306,452,000	1.8%		1	California	$6,902,807,000	9.4%
50	Alaska	107,985,000	0.1%		2	Florida	5,382,979,000	7.3%
16	Arizona	1,576,939,000	2.1%		3	Texas	4,661,488,000	6.3%
30	Arkansas	777,068,000	1.1%		4	New York	4,498,413,000	6.1%
1	California	6,902,807,000	9.4%		5	Pennsylvania	3,498,489,000	4.8%
26	Colorado	1,012,557,000	1.4%		6	Michigan	2,787,250,000	3.8%
28	Connecticut	901,648,000	1.2%		7	Ohio	2,776,912,000	3.8%
44	Delaware	263,587,000	0.4%		8	Illinois	2,758,249,000	3.7%
2	Florida	5,382,979,000	7.3%		9	North Carolina	2,448,986,000	3.3%
11	Georgia	2,072,624,000	2.8%		10	New Jersey	2,176,808,000	3.0%
42	Hawaii	320,859,000	0.4%		11	Georgia	2,072,624,000	2.8%
39	Idaho	380,772,000	0.5%		12	Virginia	1,817,456,000	2.5%
8	Illinois	2,758,249,000	3.7%		13	Tennessee	1,676,300,000	2.3%
14	Indiana	1,662,631,000	2.3%		14	Indiana	1,662,631,000	2.3%
31	Iowa	775,036,000	1.1%		15	Washington	1,630,544,000	2.2%
33	Kansas	669,240,000	0.9%		16	Arizona	1,576,939,000	2.1%
24	Kentucky	1,104,955,000	1.5%		17	Massachusetts	1,550,369,000	2.1%
27	Louisiana	970,667,000	1.3%		18	Missouri	1,518,403,000	2.1%
40	Maine	378,015,000	0.5%		19	Wisconsin	1,492,247,000	2.0%
23	Maryland	1,239,738,000	1.7%		20	South Carolina	1,319,979,000	1.8%
17	Massachusetts	1,550,369,000	2.1%		21	Alabama	1,306,452,000	1.8%
6	Michigan	2,787,250,000	3.8%		22	Minnesota	1,255,533,000	1.7%
22	Minnesota	1,255,533,000	1.7%		23	Maryland	1,239,738,000	1.7%
32	Mississippi	730,844,000	1.0%		24	Kentucky	1,104,955,000	1.5%
18	Missouri	1,518,403,000	2.1%		25	Oregon	1,025,635,000	1.4%
45	Montana	257,376,000	0.3%		26	Colorado	1,012,557,000	1.4%
38	Nebraska	407,988,000	0.6%		27	Louisiana	970,667,000	1.3%
34	Nevada	613,347,000	0.8%		28	Connecticut	901,648,000	1.2%
41	New Hampshire	374,386,000	0.5%		29	Oklahoma	899,398,000	1.2%
10	New Jersey	2,176,808,000	3.0%		30	Arkansas	777,068,000	1.1%
36	New Mexico	469,318,000	0.6%		31	Iowa	775,036,000	1.1%
4	New York	4,498,413,000	6.1%		32	Mississippi	730,844,000	1.0%
9	North Carolina	2,448,986,000	3.3%		33	Kansas	669,240,000	0.9%
48	North Dakota	148,605,000	0.2%		34	Nevada	613,347,000	0.8%
7	Ohio	2,776,912,000	3.8%		35	West Virginia	554,556,000	0.8%
29	Oklahoma	899,398,000	1.2%		36	New Mexico	469,318,000	0.6%
25	Oregon	1,025,635,000	1.4%		37	Utah	468,330,000	0.6%
5	Pennsylvania	3,498,489,000	4.8%		38	Nebraska	407,988,000	0.6%
43	Rhode Island	272,007,000	0.4%		39	Idaho	380,772,000	0.5%
20	South Carolina	1,319,979,000	1.8%		40	Maine	378,015,000	0.5%
46	South Dakota	198,746,000	0.3%		41	New Hampshire	374,386,000	0.5%
13	Tennessee	1,676,300,000	2.3%		42	Hawaii	320,859,000	0.4%
3	Texas	4,661,488,000	6.3%		43	Rhode Island	272,007,000	0.4%
37	Utah	468,330,000	0.6%		44	Delaware	263,587,000	0.4%
47	Vermont	175,425,000	0.2%		45	Montana	257,376,000	0.3%
12	Virginia	1,817,456,000	2.5%		46	South Dakota	198,746,000	0.3%
15	Washington	1,630,544,000	2.2%		47	Vermont	175,425,000	0.2%
35	West Virginia	554,556,000	0.8%		48	North Dakota	148,605,000	0.2%
19	Wisconsin	1,492,247,000	2.0%		49	Wyoming	130,787,000	0.2%
49	Wyoming	130,787,000	0.2%		50	Alaska	107,985,000	0.1%
						District of Columbia	92,474,000	0.1%

Source: U.S. Department of Health and Human Services, Social Security Administration
"Social Security Bulletin, Annual Statistical Supplement 2016" (https://www.ssa.gov/policy/docs/statcomps/supplement/)
*For December 2015. "OASDI" is Old Age, Survivors and Disability Insurance. National total includes $1,148,822,000 in payments
to recipients in U.S. territories and foreign countries.

Social Security (OASDI) Beneficiaries in 2015

National Total = 59,963,425*

ALPHA ORDER

RANK	STATE	BENEFICIARIES	% of USA
20	Alabama	1,108,543	1.8%
50	Alaska	91,960	0.2%
17	Arizona	1,241,101	2.1%
29	Arkansas	679,689	1.1%
1	California	5,651,601	9.4%
27	Colorado	813,266	1.4%
30	Connecticut	659,238	1.1%
45	Delaware	196,651	0.3%
2	Florida	4,334,337	7.2%
10	Georgia	1,714,145	2.9%
42	Hawaii	256,912	0.4%
40	Idaho	315,571	0.5%
7	Illinois	2,174,883	3.6%
14	Indiana	1,301,948	2.2%
32	Iowa	622,906	1.0%
33	Kansas	528,174	0.9%
23	Kentucky	963,497	1.6%
25	Louisiana	868,017	1.4%
39	Maine	329,559	0.5%
24	Maryland	952,251	1.6%
18	Massachusetts	1,236,248	2.1%
8	Michigan	2,141,824	3.6%
22	Minnesota	979,776	1.6%
31	Mississippi	647,420	1.1%
16	Missouri	1,258,256	2.1%
44	Montana	217,758	0.4%
38	Nebraska	330,309	0.6%
34	Nevada	492,121	0.8%
41	New Hampshire	288,891	0.5%
11	New Jersey	1,583,456	2.6%
36	New Mexico	408,931	0.7%
4	New York	3,513,125	5.9%
9	North Carolina	1,984,962	3.3%
48	North Dakota	125,786	0.2%
6	Ohio	2,290,813	3.8%
28	Oklahoma	758,912	1.3%
26	Oregon	818,228	1.4%
5	Pennsylvania	2,744,424	4.6%
43	Rhode Island	217,881	0.4%
21	South Carolina	1,066,150	1.8%
46	South Dakota	168,626	0.3%
13	Tennessee	1,392,164	2.3%
3	Texas	3,928,648	6.6%
37	Utah	375,685	0.6%
47	Vermont	142,755	0.2%
12	Virginia	1,443,127	2.4%
15	Washington	1,260,474	2.1%
35	West Virginia	468,120	0.8%
19	Wisconsin	1,170,705	2.0%
49	Wyoming	103,689	0.2%

RANK ORDER

RANK	STATE	BENEFICIARIES	% of USA
1	California	5,651,601	9.4%
2	Florida	4,334,337	7.2%
3	Texas	3,928,648	6.6%
4	New York	3,513,125	5.9%
5	Pennsylvania	2,744,424	4.6%
6	Ohio	2,290,813	3.8%
7	Illinois	2,174,883	3.6%
8	Michigan	2,141,824	3.6%
9	North Carolina	1,984,962	3.3%
10	Georgia	1,714,145	2.9%
11	New Jersey	1,583,456	2.6%
12	Virginia	1,443,127	2.4%
13	Tennessee	1,392,164	2.3%
14	Indiana	1,301,948	2.2%
15	Washington	1,260,474	2.1%
16	Missouri	1,258,256	2.1%
17	Arizona	1,241,101	2.1%
18	Massachusetts	1,236,248	2.1%
19	Wisconsin	1,170,705	2.0%
20	Alabama	1,108,543	1.8%
21	South Carolina	1,066,150	1.8%
22	Minnesota	979,776	1.6%
23	Kentucky	963,497	1.6%
24	Maryland	952,251	1.6%
25	Louisiana	868,017	1.4%
26	Oregon	818,228	1.4%
27	Colorado	813,266	1.4%
28	Oklahoma	758,912	1.3%
29	Arkansas	679,689	1.1%
30	Connecticut	659,238	1.1%
31	Mississippi	647,420	1.1%
32	Iowa	622,906	1.0%
33	Kansas	528,174	0.9%
34	Nevada	492,121	0.8%
35	West Virginia	468,120	0.8%
36	New Mexico	408,931	0.7%
37	Utah	375,685	0.6%
38	Nebraska	330,309	0.6%
39	Maine	329,559	0.5%
40	Idaho	315,571	0.5%
41	New Hampshire	288,891	0.5%
42	Hawaii	256,912	0.4%
43	Rhode Island	217,881	0.4%
44	Montana	217,758	0.4%
45	Delaware	196,651	0.3%
46	South Dakota	168,626	0.3%
47	Vermont	142,755	0.2%
48	North Dakota	125,786	0.2%
49	Wyoming	103,689	0.2%
50	Alaska	91,960	0.2%
	District of Columbia	80,546	0.1%

Source: U.S. Department of Health and Human Services, Social Security Administration
"Social Security Bulletin, Annual Statistical Supplement 2016" (https://www.ssa.gov/policy/docs/statcomps/supplement/)
*For December 2015. "OASDI" is Old Age, Survivors and Disability Insurance. National total includes 1,519,366 beneficiaries in U.S. territories and foreign countries.

Average Monthly Social Security (OASDI) Payment in 2015

National Average = $1,240 Each Month per Beneficiary*

ALPHA ORDER

RANK	STATE	PER BENEFICIARY
42	Alabama	$1,179
44	Alaska	1,174
13	Arizona	1,271
48	Arkansas	1,143
31	California	1,221
24	Colorado	1,245
2	Connecticut	1,368
3	Delaware	1,340
26	Florida	1,242
33	Georgia	1,209
20	Hawaii	1,249
34	Idaho	1,207
14	Illinois	1,268
10	Indiana	1,277
25	Iowa	1,244
15	Kansas	1,267
46	Kentucky	1,147
50	Louisiana	1,118
46	Maine	1,147
4	Maryland	1,302
18	Massachusetts	1,254
5	Michigan	1,301
8	Minnesota	1,281
49	Mississippi	1,129
34	Missouri	1,207
40	Montana	1,182
28	Nebraska	1,235
23	Nevada	1,246
6	New Hampshire	1,296
1	New Jersey	1,375
45	New Mexico	1,148
9	New York	1,280
29	North Carolina	1,234
41	North Dakota	1,181
32	Ohio	1,212
38	Oklahoma	1,185
19	Oregon	1,253
11	Pennsylvania	1,275
21	Rhode Island	1,248
27	South Carolina	1,238
42	South Dakota	1,179
36	Tennessee	1,204
37	Texas	1,187
22	Utah	1,247
30	Vermont	1,229
17	Virginia	1,259
7	Washington	1,294
38	West Virginia	1,185
11	Wisconsin	1,275
16	Wyoming	1,261

RANK ORDER

RANK	STATE	PER BENEFICIARY
1	New Jersey	$1,375
2	Connecticut	1,368
3	Delaware	1,340
4	Maryland	1,302
5	Michigan	1,301
6	New Hampshire	1,296
7	Washington	1,294
8	Minnesota	1,281
9	New York	1,280
10	Indiana	1,277
11	Pennsylvania	1,275
11	Wisconsin	1,275
13	Arizona	1,271
14	Illinois	1,268
15	Kansas	1,267
16	Wyoming	1,261
17	Virginia	1,259
18	Massachusetts	1,254
19	Oregon	1,253
20	Hawaii	1,249
21	Rhode Island	1,248
22	Utah	1,247
23	Nevada	1,246
24	Colorado	1,245
25	Iowa	1,244
26	Florida	1,242
27	South Carolina	1,238
28	Nebraska	1,235
29	North Carolina	1,234
30	Vermont	1,229
31	California	1,221
32	Ohio	1,212
33	Georgia	1,209
34	Idaho	1,207
34	Missouri	1,207
36	Tennessee	1,204
37	Texas	1,187
38	Oklahoma	1,185
38	West Virginia	1,185
40	Montana	1,182
41	North Dakota	1,181
42	Alabama	1,179
42	South Dakota	1,179
44	Alaska	1,174
45	New Mexico	1,148
46	Kentucky	1,147
46	Maine	1,147
48	Arkansas	1,143
49	Mississippi	1,129
50	Louisiana	1,118

District of Columbia	1,148

Source: CQ Press using data from U.S. Department of Health and Human Services, Social Security Administration
"Social Security Bulletin, Annual Statistical Supplement 2016" (https://www.ssa.gov/policy/docs/statcomps/supplement/)
*As of December 2015. "OASDI" is Old Age, Survivors and Disability Insurance. National average does not include beneficiaries or payments in U.S. territories or foreign countries.

Social Security Supplemental Security Income Beneficiaries in 2015

National Total = 8,309,564 Beneficiaries*

ALPHA ORDER

RANK	STATE	BENEFICIARIES	% of USA
16	Alabama	170,869	2.1%
48	Alaska	12,520	0.2%
23	Arizona	119,587	1.4%
26	Arkansas	110,094	1.3%
1	California	1,293,304	15.6%
31	Colorado	72,764	0.9%
33	Connecticut	63,740	0.8%
45	Delaware	16,869	0.2%
4	Florida	570,877	6.9%
9	Georgia	258,324	3.1%
42	Hawaii	24,775	0.3%
40	Idaho	30,735	0.4%
8	Illinois	274,742	3.3%
20	Indiana	128,774	1.5%
35	Iowa	51,020	0.6%
36	Kansas	48,374	0.6%
12	Kentucky	184,125	2.2%
15	Louisiana	178,985	2.2%
37	Maine	37,357	0.4%
22	Maryland	120,233	1.4%
11	Massachusetts	188,051	2.3%
7	Michigan	275,873	3.3%
28	Minnesota	94,147	1.1%
21	Mississippi	123,199	1.5%
19	Missouri	140,257	1.7%
44	Montana	18,315	0.2%
41	Nebraska	27,892	0.3%
34	Nevada	53,280	0.6%
43	New Hampshire	19,619	0.2%
13	New Jersey	182,460	2.2%
32	New Mexico	64,171	0.8%
3	New York	649,277	7.8%
10	North Carolina	235,607	2.8%
49	North Dakota	8,206	0.1%
6	Ohio	312,237	3.8%
27	Oklahoma	96,875	1.2%
29	Oregon	86,056	1.0%
5	Pennsylvania	367,995	4.4%
38	Rhode Island	33,137	0.4%
25	South Carolina	118,047	1.4%
47	South Dakota	14,820	0.2%
14	Tennessee	181,909	2.2%
2	Texas	666,012	8.0%
39	Utah	31,325	0.4%
46	Vermont	15,713	0.2%
17	Virginia	156,446	1.9%
18	Washington	150,981	1.8%
30	West Virginia	76,404	0.9%
24	Wisconsin	118,487	1.4%
50	Wyoming	6,701	0.1%

RANK ORDER

RANK	STATE	BENEFICIARIES	% of USA
1	California	1,293,304	15.6%
2	Texas	666,012	8.0%
3	New York	649,277	7.8%
4	Florida	570,877	6.9%
5	Pennsylvania	367,995	4.4%
6	Ohio	312,237	3.8%
7	Michigan	275,873	3.3%
8	Illinois	274,742	3.3%
9	Georgia	258,324	3.1%
10	North Carolina	235,607	2.8%
11	Massachusetts	188,051	2.3%
12	Kentucky	184,125	2.2%
13	New Jersey	182,460	2.2%
14	Tennessee	181,909	2.2%
15	Louisiana	178,985	2.2%
16	Alabama	170,869	2.1%
17	Virginia	156,446	1.9%
18	Washington	150,981	1.8%
19	Missouri	140,257	1.7%
20	Indiana	128,774	1.5%
21	Mississippi	123,199	1.5%
22	Maryland	120,233	1.4%
23	Arizona	119,587	1.4%
24	Wisconsin	118,487	1.4%
25	South Carolina	118,047	1.4%
26	Arkansas	110,094	1.3%
27	Oklahoma	96,875	1.2%
28	Minnesota	94,147	1.1%
29	Oregon	86,056	1.0%
30	West Virginia	76,404	0.9%
31	Colorado	72,764	0.9%
32	New Mexico	64,171	0.8%
33	Connecticut	63,740	0.8%
34	Nevada	53,280	0.6%
35	Iowa	51,020	0.6%
36	Kansas	48,374	0.6%
37	Maine	37,357	0.4%
38	Rhode Island	33,137	0.4%
39	Utah	31,325	0.4%
40	Idaho	30,735	0.4%
41	Nebraska	27,892	0.3%
42	Hawaii	24,775	0.3%
43	New Hampshire	19,619	0.2%
44	Montana	18,315	0.2%
45	Delaware	16,869	0.2%
46	Vermont	15,713	0.2%
47	South Dakota	14,820	0.2%
48	Alaska	12,520	0.2%
49	North Dakota	8,206	0.1%
50	Wyoming	6,701	0.1%
	District of Columbia	26,965	0.3%

Source: U.S. Department of Health and Human Services, Social Security Administration
"Social Security Bulletin, Annual Statistical Supplement 2016" (https://www.ssa.gov/policy/docs/statcomps/supplement/)
*For December 2015. National total includes1,032 beneficiaries in U.S. territories or otherwise not distributed by state. The SSI program provides income support to persons age 65 and older and blind or disabled adults and children.

Average Monthly Social Security
Supplemental Security Income Payment in 2015
National Average = $525.72 Each Month per Beneficiary*

ALPHA ORDER

RANK	STATE	AVERAGE BENEFIT
34	Alabama	$513.06
40	Alaska	505.73
11	Arizona	534.35
27	Arkansas	521.22
31	California	517.78
26	Colorado	521.29
13	Connecticut	531.29
15	Delaware	529.75
20	Florida	525.62
24	Georgia	521.75
21	Hawaii	524.32
29	Idaho	519.16
6	Illinois	546.60
8	Indiana	537.00
43	Iowa	502.70
25	Kansas	521.37
22	Kentucky	522.71
18	Louisiana	526.83
45	Maine	499.02
4	Maryland	549.81
19	Massachusetts	526.47
2	Michigan	550.64
7	Minnesota	539.54
38	Mississippi	507.18
33	Missouri	516.06
47	Montana	497.64
42	Nebraska	503.40
9	Nevada	536.29
41	New Hampshire	505.19
39	New Jersey	506.81
44	New Mexico	502.47
10	New York	534.59
35	North Carolina	509.97
50	North Dakota	475.94
5	Ohio	546.83
28	Oklahoma	520.92
13	Oregon	531.29
1	Pennsylvania	552.66
16	Rhode Island	528.07
36	South Carolina	509.93
49	South Dakota	494.18
32	Tennessee	516.99
37	Texas	507.43
23	Utah	522.18
48	Vermont	497.43
30	Virginia	518.54
3	Washington	549.98
17	West Virginia	528.04
12	Wisconsin	531.36
46	Wyoming	498.19

RANK ORDER

RANK	STATE	AVERAGE BENEFIT
1	Pennsylvania	$552.66
2	Michigan	550.64
3	Washington	549.98
4	Maryland	549.81
5	Ohio	546.83
6	Illinois	546.60
7	Minnesota	539.54
8	Indiana	537.00
9	Nevada	536.29
10	New York	534.59
11	Arizona	534.35
12	Wisconsin	531.36
13	Connecticut	531.29
13	Oregon	531.29
15	Delaware	529.75
16	Rhode Island	528.07
17	West Virginia	528.04
18	Louisiana	526.83
19	Massachusetts	526.47
20	Florida	525.62
21	Hawaii	524.32
22	Kentucky	522.71
23	Utah	522.18
24	Georgia	521.75
25	Kansas	521.37
26	Colorado	521.29
27	Arkansas	521.22
28	Oklahoma	520.92
29	Idaho	519.16
30	Virginia	518.54
31	California	517.78
32	Tennessee	516.99
33	Missouri	516.06
34	Alabama	513.06
35	North Carolina	509.97
36	South Carolina	509.93
37	Texas	507.43
38	Mississippi	507.18
39	New Jersey	506.81
40	Alaska	505.73
41	New Hampshire	505.19
42	Nebraska	503.40
43	Iowa	502.70
44	New Mexico	502.47
45	Maine	499.02
46	Wyoming	498.19
47	Montana	497.64
48	Vermont	497.43
49	South Dakota	494.18
50	North Dakota	475.94

District of Columbia 569.67

Source: U.S. Department of Health and Human Services, Social Security Administration

"Social Security Bulletin, Annual Statistical Supplement 2016" (https://www.ssa.gov/policy/docs/statcomps/supplement/)

*As of December 2015. National average includes payments to beneficiaries in U.S. territories and foreign countries. The SSI program provides income support to persons age 65 and older and blind or disabled adults and children.

Medicare Enrollees in 2016

National Total = 57,148,298 Enrollees*

ALPHA ORDER

RANK	STATE	ENROLLEES	% of USA
20	Alabama	990,834	1.7%
50	Alaska	88,333	0.2%
17	Arizona	1,180,582	2.1%
30	Arkansas	606,565	1.1%
1	California	5,826,227	10.2%
25	Colorado	817,908	1.4%
29	Connecticut	643,268	1.1%
45	Delaware	187,336	0.3%
2	Florida	4,166,079	7.3%
10	Georgia	1,575,468	2.8%
42	Hawaii	252,185	0.4%
40	Idaho	294,580	0.5%
7	Illinois	2,113,929	3.7%
16	Indiana	1,180,734	2.1%
31	Iowa	586,410	1.0%
33	Kansas	499,515	0.9%
24	Kentucky	882,123	1.5%
26	Louisiana	815,907	1.4%
39	Maine	314,834	0.6%
22	Maryland	960,975	1.7%
14	Massachusetts	1,250,755	2.2%
8	Michigan	1,943,261	3.4%
23	Minnesota	941,427	1.6%
32	Mississippi	572,164	1.0%
18	Missouri	1,162,437	2.0%
43	Montana	208,773	0.4%
38	Nebraska	322,326	0.6%
34	Nevada	472,914	0.8%
41	New Hampshire	275,097	0.5%
11	New Jersey	1,526,750	2.7%
36	New Mexico	385,898	0.7%
4	New York	3,421,064	6.0%
9	North Carolina	1,827,086	3.2%
48	North Dakota	121,933	0.2%
6	Ohio	2,206,629	3.9%
28	Oklahoma	693,893	1.2%
27	Oregon	783,986	1.4%
5	Pennsylvania	2,587,714	4.5%
44	Rhode Island	207,811	0.4%
21	South Carolina	975,927	1.7%
46	South Dakota	160,948	0.3%
13	Tennessee	1,269,219	2.2%
3	Texas	3,765,255	6.6%
37	Utah	359,472	0.6%
47	Vermont	135,668	0.2%
12	Virginia	1,391,518	2.4%
15	Washington	1,237,274	2.2%
35	West Virginia	423,634	0.7%
19	Wisconsin	1,082,446	1.9%
49	Wyoming	98,558	0.2%

RANK ORDER

RANK	STATE	ENROLLEES	% of USA
1	California	5,826,227	10.2%
2	Florida	4,166,079	7.3%
3	Texas	3,765,255	6.6%
4	New York	3,421,064	6.0%
5	Pennsylvania	2,587,714	4.5%
6	Ohio	2,206,629	3.9%
7	Illinois	2,113,929	3.7%
8	Michigan	1,943,261	3.4%
9	North Carolina	1,827,086	3.2%
10	Georgia	1,575,468	2.8%
11	New Jersey	1,526,750	2.7%
12	Virginia	1,391,518	2.4%
13	Tennessee	1,269,219	2.2%
14	Massachusetts	1,250,755	2.2%
15	Washington	1,237,274	2.2%
16	Indiana	1,180,734	2.1%
17	Arizona	1,180,582	2.1%
18	Missouri	1,162,437	2.0%
19	Wisconsin	1,082,446	1.9%
20	Alabama	990,834	1.7%
21	South Carolina	975,927	1.7%
22	Maryland	960,975	1.7%
23	Minnesota	941,427	1.6%
24	Kentucky	882,123	1.5%
25	Colorado	817,908	1.4%
26	Louisiana	815,907	1.4%
27	Oregon	783,986	1.4%
28	Oklahoma	693,893	1.2%
29	Connecticut	643,268	1.1%
30	Arkansas	606,565	1.1%
31	Iowa	586,410	1.0%
32	Mississippi	572,164	1.0%
33	Kansas	499,515	0.9%
34	Nevada	472,914	0.8%
35	West Virginia	423,634	0.7%
36	New Mexico	385,898	0.7%
37	Utah	359,472	0.6%
38	Nebraska	322,326	0.6%
39	Maine	314,834	0.6%
40	Idaho	294,580	0.5%
41	New Hampshire	275,097	0.5%
42	Hawaii	252,185	0.4%
43	Montana	208,773	0.4%
44	Rhode Island	207,811	0.4%
45	Delaware	187,336	0.3%
46	South Dakota	160,948	0.3%
47	Vermont	135,668	0.2%
48	North Dakota	121,933	0.2%
49	Wyoming	98,558	0.2%
50	Alaska	88,333	0.2%
	District of Columbia	90,520	0.2%

Source: U.S. Department of Health and Human Services, Centers for Medicare and Medicaid Services
"Medicare Enrollment Dashboard"
(https://www.cms.gov/Research-Statistics-Data-and-Systems/Statistics-Trends-and-Reports/CMSProgramStatistics/Dashboard.html)
*Includes original Medicare, Medicare Advantage, and other Medicare health plans. Includes Aged and Disabled enrollees. Total includes 1,262,151 enrollees in Puerto Rico and other outlying areas, foreign countries, or whose address is unknown.

Percent of Population Enrolled in Medicare in 2016

National Percent = 17.3% of Population*

ALPHA ORDER

RANK	STATE	PERCENT
5	Alabama	20.4
49	Alaska	11.9
34	Arizona	17.1
6	Arkansas	20.3
46	California	14.8
46	Colorado	14.8
26	Connecticut	17.9
11	Delaware	19.7
7	Florida	20.2
45	Georgia	15.3
28	Hawaii	17.7
30	Idaho	17.5
40	Illinois	16.5
27	Indiana	17.8
21	Iowa	18.7
32	Kansas	17.2
10	Kentucky	19.9
31	Louisiana	17.4
1	Maine	23.7
44	Maryland	16.0
24	Massachusetts	18.3
13	Michigan	19.6
35	Minnesota	17.0
15	Mississippi	19.2
17	Missouri	19.1
9	Montana	20.1
38	Nebraska	16.9
42	Nevada	16.1
4	New Hampshire	20.6
35	New Jersey	17.0
23	New Mexico	18.5
32	New York	17.2
25	North Carolina	18.0
42	North Dakota	16.1
19	Ohio	19.0
28	Oklahoma	17.7
15	Oregon	19.2
7	Pennsylvania	20.2
13	Rhode Island	19.6
11	South Carolina	19.7
21	South Dakota	18.7
17	Tennessee	19.1
48	Texas	13.5
50	Utah	11.8
3	Vermont	21.8
40	Virginia	16.5
35	Washington	17.0
2	West Virginia	23.2
20	Wisconsin	18.8
38	Wyoming	16.9

RANK ORDER

RANK	STATE	PERCENT
1	Maine	23.7
2	West Virginia	23.2
3	Vermont	21.8
4	New Hampshire	20.6
5	Alabama	20.4
6	Arkansas	20.3
7	Florida	20.2
7	Pennsylvania	20.2
9	Montana	20.1
10	Kentucky	19.9
11	Delaware	19.7
11	South Carolina	19.7
13	Michigan	19.6
13	Rhode Island	19.6
15	Mississippi	19.2
15	Oregon	19.2
17	Missouri	19.1
17	Tennessee	19.1
19	Ohio	19.0
20	Wisconsin	18.8
21	Iowa	18.7
21	South Dakota	18.7
23	New Mexico	18.5
24	Massachusetts	18.3
25	North Carolina	18.0
26	Connecticut	17.9
27	Indiana	17.8
28	Hawaii	17.7
28	Oklahoma	17.7
30	Idaho	17.5
31	Louisiana	17.4
32	Kansas	17.2
32	New York	17.2
34	Arizona	17.1
35	Minnesota	17.0
35	New Jersey	17.0
35	Washington	17.0
38	Nebraska	16.9
38	Wyoming	16.9
40	Illinois	16.5
40	Virginia	16.5
42	Nevada	16.1
42	North Dakota	16.1
44	Maryland	16.0
45	Georgia	15.3
46	California	14.8
46	Colorado	14.8
48	Texas	13.5
49	Alaska	11.9
50	Utah	11.8

District of Columbia   13.2

Source: CQ Press using data from U.S. Department of Health and Human Services, Centers for Medicare and Medicaid Services
"Medicare Enrollment Dashboard"
(https://www.cms.gov/Research-Statistics-Data-and-Systems/Statistics-Trends-and-Reports/CMSProgramStatistics/Dashboard.html)
*Includes original Medicare, Medicare Advantage, and other Medicare health plans. Includes Aged and Disabled enrollees. National
rate does not include enrollees or population in Puerto Rico and other outlying areas, foreign countries, or whose address is
unknown.

Medicare Actual Costs in 2015

National Total = $329,183,857,907*

<table>
<tr><th colspan="4">ALPHA ORDER</th><th colspan="4">RANK ORDER</th></tr>
<tr><th>RANK</th><th>STATE</th><th>ACTUAL COSTS</th><th>% of USA</th><th>RANK</th><th>STATE</th><th>ACTUAL COSTS</th><th>% of USA</th></tr>
<tr><td>19</td><td>Alabama</td><td>$5,976,605,277</td><td>1.8%</td><td>1</td><td>California</td><td>$29,252,903,779</td><td>8.9%</td></tr>
<tr><td>50</td><td>Alaska</td><td>656,058,136</td><td>0.2%</td><td>2</td><td>Florida</td><td>24,245,523,346</td><td>7.4%</td></tr>
<tr><td>21</td><td>Arizona</td><td>5,557,136,633</td><td>1.7%</td><td>3</td><td>Texas</td><td>23,503,459,237</td><td>7.1%</td></tr>
<tr><td>29</td><td>Arkansas</td><td>3,762,983,621</td><td>1.1%</td><td>4</td><td>New York</td><td>20,127,008,082</td><td>6.1%</td></tr>
<tr><td>1</td><td>California</td><td>29,252,903,779</td><td>8.9%</td><td>5</td><td>Illinois</td><td>14,161,706,757</td><td>4.3%</td></tr>
<tr><td>30</td><td>Colorado</td><td>3,628,015,347</td><td>1.1%</td><td>6</td><td>Pennsylvania</td><td>13,667,895,274</td><td>4.2%</td></tr>
<tr><td>26</td><td>Connecticut</td><td>4,730,529,621</td><td>1.4%</td><td>7</td><td>New Jersey</td><td>13,077,320,636</td><td>4.0%</td></tr>
<tr><td>41</td><td>Delaware</td><td>1,584,751,537</td><td>0.5%</td><td>8</td><td>Michigan</td><td>11,817,426,563</td><td>3.6%</td></tr>
<tr><td>2</td><td>Florida</td><td>24,245,523,346</td><td>7.4%</td><td>9</td><td>Ohio</td><td>10,707,852,685</td><td>3.3%</td></tr>
<tr><td>12</td><td>Georgia</td><td>8,725,252,598</td><td>2.7%</td><td>10</td><td>North Carolina</td><td>10,529,454,698</td><td>3.2%</td></tr>
<tr><td>47</td><td>Hawaii</td><td>785,230,789</td><td>0.2%</td><td>11</td><td>Massachusetts</td><td>9,480,923,702</td><td>2.9%</td></tr>
<tr><td>42</td><td>Idaho</td><td>1,398,605,480</td><td>0.4%</td><td>12</td><td>Georgia</td><td>8,725,252,598</td><td>2.7%</td></tr>
<tr><td>5</td><td>Illinois</td><td>14,161,706,757</td><td>4.3%</td><td>13</td><td>Maryland</td><td>8,670,779,538</td><td>2.6%</td></tr>
<tr><td>15</td><td>Indiana</td><td>7,928,736,958</td><td>2.4%</td><td>14</td><td>Virginia</td><td>8,458,605,328</td><td>2.6%</td></tr>
<tr><td>28</td><td>Iowa</td><td>3,846,244,037</td><td>1.2%</td><td>15</td><td>Indiana</td><td>7,928,736,958</td><td>2.4%</td></tr>
<tr><td>31</td><td>Kansas</td><td>3,569,884,417</td><td>1.1%</td><td>16</td><td>Missouri</td><td>6,902,978,212</td><td>2.1%</td></tr>
<tr><td>22</td><td>Kentucky</td><td>5,362,389,222</td><td>1.6%</td><td>17</td><td>Tennessee</td><td>6,722,643,914</td><td>2.0%</td></tr>
<tr><td>23</td><td>Louisiana</td><td>5,354,101,869</td><td>1.6%</td><td>18</td><td>Washington</td><td>6,263,687,844</td><td>1.9%</td></tr>
<tr><td>38</td><td>Maine</td><td>1,872,709,044</td><td>0.6%</td><td>19</td><td>Alabama</td><td>5,976,605,277</td><td>1.8%</td></tr>
<tr><td>13</td><td>Maryland</td><td>8,670,779,538</td><td>2.6%</td><td>20</td><td>South Carolina</td><td>5,975,047,788</td><td>1.8%</td></tr>
<tr><td>11</td><td>Massachusetts</td><td>9,480,923,702</td><td>2.9%</td><td>21</td><td>Arizona</td><td>5,557,136,633</td><td>1.7%</td></tr>
<tr><td>8</td><td>Michigan</td><td>11,817,426,563</td><td>3.6%</td><td>22</td><td>Kentucky</td><td>5,362,389,222</td><td>1.6%</td></tr>
<tr><td>32</td><td>Minnesota</td><td>3,295,953,208</td><td>1.0%</td><td>23</td><td>Louisiana</td><td>5,354,101,869</td><td>1.6%</td></tr>
<tr><td>27</td><td>Mississippi</td><td>4,474,620,725</td><td>1.4%</td><td>24</td><td>Wisconsin</td><td>5,146,365,117</td><td>1.6%</td></tr>
<tr><td>16</td><td>Missouri</td><td>6,902,978,212</td><td>2.1%</td><td>25</td><td>Oklahoma</td><td>5,029,701,630</td><td>1.5%</td></tr>
<tr><td>43</td><td>Montana</td><td>1,165,523,915</td><td>0.4%</td><td>26</td><td>Connecticut</td><td>4,730,529,621</td><td>1.4%</td></tr>
<tr><td>36</td><td>Nebraska</td><td>2,345,035,271</td><td>0.7%</td><td>27</td><td>Mississippi</td><td>4,474,620,725</td><td>1.4%</td></tr>
<tr><td>34</td><td>Nevada</td><td>2,628,418,826</td><td>0.8%</td><td>28</td><td>Iowa</td><td>3,846,244,037</td><td>1.2%</td></tr>
<tr><td>37</td><td>New Hampshire</td><td>1,973,336,160</td><td>0.6%</td><td>29</td><td>Arkansas</td><td>3,762,983,621</td><td>1.1%</td></tr>
<tr><td>7</td><td>New Jersey</td><td>13,077,320,636</td><td>4.0%</td><td>30</td><td>Colorado</td><td>3,628,015,347</td><td>1.1%</td></tr>
<tr><td>39</td><td>New Mexico</td><td>1,751,059,546</td><td>0.5%</td><td>31</td><td>Kansas</td><td>3,569,884,417</td><td>1.1%</td></tr>
<tr><td>4</td><td>New York</td><td>20,127,008,082</td><td>6.1%</td><td>32</td><td>Minnesota</td><td>3,295,953,208</td><td>1.0%</td></tr>
<tr><td>10</td><td>North Carolina</td><td>10,529,454,698</td><td>3.2%</td><td>33</td><td>Oregon</td><td>2,990,492,550</td><td>0.9%</td></tr>
<tr><td>48</td><td>North Dakota</td><td>762,604,884</td><td>0.2%</td><td>34</td><td>Nevada</td><td>2,628,418,826</td><td>0.8%</td></tr>
<tr><td>9</td><td>Ohio</td><td>10,707,852,685</td><td>3.3%</td><td>35</td><td>West Virginia</td><td>2,509,473,961</td><td>0.8%</td></tr>
<tr><td>25</td><td>Oklahoma</td><td>5,029,701,630</td><td>1.5%</td><td>36</td><td>Nebraska</td><td>2,345,035,271</td><td>0.7%</td></tr>
<tr><td>33</td><td>Oregon</td><td>2,990,492,550</td><td>0.9%</td><td>37</td><td>New Hampshire</td><td>1,973,336,160</td><td>0.6%</td></tr>
<tr><td>6</td><td>Pennsylvania</td><td>13,667,895,274</td><td>4.2%</td><td>38</td><td>Maine</td><td>1,872,709,044</td><td>0.6%</td></tr>
<tr><td>44</td><td>Rhode Island</td><td>1,138,213,119</td><td>0.3%</td><td>39</td><td>New Mexico</td><td>1,751,059,546</td><td>0.5%</td></tr>
<tr><td>20</td><td>South Carolina</td><td>5,975,047,788</td><td>1.8%</td><td>40</td><td>Utah</td><td>1,688,592,245</td><td>0.5%</td></tr>
<tr><td>45</td><td>South Dakota</td><td>982,470,459</td><td>0.3%</td><td>41</td><td>Delaware</td><td>1,584,751,537</td><td>0.5%</td></tr>
<tr><td>17</td><td>Tennessee</td><td>6,722,643,914</td><td>2.0%</td><td>42</td><td>Idaho</td><td>1,398,605,480</td><td>0.4%</td></tr>
<tr><td>3</td><td>Texas</td><td>23,503,459,237</td><td>7.1%</td><td>43</td><td>Montana</td><td>1,165,523,915</td><td>0.4%</td></tr>
<tr><td>40</td><td>Utah</td><td>1,688,592,245</td><td>0.5%</td><td>44</td><td>Rhode Island</td><td>1,138,213,119</td><td>0.3%</td></tr>
<tr><td>46</td><td>Vermont</td><td>956,757,835</td><td>0.3%</td><td>45</td><td>South Dakota</td><td>982,470,459</td><td>0.3%</td></tr>
<tr><td>14</td><td>Virginia</td><td>8,458,605,328</td><td>2.6%</td><td>46</td><td>Vermont</td><td>956,757,835</td><td>0.3%</td></tr>
<tr><td>18</td><td>Washington</td><td>6,263,687,844</td><td>1.9%</td><td>47</td><td>Hawaii</td><td>785,230,789</td><td>0.2%</td></tr>
<tr><td>35</td><td>West Virginia</td><td>2,509,473,961</td><td>0.8%</td><td>48</td><td>North Dakota</td><td>762,604,884</td><td>0.2%</td></tr>
<tr><td>24</td><td>Wisconsin</td><td>5,146,365,117</td><td>1.6%</td><td>49</td><td>Wyoming</td><td>728,535,725</td><td>0.2%</td></tr>
<tr><td>49</td><td>Wyoming</td><td>728,535,725</td><td>0.2%</td><td>50</td><td>Alaska</td><td>656,058,136</td><td>0.2%</td></tr>
<tr><td></td><td></td><td></td><td></td><td></td><td>District of Columbia</td><td>699,739,444</td><td>0.2%</td></tr>
</table>

Source: U.S. Department of Health and Human Services, Centers for Medicare and Medicaid Services
"Medicare Geographic Variation" (Public Use File)
(https://www.cms.gov/Research-Statistics-Data-and-Systems/Statistics-Trends-and-Reports/Medicare-Geographic-Variation/)
*Total actual costs not standardized for geographical variations. National figure includes payments to enrollees in Puerto Rico and other outlying areas.

Medicare Actual Costs per Beneficiary in 2015

National Rate = $6,206*

ALPHA ORDER

RANK	STATE	PER BENEFICIARY
26	Alabama	$6,286
4	Alaska	8,490
43	Arizona	5,085
23	Arkansas	6,419
38	California	5,542
47	Colorado	4,853
7	Connecticut	7,985
3	Delaware	9,026
30	Florida	6,121
36	Georgia	5,916
50	Hawaii	3,481
44	Idaho	5,045
14	Illinois	7,205
15	Indiana	6,999
17	Iowa	6,827
12	Kansas	7,536
25	Kentucky	6,354
16	Louisiana	6,941
27	Maine	6,284
1	Maryland	10,119
5	Massachusetts	8,282
28	Michigan	6,283
49	Minnesota	3,705
6	Mississippi	8,058
29	Missouri	6,210
35	Montana	5,927
10	Nebraska	7,722
30	Nevada	6,121
8	New Hampshire	7,884
2	New Jersey	9,354
46	New Mexico	4,940
24	New York	6,379
33	North Carolina	6,003
19	North Dakota	6,614
42	Ohio	5,123
11	Oklahoma	7,623
48	Oregon	4,075
37	Pennsylvania	5,578
34	Rhode Island	5,991
22	South Carolina	6,436
21	South Dakota	6,459
39	Tennessee	5,523
18	Texas	6,712
41	Utah	5,170
12	Vermont	7,536
20	Virginia	6,596
40	Washington	5,482
32	West Virginia	6,085
45	Wisconsin	4,961
9	Wyoming	7,869

RANK ORDER

RANK	STATE	PER BENEFICIARY
1	Maryland	$10,119
2	New Jersey	9,354
3	Delaware	9,026
4	Alaska	8,490
5	Massachusetts	8,282
6	Mississippi	8,058
7	Connecticut	7,985
8	New Hampshire	7,884
9	Wyoming	7,869
10	Nebraska	7,722
11	Oklahoma	7,623
12	Kansas	7,536
12	Vermont	7,536
14	Illinois	7,205
15	Indiana	6,999
16	Louisiana	6,941
17	Iowa	6,827
18	Texas	6,712
19	North Dakota	6,614
20	Virginia	6,596
21	South Dakota	6,459
22	South Carolina	6,436
23	Arkansas	6,419
24	New York	6,379
25	Kentucky	6,354
26	Alabama	6,286
27	Maine	6,284
28	Michigan	6,283
29	Missouri	6,210
30	Florida	6,121
30	Nevada	6,121
32	West Virginia	6,085
33	North Carolina	6,003
34	Rhode Island	5,991
35	Montana	5,927
36	Georgia	5,916
37	Pennsylvania	5,578
38	California	5,542
39	Tennessee	5,523
40	Washington	5,482
41	Utah	5,170
42	Ohio	5,123
43	Arizona	5,085
44	Idaho	5,045
45	Wisconsin	4,961
46	New Mexico	4,940
47	Colorado	4,853
48	Oregon	4,075
49	Minnesota	3,705
50	Hawaii	3,481
	District of Columbia	9,420

Source: CQ Press using data from U.S. Department of Health and Human Services, Centers for Medicare and Medicaid Services "Medicare Geographic Variation" (Public Use File)
(https://www.cms.gov/Research-Statistics-Data-and-Systems/Statistics-Trends-and-Reports/Medicare-Geographic-Variation/)
*Total actual costs not standardized for geographical variations. National figure includes payments and enrollees in Puerto Rico and other outlying areas.

Medicaid Enrollment in 2015

National Total = 77,846,969 Enrollees*

ALPHA ORDER

RANK	STATE	ENROLLEES	% of USA
26	Alabama	1,050,989	1.4%
46	Alaska	164,783	0.2%
13	Arizona	1,740,520	2.2%
30	Arkansas	762,166	1.0%
1	California	13,096,861	16.8%
20	Colorado	1,264,600	1.6%
31	Connecticut	746,119	1.0%
43	Delaware	227,909	0.3%
5	Florida	3,808,334	4.9%
9	Georgia	1,990,810	2.6%
37	Hawaii	340,513	0.4%
41	Idaho	283,355	0.4%
6	Illinois	3,269,999	4.2%
17	Indiana	1,295,358	1.7%
33	Iowa	618,505	0.8%
36	Kansas	403,844	0.5%
18	Kentucky	1,284,193	1.6%
16	Louisiana	1,402,212	1.8%
40	Maine	288,324	0.4%
19	Maryland	1,271,445	1.6%
11	Massachusetts	1,829,618	2.4%
4	Michigan	3,947,031	5.1%
25	Minnesota	1,052,521	1.4%
32	Mississippi	740,937	1.0%
27	Missouri	944,257	1.2%
47	Montana	139,950	0.2%
42	Nebraska	239,463	0.3%
34	Nevada	588,304	0.8%
45	New Hampshire	186,399	0.2%
14	New Jersey	1,705,594	2.2%
29	New Mexico	826,155	1.1%
2	New York	6,281,038	8.1%
10	North Carolina	1,965,805	2.5%
49	North Dakota	86,250	0.1%
7	Ohio	3,060,446	3.9%
28	Oklahoma	829,561	1.1%
23	Oregon	1,123,913	1.4%
8	Pennsylvania	2,569,232	3.3%
38	Rhode Island	308,521	0.4%
21	South Carolina	1,233,430	1.6%
48	South Dakota	124,497	0.2%
15	Tennessee	1,562,745	2.0%
3	Texas	4,273,982	5.5%
39	Utah	293,867	0.4%
44	Vermont	206,469	0.3%
24	Virginia	1,092,225	1.4%
12	Washington	1,771,679	2.3%
35	West Virginia	545,748	0.7%
22	Wisconsin	1,209,714	1.6%
50	Wyoming	66,532	0.1%

RANK ORDER

RANK	STATE	ENROLLEES	% of USA
1	California	13,096,861	16.8%
2	New York	6,281,038	8.1%
3	Texas	4,273,982	5.5%
4	Michigan	3,947,031	5.1%
5	Florida	3,808,334	4.9%
6	Illinois	3,269,999	4.2%
7	Ohio	3,060,446	3.9%
8	Pennsylvania	2,569,232	3.3%
9	Georgia	1,990,810	2.6%
10	North Carolina	1,965,805	2.5%
11	Massachusetts	1,829,618	2.4%
12	Washington	1,771,679	2.3%
13	Arizona	1,740,520	2.2%
14	New Jersey	1,705,594	2.2%
15	Tennessee	1,562,745	2.0%
16	Louisiana	1,402,212	1.8%
17	Indiana	1,295,358	1.7%
18	Kentucky	1,284,193	1.6%
19	Maryland	1,271,445	1.6%
20	Colorado	1,264,600	1.6%
21	South Carolina	1,233,430	1.6%
22	Wisconsin	1,209,714	1.6%
23	Oregon	1,123,913	1.4%
24	Virginia	1,092,225	1.4%
25	Minnesota	1,052,521	1.4%
26	Alabama	1,050,989	1.4%
27	Missouri	944,257	1.2%
28	Oklahoma	829,561	1.1%
29	New Mexico	826,155	1.1%
30	Arkansas	762,166	1.0%
31	Connecticut	746,119	1.0%
32	Mississippi	740,937	1.0%
33	Iowa	618,505	0.8%
34	Nevada	588,304	0.8%
35	West Virginia	545,748	0.7%
36	Kansas	403,844	0.5%
37	Hawaii	340,513	0.4%
38	Rhode Island	308,521	0.4%
39	Utah	293,867	0.4%
40	Maine	288,324	0.4%
41	Idaho	283,355	0.4%
42	Nebraska	239,463	0.3%
43	Delaware	227,909	0.3%
44	Vermont	206,469	0.3%
45	New Hampshire	186,399	0.2%
46	Alaska	164,783	0.2%
47	Montana	139,950	0.2%
48	South Dakota	124,497	0.2%
49	North Dakota	86,250	0.1%
50	Wyoming	66,532	0.1%
	District of Columbia	271,428	0.3%

Source: U.S. Department of Health and Human Services, Centers for Medicare and Medicaid Services
"2015 Medicaid Managed Care Enrollment Report" (https://www.medicaid.gov/medicaid/managed-care/enrollment/index.html)
*Unduplicated enrollment as of July 1, 2015. National total includes 1,458,819 Medicaid enrollees in Puerto Rico.

Percent of Population Enrolled in Medicaid in 2015

National Percent = 23.8% of Population*

RANK	STATE	PERCENT
24	Alabama	21.7
23	Alaska	22.3
13	Arizona	25.6
13	Arkansas	25.6
3	California	33.6
22	Colorado	23.2
29	Connecticut	20.8
19	Delaware	24.1
38	Florida	18.8
35	Georgia	19.5
20	Hawaii	23.9
39	Idaho	17.2
15	Illinois	25.4
33	Indiana	19.6
32	Iowa	19.8
44	Kansas	13.9
9	Kentucky	29.0
6	Louisiana	30.0
24	Maine	21.7
26	Maryland	21.2
11	Massachusetts	26.9
1	Michigan	39.8
36	Minnesota	19.2
17	Mississippi	24.8
41	Missouri	15.5
45	Montana	13.6
47	Nebraska	12.6
30	Nevada	20.4
43	New Hampshire	14.0
37	New Jersey	19.0
2	New Mexico	39.7
5	New York	31.7
33	North Carolina	19.6
48	North Dakota	11.4
12	Ohio	26.4
26	Oklahoma	21.2
10	Oregon	28.0
31	Pennsylvania	20.1
8	Rhode Island	29.2
16	South Carolina	25.2
42	South Dakota	14.6
21	Tennessee	23.7
40	Texas	15.6
50	Utah	9.8
4	Vermont	33.1
46	Virginia	13.1
17	Washington	24.8
7	West Virginia	29.7
28	Wisconsin	21.0
48	Wyoming	11.4

RANK	STATE	PERCENT
1	Michigan	39.8
2	New Mexico	39.7
3	California	33.6
4	Vermont	33.1
5	New York	31.7
6	Louisiana	30.0
7	West Virginia	29.7
8	Rhode Island	29.2
9	Kentucky	29.0
10	Oregon	28.0
11	Massachusetts	26.9
12	Ohio	26.4
13	Arizona	25.6
13	Arkansas	25.6
15	Illinois	25.4
16	South Carolina	25.2
17	Mississippi	24.8
17	Washington	24.8
19	Delaware	24.1
20	Hawaii	23.9
21	Tennessee	23.7
22	Colorado	23.2
23	Alaska	22.3
24	Alabama	21.7
24	Maine	21.7
26	Maryland	21.2
26	Oklahoma	21.2
28	Wisconsin	21.0
29	Connecticut	20.8
30	Nevada	20.4
31	Pennsylvania	20.1
32	Iowa	19.8
33	Indiana	19.6
33	North Carolina	19.6
35	Georgia	19.5
36	Minnesota	19.2
37	New Jersey	19.0
38	Florida	18.8
39	Idaho	17.2
40	Texas	15.6
41	Missouri	15.5
42	South Dakota	14.6
43	New Hampshire	14.0
44	Kansas	13.9
45	Montana	13.6
46	Virginia	13.1
47	Nebraska	12.6
48	North Dakota	11.4
48	Wyoming	11.4
50	Utah	9.8

District of Columbia   40.3

Source: CQ Press using data from U.S. Department of Health and Human Services, Centers for Medicare and Medicaid Services
"2015 Medicaid Managed Care Enrollment Report" (https://www.medicaid.gov/medicaid/managed-care/enrollment/index.html)
*Unduplicated enrollment as of July 1, 2015. National percent does not include recipients or population in U.S. territories.

Estimated Medicaid Expenditures in 2017

National Total = $574,343,000,000*

ALPHA ORDER

RANK	STATE	EXPENDITURES	% of USA
28	Alabama	$6,611,000,000	1.2%
44	Alaska	1,995,000,000	0.3%
12	Arizona	11,849,000,000	2.1%
27	Arkansas	7,166,000,000	1.2%
1	California	90,159,000,000	15.7%
24	Colorado	8,629,000,000	1.5%
26	Connecticut	7,283,000,000	1.3%
43	Delaware	2,055,000,000	0.4%
5	Florida	25,758,000,000	4.5%
18	Georgia	10,221,000,000	1.8%
40	Hawaii	2,481,000,000	0.4%
45	Idaho	1,992,000,000	0.3%
7	Illinois	20,240,000,000	3.5%
13	Indiana	11,560,000,000	2.0%
33	Iowa	5,019,000,000	0.9%
36	Kansas	3,200,000,000	0.6%
19	Kentucky	9,894,000,000	1.7%
17	Louisiana	10,284,000,000	1.8%
39	Maine	2,656,000,000	0.5%
14	Maryland	11,200,000,000	2.0%
9	Massachusetts	15,516,000,000	2.7%
8	Michigan	17,214,000,000	3.0%
15	Minnesota	11,133,000,000	1.9%
32	Mississippi	5,261,000,000	0.9%
20	Missouri	9,701,000,000	1.7%
46	Montana	1,758,000,000	0.3%
42	Nebraska	2,071,000,000	0.4%
34	Nevada	3,671,000,000	0.6%
41	New Hampshire	2,125,000,000	0.4%
10	New Jersey	14,642,000,000	2.5%
30	New Mexico	5,570,000,000	1.0%
2	New York	51,178,000,000	8.9%
11	North Carolina	14,171,000,000	2.5%
48	North Dakota	1,371,000,000	0.2%
6	Ohio	25,661,000,000	4.5%
31	Oklahoma	5,327,000,000	0.9%
22	Oregon	9,428,000,000	1.6%
4	Pennsylvania	31,343,000,000	5.5%
38	Rhode Island	2,728,000,000	0.5%
29	South Carolina	6,556,000,000	1.1%
49	South Dakota	894,000,000	0.2%
16	Tennessee	10,996,000,000	1.9%
3	Texas	40,087,000,000	7.0%
37	Utah	2,787,000,000	0.5%
47	Vermont	1,598,000,000	0.3%
23	Virginia	9,381,000,000	1.6%
25	Washington	8,263,000,000	1.4%
35	West Virginia	3,548,000,000	0.6%
21	Wisconsin	9,511,000,000	1.7%
50	Wyoming	601,000,000	0.1%

RANK ORDER

RANK	STATE	EXPENDITURES	% of USA
1	California	$90,159,000,000	15.7%
2	New York	51,178,000,000	8.9%
3	Texas	40,087,000,000	7.0%
4	Pennsylvania	31,343,000,000	5.5%
5	Florida	25,758,000,000	4.5%
6	Ohio	25,661,000,000	4.5%
7	Illinois	20,240,000,000	3.5%
8	Michigan	17,214,000,000	3.0%
9	Massachusetts	15,516,000,000	2.7%
10	New Jersey	14,642,000,000	2.5%
11	North Carolina	14,171,000,000	2.5%
12	Arizona	11,849,000,000	2.1%
13	Indiana	11,560,000,000	2.0%
14	Maryland	11,200,000,000	2.0%
15	Minnesota	11,133,000,000	1.9%
16	Tennessee	10,996,000,000	1.9%
17	Louisiana	10,284,000,000	1.8%
18	Georgia	10,221,000,000	1.8%
19	Kentucky	9,894,000,000	1.7%
20	Missouri	9,701,000,000	1.7%
21	Wisconsin	9,511,000,000	1.7%
22	Oregon	9,428,000,000	1.6%
23	Virginia	9,381,000,000	1.6%
24	Colorado	8,629,000,000	1.5%
25	Washington	8,263,000,000	1.4%
26	Connecticut	7,283,000,000	1.3%
27	Arkansas	7,166,000,000	1.2%
28	Alabama	6,611,000,000	1.2%
29	South Carolina	6,556,000,000	1.1%
30	New Mexico	5,570,000,000	1.0%
31	Oklahoma	5,327,000,000	0.9%
32	Mississippi	5,261,000,000	0.9%
33	Iowa	5,019,000,000	0.9%
34	Nevada	3,671,000,000	0.6%
35	West Virginia	3,548,000,000	0.6%
36	Kansas	3,200,000,000	0.6%
37	Utah	2,787,000,000	0.5%
38	Rhode Island	2,728,000,000	0.5%
39	Maine	2,656,000,000	0.5%
40	Hawaii	2,481,000,000	0.4%
41	New Hampshire	2,125,000,000	0.4%
42	Nebraska	2,071,000,000	0.4%
43	Delaware	2,055,000,000	0.4%
44	Alaska	1,995,000,000	0.3%
45	Idaho	1,992,000,000	0.3%
46	Montana	1,758,000,000	0.3%
47	Vermont	1,598,000,000	0.3%
48	North Dakota	1,371,000,000	0.2%
49	South Dakota	894,000,000	0.2%
50	Wyoming	601,000,000	0.1%
	District of Columbia**	NA	NA

Source: National Association of State Budget Officers
   "State Expenditure Report" (http://www.nasbo.org)
*Estimates for fiscal year 2017.
**Not available.

Percent Change in Medicaid Expenditures: 2016 to 2017

National Percent Change = 6.1% Increase*

ALPHA ORDER

RANK	STATE	PERCENT CHANGE
23	Alabama	4.0
5	Alaska	17.2
30	Arizona	2.8
13	Arkansas	9.3
11	California	10.4
49	Colorado	(4.0)
38	Connecticut	0.9
37	Delaware	1.3
10	Florida	10.7
27	Georgia	3.0
14	Hawaii	9.2
30	Idaho	2.8
3	Illinois	26.3
33	Indiana	2.6
50	Iowa	(4.6)
45	Kansas	(0.5)
42	Kentucky	0.0
2	Louisiana	28.1
42	Maine	0.0
8	Maryland	13.2
34	Massachusetts	2.5
36	Michigan	1.7
45	Minnesota	(0.5)
35	Mississippi	2.1
19	Missouri	6.0
1	Montana	35.8
22	Nebraska	4.4
6	Nevada	13.8
16	New Hampshire	8.5
26	New Jersey	3.4
28	New Mexico	2.9
17	New York	6.4
28	North Carolina	2.9
4	North Dakota	19.6
38	Ohio	0.9
44	Oklahoma	(0.2)
7	Oregon	13.6
9	Pennsylvania	12.3
18	Rhode Island	6.1
21	South Carolina	4.7
23	South Dakota	4.0
41	Tennessee	0.2
48	Texas	(3.3)
12	Utah	9.4
47	Vermont	(2.5)
20	Virginia	5.8
15	Washington	9.1
40	West Virginia	0.5
25	Wisconsin	3.6
32	Wyoming	2.7

RANK ORDER

RANK	STATE	PERCENT CHANGE
1	Montana	35.8
2	Louisiana	28.1
3	Illinois	26.3
4	North Dakota	19.6
5	Alaska	17.2
6	Nevada	13.8
7	Oregon	13.6
8	Maryland	13.2
9	Pennsylvania	12.3
10	Florida	10.7
11	California	10.4
12	Utah	9.4
13	Arkansas	9.3
14	Hawaii	9.2
15	Washington	9.1
16	New Hampshire	8.5
17	New York	6.4
18	Rhode Island	6.1
19	Missouri	6.0
20	Virginia	5.8
21	South Carolina	4.7
22	Nebraska	4.4
23	Alabama	4.0
23	South Dakota	4.0
25	Wisconsin	3.6
26	New Jersey	3.4
27	Georgia	3.0
28	New Mexico	2.9
28	North Carolina	2.9
30	Arizona	2.8
30	Idaho	2.8
32	Wyoming	2.7
33	Indiana	2.6
34	Massachusetts	2.5
35	Mississippi	2.1
36	Michigan	1.7
37	Delaware	1.3
38	Connecticut	0.9
38	Ohio	0.9
40	West Virginia	0.5
41	Tennessee	0.2
42	Kentucky	0.0
42	Maine	0.0
44	Oklahoma	(0.2)
45	Kansas	(0.5)
45	Minnesota	(0.5)
47	Vermont	(2.5)
48	Texas	(3.3)
49	Colorado	(4.0)
50	Iowa	(4.6)
	District of Columbia**	NA

Source: National Association of State Budget Officers
    "State Expenditure Report" (http://www.nasbo.org)
*Estimates for fiscal year 2017.
**Not available.

Percent of Population Receiving Public Aid in 2015

National Percent = 3.5% of Population*

ALPHA ORDER

RANK	STATE	PERCENT
7	Alabama	4.1
27	Alaska	2.8
42	Arizona	2.1
11	Arkansas	4.0
1	California	6.0
42	Colorado	2.1
38	Connecticut	2.4
20	Delaware	3.1
17	Florida	3.2
27	Georgia	2.8
20	Hawaii	3.1
46	Idaho	2.0
38	Illinois	2.4
41	Indiana	2.2
34	Iowa	2.5
42	Kansas	2.1
2	Kentucky	5.2
7	Louisiana	4.1
15	Maine	3.5
24	Maryland	2.9
13	Massachusetts	3.7
17	Michigan	3.2
34	Minnesota	2.5
4	Mississippi	4.6
17	Missouri	3.2
34	Montana	2.5
42	Nebraska	2.1
27	Nevada	2.8
47	New Hampshire	1.8
33	New Jersey	2.6
6	New Mexico	4.5
4	New York	4.6
31	North Carolina	2.7
48	North Dakota	1.4
14	Ohio	3.6
24	Oklahoma	2.9
20	Oregon	3.1
7	Pennsylvania	4.1
7	Rhode Island	4.1
24	South Carolina	2.9
34	South Dakota	2.5
12	Tennessee	3.8
31	Texas	2.7
49	Utah	1.3
15	Vermont	3.5
38	Virginia	2.4
20	Washington	3.1
3	West Virginia	5.0
27	Wisconsin	2.8
49	Wyoming	1.3

RANK ORDER

RANK	STATE	PERCENT
1	California	6.0
2	Kentucky	5.2
3	West Virginia	5.0
4	Mississippi	4.6
4	New York	4.6
6	New Mexico	4.5
7	Alabama	4.1
7	Louisiana	4.1
7	Pennsylvania	4.1
7	Rhode Island	4.1
11	Arkansas	4.0
12	Tennessee	3.8
13	Massachusetts	3.7
14	Ohio	3.6
15	Maine	3.5
15	Vermont	3.5
17	Florida	3.2
17	Michigan	3.2
17	Missouri	3.2
20	Delaware	3.1
20	Hawaii	3.1
20	Oregon	3.1
20	Washington	3.1
24	Maryland	2.9
24	Oklahoma	2.9
24	South Carolina	2.9
27	Alaska	2.8
27	Georgia	2.8
27	Nevada	2.8
27	Wisconsin	2.8
31	North Carolina	2.7
31	Texas	2.7
33	New Jersey	2.6
34	Iowa	2.5
34	Minnesota	2.5
34	Montana	2.5
34	South Dakota	2.5
38	Connecticut	2.4
38	Illinois	2.4
38	Virginia	2.4
41	Indiana	2.2
42	Arizona	2.1
42	Colorado	2.1
42	Kansas	2.1
42	Nebraska	2.1
46	Idaho	2.0
47	New Hampshire	1.8
48	North Dakota	1.4
49	Utah	1.3
49	Wyoming	1.3
	District of Columbia	6.3

Source: CQ Press using data from U.S. Department of Health and Human Services, Social Security Administration
"Social Security Bulletin, Annual Statistical Supplement 2016" (https://www.ssa.gov/policy/docs/statcomps/supplement/) and
U.S. Department of Health and Human Services, Administration for Children and Families
"TANF Caseload Data" (http://www.acf.hhs.gov/programs/ofa/programs/tanf/data-reports)
*As of December 2015. Includes recipients of Temporary Assistance to Needy Families (TANF) and/or Supplemental Security Income payments.

Recipients of Temporary Assistance to Needy Families (TANF) Payments in 2017
National Total = 2,494,100 Monthly Recipients*

ALPHA ORDER

RANK	STATE	RECIPIENTS	% of USA
25	Alabama	21,858	0.9%
42	Alaska	8,682	0.3%
28	Arizona	17,897	0.7%
44	Arkansas	7,084	0.3%
1	California	880,360	35.3%
13	Colorado	43,090	1.7%
29	Connecticut	17,417	0.7%
35	Delaware	11,216	0.4%
5	Florida	74,179	3.0%
26	Georgia	20,766	0.8%
32	Hawaii	14,646	0.6%
48	Idaho	2,738	0.1%
19	Illinois	29,486	1.2%
31	Indiana	14,671	0.6%
23	Iowa	23,578	0.9%
38	Kansas	10,310	0.4%
9	Kentucky	58,639	2.4%
34	Louisiana	13,288	0.5%
43	Maine	7,312	0.3%
11	Maryland	47,010	1.9%
10	Massachusetts	53,265	2.1%
17	Michigan	34,451	1.4%
12	Minnesota	44,792	1.8%
39	Mississippi	10,169	0.4%
22	Missouri	25,808	1.0%
40	Montana	9,989	0.4%
36	Nebraska	10,531	0.4%
24	Nevada	23,024	0.9%
47	New Hampshire	4,670	0.2%
18	New Jersey	31,509	1.3%
21	New Mexico	27,237	1.1%
2	New York	228,159	9.1%
20	North Carolina	27,869	1.1%
49	North Dakota	2,546	0.1%
4	Ohio	104,036	4.2%
30	Oklahoma	15,094	0.6%
15	Oregon	35,550	1.4%
3	Pennsylvania	127,824	5.1%
37	Rhode Island	10,479	0.4%
27	South Carolina	19,049	0.8%
45	South Dakota	5,935	0.2%
7	Tennessee	59,606	2.4%
8	Texas	59,273	2.4%
41	Utah	9,415	0.4%
46	Vermont	5,217	0.2%
14	Virginia	42,162	1.7%
6	Washington	61,670	2.5%
33	West Virginia	14,175	0.6%
16	Wisconsin	34,732	1.4%
50	Wyoming	1,379	0.1%

RANK ORDER

RANK	STATE	RECIPIENTS	% of USA
1	California	880,360	35.3%
2	New York	228,159	9.1%
3	Pennsylvania	127,824	5.1%
4	Ohio	104,036	4.2%
5	Florida	74,179	3.0%
6	Washington	61,670	2.5%
7	Tennessee	59,606	2.4%
8	Texas	59,273	2.4%
9	Kentucky	58,639	2.4%
10	Massachusetts	53,265	2.1%
11	Maryland	47,010	1.9%
12	Minnesota	44,792	1.8%
13	Colorado	43,090	1.7%
14	Virginia	42,162	1.7%
15	Oregon	35,550	1.4%
16	Wisconsin	34,732	1.4%
17	Michigan	34,451	1.4%
18	New Jersey	31,509	1.3%
19	Illinois	29,486	1.2%
20	North Carolina	27,869	1.1%
21	New Mexico	27,237	1.1%
22	Missouri	25,808	1.0%
23	Iowa	23,578	0.9%
24	Nevada	23,024	0.9%
25	Alabama	21,858	0.9%
26	Georgia	20,766	0.8%
27	South Carolina	19,049	0.8%
28	Arizona	17,897	0.7%
29	Connecticut	17,417	0.7%
30	Oklahoma	15,094	0.6%
31	Indiana	14,671	0.6%
32	Hawaii	14,646	0.6%
33	West Virginia	14,175	0.6%
34	Louisiana	13,288	0.5%
35	Delaware	11,216	0.4%
36	Nebraska	10,531	0.4%
37	Rhode Island	10,479	0.4%
38	Kansas	10,310	0.4%
39	Mississippi	10,169	0.4%
40	Montana	9,989	0.4%
41	Utah	9,415	0.4%
42	Alaska	8,682	0.3%
43	Maine	7,312	0.3%
44	Arkansas	7,084	0.3%
45	South Dakota	5,935	0.2%
46	Vermont	5,217	0.2%
47	New Hampshire	4,670	0.2%
48	Idaho	2,738	0.1%
49	North Dakota	2,546	0.1%
50	Wyoming	1,379	0.1%
	District of Columbia	8,642	0.3%

Source: U.S. Department of Health and Human Services, Administration for Children and Families
   "TANF Caseload Data" (http://www.acf.hhs.gov/programs/ofa/programs/tanf/data-reports)
*As of March 2017. National total includes 21,616 recipients in U.S. territories (19,645 in Puerto Rico).

Percent Change in TANF Recipients: 2016 to 2017

National Percent Change = 9.0% Decrease*

ALPHA ORDER				RANK ORDER		
RANK	STATE	PERCENT CHANGE		RANK	STATE	PERCENT CHANGE
40	Alabama	(13.8)		1	Wyoming	42.6
6	Alaska	6.2		2	Kentucky	40.7
37	Arizona	(10.4)		3	Montana	37.1
45	Arkansas	(16.4)		4	Utah	18.6
38	California	(11.8)		5	Rhode Island	13.8
9	Colorado	0.5		6	Alaska	6.2
48	Connecticut	(21.5)		7	Louisiana	2.1
30	Delaware	(8.2)		8	Minnesota	0.6
20	Florida	(5.8)		9	Colorado	0.5
43	Georgia	(16.3)		9	South Dakota	0.5
47	Hawaii	(19.3)		11	Nebraska	(1.0)
18	Idaho	(3.9)		12	New Hampshire	(1.2)
43	Illinois	(16.3)		13	Vermont	(2.6)
27	Indiana	(7.8)		14	Ohio	(2.7)
33	Iowa	(8.6)		15	Texas	(3.1)
27	Kansas	(7.8)		16	New Mexico	(3.3)
2	Kentucky	40.7		17	West Virginia	(3.4)
7	Louisiana	2.1		18	Idaho	(3.9)
46	Maine	(17.2)		19	North Dakota	(4.4)
32	Maryland	(8.5)		20	Florida	(5.8)
29	Massachusetts	(8.1)		21	Oklahoma	(5.9)
42	Michigan	(16.1)		22	Oregon	(6.7)
8	Minnesota	0.6		23	Virginia	(6.9)
34	Mississippi	(9.1)		24	Nevada	(7.5)
49	Missouri	(24.5)		24	New York	(7.5)
3	Montana	37.1		26	Washington	(7.7)
11	Nebraska	(1.0)		27	Indiana	(7.8)
24	Nevada	(7.5)		27	Kansas	(7.8)
12	New Hampshire	(1.2)		29	Massachusetts	(8.1)
50	New Jersey	(25.2)		30	Delaware	(8.2)
16	New Mexico	(3.3)		30	South Carolina	(8.2)
24	New York	(7.5)		32	Maryland	(8.5)
35	North Carolina	(9.2)		33	Iowa	(8.6)
19	North Dakota	(4.4)		34	Mississippi	(9.1)
14	Ohio	(2.7)		35	North Carolina	(9.2)
21	Oklahoma	(5.9)		36	Pennsylvania	(9.7)
22	Oregon	(6.7)		37	Arizona	(10.4)
36	Pennsylvania	(9.7)		38	California	(11.8)
5	Rhode Island	13.8		39	Tennessee	(12.4)
30	South Carolina	(8.2)		40	Alabama	(13.8)
9	South Dakota	0.5		41	Wisconsin	(16.0)
39	Tennessee	(12.4)		42	Michigan	(16.1)
15	Texas	(3.1)		43	Georgia	(16.3)
4	Utah	18.6		43	Illinois	(16.3)
13	Vermont	(2.6)		45	Arkansas	(16.4)
23	Virginia	(6.9)		46	Maine	(17.2)
26	Washington	(7.7)		47	Hawaii	(19.3)
17	West Virginia	(3.4)		48	Connecticut	(21.5)
41	Wisconsin	(16.0)		49	Missouri	(24.5)
1	Wyoming	42.6		50	New Jersey	(25.2)
					District of Columbia	(37.8)

Source: CQ Press using data from U.S. Department of Health and Human Services, Administration for Children and Families
  "TANF Caseload Data" (http://www.acf.hhs.gov/programs/ofa/programs/tanf/data-reports)
*March 2016 to March 2017. National percent includes recipients in U.S. territories.

TANF Work Participation Rates in 2016

National Rate = 53.4%*

ALPHA ORDER			RANK ORDER		
RANK	STATE	PERCENT	RANK	STATE	PERCENT
24	Alabama	49.3	1	Illinois	93.4
32	Alaska	45.6	2	Wyoming	83.1
46	Arizona	32.2	3	Idaho	81.0
31	Arkansas	45.7	4	Maine	75.7
15	California	56.2	5	New Hampshire	75.3
44	Colorado	33.9	6	Wisconsin	73.3
20	Connecticut	52.1	7	Oregon	67.0
45	Delaware	33.7	8	Massachusetts	65.0
35	Florida	43.3	9	Nebraska	62.5
17	Georgia	53.9	10	Ohio	61.2
23	Hawaii	50.0	11	Minnesota	60.4
3	Idaho	81.0	11	South Dakota	60.4
1	Illinois	93.4	13	Michigan	59.6
43	Indiana	34.3	14	North Dakota	59.4
16	Iowa	55.5	15	California	56.2
26	Kansas	48.9	16	Iowa	55.5
25	Kentucky	49.2	17	Georgia	53.9
48	Louisiana	28.4	18	Oklahoma	52.3
4	Maine	75.7	18	West Virginia	52.3
40	Maryland	37.6	20	Connecticut	52.1
8	Massachusetts	65.0	21	Mississippi	51.9
13	Michigan	59.6	22	Vermont	50.8
11	Minnesota	60.4	23	Hawaii	50.0
21	Mississippi	51.9	24	Alabama	49.3
49	Missouri	28.3	25	Kentucky	49.2
38	Montana	40.2	26	Kansas	48.9
9	Nebraska	62.5	27	Nevada	48.8
27	Nevada	48.8	28	South Carolina	46.1
5	New Hampshire	75.3	29	New York	46.0
41	New Jersey	37.0	30	Washington	45.9
34	New Mexico	44.6	31	Arkansas	45.7
29	New York	46.0	32	Alaska	45.6
47	North Carolina	30.1	33	Virginia	45.5
14	North Dakota	59.4	34	New Mexico	44.6
10	Ohio	61.2	35	Florida	43.3
18	Oklahoma	52.3	36	Tennessee	41.7
7	Oregon	67.0	37	Rhode Island	40.9
42	Pennsylvania	36.1	38	Montana	40.2
37	Rhode Island	40.9	39	Utah	38.0
28	South Carolina	46.1	40	Maryland	37.6
11	South Dakota	60.4	41	New Jersey	37.0
36	Tennessee	41.7	42	Pennsylvania	36.1
50	Texas	28.1	43	Indiana	34.3
39	Utah	38.0	44	Colorado	33.9
22	Vermont	50.8	45	Delaware	33.7
33	Virginia	45.5	46	Arizona	32.2
30	Washington	45.9	47	North Carolina	30.1
18	West Virginia	52.3	48	Louisiana	28.4
6	Wisconsin	73.3	49	Missouri	28.3
2	Wyoming	83.1	50	Texas	28.1

District of Columbia   54.9

Source: U.S. Department of Health and Human Services, Administration for Children and Families
"Work Participation Rates - Fiscal Year 2016" (Table 6C) (https://www.acf.hhs.gov/ofa/programs/tanf/data-reports)
*For fiscal year 2016. Work-eligible individuals with hours of participation in various work and training activities. National average includes recipients in U.S. territories.

Average Monthly TANF Assistance per Family in 2015

National Average = $398*

ALPHA ORDER

RANK	STATE	PER FAMILY
45	Alabama	$193
1	Alaska	612
39	Arizona	227
49	Arkansas	154
4	California	509
19	Colorado	368
9	Connecticut	457
36	Delaware	250
37	Florida	236
40	Georgia	223
3	Hawaii	554
27	Idaho	298
43	Illinois	210
45	Indiana	193
25	Iowa	313
33	Kansas	268
34	Kentucky	263
31	Louisiana	291
18	Maine	369
5	Maryland	501
7	Massachusetts	470
23	Michigan	323
20	Minnesota	359
50	Mississippi	139
41	Missouri	221
11	Montana	431
28	Nebraska	295
22	Nevada	343
6	New Hampshire	481
26	New Jersey	308
29	New Mexico	294
2	New York	569
42	North Carolina	218
30	North Dakota	292
21	Ohio	353
47	Oklahoma	189
10	Oregon	435
24	Pennsylvania	314
12	Rhode Island	423
44	South Carolina	205
14	South Dakota	416
48	Tennessee	168
38	Texas	233
16	Utah	385
8	Vermont	465
35	Virginia	259
17	Washington	380
32	West Virginia	284
15	Wisconsin	408
13	Wyoming	421

RANK ORDER

RANK	STATE	PER FAMILY
1	Alaska	$612
2	New York	569
3	Hawaii	554
4	California	509
5	Maryland	501
6	New Hampshire	481
7	Massachusetts	470
8	Vermont	465
9	Connecticut	457
10	Oregon	435
11	Montana	431
12	Rhode Island	423
13	Wyoming	421
14	South Dakota	416
15	Wisconsin	408
16	Utah	385
17	Washington	380
18	Maine	369
19	Colorado	368
20	Minnesota	359
21	Ohio	353
22	Nevada	343
23	Michigan	323
24	Pennsylvania	314
25	Iowa	313
26	New Jersey	308
27	Idaho	298
28	Nebraska	295
29	New Mexico	294
30	North Dakota	292
31	Louisiana	291
32	West Virginia	284
33	Kansas	268
34	Kentucky	263
35	Virginia	259
36	Delaware	250
37	Florida	236
38	Texas	233
39	Arizona	227
40	Georgia	223
41	Missouri	221
42	North Carolina	218
43	Illinois	210
44	South Carolina	205
45	Alabama	193
45	Indiana	193
47	Oklahoma	189
48	Tennessee	168
49	Arkansas	154
50	Mississippi	139
	District of Columbia	300

Source: U.S. Department of Health and Human Services, Administration for Children and Families
"Characteristics and Financial Circumstances of TANF Recipients, Fiscal Year 2015 " (Table 37)
(https://www.acf.hhs.gov/ofa/resource/characteristics-and-financial-circumstances-of-tanf-recipients-fiscal-year-2015)
*For fiscal year 2015. National average includes families in U.S. territories.

Percent of Households with Food Insecurity in 2016

National Percent = 13.0% of Households*

ALPHA ORDER

RANK ORDER

RANK	STATE	PERCENT	RANK	STATE	PERCENT
3	Alabama	18.1	1	Mississippi	18.7
25	Alaska	12.7	2	Louisiana	18.3
14	Arizona	14.6	3	Alabama	18.1
5	Arkansas	17.5	4	New Mexico	17.6
33	California	11.8	5	Arkansas	17.5
42	Colorado	10.3	6	Kentucky	17.3
29	Connecticut	12.3	7	Maine	16.4
38	Delaware	10.8	8	Indiana	15.2
32	Florida	12.0	8	Oklahoma	15.2
20	Georgia	14.0	10	North Carolina	15.1
50	Hawaii	8.7	11	West Virginia	14.9
30	Idaho	12.1	12	Ohio	14.8
36	Illinois	11.1	13	Nebraska	14.7
8	Indiana	15.2	14	Arizona	14.6
39	Iowa	10.7	14	Oregon	14.6
16	Kansas	14.5	16	Kansas	14.5
6	Kentucky	17.3	17	Michigan	14.3
2	Louisiana	18.3	17	Texas	14.3
7	Maine	16.4	19	Missouri	14.2
44	Maryland	10.1	20	Georgia	14.0
42	Massachusetts	10.3	21	Tennessee	13.4
17	Michigan	14.3	22	South Carolina	13.0
47	Minnesota	9.7	23	Montana	12.9
1	Mississippi	18.7	24	Rhode Island	12.8
19	Missouri	14.2	25	Alaska	12.7
23	Montana	12.9	25	Wyoming	12.7
13	Nebraska	14.7	27	New York	12.5
30	Nevada	12.1	27	Pennsylvania	12.5
48	New Hampshire	9.6	29	Connecticut	12.3
36	New Jersey	11.1	30	Idaho	12.1
4	New Mexico	17.6	30	Nevada	12.1
27	New York	12.5	32	Florida	12.0
10	North Carolina	15.1	33	California	11.8
49	North Dakota	8.8	34	Washington	11.6
12	Ohio	14.8	35	Utah	11.5
8	Oklahoma	15.2	36	Illinois	11.1
14	Oregon	14.6	36	New Jersey	11.1
27	Pennsylvania	12.5	38	Delaware	10.8
24	Rhode Island	12.8	39	Iowa	10.7
22	South Carolina	13.0	39	Wisconsin	10.7
41	South Dakota	10.6	41	South Dakota	10.6
21	Tennessee	13.4	42	Colorado	10.3
17	Texas	14.3	42	Massachusetts	10.3
35	Utah	11.5	44	Maryland	10.1
44	Vermont	10.1	44	Vermont	10.1
46	Virginia	9.9	46	Virginia	9.9
34	Washington	11.6	47	Minnesota	9.7
11	West Virginia	14.9	48	New Hampshire	9.6
39	Wisconsin	10.7	49	North Dakota	8.8
25	Wyoming	12.7	50	Hawaii	8.7

District of Columbia   11.4

Source: U.S. Department of Agriculture, Economic Research Service
"Household Food Security in the United States, 2016" (www.ers.usda.gov/topics/food-nutrition-assistance/food-security-in-the-us/)
*Three-year average for 2014-2016. Refers to households for which access to enough food is limited by a lack of money and other resources. About one-third of food-insecure households have very low food security, meaning that at times the food intake of some household members is reduced and their normal eating patterns are disrupted.

Supplemental Nutrition Assistance Program Benefits in 2017

National Total = $63,709,711,659*

ALPHA ORDER

RANK	STATE	BENEFITS	% of USA
15	Alabama	$1,161,155,532	1.8%
44	Alaska	191,511,906	0.3%
14	Arizona	1,335,235,066	2.1%
33	Arkansas	510,832,029	0.8%
1	California	6,732,718,937	10.6%
28	Colorado	701,946,211	1.1%
30	Connecticut	653,080,575	1.0%
43	Delaware	210,706,049	0.3%
3	Florida	4,783,367,429	7.5%
7	Georgia	2,540,245,442	4.0%
36	Hawaii	479,722,381	0.8%
42	Idaho	233,881,652	0.4%
5	Illinois	2,931,949,982	4.6%
23	Indiana	955,393,220	1.5%
34	Iowa	482,469,098	0.8%
37	Kansas	318,488,850	0.5%
24	Kentucky	943,688,786	1.5%
12	Louisiana	1,440,110,876	2.3%
41	Maine	234,520,415	0.4%
22	Maryland	987,124,235	1.5%
16	Massachusetts	1,159,027,642	1.8%
10	Michigan	2,069,172,719	3.2%
32	Minnesota	601,981,918	0.9%
27	Mississippi	742,934,749	1.2%
17	Missouri	1,116,216,424	1.8%
45	Montana	172,035,838	0.3%
40	Nebraska	241,772,391	0.4%
31	Nevada	625,062,614	1.0%
48	New Hampshire	112,555,760	0.2%
18	New Jersey	1,115,682,640	1.8%
29	New Mexico	669,640,045	1.1%
4	New York	4,737,481,756	7.4%
9	North Carolina	2,142,986,883	3.4%
49	North Dakota	77,842,534	0.1%
8	Ohio	2,225,320,253	3.5%
25	Oklahoma	879,725,084	1.4%
21	Oregon	1,009,077,892	1.6%
6	Pennsylvania	2,673,354,132	4.2%
39	Rhode Island	265,049,500	0.4%
20	South Carolina	1,065,957,607	1.7%
46	South Dakota	140,613,366	0.2%
11	Tennessee	1,586,711,088	2.5%
2	Texas	5,805,152,020	9.1%
38	Utah	286,288,642	0.4%
47	Vermont	113,015,480	0.2%
19	Virginia	1,115,536,652	1.8%
13	Washington	1,363,774,904	2.1%
35	West Virginia	481,164,948	0.8%
26	Wisconsin	877,903,936	1.4%
50	Wyoming	46,791,729	0.1%

RANK ORDER

RANK	STATE	BENEFITS	% of USA
1	California	$6,732,718,937	10.6%
2	Texas	5,805,152,020	9.1%
3	Florida	4,783,367,429	7.5%
4	New York	4,737,481,756	7.4%
5	Illinois	2,931,949,982	4.6%
6	Pennsylvania	2,673,354,132	4.2%
7	Georgia	2,540,245,442	4.0%
8	Ohio	2,225,320,253	3.5%
9	North Carolina	2,142,986,883	3.4%
10	Michigan	2,069,172,719	3.2%
11	Tennessee	1,586,711,088	2.5%
12	Louisiana	1,440,110,876	2.3%
13	Washington	1,363,774,904	2.1%
14	Arizona	1,335,235,066	2.1%
15	Alabama	1,161,155,532	1.8%
16	Massachusetts	1,159,027,642	1.8%
17	Missouri	1,116,216,424	1.8%
18	New Jersey	1,115,682,640	1.8%
19	Virginia	1,115,536,652	1.8%
20	South Carolina	1,065,957,607	1.7%
21	Oregon	1,009,077,892	1.6%
22	Maryland	987,124,235	1.5%
23	Indiana	955,393,220	1.5%
24	Kentucky	943,688,786	1.5%
25	Oklahoma	879,725,084	1.4%
26	Wisconsin	877,903,936	1.4%
27	Mississippi	742,934,749	1.2%
28	Colorado	701,946,211	1.1%
29	New Mexico	669,640,045	1.1%
30	Connecticut	653,080,575	1.0%
31	Nevada	625,062,614	1.0%
32	Minnesota	601,981,918	0.9%
33	Arkansas	510,832,029	0.8%
34	Iowa	482,469,098	0.8%
35	West Virginia	481,164,948	0.8%
36	Hawaii	479,722,381	0.8%
37	Kansas	318,488,850	0.5%
38	Utah	286,288,642	0.4%
39	Rhode Island	265,049,500	0.4%
40	Nebraska	241,772,391	0.4%
41	Maine	234,520,415	0.4%
42	Idaho	233,881,652	0.4%
43	Delaware	210,706,049	0.3%
44	Alaska	191,511,906	0.3%
45	Montana	172,035,838	0.3%
46	South Dakota	140,613,366	0.2%
47	Vermont	113,015,480	0.2%
48	New Hampshire	112,555,760	0.2%
49	North Dakota	77,842,534	0.1%
50	Wyoming	46,791,729	0.1%
	District of Columbia	200,333,265	0.3%

Source: U.S. Department of Agriculture, Food, Nutrition and Consumer Services
"Supplemental Nutrition Assistance Program" (http://www.fns.usda.gov/pd/snapmain.htm)
*Preliminary data for fiscal year 2017. National total includes $161,398,577 to U.S. territories. Costs are for benefits only and exclude administrative expenditures. Program formerly called the Food Stamp Program.

Monthly Supplemental Nutrition Assistance Program Recipients in 2017

National Total = 42,137,785 Recipients*

ALPHA ORDER

RANK	STATE	RECIPIENTS	% of USA
16	Alabama	804,336	1.9%
47	Alaska	89,113	0.2%
13	Arizona	918,728	2.2%
33	Arkansas	388,362	0.9%
1	California	4,112,066	9.8%
29	Colorado	459,247	1.1%
32	Connecticut	410,344	1.0%
43	Delaware	146,805	0.3%
3	Florida	3,186,537	7.6%
7	Georgia	1,603,845	3.8%
41	Hawaii	169,045	0.4%
40	Idaho	171,251	0.4%
5	Illinois	1,878,519	4.5%
24	Indiana	672,378	1.6%
34	Iowa	365,893	0.9%
36	Kansas	233,778	0.6%
25	Kentucky	654,873	1.6%
14	Louisiana	908,786	2.2%
38	Maine	179,734	0.4%
23	Maryland	684,282	1.6%
18	Massachusetts	763,882	1.8%
9	Michigan	1,375,434	3.3%
30	Minnesota	453,564	1.1%
27	Mississippi	537,370	1.3%
19	Missouri	758,918	1.8%
44	Montana	120,889	0.3%
39	Nebraska	175,849	0.4%
31	Nevada	440,614	1.0%
46	New Hampshire	92,457	0.2%
15	New Jersey	817,979	1.9%
28	New Mexico	460,534	1.1%
4	New York	2,910,894	6.9%
10	North Carolina	1,365,394	3.2%
49	North Dakota	53,748	0.1%
8	Ohio	1,501,795	3.6%
26	Oklahoma	603,896	1.4%
22	Oregon	686,368	1.6%
6	Pennsylvania	1,842,945	4.4%
42	Rhode Island	157,878	0.4%
20	South Carolina	719,977	1.7%
45	South Dakota	93,259	0.2%
11	Tennessee	1,047,058	2.5%
2	Texas	3,868,117	9.2%
37	Utah	206,299	0.5%
48	Vermont	76,558	0.2%
17	Virginia	775,548	1.8%
12	Washington	932,552	2.2%
35	West Virginia	340,308	0.8%
21	Wisconsin	691,635	1.6%
50	Wyoming	32,839	0.1%

RANK ORDER

RANK	STATE	RECIPIENTS	% of USA
1	California	4,112,066	9.8%
2	Texas	3,868,117	9.2%
3	Florida	3,186,537	7.6%
4	New York	2,910,894	6.9%
5	Illinois	1,878,519	4.5%
6	Pennsylvania	1,842,945	4.4%
7	Georgia	1,603,845	3.8%
8	Ohio	1,501,795	3.6%
9	Michigan	1,375,434	3.3%
10	North Carolina	1,365,394	3.2%
11	Tennessee	1,047,058	2.5%
12	Washington	932,552	2.2%
13	Arizona	918,728	2.2%
14	Louisiana	908,786	2.2%
15	New Jersey	817,979	1.9%
16	Alabama	804,336	1.9%
17	Virginia	775,548	1.8%
18	Massachusetts	763,882	1.8%
19	Missouri	758,918	1.8%
20	South Carolina	719,977	1.7%
21	Wisconsin	691,635	1.6%
22	Oregon	686,368	1.6%
23	Maryland	684,282	1.6%
24	Indiana	672,378	1.6%
25	Kentucky	654,873	1.6%
26	Oklahoma	603,896	1.4%
27	Mississippi	537,370	1.3%
28	New Mexico	460,534	1.1%
29	Colorado	459,247	1.1%
30	Minnesota	453,564	1.1%
31	Nevada	440,614	1.0%
32	Connecticut	410,344	1.0%
33	Arkansas	388,362	0.9%
34	Iowa	365,893	0.9%
35	West Virginia	340,308	0.8%
36	Kansas	233,778	0.6%
37	Utah	206,299	0.5%
38	Maine	179,734	0.4%
39	Nebraska	175,849	0.4%
40	Idaho	171,251	0.4%
41	Hawaii	169,045	0.4%
42	Rhode Island	157,878	0.4%
43	Delaware	146,805	0.3%
44	Montana	120,889	0.3%
45	South Dakota	93,259	0.2%
46	New Hampshire	92,457	0.2%
47	Alaska	89,113	0.2%
48	Vermont	76,558	0.2%
49	North Dakota	53,748	0.1%
50	Wyoming	32,839	0.1%
	District of Columbia	123,289	0.3%

Source: U.S. Department of Agriculture, Food, Nutrition and Consumer Services
"Supplemental Nutrition Assistance Program" (http://www.fns.usda.gov/pd/snapmain.htm)
*Preliminary for fiscal year 2017. National total includes 72,021 recipients in U.S. territories. Program formerly called the Food Stamp Program.

Average Monthly Supplemental Nutrition Assistance Program Benefit per Recipient in 2017
National Average = $125.99 per Recipient*

<table>
<tr><td colspan="3">ALPHA ORDER</td><td colspan="3">RANK ORDER</td></tr>
<tr><td>RANK</td><td>STATE</td><td>PER RECIPIENT</td><td>RANK</td><td>STATE</td><td>PER RECIPIENT</td></tr>
<tr><td>29</td><td>Alabama</td><td>$120.30</td><td>1</td><td>Hawaii</td><td>$236.49</td></tr>
<tr><td>2</td><td>Alaska</td><td>179.09</td><td>2</td><td>Alaska</td><td>179.09</td></tr>
<tr><td>26</td><td>Arizona</td><td>121.11</td><td>3</td><td>Rhode Island</td><td>139.90</td></tr>
<tr><td>47</td><td>Arkansas</td><td>109.61</td><td>4</td><td>California</td><td>136.44</td></tr>
<tr><td>4</td><td>California</td><td>136.44</td><td>5</td><td>New York</td><td>135.63</td></tr>
<tr><td>11</td><td>Colorado</td><td>127.37</td><td>6</td><td>Connecticut</td><td>132.63</td></tr>
<tr><td>6</td><td>Connecticut</td><td>132.63</td><td>7</td><td>Louisiana</td><td>132.05</td></tr>
<tr><td>33</td><td>Delaware</td><td>119.61</td><td>8</td><td>Georgia</td><td>131.99</td></tr>
<tr><td>16</td><td>Florida</td><td>125.09</td><td>9</td><td>North Carolina</td><td>130.79</td></tr>
<tr><td>8</td><td>Georgia</td><td>131.99</td><td>10</td><td>Illinois</td><td>130.06</td></tr>
<tr><td>1</td><td>Hawaii</td><td>236.49</td><td>11</td><td>Colorado</td><td>127.37</td></tr>
<tr><td>42</td><td>Idaho</td><td>113.81</td><td>12</td><td>Massachusetts</td><td>126.44</td></tr>
<tr><td>10</td><td>Illinois</td><td>130.06</td><td>13</td><td>Tennessee</td><td>126.28</td></tr>
<tr><td>36</td><td>Indiana</td><td>118.41</td><td>14</td><td>South Dakota</td><td>125.65</td></tr>
<tr><td>46</td><td>Iowa</td><td>109.88</td><td>15</td><td>Michigan</td><td>125.36</td></tr>
<tr><td>44</td><td>Kansas</td><td>113.53</td><td>16</td><td>Florida</td><td>125.09</td></tr>
<tr><td>31</td><td>Kentucky</td><td>120.09</td><td>17</td><td>Texas</td><td>125.06</td></tr>
<tr><td>7</td><td>Louisiana</td><td>132.05</td><td>18</td><td>Ohio</td><td>123.48</td></tr>
<tr><td>48</td><td>Maine</td><td>108.73</td><td>19</td><td>South Carolina</td><td>123.38</td></tr>
<tr><td>30</td><td>Maryland</td><td>120.21</td><td>20</td><td>Vermont</td><td>123.02</td></tr>
<tr><td>12</td><td>Massachusetts</td><td>126.44</td><td>21</td><td>Missouri</td><td>122.57</td></tr>
<tr><td>15</td><td>Michigan</td><td>125.36</td><td>22</td><td>Oregon</td><td>122.51</td></tr>
<tr><td>45</td><td>Minnesota</td><td>110.60</td><td>23</td><td>Washington</td><td>121.87</td></tr>
<tr><td>40</td><td>Mississippi</td><td>115.21</td><td>24</td><td>Oklahoma</td><td>121.40</td></tr>
<tr><td>21</td><td>Missouri</td><td>122.57</td><td>25</td><td>New Mexico</td><td>121.17</td></tr>
<tr><td>35</td><td>Montana</td><td>118.59</td><td>26</td><td>Arizona</td><td>121.11</td></tr>
<tr><td>41</td><td>Nebraska</td><td>114.57</td><td>27</td><td>Pennsylvania</td><td>120.88</td></tr>
<tr><td>37</td><td>Nevada</td><td>118.22</td><td>28</td><td>North Dakota</td><td>120.69</td></tr>
<tr><td>50</td><td>New Hampshire</td><td>101.45</td><td>29</td><td>Alabama</td><td>120.30</td></tr>
<tr><td>43</td><td>New Jersey</td><td>113.66</td><td>30</td><td>Maryland</td><td>120.21</td></tr>
<tr><td>25</td><td>New Mexico</td><td>121.17</td><td>31</td><td>Kentucky</td><td>120.09</td></tr>
<tr><td>5</td><td>New York</td><td>135.63</td><td>32</td><td>Virginia</td><td>119.87</td></tr>
<tr><td>9</td><td>North Carolina</td><td>130.79</td><td>33</td><td>Delaware</td><td>119.61</td></tr>
<tr><td>28</td><td>North Dakota</td><td>120.69</td><td>34</td><td>Wyoming</td><td>118.74</td></tr>
<tr><td>18</td><td>Ohio</td><td>123.48</td><td>35</td><td>Montana</td><td>118.59</td></tr>
<tr><td>24</td><td>Oklahoma</td><td>121.40</td><td>36</td><td>Indiana</td><td>118.41</td></tr>
<tr><td>22</td><td>Oregon</td><td>122.51</td><td>37</td><td>Nevada</td><td>118.22</td></tr>
<tr><td>27</td><td>Pennsylvania</td><td>120.88</td><td>38</td><td>West Virginia</td><td>117.83</td></tr>
<tr><td>3</td><td>Rhode Island</td><td>139.90</td><td>39</td><td>Utah</td><td>115.64</td></tr>
<tr><td>19</td><td>South Carolina</td><td>123.38</td><td>40</td><td>Mississippi</td><td>115.21</td></tr>
<tr><td>14</td><td>South Dakota</td><td>125.65</td><td>41</td><td>Nebraska</td><td>114.57</td></tr>
<tr><td>13</td><td>Tennessee</td><td>126.28</td><td>42</td><td>Idaho</td><td>113.81</td></tr>
<tr><td>17</td><td>Texas</td><td>125.06</td><td>43</td><td>New Jersey</td><td>113.66</td></tr>
<tr><td>39</td><td>Utah</td><td>115.64</td><td>44</td><td>Kansas</td><td>113.53</td></tr>
<tr><td>20</td><td>Vermont</td><td>123.02</td><td>45</td><td>Minnesota</td><td>110.60</td></tr>
<tr><td>32</td><td>Virginia</td><td>119.87</td><td>46</td><td>Iowa</td><td>109.88</td></tr>
<tr><td>23</td><td>Washington</td><td>121.87</td><td>47</td><td>Arkansas</td><td>109.61</td></tr>
<tr><td>38</td><td>West Virginia</td><td>117.83</td><td>48</td><td>Maine</td><td>108.73</td></tr>
<tr><td>49</td><td>Wisconsin</td><td>105.78</td><td>49</td><td>Wisconsin</td><td>105.78</td></tr>
<tr><td>34</td><td>Wyoming</td><td>118.74</td><td>50</td><td>New Hampshire</td><td>101.45</td></tr>
<tr><td></td><td></td><td></td><td></td><td>District of Columbia</td><td>135.41</td></tr>
</table>

Source: U.S. Department of Agriculture, Food, Nutrition and Consumer Services
"Supplemental Nutrition Assistance Program" (http://www.fns.usda.gov/pd/snapmain.htm)
*Preliminary for fiscal year 2017. National average includes recipients in U.S. territories. Program formerly called the Food Stamp Program.

Percent of Population Receiving
Supplemental Nutrition Assistance Program Benefits in 2017
National Percent = 12.9%*

ALPHA ORDER

RANK	STATE	PERCENT
6	Alabama	16.5
29	Alaska	12.0
23	Arizona	13.1
24	Arkansas	12.9
38	California	10.4
44	Colorado	8.2
34	Connecticut	11.4
10	Delaware	15.3
11	Florida	15.2
8	Georgia	15.4
31	Hawaii	11.8
40	Idaho	10.0
13	Illinois	14.7
39	Indiana	10.1
32	Iowa	11.6
46	Kansas	8.0
13	Kentucky	14.7
2	Louisiana	19.4
21	Maine	13.5
35	Maryland	11.3
36	Massachusetts	11.1
19	Michigan	13.8
45	Minnesota	8.1
4	Mississippi	18.0
27	Missouri	12.4
33	Montana	11.5
41	Nebraska	9.2
13	Nevada	14.7
48	New Hampshire	6.9
43	New Jersey	9.1
1	New Mexico	22.1
13	New York	14.7
22	North Carolina	13.3
47	North Dakota	7.1
24	Ohio	12.9
8	Oklahoma	15.4
5	Oregon	16.6
17	Pennsylvania	14.4
12	Rhode Island	14.9
18	South Carolina	14.3
37	South Dakota	10.7
7	Tennessee	15.6
20	Texas	13.7
49	Utah	6.7
28	Vermont	12.3
41	Virginia	9.2
26	Washington	12.6
3	West Virginia	18.7
30	Wisconsin	11.9
50	Wyoming	5.7

RANK ORDER

RANK	STATE	PERCENT
1	New Mexico	22.1
2	Louisiana	19.4
3	West Virginia	18.7
4	Mississippi	18.0
5	Oregon	16.6
6	Alabama	16.5
7	Tennessee	15.6
8	Georgia	15.4
8	Oklahoma	15.4
10	Delaware	15.3
11	Florida	15.2
12	Rhode Island	14.9
13	Illinois	14.7
13	Kentucky	14.7
13	Nevada	14.7
13	New York	14.7
17	Pennsylvania	14.4
18	South Carolina	14.3
19	Michigan	13.8
20	Texas	13.7
21	Maine	13.5
22	North Carolina	13.3
23	Arizona	13.1
24	Arkansas	12.9
24	Ohio	12.9
26	Washington	12.6
27	Missouri	12.4
28	Vermont	12.3
29	Alaska	12.0
30	Wisconsin	11.9
31	Hawaii	11.8
32	Iowa	11.6
33	Montana	11.5
34	Connecticut	11.4
35	Maryland	11.3
36	Massachusetts	11.1
37	South Dakota	10.7
38	California	10.4
39	Indiana	10.1
40	Idaho	10.0
41	Nebraska	9.2
41	Virginia	9.2
43	New Jersey	9.1
44	Colorado	8.2
45	Minnesota	8.1
46	Kansas	8.0
47	North Dakota	7.1
48	New Hampshire	6.9
49	Utah	6.7
50	Wyoming	5.7
	District of Columbia	17.8

Source: CQ Press using data from U.S. Department of Agriculture, Food, Nutrition and Consumer Services
  "Supplemental Nutrition Assistance Program" (http://www.fns.usda.gov/pd/snapmain.htm)
*Preliminary data for fiscal year 2017. National rate does not include recipients in U.S. territories. Program formerly called the
Food Stamp Program.

Percent of Households Receiving
Supplemental Nutrition Assistance Program Benefits in 2017
National Percent = 17.5% of Households*

ALPHA ORDER

RANK	STATE	PERCENT
11	Alabama	20.3
31	Alaska	15.5
28	Arizona	16.4
33	Arkansas	14.9
32	California	15.4
44	Colorado	10.5
24	Connecticut	17.3
10	Delaware	20.4
7	Florida	22.3
11	Georgia	20.3
17	Hawaii	18.8
40	Idaho	12.2
11	Illinois	20.3
42	Indiana	11.7
36	Iowa	13.9
46	Kansas	9.7
21	Kentucky	18.0
3	Louisiana	24.5
23	Maine	17.6
28	Maryland	16.4
25	Massachusetts	17.2
17	Michigan	18.8
45	Minnesota	10.4
6	Mississippi	22.4
34	Missouri	14.8
37	Montana	13.8
43	Nebraska	10.6
9	Nevada	21.4
47	New Hampshire	8.8
38	New Jersey	12.7
1	New Mexico	28.7
7	New York	22.3
16	North Carolina	18.9
49	North Dakota	8.0
30	Ohio	16.1
20	Oklahoma	18.6
2	Oregon	25.0
15	Pennsylvania	19.3
5	Rhode Island	23.7
21	South Carolina	18.0
39	South Dakota	12.4
14	Tennessee	20.1
26	Texas	17.1
47	Utah	8.8
27	Vermont	16.5
41	Virginia	11.8
17	Washington	18.8
4	West Virginia	23.8
34	Wisconsin	14.8
50	Wyoming	6.3

RANK ORDER

RANK	STATE	PERCENT
1	New Mexico	28.7
2	Oregon	25.0
3	Louisiana	24.5
4	West Virginia	23.8
5	Rhode Island	23.7
6	Mississippi	22.4
7	Florida	22.3
7	New York	22.3
9	Nevada	21.4
10	Delaware	20.4
11	Alabama	20.3
11	Georgia	20.3
11	Illinois	20.3
14	Tennessee	20.1
15	Pennsylvania	19.3
16	North Carolina	18.9
17	Hawaii	18.8
17	Michigan	18.8
17	Washington	18.8
20	Oklahoma	18.6
21	Kentucky	18.0
21	South Carolina	18.0
23	Maine	17.6
24	Connecticut	17.3
25	Massachusetts	17.2
26	Texas	17.1
27	Vermont	16.5
28	Arizona	16.4
28	Maryland	16.4
30	Ohio	16.1
31	Alaska	15.5
32	California	15.4
33	Arkansas	14.9
34	Missouri	14.8
34	Wisconsin	14.8
36	Iowa	13.9
37	Montana	13.8
38	New Jersey	12.7
39	South Dakota	12.4
40	Idaho	12.2
41	Virginia	11.8
42	Indiana	11.7
43	Nebraska	10.6
44	Colorado	10.5
45	Minnesota	10.4
46	Kansas	9.7
47	New Hampshire	8.8
47	Utah	8.8
49	North Dakota	8.0
50	Wyoming	6.3

| | District of Columbia | 25.2 |

Source: CQ Press using data from U.S. Department of Agriculture, Food, Nutrition and Consumer Services
"Supplemental Nutrition Assistance Program" (http://www.fns.usda.gov/pd/snapmain.htm)
*Preliminary data for fiscal year 2017. Percent calculated using 2016 estimated total households. National percent excludes households in U.S. territories. Program formerly called the Food Stamp Program.

Average Monthly Participants in Women, Infants, and Children (WIC) Special Nutrition Program in 2017
National Total = 7,285,687 Participants*

ALPHA ORDER

RANK	STATE	PARTICIPANTS	% of USA
17	Alabama	123,993	1.7%
44	Alaska	18,188	0.2%
12	Arizona	153,510	2.1%
30	Arkansas	76,518	1.1%
1	California	1,080,577	14.8%
28	Colorado	84,582	1.2%
36	Connecticut	47,830	0.7%
46	Delaware	17,077	0.2%
3	Florida	468,867	6.4%
5	Georgia	237,225	3.3%
40	Hawaii	26,856	0.4%
39	Idaho	36,526	0.5%
10	Illinois	211,367	2.9%
14	Indiana	143,975	2.0%
32	Iowa	61,996	0.9%
33	Kansas	54,135	0.7%
23	Kentucky	107,885	1.5%
19	Louisiana	119,754	1.6%
42	Maine	19,371	0.3%
16	Maryland	132,843	1.8%
21	Massachusetts	112,763	1.5%
8	Michigan	224,106	3.1%
22	Minnesota	111,120	1.5%
29	Mississippi	83,662	1.1%
20	Missouri	119,620	1.6%
45	Montana	17,444	0.2%
38	Nebraska	37,437	0.5%
31	Nevada	66,060	0.9%
47	New Hampshire	13,064	0.2%
13	New Jersey	147,937	2.0%
35	New Mexico	49,975	0.7%
4	New York	435,382	6.0%
6	North Carolina	230,658	3.2%
48	North Dakota	12,729	0.2%
9	Ohio	221,746	3.0%
24	Oklahoma	105,845	1.5%
27	Oregon	89,534	1.2%
7	Pennsylvania	226,065	3.1%
41	Rhode Island	19,501	0.3%
25	South Carolina	99,332	1.4%
43	South Dakota	18,367	0.3%
15	Tennessee	136,303	1.9%
2	Texas	821,873	11.3%
34	Utah	53,748	0.7%
49	Vermont	11,558	0.2%
18	Virginia	122,185	1.7%
11	Washington	157,476	2.2%
37	West Virginia	38,315	0.5%
26	Wisconsin	95,958	1.3%
50	Wyoming	10,159	0.1%

RANK ORDER

RANK	STATE	PARTICIPANTS	% of USA
1	California	1,080,577	14.8%
2	Texas	821,873	11.3%
3	Florida	468,867	6.4%
4	New York	435,382	6.0%
5	Georgia	237,225	3.3%
6	North Carolina	230,658	3.2%
7	Pennsylvania	226,065	3.1%
8	Michigan	224,106	3.1%
9	Ohio	221,746	3.0%
10	Illinois	211,367	2.9%
11	Washington	157,476	2.2%
12	Arizona	153,510	2.1%
13	New Jersey	147,937	2.0%
14	Indiana	143,975	2.0%
15	Tennessee	136,303	1.9%
16	Maryland	132,843	1.8%
17	Alabama	123,993	1.7%
18	Virginia	122,185	1.7%
19	Louisiana	119,754	1.6%
20	Missouri	119,620	1.6%
21	Massachusetts	112,763	1.5%
22	Minnesota	111,120	1.5%
23	Kentucky	107,885	1.5%
24	Oklahoma	105,845	1.5%
25	South Carolina	99,332	1.4%
26	Wisconsin	95,958	1.3%
27	Oregon	89,534	1.2%
28	Colorado	84,582	1.2%
29	Mississippi	83,662	1.1%
30	Arkansas	76,518	1.1%
31	Nevada	66,060	0.9%
32	Iowa	61,996	0.9%
33	Kansas	54,135	0.7%
34	Utah	53,748	0.7%
35	New Mexico	49,975	0.7%
36	Connecticut	47,830	0.7%
37	West Virginia	38,315	0.5%
38	Nebraska	37,437	0.5%
39	Idaho	36,526	0.5%
40	Hawaii	26,856	0.4%
41	Rhode Island	19,501	0.3%
42	Maine	19,371	0.3%
43	South Dakota	18,367	0.3%
44	Alaska	18,188	0.2%
45	Montana	17,444	0.2%
46	Delaware	17,077	0.2%
47	New Hampshire	13,064	0.2%
48	North Dakota	12,729	0.2%
49	Vermont	11,558	0.2%
50	Wyoming	10,159	0.1%
	District of Columbia	13,580	0.2%

Source: U.S. Department of Agriculture, Food, Nutrition and Consumer Services

"WIC Program (http://www.fns.usda.gov/pd/wicmain.htm)

*Preliminary data for fiscal year 2017. National total includes 159,113 participants in outlying areas not shown separately (Puerto Rico has 139,769 participants).

Average Monthly Benefit per Participant in Women, Infants, and Children (WIC) Special Nutrition Program in 2017
National Average = $41.22*

ALPHA ORDER

RANK	STATE	AVERAGE BENEFIT
12	Alabama	$45.10
1	Alaska	56.84
17	Arizona	42.83
14	Arkansas	43.91
10	California	45.30
36	Colorado	36.94
15	Connecticut	43.59
24	Delaware	40.91
19	Florida	42.41
31	Georgia	38.08
2	Hawaii	54.05
39	Idaho	35.37
6	Illinois	48.73
43	Indiana	34.30
45	Iowa	32.61
34	Kansas	37.20
46	Kentucky	32.36
9	Louisiana	45.60
22	Maine	41.76
21	Maryland	41.81
33	Massachusetts	37.45
35	Michigan	37.05
25	Minnesota	40.66
4	Mississippi	52.59
42	Missouri	34.34
23	Montana	41.12
30	Nebraska	38.40
38	Nevada	35.97
49	New Hampshire	30.09
3	New Jersey	53.46
37	New Mexico	36.53
5	New York	50.91
18	North Carolina	42.57
7	North Dakota	46.34
48	Ohio	30.30
40	Oklahoma	34.84
41	Oregon	34.47
13	Pennsylvania	44.79
16	Rhode Island	43.01
11	South Carolina	45.20
20	South Dakota	42.09
26	Tennessee	39.64
50	Texas	27.12
29	Utah	38.49
8	Vermont	46.15
47	Virginia	30.63
28	Washington	38.80
27	West Virginia	38.98
32	Wisconsin	37.98
44	Wyoming	33.22

RANK ORDER

RANK	STATE	AVERAGE BENEFIT
1	Alaska	$56.84
2	Hawaii	54.05
3	New Jersey	53.46
4	Mississippi	52.59
5	New York	50.91
6	Illinois	48.73
7	North Dakota	46.34
8	Vermont	46.15
9	Louisiana	45.60
10	California	45.30
11	South Carolina	45.20
12	Alabama	45.10
13	Pennsylvania	44.79
14	Arkansas	43.91
15	Connecticut	43.59
16	Rhode Island	43.01
17	Arizona	42.83
18	North Carolina	42.57
19	Florida	42.41
20	South Dakota	42.09
21	Maryland	41.81
22	Maine	41.76
23	Montana	41.12
24	Delaware	40.91
25	Minnesota	40.66
26	Tennessee	39.64
27	West Virginia	38.98
28	Washington	38.80
29	Utah	38.49
30	Nebraska	38.40
31	Georgia	38.08
32	Wisconsin	37.98
33	Massachusetts	37.45
34	Kansas	37.20
35	Michigan	37.05
36	Colorado	36.94
37	New Mexico	36.53
38	Nevada	35.97
39	Idaho	35.37
40	Oklahoma	34.84
41	Oregon	34.47
42	Missouri	34.34
43	Indiana	34.30
44	Wyoming	33.22
45	Iowa	32.61
46	Kentucky	32.36
47	Virginia	30.63
48	Ohio	30.30
49	New Hampshire	30.09
50	Texas	27.12
	District of Columbia	46.23

Source: U.S. Department of Agriculture, Food, Nutrition and Consumer Services

"WIC Program (http://www.fns.usda.gov/pd/wicmain.htm)

*Preliminary data for fiscal year 2017. National average includes outlying areas and Indian reservations not shown separately.

Percent of Public Elementary and Secondary School Students
Eligible for Free or Reduced-Price Meals in 2016
National Percent = 51.9%*

RANK	STATE	PERCENT
15	Alabama	51.0
34	Alaska	42.7
49	Arizona	0.0
3	Arkansas	63.5
10	California	58.7
35	Colorado	41.8
41	Connecticut	37.9
43	Delaware	37.4
9	Florida	58.8
4	Georgia	62.4
17	Hawaii	49.6
24	Idaho	46.9
19	Illinois	49.3
23	Indiana	48.2
37	Iowa	40.8
22	Kansas	48.4
7	Kentucky	59.4
11	Louisiana	58.3
30	Maine	44.7
28	Maryland	45.0
49	Massachusetts	0.0
32	Michigan	44.6
40	Minnesota	38.1
1	Mississippi	74.9
16	Missouri	50.0
29	Montana	44.8
33	Nebraska	44.2
13	Nevada	57.3
48	New Hampshire	28.1
45	New Jersey	36.5
2	New Mexico	71.4
21	New York	48.6
12	North Carolina	57.4
47	North Dakota	31.0
30	Ohio	44.7
5	Oklahoma	61.3
20	Oregon	49.0
25	Pennsylvania	46.7
26	Rhode Island	46.5
6	South Carolina	60.0
36	South Dakota	41.5
13	Tennessee	57.3
8	Texas	58.9
46	Utah	36.4
44	Vermont	36.8
37	Virginia	40.8
27	Washington	45.4
18	West Virginia	49.4
39	Wisconsin	39.4
42	Wyoming	37.5

RANK	STATE	PERCENT
1	Mississippi	74.9
2	New Mexico	71.4
3	Arkansas	63.5
4	Georgia	62.4
5	Oklahoma	61.3
6	South Carolina	60.0
7	Kentucky	59.4
8	Texas	58.9
9	Florida	58.8
10	California	58.7
11	Louisiana	58.3
12	North Carolina	57.4
13	Nevada	57.3
13	Tennessee	57.3
15	Alabama	51.0
16	Missouri	50.0
17	Hawaii	49.6
18	West Virginia	49.4
19	Illinois	49.3
20	Oregon	49.0
21	New York	48.6
22	Kansas	48.4
23	Indiana	48.2
24	Idaho	46.9
25	Pennsylvania	46.7
26	Rhode Island	46.5
27	Washington	45.4
28	Maryland	45.0
29	Montana	44.8
30	Maine	44.7
30	Ohio	44.7
32	Michigan	44.6
33	Nebraska	44.2
34	Alaska	42.7
35	Colorado	41.8
36	South Dakota	41.5
37	Iowa	40.8
37	Virginia	40.8
39	Wisconsin	39.4
40	Minnesota	38.1
41	Connecticut	37.9
42	Wyoming	37.5
43	Delaware	37.4
44	Vermont	36.8
45	New Jersey	36.5
46	Utah	36.4
47	North Dakota	31.0
48	New Hampshire	28.1
49	Arizona	0.0
49	Massachusetts	0.0
	District of Columbia	74.2

Source: CQ Press using data from U.S. Department of Education, National Center for Education Statistics
   "Common Core of Data (CCD) Database" (https://nces.ed.gov/ccd/elsi/)
*For school year 2015-2016.

Child Support Collections in 2016

National Total = $28,481,426,455*

ALPHA ORDER				RANK ORDER			
RANK	STATE	COLLECTIONS	% of USA	RANK	STATE	COLLECTIONS	% of USA
26	Alabama	$325,009,128	1.1%	1	Texas	$3,975,425,586	14.0%
41	Alaska	99,600,932	0.3%	2	California	2,311,471,682	8.1%
28	Arizona	312,073,959	1.1%	3	New York	1,750,878,995	6.1%
32	Arkansas	231,187,031	0.8%	4	Ohio	1,651,453,068	5.8%
2	California	2,311,471,682	8.1%	5	Florida	1,477,346,218	5.2%
27	Colorado	321,101,279	1.1%	6	Michigan	1,328,650,378	4.7%
31	Connecticut	245,530,131	0.9%	7	Pennsylvania	1,240,481,754	4.4%
46	Delaware	75,986,354	0.3%	8	New Jersey	1,154,277,540	4.1%
5	Florida	1,477,346,218	5.2%	9	Illinois	811,743,030	2.9%
10	Georgia	690,988,211	2.4%	10	Georgia	690,988,211	2.4%
42	Hawaii	99,425,230	0.3%	11	North Carolina	663,210,244	2.3%
38	Idaho	171,537,029	0.6%	12	Wisconsin	645,190,808	2.3%
9	Illinois	811,743,030	2.9%	13	Washington	640,491,685	2.2%
19	Indiana	549,292,842	1.9%	14	Massachusetts	634,750,462	2.2%
29	Iowa	307,779,154	1.1%	15	Virginia	607,383,240	2.1%
36	Kansas	187,350,486	0.7%	16	Tennessee	604,695,788	2.1%
22	Kentucky	379,507,355	1.3%	17	Missouri	596,454,203	2.1%
21	Louisiana	397,885,269	1.4%	18	Minnesota	575,056,824	2.0%
40	Maine	100,753,458	0.4%	19	Indiana	549,292,842	1.9%
20	Maryland	534,748,108	1.9%	20	Maryland	534,748,108	1.9%
14	Massachusetts	634,750,462	2.2%	21	Louisiana	397,885,269	1.4%
6	Michigan	1,328,650,378	4.7%	22	Kentucky	379,507,355	1.3%
18	Minnesota	575,056,824	2.0%	23	Oregon	359,706,112	1.3%
25	Mississippi	328,139,566	1.2%	24	Oklahoma	342,044,816	1.2%
17	Missouri	596,454,203	2.1%	25	Mississippi	328,139,566	1.2%
49	Montana	60,586,661	0.2%	26	Alabama	325,009,128	1.1%
34	Nebraska	206,148,541	0.7%	27	Colorado	321,101,279	1.1%
37	Nevada	183,853,843	0.6%	28	Arizona	312,073,959	1.1%
45	New Hampshire	76,548,067	0.3%	29	Iowa	307,779,154	1.1%
8	New Jersey	1,154,277,540	4.1%	30	South Carolina	287,578,479	1.0%
39	New Mexico	121,491,197	0.4%	31	Connecticut	245,530,131	0.9%
3	New York	1,750,878,995	6.1%	32	Arkansas	231,187,031	0.8%
11	North Carolina	663,210,244	2.3%	33	Utah	212,273,414	0.7%
43	North Dakota	96,264,449	0.3%	34	Nebraska	206,148,541	0.7%
4	Ohio	1,651,453,068	5.8%	35	West Virginia	188,496,816	0.7%
24	Oklahoma	342,044,816	1.2%	36	Kansas	187,350,486	0.7%
23	Oregon	359,706,112	1.3%	37	Nevada	183,853,843	0.6%
7	Pennsylvania	1,240,481,754	4.4%	38	Idaho	171,537,029	0.6%
47	Rhode Island	74,327,824	0.3%	39	New Mexico	121,491,197	0.4%
30	South Carolina	287,578,479	1.0%	40	Maine	100,753,458	0.4%
44	South Dakota	91,900,750	0.3%	41	Alaska	99,600,932	0.3%
16	Tennessee	604,695,788	2.1%	42	Hawaii	99,425,230	0.3%
1	Texas	3,975,425,586	14.0%	43	North Dakota	96,264,449	0.3%
33	Utah	212,273,414	0.7%	44	South Dakota	91,900,750	0.3%
50	Vermont	43,660,064	0.2%	45	New Hampshire	76,548,067	0.3%
15	Virginia	607,383,240	2.1%	46	Delaware	75,986,354	0.3%
13	Washington	640,491,685	2.2%	47	Rhode Island	74,327,824	0.3%
35	West Virginia	188,496,816	0.7%	48	Wyoming	62,578,296	0.2%
12	Wisconsin	645,190,808	2.3%	49	Montana	60,586,661	0.2%
48	Wyoming	62,578,296	0.2%	50	Vermont	43,660,064	0.2%
					District of Columbia	47,110,099	0.2%

Source: U.S. Department of Health and Human Services, Office of Child Support Enforcement
"Child Support Enforcement Annual Report to Congress" (https://www.acf.hhs.gov/css/data)
*Preliminary data for fiscal year 2016. Total does not include $352,785,644 collected in U.S. territories.

XV. Transportation

Federal Highway Funding in 2016

National Total = $39,724,000,000*

<table>
<tr><td colspan="4">ALPHA ORDER</td><td colspan="4">RANK ORDER</td></tr>
<tr><th>RANK</th><th>STATE</th><th>FUNDS</th><th>% of USA</th><th>RANK</th><th>STATE</th><th>FUNDS</th><th>% of USA</th></tr>
<tr><td>16</td><td>Alabama</td><td>$769,572,000</td><td>1.9%</td><td>1</td><td>California</td><td>$3,723,002,000</td><td>9.4%</td></tr>
<tr><td>30</td><td>Alaska</td><td>508,615,000</td><td>1.3%</td><td>2</td><td>Texas</td><td>3,501,354,000</td><td>8.8%</td></tr>
<tr><td>18</td><td>Arizona</td><td>742,166,000</td><td>1.9%</td><td>3</td><td>Florida</td><td>1,921,861,000</td><td>4.8%</td></tr>
<tr><td>28</td><td>Arkansas</td><td>525,175,000</td><td>1.3%</td><td>4</td><td>New York</td><td>1,702,650,000</td><td>4.3%</td></tr>
<tr><td>1</td><td>California</td><td>3,723,002,000</td><td>9.4%</td><td>5</td><td>Pennsylvania</td><td>1,664,297,000</td><td>4.2%</td></tr>
<tr><td>27</td><td>Colorado</td><td>542,413,000</td><td>1.4%</td><td>6</td><td>Illinois</td><td>1,442,157,000</td><td>3.6%</td></tr>
<tr><td>29</td><td>Connecticut</td><td>509,474,000</td><td>1.3%</td><td>7</td><td>Ohio</td><td>1,359,663,000</td><td>3.4%</td></tr>
<tr><td>48</td><td>Delaware</td><td>171,587,000</td><td>0.4%</td><td>8</td><td>Georgia</td><td>1,309,740,000</td><td>3.3%</td></tr>
<tr><td>3</td><td>Florida</td><td>1,921,861,000</td><td>4.8%</td><td>9</td><td>Michigan</td><td>1,067,990,000</td><td>2.7%</td></tr>
<tr><td>8</td><td>Georgia</td><td>1,309,740,000</td><td>3.3%</td><td>10</td><td>North Carolina</td><td>1,057,922,000</td><td>2.7%</td></tr>
<tr><td>49</td><td>Hawaii</td><td>171,562,000</td><td>0.4%</td><td>11</td><td>Virginia</td><td>1,032,226,000</td><td>2.6%</td></tr>
<tr><td>41</td><td>Idaho</td><td>290,128,000</td><td>0.7%</td><td>12</td><td>New Jersey</td><td>1,012,792,000</td><td>2.5%</td></tr>
<tr><td>6</td><td>Illinois</td><td>1,442,157,000</td><td>3.6%</td><td>13</td><td>Indiana</td><td>966,530,000</td><td>2.4%</td></tr>
<tr><td>13</td><td>Indiana</td><td>966,530,000</td><td>2.4%</td><td>14</td><td>Missouri</td><td>960,275,000</td><td>2.4%</td></tr>
<tr><td>32</td><td>Iowa</td><td>498,514,000</td><td>1.3%</td><td>15</td><td>Tennessee</td><td>857,163,000</td><td>2.2%</td></tr>
<tr><td>36</td><td>Kansas</td><td>383,321,000</td><td>1.0%</td><td>16</td><td>Alabama</td><td>769,572,000</td><td>1.9%</td></tr>
<tr><td>22</td><td>Kentucky</td><td>673,967,000</td><td>1.7%</td><td>17</td><td>Wisconsin</td><td>763,230,000</td><td>1.9%</td></tr>
<tr><td>19</td><td>Louisiana</td><td>711,927,000</td><td>1.8%</td><td>18</td><td>Arizona</td><td>742,166,000</td><td>1.9%</td></tr>
<tr><td>47</td><td>Maine</td><td>187,244,000</td><td>0.5%</td><td>19</td><td>Louisiana</td><td>711,927,000</td><td>1.8%</td></tr>
<tr><td>26</td><td>Maryland</td><td>609,564,000</td><td>1.5%</td><td>20</td><td>Washington</td><td>687,645,000</td><td>1.7%</td></tr>
<tr><td>25</td><td>Massachusetts</td><td>616,064,000</td><td>1.6%</td><td>21</td><td>South Carolina</td><td>679,237,000</td><td>1.7%</td></tr>
<tr><td>9</td><td>Michigan</td><td>1,067,990,000</td><td>2.7%</td><td>22</td><td>Kentucky</td><td>673,967,000</td><td>1.7%</td></tr>
<tr><td>23</td><td>Minnesota</td><td>661,442,000</td><td>1.7%</td><td>23</td><td>Minnesota</td><td>661,442,000</td><td>1.7%</td></tr>
<tr><td>33</td><td>Mississippi</td><td>490,588,000</td><td>1.2%</td><td>24</td><td>Oklahoma</td><td>643,316,000</td><td>1.6%</td></tr>
<tr><td>14</td><td>Missouri</td><td>960,275,000</td><td>2.4%</td><td>25</td><td>Massachusetts</td><td>616,064,000</td><td>1.6%</td></tr>
<tr><td>35</td><td>Montana</td><td>416,185,000</td><td>1.0%</td><td>26</td><td>Maryland</td><td>609,564,000</td><td>1.5%</td></tr>
<tr><td>40</td><td>Nebraska</td><td>293,191,000</td><td>0.7%</td><td>27</td><td>Colorado</td><td>542,413,000</td><td>1.4%</td></tr>
<tr><td>38</td><td>Nevada</td><td>368,332,000</td><td>0.9%</td><td>28</td><td>Arkansas</td><td>525,175,000</td><td>1.3%</td></tr>
<tr><td>50</td><td>New Hampshire</td><td>167,596,000</td><td>0.4%</td><td>29</td><td>Connecticut</td><td>509,474,000</td><td>1.3%</td></tr>
<tr><td>12</td><td>New Jersey</td><td>1,012,792,000</td><td>2.5%</td><td>30</td><td>Alaska</td><td>508,615,000</td><td>1.3%</td></tr>
<tr><td>37</td><td>New Mexico</td><td>372,499,000</td><td>0.9%</td><td>31</td><td>Oregon</td><td>507,004,000</td><td>1.3%</td></tr>
<tr><td>4</td><td>New York</td><td>1,702,650,000</td><td>4.3%</td><td>32</td><td>Iowa</td><td>498,514,000</td><td>1.3%</td></tr>
<tr><td>10</td><td>North Carolina</td><td>1,057,922,000</td><td>2.7%</td><td>33</td><td>Mississippi</td><td>490,588,000</td><td>1.2%</td></tr>
<tr><td>44</td><td>North Dakota</td><td>251,831,000</td><td>0.6%</td><td>34</td><td>West Virginia</td><td>443,289,000</td><td>1.1%</td></tr>
<tr><td>7</td><td>Ohio</td><td>1,359,663,000</td><td>3.4%</td><td>35</td><td>Montana</td><td>416,185,000</td><td>1.0%</td></tr>
<tr><td>24</td><td>Oklahoma</td><td>643,316,000</td><td>1.6%</td><td>36</td><td>Kansas</td><td>383,321,000</td><td>1.0%</td></tr>
<tr><td>31</td><td>Oregon</td><td>507,004,000</td><td>1.3%</td><td>37</td><td>New Mexico</td><td>372,499,000</td><td>0.9%</td></tr>
<tr><td>5</td><td>Pennsylvania</td><td>1,664,297,000</td><td>4.2%</td><td>38</td><td>Nevada</td><td>368,332,000</td><td>0.9%</td></tr>
<tr><td>45</td><td>Rhode Island</td><td>221,837,000</td><td>0.6%</td><td>39</td><td>Utah</td><td>352,225,000</td><td>0.9%</td></tr>
<tr><td>21</td><td>South Carolina</td><td>679,237,000</td><td>1.7%</td><td>40</td><td>Nebraska</td><td>293,191,000</td><td>0.7%</td></tr>
<tr><td>42</td><td>South Dakota</td><td>286,060,000</td><td>0.7%</td><td>41</td><td>Idaho</td><td>290,128,000</td><td>0.7%</td></tr>
<tr><td>15</td><td>Tennessee</td><td>857,163,000</td><td>2.2%</td><td>42</td><td>South Dakota</td><td>286,060,000</td><td>0.7%</td></tr>
<tr><td>2</td><td>Texas</td><td>3,501,354,000</td><td>8.8%</td><td>43</td><td>Wyoming</td><td>259,861,000</td><td>0.7%</td></tr>
<tr><td>39</td><td>Utah</td><td>352,225,000</td><td>0.9%</td><td>44</td><td>North Dakota</td><td>251,831,000</td><td>0.6%</td></tr>
<tr><td>46</td><td>Vermont</td><td>205,868,000</td><td>0.5%</td><td>45</td><td>Rhode Island</td><td>221,837,000</td><td>0.6%</td></tr>
<tr><td>11</td><td>Virginia</td><td>1,032,226,000</td><td>2.6%</td><td>46</td><td>Vermont</td><td>205,868,000</td><td>0.5%</td></tr>
<tr><td>20</td><td>Washington</td><td>687,645,000</td><td>1.7%</td><td>47</td><td>Maine</td><td>187,244,000</td><td>0.5%</td></tr>
<tr><td>34</td><td>West Virginia</td><td>443,289,000</td><td>1.1%</td><td>48</td><td>Delaware</td><td>171,587,000</td><td>0.4%</td></tr>
<tr><td>17</td><td>Wisconsin</td><td>763,230,000</td><td>1.9%</td><td>49</td><td>Hawaii</td><td>171,562,000</td><td>0.4%</td></tr>
<tr><td>43</td><td>Wyoming</td><td>259,861,000</td><td>0.7%</td><td>50</td><td>New Hampshire</td><td>167,596,000</td><td>0.4%</td></tr>
<tr><td></td><td></td><td></td><td></td><td></td><td>District of Columbia</td><td>161,850,000</td><td>0.4%</td></tr>
</table>

Source: U.S. Department of Transportation, Federal Highway Administration
  "Federal-aid Highway Fund Apportionments" (Table FA-4, http://www.fhwa.dot.gov/policyinformation/statistics/2015/)
*Fiscal Year 2016. National total does not include federal funds for U.S. territories.

Per Capita Federal Highway Funding in 2016

National Per Capita = $123*

ALPHA ORDER

RANK	STATE	PER CAPITA
16	Alabama	$158
1	Alaska	686
42	Arizona	107
11	Arkansas	176
46	California	95
45	Colorado	98
22	Connecticut	142
9	Delaware	180
48	Florida	93
29	Georgia	127
35	Hawaii	120
12	Idaho	173
40	Illinois	112
21	Indiana	146
15	Iowa	159
25	Kansas	132
19	Kentucky	152
19	Louisiana	152
23	Maine	141
44	Maryland	101
49	Massachusetts	90
41	Michigan	108
35	Minnesota	120
13	Mississippi	164
16	Missouri	158
3	Montana	401
18	Nebraska	154
31	Nevada	125
30	New Hampshire	126
39	New Jersey	113
10	New Mexico	179
50	New York	86
43	North Carolina	104
4	North Dakota	333
37	Ohio	117
13	Oklahoma	164
33	Oregon	124
27	Pennsylvania	130
8	Rhode Island	210
24	South Carolina	137
5	South Dakota	332
28	Tennessee	129
31	Texas	125
38	Utah	116
6	Vermont	330
34	Virginia	123
47	Washington	94
7	West Virginia	242
25	Wisconsin	132
2	Wyoming	444

RANK ORDER

RANK	STATE	PER CAPITA
1	Alaska	$686
2	Wyoming	444
3	Montana	401
4	North Dakota	333
5	South Dakota	332
6	Vermont	330
7	West Virginia	242
8	Rhode Island	210
9	Delaware	180
10	New Mexico	179
11	Arkansas	176
12	Idaho	173
13	Mississippi	164
13	Oklahoma	164
15	Iowa	159
16	Alabama	158
16	Missouri	158
18	Nebraska	154
19	Kentucky	152
19	Louisiana	152
21	Indiana	146
22	Connecticut	142
23	Maine	141
24	South Carolina	137
25	Kansas	132
25	Wisconsin	132
27	Pennsylvania	130
28	Tennessee	129
29	Georgia	127
30	New Hampshire	126
31	Nevada	125
31	Texas	125
33	Oregon	124
34	Virginia	123
35	Hawaii	120
35	Minnesota	120
37	Ohio	117
38	Utah	116
39	New Jersey	113
40	Illinois	112
41	Michigan	108
42	Arizona	107
43	North Carolina	104
44	Maryland	101
45	Colorado	98
46	California	95
47	Washington	94
48	Florida	93
49	Massachusetts	90
50	New York	86

District of Columbia	237

Source: CQ Press using data from U.S. Department of Transportation, Federal Highway Administration
"Federal-aid Highway Fund Apportionments" (Table FA-4, http://www.fhwa.dot.gov/policyinformation/statistics/2015/)
*Fiscal Year 2016. National per capita does not include population or federal funds for U.S. territories.

Public Road and Street Mileage in 2016

National Total = 4,140,108 Miles*

ALPHA ORDER

ALPHA ORDER

RANK	STATE	MILES	% of USA
18	Alabama	101,975	2.5%
46	Alaska	15,528	0.4%
33	Arizona	66,035	1.6%
17	Arkansas	102,616	2.5%
2	California	180,800	4.4%
22	Colorado	88,828	2.1%
44	Connecticut	21,531	0.5%
48	Delaware	6,427	0.2%
9	Florida	122,736	3.0%
7	Georgia	128,235	3.1%
50	Hawaii	4,469	0.1%
35	Idaho	51,342	1.2%
3	Illinois	145,892	3.5%
19	Indiana	96,616	2.3%
13	Iowa	114,741	2.8%
4	Kansas	142,047	3.4%
26	Kentucky	79,942	1.9%
34	Louisiana	61,411	1.5%
43	Maine	22,898	0.6%
41	Maryland	32,147	0.8%
40	Massachusetts	36,632	0.9%
10	Michigan	122,115	2.9%
5	Minnesota	138,794	3.4%
27	Mississippi	77,027	1.9%
6	Missouri	131,807	3.2%
30	Montana	73,610	1.8%
21	Nebraska	94,988	2.3%
37	Nevada	42,582	1.0%
45	New Hampshire	16,157	0.4%
38	New Jersey	39,071	0.9%
32	New Mexico	69,111	1.7%
14	New York	113,499	2.7%
16	North Carolina	106,522	2.6%
23	North Dakota	87,397	2.1%
8	Ohio	122,974	3.0%
15	Oklahoma	112,988	2.7%
31	Oregon	73,529	1.8%
11	Pennsylvania	120,446	2.9%
49	Rhode Island	6,052	0.1%
28	South Carolina	76,067	1.8%
24	South Dakota	82,557	2.0%
20	Tennessee	95,737	2.3%
1	Texas	313,656	7.6%
36	Utah	46,769	1.1%
47	Vermont	14,253	0.3%
29	Virginia	75,096	1.8%
25	Washington	80,392	1.9%
39	West Virginia	38,770	0.9%
12	Wisconsin	115,458	2.8%
42	Wyoming	28,326	0.7%

RANK ORDER

RANK	STATE	MILES	% of USA
1	Texas	313,656	7.6%
2	California	180,800	4.4%
3	Illinois	145,892	3.5%
4	Kansas	142,047	3.4%
5	Minnesota	138,794	3.4%
6	Missouri	131,807	3.2%
7	Georgia	128,235	3.1%
8	Ohio	122,974	3.0%
9	Florida	122,736	3.0%
10	Michigan	122,115	2.9%
11	Pennsylvania	120,446	2.9%
12	Wisconsin	115,458	2.8%
13	Iowa	114,741	2.8%
14	New York	113,499	2.7%
15	Oklahoma	112,988	2.7%
16	North Carolina	106,522	2.6%
17	Arkansas	102,616	2.5%
18	Alabama	101,975	2.5%
19	Indiana	96,616	2.3%
20	Tennessee	95,737	2.3%
21	Nebraska	94,988	2.3%
22	Colorado	88,828	2.1%
23	North Dakota	87,397	2.1%
24	South Dakota	82,557	2.0%
25	Washington	80,392	1.9%
26	Kentucky	79,942	1.9%
27	Mississippi	77,027	1.9%
28	South Carolina	76,067	1.8%
29	Virginia	75,096	1.8%
30	Montana	73,610	1.8%
31	Oregon	73,529	1.8%
32	New Mexico	69,111	1.7%
33	Arizona	66,035	1.6%
34	Louisiana	61,411	1.5%
35	Idaho	51,342	1.2%
36	Utah	46,769	1.1%
37	Nevada	42,582	1.0%
38	New Jersey	39,071	0.9%
39	West Virginia	38,770	0.9%
40	Massachusetts	36,632	0.9%
41	Maryland	32,147	0.8%
42	Wyoming	28,326	0.7%
43	Maine	22,898	0.6%
44	Connecticut	21,531	0.5%
45	New Hampshire	16,157	0.4%
46	Alaska	15,528	0.4%
47	Vermont	14,253	0.3%
48	Delaware	6,427	0.2%
49	Rhode Island	6,052	0.1%
50	Hawaii	4,469	0.1%
	District of Columbia	1,509	0.0%

Source: U.S. Department of Transportation, Federal Highway Administration
   "Highway Statistics 2016" (Table HM-20, http://www.fhwa.dot.gov/policyinformation/statistics/2016/)
*Does not include 17,184 miles of roads and streets in Puerto Rico.

Percent of Public Road and Street Mileage Federally Funded in 2016

National Percent = 24.7% of Public Road and Street Mileage*

ALPHA ORDER

RANK	STATE	PERCENT
18	Alabama	26.3
7	Alaska	29.0
43	Arizona	20.8
39	Arkansas	22.0
2	California	31.2
47	Colorado	19.8
5	Connecticut	29.4
25	Delaware	24.6
37	Florida	22.5
23	Georgia	24.8
1	Hawaii	35.0
36	Idaho	22.8
32	Illinois	23.7
24	Indiana	24.7
34	Iowa	22.9
27	Kansas	24.4
48	Kentucky	18.3
34	Louisiana	22.9
15	Maine	27.7
19	Maryland	25.4
3	Massachusetts	30.8
4	Michigan	30.0
30	Minnesota	23.9
10	Mississippi	28.5
33	Missouri	23.4
45	Montana	20.0
41	Nebraska	21.8
50	Nevada	17.6
39	New Hampshire	22.0
13	New Jersey	27.9
49	New Mexico	17.8
27	New York	24.4
38	North Carolina	22.1
42	North Dakota	21.6
26	Ohio	24.5
9	Oklahoma	28.6
20	Oregon	25.3
31	Pennsylvania	23.8
6	Rhode Island	29.1
13	South Carolina	27.9
29	South Dakota	24.1
45	Tennessee	20.0
8	Texas	28.7
43	Utah	20.8
16	Vermont	27.3
11	Virginia	28.2
20	Washington	25.3
17	West Virginia	27.2
22	Wisconsin	24.9
12	Wyoming	28.0

RANK ORDER

RANK	STATE	PERCENT
1	Hawaii	35.0
2	California	31.2
3	Massachusetts	30.8
4	Michigan	30.0
5	Connecticut	29.4
6	Rhode Island	29.1
7	Alaska	29.0
8	Texas	28.7
9	Oklahoma	28.6
10	Mississippi	28.5
11	Virginia	28.2
12	Wyoming	28.0
13	New Jersey	27.9
13	South Carolina	27.9
15	Maine	27.7
16	Vermont	27.3
17	West Virginia	27.2
18	Alabama	26.3
19	Maryland	25.4
20	Oregon	25.3
20	Washington	25.3
22	Wisconsin	24.9
23	Georgia	24.8
24	Indiana	24.7
25	Delaware	24.6
26	Ohio	24.5
27	Kansas	24.4
27	New York	24.4
29	South Dakota	24.1
30	Minnesota	23.9
31	Pennsylvania	23.8
32	Illinois	23.7
33	Missouri	23.4
34	Iowa	22.9
34	Louisiana	22.9
36	Idaho	22.8
37	Florida	22.5
38	North Carolina	22.1
39	Arkansas	22.0
39	New Hampshire	22.0
41	Nebraska	21.8
42	North Dakota	21.6
43	Arizona	20.8
43	Utah	20.8
45	Montana	20.0
45	Tennessee	20.0
47	Colorado	19.8
48	Kentucky	18.3
49	New Mexico	17.8
50	Nevada	17.6

	District of Columbia	30.1

Source: CQ Press using data from U.S. Department of Transportation, Federal Highway Administration
"Highway Statistics 2016" (Table HM-15, http://www.fhwa.dot.gov/policyinformation/statistics/2016/)
*National percent does not include federally-funded highway miles in Puerto Rico.

Interstate Highway Mileage in 2016

National Total = 48,192 Miles*

ALPHA ORDER

RANK	STATE	MILES	% of USA
18	Alabama	1,004	2.1%
17	Alaska	1,080	2.2%
15	Arizona	1,169	2.4%
33	Arkansas	749	1.6%
2	California	2,450	5.1%
20	Colorado	952	2.0%
45	Connecticut	346	0.7%
50	Delaware	41	0.1%
7	Florida	1,495	3.1%
12	Georgia	1,247	2.6%
49	Hawaii	55	0.1%
36	Idaho	612	1.3%
3	Illinois	2,185	4.5%
10	Indiana	1,264	2.6%
31	Iowa	791	1.6%
27	Kansas	874	1.8%
29	Kentucky	842	1.7%
21	Louisiana	938	1.9%
44	Maine	366	0.8%
42	Maryland	480	1.0%
38	Massachusetts	580	1.2%
11	Michigan	1,251	2.6%
24	Minnesota	914	1.9%
30	Mississippi	807	1.7%
8	Missouri	1,380	2.9%
13	Montana	1,192	2.5%
41	Nebraska	482	1.0%
37	Nevada	597	1.2%
47	New Hampshire	225	0.5%
43	New Jersey	432	0.9%
19	New Mexico	1,000	2.1%
5	New York	1,739	3.6%
9	North Carolina	1,272	2.6%
39	North Dakota	571	1.2%
6	Ohio	1,574	3.3%
23	Oklahoma	933	1.9%
34	Oregon	730	1.5%
4	Pennsylvania	1,861	3.9%
48	Rhode Island	70	0.1%
28	South Carolina	851	1.8%
35	South Dakota	679	1.4%
14	Tennessee	1,182	2.5%
1	Texas	3,436	7.1%
22	Utah	937	1.9%
46	Vermont	320	0.7%
16	Virginia	1,119	2.3%
32	Washington	764	1.6%
40	West Virginia	554	1.1%
26	Wisconsin	876	1.8%
24	Wyoming	914	1.9%

RANK ORDER

RANK	STATE	MILES	% of USA
1	Texas	3,436	7.1%
2	California	2,450	5.1%
3	Illinois	2,185	4.5%
4	Pennsylvania	1,861	3.9%
5	New York	1,739	3.6%
6	Ohio	1,574	3.3%
7	Florida	1,495	3.1%
8	Missouri	1,380	2.9%
9	North Carolina	1,272	2.6%
10	Indiana	1,264	2.6%
11	Michigan	1,251	2.6%
12	Georgia	1,247	2.6%
13	Montana	1,192	2.5%
14	Tennessee	1,182	2.5%
15	Arizona	1,169	2.4%
16	Virginia	1,119	2.3%
17	Alaska	1,080	2.2%
18	Alabama	1,004	2.1%
19	New Mexico	1,000	2.1%
20	Colorado	952	2.0%
21	Louisiana	938	1.9%
22	Utah	937	1.9%
23	Oklahoma	933	1.9%
24	Minnesota	914	1.9%
24	Wyoming	914	1.9%
26	Wisconsin	876	1.8%
27	Kansas	874	1.8%
28	South Carolina	851	1.8%
29	Kentucky	842	1.7%
30	Mississippi	807	1.7%
31	Iowa	791	1.6%
32	Washington	764	1.6%
33	Arkansas	749	1.6%
34	Oregon	730	1.5%
35	South Dakota	679	1.4%
36	Idaho	612	1.3%
37	Nevada	597	1.2%
38	Massachusetts	580	1.2%
39	North Dakota	571	1.2%
40	West Virginia	554	1.1%
41	Nebraska	482	1.0%
42	Maryland	480	1.0%
43	New Jersey	432	0.9%
44	Maine	366	0.8%
45	Connecticut	346	0.7%
46	Vermont	320	0.7%
47	New Hampshire	225	0.5%
48	Rhode Island	70	0.1%
49	Hawaii	55	0.1%
50	Delaware	41	0.1%
	District of Columbia	12	0.0%

Source: U.S. Department of Transportation, Federal Highway Administration
   "Highway Statistics 2016" (Table HM-15, http://www.fhwa.dot.gov/policyinformation/statistics/2016/)
*Does not include 282 miles of highway in Puerto Rico that are part of the interstate system.

Rural Road and Street Mileage in 2016

National Total = 2,928,054 Rural Miles*

ALPHA ORDER

RANK	STATE	MILES	% of USA
17	Alabama	74,691	2.6%
43	Alaska	12,710	0.4%
34	Arizona	39,686	1.4%
10	Arkansas	85,485	2.9%
14	California	76,013	2.6%
20	Colorado	68,258	2.3%
47	Connecticut	5,689	0.2%
48	Delaware	2,994	0.1%
35	Florida	36,440	1.2%
15	Georgia	75,978	2.6%
49	Hawaii	1,666	0.1%
32	Idaho	45,185	1.5%
6	Illinois	96,201	3.3%
21	Indiana	66,406	2.3%
5	Iowa	102,145	3.5%
2	Kansas	127,819	4.4%
23	Kentucky	64,877	2.2%
33	Louisiana	43,801	1.5%
40	Maine	19,424	0.7%
41	Maryland	13,523	0.5%
45	Massachusetts	6,509	0.2%
12	Michigan	84,153	2.9%
3	Minnesota	116,670	4.0%
25	Mississippi	64,070	2.2%
4	Missouri	107,426	3.7%
19	Montana	69,402	2.4%
9	Nebraska	87,233	3.0%
37	Nevada	32,299	1.1%
44	New Hampshire	11,093	0.4%
46	New Jersey	5,755	0.2%
27	New Mexico	60,752	2.1%
26	New York	63,794	2.2%
22	North Carolina	65,530	2.2%
11	North Dakota	84,531	2.9%
16	Ohio	75,511	2.6%
7	Oklahoma	94,824	3.2%
28	Oregon	58,592	2.0%
18	Pennsylvania	72,577	2.5%
50	Rhode Island	1,365	0.0%
30	South Carolina	56,262	1.9%
13	South Dakota	79,155	2.7%
24	Tennessee	64,335	2.2%
1	Texas	205,222	7.0%
36	Utah	35,043	1.2%
42	Vermont	12,754	0.4%
31	Virginia	48,632	1.7%
29	Washington	56,295	1.9%
38	West Virginia	32,098	1.1%
8	Wisconsin	91,666	3.1%
39	Wyoming	25,513	0.9%

RANK ORDER

RANK	STATE	MILES	% of USA
1	Texas	205,222	7.0%
2	Kansas	127,819	4.4%
3	Minnesota	116,670	4.0%
4	Missouri	107,426	3.7%
5	Iowa	102,145	3.5%
6	Illinois	96,201	3.3%
7	Oklahoma	94,824	3.2%
8	Wisconsin	91,666	3.1%
9	Nebraska	87,233	3.0%
10	Arkansas	85,485	2.9%
11	North Dakota	84,531	2.9%
12	Michigan	84,153	2.9%
13	South Dakota	79,155	2.7%
14	California	76,013	2.6%
15	Georgia	75,978	2.6%
16	Ohio	75,511	2.6%
17	Alabama	74,691	2.6%
18	Pennsylvania	72,577	2.5%
19	Montana	69,402	2.4%
20	Colorado	68,258	2.3%
21	Indiana	66,406	2.3%
22	North Carolina	65,530	2.2%
23	Kentucky	64,877	2.2%
24	Tennessee	64,335	2.2%
25	Mississippi	64,070	2.2%
26	New York	63,794	2.2%
27	New Mexico	60,752	2.1%
28	Oregon	58,592	2.0%
29	Washington	56,295	1.9%
30	South Carolina	56,262	1.9%
31	Virginia	48,632	1.7%
32	Idaho	45,185	1.5%
33	Louisiana	43,801	1.5%
34	Arizona	39,686	1.4%
35	Florida	36,440	1.2%
36	Utah	35,043	1.2%
37	Nevada	32,299	1.1%
38	West Virginia	32,098	1.1%
39	Wyoming	25,513	0.9%
40	Maine	19,424	0.7%
41	Maryland	13,523	0.5%
42	Vermont	12,754	0.4%
43	Alaska	12,710	0.4%
44	New Hampshire	11,093	0.4%
45	Massachusetts	6,509	0.2%
46	New Jersey	5,755	0.2%
47	Connecticut	5,689	0.2%
48	Delaware	2,994	0.1%
49	Hawaii	1,666	0.1%
50	Rhode Island	1,365	0.0%
	District of Columbia	0	0.0%

Source: U.S. Department of Transportation, Federal Highway Administration
"Highway Statistics 2016" (Table HM-20, http://www.fhwa.dot.gov/policyinformation/statistics/2016/)
*Does not include 3,067 miles of rural roads and streets in Puerto Rico.

Urban Road and Street Mileage in 2016

National Total = 1,212,054 Urban Miles*

ALPHA ORDER				RANK ORDER			
RANK	STATE	MILES	% of USA	RANK	STATE	MILES	% of USA
15	Alabama	27,285	2.3%	1	Texas	108,434	8.9%
47	Alaska	2,818	0.2%	2	California	104,787	8.6%
17	Arizona	26,349	2.2%	3	Florida	86,296	7.1%
27	Arkansas	17,131	1.4%	4	Georgia	52,257	4.3%
2	California	104,787	8.6%	5	New York	49,706	4.1%
22	Colorado	20,570	1.7%	6	Illinois	49,692	4.1%
28	Connecticut	15,842	1.3%	7	Pennsylvania	47,869	3.9%
44	Delaware	3,433	0.3%	8	Ohio	47,463	3.9%
3	Florida	86,296	7.1%	9	North Carolina	40,991	3.4%
4	Georgia	52,257	4.3%	10	Michigan	37,962	3.1%
49	Hawaii	2,803	0.2%	11	New Jersey	33,316	2.7%
39	Idaho	6,157	0.5%	12	Tennessee	31,402	2.6%
6	Illinois	49,692	4.1%	13	Indiana	30,210	2.5%
13	Indiana	30,210	2.5%	14	Massachusetts	30,123	2.5%
33	Iowa	12,596	1.0%	15	Alabama	27,285	2.3%
31	Kansas	14,227	1.2%	16	Virginia	26,463	2.2%
29	Kentucky	15,064	1.2%	17	Arizona	26,349	2.2%
26	Louisiana	17,610	1.5%	18	Missouri	24,382	2.0%
43	Maine	3,474	0.3%	19	Washington	24,097	2.0%
24	Maryland	18,624	1.5%	20	Wisconsin	23,791	2.0%
14	Massachusetts	30,123	2.5%	21	Minnesota	22,125	1.8%
10	Michigan	37,962	3.1%	22	Colorado	20,570	1.7%
21	Minnesota	22,125	1.8%	23	South Carolina	19,805	1.6%
32	Mississippi	12,957	1.1%	24	Maryland	18,624	1.5%
18	Missouri	24,382	2.0%	25	Oklahoma	18,164	1.5%
42	Montana	4,208	0.3%	26	Louisiana	17,610	1.5%
37	Nebraska	7,755	0.6%	27	Arkansas	17,131	1.4%
35	Nevada	10,283	0.8%	28	Connecticut	15,842	1.3%
40	New Hampshire	5,064	0.4%	29	Kentucky	15,064	1.2%
11	New Jersey	33,316	2.7%	30	Oregon	14,937	1.2%
36	New Mexico	8,359	0.7%	31	Kansas	14,227	1.2%
5	New York	49,706	4.1%	32	Mississippi	12,957	1.1%
9	North Carolina	40,991	3.4%	33	Iowa	12,596	1.0%
46	North Dakota	2,866	0.2%	34	Utah	11,726	1.0%
8	Ohio	47,463	3.9%	35	Nevada	10,283	0.8%
25	Oklahoma	18,164	1.5%	36	New Mexico	8,359	0.7%
30	Oregon	14,937	1.2%	37	Nebraska	7,755	0.6%
7	Pennsylvania	47,869	3.9%	38	West Virginia	6,672	0.6%
41	Rhode Island	4,688	0.4%	39	Idaho	6,157	0.5%
23	South Carolina	19,805	1.6%	40	New Hampshire	5,064	0.4%
45	South Dakota	3,402	0.3%	41	Rhode Island	4,688	0.4%
12	Tennessee	31,402	2.6%	42	Montana	4,208	0.3%
1	Texas	108,434	8.9%	43	Maine	3,474	0.3%
34	Utah	11,726	1.0%	44	Delaware	3,433	0.3%
50	Vermont	1,499	0.1%	45	South Dakota	3,402	0.3%
16	Virginia	26,463	2.2%	46	North Dakota	2,866	0.2%
19	Washington	24,097	2.0%	47	Alaska	2,818	0.2%
38	West Virginia	6,672	0.6%	48	Wyoming	2,813	0.2%
20	Wisconsin	23,791	2.0%	49	Hawaii	2,803	0.2%
48	Wyoming	2,813	0.2%	50	Vermont	1,499	0.1%
					District of Columbia	1,509	0.1%

Source: U.S. Department of Transportation, Federal Highway Administration
   "Highway Statistics 2016" (Table HM-20, http://www.fhwa.dot.gov/policyinformation/statistics/2016/)
*Does not include 14,116 miles of urban roads and streets in Puerto Rico.

Percent of Roadways in Mediocre or Poor Condition in 2013

National Percent = 19.9%*

ALPHA ORDER				RANK ORDER		
RANK	STATE	PERCENT		RANK	STATE	PERCENT
39	Alabama	10.7		1	Hawaii	43.2
14	Alaska	25.4		2	Connecticut	42.3
41	Arizona	9.7		3	California	38.4
29	Arkansas	16.3		4	Rhode Island	38.0
3	California	38.4		5	New Jersey	37.8
21	Colorado	21.2		6	Michigan	35.8
2	Connecticut	42.3		7	Washington	33.0
28	Delaware	16.4		8	Oklahoma	30.2
47	Florida	7.0		9	West Virginia	29.7
34	Georgia	12.1		10	New York	28.3
1	Hawaii	43.2		11	Maine	27.0
25	Idaho	18.0		12	New Hampshire	26.1
22	Illinois	20.6		13	Wisconsin	25.6
26	Indiana	17.4		14	Alaska	25.4
30	Iowa	14.4		15	New Mexico	25.3
36	Kansas	11.0		16	Louisiana	24.9
44	Kentucky	9.0		16	Mississippi	24.9
16	Louisiana	24.9		18	Vermont	24.4
11	Maine	27.0		19	Maryland	24.2
19	Maryland	24.2		20	Pennsylvania	22.8
33	Massachusetts	12.8		21	Colorado	21.2
6	Michigan	35.8		22	Illinois	20.6
40	Minnesota	10.3		23	Missouri	20.2
16	Mississippi	24.9		24	Virginia	19.8
23	Missouri	20.2		25	Idaho	18.0
43	Montana	9.1		26	Indiana	17.4
49	Nebraska	4.7		27	Utah	17.3
50	Nevada	3.6		28	Delaware	16.4
12	New Hampshire	26.1		29	Arkansas	16.3
5	New Jersey	37.8		30	Iowa	14.4
15	New Mexico	25.3		31	Texas	14.2
10	New York	28.3		32	Ohio	13.5
37	North Carolina	10.9		33	Massachusetts	12.8
37	North Dakota	10.9		34	Georgia	12.1
32	Ohio	13.5		34	South Carolina	12.1
8	Oklahoma	30.2		36	Kansas	11.0
45	Oregon	8.8		37	North Carolina	10.9
20	Pennsylvania	22.8		37	North Dakota	10.9
4	Rhode Island	38.0		39	Alabama	10.7
34	South Carolina	12.1		40	Minnesota	10.3
42	South Dakota	9.2		41	Arizona	9.7
48	Tennessee	6.8		42	South Dakota	9.2
31	Texas	14.2		43	Montana	9.1
27	Utah	17.3		44	Kentucky	9.0
18	Vermont	24.4		45	Oregon	8.8
24	Virginia	19.8		46	Wyoming	8.3
7	Washington	33.0		47	Florida	7.0
9	West Virginia	29.7		48	Tennessee	6.8
13	Wisconsin	25.6		49	Nebraska	4.7
46	Wyoming	8.3		50	Nevada	3.6

District of Columbia   94.5

Source: CQ Press using data from U.S. Department of Transportation, Bureau of Transportation Statistics
"State Transportation Statistics 2015" (Table 1-4, https://www.rita.dot.gov/bts/publications/state_transportation_statistics)
*Does not include 14,062 miles for which the condition is not reported. Road condition ratings are derived from the International Roughness Index (IRI) and the Present Serviceability Rating (PSR). States are required to report to the Federal Highway Administration (FHWA) IRI data for the Interstate system, other principal arterials, rural minor arterials, and the National Highway System regardless of functional system.

Bridges in 2016

National Total = 612,079 Bridges*

ALPHA ORDER

RANK	STATE	BRIDGES	% of USA
15	Alabama	16,098	2.6%
47	Alaska	1,488	0.2%
29	Arizona	8,154	1.3%
23	Arkansas	12,871	2.1%
4	California	25,431	4.2%
27	Colorado	8,682	1.4%
39	Connecticut	4,214	0.7%
49	Delaware	877	0.1%
24	Florida	12,313	2.0%
17	Georgia	14,835	2.4%
48	Hawaii	1,132	0.2%
37	Idaho	4,445	0.7%
3	Illinois	26,704	4.4%
11	Indiana	19,245	3.1%
7	Iowa	24,184	4.0%
5	Kansas	25,013	4.1%
18	Kentucky	14,265	2.3%
22	Louisiana	12,915	2.1%
45	Maine	2,450	0.4%
34	Maryland	5,321	0.9%
36	Massachusetts	5,171	0.8%
25	Michigan	11,156	1.8%
21	Minnesota	13,355	2.2%
14	Mississippi	17,068	2.8%
6	Missouri	24,468	4.0%
35	Montana	5,276	0.9%
16	Nebraska	15,334	2.5%
46	Nevada	1,933	0.3%
44	New Hampshire	2,486	0.4%
32	New Jersey	6,730	1.1%
40	New Mexico	3,973	0.6%
13	New York	17,462	2.9%
12	North Carolina	18,099	3.0%
38	North Dakota	4,400	0.7%
2	Ohio	28,284	4.6%
8	Oklahoma	23,053	3.8%
30	Oregon	8,118	1.3%
9	Pennsylvania	22,791	3.7%
50	Rhode Island	772	0.1%
26	South Carolina	9,358	1.5%
33	South Dakota	5,849	1.0%
10	Tennessee	20,123	3.3%
1	Texas	53,488	8.7%
42	Utah	3,039	0.5%
43	Vermont	2,766	0.5%
20	Virginia	13,892	2.3%
28	Washington	8,178	1.3%
31	West Virginia	7,217	1.2%
19	Wisconsin	14,230	2.3%
41	Wyoming	3,128	0.5%

RANK ORDER

RANK	STATE	BRIDGES	% of USA
1	Texas	53,488	8.7%
2	Ohio	28,284	4.6%
3	Illinois	26,704	4.4%
4	California	25,431	4.2%
5	Kansas	25,013	4.1%
6	Missouri	24,468	4.0%
7	Iowa	24,184	4.0%
8	Oklahoma	23,053	3.8%
9	Pennsylvania	22,791	3.7%
10	Tennessee	20,123	3.3%
11	Indiana	19,245	3.1%
12	North Carolina	18,099	3.0%
13	New York	17,462	2.9%
14	Mississippi	17,068	2.8%
15	Alabama	16,098	2.6%
16	Nebraska	15,334	2.5%
17	Georgia	14,835	2.4%
18	Kentucky	14,265	2.3%
19	Wisconsin	14,230	2.3%
20	Virginia	13,892	2.3%
21	Minnesota	13,355	2.2%
22	Louisiana	12,915	2.1%
23	Arkansas	12,871	2.1%
24	Florida	12,313	2.0%
25	Michigan	11,156	1.8%
26	South Carolina	9,358	1.5%
27	Colorado	8,682	1.4%
28	Washington	8,178	1.3%
29	Arizona	8,154	1.3%
30	Oregon	8,118	1.3%
31	West Virginia	7,217	1.2%
32	New Jersey	6,730	1.1%
33	South Dakota	5,849	1.0%
34	Maryland	5,321	0.9%
35	Montana	5,276	0.9%
36	Massachusetts	5,171	0.8%
37	Idaho	4,445	0.7%
38	North Dakota	4,400	0.7%
39	Connecticut	4,214	0.7%
40	New Mexico	3,973	0.6%
41	Wyoming	3,128	0.5%
42	Utah	3,039	0.5%
43	Vermont	2,766	0.5%
44	New Hampshire	2,486	0.4%
45	Maine	2,450	0.4%
46	Nevada	1,933	0.3%
47	Alaska	1,488	0.2%
48	Hawaii	1,132	0.2%
49	Delaware	877	0.1%
50	Rhode Island	772	0.1%
	District of Columbia	245	0.0%

Source: U.S. Department of Transportation, Federal Highway Administration
"Deficient Bridges by State and Highway System, 2016" (http://www.fhwa.dot.gov/bridge/deficient.htm)
*As of December 2016. Includes federal-aid and nonfederal-aid system bridges. National total does not include 2,308 bridges in Puerto Rico.

Structurally Deficient Bridges in 2016

National Total = 55,710 Structurally Deficient Bridges*

<table>
<tr><td colspan="4">ALPHA ORDER</td><td colspan="4">RANK ORDER</td></tr>
<tr><th>RANK</th><th>STATE</th><th>BRIDGES</th><th>% of USA</th><th>RANK</th><th>STATE</th><th>BRIDGES</th><th>% of USA</th></tr>
<tr><td>18</td><td>Alabama</td><td>1,229</td><td>2.2%</td><td>1</td><td>Iowa</td><td>4,968</td><td>8.9%</td></tr>
<tr><td>46</td><td>Alaska</td><td>144</td><td>0.3%</td><td>2</td><td>Pennsylvania</td><td>4,506</td><td>8.1%</td></tr>
<tr><td>43</td><td>Arizona</td><td>214</td><td>0.4%</td><td>3</td><td>Oklahoma</td><td>3,460</td><td>6.2%</td></tr>
<tr><td>25</td><td>Arkansas</td><td>811</td><td>1.5%</td><td>4</td><td>Missouri</td><td>3,195</td><td>5.7%</td></tr>
<tr><td>14</td><td>California</td><td>1,388</td><td>2.5%</td><td>5</td><td>Nebraska</td><td>2,361</td><td>4.2%</td></tr>
<tr><td>30</td><td>Colorado</td><td>497</td><td>0.9%</td><td>6</td><td>Illinois</td><td>2,243</td><td>4.0%</td></tr>
<tr><td>38</td><td>Connecticut</td><td>338</td><td>0.6%</td><td>7</td><td>Kansas</td><td>2,151</td><td>3.9%</td></tr>
<tr><td>49</td><td>Delaware</td><td>43</td><td>0.1%</td><td>8</td><td>Mississippi</td><td>2,098</td><td>3.8%</td></tr>
<tr><td>42</td><td>Florida</td><td>256</td><td>0.5%</td><td>9</td><td>Ohio</td><td>1,942</td><td>3.5%</td></tr>
<tr><td>27</td><td>Georgia</td><td>700</td><td>1.3%</td><td>10</td><td>New York</td><td>1,928</td><td>3.5%</td></tr>
<tr><td>48</td><td>Hawaii</td><td>64</td><td>0.1%</td><td>11</td><td>North Carolina</td><td>1,790</td><td>3.2%</td></tr>
<tr><td>34</td><td>Idaho</td><td>411</td><td>0.7%</td><td>12</td><td>Louisiana</td><td>1,739</td><td>3.1%</td></tr>
<tr><td>6</td><td>Illinois</td><td>2,243</td><td>4.0%</td><td>13</td><td>Indiana</td><td>1,533</td><td>2.8%</td></tr>
<tr><td>13</td><td>Indiana</td><td>1,533</td><td>2.8%</td><td>14</td><td>California</td><td>1,388</td><td>2.5%</td></tr>
<tr><td>1</td><td>Iowa</td><td>4,968</td><td>8.9%</td><td>15</td><td>West Virginia</td><td>1,247</td><td>2.2%</td></tr>
<tr><td>7</td><td>Kansas</td><td>2,151</td><td>3.9%</td><td>16</td><td>Michigan</td><td>1,234</td><td>2.2%</td></tr>
<tr><td>19</td><td>Kentucky</td><td>1,157</td><td>2.1%</td><td>17</td><td>Wisconsin</td><td>1,232</td><td>2.2%</td></tr>
<tr><td>12</td><td>Louisiana</td><td>1,739</td><td>3.1%</td><td>18</td><td>Alabama</td><td>1,229</td><td>2.2%</td></tr>
<tr><td>36</td><td>Maine</td><td>352</td><td>0.6%</td><td>19</td><td>Kentucky</td><td>1,157</td><td>2.1%</td></tr>
<tr><td>39</td><td>Maryland</td><td>308</td><td>0.6%</td><td>20</td><td>South Dakota</td><td>1,147</td><td>2.1%</td></tr>
<tr><td>31</td><td>Massachusetts</td><td>483</td><td>0.9%</td><td>21</td><td>Tennessee</td><td>998</td><td>1.8%</td></tr>
<tr><td>16</td><td>Michigan</td><td>1,234</td><td>2.2%</td><td>22</td><td>South Carolina</td><td>964</td><td>1.7%</td></tr>
<tr><td>26</td><td>Minnesota</td><td>800</td><td>1.4%</td><td>23</td><td>Virginia</td><td>935</td><td>1.7%</td></tr>
<tr><td>8</td><td>Mississippi</td><td>2,098</td><td>3.8%</td><td>24</td><td>Texas</td><td>900</td><td>1.6%</td></tr>
<tr><td>4</td><td>Missouri</td><td>3,195</td><td>5.7%</td><td>25</td><td>Arkansas</td><td>811</td><td>1.5%</td></tr>
<tr><td>32</td><td>Montana</td><td>465</td><td>0.8%</td><td>26</td><td>Minnesota</td><td>800</td><td>1.4%</td></tr>
<tr><td>5</td><td>Nebraska</td><td>2,361</td><td>4.2%</td><td>27</td><td>Georgia</td><td>700</td><td>1.3%</td></tr>
<tr><td>50</td><td>Nevada</td><td>31</td><td>0.1%</td><td>28</td><td>North Dakota</td><td>661</td><td>1.2%</td></tr>
<tr><td>40</td><td>New Hampshire</td><td>304</td><td>0.5%</td><td>29</td><td>New Jersey</td><td>609</td><td>1.1%</td></tr>
<tr><td>29</td><td>New Jersey</td><td>609</td><td>1.1%</td><td>30</td><td>Colorado</td><td>497</td><td>0.9%</td></tr>
<tr><td>41</td><td>New Mexico</td><td>258</td><td>0.5%</td><td>31</td><td>Massachusetts</td><td>483</td><td>0.9%</td></tr>
<tr><td>10</td><td>New York</td><td>1,928</td><td>3.5%</td><td>32</td><td>Montana</td><td>465</td><td>0.8%</td></tr>
<tr><td>11</td><td>North Carolina</td><td>1,790</td><td>3.2%</td><td>33</td><td>Oregon</td><td>429</td><td>0.8%</td></tr>
<tr><td>28</td><td>North Dakota</td><td>661</td><td>1.2%</td><td>34</td><td>Idaho</td><td>411</td><td>0.7%</td></tr>
<tr><td>9</td><td>Ohio</td><td>1,942</td><td>3.5%</td><td>35</td><td>Washington</td><td>392</td><td>0.7%</td></tr>
<tr><td>3</td><td>Oklahoma</td><td>3,460</td><td>6.2%</td><td>36</td><td>Maine</td><td>352</td><td>0.6%</td></tr>
<tr><td>33</td><td>Oregon</td><td>429</td><td>0.8%</td><td>37</td><td>Wyoming</td><td>344</td><td>0.6%</td></tr>
<tr><td>2</td><td>Pennsylvania</td><td>4,506</td><td>8.1%</td><td>38</td><td>Connecticut</td><td>338</td><td>0.6%</td></tr>
<tr><td>44</td><td>Rhode Island</td><td>192</td><td>0.3%</td><td>39</td><td>Maryland</td><td>308</td><td>0.6%</td></tr>
<tr><td>22</td><td>South Carolina</td><td>964</td><td>1.7%</td><td>40</td><td>New Hampshire</td><td>304</td><td>0.5%</td></tr>
<tr><td>20</td><td>South Dakota</td><td>1,147</td><td>2.1%</td><td>41</td><td>New Mexico</td><td>258</td><td>0.5%</td></tr>
<tr><td>21</td><td>Tennessee</td><td>998</td><td>1.8%</td><td>42</td><td>Florida</td><td>256</td><td>0.5%</td></tr>
<tr><td>24</td><td>Texas</td><td>900</td><td>1.6%</td><td>43</td><td>Arizona</td><td>214</td><td>0.4%</td></tr>
<tr><td>47</td><td>Utah</td><td>95</td><td>0.2%</td><td>44</td><td>Rhode Island</td><td>192</td><td>0.3%</td></tr>
<tr><td>45</td><td>Vermont</td><td>155</td><td>0.3%</td><td>45</td><td>Vermont</td><td>155</td><td>0.3%</td></tr>
<tr><td>23</td><td>Virginia</td><td>935</td><td>1.7%</td><td>46</td><td>Alaska</td><td>144</td><td>0.3%</td></tr>
<tr><td>35</td><td>Washington</td><td>392</td><td>0.7%</td><td>47</td><td>Utah</td><td>95</td><td>0.2%</td></tr>
<tr><td>15</td><td>West Virginia</td><td>1,247</td><td>2.2%</td><td>48</td><td>Hawaii</td><td>64</td><td>0.1%</td></tr>
<tr><td>17</td><td>Wisconsin</td><td>1,232</td><td>2.2%</td><td>49</td><td>Delaware</td><td>43</td><td>0.1%</td></tr>
<tr><td>37</td><td>Wyoming</td><td>344</td><td>0.6%</td><td>50</td><td>Nevada</td><td>31</td><td>0.1%</td></tr>
<tr><td></td><td></td><td></td><td></td><td></td><td>District of Columbia</td><td>9</td><td>0.0%</td></tr>
</table>

Source: U.S. Department of Transportation, Federal Highway Administration
   "Deficient Bridges by State and Highway System, 2016" (http://www.fhwa.dot.gov/bridge/deficient.htm)
*As of December 2016. Includes federal-aid and nonfederal-aid system bridges. National total does not include 297 structurally deficient bridges in Puerto Rico. Includes only bridges that are structurally deficient. Does not include bridges that are functionally obsolete.

Structurally Deficient Bridges as a Percent of Total Bridges in 2016

National Percent = 9.1% of Bridges Are Structurally Deficient*

ALPHA ORDER

RANK	STATE	PERCENT
30	Alabama	7.6
19	Alaska	9.7
47	Arizona	2.6
34	Arkansas	6.3
40	California	5.5
37	Colorado	5.7
28	Connecticut	8.0
43	Delaware	4.9
48	Florida	2.1
45	Georgia	4.7
37	Hawaii	5.7
21	Idaho	9.2
26	Illinois	8.4
28	Indiana	8.0
2	Iowa	20.5
25	Kansas	8.6
27	Kentucky	8.1
10	Louisiana	13.5
9	Maine	14.4
36	Maryland	5.8
20	Massachusetts	9.3
14	Michigan	11.1
35	Minnesota	6.0
12	Mississippi	12.3
11	Missouri	13.1
23	Montana	8.8
6	Nebraska	15.4
50	Nevada	1.6
13	New Hampshire	12.2
22	New Jersey	9.0
33	New Mexico	6.5
15	New York	11.0
18	North Carolina	9.9
7	North Dakota	15.0
31	Ohio	6.9
7	Oklahoma	15.0
41	Oregon	5.3
3	Pennsylvania	19.8
1	Rhode Island	24.9
17	South Carolina	10.3
4	South Dakota	19.6
42	Tennessee	5.0
49	Texas	1.7
46	Utah	3.1
39	Vermont	5.6
32	Virginia	6.7
44	Washington	4.8
5	West Virginia	17.3
24	Wisconsin	8.7
15	Wyoming	11.0

RANK ORDER

RANK	STATE	PERCENT
1	Rhode Island	24.9
2	Iowa	20.5
3	Pennsylvania	19.8
4	South Dakota	19.6
5	West Virginia	17.3
6	Nebraska	15.4
7	North Dakota	15.0
7	Oklahoma	15.0
9	Maine	14.4
10	Louisiana	13.5
11	Missouri	13.1
12	Mississippi	12.3
13	New Hampshire	12.2
14	Michigan	11.1
15	New York	11.0
15	Wyoming	11.0
17	South Carolina	10.3
18	North Carolina	9.9
19	Alaska	9.7
20	Massachusetts	9.3
21	Idaho	9.2
22	New Jersey	9.0
23	Montana	8.8
24	Wisconsin	8.7
25	Kansas	8.6
26	Illinois	8.4
27	Kentucky	8.1
28	Connecticut	8.0
28	Indiana	8.0
30	Alabama	7.6
31	Ohio	6.9
32	Virginia	6.7
33	New Mexico	6.5
34	Arkansas	6.3
35	Minnesota	6.0
36	Maryland	5.8
37	Colorado	5.7
37	Hawaii	5.7
39	Vermont	5.6
40	California	5.5
41	Oregon	5.3
42	Tennessee	5.0
43	Delaware	4.9
44	Washington	4.8
45	Georgia	4.7
46	Utah	3.1
47	Arizona	2.6
48	Florida	2.1
49	Texas	1.7
50	Nevada	1.6

District of Columbia	3.7

Source: CQ Press using data from U.S. Department of Transportation, Federal Highway Administration
   "Deficient Bridges by State and Highway System, 2016" (http://www.fhwa.dot.gov/bridge/deficient.htm)
*As of December 2016. Includes federal-aid and nonfederal-aid system bridges. National total does not include structurally deficient bridges in Puerto Rico. Includes only bridges that are structurally deficient. Does not include bridges that are functionally obsolete.

Vehicle-Miles of Travel in 2016

National Total = 3,174,407,958,000 Miles

<table>
<tr><td colspan="4">ALPHA ORDER</td><td colspan="4">RANK ORDER</td></tr>
<tr><th>RANK</th><th>STATE</th><th>MILES</th><th>% of USA</th><th>RANK</th><th>STATE</th><th>MILES</th><th>% of USA</th></tr>
<tr><td>16</td><td>Alabama</td><td>69,226,971,000</td><td>2.2%</td><td>1</td><td>California</td><td>340,114,937,000</td><td>10.7%</td></tr>
<tr><td>50</td><td>Alaska</td><td>5,258,556,000</td><td>0.2%</td><td>2</td><td>Texas</td><td>271,262,838,000</td><td>8.5%</td></tr>
<tr><td>17</td><td>Arizona</td><td>65,785,730,000</td><td>2.1%</td><td>3</td><td>Florida</td><td>215,550,749,000</td><td>6.8%</td></tr>
<tr><td>30</td><td>Arkansas</td><td>35,754,797,000</td><td>1.1%</td><td>4</td><td>New York</td><td>122,929,969,000</td><td>3.9%</td></tr>
<tr><td>1</td><td>California</td><td>340,114,937,000</td><td>10.7%</td><td>5</td><td>Georgia</td><td>122,802,186,000</td><td>3.9%</td></tr>
<tr><td>24</td><td>Colorado</td><td>52,151,611,000</td><td>1.6%</td><td>6</td><td>Ohio</td><td>118,607,622,000</td><td>3.7%</td></tr>
<tr><td>33</td><td>Connecticut</td><td>31,638,569,000</td><td>1.0%</td><td>7</td><td>North Carolina</td><td>116,748,681,000</td><td>3.7%</td></tr>
<tr><td>44</td><td>Delaware</td><td>10,177,585,000</td><td>0.3%</td><td>8</td><td>Illinois</td><td>107,314,103,000</td><td>3.4%</td></tr>
<tr><td>3</td><td>Florida</td><td>215,550,749,000</td><td>6.8%</td><td>9</td><td>Pennsylvania</td><td>101,362,493,000</td><td>3.2%</td></tr>
<tr><td>5</td><td>Georgia</td><td>122,802,186,000</td><td>3.9%</td><td>10</td><td>Michigan</td><td>99,432,538,000</td><td>3.1%</td></tr>
<tr><td>43</td><td>Hawaii</td><td>10,635,428,000</td><td>0.3%</td><td>11</td><td>Virginia</td><td>84,462,672,000</td><td>2.7%</td></tr>
<tr><td>39</td><td>Idaho</td><td>17,198,715,000</td><td>0.5%</td><td>12</td><td>Indiana</td><td>83,182,776,000</td><td>2.6%</td></tr>
<tr><td>8</td><td>Illinois</td><td>107,314,103,000</td><td>3.4%</td><td>13</td><td>New Jersey</td><td>77,092,632,000</td><td>2.4%</td></tr>
<tr><td>12</td><td>Indiana</td><td>83,182,776,000</td><td>2.6%</td><td>14</td><td>Tennessee</td><td>76,883,747,000</td><td>2.4%</td></tr>
<tr><td>31</td><td>Iowa</td><td>33,336,972,000</td><td>1.1%</td><td>15</td><td>Missouri</td><td>74,018,576,000</td><td>2.3%</td></tr>
<tr><td>32</td><td>Kansas</td><td>32,102,610,000</td><td>1.0%</td><td>16</td><td>Alabama</td><td>69,226,971,000</td><td>2.2%</td></tr>
<tr><td>25</td><td>Kentucky</td><td>49,312,718,000</td><td>1.6%</td><td>17</td><td>Arizona</td><td>65,785,730,000</td><td>2.1%</td></tr>
<tr><td>26</td><td>Louisiana</td><td>49,155,613,000</td><td>1.5%</td><td>18</td><td>Wisconsin</td><td>64,046,407,000</td><td>2.0%</td></tr>
<tr><td>40</td><td>Maine</td><td>14,838,258,000</td><td>0.5%</td><td>19</td><td>Massachusetts</td><td>61,824,851,000</td><td>1.9%</td></tr>
<tr><td>21</td><td>Maryland</td><td>59,137,327,000</td><td>1.9%</td><td>20</td><td>Washington</td><td>61,017,811,000</td><td>1.9%</td></tr>
<tr><td>19</td><td>Massachusetts</td><td>61,824,851,000</td><td>1.9%</td><td>21</td><td>Maryland</td><td>59,137,327,000</td><td>1.9%</td></tr>
<tr><td>10</td><td>Michigan</td><td>99,432,538,000</td><td>3.1%</td><td>22</td><td>Minnesota</td><td>59,028,802,000</td><td>1.9%</td></tr>
<tr><td>22</td><td>Minnesota</td><td>59,028,802,000</td><td>1.9%</td><td>23</td><td>South Carolina</td><td>54,552,642,000</td><td>1.7%</td></tr>
<tr><td>28</td><td>Mississippi</td><td>40,754,709,000</td><td>1.3%</td><td>24</td><td>Colorado</td><td>52,151,611,000</td><td>1.6%</td></tr>
<tr><td>15</td><td>Missouri</td><td>74,018,576,000</td><td>2.3%</td><td>25</td><td>Kentucky</td><td>49,312,718,000</td><td>1.6%</td></tr>
<tr><td>42</td><td>Montana</td><td>12,598,723,000</td><td>0.4%</td><td>26</td><td>Louisiana</td><td>49,155,613,000</td><td>1.5%</td></tr>
<tr><td>37</td><td>Nebraska</td><td>20,699,916,000</td><td>0.7%</td><td>27</td><td>Oklahoma</td><td>49,013,278,000</td><td>1.5%</td></tr>
<tr><td>36</td><td>Nevada</td><td>26,787,988,000</td><td>0.8%</td><td>28</td><td>Mississippi</td><td>40,754,709,000</td><td>1.3%</td></tr>
<tr><td>41</td><td>New Hampshire</td><td>13,512,597,000</td><td>0.4%</td><td>29</td><td>Oregon</td><td>36,719,189,000</td><td>1.2%</td></tr>
<tr><td>13</td><td>New Jersey</td><td>77,092,632,000</td><td>2.4%</td><td>30</td><td>Arkansas</td><td>35,754,797,000</td><td>1.1%</td></tr>
<tr><td>35</td><td>New Mexico</td><td>27,885,521,000</td><td>0.9%</td><td>31</td><td>Iowa</td><td>33,336,972,000</td><td>1.1%</td></tr>
<tr><td>4</td><td>New York</td><td>122,929,969,000</td><td>3.9%</td><td>32</td><td>Kansas</td><td>32,102,610,000</td><td>1.0%</td></tr>
<tr><td>7</td><td>North Carolina</td><td>116,748,681,000</td><td>3.7%</td><td>33</td><td>Connecticut</td><td>31,638,569,000</td><td>1.0%</td></tr>
<tr><td>45</td><td>North Dakota</td><td>9,739,209,000</td><td>0.3%</td><td>34</td><td>Utah</td><td>31,448,897,000</td><td>1.0%</td></tr>
<tr><td>6</td><td>Ohio</td><td>118,607,622,000</td><td>3.7%</td><td>35</td><td>New Mexico</td><td>27,885,521,000</td><td>0.9%</td></tr>
<tr><td>27</td><td>Oklahoma</td><td>49,013,278,000</td><td>1.5%</td><td>36</td><td>Nevada</td><td>26,787,988,000</td><td>0.8%</td></tr>
<tr><td>29</td><td>Oregon</td><td>36,719,189,000</td><td>1.2%</td><td>37</td><td>Nebraska</td><td>20,699,916,000</td><td>0.7%</td></tr>
<tr><td>9</td><td>Pennsylvania</td><td>101,362,493,000</td><td>3.2%</td><td>38</td><td>West Virginia</td><td>19,539,443,000</td><td>0.6%</td></tr>
<tr><td>48</td><td>Rhode Island</td><td>7,927,071,000</td><td>0.2%</td><td>39</td><td>Idaho</td><td>17,198,715,000</td><td>0.5%</td></tr>
<tr><td>23</td><td>South Carolina</td><td>54,552,642,000</td><td>1.7%</td><td>40</td><td>Maine</td><td>14,838,258,000</td><td>0.5%</td></tr>
<tr><td>46</td><td>South Dakota</td><td>9,506,534,000</td><td>0.3%</td><td>41</td><td>New Hampshire</td><td>13,512,597,000</td><td>0.4%</td></tr>
<tr><td>14</td><td>Tennessee</td><td>76,883,747,000</td><td>2.4%</td><td>42</td><td>Montana</td><td>12,598,723,000</td><td>0.4%</td></tr>
<tr><td>2</td><td>Texas</td><td>271,262,838,000</td><td>8.5%</td><td>43</td><td>Hawaii</td><td>10,635,428,000</td><td>0.3%</td></tr>
<tr><td>34</td><td>Utah</td><td>31,448,897,000</td><td>1.0%</td><td>44</td><td>Delaware</td><td>10,177,585,000</td><td>0.3%</td></tr>
<tr><td>49</td><td>Vermont</td><td>7,381,890,000</td><td>0.2%</td><td>45</td><td>North Dakota</td><td>9,739,209,000</td><td>0.3%</td></tr>
<tr><td>11</td><td>Virginia</td><td>84,462,672,000</td><td>2.7%</td><td>46</td><td>South Dakota</td><td>9,506,534,000</td><td>0.3%</td></tr>
<tr><td>20</td><td>Washington</td><td>61,017,811,000</td><td>1.9%</td><td>47</td><td>Wyoming</td><td>9,322,542,000</td><td>0.3%</td></tr>
<tr><td>38</td><td>West Virginia</td><td>19,539,443,000</td><td>0.6%</td><td>48</td><td>Rhode Island</td><td>7,927,071,000</td><td>0.2%</td></tr>
<tr><td>18</td><td>Wisconsin</td><td>64,046,407,000</td><td>2.0%</td><td>49</td><td>Vermont</td><td>7,381,890,000</td><td>0.2%</td></tr>
<tr><td>47</td><td>Wyoming</td><td>9,322,542,000</td><td>0.3%</td><td>50</td><td>Alaska</td><td>5,258,556,000</td><td>0.2%</td></tr>
<tr><td></td><td></td><td></td><td></td><td></td><td>District of Columbia</td><td>3,621,959,000</td><td>0.1%</td></tr>
</table>

Source: U.S. Department of Transportation, Federal Highway Administration
"Highway Statistics 2016" (Table VM-2, http://www.fhwa.dot.gov/policyinformation/statistics/2016/)

Highway Fatalities in 2015

National Total = 35,092 Fatalities

ALPHA ORDER

RANK	STATE	FATALITIES	% of USA
15	Alabama	849	2.4%
48	Alaska	65	0.2%
13	Arizona	893	2.5%
26	Arkansas	531	1.5%
2	California	3,176	9.1%
25	Colorado	546	1.6%
37	Connecticut	266	0.8%
45	Delaware	126	0.4%
3	Florida	2,939	8.4%
4	Georgia	1,430	4.1%
47	Hawaii	94	0.3%
40	Idaho	216	0.6%
9	Illinois	998	2.8%
16	Indiana	821	2.3%
32	Iowa	320	0.9%
30	Kansas	355	1.0%
17	Kentucky	761	2.2%
19	Louisiana	726	2.1%
41	Maine	156	0.4%
27	Maryland	513	1.5%
33	Massachusetts	306	0.9%
11	Michigan	963	2.7%
29	Minnesota	411	1.2%
20	Mississippi	677	1.9%
14	Missouri	869	2.5%
39	Montana	224	0.6%
38	Nebraska	246	0.7%
31	Nevada	325	0.9%
46	New Hampshire	114	0.3%
24	New Jersey	562	1.6%
34	New Mexico	298	0.8%
7	New York	1,121	3.2%
5	North Carolina	1,379	3.9%
44	North Dakota	131	0.4%
8	Ohio	1,110	3.2%
21	Oklahoma	643	1.8%
28	Oregon	447	1.3%
6	Pennsylvania	1,200	3.4%
50	Rhode Island	45	0.1%
10	South Carolina	977	2.8%
43	South Dakota	133	0.4%
12	Tennessee	958	2.7%
1	Texas	3,516	10.0%
35	Utah	276	0.8%
49	Vermont	57	0.2%
18	Virginia	753	2.1%
22	Washington	568	1.6%
36	West Virginia	268	0.8%
23	Wisconsin	566	1.6%
42	Wyoming	145	0.4%

RANK ORDER

RANK	STATE	FATALITIES	% of USA
1	Texas	3,516	10.0%
2	California	3,176	9.1%
3	Florida	2,939	8.4%
4	Georgia	1,430	4.1%
5	North Carolina	1,379	3.9%
6	Pennsylvania	1,200	3.4%
7	New York	1,121	3.2%
8	Ohio	1,110	3.2%
9	Illinois	998	2.8%
10	South Carolina	977	2.8%
11	Michigan	963	2.7%
12	Tennessee	958	2.7%
13	Arizona	893	2.5%
14	Missouri	869	2.5%
15	Alabama	849	2.4%
16	Indiana	821	2.3%
17	Kentucky	761	2.2%
18	Virginia	753	2.1%
19	Louisiana	726	2.1%
20	Mississippi	677	1.9%
21	Oklahoma	643	1.8%
22	Washington	568	1.6%
23	Wisconsin	566	1.6%
24	New Jersey	562	1.6%
25	Colorado	546	1.6%
26	Arkansas	531	1.5%
27	Maryland	513	1.5%
28	Oregon	447	1.3%
29	Minnesota	411	1.2%
30	Kansas	355	1.0%
31	Nevada	325	0.9%
32	Iowa	320	0.9%
33	Massachusetts	306	0.9%
34	New Mexico	298	0.8%
35	Utah	276	0.8%
36	West Virginia	268	0.8%
37	Connecticut	266	0.8%
38	Nebraska	246	0.7%
39	Montana	224	0.6%
40	Idaho	216	0.6%
41	Maine	156	0.4%
42	Wyoming	145	0.4%
43	South Dakota	133	0.4%
44	North Dakota	131	0.4%
45	Delaware	126	0.4%
46	New Hampshire	114	0.3%
47	Hawaii	94	0.3%
48	Alaska	65	0.2%
49	Vermont	57	0.2%
50	Rhode Island	45	0.1%
	District of Columbia	23	0.1%

Source: U.S. Department of Transportation, National Highway Traffic Safety Administration
"Traffic Safety Facts 2015" (https://crashstats.nhtsa.dot.gov/)

Highway Fatality Rate in 2015

National Rate = 1.13 Fatalities per 100 Million Vehicle-Miles of Travel

ALPHA ORDER				RANK ORDER		
RANK	**STATE**	**RATE**		**RANK**	**STATE**	**RATE**
18	Alabama	1.26		1	South Carolina	1.89
16	Alaska	1.29		2	Montana	1.81
10	Arizona	1.37		3	Mississippi	1.70
5	Arkansas	1.52		4	Kentucky	1.56
35	California	0.95		5	Arkansas	1.52
29	Colorado	1.08		6	Louisiana	1.51
45	Connecticut	0.84		6	Wyoming	1.51
17	Delaware	1.27		8	South Dakota	1.43
9	Florida	1.42		9	Florida	1.42
24	Georgia	1.21		10	Arizona	1.37
39	Hawaii	0.91		11	Texas	1.36
15	Idaho	1.30		12	Oklahoma	1.35
35	Illinois	0.95		12	West Virginia	1.35
31	Indiana	1.04		14	North Dakota	1.31
34	Iowa	0.96		15	Idaho	1.30
27	Kansas	1.13		16	Alaska	1.29
4	Kentucky	1.56		17	Delaware	1.27
6	Louisiana	1.51		18	Alabama	1.26
30	Maine	1.07		19	Nevada	1.25
42	Maryland	0.89		19	Tennessee	1.25
50	Massachusetts	0.52		21	Oregon	1.24
32	Michigan	0.98		22	North Carolina	1.23
48	Minnesota	0.72		23	Nebraska	1.22
3	Mississippi	1.70		24	Georgia	1.21
24	Missouri	1.21		24	Missouri	1.21
2	Montana	1.81		26	Pennsylvania	1.19
23	Nebraska	1.22		27	Kansas	1.13
19	Nevada	1.25		28	New Mexico	1.09
44	New Hampshire	0.87		29	Colorado	1.08
47	New Jersey	0.75		30	Maine	1.07
28	New Mexico	1.09		31	Indiana	1.04
43	New York	0.88		32	Michigan	0.98
22	North Carolina	1.23		32	Ohio	0.98
14	North Dakota	1.31		34	Iowa	0.96
32	Ohio	0.98		35	California	0.95
12	Oklahoma	1.35		35	Illinois	0.95
21	Oregon	1.24		35	Washington	0.95
26	Pennsylvania	1.19		38	Utah	0.93
49	Rhode Island	0.57		39	Hawaii	0.91
1	South Carolina	1.89		39	Virginia	0.91
8	South Dakota	1.43		39	Wisconsin	0.91
19	Tennessee	1.25		42	Maryland	0.89
11	Texas	1.36		43	New York	0.88
38	Utah	0.93		44	New Hampshire	0.87
46	Vermont	0.78		45	Connecticut	0.84
39	Virginia	0.91		46	Vermont	0.78
35	Washington	0.95		47	New Jersey	0.75
12	West Virginia	1.35		48	Minnesota	0.72
39	Wisconsin	0.91		49	Rhode Island	0.57
6	Wyoming	1.51		50	Massachusetts	0.52
					District of Columbia	0.65

Source: U.S. Department of Transportation, National Highway Traffic Safety Administration
"Traffic Safety Facts 2015" (https://crashstats.nhtsa.dot.gov/)

Percent of Traffic Fatalities That Were Speeding-Related in 2015

National Percent = 27.2%*

ALPHA ORDER

RANK	STATE	PERCENT
25	Alabama	27.8
17	Alaska	33.8
15	Arizona	34.4
45	Arkansas	16.9
22	California	30.1
8	Colorado	39.6
27	Connecticut	27.4
29	Delaware	27.0
50	Florida	10.9
42	Georgia	18.7
5	Hawaii	42.6
37	Idaho	22.7
10	Illinois	37.0
24	Indiana	28.3
46	Iowa	15.3
13	Kansas	36.1
44	Kentucky	18.4
37	Louisiana	22.7
9	Maine	38.5
34	Maryland	23.6
32	Massachusetts	26.1
27	Michigan	27.4
40	Minnesota	20.0
48	Mississippi	14.2
14	Missouri	35.7
6	Montana	40.6
47	Nebraska	15.0
16	Nevada	34.2
1	New Hampshire	49.1
36	New Jersey	22.8
4	New Mexico	43.6
21	New York	30.6
7	North Carolina	39.7
18	North Dakota	32.8
43	Ohio	18.6
30	Oklahoma	26.6
31	Oregon	26.4
2	Pennsylvania	45.0
3	Rhode Island	44.4
11	South Carolina	36.9
35	South Dakota	23.3
41	Tennessee	19.5
20	Texas	31.4
39	Utah	21.0
12	Vermont	36.8
49	Virginia	13.8
26	Washington	27.5
33	West Virginia	24.6
23	Wisconsin	29.5
19	Wyoming	31.7

RANK ORDER

RANK	STATE	PERCENT
1	New Hampshire	49.1
2	Pennsylvania	45.0
3	Rhode Island	44.4
4	New Mexico	43.6
5	Hawaii	42.6
6	Montana	40.6
7	North Carolina	39.7
8	Colorado	39.6
9	Maine	38.5
10	Illinois	37.0
11	South Carolina	36.9
12	Vermont	36.8
13	Kansas	36.1
14	Missouri	35.7
15	Arizona	34.4
16	Nevada	34.2
17	Alaska	33.8
18	North Dakota	32.8
19	Wyoming	31.7
20	Texas	31.4
21	New York	30.6
22	California	30.1
23	Wisconsin	29.5
24	Indiana	28.3
25	Alabama	27.8
26	Washington	27.5
27	Connecticut	27.4
27	Michigan	27.4
29	Delaware	27.0
30	Oklahoma	26.6
31	Oregon	26.4
32	Massachusetts	26.1
33	West Virginia	24.6
34	Maryland	23.6
35	South Dakota	23.3
36	New Jersey	22.8
37	Idaho	22.7
37	Louisiana	22.7
39	Utah	21.0
40	Minnesota	20.0
41	Tennessee	19.5
42	Georgia	18.7
43	Ohio	18.6
44	Kentucky	18.4
45	Arkansas	16.9
46	Iowa	15.3
47	Nebraska	15.0
48	Mississippi	14.2
49	Virginia	13.8
50	Florida	10.9
	District of Columbia	30.4

Source: CQ Press using data from U.S. Department of Transportation, National Highway Traffic Safety Administration
"Traffic Safety Facts 2015" (https://crashstats.nhtsa.dot.gov/)
*A speeding-related crash is if the driver was charged with a speeding-related offense or if an officer indicated that racing, driving too fast for conditions, or exceeding the posted speed limit was a contributing factor in the crash.

Percent of Vehicles Involved in Fatal Crashes That Were Large Trucks in 2015

National Percent = 8.3%*

ALPHA ORDER

RANK	STATE	PERCENT
17	Alabama	8.7
50	Alaska	1.1
32	Arizona	7.1
13	Arkansas	8.9
38	California	6.6
21	Colorado	8.4
15	Connecticut	8.8
40	Delaware	6.3
45	Florida	5.2
17	Georgia	8.7
46	Hawaii	4.8
13	Idaho	8.9
26	Illinois	7.7
7	Indiana	11.4
6	Iowa	11.9
4	Kansas	13.7
20	Kentucky	8.5
32	Louisiana	7.1
44	Maine	5.3
32	Maryland	7.1
38	Massachusetts	6.6
30	Michigan	7.3
11	Minnesota	10.3
24	Mississippi	8.1
15	Missouri	8.8
37	Montana	6.7
9	Nebraska	11.1
43	Nevada	5.7
48	New Hampshire	4.2
28	New Jersey	7.6
3	New Mexico	13.8
25	New York	7.8
41	North Carolina	6.2
1	North Dakota	25.0
8	Ohio	11.3
5	Oklahoma	12.2
21	Oregon	8.4
12	Pennsylvania	9.9
49	Rhode Island	3.4
30	South Carolina	7.3
26	South Dakota	7.7
23	Tennessee	8.3
10	Texas	10.9
19	Utah	8.6
32	Vermont	7.1
29	Virginia	7.4
47	Washington	4.3
41	West Virginia	6.2
32	Wisconsin	7.1
2	Wyoming	19.8

RANK ORDER

RANK	STATE	PERCENT
1	North Dakota	25.0
2	Wyoming	19.8
3	New Mexico	13.8
4	Kansas	13.7
5	Oklahoma	12.2
6	Iowa	11.9
7	Indiana	11.4
8	Ohio	11.3
9	Nebraska	11.1
10	Texas	10.9
11	Minnesota	10.3
12	Pennsylvania	9.9
13	Arkansas	8.9
13	Idaho	8.9
15	Connecticut	8.8
15	Missouri	8.8
17	Alabama	8.7
17	Georgia	8.7
19	Utah	8.6
20	Kentucky	8.5
21	Colorado	8.4
21	Oregon	8.4
23	Tennessee	8.3
24	Mississippi	8.1
25	New York	7.8
26	Illinois	7.7
26	South Dakota	7.7
28	New Jersey	7.6
29	Virginia	7.4
30	Michigan	7.3
30	South Carolina	7.3
32	Arizona	7.1
32	Louisiana	7.1
32	Maryland	7.1
32	Vermont	7.1
32	Wisconsin	7.1
37	Montana	6.7
38	California	6.6
38	Massachusetts	6.6
40	Delaware	6.3
41	North Carolina	6.2
41	West Virginia	6.2
43	Nevada	5.7
44	Maine	5.3
45	Florida	5.2
46	Hawaii	4.8
47	Washington	4.3
48	New Hampshire	4.2
49	Rhode Island	3.4
50	Alaska	1.1
	District of Columbia	6.7

Source: U.S. Department of Transportation, National Highway Traffic Safety Administration
   "Traffic Safety Facts: Large Trucks" (https://crashstats.nhtsa.dot.gov/)
*Large trucks are those with gross vehicle weight greater than 10,000 pounds. In 2014, 3,744 large trucks were involved in fatal crashes.

Lives Saved by Child Restraints, Seat Belts, Air Bags, and Motorcycle Helmets in 2016
National Total = 19,611 Lives

ALPHA ORDER

RANK	STATE	LIVES	% of USA
11	Alabama	533	2.7%
49	Alaska	34	0.2%
21	Arizona	357	1.8%
26	Arkansas	294	1.5%
2	California	2,035	10.4%
27	Colorado	278	1.4%
37	Connecticut	134	0.7%
42	Delaware	65	0.3%
3	Florida	1,433	7.3%
5	Georgia	864	4.4%
43	Hawaii	48	0.2%
38	Idaho	117	0.6%
8	Illinois	593	3.0%
15	Indiana	443	2.3%
29	Iowa	251	1.3%
31	Kansas	239	1.2%
16	Kentucky	424	2.2%
17	Louisiana	415	2.1%
40	Maine	96	0.5%
28	Maryland	261	1.3%
33	Massachusetts	170	0.9%
6	Michigan	641	3.3%
30	Minnesota	248	1.3%
18	Mississippi	400	2.0%
14	Missouri	461	2.4%
41	Montana	84	0.4%
39	Nebraska	116	0.6%
34	Nevada	144	0.7%
43	New Hampshire	48	0.2%
25	New Jersey	298	1.5%
32	New Mexico	206	1.1%
10	New York	535	2.7%
4	North Carolina	891	4.5%
47	North Dakota	40	0.2%
9	Ohio	538	2.7%
22	Oklahoma	352	1.8%
19	Oregon	370	1.9%
12	Pennsylvania	485	2.5%
50	Rhode Island	20	0.1%
13	South Carolina	466	2.4%
47	South Dakota	40	0.2%
7	Tennessee	624	3.2%
1	Texas	2,115	10.8%
36	Utah	139	0.7%
46	Vermont	43	0.2%
20	Virginia	364	1.9%
24	Washington	319	1.6%
35	West Virginia	142	0.7%
23	Wisconsin	344	1.8%
45	Wyoming	44	0.2%

RANK ORDER

RANK	STATE	LIVES	% of USA
1	Texas	2,115	10.8%
2	California	2,035	10.4%
3	Florida	1,433	7.3%
4	North Carolina	891	4.5%
5	Georgia	864	4.4%
6	Michigan	641	3.3%
7	Tennessee	624	3.2%
8	Illinois	593	3.0%
9	Ohio	538	2.7%
10	New York	535	2.7%
11	Alabama	533	2.7%
12	Pennsylvania	485	2.5%
13	South Carolina	466	2.4%
14	Missouri	461	2.4%
15	Indiana	443	2.3%
16	Kentucky	424	2.2%
17	Louisiana	415	2.1%
18	Mississippi	400	2.0%
19	Oregon	370	1.9%
20	Virginia	364	1.9%
21	Arizona	357	1.8%
22	Oklahoma	352	1.8%
23	Wisconsin	344	1.8%
24	Washington	319	1.6%
25	New Jersey	298	1.5%
26	Arkansas	294	1.5%
27	Colorado	278	1.4%
28	Maryland	261	1.3%
29	Iowa	251	1.3%
30	Minnesota	248	1.3%
31	Kansas	239	1.2%
32	New Mexico	206	1.1%
33	Massachusetts	170	0.9%
34	Nevada	144	0.7%
35	West Virginia	142	0.7%
36	Utah	139	0.7%
37	Connecticut	134	0.7%
38	Idaho	117	0.6%
39	Nebraska	116	0.6%
40	Maine	96	0.5%
41	Montana	84	0.4%
42	Delaware	65	0.3%
43	Hawaii	48	0.2%
43	New Hampshire	48	0.2%
45	Wyoming	44	0.2%
46	Vermont	43	0.2%
47	North Dakota	40	0.2%
47	South Dakota	40	0.2%
49	Alaska	34	0.2%
50	Rhode Island	20	0.1%
	District of Columbia	7	0.0%

Source: CQ Press using data from U.S. Department of Transportation, National Highway Traffic Safety Administration
"Traffic Safety Facts: Lives Saved in 2016" (https://crashstats.nhtsa.dot.gov/)

Safety Belt Usage Rate in 2016

National Rate = 90.1% Use Safety Belts

ALPHA ORDER

RANK ORDER

RANK	STATE	PERCENT	RANK	STATE	PERCENT
14	Alabama	92.0	1	Georgia	97.2
24	Alaska	88.5	2	California	96.5
26	Arizona	88.0	3	Oregon	96.2
48	Arkansas	75.1	4	Washington	94.7
2	California	96.5	5	Hawaii	94.5
36	Colorado	84.0	5	Michigan	94.5
21	Connecticut	89.4	7	South Carolina	93.9
18	Delaware	91.4	8	Iowa	93.8
20	Florida	89.6	9	New Jersey	93.4
1	Georgia	97.2	10	Minnesota	93.2
5	Hawaii	94.5	11	Illinois	93.0
39	Idaho	82.9	12	Indiana	92.4
11	Illinois	93.0	13	New Mexico	92.3
12	Indiana	92.4	14	Alabama	92.0
8	Iowa	93.8	15	New York	91.8
30	Kansas	87.0	16	North Carolina	91.7
33	Kentucky	86.5	17	Texas	91.6
28	Louisiana	87.8	18	Delaware	91.4
34	Maine	85.8	19	Maryland	90.8
19	Maryland	90.8	20	Florida	89.6
45	Massachusetts	78.2	21	Connecticut	89.4
5	Michigan	94.5	21	Nevada	89.4
10	Minnesota	93.2	23	Tennessee	88.9
46	Mississippi	77.9	24	Alaska	88.5
41	Missouri	81.4	25	Wisconsin	88.4
47	Montana	76.0	26	Arizona	88.0
38	Nebraska	83.3	27	Utah	87.9
21	Nevada	89.4	28	Louisiana	87.8
50	New Hampshire	70.2	29	Rhode Island	87.5
9	New Jersey	93.4	30	Kansas	87.0
13	New Mexico	92.3	31	West Virginia	86.8
15	New York	91.8	32	Oklahoma	86.6
16	North Carolina	91.7	33	Kentucky	86.5
40	North Dakota	82.8	34	Maine	85.8
37	Ohio	83.8	35	Pennsylvania	85.2
32	Oklahoma	86.6	36	Colorado	84.0
3	Oregon	96.2	37	Ohio	83.8
35	Pennsylvania	85.2	38	Nebraska	83.3
29	Rhode Island	87.5	39	Idaho	82.9
7	South Carolina	93.9	40	North Dakota	82.8
49	South Dakota	74.2	41	Missouri	81.4
23	Tennessee	88.9	42	Wyoming	80.5
17	Texas	91.6	43	Vermont	80.0
27	Utah	87.9	44	Virginia	79.0
43	Vermont	80.0	45	Massachusetts	78.2
44	Virginia	79.0	46	Mississippi	77.9
4	Washington	94.7	47	Montana	76.0
31	West Virginia	86.8	48	Arkansas	75.1
25	Wisconsin	88.4	49	South Dakota	74.2
42	Wyoming	80.5	50	New Hampshire	70.2
				District of Columbia	94.1

Source: U.S. Department of Transportation, National Highway Traffic Safety Administration
"Traffic Safety Facts: Seat Belt Use in 2016" (https://crashstats.nhtsa.dot.gov/)

Percent of Passenger Car Occupant Fatalities
Where Victim Used a Seat Belt in 2015
National Percent = 47% of Passenger Car Occupant Fatalities*

<table>
<tr><td colspan="3">ALPHA ORDER</td><td colspan="3">RANK ORDER</td></tr>
<tr><td>RANK</td><td>STATE</td><td>PERCENT</td><td>RANK</td><td>STATE</td><td>PERCENT</td></tr>
<tr><td>32</td><td>Alabama</td><td>39</td><td>1</td><td>California</td><td>60</td></tr>
<tr><td>36</td><td>Alaska</td><td>38</td><td>1</td><td>Maryland</td><td>60</td></tr>
<tr><td>39</td><td>Arizona</td><td>37</td><td>3</td><td>New Jersey</td><td>58</td></tr>
<tr><td>31</td><td>Arkansas</td><td>40</td><td>4</td><td>Minnesota</td><td>56</td></tr>
<tr><td>1</td><td>California</td><td>60</td><td>4</td><td>New York</td><td>56</td></tr>
<tr><td>29</td><td>Colorado</td><td>42</td><td>4</td><td>Washington</td><td>56</td></tr>
<tr><td>21</td><td>Connecticut</td><td>45</td><td>7</td><td>Michigan</td><td>54</td></tr>
<tr><td>14</td><td>Delaware</td><td>49</td><td>7</td><td>Texas</td><td>54</td></tr>
<tr><td>9</td><td>Florida</td><td>53</td><td>9</td><td>Florida</td><td>53</td></tr>
<tr><td>16</td><td>Georgia</td><td>48</td><td>9</td><td>North Carolina</td><td>53</td></tr>
<tr><td>44</td><td>Hawaii</td><td>30</td><td>9</td><td>Oregon</td><td>53</td></tr>
<tr><td>32</td><td>Idaho</td><td>39</td><td>12</td><td>Iowa</td><td>52</td></tr>
<tr><td>19</td><td>Illinois</td><td>47</td><td>12</td><td>Nevada</td><td>52</td></tr>
<tr><td>16</td><td>Indiana</td><td>48</td><td>14</td><td>Delaware</td><td>49</td></tr>
<tr><td>12</td><td>Iowa</td><td>52</td><td>14</td><td>Utah</td><td>49</td></tr>
<tr><td>21</td><td>Kansas</td><td>45</td><td>16</td><td>Georgia</td><td>48</td></tr>
<tr><td>21</td><td>Kentucky</td><td>45</td><td>16</td><td>Indiana</td><td>48</td></tr>
<tr><td>32</td><td>Louisiana</td><td>39</td><td>16</td><td>Maine</td><td>48</td></tr>
<tr><td>16</td><td>Maine</td><td>48</td><td>19</td><td>Illinois</td><td>47</td></tr>
<tr><td>1</td><td>Maryland</td><td>60</td><td>20</td><td>South Carolina</td><td>46</td></tr>
<tr><td>48</td><td>Massachusetts</td><td>27</td><td>21</td><td>Connecticut</td><td>45</td></tr>
<tr><td>7</td><td>Michigan</td><td>54</td><td>21</td><td>Kansas</td><td>45</td></tr>
<tr><td>4</td><td>Minnesota</td><td>56</td><td>21</td><td>Kentucky</td><td>45</td></tr>
<tr><td>28</td><td>Mississippi</td><td>43</td><td>21</td><td>Virginia</td><td>45</td></tr>
<tr><td>42</td><td>Missouri</td><td>35</td><td>21</td><td>Wisconsin</td><td>45</td></tr>
<tr><td>47</td><td>Montana</td><td>28</td><td>26</td><td>Oklahoma</td><td>44</td></tr>
<tr><td>49</td><td>Nebraska</td><td>25</td><td>26</td><td>Tennessee</td><td>44</td></tr>
<tr><td>12</td><td>Nevada</td><td>52</td><td>28</td><td>Mississippi</td><td>43</td></tr>
<tr><td>41</td><td>New Hampshire</td><td>36</td><td>29</td><td>Colorado</td><td>42</td></tr>
<tr><td>3</td><td>New Jersey</td><td>58</td><td>30</td><td>Vermont</td><td>41</td></tr>
<tr><td>36</td><td>New Mexico</td><td>38</td><td>31</td><td>Arkansas</td><td>40</td></tr>
<tr><td>4</td><td>New York</td><td>56</td><td>32</td><td>Alabama</td><td>39</td></tr>
<tr><td>9</td><td>North Carolina</td><td>53</td><td>32</td><td>Idaho</td><td>39</td></tr>
<tr><td>45</td><td>North Dakota</td><td>29</td><td>32</td><td>Louisiana</td><td>39</td></tr>
<tr><td>32</td><td>Ohio</td><td>39</td><td>32</td><td>Ohio</td><td>39</td></tr>
<tr><td>26</td><td>Oklahoma</td><td>44</td><td>36</td><td>Alaska</td><td>38</td></tr>
<tr><td>9</td><td>Oregon</td><td>53</td><td>36</td><td>New Mexico</td><td>38</td></tr>
<tr><td>42</td><td>Pennsylvania</td><td>35</td><td>36</td><td>West Virginia</td><td>38</td></tr>
<tr><td>39</td><td>Rhode Island</td><td>37</td><td>39</td><td>Arizona</td><td>37</td></tr>
<tr><td>20</td><td>South Carolina</td><td>46</td><td>39</td><td>Rhode Island</td><td>37</td></tr>
<tr><td>45</td><td>South Dakota</td><td>29</td><td>41</td><td>New Hampshire</td><td>36</td></tr>
<tr><td>26</td><td>Tennessee</td><td>44</td><td>42</td><td>Missouri</td><td>35</td></tr>
<tr><td>7</td><td>Texas</td><td>54</td><td>42</td><td>Pennsylvania</td><td>35</td></tr>
<tr><td>14</td><td>Utah</td><td>49</td><td>44</td><td>Hawaii</td><td>30</td></tr>
<tr><td>30</td><td>Vermont</td><td>41</td><td>45</td><td>North Dakota</td><td>29</td></tr>
<tr><td>21</td><td>Virginia</td><td>45</td><td>45</td><td>South Dakota</td><td>29</td></tr>
<tr><td>4</td><td>Washington</td><td>56</td><td>47</td><td>Montana</td><td>28</td></tr>
<tr><td>36</td><td>West Virginia</td><td>38</td><td>48</td><td>Massachusetts</td><td>27</td></tr>
<tr><td>21</td><td>Wisconsin</td><td>45</td><td>49</td><td>Nebraska</td><td>25</td></tr>
<tr><td>50</td><td>Wyoming</td><td>24</td><td>50</td><td>Wyoming</td><td>24</td></tr>
<tr><td></td><td></td><td></td><td></td><td>District of Columbia</td><td>83</td></tr>
</table>

Source: U.S. Department of Transportation, National Highway Traffic Safety Administration
"Traffic Safety Facts: Occupant Protection" (https://crashstats.nhtsa.dot.gov/)
*Only those fatalities where seat belts are known to have been used are counted.

Fatalities in Alcohol-Related Crashes in 2016

National Total = 12,514 Fatalities*

ALPHA ORDER

RANK	STATE	FATALITIES	% of USA
11	Alabama	321	2.6%
47	Alaska	37	0.3%
14	Arizona	289	2.3%
29	Arkansas	150	1.2%
2	California	1,247	10.0%
22	Colorado	195	1.6%
32	Connecticut	123	1.0%
45	Delaware	43	0.3%
3	Florida	987	7.9%
5	Georgia	433	3.5%
46	Hawaii	40	0.3%
37	Idaho	89	0.7%
8	Illinois	375	3.0%
18	Indiana	241	1.9%
31	Iowa	126	1.0%
35	Kansas	107	0.9%
20	Kentucky	216	1.7%
16	Louisiana	268	2.1%
40	Maine	67	0.5%
27	Maryland	156	1.2%
27	Massachusetts	156	1.2%
13	Michigan	294	2.3%
33	Minnesota	117	0.9%
26	Mississippi	164	1.3%
12	Missouri	301	2.4%
36	Montana	95	0.8%
38	Nebraska	82	0.7%
34	Nevada	114	0.9%
44	New Hampshire	49	0.4%
24	New Jersey	177	1.4%
30	New Mexico	148	1.2%
10	New York	328	2.6%
4	North Carolina	474	3.8%
42	North Dakota	55	0.4%
7	Ohio	391	3.1%
21	Oklahoma	200	1.6%
25	Oregon	172	1.4%
9	Pennsylvania	369	2.9%
50	Rhode Island	22	0.2%
6	South Carolina	396	3.2%
43	South Dakota	54	0.4%
15	Tennessee	280	2.2%
1	Texas	1,670	13.3%
41	Utah	59	0.5%
49	Vermont	31	0.2%
17	Virginia	251	2.0%
23	Washington	186	1.5%
39	West Virginia	80	0.6%
18	Wisconsin	241	1.9%
48	Wyoming	35	0.3%

RANK ORDER

RANK	STATE	FATALITIES	% of USA
1	Texas	1,670	13.3%
2	California	1,247	10.0%
3	Florida	987	7.9%
4	North Carolina	474	3.8%
5	Georgia	433	3.5%
6	South Carolina	396	3.2%
7	Ohio	391	3.1%
8	Illinois	375	3.0%
9	Pennsylvania	369	2.9%
10	New York	328	2.6%
11	Alabama	321	2.6%
12	Missouri	301	2.4%
13	Michigan	294	2.3%
14	Arizona	289	2.3%
15	Tennessee	280	2.2%
16	Louisiana	268	2.1%
17	Virginia	251	2.0%
18	Indiana	241	1.9%
18	Wisconsin	241	1.9%
20	Kentucky	216	1.7%
21	Oklahoma	200	1.6%
22	Colorado	195	1.6%
23	Washington	186	1.5%
24	New Jersey	177	1.4%
25	Oregon	172	1.4%
26	Mississippi	164	1.3%
27	Maryland	156	1.2%
27	Massachusetts	156	1.2%
29	Arkansas	150	1.2%
30	New Mexico	148	1.2%
31	Iowa	126	1.0%
32	Connecticut	123	1.0%
33	Minnesota	117	0.9%
34	Nevada	114	0.9%
35	Kansas	107	0.9%
36	Montana	95	0.8%
37	Idaho	89	0.7%
38	Nebraska	82	0.7%
39	West Virginia	80	0.6%
40	Maine	67	0.5%
41	Utah	59	0.5%
42	North Dakota	55	0.4%
43	South Dakota	54	0.4%
44	New Hampshire	49	0.4%
45	Delaware	43	0.3%
46	Hawaii	40	0.3%
47	Alaska	37	0.3%
48	Wyoming	35	0.3%
49	Vermont	31	0.2%
50	Rhode Island	22	0.2%
	District of Columbia	14	0.1%

Source: U.S. Department of Transportation, National Highway Traffic Safety Administration
"Traffic Safety Facts: Alcohol-Impaired Driving" (https://crashstats.nhtsa.dot.gov/)
*Drivers with Blood Alcohol Content (BAC) of .01 or more. "Legally Drunk" BAC differs from state to state but is often .08 or higher.

Fatalities in Alcohol-Related Crashes
as a Percent of All Highway Fatalities in 2016
National Percent = 33% of Highway Fatalities*

ALPHA ORDER				RANK ORDER		
RANK	**STATE**	**PERCENT**		**RANK**	**STATE**	**PERCENT**
31	Alabama	31		1	Montana	50
5	Alaska	44		1	Vermont	50
37	Arizona	30		3	North Dakota	49
43	Arkansas	28		4	South Dakota	47
24	California	34		5	Alaska	44
28	Colorado	32		5	Rhode Island	44
8	Connecticut	42		5	Texas	44
15	Delaware	36		8	Connecticut	42
31	Florida	31		9	Maine	41
43	Georgia	28		10	Massachusetts	40
25	Hawaii	33		10	Wisconsin	40
17	Idaho	35		12	South Carolina	39
17	Illinois	35		13	Nebraska	38
40	Indiana	29		14	New Mexico	37
31	Iowa	31		15	Delaware	36
48	Kansas	25		15	New Hampshire	36
47	Kentucky	26		17	Idaho	35
17	Louisiana	35		17	Illinois	35
9	Maine	41		17	Louisiana	35
31	Maryland	31		17	Nevada	35
10	Massachusetts	40		17	Ohio	35
43	Michigan	28		17	Oregon	35
37	Minnesota	30		17	Washington	35
49	Mississippi	24		24	California	34
28	Missouri	32		25	Hawaii	33
1	Montana	50		25	North Carolina	33
13	Nebraska	38		25	Virginia	33
17	Nevada	35		28	Colorado	32
15	New Hampshire	36		28	Missouri	32
40	New Jersey	29		28	New York	32
14	New Mexico	37		31	Alabama	31
28	New York	32		31	Florida	31
25	North Carolina	33		31	Iowa	31
3	North Dakota	49		31	Maryland	31
17	Ohio	35		31	Pennsylvania	31
40	Oklahoma	29		31	Wyoming	31
17	Oregon	35		37	Arizona	30
31	Pennsylvania	31		37	Minnesota	30
5	Rhode Island	44		37	West Virginia	30
12	South Carolina	39		40	Indiana	29
4	South Dakota	47		40	New Jersey	29
46	Tennessee	27		40	Oklahoma	29
5	Texas	44		43	Arkansas	28
50	Utah	21		43	Georgia	28
1	Vermont	50		43	Michigan	28
25	Virginia	33		46	Tennessee	27
17	Washington	35		47	Kentucky	26
37	West Virginia	30		48	Kansas	25
10	Wisconsin	40		49	Mississippi	24
31	Wyoming	31		50	Utah	21

District of Columbia   51

Source: U.S. Department of Transportation, National Highway Traffic Safety Administration
    "Traffic Safety Facts: Alcohol-Impaired Driving" (https://crashstats.nhtsa.dot.gov/)
*Drivers with Blood Alcohol Content (BAC) of .01 or more. "Legally Drunk" BAC differs from state to state but is often .08 or higher.

Percent of Fatal Traffic Accidents Involving Older Drivers in 2015

National Percent = 13.4%*

RANK	STATE	PERCENT
36	Alabama	12.2
20	Alaska	14.8
27	Arizona	13.8
33	Arkansas	12.6
47	California	10.0
33	Colorado	12.6
38	Connecticut	11.6
48	Delaware	9.5
25	Florida	14.0
24	Georgia	14.4
28	Hawaii	13.6
21	Idaho	14.6
18	Illinois	15.1
32	Indiana	12.8
12	Iowa	15.7
15	Kansas	15.3
37	Kentucky	11.8
40	Louisiana	11.3
7	Maine	16.3
16	Maryland	15.2
13	Massachusetts	15.6
35	Michigan	12.4
3	Minnesota	17.1
39	Mississippi	11.5
18	Missouri	15.1
6	Montana	16.5
44	Nebraska	10.7
40	Nevada	11.3
1	New Hampshire	19.0
8	New Jersey	16.1
44	New Mexico	10.7
23	New York	14.5
21	North Carolina	14.6
49	North Dakota	9.0
14	Ohio	15.5
31	Oklahoma	13.1
11	Oregon	15.8
4	Pennsylvania	16.7
50	Rhode Island	8.6
42	South Carolina	11.2
29	South Dakota	13.2
9	Tennessee	16.0
46	Texas	10.3
25	Utah	14.0
10	Vermont	15.9
4	Virginia	16.7
16	Washington	15.2
29	West Virginia	13.2
2	Wisconsin	18.6
43	Wyoming	11.0

RANK	STATE	PERCENT
1	New Hampshire	19.0
2	Wisconsin	18.6
3	Minnesota	17.1
4	Pennsylvania	16.7
4	Virginia	16.7
6	Montana	16.5
7	Maine	16.3
8	New Jersey	16.1
9	Tennessee	16.0
10	Vermont	15.9
11	Oregon	15.8
12	Iowa	15.7
13	Massachusetts	15.6
14	Ohio	15.5
15	Kansas	15.3
16	Maryland	15.2
16	Washington	15.2
18	Illinois	15.1
18	Missouri	15.1
20	Alaska	14.8
21	Idaho	14.6
21	North Carolina	14.6
23	New York	14.5
24	Georgia	14.4
25	Florida	14.0
25	Utah	14.0
27	Arizona	13.8
28	Hawaii	13.6
29	South Dakota	13.2
29	West Virginia	13.2
31	Oklahoma	13.1
32	Indiana	12.8
33	Arkansas	12.6
33	Colorado	12.6
35	Michigan	12.4
36	Alabama	12.2
37	Kentucky	11.8
38	Connecticut	11.6
39	Mississippi	11.5
40	Louisiana	11.3
40	Nevada	11.3
42	South Carolina	11.2
43	Wyoming	11.0
44	Nebraska	10.7
44	New Mexico	10.7
46	Texas	10.3
47	California	10.0
48	Delaware	9.5
49	North Dakota	9.0
50	Rhode Island	8.6
	District of Columbia	3.3

Source: U.S. Department of Transportation, National Highway Traffic Safety Administration
"Traffic Safety Facts: Older Population" (https://crashstats.nhtsa.dot.gov/)
*Drivers 65 years old and older. People 65 or older make up 15 percent of the total U.S. population.

Percent of Highway Fatalities Who Were Young Drivers in 2015

National Percent = 5.4% of Fatalities*

ALPHA ORDER

RANK	STATE	PERCENT
16	Alabama	6.0
48	Alaska	3.1
44	Arizona	3.8
41	Arkansas	4.1
34	California	4.6
34	Colorado	4.6
23	Connecticut	5.3
9	Delaware	6.3
33	Florida	4.7
22	Georgia	5.4
23	Hawaii	5.3
5	Idaho	7.9
9	Illinois	6.3
9	Indiana	6.3
1	Iowa	9.7
2	Kansas	8.7
30	Kentucky	5.1
31	Louisiana	5.0
44	Maine	3.8
43	Maryland	3.9
28	Massachusetts	5.2
9	Michigan	6.3
9	Minnesota	6.3
7	Mississippi	7.8
20	Missouri	5.5
4	Montana	8.0
8	Nebraska	7.7
32	Nevada	4.9
38	New Hampshire	4.4
47	New Jersey	3.2
46	New Mexico	3.7
49	New York	3.0
20	North Carolina	5.5
3	North Dakota	8.4
15	Ohio	6.2
5	Oklahoma	7.9
50	Oregon	2.9
9	Pennsylvania	6.3
38	Rhode Island	4.4
34	South Carolina	4.6
37	South Dakota	4.5
23	Tennessee	5.3
17	Texas	5.9
40	Utah	4.3
23	Vermont	5.3
28	Virginia	5.2
23	Washington	5.3
19	West Virginia	5.6
18	Wisconsin	5.7
41	Wyoming	4.1

RANK ORDER

RANK	STATE	PERCENT
1	Iowa	9.7
2	Kansas	8.7
3	North Dakota	8.4
4	Montana	8.0
5	Idaho	7.9
5	Oklahoma	7.9
7	Mississippi	7.8
8	Nebraska	7.7
9	Delaware	6.3
9	Illinois	6.3
9	Indiana	6.3
9	Michigan	6.3
9	Minnesota	6.3
9	Pennsylvania	6.3
15	Ohio	6.2
16	Alabama	6.0
17	Texas	5.9
18	Wisconsin	5.7
19	West Virginia	5.6
20	Missouri	5.5
20	North Carolina	5.5
22	Georgia	5.4
23	Connecticut	5.3
23	Hawaii	5.3
23	Tennessee	5.3
23	Vermont	5.3
23	Washington	5.3
28	Massachusetts	5.2
28	Virginia	5.2
30	Kentucky	5.1
31	Louisiana	5.0
32	Nevada	4.9
33	Florida	4.7
34	California	4.6
34	Colorado	4.6
34	South Carolina	4.6
37	South Dakota	4.5
38	New Hampshire	4.4
38	Rhode Island	4.4
40	Utah	4.3
41	Arkansas	4.1
41	Wyoming	4.1
43	Maryland	3.9
44	Arizona	3.8
44	Maine	3.8
46	New Mexico	3.7
47	New Jersey	3.2
48	Alaska	3.1
49	New York	3.0
50	Oregon	2.9

District of Columbia	0.0

Source: CQ Press using data from U.S. Department of Transportation, National Highway Traffic Safety Administration
"Traffic Safety Facts: Young Drivers" (https://crashstats.nhtsa.dot.gov/)
*Drivers 15 to 20 years old. Based on 1,886 fatalities of young drivers. An additional 2,816 passengers and nonoccupants were killed in crashes involving young drivers. Young drivers accounted for 5.4 percent of all drivers.

Licensed Drivers in 2016

National Total = 221,711,918 Licensed Drivers

ALPHA ORDER

ALPHA ORDER

RANK	STATE	DRIVERS	% of USA
22	Alabama	3,943,082	1.8%
49	Alaska	534,585	0.2%
15	Arizona	5,082,305	2.3%
30	Arkansas	2,391,103	1.1%
1	California	26,199,436	11.8%
21	Colorado	4,066,580	1.8%
28	Connecticut	2,611,007	1.2%
44	Delaware	756,328	0.3%
3	Florida	14,675,160	6.6%
10	Georgia	6,975,900	3.1%
42	Hawaii	931,703	0.4%
38	Idaho	1,160,922	0.5%
6	Illinois	8,514,644	3.8%
17	Indiana	4,553,259	2.1%
31	Iowa	2,245,640	1.0%
32	Kansas	2,030,025	0.9%
26	Kentucky	3,031,447	1.4%
24	Louisiana	3,395,095	1.5%
41	Maine	1,021,332	0.5%
18	Maryland	4,264,875	1.9%
16	Massachusetts	5,040,662	2.3%
9	Michigan	7,074,674	3.2%
25	Minnesota	3,377,910	1.5%
33	Mississippi	2,018,862	0.9%
19	Missouri	4,249,579	1.9%
43	Montana	797,145	0.4%
37	Nebraska	1,404,479	0.6%
35	Nevada	1,872,376	0.8%
40	New Hampshire	1,096,234	0.5%
11	New Jersey	6,238,436	2.8%
36	New Mexico	1,521,785	0.7%
4	New York	11,947,568	5.4%
8	North Carolina	7,267,042	3.3%
47	North Dakota	555,935	0.3%
7	Ohio	7,974,951	3.6%
29	Oklahoma	2,498,178	1.1%
27	Oregon	2,855,746	1.3%
5	Pennsylvania	8,996,815	4.1%
45	Rhode Island	753,143	0.3%
23	South Carolina	3,746,681	1.7%
46	South Dakota	622,663	0.3%
14	Tennessee	5,197,904	2.3%
2	Texas	15,879,876	7.2%
34	Utah	1,960,366	0.9%
48	Vermont	553,670	0.2%
12	Virginia	5,912,048	2.7%
13	Washington	5,635,715	2.5%
39	West Virginia	1,159,348	0.5%
20	Wisconsin	4,206,770	1.9%
50	Wyoming	421,098	0.2%

RANK ORDER

RANK	STATE	DRIVERS	% of USA
1	California	26,199,436	11.8%
2	Texas	15,879,876	7.2%
3	Florida	14,675,160	6.6%
4	New York	11,947,568	5.4%
5	Pennsylvania	8,996,815	4.1%
6	Illinois	8,514,644	3.8%
7	Ohio	7,974,951	3.6%
8	North Carolina	7,267,042	3.3%
9	Michigan	7,074,674	3.2%
10	Georgia	6,975,900	3.1%
11	New Jersey	6,238,436	2.8%
12	Virginia	5,912,048	2.7%
13	Washington	5,635,715	2.5%
14	Tennessee	5,197,904	2.3%
15	Arizona	5,082,305	2.3%
16	Massachusetts	5,040,662	2.3%
17	Indiana	4,553,259	2.1%
18	Maryland	4,264,875	1.9%
19	Missouri	4,249,579	1.9%
20	Wisconsin	4,206,770	1.9%
21	Colorado	4,066,580	1.8%
22	Alabama	3,943,082	1.8%
23	South Carolina	3,746,681	1.7%
24	Louisiana	3,395,095	1.5%
25	Minnesota	3,377,910	1.5%
26	Kentucky	3,031,447	1.4%
27	Oregon	2,855,746	1.3%
28	Connecticut	2,611,007	1.2%
29	Oklahoma	2,498,178	1.1%
30	Arkansas	2,391,103	1.1%
31	Iowa	2,245,640	1.0%
32	Kansas	2,030,025	0.9%
33	Mississippi	2,018,862	0.9%
34	Utah	1,960,366	0.9%
35	Nevada	1,872,376	0.8%
36	New Mexico	1,521,785	0.7%
37	Nebraska	1,404,479	0.6%
38	Idaho	1,160,922	0.5%
39	West Virginia	1,159,348	0.5%
40	New Hampshire	1,096,234	0.5%
41	Maine	1,021,332	0.5%
42	Hawaii	931,703	0.4%
43	Montana	797,145	0.4%
44	Delaware	756,328	0.3%
45	Rhode Island	753,143	0.3%
46	South Dakota	622,663	0.3%
47	North Dakota	555,935	0.3%
48	Vermont	553,670	0.2%
49	Alaska	534,585	0.2%
50	Wyoming	421,098	0.2%
	District of Columbia	489,831	0.2%

Source: U.S. Department of Transportation, Federal Highway Administration
"Highway Statistics 2016" (Table DL-22, http://www.fhwa.dot.gov/policyinformation/statistics/2016/)

Licensed Drivers per 1,000 Driving Age Population in 2016

National Ratio = 859 Licensed Drivers

ALPHA ORDER			RANK ORDER		
RANK	STATE	RATIO	RANK	STATE	RATIO
2	Alabama	1,012	1	Vermont	1,062
11	Alaska	930	2	Alabama	1,012
13	Arizona	926	2	Arkansas	1,012
2	Arkansas	1,012	4	New Hampshire	990
42	California	840	5	Delaware	980
17	Colorado	920	6	Tennessee	977
25	Connecticut	894	7	Washington	965
5	Delaware	980	8	Montana	949
34	Florida	866	9	Nebraska	946
36	Georgia	862	10	South Carolina	939
45	Hawaii	809	11	Alaska	930
23	Idaho	896	12	North Dakota	928
43	Illinois	833	13	Arizona	926
32	Indiana	869	14	New Mexico	924
21	Iowa	903	15	South Dakota	923
26	Kansas	893	16	Maine	921
40	Kentucky	856	17	Colorado	920
18	Louisiana	919	18	Louisiana	919
16	Maine	921	19	Wyoming	913
27	Maryland	884	20	Wisconsin	906
22	Massachusetts	900	21	Iowa	903
27	Michigan	884	22	Massachusetts	900
48	Minnesota	772	23	Idaho	896
38	Mississippi	859	23	North Carolina	896
31	Missouri	873	25	Connecticut	894
8	Montana	949	26	Kansas	893
9	Nebraska	946	27	Maryland	884
46	Nevada	801	27	Michigan	884
4	New Hampshire	990	29	Utah	880
33	New Jersey	867	30	Virginia	875
14	New Mexico	924	31	Missouri	873
49	New York	744	32	Indiana	869
23	North Carolina	896	33	New Jersey	867
12	North Dakota	928	34	Florida	866
40	Ohio	856	35	Pennsylvania	863
44	Oklahoma	814	36	Georgia	862
38	Oregon	859	36	Rhode Island	862
35	Pennsylvania	863	38	Mississippi	859
36	Rhode Island	862	38	Oregon	859
10	South Carolina	939	40	Kentucky	856
15	South Dakota	923	40	Ohio	856
6	Tennessee	977	42	California	840
50	Texas	743	43	Illinois	833
29	Utah	880	44	Oklahoma	814
1	Vermont	1,062	45	Hawaii	809
30	Virginia	875	46	Nevada	801
7	Washington	965	47	West Virginia	773
47	West Virginia	773	48	Minnesota	772
20	Wisconsin	906	49	New York	744
19	Wyoming	913	50	Texas	743

District of Columbia 858

Source: CQ Press using data from U.S. Department of Transportation, Federal Highway Administration "Highway Statistics 2016" (Table DL-22, http://www.fhwa.dot.gov/policyinformation/statistics/2016/)

Motor Vehicle Registrations in 2016

National Total = 266,799,083 Motor Vehicles*

ALPHA ORDER

RANK	STATE	VEHICLES	% of USA
19	Alabama	5,468,301	2.0%
49	Alaska	794,614	0.3%
15	Arizona	5,786,891	2.2%
31	Arkansas	2,808,138	1.0%
1	California	30,221,033	11.2%
21	Colorado	5,116,341	1.9%
30	Connecticut	2,841,842	1.1%
45	Delaware	1,003,840	0.4%
3	Florida	16,600,317	6.2%
10	Georgia	8,239,779	3.1%
43	Hawaii	1,231,728	0.5%
37	Idaho	1,842,245	0.7%
7	Illinois	10,277,182	3.8%
13	Indiana	6,140,530	2.3%
29	Iowa	3,676,290	1.4%
32	Kansas	2,649,736	1.0%
24	Kentucky	4,224,788	1.6%
26	Louisiana	3,904,962	1.5%
44	Maine	1,107,674	0.4%
25	Maryland	4,178,873	1.6%
22	Massachusetts	5,069,559	1.9%
8	Michigan	8,332,895	3.1%
20	Minnesota	5,358,317	2.0%
35	Mississippi	2,067,222	0.8%
17	Missouri	5,684,525	2.1%
39	Montana	1,794,732	0.7%
36	Nebraska	1,951,766	0.7%
33	Nevada	2,398,659	0.9%
41	New Hampshire	1,322,682	0.5%
14	New Jersey	5,940,997	2.2%
38	New Mexico	1,823,961	0.7%
4	New York	11,122,392	4.1%
9	North Carolina	8,270,643	3.1%
46	North Dakota	894,954	0.3%
6	Ohio	10,686,057	4.0%
28	Oklahoma	3,737,405	1.4%
27	Oregon	3,811,706	1.4%
5	Pennsylvania	10,748,822	4.0%
47	Rhode Island	876,228	0.3%
23	South Carolina	4,324,423	1.6%
42	South Dakota	1,246,359	0.5%
16	Tennessee	5,709,923	2.1%
2	Texas	21,766,166	8.1%
34	Utah	2,317,282	0.9%
50	Vermont	615,950	0.2%
11	Virginia	7,301,081	2.7%
12	Washington	7,047,689	2.6%
40	West Virginia	1,704,825	0.6%
18	Wisconsin	5,564,429	2.1%
48	Wyoming	855,230	0.3%

RANK ORDER

RANK	STATE	VEHICLES	% of USA
1	California	30,221,033	11.2%
2	Texas	21,766,166	8.1%
3	Florida	16,600,317	6.2%
4	New York	11,122,392	4.1%
5	Pennsylvania	10,748,822	4.0%
6	Ohio	10,686,057	4.0%
7	Illinois	10,277,182	3.8%
8	Michigan	8,332,895	3.1%
9	North Carolina	8,270,643	3.1%
10	Georgia	8,239,779	3.1%
11	Virginia	7,301,081	2.7%
12	Washington	7,047,689	2.6%
13	Indiana	6,140,530	2.3%
14	New Jersey	5,940,997	2.2%
15	Arizona	5,786,891	2.2%
16	Tennessee	5,709,923	2.1%
17	Missouri	5,684,525	2.1%
18	Wisconsin	5,564,429	2.1%
19	Alabama	5,468,301	2.0%
20	Minnesota	5,358,317	2.0%
21	Colorado	5,116,341	1.9%
22	Massachusetts	5,069,559	1.9%
23	South Carolina	4,324,423	1.6%
24	Kentucky	4,224,788	1.6%
25	Maryland	4,178,873	1.6%
26	Louisiana	3,904,962	1.5%
27	Oregon	3,811,706	1.4%
28	Oklahoma	3,737,405	1.4%
29	Iowa	3,676,290	1.4%
30	Connecticut	2,841,842	1.1%
31	Arkansas	2,808,138	1.0%
32	Kansas	2,649,736	1.0%
33	Nevada	2,398,659	0.9%
34	Utah	2,317,282	0.9%
35	Mississippi	2,067,222	0.8%
36	Nebraska	1,951,766	0.7%
37	Idaho	1,842,245	0.7%
38	New Mexico	1,823,961	0.7%
39	Montana	1,794,732	0.7%
40	West Virginia	1,704,825	0.6%
41	New Hampshire	1,322,682	0.5%
42	South Dakota	1,246,359	0.5%
43	Hawaii	1,231,728	0.5%
44	Maine	1,107,674	0.4%
45	Delaware	1,003,840	0.4%
46	North Dakota	894,954	0.3%
47	Rhode Island	876,228	0.3%
48	Wyoming	855,230	0.3%
49	Alaska	794,614	0.3%
50	Vermont	615,950	0.2%
	District of Columbia	337,100	0.1%

Source: U.S. Department of Transportation, Federal Highway Administration
"Highway Statistics 2016" (Table MV-1, http://www.fhwa.dot.gov/policyinformation/statistics/2016/)
*Includes automobiles, trucks and buses and motorcycles.

Motor Vehicles per Driving Age Population in 2016

National Rate = 1.04 Motor Vehicles*

ALPHA ORDER

RANK	STATE	RATE
7	Alabama	1.40
8	Alaska	1.38
32	Arizona	1.05
15	Arkansas	1.19
44	California	0.97
22	Colorado	1.16
44	Connecticut	0.97
10	Delaware	1.30
43	Florida	0.98
37	Georgia	1.02
29	Hawaii	1.07
6	Idaho	1.42
40	Illinois	1.01
19	Indiana	1.17
5	Iowa	1.48
19	Kansas	1.17
15	Kentucky	1.19
31	Louisiana	1.06
41	Maine	1.00
48	Maryland	0.87
46	Massachusetts	0.90
33	Michigan	1.04
11	Minnesota	1.22
47	Mississippi	0.88
19	Missouri	1.17
1	Montana	2.14
9	Nebraska	1.31
35	Nevada	1.03
15	New Hampshire	1.19
49	New Jersey	0.83
26	New Mexico	1.11
50	New York	0.69
37	North Carolina	1.02
4	North Dakota	1.49
23	Ohio	1.15
11	Oklahoma	1.22
23	Oregon	1.15
35	Pennsylvania	1.03
41	Rhode Island	1.00
27	South Carolina	1.08
2	South Dakota	1.85
29	Tennessee	1.07
37	Texas	1.02
33	Utah	1.04
18	Vermont	1.18
27	Virginia	1.08
13	Washington	1.21
25	West Virginia	1.14
14	Wisconsin	1.20
2	Wyoming	1.85

RANK ORDER

RANK	STATE	RATE
1	Montana	2.14
2	South Dakota	1.85
2	Wyoming	1.85
4	North Dakota	1.49
5	Iowa	1.48
6	Idaho	1.42
7	Alabama	1.40
8	Alaska	1.38
9	Nebraska	1.31
10	Delaware	1.30
11	Minnesota	1.22
11	Oklahoma	1.22
13	Washington	1.21
14	Wisconsin	1.20
15	Arkansas	1.19
15	Kentucky	1.19
15	New Hampshire	1.19
18	Vermont	1.18
19	Indiana	1.17
19	Kansas	1.17
19	Missouri	1.17
22	Colorado	1.16
23	Ohio	1.15
23	Oregon	1.15
25	West Virginia	1.14
26	New Mexico	1.11
27	South Carolina	1.08
27	Virginia	1.08
29	Hawaii	1.07
29	Tennessee	1.07
31	Louisiana	1.06
32	Arizona	1.05
33	Michigan	1.04
33	Utah	1.04
35	Nevada	1.03
35	Pennsylvania	1.03
37	Georgia	1.02
37	North Carolina	1.02
37	Texas	1.02
40	Illinois	1.01
41	Maine	1.00
41	Rhode Island	1.00
43	Florida	0.98
44	California	0.97
44	Connecticut	0.97
46	Massachusetts	0.90
47	Mississippi	0.88
48	Maryland	0.87
49	New Jersey	0.83
50	New York	0.69
	District of Columbia	0.59

Source: CQ Press using data from U.S. Department of Transportation, Federal Highway Administration
"Highway Statistics 2016" (Table MV-1, http://www.fhwa.dot.gov/policyinformation/statistics/2016/)
*Persons age 16 and older. Motor Vehicles include automobiles, trucks, buses, and motorcycles.

Average Travel Time to Work in 2016

National Average = 26.6 Minutes*

Source: U.S. Bureau of the Census

"2016 American Community Survey-Table DP03" (http://www.census.gov/programs-surveys/acs/)
*Workers 16 and older not working at home.

Percent of Commuters Who Drive to Work Alone in 2016

National Percent = 76.3%*

ALPHA ORDER				RANK ORDER		
RANK	STATE	PERCENT		RANK	STATE	PERCENT
1	Alabama	86.1		1	Alabama	86.1
48	Alaska	69.0		2	Mississippi	84.6
35	Arizona	76.5		3	Tennessee	83.5
5	Arkansas	83.1		4	Indiana	83.2
42	California	73.6		5	Arkansas	83.1
40	Colorado	75.0		5	Ohio	83.1
33	Connecticut	77.7		7	Louisiana	82.9
18	Delaware	81.0		8	Oklahoma	82.6
29	Florida	79.2		9	South Carolina	82.5
26	Georgia	79.3		10	Michigan	82.4
49	Hawaii	66.9		11	Kansas	82.2
26	Idaho	79.3		11	Kentucky	82.2
43	Illinois	73.1		13	Nebraska	82.0
4	Indiana	83.2		14	Missouri	81.7
17	Iowa	81.2		15	West Virginia	81.6
11	Kansas	82.2		16	North Carolina	81.3
11	Kentucky	82.2		17	Iowa	81.2
7	Louisiana	82.9		18	Delaware	81.0
26	Maine	79.3		19	Wisconsin	80.7
41	Maryland	73.8		20	Texas	80.5
47	Massachusetts	70.1		21	Rhode Island	80.3
10	Michigan	82.4		22	North Dakota	80.2
31	Minnesota	77.8		23	New Mexico	80.0
2	Mississippi	84.6		24	South Dakota	79.9
14	Missouri	81.7		25	New Hampshire	79.7
37	Montana	76.0		26	Georgia	79.3
13	Nebraska	82.0		26	Idaho	79.3
30	Nevada	78.8		26	Maine	79.3
25	New Hampshire	79.7		29	Florida	79.2
46	New Jersey	70.8		30	Nevada	78.8
23	New Mexico	80.0		31	Minnesota	77.8
50	New York	52.6		31	Wyoming	77.8
16	North Carolina	81.3		33	Connecticut	77.7
22	North Dakota	80.2		34	Virginia	76.9
5	Ohio	83.1		35	Arizona	76.5
8	Oklahoma	82.6		36	Pennsylvania	76.1
44	Oregon	72.4		37	Montana	76.0
36	Pennsylvania	76.1		38	Utah	75.8
21	Rhode Island	80.3		39	Vermont	75.6
9	South Carolina	82.5		40	Colorado	75.0
24	South Dakota	79.9		41	Maryland	73.8
3	Tennessee	83.5		42	California	73.6
20	Texas	80.5		43	Illinois	73.1
38	Utah	75.8		44	Oregon	72.4
39	Vermont	75.6		45	Washington	72.1
34	Virginia	76.9		46	New Jersey	70.8
45	Washington	72.1		47	Massachusetts	70.1
15	West Virginia	81.6		48	Alaska	69.0
19	Wisconsin	80.7		49	Hawaii	66.9
31	Wyoming	77.8		50	New York	52.6
				District of Columbia		33.0

Source: U.S. Bureau of the Census
"2016 American Community Survey-Table DP03" (http://www.census.gov/programs-surveys/acs/)
*Workers 16 and older who traveled to work by car, truck or van.

Percent of Commuters Who Drive to Work in Carpools in 2016

National Percent = 9.0%*

ALPHA ORDER

RANK	STATE	PERCENT
45	Alabama	8.0
2	Alaska	12.2
3	Arizona	11.0
6	Arkansas	10.2
5	California	10.3
25	Colorado	9.0
42	Connecticut	8.2
25	Delaware	9.0
21	Florida	9.2
13	Georgia	9.6
1	Hawaii	13.6
13	Idaho	9.6
47	Illinois	7.7
38	Indiana	8.5
42	Iowa	8.2
31	Kansas	8.9
18	Kentucky	9.3
18	Louisiana	9.3
25	Maine	9.0
25	Maryland	9.0
48	Massachusetts	7.6
31	Michigan	8.9
35	Minnesota	8.6
11	Mississippi	9.8
34	Missouri	8.7
21	Montana	9.2
25	Nebraska	9.0
6	Nevada	10.2
35	New Hampshire	8.6
39	New Jersey	8.4
17	New Mexico	9.4
50	New York	6.5
21	North Carolina	9.2
9	North Dakota	9.9
49	Ohio	7.5
15	Oklahoma	9.5
12	Oregon	9.7
39	Pennsylvania	8.4
39	Rhode Island	8.4
18	South Carolina	9.3
31	South Dakota	8.9
35	Tennessee	8.6
8	Texas	10.1
3	Utah	11.0
45	Vermont	8.0
15	Virginia	9.5
9	Washington	9.9
21	West Virginia	9.2
42	Wisconsin	8.2
25	Wyoming	9.0

RANK ORDER

RANK	STATE	PERCENT
1	Hawaii	13.6
2	Alaska	12.2
3	Arizona	11.0
3	Utah	11.0
5	California	10.3
6	Arkansas	10.2
6	Nevada	10.2
8	Texas	10.1
9	North Dakota	9.9
9	Washington	9.9
11	Mississippi	9.8
12	Oregon	9.7
13	Georgia	9.6
13	Idaho	9.6
15	Oklahoma	9.5
15	Virginia	9.5
17	New Mexico	9.4
18	Kentucky	9.3
18	Louisiana	9.3
18	South Carolina	9.3
21	Florida	9.2
21	Montana	9.2
21	North Carolina	9.2
21	West Virginia	9.2
25	Colorado	9.0
25	Delaware	9.0
25	Maine	9.0
25	Maryland	9.0
25	Nebraska	9.0
25	Wyoming	9.0
31	Kansas	8.9
31	Michigan	8.9
31	South Dakota	8.9
34	Missouri	8.7
35	Minnesota	8.6
35	New Hampshire	8.6
35	Tennessee	8.6
38	Indiana	8.5
39	New Jersey	8.4
39	Pennsylvania	8.4
39	Rhode Island	8.4
42	Connecticut	8.2
42	Iowa	8.2
42	Wisconsin	8.2
45	Alabama	8.0
45	Vermont	8.0
47	Illinois	7.7
48	Massachusetts	7.6
49	Ohio	7.5
50	New York	6.5
	District of Columbia	5.1

Source: U.S. Bureau of the Census

"2016 American Community Survey-Table DP03" (http://www.census.gov/programs-surveys/acs/)
*Workers 16 and older who traveled to work by car, truck or van.

Percent of Commuters Who Travel to Work by Public Transportation in 2016

National Percent = 5.1%*

ALPHA ORDER

RANK	STATE	PERCENT
48	Alabama	0.3
31	Alaska	1.2
21	Arizona	1.9
48	Arkansas	0.3
9	California	5.1
15	Colorado	2.9
10	Connecticut	4.9
16	Delaware	2.7
19	Florida	2.1
19	Georgia	2.1
6	Hawaii	6.7
41	Idaho	0.6
4	Illinois	9.4
35	Indiana	1.0
32	Iowa	1.1
44	Kansas	0.5
32	Kentucky	1.1
30	Louisiana	1.3
38	Maine	0.7
5	Maryland	8.5
3	Massachusetts	10.1
26	Michigan	1.4
13	Minnesota	3.6
48	Mississippi	0.3
26	Missouri	1.4
38	Montana	0.7
41	Nebraska	0.6
14	Nevada	3.4
37	New Hampshire	0.9
2	New Jersey	11.8
26	New Mexico	1.4
1	New York	28.4
35	North Carolina	1.0
44	North Dakota	0.5
23	Ohio	1.6
44	Oklahoma	0.5
11	Oregon	4.4
8	Pennsylvania	5.6
18	Rhode Island	2.4
41	South Carolina	0.6
44	South Dakota	0.5
38	Tennessee	0.7
26	Texas	1.4
16	Utah	2.7
24	Vermont	1.5
12	Virginia	4.1
7	Washington	6.4
32	West Virginia	1.1
22	Wisconsin	1.7
24	Wyoming	1.5

RANK ORDER

RANK	STATE	PERCENT
1	New York	28.4
2	New Jersey	11.8
3	Massachusetts	10.1
4	Illinois	9.4
5	Maryland	8.5
6	Hawaii	6.7
7	Washington	6.4
8	Pennsylvania	5.6
9	California	5.1
10	Connecticut	4.9
11	Oregon	4.4
12	Virginia	4.1
13	Minnesota	3.6
14	Nevada	3.4
15	Colorado	2.9
16	Delaware	2.7
16	Utah	2.7
18	Rhode Island	2.4
19	Florida	2.1
19	Georgia	2.1
21	Arizona	1.9
22	Wisconsin	1.7
23	Ohio	1.6
24	Vermont	1.5
24	Wyoming	1.5
26	Michigan	1.4
26	Missouri	1.4
26	New Mexico	1.4
26	Texas	1.4
30	Louisiana	1.3
31	Alaska	1.2
32	Iowa	1.1
32	Kentucky	1.1
32	West Virginia	1.1
35	Indiana	1.0
35	North Carolina	1.0
37	New Hampshire	0.9
38	Maine	0.7
38	Montana	0.7
38	Tennessee	0.7
41	Idaho	0.6
41	Nebraska	0.6
41	South Carolina	0.6
44	Kansas	0.5
44	North Dakota	0.5
44	Oklahoma	0.5
44	South Dakota	0.5
48	Alabama	0.3
48	Arkansas	0.3
48	Mississippi	0.3
	District of Columbia	36.0

Source: U.S. Bureau of the Census
"2016 American Community Survey-Table DP03" (http://www.census.gov/programs-surveys/acs/)
*Workers 16 and older.

Annual Miles per Vehicle in 2016

National Annual Average = 11,864 Miles*

ALPHA ORDER

RANK	STATE	MILES
15	Alabama	12,660
50	Alaska	6,618
27	Arizona	11,368
14	Arkansas	12,733
28	California	11,254
39	Colorado	10,193
30	Connecticut	11,133
40	Delaware	10,139
12	Florida	12,985
3	Georgia	14,904
47	Hawaii	8,635
43	Idaho	9,336
37	Illinois	10,442
7	Indiana	13,547
44	Iowa	9,068
20	Kansas	12,115
23	Kentucky	11,672
17	Louisiana	12,588
9	Maine	13,396
4	Maryland	14,152
19	Massachusetts	12,195
22	Michigan	11,933
33	Minnesota	11,016
1	Mississippi	19,715
11	Missouri	13,021
49	Montana	7,020
36	Nebraska	10,606
29	Nevada	11,168
38	New Hampshire	10,216
13	New Jersey	12,976
2	New Mexico	15,288
32	New York	11,052
5	North Carolina	14,116
35	North Dakota	10,882
31	Ohio	11,099
10	Oklahoma	13,114
41	Oregon	9,633
42	Pennsylvania	9,430
45	Rhode Island	9,047
16	South Carolina	12,615
48	South Dakota	7,627
8	Tennessee	13,465
18	Texas	12,463
6	Utah	13,571
21	Vermont	11,985
24	Virginia	11,569
46	Washington	8,658
26	West Virginia	11,461
25	Wisconsin	11,510
34	Wyoming	10,901

RANK ORDER

RANK	STATE	MILES
1	Mississippi	19,715
2	New Mexico	15,288
3	Georgia	14,904
4	Maryland	14,152
5	North Carolina	14,116
6	Utah	13,571
7	Indiana	13,547
8	Tennessee	13,465
9	Maine	13,396
10	Oklahoma	13,114
11	Missouri	13,021
12	Florida	12,985
13	New Jersey	12,976
14	Arkansas	12,733
15	Alabama	12,660
16	South Carolina	12,615
17	Louisiana	12,588
18	Texas	12,463
19	Massachusetts	12,195
20	Kansas	12,115
21	Vermont	11,985
22	Michigan	11,933
23	Kentucky	11,672
24	Virginia	11,569
25	Wisconsin	11,510
26	West Virginia	11,461
27	Arizona	11,368
28	California	11,254
29	Nevada	11,168
30	Connecticut	11,133
31	Ohio	11,099
32	New York	11,052
33	Minnesota	11,016
34	Wyoming	10,901
35	North Dakota	10,882
36	Nebraska	10,606
37	Illinois	10,442
38	New Hampshire	10,216
39	Colorado	10,193
40	Delaware	10,139
41	Oregon	9,633
42	Pennsylvania	9,430
43	Idaho	9,336
44	Iowa	9,068
45	Rhode Island	9,047
46	Washington	8,658
47	Hawaii	8,635
48	South Dakota	7,627
49	Montana	7,020
50	Alaska	6,618

District of Columbia	10,744

Source: CQ Press using data from U.S. Department of Transportation, Federal Highway Administration
   "Highway Statistics 2016" (Tables MV-1 and VM-2, http://www.fhwa.dot.gov/policyinformation/statistics/2016/)
*Includes automobiles, trucks, buses and motorcycles.

Average Miles per Gallon in 2015

National Average = 17.9 Miles per Gallon*

<table>
<tr><td colspan="3">ALPHA ORDER</td><td colspan="3">RANK ORDER</td></tr>
<tr><td>RANK</td><td>STATE</td><td>MILES PER GALLON</td><td>RANK</td><td>STATE</td><td>MILES PER GALLON</td></tr>
<tr><td>5</td><td>Alabama</td><td>20.2</td><td>1</td><td>Florida</td><td>21.6</td></tr>
<tr><td>49</td><td>Alaska</td><td>13.2</td><td>2</td><td>Hawaii</td><td>21.4</td></tr>
<tr><td>12</td><td>Arizona</td><td>19.1</td><td>3</td><td>North Carolina</td><td>21.0</td></tr>
<tr><td>25</td><td>Arkansas</td><td>18.0</td><td>4</td><td>Vermont</td><td>20.4</td></tr>
<tr><td>9</td><td>California</td><td>19.5</td><td>5</td><td>Alabama</td><td>20.2</td></tr>
<tr><td>19</td><td>Colorado</td><td>18.4</td><td>6</td><td>Delaware</td><td>19.9</td></tr>
<tr><td>17</td><td>Connecticut</td><td>18.8</td><td>7</td><td>New York</td><td>19.6</td></tr>
<tr><td>6</td><td>Delaware</td><td>19.9</td><td>7</td><td>Utah</td><td>19.6</td></tr>
<tr><td>1</td><td>Florida</td><td>21.6</td><td>9</td><td>California</td><td>19.5</td></tr>
<tr><td>12</td><td>Georgia</td><td>19.1</td><td>9</td><td>Wisconsin</td><td>19.5</td></tr>
<tr><td>2</td><td>Hawaii</td><td>21.4</td><td>11</td><td>Minnesota</td><td>19.2</td></tr>
<tr><td>33</td><td>Idaho</td><td>17.4</td><td>12</td><td>Arizona</td><td>19.1</td></tr>
<tr><td>40</td><td>Illinois</td><td>16.1</td><td>12</td><td>Georgia</td><td>19.1</td></tr>
<tr><td>19</td><td>Indiana</td><td>18.4</td><td>14</td><td>Massachusetts</td><td>19.0</td></tr>
<tr><td>44</td><td>Iowa</td><td>15.4</td><td>14</td><td>Tennessee</td><td>19.0</td></tr>
<tr><td>19</td><td>Kansas</td><td>18.4</td><td>16</td><td>New Mexico</td><td>18.9</td></tr>
<tr><td>35</td><td>Kentucky</td><td>17.1</td><td>17</td><td>Connecticut</td><td>18.8</td></tr>
<tr><td>37</td><td>Louisiana</td><td>16.6</td><td>17</td><td>Nevada</td><td>18.8</td></tr>
<tr><td>42</td><td>Maine</td><td>16.0</td><td>19</td><td>Colorado</td><td>18.4</td></tr>
<tr><td>31</td><td>Maryland</td><td>17.7</td><td>19</td><td>Indiana</td><td>18.4</td></tr>
<tr><td>14</td><td>Massachusetts</td><td>19.0</td><td>19</td><td>Kansas</td><td>18.4</td></tr>
<tr><td>19</td><td>Michigan</td><td>18.4</td><td>19</td><td>Michigan</td><td>18.4</td></tr>
<tr><td>11</td><td>Minnesota</td><td>19.2</td><td>23</td><td>Rhode Island</td><td>18.3</td></tr>
<tr><td>29</td><td>Mississippi</td><td>17.8</td><td>24</td><td>Missouri</td><td>18.1</td></tr>
<tr><td>24</td><td>Missouri</td><td>18.1</td><td>25</td><td>Arkansas</td><td>18.0</td></tr>
<tr><td>38</td><td>Montana</td><td>16.4</td><td>25</td><td>Oregon</td><td>18.0</td></tr>
<tr><td>43</td><td>Nebraska</td><td>15.9</td><td>25</td><td>Washington</td><td>18.0</td></tr>
<tr><td>17</td><td>Nevada</td><td>18.8</td><td>28</td><td>Oklahoma</td><td>17.9</td></tr>
<tr><td>34</td><td>New Hampshire</td><td>17.3</td><td>29</td><td>Mississippi</td><td>17.8</td></tr>
<tr><td>40</td><td>New Jersey</td><td>16.1</td><td>29</td><td>Ohio</td><td>17.8</td></tr>
<tr><td>16</td><td>New Mexico</td><td>18.9</td><td>31</td><td>Maryland</td><td>17.7</td></tr>
<tr><td>7</td><td>New York</td><td>19.6</td><td>32</td><td>West Virginia</td><td>17.5</td></tr>
<tr><td>3</td><td>North Carolina</td><td>21.0</td><td>33</td><td>Idaho</td><td>17.4</td></tr>
<tr><td>50</td><td>North Dakota</td><td>12.7</td><td>34</td><td>New Hampshire</td><td>17.3</td></tr>
<tr><td>29</td><td>Ohio</td><td>17.8</td><td>35</td><td>Kentucky</td><td>17.1</td></tr>
<tr><td>28</td><td>Oklahoma</td><td>17.9</td><td>35</td><td>Virginia</td><td>17.1</td></tr>
<tr><td>25</td><td>Oregon</td><td>18.0</td><td>37</td><td>Louisiana</td><td>16.6</td></tr>
<tr><td>39</td><td>Pennsylvania</td><td>16.3</td><td>38</td><td>Montana</td><td>16.4</td></tr>
<tr><td>23</td><td>Rhode Island</td><td>18.3</td><td>39</td><td>Pennsylvania</td><td>16.3</td></tr>
<tr><td>45</td><td>South Carolina</td><td>15.2</td><td>40</td><td>Illinois</td><td>16.1</td></tr>
<tr><td>47</td><td>South Dakota</td><td>14.0</td><td>40</td><td>New Jersey</td><td>16.1</td></tr>
<tr><td>14</td><td>Tennessee</td><td>19.0</td><td>42</td><td>Maine</td><td>16.0</td></tr>
<tr><td>47</td><td>Texas</td><td>14.0</td><td>43</td><td>Nebraska</td><td>15.9</td></tr>
<tr><td>7</td><td>Utah</td><td>19.6</td><td>44</td><td>Iowa</td><td>15.4</td></tr>
<tr><td>4</td><td>Vermont</td><td>20.4</td><td>45</td><td>South Carolina</td><td>15.2</td></tr>
<tr><td>35</td><td>Virginia</td><td>17.1</td><td>46</td><td>Wyoming</td><td>14.4</td></tr>
<tr><td>25</td><td>Washington</td><td>18.0</td><td>47</td><td>South Dakota</td><td>14.0</td></tr>
<tr><td>32</td><td>West Virginia</td><td>17.5</td><td>47</td><td>Texas</td><td>14.0</td></tr>
<tr><td>9</td><td>Wisconsin</td><td>19.5</td><td>49</td><td>Alaska</td><td>13.2</td></tr>
<tr><td>46</td><td>Wyoming</td><td>14.4</td><td>50</td><td>North Dakota</td><td>12.7</td></tr>
<tr><td></td><td></td><td></td><td></td><td>District of Columbia</td><td>29.1</td></tr>
</table>

Source: CQ Press using data from U.S. Department of Transportation, Federal Highway Administration
"Highway Statistics 2015" (Table VM-2, http://www.fhwa.dot.gov/policyinformation/statistics/2015/)
*Total vehicle-miles for 2015 divided by total highway motor-fuel use. Includes gasoline, gasohol, diesel, and other "special fuels."

Percent of Traffic Fatalities That Were Pedestrians in 2015

National Percent = 15.3%*

ALPHA ORDER

RANK	STATE	PERCENT
29	Alabama	11.5
9	Alaska	18.5
14	Arizona	17.1
40	Arkansas	8.1
6	California	23.4
31	Colorado	10.8
15	Connecticut	16.9
2	Delaware	27.8
7	Florida	21.4
22	Georgia	13.5
4	Hawaii	26.6
49	Idaho	3.7
19	Illinois	15.0
28	Indiana	11.7
41	Iowa	7.8
45	Kansas	6.8
38	Kentucky	8.8
21	Louisiana	14.0
26	Maine	12.2
11	Maryland	17.9
5	Massachusetts	23.5
13	Michigan	17.2
36	Minnesota	9.5
37	Mississippi	9.3
27	Missouri	12.0
46	Montana	6.3
42	Nebraska	7.7
8	Nevada	20.3
44	New Hampshire	7.0
1	New Jersey	30.2
10	New Mexico	18.1
3	New York	27.4
23	North Carolina	13.2
47	North Dakota	5.3
33	Ohio	10.5
32	Oklahoma	10.7
17	Oregon	15.4
24	Pennsylvania	12.6
12	Rhode Island	17.8
24	South Carolina	12.6
48	South Dakota	3.8
30	Tennessee	10.9
18	Texas	15.3
16	Utah	16.7
38	Vermont	8.8
34	Virginia	10.2
19	Washington	15.0
43	West Virginia	7.1
35	Wisconsin	10.1
50	Wyoming	3.4

RANK ORDER

RANK	STATE	PERCENT
1	New Jersey	30.2
2	Delaware	27.8
3	New York	27.4
4	Hawaii	26.6
5	Massachusetts	23.5
6	California	23.4
7	Florida	21.4
8	Nevada	20.3
9	Alaska	18.5
10	New Mexico	18.1
11	Maryland	17.9
12	Rhode Island	17.8
13	Michigan	17.2
14	Arizona	17.1
15	Connecticut	16.9
16	Utah	16.7
17	Oregon	15.4
18	Texas	15.3
19	Illinois	15.0
19	Washington	15.0
21	Louisiana	14.0
22	Georgia	13.5
23	North Carolina	13.2
24	Pennsylvania	12.6
24	South Carolina	12.6
26	Maine	12.2
27	Missouri	12.0
28	Indiana	11.7
29	Alabama	11.5
30	Tennessee	10.9
31	Colorado	10.8
32	Oklahoma	10.7
33	Ohio	10.5
34	Virginia	10.2
35	Wisconsin	10.1
36	Minnesota	9.5
37	Mississippi	9.3
38	Kentucky	8.8
38	Vermont	8.8
40	Arkansas	8.1
41	Iowa	7.8
42	Nebraska	7.7
43	West Virginia	7.1
44	New Hampshire	7.0
45	Kansas	6.8
46	Montana	6.3
47	North Dakota	5.3
48	South Dakota	3.8
49	Idaho	3.7
50	Wyoming	3.4
	District of Columbia	56.5

Source: U.S. Department of Transportation, National Highway Traffic Safety Administration
"Traffic Safety Facts: Pedestrians" (https://crashstats.nhtsa.dot.gov/)
*A pedestrian fatality is any person on foot, walking, running, jogging, hiking, sitting, or lying down who is involved in a motor vehicle traffic crash.

Percent of Traffic Fatalities That Were Bicyclists in 2015

National Percent = 2.3%*

ALPHA ORDER

RANK	STATE	PERCENT
33	Alabama	1.1
46	Alaska	0.0
6	Arizona	3.2
43	Arkansas	0.6
4	California	4.1
15	Colorado	2.4
33	Connecticut	1.1
15	Delaware	2.4
2	Florida	5.1
26	Georgia	1.6
20	Hawaii	2.1
46	Idaho	0.0
12	Illinois	2.6
30	Indiana	1.5
26	Iowa	1.6
39	Kansas	0.8
37	Kentucky	0.9
3	Louisiana	4.7
46	Maine	0.0
20	Maryland	2.1
10	Massachusetts	2.9
5	Michigan	3.4
15	Minnesota	2.4
42	Mississippi	0.7
35	Missouri	1.0
44	Montana	0.4
26	Nebraska	1.6
9	Nevada	3.1
12	New Hampshire	2.6
6	New Jersey	3.2
18	New Mexico	2.3
6	New York	3.2
25	North Carolina	1.7
39	North Dakota	0.8
18	Ohio	2.3
37	Oklahoma	0.9
23	Oregon	1.8
32	Pennsylvania	1.3
46	Rhode Island	0.0
26	South Carolina	1.6
39	South Dakota	0.8
35	Tennessee	1.0
31	Texas	1.4
23	Utah	1.8
1	Vermont	7.0
22	Virginia	2.0
14	Washington	2.5
44	West Virginia	0.4
11	Wisconsin	2.7
46	Wyoming	0.0

RANK ORDER

RANK	STATE	PERCENT
1	Vermont	7.0
2	Florida	5.1
3	Louisiana	4.7
4	California	4.1
5	Michigan	3.4
6	Arizona	3.2
6	New Jersey	3.2
6	New York	3.2
9	Nevada	3.1
10	Massachusetts	2.9
11	Wisconsin	2.7
12	Illinois	2.6
12	New Hampshire	2.6
14	Washington	2.5
15	Colorado	2.4
15	Delaware	2.4
15	Minnesota	2.4
18	New Mexico	2.3
18	Ohio	2.3
20	Hawaii	2.1
20	Maryland	2.1
22	Virginia	2.0
23	Oregon	1.8
23	Utah	1.8
25	North Carolina	1.7
26	Georgia	1.6
26	Iowa	1.6
26	Nebraska	1.6
26	South Carolina	1.6
30	Indiana	1.5
31	Texas	1.4
32	Pennsylvania	1.3
33	Alabama	1.1
33	Connecticut	1.1
35	Missouri	1.0
35	Tennessee	1.0
37	Kentucky	0.9
37	Oklahoma	0.9
39	Kansas	0.8
39	North Dakota	0.8
39	South Dakota	0.8
42	Mississippi	0.7
43	Arkansas	0.6
44	Montana	0.4
44	West Virginia	0.4
46	Alaska	0.0
46	Idaho	0.0
46	Maine	0.0
46	Rhode Island	0.0
46	Wyoming	0.0

| | District of Columbia | 4.3 |

Source: U.S. Department of Transportation, National Highway Traffic Safety Administration
   "Traffic Safety Facts: Bicyclists and Other Cyclists" (https://crashstats.nhtsa.dot.gov/)
*A bicyclist fatality includes any person on a bicycle, tricycle, or unicycle powered solely by pedals that is involved in a vehicle traffic crash.

Percent of Recreational Boating Accidents Involving Alcohol in 2016

National Percent = 7.9% of Accidents*

ALPHA ORDER

RANK	STATE	PERCENT
6	Alabama	15.2
42	Alaska	3.8
13	Arizona	12.2
40	Arkansas	4.3
45	California	2.8
30	Colorado	7.0
32	Connecticut	6.4
40	Delaware	4.3
38	Florida	4.5
16	Georgia	10.7
47	Hawaii	0.0
35	Idaho	6.0
8	Illinois	13.5
19	Indiana	10.0
2	Iowa	18.9
3	Kansas	18.8
9	Kentucky	13.0
33	Louisiana	6.3
13	Maine	12.2
26	Maryland	8.0
29	Massachusetts	7.6
26	Michigan	8.0
3	Minnesota	18.8
5	Mississippi	18.6
17	Missouri	10.2
9	Montana	13.0
38	Nebraska	4.5
33	Nevada	6.3
46	New Hampshire	2.6
43	New Jersey	3.7
47	New Mexico	0.0
20	New York	9.6
24	North Carolina	8.4
47	North Dakota	0.0
26	Ohio	8.0
22	Oklahoma	9.1
43	Oregon	3.7
11	Pennsylvania	12.7
25	Rhode Island	8.3
31	South Carolina	6.6
7	South Dakota	15.0
21	Tennessee	9.5
15	Texas	11.9
37	Utah	5.3
47	Vermont	0.0
35	Virginia	6.0
17	Washington	10.2
1	West Virginia	25.0
23	Wisconsin	8.7
12	Wyoming	12.5

RANK ORDER

RANK	STATE	PERCENT
1	West Virginia	25.0
2	Iowa	18.9
3	Kansas	18.8
3	Minnesota	18.8
5	Mississippi	18.6
6	Alabama	15.2
7	South Dakota	15.0
8	Illinois	13.5
9	Kentucky	13.0
9	Montana	13.0
11	Pennsylvania	12.7
12	Wyoming	12.5
13	Arizona	12.2
13	Maine	12.2
15	Texas	11.9
16	Georgia	10.7
17	Missouri	10.2
17	Washington	10.2
19	Indiana	10.0
20	New York	9.6
21	Tennessee	9.5
22	Oklahoma	9.1
23	Wisconsin	8.7
24	North Carolina	8.4
25	Rhode Island	8.3
26	Maryland	8.0
26	Michigan	8.0
26	Ohio	8.0
29	Massachusetts	7.6
30	Colorado	7.0
31	South Carolina	6.6
32	Connecticut	6.4
33	Louisiana	6.3
33	Nevada	6.3
35	Idaho	6.0
35	Virginia	6.0
37	Utah	5.3
38	Florida	4.5
38	Nebraska	4.5
40	Arkansas	4.3
40	Delaware	4.3
42	Alaska	3.8
43	New Jersey	3.7
43	Oregon	3.7
45	California	2.8
46	New Hampshire	2.6
47	Hawaii	0.0
47	New Mexico	0.0
47	North Dakota	0.0
47	Vermont	0.0
	District of Columbia	0.0

Source: CQ Press using data from United States Coast Guard
"Boating Statistics 2016" (http://www.uscgboating.org/statistics/accident_statistics.php)
*Alcohol involvement in a boating accident includes any accident in which alcoholic beverages are consumed in the boat and the investigating official has determined that the operator was impaired or affected while operating the boat.

Railroad Accidents and Incidents in 2016

National Total = 11,200*

ALPHA ORDER

RANK	STATE	ACCIDENTS	% of USA
20	Alabama	169	1.5%
42	Alaska	53	0.5%
31	Arizona	120	1.1%
30	Arkansas	122	1.1%
2	California	954	8.5%
26	Colorado	155	1.4%
21	Connecticut	167	1.5%
35	Delaware	88	0.8%
7	Florida	344	3.1%
10	Georgia	304	2.7%
50	Hawaii	0	0.0%
41	Idaho	56	0.5%
3	Illinois	847	7.6%
9	Indiana	318	2.8%
24	Iowa	161	1.4%
17	Kansas	176	1.6%
29	Kentucky	128	1.1%
11	Louisiana	263	2.3%
47	Maine	16	0.1%
22	Maryland	166	1.5%
14	Massachusetts	194	1.7%
17	Michigan	176	1.6%
16	Minnesota	180	1.6%
34	Mississippi	107	1.0%
13	Missouri	206	1.8%
38	Montana	77	0.7%
24	Nebraska	161	1.4%
44	Nevada	32	0.3%
49	New Hampshire	6	0.1%
5	New Jersey	669	6.0%
35	New Mexico	88	0.8%
1	New York	1,275	11.4%
19	North Carolina	174	1.6%
39	North Dakota	68	0.6%
8	Ohio	333	3.0%
33	Oklahoma	114	1.0%
28	Oregon	129	1.2%
6	Pennsylvania	626	5.6%
48	Rhode Island	15	0.1%
32	South Carolina	117	1.0%
46	South Dakota	21	0.2%
23	Tennessee	162	1.4%
4	Texas	766	6.8%
42	Utah	53	0.5%
45	Vermont	30	0.3%
15	Virginia	181	1.6%
12	Washington	235	2.1%
37	West Virginia	79	0.7%
27	Wisconsin	137	1.2%
40	Wyoming	59	0.5%

RANK ORDER

RANK	STATE	ACCIDENTS	% of USA
1	New York	1,275	11.4%
2	California	954	8.5%
3	Illinois	847	7.6%
4	Texas	766	6.8%
5	New Jersey	669	6.0%
6	Pennsylvania	626	5.6%
7	Florida	344	3.1%
8	Ohio	333	3.0%
9	Indiana	318	2.8%
10	Georgia	304	2.7%
11	Louisiana	263	2.3%
12	Washington	235	2.1%
13	Missouri	206	1.8%
14	Massachusetts	194	1.7%
15	Virginia	181	1.6%
16	Minnesota	180	1.6%
17	Kansas	176	1.6%
17	Michigan	176	1.6%
19	North Carolina	174	1.6%
20	Alabama	169	1.5%
21	Connecticut	167	1.5%
22	Maryland	166	1.5%
23	Tennessee	162	1.4%
24	Iowa	161	1.4%
24	Nebraska	161	1.4%
26	Colorado	155	1.4%
27	Wisconsin	137	1.2%
28	Oregon	129	1.2%
29	Kentucky	128	1.1%
30	Arkansas	122	1.1%
31	Arizona	120	1.1%
32	South Carolina	117	1.0%
33	Oklahoma	114	1.0%
34	Mississippi	107	1.0%
35	Delaware	88	0.8%
35	New Mexico	88	0.8%
37	West Virginia	79	0.7%
38	Montana	77	0.7%
39	North Dakota	68	0.6%
40	Wyoming	59	0.5%
41	Idaho	56	0.5%
42	Alaska	53	0.5%
42	Utah	53	0.5%
44	Nevada	32	0.3%
45	Vermont	30	0.3%
46	South Dakota	21	0.2%
47	Maine	16	0.1%
48	Rhode Island	15	0.1%
49	New Hampshire	6	0.1%
50	Hawaii	0	0.0%
	District of Columbia	123	1.1%

Source: U.S. Department of Transportation, Federal Railroad Administration, Office of Safety Analysis
"Railroad Accidents and Incidents" (Table 1.11, http://safetydata.fra.dot.gov/OfficeofSafety/Default.aspx)
*Accidents or incidents include all events reportable to the U.S. Department of Transportation. These include train accidents causing damage above an established threshold; highway-rail grade crossing incidents involving impact between railroad equipment and highway users at crossings; and all other reportable incidents that cause a fatality or injury to any person or an occupational illness to a railroad employee. There were 774 fatalities involving railroads.

Railroad Mileage Operated in 2015

National Total = 137,465 Miles of Railroad*

RANK	STATE	MILES	% of USA
18	Alabama	3,211	2.3%
46	Alaska	470	0.3%
35	Arizona	1,780	1.3%
29	Arkansas	2,417	1.8%
5	California	4,803	3.5%
27	Colorado	2,452	1.8%
47	Connecticut	438	0.3%
48	Delaware	367	0.3%
24	Florida	2,818	2.0%
7	Georgia	4,422	3.2%
50	Hawaii	0	0.0%
37	Idaho	1,604	1.2%
2	Illinois	7,119	5.2%
9	Indiana	4,274	3.1%
11	Iowa	3,818	2.8%
6	Kansas	4,768	3.5%
25	Kentucky	2,608	1.9%
22	Louisiana	3,041	2.2%
41	Maine	1,091	0.8%
43	Maryland	937	0.7%
39	Massachusetts	1,327	1.0%
16	Michigan	3,234	2.4%
8	Minnesota	4,292	3.1%
30	Mississippi	2,384	1.7%
10	Missouri	3,858	2.8%
12	Montana	3,781	2.8%
17	Nebraska	3,228	2.3%
40	Nevada	1,193	0.9%
45	New Hampshire	489	0.4%
42	New Jersey	984	0.7%
34	New Mexico	1,860	1.4%
15	New York	3,378	2.5%
23	North Carolina	2,879	2.1%
14	North Dakota	3,389	2.5%
4	Ohio	4,903	3.6%
19	Oklahoma	3,196	2.3%
28	Oregon	2,423	1.8%
3	Pennsylvania	5,165	3.8%
49	Rhode Island	60	0.0%
32	South Carolina	2,277	1.7%
36	South Dakota	1,736	1.3%
26	Tennessee	2,598	1.9%
1	Texas	10,539	7.7%
38	Utah	1,351	1.0%
44	Vermont	613	0.4%
20	Virginia	3,123	2.3%
21	Washington	3,056	2.2%
31	West Virginia	2,376	1.7%
13	Wisconsin	3,438	2.5%
33	Wyoming	1,877	1.4%

RANK	STATE	MILES	% of USA
1	Texas	10,539	7.7%
2	Illinois	7,119	5.2%
3	Pennsylvania	5,165	3.8%
4	Ohio	4,903	3.6%
5	California	4,803	3.5%
6	Kansas	4,768	3.5%
7	Georgia	4,422	3.2%
8	Minnesota	4,292	3.1%
9	Indiana	4,274	3.1%
10	Missouri	3,858	2.8%
11	Iowa	3,818	2.8%
12	Montana	3,781	2.8%
13	Wisconsin	3,438	2.5%
14	North Dakota	3,389	2.5%
15	New York	3,378	2.5%
16	Michigan	3,234	2.4%
17	Nebraska	3,228	2.3%
18	Alabama	3,211	2.3%
19	Oklahoma	3,196	2.3%
20	Virginia	3,123	2.3%
21	Washington	3,056	2.2%
22	Louisiana	3,041	2.2%
23	North Carolina	2,879	2.1%
24	Florida	2,818	2.0%
25	Kentucky	2,608	1.9%
26	Tennessee	2,598	1.9%
27	Colorado	2,452	1.8%
28	Oregon	2,423	1.8%
29	Arkansas	2,417	1.8%
30	Mississippi	2,384	1.7%
31	West Virginia	2,376	1.7%
32	South Carolina	2,277	1.7%
33	Wyoming	1,877	1.4%
34	New Mexico	1,860	1.4%
35	Arizona	1,780	1.3%
36	South Dakota	1,736	1.3%
37	Idaho	1,604	1.2%
38	Utah	1,351	1.0%
39	Massachusetts	1,327	1.0%
40	Nevada	1,193	0.9%
41	Maine	1,091	0.8%
42	New Jersey	984	0.7%
43	Maryland	937	0.7%
44	Vermont	613	0.4%
45	New Hampshire	489	0.4%
46	Alaska	470	0.3%
47	Connecticut	438	0.3%
48	Delaware	367	0.3%
49	Rhode Island	60	0.0%
50	Hawaii	0	0.0%
	District of Columbia	23	0.0%

Source: Association of American Railroads
"Railroads and States" (https://www.aar.org/data-center/railroads-states)
*Includes Class I and non-Class I miles. Excludes trackage rights. Synonymous with route-miles, so that a mile of single track is counted the same as a mile of double track.

Sources

ACT, Inc.
500 ACT Drive, P.O. Box 168
Iowa City, IA 52243-0168
319-337-1000
www.act.org

Administration for Children and Families
U.S. Department of Health and Human Services
330 C Street, SW
Washington, DC 20201
202-401-9215
www.acf.hhs.gov

American Cancer Society, Inc.
250 Williams Street, NW
Atlanta, GA 30303
800-227-2345
www.cancer.org

American Hospital Association
155 N. Wacker Drive
Chicago, IL 60606
312-422-3000
www.aha.org

Association of American Railroads
425 Third Street, SW, Suite 1000
Washington, DC 20024
202-639-2100
www.aar.org

Bureau of Economic Analysis
U.S. Department of Commerce
4600 Silver Hill Road
Washington, DC 20233
301-278-9004
www.bea.gov

Bureau of Justice Statistics
U.S. Department of Justice
810 Seventh Street, NW
Washington, DC 20531
202-307-0765
www.bjs.gov

Bureau of Labor Statistics
U.S. Department of Labor
2 Massachusetts Avenue, NE
Washington, DC 20212-0001
202-691-5200
www.bls.gov

Bureau of Transportation Statistics
U.S. Department of Transportation
1200 New Jersey Avenue, SE
Washington, DC 20590
800-853-1351
www.rita.dot.gov

Census Bureau
4600 Silver Hill Road
Washington, DC 20233-0001
800-923-8282
www.census.gov

Centers for Disease Control and Prevention
1600 Clifton Road
Atlanta, GA 30329-4027
800-232-4636
www.cdc.gov

Centers for Medicare and Medicaid Services
7500 Security Boulevard
Baltimore, MD 21244-1850
877-267-2323
www.cms.hhs.gov

College Board
250 Vesey Street
New York, NY 10281
212-713-8000
www.collegeboard.org

Economic Research Service
U.S. Department of Agriculture
1400 Independence Avenue, SW
Mail Stop 1800
Washington, DC 20250-0002
202-694-5139
www.ers.usda.gov

Energy Information Administration
U.S. Department of Energy
1000 Independence Avenue, SW
Washington, DC 20585
202-586-8800
www.eia.doe.gov

Environmental Protection Agency
Ariel Rios Building
1200 Pennsylvania Avenue, NW
Washington, DC 20460
202-272-0167
www.epa.gov

Federal Bureau of Investigation
J Edgar Hoover Building
935 Pennsylvania Avenue, NW
Washington, DC 20535-0001
202-324-3000
www.fbi.gov

Federal Highway Administration
U.S. Department of Transportation
1200 New Jersey Avenue, SE
Washington, DC 20590
202-366-4000
www.fhwa.dot.gov

Federation of Tax Administrators
444 North Capitol Street, NW, Suite 348
Washington, DC 20001
202-624-5890
www.taxadmin.org

Food and Nutrition Service
U.S. Department of Agriculture
3101 Park Center Drive
Alexandria, VA 22302
703-305-2062
www.fns.usda.gov

General Services Administration
1800 F Street, NW
Washington, DC 20450
844-472-43111
www.gsa.gov

Health Resources and Services Administration
Division of Practitioner Data Banks
5600 Fishers Lane
Rockville, MD 20857
301-443-3376
www.hrsa.gov

Institute of Museum and Library Services
955 L'Enfant Plaza North, SW, Suite 4000
Washington, DC 20024-2135
202-653-4657
www.imls.gov

Internal Revenue Service
U.S. Department of the Treasury
1111 Constitution Avenue, NW
Washington, DC 20224
202-283-1710
www.irs.gov

Medical Expenditure Panel Survey
Agency for Healthcare Research and Quality
5600 Fishers Lane
Rockville, MD 20857
301-427-1364
www.meps.ahrq.gov

National Agricultural Statistics Service
1400 Independence Avenue, SW
Washington, DC 20250
800-727-9540
www.nass.usda.gov

National Assembly of State Arts Agencies
1200 18th Street, NW, Suite 1100
Washington, DC 20036
202-347-6352
www.nasaa-arts.org

National Center for Education Statistics
U.S. Department of Education
550 12th Street, SW
Washington, DC 20036
202-403-5551
https://nces.ed.gov/

National Center for Health Statistics
U.S. Department of Health and Human Services
3311 Toledo Road
Hyattsville, MD 20782
800-232-4636
www.cdc.gov/nchs/

National Conference of State Legislatures
7700 E. First Place
Denver, CO 80230
303-364-7700
www.ncsl.org

National Education Association
1201 16th Street, NW
Washington, DC 20036-3290
202-833-4000
www.nea.org

National Highway Traffic Safety Administration
1200 New Jersey Avenue, SE
Washington, DC 20590
888-327-4236
www.nhtsa.gov

National Institute on Alcohol Abuse and Alcoholism
5635 Fishers Lane, MSC 9304
Bethesda, MD 20892-9304
301-443-3860
www.niaaa.nih.gov

National Oceanic & Atmospheric Administration
U.S. Department of Commerce
1401 Constitution Avenue, NW, Room 5128
Washington, DC 20230
202-482-6090
www.noaa.gov

Office of Management and Budget
725 17th Street, NW
Washington, DC 20503
202-395-3080
www.USAspending.gov

Project on Student Debt
Institute for College Access and Success
405 14th Street, 11th Floor
Oakland CA 94612
510-318-7900
http://ticas.org/posd/home

Social Security Administration
Office of Public Inquiries
1100 West High Rise
6401 Security Boulevard
Baltimore, MD 21235
800-772-1213 (information)
www.ssa.gov

Storm Prediction Center
National Weather Service
120 David Boren Boulevard
Norman, OK 73072
405-579-0771
www.spc.noaa.gov

Tax Foundation
1325 G Street, NW, Suite 950
Washington, DC 20005
202-464-6200
www.taxfoundation.org

U.S. Department of Defense
Directorate for Public Inquiry and Analysis
Room 2E565 The Pentagon
1400 Defense Pentagon
Washington, DC 20301-1400
703-571-3343
www.defense.gov

U.S. Department of Veterans Affairs
810 Vermont Avenue, NW
Washington, DC 20420
800-827-1000
www.va.gov

U.S. Geological Survey
12201 Sunrise Valley Drive
Reston, VA 20192
888-275-8747
www.usgs.gov

Index